WILEY

Practitioner's Guide to GAAP 2021

Subscriber
Update
Service

BECOME A SUBSCRIBER!

Did you purchase this product from a bookstore?

If you did, it's important for you to become a subscriber. John Wiley & Sons, Inc. may publish, on a periodic basis, supplements and new editions to reflect the latest changes in the subject matter that you ***need to know*** in order to stay competitive in this ever-changing industry. By contacting the Wiley office nearest you, you'll receive any current update at no additional charge. In addition, you'll receive future updates and revised or related volumes on a 30-day examination review.

If you purchased this product directly from John Wiley & Sons, Inc., we have already recorded your subscription for this update service.

To become a subscriber, please call **1-877-762-2974** or send your name, company name (if applicable), address, and the title of the product to

mailing address: **Supplement Department**
John Wiley & Sons, Inc.
One Wiley Drive
Somerset, NJ 08875
e-mail: **subscriber@wiley.com**
fax: **1-732-302-2300**
online: **www.wiley.com**

For customers outside the United States, please contact the Wiley office nearest you:

Professional & Reference Division
John Wiley & Sons Canada, Ltd.
22 Worcester Road
Etobicoke, Ontario M9W 1L1
CANADA
Phone: 416-236-4433
Phone: 1-800-567-4797
Fax: 416-236-4447
Email: canada@jwiley.com

John Wiley & Sons, Ltd.
The Atrium
Southern Gate, Chichester
West Sussex, PO19 8SQ
ENGLAND
Phone: 44-1243 779777
Fax: 44-1243 775878
Email: customer@wiley.co.uk

John Wiley & Sons Australia, Ltd.
33 Park Road
P.O. Box 1226
Milton, Queensland 4064
AUSTRALIA
Phone: 61-7-3859-9755
Fax: 61-7-3859-9715
Email: brisbane@johnwiley.com.au

John Wiley & Sons (Asia) Pte. Ltd.
2 Clementi Loop #02-01
SINGAPORE 129809
Phone: 65-64632400
Fax: 65-64634604/5/6
Customer Service: 65-64604280
Email: enquiry@wiley.com.sg

WILEY

Practitioner's Guide to GAAP 2021

Interpretation and Application of
GENERALLY ACCEPTED
ACCOUNTING PRINCIPLES

Joanne M. Flood

WILEY

Published by John Wiley & Sons, Inc., Hoboken, New Jersey.
Published simultaneously in Canada.

Library of Congress Cataloging-in-Publication Data is Available:

ISBN 978-1-119-73617-2 (Paperback)
ISBN 978-1-119-73619-6 (ePDF)
ISBN 978-1-119-73618-9 (ePub)

Cover design and image: Wiley

SKY10024657_020321

CONTENTS

PREFACE

Wiley GAAP 2021: Interpretation and Application provides analytical explanations, copious illustrations, and nearly 300 examples of all current generally accepted accounting principles. The book integrates principles promulgated by the FASB in its *Accounting Standards Codification.TM* *Wiley GAAP* is organized to align fully with the structure of the FASB Codification. Each chapter begins with a list of the subtopics included within the topic, scope, scope exceptions, technical alerts of any FASB Updates, and an overview of the topic. The remainder of each chapter contains a detailed discussion of the concepts and practical examples and illustrations. This organization facilitates the primary objective of the book—to assist financial statement preparers and practitioners in resolving the myriad practical problems faced in applying GAAP.

Hundreds of meaningful, realistic examples guide users in the application of GAAP to the complex fact situations that must be dealt with in the real world practice of accounting. In addition to this emphasis, a major strength of the book is that it explains the theory of GAAP in sufficient detail to serve as a valuable adjunct to accounting textbooks. Much more than merely a reiteration of currently promulgated GAAP, it provides the user with the underlying conceptual bases for the rules. It facilitates the process of reasoning by analogy that is so necessary in dealing with the complicated, fast-changing world of commercial arrangements and transaction structures. It is based on the author's belief that proper application of GAAP demands an understanding of the logical underpinnings of all its technical requirements.

As a bonus, a comprehensive presentation and disclosure checklist, available online to all *Wiley GAAP* purchasers, offers practical guidance on preparing financial statements for commercial entities in accordance with GAAP. For easy reference and research, the checklist also follows the order of the Codification. Go to www.wiley.com/go/GAAP2021 (password: Flood).

The author's wish is that this book will serve preparers, practitioners, faculty, and students as a reliable reference tool to facilitate their understanding of, and ability to apply, the complexities of the authoritative literature.

ASUs Issued Since Previous Edition. The following FASB Accounting Standards Updates (ASUs) were issued since *Wiley GAAP 2020* and through June 2021. Their requirements are incorporated into this edition of *Wiley GAAP*, as and where appropriate, and/or in the Technical Alert section at the beginning of the topic referenced in the ASU title.

- Update 2019-07—Codification Updates to SEC Sections—Amendments to SEC Paragraphs Pursuant to SEC Final Rule Releases No. 33-10532, Disclosure Update and Simplification, and Nos. 33-10231 and 33-10442, Investment Company Reporting Modernization, and Miscellaneous Updates (SEC Update)
- Update 2019-08—Compensation—Stock Compensation (Topic 718) and Revenue from Contracts with Customers (Topic 606): Codification Improvements—Share-Based Consideration Payable to a Customer Update 2019-09—Financial Services—Insurance (Topic 944): Effective Date
- Update 2019-10—Financial Instruments—Credit Losses (Topic 326), Derivatives and Hedging (Topic 815), and Leases (Topic 842): Effective Dates
- Update 2019-11—Codification Improvements to Topic 326, Financial Instruments—Credit Losses

- Update 2019-12—Income Taxes (Topic 740): Simplifying the Accounting for Income Taxes
- Update 2020-01—Investments—Equity Securities (Topic 321), Investments—Equity Method and Joint Ventures (Topic 323), and Derivatives and Hedging (Topic 815)—Clarifying the Interactions between Topic 321, Topic 323, and Topic 815 (a consensus of the FASB Emerging Issues Task Force)
- Update 2020-02—Financial Instruments—Credit Losses (Topic 326) and Leases (Topic 842)—Amendments to SEC Paragraphs Pursuant to SEC Staff Accounting Bulletin No. 119 and Update to SEC Section on Effective Date Related to Accounting Standards Update No. 2016-02, Leases (Topic 842) (SEC Update)
- Update 2020-03—Codification Improvements to Financial Instruments
- Update 2020-04—Reference Rate Reform (Topic 848): Facilitation of the Effects of Reference Rate Reform on Financial Reporting
- Update 2020-05—Revenue from Contracts with Customers (Topic 606) and Leases (Topic 842): Effective Dates for Certain Entities
- Update 2020-06—Debt—Debt with Conversion and Other Options (Subtopic 470-20) and Derivatives and Hedging—Contracts in Entity's Own Equity (Subtopic 815-40): Accounting for Convertible Instruments and Contracts in an Entity's Own Equity

On the Horizon. Significant accounting changes are on the horizon. In the next year, the FASB is expected to make strides on the following major projects and others:

- Conceptual framework projects on elements, measurement, and presentation
- Identifiable intangible assets
- Disclosure framework revisions on income taxes, inventory, interim reporting, government acquisitions
- Disaggregation of performance information
- Not-for-profit reporting of gifts-in-kind
- Segment reporting
- Numerous narrow scope projects

Readers are encouraged to check the FASB website for status updates to the above and other FASB projects.

Joanne M. Flood
June 2020

ABOUT THE AUTHOR

Joanne M. Flood, CPA, is an author and independent consultant on accounting and auditing technical topics and e-learning. She has experience as an auditor in both an international firm and a local firm and worked as a senior manager in the AICPA's Professional Development group. She received her MBA summa cum laude in accounting from Adelphi University and her bachelor's degree in English from Molloy College.

While in public accounting, Joanne worked on major clients in retail, manufacturing, and finance and on small business clients in construction, manufacturing, and professional services. At the AICPA, she developed and wrote e-learning, text, and instructor-led training courses on U.S. and international standards. She also produced training materials in a wide variety of media, including print, video, and audio, and pioneered the AICPA's e-learning product line. Joanne resides on Long Island, New York, with her daughter, Elizabeth. Joanne is the author of the following Wiley publications:

Financial Disclosure Checklist

Wiley GAAP 2021: Interpretation and Application of Generally Accepted Accounting Principles

Wiley Practitioner's Guide to GAAS 2021: Covering all SASs, SSAEs, SSARSs, and Interpretations

Wiley GAAP: Financial Statement Disclosures Manual (Wiley Regulatory Reporting)

Wiley Revenue Recognition

CODIFICATION TAXONOMY

Topic # and title		Subtopic # and title	
I. General Principles and Objectives			
105	Generally Accepted Accounting	105-10	Overall Principles
II. Overall Financial Reporting, Presentation, and Display Matters			
A. Overall Presentation of Financial Statements			
205	Presentation of Financial Statements	205-10	Overall
		205-20	Discontinued Operations
		205-30	Liquidation Basis of Accounting
		205-40	Going Concern
210	Balance Sheet	210-10	Overall
		210-20	Offsetting
215	Statement of Shareholders' Equity	215-10	Overall
220	Income Statement-Reporting Comprehensive Income	220-10	Overall
		220-20	Unusual or Infrequently Occurring Items
		220-30	Business Interruption Insurance
230	Statement of Cash Flows	230-10	Overall
235	Notes to Financial Statements	235-10	Overall
B. Various Financial Reporting, Presentation, and Display Matters			
250	Accounting Changes and Error Corrections		
		250-10	Overall
255	Changing Prices	255-10	Overall
260	Earnings Per Share	260-10	Overall
270	Interim Reporting	270-10	Overall
272	Limited Liability Entities	272-10	Overall
274	Personal Financial Statements	274-10	Overall
275	Risks and Uncertainties	275-10	Overall
280	Segment Reporting	280-10	Overall
III. Transaction-Related Topics			
A. Financial Statement Accounts			
310	Receivables	310-10	Overall
		310-20	Nonrefundable Fees and Other Costs
		310-30	Loans and Debt Securities Acquired with Deteriorated Credit Quality
		310-40	Troubled Debt Restructurings by Creditors

Topic # and title		Subtopic # and title	
320	Investments—Debt and Equity Securities	320-10	Overall Securities
321	Investments—Equity Securities	321-10	Overall
323	Investments—Equity Method and Joint Ventures	323-10	Overall Joint Ventures
		323-30	Partnerships, Joint Ventures, and Limited Liability Entities
325	Investments—Other	325-10	Overall
		325-20	Cost Method Investments
		325-30	Investments in Insurance Contracts
		325-40	Beneficial Interests in Securitized Financial Assets
326	Financial Instruments—Credit Losses	326-10	Overall
		326-20	Measured at Amortized Cost
		326-20-30	Available-for-Sale Securities
330	Inventory	330-10	Overall
340	Other Assets and Deferred Costs	340-10	Overall
		340-20	Capitalized Advertising Costs
		340-30	Insurance Contracts That Do Not Transfer Insurance Risk
		340-40	Contracts with Customers
350	Intangibles—Goodwill and Other	350-10	Overall
		350-20	Goodwill
		350-30	General Intangibles Other Than Goodwill
		350-40	Internal-Use Software
		350-50	Website Development Costs
360	Property, Plant, and Equipment	360-10	Overall
		360-20	Real Estate Sales
405	Liabilities	405-10	Overall
		405-20	Extinguishment of Liabilities
		405-30	Insurance-Related Assessments
		405-40	Obligations Resulting from Joint and Several Liabilities
410	Asset Retirement and Environmental Obligations		
		410-20	Asset Retirement Obligations
		410-30	Environmental Obligations
420	Exit or Disposal Cost Obligations	420-10	Overall
430	Deferred Revenue	430-10	Overall
440	Commitments	440-10	Overall
450	Contingencies	450-10	Overall
		450-20	Loss Contingencies

Topic # and title		*Subtopic # and title*	
		450-30	Gain Contingencies
460	Guarantees	460-10	Overall
470	Debt	470-10	Overview
		470-20	Debt with Conversion and Other Options
		470-30	Participating Mortgage Loans
		470-40	Product Financing Arrangements
		470-50	Modifications and Extinguishments
		470-60	Troubled Debt Restructurings by Debtors
480	Distinguishing Liabilities from Equity	480-10	Overall
505	Equity	505-10	Overall
		505-20	Stock Dividends and Stock Splits
		505-30	Treasury Stock
		505-50	Equity-Based Payments to Non-Empoyees
		505-60	Spin-offs and Reverse Spin-offs
605	Revenue Recognition	605-10	Overall
		605-15	Products
		605-20	Services
		605-25	Multiple-Element Arrangements
		605-28	Milestone Method
		605-30	Rights to Use
		605-35	Construction-Type and Production-Type Contracts
		605-40	Gains and Losses
		605-45	Principal Agent Considerations
		605-50	Customer Payments and Incentives
606	Revenue from Contracts with Customers	606-10	Overall
610	Other Income	610-10	Overall
		610-20	Gains and Losses from the Derecognition of Nonfinancial Assets
		610-30	Gains and Losses on Involuntary Conversions
705	Cost of Sales and Services	705-10	Overall
		705-20	Accounting for Consideration Received from a Vendor[1]
710	Compensation—General	710-10	Overall
712	Compensation—Nonretirement Postemployment Benefits	712-10	Overall

Topic # and title		Subtopic # and title	
715	Compensation—Retirement Benefits	715-10	Overall
		715-20	Defined Benefit Plans—General
		715-30	Defined Benefit Plans—Pensions
		715-60	Defined Benefit Plans—Other Postretirement
		715-70	Defined Contribution Plans
		715-80	Multiemployer Plans
718	Compensation—Stock Compensation	718-10	Overall
		718-20	Awards Classified as Equity
		718-30	Awards Classified as Liabilities
		718-40	Employee Stock Ownership Plans
		718-50	Employee Share Purchase Plans
		718-740	Income Taxes
720	Other Expenses	720-10	Overall
		720-15	Start-Up Costs
		720-20	Insurance Costs
		720-25	Contributions Made
		720-30	Real and Personal Property Taxes
		720-35	Advertising Costs
		720-40	Electronic Equipment Waste Obligations
		720-45	Business and Technology Reengineering
		720-50	Fees Paid to the Federal Government by Pharmaceutical Manufacturers and Health Insurer
730	Research and Development	730-10	Overall
		730-20	Research and Development Arrangements
740	Income Taxes	740-10	Overall
		740-20	Intraperiod Tax Allocation
		740-30	Other Considerations or Special Areas

B. Broad Transactional Categories

805	Business Combinations	805-10	Overall
		805-20	Identifiable Assets and Liabilities, and Any Noncontrolling Interest
		805-30	Goodwill or Gain from Bargain Purchase, Including Consideration Transferred
		805-40	Reverse Acquisitions
		805-50	Related Issues
		805-740	Income Taxes
808	Collaborative Arrangements	808-10	Overall

Topic # and title		Subtopic # and title	
810	Consolidation	810-10	Overall
		810-20	Control of Partnerships and Similar Entities
		810-30	Research and Development Arrangements
815	Derivatives and Hedging	815-10	Overall
		815-15	Embedded Derivatives
		815-20	Hedging—General
		815-25	Fair Value Hedges
		815-30	Cash Flow Hedges
		815-35	Net Investment Hedges
		815-40	Contracts in Entity's Own Equity
		815-45	Weather Derivatives
820	Fair Value Measurements	820-10	Overall
825	Financial Instruments	825-10	Overall
		825-20	Registration Payment Arrangements
830	Foreign Currency Matters	830-10	Overall
		830-20	Foreign Currency Transactions
		830-30	Translation of Financial Statements
		830-230	Statement of Cash Flows
		830-740	Income Taxes
835	Interest	835-10	Overall
		835-20	Capitalization of Interest
		835-30	Imputation of Interest
840	Leases	840-10	Overall
		840-20	Operating Leases
		840-30	Capital Leases
		840-40	Sale-Leaseback Transactions
845	Nonmonetary Transactions	845-10	Overall
		848-10	Overall
		848-20	Contract Modifications
		848-30	Hedging-General
		848-40	Fair Value Hedges
		848-50	Cash Flow Hedges
850	Related-Party Disclosures	850-10	Overall
852	Reorganization	852-10	Overall
		852-20	Quasi-Reorganization
		852-740	Income Taxes
853	Service Concession Arrangements	853-10	Overall
855	Subsequent Events	855-10	Overall

	Topic # and title		*Subtopic # and title*
860	Transfers and Servicing	860-10	Overall
		860-20	Sales of Financial Assets
		860-30	Secured Borrowings and Collateral
		860-40	Transfers to Qualifying Special-Purpose Entities
		860-50	Servicing Assets and Liabilities
IV.	**Industry/Unique Topics**		
905	Agriculture	905-10	Overall
908	Airlines	908-10	Overall
910	Contractors—Construction	910-10	Overall
		910-20	Contract Costs
912	Contractors—Federal Government	912-10	Overall
		912-20	Contract Costs
915	Development Stage Entities	915-10	Overall
920	Entertainment—Broadcasters	920-10	Overall
922	Entertainment—Cable Television	922-10	Overall
924	Entertainment—Casinos	924-10	Overall
926	Entertainment—Films	926-10	Overall
		926-20	Other Assets—Film Costs
928	Entertainment—Music	928-10	Overall
930	Extractive Activities—Mining	930-10	Overall
932	Extractive Activities—Oil and Gas	932-10	Overall
940	Financial Services—Brokers	940-10	Overall and Dealers
942	Financial Services—Depository	942-10	Overall and Lending
944	Financial Services—Insurance	944-10	Overall
		944-20	Insurance Activities
		944-30	Acquisition Costs
		944-40	Claim Costs and Liabilities for Future Policy Benefits
		944-50	Policyholder Dividends
		944-60	Recognition
		944-80	Separate Accounts
946	Financial Services—Investment	946-10	Overall Companies
		946-20	Investment Company Activities
948	Financial Services—Mortgage	948-10	Overall Banking
950	Financial Services—Title Plant		
952	Franchisors	952-10	Overall
954	Health Care Entities	954-10	Overall
958	Not-for-Profit Entities	958-10	Overall
		958-20	Financially Interrelated Entities
		958-30	Split-Interest Agreements

	Topic # and title		Subtopic # and title
960	Plan Accounting—Defined Benefit	960-10	Overall Pension Plans
		960-20	Accumulated Plan Benefits
		960-30	Net Assets Available for Plan Benefits
		960-40	Terminating Plans
962	Plan Accounting—Defined	962-10	Overall Contribution Pension Plans
		962-40	Terminating Plans
965	Plan Accounting—Health and Welfare	965-10	Overall Benefit Plans
		965-20	Net Assets Available for Plan Benefits
		965-30	Plan Benefits Obligations
		965-40	Terminating Plans
970	Real Estate—General	970-10	Overall
972	Real Estate—Common Interest	972-10	Overall Realty Associations
974	Real Estate—Real Estate	974-10	Overall Investment Trusts
976	Real Estate—Retail Land	976-10	Overall
978	Real Estate—Time-Sharing Activities	978-10	Overall
980	Regulated Operations	980-10	Overall
		980-20	Discontinuation of Rate-Regulated Accounting
985	Software	985-10	Overall
		985-20	Costs of Software to Be Sold, Leased, or Marketed

V. Glossary

WILEY

Practitioner's Guide to GAAP 2021

1 ASC 105 GENERALLY ACCEPTED ACCOUNTING PRINCIPLES

PERSPECTIVES AND ISSUES

What Is GAAP?

The FASB Accounting Standards Codification™ (ASC) is the:

> *. . . source of authoritative generally accepted accounting principles (GAAP) recognized by the FASB to be applied by nongovernmental entities. Rules and interpretive releases of the Securities and Exchange Commission (SEC) under authority of federal securities laws are also sources of authoritative GAAP for SEC registrants. In addition to the SEC's rules and interpretive releases, the SEC staff issues Staff Accounting Bulletins that represent practices followed by the staff in administering SEC disclosure requirements, and it utilizes SEC Staff Announcements and Observer comments made at Emerging Issues Task Force meetings to publicly announce its views on certain accounting issues for SEC registrants. ASC 105-10-05-1*

In the absence of authoritative guidance, the FASB Codification (the Codification) offers the following approach:

> *If the guidance for a transaction or event is not specified within a source of authoritative GAAP for that entity, an entity shall first consider accounting principles for similar transactions or events within a source of authoritative GAAP for that entity and then consider nonauthoritative guidance from other sources. An entity shall not follow the accounting treatment specified in accounting guidance for similar transactions or events in cases in which those accounting principles either prohibit the application of the accounting treatment to the particular transaction or event or indicate that the accounting treatment should not be applied by analogy. ASC 105-10-05-2*

GAAP establishes:

- The measurement of economic activity,
- The time when such measurements are to be made and recorded,
- The disclosures surrounding this activity, and
- The preparation and presentation of summarized economic information in the form of financial statements.

GAAP develops when questions arise about how best to accomplish those items. In response to those questions, GAAP is either prescribed in official pronouncements of authoritative bodies empowered to create it, or it originates over time through the development of customary practices that evolve when authoritative bodies fail to respond. Thus, GAAP is a reaction to and a product of the economic environment in which it develops. As such, the development of accounting and financial reporting standards has lagged the development and creation of increasingly intricate economic structures and transactions.

There are two broad categories of accounting principles—recognition and disclosure.

Recognition Principles Recognition principles determine the timing and measurement of items that enter the accounting cycle and impact the financial statements. These are reflected in quantitative standards that require economic information to be reflected numerically.

Disclosure Principles Disclosure principles deal with factors that are not always quantifiable. Disclosures involve qualitative information that is an essential ingredient of a full set of financial statements. Their absence would make the financial statements misleading by omitting information relevant to the decision-making needs of the reader. Disclosure principles also complement recognition principles by dictating that disclosures

- expand on some quantitative data,
- explain assumptions underlying the numerical information, and
- provide additional information on accounting policies, contingencies, uncertainties, etc., which are essential to fully understand the performance and financial condition of the reporting enterprise.

DEFINITIONS OF TERMS

See Appendix A, *Definitions of Terms*, for terms related to this topic: Conduit Debt Securities, Financial Statements Are Available to Be Issued, Nongovernmental Entity, Nonpublic Entity, Not-for-Profit Entity, and Public Business Entity.

CONCEPTS, RULES, AND EXAMPLES

History of GAAP

From time to time, the bodies given responsibility for the promulgation of GAAP have changed, and indeed more than a single such body has often shared this responsibility. In response to the stock market crash of 1929, the AICPA appointed the Committee on Accounting Procedure. This was superseded in 1959 by the Accounting Principles Board (APB) created by the AICPA. Because of operational problems, in 1972 the profession replaced the APB with a three-part organization consisting of the Financial Accounting Foundation (FAF), Financial Accounting Standards Board (FASB), and the Financial Accounting Standards Advisory Council (FASAC). Since 1973 the FASB has been the organization designated to establish standards of financial reporting.

GAAP Codification

In 2009, FASB's Codification became the single official source of authoritative, non-governmental U.S. generally accepted accounting principles. It superseded all nongrandfathered (see ASC 105-10-70-2 for a list of grandfathered guidance), non-SEC accounting guidance. Only one level of authoritative GAAP exists, excluding the guidance issued by the Securities and Exchange Commission (SEC). All other literature is nonauthoritative.

Other and Nonauthoritative Sources Not all GAAP resulted from the issuance of pronouncements by authoritative bodies, and not all GAAP is found in the codification. For example, depreciation methods such as straight-line and declining balance have long been accepted. There are, however, no definitive pronouncements that can be found to state this. Furthermore, there are many disclosure principles that evolved into general accounting practice because they were originally required by the SEC in documents submitted to them. Much of the content of statements of financial position and income statements has evolved over the years in the absence of adopted standards.

The Codification lists some possible nonauthoritative sources:

- Practices that are widely recognized and prevalent either generally or in the industry,
- FASB Concepts Statements,
- American Institute of Certified Public Accountants (AICPA) Issues Papers,
- International Financial Reporting Standards of the International Accounting Standards Board,
- Pronouncements of professional associations or regulatory agencies,
- Technical Information Service Inquiries and Replies included in AICPA Technical Practice Aids,
- Accounting textbooks, handbooks, and articles. (ASC 105-10-05-3)

SEC Guidance in the Codification To increase the utility of the Codification for public companies, relevant portions of authoritative content issued by the SEC and selected SEC staff interpretations and administrative guidance are included for reference in the Codification. The sources include:

- Regulation S-X,
- Financial Reporting Releases (FRR)/Accounting Series Releases (ASR),
- Interpretive Releases (IR), and
- SEC staff guidance in:
    - Staff Accounting Bulletins (SAB),
    - EITF Topic D and SEC Staff Observer comments.

The Codification does not, however, incorporate the entire population of SEC rules, regulations, interpretive releases, and staff guidance. SEC guidance not incorporated in the codification includes content related to auditing or independence matters or matters outside of the basic financial statements, including Management's Discussion and Analysis (MD&A).

The Standards-Setting Process

The FASB has long adhered to rigorous "due process" when creating new guidance. The goal is to involve constituents who would be affected by the newly issued guidance so that the standards created will result in information that reports economic activity as objectively as possible without attempting to influence behavior in any particular direction. Ultimately, however, the guidance is the judgment of the FASB, based on research, public input, and deliberation.

The Board issues guidance through Accounting Standards Updates (ASU) which describe amendments to the Accounting Standards Codification. Once issued, the provisions become GAAP after the stated effective date.

Accounting Standards Updates Accounting Standards Updates (ASUs) are composed of:

- A summary of the key provisions of the project that led to the changes,
- The specific changes to the Codification, and
- The Basis for Conclusions.

The title of the combined set of new guidance and instructions is *Accounting Standards Update YY-XX*, where YY is the last two digits of the year and XX is the sequential number for each update. All authoritative GAAP issued by the FASB is issued in this format.

The FASB organizes the content of ASUs using the same Section headings as those used in the Codification. ASUs are not deemed authoritative in their own right; instead, they serve only to update the Codification and provide the historical basis for conclusions.

The content from updates that is not yet fully effective for all reporting entities appears in the Codification as boxed text and is labeled "pending content." The pending content text box includes the earliest transition date and a link to the related transition guidance, also found in the Codification.

Maintenance Updates As with any publishing practice, irregularities occur. To make necessary corrections, the FASB staff issues Maintenance Updates. These are not addressed by the Board and contain nonsubstantive editorial changes and link-related changes.

American Institute of Certified Public Accountants Although it currently plays a greatly reduced standard-setting role, the American Institute of Certified Public Accountants (AICPA) has authorized the Financial Reporting Executive Committee (FinREC) to determine the AICPA's policies on financial reporting standards and to speak for the AICPA on accounting matters. FinREC, formerly the Accounting Standards Executive Committee (AcSEC), is the senior technical committee at the AICPA. It is composed of seventeen volunteer members, representative of industry, analysts, and both national and regional public accounting firms.

Researching GAAP Problems

These procedures should be refined and adapted to each individual fact situation.

Codification Structure The FASB Codification is located on fasb.org. The site is intended to be easily searchable for research purposes. This section provides an overview of the site's contents and search functionality.

Areas On all pages of the site, all categories of the Codification are listed down the vertical menu bar on the left side of the page, revealing the following Areas, and the numbering series for each one:

- General Principles (100). (Establishes the Codification as the source of GAAP.)
- Presentation (200). (Topics in this area relate only to presentation matters; they do not address recognition, measurement, and derecognition matters. Examples of these topics are income statement, balance sheet, and earnings per share.)
- Assets (300).
- Liabilities (400).
- Equity (500).
- Revenue (600).
- Expenses (700). (Clusters all types of expense-related GAAP into five broad categories, which are cost of goods sold, research and development, compensation, income taxes, and other expenses.)
- Broad Transactions (800). (Contains the major transactional topics, such as business combinations, derivatives, and foreign currency matters.)
- Industry (900). (Itemizes GAAP for specific industries, such as entertainment, real estate, and software.)
- Master Glossary.

Topics Areas are further divided by topics, subtopics, sections, and subsections. FASB has developed a classification system specifically for the Codification. The following is the structure of the classifications system: XXX-YY-ZZ-PP, where:

- XXX = topic,
- YY = subtopic,
- ZZ = section, and
- PP = paragraph.

An "S" preceding the section number denotes SEC guidance. At the most granular level of detail, the Codification has a two-digit numerical code for a standard set of categories.

The Codification Taxonomy can be found in the section that precedes Chapter 1.

Subtopics Subtopics represent subsets of a topic and are typically identified by type or by scope. For example, lessees and lessors are two separate subtopics of leases Topic 842. Each topic contains an "overall subtopic" (designated "-10") that generally represents the pervasive guidance for the topic, which includes guidance that applies to all other subtopics. Each additional subtopic represents incremental or unique guidance not contained in the overall subtopic.

Exhibit-Sections

Title	Number	Description
Status	00	Includes references to the Accounting Standards Updates that affect the subtopic.
Overview and background	05	Provides overview and background material.
Objectives	10	States the high-level objectives of the topic.
Scope and scope exceptions	15	Outlines the transactions, events, and other occurrences to which the subtopic guidance does or does not apply.
Glossary	20	Contains definitions for terms found within the subtopic guidance.
Recognition	25	Defines the criteria, timing, and location for recording an item in the financial statements.
Initial measurement	30	Provides guidance on the criteria and amounts used to measure a transaction at the initial date of recognition.
Subsequent measurement	35	Provides guidance on the measurement of an item after the recognition date.
Derecognition	40	Relates almost exclusively to assets, liabilities, and equity. Provides criteria, the method to determine the amount of basis, and the timing to be used when derecognizing a particular item for purposes of determining gain or loss.
Other presentation matters	45	Provides guidance on presenting items in the financial statements.
Disclosure	50	Provides guidance regarding disclosure in the notes to or on the face of the financial statements.
Implementation guidance and illustrations	55	Contains illustrations of the guidance provided in the preceding sections.
Relationships	60	Contains links to guidance that may be helpful to the reader of the subtopic.

Transition and Open Effective Date Information	65	Contains references to paragraphs within the subtopic that have open transition guidance.
Grandfathered Guidance	70	Contains descriptions, references, and transition periods for content grandfathered after July 1, 2009, by an Accounting Standards Update.[1]
XBRL Elements	75	Contains the related XBRL elements for the subtopic.
SEC Materials	S99	Contains selected SEC content for use by public companies.

Sections Sections represent the nature of the content in a subtopic—for example, recognition, measurement, and disclosure. The sectional organization for all subtopics is the same. In a manner similar to that used for topics, sections correlate closely with sections of individual International Accounting Standards. Sections are further broken down into *subsections, paragraphs*, and *subparagraphs*, depending on the specific content of each section.

Finding Information By drilling down through the various topics and subtopics in the sidebar of the online Codification, a researcher can eventually locate the relevant GAAP information. When searching for specific words or phrases, the best search tool is the Codification search function.

Codification Terminology The FASB standardized on the term "entity" to replace terms such as company, organization, enterprise, firm, preparer, etc. So, too, the Codification uses "shall" throughout to replace "should," "is required to," "must," etc. The FASB believes these terms all represent the same concept—the requirement to apply a standard. "Would" and "should" are used to indicate hypothetical situations. To reduce ambiguity, the Codification also eliminated qualifying terminology, such as *usually*, *ordinarily*, *generally*, and similar terms.

Research Procedures

Step 1: Identify the Problem Incorrect answers (e.g., regarding the proper way to report revenue-producing activities) commonly flow from improper definition of the actual question to be resolved. Consider the following:

- Gain an understanding of the problem or question.
- Challenge the tentative definition of the problem and revise, as necessary.
- Problems and research questions can arise from new authoritative pronouncements, changes in a firm's economic operating environment, or new transactions, as well as from the realization that the problem had not been properly defined in the past.
- If proposed transactions and potential economic circumstances are anticipated, more deliberate attention can be directed at finding the correct solution, and certain proposed transactions having deleterious reporting consequences might be avoided altogether or structured more favorably.

[1] Certain accounting standards allowed for the continued application of superseded accounting standards for transactions that have an ongoing effect in an entity's financial statements. That superseded guidance has not been included in the Codification is considered grandfathered and continues to remain authoritative for those transactions after the effective date of the Codification. (ASC 105-10-70-2)

- If little is known about the subject area, it may be useful to consult general reference sources to become more familiar with the topic, that is, the basic what, why, how, when, who, and where. Web-based research vastly expands the ability to gather useful information.
- Determine whether the issue you are researching is a GAAP issue or an auditing issue so that your search is directed to the appropriate literature.

Step 2: Analyze the Problem

- Identify critical factors, issues, and questions that relate to the research problem.
- What are the options? Brainstorm possible alternative accounting treatments.
- What are the goals of the transaction? Are these goals compatible with full and transparent disclosure and recognition?
- What is the economic substance of the transaction, irrespective of the manner in which it appears to be structured?
- What limitations or factors can affect the accounting treatment?

Step 3: Refine the Problem Statement

- Clearly articulate the critical issues in a way that will facilitate research and analysis.

Step 4: Identify Plausible Alternatives

- Plausible alternative solutions are based upon prior knowledge or theory.
- Additional alternatives may be identified as Steps 5–7 are completed.
- The purpose of identifying and discussing different alternatives is to be able to respond to key accounting issues that arise out of a specific situation.
- The alternatives are the potential methods of accounting for the situation from which only one will ultimately be chosen.
- Exploring alternatives is important because many times there is no single cut-and-dried financial reporting solution to the situation.
- Ambiguity often surrounds many transactions and related accounting issues and, accordingly, the accountant and business advisor must explore the alternatives and use professional judgment in deciding on the proper course of action.

Step 5: Develop a Research Strategy

- Determine which literature to search.
- Generate keywords or phrases that will form the basis of an electronic search.
- Consider trying a broad search to:
  - Assist in developing an understanding of the area,
  - Identify appropriate search terms, and
  - Identify related issues and terminology.
- Consider trying very precise searches to identify whether there is authoritative literature directly on point.

Step 6: Search Authoritative Literature (Described in Additional Detail Below) This step involves implementation of the research strategy through searching, identifying, and locating applicable information:

- Research the Codification.
- Research using *Wiley GAAP*.
- Research other literature.
- Research practice.

- Use theory.
- Find analogous events and/or concepts that are reasonably similar.

Step 7: Evaluation of the Information Obtained

- Analyze and evaluate all of the information obtained.
- This evaluation should lead to the development of a solution or recommendation. Again, it is important to remember that Steps 3–7 describe activities that will interact with each other and lead to a more refined process in total, and a more complete solution. These steps may involve several iterations.

Search Authoritative Literature (Step 6)—Further Explanation

The following sections discuss in more detail how to search authoritative literature as outlined in Step 6.

Researching *Wiley GAAP* This publication can assist in researching GAAP for the purpose of identifying technical answers to specific inquiries. You can begin your search by using the contents page at the front of this book or by using the index at the back of this publication. The path chosen depends in part on how specific the question is. An initial reading of the chapter or relevant section will provide a broader perspective on the subject. However, if one's interest is more specific, it might be more efficient to search the index.

Each chapter in this publication is organized in the following manner:

- Table of contents on the first page of the chapter.
- Perspective and Issues, providing an overview of the chapter contents (noting any current controversy or proposed GAAP changes affecting the chapter's topics), scope of the topic, and a list of major topics and subtopics in the FASB Accounting Standards Codification relevant to the chapter's topics.
- Concepts, Rules, and Examples, setting forth the detailed guidance and examples.

The appendices in this publication are *Definitions of Terms* and *Disclosure and Presentation Checklist for Commercial Businesses* (www.wiley.com/go/GAAP2021). After reading the relevant portions of this publication, the list of major topics and subtopics in the Codification can be used to find the sections in the Codification that are related to the topic, so that these can be appropriately understood and cited in documenting your research findings and conclusions. Readers familiar with the professional literature can use the Codification Taxonomy that precedes this chapter to quickly locate the pages in this publication relevant to each specific pronouncement.

Researching Nonpromulgated GAAP Researching nonpromulgated GAAP consists of reviewing pronouncements in areas similar to those being researched, reading accounting literature mentioned in ASC 105-10-05-3 and earlier in this chapter as "other and nonauthoritative sources," and carefully reading the relevant portions of the FASB Conceptual Framework (summarized later in this chapter). Concepts and intentions espoused by accounting experts offer essential clues to a logical formulation of alternatives and conclusions regarding problems that have not yet been addressed by the standard-setting bodies.

Both the AICPA and FASB publish a myriad of nonauthoritative literature. FASB publishes the documents it uses in its due process: Discussion Papers, Invitations to Comment, Exposure Drafts, and Preliminary Views as well as minutes from its meetings. It also publishes research reports, newsletters, and implementation guidance. The AICPA publishes Technical Practice Aids, Issues Papers, Technical Questions and Answers, Audit and Accounting Guides, as well as comment letters on proposals of other standard-setting bodies, and the monthly periodical, *Journal of Accountancy*. Technical Practice Aids are answers published by the AICPA to questions about accounting and auditing standards. AICPA Issues Papers are research documents about accounting and reporting problems that the AICPA believes should be resolved by FASB. They provide information about alternative accounting treatments used in practice.

The Securities and Exchange Commission issues Staff Accounting Bulletins and makes rulings on individual cases that come before it. These rulings create and impose accounting standards on those whose financial statements are to be submitted to the Commission.

Governmental agencies such as the Government Accountability Office, the Federal Accounting Standards Advisory Board, and the Cost Accounting Standards Board have certain publications that may assist in researching written standards. Also, industry organizations and associations may be other helpful sources.

Certain publications are helpful in identifying practices used by entities that may not be promulgated as standards. Wiley is publishing a new volume on Financial Statement Disclosures, which is scheduled for 2020 publication. EDGAR (Electronic Data Gathering, Analysis, and Retrieval) publishes the SEC filings of public companies, which includes the companies' financial statements. Through selection of keywords and/or topics, this service can provide information on how other entities resolved similar problems.

Internet-Based Research Sources There has been and continues to be an information revolution affecting the exponential growth in the volume of materials, authoritative and non-authoritative, that are available on the Internet. A listing of just a small cross-section of these sources follows:

Accounting Websites		
AICPA	www.aicpa.org	Includes the Financial Reporting Center for accounting and assurance information and resources; CPE information; Professional Ethics and Peer Review releases and information; information on relevant congressional/executive actions; online publications, such as the Journal of Accountancy; also has links to other organizations; includes links to standard-setting bodies and their authoritative standards for nonissuers including auditing standards, attestation standards, and quality control standards
FASB	www.fasb.org	Information on FASB; Access to the Codification and ASUs, Project Status reports with EDs, research papers, and meeting notes; webcasts
FASB Codification	asc.fasb.org/home	Database using the accounting Codification; includes cross-referencing and tutorials
GASB	www.gasb.org	Information on GASB; new GASB documents; summaries/status of all GASB statements; proposed Statements; Technical Bulletins; Interpretations
International Accounting Standards Board (IASB)	www.ifrs.org	Information on the IASB; lists of Pronouncements, Exposure Drafts, project summaries, and conceptual framework

PCAOB	www. pcaobus.org	Sections on rulemaking, standards (including the auditing, attestation, quality control, ethics, and independence standards), enforcement, inspections and oversight activities
SEC	www.sec.gov	SEC digest and statements; EDGAR searchable database; information on current SEC rulemaking

The Concept of Materiality

Technical Alert In August 2018, the FASB issued changes to the Concepts Statements. Chapter 3 of Concepts Statement 8 (CON 8) reinstates the definition of materiality that was in CON 2 and was superseded in 2010 by CON 8. The Board, aware that the CON 8 description of the legal concept of materiality might be inconsistent with the U. S. Supreme Court's definition decided to remove the CON 8 description and replace it. In addition to the reinstatement of the CON 2 definition of materiality, the amendments to Chapter 3 of CON 8 discusses how materiality differs from relevance and that materiality assessments can be properly made only by those with an understanding of the entity's facts and circumstances. Below are the relevant changes.

> QC11. Relevance and materiality are defined by what influences or makes a difference to an investor or other decision maker; however, these two concepts can be distinguished from each other. Relevance is a general notion about what type of information is useful to investors. Materiality is entity specific. The omission or misstatement of an item in a financial report is material if, in light of surrounding circumstances, the magnitude of the item is such that it is probable that the judgment of a reasonable person relying upon the report would have been changed or influenced by the inclusion or correction of the item.
>
> QC11A. A decision not to disclose certain information or recognize an economic phenomenon may be made, for example, because the amounts involved are too small to make a difference to an investor or other decision maker (they are immaterial). However, magnitude by itself, without regard to the nature of the item and the circumstances in which the judgment has to be made, generally is not a sufficient basis for a materiality judgment.
>
> QC11B. No general standards of materiality could be formulated to take into account all the considerations that enter into judgments made by an experienced reasonable provider of financial information. This is because materiality judgments can properly be made only by those that understand the reporting entity's pertinent facts and circumstances. Whenever an authoritative body imposes materiality rules or standards, it is substituting generalized collective judgments for specific individual judgments, and there is no reason to suppose that the collective judgments always are superior.

Descriptions of Materiality

Materiality has great significance in understanding, researching, and implementing GAAP and affects the entire scope of financial reporting. Disputes over financial statement presentations often turn on the materiality of items that were, or were not, recognized, measured, and presented in certain ways.

Materiality is described by the FASB in Statement of Financial Concepts 8 (CON 8),

Qualitative Characteristics of Accounting Information:

Information is material if omitting it or misstating it could influence decisions that users make on the basis of the financial information of a specific reporting entity. In other words, materiality is an entity-specific aspect of relevance based on the nature or magnitude or both of the items to which the information relates in the contest of an individual entity's financial report.

The Supreme Court has held that a fact is material if there is:

a substantial likelihood that the disclosure of the omitted fact would have been viewed by the reasonable investor as having significantly altered the "total mix" of information made available.

Due to its inherent subjectivity, the FASB definition does not provide specific or quantitative guidance in distinguishing material information from immaterial information. The individual accountant must exercise professional judgment in evaluating information and concluding on its materiality. Materiality as a criterion has both quantitative and qualitative aspects, and items should not be deemed *immaterial* unless all potentially applicable quantitative and qualitative aspects are given full consideration and found not relevant.

SAB Topics 1.M (SAB 99) and 1.N (SAB 108) contain guidance from the SEC staff on assessing materiality during the preparation of financial statements. That guidance references the Supreme Court opinion and the definition in CON 2, which has been superseded by CON 8. The SEC in Staff Accounting Bulletin (SAB) Topics 1.M (SAB 99) and 1.N (SAB 108) provides useful discussions of this issue. SAB Topic 1.M indicates that:

a matter is material if there is a substantial likelihood that a reasonable person would consider it important.

Although not strictly applicable to nonpublic preparers of financial statements, the SEC guidance is worthy of consideration by all accountants and auditors. Among other things, Topic notes that deliberate application of nonacceptable accounting methods cannot be justified merely because the impact on the financial statements is deemed to be immaterial. Topic 1.N also usefully reminds preparers and others that materiality has both quantitative and qualitative dimensions, and both must be given full consideration. Topic 1.N has added to the literature of materiality with its discussion of considerations applicable to prior period restatements.

Quantitative Factors Quantitatively, materiality has been defined in relatively few pronouncements, which speaks to the great difficulty of setting precise measures for materiality. For example, in ASC 280-10-50, which addresses segment disclosures, a material segment or customer is defined in ASC 280-10-50-12 as representing 10% or more of the reporting entity's revenues (although, even given this rule, qualitative considerations may cause smaller segments to be deemed reportable). The Securities and Exchange Commission has, in several of its pronouncements, defined materiality as 1% of total assets for receivables from officers and stockholders, 5% of total assets for separate balance sheet disclosure of items, and 10% of total revenue for disclosure of oil and gas producing activities.

Qualitative Factors In addition to quantitative assessments, preparers should consider qualitative factors, such as company-specific trends and performance metrics. Information from analysts' reports and investor calls may provide an indication of what is important to reasonable investors and should be considered.

Although materiality judgments have traditionally been primarily based on quantitative assessments, the nature of a transaction or event can affect a determination of whether that transaction or event is material. Examples of items that involve an otherwise immaterial amount but that would be material include:

- A transaction that, if recorded, changes a profit to a loss or changes compliance with ratios in a debt covenant to noncompliance,
- A transaction that might be judged immaterial if it occurred as part of routine operations may be material if its occurrence helps meet certain objectives. For example, a transaction that allows management to achieve a target or obtain a bonus that otherwise would not become due would be considered material, regardless of the actual amount involved.
- Offers to buy or sell assets for more or less than book value, and
- Litigation proceedings against the company pursuant to price-fixing or antitrust allegations, and active negotiations regarding their settlement.

Degree of Precision Another factor in judging materiality is the degree of precision that may be attained when making an estimate. For example, accounts payable can usually be estimated more accurately than a possible loss from the incurrence of an asset retirement obligation. An error amount that would be material in estimating accounts payable might be acceptable in estimating the retirement obligation.

The Conceptual Framework

The conceptual framework is designed to prescribe the nature, function, and limits of financial accounting and reporting and is to be used as a guideline that will lead to consistent standards. FASB has issued eight pronouncements (five of which remain extant) called Statements of Financial Accounting Concepts (CON). These conceptual statements do *not* establish accounting standards or disclosure practices for particular items and are not enforceable under the AICPA Code of Professional Conduct. Since GAAP may be inconsistent with the principles set forth in the conceptual framework, the FASB expects to reexamine existing accounting standards. Until that time, a CON does not require a change in existing GAAP. CON do not amend, modify, or interpret existing GAAP, nor do they justify departing from GAAP based upon interpretations derived from them.

The conceptual framework is a set of interrelated principles that are deduced from a set of foundational assumptions. The objective of financial reporting is the most important because until standards setters know what financial reports are intended to do, they cannot create any other aspect of the framework in a meaningful way. Once standards setters have an objective, then there is a need for other foundational concepts, for example, the going concern assumption. The conceptual framework directs measurement and recognition principles in a particular way. With assumptions in place, the principle can be deduced. Principles are the tools that the Board uses in deciding what items belong in the financial statements; what items should be recognized, presented, and disclosed; and for defining the boundaries of the reporting entity. Using those principles in the creation of accounting standards produces financial reports that meet the objectives of financial reporting.

CON #	Title	Status[2]
1	Objectives of Financial Reporting by Business Enterprises	Replaced by CON 8, Ch. 1
2	Qualitative Characteristics of Accounting Information	Replaced by CON 8, Ch. 3
3	Elements of Financial Statements of Business Enterprises	Replaced by CON 6
4	Objectives of Financial Reporting by Nonbusiness Organizations	Extant
5	Recognition and Measurement in Financial Statements of Business Enterprises	Extant
6	Elements of Financial Statements—A Replacement of FASB Concepts Statement No. 3 (incorporating an amendment of FASB Concepts Statement No. 2)	Extant
7	Using Cash Flow Information and Present Value in Accounting Measurement	Extant
8	Ch. 1—The Objectives of General Preparation of Financial Reporting	Extant
	Ch. 2—Reserved for a chapter on the reporting entity	Reserved
	Ch. 3—Qualitative Characteristics of Useful Financial Information	Extant

FASB's conceptual framework is intended to serve as the foundation upon which the Board can construct standards that are both sound and internally consistent. The fact that the framework was intended to guide FASB in establishing standards is embodied in the preface to CON 8, which states:

> *The Board itself is likely to be the most direct beneficiary of the guidance provided by Concepts Statements. They will guide the Board in developing accounting and reporting standards by providing the Board with a common foundation and basic reasoning on which to consider merits of alternatives.*

The conceptual framework is also intended for use by the business community to help understand and apply standards and to assist in their development. This goal is also mentioned in the preface to CON 8:

> *However, knowledge of the objectives and concepts the Board will use in developing new guidance also should enable those who are affected by or interested in generally accepted accounting standards (GAAP) to understand better the purposes, content, and characteristics of information provided by financial accounting and reporting.*

[2] Ibid.

That knowledge is expected to enhance the usefulness of, and confidence in, financial accounting and reporting. The objectives and fundamental concepts also may provide some guidance in analyzing new or emerging problems of financial accounting and reporting in the absence of applicable authoritative pronouncements.

The FASB Special Report, *The Framework of Financial Accounting Concepts and Standards* (1998), states that the conceptual framework should help solve complex financial accounting or reporting problems by:

- Providing a set of common premises as a basis for discussion;
- Providing precise terminology;
- Helping to ask the right questions;
- Limiting areas of judgment and discretion and excluding from consideration potential solutions that are in conflict with it; and
- Imposing intellectual discipline on what traditionally has been a subjective and ad hoc reasoning process.

Components of the Conceptual Framework The components of the conceptual framework for financial accounting and reporting include objectives, qualitative characteristics, elements, recognition, measurement, and disclosure concepts.

Elements of financial statements are the components from which financial statements are created. They include assets, liabilities, equity, investments by owners, distributions to owners, comprehensive income, revenues, expenses, gains, and losses. In order to be included in financial statements, an element must meet criteria for recognition and possess a characteristic that can be reliably measured. Reporting or display considerations are concerned with what information should be provided, who should provide it, and where it should be displayed. How the financial statements (financial position, earnings, and cash flow) are presented is the focal point of this part of the conceptual framework project.

Of the five extant Concepts Statements, the fourth, *Objectives of Financial Reporting by Nonbusiness Organizations*, is not covered here due to its specialized nature. Because the topics in CON 8 are foundational, this discussion begins with CON 8.

CON 8 is a result of a joint FASB/IASB project to improve and converge their frameworks. The current status of the project can be found on FASB.org.[3]

CON 8—Chapter 1: The Objective of General Purpose Financial Reporting

Chapter 1 identifies the objective of financial reporting and indicates that this objective applies to all financial reporting. It is not limited to financial statements. The objective is to provide information that is useful in making decisions about providing resources to the entity. Users of financial information are identified as existing and potential investors, lenders, and other creditors. Chapter 1 is directed at general-purpose external financial reporting by a business enterprise as it relates to the ability of that enterprise to generate favorable cash flows.

Investors and creditors need financial reports that provide understandable information that will aid in predicting the future cash flows of an entity. The expectation of cash flows affects an

[3] Ibid.

entity's ability to meet the obligations of loans and other forms of credit and to pay interest and dividends, which in turn affects the market price of that entity's stocks and bonds.

To assess cash flows, financial reporting should provide information relative to an enterprise's economic resources, the claims against the entity, and the effects of transactions, events, and circumstances that change resources and claims to resources. A description of these informational needs follows:

- *Economic resources, claims against the entity, and owners' equity*. This information provides the users of financial reporting with a measure of future cash flows and an indication of the entity's strengths, weaknesses, liquidity, and solvency.
- *Economic performance and earnings*. Past performance provides an indication of an entity's future performance. Furthermore, earnings based upon accrual accounting provide a better indicator of economic performance and future cash flows than do current cash receipts and disbursements. Accrual basis earnings are a better indicator because a charge for recovery of capital (depreciation/amortization) is made in determining these earnings. The relationship between earnings and economic performance results from matching the costs and benefits (revenues) of economic activity during a given period by means of accrual accounting. Over the life of an enterprise, economic performance can be determined by net cash flows or by total earnings since the two measures would be equal.
- *Liquidity, solvency, and funds flows*. Information about cash and other funds flows from borrowings, repayments of borrowings, expenditures, capital transactions, economic resources, obligations, owners' equity, and earnings may aid the user of financial reporting information in assessing a firm's liquidity or solvency.
- *Management stewardship and performance*. The assessment of a firm's management with respect to the efficient and profitable use of the firm's resources is usually made on the basis of economic performance as reported by periodic earnings. Because earnings are affected by factors other than current management performance, earnings may not be a reliable indicator of management performance.
- *Management explanations and interpretations*. Management is responsible for the efficient use of a firm's resources. Thus, it acquires knowledge about the enterprise and its performance that is unknown to the external user. Explanations by management concerning the financial impact of transactions, events, circumstances, uncertainties, estimates, judgments, and any effects of the separation of the results of operations into periodic measures of performance enhance the usefulness of financial information.

CON 8—Chapter 3: Qualitative Characteristics of Useful Financial Information

The purpose of financial reporting is to provide decision makers with useful information. Individuals or standard-setting bodies should make accounting choices based upon the usefulness of that information to the decision-making process. CON 8—Chapter 3 identifies the qualities or characteristics that make information useful in the decision-making process. It also establishes a terminology to provide a greater understanding of the characteristics.

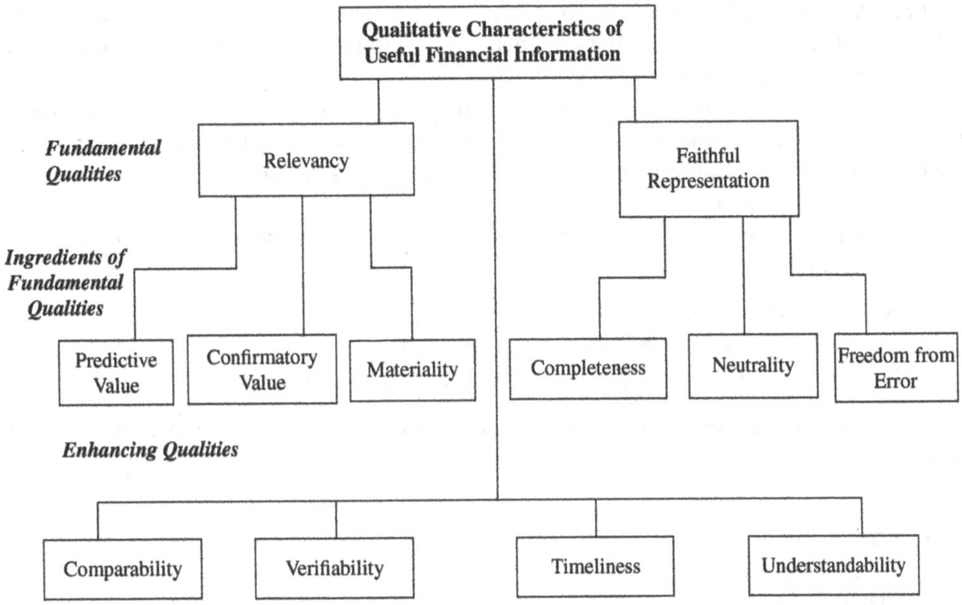

Fundamental Qualitative Characteristics Information must be useful to be beneficial to the user. To be useful, accounting information must both be *relevant* and *faithfully represent* what it claims to represent.

Relevance Information is relevant to a decision if it makes a difference to the decision maker's ability to predict events or to confirm or correct expectations. Relevant information will reduce the decision maker's assessment of the uncertainty of the outcome of a decision even though it may not change the decision itself. Information is relevant if it provides knowledge concerning:

- Past events (confirmatory value). Disclosure information is relevant because it provides information about past events.
- Future events (predictive value) and if it is timely. The predictive value of accounting information does not imply that such information is a prediction. The predictive value refers to the utility that a piece of information has as an input into a predictive model.

An item of information is material and should be reported if it is significant enough to have an effect on the decision maker. Materiality is entity specific. It is dependent upon the relative size of an item and nature of the item. Because materiality is evaluated in the context of an individual entity's financial report, the FASB could not offer quantitative standards of materiality.

Faithful representation Financial statements are an abstraction of the activities of a business enterprise. They simplify the activities of the actual entity. To be faithfully representative, financial statements must portray the important financial relationships of the entity itself. Information is faithfully representative if it is:

Complete,
Neutral, and
Free from errors.

Complete A complete representation contains all the information that would enable users to understand the information. In addition to quantitative information, a particular item may need to include a description and explanation.

Neutral Neutral means that accounting information should serve to communicate without attempting to influence behavior in a particular direction. This does not mean that accounting should not influence behavior or that it should affect everyone in the same way. It means that information should not favor certain interest groups.

Free from error Free from error does not mean perfectly accurate. However, it does mean that a description is:

- Accurately described,
- The explanation of the phenomenon is explained, and
- No errors have been made in selecting and reporting the process.

Enhancing Qualities Information that is relevant and faithfully represented can be enhanced by:

- Comparability,
- Verifiability,
- Timeliness, and
- Understandability.

These enhancing characteristics also may be the determinative factors when considering how to present information that is equally relevant and faithfully represented.

Comparability To be useful, accounting information should be comparable. The characteristic of comparability allows the users of accounting information to assess the similarities and differences either among different entities for the same time period or for the same entity over different time periods. Comparisons are usually made on the basis of quantifiable measurements of a common characteristic. Therefore, to be comparable, the measurements used must be reliable with respect to the common characteristic. Noncomparability can result from the use of different inputs, procedures, or systems of classification.

Related to comparability, consistency is an interperiod comparison that requires the use of the same accounting principles from one period to another. Although a change of an accounting principle to a more preferred method results in inconsistency, the change is acceptable if the effect of the change is disclosed. Consistency, however, does not ensure comparability. If the measurements used are not representationally faithful, comparability will not be achieved.

Verifiability Verifiability means that several independent measures will obtain the same accounting measure. An accounting measure that can be repeated with the same result (consensus) is desirable because it serves to detect and reduce measurer bias. Cash is highly verifiable. Inventories and depreciable assets tend to be less verifiable because alternative valuation methods exist. The direct verification of an accounting measure would serve to minimize measurer bias and measurement bias. The verification of the procedures used to obtain the measure would minimize measurer bias only. Finally, verifiability does not guarantee representational faithfulness or relevance.

Timeliness Although timeliness alone will not make information useful, information must be timely to be useful.

Understandability Financial reports must be understandable for users who have a "reasonable knowledge of business and economic activities and who review and analyze the information diligently" (CON 8, QC 32).

Trade-Offs Although it is desirable that accounting information contains the characteristics that have been identified above, not all of these characteristics are compatible. Often, one characteristic may be obtained only by sacrificing another. The trade-offs that must be made are determined on the basis of the relative importance of the characteristics. This relative importance, in turn, is dependent upon the nature of the users and their particular needs.

Cost Constraint The qualitative characteristics of useful accounting information are subject to a constraint: the relative cost-benefit of that information. Associated with the benefits to the user of accounting information is the cost of using that information and of providing it to the user. Information should be provided only if its benefits exceed its cost. Unfortunately, it is difficult to value the benefit of accounting information. It is also difficult to determine whether the burden of the cost of disclosure and the benefits of such disclosure are distributed fairly.

CON 8—Chapter 8: Notes to Financial Statements

In August 2018, the FASB added a new chapter to CON 8: Chapter 8, *Notes to Financial Statements*. Chapter 8 gives the Board a framework for setting disclosure requirements on individual standards-level projects. This new chapter is designed to improve the Board's process for setting requirements and describes

- the purpose of notes,
- the nature of appropriate content, and
- general limitations on disclosures, such as cost constraints and unintended consequences.

CON 5: Recognition and Measurement in Financial Statements of Business Enterprises

CON 5 indicates that financial statements are the principal means of communicating useful financial information. A full set of such statements contains:

- Financial position at end of the period
- Earnings for the period
- Comprehensive income for the period
- Cash flows during the period
- Investments by and distributions to owners during the period.

Financial statements result from simplifying, condensing, and aggregating transactions. Therefore, no one financial statement provides sufficient information by itself and no one item or part of each statement can summarize the information.

A statement of financial position provides information about an entity's assets, liabilities, and equity. Earnings are a measure of entity performance during a period. Earnings are similar to net income but exclude accounting adjustments from earlier periods such as cumulative effect changes in accounting principles. Comprehensive income comprises all recognized changes in equity other than those arising from investments by and distributions to owners. A statement of cash flows reflects receipts and payments of cash by major sources and uses including operating, financing, and investing activities. The investments by and distributions to owners reflect the capital transactions of an entity during a period.

Income is determined by the concept of financial capital maintenance, which means that only if the money amount of net assets increases during a period (excluding capital transactions) is there a profit. For recognition in financial statements, subject to both cost-benefit and materiality constraints, an item must meet the following criteria:

1. Definition—Meet the definition of an element in financial statements
2. Measurability—Have a relevant attribute measurable with sufficient reliability
3. Relevance
4. Reliability

Items reported in the financial statements are based on historical cost, replacement cost, market value, net realizable value, and present value of cash flows. Price level changes are not recognized in these statements and conservatism guides the application of recognition criteria.

CON 6: Elements of Financial Statements

CON 3 was replaced by CON 6. CON 6 carried forward essentially all of the concepts in CON 3 and added the elements unique to the financial statements of not-for-profit organizations. CON 6 defines ten interrelated elements that are used in the financial statements of business enterprises:

1. *Assets*—Probable future economic benefits obtained or controlled by a particular entity as a result of past transactions or events.
2. *Liabilities*—Probable future sacrifices of economic benefits arising from present obligations of a particular entity to transfer assets or provide services to other entities in the future as a result of past transactions or events.
3. *Equity (Net Assets)*—The residual interest in the assets that remains after deducting its liabilities. In a business enterprise, equity is the ownership interest.
4. *Revenues*—Inflows or other enhancements of assets of an entity or settlement of its liabilities (or a combination of both) from delivering or producing goods, rendering services, or other activities that constitute the entity's ongoing major and central operations.
5. *Expenses*—Outflows or other using up of assets or incurrences of liabilities (or a combination of both) from delivering or producing goods, rendering services, or carrying out other activities that constitute the entity's ongoing major and central operations.
6. *Gains*—Increases in equity (net assets) from peripheral or incidental transactions of an entity and from all other transactions and other events and circumstances affecting the entity except those that result from revenues or investments by owners.
7. *Losses*—Decreases in equity (net assets) from peripheral or incidental transactions of an entity and from all other transactions and other events and circumstances affecting the entity except those that result from expenses or distributions to owners.
8. *Comprehensive Income*—The change in equity of a business enterprise during a period from transactions and other events and circumstances from sources other than investments by owners or distributions to owners.
9. *Investments by Owners*—Increases in equity of a particular business enterprise resulting from transfers to it for the purpose of increasing ownership interests.
10. *Distributions to Owners*—Decreases in the equity of a particular business enterprise resulting from transferring assets, rendering services, or incurring liabilities to owners.

Revenues are commonly distinguished from gains for three reasons. See the table below:

Revenues	**Gains**
Result from an entity's central operations	Result from incidental or peripheral activities of the entity
Are usually earned	Result from nonreciprocal transactions (such as winning a lawsuit or receiving a gift) or other economic events for which there is no earnings process
Are reported gross	Are reported net

Expenses are commonly distinguished from losses for three reasons:

Expenses	**Losses**
Result from an entity's central operations	Result from incidental or peripheral activities of the entity
Often incurred during the earnings process	Often result from nonreciprocal transactions (such as thefts or fines) or other economic events unrelated to an earnings process
Reported gross	Reported net

Definitions of Terms CON 6 also defines several significant financial accounting and reporting terms that are used in the Concepts Statements (and FASB pronouncements issued after the Concepts Statements).

An *event* is a happening of consequence to an entity. It can be an internal event (the use of raw materials) or an external event with another entity (the purchase of labor) or with the environment in which the business operates (a technological advance by a competitor).

A *transaction* is a particular kind of event. It is an external event that involves transferring something of value to another entity.

Circumstances are a condition, or set of conditions, that create situations that might otherwise not have occurred and might not have been anticipated.

Accrual is the accounting process of recognizing the effects of future cash receipts and payments in the current period. Accrual accounting attempts to record the financial effects on an entity of transactions and of other events and circumstances that have consequences for the entity in the periods in which those transactions, events, and circumstances occur rather than in the periods in which cash is received or paid by the entity.

Deferral is the accounting process of recognizing a liability resulting from a current cash receipt or an asset resulting from a current cash payment.

Realization is the process of converting noncash assets into cash.

Recognition is the process of formally incorporating a transaction or other event into the financial statements.

Matching is the simultaneous recognition of the revenues and expenses that result directly and jointly from the same transaction or other event.

Allocation is the process of assigning expenses to periods when the transactions or events that cause the using up of the benefits cannot be identified or when the cause can be identified but the actual amount of benefit used up cannot be reliably measured.

Elements of Not-for-Profit Financial Statements Of the ten elements listed previously, seven are used by not-for-profit organizations. The three elements omitted are investments by owners, distributions to owners, and comprehensive income. The net assets (equity) of not-for-profit organizations is divided into three classes—unrestricted, temporarily restricted, and permanently restricted— based on the existence or absence of donor-imposed restrictions.

CON 7: Using Cash Flow Information and Present Value in Accounting Measurements

CON 7 provides a framework for using estimates of future cash flows as the basis for accounting measurements either at initial recognition or when assets are subsequently remeasured at fair value and for using the interest method of amortization. It provides the principles that govern measurement using present value, especially when the amount of future cash flows, their timing, or both are uncertain. However, it does not address recognition questions, such as which transactions and events should be valued using present value measures. Fair value is the objective for most measurements at initial recognition and for fresh-start measurements in subsequent periods. At initial recognition, the cash paid or received (historical cost or proceeds) is usually assumed to be fair value, absent evidence to the contrary. For fresh-start measurements, a price that is observed in the marketplace for an essentially similar asset or liability is fair value. If purchase prices and market prices are available, there is no need to use alternative measurement techniques to approximate fair value. However, if alternative measurement techniques must be used for initial recognition and for fresh-start measurements, those techniques should attempt to capture the elements that when taken together would comprise a market price if one existed. The objective is to estimate the price likely to exist in the marketplace if there were a marketplace fair value.

CON 7 states that the only objective of using present value in accounting measurements is fair value. It is necessary to capture, to the extent possible, the economic differences in the marketplace between sets of estimated future cash flows. A present value measurement that fully captures those differences must include the following elements:

1. An estimate of the future cash flow, or in more complex cases, series of future cash flows at different times;
2. 2 Expectations about possible variations in the amount or timing of those cash flows;
3. The time value of money, represented by the risk-free rate of interest;
4. The risk premium—the price for bearing the uncertainty inherent in the asset or liability;
5. Other factors, including illiquidity and market imperfections.

How CON 7 Measures Differ from Previously Utilized Present Value Techniques Previously employed present value techniques typically used a single set of estimated cash flows and a single discount (interest) rate. In applying those techniques, adjustments for factors 2 through 5 described in the previous section are incorporated in the selection of the discount rate. In the CON 7 approach, only the third factor listed (the time value of money) is included in the discount rate; the other factors cause adjustments in arriving at risk-adjusted expected cash flows. CON 7 introduces the probability-weighted, expected cash flow approach, which focuses on the range of possible estimated cash flows and estimates of their respective probabilities of occurrence.

Previous techniques used to compute present value used estimates of the cash flows most likely to occur. CON 7 refines and enhances the precision of this model by weighting different cash flow scenarios (regarding the amounts and timing of cash flows) by their estimated probabilities of occurrence and factoring these scenarios into the ultimate determination of fair value.

The difference is that values are assigned to the cash flows other than the most likely one. To illustrate, a cash flow might be $100, $200, or $300, with probabilities of 10%, 50%, and 40%, respectively. The most likely cash flow is the one with 50% probability, or $200. The expected cash flow is $230 [=($100 × .1) + ($200 × .5) + ($300 × .4)].

The CON 7 method, unlike previous present value techniques, can also accommodate uncertainty in the timing of cash flows. For example, a cash flow of $10,000 may be received in one year, two years, or three years, with probabilities of 15%, 60%, and 25%, respectively. Traditional present value techniques would compute the present value using the most likely timing of the payment—two years. The example below shows the computation of present value using the CON 7 method. Again, the expected present value of $9,030 differs from the traditional notion of a best estimate of $9,070 (the 60% probability) in this example:

Present value of $10,000 in 1 year discounted at 5%	$9,523	
Multiplied by 15% probability		$1,428
Present value of $10,000 in 2 years discounted at 5%	$9,070	
Multiplied by 60% probability		5,442
Present value of $10,000 in 3 years discounted at 5%	$8,638	
Multiplied by 25% probability		2,160
Probability weighted expected present value		$9,030

Measuring Liabilities The measurement of liabilities involves different problems from the measurement of assets; however, the underlying objective is the same. When using present value techniques to estimate the fair value of a liability, the objective is to estimate the value of the assets required currently to (1) settle the liability with the holder or (2) transfer the liability to an entity of comparable credit standing. To estimate the fair value of an entity's notes or bonds payable, accountants look to the price at which other entities are willing to hold the entity's liabilities as assets. For example, the proceeds of a loan are the price that a lender paid to hold the borrower's promise of future cash flows as an asset.

The most relevant measurement of an entity's liabilities should always reflect the credit standing of the entity. An entity with a good credit standing will receive more cash for its promise to pay than an entity with a poor credit standing. For example, if two entities both promise to pay $750 in three years with no stated interest payable in the interim, Entity A, with a good credit standing, might receive about $630 (a 6% interest rate). Entity B, with a poor credit standing, might receive about $533 (a 12% interest rate). Each entity initially records its respective liability at fair value, which is the amount of proceeds received—an amount that incorporates that entity's credit standing.

Present value techniques can also be used to value a guarantee of a liability. Assume that Entity B in the above example owes Entity C. If Entity A were to assume the debt, it would want to be compensated $630—the amount that it could get in the marketplace for its promise to pay $750 in three years. The difference between what Entity A would want to take the place of Entity B ($630) and the amount that Entity B receives ($533) is the value of the guarantee ($97).

Interest Method of Allocation CON 7 describes the factors that suggest that an interest method of allocation should be used. It states that the interest method of allocation is more relevant than other methods of cost allocation when it is applied to assets and liabilities that exhibit one or more of the following characteristics:

1. The transaction is, in substance, a borrowing and lending transaction.
2. Period-to-period allocation of similar assets or liabilities employs an interest method.
3. A particular set of estimated future cash flows is closely associated with the asset or liability.
4. The measurement at initial recognition was based on present value.

Accounting for Changes in Expected Cash Flows If the timing or amount of estimated cash flows changes and the asset or liability is not remeasured at a fresh-start measure, the interest method of allocation should be altered by a catch-up approach. That approach adjusts the carrying amount to the present value of the revised estimated future cash flows, discounted at the original effective interest rate.

Application of Present Value Tables and Formulas *Present value of a single future amount.* To take the present value of a single amount that will be paid in the future, apply the following formula, in which PV is the present value of $1 paid in the future, r is the interest rate per period, and n is the number of periods between the current date and the future date when the amount will be realized:

$$PV = 1/(1+r)^n$$

In many cases the results of this formula are summarized in a present value factor table:

(*n*) Periods	2%	3%	4%	5%	6%	7%	8%	9%	10%
1	0.9804	0.9709	0.9615	0.9524	0.9434	0.9346	0.9259	0.9174	0.9091
2	0.9612	0.9426	0.9246	0.9070	0.8900	0.8734	0.8573	0.8417	0.8265
3	0.9423	0.9151	0.8890	0.8638	0.8396	0.8163	0.7938	0.7722	0.7513
4	0.9239	0.8885	0.8548	0.8227	0.7921	0.7629	0.7350	0.7084	0.6830
5	0.9057	0.8626	0.8219	0.7835	0.7473	0.7130	0.6806	0.6499	0.6209

Example of a Present Value Calculation

Suppose one wishes to determine how much would need to be invested today to have $10,000 in 5 years if the sum invested would earn 8%. Looking across the row with $n = 5$ and finding the present value factor for the $r = 8\%$ column, the factor of 0.6806 would be identified. Multiplying $10,000 by 0.6806 results in $6,806, the amount that would need to be invested today to have $10,000 at the end of 5 years. Alternatively, using a calculator and applying the present value of a single sum formula, one could multiply $10,000 by $1/(1 + .08)^5$, which would also give the same answer—$6,806.

Present value of a series of equal payments (an annuity) Many times in business situations a series of equal payments paid at equal time intervals is required. Examples of these include payments of semiannual bond interest and principal or lease payments. The present value of each of these payments could be added up to find the present value of this annuity, or alternatively a much simpler approach is available. The formula for calculating the present value of an annuity of $1 payments over *n* periodic payments at a periodic interest rate of *r* is:

$$PV\ Annuity = \frac{\left(1 - \frac{1}{(1+r)^n}\right)}{r}$$

The results of this formula are summarized in an annuity present value factor table:

(*n*) Periods	2%	3%	4%	5%	6%	7%	8%	9%	10%
1	0.9804	0.9709	0.9615	0.9524	0.9434	0.9346	0.9259	0.9174	0.9091
2	1.9416	1.9135	1.8861	1.8594	1.8334	1.8080	1.7833	1.7591	1.7355
3	2.8839	2.8286	2.7751	2.7233	2.6730	2.6243	2.5771	2.5313	2.4869
4	3.8077	3.7171	3.6299	3.5460	3.4651	3.3872	3.3121	3.2397	3.1699
5	4.7135	4.5797	4.4518	4.3295	4.2124	4.1002	3.9927	3.8897	3.7908

Example of an Annuity Present Value Calculation

Suppose four annual payments of $1,000 will be needed to satisfy an agreement with a supplier. What would be the amount of the liability today if the interest rate the supplier is charging is 6% per year? Using the table to get the present value factor, the $n = 4$ periods row, and the 6% column, gives you a factor of 3.4651. Multiply this by $1,000 and you get a liability of $3,465.10 that should be recorded. Using the formula would also give you the same answer with $r = 6\%$ and $n = 4$.

Caution must be exercised when payments are not to be made on an annual basis. If payments are on a semiannual basis, $n = 8$, but *r* is now 3%. This is because *r* is the periodic interest rate, and the semiannual rate would not be 6%, but half of the 6% annual rate. Note that this is somewhat simplified, since due to the effect of compound interest 3% semiannually is slightly more than a 6% annual rate.

Example of the Relevance of Present Values

A measurement based on the present value of estimated future cash flows provides more relevant information than a measurement based on the undiscounted sum of those cash flows. For example, consider the following four future cash flows, all of which have an undiscounted value of $100,000:

1. Asset A has a fixed contractual cash flow of $100,000 due tomorrow. The cash flow is certain of receipt.
2. Asset B has a fixed contractual cash flow of $100,000 due in 20 years. The cash flow is certain of receipt.
3. Asset C has a fixed contractual cash flow of $100,000 due in 20 years. The amount that ultimately will be received is uncertain. There is an 80% probability that the entire $100,000 will be received. There is a 20% probability that $80,000 will be received.
4. Asset D has an *expected* cash flow of $100,000 due in 20 years. The amount that ultimately will be received is uncertain. There is a 25% probability that $120,000 will be received. There is a 50% probability that $100,000 will be received. There is a 25% probability that $80,000 will be received.

Assuming a 5% risk-free rate of return, the present values of the assets are:

1. Asset A has a present value of $99,986. The time value of money assigned to the one-day period is $14 [$100,000 × .05/365 days].
2. Asset B has a present value of $37,689 [$100,000/(1 + .05)^{20}].
3. Asset C has a present value of $36,181 [(100,000 × .8 + 80,000 × .2)/(1 + .05)^{20}].
4. Asset D has a present value of $37,689 [($120,000 × .25 + 100,000 × .5 + 80,000 × .25)/ (1 + .05)^{20}].

Although each of these assets has the same undiscounted cash flows, few would argue that they are economically the same or that a rational investor would pay the same price for each. Investors require compensation for the time value of money. They also require a risk premium. That is, given a choice between Asset B with expected cash flows that are certain and Asset D with cash flows of the same expected amount that are uncertain, investors will place a higher value on Asset B, even though they have the same expected present value. CON 7 says that the risk premium should be subtracted from the expected cash flows before applying the discount rate. Thus, if the risk premium for Asset D was $500, the risk-adjusted present values would be $37,500 {[($120,000 × .25 + 100,000 × .5 + 80,000 × .25) – 500]/(1 + .05)^{20}}.

Practical Matters Like any accounting measurement, the application of an expected cash flow approach is subject to a cost-benefit constraint. The cost of obtaining additional information must be weighed against the additional reliability that information will bring to the measurement. As a practical matter, an entity that uses present value measurements often has little or no information about some or all of the assumptions that investors would use in assessing the fair value of an asset or a liability. Instead, the entity must use the information that is available to it without undue cost and effort when it develops cash flow estimates. The entity's own assumptions about future cash flows can be used to estimate fair value using present value techniques, as long as there are no contrary data indicating that investors would use different assumptions. However, if contrary data exist, the entity must adjust its assumptions to incorporate that market information.

2 ASC 205 PRESENTATION OF FINANCIAL STATEMENTS

PERSPECTIVE AND ISSUES

Subtopics

ASC 205, *Presentation of Financial Statements*, is divided into four subtopics:

- ASC 205-10, *Overall*, which emphasizes the value of comparative financial statements.
- ASC 205-20, *Discontinued Operations*, which provides guidance on reporting the results of operations when:
  - A component of an entity has been disposed of or is classified as held for sale, and
  - A business or nonprofit activity that, on acquisition, is classified as held for sale.
- ASC 205-30, *Liquidation Basis of Accounting*, provides guidance on when and how to prepare liquidation basis of accounting financial statements and the related disclosures.
- ASC 204-40, *Going Concern*, which provides guidance for evaluating whether there is substantial doubt about an entity's ability to continue as a going concern.

Scope and Scope Exceptions

ASC 205-10 The guidance in ASC 205-10 applies to

- All subtopics in ASC 205-10 unless explicitly excluded
- Business entities and not-for-profit entities
(ASC 205-10-15-1)

ASC 205-20 The guidance in 205-20 applies to either:

- A component of an entity or a group of components that is disposed of or is classified as held for sale, *or*
- A business or nonprofit entity that, on acquisition, is classified as held for sale.
(ASC 205-20-15-2)

The guidance does *not* apply to oil and gas properties that use the full-cost method of accounting prescribed by the SEC. (ASC 205-20-15-3)

ASC 205-30 ASC 205-30 does not apply to companies registered under the Investment Company Act of 1945. (ASC 205-30-15-1)

ASC 205-40 ASC 205-40 applies to all entities. (ASC 205-40-15-1)

DEFINITIONS OF TERMS

Source: ASC 205, *Glossaries*. Also see Appendix A, *Definitions of Terms*, for other terms related to this topic: Business, Component of an Entity, Comprehensive Income, Disposal Group, Fair Value, Financial Statements Are Available to Be Issued, Financial Statements Are Issued, Firm Purchase Commitment, Market Participants, Net Income, Nonprofit Activity, Not-for-Profit Entity, Operating Segment, Orderly Transactions, Other Comprehensive Income, Probable, Public Business Entity, Related Parties, Remote, Reporting Unit.

Asset Group. An asset group is the unit of accounting for a long-lived asset or assets to be held and used, which represents the lowest level for which identifiable cash flows are largely independent of the cash flows of other groups of assets and liabilities.

Liquidation. The process by which an entity converts its assets to cash or other assets and settles its obligations with creditors in anticipation of the entity ceasing all activities. Upon cessation of the entity's activities, any remaining cash or other assets are distributed to the entity's investors or other claimants (albeit sometimes indirectly). Liquidation may be compulsory or voluntary. Dissolution of an entity as a result of that entity being acquired by another entity or merged into another entity in its entirety and with the expectation of continuing its business does not qualify as liquidation.

Settlement of a Pension or Postretirement Benefit Obligation. A transaction that is an irrevocable action, relieves the employer (or the plan) of primary responsibility for a pension or postretirement benefit obligation, and eliminates significant risks related to the obligation and the assets used to effect the settlement.

Statement of Changes in Net Assets in Liquidation. A statement that presents the changes during the period in net assets available for distribution to investors and other claimants during liquidation.

Statement of Net Assets in Liquidation. A statement that presents a liquidating entity's net assets available for distribution to investors and other claimants as of the end of the reporting period.

Substantial Doubt About an Entity's Ability to Continue as a Going Concern. Substantial doubt about an entity's ability to continue as a going concern exists when conditions and events, considered in the aggregate, indicate that it is probable that the entity will be unable to meet its obligations as they become due within one year after the date that the financial statements are issued (or within one year after the date that the financial statements are available to be issued when applicable). The term *probable* is used consistently with its use in Topic 450 on contingencies.

CONCEPTS, RULES, AND EXAMPLES

ASC 205-10, *Overall*

Comparative Statements To increase the usefulness of financial statements, many entities include financial statements for one or more prior years in their annual reports. Some also include five- or ten-year summaries of condensed financial information. Comparative financial statements allow investment analysts and other interested readers to perform comparative analysis of pertinent information. ASC 205-10-45-1 explains that the presentation of comparative financial statements in annual reports enhances the usefulness of such reports and brings out more clearly the nature and trends of current changes affecting the enterprise. Comparative presentation emphasizes the fact that the statements for a series of periods are far more significant than those for a single period and that the accounts for one period are but an installment of what is essentially a continuous history. The full set of financial statements is listed in Appendix B.

Changes Affecting Comparability ASC 205 emphasizes the principle of comparability and the importance of consistency to comparability. To the extent they remain significant, notes to financial statements should be repeated in comparative statements or at least referred to. Any exceptions to comparability must be disclosed as described in ASC 250. (ASC 205-10-45-3) If because of reclassification or other reasons the manner of or basis for presenting corresponding items has changed, that change must be explained. (ASC 205-10-50-1)

Reclassifications Occasionally, a company will choose to change the way it applies an accounting principle, resulting in a change in the way that a particular financial statement caption is displayed or in the individual general ledger accounts that comprise a caption. These reclassifications may occur for a variety of reasons, including:

- In the entity's judgment, the revised methodology more accurately reflects the economics of a type or class of transaction.
- An amount that was immaterial in previous periods and combined with another number has become material and warrants presentation as a separately captioned line item.
- Due to changes in the business or the manner in which the financial statements are used to make decisions, the entity deems a different form of presentation to be more useful or informative.

To maintain comparability of financial statements when such changes are made, the financial statements of all periods presented must be reclassified to conform to the new presentation.

Such reclassifications, which usually affect only the statement of income, do not affect reported net income or retained earnings for any period since they result in simply recasting amounts that were previously reported. Normally, a reclassification will result in an increase in one or more reported numbers with a corresponding decrease in one or more other numbers. In addition, these changes reflect changes in the application of accounting principles either for which there are multiple alternative treatments or for which GAAP is silent, and thus the entity has discretion in presentation.

Reclassifications are not explicitly dealt with in GAAP, but as mentioned in the chapter on ASC 205, the Codification emphasizes the need for comparability (ASC 205-10-45-3) and reclassifications do commonly occur in practice.

ASC 205-20, *Discontinued Operations*

The Codification requires entities to report discontinued operations separately on the balance sheet. The objective of this rule is to provide comparability for an entity's continuing operations. ASC 205-20 provides guidance on which disposals can be presented as discontinued operations.

Determining When a Disposal Should Be Presented as a Discontinued Operation The unit of account for a discontinued operation is:

- A component of an entity,
- A group of components of an entity, or
- A business or nonprofit entity.

The guidance describes a discontinued operation as a disposal of a component or group of components that:

- Is disposed of by sale, classified as held for sale, or disposed by other than sale (for example, by abandonment, exchange, or distribution to owner), *and*
- Represents a strategic shift that has (or will have) a major effect on an entity's operations and financial results.

(ASC 205-20-45-1B)

Exhibit—Classification as a Discontinued Operation

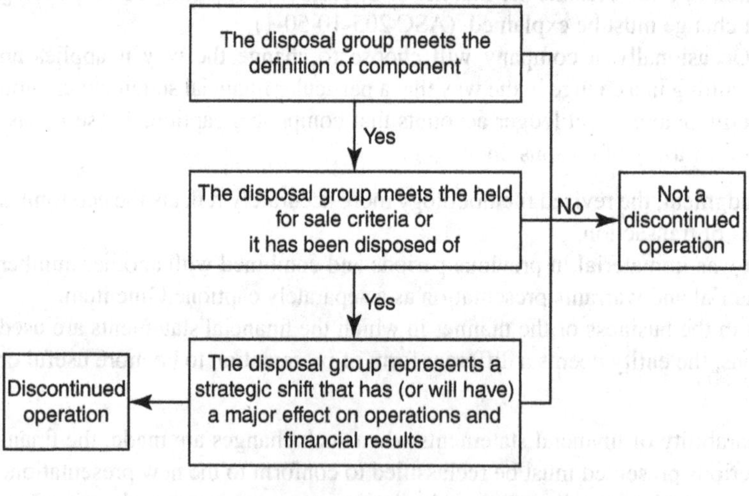

The Concept of a Strategic Shift The guidance states that a strategic shift could include:

- A major geographical area of operations,
- A major line of business,
- A major equity method investment, or

- Other major parts of an entity.
(ASC 205-20-45-1C)

Strategic shift is an entity-specific concept, based on the qualitative and quantitative conditions of a particular entity. Entities need to use considerable judgment to determine whether a strategic shift has occurred. The guidance does not define "major" in the phrase "strategic shift that has (or will have) a major effect on an entity's operations and financial results" and avoids using a bright line quantitative threshold measurement when determining whether a strategic shift exists. The guidance does provide several detailed case studies with the following sales measures:

- Product line that represents 15% of a reporting entity's total revenues
- Geographical area that represents 20% of a reporting entity's total assets
- All stores in one of its two types of formats that represents 30% of historic net income and 15% of current period net income
- Component that is an equity method investment representing 20% of the entity's total assets
- 80% of a product line that accounts for 40% of total revenue

Even with reference to the examples, there is a degree of judgment involved in making the determination of whether a major shift has occurred.

Classification as Held for Sale A component or group of components is classified as held for sale in the period in which *all* of the following occur:

a. Management commits to a plan to sell the entity.
b. The entity to be sold is available for immediate sale.
c. The entity has taken action to complete the plan, including a program to find a buyer or other actions.
d. The sale or transfer of the entity to be sold is probable and is expected to be recognized as a completed sale within one year, unless events beyond the entity's control occur.
e. The entity to be sold is being actively marketed at a price that is reasonable in relation to its current fair value, indicating the entity's intent and ability to sell the entity, and the entity to be sold is available for immediate sale.
f. Actions required to complete the plan to sell make it unlikely that the plan will be withdrawn or changed in any significant way.
(ASC 205-20-45-1E)

These criteria mirror those in ASC 360-10-45-9. For those components that have been disposed of or classified as held for sale, but that do not meet the requirements for reporting as discontinued operations, the entity should look to ASC 360-10-45 on long-lived assets classified as held for sale or to be disposed of for guidance. (ASC 205-10-05-3A)

If at any time the criteria for held for sale are no longer met, the entity to be sold is reclassified as held and used and accounted for using the guidance in ASC 360. (ASC 205-20-45-1F)

Any business or nonprofit activity that on the date of acquisition meets the held for sale criteria must be presented as a discontinued operation whether or not it meets the strategic shift criteria. (ASC 205-20-45-1D) This avoids including in operations an activity that will never be part of continuing operations.

Entities may be excepted from the one-year requirement if:

- When the entity commits to a plan to sell, the entity expects that other than the buyer will impose conditions that will extend the tie required to sell and:
  - A firm purchase commitment must be obtained to respond to those conditions and
  - The firm purchase commitment is probable within one year.
- The entity obtains a firm purchase commitment and the buyer or others impose conditions on the transfer of an entity previously classified as held for sale and those conditions will extend the sale completion period. In this situation, both of the following conditions must be met:
  - Actions necessary to respond to the conditions have been or will be timely initiated.
  - The entity expects a favorable resolution of the delaying factors.
- During the one-year period unexpected circumstances arise that delay the sale beyond one year. The following conditions must be met:
  - The entity initiated actions during the one-year period to respond to the change.
  - The entity is actively marketing the entity to be sold at a reasonable price.
  - The criteria in ASC 205-20-45-1E above are met. (ASC 205-20-45-1G)

Example—Determination of Whether to Report Discontinued Operations

Software Solutions Plus offers four major product lines. It has a children's educational line, a children's game line, a business office line, and a desktop publishing line. The product line is the lowest level at which the operations and cash flows can be clearly distinguished by management. Each line is branded and has distinguishable operations and cash flow. Therefore, each product line includes a group of components of the entity.

Case 1—Software Solutions Plus decides to shift its strategy and exit the game business and commits to a plan to sell the children's game line. The assets and liabilities of the product line are classified as held for sale at that date. Software Solutions Plus has decided that it will not develop any new computer games for the children's market. In this case, the conditions are met to report the children's game line as a discontinued operation.

Case 2—Instead of exiting the children's game business entirely as in Case 1, Software Solutions Plus decides to keep its game programmers on its staff and have them develop new children's games. However, instead of selling the games to the home market via distributors as it had been doing, each existing and newly developed game will be marketed and sold to other software game companies. Software Solutions Plus will not provide technical support for any particular game software after it is sold. It will continue to have revenues and expenses related to the children's game product line. Thus, management concludes there is not a major strategic shift. The change in the manner of marketing the line cannot be reported in discontinued operations.

Case 3—Discontinued Product Not a Component of the Entity. Software Solutions Plus decides to discontinue developing and selling its graphics drawing program product, which is part of the desktop publishing product line. In this case, because the graphics drawing program product is not a component of the entity on its own, but instead is part of the component desktop publishing product line, the sale of the graphics drawing program cannot be reported in discontinued operations.

Presentation—Balance Sheet In the period that a discontinued operation is classified as held for sale or is disposed of and for all prior reporting periods, entities must separately present assets and liabilities of the discontinued operation on the face of the balance sheet. Those assets and liabilities should not be offset and presented as a single line item. Disposal groups may meet the held-for-sale criteria of a discontinued operation but not meet the definition of a discontinued operation. In those cases, the entity must separately present assets and liabilities on the face of the balance sheet in the period in which the disposal group is classified as held for sale and the entity does not have to reclassify previously reported amounts. (ASC 205-20-45-10)

The entity must also disclose the major classes of assets and liabilities of a discontinued operation on the face of the balance sheet or in the notes. (ASC 205-20-45-11 and 205-20-50-5B(e)) Guidance does not specify the major classes, but one of the examples includes cash, trade receivables, inventories, property, plant and equipment, trade payables, and short-term borrowings.

Presentation—Income Statement In the period in which a component of an entity is reported as a discontinued operation, the results of operations of that component are reported as a separate component of income, before the cumulative effect of accounting changes. Any gain or loss recognized on disposal is reported separately on the face of the income statement or disclosed in the notes. The income statements of any prior periods being presented should be restated to also reflect the results of operations of the component as discontinued operations. All amounts should be reported less applicable income taxes (benefits), as shown in the example below. If a disposal does not qualify as a discontinued operation, it should be included in income from continuing operations. (ASC 205-20-45-3, 45-3A, and 45-3B)

The gain or loss is calculated based on guidance in other topics. For example, if the discontinued operation is within the scope of ASC 360, *Property, Plant and Equipment*, guidance can be found in that topic and in the related chapter in this book. (ASC 205-20-45-3C)

Example of Income Statement Presentation for Discontinued Operations

	20X2	*20X1*
Income from continuing operations before income taxes	$ 598	$ 583
Income taxes	239	233
Income from continuing operations	359	350
Discontinued operations (Note ___)		
Loss from operations of discontinued component	1,165	1,045
Loss on disposal of discontinued component	167	
Income tax benefit	532	418
Loss on discontinued operations	800	277
Net income	$ (441)	$ (282)

Treatment of Other Items	
Allocation of overhead	General corporate overhead may not be allocated to discontinued operations. (ASC 205-20-45-9)
Interest—buyer assumes debt of the entity or the entity is required to repay debt	Allocated to discontinued operations. (ASC 205-20-45-6)
Interest—other consolidated interest	Allocation to discontinued operations is permitted but not required. (ASC 205-20-45-7) If allocated, look to guidance in ASC 205-20-55.

Adjustments to Amounts Previously Reported Circumstances may be such that amounts previously reported in discontinued operations may need to be adjusted in a subsequent period. If so, those adjustments should be presented separately in the discontinued operations section of the income statement. Adjustments may result from such events as resolution of contingencies or settlement of employee benefit plan obligations. (ASC 205-20-45-4 and 45-5)

ASC 205-30, *Liquidation Basis of Accounting*

Guidance requires financial statements to be prepared using the liquidation basis of accounting (see "Definitions of Terms" section in this chapter) when liquidation is imminent. Liquidation is considered imminent when either of the following occurs:

- A plan for liquidation is approved by the person or persons with the authority to make such a plan effective, and the likelihood is remote that either of the following will occur:
  - The execution of the plan will be blocked by other parties.
  - The entity will return from liquidation.
- A plan for liquidation is being imposed by other forces, such as involuntary bankruptcy, and the likelihood is remote that the entity will return from liquidation.
  (ASC 205-30-25-2)

Measurement The financial statements prepared under the liquidation basis of accounting are intended to "report the amount of cash or other consideration that an investor might reasonably be expected to receive after liquidation." (ASU 2013-07, BC13) Assets should be measured at the amount the entity expects to collect upon sale. This may or may not be fair value. Fair value assumes an orderly sale.

An entity using the liquidation basis of accounting may have items that it now intends to sell or use to settle liabilities, but that were previously recognized, e.g., trademarks. Those items may be recognized in the aggregate and should be recognized for the amount expected to be realized. (ASC 205-30-25-4)

Liabilities should be recognized in accordance with relevant guidance in other Topics. However, the entity should not anticipate being legally released from its debt. (ASC 205- 30-30-2)

Estimated costs to dispose of assets or other items to be sold in liquidation should be accrued, but discount provisions should not be applied. (ASC 205-30-25-6 and 205-30-30-3) Those costs should be presented in the aggregate, but separate from the related assets or items. If and when it has a reasonable basis for estimation, the entity should accrue costs and income expected to be incurred or earned through the end of the liquidation. (ASC 205-30-25-46 and 47)

The entity must remeasure its assets, liabilities, and disposal cost and income accruals at each measurement date.

Financial Statements The entity must at least prepare:

- A statement of net assets in liquidation, and
- A statement of changes in net assets in liquidation.
  (ASC 205-30-45-1)

The liquidation basis of accounting should be applied prospectively from the day the liquidation becomes imminent. The initial statement of changes in net assets in liquidation should present changes that occurred only during the period since liquidation became imminent. (ASC 205-30-45-2)

ASC 205-40, *Going Concern*

The FASB's guidance, with some exceptions, mirrors going concern requirements for auditors currently found in PCAOB and AICPA standards. Management must perform at least annually an evaluation of the entity's ability to continue as a going concern within one year after the financial statements issuance date. The assessment should be performed for each annual and interim period and involves a two-step process. (ASC 205-40-50-1)

Step 1: Evaluating Conditions and Events That May Raise Substantial Doubts Management must evaluate, in the aggregate, conditions and events that are known or reasonably knowable at the evaluation date. Guidance includes the term "reasonably knowable" to emphasize that an entity may not know all events that could cause doubt, but must make a reasonable effort to assess the situation. The initial assessment should *not* take into account the mitigating effect of management's potential actions. Substantial doubt typically revolves around an entity's ability to meet its obligations and exists if it is probable that the entity will not be able to meet those obligations within one year after the issuance date of the financial statements or the date when the financial statements are available to be issued. Probable is consistent with the use of the term in ASC 450, that is, a future event is likely to occur. When making this evaluation, management should consider quantitative and qualitative information about:

- The entity's current financial condition, including its liquidity sources.
- The entity's conditional and unconditional obligation due within the year.
- The fund's required to maintain operations.
- Other conditions, when considered with the items above, may adversely affect the entity's ability to meet its obligations.
  (ASC 205-40-50-5)

Indicators of adverse conditions or events include:

- Negative financial trends
- Default on obligations
- Denial of credit from suppliers
- A need to restructure debt
- A need to find new financing sources
- A need to dispose of substantial assets
- Work stoppages
- Labor difficulties
- Substantial dependence on success of a particular project
- Unprofitable long-term commitments
- Legal proceedings
- Legislation that might jeopardize the entity's ability to operate
- Loss of a key patent or franchise
- Loss of a major customer or supplier
- Underinsured natural catastrophe

For potential adverse conditions or events, management should consider

- Timing,
- Likelihood, and
- Magnitude.

Step 2: Consideration of Management's Plans When Substantial Doubt Is Raised If the conditions raise substantial doubt about going concern, management must assess its plans to mitigate the issues and whether they will alleviate the substantial doubt. (ASC 205-40-50-6) The table below lists types of plans to alleviate substantial doubt and the information to consider when evaluating each type of plan.

Plan	Types of Information to Consider
Disposing of an asset or business	• Restrictions on disposal of an asset or business • Marketability of the asset or business • Possible direct or indirect effects of disposal of the asset or business
Borrowing money or restructuring debt	• Availability and terms of new debt financing, or availability and terms of existing debt refinancing • Existing or committed arrangements to restructure or subordinate debt or to guarantee loans to the entity • Possible effects on management's borrowing plans of existing restrictions on additional borrowing or the sufficiency of available collateral
Reducing or delaying expenditures	• Feasibility of plans to reduce overhead or administrative expenditures, to postpone maintenance or research and development projects, or to lease rather than purchase assets • Possible direct or indirect effects on the entity and its cash flows of reduced or delayed expenditures
Increasing ownership equity	• Feasibility of plans to increase ownership equity, including existing or committed arrangements to raise additional capital • Existing or committed arrangements to reduce current dividend requirements or to accelerate cash infusions from affiliates or other investors
(ASC 205-40-55-3)	

These plans can be considered only if *both* of the following conditions are met:

- It is probable that the plans will be effectively implemented within the year.
- It is probable that the plans when implemented will mitigate the conditions or events that raise substantial doubt about a going concern.
  (ASC 205-40-50-7)

In order for these plans to be considered, generally, management or those with authority must approve the plans before the issuance date of the financial statements. (ASC 205-40-50-8) In considering whether the plan will mitigate doubt about going concern, management should consider the anticipated timing and magnitude of the mitigating effect.

Disclosure Requirements

Management Conclusion	**Disclosures**
Conditions do not give rise to substantial doubt	No specific disclosures are required.
Substantial doubt that is alleviated by management's plans	• In a separate note or part of another note, for example, on debt: ◦ Principal conditions or events that raised substantial doubt, ◦ Management's evaluation of the significance of those conditions or events in relation to the entity's ability to meet its obligations, and ◦ Management's plans that alleviated those concerns. (ASC 205-40-50-12)
After considering all the facts and management's plans, management concludes that substantial doubt remains	• A separate note with: ◦ A statement that there is substantial doubt about the entity's ability to continue as a going concern within one year after the date that the financial statements are issued or available to be issued. • Disclosures that allow users to understand: ◦ Principal conditions or events that raised substantial doubt, ◦ Management's evaluation of the significance of those conditions or events in relation to the entity's ability to meet its obligations. And ◦ Management's plans to mitigate the conditions or events. (ASC 205-40-50-13)
In subsequent years	Present the above disclosures in subsequent financial statements as long as substantial doubt exists. If any changes in conditions or events occur, they should be explained. It is expected that as more is known, the disclosure will become more extensive. If the substantial doubt is resolved in a subsequent period, the entity must disclose how it was resolved. (ASC 205-40-50-14)

Example—Substantial Doubts About Going Concern Are Raised but Alleviated

Carolina Furniture is an established business without any significant changes over the last several years. Despite changes in the industry, Carolina has positive financial trends and the industry overall has positive trends. Carolina built a new factory nine years ago and has a loan balloon payment due in six months. Carolina does not have sufficient cash to repay the loan. However, the company has a history of being able to successfully obtain financing and has no other significant debt.

Management evaluates whether conditions in the aggregate raise substantial doubt about Carolina continuing as a going concern. Management considers only conditions that are relevant, known, and reasonably knowable at the date the financial statements are issued.

In Step One of the analysis, management can only consider the conditions and not plans to mitigate any concerns. Management concludes that events and conditions indicate that Carolina will not be able to meet its loan obligation when due. Management then moves to Step Two and considers its plans to mitigate significant doubt about going concern. Because of its positive financial trends, stable history, and past ability to finance debt, management is confident that it will be able to obtain new financing. Management concludes that its plan will be implemented and substantial doubt will be alleviated.

Carolina discloses that it has significant debt coming due within six months and that it is probable that it will be able to refinance the loan prior to maturity. Carolina also discloses the details related to its plan. Carolina has the option of disclosing this information in a separate note or in a related note, for example, a note on debt.

Example—Substantial Doubts About Going Concern Are Raised and Not Alleviated by Management's Plans

Assume similar facts as above except that Carolina's has had negative sales over the past five years. When it recently attempted to finance supplies, it was unsuccessful. In its Step Two assessment management is not confident that it will be able to obtain new financing. Management concludes that its plan will not be implemented and substantial doubt will not be alleviated. Management discloses that there is substantial doubt about Carolina's ability to continue as a going concern, that there is significant debt coming due, and that Carolina does not currently have the funds to repay the debt. Carolina also discloses that because of its economic conditions and trends, it is not probable that its plans to finance the debt will be successful. These disclosures appear in a separate going concern note.

3 ASC 210 BALANCE SHEET

PERSPECTIVE AND ISSUES

Subtopics

ASC 210, *Balance Sheet*, is divided into two subtopics:

- ASC 210-10, *Overall,* which focuses on the presentation of the balance sheet, particularly the operating cycle and classification of current assets and liabilities, and
- ASC 210-20, *Offsetting,* which offers guidance on offsetting amounts for certain contracts and repurchase agreements accounted for as collateralized borrowings and reverse repurchase agreements accounted for as collateralized borrowings.

Scope and Scope Exceptions

ASC 210-10 The guidance in ASC 210-10 applies to all entities. However, the guidance related to classification of current assets and current liabilities does not apply if the entity does not present a classified balance sheet.

ASC 210-20 The guidance in ASC 210-20 does not apply to:

> The derecognition or nonrecognition of assets and liabilities. Derecognition by sale of an asset or extinguishment of a liability results in removal of a recognized asset or liability and generally results in the recognition of gain or loss. Although conceptually different, offsetting that results in a net amount of zero and derecognition with no gain or loss are indistinguishable in their effects on the statement of financial position. Likewise, not recognizing assets and liabilities of the same amount in financial statements achieves similar reported results. (ASC 210-10-15-2)

Generally, right of setoff involves only two parties. Exceptions to this two-party principle are limited to the guidance in these subtopics and paragraphs:

- ASC 840-30, paragraphs 32 through 52 (leveraged leases)
- Upon implementation of ASU 2016-02, *Leases*—ASC 842-50 (leveraged leases)
- ASC 715-30 (accounting for pension plan assets and liabilities)
- ASC 715-60 (accounting for plan assets and liabilities)
- ASC 740-10 (net tax asset or liability amounts reported)
- ASC 815, paragraphs 815-10-45-1 through 45-7 (derivative instruments with the right to reclaim cash collateral or the obligation to return cash collateral)
- ASC 940-320 (trade date accounting for trading portfolio positions) and 910-405 (advances received on construction contracts)
- ASC 942-210-45-3A.
  (ASC 210-20-15-3)

Scope of Disclosures The scope of the disclosures required by ASC 210-20 is limited to:

- Recognized derivative instruments accounted for in accordance with Topic 815, including bifurcated embedded derivatives, repurchase agreements and reverse repurchase agreements, and securities borrowing and securities lending transactions that are offset in accordance with either Section 210-20-45 or Section 815-10-45.
- Recognized derivative instruments accounted for in accordance with Topic 815, including bifurcated embedded derivatives, repurchase agreements and reverse repurchase agreements, and securities borrowing and securities lending transactions that are subject to an enforceable master netting arrangement or similar agreement, irrespective of whether they are offset in accordance with either Section 210-20-45 or Section 815-10-45.
  (ASC 210-20-50-1)

The FASB has made it clear that the disclosure requirements do not apply to:

- Loan and customer deposits at the same financial institution.
- Financial instruments only subject to collateral agreement. The FASB views these as primarily credit enhancements.
- Trade receivables and payables with a counterparty to be netted in the event of default. The FASB views these as primarily credit enhancements. In addition, requiring these to be disclosed would cause an undue burden on financial statement preparers.
- Receivables and payables of broker dealers resulting from unsettled regular-way trades.

Overview

Statements of financial positions (also commonly known as balance sheets or statements of financial condition) present information about assets, liabilities, and owners' equity and their relationships to each other. They reflect an entity's resources (assets) and its financing structure (liabilities and equity) in conformity with generally accepted accounting principles. The statement of financial position reports the aggregate effect of transactions at a point in time, whereas the statements of income, retained earnings, comprehensive income, and cash flows all report the effect of transactions occurring during a specified period of time such as a month, quarter, or year.

It is common for the statement of financial position to be divided into classifications based on the length of the entity's operating cycle. Assets are classified as current if they are reasonably expected to be converted into cash, sold, or consumed either within one year or within one operating cycle, whichever is longer. Liabilities are classified as current if they are expected to be liquidated through the use of current assets or incurring other current liabilities. The excess or deficiency of current assets over or under current liabilities, which is referred to as net working capital, identifies, if positive, the relatively liquid portion of the entity's capital that is potentially available to serve as a buffer for meeting unexpected obligations arising within the ordinary operating cycle of the business.

DEFINITIONS OF TERMS

Source: ASC 210, *Glossaries*. Also see Appendix A, *Definitions of Terms*, for additional terms relevant to this section: Cash, Cash Equivalents, Commencement Date of the Lease, Contract, Derivative Instrument, Lease, Lessee, Lessor, Leveraged Lease, Underlying Asset, Working Capital.

Current Assets. Current assets is used to designate cash and other assets or resources commonly identified as those that are reasonably expected to be realized in cash or sold or consumed during the normal operating cycle of the business.

Current Liabilities. Current liabilities is used principally to designate obligations whose liquidation is reasonably expected to require the use of existing resources properly classifiable as current assets, or the creation of other current liabilities.

Daylight Overdraft. Daylight overdraft or other intraday credit refers to the accommodation in the banking arrangements that allows transactions to be completed even if there is insufficient cash on deposit during the day provided there is sufficient cash to cover the net cash requirement at the end of the day. That accommodation may be through a credit facility, including a credit facility for which a fee is charged, or from a deposit of collateral.

Operating Cycle. The average time intervening between the acquisition of materials or services and the final cash realization constitutes an operating cycle.

Repurchase Agreement Accounted for as a Collateralized Borrowing. A repurchase agreement (repo) refers to a transaction in which a seller-borrower of securities sells those securities to a buyer-lender with an agreement to repurchase them at a stated price plus interest at a specified date or in specified circumstances. A repurchase agreement accounted for as a collateralized borrowing is a repo that does not qualify for sale accounting under Topic 860. The payable under a repurchase agreement accounted for as a collateralized borrowing refers to the amount of the seller-borrower's obligation recognized for the future repurchase of the securities from the buyer-lender. In certain industries, the terminology is reversed; that is, entities in those industries refer to this type of agreement as a reverse repo.

Reverse Repurchase Agreement Accounted for as a Collateralized Borrowing. A reverse repurchase agreement accounted for as a collateralized borrowing (also known as a reverse repo) refers to a transaction that is accounted for as a collateralized lending in which a buyer-lender buys securities with an agreement to resell them to the seller-borrower at a stated price plus interest at a specified date or in specified circumstances. The receivable under a reverse repurchase agreement accounted for as a collateralized borrowing refers to the amount due from the seller-borrower for the repurchase of the securities from the buyer-lender. In certain industries, the terminology is reversed; that is, entities in those industries refer to this type of agreement as a repo.

Right of Setoff. A right of setoff is a debtor's legal right, by contract or otherwise, to discharge all or a portion of the debt owed to another party by applying against the debt an amount that the other party owes to the debtor.

Securities Custodian. The securities custodian for a securities transfer system may be the bank or financial institution that executes securities transfers over the securities transfer system, and book entry securities exist only in electronic form on the records of the transfer system operator for each entity that has a security account with the transfer system operator.

Short-Term Obligations. Short-term obligations are those that are scheduled to mature within one year after the date of an entity's balance sheet or, for those entities that use the operating cycle concept of working capital, within an entity's operating cycle that is longer than one year.

CONCEPTS, RULES, AND EXAMPLES

Form of the Statement of Financial Position

The format of a statement of financial position is not specified by any authoritative pronouncement. Instead, formats and titles have developed as a matter of tradition and, in some cases, through industry practice.

Two basic formats are used:

1. The balanced format, in which the sum of the amounts for liabilities and equity are added together on the face of the statement to illustrate that assets equal liabilities plus equity.
2. The less frequently presented equity format, which shows totals for assets, liabilities, and equity, but no sums illustrating that assets less liabilities equal equity.

Those two formats can take one of two forms:

1. The account form, presenting assets on the left-hand side of the page and liabilities and equity on the right-hand side.
2. The report form, which is a top-to-bottom or running presentation.

The three elements customarily displayed in the heading of a statement of financial position are:

1. The legal name of the entity whose financial position is being presented
2. The title of the statement (e.g., statement of financial position or balance sheet)
3. The date of the statement (or statements, if multiple dates are presented for comparative purposes).

Entity's Name The entity's legal name appears in the heading exactly as specified in the document that created it (e.g., the certificate of incorporation, partnership agreement, LLC operating agreement, etc.). The legal form of the entity is often evident from its name when the name includes such designations as "incorporated," "LLP," or "LLC." Otherwise, the legal form is either captioned as part of the heading or disclosed in the notes to the financial statements. A few examples are as follows:

ABC Company
(a general partnership)
ABC Company
(a sole proprietorship)
ABC Company
(a division of DEF, Inc.)

The use of the titles "statement of financial position," "balance sheet," or "statement of financial condition" infers that the statement is presented using generally accepted accounting principles. If, instead, some financial reporting framework, such as income tax basis or cash basis is used, the financial statement title must be revised to reflect this variation. The use of a title such as "Statements of Assets and Liabilities—Income Tax Basis" is necessary to differentiate the financial statement being presented from a GAAP statement of financial position.

Date The last day of the fiscal period is used as the statement date. Usually, this is a month-end date unless the entity uses a fiscal reporting period always ending on a particular day of the week such as Friday or Sunday. In these cases, the statement of financial position would be dated accordingly (i.e., December 26, October 1, etc.).

Consistency of Format Statements of financial position generally are uniform in appearance from one period to the next with consistently followed form, terminology, captions, and patterns of combining insignificant items. If changes in the manner of presentation are made when comparative statements are presented, the prior year's information must be restated to conform to the current year's presentation.

ASC 210-10, *Overall*

Assets, liabilities, and shareholders' equity are separated in the statement of financial position so that important relationships can be shown and attention can be focused on significant subtotals.

Current Assets Current assets are cash and other assets that are reasonably expected to be realized in cash or sold or consumed during the normal operating cycle of the business. (ASC 210- 10-05-4) When the normal operating cycle is less than one year, a one-year period is used to distinguish current assets from noncurrent assets. When the operating cycle exceeds one year, the operating cycle will serve as the proper period for purposes of current asset classification. (ASC 210-10-45-3) When the operating cycle is very long, the usefulness of the concept of current assets diminishes. The following items are classified as current assets:

- *Cash and cash equivalents* include cash on hand consisting of coins, currency, undeposited checks; money orders and drafts; demand deposits in banks; and certain short-term, highly liquid investments. Any type of instrument accepted by a bank for deposit would be considered to be cash. Cash must be available for withdrawal on demand. Cash that is restricted as to withdrawal, such as certificates of deposit, would not be included with cash because of the time restrictions. Cash must be available for current use in order to be classified as a current asset. Cash that is restricted in use would not be included in cash unless its restrictions will expire within the operating cycle. Cash restricted for a noncurrent use, such as cash designated for the purchase of property or equipment, would not be included in current assets. (ASC 210-10-45-4) Cash equivalents include short-term, highly liquid investments that:
    - are readily convertible to known amounts of cash, and
    - are so near their maturity (maturities of three months or less from the date of purchase by the entity) that they present negligible risk of changes in value because of changes in interest rates.

  U.S. Treasury bills, commercial paper, and money market funds are all examples of cash equivalents. Only instruments with original maturity dates of three months or less qualify as cash equivalents. (ASC 210-10-45-1)

- *Marketable securities* representing the investment of cash available for current operations.
- *Receivables* include accounts and notes receivable, receivables from affiliated entities, and officer and employee receivables. The term "accounts receivable" is generally understood to represent amounts due from customers arising from transactions in the ordinary course of business (sometimes referred to as "trade receivables").
- *Inventories* are goods on hand and available-for-sale, raw materials, work in process, operating supplies, and ordinary maintenance materials and parts. The basis of valuation and the method of pricing are to be disclosed.
- *Prepaid expenses* are amounts paid in advance to secure the use of assets or the receipt of services at a future date. Prepaid expenses will not be converted to cash, but they are classified as current assets because, if not prepaid, they would have required the use of current assets during the coming year or operating cycle, if longer. (ASC 210-10- 45-2) Prepaid rent and prepaid insurance are the most common examples of prepaid expenses.

Noncurrent Assets ASC 210-10-45-4 excludes the following from current assets:

- Cash and claims to cash that are:
  - restricted as to withdrawal or use for other than current operations,
  - designated for expenditure in the acquisition or construction of noncurrent assets, or
  - segregated for the liquidation of long-term debts.

  Even though not actually set aside in special accounts, funds that are clearly to be used in the near future for the liquidation of long-term debts, payments to sinking funds, or for similar purposes shall also, under this concept, be excluded from current assets. However, if such funds are considered to offset maturing debt that has properly been set up as a current liability, they may be included within the current asset classification.
- Receivables arising from unusual transactions (such as the sale of capital assets, or loans or advances to affiliates, officers, or employees) that are not expected to be collected within 12 months.
- Investments that are intended to be held for an extended period of time (longer than one operating cycle). The following are the three major types of long-term investments:
  1. *Investments in securities*—stocks, bonds, and long-term notes receivable. Securities that are classified as available-for-sale or held-to-maturity investments are classified as long term if management intended to hold them for more than one year.
  2. *Tangible assets* not currently used in operations (e.g., land purchased as an investment and held for sale).
  3. *Investments held in special funds* (e.g., sinking funds, pension funds, amounts held for plant expansion, and cash surrender values of life insurance policies).
- Depreciable assets
  - *Property, plant, and equipment*. These are disclosed with related accumulated depreciation/depletion.
  - *Intangible assets* include legal and/or contractual rights that are expected to provide future economic benefits and purchased goodwill. Patents, copyrights, logos, and trademarks are examples of rights that are recognized as intangible assets.
- Other assets. An all-inclusive heading that incorporates assets that do not fit neatly into any of the other asset categories (e.g., long-term prepaid expenses, deposits made to

purchase equipment, deferred income tax assets (net of any required valuation allowance), bond issue costs, noncurrent receivables, and restricted cash).

Liabilities

Liabilities are displayed on the statement of financial position in the order of expected payment.

Current Liabilities Obligations are classified as current if their liquidation is reasonably expected to require the use of existing resources properly classifiable as current assets or to create other current obligations. (ASC 210-10-45-6) Current liabilities also includes obligations that are due on demand or that are callable at any time by the lender and are classified as current regardless of the intent of the entity or lender. ASC 470-10-45 includes more guidance on those and on short-term debt expected to be refinanced. (ASC 210-10-45-7) The following items are classified as current liabilities:

- *Accounts payable.* Accounts payable is normally comprised of amounts due to suppliers (vendors) for the purchase of goods and services used in the ordinary course of running a business.
- *Trade notes payable* are also obligations that arise from the purchase of goods and services. They differ from accounts payable because the supplier or vendor finances the purchase on terms longer than the customary period for trade payables. The supplier or vendor generally charges interest for this privilege. If interest is not charged, it is imputed in accordance with ASC 835.
  A valuation allowance is used to reduce the carrying amount of the note for the resulting discount.
- *Accrued expenses* represent estimates of expenses incurred on or before the date of the statement of financial position that have not yet been paid and that are not payable until a succeeding period within the next year.
- *Dividends payable* are obligations to distribute cash or other assets to shareholders that arise from the declaration of dividends by the entity's board of directors.
- *Advances and deposits* are collections of cash or other assets received in advance to ensure the future delivery of goods or services. Advances and deposits are classified as current liabilities if the goods and services are to be delivered within the next year (or the operating cycle, if longer). Advances and deposits include such items as advance rentals and customer deposits. Certain advances and deposits are sometimes captioned as deferred or unearned revenues.
- *Agency collections and withholdings* are liabilities that arise because the entity acts as an agent for another party. Employee tax withholdings, sales taxes, and wage garnishments are examples of agency collections. (ASC 210-10-45-9d)
- *Current portion of long-term debt* is the portion of a long-term obligation that will be settled during the next year (or operating cycle, if longer) by using current assets. (ASC 210-10-45-9b) Generally, this amount includes only the payments due within the next year under the terms of the underlying agreement. However, if the entity has violated a covenant in a long-term debt agreement and, as a result, the investor is legally entitled to demand payment, the entire debt amount is classified as current unless the lender formally (in writing) waives the right to demand repayment of the debt for a period in excess of one year (or one operating cycle, if longer). In two cases, obligations to be paid in the

next year are not classified as current liabilities because the liquidation does not require the use of current assets or the creation of other current liabilities:

- Debt expected to be refinanced through another long-term issue, and
- Debt that will be retired through the use of noncurrent assets, such as a bond sinking fund, are treated as noncurrent liabilities.

(See additional guidance in the chapter on ASC 470.)

Noncurrent Liabilities

Obligations that are not expected to be liquidated within one year (or the current operating cycle, if longer) are classified as noncurrent. The following items would be classified as noncurrent:

- *Notes and bonds payable* are obligations that will be paid in more than one year (or one operating cycle, if longer).
- *Lease obligations* are contractual obligations that arise from obtaining the use of property or equipment via a lease contract.
- *Written put options on the option writer's (issuer's) equity shares and forward contracts to purchase an issuer's equity shares that require physical or net cash settlement* are classified as liabilities on the issuer's statement of financial position. The obligation is classified as noncurrent unless the date at which the contract will be settled is within the next year (or operating cycle, if longer).
- *Certain financial instruments that embody an unconditional obligation to issue a variable number of equity shares and financial instruments other than outstanding shares that embody a conditional obligation to issue a variable number of equity shares* are classified as a liability in the issuer's statement of financial position. The obligation is classified as noncurrent unless the date at which the financial instrument will be settled is within the next year (or operating cycle, if longer).
- *Contingent obligations* are recorded when it is probable that an obligation will occur as the result of a past event. In most cases, a future event will eventually confirm the amount payable, the payee, or the date payable. The classification of a contingent liability as current or noncurrent depends on when the confirming event will occur and how soon afterwards payment must be made.
- *Mandatorily redeemable shares* are recorded as liabilities per ASC 480. A mandatory redemption clause requires common or preferred stock to be redeemed (retired) at a specific date(s) or upon occurrence of an event which is uncertain as to timing although ultimately certain to occur. The obligation is classified as noncurrent unless the date at which the shares must be redeemed is within the next year (or operating cycle, if longer).
- *Other noncurrent liabilities* include defined benefit pension obligations, postemployment obligations, and postretirement obligations.

Presentation

The classification and presentation of information in a statement of financial position may be highly aggregated, highly detailed, or anywhere in between. In general, highly aggregated statements of financial position are used in annual reports and other presentations provided to the public. Highly detailed statements of financial position are used internally by management.

A highly aggregated statement of financial position includes only a few line items. The additional details required by GAAP are found in the notes to the financial statements.

A more detailed statement of financial position includes more line items (for details about specific assets and liabilities) than are found in most statements of financial position.

ASC 210-20, *Offsetting*

Offsetting is the practice of netting assets and liabilities on the balance sheet as opposed to presenting them gross as assets and liabilities. In general, assets and liabilities are not permitted to be offset against each other unless certain specified criteria are met. The Codification permits offsetting only when *all* of the following conditions are met that constitute a right of setoff:

1. Each of the two parties owes the other determinable amounts (although they may be in different currencies and bear different rates of interest).
2. The reporting party has the right to set off the amount it owes against the amount owed to it by the other party.
3. The reporting party intends to set off the two amounts. If the entity does not intend to offset the amounts, offsetting presentation is not representationally faithfully. (ASC 210- 20-45-4)
4. The right of setoff is legally enforceable.
   (ASC 210-20-45-1)

Criterion 3 above is subjective and requires judgment. When making the judgment, entities may want to consider historical precedent. For example, if a settlement by offsetting balances with the other party has occurred in prior transactions, the reporting entity appropriately may expect a similar offset in the future.

Furthermore, when maturities differ, only the party with the nearest maturity can offset, because the party with the later maturity must settle in the manner determined by the party with the earlier maturity. (ASC 210-20-45-3)

Entities must apply their choices to offset consistently. Net receivables arising from application of ASC 210-20 cannot be offset against net payables. (ASC 210-20-45-12)

Bankruptcy In particular cases, state laws or bankruptcy laws may impose restrictions or prohibitions against the right of setoff. (ASC 210-20-45-8)

Taxes Payable Cash or the offsetting of other assets against a tax liability or other amounts due to governmental bodies is acceptable only under the following, limited circumstances:

- When it is clear that a purchase of securities is in substance an advance payment of taxes payable in the near future, and
- The securities are acceptable for the payment of taxes.

Primarily this occurs as an accommodation to governmental bodies that issue tax anticipation notes in order to accelerate the receipt of cash from future taxes. (ASC 210-20-45-6 and 45-7)

Repurchase and Reverse Repurchase Agreements ASC 210-20-45-11 permits the offset of amounts recognized as payables in repurchase agreements accounted for as collateralized borrowings against amounts recognized as receivables in reverse repurchase agreements accounted for as collateralized borrowings with the same counterparty. If certain conditions are met, an entity may, but is not required to, offset the amounts recognized. The additional conditions for offsetting repurchase and reverse repurchase agreements are:

- The agreements must have the same explicit settlement date.
- The agreements must be executed in accordance with a master netting agreement.

- The securities underlying the agreements exist in "book entry" form and can be transferred only by means of entries in the records of the transfer system operator or the security custodian.
- The agreements will be settled on a securities transfer system that transfers ownership of "book entry" securities, and banking arrangements are in place so that the entity must only keep cash on deposit sufficient to cover the net payable.
- Cash settlements for securities transferred are made under established bank arrangements that provide that an entity to have cash on deposit for net amounts due at close of business. The entity uses the same account for cash inflows and outflows related to the settlement. (Also see ASC 210-20-45-14 through 17 for additional details.)
- The same account at the clearing bank is used for the cash inflows of the settlement of the reverse repurchase agreements and the cash outflows in the settlement of the repurchase agreements.

These conditions do not apply to amounts recognized for other types of repurchase and reverse repurchase agreements executed under a master netting arrangement. This does not mean that those amounts could not otherwise meet the conditions for a right of setoff. (ASC 210-20-45-13)

Disclosures and Presentation For information on disclosures and more information on presentation, please see the Scope and Scope Exceptions section earlier in this chapter and the *Disclosure and Presentation Checklist for Commercial Businesses* at www.wiley.com/go/GAAP2021.

Other Sources

See ASC Location—*Wiley GAAP* Chapter	*For information on . . .*
ASC 310-10-45-8	Presentation of unearned discounts (other than cash or quantity discounts and the like), finance charges, and interest.
ASC 605-35-45-2	Presentation of provisions for losses on contracts.
ASC 715-30	Accounting for pension plan assets and liabilities.
ASC 715-60	Accounting for plan assets and liabilities.
ASC 740-10	Amounts reported for net tax assets or liabilities or both.
ASC 815-10-45-1 through 45-7	Derivative instruments with the right to reclaim cash collateral or the obligation to return cash collateral.
ASC 842-50-35-32 through 35-52	Leveraged leases.
ASC 852-10-45-4	Presentation of liabilities subject to compromise and those not subject to compromise during reorganization proceedings.
ASC 910-405	Advances received on construction contracts with the federal government.
ASC 926-20-45-1	Presentation of film costs in a classified balance sheet.
ASC 940-320	Trade date accounting for trading portfolio positions for brokers and dealers.
ASC 942-310-45-3A	For depository and lending institutions, reciprocal balances with other banks.

4 ASC 215 STATEMENT OF SHAREHOLDER EQUITY

PERSPECTIVE AND ISSUES

ASC 215, *Statement of Shareholder Equity*, contains one subtopic: ASC 215-10, *Overall*

That subtopic merely provides a referral to ASC 505, *Equity*.

5 ASC 220 INCOME STATEMENT—REPORTING COMPREHENSIVE INCOME

PERSPECTIVE AND ISSUES

Subtopics

ASC 220, Income Statement Reporting—Comprehensive Income, contains the following subtopics:

- ASC 220-10, *Overall*, which provides guidance on the reporting, presentation, and disclosure of comprehensive income.
- ASC 220-20, *Unusual Items or Infrequently Occurring Items*, which addresses the classification, presentation, and disclosure of unusual or infrequently occurring items.
- ASC 220-30, *Business Interruption Insurance*, which provides presentation and disclosure requirements for business interruption insurance.

The three subtopics provide discrete information and are not interrelated. (ASC 220-10-05-1 through 5)

Scope

ASC 220 applies to all entities except it does *not* apply to the following:

- Those that do not have any items of comprehensive income.
- Those not-for-profit entities that are required to follow the guidance in ASC 958-205. (ASC 220-10-15-3)

It applies to general purpose financial statements that present results of operations according to GAAP. (ASC 220-10-15-5)

ASC 220 focuses on presentation and disclosure and does not address recognition and measurement requirements.

Overview

In financial reporting, performance is primarily measured by net income and its components, which are presented in the income statement. A second performance measure—comprehensive income—is a more inclusive notion of performance than net income. It includes all recognized changes in equity that occur during a period except those resulting from investments by owners and distributions to owners.

Because comprehensive income includes the effects on an entity of economic events largely outside of management's control, some have said that net income is a measure of management's performance and comprehensive income is a measure of entity performance.

In contrast to the statement of financial position, which provides information about an entity at a point in time, an income statement provides information about a period of time. It reflects information about the transactions and other events occurring within the period. Most of the weaknesses of an income statement are a result of its periodic nature. Entities are continually creating and selling goods and services, and at any single point in time some of those processes will be incomplete.

DEFINITIONS OF TERMS

Source: ASC 220 glossaries. Also see Appendix A, *Definitions of Terms*, for definitions relevant to this chapter: Available-for-Sale Securities, Comprehensive Income, Conduit Debt Security,

Holding Gain or Loss, Market Risk Benefit, Net Income, Noncontrolling Interest, Nonpublic Entity, Other Comprehensive Income, Parent, Publicly Traded Company, and Subsidiary.

Business Interruption Insurance. Insurance that provides coverage if business operations are suspended due to the loss of use of property and equipment resulting from a covered cause of loss. Business interruption insurance coverage generally provides for reimbursement of certain costs and losses incurred during the reasonable period required to rebuild, repair, or replace the damaged property.

Gross Margin. The excess of sales over cost of goods sold. Gross margin does not consider all operating expenses.

Infrequency of Occurrence. The underlying event or transaction should be of a type that would not reasonably be expected to recur in the foreseeable future, taking into account the environment in which the entity operates.

Reclassification Adjustments. Adjustments made to avoid double counting in comprehensive income items that are displayed as part of net income for a period that also had been displayed as part of other comprehensive income in that period or earlier periods. (ASC 220-10-20)

Unusual Nature. The underlying event or transaction should possess a high degree of abnormality and be of a type clearly unrelated to, or only incidentally related to, the ordinary and typical activities of the entity, taking into account the environment in which the entity operates.

CONCEPTS, RULES, AND EXAMPLES

ASC 220-10, *Overall*—Comprehensive Income

Comprehensive income is the change in equity that results from revenue, expenses, gains, and losses during a period, as well as any other recognized changes in equity that occur for reasons other than investments by owners and distributions to owners. Comprehensive income consists of:

- All components of net income and
- All components of other comprehensive income.
  (ASC 220-10-20)

Format of Statement of Income and Comprehensive Income

Entities must present in the period they are recognized all items that meet the definition of comprehensive income:

- In a combined statement of income and comprehensive income, or
- In two separate, but consecutive statements.
  (ASC 220-10-45-1(C))

Exhibit—Items Required to Be Displayed in Either Acceptable Format of the Statement of Comprehensive Income

Reporting Comprehensive Income	
Single Continuous Statement of Net Income and Comprehensive Income	**Two Separate but Consecutive Statements**
Show: • Components of net income • Total net income • Components of other comprehensive income • Total of other comprehensive income • Total comprehensive income	In the statement of net income show: • Components of net income • Total of net income In the statement of comprehensive income presented immediately after the statement of net income, begin with net income and show: • Components of other comprehensive income • Total of other comprehensive income • Total of comprehensive income
(ASC 220-10-45-1A)	(ASC 220-10-45-1B)

Basic Order of Income and Comprehensive Income Statements The basic order of presentation of information in an income statement (or statement of income and comprehensive income) is defined by accounting standards, as shown by the diagram below. Other than in the section "Income from Continuing Operations," the display of revenues, expenses, gains, losses, and other comprehensive income is predetermined by the Codification guidance. Only within income from continuing operations do tradition and industry practice determine the presentation.

The three items that are shown in the heading of an income statement are:

1. The name of the entity whose results of operations is being presented
2. The title of the statement
3. The period of time covered by the statement

Exhibit—Basic Order of Income Statement and Comprehensive Income Statement

Statement of Income
Income from continuing operations Sales or service revenues Costs of goods sold Operating expenses Remaining excess of fair value over cost of acquired net assets in a business combination Gains and losses Other revenues and expenses Items that are unusual or infrequent, gross Income tax expense related to continuing operations
Results from discontinued operations Income (loss) from operations of a discontinued component Gain (loss) from disposal of a discontinued component

Net income
Earnings per share information
Other comprehensive income Foreign currency translation adjustments Unrealized gains (losses) on securities Adjustments related to pension liabilities or assets Gains/losses on cash-flow hedging items Gains/losses on hedges of forecasted foreign-currency-denominated transactions Reclassification adjustment (may be shown gross or net of tax, details may be disclosed in note) Income tax related to other comprehensive income (if components are not shown net of tax)
Comprehensive income
Earnings per share information

Entity Name The entity's legal name should be used and supplemental information could be added to disclose the entity's legal form as a corporation, partnership, sole proprietorship, or other form if that information is not apparent from the entity's name.

Statement Titles The use of the titles "Income Statement," "Statement of Income and Comprehensive Income," "Statement of Operations," or "Statement of Earnings" denotes preparation in accordance with GAAP. If another comprehensive basis of accounting were used, such as the cash or income tax basis, the title of the statement would be modified accordingly. "Statement of Revenue and Expenses—Income Tax Basis" or "Statement of Revenue and Expenses—Modified Cash Basis" are examples of such titles.

Statement Date The date of an income statement must clearly identify the time period involved, such as "Year Ending March 31, 20X1." That dating informs the reader of the length of the period covered by the statement and both the starting and ending dates. Dating such as "The Period Ending March 31, 20X1" or "Through March 31, 20X1" is not useful because of the lack of precision in those titles. Income statements are rarely presented for periods in excess of one year but are frequently seen for shorter periods such as a month or a quarter. Entities whose operations form a natural cycle may have a reporting period end on a specific day (e.g., the last Friday of the month). These entities should head the income statement "For the 52 Weeks Ended March 29, 20X1" (each week containing seven days, beginning on a Saturday and ending on a Friday). Although that fiscal period includes only 364 days (except for leap years), it is still considered an annual reporting period.

Consistency of Form Income statements generally should be uniform in appearance from one period to the next. The form, terminology, captions, and pattern of combining insignificant items should be consistent. If comparative statements are presented, the prior year's information should be restated to conform to the current year's presentation if changes in presentation are made.

Aggregation The level of disaggregation is a matter of judgment. It should be efficient to give to readers meaningful information. Aggregation of items should not serve to conceal significant information, such as netting revenues against expenses or combining dissimilar types of revenues, expenses, gains, or losses. Although the Codification does not offer benchmarks for disaggregation of income items, the SEC's Division of Corporate Finance's Form and content of and requirements for financial statements regulation S-X 5-03(1) does require separate presentation for some items that exceed 10% of total revenue. Those items include net sales of tangible products, service revenue, rental income operating revenue of public utilities, and other revenues. The SEC also requires the costs and expenses related to those items to be presented separately.[1] Non SEC preparers may want to consider those thresholds when deciding which amounts to disaggregate. Any benchmarks used should be applied consistently.

The category "other or miscellaneous expense" should contain, at maximum, an immaterial total amount of aggregated insignificant items. Once this total approaches a material amount of total expenses, some other aggregations with explanatory titles should be selected.

Income from Continuing Operations

The section "income from continuing operations" includes all revenues, expenses, gains, and losses that are not required to be reported in other sections of an income statement.

There are two generally accepted formats for the presentation of income from continuing operations:

1. The single-step format
2. The multiple-step format

Single-Step Format In the single-step format, items are classified into two groups: revenues and expenses. The operating revenues and other revenues are itemized and summed to determine total revenues. The cost of goods sold, operating expenses, and other expenses are itemized and summed to determine total expenses. The total expenses (including income taxes) are deducted from the total revenues to arrive at income from continuing operations.

Example—A Single-Step Format for Income from Continuing Operations

Revenues:		
Sales (net of discounts and returns and allowances)	$xxx	
Gain on sale of equipment	xxx	
Interest income	xxx	
Dividend income	xxx	$xxx
Expenses:		
Cost of goods sold	$xxx	
Selling expenses	xxx	
General and administrative expenses	xxx	
Interest expense	xxx	(xxx)
Income from continuing operations		xxx

Multiple-Step Format Some believe that a multiple-step format enhances the usefulness of information about an entity's performance by reporting the interrelationships of revenues and expenses, using subtotals to report significant amounts. In a multiple-step format, operating revenues and expenses are separated from nonoperating revenues and expenses to provide more information concerning the firm's primary activities. This format breaks the revenue and expense

[1] Application of Regulation S-X (17 CFR Part 210) can be found on the eccr.gov website.

items into various intermediate income components so that important relationships can be shown and attention can be focused on significant subtotals. Some examples of common intermediate income components are as follows:

- Gross profit (margin)—The difference between net sales and cost of goods sold.
- Operating income—Gross profit less operating expenses.
- Income before income taxes—Operating income plus any other revenue items and less any other expense items.

Example of a Multiple-Step Format for Income from Continuing Operations

Sales:			
Sales			$xxx
Less: Sales discounts		$xxx	
Sales returns and allowances		xxx	(xxx)
Net sales			$xxx
Cost of goods sold		xxx	
Gross profit			$xxx
Operating expenses:			
Selling expenses			
Sales salaries	$xxx		
Commissions	xxx		
Advertising expense	xxx		
Delivery expense	xxx		
Selling supplies expense	xxx		
Depreciation of store furniture and equipment	xxx	$xxx	
General and administrative expenses			
Officers' salaries	$xxx		
Office salaries	xxx		
Bad debts expense	xxx		
Office supplies expense	xxx		
Depreciation of office furniture and fixtures	xxx		
Depreciation of building	xxx		
Insurance expense	xxx		
Utilities expense	xxx	xxx	
Total operating expense			
Operating income			(xxx)
Other revenues:			$xxx
Dividend income		$xxx	
Gain on business acquisition ("bargain purchase")		xxx	
Interest income		xxx	xxx
Other expenses:		$xxx	
Interest expense			(xxx)
Income from continuing operations			$xxx

Items Included in Income from Continuing Operations The following items of revenue, expense, gains, and losses are included within income from continuing operations:

- *Sales or service revenues* are charges to customers for the goods and/or services provided during the period. This section should include information about discounts, allowances, and returns in order to determine net sales or net revenues.

- *Cost of goods sold* is the cost of the inventory items sold during the period. In the case of a merchandising firm, net purchases (purchases less discounts, returns, and allowances plus freight-in) are added to the beginning inventory to obtain the cost of goods available-for-sale. From the cost of goods available-for-sale amount, the ending inventory is deducted to obtain the cost of goods sold.
- *Operating expenses* are primary recurring costs associated with central operations (other than cost of goods sold) that are incurred in order to generate sales. Operating expenses are normally reported in the following two categories:

  1. Selling expenses
  2. General and administrative expenses.

  Selling expenses are those expenses directly related to the company's efforts to generate sales (e.g., sales salaries, commissions, advertising, delivery expenses, depreciation of store furniture and equipment, and store supplies). General and administrative expenses are expenses related to the general administration of the company's operations (e.g., officers and office salaries, office supplies, depreciation of office furniture and fixtures, telephone, postage, accounting and legal services, and business licenses and fees).

- *Gains and losses* result from the peripheral transactions of the entity. If immaterial, they are usually combined and shown with the normal, recurring revenues and expenses. If they are individually material, they should be disclosed on a separate line. Examples are write-downs of inventories and receivables, effects of a strike, gains and losses on the disposal of equipment, and gains and losses from exchange or translation of foreign currencies. Holding gains on available-for-sale securities are included in other comprehensive income rather than income from continuing operations.
- *Other revenues and expenses* are revenues and expenses not related to the central operations of the company (e.g., interest revenues and expenses, and dividend revenues).
- *Unusual and/or infrequent items* should be reported as a separate component of income from continuing operations.
- *Goodwill impairment losses* are presented as a separate line item in the income from continuing operations section of the income statement.
- *Exit or disposal activity costs* are included in income from continuing operations before income taxes.
- *Income tax expense* related to continuing operations is that portion of the total income tax expense applicable to continuing operations.

Net Income The section ends in a subtotal that varies depending upon the existence of discontinued operations. Net income reflects all items of profit and loss recognized during the period, except for error corrections. (ASC 220-10-45-7A) The effects of changes in accounting principles (under ASC 250) are dealt with by retrospective application to all prior periods being presented. For example, the subtotal is usually titled "income from continuing operations" only when there is a section for discontinued operations in one of the years presented. The titles are adjusted accordingly if more than one of these additional sections are necessary. If there are no discontinued operations, the subtotal is titled "net income."

The requirement that net income be presented as one amount does not apply to those entities that have statements different in format from commercial enterprises:

- Investment companies
- Insurance entities
- Certain not-for-profit entities (NFPs)
(ASC 220-10-45-7A)

Entities with an Outstanding Noncontrolling Interest In addition to presenting consolidated net income and comprehensive income, entities with an outstanding noncontrolling interest are required to report the following items in the financial statement in which net income and comprehensive income are presented:

- Amount of net income and comprehensive income attributable to the parent
- Amount of net income and comprehensive income attributable to the noncontrolling interest in a less-than-wholly-owned subsidiary
(ASC 220-10-45-5)

Items of Other Comprehensive Income

ASC 220-10-45-10A lists the following as items currently within other comprehensive income:

- Foreign currency translation adjustments (see paragraph 830-30-45-12).
- Gains and losses on foreign currency transactions that are designated as, and are effective as, economic hedges of a net investment in a foreign entity, commencing as of the designation date (see paragraph 830-20-35-3(a)).
- Gains and losses on intra-entity foreign currency transactions that are of a long-term investment nature (that is, settlement is not planned or anticipated in the foreseeable future), when the entities to the transaction are consolidated, combined, or accounted for by the equity method in the reporting entity's financial statements (see paragraph 830-20-35-3(b)).
- Gains and losses (effective portion) on derivative instruments that are designated as, and qualify as, cash flow hedges (see paragraph 815-20-35-1(c)).
- The difference between changes in fair value of the excluded components of derivatives designated in qualifying hedges and the initial value of the excluded components recognized in earnings under a systematic and rational method.[2]
- Unrealized holding gains and losses on available-for-sale debt securities (see paragraph 320-10-45-1).[3]
- Unrealized holding gains and losses that result from a debt security being transferred into the available-for-sale category from the held-to-maturity category (see paragraph 320-10-35-10(c)).
- Amounts recognized in other comprehensive income for debt securities classified as available-for-sale and held-to-maturity related to another-than-temporary impairment recognized in accordance with Section 320-10-35 if a portion of the impairment was not recognized in earnings.[4]

---

[2] This bulleted item is effective upon implementation of ASU 2017-12.

[3] Upon implementation of ASU 2016-13, this reference will change to ASC 326-30-35-2. See the Chapter on ASC 326 for information on ASC 2016-13.

[4] Upon implementation of ASU 2016-13, this bullet point is superseded.

- Subsequent decreases (if not another-than-temporary impairment) or increases in the fair value of available-for-sale securities previously written down as impaired (see paragraph 320-10-35-18).[5]
- Gains or losses associated with pension or other postretirement benefits (that are not recognized immediately as a component of net periodic benefit cost) (see paragraph 715- 20-50-1(j)).
- Prior service costs or credits associated with pension or other postretirement benefits (see paragraph 715-20-50-1(j)).
- Transition assets or obligations associated with pension or other postretirement benefits (that are not recognized immediately as a component of net periodic benefit cost) (see paragraph 715-20-50-1(j)).
- Changes in fair value attributable to instrument-specific credit risk of liabilities for which the fair value option is elected (see paragraph 825-10-45-5).
- The effect of changes in the discount rates used to measure traditional and limited-payment long-duration insurance contracts (see ASC 944-40-35-6A(b)(1).
- The effect of changes in the fair value of a market risk benefit attributable to a change in the instrument-specific credit risk (see ASC 9440-40-35-8A).

The following items do not quality as comprehensive income:

- Changes in equity resulting from investment by and distributions to owners
- Items that are required to be reported as direct adjustments to paid-in-capital, retained earnings, or other non-income equity accounts
  (ASC 220-10-45-10B)

Other comprehensive income is recognized and measured in accordance with the accounting pronouncement that deems it part of other comprehensive income.

Income Tax Effects (ASC 220-10-45-12) The items of other comprehensive income can be reported either:

- Net of related tax effects in the statement, or
- Gross with the tax effects related to all components reported on a single, separate line.
  (ASC 220-10-45-11)

The tax effects of each component of other comprehensive income must be presented in the statement in which those components are presented or in the notes of the financial statements. (ASC 220-10-45-12) If gross reporting is used, the notes to the financial statements must disclose the tax effects related to each component (if there is more than one component). The examples below illustrate the two presentations.

The Codification also has guidance on the reclassification of certain tax effects from AOCI. The guidance is intended to help entities address certain stranded income tax effects in accumulated other comprehensive income (AOCI) resulting from the Tax Cuts and Jobs Act. Under the guidance, entities have an option to reclassify stranded tax effects within AOCI to retained earnings in each period in which the effect of the change in the U.S. federal corporate income tax rate in the Tax Cuts and Jobs Act (or portion thereof) is recorded. If the entity elects to reclassify the income tax effects of the Tax Cuts and Jobs Act from AOCI to retained earnings, the reclassification includes:

---

[5] Ibid.

a. The effects of the change in the U.S. federal corporate income tax rate as the gross defined tax amounts and related valuation allowances.
b. Other income tax effects that the entity elects to reclassify.
(ASC 220-10-45-12A)

The guidance recommends financial statement preparers disclose:

- A description of the accounting policy for releasing income tax effects from AOCI.
- Whether they elect to reclassify the stranded income tax effects from the Tax Cuts and Jobs Act, and information about the other income tax effects that are reclassified. If the preparers elect not to reclassify the effects, they must disclose that fact in the period of adoption.
(ASC 220-10-50-1 through 50-3)

The guidance affects any organization that

- is required to apply the provisions of Topic 220, Income Statement—Reporting Comprehensive Income, and
- has items of other comprehensive income for which the related tax effects are presented in other comprehensive income as required by GAAP.

Accumulated Other Comprehensive Income At the end of the reporting period, that reporting period's total of other comprehensive income is transferred to a component of equity. It is presented separately from retained earnings and additional paid-in capital on the balance sheet. (ASC 220-10-45-14) On the face of the financial statements, or as a note, the entity must present:

- The changes in the accumulated balances of each component of other comprehensive income and
- Current period reclassifications out of accumulated other comprehensive income and other amounts of other comprehensive income, either before-tax or net-of-tax.
(ASC 220-10-45-14A)

Reclassification Adjustments Some items impact other comprehensive income in one period and then affect net income in the same or a later period. For example, an unrealized holding gain on an available-for-sale debt security is included in other comprehensive income in the period in which the market fluctuation occurs. Later, perhaps years later, the security is sold, and the realized gains are included in net income. An adjustment to the unrealized holding gain component of other comprehensive income is necessary to avoid double counting the gain—once in net income in the current year and once in other comprehensive income in the earlier period. Adjustments of that type are called reclassification adjustments. (ASC 220-10-45-15)[6] The process of including in net income an item previously reported in other comprehensive income is often referred to as "recycling."

The entity determines the reclassification adjustments for each component of other comprehensive income. The sale of an investment in a foreign entity may trigger an adjustment for foreign currency items that had been included in other comprehensive income previously. In such a case, the requirement for a reclassification is limited to accumulated foreign currency translation

---

[6] Life insurers should exclude from amounts reclassified out of accumulated other comprehensive income changes in unrealized gains and losses on available-for-sale debt securities associated with direct adjustments made to policy liabilities necessary to reflect these balances as if such unrealized gains and losses were realized. (ASC 220-10-55-15C)

gains or losses). An adjustment is also necessary upon the complete (or substantially complete) liquidation of an investment in a foreign entity. See ASC 830-30-40-1 through 40-1A for more information. (ASC 220-10-45-16)

Amounts accumulated in other comprehensive income from cash flow hedges are reclassified into earnings in the same period(s) in which the hedged forecasted transactions (such as a forecasted sale) affect earnings. If it becomes probable that the forecasted transaction will not occur, the net gain or loss in accumulated other comprehensive income must be immediately reclassified.

Only minimum pension liabilities will not require reclassification adjustments (because they will not be reported in net income in any future period).

Disclosures for items reclassified out of AOCI include:

- The effect of significant amounts reclassified from each component of AOCI based on its source, and
- The income statement line items affected by the reclassification. (ASC 220-10-45-17A)

If an entity uses a separate line item in the income statement to present pension or other postretirement benefit cost components reclassified out of AOCI, the entity is not required to present those items parenthetically. Entities with defined benefit pension costs reclassified out of accumulated other comprehensive income must identify the amount of each reclassified pension cost component and put in a reference to the relevant disclosure that provides more detail. (ASC 220-10-45-17A and 17B)

If a component is only partially reclassified to net income, entities must cross-reference to the related footnote for additional information. (ASC 220-10-45-17B)

Interim Reporting For interim reporting, entities must present a total for comprehensive income but are *not* required to present the individual components of OCI. Entities that present two statements in their annual financial reports have the option of using a single-statement approach in their condensed interim financial statements. Using one statement avoids the presentation of a separate statement of comprehensive income that contains only one line item for total comprehensive income. (ASC 220-10-45-18) Nonpublic entities are not required to meet the requirements for reclassifications in interim reporting. (ASC 220-10-45-18B)

Reporting Comprehensive Income in a Combined Statement of Income and Comprehensive Income

As noted previously, entities have the option of two presentations. The first is illustrated in the two exhibits that follow.

Example of a Combined Statement of Income and Comprehensive Income with "Net of Tax" Presentation

Hypothetical Corporation
Statement of Comprehensive Income
for the Year Ended December 31, 20X1
($000 omitted)

Revenues	$395,400
Expenses	(251,220)
Other gains and losses	1,500

Income from operations before tax		145,680
Income tax expense		(62,430)
Net income		83,250
Earnings per share		
Basic and diluted 0.73		
Other comprehensive income		
Foreign currency translation adjustment, net of $5,100 tax		11,900
Unrealized gain on securities:		
Unrealized holding gains arising during period, net of $7,500 tax	17,500	
Less: Reclassification adjustment, net of $1,500 tax, for gain included currently in net income	(3,500)	14,000
Cash flow hedges		
Net derivative losses arising during the period, net of $4,800 tax	(11,200)	
Less: Reclassification adjustment for losses included currently in net income, net of $7,762 tax	18,113	6,913
Defined benefit pension plans:		
Prior service cost arising during period	(3,900)	
Net loss arising during period	(2,900)	
Less: Amortization of prior service cost included with net period pension cost	300	
Less: Tax effects		
	1,950	(4,550)
Other comprehensive income		(28,263)
Comprehensive income		$111,513

Example of a Combined Statement of Income and Comprehensive Income with "Gross of Tax" Presentation

Hypothetical Corporation
Statement of Comprehensive Income
for the Year Ended December 31, 20X1
($000 omitted)

Sales		$395,400
Expenses		(251,220)
Other gains and losses		1,500
Income from operations before tax		145,680
Income tax expense		(62,430)
Net earnings		83,250
Earnings per share		
Basic and diluted 0.73		
Other comprehensive income		
Foreign currency translation adjustment		17,000
Unrealized gains on securities:		
Unrealized holding gains arising during period	25,000	
Less: Reclassification adjustment for gain included currently in net income	(5,000)	20,000
Cash flow hedges		
Net derivative losses arising during the period	(16,000)	

Less: Reclassification adjustment for losses included currently in net income	25,875	9,875
Defined benefit plans adjustment[7]		
Prior service cost arising during period	(3,900) (a)	
Net loss arising during period	(2,900) (a)	
Less: Amortization of prior service cost included with net period pension cost	300 (a)	(6,500)
Other comprehensive income, before tax		40,375
Income tax expense related to items of other comprehensive income		(12,112)
Other comprehensive income, net of tax		28,263
Comprehensive income		$111,513

(a) These AOCI components are components of net periodic pension cost (see pension note for additional details).

If the "gross" approach illustrated above is used, it is also necessary to present in the notes to the financial statements details regarding the allocation of the tax effects to the several items included in other comprehensive income.

Reporting Comprehensive Income in Two Separate but Consecutive Statements of Income and Comprehensive Income

Entities are not required to present information about comprehensive income in a continuous statement of income and comprehensive income. Instead, they can present the components of other comprehensive income, the totals of other comprehensive income, and a total for comprehensive income in a statement which must immediately follow a statement of net income.

Example of Two Separate but Consecutive Statements of Income and Comprehensive Income—Net of Tax Presentation

Hypothetical Corporation
Statement of Income
for the Year Ended December 31, 20X1
($000 omitted)

Revenues, (includes $12,000 accumulated other comprehensive income reclassifications for net gains in cash flow hedges)	
Expenses, (includes ($10,000) accumulated other comprehensive income reclassifications for net loss in cash flow hedges)	$395,400 (251,220)
Other gains and losses	1,500
Income from operations before tax	145,680
Income tax expense	(62,430)
Net income	83,250
Earnings per share	
Basic and diluted 0.73	

Hypothetical Corporation Statement of Comprehensive Income
for the Year Ended December 31, 20X1 ($000 omitted)

[7] Ibid.

Net income		83,250
Other comprehensive income		
Foreign currency translation adjustment, net of $5,100 tax		11,900
Unrealized gain on securities:		
Unrealized holding gains arising during period, net of $7,500 tax	17,500	
Less: Reclassification adjustment, net of $1,500 tax, for gain included currently in net income	(3,500)	14,000
Cash flow hedges		
Net derivative losses arising during the period, net of $4,800 tax	(11,200)	
Less: Reclassification adjustment for losses included currently in net income, net of $7,762 tax	18,113	6,913
Defined benefit pension plans: tax[8]		
Prior service cost arising during period	(3,900) (a)	
Net loss arising during period	(2,900) (a)	
Less: Amortization of prior service cost included with net period pension cost	300 (a)	
Less: Tax effects	1,950	(4,550)
Other comprehensive income		28,263
Comprehensive income		$111,513

(a) These AOCI components are components of net periodic pension cost (see pension note for additional details).

Pro Forma Earnings

Companies have made reference in press releases and published materials to an alternative measure of performance, referred to as "pro forma earnings." This practice has generated confusion because there is no standard definition for "pro forma earnings." Different reporting entities can, and have, defined pro forma earnings on a wide range of ad hoc bases, and sometimes a given entity fails even to consistently define this amount from period to period.

Often, even when GAAP-basis earnings are stated in the same announcement as the pro forma measure, it is the latter that receives most of the attention. In a number of instances, pro forma earnings have been based on very aggressive exclusions of operating costs and, sometimes, the inclusion of onetime gains. Such practices ultimately came to be widely recognized as being misleading and inappropriate, and popular sentiment turned against employment of such devices.

The SEC adopted Regulation G to curtail the use of pro forma earnings statements. Regulation G states that a public company, or a person acting on its behalf, is not to make public a non-GAAP financial measure that, taken together with the information accompanying that measure, either contains an untrue statement of a material fact or omits a material fact that would be necessary to make the presentation of the non-GAAP financial measure not misleading. Further, Regulation G requires a public company that discloses or releases a non-GAAP financial measure to include in that disclosure or release a presentation of the most directly comparable GAAP financial measure and a reconciliation of the disclosed non- GAAP measure to that directly comparable GAAP financial measure. (Regulation G, Section II A, paragraph 3a)

The regulations also prohibit certain non-GAAP measures from inclusion in SEC filings. Public companies must not:

- Exclude from non-GAAP liquidity measures charges or liabilities that required, or will require, cash settlement, or would have required cash settlement absent an ability to settle

[8] Ibid.

in another manner. However, earnings before interest and taxes (EBIT) and earnings before interest, taxes, depreciation, and amortization (EBITDA) are permissible.

- Create a non-GAAP performance measure that eliminates items identified as nonrecurring, infrequent, or unusual if the nature of the excluded item is such that it is reasonably likely to recur within two years or (b) similar to a charge or gain that occurred within the prior two years.
- Present non-GAAP financial measures on the face of the registrant's financial statements prepared in accordance with GAAP or in the accompanying notes.
- Present non-GAAP financial measures on the face of any pro forma financial information required to be disclosed by Article 11 of Regulation S-X (e.g., business combinations or disposals).
- Use titles or descriptions of non-GAAP financial measures that are the same as, or confusingly similar to, titles or descriptions used for GAAP measures.
(Regulation G, Section II B, paragraph 2)

ASC 220-20, *Unusual Items or Infrequently Occurring Items*

Items that are unusual or infrequent or both should be reported as a separate component of income from continuing operations. The EPS effect of these items should not be separated on the face of the income statement. (ASC 220-20-45-1 and 50-1)

In addition, the entity should disclose the nature and financial effects of each event or transaction on the face of the income statement as a separate component of continuing operations, or alternatively, in notes to financial statements. (ASC 220-20-50-3 and 45-16)

Unusual Nature To meet this criterion, the underlying event or transaction should:

- Possess a high degree of abnormality, and
- Be clearly unrelated to, or only incidentally related to, the ordinary and typical activities of the reporting entity, taking into account the environment in which it operates.

In determining whether an event or transaction is of an unusual nature, the following special characteristics of the reporting entity are considered:

- Type and scope of operations
- Lines of business
- Operating policies
- Industry (or industries) in which the reporting entity operates
- Geographic locations of its operations
- Nature and extent of government regulation.

An event that is of an unusual nature for one reporting entity can be an ordinary and usual activity of another because of the above characteristics. Whether an event or transaction is beyond the control of management is irrelevant in the determination of whether it is of an unusual nature. (ASC 220-20-55-1)

Infrequency of Occurrence To satisfy this requirement, the underlying event or transaction should be of a type that would not reasonably be expected to recur in the foreseeable future, again taking into account the environment in which the reporting entity operates. (ASC 220-20-55-2)

ASC 220-30, *Business Interruption Insurance*

In general, proceeds from insurance claims are classified based on the nature of the loss and requires judgment. ASC 220-30 provides guidance on presentation and disclosure of business interruption insurance. This type of insurance may cover:

- Gross margin lost because of the suspension of normal operations,
- Fixed charges,
- Expenses related to gross margin, and
- Expenses incurred to reduce the loss from business interruption, etc.
(ASC 220-30-05-2)

Entities may choose how to record proceeds from business interruption insurance in the statement of operations as long as it does not conflict with other standards. (ASC 220-30-45-1) The proceeds related to lost assets should not be recorded as reductions of the costs to rebuild or replace the insured asset.

Disclosures and Presentation Disclosure requirements can be found in the *Disclosure and Presentation Checklist for Commercial Businesses* at www.wiley.com/go/GAAP2021.

Other Sources

See ASC Location—*Wiley GAAP* Chapter	***For information on . . .***
ASC 740-270-30-8 through 30-12	The computation of interim period income taxes applicable to significant unusual or infrequently occurring items.

6 ASC 230 STATEMENT OF CASH FLOWS

PERSPECTIVE AND ISSUES

Technical Alert

In August 2018, the FASB issued ASC 2018-15, *Intangibles—Goodwill and Other Internal-Use Software (Topic 350-40): Customer's Accounting for Implementation Costs Incurred in a Cloud Computing Arrangement That Is a Service Contract.* This ASU requires an entity to classify payments made for capitalized implementation costs in the same category as payments made for fees associated with the hosting element. This category is typically cash flows from operating activities. (ASC 350-40-45-3) The ASU is effective:

- For public business entities—fiscal years beginning after December 15, 2019, and interim periods within those fiscal years.
- For all other entities—for fiscal years beginning after December 15, 2020, and interim periods within annual periods beginning after December 15, 2021.

Early adoption is permitted. The changes can be applied retrospectively or prospectively to implementation costs incurred after the date of adoption.

Subtopic

ASC 230, *Statement of Cash Flows*, contains one subtopic:

- ASC 230-10, *Overall*, that establishes standards for cash flow reporting in general purpose financial statements.

Scope and Scope Exceptions

A statement of cash flows is a required part of a complete set of financial statements for business enterprises and not-for-profit organizations. The following are *not* required to present a statement of cash flows:

- Defined pension plans that present financial information under Topic 960
- Other employee plans that present information similar to ASC 960 (ASC 962-205-45-9)
- A common trust fund, variable annuity account, or similar fund maintained by a bank, insurance entity, or other entity in its capacity as a trustee, administrator, or guardian for the collective investment and reinvestment of moneys
- Investment companies within the scope of ASC 946 if the following conditions are met:
  - Substantially all of the entity's investments are highly liquid,
  - The entity's investments are carried at fair value and classified in accordance with ASC 820 as Level 1 or Level 2 or were measured using the practical expedient to determine fair value and are redeemable in the near term,
  - The entity has little or no debt, based on average debt outstanding during the period, in relation to average total assets, and
  - The entity provides a statement of changes in net assets.

  (ASC 230-10-15-4)

DEFINITIONS OF TERMS

Source: ASC 230-10-20, *Glossary*, except for "direct method" and "indirect method." See also Appendix A, *Definitions of Terms*, for additional terms relevant to this topic: Cash, Cash Equivalents, Conditional Contribution, Contract, Contribution, Donor-imposed Condition, Donor-imposed Restriction, Effective Interest Rate, Fair Value (3rd definition), Financial Asset (Def. 2), Inherent Contribution, Lease, Lease Liability, Lease Payments, Lessee, Lessor, Market Participants, Net Assets, Net Assets with Donor Restrictions, Net Assets without Donor Restrictions, Promise to Give, Public Business Entity, Underlying Asset.

Direct Method. A method that derives the net cash provided by operating activities from the components of operating cash receipts and payments as opposed to adjusting net income for items not affecting cash.

Financing Activities. Financing activities include obtaining resources from owners and providing them with a return on, and a return of, their investment; receiving restricted resources that by donor stipulation must be used for long-term purposes; borrowing money and repaying amounts borrowed, or otherwise settling the obligation; and obtaining and paying for other resources obtained from creditors on long-term credit.

Indirect (Reconciliation) Method. A method that derives the net cash provided by operating activities by adjusting net income for revenue and expense items not resulting from cash transactions.

Investing Activities. Investing activities include making and collecting loans and acquiring and disposing of debt or equity instruments and property, plant, and equipment and other productive assets, that is, assets held for or used in the production of goods or services by the entity (other than materials that are part of the entity's inventory). Investing activities exclude acquiring and disposing of certain loans or other debt or equity instruments that are acquired specifically for resale, as discussed in paragraphs ASC 230-10-45-12 and 230-10- 45-21.

Operating Activities. Operating activities include all transactions and other events that are not defined as investing or financing activities (see paragraphs 230-10-45-12 through 45-15). Operating activities generally involve producing and delivering goods and providing services. Cash flows from operating activities are generally the cash effects of transactions and other events that enter into the determination of net income.

CONCEPTS, RULES, AND EXAMPLES

Cash Focus

The statement of cash flows includes only inflows and outflows of cash and cash equivalents and amounts generally described as restricted cash or unrestricted cash equivalents. (ASC 230-10-45-4) To prepare a statement of cash flows, the preparer must understand what qualifies as cash and cash equivalents. The next challenge for the preparer is the classification of the cash flows, especially for nonrecurring transactions.

Cash equivalents include any short-term, highly liquid investments (see definition in Appendix A for criteria) used as a temporary investment of idle cash. Entities usually purchase and sell cash equivalents as part of their cash management activities. Those transactions do not need to be reported in the statement of cash flow. (ASC 230-10-45-5) The entity should establish a policy stating which items that satisfy the definition of cash equivalents are treated as such. (ASC 230-10-45-6)

The effects of investing and financing activities that do not result in receipts or payments of cash should be reported in a separate schedule immediately following the statement of cash flows or in the notes to the financial statements. This is to preserve the statement's primary focus on cash flows from operating, investing, and financing activities. If a transaction is part cash and part noncash, only the cash portion is reported in the body of the statement of cash flows.

The primary purpose of the statement of cash flows is to provide information about cash receipts and cash payments of an entity during a period. A secondary purpose is to provide information about the entity's investing and financing activities during the period.

Specifically, the statement of cash flows helps investors and creditors assess:

- The entity's ability to generate future positive cash flows
- The entity's ability to meet obligations and pay dividends
- The reasons for differences between net income and net cash receipts and payments
- The cash and noncash aspects of investing and financing transactions on an entity's financial position
  (ASC 230-10-10-2)

The ultimate objective of investment and credit decisions is the maximization of net cash inflows, so information for assessing the amounts, timing, and uncertainty of prospective cash flows is needed.

Classification of Cash Receipts and Disbursements

ASC 230-10-45-10 through 17 discuss classification of cash receipts and disbursements. The statement of cash flows requires classification of cash receipts and cash disbursements into three categories:

1. Investing activities
2. Financing activities
3. Operating activities

See the "Definitions of Terms" section above for more information on these categories.

Some cash receipts and payments may have aspects of more than one category. In those cases, the preparer should apply the predominance principle. That is, first, the preparer should apply the guidance in this Topic and others. If guidance is not available, the preparer should then classify each cash flow on the basis of the activity likely to be the predominant source or use of cash flows for the item. (ASC 230-10-45-22 and 22A)

The following exhibit contains examples of the classification of cash inflows and outflows within the statement of cash flows.

Exhibit—Classification of Inflows and Outflows[1]

• Topics 255 and 940 offer guidance on securities and other assets held in trading accounts carried by banks, brokers, and dealers in securities.
• Cash receipts and payments from purchases and sales of securities classified as trading debt securities in accordance with Topic 320 and equity securities accounted for in accordance with Topic 321 are classified as cash flows based on the nature and purpose for which the securities were acquired. (ASC 230-10-45-19)
• Classify proceeds from the settlement of insurance claims (not proceeds from corporate-owned life insurance policies (COLI), including bank-owned life insurance (BOLI) policies) based on the nature of each component loss. (ASC 230-10-45-21B)
• Classify cash payments for premiums of corporate-owned life insurance policies (COLI), including bank-owned life insurance (BOLI) policies as cash flows for investing, operating, or a combination of investing or operating activities. (ASC 230-10-45-21C)
• For distributions received from equity method investees: Choose one of two approaches and make an accounting policy election: 1. **The cumulative earnings approach.** In this approach, the investor compares the distribution received with its cumulative equity method earnings since inception. Distributions received up to the amount of cumulative earnings are a return on investment classified in operating activities. Excess distributions are considered a return on interest, classified as investing activities. 2. **Nature of distribution approach.** The entity classifies distributions based on the nature of the investee's activities that generated the distribution. If the information necessary to implement this approach is not available, the investor should use the cumulative earnings approach and report a change in accounting principle. (ASC 230-10-45-21D) • Classify lessee's interest on a lease liability according to ASC 230's requirements for interest paid. (842-20-25-5b)

[1] See the Technical Alert section at the beginning of this chapter for new guidance on classification of certain items not included herein.

	Operating	Investing	Financing
Cash Inflows	• Receipts from sale of goods or services • Returns on loans, other debt instruments of other entities, and equity securities (interest and dividends) (ASC 230-10-45-16) • Sales of other securities and other assets if acquired for resale and carried at fair value in a trading account (ASC 230-10-45-20) • Acquisitions and sales of loans acquired specifically for resale and carried at fair value at the lower of cost or fair value[2] (ASC 230-10-45-21)	• Cash flows from purchases, sales, and maturities of available-for-sale debt securities (ASC 230-10-45-11) • Collections or sales of loans and sales of other entities' debt instruments, except, per ASC 230-10-45-21A, for cash equivalents and certain debt instruments acquired specifically for resale, and donated debt instruments received by not-for-profit entities • Collections on a transferor's beneficial interest in a securitization of the transferor's trade receivables • Sales of equity instruments, held in available-for-sale or held-to-maturity portfolios, of other enterprises, except for donated debt instruments received from NFPs, and from returns of investment in those instruments	• Proceeds from issuing equity instruments • Proceeds from issuing debt (short-term or long-term), including bonds, mortgages, and notes • Not-for-profits' cash receipts from contributions and investment income the donor restricts to the purposes of acquiring, constructing or improving long-lived assets or establishing or increasing a donor-restricted endowment fund
		• Sales of property, plant, and equipment and other productive assets • Sales of loans not specifically acquired for resale • Proceeds from insurance settlements related to the sale or disposal of loans, investments, or property, plant, or equipment (ASC 230-10-45-12)	• Proceeds from derivative instruments that include, at inception, financing elements. The proceeds may be received at inception or over the term of the instrument. Not included are a financing element inherently included in an at-the-market derivative instrument (ASC 230-10-45-14)

[2] Upon implementation of ASU 2016-13, this language changes to "carried at fair value or at the lower of an amortized cost basis or fair value."

	Operating	Investing	Financing
	• Not-for-profits' sale of donated financial assets that on receipt had no donor-imposed limitations on sale and were converted immediately into cash (ASC 230-10-45-21A)		• Not-for-profits' donor-restricted cash gifts that are limited to long-term purposes (ASC 230-10-45-21A)
	• For lessors—cash receipts from lease payments (ASC 842-30-45-5)		
	• All other cash receipts not from inventory or financing activities (ASC 230-10-45-16a)		
Cash Outflows	• Payments for inventory • Payments to employees and other suppliers for goods and services • Payments to government for taxes, duties, fines, and other fees or penalties • Payments of interest • For settlement of zero-coupon debt instruments, including other debt instruments, with insignificant coupon rates relative to the effective interest rate of the borrowing, the interest portion • Payments of asset retirement obligations	• Loans made and acquisitions of other entities' debt instruments other than cash equivalents and certain debt instruments acquired for resale • Purchase of equity instruments other than certain instruments, carried in a trading account, of other enterprises • Purchase of property, plant, and equipment and other productive assets, including interest capitalized as part of the cost of those assets • Contingent consideration cash payments made by an acquirer soon after a business combination. (Soon is defined as three months or less.) (ASC 230-10-45-13)	• Payment of dividends or other distributions to owners, including repurchase of entity's stock • Cash paid to a tax authority when the employer is withholding shares from an employee's award for tax-withholding purposes is an outlay to reacquire the entity's equity instruments • Repayment of debt principal • For settlement of zero-coupon debt instruments, including other debt instruments, with insignificant coupon rates relative to the effective interest rate of the borrowing, the principal portion

	• Payment not made soon after the acquisition date of a business combination by an acquirer to settle a contingent consideration liability, where the payment exceeds the original amount of the contingent consideration liability (ASC 230-10-45-17) • Purchase of trading debt and equity securities and assets acquired specifically for resale carried at fair value in a trading account (ASC 230-10-45-19 and 45-20)		• Other principal payments to creditors for long-term credit • Distributions, to counterparties of derivative instruments that include financing elements at inception. These may be received at inception or over the term of the instrument. Not included are a financing element inherently included in an at-the-market derivative instrument with no prepayments.
	• Loans acquired specifically for resale and carried at fair value at the lower of cost or fair value (ASC 230-10-45-21)		• Payments for debt issue costs • Contingent consideration payments by an acquirer not made soon after a business combination up to the amount of the original contingent consideration liability. (Soon is defined as three months or less.) (ASC 230-10-45-15) • Debt prepayment or debt extinguishment costs (ASC 230-10-45-16)

	Operating	*Investing*	*Financing*
	• Payments from operating leases, except to the extent that those payments represent costs to bring another asset for its intended use • Variable lease payments and short-term payments not included in the lease liability (ASC 842-20-45-5-c)	• Loan payments associated with the costs to bring another asset for its intended use that are capitalized as part of a lease sale (ASC 842-20-45-5b)	• Repayments for the principal portion of the lease liability from a financing lease (ASC 842-20-45-5a)
	• All other cash payments that are not from investing or financing activities (ASC 230-10-45-17f)		

Exhibit—Statement of Cash Flows (Without Details of Operating Activities)

The following exhibit demonstrates the classification of cash receipts and disbursements in the investing and financing activities of a statement of cash flows (though without detail of the required operating activities section):

Liquid Corporation
Statement of Cash Flows
for the Year Ended December 31, 20X1

Net cash flows from operating activities		$ xxx
Cash flows from investing activities:		
Purchase of property, plant, and equipment	$(xxx)	
Sale of equipment	xx	
Collection of notes receivable	xx	
Net cash used in investing activities		
Cash flows from financing activities:		(xx)
Sale of common stock	xxx	
Repayment of long-term debt	(xx)	
Reduction of notes payable	(x)	
Net cash provided by financing activities		xx
Effect of exchange rate changes on cash		xx
Net increase (decrease) in cash		xxx
Cash, cash equivalents, and restricted cash at beginning of year		xxx
Cash, cash equivalents, and restricted cash at end of year		$ xxx
Schedule of noncash financing and investing activities:		
Conversion of bonds into common stock		$ xxx
Property acquired under finance leases		xxx
		$ xxx

Operating Activities Presentation

The operating activities section of the statement of cash flows can be presented under the direct method or the indirect method. The FASB has long expressed a preference for the direct method of presenting net cash from operating activities, that is, presenting major classes of gross cash receipts and payments and their sum. Conversely, the indirect method has always been vastly preferred by preparers.

The Direct Method The direct method shows the items that affected cash flow during the reporting period. Cash received and cash paid are presented, as opposed to converting accrual-basis income to cash flow information. At a minimum, entities using the direct method are required to report the following classes of operating cash receipts and payments:

- Cash collected from customers
- Interest and dividends received
- Other operating cash receipts
- Cash paid to employees and other suppliers
- Interest paid
- Income taxes paid including separate identification of the cash that would have been paid if the reporting entity had not received an income tax benefit resulting from increases in the fair value of its shares associated with share-based compensation arrangements
- Other operating cash payments
  (ASC 230-10-45-25)

Entities are encouraged to make further breakdowns that would be useful to financial statement users. For example, disaggregating "cash paid to employees and suppliers" might reveal useful information.

The direct method allows the user to clarify the relationship between the company's net income and its cash flows. For example, payments of expenses are shown as cash disbursements and are deducted from cash receipts. In this way, the user is able to understand the cash receipts and cash payments for the period. The information needed to prepare the operating activities section using the direct method can often be obtained by converting information already appearing in the statement of financial position and income statement. Formulas for conversion of various income statement amounts for the direct method of presentation from the accrual basis to the cash basis are summarized below.

The Indirect Method The indirect method is the most widely used presentation of cash from operating activities, because it is easier to prepare. It focuses on the differences between net income and cash flows. The indirect format begins with net income, which is obtained directly from the income statement. Revenue and expense items not affecting cash are added or deducted to arrive at net cash provided by operating activities. For example, depreciation and amortization would be added back because they reduce net income without affecting cash.

The statement of cash flows prepared using the indirect method emphasizes changes in the components of most current asset and current liability accounts. Changes in inventory, accounts receivable, and other current accounts are used to determine the cash flow from operating activities. Preparers calculate the change in accounts receivable using the balances net of the allowance account in order to ensure that write-offs of uncollectible accounts are treated properly. Other adjustments under the indirect method include changes in the account balances of deferred income taxes and the income (loss) from investments reported using the equity method. However, short-term borrowing used to purchase equipment is classified as a financing activity.

Exhibit—Converting Income Statement Amounts from the Accrual Basis to the Cash Basis—Direct Method

Accrual basis		*Additions*		*Deductions*		*Cash basis*
Net sales	+	Beginning A/R	–	Ending A/R A/R written off	=	Cash received from customers
Cost of goods sold	+	Ending inventory Beginning A/P	–	Manufacturing depreciation and amortization Beginning inventory Ending A/P	=	Cash paid to suppliers
Operating expenses	+	Ending prepaid expenses Beginning accrued expenses	–	Sales and administrative depreciation and amortization Beginning prepaid expenses Ending accrued expenses payable Bad debts expense	=	Cash paid for operating expenses

The following diagram shows the adjustments to net income necessary for converting accrual-based net income to cash-basis net income when using the indirect method. The diagram is simply an expanded statement of financial position equation.

Exhibit—Converting Accrual-Based Net Income to Cash-Basis Net Income—Indirect Method

	*Current assets**	+	*Noncurrent assets*	=	*Current liabilities*	+	*Long-term liabilities*	+	*Income*	*Accrual income adjustment to convert to cash flow*
1.	Increase			=					Increase	Decrease
2.	Decrease			=					Decrease	Increase
3.				=	Increase				Decrease	Increase
4.				=	Decrease				Increase	Decrease

* Other than cash and cash equivalents

For example, using Row 1, a credit sale would increase accounts receivable and accrual-basis income but would not affect cash. Therefore, its effect must be removed from the accrual income in order to convert to cash income. The last column indicates that the increase in a current asset balance must be deducted from income to obtain cash flow. Using Row 2, a decrease in a current asset, such as prepaid rent, indicates that net income was decreased by rent expense, without a cash outflow in the current period. Thus, the decrease in prepaid rent would be added back to convert to cash income.

Similarly, using Row 3, an increase in a current liability must be added to income to obtain cash flows (e.g., accrued wages are on the income statement as an expense, but they do not require cash; the increase in wages payable must be added back to remove this noncash expense from accrual-basis income). Using Row 4, a decrease in a current liability, such as accounts payable, indicates that cash was used but the expense was incurred in an earlier period. Thus, the decrease in accounts payable would be subtracted to include this disbursement in cash income.

If the indirect method is chosen, then the amount of interest and income tax paid must be included in the related disclosures.

Reconciliation of Net Income and Net Cash Flow from Operating Activities If an entity uses the indirect method to provide information about major classes of operating cash receipts and payments, it must report the same amount of net cash flow from operating activities indirectly. This is done with an adjustment to net income to reconcile it to net cash from operating activities by removing:

- The effects of all deferrals of past operating activities, and
- All items included in net income that do not affect cash provided for or used for operating activities.
  (ASC 230-10-45-28)

When the direct method is used by an entity other than a not-for-profit, a separate schedule reconciling net income to net cash flows from operating activities must also be provided. (ASC 230-10-45-30) That schedule reports the same information as the operating activities section prepared using the indirect method. Therefore, a firm must prepare and present both the direct and indirect methods when using the direct method for reporting cash from operating activities.

If the indirect method is used, the reconciliation may be presented with the statement of cash flow or in a separate schedule. If presented separately, the statement of cash flow reports only the net cash flow from operating activities. If the reconciliation is presented in the statement of cash flows, adjustments to net income to determine net cash flow from operating activities must be identified as reconciling items. (ASC 230-10-45-31 and 45-32)

Comparison of Methods The major drawback to the indirect method involves the user's difficulty in comprehending the information presented. This method does not show the sources or uses of cash. Only adjustments to accrual-basis net income are shown. In some cases, the adjustments can be confusing. For instance, the sale of equipment resulting in an accrual-basis loss would require that the loss be added to net income to arrive at net cash from operating activities. (The loss was deducted in the computation of net income, but because the sale will be shown as an investing activity, the loss must be added back to net income.)

The direct method portrays the amounts of cash both provided by and used in the reporting entity's operations, instead of presenting net income and reconciling items. The direct method reports only the items that affect cash flow (inflows/outflows of cash) and ignores items that do not affect cash flow (depreciation, gains, etc.). The general formats of both the direct method and the indirect method are shown below.

Exhibit—Operating Activities: Formats for Direct and Indirect Methods

Direct method

Cash flows from operating activities:		
Cash received from sale of goods	$ xxx	
Cash interest received	xxx	
Cash dividends received	xxx	
Cash provided by operating activities		$ xxx
Cash paid to suppliers	(xxx)	
Cash paid for operating expenses	(xxx)	
Cash interest paid	(xxx)	
Cash paid for taxes	(xxx)	
Cash disbursed for operating activities		(xxx)
Net cash flows from operating activities		$ xxx

Indirect method

Cash flows from operating activities:	
Net income	$ xx
Add/deduct items not affecting cash:	
Decrease (increase) in accounts receivable	(xx)
Depreciation and amortization expense	xx
Increase (decrease) in accounts payable	xx
Decrease (increase) in inventories	xx
Loss on sale of equipment	
Net cash flows from operating activities	$ xx

Other Requirements

Gross versus Net Basis The emphasis in the statement of cash flows is on gross cash receipts and payments. For instance, reporting the net change in bonds payable would obscure the financing activities of the entity by not disclosing separately cash inflows from issuing bonds and cash outflows from retiring bonds. In a few circumstances, netting of cash flows is allowed. The items must have these characteristics:

- Quick turnovers,
- Large amounts, and
- Short maturities (maturities of three months or less).
  (ASC 230-10-45-8)

Net reporting for the following assets and liabilities is allowed provided the original maturity is three months or less:

- Investments (other than cash equivalents),
- Loans receivable, and
- Debts.
  (ASC 230-10-45-9)

Discontinued Operations The disclosure requirements relevant to discontinued operations and related cash flows can be found in the disclosure checklist at www.wiley.com/go/ GAAP2021—reference ASC 205-20-50-5B(c).

Cash Flow per Share This information may *not* be displayed in the financial statements of a reporting entity.

Net Reporting by Financial Institutions

Banks, savings institutions, and credit unions are allowed to report net cash receipts and payments for the following:

- Deposits placed with other financial institutions
- Withdrawals of those deposits
- Time deposits accepted
- Repayments of time deposits
- Loans made to customers
- Principal collections of loans made to customers.
  (ASC 942-230-45-1)

Reporting Hedging Transactions

Per ASC 230-10-45-27, the cash flows resulting from derivative instruments that are accounted for as fair value hedges or cash flow hedges may be classified as the same type of cash flows as the hedged items provided that the accounting policy is disclosed. There is an exception for hedges considered to have a financing element at inception. If the derivative instrument used to hedge includes at inception an other-than-insignificant financing element, all cash inflows and outflows associated with the derivative instrument are reported by the borrower as cash flows from financing activities. (ASC 230-10-45-27) A derivative that at inception includes off-market terms, or requires up-front cash payment, or both, often contains a financing element. A derivative instrument is viewed as including a financing element if its contractual terms have been structured to ensure that net payments will be made by one party in the earlier periods of the derivative's term and subsequently returned by the counterparty in the later periods (other than elements that are inherent in at-the-money derivative instruments with no prepayments). If for any reason hedge accounting for an instrument is discontinued, then any cash flows subsequent to the date of discontinuance are classified consistent with the nature of the instrument.

Reporting Foreign Currency Cash Flows

If an entity has foreign currency transactions or foreign operations, it should look to ASC 830 for guidance.

Preparation of the Statement—Comprehensive Example

Objective Under a cash and cash equivalents basis, the changes in the cash account and any cash equivalent account is the "bottom line" figure of the statement of cash flows. Using the 20X1 and 20X2 statements of financial position in this example, there is an increase of $25,000 in cash and cash equivalents. This is the difference between the totals for cash and treasury bills between 20X1 and 20X2 ($41,000 – $16,000).

Direct Method When preparing the statement of cash flows using the direct method, gross cash inflows from revenues and gross cash outflows to suppliers and for expenses are presented in the operating activities section.

Indirect Method In preparing the reconciliation of net income to net cash flow from operating activities (indirect method), changes in all accounts (other than cash and cash equivalents) that are related to operations are additions to or deductions from net income to arrive at net cash provided by operating activities.

Using T-Accounts A T-account analysis may be helpful when preparing the statement of cash flows. A T-account is set up for each account and beginning (20X1) and ending (20X2) balances are taken from the appropriate statement of financial position. Additionally, a T-account for cash and cash equivalents from operating activities and a master or summary T-account of cash and cash equivalents should be used.

Example of Preparing a Statement of Cash Flows

The financial statements below will be used to prepare the statement of cash flows.

Johnson Company
Statements of Financial Position
December 31, 20X2 and 20X1

	20X2	*20X1*
Assets		
Current assets:		
Cash	$ 37,000	$ 10,000
Treasury bills	4,000	6,000
Accounts receivable—net	9,000	11,000
Inventory	14,000	9,000
Prepaid expenses	10,000	13,000
Total current assets	$ 74,000	$ 49,000
Noncurrent assets:		
Investment in available-for-sale securities	7,500	15,000
Add (less) adjustment for changes in fair value	1,000	(3,000)
Investment in XYZ (35%)	16,000	14,000
Patent	5,000	6,000
Leased asset	5,000	–
Property, plant, and equipment	39,000	37,000
Less accumulated depreciation	(7,000)	(3,000)
Total assets	$140,500	$115,000
Liabilities		
Current liabilities:		
Accounts payable	$ 2,000	$ 12,000
Notes payable—current	9,000	–
Interest payable	3,000	2,000
Dividends payable	5,000	2,000
Income taxes payable	2,180	1,000
Lease obligation	700	–

Total current liabilities	21,880	17,000
Noncurrent liabilities:		
Deferred tax liability	9,360*	4,920*
Bonds payable	10,000	25,000
Lease obligation	4,300	
Total liabilities	$ 45,540	$ 46,920
Stockholders' equity		
Common stock, $10 par value	$ 33,000	$ 26,000
Additional paid-in capital	16,000	3,000
Retained earnings	45,320	41,000
Accumulated other comprehensive income		
Net unrealized loss on available-for-sale securities	640	(1,920)
Total stockholders' equity	$ 94,960	$ 68,080
Total liabilities and stockholders' equity	$140,500	$115,300

* *Net of deferred tax asset ($540) and ($1,080) respectively.*

Johnson Company
Statement of Earnings and Comprehensive Income
for the Year Ended December 31, 20X2

Sales		$100,000
Other income		8,500
		$108,500
Cost of goods sold, excluding depreciation		60,000
Selling, general, and administrative expenses		12,000
Depreciation		8,000
Amortization of patents		1,000
Interest expense		2,000
		$ 83,000
Income before taxes		$ 25,500
Income taxes:		
Current	$6,180	
Deferred	3,000	9,180
Net income		$ 16,320
Other comprehensive income, net of tax		
Unrealized gains on securities:		
Unrealized holding gains (less applicable income taxes of $900)		1,600
Add reclassification adjustment (less applicable income taxes of $540)		960
Total other comprehensive income		$ 2,560
Comprehensive income		$ 18,880

Additional information (all relating to 20X2)

1. Equipment costing $6,000 with a book value of $2,000 was sold for $5,000.
2. The company received a $3,000 dividend from its investment in XYZ, accounted for under the equity method and recorded income from the investment of $5,000 that is included in other income.
3. The company issued 200 shares of common stock for $5,000.
4. The company signed a note payable for $9,000.
5. Equipment was purchased for $8,000.
6. The company converted $15,000 bonds payable into 500 shares of common stock. The book value method was used to record the transaction.
7. A dividend of $12,000 was declared.
8. Equipment was leased on December 31, 20X2. The principal portion of the first payment due December 31, 20X3, is $700.
9. The company sold half of their available-for-sale investments during the year for $8,000. The fair value of the remaining available-for-sale investments was $8,500 on December 31, 20X2.
10. The income tax rate is 36%.

Summary of Cash and Cash Equivalents

Inflows	Outflows	
(d) 5,000		
	8,000 (g)	
	9,000 (i)	
(h) 5,000		
(n) 9,000		
(s) 8,000		
(t) 15,000		
42,000	17,000	
	25,000	Net increase in cash
42,000	42,000	

Cash and Cash Equivalents—Operating

(a) 16,320	
(b) 8,000	
(c) 1,000	3,000 (d)
(e) 3,000	5,000 (f)
(f) 3,000	
(j) 2,000	5,000 (k)
(l) 3,000	10,000 (m)
(o) 1,000	
(p) 1,180	500 (s)
38,500	23,500
	15,000 (t)
38,500	38,500

Accounts Receivable (Net)

11,000	
	2,000 (j)
9,000	

Inventory

9,000	
(k) 5,000	
14,000	

Prepaid Expenses

13,000	
	3,000 (l)
10,000	

Investment in AFS Securities

15,000	
	7,500 (s)
7,500	

Adjustment for Changes in FV of AFS Securities

	3,000
(s) 1,500	
(s) 2,500	
1,000	

Investment in XYZ

14,000	
(f) 5,000	3,000 (f)
16,000	

Patent

6,000	
	1,000 (c)
5,000	

Leased Equipment

(r) 5,000	
5,000	

Property, Plant & Equipment	
37,000	
	6,000 (d)
(g) 8,000	
39,000	

Accumulated Depreciation	
	3,000
	8,000 (b)
(d) 4,000	
	7,000

Accounts Payable	
	12,000
(m) 10,000	
	2,000

Notes Payable	
	9,000 (n)
	9,000

Interest Payable	
	2,000
(o) 1,000	2,000 (o)
	3,000

Dividends Payable	
	2,000
(i) 9,000	12,000 (i)
	5,000

Income Taxes Payable	
	1,000
(p) 5,000	6,180 (p)
	2,180

Deferred Tax Liability (Net)	
	4,920
	3,000 (e)
	540 (s)
	900 (s)
	9,360

Bonds Payable	
	25,000
(q) 15,000	
	10,000

Lease Obligation	
	5,000 (r)
	5,000

Common Stock	
	26,000
	2,000 (h)
	5,000 (q)
	33,000

Addl. Paid-in Capital	
	3,000
	3,000 (h)
	10,000 (q)
	16,000

Retained Earnings	
	41,000
	16,320 (a)
(i) 12,000	
	45,320

Unrealized Gain (Loss) on AFS Securities	
1,920	
	960 (s)
	1,600 (u)
	640

Explanation of entries to compile the statement of cash flows

a. Cash and Cash Equivalents—Operating Activities is debited for $16,320 (net income) and the credit is to Retained Earnings.

b. Depreciation is not a cash flow; however, depreciation expense was deducted to arrive at net income. Therefore, Accumulated Depreciation is credited and Cash and Cash Equivalents—Operating Activities is debited.

c. Amortization of patents is another expense not requiring cash; therefore, Cash and Cash Equivalents—Operating Activities is debited and Patent is credited.

d. The sale of equipment (additional information, item 1) resulted in a $3,000 gain. The gain is computed by comparing the book value of $2,000 with the sales price of $5,000. Cash proceeds of $5,000 are an inflow of cash. Since the gain was included in net income, it must be deducted from net income to determine cash provided by operating activities. This is necessary to avoid counting the $3,000 gain both in cash provided by operating activities and in investing activities. The following entry would have been made on the date of sale:

Cash	5,000	
Accumulated depreciation ($6,000 – $2,000)	4,000	
Property, plant, and equipment		6,000
Gain on sale of equipment ($5,000 – $2,000)		3,000

Adjust the T-accounts as follows: debit Summary of Cash and Cash Equivalents for $5,000, debit Accumulated Depreciation for $4,000, credit Property, Plant, and Equipment for $6,000, and credit Cash and Cash Equivalents—Operating Activities for $3,000.

e. The deferred income tax liability account shows an increase of $4,440. The $3,000 increase that pertains to amounts reported in the income statement must b added to income from operations. Although the $3,000 was deducted as part of income tax expense in determining net income, it did not require an outflow of cash. Therefore, debit Cash and Cash Equivalents—Operating Activities and credit Deferred Taxes. The other two amounts in the deferred tax liability account are covered below, under paragraph "p."

f. Item 2 under additional information indicates that the investment in XYZ is accounted for under the equity method. The investment in XYZ had a net increase of $2,000, which is the result of the equity in the earnings of XYZ of $5,000 and the receipt of a $3,000 dividend. Dividends received (an inflow of cash) would reduce the investment in XYZ, while the equity in the income of XYZ would increase the investment without affecting cash. The journal entries would have been:

Cash (dividend received)	3,000	
Investment in XYZ		3,000
Investment in XYZ	5,000	
Equity in earnings of XYZ		5,000

The dividend received ($3,000) is an inflow of cash, and the equity earnings are not. Debit Investment in XYZ for $5,000, credit Cash and Cash Equivalents—Operating Activities for $5,000, debit Cash and Cash Equivalents—Operating Activities for $3,000, and credit Investment in XYZ for $3,000.

g. The Property, Plant, and Equipment account increased because of the purchase of $8,000 (additional information, item 5). The purchase of assets is an outflow of cash. Debit Property, Plant, and Equipment for $8,000 and credit Summary of Cash and Cash Equivalents.

h. The company sold 200 shares of common stock during the year (additional information, item 3). The entry for the sale of stock was:

Cash	5,000	
Common stock (200 shares × $10)		2,000
Additional paid-in capital		3,000

This transaction resulted in an inflow of cash. Debit Summary of Cash and Cash Equivalents $5,000, credit Common Stock $2,000, and credit Additional Paid-in Capital $3,000.

i. Dividends of $12,000 were declared (additional information, item 7). Only $9,000 was actually paid in cash, resulting in an ending balance of $5,000 in the Dividends Payable account. Therefore, the following entries were made during the year:

Retained earnings	12,000	
Dividends payable		12,000
Dividends payable	9,000	
Cash		9,000

These transactions result in an outflow of cash. Debit Retained Earnings $12,000 and credit Dividends Payable $12,000. Additionally, debit Dividends Payable $9,000 and credit Summary of Cash and Cash Equivalents $9,000 to indicate the cash dividends paid during the year.

j. Accounts Receivable (net) decreased by $2,000. This is added as an adjustment to net income in the computation of cash provided by operating activities. The decrease of $2,000 means that an additional $2,000 cash was collected on account above and beyond the sales reported in the income statement. Debit Cash and Cash Equivalents—Operating Activities and credit Accounts Receivable for $2,000.

k. Inventories increased by $5,000. This is subtracted as an adjustment to net income in the computation of cash provided by operating activities. Although $5,000 additional cash was spent to increase inventories, this expenditure is not reflected in accrual-basis cost of goods sold. Debit Inventory and credit Cash and Cash Equivalents—Operating Activities for $5,000.
l. Prepaid Expenses decreased by $3,000. This is added back to net income in the computation of cash provided by operating activities. The decrease means that no cash was spent when incurring the related expense. The cash was spent when the prepaid assets were purchased, not when they were expensed on the income statement. Debit Cash and Cash Equivalents—Operating Activities and credit Prepaid Expenses for $3,000.
m. Accounts Payable decreased by $10,000. This is subtracted as an adjustment to net income. The decrease of $10,000 means that an additional $10,000 of purchases were paid for in cash; therefore, income was not affected but cash was decreased. Debit Accounts Payable and credit Cash and Cash Equivalents—Operating Activities for $10,000.
n. Notes Payable increased by $9,000 (as listed under additional information, item 4). This is an inflow of cash and would be included in the financing activities. Debit Summary of Cash and Cash Equivalents and credit Notes Payable for $9,000.
o. Interest Payable increased by $1,000, but interest expense reported on the income statement was $2,000. Therefore, although $2,000 was expensed, only $1,000 cash was paid ($2,000 expense – $1,000 increase in interest payable). Debit Cash and Cash Equivalents—Operating Activities for $1,000 for the noncash portion, debit Interest Payable for $1,000 for the cash portion, and credit Interest Payable for $2,000 for the expense.
p. The following entry was made to record the incurrence of the tax liability:

Income tax expense	9,180	
Income taxes payable		6,180
Deferred tax liability		3,000

Therefore, $9,180 was deducted in arriving at net income. The $3,000 credit to Deferred Income Taxes was accounted for in entry e above. The $6,180 credit to Taxes Payable does not, however, indicate that $6,180 cash was paid for taxes. Since Taxes Payable increased $1,180, only $5,000 must have been paid and $1,180 remains unpaid. Debit Cash and Cash Equivalents—Operating Activities for $1,180, debit Income Taxes Payable for $5,000, and credit Income Taxes Payable for $6,180.

q. Item 6 under the additional information indicates that $15,000 of bonds payable were converted to common stock. This is a *noncash* financing activity and should be reported in a separate schedule. The following entry was made to record the transaction:

Bonds payable	15,000	
Common stock (500 shares × $10 par)		5,000
Additional paid-in capital		10,000

Adjust the T-accounts with a debit to Bonds Payable, $15,000; a credit to Common Stock, $5,000; and a credit to Additional Paid-in Capital, $10,000.

r. Item 8 under the additional information indicates that leased equipment was acquired on the last day of 20X2. The entity classified that lease as a finance lease. This is also a noncash financing activity and should be reported in a separate schedule. The following entry was made to record the lease transaction:

Leased asset	5,000	
Lease obligation		5,000

s. The company sold half of its available-for-sale investments during the year for $8,000 (additional information, item 9). The entry for the sale of the investments was:

Cash	8,000	
Investment in available-for-sale securities		7,500
Gain on sale of investments		500

This transaction resulted in an inflow of cash. Debit Summary of Cash and Cash Equivalents $8,000, credit Investment in Available-for-Sale Securities $7,500, and credit Cash and Cash Equivalents—Operating Activities $500. The following additional journal entries were made:

Adjustment for changes in FV	1,500	
Other comprehensive income ($1,500 × 64%)		960
Deferred tax liability ($1,500 × 36%)		540

To adjust the allowance account for the sale, one-half of the amounts provided at the end of 20X2 must be taken off the books when the related securities are sold.

Adjustment for changes in FV	2,500	
Unrealized gain on available-for-sale securities ($2,500 × 64%)		1,600
Deferred tax liability ($2,500 × 36%)		900

The change in fair value of the remaining securities at year-end (as listed under additional information, item 9) must be adjusted. The book value of the securities before the adjustment above is $6,000 ($7,500 – $1,500). The fair value of the securities is $8,500. An adjustment of $2,500 is necessary.

t. The cash and cash equivalents from operations ($15,000) is transferred to the Summary of Cash and Cash Equivalents.

All of the changes in the noncash accounts have been accounted for and the balance in the Summary of Cash and Cash Equivalents account of $25,000 is the amount of the year-to-year increase in cash and cash equivalents. The formal statement may now be prepared using the T- account, Summary of Cash and Cash Equivalents. The alphabetic characters in the statement below refer to the entries in that T-account. The following statement of cash flows is prepared under the direct method. The calculations for gross receipts and gross payments needed for the direct method are shown below the statement.

Johnson Company
Statement of Cash Flows
for the Year Ended December 31, 20X2

Cash flow from operating activities			
Cash received from customers	$102,000		
Dividends received	3,000		
Cash provided by operating activities			$105,000
Cash paid to suppliers	$ 75,000		
Cash paid for expenses	9,000		
Interest paid	1,000		
Income taxes paid			
Cash paid for operating activities	5,000		(90,000)
Net cash flow provided by operating activities		(t)	$ 15,000

Cash flow from investing activities			
Sale of equipment	5,000	(d)	
Sale of investments	8,000	(s)	
Purchase of property, plant, and equipment	(8,000)	(g)	
Net cash provided by investing activities			5,000
Cash flow from financing activities			
Sale of common stock	$ 5,000	(h)	
Increase in notes payable	9,000	(n)	
Dividends paid	(9,000)	(i)	
Net cash provided by financing activities			5,000
Net increase in cash and cash equivalents			$ 25,000
Cash and cash equivalents at beginning of year			16,000
Cash and cash equivalents at end of year			$ 41,000

Calculation of amounts for operating activities section

Cash received from customers = Net sales + Beginning A / R − Ending A / R

$$\$100,000 + \$11,000 - \$9,000 = \$102,000$$

Cash paid to suppliers = Cost of goods sold + Beginning A / P − Ending A / P + Ending inventory − Beginning inventory

$$\$60,000 + \$12,000 - \$2,000 + \$14,000 - \$9,000 = \$75,000$$

Cash paid for operating expenses = Operating expenses + Ending prepaid expenses − Beginning prepaid expenses − Depreciation expense (and other noncash operating expenses)

$$\$12,000 + \$8,000 + \$1,000 + \$10,000 - \$13,000 \boxtimes \$8,000 - \$1,000 = \$9,000$$

Interest paid = Interest expense + Beginning interest payable − Ending interest payable

$$\$2,000 + \$2,000 - \$3,000 = \$1,000$$

Taxes paid = Income taxes + Beginning income taxes payable − Ending income taxes payable − Change in deferred income taxes — operating portion

$$\$9,180 + \$1,000 - \$2,180 - \$3,000 = \$5,000$$

When a statement of cash flows is prepared using the direct method of reporting operating cash flows, the reconciliation of net income to operating cash flows must also be provided. The T-account, Cash and Cash Equivalents—Operating Activities is used to prepare the reconciliation. The alphabetic characters in the reconciliation below refer to the entries in the T-account.

Reconciliation of net income to net cash provided by operating activities

Net income		(a)	$16,320
Add (deduct) items not using (providing) cash:			
Depreciation	8,000	(b)	
Amortization	1,000	(c)	
Gain on sale of equipment	(3,000)	(d)	
Increase in deferred taxes	3,000	(e)	
Equity in XYZ	(2,000)	(f)	
Decrease in accounts receivable	2,000	(j)	
Increase in inventory	(5,000)	(k)	
Decrease in prepaid expenses	3,000	(l)	
Decrease in accounts payable	(10,000)	(m)	
Increase in interest payable	1,000	(o)	
Increase in income taxes payable	1,180	(p)	
Gain on sale of AFS securities	(500)	(s)	(1,320)
Net cash flow provided by operating activities		(t)	$15,000
Schedule of noncash investing and financing activities transactions			
Conversion of bonds into common stock		(q)	$15,000
Acquisition of leased equipment		(r)	$ 5,000

Statement of Cash Flows for Consolidated Entities

A consolidated statement of cash flows must be presented when a complete set of consolidated financial statements is issued. The consolidated statement of cash flows would be the last statement to be prepared, as the information to prepare it will come from the other consolidated statements (consolidated statement of financial position, income statement, and statement of retained earnings). The preparation of a consolidated statement of cash flows involves the same analysis and procedures as the statement for an individual entity with a few additional items. When the indirect method is used, the additional noncash transactions relating to the business combination, such as the differential amortization, must also be reversed, and all transfers to affiliates must be eliminated, as they do not represent cash inflows or outflows of the consolidated entity.

All unrealized intercompany profits should have been eliminated in preparation of the other statements. Any income or loss allocated to noncontrolling parties would need to be added back, as it would have been eliminated in computing consolidated net income but does not represent a true cash outflow or inflow. Finally, only dividend payments that are not intercompany should be recorded as cash outflows in the financing activities section.

In preparing the operating activities section of the statement by the indirect method following a purchase business combination, the changes in assets and liabilities related to operations since acquisition should be derived by comparing the consolidated statement of financial position as of the date of acquisition with the year-end consolidated statement of financial position. These changes will be combined with those for the acquiring company up to the date of acquisition as adjustments to net income. The effects due to the acquisition of these assets and liabilities are reported under investing activities.

Disclosures

Disclosures related to this topic can be found in the disclosure checklist at www.wiley.com/go/GAAP2021.

Other Sources (ASC 230-10-60)

See ASC Location—*Wiley GAAP* Chapter	***For information on . . .***
ASC 320	Classification and reporting in the statement of cash flows of cash flows from available-for-sale, held-to-maturity, and trading debt securities.
ASC 321	Classification and reporting in the statement of cash flows from equity securities.
ASC 325-30-45	Classification in the statement of cash flows of cash receipts and cash payments related to life settlement contracts.
ASC 830	Reporting and implementation guidance for presenting a statement of cash flows of an entity with foreign currency transactions or foreign currency operations.

7 ASC 235 NOTES TO FINANCIAL STATEMENTS

PERSPECTIVE AND ISSUES

Subtopic

ASC 235, *Notes to Financial Statements*, contains one subtopic:

- ASC 235-10, *Overall*, which addresses "the content and usefulness of the accounting policies judged by management to be most appropriate to fairly present the entity's financial statement."

The topic does not address specific disclosures. Those are addressed in the related topics. The topic does, however, list accounting policy disclosures commonly required:

- Basis of consolidation
- Depreciation methods
- Amortization of intangibles
- Inventory pricing
- Recognition of revenue from contracts with customers
- Recognition of revenue from leasing operations (ASC 235-10-50-4)

Scope

ASC 235 applies to all entities and has no scope exceptions.

Technical Alert

Disclosures have drawn the attention of both the FASB and the SEC. As the disclosure requirements have accumulated over the years, there has been a growing concern about information overload and whether more is necessarily better. Both the FASB and the SEC have initiatives to improve disclosures.

FASB Initiatives The FASB currently has projects on:

- Financial performance reporting—disaggregation of deb
- Income taxes
- Interim reporting
- Inventory
- Government assistance
- Disaggregation of performance information
- Not-for-profit reporting of gifts in kind
- Segment reporting
- Simplifying the balance sheet classification of debt

The framework project will address the process for establishing disclosure and for determining which disclosures to make. As part of its Framework project, the FASB issued an Exposure Draft in September 2015, *Proposed Amendments to Statement of Financial Accounting Concepts*, to amend CON 8. As part of its second project, the Disclosure Framework project, the FASB issued an Exposure Draft in September 2015, *Proposed Accounting Standards Update: Notes to Financial Statements: Assessing Whether Disclosures Are Material (Topic 235)*. As this volume goes to press, the FASB is redeliberating. More information can be found in the Technical Alert section of the chapter on ASC 105 and on the FASB's website.

SEC Initiative In an April 2014 speech by Keith Higgins, SEC Division of Corporation Finance Director, Mr. Higgins suggested ways that entities can improve disclosure effectiveness:

- Reduce repetition
- Focus the disclosure
- Eliminate outdated information

The full speech is available on the SEC's website, sec.gov.

In December 2015, the Fixing America's Surface Transportation (FAST) Act directed the SEC to modernize and simplify form S-K requirements. The SEC is reviewing specific sections of regulations S-K and S-X, with a goal of updating requirements and eliminating duplicate disclosures. The Commission also wants to continue to provide material information and reduce cost burdens on companies. As part of the project, the SEC amended its rules in August 2018 and March 2019. In January 2020, the SEC, in response to a study mandated by the Jumpstart Our Business Startups Act, proposed amendments to modernize, simplify, and enhance certain financial disclosures required by Regulation S-K. These proposed changes are designed to eliminate duplicative disclosures and modernize and enhance Management's Discussion and Analysis disclosures. Those interested in the SEC's disclosure project should visit sec.gov.

DEFINITIONS OF TERMS

See Appendix A, *Definitions of Terms*, for definitions of terms related to this topic: Contract, Customer, and Revenue.

CONCEPTS, RULES, AND EXAMPLES

Accounting Policies

There are different methods of valuing assets, recognizing revenues, and assigning costs. Financial statement users must be aware of the accounting policies selected by an entity so that sound economic decisions can be made. The reporting entity is responsible for adopting and adhering to the highest-quality accounting policies possible. ASC 235 requires management, in discharging this responsibility, to adopt accounting principles and methods of applying them that are the most appropriate in the circumstances to present fairly financial position, cash flows, and results of operations, in accordance with generally accepted accounting principles. (ASC 235-10-50-1)

This requirement applies even in reporting situations where one or more of the basic financial statements have been omitted. However, it does not apply to unaudited interim statements where the accounting policies have not changed since the issuance of the last annual statements. (ASC 235-10-50-2)

The accounting policies disclosures should encompass those accounting principles and methods that involve the following:

- Selection from acceptable alternatives
- Principles and methods peculiar to the industry
- Unique applications of GAAP
  (ASC 235-10-50-3)

In theory, if only one method of accounting for a type of transaction is acceptable under GAAP, it is not necessary to explicitly cite it in the accounting policies note. However, many entities do routinely identify all accounting policies affecting the major financial statement captions.

In the accounting policy disclosure, it is not necessary to repeat details that are provided in other disclosures. Many preparers simply cross-reference accounting policy disclosures to relevant details provided in other notes to the financial statements.

The "summary of significant accounting policies" is customarily, but not necessarily, the first note disclosure included in the financial statements. A more all-encompassing title such as "Nature of business and summary of significant accounting policies" is frequently used.

Commonly Disclosed Accounting Policies A listing of accounting policies commonly disclosed by reporting entities follows (the listing is not intended to be all-inclusive):

- Accounting period
- Advertising costs
- Capitalization of interest
- Cash equivalents
- Changes in accounting policies
- Combined financial statements—principles of combination
- Comprehensive income
- Concentrations of credit risk, major customers, and/or suppliers
- Consolidation policy
- Contingencies
- Derivatives and hedging activities
- Earnings per share
- Environmental costs
- Fair value elections, methods, assumptions, inputs used
- Financial instruments
- Foreign operations
- Goodwill
- Going concern issues
- Impairment of long-lived assets, goodwill, other intangibles, investments, etc.
- Income taxes

- Intangibles—amortizable and/or nonamortizable
- Inventories
- Investments
- Nature of operations
- New accounting pronouncements
- Pension and other postretirement or postemployment plans
- Property and equipment, depreciation and amortization
- Reclassifications
- Research and development costs
- Revenue from contracts with customers
- Revenue recognition from leasing operations
- Shipping and handling costs
- Start-up costs
- Use of estimates
- Warranties

Timing of Adoption Decisions Upon formation of a business or nonprofit organization, an entity makes decisions regarding the adoption of accounting policies, based on the types of activities in which the entity engages and the industry and environment in which it operates. Certain ASC Topics permit choices to be made from among alternative, acceptable accounting treatments. The principles selected from among the available alternatives and the methods of applying those principles constitute the reporting entity's accounting policies.

Management initially adopts accounting principles at two distinct times:

1. Upon formation of the reporting entity
2. Upon the occurrence of a new type of event or transaction that had either not happened in the past or had previously been judged to be immaterial

Once the initial adoption decisions are made, the users of the financial statements expect a reporting entity's financial statements to be prepared consistently over time. This facilitates comparisons across periods and among different reporting entities.

Disclosure Techniques

When preparing disclosure notes, entities should consider the purpose of the disclosure—to provide users with information that assists them in assessing the entity's performance and cash flow. The notes should enhance the information presented on the face of the financial statements, provide clarity, and be organized in a logical manner. Entities should also word notes in plain English, consider tabular formats, and cross referencing.

The following five disclosure techniques are used in varying degrees in contemporary financial statements:

1. Parenthetical explanations
2. Notes to the financial statements
3. Cross-references
4. Valuation allowances (sometimes referred to as "contra" amounts)
5. Supporting schedules

Parenthetical Explanations Information is sometimes disclosed by means of parenthetical explanations appended to the appropriate statement of financial position caption. For example:

Common stock ($10 par value, 200,000 shares authorized, 150,000 issued) $1,500,000

Parenthetical explanations have an advantage over both notes to the financial statements and supporting schedules. Parenthetical explanations place the disclosure prominently in the body of the statement instead of in a note or schedule where it is more likely to be overlooked.

Notes to Financial Statements If the information cannot be disclosed in a relatively short and concise parenthetical explanation, a note disclosure is used. For example:

Inventories (see note 1) $2,550,000

The notes to the financial statements would contain the following:

Note 1: *Inventories are stated at the lower of cost or market. Cost is determined using the first-in, first-out (FIFO) method.*

Cross-References Cross-referencing is used when there is a direct relationship between two accounts on the statement of financial position. For example, among the current assets, the following might be shown if $1,500,000 of accounts receivable were pledged as collateral for a $1,200,000 bank loan:

Accounts receivable pledged as collateral on bank loan payable $1,500,000

Included in the current liabilities would be the following:

Bank loan payable—collateralized by accounts receivable $1,200,000

Valuation Allowances Valuation allowances are used to reduce or increase the carrying amounts of certain assets and liabilities. Accumulated depreciation reduces the carrying value of property, plant, and equipment, and a bond premium (discount) increases (decreases) the face value of a bond payable as shown in the following illustration:

Equipment	$18,000,000	
Less accumulated depreciation	(1,625,000)	$16,375,000
Bonds payable	$20,000,000	
Less discount on bonds payable	(1,300,000)	$18,700,000
Bonds payable	$20,000,000	
Add premium on bonds payable	1,300,000	$21,300,000

8 ASC 250 ACCOUNTING CHANGES AND ERROR CORRECTIONS

PERSPECTIVE AND ISSUES

Subtopics

ASC 250, *Accounting Changes and Error Corrections*, contains one subtopic: ASC 250-10, *Overall*, which:

- Provides guidance on accounting for and reporting on accounting changes and error corrections
- Requires, unless impractical, retrospective application of a change in accounting principle
- Provides guidance on when retrospective application is impractical and how to report on the impracticability
(ASC 250-10-05-2 and 05-3)

ASC 250-10 also:

- Specifies the method of treating error correction in comparative statements
- Specifies the disclosures required upon restatement of previously issued statements of income
- Recommends methods of presentation of historical, statistical-type financial summaries affected by error corrections
(ASC 250-10-05-5)

Scope

ASC 250 applies to all entities' financial statements and summaries of information that reflect an accounting period affected by an accounting change or error. (ASC 250-10-15-2)

Overview

Changes in accounting for given transactions can have a profound influence on investing and operational decisions. Financial statement analysts and the entity's decision makers both generally presume that financial statements are comparable and consistent across periods and among entities within industry groupings. Any type of accounting change potentially can create inconsistency. The challenge is to present the effects of the change in a manner that is most readily understood by users of financial statements.

ASC 250 contains the underlying presumption that in preparing financial statements an accounting principle, once adopted, should not be changed when accounting for events and transactions of a similar type. There are generally four scenarios that result in an accounting change:

1. Change in accounting principle
2. Change in estimate
3. Change in entity
4. Correction of an error

In order to apply the proper accounting guidance, preparers must be able to determine the reasons for the change.

Technical Alert

In January 2017, the FASB issued ASU 2017-03, *Accounting Changes and Error Corrections (Topic 250) and Investments—Equity Method and Joint Ventures* (Topic 323) Amendments to SEC Paragraphs Pursuant to Staff Announcements at the September 22, 2016 and November 17, 2016 EITF Meetings. The ASU amends the Codification to reflect SEC staff comments made at EITF meetings. At a September 2016 meeting, the SEC staff expressed its expectations about disclosures on the effects of new FASB guidance, specifically:

- ASU 2014-09 on revenue,
- ASU 2016-02 on leases, and
- ASU 2016-13 on credit losses on financial instruments.

As referenced later in this chapter SEC SAB Topic 11.M requires registrants to disclose the effect of recently issued accounting standards on their financial statements when adopted in the future. The ASU incorporates the SEC Staff views as follows:

- Registrants should determine the appropriate financial statement disclosures about the potential material effects of the ASUs listed above on the financial statements when adopted.

- If a registrant does not know or cannot reasonably estimate the impact that adoption of the ASUs referenced is expected to have, the registrants should make a statement to that effect and consider additional qualitative disclosures that will assist the reader in assessing the significance of the impact that the standard will have when adopted.
- The additional qualitative disclosures should include a description of the effect of the accounting policies that the registrant expects to apply, if determined, and a comparison to the registrant's current accounting policies.
- Registrant should describe the status of their process to implement the new standards and the significant implementation matters yet to be addressed.

The SEC announcement also applies to any subsequent amendments to guidance in the ASUs above that are issued prior to a registrant's adoption of the ASUs.

DEFINITIONS OF TERMS

Source: ASC 250-10-20

Accounting Change. A change in an accounting principle, an accounting estimate, or the reporting entity. The correction of an error in previously issued financial statements is not an accounting change.

Change in Accounting Estimate. A change that has the effect of adjusting the carrying amount of an existing asset or liability or altering the subsequent accounting for existing or future assets or liabilities. A change in accounting estimate is a necessary consequence of the assessment, in conjunction with the periodic presentation of financial statements, of the present status and expected future benefits and obligations associated with assets and liabilities. Changes in accounting estimates result from new information. Examples of items for which estimates are necessary are uncollectible receivables, inventory obsolescence, service lives and salvage values of depreciable assets, and warranty obligations.

Change in Accounting Estimate Effected by a Change in Accounting Principle. A change in accounting estimate that is inseparable from the effect of a related change in accounting principle. An example of a change in estimate effected by a change in principle is a change in the method of depreciation, amortization, or depletion for long-lived, nonfinancial assets.

Change in Accounting Principle. A change from one generally accepted accounting principle to another generally accepted accounting principle when there are two or more generally accepted accounting principles that apply or when the accounting principle formerly used is no longer generally accepted. A change in the method of applying an accounting principle is also considered a change in accounting principle.

Change in the Reporting Entity. A change that results in financial statements that, in effect, are those of a different reporting entity. A change in the reporting entity is limited mainly to the following:

a. Presenting consolidated or combined financial statements in place of financial statements of individual entities
b. Changing specific subsidiaries that make up the group of entities for which consolidated financial statements are presented
c. Changing the entities included in combined financial statements.

Neither a business combination accounted for by the acquisition method nor the consolidation of a variable interest entity (VIE) pursuant to Topic 810 is a change in reporting entity.

Direct Effects of a Change in Accounting Principle. Those recognized changes in assets or liabilities necessary to effect a change in accounting principle. An example of a direct effect is an adjustment to an inventory balance to effect a change in inventory valuation method. Related changes, such as an effect on deferred income tax assets or liabilities or an impairment adjustment resulting from applying the subsequent measurement guidance in Subtopic 330-10 to the adjusted inventory balance, are also examples of direct effects of a change in accounting principle.

Error in Previously Issued Financial Statements. An error in recognition, measurement, presentation, or disclosure in financial statements resulting from mathematical mistakes, mistakes in the application of generally accepted accounting principles (GAAP), or oversight or misuse of facts that existed at the time the financial statements were prepared. A change from an accounting principle that is not generally accepted to one that is generally accepted is a correction of an error.

Indirect Effects of a Change in Accounting Principle. Any changes to current or future cash flows of an entity that result from making a change in accounting principle that is applied retrospectively. An example of an indirect effect is a change in a nondiscretionary profit sharing or royalty payment that is based on a reported amount such as revenue or net income.

Restatement. The process of revising previously issued financial statements to reflect the correction of an error in those financial statements.

Retrospective Application. The application of a different accounting principle to one or more previously issued financial statements, or to the statement of financial position at the beginning of the current period, as if that principle had always been used, or a change to financial statements of prior accounting periods to present the financial statements of a new reporting entity as if it had existed in those prior years.

CONCEPTS, RULES, AND EXAMPLES

Accounting Changes

There are legitimate reasons for a reporting entity to change its accounting, including to:

- Change an accounting principle. Adopt a newly issued accounting principle or change to an existing alternative accounting principle that the entity deems to be preferable to the one it is currently following.
- Change an estimate from refining an estimate made in the past as a result of further experience and better information.
- Change a reporting entity.
- Correct an error made in previously issued financial statements. Although technically not an "accounting change" as defined in GAAP literature, correcting an error involves restating previously issued financial statements and is also governed by ASC 250.

It is important for the reporting entity to adequately inform financial statement users when one or more of these changes are made and to provide sufficient information to enable the reader to distinguish the effects of the change from other factors affecting results of operations.

There are two methods for presenting and disclosing accounting changes or errors:

1. Retrospective application, where the entity
   - Restates the financial statements presented to apply the new principle as if the new principle had always been used and,
   - Includes the cumulative effect from prior years presented in the opening balance of retained earnings and the carrying amounts of assets and liabilities in the earliest year presented. (ASC 250-10-45-5)
2. Currently and prospectively, where the entity
   - Reflects the change in current and future financial statements without restating prior years.

Each of the types of accounting changes and the proper treatment prescribed for them is summarized in the following chart and discussed in detail in the sections that follow.

Exhibit—Summary of Accounting for Changes and Error Corrections

	Treatment in financial statements, historical summaries, financial highlights, and other similar presentations of businesses and not-for-profit organizations		
Type and description of change or correction	***Retrospective application to all periods presented unless impracticable***	***Affects period of change and, if applicable, future periods***	***Restatement of all prior period financial statements presented***
• Change in accounting principle New principle required to be preferable	✓		
• Change in accounting estimate		✓	
• Change in accounting estimate effected by a change in accounting principle New principle required to be preferable		✓	
• Change in reporting entity	✓		
			Restatements: Note: The word "restatement" is only to be used to describe and/ or present corrections of prior period errors.
• Correction of errors in previously issued financial statements			✓

Change in Accounting Principle

A change in accounting principle is a change from one acceptable method to another. The following are *not* considered changes in accounting principle:

- Initial adoption of an accounting principle for events occurring for the first time or that were previously immaterial
- Adoption or modification of an accounting principle for transactions or events substantially different from previous transactions
  (ASC 250-45-1)

Entities must apply all voluntary changes in accounting principles retrospectively to prior period financial statements unless it is impracticable to do so or guidance mandates another approach. The entity is permitted to change from one generally accepted accounting principle to another only when:

- It voluntarily decides to do so and can justify the use of the alternative accounting principle as being preferable to the principle currently being followed, or
- It is required to make the change as a result of a newly issued accounting pronouncement.
  (ASC 250-10-45-2)

The Codification grants entities the flexibility of choosing among alternative methods of accounting for the same economic transactions. Examples include such diverse areas as alternative cost-flow assumptions used to account for inventory and cost of sales, different methods of depreciating long-lived assets, and varying methods of identifying operating segments. In choosing among the various alternatives, the entity should select principles and apply them in a manner that results in financial statements that faithfully represent economic substance over form and that are fully transparent to the user.

According to ASC 250, the term "accounting principle" includes not only the accounting principles and practices used by the reporting entity, but also its methods of applying them. A change in the components used to cost a firm's inventory is considered a change in accounting principle and, therefore, is only permitted when the new inventory costing method is preferable to the former method.

For disclosures related to a change in accounting principle, see the *Disclosure and Presentation Checklist for Commercial Businesses* at www.wiley.com/go/GAAP2021.

Preferability The entity is only permitted to voluntarily change the reporting entity's accounting principles when the newly employed principle is preferable to the principle it is replacing. This may be difficult to justify.

The preferability assessment should be made from the perspective of financial reporting and not solely from an income tax perspective. Thus, favorable income tax consequences alone do not justify making a change in financial reporting practices. ASC 250 does not provide a definition of preferability or criteria by which to make such assessments, so this remains a matter of professional judgment. What is preferable for one industry or company is not necessarily considered preferable for another.

Retrospective Application Changes in accounting principle must be reflected in financial statements by retrospective application to all prior periods presented unless it is impracticable to do so. (ASC 250-10-45-5) (See impracticability exception section below.)

Accounting Standards Updates include specific provisions regarding transitioning to the new principles. Adopting entities must follow these provisions. The default method is retrospective restatement. Updates may provide for adoption using cumulative effect or catch-up adjustments, if the FASB believes that is the most beneficial method of transition. (ASC 250-10-45-3)

Exhibit—Application of Retrospective Method Retrospective application is accomplished by the steps in the following exhibit. (ASC 250-10-45-5)

At the beginning of the first period presented in the financial statements:

↓

Step 1
Adjust the carrying amounts of assets and liabilities for the cumulative effect of changing to the new accounting principle on periods prior to those presented in the financial statements.

↓

Step 2
Offset the effect of the adjustment in Step 1 (if any) by adjusting the opening balance of retained earnings (or other components of equity or net assets, as applicable to the reporting entity).

↓

For each individual prior period presented in the financial statements:

↓

Step 3
Adjust the financial statements for the effects of applying the new accounting principle to that specific period.

Impracticability Exceptions All prior periods presented in the financial statements are required to be adjusted for the retroactive application of the newly adopted accounting principle, unless it is impracticable to do so. The Codification recognizes that there are certain circumstances when there is a change in accounting principle when it will not be feasible to compute the retroactive adjustment to the prior periods affected or (2) the period-specific adjustments relative to periods presented in the financial statements.

For the entity to assert that it is impracticable to retrospectively apply the new accounting principle, one or more of the following conditions must be present:

1. The entity has made a reasonable effort to determine the retrospective adjustment and is unable to do so.
2. If it were to apply the new accounting principle retrospectively, the entity would be required to make assumptions regarding its intent in a prior period that would not be able to be independently substantiated.

3. If it were to apply the new accounting principle retrospectively, the entity would be required to make significant estimates of amounts for which it is impossible to distinguish objective information that:
   - Would have been available at the time the original financial statements for the prior period (or periods) were issued and
   - Provides evidence of circumstances that existed at that time regarding the amounts to be measured, recognized, and/or disclosed by retrospective application.

   (ASC 250-10-45-9)

Impracticable to determine period-specific effects when cumulative effects can be determined The entity may be able to determine the cumulative effect of applying the new accounting principle to prior periods, but unable to determine the period-specific effects of the change on all of the prior periods presented in the financial statements. In that case, the entity must follow these steps to adopt the new accounting principle:

1. Adjust the carrying amounts of the assets and liabilities for the cumulative effect of applying the new accounting principle at the beginning of the earliest period presented for which it is practicable to make the computation.
2. Any offsetting adjustment required by applying Step 1 is made to beginning retained earnings (or other applicable components of equity or net assets) of that period. (ASC 250-10-45-6)

Impracticable to determine effects on any prior periods If it is impracticable to determine the cumulative effect of adoption of the new accounting principle on any prior periods, the entity must apply the new principle prospectively as of the earliest date that it is practicable to do so. (ASC 250-10-45-7) The most common example of this occurs when the entity of a reporting entity decides to change its inventory costing assumption from first-in, first-out (FIFO) to last-in, first-out (LIFO).

Example of Change from FIFO to LIFO

During 20X3 Warady Inc. decided to change the method used for pricing its inventories from FIFO to LIFO. The inventory values are as listed below using both FIFO and LIFO methods. Sales for the year were $15,000,000 and the company's total purchases were $11,000,000. Other expenses were $1,200,000 for the year. The company had 1,000,000 shares of common stock outstanding throughout the year.

Inventory values

	FIFO	*LIFO*	*Difference*
12/31/X2 Base year	$2,000,000	$2,000,000	$ —
12/31X3	4,000,000	1,800,000	2,200,000
Variation	$2,000,000	$ 200,000	$2,200,000

The computations for 20X3 would be as follows:

	FIFO	*LIFO*	*Difference*
Sales	$15,000,000	$15,000,000	$ –
Cost of goods sold			
Beginning inventory	2,000,000	2,000,000	–
Purchases	11,000,000	11,000,000	–
Goods available for sale	13,000,000	13,000,000	–
Ending inventory	4,000,000	1,800,000	2,200,000
	9,000,000	11,200,000	(2,200,000)
Gross profit	6,000,000	3,800,000	2,200,000
Other expenses	1,200,000	1,200,000	–
Net income	$ 4,800,000	$ 2,600,000	$ 2,200,000

Indirect Effects of a Change in Accounting Principle A change in accounting principle sometimes results in indirect effects from legal or contractual obligations of the reporting entity, such as profit sharing or royalty arrangements that contain monetary formulas based on amounts in the financial statements. Contracts and agreements are often silent regarding how such a change might affect amounts that were computed (and distributed) in prior years. ASC 250 specifies that irrespective of whether the indirect effects arise from an explicit requirement in the agreement or are discretionary, if incurred they should be recognized in the period in which the reporting entity makes the accounting change. (ASC 250-10-45-8)

Disclosure of Effect of ASUs Not Yet in Effect

There is no requirement in GAAP to disclose information about new accounting principles not yet adopted. The accounting principles used in the reporting entity's financial statements may comply with GAAP as of the reporting date, but those principles may become unacceptable at a specified future date due to the issuance of a new accounting standard that is not yet effective. If the new GAAP, when adopted, is expected to materially affect the future financial statements, the users of the current financial statements may find it helpful to be informed about the future change. The objective of such a disclosure is to ensure that the financial statements are not misleading and that the users are provided with adequate information to assess the significance of adopting the new GAAP on the reporting entity's future financial statements.

In some cases, the effect of the future change will be so pervasive that the presentation of pro forma financial data to supplement the historical financial statements would be useful. The pro forma data would present the effects of the future adoption as if it had occurred at the date of the statement of financial position. The pro forma data may be presented in a column next to the historical data, in the notes to the financial statements, or separately accompanying the basic historical financial statements. Disclosure may also be useful regarding other future effects that may be triggered by the adoption of the new GAAP, such as adverse effects on the reporting entity's compliance with its debt covenants.

The best source of guidance in determining the form and content of these disclosures is ASC 250-10-S99. While this guidance is applicable to public companies, entities who decide to disclose prospective changes may want to consider applying it. Under the SEC requirement, the entity should disclose:

- A brief description of the new standard.
- The date the reporting entity is required to adopt the new standard.
- If the new standard permits early adoption and the reporting entity plans to do so, the date that the planned adoption will occur.
- The method of adoption that the entity expects to use. If this determination has not yet been made, then a description of the alternative methods of adoption that are permitted by the new standard.
- The impact that the new standard will have on the financial statements, unless not known or reasonably estimable. If the entity has quantified the impact, then it is to disclose the estimated amount. If the entity has not yet determined the impact or if the impact is not expected to be material, this is to be disclosed.

The SEC staff also encourages the following additional disclosures:

- The potential impact of adoption on such matters as loan covenant compliance, planned or intended changes in business practices, changes in availability of or cost of capital, and the like.
- Newly issued standards that are not expected to materially affect the reporting entity should nevertheless be disclosed with an accompanying statement that adoption is not expected to have a material effect on the reporting entity.
- When the newly issued standard only affects disclosure and the future disclosures are expected to be significantly different from the current disclosures, it is desirable to provide the reader with details.

(See also the Technical Alert at the beginning of the chapter.)

Disclosure of Proposed GAAP

There is no requirement under GAAP or under SEC rules to disclose the potential effects of standards that have been proposed but not yet issued. If the entity wishes to voluntarily disclose information that it believes will provide the financial statement users with useful, meaningful information, the SEC provides guidance (SAB Topic 11-M) that may be helpful on how to present this information.

Change in Accounting Estimate

The preparation of financial statements requires frequent use of estimates for such items as asset service lives, salvage values, asset impairments, and collectability of accounts receivable. Future conditions and events that affect these estimates cannot be estimated with certainty. Therefore, changes in estimates will be inevitable as new information and more experience is obtained. Changes in estimates must be recognized currently and prospectively. (ASC 250-10-45-17) The effect of the change in accounting estimate is accounted for currently and prospectively in

- The period of change if the change affects that period only
- The period of change and future periods if the change affects both

The reporting entity may not account for a change in estimate retrospectively, through restatement of prior periods, or by presentation of pro forma amounts as a result of a change in accounting estimate.

Entities should document the reasons for the change in estimate and the timing of the change.

Example of a Change in Accounting Estimate—Accounted for Currently and Prospectively

On January 1, 20X1, a machine purchased for $10,000 was originally estimated to have a ten-year useful life and a salvage value of $1,000. On January 1, 20X6 (five years later), the asset is expected to last another ten years and have a salvage value of $800. As a result, both the current period (the year ending December 31, 20X6) and subsequent periods are affected by the change. Annual depreciation expense over the estimated remaining useful life is computed as follows:

Original cost	$10,000
Less estimated salvage (residual) value	(1,000)
Depreciable amount	9,000
Accumulated depreciation, based on original assumptions (10-year life)	
20X1	900
20X2	900
20X3	900
20X4	900
20X5	900
	4,500
Carrying value at 1/1/20X6	5,500
Revised estimate of salvage value	(800)
Depreciable amount	4,700
Remaining useful life at 1/1/20X6	10 years
	$ 470 depreciation per year
Effect on 20X6 net income	$ 470 – $900 = $430 increase

Example of a Change in Accounting Estimate Accounted for Currently

The industry in which ABC Company operates suffers a significant downturn, resulting in a decline in the financial condition of its customers and a noticeable worsening of the days required to collect its accounts receivable. ABC had formerly provided an amount equal to 2% of its credit sales as an increment to the bad debt allowance, resulting in a current balance in the allowance of $105,000. However, the new economic conditions mandate an immediate change to a 4% allowance. Accordingly, ABC provides an additional $105,000 in the current period to increase the previously recorded allowance to meet the new 4% estimate, and also begins providing 4% in the bad debt allowance on all new credit sales. Both of these adjustments are reflected in current period expense, even though the increased allowance on existing receivables pertains to sales made (in part) in a prior reporting period, because the change in estimate was made in the current period based on new circumstances that arose in that period—specifically, the declining credit standing of its customers.

Change in Accounting Estimate Affected by a Change in Accounting Principle

To change certain accounting estimates, the entity must adopt a new accounting principle or change the method it uses to apply an accounting principle. In contemplating such a change, the entity would not be able to separately determine the effects of changing the accounting principle from the effects of changing its estimate. The change in estimate is accomplished by changing the method.

A change in accounting estimate that is affected by a change in accounting principle is accounted for in the same manner as a change in accounting estimate, that is, currently and prospectively in the current and future periods affected. However, because the entity is changing the company's accounting principle or method of applying it, the new accounting principle, as previously discussed, must be preferable to the accounting principle being superseded. (ASC 250-10-45-18)

The entity may decide, for example, to change its depreciation method for certain types of assets from straight-line to an accelerated method, such as double-declining balance to recognize the fact that those assets are more productive in their earlier years of service because they require less downtime and do not require repairs as frequently. Such a change is permitted only if the entity justifies it based on the fact that using the new method is preferable to the old one, in this case because it more accurately matches the costs of production to periods in which the units are produced. (ASC 250-10-45-19)

Guidance makes a distinction, however, for entities that elect to apply a depreciation method that results in accelerated depreciation until the point during the useful life of the depreciable asset when it is useful to change to straight-line depreciation in order to fully depreciate the asset over the remaining term. At this point, the remaining carrying value (net book value) is depreciated using the straight-line method over its remaining useful life. If this method is consistently followed by the reporting entity, the changeover to straight-line depreciation is not considered to be an accounting change. (ASC 250-10-45-20)

Change in Reporting Entity

A change in reporting entity is a special type of change in accounting principle. Changes in reporting entity include:

- Consolidated or combined financial statements in place of individual entities' statements
- A change in the members of the group of subsidiaries that comprise the consolidated financial statements
- A change in the companies included in combined financial statements

Specifically *excluded* from qualifying as a change in reporting entity are:

- A business combination accounted for under the acquisition method in ASC 805, and
- Consolidation of a variable interest entity accounted for under ASC 810.

An accounting change resulting in financial statements that are, in effect, of a different reporting entity than previously reported on, is retrospectively applied to the financial statements of all prior periods presented in order to show financial information for the new reporting entity for all periods (ASC 250-10-45-21). One exception is that interest cost previously capitalized under ASC 835-20 is not changed when retrospectively applying the change to prior periods. The change is also retrospectively applied to previously issued interim financial information.

Error Corrections

Errors are sometimes discovered after financial statements have been issued. Errors result from mathematical mistakes, mistakes in the application of GAAP, or the oversight or misuse of facts known or available to the accountant at the time the financial statements were prepared. Errors can occur in recognition, measurement, presentation, or disclosure. A change from an unacceptable (or incorrect) accounting principle to a correct principle is also considered a correction of an error and not a change in accounting principle. Such a change should not be confused with the preferability determination discussed earlier that involves two or more acceptable principles. An error correction pertains to the recognition that a previously used method was not an acceptable method at the time it was employed.

The essential distinction between a change in estimate and the correction of an error depends upon the availability of information. An estimate requires revision because by its nature it is based upon incomplete information. Later data will either confirm or contradict the estimate and any contradiction will require revision of the estimate. An error results from the misuse of existing information available at the time which is discovered at a later date. However, this discovery is not as a result of additional information or subsequent developments.

Correction of a material misstatement is done through the entity issuing corrected financial statements that have been restated. If comparative financial statements are soon to be issued, the entity may reflect the correction of the error in those statements, indicating that the prior period has been restated. Users of the previously issued financial statements must be notified to no longer rely on those financial statements. If only a single period is presented, the entity makes an adjustment to beginning retained earnings for the cumulative effect of the error.

ASC 250 specifies that, when correcting an error in prior period financial statements, the term "restatement" should be used. That term is exclusively reserved for this purpose so as to effectively communicate to users of the financial statements the reason for a particular change in previously issued financial statements.

Restatement consists of the following steps:

Step 1 Adjust the carrying amounts of assets and liabilities at the beginning of the first period presented in the financial statements for the cumulative effect of correcting the error on periods prior to those presented in the financial statements.

Step 2 Offset the effect of the adjustment in Step 1 (if any) by adjusting the opening balance of retained earnings (or other components of equity or net assets, as applicable to the reporting entity) for that period.

Step 3 Adjust the financial statements of each individual prior period presented for the effects of correcting the error on that specific period (referred to as the period-specific effects of the error).
(ASC 250-10-45-23)

Example of a Correction of an Error in Previously Issued Financial Statements

Assume that Truesdell Company had overstated its depreciation expense by $50,000 in 20X0 and $40,000 in 20X2. Both overstatements are the result of mathematical mistakes. The errors affected both the financial statements and the income tax returns in 20X1 and 20X2 and are discovered in 20X3.

Truesdell's statements of financial position and statements of income and retained earnings as of and for the year ended December 31, 20X2, prior to the restatement were as follows:

Truesdell Company
Statement of Income and Retained Earnings
Prior to Restatement
Year Ended December 31, 20X2

	20X2
Sales	$2,000,000
Cost of sales	
Depreciation	750,000
Other	390,000
	1,140,000
Gross profit	860,000
Selling, general, and administrative expenses	450,000
Income from operations	410,000
Other income (expense)	10,000
Income before income taxes	420,000
Income taxes	168,000
Net income	252,000
Retained earnings, beginning of year	6,463,000
Dividends	(1,200,000)
Retained earnings, end of year	$5,515,000

Truesdell Company
Statement of Financial Position
Prior to Restatement
December 31, 20X2

	20X2
Assets	
Current assets	$2,540,000
Property and equipment	
Cost	3,500,000
Accumulated depreciation and amortization	(4,30,000)
	3,070,000
Total assets	$5,610,000
Liabilities and stockholders' equity	
Income taxes payable	$ –
Other current liabilities	12,000
Total current liabilities	12,000
Noncurrent liabilities	70,000
Total liabilities	82,000
Stockholders' equity	
Common stock	13,000
Retained earnings	5,515,000
Total stockholders' equity	5,528,000
Total liabilities and stockholders' equity	$5,610,000

The following steps are followed to restate Truesdell's prior period financial statements:

Step 1 Adjust the carrying amounts of assets and liabilities at the beginning of the first period presented in the financial statements for the cumulative effect of correcting the error on periods prior to those presented in the financial statements.

The first period presented in the 20X3 financial report is 20X2. At the beginning of that year, $50,000 of the mistakes had been made and reflected on both the income tax return and financial statements. Assuming a flat 40% income tax rate and ignoring the effects of penalties and interest that would be assessed on the amended income tax returns, the following adjustment would be made to assets and liabilities at January 1, 20X2:

Decrease in accumulated depreciation	$50,000
Increase in income taxes payable	(20,000)
	$30,000

Step 2 Offset the effect of the adjustment in Step 1 by adjusting the opening balance of retained earnings (or other components of equity or net assets, as applicable to the reporting entity) for that period.

Retained earnings at the beginning of 20X2 will increase by $30,000 as the offsetting entry resulting from Step 1.

Step 3 Adjust the financial statements of each individual prior period presented for the effects of correcting the error on that specific period (referred to as the period- specific effects of the error).

The 20X2 prior period financial statements will be corrected for the period-specific effects of the restatement as follows:

Decrease in depreciation expense and accumulated depreciation	$40,000
Increase in income tax expense and income taxes payable	(16,000)
Increase 20X2 net income	$24,000

The restated financial statements are presented below.

Truesdell Company
Statements of Income and Retained Earnings
As Restated
Years Ended December 31, 20X3 and 20X2

	20X3	*20X2 restated*
Sales	$ 2,100,000	$ 2,000,000
Cost of sales		
Depreciation	740,000	710,000
Other	410,000	390,000
	1,150,000	1,100,000
Gross profit	950,000	900,000
Selling, general, and administrative expenses	460,000	450,000
Income from operations	490,000	450,000
Other income (expense)	(5,000)	10,000
Income before income taxes	485,000	460,000
Income taxes	2,00,000	184,000
Net income	285,000	276,000
Retained earnings, beginning of year, as originally reported	5,569,000	6,463,000
Restatement to reflect correction of depreciation (Note X)	—	30,000
Retained earnings, beginning of year, as restated	5,569,000	6,493,000
Dividends	(800,000)	(1,200,000)
Retained earnings, end of year	$ 5,054,000	$ 5,569,000

Truesdell Company
Statements of Financial Position
As Restated
December 31, 20X3 and 20X2

	20X3	*20X2 restated*
Assets		
Current assets	$ 2,840,000	$2,540,000
Property and equipment		
Cost	3,750,000	3,500,000
Accumulated depreciation and amortization	(1,050,000)	(340,000)
	2,700,000	3,160,000
Total assets	$ 5,540,000	$5,700,000
Liabilities and stockholders' equity		
Income taxes payable	$50,000	$35,000
Other current liabilities	110,000	12,000
Total current liabilities	160,000	48,000
Noncurrent liabilities	313,000	70,000
Total liabilities	473,000	118,000
Stockholders' equity		
Common stock	13,000	13,000
Retained earnings	5,054,000	5,569,000
Total stockholders' equity	5,067,000	5,582,000
Total liabilities and stockholders' equity	$ 5,540,000	$5,700,000

For disclosures related to restatements of financial statements previously issued, see the *Disclosure and Presentation Checklist for Commercial Businesses* at www.wiley.com/go/ GAAP2021. The disclosures need not be repeated in subsequent periods.

The correction of an error in the financial statements of a prior period discovered subsequent to their issuance is reported as a prior period adjustment in the financial statements of the subsequent period.

Evaluating Uncorrected Misstatements

Misstatements, particularly if detected after the financial statements have been produced and distributed may, under certain circumstances, be left uncorrected. This decision is directly impacted by judgments about materiality, discussed in Chapter 1. The financial statement preparer is expected to exercise professional judgment in determining the level of materiality to apply in order to cost-effectively prepare full, complete, and accurate financial statements in a timely manner.

There have been instances where the materiality concept has been used to rationalize the noncorrection of errors that should have been dealt with, and even to excuse errors known when first committed. The fact that the concept of materiality has sometimes been abused led to the promulgation of further guidance relative to error corrections. For purposes of correcting an error, the entity should evaluate the error in relation to estimated income for the year and its effect on earnings trends. (ASC 250-10-45-27)

Types of Misstatements Misstatements may be characterized as known or likely. Known misstatements arise from:

- Incorrect selection or application of accounting principles
- Errors in gathering, processing, summarizing, interpreting, or overlooking relevant data
- An intent to mislead the financial statement user to influence their decisions
- Concealment of theft

Likely misstatements arise from:

- Differences in judgment between the entity and the auditor regarding accounting estimates where the amount presented in the financial statements is outside the range of what the auditor believes is reasonable
- Amounts that the auditor has projected based on the results of performing statistical or nonstatistical sampling procedures on a population

In assessing the impact of uncorrected misstatements, the entity should assess materiality both quantitatively and qualitatively from the standpoint of whether a financial statement user would be misled if a misstatement were not corrected or if, in the case of informative disclosure errors, full disclosure was not made. Qualitative considerations include (but are not limited to) whether the misstatement:

- Arose from estimates or from items capable of precise measurement and, if the misstatement arose from an estimate, the degree of precision inherent in the estimation process
- Masks a change in earnings or other trends
- Hides a failure to meet analysts' consensus expectations for the reporting entity
- Changes a loss to income or vice versa
- Concerns a segment or other portion of the reporting entity's business that has been identified as playing a significant role in operations or profitability
- Affects compliance with loan covenants or other contractual commitments
- Increases the entity's compensation by affecting a performance measure used as a basis for computing it
- Involves concealment of an unlawful transaction

Misstatements from Prior Years The entity may have decided to not correct misstatements that occurred in one or more prior years because, in its judgment at the time, the financial statements were not materially misstated. Two methods of making that materiality assessment—sometimes referred to as the "rollover" and the "iron curtain" methods—have been widely used in practice.

The *rollover method* quantifies a misstatement as its originating or reversing effect on the *current period's* statement of income, irrespective of the potential effect on the statement of financial position of one or more prior periods' accumulated uncorrected misstatements.

The *iron curtain method*, on the other hand, quantifies a misstatement based on the *accumulated uncorrected amount* included in the current, end-of-period statement of financial position, irrespective of the year (or years) in which the misstatement originated.

Each of these methods, when considered separately, has strengths and weaknesses, as follows:

Method	*Focuses on*	*Strength*	*Weakness*
Rollover	Current period income statement	Focuses on whether the income statement of the current period is materially misstated, assuming that the statement of financial position is not materially misstated	Material misstatement of the statement of financial position can accumulate over multiple periods
Iron curtain	End of period statement of financial position	Focuses on ensuring that the statement of financial position is not materially misstated, irrespective of the year or years in which a misstatement originated	Does not consider whether the effect of correcting a statement of financial position misstatement that arose in one or more periods is material to the current period income statement

Guidance for SEC Registrants The SEC staff issued Staff Accounting Bulletin (SAB) 108, *Considering the Effects of Prior Year Misstatements in Current Year Financial Statements*, to address how registrants (i.e., publicly held corporation) are to evaluate misstatements. SAB 108 prescribes that if a misstatement is material to *either* the income statement or the statement of financial position, it is to be corrected in a manner set forth in the bulletin and illustrated in the example and diagram below.

Example—Analysis of Materiality of Misstatements Using the Rollover and Iron Curtain Approaches

Lenny Payne, the CFO of Flamingo Industries, is preparing the company's 20X3 financial statements. The company has consistently overstated its accrued liabilities by following a policy of accruing the entire audit fee it will pay its independent auditors for auditing the financial statements for the reporting year, even though approximately 80% of the work is performed in, and is thus an expense of, the following year.

Due to regular increases in audit fees, the overstatement of liabilities at 12/31/20X5 has accumulated as follows:

Year ended 12/31	*Amount of misstatement originating during year*	*End-of-year accumulated misstatement*
20X1	$15	$15
20X2	5	20
20X3	5	25
20X4	5	30
20X5	10	40

Lenny has consistently used the rollover approach to assess materiality and, in all previous years, had judged the amount of the misstatement that originated during that year to be immaterial. The guidance in SAB 108 is illustrated in the following decision diagram:

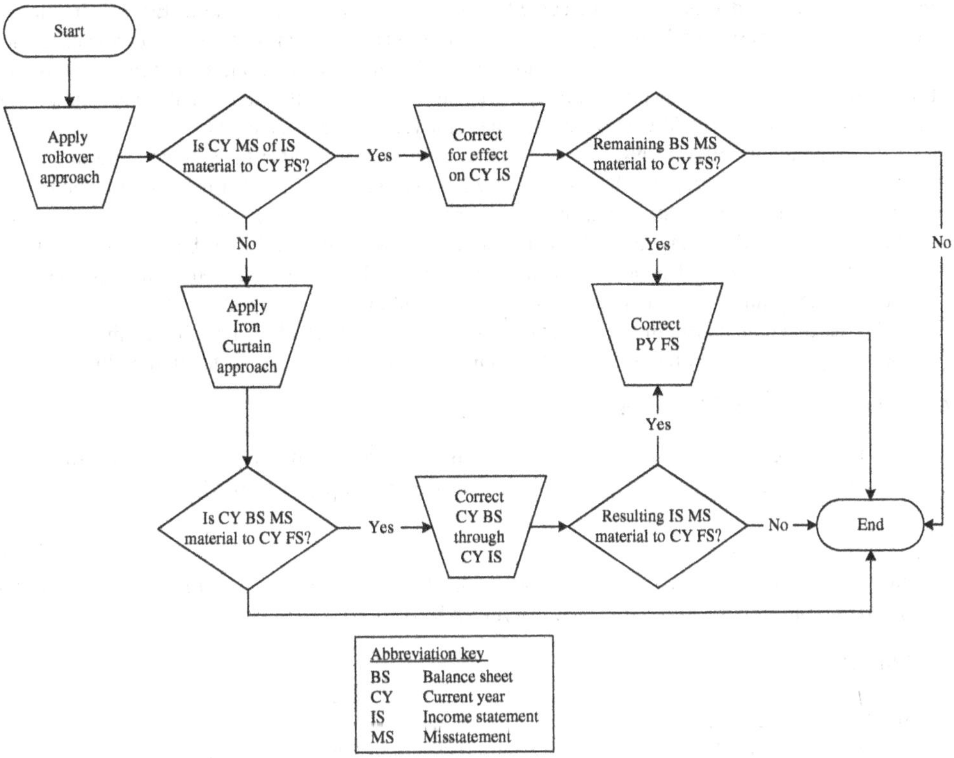

Following the decision tree, Lenny analyzes the misstatement as follows:

1. Applying the *rollover* approach, as he had done consistently in the past, Lenny computes the misstatement as the $10 that originated in 20X5. In his judgment, this amount is immaterial to the 20X5 income statement.
2. Applying the *iron curtain* approach, Lenny evaluates whether the accumulated misstatement of $40 materially misstates the statement of financial position at 12/31/20X5. Lenny believes that, considering both quantitative and qualitative factors, the misstatement has grown to the point where it does result in a materially misstated statement of financial position.

   According to SAB 108 and as shown on the diagram, Lenny would record an adjustment to correct the statement of financial position as follows:

	Debit	***Credit***
Accrued professional fees	40,000	
Professional fees (general and administrative expenses)		40,000

To correct the statement of financial position by reversing misstated accrual for audit fees not yet incurred.

Upon review of the effect of the correcting entry, Lenny believes that recording the entry will result in a material misstatement to the 20X5 income statement. Consequently, to avoid this result, the prior years' financial statements of Flamingo Industries would, under normal circumstances, be required to be restated as previously discussed in the section of this chapter titled "Error Corrections." This would be the case even if the adjustment to the prior year financial statements was, and continues to be, immaterial to those financial statements. The SEC would not, however, require Flamingo Industries to amend previously filed reports; instead, registrants are permitted to make the correction in the next filing submitted to the SEC that includes the prior year financial statements.

If the cumulative effect adjustment occurs in an interim period other than the first interim period, the SEC waived the requirement that previously filed interim reports for that fiscal year be amended. Instead, comparative information presented for interim periods of the first year subsequent to initial application is to be adjusted to reflect the cumulative effect adjustment as of the beginning of the fiscal year of initial application. The adjusted results are also required to be included in the disclosures of selected quarterly information that are required by Regulation S-K, Item 302.

Entities that do not meet the criteria to use the cumulative effect adjustment are required to follow the provisions of ASC 250 that require restatement of all prior periods presented in the filing.

Interim Reporting Considerations

For interim reporting considerations regarding changes in accounting principles, accounting estimates, and reporting entities and corrections of errors, see Chapter 11 on ASC 270.

Disclosures

Disclosures related to ASC 250 can be found in the *Disclosure and Presentation Checklist for Commercial Businesses* at www.wiley.com/go/GAAP2021.

Other Sources

See ASC Location—*Wiley GAAP* Chapter	***For information on . . .***
ASC 260-10-55-15 through 55-16	The effect of restatements expressed in per-share terms.
ASC 323-10-45-1 through 45-2	The classification of an investor's share of error corrections reported in the financial statements of the investee.

9 ASC 255 CHANGING PRICES

PERSPECTIVE AND ISSUES

Subtopic

ASC 255, *Changing Prices*, contains one subtopic:

- ASC 255-10, *Overall*, that provides guidance on reporting the effects of changing prices or inflation

Scope

The topic applies to business entities that prepare U.S. GAAP financial statements and "foreign entities that prepare financial statements in the currency for which the operations and that operate in countries with hyperinflationary economies."

The ASC disclosures are encouraged, but not required.

DEFINITIONS OF TERMS

Source: ASC 255-10-20. Also see Appendix A, *Definitions of Terms*, for the terms Commencement Date of the Lease (Commencement Date), Contract, Direct Financing Lease, Fair Value (Def. 3), Income from Continuing Operations, Lease, Lase Payments, Lease Receivable, Lease Term, Lessee, Lessor, Leveraged Lease, Net Investment in the Lease, Sales-Type Lease, Underlying Asset, and Unguaranteed Residual Asset.

Consumer Price Index for All Urban Consumers. An index of price level changes affecting consumers generally often used to measure changes in the general purchasing power of the monetary unit itself.

Current Cost-Constant Purchasing Power Accounting. A method of accounting based on measures of current cost or lower recoverable amount in units of currency, each of which has the same general purchasing power. For operations in which the dollar is the functional currency, the general purchasing power of the dollar is used and the Consumer Price Index for All Urban Consumers is the required measure of purchasing power. For operations in which the functional currency is other than the dollar, the general purchasing power of either the dollar or the functional currency is used (see paragraphs 255-10-50-45 through 50-47).

Historical Cost. The generally accepted method of accounting used in the primary financial statements that is based on measures of historical prices without restatement into units, each of which has the same general purchasing power.

Historical Cost-Constant Purchasing Power Accounting. A method of accounting based on measures of historical prices in units of a currency, each of which has the same general purchasing power.

Income-Producing Real Estate. Properties that meet all of the following criteria:

- Cash flows can be directly associated with a long-term leasing agreement with unaffiliated parties.
- The property is being operated. (It is not in a construction phase.)
- Future cash flows from the property are reasonably estimable.
- Ancillary services are not a significant part of the lease agreement.

Hotels, which have occupancy rates and related cash flows that may fluctuate to a relatively large extent, do not meet the criteria for income-producing real estate.

Mineral Resource Assets. Assets that are directly associated with and derive value from all minerals that are extracted from the earth. Such minerals include oil and gas, ores containing ferrous and nonferrous metals, coal, shale, geothermal steam, sulphur, salt, stone, phosphate, sand, and gravel. Mineral resource assets include mineral interests in properties, completed and uncompleted wells, and related equipment and facilities and other facilities required for purposes of extraction. This definition does not cover support equipment because that equipment is included in the property, plant, and equipment for which current cost measurements are required.

Monetary Assets. Money or a claim to receive a sum of money the amount of which is fixed or determinable without reference to future prices of specific goods or services.

Monetary Liability. An obligation to pay a sum of money the amount of which is fixed or determinable without reference to future prices of specific goods and services.

Motion Picture Films. All types of film, including feature films, television specials, television series, or similar products (including animated films and television programming) that are sold, licensed, or exhibited, whether produced on film, video tape, digital, or other video recording format.

Parity Adjustment. The effect of the difference between local and U.S. inflation for the year on net assets (that is, shareholders' equity) measured in nominal dollars. If only the differential rates of U.S. and local inflation are reflected in the exchange rates (parity), the parity adjustment and the translation adjustment net to zero. Therefore, the sum of the parity adjustment and the translation adjustment represents the effect of exchange rate changes in excess of (or less than) that needed to maintain purchasing power parity between the functional currency and the dollar.

Probable Reserves. Probable reserves are reserves for which quantity and grade and/or quality are computed from information similar to that used for proven reserves, but the sites for inspection, sampling, and measurement are farther apart or are otherwise less adequately spaced. The degree of assurance, although lower than that for proven (measured) reserves, is high enough to assume continuity between points of observation.

Proven Reserves. Proven reserves are reserves for which both of the following conditions are met:

- Quantity is computed from dimensions revealed in outcrops, trenches, workings, or drill holes; grade and/or quality are computed from the results of detailed sampling.

- The sites for inspection, sampling, and measurement are spaced so closely and the geologic character is so well defined that size, shape, depth, and mineral content of reserves are well established.

Purchasing Power Gain or Loss. The net gain or loss determined by restating in units of constant purchasing power the opening and closing balances of, and transactions in, monetary assets and liabilities.

Recoverable Amount. Current worth of the net amount of cash expected to be recoverable from the use or sale of an asset.

Restate-Translate. An approach to converting current cost-nominal functional currency data of a foreign operation into units of constant purchasing power expressed in dollars. Using this approach, the current cost-nominal functional currency data are restated into units of constant purchasing power using a general price index for the foreign currency. After restatement into units of constant functional currency purchasing power, the current cost data are translated into dollars. This approach often necessitates a parity adjustment.

Translate-Restate. An approach to converting current cost-nominal functional currency data of a foreign operation into units of constant purchasing power expressed in dollars. Using this approach, the current cost-nominal functional currency data are first translated into dollars and then restated into units of constant purchasing power using the Consumer Price Index for All Urban Consumers.

Translation Adjustments. Translation adjustments result from the process of translating financial statements from the entity's functional currency into the reporting currency.

Value in Use. The amount determined by discounting the future cash flows (including the ultimate proceeds of disposal) expected to be derived from the use of an asset at an appropriate rate that allows for the risk of the activities concerned.

CONCEPTS, RULES, AND EXAMPLES

Elective Disclosures

Business entities are encouraged, but not required, to present supplementary information on the effects of changing prices. See www.wiley.com/go/GAAP2021, for a list of selected elective disclosures.

Other Sources

See ASC 912-255-50-1 for guidance on supplementary information provided by federal government contractors on the effects of changing prices when calculating the purchasing power gain or loss on net monetary items.

10 ASC 260 EARNINGS PER SHARE

PERSPECTIVE AND ISSUES

Subtopic

ASC 260, *Earnings per Share*, consists of one subtopic:

- ASC 260-10, *Overall*, that provides the guidance for computation, presentation, and disclosure for earnings per share (EPS) for entities with publicly held common stock or potential common stock.

This subtopic also offers guidance on EPS and recognition and measurement of the effect of a down round feature when it is triggered.
(ASC 260-10-05-1 and 05-1A)

The subtopic also includes master limited partnership subsections that clarify the application to master limited partnership of the Other Presentation Matters subsection.

Scope and Scope Exceptions

ASC 260 applies to all entities:

- Whose common stock or potential common stock is traded in a public market, or
- Who have made a filing or are in the process of making a filing to trade their stock publicly.

Notice that nonpublic companies are not required to report earnings per share. The guidance also does not apply to investment companies who comply with ASC 946 or in statements of wholly owned subsidiaries. If an entity not required to report under ASC 260 chooses to provide EPS information, the entity must comply with the ASC 260 guidance. (ASC 260-10-45-5)

Overview

Earnings per share (EPS) is an indicator widely used by investors to gauge the profitability of a corporation. Its purpose is to indicate how effective an enterprise has been in using the resources provided by its common stockholders through measuring the income earned by each share of common stock.

In its simplest form, EPS is net income (loss) divided by the weighted-average number of shares of outstanding common stock. The EPS computation becomes more complex with the existence of securities that are not common stock but have the potential of causing additional shares of common stock to be issued and, therefore, to dilute EPS upon conversion or exercise. Diluted EPS (DEPS) includes the potential dilution that could occur from other financial instruments that would increase the total number of outstanding shares of common stock. Examples of potentially dilutive securities are convertible preferred stock, convertible debt, options, and warrants. An EPS number that does not take into account the potential dilutive effects of such securities would be misleading. In addition, a lack of standardization in the way in which these securities are included in such an EPS computation would make comparability among corporations extremely difficult.

DEFINITIONS OF TERMS

Source: ASC 260-10-20, *Glossary*. See also Appendix A, *Definitions of Terms*, for definitions of: Call Option, Down Round Feature, Employee Stock Ownership Plan, Equity Restructuring, Fair Value, Financial Instrument, Noncontrolling Interest, Not-for-Profit Entity, Option, Public

Business Entity, Put Option, Security, Share-Based Equity Payments, Standard Antidilution Provisions, Stock Dividend, Subsidiaries, and Warrants.

Antidilution. An increase in earnings per share amounts or a decrease in loss per share amounts.

Basic Earnings Per Share. The amount of earnings for the period available to each share of common stock outstanding during the reporting period.

Consolidated Financial Statements. The financial statements of a consolidated group of entities that include a parent and all its subsidiaries presented as those of a single economic entity.

Consolidated Group. A parent and all its subsidiaries.

Contingent Issuance. A possible issuance of shares of common stock that is dependent on the satisfaction of certain conditions.

Contingent Stock Agreement. An agreement to issue common stock (usually in connection with a business combination) that is dependent on the satisfaction of certain conditions. See Contingently Issuable Shares.

Contingently Convertible Instruments. Contingently convertible instruments are instruments that have embedded conversion features that are contingently convertible or exercisable based on either of the following:

- A market price trigger
- Multiple contingencies if one of the contingencies is a market price trigger and the instrument can be converted or share settled based on meeting the specified market condition

A market price trigger is a market condition that is based at least in part on the issuer's own share price. Examples of contingently convertible instruments include contingently convertible debt, contingently convertible preferred stock, and the instrument described by paragraph 260-10-45-43, all with embedded market price triggers.

Contingently Issuable Shares. Shares issuable for little or no cash consideration upon the satisfaction of certain conditions pursuant to a contingent stock agreement. Also called contingently issuable stock. See Contingent Stock Agreement.

Conversion Rate. The ratio of the number of common shares issuable upon conversion to a unit of a convertible security. For example, $100 face value of debt convertible into 5 shares of common stock would have a conversion ratio of 5:1. Also called conversion ratio.

Convertible Security. A security that is convertible into another security based on a conversion rate. For example, convertible preferred stock that is convertible into common stock on a two-for-one basis (two shares of common for each share of preferred).

Diluted Earnings Per Share. The amount of earnings for the period available to each share of common stock outstanding during the reporting period and to each share that would have been outstanding assuming the issuance of common shares for all dilutive potential common shares outstanding during the reporting period.

Dilution. A reduction in EPS resulting from the assumption that convertible securities were converted, that options or warrants were exercised, or that other shares were issued upon the satisfaction of certain conditions.

Dropdown. A transfer of certain net assets from a sponsor or general partner in exchange for consideration. (Effective upon implementation of ASU 2015-06.)

Earnings Per Share. The amount of earnings attributable to each share of common stock. For convenience, the term is used to refer to either earnings or loss per share.

Equity Restructuring. A nonreciprocal transaction between an entity and its shareholders that causes the per-share fair value of the shares underlying an option or similar award to change, such as a stock dividend, stock split, spinoff, rights offering, or recapitalization through a large, nonrecurring cash dividend.

Exercise Price. The amount that must be paid for a share of common stock upon exercise of an option or warrant.

If-Converted Method. A method of computing EPS data that assumes conversion of convertible securities at the beginning of the reporting period (or at time of issuance, if later).

Income Available to Common Stockholders. Income (or loss) from continuing operations or net income (or net loss) adjusted for preferred stock dividends.

Participating Security. A security that may participate in undistributed earnings with common stock, whether that participation is conditioned upon the occurrence of a specified event or not. The form of such participation does not have to be a dividend—that is, any form of participation in undistributed earnings would constitute participation by that security, regardless of whether the payment to the security holder was referred to as a dividend.

Potential Common Stock. A security or other contract that may entitle its holder to obtain common stock during the reporting period or after the end of the reporting period.

Preferred Stock. A security that has preferential rights compared to common stock.

Purchased Call Option. A contract that allows the reporting entity to buy a specified quantity of its own stock from the writer of the contract at a fixed price for a given period. See Call Option.

Reverse Treasury Stock Method. A method of recognizing the dilutive effect on EPS of satisfying a put obligation. It assumes that the proceeds used to buy back common stock (pursuant to the terms of a put option) will be raised from issuing shares at the average market price during the period. See Put Option.

Rights Issue. An offer to existing shareholders to purchase additional shares of common stock in accordance with an agreement for a specified amount (which is generally substantially less than the fair value of the shares) for a given period.

Treasury Stock Method. A method of recognizing the use of proceeds that could be obtained upon exercise of options and warrants in computing diluted EPS. It assumes that any proceeds would be used to purchase common stock at the average market price during the period.

Weighted-Average Number of Common Shares Outstanding. The number of shares determined by relating the portion of time within a reporting period that common shares have been outstanding to the total time in that period. In computing diluted EPS, equivalent common shares are considered for all dilutive potential common shares.

CONCEPTS, RULES, AND EXAMPLES

Presentation on the Income Statement

Simple and Complex Capital Structure Simple capital structures are those with only common stock outstanding and having no potential common shares that upon conversion or exercise could dilute EPS. (ASC 260-10-45-2) Simple capital structures only have basic EPS. All other entities are considered to have complex capital structures. Entities with a complex capital structure have potential common stock in the form of potentially dilutive securities, options, warrants, or other rights that upon conversion or exercise have the potential to dilute earnings per common share. Basic EPS must be presented on the face of the income statement. If an entity has complex EPS, both basic and complex EPS must be presented on the face of the statement with equal prominence. (ASC 260-10-45-2) EPS must be presented for all periods where an income statement or summary of earnings is presented. If DEPS is presented in one period, it must be presented for all periods. (ASC 260-10-45-2) If basic and diluted EPS are the same, dual presentation can be shown on one line on the income statement. (ASC 260-10-45-7)

The reason for the differentiation between simple and complex capital structures is that ASC 260 requires different financial statement presentation for each. ASC 260 mandates that EPS be shown on the face of the income statement for each of the following items (when applicable):

- Income from continuing operations
- Net income

EPS data is to be presented for all periods for which an income statement or summary of earnings is presented. If DEPS is reported for at least one period, it is to be reported for all periods presented, regardless of whether DEPS differs from basic EPS. (ASC 260-10-45-7) However, if basic and diluted EPS are the same amounts for all periods presented, dual presentation may be accomplished in one line on the face of the income statement.

Discontinued Operations An entity that reports a discontinued operation or the cumulative effect of a change in accounting principle presents basic and diluted EPS amounts for these line items either on the face of the income statement or in the notes to the financial statements. (ASC 2160-10-45-3) These requirements must be fulfilled regardless of whether the capital structure is simple or complex. The difference in the two structures is that a simple capital structure requires presentation of only a single EPS number for each item, while a complex structure requires the dual presentation of basic EPS and DEPS for each item.

Year-to-Date Diluted EPS ASC 260-10-45 addresses the matter of how to compute year-to-date diluted EPS (1) when a company has a year-to-date loss from continuing operations including one or more quarters with income from continuing operations, and (2) when in-the-money options or warrants were not included in one or more quarterly diluted EPS computations because there was a loss from continuing operations in those quarters.

ASC 260 directs that in applying the treasury stock method in year-to-date computations, the number of incremental shares to be included in the denominator is to be determined by computing a year-to-date weighted-average of the number of incremental shares included in each quarterly diluted EPS computation.

However, ASC 260 includes a prohibition against antidilution, which states that the computation of diluted EPS is not to assume conversion, exercise, or contingent issuance of securities that would have an antidilutive effect on EPS. There may be a conflict between these provisions when a period longer than three months has an overall loss but includes quarters with income. For periods with year-to-date income (as in quarterly filings on Form 10-Q), in computing year-to-date diluted EPS, SEC staff believes that year-to-date income (or loss) from continuing operations should be the basis for determining whether or not dilutive potential common shares not included in one or more quarterly computations of diluted EPS should be included in the year-to-date computation.

According to ASC 260-10-45, (1) when there is a year-to-date loss, potential common shares should never be included in the computation of diluted EPS, because to do so would be antidilutive, and (2) when there is year-to-date income, if in-the-money options or warrants were excluded from one or more quarterly diluted EPS computations because the effect was antidilutive (there was a loss from continuing operations in those periods), then those options or warrants should be included in the diluted EPS denominator (on a weighted-average basis) in the year-to-date computation as long as the effect is not antidilutive. (ASC 260-10-45-20) Similarly, contingent shares that were excluded from a quarterly computation solely because there was a loss from continuing operations should be included in the year-to-date computation unless the effect is antidilutive.

Other Presentation and Disclosure Requirements The additional items required to be disclosed for all periods for which an income statement is presented can be found in the *Disclosure and Presentation Checklist for Commercial Businesses* at www.wiley.com/go/GAAP2021.

Basic EPS Calculation

The basic EPS formula contains three elements:

- Net income
- Preferred dividends
- Weighted-average of common shares outstanding

$$\text{EPS} = \frac{\text{Net income} - \text{preferred dividends}}{\text{Weighted-average number of common shares outstanding}}$$

Shares are weighted for the portion of the fiscal period for which they were outstanding. (ASC 260-10-45-10)

This calculation becomes complex when net income does not necessarily represent the earnings available to the common stockholder, and a simple weighted-average of common shares outstanding does not necessarily reflect the true nature of the situation.

If an entity is presenting consolidated financial statements with less than wholly owned subsidiaries, then it should exclude from net income the income attributable to the noncontrolling interest in subsidiaries. (ASC 260-10-45-11A)

Effect of Preferred Dividends The basic EPS calculation is income available to common stockholders (the numerator) divided by the weighted-average number of common shares EPS calculation is to measure the performance of the entity over the reporting period. The net income available to common stockholders used as the numerator in any of the EPS computations must be reduced by any preferential claims against it by other securities. The justification for this reduction is that the preferential claims of the other securities must be satisfied before any income is available to the common stockholder. These other securities are usually in the form of preferred stock, and the deduction from income is the amount of the dividend declared (whether or not paid) during the year on the preferred stock. If the preferred stock is cumulative,[1] the dividend is deducted from income (added to the loss) whether or not declared. If the preferred stock dividends are cumulative only if earned, they should be deducted only to the extent that they are earned. (ASC 260-10-45-11) At the option of the issuer, preferred stock dividends are sometimes payable in either cash or common stock. The form of payment is not a determinant in accounting for the effect of the preferred dividend on net income available to common stockholders. Therefore, for the purposes of the numerator in EPS computations, net income or loss is adjusted to compute the portion available to common stockholders.

[1] Cumulative preferred stock requires that if the entity fails to pay a dividend in any year, it must make it up in a later year before paying any dividends to holders of common stock.

Preferred Stock Dividends Payable in Common Shares All dividends represent distributions of accumulated earnings, and accordingly are not reported as expenses on the income statement under GAAP. However, as discussed above, for purposes of computing EPS, preferred dividends must be deducted in order to ascertain how much income is available for common stockholders. In some cases, preferred dividends are not payable in cash, but rather in common shares (based on market value as of the date of declaration, typically). In certain cases, the dividends may be payable in common shares or cash at the issuer's option.

ASC 260 defines income available to common stockholders as "income (or loss) from continuing operations or net income (or net loss) adjusted for preferred stock dividends." This adjustment in computing income available to common stockholders is consistent with the treatment of common stock issued for goods or services. (ASC 260-10-45-12)

Example of Preferred Stock Dividends Payable in Common Shares

Delta Corporation has three classes of preferred stock outstanding, as noted in the following table:

Stock type	Preferred stock description	Total $ issued
Series A	7% preferred stock, $100 par value, 3,000 shares outstanding, payable in common stock priced at market value on declaration date	$300,000
Series B	5% preferred stock, $100 par value, 2,000 shares outstanding, payable in common stock at fixed price of $2.00/share	200,000
Series C	8% preferred stock, $100 par value, 1,000 shares outstanding, payable in cash or in common stock at market price on declaration date, at Delta's option	100,000

On the dividend declaration date, the price of a share of common stock is $2.50. Delta's Board of Directors approves the payment of the Series C dividend as 50% cash, 50% common stock. The following table shows the types and amounts of dividends due for all types of preferred stock:

Stock type	Total dividend due	Applicable common stock price	Number of common shares issued	Cash issued
Series A	$ 21,000	$2.50	8,400	
Series B	10,000	2.00	5,000	
Series C	8,000	2.50	1,600	$ 4,000
	$ 39,000		15,000	$ 4,000

Delta has net income of $110,000, from which the total dividend due, regardless of the form of payment, must be subtracted. The calculation follows:

$$\frac{\$110,000\text{ net income} - \$39,000\text{ dividend}}{\text{Common shares outstanding}}$$

Delta's fiscal year is the calendar year. Delta had 200,000 shares of common stock outstanding on January 1, issued an additional 30,000 common shares on May 1, and declared the previously described preferred stock dividends on 12/31. Based on this information, the weighted-average number of shares outstanding follows:

Description	Number of shares	Weighted-average shares outstanding	Fraction of the year deemed outstanding
Number of shares as of 1/1	200,000	12/12	200,000
Common stock issuance on 5/1	30,000	8/12	20,000
Common stock issued on 12/31 as part of preferred stock dividend	15,000	12/12	15,000
Weighted-average number of common shares outstanding			235,000

Delta divides the 235,000 common shares outstanding into the adjusted net income to arrive at the following EPS calculation:

$$\frac{\$110{,}000-\$39{,}000}{235{,}000\,\text{common shares}}=\$0.30$$

Down Round Feature Down round features are found in certain equity-linked instruments (or embedded features) that result in reduced strike price based on the pricing of future equity offerings. Because of the complexity and resulting increased costs of accounting for these instruments, the entity is not required to consider down round features' equity classification when assessing whether those instruments are indexed to an entity's own stock.

The effect of the feature is the difference between the fair value of the financial instrument without the down round feature with a strike price corresponding to the related instrument's:

- current strike price and
- a strike price corresponding to the reduced strike price.
  (ASC 260-10-30-1)

Entities that present EPS should recognize the effect of the down round feature only when it is triggered. (ASC 260-10-45-12B) The effect is treated as a dividend and as a reduction of income available to common shareholders in the basic EPS. (ASC 260-10-25-1) Convertible instruments with included conversion options that have down round features should follow the guidance in ASC 470-20.

Contingently Issuable Shares The computation of the weighted-average of common stock outstanding is complicated by the effect that various transactions have on the computation of common shares outstanding. For example, an entity involved in a purchase business combination may have a contractual obligation to issue common shares when certain conditions are met. These contingently issued shares should be included in the denominator only when there is no circumstance under which those shares would not be issued. (ASC 260-10-45-12C)

While it is impossible to analyze all the possibilities, ASC 260 provides discussion of some of the more common transactions affecting the number of common shares outstanding. By analogy, the theoretical model set forth in these relatively simple examples can be applied to situations that are not explicitly discussed.

Stock Dividend or Stock Split When an entity issues a dividend in the form of its own stock or splits its stock, it does not receive any consideration, but it does increase the number of shares outstanding. ASC 260 states that the increase in shares as a result of a stock split or dividend, or decrease in shares as a result of a reverse split, should be given retroactive recognition as an appropriate equivalent charge for all periods presented. Thus, even if a stock dividend or split occurs at the end of the period, it is considered outstanding for the entirety of each period presented. The reasoning is that a stock dividend or split has no effect on the ownership percentage of the common stockholder. To show a dilution in the EPS reported would erroneously give the impression of a decline in profitability when in fact it was merely an increase in the shares out- standing due to the stock dividend or split. ASC 260 carries this principle one step further by requiring the retroactive adjustment of outstanding shares for stock dividends or splits occurring after the end of the period, but before the release of the financial statements. The rationale for this adjustment is that the primary interest of the financial statement user is considered to be the company's current capitalization. (ASC 260-10-55-12) If this situation occurs, disclosure of both the end-of-year outstanding shares and those used to compute EPS is required. (ASC 260-10-55-17)

When shares are issued in connection with a business combination that occurs during the period, they are treated as issued and outstanding as of the date of the acquisition.

Exhibit—Effect of Certain Transactions or Amounts on the Weighted-Average Computation

Weighted-Average Computations

Transaction/Amount	*Effect on weighted-average computation*
• Common stock outstanding at the beginning of the period	• Included in number of shares outstanding
• Issuance of common stock	• Increase number of shares outstanding by the number of shares issued times the portion of the year outstanding
• Conversion into common stock	• Increase number of shares outstanding by the number of shares converted times the portion of the year outstanding
• Reacquisition of common stock	• Decrease number of shares outstanding by number of shares reacquired times portion of the year since reacquisition
• Contingently issuable shares	• Include only when the contingency has been met and there is no circumstance under which those shares would not be issued
• Stock dividend or split	• Increase number of shares outstanding by number of shares issued for the dividend or resulting from the split retroactively as of the beginning of the earliest period presented
• Reverse split	• Decrease number of shares outstanding by decrease in shares retroactively as of the beginning of the earliest period presented
• Business combination	• Increase number of shares outstanding by number of shares issued times portion of year since acquisition
• Triggering of down round feature	• Deduct the value of the effect on calculating income available to common stock hedges

The exhibit above does not provide for all of the possible complexities arising in the EPS computation; however, most of the others occur under a complex capital structure. The complications arising under a complex capital structure are discussed and illustrated in detail later in this chapter and in the final section, "Comprehensive Example." The illustration below applies some of the foregoing concepts to a simple capital structure.

Example of EPS Computation—Simple Capital Structure

Assume the following information:

	Numerator information			*Denominator information*	
a.	Income from continuing operations	$130,000	a.	Common shares outstanding	100,000
b.	Loss from discontinued operations (net of income tax)	(30,000)	b.	Shares issued for cash 4/1/ /X1	20,000
c.	Net income	100,000	c.	Shares issued in 10% stock dividend declared in July 20X1	12,000
d.	6% cumulative preferred stock, $100 par, 1,000 shares issued and outstanding	100,000	d.	Shares of treasury stock reacquired 10/1/X1	10,000

When calculating the numerator, the claims related to the preferred stock are deducted to arrive at the income available to the common stockholders. In this example, the preferred stock is cumulative. Thus, regardless of whether or not the board of directors declares a preferred dividend, holders of the preferred stock have a claim of $6,000 (= 1,000 shares × $100 par × 6%) against 20X1 earnings. Therefore, $6,000 must be deducted from the numerator to arrive at the income available to common stockholders. Note that any cumulative preferred dividends in arrears are ignored in computing this period's EPS since they would have been incorporated into previous periods' EPS calculations. Also note that this $6,000 would have been deducted for *non*cumulative preferred stock only if a dividend of this amount had been declared during the period.

The EPS calculations follow.

Earnings per common share:

On income from continuing operations before loss from discontinued operation

$$\frac{\$130{,}000 - \$6{,}000}{\text{Common shares outstanding}}$$

On net income

$$\frac{\$100{,}000 - \$6{,}000}{\text{Common shares outstanding}}$$

The computation of the denominator is based upon the weighted-average number of common shares outstanding. A simple weighted-average is not considered appropriate because of the various complexities. Table 10.1 illustrates one way of computing the weighted-average number of shares outstanding.

Table 10.1

Item	**Actual number of shares**	**Retroactive effects of July stock dividend**	**Subtotal number of shares deemed outstanding**	**Fraction of the year deemed outstanding**	**Shares times fraction of the year deemed outstanding**
Number of shares as of beginning of the year 1/1/X1	100,000	10,000			
[10%(100,000)]	110,000	12/12	110,000		
Shares issued 4/1/X1	20,000	2,000			
[10%(20,000)]	22,000	9/12	16,500		
Treasury shares reacquired 10/1/X1	(10,000)	–	(10,000)	3/12	(2,500)
Weighted-average number of common shares outstanding				124,000	

The stock dividend declared in July is treated as being retroactive to the beginning of the year. Thus, for the period 1/1 through 4/1, 110,000 shares are considered to be outstanding. When shares are issued, they are included in the weighted-average beginning with the date of issuance. The shares issued as a result of the stock dividend applicable to the 20,000 newly issued shares are also assumed to have been outstanding for the same period as the 20,000 shares. Thus, we can see that of the 12,000-share stock dividend, 10,000 shares relate to the beginning balance and 2,000 shares to the new issuance (10% of 100,000 and 20,000, respectively). The reacquisition of the treasury stock requires that these shares be excluded from the calculation for the remainder of the period after their reacquisition date. This amount is subtracted from the calculation because the shares were reacquired from shares outstanding prior to their reacquisition.

To complete the example, we divide the previously computed numerator by the weighted-average number of common shares outstanding to arrive at EPS.

Earnings per common share:

On income from continuing operations before loss from discontinued operation	$\frac{\$130{,}000 - \$6{,}000}{124{,}000 \text{ common shares}}$	= $1.00
On net income	$\frac{\$100{,}000 - \$6{,}000}{124{,}000 \text{ common shares}}$	= $0.76

The numbers computed above are required to be presented on the face of the income statement. Reporting a $.24 loss from discontinued operation per share ($30,000 loss on discontinued operation ÷ 124,000 common shares) is required either on the face of the income statement or in the notes to the financial statements.

Diluted Earnings Per Share (DEPS)

The computation of EPS under a complex capital structure involves all of the complexities discussed under the simple structure and many more.

Computation of DEPS A complex capital structure is one that includes securities that grant rights with the potential to be exercised and reduce EPS, that is, dilutive securities. In the calculation of DEPS:

- The denominator is increased to include the number of additional shares that would have been outstanding had the dilutive shares been issued.
- The numerator is also adjusted for any change in income or loss that would have resulted from the conversion.
- Any antidilutive securities (those that increase EPS) are not included in the computation of EPS.
- The common stock outstanding and all other dilutive securities are used to compute diluted earnings per share (DEPS).
(ASC 260-10-45-16)

DEPS represents the earnings attributable to each share of common stock after giving effect to all potentially dilutive securities which were outstanding during the period. When calculating DEPS, the entity should not assume conversion, exercise, or contingent issuance of securities that would have an antidilutive effect on EPS. Actual shares issued should be evaluated to determine if they are dilutive or antidilutive. Each user should be evaluated separately. (ASC 260-10-45-17)

The computation of DEPS requires the entity to:

1. Identify all potentially dilutive securities.
2. Compute dilution, the effects that the other dilutive securities have on net income and common shares outstanding.

Step 1: Identification of potentially dilutive securities Dilutive securities are those that have the potential of being exercised and reducing the EPS figure. Some examples of dilutive securities identified by ASC 260 are convertible debt, convertible preferred stock, options, warrants, participating securities, two-class common stocks, and contingent shares.

Convertible securities. A convertible security is one type of potentially dilutive security. A security of this type has an inherent dual nature. Convertibles are comprised of two distinct elements:

1. The right to receive dividends or interest, and
2. The right to potentially participate in earnings by becoming a common stockholder.

This security is included in the DEPS computation because of element number 2 above.

Options and warrants. Options, warrants, and their equivalents generally derive their value from the right to obtain common stock at specified prices over an extended period of time.

Participating securities and two-class common stocks. The capital structure of some entities includes securities that may participate in dividends with common stocks according to a predetermined formula, or a class of common stock with different dividend rates from those of another class of common stock but without prior or senior rights. If the effect is dilutive, entities do not have the option of using the if-converted method for those securities that are convertible into common stock. For these securities, participating securities, and two-class common stocks, the two-class method of computing EPS, as described later on, is used.

Financial instruments with characteristics of both liabilities and equity. ASC 480 specifies that certain freestanding financial instruments (as distinguished from compound financial instruments) that may resemble equity are nevertheless required to be classified as liabilities on the issuer's statement of financial position. Such instruments include mandatorily redeemable financial instruments (including mandatorily redeemable common or preferred stock) and certain forward contracts that require physical settlement by repurchase of a fixed number of the issuer's equity shares. Issuers of these instruments are required to:

- Exclude any shares of common stock that are required to be redeemed or repurchased from the denominator of the EPS and DEPS computations, and
- Apply the two-class method described in ASC 260-10-45-60, described later in this chapter, to deduct from income available to common stockholders any amounts attributable to shares that are to be redeemed or repurchased, including contractual dividends and participation rights in undistributed earnings. This deduction is limited to amounts not recognized in the issuer's financial statements as interest expense.
(ASC 480-10-45-4)

Contingent issuances of common stock. Contingently convertible instruments are those that have embedded conversion features that are contingently convertible or exercisable based either on a market price trigger or on multiple contingencies, if one of the contingencies is a market price trigger and the instrument can be converted or share settled based on meeting the specified market condition. A market price trigger is a condition that is based at least in part on the reporting entity's share price. Examples include contingently convertible debt and contingently convertible preferred stock. A typical trigger occurs when the market price exceeds a defined conversion price by a specified percentage (e.g., when the market price first equals or exceeds 20% more than the conversion price of $33 per share). Others have floating market price triggers for which conversion is dependent upon the market price of the reporting entity's stock exceeding the conversion price by a specified percentage(s) at specified times during the term of the debt. Yet other contingently convertible instruments require that the market price of the issuer's stock exceed a specified level for a specified period (for example, 20% above the conversion price for a 30-day period). In addition, these instruments may have additional features such as parity features, issuer call options, and investor put options.

Contingently convertible instruments must be included in diluted EPS, if dilutive, regardless of whether the market price trigger has been met. The reasoning is that there is no substantive economic difference between contingently convertible instruments and conventional convertible instruments with a market price conversion premium. ASC 260-10-45-44 is to be applied to instruments that have multiple contingencies, if one of these is a market price trigger and the instrument is convertible or settleable in shares based on a market condition being met—that is, the conversion is not dependent on a substantive non-market-based contingency.

Example—Contingently Convertible Debt with a Market Price Trigger

The holder of the Frye Corp. 4% interest-bearing bonds, amounting to $100,000 face value, may convert the debt into shares of Frye common stock when the share price exceeds the market price trigger; otherwise, the holder is only entitled to the par value of the debt. The conversion ratio is 20 shares per bond, or a total of 2,000 shares of stock. The implicit conversion price, therefore, is $50 per share. At the time of issuance of the bonds, Frye common stock has a market price of $40. Frye's effective tax rate is 35%. Frye has 20,000 shares of its common shares outstanding. The bonds become convertible when the average share price for the year exceeds $65 (130% of conversion price).

The contingently convertible bonds are issued on January 1, 20X1. Income available to common shareholders for the year ended December 31, 20X1, is $80,000, and the average share price for the year is $55. The issuer of the contingently convertible debt would apply ASC 260-10-45, which requires the reporting entity to include the dilutive effect of the convertible debt in diluted EPS even though the market price trigger of $65 has not been met.

Basic EPS is ($80,000 ÷ 20,000 shares =) $4.00 per share. Applying the if-converted method to the debt instrument dilutes EPS to $3.77. (To compute DEPS, net income is increased by the after-tax effect of interest, and this is then divided by the total of outstanding plus potential common shares.)

Another consideration is contingent issuances of common stock (e.g., stock subscriptions). If shares are to be issued in the future with no restrictions on issuance other than the passage of time, as of the beginning of the period in which the conditions were satisfied, they are considered issued and treated as outstanding in the computation of DEPS. (ASC 260-10-45-48a) For year-to-date DEPS the contingent shares are weighted. (ASC 260-10-45-49)

Other issuances that are dependent upon certain conditions being met should be evaluated in a different manner. ASC 260 uses as examples the maintenance of current earnings levels and the attainment of specified earnings increases. The following table lists examples and the accounting treatment for each.

Exhibit—Issuances Contingent on Certain Conditions

Shares Issued Contingent Upon:	Treatment
Merely maintaining the earnings levels currently being attained	The DEPS computation should include the number of shares that would be issued based on the assumption that the current amount of earnings will remain unchanged if the effect is dilutive.
The market price at a future date	The DEPS computation should include the number of shares that would be issued based on market price at the end of the reporting period if the effect is dilutive.
The lapsing of time *and* the market price of the stock (which generally affects the number of shares issued)	Both conditions must be met to include the contingently issuable shares in the DEPS computation.
Conditions other than changes in market price	Assume the current status of the conditions remains unchanged until the end of the contingency period and calculate accordingly
(ASC 260-10 45-51 through 45-54)	

Example of the Impact of Contingent Stock Issuances on EPS

Arturo Corporation offers its management team the following set of stock-based incentives that apply to the current year of operations:

- A stock grant of 25,000 common shares if the company attains full-year net income of at least $1 million.
- An additional stock grant of 1,000 common shares for every additional $100,000 of net income recorded above $1 million.
- A stock grant of 50,000 common shares if the company is granted ISO 9001 certification, to be issued immediately upon completion of the certification.

Arturo has 500,000 shares of common stock outstanding throughout the calendar year, which is its fiscal year. It obtains the ISO 9001 certification on April 1. Arturo's full-year net income is $1,300,000. It records the following basic EPS:

$$\frac{\$1,300,000 \text{ net income}}{537,500 \text{ common shares}} = \$2.42$$

The denominator incurs 3/4 of the 50,000 stock grant (e.g., 37,500 shares) associated with completion of the ISO 9001 certification, since the grant occurs after 1/4 of the fiscal year had been completed. The stock grant that is contingent on full-year earnings is not included in the basic EPS calculation, since the grant cannot occur until the last day of the year, and therefore has a negligible impact on the calculation.

For the DEPS calculation, the contingent stock grant of 25,000 shares associated with the $1 million net income goal is included in the full-year weighted-average, as well as the 3,000 shares associated with the incremental increase in net profits above $1 million and the 50,000 shares associated with the ISO 9001 project completion. The calculation of shares to include in the DEPS denominator follows:

Common stock outstanding	500,000
Stock grant associated with ISO 9001 project completion	50,000
Stock grant associated with attainment of $1 million net income goal	25,000
Stock grant associated with attainment of incremental $300,000 net income goal	3,000
Total DEPS shares	578,000

By including these shares in the denominator of the DEPS calculation, Arturo arrives at the following diluted EPS:

$$\frac{\$1,300,000 \text{ net income}}{578,000 \text{ common shares}} = \$2.25$$

Step 2: Computation of DEPS The second step in the process is the actual computation of DEPS. There are basically two methods used to incorporate the effects of other dilutive securities on EPS (excluding participating and two-class common securities for which the two-class method described above is used):

1. The treasury stock method, and
2. The if-converted method.

The treasury stock method for computing DEPS. The treasury stock method, used for the exercise of most warrants or options, requires that DEPS be computed as if:

- The options or warrants were exercised at the beginning of the period (or actual date of issuance, if later), and

- That the funds obtained from the exercise were used to purchase (reacquire) the company's common stock at the average market price for the period. (ASC 260-10-45-23)

The incremental shares (the difference between the number of shares assumed issued and the number of shares assumed purchased) is included in the denominator of the diluted EPS computation. (ASC 260-10-45-23)

Example—Treasury Stock Method: Simple Capital Structure

An example of the requirements under ASC 260 follows. If a corporation has warrants outstanding for 1,000 shares of common stock exercisable at $10 per share, and the average market price of the common stock is $16 per share, the following occurs: The company receives $10,000 (1,000 × $10) and issue 1,000 shares from the exercise of the warrants which would enable it to repurchase 625 shares ($10,000 ÷ $16) in the open market. The net increase in the denominator (which effects a dilution in EPS) is 375 shares (1,000 issued less 625 repurchased). If the exercise price is greater than the average market price, the exercise is not assumed since the result would be antidilutive. In that case, DEPS of prior periods presented in comparative form are not restated to reflect the change in market price.

Treasury Stock Method

Denominator must be increased by net dilution, as follows:

Net dilution	= Shares issued – Shares assumed to be repurchased
where:	
Shares issued	= Proceeds received ÷ Exercise price per share
Shares assumed to be repurchased share	= Proceeds received ÷ Average market price per

(ASC 260-10-45-23)

The if-converted method for computing DEPS. The if-converted method is used for those convertible securities that are currently sharing in the earnings of the company through the receipt of interest or dividends as preferential securities, but that have the potential for sharing in the earnings as common stock (e.g., convertible bonds or convertible preferred stock). The if-converted method logically recognizes that the convertible security can only share in the earnings of the company as one or the other, not both. Thus, the dividends or interest less income tax effects applicable to the convertible security as a preferential security are not recognized in income available to common stockholders used to compute DEPS, and the weighted-average number of shares is adjusted to reflect the assumed conversion as of the beginning of the year (or actual date of issuance, if later). (ASC 260-10-45-40)

If-Converted Method Computation for DEPS

Numerator

Income available to common stockholders recomputed to reflect assumed and/or actual conversion

- Add back interest expense less income tax effects
- Convertible preferred dividends are no longer subtracted
- Add back other expenses attributable to convertible issues

Denominator

Weighted-average number of shares of common stock outstanding adjusted to reflect the assumed and/or actual conversion of convertible securities at the beginning of the period or actual date of issuance, if later

Exceptions. Generally, the if-converted method is used for convertible securities, while the treasury stock method is used for options and warrants. There are some situations specified by ASC 260 for which this does not hold true:

- If options or warrants permit or require that debt or other securities of the issuer be tendered for all or a portion of the exercise price, the if-converted method is used.
- If options or warrants require that the proceeds from the exercise are to be used to retire existing debt, the if-converted method is used.
- If convertible securities require cash payment upon conversion, and are, therefore, considered equivalent to warrants, the treasury stock method is used.
(ASC 260-10-55-9 through 55-11)

Examples of EPS Computation

Each of the following independent examples is presented to illustrate the principles discussed above. The procedural guidelines are detailed to enable the reader to understand the computation without referring back to the preceding explanatory text.

Example of the Treasury Stock Method—Complex Capital Structure

Assume that net income is $50,000 and the weighted-average number of common shares outstanding has been computed as 10,000. Additional information regarding the capital structure is:

- 4% nonconvertible, cumulative preferred stock, par value of $100 per share, 1,000 shares issued and outstanding the entire year
- Options and warrants to purchase 1,000 shares of common stock at $8 per share were outstanding all year.
- The average market price of common stock during the year was $10.

The first step in applying this method is the determination of basic EPS. This calculation appears as follows:

$$\frac{\text{Net income} - \text{Preferred dividends}}{\text{Weighted-average number of common shares outstanding}}$$

$$= \frac{\$50{,}000 - \$4{,}000}{10{,}000 \text{ shares}}$$

$$= \$4.60$$

The second step is the calculation of DEPS, which is based upon outstanding common stock and other dilutive securities. The options and warrants are the only potentially dilutive securities in the example. However, remember that only dilutive options (Market price > Exercise price) are included in the computation. The treasury stock method is used to compute the number of shares to be added to the denominator as illustrated below.

Proceeds from assumed exercise of options and warrants (1,000 shares × $8 per share)	$8,000
Number of shares issued	1,000
Number of shares assumed to be reacquired ($8,000 ÷ $10 average market price per share)	800
Number of shares assumed issued and not reacquired	200*

* *An alternative approach that can be used to calculate this number for DEPS is demonstrated below.*

$$\frac{\text{Average market price} - \text{Exercise price}}{\text{Average market price}}$$

$$\times \text{Number of shares under options warrants} = \text{Shares not reacquired}$$

$$\frac{\$10 - \$8}{\$10} \times 1{,}000\,\text{shares} = 200\,\text{shares}$$

DEPS can now be calculated as follows, including the effects of applying the treasury stock method:

$$\frac{\text{Net income} - \text{Preferred dividends}}{\text{Weighted-average number of common shares outstanding} + \text{Number of shares assumed issued and not reacquired with proceeds from options and warrants}}$$

$$= \frac{\$50{,}000 - \$4{,}000}{10{,}000 + 200\,\text{shares}}$$

$$= \$4.51$$

Note the dilutive effect of the options and warrants shown in Table 10.2, as EPS of $4.60 is reduced to DEPS of $4.51.

Table 10.2
Computations of Basic EPS and Diluted EPS

	EPS on outstanding common stock (Basic EPS)			*DEPS*		
Item	*Numerator*		*Denominator*	*Numerator*		*Denominator*
Net income	$50,000			$50,000		
Preferred dividends	(4,000)			(4,000)		
Common shares outstanding			10,000 shs			10,000 shs
Options and warrants						200
Totals	$46,000	÷	10,000 shs	$46,000	÷	10,200 shs
EPS		$4.60			$4.51	

Example of the If-Converted Method—Complex Capital Structure

Assume net income of $50,000 and weighted-average common shares outstanding of 10,000. Additional information regarding capital structure is:

- 7% convertible debt, 200 bonds each convertible into forty common shares. The bonds were outstanding the entire year. The income tax rate is 40%. The bonds were issued at par ($1,000 per bond). No bonds were converted during the year.

- 4% convertible, cumulative preferred stock, par value of $100 per share, 1,000 shares issued and outstanding. Each preferred share is convertible into two common shares. The preferred stock was issued at par value and was outstanding the entire year. No shares were converted during the year.

The first step is to compute basic EPS. As in the previous example, this is $4.60. The next step is the computation of DEPS, assuming conversion of the convertible debt in order to determine whether their conversion would be dilutive. The convertible bonds are assumed to have been converted to common stock at the beginning of the year, since no bonds were actually converted during the year. The effects of this assumption are twofold. One, if the bonds are converted, interest expense would be reduced by $14,000 (= 7% × 200 bonds × $1,000 par value per bond); and two, there will be an additional 8,000 shares of common stock outstanding during the year (= 200 bonds × 40 common shares per bond). The effect of avoiding $14,000 of interest expense will increase net income, but it will also increase income tax expense due to the lost income tax deduction. Consequently, the net after-tax effect of avoiding interest expense of $14,000 is $8,400 [= (1 – .40) × $14,000]. DEPS is computed as follows:

$$\frac{\text{Net income} - \text{Preferred dividends} + \text{Interest expense (net of tax)}}{\text{Weighted-average number of common shares outstanding} + \text{Shares issued upon conversion of bonds}}$$

$$= \frac{\$50,000 - \$4,000 + \$8,400}{10,000 + 8,000\text{shares}}$$

$$= \$3.02$$

The convertible debt is dilutive because EPS of $4.60 is reduced to DEPS of $3.02.

To determine the dilutive effect of the preferred stock, the preferred stock is assumed to have been converted to common stock at the beginning of the year, since no shares of preferred stock were actually converted during the year. The effects of this assumption are twofold. One, if the preferred stock is converted, there will be no preferred dividends of $4,000 for the year; and two, there will be an additional 2,000 shares of common stock outstanding during the year (the conversion rate is 2 for 1 on 1,000 shares of outstanding preferred stock). DEPS considering the preferred stock is computed, as follows, reflecting these two assumptions:

$$\frac{\text{Net income} + \text{Interest expense (net of tax)}}{\text{Weighted-average number of common shares outstanding} + \text{Shares issued upon conversion of bonds} + \text{Shares issued upon conversion of preferred stock}}$$

$$= \frac{\$50,000 + \$8,400}{10,000 + 8,000 + 2,000\,\text{shares}}$$

$$= \$2.92$$

The convertible preferred stock is also dilutive because DEPS of $3.02 is reduced to DEPS of $2.92.

Together, the effect of the convertible bonds and preferred stock reduces EPS of $4.60 to DEPS of $2.92. In this example, the convertible bonds must be considered first, prior to the inclusion of the convertible preferred stock in the computation. For a complete explanation of the sequencing process of including multiple dilutive securities in the computations of DEPS, see the comprehensive example at the end of the chapter. Table 10.3 summarizes the computations made for this example.

Table 10.3
Computations of Basic EPS and Diluted EPS

	EPS on outstanding common stock (Basic EPS)			*DEPS*		
Item	*Numerator*		*Denominator*	*Numerator*		*Denominator*
Net income	$50,000			$50,000		
Preferred dividend	(4,000)					
Common shares outstanding			10,000 shs			10,000 shs
Conversion of preferred						2,000
Conversion of bonds				8,400		8,000
Totals	$46,000	÷	10,000 shs	$58,400	÷	20,000 shs
EPS		$4.60			$2.92	

In the preceding example, all of the potentially dilutive securities were outstanding the entire year and no conversions or exercises were made during the year. If a potentially dilutive security was not outstanding the entire year, then the numerator and denominator effects would have to be *time-weighted*. For instance, suppose the convertible bonds in the above example were issued during the current year on July 1. If all other facts remain unchanged, DEPS would be computed as follows:

$$\frac{\text{Net income} + \text{Interest expense (net of tax)}}{\begin{array}{l}\text{Weighted-average number of common shares outstanding} + \\ \text{Shares issued upon conversion of preferred stock} + \\ \text{Shares issued upon conversion of bonds}\end{array}}$$

$$= \frac{\$50{,}000 + 1/2(8{,}400)}{10{,}000 + 2{,}000 + 1/2(8{,}000)}$$

$$= \$3.39$$

Since the DEPS of $3.39 is still less than the EPS of $4.60, the convertible debt is dilutive whether or not it is outstanding the entire year.

If actual conversions or exercises take place during a period, the common shares issued upon conversion will be outstanding from their date of issuance and therefore will be included in the computation of the weighted-average number of common shares outstanding. These shares are then weighted from their respective dates of issuance. Assume that all the bonds in the above example are converted on July 1 into 8,000 common shares; the following effects should be noted:

- For basic EPS, the weighted-average of common shares outstanding will be increased by (8,000 shares) (6 months outstanding/12 months in the period) or 4,000. Income will increase $4,200 net of income tax, because the bonds were only outstanding for the first half of the year.
- For DEPS, the if-converted method is applied to the period January 1 to June 30 because it was during this period that the bonds were potentially dilutive. The interest expense, net

of income tax, of $4,200 is added to the net income in the numerator, and 4,000 shares are added to the denominator.

- Interestingly, the net effect of items 1 and 2 is the same for the period, whether these dilutive bonds were outstanding the entire period or converted during the period.

Participating Securities and the Two-Class Method

Reporting entities that issue securities that are entitled to participate in dividends with common shares (participating shares) will report lower EPS under the guidance in ASC 260-10-55. This issue addresses the computation of EPS by entities that have issued securities, other than common stock, that entitle the holder to participate in dividends when, and if, dividends are declared on common stock. In addition, ASC 260-10-45-59A through 70 provides further guidance on calculating EPS using a two-class method and requires companies to retroactively restate EPS amounts presented. (ASC 260-10-45-59A)

Participation rights are defined based solely on whether the holder is entitled to receive any dividends if the entity declares them during the period. The codification also requires the use of the two-class method for computing basic EPS when participating convertible securities exist. The use of the two-class method encompasses other forms of participating securities, including options, warrants, forwards, and other contracts to issue an entity's common shares (including unvested share-based compensation awards).

Presentation and Disclosure For other than common stock, presentation of participating securities' basic and diluted EPS is not required, but is permitted. What is required by ASC 260-10-55 is adjustment to the earnings that are used to compute EPS for the common stock.

Participating Security Defined Participating securities are defined in the "Definitions of Terms" section at the beginning of this chapter as any "security that may participate in undistributed earnings with common stock, whether that participation is conditioned upon the occurrence of a specified event or not . . . regardless of the whether the payment to the security holder was referred to as a dividend." Also not considered to be participation rights are dividends, or their equivalents, that can be transferred to the holder of a share-based payment award as a reduction in the exercise price of the award. (ASC 260-10-45-62)

Additional guidance clarifies that instruments granted in share-based payment transactions can be participating securities prior to the requisite service having been rendered. However, the right to receive dividends or dividend equivalents that the holder will forfeit if the award does not vest does not qualify as a participation right, as the award does not meet the definition of a participation security.

In addition to the amount of dividends declared in the current period, net dividends must be reduced by the contractual amount of dividends or other participation payments that are paid or accumulated for the current period. The allocation of undistributed earnings for a period should be done for a participating security based on the contractual participation rights of the security to share in the current earnings assuming all earnings for the period are distributed. The allocation process is not based on a fair-value analysis, but is based on the term of the securities. For losses, an entity would allocate to the participating securities a portion of the net losses of the entity in accordance with the contractual provisions that may require the security to have an obligation to share in the issuing entity's losses. This occurs when the participating security holder has an obligation to share in the losses of the issuing entity if the holder is obligated to fund the issuing authority's losses or if losses incurred by the issuing entity reduce the security's principal or mandatory redemption amount.

Two-Class Method This is an earnings allocation formula for computing EPS. It determines EPS for each class of common stock and participating securities according to dividends declared/ accumulated and participation rights in undistributed earnings. (ASC 260-10-45-60) The codification requires that the two-class method be applied for participating convertible securities when computing basic EPS. (ASC 260-10-45-60A)

Use of the two-class method is dependent upon having no unsatisfied *contingencies* or objectively determinable contingent events. Thus, if preferred shares are entitled to participate in dividends with common shareholders only if management declares the distribution to be "extraordinary," this would not invoke the use of the two-class computation of EPS. However, if classification of dividends as extraordinary is predetermined by a formula, then undistributed earnings would be allocated to common stock and the participating security based on the assumption that all of the earnings for the period are distributed, with application of the defined sharing formula used for the determination of the allocation to the participating security.

If the participating security participates with common stock in earnings for a period in which a specified event occurs, regardless of whether a dividend is actually paid during the period (e.g., achievement of a target market price or achievement of threshold earnings), then undistributed earnings would be allocated to common stock and the participating security based on the assumption that all of the earnings for the period are distributed. Undistributed earnings would be allocated to the participating security if the contingent condition would have been satisfied at the reporting date, even if no actual distribution were made.

Example—Participating Convertible Preferred Stock

Assume that Struthers Corp. had 20,000 shares of common stock and 5,000 shares of preferred stock outstanding during 20X1, and reported net income of $65,000 for 20X1. Each share of preferred stock is convertible into two shares of common stock. The preferred stock is entitled to a noncumulative annual dividend of $5 per share. After the common has been paid a dividend of $1 per share, the preferred stock then participates in any additional dividends on a 2:3 per share ratio with the common. For 20X1, the common shareholders have been paid $26,000 (or $1.30 per share), and the preferred shareholders have been paid $26,000 (or $5.20 per share). Basic EPS under the two-class method for 20X1 would be computed as follows:

Net income		65,000
Less dividends paid:		
Common	$26,000	
Preferred stock	26,000	52,000
Undistributed 20X1 earnings		$13,000

Allocation of undistributed earnings

To preferred

$$0.2(5{,}000) \div \left[0.2(5{,}000) + 0.3(20{,}000)\right] \times \$13{,}000 = \$1{,}857$$

$$\$1{,}857 \div 5{,}000\,\text{shares} = \$0.37\,\text{per share}$$

To common

$$0.3(20{,}000) \div [0.2(5{,}000) + 0.3(20{,}000)] \times \$13{,}000 = \$11{,}143$$

$$\$11{,}143 \div 20{,}000 \text{ shares} = \$0.56 \text{ per share}$$

Basic EPS amounts for 20X1

	Preferred	*Common*
Distributed earnings	$ 5.20	$ 1.30
Undistributed earnings	0.37	0.56
Total	$ 5.57	$ 1.86

Example—Participating Convertible Debt Instrument

Assume that Wincomp, Inc. had 20,000 shares of common stock outstanding during 20X1 and reported net income of $85,000 for the year. On January 1, 20X1, Wincomp issues 1,000 30-year, 3% convertible bonds with an aggregate par value of $1,000,000. Each bond is convertible into eight shares of common stock. After the common has been paid a dividend of $1 per share, the bondholders then participate in any additional dividends on a 2:3 per share ratio with common shareholders. The bondholders receive common stock dividends based on the number of shares of common stock into which the bonds are convertible. The bondholders do not have any voting rights prior to conversion into common stock. For 20X1, the Wincomp common shareholders have been paid $20,000 (or $1.00 per share). Basic EPS under the two class method for 20X1 would be computed as follows:

Net income		$85,000
Less dividends paid:		
Common	$20,000	20,000
Undistributed 20X1 earnings		$65,000

Allocation of undistributed earnings

To convertible bonds

$$0.2(8{,}000) \div [0.2(8{,}000) + 0.3(20{,}000)] \times \$65{,}000 = \$13{,}684$$

$$\$13{,}684 \div 8{,}000 \text{ shares} = \$1.71 \text{ per share}$$

To common

$$0.3(20{,}000) \div [0.2(8{,}000) + 0.3(20{,}000)] \times \$65{,}000 = \$51{,}316$$

$$\$51{,}316 \div 20{,}000 \text{ shares} = \$2.57 \text{ per share}$$

Basic EPS amounts for 20X1

	Convertible bonds	Common
Distributed earnings	$–	$1.00
Undistributed earnings	1.71	2.57
Total	$1.71	$3.57

Example—Participating Warrants

Assume that SmithCo. had 15,000 shares of common stock and 1,000 warrants to purchase shares of common stock outstanding during 20X1. SmithCo. reported net income of $75,000 for the year. Each warrant entitles the holder to purchase one share of common stock at $10 per share. In addition, the warrant holders receive dividends on the underlying common stock to the extent they are declared. For 20X1, common shareholders have been paid $30,000 ($2.00 per share), and the warrant holders have been paid $2,000 (also $2.00 per share). Basic EPS under the two-class method for 20X1 would be computed as follows:

Net income		$75,000
Less dividends paid:		
Common stock	$30,000	
Warrants	2,000	32,000
Undistributed 20X1 earnings		$43,000

Allocation of undistributed earnings

To warrants

$$0.5(1{,}000) \div \left[0.5(1{,}000) + 0.5(15{,}000)\right] \times \$43{,}000 = \$2{,}687.50$$

$$\$2{,}687.50 \div 1{,}000 \text{ shares} = \$2.69 \text{ per share}$$

To common

$$0.5(15{,}000) \div \left[0.5(1{,}000) + 0.5(15{,}000)\right] \times \$43{,}000 = \$40{,}312.50$$

$$\$40{,}312.50 \div 15{,}000 \text{ shares} = \$2.69 \text{ per share}$$

Basic EPS amounts for 20X1

	Common	*Warrants*
Distributed earnings	$2.00	$2.00
Undistributed earnings	2.69	2.69
Total	$4.69	$4.69

Effect of Contracts That May Be Settled in Stock or Cash on the Computation of DEPS

In calculating EPS, adjustments should be made to the numerator for contracts that are classified, in accordance with ASC 815-40-15, as equity instruments, but for which the company has a stated policy or for which past experience provides a reasonable basis to believe that such contracts will be paid partially or wholly in cash (in which case there will be no potential common shares included in the denominator). (ASC 260-10-45-45) Thus, a contract that is reported as an equity instrument for accounting purposes may require an adjustment to the numerator for any changes in income or loss that would result if the contract had been reported as an asset or liability for accounting purposes during the period.

For purposes of computing diluted EPS, the adjustments to the numerator described above are only permitted for instruments for which the effect on net income (the numerator) is different depending on whether the instrument is accounted for as an equity instrument or as an asset or liability (e.g., those that are within the scope of ASC 480 or ASC 815-40-15). (ASC 260-10-55-32) The provisions of ASC 260 require that for contracts that provide the company with a choice of settlement methods, the company should assume that the contract will be settled in shares. That presumption may be overcome if past experience or a stated policy provides a reasonable basis to believe that it is probable that the contract will be paid partially or wholly in cash.

ASC 260-10-55-36 also states that, for contracts in which the holder controls the means of settlement, past experience or a stated policy is not determinative. In those situations, the more dilutive of cash or share settlement should be used. (ASC 260-10-45-460)

Adjustment to the numerator in year-to-date diluted EPS calculations may be required in certain circumstances. ASC 260-10-55-34 cites the example of contracts in which the holder controls the method of settlement and that would have a more dilutive effect if settled in shares, where the numerator adjustment is equal to the earnings effect of the change in the fair value of the asset/liability recorded during the year-to-date period. In that situation, the number of incremental shares included in the denominator is to be determined by calculating the number of shares that would be required to settle the contract using the average share price during the year-to-date period.

ASC 480 requires entities that issue mandatorily redeemable financial instruments or that enter into forward purchase contracts that require physical settlement by repurchase of a fixed number of shares in exchange for cash to exclude the common shares that are to be redeemed or repurchased in calculating EPS and DEPS. Amounts attributable to shares that are to be redeemed or repurchased that have not been recognized as interest costs (e.g., amounts associated with participation rights) are deducted in computing the income available to common shareholders (the numerator of the EPS calculations) consistently under the "two-class" method. Therefore, ASC 480's requirements for calculating EPS partially nullify ASC 260-10-55 for those financial instruments. For other financial instruments, including those that are liabilities under ASC 480, the guidance in ASC 260-10-55 remains applicable.

Inclusions/Exclusions from Computation of DEPS

The computations of DEPS also does not include contracts such as purchased put options and purchased call options (options held by the entity on its own stock). The inclusion of such contracts would be antidilutive. If the outstanding call options or warrants are issued by the reporting entity, they should be accounted for in EPS using the treasury method. (ASC 260-10-45-3) (ASC 260-10-55-3B)

Sometimes entities issue contracts that may be settled in common stock or in cash at the election of either the issuing entity or the holder. The determination of whether the contract is reflected in the computation of DEPS is based on the facts available each period. It is presumed that the contract will be settled in common stock and the resulting common shares will be included in DEPS if the effect is dilutive. This presumption may be overcome if past experience or a stated policy provides a reasonable basis to believe that the contract will be paid partially or wholly in cash. If during the reporting period the exercise price exceeds the average market price for that period, the potential dilutive effect of the contract on EPS is computed using the reverse treasury stock method. Under this method:

- Issuance of sufficient common shares is assumed to have occurred at the beginning of the period (at the average market price during the period) to raise enough proceeds to satisfy the contract.
- The proceeds from issuance of the shares are assumed to have been used to satisfy the contract (i.e., to buy back shares).
- The denominator of the DEPS calculation includes the incremental number of shares (the difference between the number of shares assumed issued and the number of shares assumed received from satisfying the contract).

(ASC 260-10-45-35)

Partially Paid Shares

If an entity has common shares issued in a partially paid form and the shares are entitled to dividends in proportion to the amount paid, the common-share equivalent of those partially paid shares is included in the computation of basic EPS to the extent that they were entitled to participate in dividends. Partially paid stock subscriptions that do not share in dividends until paid in full are considered the equivalent of warrants and are included in the calculation of DEPS using the treasury stock method. (ASC 260-10-45-22 and 55-23)

Example of Impact of Partially Paid Shares on EPS

Orion Corporation has 200,000 shares of common stock outstanding. In addition, under a stock subscription plan, investors have paid $30,000 toward the purchase of 4,000 common shares at the fixed price of $15 per share. Investors purchasing shares under the plan are entitled to dividends in proportion to the amount paid. Thus, there are 2,000 shares in the stock subscription plan for the purpose of calculating basic EPS, calculated as follows:

$$\frac{4{,}000 \text{ common shares}}{(4{,}000 \text{ common shares} \times \$15/\text{share})/\$30{,}000 \text{ paid}}$$
$$= 2{,}000 \text{ shares}$$

Orion records net income of $50,000 for the fiscal year. Its calculation of basic EPS follows:

$$\frac{\$50{,}000 \text{ net income } 2{,}000}{\text{existing common shares} + 2{,}000 \text{ stock subscription shares}}$$
$$= \$0.25$$

Once the stock subscription plan is completed, with all shares paid for and issued under that earlier plan, Orion creates another plan, which is one that does not allow participants to share in dividends until all payments are completed. Again, participants have thus far paid $30,000 to acquire

4,000 common shares at a fixed price of $15 each. Orion has 204,000 shares of common stock outstanding, and its net income for the current fiscal year is $80,000. The average market price of Orion's stock during the period is $20. Orion calculates the number of additional common shares with the following calculation, which is the same approach used to calculate the number of shares associated with warrants:

Proceeds from assumed purchase of shares in subscription plan (4,000 shares × $15/share)	$60,000
Number of shares to be issued	4,000
Number of shares assumed to be reacquired ($60,000/$20 average market price)	3,000
Number of shares assumed issued and not reacquired	1,000

Orion's DEPS calculation follows:

$$\frac{80,000 \text{ net income}}{204,000 \text{ existing common shares} + 1,000 \text{ shares from stock purchase plan}}$$

$= \$0.39$

Note that Orion's basic EPS is not affected by the shares to be issued under this plan, since no right to dividends exists until the subscription has been fully paid.

Effect of Certain Derivatives on EPS Computations

ASC 260 did not contemplate certain complex situations having EPS computation implications. In ASC 815-40-15, the accounting for derivative financial instruments that are indexed to, and potentially to be settled in, the reporting entity's own shares has been addressed. It establishes a model for categorization of a range of such instruments and deals with the EPS effects of each of these. This approach assumes that when the entity can elect to settle these instruments by payment of cash or issuance of shares, the latter will be chosen; if the holder (counterparty) has that choice, payment of cash must be presumed. (Certain exceptions exist when the settlement alternatives are not economically equivalent; in those instances, accounting is to be based on the economic substance of the transactions.) Statement of financial position classification of such instruments is based on consideration of a number of factors, and classification may change from period to period if there are certain changes in circumstances.

For EPS computation purposes, for those contracts that provide the company with a choice of either cash settlement or settlement in shares, ASC 815-40-15 states that settlement in shares should be assumed, although this can be overcome based on past experience or stated policy. If the counterparty controls the choice, however, the more dilutive assumption must be made, irrespective of past experience or policy.

ASC 260-10-45-35 requires the use of the "reverse treasury stock method" to account for the dilutive impact of written put options and similar derivative contracts, if they are "in the money" during the reporting period. Using this method, an incremental number of shares is determined to be the excess of the number of shares that would have to be sold for cash, at the average market price during the period, to satisfy the put obligation over the number of shares obtained via the put exercise. ASC 815-40-15 states that, for contracts giving the reporting entity a choice of settlement methods (stock or cash), it should assume share settlement, although this can be overcome if past behavior makes it reasonable to presume cash settlement.

If the holder controls the settlement method, however, the more dilutive method of settlement must be presumed.

Effect on EPS of Redemption or Induced Conversion of Preferred Stock

Companies may redeem shares of their outstanding preferred stock for noncash consideration such as by exchanges for other securities. Sometimes the company induces conversion by offering additional securities or other consideration to the holders. Such offers are sometimes referred to as "sweeteners." The accounting for "sweeteners" offered to convertible debt holders was addressed by ASC 470-20-05, and is explained in the chapter on ASC 470. ASC 260-10-S99 deals with the anomalous situation of "sweeteners" offered to induce conversion of convertible preferred shares.

The position of the SEC staff is that any excess of the fair value of consideration given over the book value of the preferred stock represents a return to the preferred stockholder and, consequently, is to be accounted for similar to dividends paid to the preferred stockholders for purposes of computing EPS. This means that the excess should be deducted from earnings to compute earnings available for common stockholders in the calculation of EPS.

If the converse is true, with consideration given being less than carrying value, including when there is an excess of the carrying amount of the preferred stock over the fair value of the consideration transferred, this should be added to net income to derive earnings available for common stockholders in the calculation of EPS.

This SEC staff position applies to redemptions of convertible preferred stock, whether or not the embedded conversion feature is "in the money" or not at the time of redemption.

If the redemption or induced conversion is affected by offering other securities, rather than cash, fair values would be the referent to determine whether an excess was involved. If the conversion includes the reacquisition of a previously recognized beneficial conversion feature, then reduce the fair value of the consideration by the intrinsic value of the conversion option on the commitment date.

Furthermore, per ASC 260-10-S99, in computing the carrying amount of preferred stock that has been redeemed or been subject to an induced conversion, the carrying amount of the preferred stock is to be reduced by the related issuance costs irrespective of how those costs were classified in the stockholders' equity section of the statement of financial position upon initial issuance.

Since ASC 480-10-25-4 defines mandatorily redeemable preferred stock as a liability, not as equity, the guidance in ASC 260-10-S99 would not apply. Rather, any excess or shortfall offered in an induced conversion situation involving mandatorily redeemable preferred stock would be reported as gain or loss on debt extinguishment, not as a dividend.

In a related matter, ASC 260-10-S99 discusses the accounting required when a reporting entity effects a redemption or induced conversion of only a portion of the outstanding securities of a class of preferred stock. Reflecting an SEC staff position, any excess consideration should be attributed to those shares that are redeemed or converted. Thus, for the purpose of determining whether the "if-converted" method is dilutive for the period, the shares redeemed or converted should be considered separately from those shares that are not redeemed or converted. It would be inappropriate to aggregate securities with differing effective dividend yields when determining whether the "if-converted" method is dilutive, which would be the result if a single, aggregate computation was made for the entire series of preferred stock.

Example of Partial Conversion

Hephaestus Construction has 1,000 shares of convertible preferred stock outstanding at the beginning of the reporting period. Hephaestus issued the preferred stock at its fair value, which matched its $15/share par value. The shares have a stated dividend of 7% ($1.05), and each convertible preferred share converts into one share of Hephaestus common stock. During the reporting period, Hephaestus redeemed 250 shares for $18/share.

Hephaestus should determine whether the conversion is dilutive for the remaining 750 shares by applying the "if-converted" method for the entire period, comparing the $1.05 stated dividend to the effect of assuming their conversion into 750 shares of Hephaestus common stock.

Hephaestus should use the same calculation for the converted 250 shares, weighted from the beginning of the period to their redemption date. In this case, Hephaestus should apply the "if-converted" method using the $1.05 stated dividend and redemption premium of $3/share, in comparison to the effect of assuming their conversion into 250 shares of Hephaestus common stock.

EPS Impact of Tax Effect of Dividends Paid on Unallocated ESOP Shares

Under the provisions of ASC 718-40, dividends paid on unallocated shares are not charged to retained earnings. Since the employer controls the use of dividends on unallocated shares, these dividends are not considered dividends for financial reporting purposes. Consequently, the dividends do not affect the DEPS computation.

Earnings Per Share Implications of ASC 718

ASC 718 mandates that share-based employee compensation arrangements must, with very few exceptions, be recognized as expenses over the relevant employee service period. ASC 260-10-45- 28A requires that employee equity share options, nonvested shares, and similar equity instruments granted to employees be treated as potential common shares in computing diluted EPS. DEPS should be based on the actual number of options or shares granted and not yet forfeited, unless doing so would be antidilutive. If vesting in or the ability to exercise (or retain) an award is contingent on a performance or market condition (e.g., as the level of future earnings), the shares or share options shall be treated as contingently issuable shares. If equity share options or other equity instruments are outstanding for only part of a reporting period, the shares issuable are to be weighted to reflect the portion of the period during which the equity instruments are outstanding.

ASC 260 provides guidance on applying the treasury stock method for equity instruments granted in share-based payment transactions in determining DEPS.

Master Limited Partnerships—Dropdown Transactions

General partners, limited partners, and incentive distribution rights holders have different rights to participate in distributable cash flow under the guidance in ASC 260. This results in a two-class method of calculating earnings per unit. (ASC 260-10-45-72)

A general partner may transfer or "drop down" net assets to a master limited partnership. If that transaction is accounted for as a transaction between entities under common control, the statements of operations of the master limited partnership are adjusted retrospectively to reflect the dropdown transaction as if it occurred on the earliest date during which the entities were under common control. If a dropdown transaction occurs after the formation of a master limited partnership, ASC 260 requires that all earnings or losses of a transferred business related to periods prior to the date of the dropdown transaction be allocated entirely to the general partner. (ASC 260-10-55-111)

COMPREHENSIVE EXAMPLE

The previous examples used a simplified approach for determining whether or not options, warrants, convertible preferred stock, or convertible bonds have a dilutive effect on DEPS. If the DEPS number computed was lower than basic EPS, the security was considered dilutive. This approach is adequate when the company has only one potentially dilutive security. If the firm has more than one potentially dilutive security, a more complex ranking procedure must be employed. (ASC 260) For example, assume the following facts concerning the capital structure of a company:

- Income from continuing operations and net income are both $50,000. Income from continuing operations is not displayed on the firm's income statement.
- The weighted-average number of common shares outstanding is 10,000 shares.
- The income tax rate is a flat 40%.
- Options to purchase 1,000 shares of common stock at $8 per share were outstanding all year.
- Options to purchase 2,000 shares of common stock at $13 per share were outstanding all year.
- The average market price of common stock during the year was $10.
- 200 7% convertible bonds, each convertible into 40 common shares, were outstanding the entire year. The bonds were issued at par value ($1,000 per bond) and no bonds were converted during the year.
- 4% convertible, cumulative preferred stock, par value of $100 per share, 1,000 shares issued and outstanding the entire year. Each preferred share is convertible into one common share. The preferred stock was issued at par value and no shares were converted during the year.

Note that reference is made below to some of the tables included in the body of the chapter because the facts above represent a combination of the facts used for the examples in the chapter.

To determine both basic EPS and DEPS, the following procedures must be performed:

1. Calculate basic EPS as if the capital structure were simple.
2. Identify other potentially dilutive securities.
3. Calculate the per-share effects of assuming issuance or conversion of each potentially dilutive security on an individual basis.
4. Rank the per-share effects from smallest to largest.
5. Recalculate EPS (Step 1 above) adding the potentially dilutive securities one at a time in order, beginning with the security with the *smallest* per-share effect.
6. Continue adding potentially dilutive securities to each successive calculation until all have been added or until the addition of a security increases EPS (antidilution) from its previous level.

Applying these procedures to the facts above:

1. Basic EPS

$$\frac{\text{Net income} - \text{Preferred dividends}}{\text{Weighted-average number of common shares outstanding}}$$

$$= \frac{\$50{,}000 - \$4{,}000}{10{,}000\,\text{shares}}$$

$$= \$4.60$$

2. Identification of other potentially dilutive securities:

   a. Options (two types)
   b. 7% convertible bonds
   c. 4% convertible cumulative preferred stock.

Diluted EPS (DEPS)

3. Per-share effects of conversion or issuance of other potentially dilutive securities calculated individually:

   a. Options—Only the options to purchase 1,000 shares at $8.00 per share are potentially dilutive. The options to purchase 2,000 shares of common stock are antidilutive because the exercise price is greater than the average market price. Thus, they are not included in the computation.

   Proceeds if options exercised:

$$1{,}000\,\text{shares} \times \$8\,\text{per share} = \underline{\underline{8{,}000}}$$

Shares that could be acquired:

$$\$8{,}000 \div \$10 = 800$$
$$\text{Dilutive shares: } 1{,}000 - 800 = 200$$

$$\frac{\text{Increase / decrease in net income}}{\text{Increase in weighted-average number of common shares outstanding}}$$

$$= \frac{\$0}{200\text{ shares}} = \$0$$

   b. 7% convertible bonds (see Table 10.3).

$$\frac{\text{Increase / decrease in net income}}{\text{Increase in weighted-average number of common shares outstanding}}$$

$$= \frac{\$8{,}400}{8{,}000\text{ shares}}$$
$$= \$1.05$$

   c. 4% convertible cumulative preferred stock—the outstanding common shares increase by 1,000 when all shares are converted. This results in total dividends of $4,000 not being paid.

$$\frac{\text{Increase decrease in net income}}{\text{Increase in weighted-average number of common shares outstanding}}$$

$$= \frac{\$4{,}000}{1{,}000\,\text{shares}}$$
$$= \$4.00$$

2. Rank the per-share effects from smallest to largest:

a. Options	$ 0	
b. 7% convertible bonds		1.05
c. 4% convertible cumulative preferred stock		4.00

3. Recalculate the EPS in rank order starting from the security with the smallest per-share dilution and adding one potentially dilutive security at a time:

   a. DEPS—options added:

$$\frac{\text{Net income} - \text{Preferred dividends}}{\text{Weighted-average number of common shares outstanding} + \text{Shares not acquired with proceeds of options}}$$

$$= \frac{\$50{,}000 - \$4{,}000}{10{,}000 + 200 \text{ shares}}$$
$$= \$4.51$$

   b. DEPS—options and 7% convertible bonds added:

$$\frac{\text{Net income} - \text{Preferred dividends} + \text{Interest expense (net of tax)}}{\text{Weighted-average number of common shares outstanding} + \text{Shares not acquired with proceeds of options} + \text{Shares issued upon conversion of bonds}}$$

$$= \frac{\$50{,}000 - \$4{,}000 + \$8{,}400}{10{,}000 + 200 + 8{,}000 \text{shares}}$$
$$= \$2.99$$

   c. DEPS—options, 7% convertible bonds, and 4% convertible cumulative preferred stock added:

$$\frac{\text{Net income} + \text{Interest expense (net of tax)}}{\text{Weighted-average number of common shares outstanding} + \text{Shares not acquired with proceeds of options} + \text{Shares issued upon conversion of bonds} + \text{Shares issued upon conversion of preferred stock}}$$

$$= \frac{\$50{,}000 + \$8{,}400}{10{,}000 + 200 + 8{,}000 + 1{,}000 \text{ shares}}$$
$$= \$3.04$$

   DEPS = $2.99

Since the addition of the 4% convertible cumulative preferred stock raises DEPS from $2.99 to $3.04, the preferred stock is antidilutive and is therefore excluded from the computation of DEPS.

A dual presentation of basic EPS and DEPS is required. The dual presentation on the face of the income statement would appear as follows:

Net income	$50,000
Earnings per common share* (Note X)	$ 4.60
Earnings per common share, assuming dilution* (Note X)	$ 2.99

* *The captions "Basic EPS" and "Diluted EPS" may be substituted, respectively.*

Note X: Earnings per Share (Illustrative Disclosure Based on Facts from the Example)

The following adjustments were made to the numerators and denominators of the basic and diluted EPS computations:

	Year Ended December 31, 20X1		
	Income (numerator)	*Weighted-average number of outstanding shares (denominator)*	*Amount per share*
Net income	$50,000		
Less: Preferred stock dividends	(4,000)		
Basic EPS			
Income available to common stockholders	46,000	10,000	$4.60
Effects of Dilutive Securities			
Options to purchase common stock		200	
7% convertible bonds	8,400	8,000	
Diluted EPS			
Income available to common stockholders adjusted for the effects of assumed exercise of options and conversion of bonds	$54,400	18,200	$2.99

There were 1,000 shares of $100 par value, 4% convertible, cumulative preferred stock issued and outstanding during the year ended December 31, 20X1, that were not included in the above computation because their conversion would not have resulted in a dilution of EPS.

Example of the Presentation and Computation of Earnings per Share

Assume that 100,000 shares were outstanding throughout the year.

ABC Company
Income Statement
for the Year Ended December 31, 20X1

Sales		$2,000,000
Cost of goods sold		750,000
Gross profit		$1,250,000
Selling and administrative expenses		500,000
Income from operations		$ 750,000
Other revenues and expense		
Interest income	$40,000	
Interest expense	(30,000)	10,000
Income before unusual or infrequent items and income taxes		$ 760,000
Unusual or infrequent items:		
Loss from permanent impairment of value of manufacturing facilities		(10,000)
Income from continuing operations before income taxes		$ 750,000
Income taxes		300,000
Income from continuing operations		$ 450,000
Discontinued operations:		

Loss from operations of Division X, including loss on disposal of $100,000 and income tax benefit of $58,000	$ 102,000
Net income	$ 348,000
Basic EPS computation	
Income from continuing operations ($450,000/100,000)	$4.50
Discontinued operations* ($30,000/100,000)	(0.30)
Net income available for common stockholders	$4.20

* *May instead be shown in the notes to the financial statements.*

Other Sources

See ASC Location—*Wiley GAAP* Chapter	*For information on . . .*
ASC 710-10-45	The effects of employer shares held by a rabbi trust in computing basic and diluted EPS.
ASC 718-10-45	The effects of equity share options granted in share-based payment arrangements, nonvested shares, and similar equity instruments in computing diluted EPS.
ASC 718-40-45 and 718-40-50	The effects of issues resulting from the existence of employee stock ownership plans in computing basic and diluted EPS and the related disclosure requirements.

11 ASC 270 INTERIM REPORTING

PERSPECTIVE AND ISSUES

Subtopic

ASC 270, *Interim Reporting*, contains one subtopic:

- ASC 270-10, *Overall*, that provides guidance on:
  - Accounting and disclosure issues for reporting on periods less than one year, and
  - Minimum disclosure requirements for interim reporting for publicly traded companies.

Overview

The term "interim reporting" refers to financial reporting for periods of less than a year. The Codification does not mandate interim reporting. However, the SEC requires public companies to file quarterly summarized interim financial data on its Form 10-Q. The level of detail of the information required in those interim reports is substantially less than is specified under the Codification for annual financial statements.

Objective The objective of interim reporting is to provide current information regarding enterprise performance to existing and prospective investors, lenders, and other financial statement users. This enables users to act upon relevant information in making informed decisions in a timely manner. SEC filings on Form 10-Q are due in no more than 45 days after period end. The demand for timely information means that interim data will often be more heavily impacted by estimates and assumptions.

Integral Approach Historically, there have been two competing views of interim reporting. Under the *integral* view, the interim period is considered an integral part of the annual accounting period. It thus follows that annual operating expenses are to be estimated and allocated to the interim periods based on forecasted annual activity levels such as sales volume. The results of subsequent interim periods are adjusted to reflect the effect of estimation errors in earlier interim periods of the same fiscal year. ASC 270-10-45-1 prefers the integral view.

Discrete Approach Under the *discrete* view, each interim period is considered a discrete accounting period. Thus, estimations and allocations are made using the same methods used for annual reporting. It follows that the same expense recognition rules apply as under annual reporting, and no special interim accruals or deferrals would be necessary or permissible. Annual operating expenses are recognized in the interim period incurred, irrespective of the number of interim periods benefited (i.e., no special deferral rules would apply to interim periods).

Integral/Discrete Pros and Cons Proponents of the integral view argue that unique interim expense recognition procedures are necessary to avoid fluctuations in period-to-period results that might be misleading to financial statement users. Applying the integral view results in interim earnings which are indicative of annual earnings and, thus, arguably more useful for predictive purposes. Proponents of the discrete view argue that the smoothing of interim results for purposes of forecasting annual earnings has undesirable effects. For example, a turning point during the year in an earnings trend could be obscured if smoothing techniques implied by the integral view were to be employed.

The debate between integral and discrete views of interim reporting can result in very different interim measures of results of operations. This can occur, for example, because certain annual expenses may be concentrated in one interim period, yet benefit the entire year's operations. Examples include advertising expenses and major repairs and maintenance of equipment. Also, in the United States (and many other jurisdictions) progressive (graduated) income tax rates are applied to total annual income and various income tax credits may arise, all of which are computed on annual pretax earnings, often adding complexity to the determination of quarterly income tax expense.

Other Issues Interim reporting is problematic for reasons other than the choice of an underlying measurement philosophy. As reporting periods are shortened, the effects of errors in estimation and allocation are magnified, and randomly occurring events which might not be material in the context of a full fiscal year could create major distortions in short interim period summaries of reporting entity performance. The effects of seasonal fluctuations and temporary market conditions further limit the reliability, comparability, and predictive value of interim reports.

DEFINITIONS OF TERMS

See Appendix A, *Definitions of Terms*, for definitions of Acquiree, Acquirer, Acquisition by a Not-for-Profit Entity, Business, Business Combination, Contract, Contract Asset, Contract Liability, Financial Asset, Financing Receivable, Lease, Legal Entity, Lessee, Lessor, Net Realizable Value, Not-for-Profit Entity, Performance Obligation, Public Business Entity, Transaction Price, Underlying Asset, and Variable Interest Entity.

CONCEPTS, RULES, AND EXAMPLES

Differentiation between Public and Nonpublic Entities

The explanations and interpretations in this chapter have been divided into two sections. The first part discusses issues applicable to *both* public and nonpublic reporting entities (including, where applicable, not-for-profit organizations). The second part discusses issues applicable *only* to publicly traded companies.

The usefulness of interim reports rests on the relationship to annual reports. Therefore, ASC 270-10-45-1 states that "each interim period should be viewed primarily as an integral part of an annual period," and the accounting should be based on the principles and practices used in the entity's annual reporting. The exception to this is if the entity has adopted a change in accounting in the interim period. Certain principles and practices may also have to be modified so that the interim reporting better relates to the annual results. The modifications are detailed in ASC 270-10-45-4 through 45-11 and are discussed in the sections below.

REQUIREMENTS APPLICABLE TO ALL REPORTING ENTITIES

Revenues

Revenues are recognized as earned during an interim period using the same principles followed in annual reports, that is, "as the entity satisfies a performance obligation by transferring a promised good or service to a customer." (ASC 270-10-45-3) This rule applies to both product sales and service revenues. For example, product sales cutoff procedures are applied at the end of each interim period in the same manner that they are applied at year-end, and revenue from long term construction contracts is recognized at interim dates using the same method used at year-end.

Product Costs and Direct Costs

Product costs and costs directly associated with service revenues are treated in interim reports in the same manner as in annual reports. (ASC 270-20-45-5) The Codification provides four integral view exceptions:

1. The gross profit or other method that is not the method used at annual dates may be used to estimate cost of goods sold and ending inventory for interim periods. The method used must be disclosed.
2. When inventory consists of LIFO layers, and a portion of the base period layer is liquidated at an interim date, and it is expected that this inventory will be replaced by year-end, the anticipated cost of replacing the liquidated inventory is included in cost of sales of the interim period.
3. Inventory losses from the application of subsequent measurement guidance in ASC 330-10 should not be deferred beyond the interim period. Recoveries from such losses on the same inventory are recognized as a gain in the subsequent interim period. Recognition of this gain in the later interim period is limited to the extent of loss previously recognized. If the entity reasonably expects to restore the market value or net realizable value, it does not have to recognize that temporary decline in the interim financial statements.
4. Entities using standard cost accounting systems ordinarily report purchase price, wage rate, and usage or efficiency variances in the same manner as year-end. Planned purchase price and volume or capacity cost variances, are deferred if expected to be absorbed by year-end. (ASC 270-10-45-6)

The first exception above eliminates the need for a physical inventory count at the interim date. The other three exceptions attempt to synchronize the quarterly financial statements with the annual report. For example, consider the LIFO liquidation exception. Without this exception, interim cost of goods sold could include low earlier year or base-period costs, while annual cost of goods sold would include only current year costs.

Example of Interim Reporting of Product Costs

Dakota Corporation encounters the following product cost situations as part of its quarterly reporting:

- It takes physical inventory counts at the end of the second quarter and end of the fiscal year. Its typical gross profit is 30% of sales. The actual gross profit applicable to the first six months of the year is 32%. The actual full-year gross profit is 29%.
- It carries one type of its inventory at LIFO and the remaining inventory at first-in, first-out (FIFO).
- It suffers a clearly temporary decline of $10,000 in the market value of a specific part of its FIFO inventory in the first quarter, which it recovers in the second quarter.
- It liquidates earlier-period, lower-cost LIFO inventories during the second quarter. The liquidation results in second quarter cost of goods sold being $90,000 less (and, of course, second quarter gross profit being $90,000 more) than it would have been absent the LIFO liquidation. Dakota expects to, and does, restore these inventory levels by year-end.
- It suffers a decline of $65,000 in the market value of its FIFO inventory during the third quarter. The inventory value increases by $75,000 in the fourth quarter.

Dakota computes interim cost of goods sold to reflect the effect of these situations as follows:

	Quarter 1	*Quarter 2*	*First 6 months*	*Quarter 3*	*Quarter 4*	*Full year*
Sales	$10,000,000	$ 8,500,000	$ 18,500,000	$7,200,000	$11,800,000	$37,500,000
Complement of normal gross profit percentage	70%			70%		
Cost of goods sold using gross profit method	7,000,000			5,040,000		
Complement of year-to-date gross profit percentage based on actual count			68%			70%
Cost of goods sold based on actual count			12,580,000			26,625,000
Sales	$10,000,000	$ 8,500,000	$ 18,500,000	$7,200,000	$11,800,000	$37,500,000
Adjustment for effect of temporary LIFO liquidation[1]			90,000			
Decline in inventory value[2]				65,000		
Adjusted cost of goods sold	$ 7,000,000	$5,670,000[3]	$ 12,670,000	$5,105,000	$ 8,850,000[4]	$26,625,000

[1] Full recognition of replacement of earlier period LIFO layer in the period that the temporary liquidation was incurred.
[2] No recognition is given to the first quarter temporary decline in value or the subsequent increase because, at the time it occurred, it was expected to be temporary. Full recognition is given to the third quarter market value decline

assuming that it was not expected to be temporary. This is followed by recognition of the market value increase, but only to offset the amount of the initial decline.
[3] Calculated as: Adjusted cost of goods sold for first six months based on actual inventory count – Cost of goods sold recognized during the first quarter using the gross profit method.
[4] Calculated as: Full year cost of goods sold of $26,625,000 – $12,670,000 cost of goods sold for first half of year –$5,105,000 cost of goods sold recognized during the third quarter.

To illustrate that the fourth quarter is appropriately adjusted for the effects of applying the interim costing rules to the other quarters, the fourth quarter cost of goods sold is proved as follows:

	Fourth quarter
Fourth quarter sales × actual annual gross profit complement (100% – 29% = 71%)	$8,378,000
Adjustment for the difference between the 68% complement based on the second quarter physical inventory count and the 71% annual complement multiplied by sales for the first six months	555,000
Adjustment for the difference between the 70% complement used under the gross profit method in the third quarter and the actual 71% annual complement multiplied by sales for the third quarter	72,000
Fourth quarter recovery of the third quarter FIFO market decline	(65,000)
Effect of replacing the second quarter temporary decline in LIFO inventory levels	(90,000)
	$8,850,000

Other Costs and Expenses

The integral view is evident in how the Codification treats costs incurred in interim periods. Most costs and expenses are recognized in interim periods as incurred. However, a cost that clearly benefits more than one interim period (e.g., annual repairs or property taxes) is allocated among the periods benefited. (ASC 270-10-45-8) The allocation is based on:

- Estimates of time expired,
- Benefit received, or
- Activity related to the specific periods.

Allocation procedures are to be consistent with those used at year-end reporting dates. However, if a cost incurred during an interim period cannot be readily associated with other interim periods, it is not arbitrarily assigned to those periods. The following parameters (ASC 270-45-10-9) are used in interim periods to account for certain types of expenses incurred in those periods:

- Costs that benefit two or more interim periods (e.g., annual major repairs) are assigned to interim periods through the use of deferrals or accruals.
- Quantity discounts given to customers based on annual sales volume are allocated to interim periods on the basis of sales to customers during the interim period relative to estimated annual sales.
- Property taxes (and like costs) are deferred or accrued at a year-end date to reflect a full year's charge to operations. Charges to interim periods follow similar procedures.
- Advertising costs are permitted to be deferred to subsequent interim periods within the same fiscal year if the costs clearly benefit those later periods. Prior to actually receiving

advertising services, advertising costs may be accrued and allocated to interim periods on the basis of sales if the sales arrangement implicitly includes the advertising program.

Costs and expenses subject to year-end determination, such as discretionary bonuses and profit-sharing contributions, are assigned to interim periods in a reasonable and consistent manner to the extent they can be reasonably estimated. (ASC 270-10-45-10)

Application of interim expense reporting principles is illustrated in the following examples.

Example of Interim Reporting of Other Expenses

Dakota Corporation encounters the following expense scenarios as part of its quarterly reporting (for illustrative purposes, all amounts are considered to be material):

- Its largest customer, Floor-Mart, placed firm orders for the year that will result in sales of $1,500,000 in the first quarter, $2,000,000 in the second quarter, $750,000 in the third quarter, and $1,650,000 in the fourth quarter. Dakota gives Floor-Mart a 5% rebate if Floor-Mart buys at least $5 million of goods each year. Floor-Mart exceeded the $5 million goal in the preceding year and is expected to do so again in the current year.
- It incurs $24,000 of trade show fees in the first quarter for a trade show that will occur in the third quarter.
- It pays $64,000 in advance in the second quarter for a series of advertisements that will run during the third and fourth quarters.
- It receives a $32,000 property tax bill in the second quarter that applies to the following twelve-month period (July 1 to June 30).
- It incurs annual air filter replacement costs of $6,000 in the first quarter.
- Its management team is entitled to a year-end cash bonus of $120,000 if it meets an annual sales target of $40 million, prior to any sales rebates, with the bonus dropping by $10,000 for every million dollars of sales not achieved.

Dakota used the following calculations to record these scenarios:

	Quarter 1	*Quarter 2*	*Quarter 3*	*Quarter 4*	*Full year*
Sales	$10,000,000	$8,500,000	$7,200,000	$11,800,000	$37,500,000
Deduction from sales	(75,000)[1]	(100,000)	(37,500)	(82,500)	(295,000)
Marketing expense			24,000[2]		24,000
Advertising expense			32,000[3]	32,000	64,000
Property tax expense			8,000[4]	8,000	16,000
Maintenance expense	1,500[5]	1,500	1,500	1,500	6,000
Bonus expense	30,000[6]	25,500	21,600	17,900	95,000

[1] The sales rebate is based on 5% of actual sales to the customer in the quarter when the sale is made. The actual payment back to the customer does not occur until the end of the year when the $5 million goal is definitively reached.

[2] The $24,000 trade show payment is initially recorded as a prepaid expense and then charged to marketing expense when the trade show occurs in the third quarter.

[3] The $64,000 advertising payment is initially recorded as a prepaid expense and then charged to advertising expense when the advertisements run.

[4] The $32,000 property tax payment is initially recorded as a prepaid expense and then charged to property tax expense on a straight-line basis over the next four quarters.

[5] The $6,000 air filter replacement payment is initially recorded as a prepaid expense and then charged to maintenance

expense over the one-year life of the air filters.
[6] The management bonus is recognized in proportion to the amount of revenue recognized in each quarter. Once it becomes apparent that the full sales target will not be reached, the bonus accrual is adjusted downward. In this case, the downward adjustment is assumed to be in the fourth quarter, since past history and seasonality factors made achievement of the full goal unlikely until fourth quarter results were known.

Seasonality

The operations of many businesses are subject to recurring material seasonal variations. Such businesses are required to disclose the seasonality of their activities to avoid the possibility of misleading interim reports. ASC 270-10-45-11 also recommends that such businesses present results of operations for twelve-month periods ending at the interim date of the current and preceding year.

Fair Value of Financial Instruments

ASC 825-10-50 requires disclosures about the fair value of financial instruments in interim reporting periods, as well as in annual financial statements. Those requirements can be found in the disclosure checklist at www.wiley.com/go/GAAP2021.

Unusual or Infrequent Items and Disposals of Components

The effects of the disposal of a component of the entity and unusual or infrequently occurring transactions or events that are material to operating results of the interim period are reported separately in the interim period in which they occur. (ASC 270-10-45-11A) The same treatment is given to other unusual or infrequently occurring events. No attempt is made to allocate the effects of these items over the entire fiscal year in which they occur.

Example of Disposal of a Component and Unusual or Infrequently Occurring Items

Dakota Corporation's Helena, Montana, facility suffers a direct hit from a tornado during the second quarter. Dakota's management believes the loss warrants treatment as an unusual and infrequently occurring item since the state of Montana does not typically experience tornadoes. Dakota's insurance does not cover tornadoes, and the loss resulting from cleanup costs and writing down the net book value of the damaged portion of the building is $620,000, or $403,000 net of applicable income taxes computed at a flat 35% rate. As required by ASC 360-10-35, Dakota's management estimates the expected future cash flows from the use and ultimate disposition of the property and determines that the building does not require any further write-down for impairment.

In the third quarter, before the tornado repairs are completed, this unfortunate facility is subjected to a flood; however, the unreimbursed damage is only $68,000, or $44,200 net of applicable income taxes. The flood damage is considered material in the third quarter, but subsequently, during the fourth quarter, is determined to be immaterial for annual reporting purposes.

Finally, in the fourth quarter, management declares the facility too damaged to repair, and reclassifies it as held-for-sale. The facility meets the criteria of ASC 360-10-35 to be classified as a component of the entity since its operations and cash flows are clearly distinguishable from the rest of Dakota

Corporation. Activities conducted at the facility generated income from operations of $82,000 in the first quarter, followed by losses of $102,000, $129,000, and $104,000 in the succeeding quarters, prior to 35% income taxes. Upon classification of the facility as held for sale, the carrying value is written down to its fair value less cost to sell resulting in a further loss of $117,000, which is net of $63,000 in applicable income taxes.

Dakota includes these circumstances in its quarterly and annual financial statement in the following manner:

	Quarter 1	*Quarter 2*	*Quarter 3*	*Quarter 4*	*Full year*
Income from continuing operations	$814,000	$629,000	$483,000		$2,483,650[1]
Discontinued operations:					
Loss from operations of discontinued component, net of applicable income taxes of $36,400			(67,600)[2]		
Loss from operations of discontinued component, net of applicable income taxes of $88,550					(164,450)[3]
Income from continuing operations	$814,000	$629,000	$483,000	$505,000	$2,483,650[1]
Loss from reclassification of Montana facility as held for sale and adjusting the carrying value to fair value less costs to sell, net of applicable income taxes of $63,000				(117,000)	(117,000)
Loss from discontinued operations				(184,600)	(281,450)
Unusual and infrequently occurring items:					
Tornado loss (less applicable income taxes of $217,000)		(403,000)			(403,000)
Flood loss (less applicable income taxes of $23,800)			(44,200)		0[1]
Net income	$814,000	$226,000	$438,800	$320,400	$1,799,200

[1] The full-year income from continuing operations does not match the total of quarterly income from continuing operations, because the third-quarter classification of flood damage is not considered unusual or infrequent for annual reporting purposes, and so is added back into annual income from continuing operations. Annual income is also reduced by operating losses in the discontinued facility for the full year, which were retained in income from continuing operations for the first three quarters. Full-year income from continuing operations is computed as follows:

[2] The facility is classified as discontinued in the fourth quarter; there is no requirement to restate prior interim statements to show the loss from operations of the facility in earlier quarters.

[3] The full-year financial statement reflects the full-year loss from discontinued operations.

Sum of operating income for four quarters	$2,431,000
– Unusual or infrequent loss shifted back to operating income	(44,200)
+ After-tax effect of first three quarters of losses on discontinued operations	96,850
= Full-year income from continuing operations	$2,483,650

Note that classification as an unusual or infrequently occurring item is based on facts and circumstances, given the requirement under the Codification that the event be infrequent in occurrence or unusual in nature. If the plant were located in Kansas, for example, and tornado damage did not qualify under both criteria given its location, then this would not have been presented as an unusual or infrequently occurring item.

Contingencies

In general, contingencies and uncertainties that exist at an interim date are accrued or disclosed in the same manner required for annual financial statements. For example, contingent liabilities that are probable and subject to reasonable estimation are to be accrued. The materiality of the contingency is evaluated in relation to the expected annual results. Disclosures regarding material contingencies and uncertainties are to be repeated in all interim and annual financial statements until they have been settled, adjudicated, transferred, or judged to be immaterial.

The following adjustments or settlements are accorded special treatment in interim reports if they relate to prior interim periods of the current fiscal year:

- Litigation or similar claims
- Income taxes (except for the effects of retroactive tax legislation enacted during an interim period)
- Renegotiation proceedings associated with government contracts
- Utility revenue under rate-making processes.

If the item is material, directly related to prior interim periods of the current fiscal year in full or in part, and becomes reasonably estimable in the current interim period, it is reported as follows:

- The portion directly related to the current interim period is included in that period.
- Prior interim periods are restated to reflect the portions directly related to those periods.
- The portion directly related to prior years is recognized in the restated first interim period of the current year.
  (ASC 270-10-45-17 and 45-18)

Example of Interim Reporting of Contingencies

Dakota Corporation is sued over its alleged violation of a patent in one of its products. Dakota settles the litigation in the fourth quarter. Under the settlement terms, Dakota must retroactively pay a 3% royalty on all sales of the product to which the patent applies. Sales of the product are $150,000 in the first quarter, $82,000 in the second quarter, $109,000 in the third quarter, and $57,000 in the fourth quarter. In addition, the cumulative total of all sales of the product in prior years is $1,280,000. Dakota restates its quarterly financial results to include the following royalty expense:

	Quarter 1	*Quarter 2*	*Quarter 3*	*Quarter 4*	*Full year*
Sales related to lawsuit	$150,000	$82,000	$109,000	$57,000	$398,000
Royalty expense	4,500	2,460	3,270	1,710	11,940
Royalty expense related to prior years' sales	38,400				38,400

Accounting Changes

The Codification recommends making a change in accounting principle in the first interim report of a fiscal year wherever possible. (ASC 270-10-45-15)

Change in Accounting Principle Entities must disclose in interim financial statements any changes in accounting principles or the methods of applying them from those that were followed in:

- The prior fiscal year,
- The comparable interim period of the prior fiscal year, and
- The preceding interim periods of the current fiscal year. (ASC 270-10-45-12)

The information to be included in these disclosures is the same as is required to be included in annual financial statements and is to be provided in the interim period in which the change occurs, subsequent interim periods of that same fiscal year, and the annual financial statements that include the interim period of change.

ASC 250 requires changes in accounting principles to be adopted through retrospective application to all prior periods presented. This accounting treatment is the same in both interim and annual financial statements. The entity is precluded from using the impracticability exception to avoid retrospective application to pre-change interim periods of the same fiscal year in which the change is made. Thus, if it is impracticable to apply the change to those pre-change interim periods, the change can only be made as of the beginning of the following fiscal year. (ASC 250-10-45-14) The FASB believes this situation will rarely occur in practice.

Change in Accounting Estimate A change in accounting estimate is accounted for in the period of change. ASC 250 requires that changes in accounting estimate be accounted for currently and prospectively. Retroactive restatement and presentation of pro forma amounts are not permitted. This accounting is the same whether the change occurs at the end of a year or during an interim reporting period. (ASC 270-10-45-14)

Change in Reporting Entity When an accounting change results in the financial statements presenting a different reporting entity than was presented in the past, all prior periods presented in the new financial statements, including all previously issued interim financial information, are to be retroactively restated to present the financial statements of the new reporting entity. In restating the previously issued information, however, interest previously capitalized under ASC 835, with respect to equity-method investees that have not yet commenced their planned principal operations, is not to be changed.

Corrections of Errors Adjustments related to prior interim periods of the current year arise from:

- Settlement of litigation or similar claims
- Income taxes
- Renegotiation procedures
- Utility revenue governed by rate-making processes (ASC 250-10-45-25)

The term "restatement" is only used to describe a correction of an error from a prior period. When a restatement is made, the financial statements of each individual prior period presented (whether interim or annual) must be adjusted to reflect correction of the effects of the error that relate to that period. Full disclosure of the restatement must be provided in the financial statements of the:

- Interim period in which the restatement is first made,
- Subsequent interim periods during the same fiscal year that includes the interim period in which the restatement is first made, and
- Annual period that includes the interim period in which the restatement is first made.

If the item occurs after the first interim period and affects prior interim periods of the current year, the entity:

- Restates prior interim periods
- For portions of the item affecting prior years, includes in the determination of net income of the first interim period of the current year
  (ASC 270-10-45-18)

REQUIREMENTS APPLICABLE TO PUBLIC REPORTING ENTITIES

Quarterly Reporting to the SEC

Summarized Interim Financial Data The SEC does not require registrants to file complete sets of quarterly financial statements. Rather, on a quarterly basis, condensed (summarized) unaudited interim financial statements are required to be filed with the SEC on its Form 10-Q (Regulation S-X, Rule 10-01—ASC 270-10-S99-1). There are minimum captions and disclosures required to be included in these financial statements. For detailed guidance, entities should look to ASC 270-10-S99 SEC Materials and Regulation S-X Rule 10-02, Interim Financial Statements.

Other Sources

See ASC Location—*Wiley GAAP* Chapter	*For information on . . .*
220-10-45-18	Comprehensive income
250-10-45-12 through 14	Accounting changes
330-10-55-2 and 610-30-25-3	Inventory
720-20-35-3 through 35-5 and 720-20-35-8	Incurred but not reported liability
715-20-55-18 and 55-19 and 715-60-35-40	Pensions and other post-retirement benefits
740-270	Income tax provisions
820-10-50	Additional disclosure guidance on fair value measurements and disclosures for the reporting entity

12 ASC 272 LIMITED LIABILITY ENTITIES

PERSPECTIVE AND ISSUES

Subtopic

ASC 272, *Limited Liability Entities*, contains one subtopic:

- ASC 272-10, *Overall*, that contains guidance for limited liability entities organized in the United States that prepare financial statements under U.S. GAAP.

DEFINITIONS OF TERMS

ASC 272 does not contain a glossary. However, it does define a limited liability company as having the following characteristics:

- It is an unincorporated association of two or more persons
- Its members have limited personal liability for the obligations or debts of the entity
- It is classified as a partnership for federal income tax purposes.

Further, ASC 272 states that for a limited liability company to be classified as a partnership for federal tax purposes, it must *lack* at least two of the following characteristics:

- Limited liability
- Free transferability of interests
- Centralized management
- Continuity of life.
  (ASC 272-10-5-6)

CONCEPTS, RULES, AND EXAMPLES

Reporting by Limited Liability Companies and Partnerships

Accounting theory and practice have overwhelmingly developed within the context of businesses organized as traditional corporations. Accordingly, there is little official guidance to entities organized as partnerships or other forms of business, which is generally not a serious concern given that most transactions entered into by such entities do not differ generically from those conducted by corporations. The primary differences relate to equity transactions and to the display of the equity section of the statement of financial position.

ASC 272 addresses certain issues pertaining to accounting and reporting by limited liability entities: either a limited liability company or a limited liability partnership. This Topic establishes that, when an entity restructures itself as a limited liability entity, the basis of all assets and liabilities from its predecessor entity are carried forward. Also, as suggested by ASC 740, *Income Taxes*, if the new entity is not a taxable one, any deferred tax assets or liabilities existing previously should be written off at the time the change in tax status becomes effective; with the elimination of any debit or credit balance being effected by a charge or credit to current period tax expense.

Presentation With regard to financial statement display issues, the Codification requires that the headings of each statement identify the entity as being a limited liability company or a limited liability partnership, similar to the common practice of identifying partnership entities. This alerts the user to certain anomalies, such as (most commonly) an absence of income tax expense and a related liability, and the use of somewhat distinctive captions in the equity section of the statement of financial position. In the case of limited liability entities, the term "members' equity" has been prescribed, and the changes in members' equity should be communicated in:

- a separate financial statement,
- a combined statement of operations and changes in members' equity, or
- the notes to the financial statements.

Members' Equity A limited liability company (LLC) presents its equity using the caption "members' equity." In accordance with ASC 272-10-45-3, the equity attributable to each class of member should be separately stated on the face of the statement of financial position or disclosed in the notes to the financial statements.

A deficit, if one exists, should be reported in the members' equity account(s), even if there is limited liability for the members. This is consistent with the "going concern" assumption that underlies GAAP. There is no requirement to disaggregate members' equity into separate components (undistributed earnings, unallocated capital, etc.) on the face of the statement of financial position or in the notes, although this is of course permissible. (ASC 272-10-45-4)

Amounts due from members for capital contributions, if any remain unpaid at the date of the statement of financial position, should be shown as deductions from members' equity. This is entirely consistent with practice for unpaid stock subscriptions receivable. (ASC 272-10-45-5)

Comparative Statements GAAP presumes that comparative financial statements are more useful than those for a single period, and accordingly that comparative statements should normally be presented. However, for such financial statements to be meaningful, the information for the earlier period must be truly comparable to that of the more recent period. (ASC 272-10-45-6)

If the formation of the limited liability company or the limited liability partnership results in a new reporting entity being created, the guidance of ASC 250 dealing with changes in accounting entities should be consulted. (ASC 272-10-45-7)

Disclosures ASC 272 sets forth certain disclosures to be made in the financial statements of limited liability companies. These disclosures are listed in the *Disclosure and Presentation Checklist for Commercial Businesses* at www.wiley.com/go/GAAP2021.

Other Sources

See ASC Location—*Wiley GAAP* Chapter	***For information on . . .***
ASC 740-10-25-6	Recognizing the financial statement effects of a tax position.
ASC 740-10-25-32	Recognizing a deferred tax liability or asset for temporary differences at the date that a nontaxable entity becomes a taxable entity.
ASC 740-10-50-9	Adjustments of a deferred tax liability or asset for enacted changes in tax laws or rates or a change in the tax status of the entity.
ASC 805-50	Common control transactions in business combinations.

13 ASC 274 PERSONAL FINANCIAL STATEMENTS

PERSPECTIVE AND ISSUES

Subtopic

ASC 274, *Personal Financial Statements*, consists of one subtopic:

- ASC 274-10, *Overall*, that addresses the preparation and presentation of financial statements of individuals or groups of related individuals (i.e., families).

Overview

Personal financial statements are generally prepared to organize and plan an individual's financial affairs on a more formal basis. Specific purposes that might require the preparation of personal financial statements include

- Obtaining credit,
- Income tax planning,
- Retirement planning,
- Gift and estate planning, or
- Public disclosure of financial affairs for public officials and candidates for public office.

Estimated current values of assets and liabilities are almost always specified for use in the preparation of personal financial statements because this information is more relevant to users than historical cost.

DEFINITIONS OF TERMS

Source: ASC 274-10-20

Estimated Current Value. The amount for which an item could be exchanged between a buyer and a seller, each of whom is well informed and willing, and neither of whom is compelled to buy or sell.

Net Worth. The difference between total assets and total liabilities, after deducting estimated income taxes on the differences between the estimated current values of assets and the estimated current amounts of liabilities and their income tax bases.

CONCEPTS, RULES, AND EXAMPLES

Personal financial statements can be prepared for an individual, jointly for a husband and wife, or collectively for a family. Personal financial statements consist of:

- *Statement of financial condition*—The only required financial statement, the statement of financial condition, presents the estimated current values of assets and the estimated current amounts of liabilities. A liability is recognized for estimated income taxes on the difference between the asset and liability amounts set forth in the statement of financial condition and their respective income tax bases. Naturally, the residual amount after deducting the liabilities (including the estimated income tax liability) from the assets is presented as net worth at that date.
- *Statement of changes in net worth*—An optional statement that presents the primary sources of increases and decreases in net worth over a period of time. (ASC 274-10-45-4)
- *Comparative financial statements*—The inclusion of a comparison of the current period's financial statements with one or more previous period's financial statements is optional. (ASC 274-10-45-5)

Basis of Presentation The accrual basis, rather than the cash basis, of accounting is used in preparing personal financial statements. (ASC 274-10-35-2) The presentation of personal financial statements does not require the classification of assets and liabilities as current and noncurrent. Instead, assets and liabilities are presented in order of liquidity and maturity. (ASC 274-10-45-7)

Measurement

Assets In personal financial statements, assets are presented at their estimated current values. (ASC 274-10-45-4) This is defined by ASC 274 as the amount at which the item could be exchanged between a buyer and a seller, assuming both parties are well informed, and neither party is compelled to buy or sell. Disposal costs, if material, are deducted to arrive at current values. (ASC 274-10-55-2)

Liabilities Liabilities are presented at the lesser of the discounted amount of cash to be paid or the current cash settlement amount. The discount rate should be the rate implicit in the transaction that gave rise to the liability. (ASC 274-10-35-12)

Use of a Specialist A specialist may need to be consulted to determine the current value of certain types of assets (e.g., works of art, jewelry, restricted securities, investments in closely held businesses, and real estate). (ASC 274-10-55-3) If property is held in joint tenancy, as community property, or through a similar joint ownership arrangement, the financial statement preparer may require the advice of an attorney to determine, under applicable state law, the portion of the property interest that should be included in the individual's assets.

Use of Information About Recent Transactions The use of information about recent transactions involving similar types of assets and liabilities, in similar circumstances, constitutes a satisfactory means of determining the estimated current value of an asset and the estimated current amount of a liability. If recent transactional information cannot be obtained, it is permissible to use other methods:

- capitalization of past or prospective earnings,
- liquidation values, the adjustment of historical cost based on changes in a specific price index,
- appraisals, and
- discounted amounts of projected cash receipts and payments).
  (ASC 274-10-55-1)

The methods used should be followed consistently from period to period unless the facts and circumstances dictate a change to different methods.

The table below summarizes the methods of determining "estimated current values" for assets and "estimated current amounts" for liabilities. Some of the items are expanded upon after the table

Exhibit—Valuing Assets and Liabilities

Item	*Discounted Cash Flow*	*Quoted Market Price*	*Appraised Value*	*Other*
Assets				
Receivables	✓			
Marketable securities		✓		
Over-the-counter securities				Bid and asked prices
Options				Published prices
Investments in a closely held business				Several methods
Life insurance				The cash value of the policy less the amount of any loans against it
Intangible assets	✓			
Future interests and similar assets	✓			
Other assets, e.g., personal possessions			✓	
Real estate, including leaseholds				Variety of information sources for determining value
Liabilities				
Payables and other liabilities	✓			
Noncancelable commitments	✓			

Item	Discounted Cash Flow	Quoted Market Price	Appraised Value	Other
Income taxes payable				Estimate based on the relationship of taxable income earned to date to total estimated taxable income for the year, net of taxes withheld or paid with estimated tax returns.
Estimated income taxes				Calculated based on estimated current values of all assets had been realized and the estimated current amounts of all liabilities had been liquidated on the statement date

Income taxes payable Income taxes payable should include unpaid income taxes for completed tax years and the estimated amount for the elapsed portion of the current tax year. Additionally, personal financial statements are required to include estimated income tax on the difference between the current value (amount) of assets (liabilities) and their respective income tax bases as if they had been realized or liquidated. (ASC 274-10-35-14)

Business interests Business interests that comprise a large portion of a person's total assets should be presented separately from other investments. An investment in a separate entity that is marketable as a going concern (e.g., a closely held corporation) should be presented as one amount. (ASC 274-10-45-9) If the investment is a limited business activity, not conducted in a separate legal entity, separate asset and liability amounts should be shown (e.g., investment in real estate and related mortgage; only the person's beneficial interest in the investment is included in his/her personal financial statements). (ASC 274-10-45-10)

The preparer must decide whether to value the net investment him/herself or to engage a qualified specialist. The possible valuation methods available are discounted cash flow, appraised value, liquidation value, multiple of earnings, reproduction value, adjustment of book value (e.g., equity method), or cost. In some cases, it is appropriate to use a combination of approaches to reasonably estimate the current value.

Investor holding large blocks of securities ASC 274 specifically provides for adjustment of the current value of securities for the effects of transferability restrictions or the effects of the investor holding a large block of securities (blockage factor). Adjustments for blockage factors are specifically prohibited by ASC 820. (ASC 274-20-35-7)

Disclosures The disclosures are typically made in either the body of the financial statements or in the accompanying notes. A full list can be found in the *Disclosure and Presentation Checklist for Commercial Businesses* at www.wiley.com/go/GAAP2021.

Example—Hypothetical Set of Personal Financial Statements

Marcus and Kelly Imrich
Statements of Financial Condition
December 31, 20X2 and 20X1

Assets	**20X2**	**20X1**
Cash	$ 381,437	$ 207,621
Certificate of deposit	20,000	10.000
Securities		
Marketable (Note 2)	128,787	260,485
Tax-exempt bonds (Note 3)	1,890,222	986,278
Loans receivable (Note 4)	262,877	362,877
Partnership and joint venture interests (Note 5)	935,000	938,000
Real estate interests (Note 6)	890,000	2,500,000
David Corporation (Note 7)	2,750,687	2,600,277
Cash surrender value of life insurance (Note 8)	388,000	265,000
Personal residences (Note 9)	2,387,229	2,380,229
Deferred losses from partnerships	68,570	60,830
Vested interest in David Corporation benefit plan	545,960	530,960
Personal jewelry and furnishings (Note 10)	513,000	6,700
Total assets	$11,161,769	$11,109,257
Liabilities		
Mortgage payable (Note 11)	$ 254,000	$ 267,000
Security deposits—rentals		5,700
Income taxes payable—current year balance	9,800	10,680
Total liabilities	263,800	283,380
Estimated income taxes on difference between estimated current values of assets and estimated current amounts of liabilities and their tax bases (Note 12)	555,400	731,000
Net Worth	10,342,569	10,094,877
Total liabilities and net worth	$11,161,769	$11,109,257

Marcus and Kelly Imrich
Statement of Changes in Net Worth for the Years
Ended December 31, 20X2 and 20X1

Realized increases in net worth	*20X2*	*20X1*
Salary and bonus	$ 200,000	$ 175,000
Dividends and interest income	184,260	85,000

Distribution from limited partnerships	280,000	260,000
Gain on sales of marketable securities	58,240	142,800
	722,500	662,800
Realized decreases in net worth		
Income taxes	180,000	140,000
Interest expense	25,000	26,000
Real estate taxes	21,000	18,000
Personal expenditures	242,536	400,000
	468,536	584,000
Net realized increase in net worth	253,964	78,800
Unrealized increases in net worth		
Marketable securities (net of realized gains on securities sold)	37,460	30,270
Benefit plan—David Corporation	15,000	14,000
Personal jewelry and furnishings	20,000	18,000
	72,460	62,270
Unrealized decreases in net worth		
Estimated income taxes on the difference between the estimated current values of assets and the estimated current amounts of liabilities and their tax bases	78,732	64,118
Net unrealized decrease in net worth	(6,272)	(1,848)
Net increase in net worth	247,692	76,952
Net worth at the beginning of year	10,094,877	10,017,925
Net worth at the end of year	$10,342,569	$10,094,877

Marcus and Kelly Imrich
Notes to Financial Statements

Note 1: The accompanying financial statements include the assets and liabilities of Marcus and Kelly Imrich. Assets are stated at their estimated current values, and liabilities at their estimated current amounts.

Note 2: The estimated current values of marketable securities are either (1) their quoted closing prices or (2) for securities not traded on the financial statement date, amounts that fall within the range of quoted bid and asked prices.

Marketable securities consist of the following:

Stocks	*Number of shares*	*Estimated current values*	*Number of shares*	*Estimated current values*
Susan Schultz, Inc.		1,000	$ 122,000	
Ripley Robotics Corp.	500	$ 51,927	1,000	120,485

L.A.W. Corporation	300	20,700	100	5,000
Jay & Kelly Corp.	300	20,700	200	5,000
J.A.Z. Corporation	200	35,460	200	8,000
		$ 128,787		$ 260,485

Note 3: The interest income from state and municipal bonds is generally not subject to federal income taxes but is, except in certain cases, subject to state income tax and federal alternative minimum tax.

Note 4: The loan receivable from Carol Parker, Inc. matures January 2020 and bears interest at the prime rate.

Note 5: Partnership and joint venture interests consist of the following:

	Percent owned	*Cost*	*Estimated current value 12/31/20X2*	*Estimated current value 12/31/20X2*
East Third Partnership	50.0%	$50,000	100,000	100,000
631 Lucinda Joint Venture	20.0	10,000	35,000	38,000
27 Wright Partnership	22.5	10,000	40,000	50,000
Eannarino Partnership	10.0	40,000	60,000	50,000
Sweeney Joint Venture	30.0	100,000	600,000	600,000
Kelly Parker Group	20.0	20,000	100,000	100,000
707 Lucinda Joint Venture	50.0	(11,000)	--	--
			$935,000	$938,000

Note 6: Marcus and Kelly Imrich own a one-half interest in an apartment building in DeKalb, Illinois. The estimated current value was determined by Marcus and Kelly Imrich. Their income tax basis in the apartment building was $1,000,000 for both 20X2 and 20X1.

Note 7: Kelly Imrich owns 75% of the common stock of the David Corporation. A condensed statement of assets, liabilities, and stockholders' equity (income tax basis) of David Corporation as of December 31, 20X2 and 20X1 is summarized below.

	20X2	*20X1*
Current assets	$2,975,000	$3,147,000
Investments	200,000	200,000
Property and equipment (net)	145,000	165,000
Loans receivable	110,000	120,000

Total assets	$3,430,000	$3,632,000
Current liabilities	$2,030,000	$2,157,000
Other liabilities	450,000	400,000
Total liabilities	2,480,00	2,557,000
Stockholders' equity	950,000	1,075,000
Total liabilities and stockholders' equity	$3,430,000	$3,632,000

Note 8: At December 31, 20X2 and 20X1, Marcus Imrich owned a $1,000,000 whole life insurance policy. Kelly Imrich is the sole beneficiary under the policy.

Note 9: The estimated current values of the personal residences are their appraisal value based on an estimate of selling price, net of estimated selling costs obtained from an independent real estate agent familiar with similar properties in similar locations. Both residences were purchased in 20X0.

Note 10: The estimated current values of personal effects and jewelry are the appraised values of those assets, determined by an independent appraiser for insurance purposes.

Note 11: The mortgage (collateralized by the residence) is payable in monthly installments of $2,479, including interest at an annual rate of 6% through 20X5.

Note 12: The estimated current amounts of liabilities at December 31, 20X2, and December 31, 20X1, equaled their income tax bases. Estimated income taxes have been provided on the excess of the estimated current values of assets over their tax bases as if the estimated current values of the assets had been realized on the dates of the statements of financial condition, using applicable income tax laws and regulations. The provision will probably differ from the amounts of income taxes that eventually will be paid because those amounts are determined by the timing and the method of disposal or realization and the income tax laws and regulations in effect at the time of disposal or realization.

The excess of estimated current values of major assets over their income tax bases are:

	December 31	
	20X2	*20X1*
Investment in David Corporation	$1,400,000	$1,350,000
Vested interest in benefit plan	350,000	300,000
Investment in marketable securities	100,000	120,300
	$1,850,000	$1,770,300

14 ASC 275 RISKS AND UNCERTAINTIES

PERSPECTIVE AND ISSUES

Subtopic

ASU 275, *Risks and Uncertainties*, contains one subtopic:

- ASU 275-10, *Overall*, that provides guidance on disclosures of risks and uncertainties inherent in entity's operations and activities in cases where principal operations have not begun.

This topic recognizes that all entities face risk and uncertainty. This topic is meant to provide users with an early warning about any issues with key information. The objective of ASC 275 is to provide guidelines that will enable the preparer to screen the many risks and uncertainties faced by entities and focus on those most useful to the readers of the particular entity's report—those that will enable the readers to assess the future cash flows and result of operations. Thus, the topic focuses on screening criteria for risks and uncertainties and the resulting required disclosures. It looks at risks and uncertainties arising internally as well as those arising from changes in the industry and economic environment.

Scope and Scope Exceptions

The guidance applies to all GAAP financial statements, interim and annual, but not to condensed or summarized financial statements. The guidance does not apply to risks and uncertainties associated with:

- Management or key personnel
- Proposed changes in accounting principles
- Deficiencies in the internal control structure
- The possible effects of acts of God, war, or sudden catastrophes.
(ASC 275-10-15-4)

The Codification points out that there is overlap between this topic and the requirements of the SEC and other Codification topics, particularly ASC 450. The guidance in ASC 275 does not alter any of those requirements. (See the "Other Sources" section at the end of this chapter for other references.)

DEFINITIONS OF TERMS

Source: ASC 275-10-20. Also see Appendix A, *Definitions of Terms*, for the definitions of Contract, Customer, Fair Value, Performance Obligation, Net Realizable Value, Reasonably Possible, Revenue, and Transaction Price.

Near Term. A period of time not to exceed one year from the date of the financial statements.

Severe Impact. (Used in reference to current vulnerability due to certain concentrations.) A significant financially disruptive effect on the normal functioning of an entity. Severe impact is a higher threshold than material. Matters that are important enough to influence a user's decisions are deemed to be material, yet they may not be so significant as to disrupt the normal functioning of the entity. Some events are material to an investor because they might affect the price of an entity's capital stock or its debt securities, but they would not necessarily have a severe impact on (disrupt) the entity itself. The concept of severe impact, however, includes matters that are less than catastrophic. Matters that are catastrophic include, for example, those that would result in bankruptcy.

CONCEPTS, RULES, AND EXAMPLES

ASC 275-10-50, *Risks and Uncertainties*, requires disclosure in financial statements about risks and uncertainties existing as of the date of those statements that could significantly affect the amounts reported in the near term. The four areas of disclosure required by ASC 275-10-50 are risks and uncertainties relating to:

1. The nature of the entity's operations, including the activities in which the entity is currently engaged even if principal operations have not commenced,
2. Use of estimates in the preparation of financial statements,
3. Certain significant estimates, and
4. Vulnerability due to certain concentrations.

These areas are not mutually exclusive and may overlap with other requirements. The disclosures may be:

- Grouped together,
- Placed in other parts of the financial statements, or
- Made as part of the disclosures required by other ASC Topics.
  (ASC 275-10-50-1)

Nature of Operations or Activities

ASC 275-10-50-2 requires that entities that have commenced planned principal operations disclose:

- The major products or services that they sell or provide,
- The principal markets that they serve, and
- The location of those markets.

If an entity has not commenced principal operations, it should also disclose what activities are being planned. (ASC 275-10-50-2A) Quantification is not required in disclosures about the nature of operations.

An entity operating in more than one industry must disclose:

- All industries it is operating within.
- The relative importance of each industry. (This can be conveyed by the use of words such as "predominantly," "about equally," or "major.")
- The basis for determining the relative importance of each industry (assets, revenue, or earnings).

Not-for-profit entities should disclose the nature of their principal services and the revenue sources for those services.

For details of the required disclosures, see the *Disclosure and Presentation Checklist for Commercial Businesses* at www.wiley.com/go/GAAP2021. (Note these disclosures apply to all entities.)

Use of Estimates in the Preparation of Financial Statements

Financial statements must include an explanation that the preparation of financial statements in accordance with GAAP requires the use of estimates by management. The purpose of this disclosure is to clearly alert users to the pervasiveness of estimates. (ASC 275-10-50-4)

Certain Significant Estimates

Under certain circumstances, ASC 275-10-50 requires disclosures regarding estimates used. See the *Disclosure and Presentation Checklist for Commercial Businesses* at www.wiley.com/go/ GAAP2021, for details.

Examples of Items That May Be Based on Estimates That Are Particularly Sensitive to Change in the Near Term (ASC 275-10-50-15)

- Inventory subject to rapid technological obsolescence
- Specialized equipment subject to technological obsolescence
- Valuation allowances for deferred income tax assets based on future taxable income
- Capitalized motion picture film production costs
- Capitalized computer software costs
- Deferred policy acquisition costs of insurance entities
- Valuation allowances for commercial and real estate loans
- Environmental remediation-related obligations
- Litigation-related obligations
- Contingent liabilities for guarantees of other entities' obligations
- Amounts reported for long-term obligations, such as amounts reported for pensions and postemployment benefits
- Net proceeds recoverable, the provisions for expected loss to be incurred, or both, on disposition of a business or assets
- Amounts reported for long-term contracts

Current Vulnerability Due to Concentrations

Vulnerability from concentrations occurs when entities fail to diversify in order to mitigate risk. See the *Disclosure and Presentation Checklist for Commercial Businesses* at www.wiley.com/go/GAAP2021, for details of disclosures required from concentration vulnerability.

Examples of Concentrations That Require Disclosure (ASC 275-10-50-18)

- Concentrations in the volume of business transacted with a particular customer, supplier, lender, grantor, or contributor
- Concentrations in revenue from particular products, services, or fundraising events
- Concentrations in the available sources of supply of materials, labor, services, or of licenses or other rights used in the entity's operations
- Concentrations in the market or geographic area in which an entity conducts its operations

The potential for severe impact can occur as the result of the total or partial loss of a business relationship, price or demand changes, loss of patent protection, changes in the availability of a resource or right, or the disruption of operations in a market or geographic area. For purposes of ASC 275-10-50, it is always considered reasonably possible in the near term that any customer, grantor, or contributor will be lost and that operations located outside an entity's home country will be disrupted.

For concentrations of labor subject to collective bargaining agreements and concentrations of operations outside an entity's home country, the following additional disclosures are required (ASC 275-10-50-20):

1. For labor subject to collective bargaining agreements, disclosure is to include both the percentage of the labor force covered by collective bargaining agreements and the percentage of the labor force covered by collective bargaining agreements that will expire within one year.
2. For operations located outside the entity's home country, disclosure is to include the carrying amounts of net assets and the geographic areas in which they are located.

Other Sources

See ASC Location—*Wiley GAAP* Chapter	*For illustrations and guidance on . . .*
ASC 270-10-50-6	Disclosure of contingencies in summarized interim financial information of publicly traded entities.
ASC 270-10-50-6	Disclosure of contingencies in summarized interim financial information of publicly traded entities.
ASC 330-10-55-8	The kinds of disclosures required for risks and uncertainties related to inventory.
ASC 360-10-55-50 through 55-54	The kinds of disclosures required for risks and uncertainties related to specialized manufacturing equipment.
ASC 410-30-55-7	The kinds of disclosures required for risks and uncertainties related to environmental remediation liabilities.
ASC 450-20-55-36	The kinds of disclosures required for risks and uncertainties related to loss contingencies.
ASC 460-10-55-25	The kinds of disclosures required for risks and uncertainties related to guarantees of debt.
ASC 605-35-55-2	The kinds of disclosures for risks and uncertainties related to long-term construction contracts.

See ASC Location—*Wiley GAAP* Chapter	***For illustrations and guidance on . . .***
ASC 606-50-1 through 50-23	Disclosures of revenue and contracts with customers.
ASC 740-10-55-218	The kinds of disclosures required for risks and uncertainties related to income taxes.
ASC 958-605-55-69	The kinds of disclosures required for risks and uncertainties related to contributions.
ASC 985-20-55-23	The kinds of disclosures required for risks and uncertainties related to capitalized software costs.

15 ASC 280 SEGMENT REPORTING

PERSPECTIVE AND ISSUES

Subtopic

ASC 280, *Segment Reporting*, has one subtopic:

- ASC 280-10, *Overall*, that provides guidance to public business entities on how to report certain information about:
  - Operating segments in complete sets of financial statements, and in
  - Condensed financial statements of interim periods issued to shareholders.

ASC 280 also requires public entities to disclose certain information about:

- Their products and services,
- The geographic areas in which they operate, and
- Their major customers.

Scope and Scope Exceptions

ASC 280 applies to public entities. The statement does not mandate application to not-for-profit organizations or to nonpublic entities—which are, nevertheless, encouraged to voluntarily provide the segment disclosures prescribed by ASC 280. It also does not apply to "parent entities, subsidiaries, joint ventures, or investees accounted for by the equity method if those entities' separate company statements also are consolidated or combined in a complete set of financial statements and both the separate company statements and the consolidated or combined statements are included in the same financial report." However, ASC 280 does apply to those entities if they are public entities, whose financial statements are issued separately. (ASC 280-10-15-2 and 3)

Overview

With many companies organized as conglomerates, the presentation of basic consolidated financial statements on an aggregated basis does not provide users with sufficient information for decision-making purposes. The primary benefit of segment reporting is the release of "hidden data" from consolidated financial information. Different segments may possess different levels of profitability, risk, and growth. Assessing future cash flows and their associated risks can be aided by segment data. For example, knowledge of the level of reporting entity operations in growing or declining product lines can help in the prediction of cash flow, while knowledge of the scope of reporting entity operations in an unstable geographic area can help in the assessment of risk. In general, information about the nature and relative size of an enterprise's various business operations is considered useful by decision makers.

Objective The objective of segment reporting, is to

> *. . . Provide information about the different types of business activities in which an enterprise engages and the different economic environments in which it operates to help users of financial statements:*
>
> a. *Better understand the enterprise's performance*
> b. *Better assess its prospects for future net cash flows*
> c. *Make more informed judgments about the enterprise as a whole.*
>
> (ASC 280-10-10-1)

Management Approach The disaggregation approach adopted by ASC 280-10-05-03 and 04 is the "management approach," meaning it is based on the way management organizes segments internally to make operating decisions and assess performance. The management approach, in general, provides that external financial reporting will closely conform to internal reporting, thus giving financial statement users the ability to view the reporting entity's segments in the same manner as internal decision makers.

Financial information can be segmented in several ways:

- By types of products or services,
- By geography, by legal entity, or
- By type of customer.

ASC 280 provides a methodology to identify the operating segments that are separately reportable (referred to as "reportable segments") and requires that each reportable segment disclose, among other items,

- Its profit or loss,
- Certain specific revenues and expenses, and
- Its assets.

Management is also required to reconcile segment information with its consolidated general- purpose financial statements. Even if the following information is not used by management in making operating decisions ASC 280 requires that all public companies report information on a company-wide basis about

- Revenues for each product and service,
- Countries in which revenues are recognized and assets are held, and
- Its major customers.

The Codification does not limit segment reporting to purely financial information. It also requires a description of the company's rationale or methods employed in determining the composition of the segments. This description includes

- The products or services produced by each segment,
- Differences in measurement practices between segments and the consolidated entity, and
- Differences in the segments' measurement practices between periods.

DEFINITIONS OF TERMS

Source: ASC 280, *Glossaries*. Also see Appendix A, *Definitions of Terms*, for definitions of Conduit Debt Securities and Public Entity.

Chief Operating Decision Maker (CODM). The person(s) at the reporting entity level whose general function (not specific title) is to allocate resources to, and assess the performance of, the segments. Within a reporting entity, this authority does not necessarily need to be vested in a single individual, rather, the responsibilities can be fulfilled by a group of individuals.

Operating Segment. A component of a public entity that has all of the following characteristics:

a. It engages in business activities from which it may recognize revenues and incur expenses (including revenue and expenses relating to transactions with other components of the same public entity).

b. Its operating results are regularly reviewed by the public entity's chief operating decision maker to make disclosures about resources to be allocated to the segment and assess its performance.

c. Its discrete financial information is available.

Segment Manager. The person(s) accountable to the reporting entity's CODM (defined earlier) for one or more operating segment's activities, financial results, budgets, forecasts, and operating plans. The reporting entity's CODM can also serve as segment manager for one or more operating segments. (ASC 280-10-50-7 and 8)

CONCEPTS, RULES, AND EXAMPLES

Operating Segments

Operating segments frequently have a segment manager function that communicates on an ongoing basis with the reporting entity's CODM. The CODM is the person responsible for allocating resources and assessing performance. The CODM may be the CEO or COO, but is not necessarily a single individual but rather the segment management responsibility can vest functionally in a committee or group of designated individuals. (ASC 280-10-50-7) Additionally, an operating segment may not be revenue generating from its inception, because it may be in a start-up phase. (ASC 280-10-50-3)

Not all activities that occur within the reporting entity are allocable to its operating segments. Activities that are non-revenue-producing or that are incidental to the reporting entity, such as corporate headquarters or certain service or support departments, should not be attributed to operating segments. ASC 280 specifies that the reporting entity's pension and other postretirement benefit plans are not considered to be operating segments. (ASC 280-10-50-4)

Reportable Segments An operating segment is considered to be a reportable segment if it meets the description above and is significant to the enterprise as a whole because it satisfies one of the three quantitative 10% tests described below. If a segment does not meet the tests below, but management believes the information may be useful, the operating segments may be reportable. (ASC 280-10-50-12)

Revenue Test Segment revenue (unaffiliated and intersegment) is at least 10% of the combined revenue (unaffiliated and intersegment) of all operating segments. (ASC 280-10-50-12a)

Profit and Loss Test The absolute amount of segment profit or loss is at least 10% of the greater, in absolute amount, of:

1. Combined profits of all operating segments reporting a profit
2. Combined losses of all operating segments reporting a loss
   (ASC 280-10-50-12b)

ASC 280-10-55 clarifies that, if the CODM uses different measures of profit or loss to evaluate the performance of different segments (e.g., net income versus operating income), the reporting entity must use a single, consistent measure for the purposes of this profit and loss test. This does not, however, affect the requirement that the reporting entity disclose the measure of profit or loss used by the CODM for the purposes of decision making regarding the segment's performance and resources to be allocated to the segment.

Assets Test Segment assets are at least 10% of the combined assets of all operating segments. (ASC 280-10-50-12c) Segment assets include those assets used exclusively by the segment and the allocated portion of assets shared by two or more segments. Assets held for general corporate purposes are not assigned to segments.

Comparability Interperiod comparability must be considered in conjunction with the results of the 10% tests. If a segment fails to meet the tests in the current reporting period but has satisfied the tests in the past and is expected to in the future, it is considered as being reportable in the current year for the sake of comparability. Similarly, if a segment which rarely passes the tests does so in the current year as the result of an unusual event, that segment may be excluded to preserve comparability.

75% Test After the 10% tests are completed, a 75% test must be performed. (ASC 280-10-50-14) The combined external revenue of all reportable segments must be at least 75% of the combined unaffiliated revenue of all operating segments. If the 75% test is not satisfied, additional segments must be designated as reportable until the test is satisfied. The purpose of this test is to ensure that reportable segments account for a substantial portion of the entity's operations.

Example of Segment Testing

The following example illustrates the three 10% tests and the 75% test.

Operating segment	*External revenue*	*Intersegment revenue*	*Total Revenue*	*Segment profit*	*Segment (loss)*	*Assets*
A	90	$ 12	$ 102	$11	$–	$ 70
B	120	–	120	10	–	50
C	110	20	130	–	(40)	90
D	200	–	200	–	–	140
E	140	300	440	–	(100)	230
F	380	–	380	60	–	260
G	144	–	144	8	–	30
Total	$1,184	$332	$1,516	$89	($140)	$870

NOTE: Because the $140 total segment losses exceed the $89 total segment profits, the $140 is used for the 10% test.

Summary of Test Results

x = Passed test – Reportable segment

Operating Segment	*Total revenues (10% of $1,516 = $152)*	*Segment profit/loss (10% of $140 = $14)*	*Assets (10% of $870 = $87)*	*75% of unaffiliated revenues test*
A				
B				
C		X	X	$ 110
D	X		X	200
E	X	X	X	140
F	X	X	X	380
G				—
				830
			75% of $1,184	888
			Revenue shortfall	$(58)

Note that the aggregate revenues of the reportable segments that passed the 10% tests are $58 short of providing the required coverage of 75% of external revenues. Consequently, an additional operating segment (A, B, or G) will need to be added to the reportable segments in order to obtain sufficient coverage.

Aggregating Segments Certain other factors must be considered when identifying reportable segments. Management may consider aggregating two or more operating segments if:

1. They have similar economic characteristics,
2. Aggregation is consistent with the objective and basic principles of ASC 280, and
3. The segments are similar in all of the following areas:
   a. The nature of the products and services
   b. The nature of the production processes
   c. The type of customer for their products and services
   d. The methods used to distribute their products or provide their services
   e. The nature of the regulatory environment.

   (ASC 280-10-50-11)

At the discretion of management, this aggregation can occur prior to performing the 10% tests. Generally, aggregation should be consistent with a reasonable investor's expectation and external communications, such as filings, press releases, and website information. Management may *optionally* combine information on operating segments that do not meet any of the 10% tests to produce a reportable segment, but only if the segments being combined have similar economic characteristics and also share a majority of the five aggregation criteria listed above. (ASC 280-10-50-13)

Note that information about operating segments that does not meet any of the 10% thresholds may still be disclosed separately. (ASC 280-10-50-15) By utilizing the aggregation criteria and quantitative thresholds (10% tests) for determining reportable segments, ASC 280 uses what should be considered a modified management approach.

The number of reportable segments should not be so great as to decrease the usefulness of segment reporting. As a rule of thumb, FASB suggests that if the number of reportable segments exceeds ten, segment information may become too detailed. In this situation, the most closely related operating segments should be combined into broader reportable segments, again, however, subject to the objectives inherent in ASC 280's requirements. (ASC 280-10-50-18)

The following diagram is an example of the different components of a reporting entity used for various accounting and reporting purposes.

Exhibit—Alternative Balance Sheet Segmentation

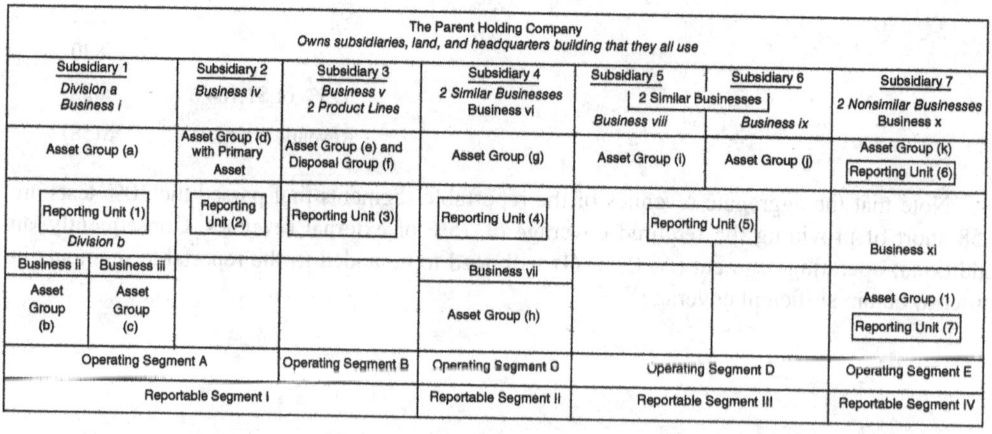

Reassessment of Segments

Entities may want to consider changes that may indicate segments should be reassessed, including:

- Information communicated to the entity's board of directors or to external parties
- CODM
- Staff who regularly meet with the CODM
- Information regularly reviewed by the CODM
- Structure of the organization
- Budgeting process
- Level at which budgets are reviewed

Measurement Issues

Transfer Pricing Since segment revenue as defined by ASC 280 includes intersegment sales, transfer pricing becomes an issue. Rather than establishing a basis for setting transfer prices, FASB requires companies to use the same transfer prices for segment reporting purposes as are used internally. Since most segments are organizational profit centers, internal transfer prices would generally reflect market prices, but even if this is not the case, these same transfer prices must be used for segment disclosures.

Common Costs Another issue in determining profit or loss is the allocation of common costs. Common costs are expenses incurred by the reporting entity for the benefit of more than one operating segment. Again, segment reporting is required to conform to internal management reporting. Accordingly, these costs are only allocated to a segment for external reporting purposes if they are included in the measure of the segment's profit or loss that is used internally by the CODM.

General Corporate Expense Difficulties can arise in distinguishing common costs from general corporate expenses. General corporate expenses are not direct expenses from the point of view of any operating segment; they are incurred for the benefit of the corporation as a whole and cannot be reasonably attributed to any operating segment. Common costs, on the other hand, benefit two or more segments and can be allocated to those segments in a manner determined by management to support internal decision making by the reporting entity.

Corporate Assets Similarly, only those assets that are included internally in the measure of the segment's assets used to make operating decisions are reported as assets of the segment in external financial reports. If management allocates amounts to segment profit or assets internally and those amounts are used by the CODM, then those amounts are to be allocated on a reasonable basis and disclosed.

Segment and Entity-Wide Disclosures

ASC 280 requires disclosures regarding the reporting entity's reportable segments. In addition to segment data, ASC 280-10-50-38 through 42 mandates that certain entity-wide disclosures be made. The entity-wide disclosures are required for all reporting entities subject to ASC 280, even those that have only a single reportable segment. Those disclosures are listed in the *Disclosure and Presentation Checklist for Commercial Businesses* at www.wiley.com/go/GAAP2021.

Restatement of Previously Reported Segment Information

ASC 280-10-50-34 requires segment reporting on a comparative basis when the associated financial statements are comparative. Therefore, the entities should restate the information to preserve comparability whenever the reporting entity has changed the structure of its internal organization in a manner that causes a change to its reportable segments. The entity must explicitly disclose that it has restated the segment information of earlier periods.

Example—Comprehensive Illustration of the Application of Segment Reporting

The following illustration is provided for a hypothetical company, Resources Unlimited. The illustration provides segment disclosures by legal entity.

NOTE: ASC 280 provides illustrative segment disclosures by product line.

Description of the Types of Products and Services from Which Each Reportable Segment Derives Its Revenues Resources Unlimited has four reportable segments: Wholesale Corporation, Retail Corporation, Library Corporation, and Software Corporation. Wholesale Corporation buys and resells used elementary and college textbooks. Retail Corporation operates 200 college bookstores and a related e-commerce website selling both new and used college textbooks, trade books, sports apparel, and other sundries. Library Corporation sells library books primarily to elementary school libraries. Software Corporation develops and sells library systems application software.

Measurement of Segment Profit or Loss and Segment Assets The accounting policies of the segments are the same as those described in the summary of significant accounting policies except the first-in, first-out (FIFO) method of inventory valuation is used for segment reporting. In addition, Resources Unlimited allocates interest expense to each segment based on the segment's average borrowings from the corporate office. However, the related debt is not allocated to the segments and remains on the corporate statement of financial position. Resources Unlimited evaluates performance based on profit or loss before income taxes not including nonrecurring gains and losses.

Resources Unlimited accounts for intersegment sales and transfers as if the sales or transfers were transacted with third parties (i.e., at current market prices).

Factors Management Used to Identify Reportable Segments Resources Unlimited's business is conducted through four separate legal entities that are wholly owned subsidiaries. At the company's inception, each entity was founded and managed by a different Resources Unlimited stockholder/family member. Each corporation is still managed separately, as each business has a distinct customer base and requires different strategic and marketing efforts.

Information About Profit and Loss and Assets The amounts in the illustration are assumed to be the amounts in reports used by the CODM. Resources Unlimited allocates interest expense to the segments; however, it does not allocate income taxes and unusual items to them.

($000 omitted)

	Wholesale Corporation	**Retail Corporation**	**Library Corporation**	**Software Corporation**	**Totals**
Revenues from external customers	$197,500	$263,000	$182,300	$102,200	$745,000
Intersegment revenues	23,000	–	–	–	23,000
Interest revenue	250	150	–	–	400
Interest expense	1,570	2,150	1,390	2,700	7,810

Depreciation and amortization*	8,600	13,100	7,180	6,070	34,950
Segment profit	12,100	13,500	9,900	5,100	40,600
Segment assets	121,200	153,350	100,600	85,000	460,150
Expenditures for segment assets	7,200	12,700	5,600	6,700	32,200

* *Depreciation and amortization are required to be disclosed for each operating segment even if the CODM evaluates segment performance using pre-depreciation measures such as earnings before income taxes, depreciation, and amortization (EBITDA). (ASC 280-10-55)*

Reconciliations An illustration of reconciliations for revenues, profit and loss, assets, and other significant items is shown below. In general, this illustration assumes that there are no unreported operating segments, but there is a corporate headquarters, thus most reconciling items relate to corporate revenues and expenses.

As discussed previously, the company recognizes and measures inventory based on FIFO valuation for segment reporting. The consolidated financial statements are assumed not to include discontinued operations or the cumulative effect of a change in accounting principle.

	($000 omitted)
Revenue	
Total revenues for reportable segments	$768,000
Elimination of intersegment revenue	(23,000)
Total consolidated revenue	$745,000
Profit and loss	
Total profit for reportable segments	$ 40,600
Elimination of intersegment profits	(6,100)
Unallocated amounts relating to corporate operations:	
Interest revenue	500
Interest expense	(800)
Depreciation and amortization	(1,900)
Unrealized gain on trading securities	1,865
Income before income taxes and extraordinary items	$ 34,165
Assets	
Total assets for reportable segments	$460,150
Corporate short-term investments, land and building	25,100
Adjustment for LIFO reserve in consolidation	(9,200)
	$476,050

Other significant items

	Segment totals	*Adjustments*	*Consolidated totals*
Expenditures for segment assets	$32,200	800	$33,000

The reconciling adjustment is the amount of expenditures incurred for additions to the corporate headquarters building, which is not included in the segment information.

Products and services

Used textbooks	$296,125
New textbooks	72,150
Trade books	45,700
Sports apparel	41,325
Sundries	5,200
Library books	182,300
Library software	102,200
Total consolidated revenue	$745,000

Geographic information

	*Revenues**	*Long-lived assets*
United States	$687,400	$253,200
Foreign countries	57,600	18,800
Total	$745,000	$272,000

* *Revenues are attributed to countries as follows: For Wholesale Corporation and Library Corporation, the country in which the customer takes delivery. For Retail Corporation, the country in which the retail store is located or, for Internet sales, the country to which the merchandise is delivered. For Software Corporation, the country where the host server on which the software is installed is located.*

Major Customers No single customer represents 10% or more of the consolidated revenues. Consequently, management believes that the companies' sales are appropriately diversified.

Other Sources

See ASC Location—*Wiley GAAP* Chapter	*For information on . . .*
ASC 350	Information to be disclosed about goodwill in each reportable segment and significant changes in the allocation of goodwill by reportable segments.
ASC 350	Segment disclosures related to each impairment loss recognized related to an intangible asset.
ASC 420-10-50-1	Segment information to be disclosed in the period in which an exit or disposal activity is initiated.
ASC 908-280	Segmentation in the airline industry.
ASC 924-280	Segment guidance in the casino industry.

16 ASC 310 RECEIVABLES

PERSPECTIVE AND ISSUES

Technical Alert

ASU 2019-10

Guidance regarding effective dates In November 2019, the FASB issued ASU 2019-10, *Financial Instruments—Credit Losses (Topic 326), Derivatives and Hedging (Topic 815), and Leases (Topic 842: Effective Dates*. The ASU grants private companies, not-for-profit organizations, and certain small public company SEC filers additional time to implement recent FASB standards on current expected credit losses (CECL).

ASU 2019-10 Effective Date Changes		
Topic	**Public business entities that meet the definition of SEC Filers, except Smaller Reporting Companies (SRCs) as defined by the SEC**	**All Other Entities**
CECL (ASC 326)	Fiscal years beginning after December 15, 2019	Fiscal years beginning after December 15, 2022

* *Includes Employee Benefit Plans and NFP Conduit Bond Obligors that file with the SEC or furnish financial statements to the SEC.*

The ASUs in this chapter that are affected are:

- ASU. 2016-13, *Financial Instruments—Credit Losses (Topic 326): Measurement of Credit Losses on Financial Instruments,*
- ASU 2018-19, *Codification Improvements to Topic 326, Financial Instruments—Credit Losses,*
- ASU 2019-04, *Codification Improvements to Topic 326, Financial Instruments—Credit Losses, Topic 815, Derivatives and Hedging, and Topic 825, Financial Instruments, and*
- ASU 2019-05, *Financial Instruments—Credit Losses (Topic 326): Targeted Transition Relief*

ASU 2016-13

In June 2016, the FASB issued ASU 2016-13, *Financial Instruments—Credit Losses (Topic 326) Measurement of Credit Losses on Financial Instruments.* This ASU makes changes to several topics, and adds a new topic—ASC 326.

Effective Dates See information on ASU 2019-10 for changes in effective dates.

Early adoption is allowed for all entities for fiscal years beginning after December 15, 2018, including interim periods therein. (ASC 326-10-65-1)

Also, please see the information below on ASU 2019-05.

Transition Except where noted in the following table, entities should use the modified-retrospective approach and record a cumulative-effect adjustment to retained earnings as of the beginning of the first reporting period that the entity adopts the guidance. For example, a calendar-year private company that adopts the standard in 2021 records the cumulative effect adjustment on January 1, 2021.

Guidance The new guidance affects several topics. Readers should look to those topics for more information. This chapter will outline how ASU 2016-13 affects ASC 310.

ASU 2016-13 changes the accounting for credit impairments for trade and other receivables and purchased-credit impaired (PCD) financial assets. The guidance on the latter is being deleted from ASC 310 and moved to ASC 326. Further information on accounting for PCDs under the ASU 2016-13 amendments can be found in the chapter on ASC 326.

Under the new guidance, ASC 326's current expected credit loss (CECL) model replaces the expected loss model in ASC 310-10. Under the CECL model, entities will have to estimate expected credit losses for trade receivables and other financing receivables. Currently, an allowance or loss is recognized when it is probable. Under the new model, an allowance or loss will be recognized upon initial recognition of the asset and will reflect all future events that will lead to a recognized loss, regardless of whether it is probable that future event will occur. The extant guidance looks at past events and current conditions, whereas the new guidance is forward looking and requires estimates for future expectations.

To assess credit risk, the new guidance allows entities to continue to pool assets with similar characteristics. However, entities will want to take a second look at the receivables in a pool and make sure they have similar risk characteristics.

If an entity is not able to develop a reasonable and supportable forecast for the full remaining life of a financial asset, it should go back to using historical loss information.

Perhaps the best way to understand how the new guidance works is to look at a simple example based on an example in the ASU.

Example—Estimating ECLs for Trade Receivables Using an Aging Schedule

Entity A manufactures t-shirts and sells them to retailers. The typical payment terms include a 2% discount if payment is received in 60 days, with payment required in 90 days. Entity A's aging schedule is based on historical loss information, and the historical credit loss percentages. The economic forecast has improved, specifically the unemployment rate, which affects Entity A's ultimate customers, has decreased and further improvement is expected in the next year. This information leads Entity A to decrease its historical loss rate by 10%.

Past-Due Status	Historical Credit Rate	Amortized Cost Basis	Expected Credit Loss Rate—Factoring in a 10% Improvement	Expected Credit Loss Estimate
Current	.3%	6,200,328	.27%	$16,741
1–30 days past due	8%	9,200	7.2%	662
31–60 days past due	26%	2,300	23.4%	538
61–90 days past due	58%	1,500	52.2%	783
More than 90 days past due	82%	750	73.8%	554
Total				$19,278

Entities are expected to reflect a risk of loss even if the risk is remote. The entity would not reflect a credit loss if historical experience and reasonable and supportable forecast expect nonpayment of the amortized cost basis is zero. The ASU uses U.S. Treasury securities as an example of this situation.

For assets secured by collateral, the ASU provides a practical expedient. Under certain conditions, entities are permitted to estimate credit losses on collateral-dependent financial assets as the difference between the collateral's fair value and the amortized cost basis of the financial asset.

Investors must amortize the purchase premium of a callable debt security to the first call date. This provides the following benefits:

- Better aligns interest income recognition with market participant price assumptions
- Affects interest income and gain or loss when the debt is called
- If the security is not called at first call date, resets the effective yield.

Example

ABC Company purchases a bond for $104, with a par of $100, coupon rate of 5%, ten years to maturity, and callable five years before maturity. Under extant guidance, the $4 premium would be amortized over ten years. This would result in cumulative amortization of $1.78 at the first call date and recognition of a $2.22 loss if the call was exercised. Under the ASU, the premium is amortized over five years. This would result in no loss related to the premium recognized if the call was exercised at the first call date. If the call was not exercised, then ABC would reset the effective yield based on the current amortized cost and the future payment terms.

ASU 2018-19

In November 2018, the FASB issued ASU 2018-19, *Codification Improvements to Topic 326, Financial Instruments—Credit Losses*. This update affects this chapter by changing the effective date of ASU 2016-13 for nonpublic entities. Those changes are reflected in the effective dates above. Also, for an option to use the fair value option, see the information on ASU 2019-05 below.

ASU 2019-04

In April 2019, the FASB issued Codification Improvements to Topic 326, *Financial Instruments—Credit Losses*, Topic 815, *Derivatives and Hedging*, and Topic 825, *Financial Instruments*. Issue 1B of the ASU provides revised guidance on how an entity should account for loans with various classifications. The changes require that an entity:

- Reverse in earnings any allowance for credit losses or valuation allowances that had been previously measured on a loan,
- Reclassify the loan to the new classification, and
- Apply the applicable measurement guidance in accordance with the new classification.

The ASC 310 amendments in ASU 2019-04 are incorporated in this chapter.

ASU 2019-05

In May 2019, the FASB issued ASU 2019-05, *Financial Instruments—Credit Losses (Topic 326)—Targeted Transition Relief.*

Guidance This Update provides an option to irrevocably elect the fair value option for certain financial assets previously measured at amortized cost basis. The FASB expects this amendment to increase comparability because it aligns measurement methodologies for similar financial assets. This option is available to reporting entities within the scope of ASC 326. The new option may be applied on an instrument-by-instrument basis for eligible instruments. Note that this option *does not* apply to held-to-maturity debt securities. An entity that applies the fair value option should then apply the guidance in ASC 820-10 and ASC 825-10. (ASC 326-10-65-3)

Effective Dates For entities that have adopted ASU 2016-13, ASU 2019-05 is effective for fiscal years beginning after December 15, 2019, including interim periods within those fiscal years. Those entities may early adopt in any of the interim periods.

For entities that have not yet implemented ASU 2016-13, see the information on ASU 2019-10 at the beginning of this chapter.

Transition Entities should adopt the changes using a modified-retrospective basis by means of a cumulative-effect adjustment to the opening balance of retained earnings balance as of the date the entity adopted ASU 2016-13.

Subtopics

ASC 310, *Receivables,* consists of four subtopics:

- ASC 310-10, *Overall,* which provides general guidance for receivables and has two subsections:
  - *General,* which provides guidance on receivables in general and standby commitments to purchase loans, factoring arrangements, and rebates,

  - *Acquisition, Development, and Construction Arrangements*, which provides guidance on whether a lender should account for the arrangement as a loan or as an investment in real estate or in a joint venture.
- ASC 310-20, *Nonrefundable Fees and Other Costs*, which provides guidance on nonrefundable fees, origination costs, and acquisition costs associated with lending activities and loan purchases.
- ASC 310-30, *Loans and Debt Securities Acquired with Deteriorated Credit Quality*,[1] which provides guidance regarding loans acquired with evidence of deterioration of credit quality since origination acquired by completion of a transfer for which it is probable, at acquisition, that the investor will be unable to collect all contractually required payments receivable.
- ASC 310-40, *Troubled Debt Restructurings by Creditors*, which provides guidance focused on the creditor's records. Guidance for the debtor's accounting in a troubled debt restructuring (TDR) is found in ASC 470-60.

Scope and Scope Exceptions

The scope and scope exceptions for this topic are presented at the beginning of the section on each subtopic.

DEFINITIONS OF TERMS

Source: ASC 310, *Glossary* Sections. Also see Appendix A, *Definitions of Terms*, for definitions of Acquisition, Development, and Construction Arrangement, Amortized Cost Basis, Bargain Purchase Option, Bargain Renewal Option, Commencement Date of the Lease (Commencement Date), Commitment Fees, Contract, Control, Current Assets, Debt, Debt Security, Direct Financing Lease, Loan Origination Costs, Effective Interest Rates, Fair Value, Financial Asset, Financing Receivable, Indirectly Related to the Leased Property, Initial Investment, Lease, Lease Modification, Lease Payments, Lease Receivable, Lease Term, Lending Activities, Lessee, Lessor, Leveraged Lease, Loan Origination Fees, Market Participants, Not-for-Profit Entity, Noncancelable Lease Term, Orderly Transaction, Penalty, Probable, Public Business Entity, Recorded Investment, Purchased Financial Asset with Credit Deterioration, Recourse, Related Parties, Sales-type Lease, Standby Letter of Credit, Time of Restructuring, Troubled Debt Restructuring, and Underlying Asset.

Accretable Yield. The excess of a loan's cash flows expected to be collected over the investor's initial investment in the loan.

Blended-rate Loans. Blended-rate loans involve lending new funds at market interest rates combined with existing loans at rates currently lower than market rates. (Those funds are not advanced under a line of credit.)

Carrying Amount. For a receivable, the face amount increased or decreased by applicable accrued interest and applicable unamortized premium, discount, finance charges, or issue costs and also an allowance for uncollectible amounts and other valuation accounts. For a payable, the face amount increased or decreased by applicable accrued interest and applicable unamortized premium, discount, finance charges, or issue costs.

[1] Upon implementation of ASU 2016-13, this subtopic will be superseded, and entities should look to ASC 326 for the related guidance.

Cash Flows Expected at Acquisition. The investor's estimate, at acquisition, of the amount and timing of undiscounted principal, interest, and other cash flows expected to be collected. This would be the investor's best estimate of cash flows, including the effect of prepayments if considered, that is used in determining the acquisition price, and, in a business combination, the investor's estimate of fair value for purposes of acquisition price assignment in accordance with subtopic 805-20. One acceptable method of making this estimate is described in paragraphs 820-10-55-3F through 55-3G and 820-10-55-4 through 55-20, which provide guidance on present value techniques.

Class of Financing Receivable. A group of financing receivables determined on the basis of all of the following:

- Initial measurement attribute (for example, amortized cost or purchased credit impaired)
- Risk characteristics of the financing receivable
- An entity's method for monitoring and assessing credit risk

See paragraphs 310-10-55-16 through 55-18 and 310-10-55-22.

Upon implementation of ASU 2016-13, this language changes to: a group of financing receivables determined on the basis of both of the following:

- Risk characteristics of the financing receivable
- An entity's method for monitoring and assessing credit risk

See paragraphs 310-10-55-16 through 55-18 and 310-10-55-22.

Collateral-Dependent Loan. A loan for which the repayment is expected to be provided solely by the underlying collateral.

Common Risk Characteristics. Loans with similar credit risk (for example, evidenced by similar Fair Isaac Company [FICO] scores, an automated rating process for credit reports) or risk ratings, and one or more predominant risk characteristics, such as financial asset type, collateral type, size, interest rate, date of origination, term, and geographic location.

Completion of a Transfer. A completion of a transfer occurs for a transaction with any of the following characteristics:

- It satisfies the conditions in paragraph 860-10-40-5 to be accounted for as a sale.
- It is in a business combination.
- It is to a newly created subsidiary if the transferee has written the loan down to its fair value with the intent of transferring the stock of the subsidiary as a dividend to the shareholders of the parent entity.
- It is a contribution receivable or a transfer that satisfies a prior promise to give.

Contractually Required Payments Receivable. The total undiscounted amount of all uncollected contractual principal and contractual interest payments both past due and scheduled for the future, adjusted for the timing of prepayments, if considered, less any reduction by the investor. For an acquired asset-backed security with required contractual payments of principal and interest, the contractually required payments receivable is represented by the contractual terms of the security. However, when contractual payments of principal and interest are not specified by the security, it is necessary to consider the contractual terms of the underlying loans or assets.

Credit Card Fees. The periodic uniform fees that entitle cardholders to use credit cards. The amount of such fees generally is not dependent upon the level of credit available or frequency of usage. Typically, the use of credit cards facilitates the cardholder's payment for the purchase of goods and services on a periodic, as-billed basis (usually monthly), involves the extension of credit, and, if payment is not made when billed, involves imposition of interest or finance charges. Credit card fees include fees received in similar arrangements, such as charge card and cash card fees.

Credit Quality Indicator. A statistic about the credit quality of a financial asset.

Expected Residual Profit. The amount of profit, whether called interest or another name, such as equity kicker, above a reasonable amount of interest and fees expected to be earned by a lender.

Idle Time. Idle time represents the time that a lender's employees are not actively involved in performing origination activities for specific loans. Idle time can be caused by many factors, including lack of work, delays in work flow, and equipment failure. Idle time can be measured through the establishment of standard costs, time studies, ratios of productive and nonproductive time, and other methods.

Incremental Direct Costs. Costs to originate a loan that have both of the following characteristics:

- Result directly from and are essential to the lending transaction
- Would not have been incurred by the lender had that lending transaction not occurred

Initial Investment. The amount paid to the seller plus any fees paid or less any fees received.

Lending Activities. Lending, committing to lend, refinancing or restructuring loans, arranging standby letters of credit, syndicating loans, and leasing activities are lending activities.

Loan. A contractual right to receive money on demand or on fixed or determinable dates that is recognized as an asset in the creditor's statement of financial position. Examples include but are not limited to accounts receivable (with terms exceeding one year) and notes receivable.

Loan Participation. A transaction in which a single lender makes a large loan to a borrower and subsequently transfers undivided interests in the loan to groups of banks or other entities.

Loan Syndication. A transaction in which several lenders share in lending to a single borrower. Each lender loans a specific amount to the borrower and has the right to repayment from the borrower. It is common for groups of lenders to jointly fund those loans when the amount borrowed is greater than any one lender is willing to lend.

Net Investment in an Original Loan. The net investment in an original loan includes the unpaid loan principal, any remaining unamortized net fees or costs, any remaining unamortized purchase premium or discount, and any accrued interest receivable.

Nonaccretable Difference. A loan's contractually required payments receivable in excess of the amount of its cash flows expected to be collected.

Portfolio Segment. The level at which an entity develops and documents a systematic methodology to determine its allowance for credit losses. See paragraphs 310-10-55-21 through 55-22.

Private Label Credit Cards. Private label credit cards are those credit cards that are issued by, or on behalf of, a merchandising entity for the purchase of goods or services that are sold at that entity's place(s) of business.

Recorded Investment. The amount of the investment in a loan, which is not net of a valuation allowance, but which does reflect any direct write-down of the investment.

Recorded Investment in the Receivable. The recorded investment in the receivable is the face amount increased or decreased by applicable accrued interest and unamortized premium, discount, finance charges, or acquisition costs and may also reflect a previous direct write-down of the investment.

Recourse. The right of a transferee of receivables to receive payment from the transferor of those receivables for any of the following:

- Failure of debtors to pay when due
- The effects of prepayments
- Adjustments resulting from defects in the eligibility of the transferred receivables

Revolving Privileges. A feature in a loan that provides the borrower with the option to make multiple borrowings up to a specified maximum amount, to repay portions of previous borrowings, and to then reborrow under the same loan.

CONCEPTS, RULES, AND EXAMPLES

Scope

ASC 310-10, *Overall*

ASC 310-10-15-3 lists two exceptions to the guidance in the General Subsections of ASC 310-10:

- Mortgage banking activities and
- Contracts accounted for as derivative instruments under ASC 815-10.

ASC 310-10-15-5 states that the Acquisition, Development, and Construction Subsections' guidance applies to all entities, but not all arrangements. It applies only to those acquisition, development, and construction arrangements in which the lender participates in expected residual profit.

Overview

Receivables exist in nearly every entity. They come from credit sales, loans, or other transactions and may be in the form of loans, notes, or other type of financial instruments. (ASC 310-10-05-4)

Types of Receivables Financing receivables are contractual rights to receive cash either on demand or on fixed or determinable dates. They are recognized as assets on the statement of financial position. Financing receivables include:

- Trade accounts receivable.
- Loans.
- Lease receivables arising from sales-type leases or direct financing leases. (This bullet is added by ASU 2016-02 on *Leases*.)
- Credit cards.
- Notes receivable.
- Receivables relating to a lessor's right to payments from a lease other than an operating lease that should be recognized as assets.[2]
  (ASC 310-10-55-14)

Accounts receivable, open accounts, or trade accounts are agreements by customers to pay for services received or merchandise obtained.

[2] Upon implementation of ASU 2016-02, Leases, this bullet point will change to "Receivables relating to a lessor's right to payments from a leveraged lease that should be recognized in accordance with ASC 842-10-65-1(z)."

Notes receivable are formalized obligations evidenced by written promissory notes. Notes receivable generally arise from cash advances but could result from sales of merchandise or the provision of services.

Entities may enter into forward standby commitments to purchase loans at a stated price in return for a standby commitment fee. Settlement is in the hands of the seller. The seller would deliver the loans only when and if the contract price is equal to or executes the market price on the settlement date. This arrangement is, in effect, a written put option. (ASC 310-10- 05-05)

Factored receivables are sold to a third party, usually a factor. The factor assumes the risk of collection, without recourse to the transferor. Debtors pay the factor directly. (ASC 310-10-05-06)

Rebates in this context are refunds of portions of precomputed finance charges on installment loans or trade receivables. Rebate calculations are often governed by law. (ASC 310-10-05-7)

The following are not financing receivables:

- Debt securities in the scope of ASC 320
- Unconditional promises to give recognized in accordance with ASC 958-605-25-7 through 25-15
- A transferor's interest in securitization transactions accounted for as sales in ASC 860
- Purchased beneficial interest in securitized financial assets within the scope of ASC 325-40 (ASC 310-10-55-15)

Valuation Allowance for Uncollectible Amounts[3]

The recording of a valuation allowance for anticipated uncollectible amounts is almost always necessary. The *direct write-off method*, in which a receivable is charged off only when it is clear that it cannot be collected, is unsatisfactory since it overstates assets and also results in a mismatching of revenues and expenses. (Note that the direct write-off method may be required for tax purposes, but if so, this results in temporary differences for which interperiod tax allocation will generally be required.) Proper matching, which remains a valid financial reporting objective, can only be achieved if bad debts are recorded in the same fiscal period as the revenues to which they are related. Since the amount of uncollectible accounts is not known with certainty, an estimate must generally be made.

There are two popular estimation techniques, both acceptable under GAAP:

1. The *percentage-of-sales method* is principally oriented toward achieving the best possible matching of revenues and expenses.
2. The *aging the accounts* method is more inclined toward the presentation of the correct net realizable value of the trade receivables in the statement of financial position.

Percentage-of-Sales Method For the percentage-of-sales method, historical data are analyzed to ascertain the relationship between bad debts and credit sales. The derived percentage is then applied to the current period's sales revenues to arrive at the appropriate debit to bad debts expense for the year. The offsetting credit is made to allowance for uncollectible accounts. When specific customer accounts are subsequently identified as uncollectible, they are written off against this allowance.

[3] See the Technical Alert on ASU 2016-13 at the beginning of this chapter for updated information.

Example of Percentage-of-Sales Method

Total credit sales for year:	$7,500,000	
Bad debt ratio from prior years or other data source:	1.75%	of credit sales
Computed year-end adjustment for bad debts expense:	$ 131,250	($7,500,000 × .0175)
The entry required is		
Bad debts expense	131,250	
Allowance for uncollectible receivables		131,250

Care must be taken to ensure that the bad debt ratio computed will be representative of uncollectibility of the current period's credit sales. A ratio based on historical experience may require an adjustment to reflect the current economic climate. For example, if a large percentage of customers are concentrated in a geographic area that is experiencing an economic downturn, the rate of default may increase over that previously suffered. Changes in credit terms and in customer mix may also affect the relationship between sales and bad debts, and should be given consideration in determining the bad debt percentage to be applied to current period credit sales. In practice, these relationships evolve slowly over time and may not always be observed over the short term.

Aging the Accounts Method When aging the accounts, an analysis is prepared of the customer receivables at the date of the statement of financial position. Each customer's balance is categorized by the number of days or months the underlying invoices have remained outstanding. Based on the reporting entity's past experience or on other available statistics, such as industry trends, historical bad debts percentages are applied to each of these aggregate amounts, with larger percentages being applied to the older accounts. The end result of this process is a computed total dollar amount that implies the proper ending balance in the allowance for uncollectible receivables at the date of the statement of financial position. The computed amount is compared to the balance in the valuation account, and an adjustment is made for the differences.

Example of the Aging Method

	Age of accounts			
	Under 30 days	*30–90 days*	*Over 90 days*	*Total*
Gross receivables	$1,100,000	$425,000	$360,000	
Bad debt percentage	0.5%	2.5%	15%	
Provision required	$ 5,500	$ 10,625	$ 54,000	$70,125

The credit balance required in the allowance account is $70,125. A debit balance of $58,250 already exists in the allowance account because charge-offs during the year that exceeded the credit balance in the allowance account at the previous year-end. The necessary entry is

Bad debts expense ($58,250 + 70,1250)	128,375	
Allowance for uncollectible receivables		128,375

Change in Estimate Both of the estimation techniques should produce approximately the same result over the course of a number of years. Nonetheless, these adjustments are based upon estimates and will never precisely predict ultimate results. There are two possible accounting treatments for adjustments, depending on the circumstances.

- When facts subsequently become available to indicate that the amount provided as an allowance for uncollectible accounts was incorrect, an adjustment classified as a change in estimate is made.
- If the amount is incorrect because of a failure to consider facts available at the time the estimate was made, a correction of an accounting error is recognized.

Imputed Interest The proper valuation of a receivable is the present value of future payments to be received, determined by using an interest rate commensurate with the risks involved at the date of the receivable's creation. (ASC 310-10-30-3) In many situations the interest rate commensurate with the risks involved is the rate stated in the agreement between the payee and the debtor. However, if the receivable is noninterest-bearing or if the rate stated in the agreement is not indicative of the market rate for a debtor of similar creditworthiness under similar terms, interest is imputed at the market rate. ASC 835-30 specifies when and how interest is to be imputed when the receivable is noninterest-bearing or the stated rate on the receivable is not reasonable.

Lending and Financing Activities, Including Trade Receivables Receivables generally arise from extending credit to others.

If the reporting entity has the intent and ability to hold trade receivables or loans for the foreseeable future or until maturity or payoff, those receivables are reported in the statement of financial position at their outstanding principal (face) amounts less any write-offs and allowance for uncollectible receivables or at fair value. Loans originated by the reporting entity are reported net of deferred fees or costs of originating them, and purchased loans are reported net of any unamortized premium or discount. If a decision has been made to sell loans, those loans are transferred to a held-for-sale category on the statement of financial position and reported at the lower of cost or fair value. Any amount by which cost exceeds fair value is accounted for as a valuation allowance.

When a trade receivable or loan is deemed uncollectible, the balance is written off against the allowance for uncollectible receivables. Recoveries of loans and trade receivables that were previously written off are recorded when received—either by a credit directly to earnings or by a credit to the allowance for uncollectible receivables.

ASC 310-10-25 also includes standards for recognizing fees related to receivables. Delinquency fees are recognized when chargeable, provided that collectibility is reasonably assured. Prepayment fees are not recognized until prepayments have occurred. Rebates of finance charges due because payments are made earlier than required are recognized when the receivables are prepaid and are accounted for as adjustments to interest income. (ASC 310-10-25-11 through 25-13)

Example of Delinquency Fees, Prepayment Fees, and Rebates

The DitchWay Company sells a ditch-digging machine called the DitchMade that contractors use to lay utility lines and pipes. DitchWay invoices customers a standard monthly fee for two years, after which they receive title to their DitchMade machines. The DitchMade machine is patent-protected and unique, so contractors must purchase from DitchWay. If a contractor makes a late payment, DitchWay bills them a $150 late fee. Since DitchWay can withhold title to the equipment if all fees are not received, the collection of these fees is reasonably assured. DitchWay's entry to record a late fee follows:

Accounts receivable	150	
Income—delinquency fees		150

One contractor enters bankruptcy proceedings. It has accumulated $450 of unpaid delinquency fees by the time it enters bankruptcy. DitchWay uses the following entry to eliminate the fees from its accounts receivable:

Bad debt allowance	450	
Accounts receivable		450

DitchWay's sale agreement recognizes that its billing schedule is essentially a series of loan payments with an implied interest rate of 12%. About 20% of all contractors obtain better financing elsewhere and prepay their invoices in order to reduce the interest payment. DitchWay charges a flat $500 prepayment fee when a prepayment occurs. Though the proportion of early payments is predictable, DitchWay cannot recognize prepayment fees until each prepayment actually occurs. One contractor makes a prepayment, so DitchWay records the receivable for the prepayment fee with the following entry:

Accounts receivable	500	
Income—prepayment fees		500

The DitchWay sales agreement also states that, when a contractor prepays an invoice, it should pay the full amount of the invoice, even if paid early, and DitchWay will rebate the unearned portion of the interest expense associated with the early payment. In one case, a contractor prepays a single $2,500 invoice for which the original sales entry was as follows:

Accounts receivable	2,500	
Interest income		450
Revenue		2,050

The amount of interest to be rebated back to the contractor is $225, which DitchWay records with the following entry:

Interest income—rebated	225	
Cash		225

In this case, the use of the contra account, interest income—rebated, provides the reporting entity with greater control and information for management purposes. However, the debit could be made directly to interest income if these enhancements are not useful.

Pledging, Assigning, and Factoring Receivables

An organization can alter the timing of cash flows resulting from sales to its customers by using its accounts receivable as collateral for borrowings or by selling the receivables outright. A wide variety of arrangements can be structured by the borrower and lender, but the most common are pledging, assignment, and factoring.

Pledging Accounts receivable pledging is an agreement in which accounts receivable are used as collateral for loans. The customers whose accounts have been pledged are not aware of this event, and their payments are still remitted to the original entity to which the debt was owed. The pledged accounts merely serve as security to the lender, giving comfort that sufficient assets exist to generate cash flows adequate in amount and timing to repay the debt. However, the debt is paid by the borrower whether or not the pledged receivables are collected and whether or not the pattern of their collection matches the payments due on the debt.

Assignment Accounts receivable assignment is a more formalized transfer of the receivables to the lending institution. The lender investigates the specific receivables that are being proposed for assignment and will approve those that it deems worthy as collateral. Usually customers are not aware that their accounts have been assigned and they continue to forward their payments to the original obligee (the borrowing entity). In some cases, the assignment agreement requires that collection proceeds be immediately delivered to the lender. The borrower is, however, the primary obligor of the debt and is required to make timely payment on the debt whether or not the receivables are collected as anticipated. The borrowing is with recourse, and the general credit of the borrower is pledged to the payment of the debt.

Since the lender knows that not all the receivables will be collected on a timely basis by the borrower, only a fraction of the face value of the receivables will be advanced as a loan to the borrower. Typically, this amount ranges from 70 to 90%, depending upon the credit history and collection experience of the borrower.

Assigned accounts receivable remain the assets of the borrower and continue to be presented in its financial statements, with appropriate disclosure. Prepaid finance charges would be recorded as a prepaid expense and amortized to expense over the period to which the charges apply.

In the typical case involving the assignment of receivables, the borrower retains control of the receivables, and it is clear that the transaction is a secured borrowing rather than a sale. If it is unclear whether the borrower has retained control of the receivables, a determination must be made as to whether to account for the transfer as a sale or as a secured borrowing. Making that determination is discussed in the chapter on ASC 860, *Transfers of Financial Assets under ASC 860.*

Factoring Accounts receivable factoring traditionally involves the outright sale of receivables to a finance company known as a factor. These arrangements involve (1) notification to the customer to remit future payments to the factor and (2) the transfer of receivables to the factor without recourse to the transferor. The factor assumes the risk of an inability to collect. Thus, once a factoring arrangement is completed, the transferor has no further involvement with the accounts, except for a return of merchandise.

In its simplest form, the receivables are sold and the difference between the cash received and the carrying value is recognized as a gain or loss.

The classic factoring arrangement provides two financial services to the business:

1. It permits the reporting entity to obtain cash earlier than waiting for customers to pay, and
2. It transfers the risk of bad debts to the factor.

The factor is compensated for each of these services. Interest is charged based on the anticipated length of time between the date the factoring arrangement is consummated and the expected collection date of the receivables sold. A fee is charged based upon the factor's anticipated bad debt losses.

Some companies factor receivables as a means of transferring bad debt risk, but leave the cash on deposit with the factor until the weighted-average due date of the receivables, thereby avoiding interest charges. This arrangement is still referred to as factoring, since the customer receivables have been sold. However, the borrowing entity does not receive cash but instead records a new receivable, usually captioned "Due from Factor." This receivable, in contrast to the original customer receivables, is essentially without risk and is presented in the statement of financial position without a deduction for estimated uncollectible receivables.

Merchandise returns are normally the responsibility of the transferor, who must then make the appropriate settlement with the factor. To protect against the possibility that merchandise returns will diminish the total of receivables to be collected, a factor will frequently advance only a portion of the face amount of the factored receivables (less any interest and factoring fee deductions). The factor will retain a certain fraction of the total proceeds relating to the portion of sales that are anticipated to be returned by customers. This sum is known as the factor's *hold-back*. When merchandise is returned to the transferor, an entry is made off-setting the receivable from the factor. At the end of the return privilege period, any remaining holdback will become due and payable to the transferor.

Example of Accounting for the Factoring of Receivables without Recourse

1. Thirsty Corp. enters into an agreement with Rich Company to sell a group of its receivables without recourse. The receivables have a total face value of $200,000 (against which a 5% allowance had been recorded). The factor will charge 20% interest computed on the weighted-average time to maturity of the receivables of 36 days plus a 3% fee. A 5% holdback will also be retained.
2. Thirsty's customers return for credit $4,800 of merchandise.
3. The customer return privilege period expires and the remaining holdback is paid to the transferor.

The entries required are as follows:

1. Cash	180,055	
Allowance for bad debts (200,000 × .05)	10,000	
Interest expense (or prepaid) (200,000 × .20 × 36/365)	3,945	
Factoring fee (200,000 × .03)	6,000	
Factor's holdback receivable [$10,000/($10,000+ $190,000) × $190,000]	9,500	
Loss on sale of receivables	500	
Bad debts expense		10,000
Accounts receivable		200,000

The interest expense, factor's fee, and loss can be combined into a $10,445 charge to loss on the sale of receivables.

2. Sales returns and allowances	4,800	
Factor's holdback receivable		4,800
3. Cash	5,200	
Factor's holdback receivable		4,700
Loss on sale of receivables		500

The factor's holdback receivable recorded by the seller is required by ASC 860 to be an allocation of the carrying value of the receivables ($190,000) between the assets sold (the receivables) and the assets retained (the holdback) based on their relative fair values at the date of the factoring agreement. The factor holds back 5% of the face value ($200,000) for a total of $10,000. Upon settlement the loss or gain recorded at the origination of the factoring arrangement needs to be adjusted because the factor pays the remaining holdback of $5,200 ($10,000 holdback – $4,800 returns) in settlement of an asset with a carrying value of $4,700 ($9,500 – $4,800).

Factoring results in a transfer of title to the factored receivables. Where there is a no recourse provision or other continuing involvement with the receivables, the removal of the receivables from the borrower's statement of financial position is clearly warranted.

Another variation is known as factoring with recourse. Accounting for factoring with recourse requires a determination of whether the transfer is a sale or a secured borrowing. That determination is made by applying ASC 860. See the chapter on ASC 860 for more information.

Subsequent Measurement

Technical Alert – ASU 2016-13 Note: The section in ASC 310-10-35 on subsequent measurement of specific types of receivables remains in effect, with some changes, after implementation of ASU 2016-13. The guidance in ASC 310 on impairment of loans and receivables is superseded upon implementation of ASU 2016-13, including paragraphs ASC 310-10-35-1 through 35-43. Those paragraphs apply to:

- Loan impairments
- Credit losses for loans and trade receivables
- Credit losses for certain standby letters of credit and certain loan commitments
- Subsequent measurement of specific types of receivables.
  (ASC 310-10-35-1)

The superseded guidance addresses the impairment concepts related to:

- All receivables and points to the guidance in ASC 450-20, and
- Loans identified for evaluation and are individually deemed to be impaired.
  (ASC 310-10-35-3)

The information on subsequent measurement that follows reflects the guidance in effect before the implementation of ASU 2016-13, with references to the ASU 2016-13 changes. For more information and an example of the guidance after implementation of ASU 2016-13, see the Chapter on ASC 326.

Technical Alert – ASU 2019-04 As noted earlier in this chapter, in April 2019, the FASB issued ASU 2019-04 to clarify certain questions regarding subsequent measurement of loans. Those changes are noted below.

Impairment of Loans and Receivables

ASC 310-10-35 applies to all creditors and to all loans except:

- Large groups of similar small balance loans that are collectively evaluated for impairment
- Loans measured at fair value or lower of cost or fair value.
- Leases ASC 840, *Leases*. (This bullet is superseded upon adoption of ASU 2016-02 on *Leases*.)
- ASC 320 debt securities.
  (ASC 310-10-35-13)

If it is probable that a creditor will not collect all amounts (principal and interest) owed to the degree specified in the loan agreement, a loan is considered impaired. (ASC 310-10-35-16) A delay does not impair the loan if the creditor collects all amounts due, including interest accrued during the delay, at the contractual rate.

Measurement An impaired loan can be measured on a loan-by-loan basis or aggregated with other loans with common risk factors. The impaired loan can be measured in any of the following ways:

- Present value of expected future cash flows using the loan's original effective interest rate (the contractual interest rate adjusted for premium or discount and net deferred loan costs or fees at acquisition or origination).
- Loan's observable market price.
- Fair value of the collateral if the loan is collateral dependent, that is, repayment is expected to be provided by the collateral. (If this method is used, ASC 820 on fair value applies.) (ASC 310-10-35-22)

When foreclosure becomes probable, the creditor must measure impairment based on the fair value of the collateral. This must be done so that the impairment is not delayed until actual impairment occurs. (ASC 310-10-35-32)

Other measurement considerations include:

- Costs to sell, on a discounted basis, if they will reduce cash flows to satisfy the loan, (ASC 310-10-35-24)
- Creation of or adjustment to a valuation allowance account with the offset to bad-debt expense if the recorded investment is greater than:
  - The impaired loan measurement,
  - The observable market price of the loan, or
  - The fair value of the collateral,
- If the contractual interest rate varies based on changes in an independent factor, the creditor can choose between:

  a. Calculating the effective interest on the factor as it changes over the loan's life, or
  b. Calculating the effective interest as fixed at the rate in effect at the date of impairment. (ASC 310-10-35-25)

- Cash flow estimates should be the creditors' best estimate based on reasonable and supportable assumptions. (ASC 310-10-35-26)

The choice must be consistently applied. Projections of factor changes should not be made. (ASC 310-10-35-28)

After impairment, creditors should use the methods described above to record, measure, and present impairment. If the existing policy results in a recorded investment less than fair value, no additional impairment is recognized. (ASC 310-10-35-37)

Significant changes occurring in measurement values require recalculation and adjustment of the valuation allowance. Net carrying amount of the loan should not exceed the recorded investment. (ASC 310-10-35-38)

Subsequent Measurement for Specific Types of Receivables

The guidance for subsequent measurement of receivables remains in effect after the implementation of ASU 2016-13, with some changes, for these specific types of receivables:

- Financial assets subject to prepayment
- Standby commitments to purchase loans
- Loans and trade receivables not held for sale

- Nonmortgage loans held for sale
- Loans not previously held for sale
- Amortization of discount or premium on notes
- Premiums allocated to loans purchased in a credit card portfolio
- Hedged portfolios of loans
- Interest income (This bullet is added by ASU 2016-13)
  (ASC 310-10-35-44)

Financial Assets Subject to Prepayment These should be measured like investments in available for sale or trading debt securities. Instruments within the scope of ASC 815-10-15 are an exception to this treatment. (ASC 310-10-35-45)

Standby Commitments to Purchase Loans If the standby commitment is accounted for as a written put option as per ASC 310-10-25-6, entities should subsequently account for it at the greater of the initial standby commitment fee or the fair value of the written put options. Unrealized gains or losses should be accounted for in current operations. (ASC 310-10-35-46) Note: Upon implementation of ASU 2016-13, in this paragraph, "accounted for as a written put option" changes to "recorded as the amount of the option."

Loans and Trade Receivables Not Held for Sale If management has the intent and ability to hold the loan or trade receivable for the foreseeable future or until maturity or payoff, it should be reported in the balance sheet at outstanding principal adjusted for write offs, allowances, deferred fees or costs on originated loans, and unamortized premiums or discounts. (ASC 310-10-35-47) Note that upon implementation of ASU 2019-04, the heading of this paragraph deletes "Loans and," the basis for reporting changes to amortized cost basis, and entities are referred to ASC 326-10 for guidance on financial instruments measured at amortized cost basis.

Nonmortgage Loans Not Held for Sale ASU 2019-04 clarifies that a nonmortgage loan with the intent to hold for the foreseeable future or until maturity or payoff should be reported at amortized cost basis. Entities are referred to ASC 326-10 for guidance on financial instruments measured at amortized cost basis. (ASC 310-10-35-47A)

Nonmortgage Loans Held for Sale Nonmortgage loans held for sale are reported at the lower of cost or fair value. After the implementation of ASU 2016-13, this language changes to lower of amortized cost basis or fair value. ASU 2019-04 clarifies that the amount by which the amortized cost basis exceeds fair value is accounted for as valuation allowance and changes in the valuation allowance should be reflected in net income in the period of change. (ASC 310- 10-35-48)

Transfers of Nonmortgage Loans between Classifications ASU 2019-04 clarifies that if a nonmortgage loan is transferred from the not-for-sale classification to the held-for-sale classification, the entity should reverse any allowance for credit losses previously recorded at the transfer date. The nonmortgage loan is then transferred at its amortized cost basis. This basis is reduced by any amounts previously written off, but excludes an allowance for credit losses. Next the entity determines if a valuation allowance is needed by following the guidance in ASC 310-10. (ASC 310-10-35-48A)

If a nonmortgage loan is transferred from the held-for-sale to not-held-for-sale, the entity should reverse any valuation allowance previously recorded on the transfer date. The nonmortgage loan is then transferred at its amortized cost basis. This basis is reduced by any amounts previously written off, but excludes an allowance for credit losses. Next the entity determines if a valuation allowance is needed by following the guidance in ASC 310-10. (ASC 310-10-35-48B)

Loans Not Previously Held for Sale When management decides to sell loans, those loans should be transferred to the held-for-sale classification and carried at the lower of cost or fair value. This paragraph is superseded upon implementation of ASU 2016-13. (ASC 310-10-35-49)

Amortization of Discount or Premium on Notes Practitioners should look to ASC 835-for guidance on this item. (ASC 310-10-35-50)

Premiums Allocated to Loans Purchased in a Credit Card Portfolio Management should amortize, over the life of the loan, the premium allocated to loans acquired when the entity purchased a credit card portfolio at an amount that exceeds the sum of the amounts due under the credit card receivables. (ASC 310-10-35-52)

Hedged Portfolios of Loans Entities should look to ASC 815-20-55 for guidance on hedges associated with portfolios of loans or specific loan cash flows. (ASC 310-10-35-52)

Interest Income This guidance is effective upon implementation of ASU 2016-13. If an entity recognizes per ASC 326 interest income on purchased financial assets with credit deterioration, the entity should not recognize the discount embedded in the purchase price attribution of the acquirer's assessment of expected credit losses at the date of acquisition as interest income. The noncredit-related interest discount or premium should be accreted or amortized as interest income. (ASC 310-10-35-53B)

Recognition of income on purchased financial assets with credit deterioration depends on having a reasonable expectation about the amount expected to be collected. Subsequent to purchase, an entity is not prohibited from placing financial assets on nonaccrual status. Management cannot, however, place a financial asset on nonaccrual to manipulate income by circumventing recognition of a credit loss. When the entity acquires the financial asset for the rewards of ownership of the underlying collateral, accrual of income is not appropriate. Interest income must not be recognized to the extent that the net investment in the financial asset would increase to an amount greater than the payoff amount. (ASC 3120-10-35-53C)

ASC 310-20, *Nonrefundable Fees and Other Costs*

Scope and Scope Exceptions

Transactions The following transactions are included in ASC 315-20:

- Recognition and the balance sheet classification of nonrefundable fees and costs associated with lending activities;
- Accounting for discounts, premiums, and commitment fees associated with the purchase of loans and other debt securities; and
- Loans designated as a hedged item in a fair value hedge ASC 815 (ASC 310-20-15-2)

Specifically excluded from ASC 310-20 guidance are:

- Loan origination or commitment fees that are refundable; however, the guidance does apply when such fees subsequently become nonrefundable.
- Costs that are incurred by the lender in transactions with independent third parties if the lender bills those costs directly to the borrower.
- Nonrefundable fees and costs associated with originating or acquiring loans that are carried at fair value if the changes in fair value are included in earnings of a business entity or change in net assets of a not-for-profit entity (NFP). The exclusion provided in this paragraph and the preceding paragraph applies to nonrefundable fees and costs associated

with originating loans that are reported at fair value and premiums or discounts associated with acquiring loans that are reported at fair value. Loans that are reported at cost or the lower of cost[4] or fair value, loans or debt securities reported at fair value with changes in fair value reported in other comprehensive income (includes financial assets subject to prepayment as defined in paragraph 860-20-35-2, and debt securities classified as available-for-sale under Topic 320), and loans that have a market interest rate, or adjust to a market interest rate, are not considered to be loans carried at fair value.

- Fees and costs related to a commitment to originate, sell, or purchase loans that is accounted for as a derivative instrument under Subtopic 815-10.
- Fees and costs related to a standby commitment to purchase loans if the settlement date of that commitment is not within a reasonable period or the entity does not have the intent and ability to accept delivery without selling assets. For guidance on fees and costs related to such a commitment, see paragraph 310-10-30-7. (ASC 310-20-15-3)

The following table outlines the applicability of this Subtopic to various types of assets.

Types of Assets	Basis of Accounting	Does ASC 310-20 Apply?
Loans or debt securities held in an investment portfolio	Historical or amortized cost basis	Yes
Loans held for sale	Lower of cost or when ASC 2016-13 is implemented amortized cost basis or fair value	Yes
Loans or debt securities held in trading securities by certain financial institutions	Fair value, changes in value are included in earnings	No
Loans or debt securities, available for sale	Fair value, changes in value reported in OCI	Yes
ASC 310-20-15-4)		

Loan Origination Fees These fees should be deferred and recognized over the life of the loan as an adjustment of interest income. (ASC 310-20-25-2) If there are any related direct loan origination costs, the origination fees and origination costs should be netted, and only the net amount should be deferred and amortized via the interest method. Origination costs include those incremental costs such as credit checks and security arrangements, among others, pertaining to a specific loan.

The only exception to the foregoing rule would be in the instance of certain loans that also qualify as debt instruments under ASC 320. For those carried in the "trading securities" portfolio, related loan origination fees should be charged to expense when incurred; the requirement that these be carried at fair value would make adding these costs to the asset carrying amounts a useless exercise.

[4] Upon implementation of ASU 2016-13, "cost" becomes "amortized cost basis."

Example of a Loan Origination Fee

Debtor Corp. wishes to take out a loan with Klein Bank for the purchase of new machinery. The fair value of the machinery is $614,457. The loan is for ten years, designed to give Klein an implicit return of 10% on the loan. The annual payment is calculated as follows:

$$\text{Annual payment} = \frac{\$614,457}{PV^{10},10\%} = \frac{614,457}{6.14457} = \$100,000$$

Unearned interest on the loan would be $385,543 [(10 × $100,000) – $614,457].

Klein also is to receive a "nonrefundable origination fee" of $50,000. Klein incurred $20,000 of direct origination costs (for credit checks, etc.). Thus, Klein has *net* nonrefundable origination fees of $30,000. The new net investment in the loan is calculated below.

Gross investment in loan (10 × $100,000)	$1,000,000
Less: Unamortized net nonrefundable origination fees	(30,000)
	970,000
Less: Unearned interest income (from above)	385,543
Net investment in loan	$ 584,457

The new net investment in the loan can be used to find the new implicit interest rate.

$$\frac{100,000}{(1+i)^1} + \frac{100,000}{(1+i)^2} + \ldots + \frac{100,000}{(1+i)^{10}}$$

$$= 584,457$$

where i = implicit rate

Thus, the implicit interest rate is 11.002%. The amortization table for the first three years is set up as follows:

(a) *Loan payments*	*(b)* *Reduction in unearned interest*	*(c)* *Interest revenue (PV × implicit rate of 11.002%)*	*(d)* *Reduction in net orig. fees (c–b)*	*(e)* *Reduction in PV of net invest (a–c)*	*(f)* *PV of net loan investment*
					$584,457
$100,000	$61,446*	$64,302	$2,856	$35,689	548,759
100,000	57,590**	60,374	2,784	39,626	509,133
100,000	53,349***	56,015	2,666	43,985	465,148

* ($614,457 × 10%) = $61,446

** [$614,457 – ($100,000 – $61,446)] × 10% = $57,590

*** [$575,900 – ($100,000 – $57,590)] × 10% = $53,349

Commitment Fees and Costs Often fees are received in advance in exchange for a commitment to originate or purchase a loan. These fees should be deferred and recognized upon exercise of the commitment as an adjustment of interest income over the life of the loan (ASC 310-20-35-2), as in Example 1 for origination costs and fees. If a commitment expires unexercised, the fees should be recognized as income upon expiration. (ASC 310-20-35-3)

As with loan origination fees and costs, if both commitment fees are received and commitment costs are incurred relating to a commitment to originate or purchase a loan, the net amount of fees or costs should be deferred and recognized over the life of the loan. (ASC 310-20-25-12)

If there is a remote possibility of exercise, the commitment fees may be recognized on a straight-line basis over the commitment period as "service fee income." If there is a subsequent exercise, the unamortized fees at the date of exercise should be recognized over the life of the loan as an adjustment of interest income, as in the previous example. (ASC 310-20-35-3a)

In certain cases, commitment fees are determined retroactively as a percentage of available lines of credit. If the commitment fee percentage is nominal in relation to the stated rate on the related borrowing, with the borrowing earning the market rate of interest, the fees shall be recognized in income as of the determination date. (ASC 310-20-35-3b)

Example of a Commitment Fee

Glass Corp. has a $2 million, 10% line of credit outstanding with Ritter Bank. Ritter charges its annual commitment fee as 0.1% of any available balance as of the end of the prior period. Ritter will report $2,000 ($2 million × 0.1%) as service fee income in its current income statement.

Loan Refinancing or Restructuring That Is Not a TDR When the terms of a refinanced/restructured loan are as favorable to the lender as the terms for loans to customers with similar risks who are not in a troubled debt restructuring, the refinanced loan is treated as a new loan, and all prior fees of the old loan are recognized in interest income when the new loan is made. This condition is met if:

- The new loan's effective yield at least equals the effective yield for similar loans, and
- Modifications of the original debt are more than minor.
  (ASC 310-20-35-9)

When the above situation is not satisfied, the fees or costs from the old loan become part of the net investment in the new loan.

If the refinancing or restructuring does not meet the conditions above in ASC 310-20-35-9 or if the modifications are minor, the unamortized net fees or costs of the original loan and any prepayment fees are carried forward as part of the net investment in the loan. Thus, the investment in the new loan consists of:

- The remaining net investment in the original loan,
- Additional amounts loaned,
- Fees received, and
- Direct loan origination costs associated with the refinancing or restructuring.
  (ASC 310-20-35-10)

A modification of debt is more than minor if the difference between the present value of the cash flows under the new terms is 10% or more different than the present value of the remaining cash flows under the original debt instrument. If less than 10%, the debtor should consider specific facts and circumnstances to determine if the modification is more than minor. (ASC 310-20-35-11)

Example of a Refinanced Loan—Favorable Terms: Origination Fees

Jeffrey Bank refinanced a loan receivable to $1,000,000, at 10% interest, with annual interest receipts for ten years. Jeffrey's "normal" loan in its portfolio to debtors with similar risks is for

$500,000 at 9% interest for five years. Jeffrey had loan origination fees from the original loan of $20,000. These fees are recognized in income *immediately* because the terms of the restructuring are as favorable to Jeffrey as a loan to another debtor with similar risks.

Example of a Refinanced Loan—Unfavorable Terms: Origination Fees

Assume the same facts as in Example 3 except that the refinanced terms are $500,000 principal, 7% interest for three years. Since the terms are not as favorable to Jeffrey as a loan to another debtor with similar risks, the $20,000 origination fees become part of the new investment in the loan and recognized in interest income over the life of the new loan, as in Example 1.

Purchase of a Loan or Group of Loans Fees paid or fees received when purchasing a loan or group of loans should normally be considered part of the initial investment, to be recognized in income over the lives of the loans. (ASC 310-20-35-15) However, if the loans qualify as debt securities under ASC 320 and are held in the lender's "trading securities" portfolio, these fees should be reported in income when paid or received, and not added to the cost of the loans.

Estimating Principal Prepayments In calculating the constant effective yield necessary to apply the interest method, the entity should use the loan's payment terms. If the entity holds a large number of similar loans with prepayment probable and reasonably estimable timing and amounts, the entity may consider estimating future payments when calculating the yield. (ASC 310-20-35-26)

Investors must amortize the purchase premium of a callable debt security to the first call date. This provides the following benefits:

- Better aligns interest income recognition with market participant price assumptions
- Affects interest income and gain or loss when the debt is called
- If the security is not called at first call date, resets the effective yield.
  (ASC 310-20-35-33)

Example

ABC Company purchases a bond for $104, with a par of $100, coupon rate of 5%, ten years to maturity, and callable five years before maturity. Under extant guidance, the $4 premium would be amortized over ten years. This would result in cumulative amortization of $1.78 at the first call date and recognition of a $2.22 loss if the call was exercised. Under the ASU, the premium is amortized over five years. This would result in no loss related to the premium recognized if the call was exercised at the first call date. If the call was not exercised, then ABC would reset the effective yield based on the current amortized cost and the future payment terms.

Special Arrangements Often lenders provide demand loans (loans with no scheduled payment terms). In this case, any net fees or costs should be recognized on a straight-line basis over a period determined by mutual agreement of the parties, usually over the estimated length of the loan.

Under a revolving line of credit, any qualifying costs are recognized in income on a straight-line basis over the period that the line of credit is active. (ASC 310-10-55-3) If the line of credit is terminated due to the borrower's full payment, any unamortized net fees or costs are recognized in income.

Example of a Line of Credit—Origination Fee

Green Bank received $50,000 as a nonrefundable origination fee on a $2 million demand loan. Green's loan dictates that any fees are to be amortized over a period of ten years. Therefore, $5,000 (= $50,000 × 1/10) of origination fees will be recognized as an addition to interest income each year for the next ten years.

Other Lending-Related Costs Some ancillary costs do not qualify for deferral and should be expensed. The following exhibit lists some of those costs and others that do qualify for deferral.

Exhibit—Other Lending-Related Costs Incurred by Lender

Cost	Treatment
Advertising	Expense as incurred
Soliciting potential borrowers	Expense as incurred
Servicing existing loans	Expense as incurred
Establishing and monitoring credit policies, supervision, and administration	Expense as incurred
(ASC 320-20-25-3)	
Software for loan processing and origination	Expense as incurred
(ASC 320-20-25-4)	
Fees paid to service loans for loan processing and origination	Expense as incurred
(ASC 320-20-25-5)	
Employee bonuses related to loan origination activities	Portions directly related are deferrable
(ASC 320-20-25-6)	
Commission-based compensation directly related to time spent	Deferrable
Allocation of total compensation between origination and other activities so that costs associated with lending activities deferred for completed loans	Deferrable
(ASC 320-20-25-7)	

ASC 310-30, *Certain Loans and Debt Securities Acquired with Deteriorated Credit Quality*[5]

Scope and Scope Exceptions This subtopic applies to loans acquired by completion of a transfer for which it is probable at the time of acquisition that the new investor will not be able to collect all the contractually required payments. The loans have evidence of deterioration of credit quality since their origination. ASC 310-30-15-2 excludes the following transactions from ASC 310-30 guidance:

- Loans that are measured at fair value if all changes in fair value are included in earnings or, for an NFP, loans that are measured at fair value if all changes in fair value are included in the statement of activities and included in the performance indicator if a performance indicator is presented. Examples include those loans classified as trading securities under Topic 320 and Subtopic 948-310.

[5] ASC 310-30 is superseded upon implementation of ASU 2016-13. Financial assets for which this guidance has been applied currently should look to the new guidance in ASU 2016-13 on PCD asset.

- Mortgage loans classified as held for sale under paragraph 948-310-35-1.
- Leases as defined in Topic 840. Only contracts that are classified by the purchaser as leases under that topic meet this exclusion. The distinction between purchasing a lease and purchasing a stream of cash flows must be drawn to determine applicability of this Section. (This bullet is superseded by ASU 2016-02.)
- Loans acquired in a business combination accounted for at historical cost, including business combinations of two or more NFPs, the acquisition of a for-profit business entity by an NFP, and combinations of two or more mutual entities.
- Loans held by liquidating banks (financial reporting by liquidating banks is discussed in Topic 942).
- Revolving credit agreements, such as credit cards and home equity loans, if at the acquisition date the borrower has revolving privileges.
- Loans that are a transferor's interests (see Subtopic 325-40).

ASC 310-30-15-4 further excludes the following transactions and activities:

- Loans that are derivative instruments subject to the requirements of Topic 815. If a loan would otherwise be in the scope of this paragraph of this Section and has within it an embedded derivative that is subject to that topic, the host instrument (as described in that topic) remains within the scope of this paragraph of this Section if it satisfies the conditions in this paragraph.
- Loans for which it is possible, but not probable, that the investor will be unable to collect all amounts due according to the contractual terms of the loan.
- Situations in which credit is still being offered, and the entire relationship is excluded if, at the acquisition date, the borrower has revolving privileges. This scope exclusion is appropriate because lenders generally will not continue to make credit available to borrowers from whom it is probable that the lender will not collect all contractually required payments receivable.

Overview ASC 310-30 requires the preparer to differentiate between securities investments acquired directly from the issuer and those obtained on the secondary market. It imposes accounting requirements for debt instruments acquired in transfers when the purchase price reflects a change in the debtor's credit standing since the original issuance of the instrument. This guidance is applicable to all acquirers of loans or debt securities (bonds, securitized loans, etc.), not merely financial institutions, although fewer commercial or industrial entities would tend to be making such purchases.

Market conditions Debt instruments (whole loans or loan participations, as well as securities) will generally trade in the secondary market at prices that vary from the amount at which they were issued originally. The prices may be higher or lower than the face amount, depending on the confluence of several factors. Because interest rates change almost continually, it is rare that market rates will correspond to the nominal rate on any given loan or debt security, even if the loan or instrument originally carried a market yield. Furthermore, many instruments are issued at premiums or discounts at inception, for various reasons. In the secondary market, prices will be adjusted continually to reflect current market conditions related to the loan's (or security's) coupon rate and the credit standing of the issuer/borrower, within the context of market rates of interest and other factors. If current rates are higher than the instrument's coupon (i.e., contractual) rate, it will trade at a discount from par value, while if the current rates are below the coupon rate, it will sell for a premium, if other variables are held constant.

Changes in creditworthiness Furthermore, the borrower's creditworthiness may have changed since the loan was originated or the debt instrument was issued. This also impacts the price at which the loan or security will trade. A decline in credit standing results in a drop in value, while an improvement in credit standing causes a rise in the value of the entity's debt. Creditworthiness pertains to the risk of default, and a number of well-regarded private sector companies closely monitor the outstanding debt of publicly held and private corporations and various governmental agencies and political subdivisions. Examples of rating agencies or measures are Moody's, Standard & Poor's, and Fitch's for publicly held companies and the Fair Isaac credit score (FICO) for private companies.

Loans or debt securities may trade in the secondary market at their original issuance prices as the coincidental result of offsetting changes in the variables noted above. Thus, market yields may have declined—which would cause a rise in the price of fixed coupon debt instruments, but concurrently the issuer's creditworthiness may have been downgraded by rating agencies, which would cause the price of the debt to decline. In tandem, the credit downgrade may have essentially negated the price increase from lower market interest rates. In applying ASC 310-30, entities must:

- Refer to the price at which the loan or security has been transferred, in relation to its "par" or original issuance price, and
- Examine whether there is information to suggest that there has been a change in the issuer's credit quality since inception of the obligation.

ASC 310-30 only applies if there has been a change in the issuer's credit quality since the inception of the debt.

ASC 310-30 in Greater Detail The purpose of ASC 310-30 is to prescribe the accounting for debt instruments (comprising most loans and debt securities, with certain exceptions) which are acquired via a transfer (i.e., in the secondary market) and which have been affected by changes in credit quality. The guidance requires that the accretable yield be determined. The accretable yield is derived from:

- The relationship between the future cash flows expected to be collected, and
- The price paid by the investor for the acquired instrument.

The accretable yield is distinguished from the nonaccretable difference, which is generally the excess of the total of contractual future cash flows over the expected cash flows.

Neither the accretable yield nor the nonaccretable difference can be displayed in the financial statements. For example, consider a loan that contractually is obligated to pay a total of $85,000 in future interest and principal, but which can be purchased for $50,00 and is expected to provide future cash flows of only $73,500. The $23,500 ($73,500 – 50,000) spread between the purchase price and the undiscounted expected future cash flows is the accretable yield. The further $11,500 ($85,000 – 73,500) spread between expected and contractual cash flows, however, is the nonaccretable difference, which cannot be given accounting recognition under ASC 310-30. That is, the loan (which is an investment in the hands of the transferee) cannot be recorded or displayed at the higher $85,000 amount, with a contra account or valuation allowance pertaining to the pretransfer estimated uncollectible amount being reported. Instead, the purchase cost, $50,000, must be the initial representation of this acquired asset, which is later increased by virtue of the accretion of yield (and reduced by collections).

Upon acquisition, the effective yield is computed based on the expected pattern (i.e., timings and amounts) of future cash flows, so that interest can be accreted on the level-yield basis (a constant rate on a changing base). Over the holding term of the investment, expected cash flows may change. They may:

- Decline due to perceived impairment, or
- Increase due to upgrading of creditworthiness.

The accounting for such changes varies, with decreases in expectations triggering immediate impairment loss recognition, while increases will generally be reported prospectively over the holding period of the instrument. The precise accounting for changes in expected future cash flows also depends, per ASC 310-30, on whether the instrument is accounted for as a:

- Loan (under ASC 310-30), or
- A debt security (under ASC 320).

Under ASC 310-30, reductions in expected future cash flows trigger the recognition of a loss in the current reporting period.

Accounting for Investments in Loans with Deteriorated Credit Quality Acquired by Transfer.

Initial measurement Loans acquired by transfer (i.e., in the secondary market) are recorded initially at acquisition cost. If the acquisition price differs from the par or face amount (i.e., there is a premium or a discount), the effective yield has to be computed and used to accrete the discount (or, if a premium, amortize it) over the expected term of the instrument. The estimation of the amounts of expected future cash flows, and the timing of those cash flows, is obviously a matter of some complexity and inevitable subjectivity. For example, if payments from a credit-impaired obligor are expected to be made, say, fifteen days late on average, this will impact the computed effective yield on the loan and is to be given explicit consideration in ascertaining the effective yield, subject to the usual materiality threshold concerns. The calculation of accretable yield is made at the acquisition date, but it may later have to be adjusted as expectations regarding future cash flow amounts change. Subsequent reduced expectations of cash flows will result in the recognition of impairment, while expectations of enhanced or improved cash flows may result in reversal of previously recognized impairment (if any), or increased effective yield over the instrument's remaining holding period.

Subsequent measurement—loans not accounted for as a debt security At the date of transfer, if there is evidence of a decline in creditworthiness since the instrument's inception, such that the full amount of contractual cash flows will not be received, the provisions of ASC 310-30 must be applied. In this context, the loan is considered impaired for purposes of applying ASC 450 or, if applicable, ASC 310-10. To apply the guidance in ASC 310-10-35-10 through 35-11, the investor must meet certain criteria. It must be unable to collect all cash flows expected to be collected by the investor plus any additional cash flows expected to collected arising from a change in estimate after acquisition.

In such cases, the investor must estimate cash flows to be received, and accrete the initial carrying amount to that amount, rather than to the gross amount of future contractual cash flows. An uncertainty regarding future cash flows that suggests only a possible shortfall versus contractual amounts owed would not qualify for the accounting in Subtopic ASC 310-30. In such a situation, there would be disclosure of reasonably possible contingent losses, and if at a later date the loss is deemed to have become probable, a loss accrual would be recognized per ASC 450 as a change in estimate. (ASC 310-30-35-10)

Example—Loan Acquired with Deteriorated Credit Quality at Transfer

Assume that Investor Co. acquires a loan with a remaining principal balance of $650,000 on January 1, 20X1. The contractual terms of the loan call for interest-only payments, at 9%, annually through December 31, 20X5, at which time the full principal balance is due. The debtor's credit rating has been reduced subsequent to the initiation of the borrowing, and the 20X0 interest payment was not made when due. Investor Co. pays $500,000 (flat) for the loan and any unpaid interest. The expectation is that the debtor will pay $40,000 at the end of 20X1, $60,000 at the end of years 20X2 and 20X1 (each year), $70,000 at the end of 20X4, and $600,000 at the end of 20X5. These total projected cash inflows of $830,000, are lower than the contractually due amount, $1,001,000 (including the amount in arrears for 20X0). The effective yield will be about 12.6%. At transfer, the investment is recorded at cost, as follows:

Investment in loan receivable	500,000	
Cash		500,000
(500,000 × 12.6%)		

At the end of 20X1, immediately prior to receipt of the payment, the entry to record the accretion for the year, at the effective yield, is:

Investment in loan receivable	62,974	
Accretion (interest income)		62,974

The collection of the anticipated amount at December 31, 20X1, is recorded as follows:

Cash	40,000	
Investment in loan receivable		40,000

Entries for subsequent years' accretion and collections would follow in the same manner. This presumes, of course, that amounts expected to be received indeed are received, and that expectations about the future receipts do not depart from what had been anticipated when the loan was purchased.

The changes in carrying amount and recognition of income over the full five-year period are illustrated in the following chart.

Year ending December 31	A *Beginning carrying amount*	B *Cash flows expected to be collected*	C *Interest income*	D *Reduction (increase) in carrying amount (B–C)*	E *Ending carrying amount of loan (A–D)*
20X1	$500,000	$ 40,000	$ 62,974	$ (22,974)	$522,974
20X2	522,974	60,000	65,867	(5,867)	528,841
20X3	528,841	60,000	66,606	(6,606)	535,447
20X4	535,447	70,000	67,438	2,56	532,885
20X5	532,885	600,000	67,115	532,885	–
		$830,000	$330,00	$ 500,000	

In the foregoing chart, the $830,000 total cash collected consists of $330,000 in interest, accreted at the 12.6% computed yield, and $500,000 return of investment in the loan receivable.

Contrast this result with the examples that follow.

Example—Subsequent Decrease in Expected Cash Flows

If, subsequent to acquisition and computation of effective yield, the expected cash flows associated with a loan are revised downward, ASC 310-30 directs that this be accounted for as an impairment. The adjustment results in the previously determined yield percentage being maintained in future periods by applying the constant return to the reduced carrying value of the loan. While some might argue that a diminished expectation of cash flows would imply a new lower rate of return, ASC 310-30 instead opts for recognizing an immediate impairment, measured as the then-present value of the stream of cash flow shortfalls being projected. This results in a continuing rate of return equal to the original estimate, but with a step-down in the carrying value of the loan.

To illustrate, using the same basic facts above, assume now that immediately after the 20X3 payment is made, Investor Co. revises its expectation of cash flows to be received in 20X4 and 20X5. It now anticipates zero cash collection in 20X3, and only $500,000 at year-end 20X5. The present value of these shortfalls—a $70,000 shortage one year hence, followed by a $100,000 shortfall two years later—discounted at the 12.6% yield on the investment computed at the date of transfer, reveals an impairment of $141,039 as of the start of 20X4. The entry to record this, given that the investment is treated as a loan rather than as a debt security, is as follows:

Bad debt expense	141,039	
Allowance for uncollectible loan receivable		141,039

The reduced net carrying value of the loan receivable, which is $394,408 immediately following this adjustment, will continue to accrete at 12.6%, as the following table illustrates:

Year ending December 31	*A Beginning carrying amount of loan*	*B Cash flows expected to be collected*	*C Interest income*	*D Reduction (increase) in carrying amount (B–C)*	*E Ending carrying amount of loan (A–D)*
20X1	$500,000	$ 40,000	$ 62,974	$ (22,974)	$522,974
20X2	522,974	60,000	65,867	(5,867)	528,841
20X3	528,841	60,000	66,606	(6,606)	
20X4*		141,039	394,408		
20X5	394,408	–	49,675	(49,675)	444,083
20X6	444,083	500,000	55,917	444,083	–
		$660,000	$301,039	$500,000	

* Provision of allowance for estimated uncollectible future cash flows, computed at present value using the effective yield of the loan.

Observe in the foregoing chart that total cash collected, $660,000, consists of $301,039 in interest, accreted at the 12.6% computed yield, and the recovery of only $358,961 of the $500,000 investment in the loan receivable. In other words, the guidance treats the decrease in expected cash flows as a loss of principal, accounted for as a bad debt and a provision of a valuation allowance against the $500,000 loan receivable. Note that the decreased cash flow expectation was *not* accounted for as a lowered future return on the investment (which would have resulted in lower interest income recognition in years 20X4 and 20X5 coupled with a full recovery of the principal invested).

Example with Decrease in Expected Cash Flows Followed by Increase in Expected Cash Flows (Recovery of Uncollectible Loan Receivable)

If Investor Co., above, first lowers its expectation regarding future cash flows and then partially reverses its estimate, so that some or all (but not more than all) of the allowance of the uncollectible loan receivable proves unneeded, this is accounted for under ASC 310-30 as a reversal of the valuation allowance account (i.e., as a change in an accounting estimate).

To illustrate, consider again the facts in the basic example, and now assume that in 20X3 Investor Co. has the expectation that no interest will be collected in 20X4 and that only $500,000 will be collected in 20X5. In 20X4, however, $20,000 is in fact collected, and Investor Co. then expects a full collection of the $600,000 in 20X5 (but no recovery of the $50,000 missed payment in 20X4).

The entry to record the reduced expectation of future cash flows at the end of 20X2 or beginning of 20X3 is as shown previously.

Bad debt expense	141,039	
Allowance for uncollectible loan receivable		141,039

In 20X4, the collection of the $20,000 (when no collection at all was anticipated) coupled with the renewed expectation of collecting $600,000 in 20X5 required that some of the previously provided valuation allowance be reversed. The amount of valuation allowance to be restored, per ASC 310-30, is that amount which will result in interest accretion thereafter at the previously determined 12.6% yield through the final collection of the loan. Assuming that the $20,000 collection in December 20X4 came as a surprise, the adjustment will be computed with reference to the final remaining collection, $600,000, expected in December 20X5, and to the $20,000 unexpected 20X6 collection.

The entry to partially restore the carrying value of the loan, net of the valuation allowance, is as follows:

Allowance for uncollectible loan receivable	108,802	
Bad debt expense		108,802

The computation of the foregoing amount may be somewhat confusing, unless one keeps in mind that the objective of ASC 310-30 is to provide for the reporting of interest income over the full carrying term of the loan receivable, at a constant rate on a changing balance, with that rate being the rate computed at the date of transfer. The only exception, which will be illustrated later in this section, is for situations where the total cash to be collected exceeds the estimate made at the date of transfer; in that case, a higher rate of return is reported in periods after the change in estimate, to avoid the alternative of reporting a gain at the date the new estimate is made. In this example, the anticipated "extra" 20X5 collection of $100,000 ($600,000 – $500,000) has a present value at the end of 20X14 of $88,802, so this previously provided valuation allowance is no longer needed. Furthermore, the $20,000 collection in 20X4 was unexpected, and had previously been fully included in the valuation allowance as being uncollectible, so this too must be reversed. Therefore, the total reversal of valuation allowance is the sum of these two amounts, or $108,802. Alternatively, this can be computed as the adjustment necessary to bring the net carrying value of the loan receivable to the amount of "principal" to be collected in December 20X5 (i.e., the present value, discounting at 12.6%, of the expected $600,000 collection).

The net carrying value of the loan receivable will continue to accrete at 12.6%, both after the recognition of the valuation allowance at the end of 20X3 and after the partial elimination of the valuation allowance in 20X4, as the following table illustrates:

Year ending December 31	A *Beginning carrying amount of loan*	B *Cash flows expected to be collected*	C *Interest Income*	D *Reduction (increase) in carrying amount (B–C)*	E *Ending carrying amount of loan (A–D)*
20X1	$500,000	$ 40,000	$ 62,974	$ (22,974)	$522,974
20X2	522,974	60,000	65,867	(5,867)	528,841
20X3	528,841	60,000	66,606	(6,606)	
20X3*		141,039	394,408		
20X4	394,408	20,000	49,675	(29,675)	
20X4**				(108,802)	532,885
20X5	532,885	6,00,000	67,115	532,885	–
		$780,000	$312,237	$500,000	

* Provision of allowance for estimated uncollectible future cash flows, computed at present value using the effective yield on the loan.

** Restoration of a portion of the previously provided allowance, computed at present value using the effective yield on the loan, relative to expected 20X5 collection, plus the $20,000 unanticipated collection in 20X4 at full accreted amount.

Observe in the foregoing chart that total cash collected, $780,000, consisted of $312,237 in interest, accreted at the 12.6% computed yield, and the recovery of only $467,763 of the $500,000 investment in the loan receivable. As in the immediately preceding example, ASC 310-30 treats the decrease in expected cash flows as a loss of principal, accounted for as a bad debt and a provision of a valuation allowance against the $500,000 loan receivable. In this case, $32,237 of "principal" (i.e., of the amount recognized at the time of transfer) was lost, which is the net of the $141,039 valuation allowance provision in 20X3 and the $108,802 recovery recognized in 20X4.

Note that in all of the preceding examples the carrying value of the loan receivable continues to earn the computed 12.6% yield throughout the holding period. This was true if the initially estimated future cash flows were all collected as planned, or if changes to the estimated amounts or timings later were made—as long as the total cash to be collected did not exceed the amount originally (i.e., upon transfer to Invest Co.) estimated. In the next example, the collections exceed what was anticipated when the loan was acquired, and this necessitates a different approach to accounting for the interest yield on the investment.

In all cases where an allowance for uncollectible loan amounts has been provided, if the loan is subsequently foreclosed, the lender must measure the long-lived asset received in full satisfaction of a receivable at fair value less cost to sell as prescribed by ASC 310-40. That subtopic prescribes that after a troubled debt restructuring, the creditor must account for assets received in satisfaction of a receivable the same as if the assets had been acquired for cash. Accordingly there will be a new cost basis for the long-lived asset received in full satisfaction of a receivable; the valuation allowance would not be carried over as a separate element of the cost basis for purposes of accounting for the long-lived asset under ASC 360 subsequent to foreclosure.

Example—Increase in Expected Cash Flows

Assume again the basic facts of the investment in the loan receivable made by Investor Co. However, after fully collecting the anticipated amounts in 20X1 and 20X2, Investor revises its estimates of the amounts to be collected in 20X3, 20X4, and 20X5. Specifically, it now expects to receive $75,000 at the end of 20X3 and again at the end of 20X4, and to collect the full remaining balance, $650,000, at the end of 20X5. ASC 310-30 does not permit recognition of a gain or other income upon making this new estimate, but does instead require that the effective yield be recomputed and that future receipts be allocated between interest income and principal reduction consistent with the new accretable yield.

Note that no entry is required at the time of the new estimate of future cash flows because no gain or loss (or reversal of previously recognized loss) is being affected. As with changes in accounting estimates under ASC 250, this is handled strictly on a prospective basis.

Year ending December 31	A *Beginning carrying amount of loan*	B *Cash flows expected to be collected*	C *Interest income*	D *Reduction (increase) in carrying amount (B–C)*	E *Ending carrying amount of loan (A–D)*
20X1	$500,000	$ 40,000	$ 62,974	$ (22,974)	$522,974
20X2	522,974	60,000	65,867	(5,867)	528,841
20X3*					
20X4	528,841	75,000	88,086	(13,086)	541,927
20X5	541,927	75,000	90,265	(15,265)	557,192
20X6	557,192	650,000	92,808	557,192	–
		$9,00,000	$4,00,000	$5,00,000	

* Based on new expectations regarding future cash flows, a new yield is computed in an amount that equates the present value of expected receipts in 20X3–X5 to the carrying value at the end of 20X2, $528,841. This yield is about 16.7%.

In the foregoing example, $900,000 in cash is ultimately collected, allocated $400,000 to interest income and $500,000 to recovery of the amount recorded at the date of transfer, which was the sum paid for the loan receivable.

Accounting for Investments in Pools of Loans Acquired by Transfer Loans that are acquired as a pool present special accounting considerations. Each individual loan must meet the criteria of ASC 310-30 in order to apply the accounting set forth in this standard. Thus, if a group of loans are acquired together and in the aggregate have expected future cash flows in an amount lower than the aggregate contractual cash flows, this does not qualify each of the loans to be accounted for under ASC 310-30. Rather, each loan must be reviewed for impairment due to credit quality, and only those individual loans exhibiting the defined characteristic would be subject to the specified accounting.

After making a determination that each loan in a proposed pool has met the threshold conditions set forth under ASC 310-30 (i.e., that there has been evidence of credit quality deterioration subsequent to the origination, and that it is probable that, as of the transfer date, the transferee will not collect all the contractually required payments), a further determination must be made that the loans share common risk characteristics. Under provisions of ASC 310-30, loans with similar credit risk or risk ratings, and one or more predominant risk characteristics, such as financial asset type, collateral type, 9size, interest rate, date of origination, term, and geographic location, will be considered to have common risk characteristics. Credit risk can be assessed by reference to publicly available ratings of publicly held companies or by automated ratings such as that produced by FICO.

The aggregate cost of the loans to be aggregated is apportioned to the loans in the pool in proportion to their respective fair values at date of acquisition. The aggregate accretable yield of the pool is allocated among the loans in this same manner.

Only loans acquired in a given fiscal *quarter* (not year!) are subject to aggregation for financial reporting purposes. Once a pool is established, its integrity must be maintained, and thus loans can only be removed from the pool upon sale, foreclosure, write-off, or settlement. (ASC 330-30-40-1) New loans cannot be added to an existing pool. The excess of contractually required cash flows over the acquisition cost of the pool may not be used to offset or absorb changes to anticipated cash flows associated with other loans or pools of loans having other common risk characteristics.

Removal of a loan from a portfolio is effected at the loan's then-carrying value (ASC 330-30-40-2), and accordingly a gain or loss would be reflected in income of the period, measured as the difference between the carrying value and the fair value of the amount received in settlement (e.g., cash or collateral). Any difference between the carrying amount of the loan being removed from the pool and the fair value of the amount received will not impact the percentage yield being used to accrete value on the remainder of the pool. (ASC 330-30-35-15)

Example of an Investment in a Pool of Loans Acquired by Transfer

Garfield Corporation acquires the following seven loans for $600,000 during the same fiscal quarter:

Loan no.	*Fair value*	*Remaining term*	*Interest rate*	*FICO score*
1	$ 53,000	4 years	9%	450
2	260,000	4 years	6%	800
3	125,000	4 years	10%	600
4	78,000	4 years	8%	480
5	50,000	4 years	7%	730
6	92,000	4 years	10%	390
7	67,000	4 years	9%	340
	$725,000			

Garfield elects to split these loans into two groups—those having FICO scores below the minimum Fannie Mae acceptance score of 620, and those above it. Accordingly, loan numbers 2 and 5 are shifted into a separate Pool A, with the remaining loans in Pool B. The $600,000 acquisition cost is allocated to the two pools based on the relative fair values of the loans within the pools, as shown below.

Pool no.	*Aggregate fair value*	*Proportion of total fair value*	*Cost allocation*
A	$310,000	43%	$258,000
B	415,000	57%	342,000
	$725,000	100%	$600,000

Garfield expects $117,376 annual payments from the Pool B loans. It determines that the discount rate equating all cash flows expected to be collected with the $342,000 allocated purchase price is 14%. Using the 14% rate, Garfield constructs the following amortization table for Pool B:

Year	*Expected cash receipts*	*Interest income (14%)*	*Reduction of carrying amount*	*Carrying amount*
Inception				$342,000
1	$117,376	$ 47,880	$ 69,496	272,504
2	117,376	38,151	79,225	193,279
3	117,376	27,059	90,317	102,962
4	117,376	14,414	102,962	0
	$469,504	$127,504	$342,000	

At the beginning of Year 3, Garfield writes off the remaining balance of Loan 7. Prior to the final payment, Loan 7 has a carrying value of $31,204, as determined by apportioning the carrying amount of Pool B at the end of Year 2 amongst the five loans in the pool based on their relative fair values at the date of acquisition. This apportionment calculation is shown in the following table:

Loan no.	Fair value at inception	Relative values	Apportionment of year 2 carrying amount
1	$ 53,000	12.77%	$ 24,684
3	125,000	30.12%	58,217
4	78,000	18.80%	36,327
6	92,000	22.17%	42,847
7	67,000	16.14%	1,204
	$415,000	100.00%	$193,279

Garfield records the loan write-off with the following entry:

Loss on loan write-off	31,204	
Investment in loan receivable		31,204

The following amortization table reflects the removal of Loan 7 from Pool B, along with its proportionate share of the expected cash receipts in Years 3 and 4.

Year	Expected cash receipts	Interest income (14%)	Reduction of carrying amount	Carrying amount
Inception				$ 342,000
1	$117,376	$ 47,880	$ 69,496	272,504
2	117,376	38,151	79,225	193,279
Write-off	31,204	162,075		
3	98,426	22,690	75,736	86,339
4	98,426	12,087	86,339	0
	$431,604	$ 120,808	$342,000	

If loans are accounted for in a pool and you subsequently modify one or more of these loans, do not remove the loans from the pool even if the modification would otherwise be considered a troubled debt restructuring. The entity must continue to evaluate whether the pool is impaired if the expected cash flows associated with the pool change.

Subsequent measurement—loans accounted for as debt securities If the debt instrument acquired in a transfer to be accounted for under ASC 310-30 meets the definition of a security, as set forth in ASC 320 (namely, that it constitutes a share, participation, or other interest that is represented by a registered or bearer instrument or by book entry, and is one of a class or series of participations, interests, or obligations), then ASC 310-30 prescribes a slightly different mode of accounting for changes in expected cash flows.

If the fair value of the debt security is less than its amortized cost, the entity should apply the impairment guidance in ASC 320-10-35. To conform to ASC 320's requirements, an anticipated downward change in expected future cash flows must be examined to determine whether the change is merely a temporary change or whether an other than temporary decline has occurred. While temporary impairment is not impossible, if in fact the transferee of debt securities now anticipates further reduced cash flows from the security, there is a substantial likelihood that the impairment in value is other than temporary. Under ASC 320, other-than-temporary impairment must be recognized by writing down the carrying value of the investment and reflecting the change in current earnings, whether the security is being held in the available-for-sale portfolio or is being held to maturity.

If, on the other hand, the entity expects the debt security's cash flows to increase from the amounts anticipated at transfer, then similar to what was illustrated above, the accretable yield must be recomputed and periodic interest income thereafter appropriately adjusted. This is considered a change in accounting estimate under ASC 250. (ASC 330-30-35-8 and 35-9)

To illustrate, consider the same facts as set forth above, except now assume that the loan is a debt security meeting the definition set forth in ASC 320. When acquired, it was treated as being available-for-sale, but for this example no changes in value are addressed other than that associated with the changed expectation of cash flows.

Example of Reduction in Cash Flow Expectations

The anticipated cash flows occurred in 20X1, 20X2, and 20X3, but at the beginning of 20X4 Investor Co. revises its expectations, and now believes that there will be a zero cash collection in 20X4, and only $500,000 at year-end 20X5. The present value of these shortfalls—a $70,000 shortage at year- end 20X4, followed by a $100,000 gap at year-end 20X5—discounted at the same 12.6% rate computed as the yield on the investment at transfer, reveals an impairment of $141,039 as of the start of 20X4. The entry to record this, given that the investment is treated as a debt security, rather than as a loan, is as follows:

Loss on impairment of investment	141,039	
Investment in available-for-sale debt securities		141,039

Apart from the bookkeeping (writing down the investment directly rather than crediting a contra asset account), the treatment is very similar to that previously presented. Most importantly, the reduced net carrying value of the debt security held as an available-for-sale security will continue to accrete at 12.6%, as the following table illustrates:

Year ending December 31	*A Beginning carrying amount of investment*	*B Cash flows expected to be collected*	*C Interest income*	*D Reduction (increase) in carrying amount (B–C)*	*E Ending carrying amount of investment (A–D)*
20X1	$500,000	$ 40,000	$ 62,974	$ (22,974)	$522,974
20X2	522,974	60,000	65,867	(5,867)	528,841
20X3	528,841	60,000	66,606	(6,606)	
20X3*		141,039	394,408		
20X4	394,408	–	49,675	(49,675)	444,083
20X5	444,083	5,00,000	55,917	444,083	–
		$660,000	$301,039	$500,000	

* Write-down of carrying value of investment in debt security, due to reduced expectation of future cash flows, which is judged to be an OTTI, computed at present value using the effective yield on the loan.

The total cash collected, $660,000, is accounted for as interest income, in the total amount $301,039, and recovery of the "principal" of the investment, net of the impairment recorded in 20X3, amounting to $358,961.

Example with Decrease in Expected Cash Flows Followed by Increase in Expected Cash Flows

Unlike in the earlier examples, where the investment was accounted for as a loan receivable, here the investment is in a debt security accounted for under ASC 320, which prohibits restoring an other-than-temporary decline in value. For this reason, the write-down was not reflected through a contra asset (allowance) account, and a later improvement in the outlook for future cash flows must instead be accounted for prospectively as a yield adjustment.

Assume, therefore, that Investor Co. first lowers its expectation regarding future cash flows and then partially reverses its estimate, so that some or all of the amount of future cash flow thought not to be forthcoming now again is expected to be received. Specifically, assume that in 20X3 Investor Co. has the expectation that no interest will be collected in 20X4 and that only $500,000 will be collected in 20X5. In 20X4, however, $20,000 is in fact collected, and Investor Co. then expects a full collection of the $600,000 in 20X5 (but no recovery of the $50,000 missed payment in 20X4).

The entry to record the reduced expectation of future cash flows at the end of 20X2 or beginning of 20X3 is as shown below.

Loss on impairment of investment	141,039	
Investment in available-for-sale debt securities		141,039

In 20X4, the collection of the $20,000 (when no collection at all was anticipated), coupled with the renewed expectation of collecting $600,000 in 20X5, requires that the yield through the end of the expected holding period (final payoff, in this case) be recomputed. Assuming that the $20,000 payment for 20X4 is received before the financial statements for 20X4 have been prepared, it would be appropriate to recompute accretable yield as of the beginning of that year, so that both 20X4 and 20X5 will report interest income consistent with the pattern of cash flows over that two-year period. The calculated yield on an investment equal to the carrying value at the beginning of 20X4 ($394,408), which is expected to generate cash inflows of $20,000 at the end of that year and $600,000 at the end of the next year, is 25.9%, and this is used to accrete yield over the remaining term.

Since this will be reported prospectively, no entry is made as of the beginning of the year (nor would the necessary information have been available), but the entry to record interest income and the accretion for uncollected interest would be as follows:

Cash	20,000	
Investment in available-for-sale debt securities	82,156	
Interest income		102,156

The accretion of value is akin to an amortization of discount, and represents interest earned but not received, based on the most recent estimates of future cash flows. It does not represent a recovery of the previously written down carrying value of the investment because of permanent impairment. The complete analysis can be seen in the chart that follows:

Year ending December 31	A *Beginning carrying amount of investment*	B *Cash flows expected to be collected*	C *Interest income*	D *Reduction (increase) in carrying amount (B–C)*	E *Ending carrying amount of investment (A–D)*
20X1	$500,000	$ 40,000	$ 62,974	$ (22,974)	$ 522,974
20X2	522,974	60,000	65,867	(5,867)	528,841
20X3	528,841	60,000	66,606	(6,606)	
20X3*		141,039	394,408		
20X4**	394,408	20,000	102,156	(82,156)	476,564
20X5	476,564	600,000	123,436	476,564	–
		$780,000	$421,039	$500,000	

* Write-down of carrying value of investment in debt security, due to reduced expectation of future cash flows, which is judged to be an OTTI computed at present value using the effective yield on the loan.

** Interest is accreted at the new rate of 25.9% hereafter.

It will be observed in the foregoing chart that total cash collected, $780,000, consisted of $421,039 in interest, accreted first at the 12.6% computed yield through the end of 20X3, and then at the 25.9% computed yield in light of higher expected cash flows for 20X4 and 20X5. The remainder of the cash flows, totaling $358,961, was attributable to the recovery of the investment, net of the write-down for impairment in 20X3.

In contrast to the example where the investment was accounted for as a loan receivable, here the yield is adjusted prospectively when a recovery in value is observed, and this causes relatively more of the future cash flows to be treated as interest income, and relatively less as recovery of the investment principal.

Note that if no reduction in future cash flows had been anticipated, but if an increase in cash flows was expected at some point during the holding period of the investment, the result, from an accounting standpoint, would be as shown immediately above. The accretable yield would have been computed and recognized prospectively over the remaining holding period of the security.

ASC 310-40, *Troubled Debt Restructurings by Creditors* A TDR occurs under specific circumstances: when a creditor "for economic or legal reasons related to the debtor's financial difficulties grants a concession to the debtor that it would not otherwise consider." Therefore, a TDR does not apply to restructurings that merely reflect general economic conditions that may lead to a reduction in interest rates. It also does not apply if a debt is refunded with new debt having an effective interest rate that approximates that of similar debt issued by nontroubled debtors.

ASC 310-40 focuses on the substance of debt modifications—their effect on future cash receipts or payments. Timing, interest, or principal may be modified under a TDR. These all affect cash flows and a creditor's total return on the receivable. Evaluating whether a modification of debt terms is in substance a TDR is critical to determining whether ASC 310-40 applies. Therefore, the scope and scope exceptions of this subtopic take on added significance.

Scope and Scope Exceptions

ASC 310-40 applies to all troubled debt restructurings by creditors. Accounting by debtors is found in ASC 470-60. Interestingly the two subtopics use different applicability tests and so creditors and debtors applying the same facts and circumstances may not reach the same conclusion as to whether a troubled debt restructuring (TDR) has occurred. (ASC 310-40-15-3)

Examples of TDRs TDRs may include, but are not limited to, one or a combination of two basic transaction types:

1. Settling the debt for less than its recorded investment in the receivable through:
   - Transfer from the debtor to the creditor of receivables from third parties, real estate, or other assets to satisfy fully or partially a debt.
   - Granting of an equity interest to the creditor by the debtor to satisfy fully or partially a debt. This does not apply if the equity interest is granted pursuant to existing terms for converting the debt into an equity interest. (ASC 310-40-15-6b)
2. Continuing to carry the debt, but modifying the terms through, for instance,
   - Reduction of the stated interest rate, accrued interest, face amount of the debt, or maturity amount of the debt.
   - Extension of the maturity date at a stated interest rate lower than the current market rate. ASC 310-40-15-9)

Excluded from TDR Guidance The following are *excluded* for consideration under the TDR guidance:

- Lease modifications
- Changes in employment-related agreements
- Unless they involve an agreement between debtor and creditor to restructure:
  - Debtors' failures to pay trade accounts according to their terms, or
  - Creditors' delays in taking legal action to collect overdue amounts of interest and principal
- Modifications of loans within a pool accounted for as impaired loans[6]
- Changes in expected cash flows of a pool of loans accounted for as impaired loans resulting from the modification of one or more loans within the pool.[7]

  (ASC 310-40-15-11)

Even if a debtor is experiencing some financial difficulties, a debt restructuring may not be a troubled debt restructuring for the purposes of ASC 310-40. None of the following situations are considered TDRs:

- The fair value of assets or equity accepted by a creditor from a debtor in full satisfaction of its receivable at least equals the creditor's amortized cost basis in the receivable.
- The fair value of assets or equity transferred by a debtor to a creditor in full settlement of its payable at least equals the debtor's carrying amount of the payable.
- The creditor reduces the effective interest rate on the debt primarily to reflect a decrease in market interest rates in general or a decrease in the risk so as to maintain a relationship with a debtor that can readily obtain funds from other sources at the current market interest rate.
- The debtor issues, in exchange for its debt, new marketable debt having an effective interest rate based on its market price that is at or near the current market interest rates of debt with similar maturity dates and stated interest rates issued by nontroubled debtors.

  (ASC 310-40-15-12)

Determining Whether a Troubled Debt Restructuring Has Occurred The first thing the creditor should consider in determining whether a TDR has occurred is whether it expects to collect all amounts due. A TDR receivable is one that is restructured or modified for economic or legal reasons where these conditions are present:

- The creditor grants a concession that it otherwise would not consider, and
- The borrower is having financial difficulties. (ASC 310-40-15-5)

[6] This bullet is superseded by ASU 2016-03.

[7] Ibid.

Exhibit—Determining Whether a Refinancing or Restructuring Is a TDR (ASC 310-40-15-5)

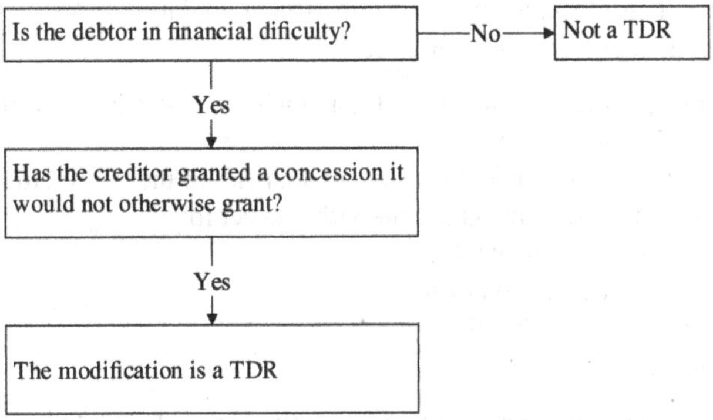

The creditor's motivation is to recoup as much of the debt as possible. A TDR may be a result of negotiation between the parties or may be imposed by a court, for example, in an arrangement under the Federal Bankruptcy Protection Act. "Concession" and "financial difficulties" have specific meanings under the guidance.

Determining Whether a Concession Has Been Granted The Codification offers specific instances describing when concessions have occurred.

Amounts due A concession has been granted as a result of a restructuring when the creditor does not expect to collect all amounts due, including interest accrued at the original contract rate. The creditor should also consider changes to underlying collateral if the principal payment is dependent on the value of the collateral. (ASC 310-40-15-13)

The Codification does not specify how a creditor should determine that it will be unable to collect all amounts due according to the contractual terms of a loan. A creditor should apply its normal loan review procedures in making that judgment. (ASC 310-40-35-9) However, the Codification does specifically prohibit creditors from using the borrower's effective rate test in ASC 470-60-55-10 in evaluating whether a concession has been granted to a borrower. (ASC 310-40-15-8A)

Additional collateral and guarantees A creditor may restructure a debt in exchange for additional collateral or guarantees from the debtor. If the nature and amount of that additional collateral or guarantees received as part of a restructuring do not serve as adequate compensation for other terms of the restructuring, the creditor needs to consider whether a concession has occurred. (ASC 310-40-15-14)

Access to market-rate funds In a declining-rate environment, the loan may be restructured with a lower interest rate. The creditor needs to evaluate whether the debtor would be able to get the same terms and market rate from another lender. If so, a concession has not occurred. If not, the restructuring would be considered to be at a below-market rate and this may indicate that the creditor has granted a concession. (ASC 310-40-15-15)

Temporary/permanent increases in interest rate The borrower cannot assume that a temporary or permanent increase in the contractual interest rate as a result of a restructuring is not a concession. The new contractual interest rate could still be below market interest rates for new debt with similar risk characteristics. Borrowers have to perform the TDR evaluation based on consideration of any other changes as a result of the restructuring. (ASC 310-40-15-16)

Evaluating an insignificant delay A delay in payments is not considered a concession if the delay is insignificant. This is aligned with the impairment guidance in ASC 310-10. A delay may be insignificant depending on the following factors:

- The amount of payment subject to delay is insignificant relative to the unpaid principal or collateral value of the debt.
- The restructuring results in an insignificant shortfall in the contractual amount due.
- The delay in the timing is insignificant with respect to:
  a. The frequency of payments due
  b. The original contractual maturity
  c. The original expected duration.
  (ASC 310-40-15-17)

The preparer should use judgment in evaluating the factors listed. Other factors may also be considered in evaluating whether an insignificant delay has occurred, including the cumulative effect of past restructurings.

Determining Whether a Debtor Is Experiencing Financial Difficulty Lenders should consider the following factors when evaluating the first condition for a TDR—borrower's financial difficulty:

- Borrower is in payment default on any of its debt; or it is probable the debtor will be in payment default on any of its debt in the foreseeable future without the modification.
- The borrower has declared or is in the process of declaring bankruptcy.
- There is substantial doubt about the borrower's business continuing as a going concern.
- Borrower has securities that have been delisted or are in the process or threat of being delisted from an exchange.
- Based on estimates and projections that encompass only the current business capabilities, the creditor forecasts that the debtor's entity-specific cash flows will be insufficient to service any of its debt in accordance with contractual terms for the foreseeable future.
- Without the modification, the borrower cannot obtain funds from sources other than the existing creditors at an effective interest rate equal to the current market interest rate for similar debt for a nontroubled debtor.
  (ASC 310-40-15-20)

Measurement and Derecognition[8]

Accounting treatment of a TDR depends on the facts and circumstances, that is, the type of restructuring.

Substituted Debtors in a Troubled Debt Restructuring ASC 310-40-40-1 addresses the situation of a sale of real estate collateral by a debtor in a troubled debt situation, with the acquirer assuming the obligation to the creditor (the reporting entity) such that the fair value of the obligation (the present value of payments, less than the net investment) was less than the creditor's

[8] Recorded investment in the receivable is used in this section instead of carrying amount of the receivable because the carrying amount is net of an allowance for estimated uncollectible amounts or other valuation account, if any, while the recorded investment in the receivable is not. Upon implementation of ASU 2016-13, "recorded investment" in the receivable will change to "amortized cost basis."

carrying value of the loan receivable. In such circumstances, the creditor would be required to recognize a loss on the original loan in the amount by which the net investment in the loan exceeds the fair value of the assets received. The fair value of the payments should be recorded as an asset by the creditor.

Receipt of Assets in Full Satisfaction of a Receivable A creditor may receive from the debtor receivables from third parties, real estate, or other assets or equity interest in the debtor.

- If the assets received represent full satisfaction of a receivable, the creditor should record those items at their fair value at the time of the restructuring.
- If the creditor intends to sell long-lived assets received, it should deduct costs to sell from fair value. The creditor may also use the fair value of the receivable satisfied, if this more clearly evident.
- The difference between the recorded investment in the receivable and the fair value of the amounts received in settlement of the debt less costs to sell is recorded as a loss for the period.
  (ASC 310-40-40-2 through 40-4)

Partial Satisfaction of a Receivable The creditor may receive assets in partial satisfaction of a receivable and agree to modify the terms of the remaining receivable. The recorded investment in the receivable is reduced by the fair value less cost to sell of the assets received. If the creditor receives cash, it reduces the investment in the receivable by the amount of cash received. This treatment is used even if the terms of the remaining receivable are not modified. (ASC 310- 40-35-7)

Impairment of a Loan Often a loan whose terms are modified in a TDR has already been treated as an impaired loan under ASC 310-10. However, if it has not, the creditor should use the effective interest rate based on the original contract rate to discount cash flows. (ASC 310-40-35-12) The creditor should recognize a loss on the original loan and an asset at fair value for the payment to be received. The creditor measures the loss in the same way as in receipt of asset in full satisfaction of a receivable (see above). (ASC 310-40-40-1)

Foreclosure A TDR may be an in-substance repossession or foreclosure whether or not a formal foreclosure has taken place. The creditor may have received the debtor's assets in full or partial satisfaction of the receivable. In that case, the creditor treats the transaction in the same way as receipts of asset in full satisfaction of a receivable (see above). (ASC 320-40-40-6) The creditor is considered to have physical possession of the property and the receivable should be derecognized and the real property recognized only when either:

- The creditor obtains legal title to the property upon completion of foreclosure, or
- The borrower conveys all interest in the property to the creditor to satisfy the loan through completion of a deed in lieu of foreclosure or a similar legal agreement.
  (ASC 310-40-55-10A)

Classification of certain government-guaranteed mortgage loans upon foreclosure This is a narrow-scope topic designed to eliminate inconsistencies in financial reporting.

Certain government-sponsored loan guarantee programs, such as those offered by the FHA, HUD, and the VA, allow qualifying creditors to extend mortgage loans to borrowers with a guarantee that entitles the creditor to recover all or a portion of the unpaid principal balance from the government if the borrower defaults. The Codification offers specific guidance on how to classify or measure foreclosed mortgage loans that are government guaranteed.

ASC 310-40 requires that the entity derecognize a mortgage loan and recognize a separate other receivable upon foreclosure if *all* the following conditions are met:

- The loan has a government guarantee that is not separable from the loan before foreclosure.
- At the time of foreclosure, the creditor has the intent to convey the real estate property to the guarantor and make a claim on the guarantee, and the creditor has the ability to recover under that claim.
- At the time of foreclosure, any amount of the claim that is determined on the basis of the fair value of the real estate is fixed.
  (ASC 310-40-40-7B)

Upon foreclosure, the entity should measure the separate other receivable based on the amount of the loan balance (principal and interest) expected to be recovered from the guarantor. (ASC 310-40-40-7A)

Example 1—Settlement of a Troubled Debt by Transfer of Assets

Assume the debtor company transfers land having a book value of $70,000 and a fair market value of $80,000 in full settlement of its note payable. The note has a remaining life of five years, a principal balance of $90,000, and related accrued interest of $10,000 is recorded. The creditor makes the following entries to record the settlement:

Land	80,000	
Bad debt expense	20,000	
Note receivable		90,000
Interest receivable		10,000

Example 2—Modification of Terms: Restructuring with Gain/Loss Recognized (Payments Are Less Than the Recorded Investment in the Receivable)

Assume that a note has a principal balance of $90,000, accrued interest of $10,000, an interest rate of 5%, and a remaining life of five years. The interest rate is reduced to 4%, the principal is reduced to $72,500, and the accrued interest at date of restructure is forgiven.

Future cash flows (after restructuring) at the agreement's original effective interest rate:

		5% 5 yrs PV Factor
Principal	$56,806	($72,500 × .78353)
Interest	<u>12,555</u>	($2,900 × 4.32948)
Total present value	$ 69,361	
Amount prior to restructure ($90,000 principal + $10,000 accrued interest)	<u>(100,000)</u>	
Creditor's loss	<u>$ (30,639)</u>	

Beginning of Year 1		
Bad debt expense	30,639	
Interest receivable		10,000
Valuation allowance		20,639
End of Year 1		
Cash	2,900	
Valuation allowance	568	
Bad debt expense (or interest income)		3,468 (69,361 × .05)

End of Year 2		
Cash	2,900	
Valuation allowance	596	
Bad debt expense (or interest income)		3,496 [(69,361 + 568) = 69,929 × .05]
End of Year 3		
Cash	2,900	
Valuation allowance	626	
Bad debt expense (or interest income)		3,526 [(69,929 + 596) = 70,525 × .05]
End of Year 4		
Cash	2,900	
Valuation allowance	658	
Bad debt expense (or interest income)		3,558 [(70,525 + 626) = 71,151 × .05]
End of Year 5		
Cash	2,900	
Valuation allowance	691	
Bad debt expense (or interest income)		3,591 [(71,151 + 658) = 71,809 × .05]
Cash	72,500	
Valuation allowance	17,500	
Note receivable		90,000

Example 3—Restructuring with No Gain/Loss Recognized (Payments Exceed the Recorded Investment in the Receivable)

Modify Example 2 as follows:

Assume the $100,000 owed is reduced to a principal balance of $95,000. The interest rate of 5% is reduced to 4%.

Future cash flows (after restructuring) at the agreement's original effective interest rate:

		5% 5 yrs PV Factor
Principal	$74,435	($95,000 × .78353)
Interest	16,452	($3,800 × 4.32948)
Total present value	$ 90,887	
Amount prior to restructure ($90,000 principal + $10,000 accrued interest)	(1,000,000)	
Creditor's loss	$ (9,113)	

Beginning of Year 1		
Bad debt expense	9,113	
Note receivable—new	95,000	
Note receivable—old		90,000
Interest receivable		10,000
Valuation allowance		4,113
End of Year 1		
Cash	3,800	
Valuation allowance	744	
Bad debt expense (or interest income)		4,544 (90,887 × .05)
End of Year 2		
Cash	3,800	
Valuation allowance	781	
Bad debt expense (or interest income)		4,581 [(90,887 + 744) = 91,631 × .05]
End of Year 3		
Cash	3,800	
Valuation allowance	821	
Bad debt expense (or interest income)		4,621 [(91,631 + 781) = 92,412 × .05]

End of Year 4		
Cash	3,800	
Valuation allowance	862	
Bad debt expense (or interest income)		4,662 [(92,412 + 821) = 93,233 × .05]
End of Year 5		
Cash	3,800	
Valuation allowance	905	
Bad debt expense (or interest income)		4,705 [(93,233 + 862) = 94,095 × .05]
Cash	95,000	
Note receivable		95,000

Presentation and Disclosures

For presentation and disclosure information for the guidance covered in this chapter, see the *Disclosure and Presentation Checklist for Commercial Businesses* at www.wiley.com/go/ GAAP2021.

Other Sources

See ASC Location—*Wiley GAAP* Chapter	*For information on . . .*
ASC 405-30-25-8	Receivables related to recovery of insurance-related assessments.
ASC 450-20	Loss contingencies, including accrual of an estimated loss from a loss contingency.
ASC 460	Accounting by a guarantor at the inception of a guarantee issued.
ASC 460 on guarantees and ASC 815 on guarantees accounted for as a derivative.	Loan guarantees, in which an entity lends its creditworthiness to another party for a fee and enhances the other party's ability to borrow funds. Upon implementation of ASU 2014-09 on revenue recognition, this item changes to: Loan guarantees, in which an entity (guarantor) lends its creditworthiness to another party (borrower) for a fee, thereby enhancing that other party's ability to borrow funds. See Topic 460 on guarantees.
ASC 860-20	Transfers of all financial assets, including receivables.
ASC 860-50	Servicing assets and liabilities related to loans and other receivables.
Source: (ASC 310-10-60)	
ASC 320-10-15	The determination of whether an other-than-temporary impairment of beneficial interests exists and on interest income recognition on beneficial interests.[9]

[9] This paragraph is superseded by ASU 2016-13.

ASC 325-40-15	Determination of whether an other-than-temporary impairment of beneficial interests exists and on interest income recognition on beneficial interests.[10]
Source: (ASC 310-20-60)	
ASC 325-40	Transferor's interests in securitized transactions accounted for as sales and purchased beneficial interests.[11]
ASC 470	Borrower's accounting for a participating mortgage loan if the lender is entitled to participate in appreciation in the fair value of the mortgaged real estate project, the results of operations of the mortgaged real estate project, or in both.[12]
ASC 470-60	Troubled debt restructurings by debtors.[13]
(ASC 310-30-60)	

[10] Upon implementation of ASU 2016-13, this paragraph is changed to: Determination of whether a credit loss on beneficial interests exists and on interest income recognition beneficial interest.

[11] This paragraph is superseded by ASU 2016-13.

[12] Ibid.

[13] Ibid.

17 ASC 320 INVESTMENTS—DEBT SECURITIES

PERSPECTIVE AND ISSUES

Technical Alerts

The FASB has an ongoing financial instruments project. As part of this project, the FASB issued the following Updates:

- ASU 2016-13, *Financial Instruments—Credit Losses (Topic 326) Measurement of Credit Losses on Financial Instruments*
- ASU 2018-09, *Codification Improvements to Topic 326, Financial Instruments—Credit Losses*
- ASU 2019-04, *Codification Improvements to Topic 326, Financial Instruments—Credit Losses, Topic 815, Derivatives and Hedging, and Topic 825, Financial Instruments*
- ASU 2019-05. *Financial Instruments—Credit Losses (Topic 326)—Targeted Transition Relief*
- ASU 2019-10, *Financial Instruments—Credit Losses (Topic 326), Derivatives and Hedging (Topic 815), and Leases (Topic 842): Effective Dates*

These are discussed below.

ASU 2019-10

Guidance regarding effective dates In November 2019, the FASB issued ASU 2019-10, *Financial Instruments—Credit Losses (Topic 326), Derivatives and Hedging (Topic 815), and Leases (Topic 842): Effective Dates*. The ASU grants private companies, not-for-profit organizations, and certain small public company SEC filers additional time to implement recent FASB standards on current expected credit losses (CECL).

ASU 2019-10 Effective Dates

Topic	**Public business entities that meet the definition of SEC Filers, except Smaller Reporting Companies (SRCs) as determined by the SEC as of November 15, 2019**	**All Other Entities**
CECL (ASC 326)	Fiscal years beginning after December 15, 2019	Fiscal years beginning after December 15, 2022

** Includes Employee Benefit Plans and NFP Conduit Bond Obligors that file with the SEC or furnish financial statements to the SEC.*

The ASUs in this chapter that are affected are:

- ASU. 2016-13, *Financial Instruments—Credit Losses (Topic 326): Measurement of Credit Losses on Financial Instruments,*
- ASU 2018-19, *Codification Improvements to Topic 326, Financial Instruments—Credit Losses,*
- ASU 2019-04, *Codification Improvements to Topic 326, Financial Instruments—Credit Losses, Topic 815, Derivatives and Hedging, and Topic 825, Financial Instruments, and*
- ASU 2019-05, *Financial Instruments—Credit Losses (Topic 326): Targeted Transition Relief*

ASU 2016-13 In June 2016, the FASB issued ASU 2016-13, *Financial Instruments—Credit Losses (Topic 326) Measurement of Credit Losses on Financial Instruments*. This ASU makes changes to several topics, and adds a new topic—ASC 326. The primary coverage can be found in the chapter on ASC 326. This Technical Alert covers the changes related to ASC 320.

Guidance related to ASC 320 The ASU created a current expected credit loss (CECL) model in ASC 326-20 that replaces the impairment guidance in ASC 310-10. However, the FASB decided that the CECL model should not apply to available-for-sale (AFS) debt securities. The ASU instead made targeted amendments to the current AFS debt security impairment model and placed the new guidance in a new subtopic, ASC 326-30. This will result in entities using different impairment models for AFS debt securities and those that are classified as held to maturity.

The amendments do not apply to an AFS debt security that the entity intends to sell or will likely be required to sell before the recovery of the amortized cost basis. In those cases, the entity would write down the debt security's amortized cost to the debt security's fair value as required under existing GAAP.

AFS Debt Securities

Item	*Existing Guidance*	*New, ASU 2016-13 Guidance*
Credit losses	Recognize impairment as a reduction of the cost basis of the investment.	Recognize an allowance for credit losses. The allowance is limited by the amount that the fair value is less than the amortized cost basis.
Improvements in estimated credit losses	Recognize improvements in earnings as a reduction in the allowance and credit loss expense.	Prospectively recognize as interest income over time.

In addition, the ASU eliminates "other-than-temporary" impairment (OTTI). The new guidance focuses on determining whether unrealized losses are credit losses or whether they are caused by other factors. Therefore, the entity cannot use the length of time a security has been in an unrealized loss position as a factor to conclude that a credit loss does not exist. Also, when assessing whether a credit loss exists, the entity may not consider recoveries in fair value after the balance sheet date.

Disclosures The ASU retains the existing AFS debt security disclosure requirements, but amends them to reflect the use of an allowance for credit losses and the elimination of the OTTI concept. The new guidance also requires some new disclosures. Entities will have to disclose a tabular roll forward of the allowance account and to disclose their accounting policy for recognizing write-offs.

Transition Method Except where noted in the table below, entities should use a modified-retrospective approach and record a cumulative-effect adjustment to retained earnings as of the beginning of the first reporting period that the entity adopts the guidance. For example, a calendar-year private company that adopts the standard in 2022 records the cumulative effect adjustment on January 1, 2022. The transition adjustment includes those adjustments made as a result of an entity amending its accounting policy if it adopts the amendments in ASU 2019-04 related to determining when accrued interest receivables are deemed uncollectible and written off. Also, see the information below on ASU 2019-05 for an option to select the fair value option.

Prospective Transition Approach Required

Circumstance	*Accounting treatment*
Debt securities for which an OTTI was recognized before the adoption date	If amounts relate to improvements in cash flows expected to be collected, continue to accrete into income over the remaining life of the asset. If cash flows improve because of improvements in credit after the adoption date, record in the income statement in the period received. If cash flows are expected to decrease because of deterioration in credit expectations, record an allowance.

Assets previously accounted for as PCD (purchased financial assets with credit deterioration)	Adjust the amortized cost basis on adoption to reflect the addition of the allowance for credit losses on the transition date. Continue to accrete or amortize, at the effective interest rate at the adoption date, the remaining noncredit discount or premium. Apply the same transition requirements to beneficial interests that previously applied the PCD model or have a significant difference between contractual cash flows and expected cash flows.

(ASC 326-10-65-1)

Effective date See the information in ASU 2019-10 above.

Early adoption is allowed for all entities for fiscal years beginning after December 15, 2018, including interim periods therein. (ASC 326-10-65-1)

Also, please see the information below on ASU 2019-05.

ASU 2018-19 In November 2018, the FASB issued ASU 2018-19, *Codification Improvements to Topic 326, Financial Instruments—Credit Losses*. ASU 2018-19 affects this chapter by changing the effective date of ASU 2016-13 for nonpublic entities. Those changes are reflected in the effective dates above. Also, for an option to use the fair value option, see the information on ASU 2019-05 below.

ASU 2019-04 In April 2019, the FASB issued *Codification Improvements to Topic 326, Financial Instruments—Credit Losses, Topic 815, Derivatives and Hedging, and Topic 825, Financial Instruments*. Issue 1B of the ASU provides revised guidance on how an entity should account for transfer of debt securities between categories. The changes require that an entity:

- Reverse in earnings any allowance for credit losses or valuation allowances that had been previously measured on a debt security category,
- Reclassify and transfer the debt security to the new category, and
- Apply the applicable measurement guidance in accordance with the new category.

ASU 2019-04 has the same effective dates as ASU 2016-13 explained above. The ASC 320 amendments in ASU 2019-04 are noted in this chapter.

ASU 2019-05 In May 2019, the FASB issued ASU 2019-05, *Financial Instruments—Credit Losses (Topic 326)—Targeted Transition Relief.*

Guidance This Update provides an option to irrevocably elect the fair value option for certain financial assets previously measured at amortized cost basis. The FASB expects this amendment to increase comparability because it aligns measurement methodologies for similar financial assets. This option is available to reporting entities within the scope of ASC 326. The new option may be applied on an instrument-by-instrument basis for eligible instruments. Note that this option *does not* apply to held-to-maturity debt securities. An entity that applies the fair value option should then apply the guidance in ASC 820-10 and ASC 825-10. (ASC 326-10-65-3)

For entitles that have not yet adopted ASU 2016-13, provisions of ASU 2019-04 related to ASC 320 have the same effective dates as ASU 2016-13. For those entities that have adopted ASU 2016-13, the provisions are effective for fiscal years beginning after December 15, 2019, including interim periods within those fiscal years. Early adoption is permitted in any interim period if the entity has adopted ASU 2016-13.

Transition For entities that have not yet implemented ASU 2016-13, the effective date and transition methodology in ASU 2019-05 are the same as ASU 2016-13. For entities that have adopted ASU 2016-13, ASU 2019-05 is effective for fiscal years beginning after December 15, 2019, including interim periods within those fiscal years. Those entities may early adopt in any of the interim periods.

Entities should adopt the changes using a modified-retrospective basis by means of a cumulative-effect adjustment to the opening balance of retained earnings balance as of the date the entity adopted ASU 2016-13.

Investment Topics

The Codification contains several topics dealing with investments, including:

- ASC 320, *Investments—Debt Securities*
- ASC 321, *Investments—Equity Securities*
- ASC 323, *Investments—Equity Method and Joint Ventures*
- ASC 325, *Investments—Other*
  (ASC 320-10-05-01)
- ASC 326-30, Financial Instruments—*Credit Losses—Available-for-Sale Debt Securities*

Subtopics

ASC 320, *Investments—Debt Securities*, contains one subtopic:

- ASC 320-10, *Overall*, that contains guidance for all investments in debt securities (ASC 320-10-05-1)

Scope and Scope Exceptions

ASC 320 applies to all entities that do not belong to specialized industries for purposes of ASC 320. The entities deemed by ASC 320 *not* to be specialized industries include:

- Cooperatives,
- Mutual entities, and
- Trusts that do not report substantially all their debt securities at fair value.
  (ASC 320-10-15-2)

ASC 320 does *not* apply to "entities whose specialized accounting practices include accounting for substantially all investments in debt securities at fair value, with changes in value recognized in earnings (income) or in the change in net assets," such as

- Brokers and dealers in securities,
- Defined benefit and other postretirement plans (upon implementation of ASC 2019-04, this bullet changes to defined benefit pension and health and welfare plans), and
- Investment companies.
  (ASC 320-15-3)

Upon implementation of ASU 2016-13, this Topic does not apply to not-for-profit entities. Until an entity adopts ASU 2016-13, the guidance in ASC 320-10-35-17 through 35-34 provides guidance on impairment and the application to not-for-profit entities. (ASC 320-15-4) ASC 320 also does not apply to:

- Derivative instruments subject to ASC 815. In the case of an investment subject to ASC 320 with an embedded derivative, the host instrument is accounted for under ASC 320, and the embedded derivative is accounted for under ASC 815.
- Investments in consolidated subsidiaries.
  (ASC 320-10-15-7)

Overview

ASC 320 classifies debt securities into one of three categories:

1. Held-to-maturity,
2. Trading, or
3. Available-for-sale.

These categories are explored in depth in this chapter and summarized in the exhibit "Classification of Debt Securities" later in this chapter.

DEFINITIONS OF TERMS

Source: ASC 320-10-20, *Glossary*. Also see Appendix A, *Definitions of Terms*, for additional terms related to this topic: Amortized Cost Basis, Available-for-Sale Securities, Cash Equivalents, Component of an Entity, Debt Security (Def. 1), Equity Security (Def. 1), Fair Value, Holding Gain or Loss, Market Participants, Not-for-Profit Entity, Operating Segment, Orderly Transaction, Public Business Entity, Readily Determinable Fair Value (Def. 2), Recorded Investment, Related Parties, Reporting Unit, and Security (Def. 2).

Asset Group. An asset group is the unit of accounting for a long-lived asset or assets to be held and used that represents the lowest level for which identifiable cash flows are largely independent of the cash flows of other groups of assets and liabilities.

Retrospective Interest Method. A method of interest income recognition under which income for the current period is measured as the difference between the amortized cost at the end of the period and the amortized cost at the beginning of the period, plus any cash received during the period.

Structured Note. A debt instrument whose cash flows are linked to the movement in one or more indexes, interest rates, foreign exchange rates, commodities prices, prepayment rates, or other market variables. Structured notes are issued by U.S. government-sponsored enterprises, multilateral development banks, municipalities, and private entities. The notes typically contain embedded (but not separable or detachable) forward components or option components such as caps, calls, and floors. Contractual cash flows for principal, interest, or both can vary in amount and timing throughout the life of the note based on nontraditional indexes or nontraditional uses of traditional interest rates or indexes.

Trading. An activity involving securities sold in the near term and held for only a short period of time. The term trading contemplates a holding period generally measured in hours and days rather than months or years. See paragraph 948-310-40-1 for clarification of the term trading for a mortgage banking entity.

Trading Securities. Securities that are bought and held principally for the purpose of selling them in the near term and therefore held for only a short period of time. Trading generally reflects active and frequent buying and selling, and trading securities are generally used with the objective of generating profits on short-term differences in price.

CONCEPTS, RULES, AND EXAMPLES

Classification of Debt Securities

Classification is made and documented at the time of the initial acquisition of each investment. (ASC 320-10-25-1 and 2) The appropriateness of classification is reassessed at each reporting date. (ASC 320-10-35-5) ASC 320 requires all debt securities to be placed into one of three categories. Their characteristics and accounting and reporting requirements are summarized in the exhibit below and the discussion that follows.

Exhibit—Classification and Measurement of Debt Securities

Category	Characteristics	Reported subsequently on statement of financial position	Reported in income
Held-to-maturity	Positive intent and ability to hold until maturity	Amortized cost.	Interest and dividends, including amortization of premiums and discounts arising at acquisition. Realized gains and losses. (Unrealized gains and losses are not recognized.) A transaction gain or loss on a foreign-currency-denominated held-to-maturity security is accounted for according to ASC 830-20
Trading	Bought and held principally to sell short-term	Fair value.	Interest and dividends, including amortization of premium and discount arising at acquisition. Realized gains and losses. Unrealized gains and losses when realized. Changes in fair value.
Available-for-sale	Neither held-to-maturity nor trading securities Have readily determinable fair value	Fair value as current assets. Unrealized gains and losses in accumulated other comprehensive income as a component of equity. If designated as a fair value hedge, all or a portion of the unrealized gain or loss should be recognized in earnings.	Interest and dividends, including amortization of premium and discount arising at acquisition. Realized gains and losses. Unrealized holding gains and losses in OCI, except for those designated as a hedged in a fair value ledge.

Source: (ASC 320-10-25-4, 35-1, and 35-4)

Held-to-Maturity Debt Securities

If an entity has both the *positive intent* and the *ability* to hold debt securities to maturity, those maturities are classified at acquisition and measured and presented at amortized cost. (ASC 320-10-25-1 and 25-2) For these securities, fair value is not relevant to measuring the cash flow and there is no benefit to financial statement users of introducing the potential volatility associated with fair value. Each investment in a debt security is evaluated separately.

An entity should reassess, at each reporting period, the classification if its intent and ability to hold the security changes. Because the intent is not expected to change, the reassessment generally focuses on the ability to hold the security. (ASC 320-10-25-6)

Circumstances Inconsistent with the Held-to-Maturity Category Held-to-maturity securities are accounted for at amortized cost. To justify that accounting treatment, the held-to-maturity category does not include securities available for sale in response to a need for liquidity or changes in:

- Market interest rates
- Foreign currency risk
- Funding sources and terms
- Yield and availability of alternative investments
(ASC 320-10-25-4)

For asset-liability management purposes, similar or identical securities may be classified differently depending upon intent and ability to hold. (ASC 320-10-25-5)

Under ASC 860-20-35-2 and 35-3, securities, which can be settled in a manner that could cause the recorded amounts not to be substantially recovered, cannot be classified as held-to-maturity. Depending upon the circumstances, those securities are categorized as either trading or available-for-sale.

Certain conditions may indicate that an entity does not have either or both the intent and ability to hold the security to maturity. There are also specific scenarios where a debt security should *not* be classified as held-to-maturity or where stated intent will be called into question in the future:

- Contractually, the security can be prepaid or settled in a way that the holder would not recover all or substantially all of its investment.
- The debt security is available to be sold in response to:
    - Changes in market interest rates or the security's prepayment risk or foreign exchange risk
    - Need for liquidity.
- The security may need to be sold to implement tax strategies.
- Security sold based on speculative analysis before any actual deterioration of the issuer's creditworthiness.
- Security sold to meet regulatory capital requirements.
- Exercise of a put option.
- Convertible debt securities classified as held-to-maturity.
- The entity has a policy to initially classify all debt securities as held-to-maturity and then transfer all securities to available-for-sale at a trigger point.
- An insurance or other regulated entity clarifies a security as held-to-maturity while at the same time telling regulators that the security could be sold to meet liquidity needs.
(ASC 320-10-25-5)

Transfers In general, transfers to or from the held-to-maturity category are not permitted. In those rare circumstances where there are transfers or sales of securities in this category, certain disclosures must be made in the notes to the financial statements for each period for which the results of operations are presented. For those disclosures, see the *Disclosure and Presentation Checklist for Commercial Businesses* at www.wiley.com/go/GAAP2021.

The following changes in circumstances are not considered inconsistent with the transfer, including:

- Significant deterioration in creditworthiness of the issuer
- Elimination or reduction of tax-exempt status of interest through a change in tax law
- Major business disposition or combination
- Statutory or regulatory changes that significantly modify what a permissible investment is or the maximum level of the security to be held
- Downsizing in response to a regulatory increase in the industry's capital requirements
- A significant increase in risk weights for regulatory risk-based capital purposes (ASC 320-10-25-6)

Other events may prompt a sale or transfer of a held-to-maturity security before maturity. These events should be:

1. Isolated
2. Nonrecurring
3. Unusual for the reporting entity
4. Not able to be reasonably anticipated (ASC 320-10-25-9)

If a sale meets *all* four of the conditions above, it may be considered not "tainted" and not call into question the entity's intent to hold other debt to maturity in the future. Note that meeting all four conditions should be extremely rare. (See section later in this chapter on "Transfers between Categories" for more information on "tainted" transfers.)

Sales after a Substantial Portion of Principal Is Collected The sale of a security near enough to its maturity date, for example, within three months of its maturity, meets the requirement to hold to maturity, since the interest rate risk is substantially diminished. Likewise, if a call is considered probable, a sale within three months of that date meets the requirement. The sale of a security after collection of at least 85% of the principal outstanding at acquisition (due to prepayments or to scheduled payments of principal and interest in equal installments) also qualifies, since the "tail" portion no longer represents an efficient investment due to the economic costs of accounting for the remnants. Scheduled payments are not required to be equal for variable-rate debt. (ASC 320-10-25-14)

Example of Held-to-Maturity Debt Securities

The 12/31/X1 debt security portfolio categorized as held-to-maturity is as follows:

Security	Maturity value	Amortized cost	Assumed fair value
DEF 12% bond, due 12/31/X2	$ 10,000	$10,320	$10,200
PQR mortgage-backed debt, due 12/31/X4	$100,000	$92,000	$90,000
JKL 8% bond, due 12/31/X8	$ 10,000	$ 8,929	$ 9,100

The statement of financial position would report all the securities in this category at amortized cost and would classify them as follows:

Security	*Maturity date*	*Statement of financial position*	*Classification*
DEF	12/31/X2	$10,320	Current
PQR	12/31/X4	92,000	Noncurrent
JKL	12/31/X8	8,929	Noncurrent

Interest income, including premium and discount amortization, is included in income. (ASC 320-10-35-4) Any realized gains or losses are also included in income. Unless another basis yields a similar result, entities must amortize the premium or discount on debt securities using the effective-interest method. Interest income is calculated using the effective-interest rate applied to the beginning carrying amount for each period.

Trading Debt Securities

If an entity has debt securities that it intends to actively and frequently buy and sell for short-term profits, those securities are classified as trading securities and carried at fair value on the statement of financial position as current assets. All applicable interest and dividends, realized gains and losses, and unrealized gains and losses on changes in fair value are included in income. (ASC 320-10-25-1) Mortgage-backed interest-only certificates held for sale require classification as trading securities. (ASC 320-10-25-5)

Example of Accounting for Trading Securities

The Year 1 current trading securities portfolio is as follows:

Security	*Cost*	*Fair value*	*Difference (fair value minus cost)*
ABC	$1,000	$ 900	$(100)
MNO calls	1,500	1,700	200
STU	2,000	1,400	(600)
XYZ 7% bond	2,500	2,600	100
	$7,000	$6,600	$(400)

A $400 adjustment is required in order to recognize the decline in fair value. The entry required is

Unrealized loss on trading securities	400	
Trading securities—MNO calls	200	
Trading securities—XYZ 7% bond	100	
Trading securities—ABC		100
Trading securities—STU		600

The unrealized loss would appear on the income statement as part of other expenses and losses. (ASC 320-10-35-1) Dividend and interest income (including premium and discount amortization arising at acquisition) is included in income. Any realized gains or losses from the sale of securities are also included in income.

An alternative to direct write-up and write-down of securities is the use of an asset valuation allowance account to adjust the portfolio totals. In the above example, the entry would be:

Unrealized loss on trading securities	400	
Valuation allowance (contra asset)		400

The valuation allowance of $400 would be deducted from historical cost to obtain a fair value of $6,600 for the trading securities on the statement of financial position.

All trading securities are classified as current assets and the statement of financial position would appear as follows:

Current assets:

Trading securities at fair value (cost = $7,000)	$6,600

The Year 2 current trading portfolio is as follows:

Security	*New securities cost*	*Old securities Year 1 fair value*	*Year 2 fair value*	*Difference**
ABC		$ 900	$1,000	$100
DEF Puts	$1,500		1,500	0
STU		1,400	1,800	400
VWX	2,700		2,800	100
	$4,200	$2,300	$7,100	$600

* *Difference = Year 2 fair value – (Cost or Year 1 fair value)*

A $600 adjustment is required in order to recognize the increase in fair value. The entry required is:

Trading securities—ABC	100	
Trading securities—STU	400	
Trading securities—VWX	100	
Unrealized gain on trading securities		600

The unrealized gain would appear on the income statement as part of other income.

Example of Accounting for a Realized Gain on Trading Securities

Assume:

1. The same information as given in the above example for Year 1
2. In Year 2, the MNO calls are sold for $1,600 and the XYZ 7% bonds are sold for $2,700. The entry required to record the sale is:

Cash	4,300	
Realized loss on sale of trading securities	100	
Realized gain on sale of trading securities		100
Trading securities—MNO calls (Year 1 fair value)		1,700
Trading securities—XYZ 7% bonds (Year 1 fair value)		2,600

Under the valuation allowance method, the current trading portfolio would appear as follows:

Security	*Cost*	*Year 2 fair value*
ABC	$1,000	$1,000
DEF Puts	1,500	1,500
STU	2,000	1,800
VWX	2,700	2,800
	$7,200	$7,100

The required entries to recognize the increase in fair value and the realized gain are:

Valuation allowance	300	
Unrealized gain on trading securities		300

To adjust the valuation allowance to reflect the unrealized loss of $100 at the end of year 2 on the remaining trading portfolio:

Cash	4,300	
Trading securities—MNO calls (Cost)		1,500
Trading securities—XYZ 7% bonds (Cost)		2,500
Realized gain on sale of trading securities		300

The statement of financial position under both methods would appear as follows:

Current assets:	
Trading securities at fair value (cost = $7,200)	$7,100

Available-for-Sale Securities

Investments in debt securities that are *not* classified as either trading securities or held-to-maturity are classified as available-for-sale. The securities in this category are required to be carried at fair value on the statement of financial position. (ASC 320-10-35-1) The determination of current or noncurrent status for individual securities depends on whether the securities are considered working capital. (ASC 210-10-45)

All applicable interest (including premium and discount amortization arising at acquisition) and any realized gains or losses from the sale of securities are included in income from continuing operations. Other than the possibility of having some noncurrent securities on the statement of financial position, the major difference between trading securities and available-for-sale securities is the handling of unrealized gains and losses. Unlike trading securities, the *unrealized* gains and losses of available-for-sale securities are excluded from net income. Instead, they are reported in other comprehensive income. An exception to this is if all or part of the gain or loss is designated as a fair value hedge. In that case, the unrealized gain or loss is recognized in earnings. (ASC 320-10-35-1 and ASC 320-10-45-8)

Example of Available-for-Sale Debt Securities

Bonito Corporation purchases 10,000 bonds of Easter Corporation maturing in six years, at a price of $95.38, and classifies them as available-for-sale. The bonds have a par value of $100 and pay interest of 7% annually. At the price Bonito paid, the effective interest rate is 8%. The calculation of the bond discount follows:

Maturity value of bonds receivable		$1,000,000
Present value of $1,000,000 due in 6 years at 8% (multiplier = 0.6302)	630,200	
Present value of $70,000 interest payable annually for 6 years at 8% annually (multiplier = 4.6229)	323,600	
Purchase price of bonds		953,800
Discount on bonds payable		46,200

The complete table of interest income and discount amortization calculations for the remaining life of the bonds follows:

Year	*Beginning value*	*Interest received*	*Recognized interest income**	*Discount amortization*	*Ending value*
1	$953,800	$70,000	$76,304	6,304	960,104
2	960,104	70,000	76,808	6,808	966,912
3	966,912	70,000	77,353	7,353	974,265
4	974,265	70,000	77,941	7,941	982,206
5	982,206	70,000	78,576	8,576	990,782
6	990,782	70,000	79,218	9,218	1,000,000
				46,200	

* *(Beginning value) × (effective interest rate of 8%)*

At the end of Year 1, the quoted market price of the bonds is $98, and it is $94 at the end of Year 2. The company has an incremental tax rate of 25%. The following table calculates the before-tax and after-tax holding gains and losses on the investment.

Year	*Ending carrying value*	*Ending fair value*	*Holding gain/(loss)*	*Income tax*	*Net of tax*
1	$960,104	$980,000	$19,896	4,974	14,922
2	966,912	940,000	(26,912)	(6,728)	(20,184)
Net			(7,016)	(1,754)	(5,262)

Bonito sells the bonds at the end of Year 2, and reports these gains and losses in net income and other comprehensive income in the indicated years as follows:

	Year 1	*Year 2*
Net income:		
Interest income	76,304	76,808
Loss on sale of bonds		(7,016)
Income tax expense	(19,076)	(17,448)
Net gain/(loss) realized in net income	57,228	52,344
Other comprehensive income:		
Gain/(loss) on available-for-sale securities arising during period, net of tax	14,922	(20,184)
Reclassification adjustment, net of tax		5,262
Other comprehensive income net gain/(loss)	14,922	(14,922)

Notice that the changes in fair value are reflected in net income *after* the sale of available-for-sale securities, thus reducing volatility in net income.

Transfers between Categories

ASC 320 includes provisions intended to curtail management manipulation of income through careful selection of portfolio securities to be sold, a practice commonly known as "gains trading" and primarily used by financial institutions. Transfers from one of the three portfolio classifications to any other are expected to be rare. ASC 320 imposes limitations on situations in which it would be permissible to transfer investments between portfolios. ASC 320 prohibits an entity the use of the "held-to-maturity" classification once it has been "tainted" by sales of securities that had been classified in that portfolio. (ASC 320-10-35-8 and 9) This is because a taint calls into question management's credibility. (See the discussion earlier in this chapter in the section "Held-to-Maturity Debt Securities—Transfer" for more information.)

Securities purchased for the trading portfolio are so classified because it is management's intent to seek advantage in short-term price movements. The fact that management does not dispose of those investments quickly does not necessarily mean that the original categorization was improper or that an expressed changed intent calls for an accounting entry. While transfers out of the trading category are not completely prohibited, they would have to be supported by facts and circumstances making the assertion of changed intent highly credible.

Measurement Transfers among portfolios are accounted for at fair value as of the date of the transfer. (ASC 320-10-35-10)[1] Generally, investments in the trading category transferred to the available-for-sale category warrant no further recognition of gain or loss, as the carrying value of the investments already reflects any unrealized gains or losses experienced since their original acquisition. The only caveat is that, if the reporting entity's accounting records of its investments, as a practical matter, have not been updated for fair values since the date of the most recently issued statement of financial position, any changes occurring since that time need to be recognized at the date the transfer occurs. The fair value at the date of transfer becomes the new "cost" of the security in the available-for-sale portfolio.

When the security is transferred, any unrealized holding gains and losses are accounted for as shown in the following exhibit.

Exhibit—Transfers of Debt Securities between Categories: Accounting Treatment for Unrealized Holding Gains or Losses—*Before* Implementation of ASU 2019-04

From	To	Accounting Treatment for Unrealized Holding Gains or Losses
Trading	AFS or HTM	Fair value at date of transfer Do not reverse unrealized gain or loss already recognized.
AFS or HTM	Trading	Recognize in income those not already recognized. Transfers into or from the trading category should be rare.
HTM	AFS	Recognize in OCI per ASC 220. 320-10-35-10c Few transfers are expected from the HTM category.
AFS	HTM	Continue to report in a separate component of shareholders' equity, such as AOCI, but amortize over the remaining life of the security as an adjustment of yield.
(ASC 320-10-35-10)		

[1] Upon implementation of ASU 2019-04, this language changes to "transfer of a debt security from or into a trading category is accounted for at fair value."

Exhibit—Transfers of Debt Securities between Categories *After* Implementation of ASU 2019-04

From	To	Accounting Treatment
Trading	AFS or HTM	Fair value at date of transfer Do not reverse unrealized gain or loss already recognized
AFS or HTM	Trading	Recognize in earnings any unrealized gain or loss not previously recognized in earnings
HTM	AFS	• Reverse in earnings any allowance for credit losses on the HTM security previously recorded • Transfer at amortized port • Determine if an allowance for credit losses is necessary under ASC 326-30 • Report in AOCI any unrealized gain or loss on the AFS security, excluding the amount recorded for credit losses • Consider whether the transfer calls into question management's intent to hold to maturity the remaining securities
AFS	HTM	• Reverse in earnings any allowance for credit losses previously recorded on the AFS security • Transfer the AFS security at amortized cost basis net of any unrealized gain or loss reported in AOCI • Determine if an allowance for credit losses is necessary under ASC 326-30 • Continue to report the holding gain or loss in a separate component of stockholders' equity such as AOCI • Amortize unrealized holding gain or loss over the life of the security as arrangements of yield
(ASC 320-10-35-10, 10A, 10B)		

A security transferred from HTM to AFS brings over its amortized cost basis. (ASC 320-10-35-15) For a security transferred from AFS to HTM, the difference between the par value at transfer date is amortized as a yield adjustment. Entities should conclude whether the transfer of a security from the HTM category to the AFS category raises questions about the entity's intent and ability to hold to maturity the securities remaining in the HTM category. (ASC 320-10-35-10A(e)) The adjusted cost basis is the fair value adjusted for subsequent amortization. (ASC 320-10-35-16)[2]

Impairment of AFS and HTM Securities[3]

ASC 320 addresses the impairment of individual available-for-sale and held-to-maturity securities. Impairment of trading securities is generally not relevant because trading securities are measured at fair value in income.

---

2 Upon implementation of ASU 2019-04, this provision is changed to transferring a security from AFS to HTM may create a premium or discount that should be amortized as a yield adjustment under the guidance of ASC 310-20. The basis is determined at the transfer date, reduced by any previous writeoffs, but excluding any allowance for credit losses, plus or minus the amount of any remaining unrealized holding gain or loss reported in AOCI. (ASC 320-10-35-16)

3 Upon implementation of ASU 2016-13, this section on impairment will be superseded and guidance on impairment can be found in ASC 326.

Scope The guidance on impairment of individual available-for-sale and held-to-maturity securities applies to:

- Debt securities within the scope of ASC 320 with the following clarification:
  - If the application of ASC 815-15-25 (recognition of embedded derivatives) results in bifurcating an investment into a host instrument and an embedded derivative, the host instrument would be evaluated for impairment under this guidance if it falls within its scope.
  - The standard applies to debt securities that are (a) within the scope of ASC 958-320 (not-for-profit entities' investments in debt and equity securities) and (b) held by an investor that reports a performance indicator as defined in ASC 954-220-45.

  (ASC 320-10-35-17)

Steps to Determine Existence and Accounting for Impairment ASC 320-10-35 establishes a two-step decision process to determine if an investment classified as available for sale or held to maturity has been impaired:

Step 1. Determine whether the investment is impaired, and if so,
Step 2. Evaluate whether the impairment is other than temporary.

The guidance also establishes a discrete model for assessing impairment of cost-method investments that present unique challenges since reasonable estimation of their fair value is often not practical or cost effective.

In considering whether the issuer (i.e., borrower or debtor) of a debt security can prepay or settle the security in a manner that would result in the investor not recovering substantially all of its cost, the investor is not permitted to combine separate contracts such as a debt security and a guarantee or other credit enhancement.

Step 1—Determine whether the investment is impaired The unit of accounting for the purpose of performing these steps is the individual security level. This is defined as the level and method of aggregation used by the reporting entity to measure realized and unrealized gains and losses on its debt and equity securities. An example of an acceptable method of aggregation would be for the reporting entity to consider equity securities of an issuer that carry the same Committee on Uniform Security Information Procedures (CUSIP) number that were purchased in separate trade lots to be considered together on an average cost basis. (ASC 320-10-35-20)

An investment is impaired if its fair value is less than its cost. (ASC 320-10-35-21) Cost is defined for this as amortized cost basis (ACB) and includes adjustments made to the original cost of the investment for such items as:[4]

- Accretion
- Amortization
- Cash collections
- Foreign exchange
- Previous OTTI recognized as charges to net income less any accumulative effect adjustments
- Fair value hedge accounting adjustments

  (ASC 323-10-35-20)

[4] ASC 815-25-35-1 indicates that, with respect to a qualifying fair value hedge, the change in fair value of the hedged item that is attributable to the hedged risk is recorded as an adjustment to the carrying amount of the hedged item and is recognized currently in net income

The assessment of whether an investment is impaired must be made for each interim and annual reporting period. In assessing impairment of debt securities, the investor is not permitted to combine separate contracts such as guarantees or other credit enhancements. (ASC 320-10-35-22 and 35-23)

If the investment is impaired, proceed to Step 2.

Step 2—evaluate whether the impairment is other-than-temporary If the fair value of the investment is less than its amortized cost at the ending date of a reporting period (the date of the latest statement of financial position), management is tasked with evaluating whether the impairment is temporary, or whether it is "other-than-temporary." While the term "other-than-temporary" is not defined, the FASB affirmatively states that it *does not mean permanent.* (ASC 320-10-35-30) Thus, a future recovery of all or a portion of the decline in fair value is not necessarily indicative that an assessment of OTTI made in prior periods was incorrect.

Intent to sell If an entity intends to sell the security, an OTTI is considered to have occurred. (ASC 320-10-35-33A)

Required to sell Even if an entity does not intend to sell the security, it may be required to sell the security. The entity should use all available evidence to assess whether it is more likely than not that it will be required to sell the security prior to recovery of its amortized cost basis. This may be the case, for example, if the entity has cash or working capital requirements or contractual or regulatory obligations that will require sale of the security prior to a forecasted recovery. If it is more likely than not that a sale will be required prior to recovery of the security's amortized cost basis, OTTI is considered to have been incurred. (ASC 320-10-35-33B) If, at the measurement date, the entity does not expect to recover the *entire* amortized cost basis, then the entity cannot assert that it will recover the amortized cost basis regardless of any intent to continue holding the security or to sell the security. Therefore, if an entity is required to sell a security, OTTI is considered to have been incurred and a credit loss exists. (ASC 320-10-35-33C)

Calculation of amount of expected recovery In assessing whether a credit loss exists, an entity compares the present value of cash flows expected to be collected (PVCF) from the security to the security's amortized cost basis. The computation, in simple terms, is made by discounting the expected cash flows at the effective interest rate implicit in the security at the date of its acquisition. A methodology for estimation of that amount is described in ASC 310, which is codified in the ASC as follows:

- ASC 310-10-35-21 through 35-37
- ASC 310-30-30-2
- ASC 310-40-35-12
  (ASC 320-10-35-33D)

Many factors influence the estimate of whether a credit loss has occurred and the period over which the debt security is expected to recover. (ASC 320-10-35-33F) Examples of these factors include, but are not limited to:

- The length of time and the extent to which the fair value of the security has been less than its amortized cost basis.
- Adverse conditions that relate specifically to the security, an industry, or a geographic locale such as:
  - Changes in the financial condition of the issuer of the security or, in the case of asset-backed securities, changes in the financial condition of the underlying loan obligors.
  - Changes in technology.

  - Discontinuance of a segment of the business that may affect the future earnings potential of the issuer or underlying loan obligors of the security.
  - Changes in the quality of a credit enhancement.
- The historical and implied volatility of the fair value of the security.
- The payment structure of the debt security and the likelihood of the issuer being able to make payments that are scheduled to increase in the future; examples of nontraditional loan terms are described in ASC 310-10-50-25, ASC 825-10-55-1, and ASC 825-10-55-2.
- Failure of the security's issuer to make scheduled interest or principal payments.
- Changes in the rating of the security by a ratings agency.
- Recoveries or additional declines in fair value that occur subsequent to the date of the statement of financial position.
(ASC 320-10-35-33F)

In developing the estimate of PVCF for the purpose of assessing whether OTTI has occurred (or recurred), the entity should consider all available information relevant to the collectibility of sums due under the terms of the security, including information about past events, current conditions, and reasonable and supportable forecasts. That information generally should include:

- The remaining payment terms of the security,
- Prepayment speeds,
- The financial condition of the issuer(s),
- Expected defaults, and
- The value of the collateral.
(ASC 320-10-35-33G)

To accomplish this objective, the entity should consider, for example:

- Industry analyst reports and forecasts,
- Sector credit ratings, and
- Other market data relevant to the collectibility of the security.
(ASC 320-10-35-33H)

The entity must also consider how other credit enhancements affect the expected performance of the security, including:

- The current financial condition of the guarantor of the security (unless the guarantee is a separate contract under ASC 320-10-35-23), and/or
- Whether any subordinated interests are capable of absorbing estimated losses on the loans underlying the security.
(ASC 320-10-35-33I)

The remaining payment terms of the security could differ significantly from the payment terms in prior periods, such as when securities are backed by nontraditional loans (e.g., reverse mortgages, interest-only debt, adjustable-rate products). As a result, management must consider whether currently performing loans that back a security will continue to perform when required payments increase in the future, including any required "balloon" payments. Management should also consider how the value of any collateral would affect the security's expected performance. If there has been a decline in the fair value of the collateral, management is to assess the effect of that decline on the ability of the entity to collect the balloon payment. (ASC 320-10-35-33I)

Recognition of an OTTI If, as a result of Step 2, the entity judges the impairment to be other than temporary, the amount of the loss depends on whether the entity intends to sell the security or will be, more likely than not, required to sell the security. (ASC 320-10-35-34A) If the entity intends to sell, or more likely than not will be required to sell the investment before recovery of the AC less any current period credit loss, the reporting entity recognizes an impairment loss as a charge to net income for the entire difference between the investment's amortized cost basis and its fair value at the date of the statement of financial position. (ASC 320-10-35-34B)

If the entity does *not* intend to sell or likely will not be required to sell the investment, the entity splits the OTTI into two components:

- The amount related to the credit loss is recognized in net income when incurred.
- The remaining portion is accounted for through other comprehensive income.
  (ASC 320-10-35-34C and 35-34D)

Exhibit—Determining OTTI of Debt Securities to Be Recognized in Net Income and in Other Comprehensive Income (OCI)

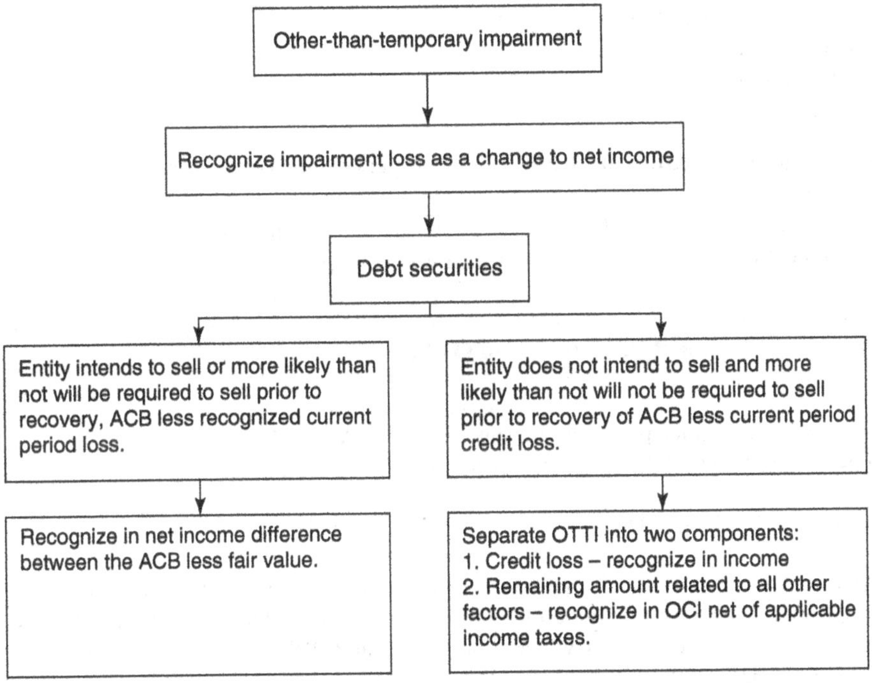

The previous ACB less OTTI recognized in earnings that represents the current period credit loss becomes the new amortized cost basis of the investment prospectively. That new ACB is not adjusted for subsequent recoveries in fair value. The amortized cost basis is adjusted, however, for accretion and amortization, as described in the next section. (ASC 320-10-35-34E)

Subsequent Measurement after Recognition of an OTTI After recognition of an OTTI, the impaired security is accounted for as follows. The entity accounts for a debt security subject to OTTI as if that security had been purchased on the measurement date of the OTTI at an amortized cost basis equal to the previous amortized cost basis less than the OTTI (recognized as a charge to net income as a current period credit loss). (ASC 320-10-35-35)

Debt securities classified as available-for-sale (AFS) Subsequent increases and decreases in the fair value of AFS securities, if not caused by an additional OTTI, are included in OCI. (ASC 320-10-35-35)

Debt securities classified as held-to-maturity The OTTI recognized in OCI for held-to-maturity securities is prospectively accreted (sometimes referred to as "recycling") from other comprehensive income (OCI) to the amortized cost of the debt security over its remaining life based on the amount and timing of future estimated cash flows. That accretion is to increase the security's carrying value and continues until the security is sold, matures, or there is an additional OTTI charged to net income. If the security is sold, guidance on the effect of changes in circumstances that would not call into question management's intent to hold other debt securities to maturity in the future is discussed in a previous section of this chapter and is provided in the following authoritative literature:

- ASC 320-10-25-6, and 25-9
- ASC 320-10-25-14
- ASC 320-10-50-11
  (ASC 320-10-35-35A)

Income Statement Presentation of an OTTI In periods in which management determines that a decline in the fair value of a security below its amortized cost basis is other than temporary, management presents the total OTTI in the income statement with an offset for the amount of the total OTTI that is recognized in OCI, if any (Component 2).

Example of Income Statement Presentation of OTTI

Total losses from other-than-temporary impairment	$(30,000)
Portion of loss recognized in other comprehensive income (before income taxes)	22,000
Net impairment losses recognized in net income	$ (8,000)

When reporting the components of accumulated other comprehensive income (AOCI), management must present separately the amounts recognized in AOCI related to held-to-maturity and available-for-sale debt securities for which a portion of an OTTI has been recognized as a charge to net income. (ASC 320-10-45-9A)

Structured Notes ASC 320-10-35-38 through 35-43 deals with the complex area of "structured notes," in particular with the matters of the recognition of interest income and of the statement of financial position classification of such instruments. When recognizing interest income on structured note securities in an available-for-sale or held-to-maturity portfolio, the retrospective interest method is used if three conditions are satisfied. These conditions are:

1. Either the original investment amount or the maturity amount of the contractual principal is at risk.

2. Return of investment on note is subject to volatility arising from either:
    - No stated rate or stated rate that is not a constant percentage or in the same direction as changes in market-based interest rates or interest rate index, or
    - Fixed or variable coupon rate lower than that for interest for traditional notes with similar maturity, and a portion of potential yield based on occurrence of future circumstances or events.
3. Contractual maturity of bond is based on a specific index or on occurrence of specific events or situations outside the control of contractual parties.
   (ASC 320-10-35-40)

This does not apply to structured note securities that, by their nature, subject the holder to reasonably possible loss of all, or substantially all, of the original invested amount (other than due to debtor failure to pay amount owed). In those instances, the investment is to be carried at fair value with changes in value recognized in current earnings. (ASC 320-10-35-38)

If certain conditions are satisfied, interest income on AFS or HTM structured securities for a reporting period is measured by reference to the change in amortized cost from period beginning to period end, plus any cash received during the period. Amortized cost is determined with reference to the conditions applicable as of the respective date of the statement of financial position. Other-than-temporary declines in fair value would also have to be recognized in earnings, consistent with ASC 320 requirements for held-to-maturity investments. (ASC 320-10-35-41)

18 ASC 321 INVESTMENTS—EQUITY SECURITIES

PERSPECTIVE AND ISSUES

Investment Topics

The Codification contains several topics dealing with investments, including:

- ASC 320, *Investments—Debt Securities.*
- ASC 321, *Investments—Equity Securities* (added by ASU 2016-01).
- ASC 323, *Investments—Equity Method and Joint Ventures.*
- ASC 325, *Investments—Other.*
- ASC 326, *Financial Instruments—Credit Losses.* See the chapter on ASC 326 for more information.
(ASC 321-10-05-1)

Subtopic

ASC 321, *Investments—Equity Securities,* contains one subtopic:

- ASC 321-10, *Overall,* which provides accounting and reporting guidance for investments in equity securities.
(ASC 321-10-05-2)

Scope and Scope Exceptions

Scope—Entities The guidance in ASC 321 applies to all entities, including entities that are not deemed specialized industries for purposes of this Topic:

- Cooperatives and mutual entities, such as credit unions and mutual insurance entities
- Trusts that do not report substantially all of their securities at fair value
  (ASC 321-10-15-2)

Note: The disclosures required by ASC 321-10-50-4 are not required for entities within the scope of ASC 958 on not-for-profit entities.

The guidance does *not* apply to entities in specialized industries that account for substantially all investments at fair value, with changes in value recognized in earnings (income) or in the change in net assets. Examples of those entities are:

- Brokers and dealers in securities (Topic 940)
- Defined benefit pension, other postretirement plans, and health and welfare plans (Topics 960, 962, and 965)
- Investment companies (Topic 946)
  (ASC 321-10-15-3)

Scope—Instruments Included in the scope, as if the ownership interests are equity securities, are ownership interests in an entity, including:

- Investments in partnerships,
- Unincorporated joint ventures, and
- Limited liability corporations.
  (ASC 321-10-15-4)

It also applies to forwards and purchased options to acquire and dispose of ownership interests that are not treated as derivatives in ASC 815, but are accounted for under ASC 321. ASC 815-10-15-141A offers guidance on applying the guidance in ASC 815-10-15-141. (ASC 321-10-15-6)

ASC 321 does *not* apply to any of the following items:

- Derivative instruments subject to the requirements of ASC 815, including those that have been separated from a host contract as required by ASC 815-15-25
- Investments accounted for under the equity method (ASC 323)
- Investments in consolidated subsidiaries
- An ownership interest in an exchange, usually held by broker-dealers and by depository and lending institutions
- Federal Home Loan Bank Stock (ASC 942-325)
- Federal Reserve Bank Stock (ASC 942-325)
  (ASC 321-10-15-5)

DEFINITIONS OF TERMS

Source: ASC 321-20. See Appendix A, *Definitions of Terms*, for terms related to this topic: Equity Security (Def. 1), Fair Value (Def. 2), Holding Gain or Loss, Market Participants, Orderly Transaction, Readily Determinable Fair Values, Related Parties, and Security (Def. 2).

CONCEPTS, RULES, AND EXAMPLES

Initial Measurement—Investments That No Longer Qualify for the Equity Method

There may be circumstances where the investor's share of the investment no longer qualifies for the equity method. For instance, the level of investment may decline. In those cases, the security's initial basis becomes the carrying value. Any losses accrued remain as part of the carrying value and those related to the investment account are not adjusted retroactively. If the equity method is discontinued, the equity security is remeasured following the guidance in ASC 321-10-35-1 or 35-2. In applying ASC 321-10-35-2 to the investment retained, if the investor identifies observable price changes in transactions for the same or a similar investment by the same issuer that results in the entity discontinuing the equity method, the entity remeasures the retained investment at fair value once it no longer applies ASC 323. (ASC 323-10-30-1)

Subsequent Measurement

The chart that follows gives an overview of the subsequent measurement of equity securities. Details follow.

Equity Securities *with* Readily Determinable Fair Value Because, unlike debt securities, equity securities do not have a maturity date, the entity primarily realizes the value of an equity investment through a sale. So, fair value is the most appropriate measure. All equity investments in the scope of ASC 321, with readily determinable fair value, are measured at fair value, using the guidance in ASC 820, with changes in fair value reflected in income. (ASC 321-10-35-1)

Exhibit—Subsequent Measurement of Equity Securities—Overview

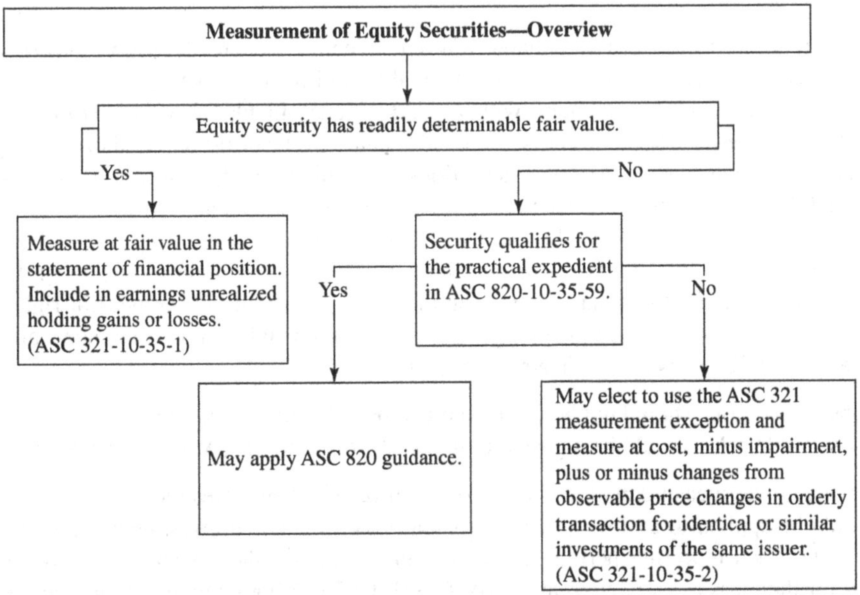

Equity Securities *without* Readily Determinable Fair Values—ASC 820-20 Practical Expedient Some investments that do not have readily determinable fair value as defined in ASC 820-20 may qualify for a practical expedient under ASC 820-10-35-59. If so, they are measured at net asset value, that is, cost minus impairment, plus or minus observable price changes in an orderly transaction for an identical or similar instrument from the same issuer.

This expedient is available to:

- Investment companies within the scope of ASC 946, or
- Real estate funds that use measurement principles consistent with those in ASC 946;

If the investment meets those qualifications, the entity may value them at net asset value per share, that is, the amount of net assets attributable to each share of common stock.
(ASC 820-10-35-59)

Equity Securities *without* Readily Determinable Fair Values—ASC 321 Measurement Alternative Fair value through current income is ASC 321's default accounting for equity investments not accounted for using the equity method. However, ASC 321 offers a measurement exception for equity investments without readily determinable fair values. ASC 321 allows some entities to elect the cost method. This method is intended to reflect the fair value of the security as of the date that the observable transaction took place.

Entities following specialized accounting models, such as investment companies and broker-dealers, do not have that option. All others may elect to record these investments at cost, less impairment, adjusted for subsequent price changes. Entities that elect the cost-method option must make changes in the carrying value of the equity investment as of the date that observable price changes occurred:

- In orderly transactions
- For the identical or similar investment
- Of the same issuer.
  (ASC 321-10-35-2)

Entities are required to make a reasonable effort to identify reasonably knowable price changes. (ASC 321-10-55-8) This approach eliminates the need for entities to get a valuation every reporting period for equity investments without readily determinable fair values. However, in making its measurement election, the entity should also consider the effort required to identify known or reasonably knowable observable transactions, determine whether those transactions were orderly, and determine if those transactions were for similar investments.

The entity should adjust the observable price of the similar security as of the date the observable transaction took place. Determining whether an equity security is similar requires significant judgment. When making the determination, entities should consider differences in rights and obligations of the securities, such as voting rights, distribution rights and preferences, and conversion features. Differences may indicate either that:

- The observable price should not be used to adjust the value of the security, or
- The observable price should be adjusted to reflect the differences. (ASC 321-10-55-9)

An entity elects the measurement exception on an investment by investment basis. Once elected, it should be applied to an investment consistently as long as the investment meets the qualifying criteria. Each reporting period, the entity must reassess whether an equity investment qualifies for the measurement alternative. (ASC 321-10-35-2) For example, if an investee goes public and there is a readily determinable fair value, the investment must be measured prospectively at fair value using the guidance in ASC 820.

The application of the measurement exception requires professional judgment. Entities would be prudent to document their assessments.

Changes in Measurement Approach An entity that measures an equity security without readily determinable fair value using the ASC 321 measurement exception may change to the ASC 820 expedient through an election. That election is irrevocable and the entity must measure all future purchases of identical or similar investments of the same issuer using the ASC 820 fair value expedient. (ASC 321-10-35-2) To avoid manipulation, the Board believes that just because of difference in purchase dates an entity should not measure the same equity in different ways.

Impairment Model for Equity Securities *without* Readily Determinable Fair Values An entity must follow the impairment guidance in ASC 321 for an investment without readily determinable fair value if:

- The investment does not qualify for the practical expedient in ASC 820-10-35-59, and
- The entity uses the ASC 321 measurement exception to measure the investment. (ASC 321-10-35-3)

ASC 321 has a single-step, impairment model for equity investments without readily determinable fair values. The single-step model requires the entity to perform a qualitative assessment of impairment each reporting period. If the entity determines impairment exists, it then turns to a quantitative assessment and estimates the fair value of the investment the loss is the difference between the carrying value and the fair value of the investment and is recognized in net income. (ASC 321-10-35-4) Using the single-step model, the entity does not have to predict whether the investment will recover its value.

Impairment indicators ASC 321 includes the following impairment indicators:

- A significant deterioration in the investee's:
  - Earnings performance,
  - Credit rating,
  - Asset quality, or
  - Business prospects.
- A significant adverse change in the investee's:
  - Regulatory,
  - Economic, or
  - Technological environment.
- A significant adverse change in the general market condition of either the geographical area or the industry in which the investee operates.
- For an amount less than the carrying amount of that investment:
  - A bona fide offer to purchase,
  - An offer by the investee to sell, or
  - A completed auction process for the same or similar investment.
- Factors that raise significant concerns about the investee's ability to continue as a going concern, much as negative cash flows from operations, working capital deficiencies, or noncompliance with statutory capital requirements or debt covenants. (ASC 323-10-35-3)

The guidance does not assign a probability threshold to the indicators. The presence of any one of these or other indicators does not mean impairment exists. It does mean that the entity needs a quantitative valuation of the investment.

Dividend Income

Dividend income from investments in equity securities is included in income of the investor. (ASC 321-10-35-6)

Presentation and Disclosure

For ASC 321-45 presentation and disclosure requirements, see Appendix B, *Disclosure and Presentation Checklist for Commercial Businesses* at www.wiley.com/go/GAAP2021.

19 ASC 323 INVESTMENTS—EQUITY METHOD AND JOINT VENTURES

PERSPECTIVE AND ISSUES

Investment Topics

The Codification contains several topics dealing with investments, including:

- ASC 320, *Investments—Debt and Equity Securities.* ASU 2016-01 changes the name of ASC 320 to Investments—Debt Securities.
- ASC 321, *Investments—Equity Securities.* This topic was added by ASU 2016-01. See the chapter on ASC 321 for more information.
- ASC 323, *Investments—Equity Method and Joint Ventures*
- ASC 325, *Investments—Other*
- ASC 326, *Financial Instruments—Credit Losses.* See the chapter on ASC 326 for more information.

Technical Alert

ASU 2020-01 In January 2020, the FASB's Emerging Issues Task Force (EITF) issued ASU 2020-01, *Investments—Equity Securities (Topic 321), Investment Equity Method and Joint Ventures (Topic 323), and Derivatives and Hedging (Topic 815).* The purpose of the ASU is to clarify the interactions between Topics 321, 323, and 815.

Guidance Issue 1 of the ASU addresses what happens when an entity applies or discontinues the equity method of accounting. The changes are noted in this chapter.

Issue 2 addresses whether to apply the guidance in ASC 321 or 815 to forward contracts and purchased options to purchase securities that, upon settlement of the forward contract or exercise of the purchased option, should be accounted for under the equity method in ASC 323 or under ASC 321. The investments under question are not derivatives or in-substance common stock in the scope of ASC 323. The EITF decided that:

- For the purpose of applying ASC 815-10-15-141(a), entities should not consider whether, upon the settlement of the forward contract or service of the purchased option either individually or with existing investments, the underlying securities should be accounted for under ASC 323 or the fair value option in ASC 825.
- Entities should evaluate the remaining ASC 815-10-15-141 characteristics to determine how to account for the forward contracts and purchased options.

Effective Date The ASU is effective:

- For public business entities—fiscal years beginning after December 15, 2020, and interim periods within those fiscal years.
- For all other entities—fiscal years beginning after December 15, 2020, and interim periods within those fiscal years.

Early adoption is permitted.
Transition The ASU should be applied prospectively.

Subtopics

ASC 323, *Investments—Equity Method and Joint Ventures*, contains three subtopics:

- ASC 323-10, *Overall,* which addresses the application of the equity method to entities within its scope,
- ASC 323-30, *Partnerships, Joint Ventures, and Limited Liability Entities*, which provides guidance on applying the equity method to partnerships, joint ventures, and limited liability entities, and
- ASC 323-740, *Income Taxes,* which provides stand-alone guidance on a specific type of real estate investment, Qualified Affordable Housing Project Subsections.
(ASC 323-10-15-2)

DEFINITIONS OF TERMS

Source: ASC 323, *Glossaries*. Also see Appendix A, *Definitions of Terms*, for other terms relevant to this topic: Common Stock, Corporate Joint Venture, Current Tax Expense, Dividends, Event, Income Tax Expense (or Benefits), Income Taxes, Investee, Investor, Noncontrolling Interest, Not-for-Profit Entity, Parent, Public Business Entity, Public Business, and Subsidiary.

Earnings or Losses of an Investee. Net income (or net loss) of an investee determined in accordance with U.S. GAAP.

In-Substance Common Stock. An investment in an entity that has risk and reward characteristics that are substantially similar to that entity's common stock.

Significant Influence. See ASC 323-10-15-6 through 15-11 and information on "Significant Influence" in the next section of this chapter.

Standstill Agreement. An agreement signed by the investee and investor under which the investor agrees to limit its shareholding in the investee.

CONCEPTS, RULES, AND EXAMPLES—ASC 323-10, *OVERALL*: THE EQUITY METHOD OF ACCOUNTING FOR INVESTMENTS

Scope and Scope Exceptions

ASC 323 applies to all entities and their investments in common stock or in-substance common stock, including common stock of corporate joint ventures. (ASC 323-10-15-3)

The guidance in ASC 323 guidance does not apply to an investment:

- Accounted for in accordance with ASC 815-10, *Derivatives and Hedging—Overall*
- In common stock held by a nonbusiness entity, such as an estate, trust, or individual

- In common stock within the scope of ASC 810, *Consolidation*
- Held by an investment company within the scope of ASC 946, except as discussed in paragraph 946-323-45-2, an entity that provides services to the investment company (ASC 323-10-15-4)

ASC 323-10 does not apply to an investment in a partnership or unincorporated joint venture (covered in ASC 323-30) or an investment in a limited liability company that maintains specific ownership accounts for each investor (discussed in ASC 272). (ASC 323-10-15-5) Additional information regarding scope can be found in the section in this chapter on significant influence.

Overview

ASC 323-10-05-4 explains that investments in the stock of joint ventures and other noncontrolled entities are usually accounted for by either:

- The recognition and measurement guidance in ASC 321 or
- The equity method in this Topic.

When an investor has significant influence over an investee, the investor is no longer considered to be a passive investor, and the equity method is an appropriate way to reflect that fact and to account for the investment. If an investor has the ability to exert significant influence over the operations and financial policies of an investee, it is appropriate for the investor to reflect that responsibility in the investor's financial statements. The advantages of the equity method are that it:

- Recognizes changes to the underlying economic resources
- More closely meets the objectives of accrual accounting than the cost method
- Best enables investors in corporate joint ventures to reflect their investment in those ventures

The equity method of accounting has been referred to as a "one-line consolidation," because the net result of applying ASC 323 on reported net income and on net worth should be identical to what would have occurred had full consolidation been applied. However, rather than include its share of each component (e.g., sales, cost of sales, operating expenses, etc.) in its financial statements, the investor only includes its share of the investee's net income as a separate line item in its income. (Note that there is an exception to this one-line rule for prior period adjustments.) It should be noted that the final bottom-line impact on the investor's financial statements is identical whether the equity method or full consolidation is employed; only the amount of detail presented within the financial statements differs.

Significant Influence

The equity method recognizes a substantive economic relationship between the investor and investee. The equity method is not, however, a substitute for consolidation. It is employed where the investor has significant influence over the operations of the investee but lacks control. In general, significant influence is inferred when the investor owns between 20% and 50% of the investee's voting common stock. Any ownership percentage over 50% presumably gives the investor actual voting control, making full consolidation of financial statements necessary. Indications of significant influence are:

- Representation on the board of directors
- Participation in policy-making processes
- Material intra-entity transactions

- Interchange of managerial personnel
- Technological dependency
- Extent of ownership in relation to other investors
  (ASC 323-10-15-6)

The 20% threshold stipulated in ASC 323 is presumptive, but not absolute. Circumstances may suggest that significant influence exists even though the investor's level of ownership is less than 20% or, conversely, that it is absent despite a level of ownership above 20%. (ASC 323-10-15-7 and 15-8)

Whether sufficient contrary evidence exists to negate the presumption of significant influence is a matter of judgment. Judgment requires a careful evaluation of all pertinent facts and circumstances, and significant influence may change over time. For more information, see the section below on "Change in Ownership Level or Influence."

In determining whether significant influence may not exist, the entity should consider the following factors:

- Opposition by the investee
- Agreements, such as standstill agreements, under which the investor surrenders shareholder rights
- Majority ownership by a small group of shareholders
- Inability to obtain desired information from the investee
- Inability to obtain representation on investee board of directors, etc. (ASC 323-10-15-10)

As a practical matter, absence of control by the parent is the only remaining reason to not consolidate a majority-owned investee. (ASC 323-10-15-11)

Change in Ownership Level or Influence Changes in the level of ownership or influence may mean that an investment qualifies for the equity method. (ASC 323-10-15-12) For a fuller discussion see the section later in this chapter on "Changes in Level of Ownership or Degree of Influence."

In-substance Common Stock—Significant Influence in the Absence of Ownership of Voting Common Stock ASC 323 was written to apply the accounting for investments to investments in voting common stock of an investee. A reporting entity that has the ability to exercise significant influence over the operating and financial policies of an investee should apply the equity method only when it has

- An investment(s) in common stock and/or
- An investment that is in-substance common stock

ASC 323-10-15-13 addresses the accounting for investments in other investment vehicles that may be in-substance common stock, such as preferred stock, options and warrants, and complex licensing and/or management agreements, where significant influence might also be present.

In-substance common stock is an investment in an entity that has risk and reward characteristics that are substantially similar to the investee's common stock. Whether or not significant influence is wielded is a fact question, and suggested criteria are not provided in the ASC.

Management must consider certain characteristics when determining whether an investment in an entity is substantially similar to an investment in that entity's common stock.

- *Subordination.* It must be determined whether the investment has subordination characteristics substantially similar to the investee's common stock. If there are substantive liquidation preferences, the instrument would not be deemed substantially similar to common stock. On the other hand, certain liquidation preferences are not substantive

(e.g., when the stated liquidation preference that is not significant in relation to the purchase price of the investment), and would be discounted in this analysis.
- *Risks and rewards of ownership.* A reporting entity must determine whether the investment has risks and rewards of ownership that are substantially similar to an investment in the investee's common stock. If an investment is not expected to participate in the earnings (and losses) and capital appreciation (and depreciation) in a manner that is substantially similar to common stock, this condition would not be met. Participating and convertible preferred stocks would likely meet this criterion, however.
- *Obligation to transfer value.* An investment is not substantially similar to common stock if the investee is expected to transfer substantive value to the investor and the common shareholders do not participate in a similar manner. For example, if the investment has a substantive redemption provision (for example, a mandatory redemption provision or a non-fair-value put option) that is not available to common shareholders, the investment is not substantially similar to common stock.
(ASC 323-10-15-13)

These are conjunctive constraints. If the entity determines that *any one* of the following characteristics indicates that an investment in an entity is not substantially similar to an investment in that entity's common stock, the investment is not in-substance common stock. (ASC 323-10-15-14) This analysis should be performed on all classes of stock the investee has.

In some instances it may be difficult to assess whether the foregoing characteristics are present or absent. The Codification suggests that, in such circumstances, management of the reporting entity (the investor) should also analyze whether the future changes in the fair value of the investment are expected to be highly correlated with the changes in the fair value of the investee's common stock. If the changes in the fair value of the investment are not expected to be highly correlated with the changes in the fair value of the common stock, then the investment is not in-substance common stock. (ASC 323-10-15-15)

Reassessment of significant influence for in-substance common stock The initial assessment of in-substance common stock is based on the ability of the entity to exercise significant influence. The assessment should be revisited if one or more of these occur:

- The contractual terms of the investment are changed resulting in a change to any of its characteristics described above.
- There is a significant change in the capital structure of the investee, including the investee's receipt of additional subordinated financing.
- The reporting entity obtains an additional interest in an investment in which the investor has an existing interest. As a result, the method of accounting for the cumulative interest is based on the characteristics of the investment at the date at which the entity obtains the additional interest (that is, the characteristics that the entity evaluated in order to make its investment decision), and will result in the reporting entity applying one method of accounting to the cumulative interest in an investment of the same issuance. (ASC 323-10-15-16)

The mere fact that the investee is suffering losses is not a basis for reconsideration of whether the investment is in-substance common stock. (ASC 323-10-15-17) For investments in which the entity has the ability to exercise significant influence over the operating and financial policies of the investee, the reporting entity makes an initial determination about whether existing investments are in-substance common stock. The initial determination is based on circumstances that exist on the date the investor obtains significant influence over the investee, rather than on the date that the investment is made. (ASC 323-10-15-18)

Recognition and Initial Measurement

The investor measures its initial equity method investment at cost in accordance with the guidance on business combinations in ASC 805-50-30, except that the entity measures at fair value:

a. A retained investment in the common stock of an investee in a deconsolidation transaction in accordance with paragraphs 810-10-40-3A through 40-5
b. An investment in the common stock of an investee recognized in accordance with ASC 610-20 upon the derecognition of a distinct
    a. Nonfinancial asset or
    b. In-substance nonfinancial asset

    (ASC 323-10-30-2)

Contingent Consideration Arrangements—Initial Recognition All business combinations are required to be accounted for using the acquisition method as prescribed in ASC 805. Contingent consideration should, in general, only be included in the initial measurement of an equity method investment if required to be so included by guidance contained in other than ASC 805. (ASC 323-10-30-2A)

If an equity method investment agreement involves a contingent consideration arrangement in which the fair value of the investor's share of the investee's net assets exceeds the investor's initial cost (referred to as the "differential"), a liability is recognized. (ASC 323-10-25-2A) The liability is the *lesser* of the:

- Excess of the investor's share of the investee's net assets over the measurement of initial cost (including contingent consideration otherwise recognized), *or*
- Maximum amount of contingent consideration not otherwise recognized. (ASC 323-10-30-2B)

Example of the Equity Method—A Simple Case That Ignores Deferred Income Taxes

On January 2, 20X1, R Corporation (the investor) acquired 40% of E Company's (the investee) voting common stock from the former owner for $100,000. Unless demonstrated otherwise, it is presumed that R Corporation can exercise significant influence over E Company's operating and financing policies. On January 2, E's stockholders' equity consists of the following:

Common stock, $1.00 par value per share; 100,000 shares authorized, 50,000 shares issued and outstanding	$ 50,000
Additional paid-in capital	150,000
Retained earnings	50,000
Total stockholders' equity	$ 250,000

Note that, although improbable in practice, for this simple example, the cost of E Company common stock was exactly equal to 40% of the book value of E's net assets. Assume also that there is no difference between the book value and the fair value of E Company's assets and liabilities. Accordingly, the balance in the investment account in R's records represents exactly 40% of E's stockholders' equity ($100,000/40%). Assume further that E Company reported net income for 20X1 of $30,000 and paid cash dividends of $10,000. Its stockholders' equity at year-end 20X1would be as follows:

Common stock, $1.00 par value per share; 100,000 shares authorized, 50,000 shares issued and outstanding	$ 50,000
Additional paid-in capital	150,000
Retained earnings *($50,000 beginning of year + 30,000 net income – 10,000 cash dividends)*	70,000
Total stockholders' equity	$ 270,000

R Corporation would record its share of the increase in E Company's net assets during 20X1 as follows:

Investment in E Company	12,000	
Equity in E income *($30,000 × 40%)*		12,000
To record net income of E Company		
Cash	4,000	
Investment in E Company *($10,000 cash dividend × 40%)*		4,000
To record the cash dividend		

When R's statement of financial position is prepared at December 31, 20X1, the balance reported as the carrying value of the equity method investment in E Company would be $108,000 (= $100,000 + $12,000 – $4,000). This amount continues to represent 40% of the book value of E's net assets at the end of the year (40% × $270,000). The equity in E income is reported as a separate caption in R's income statement, typically as a component of income from continuing operations before income taxes.

Stock-Based Compensation Granted to Employees and Nonemployees of an Equity Method Investor An investor may grant share-based payment awards to employees or nonemployees of an equity method investee if those grantees provide goods or services to the investee that are used or consumed in the investee's operations. The investor should follow the guidance below if:

- There is no proportional funding by other investors,
- The investor does not receive any increase in relative ownership percentage, and
- The investor's grant was not agreed to in connection with the investor's acquisition of an interest in the investee.
(ASC 323-10-25-3)

To the extent the investor's claim on the investee's book value has not been increased, a contributing investor should expense the cost of share-based payment awards as incurred in the same period the costs are recognized by the investee. (ASC 323-10-25-4)

For the amount that the other equity method investors' net book value has increased as a result of the funding by the contributing investor, the other investors should report income. (ASC 323-10-25-5) The compensation cost recognized should be measured initially at fair value per the guidance in ASC 718. (ASC 323-10-30-3)

Subsequent Accounting

Overall Guidance Before discussing the procedures involved in subsequent accounting for equity method accounting, entities should note the guidance when investor and investee have different fiscal years. In such cases, the Codification permits the investor to use the most recent financial statements available as long as the lag in reporting is consistent from period to period. (ASC 323-10-35-6) Analogizing from ASC 810, the lag period should not exceed three months. (ASC 810-10-45-12)

If the investee changes its fiscal year-end to reduce or eliminate the lag period, ASC 810-10-45-13 stipulates that the change should be treated as a voluntary change in accounting principle under ASC 250 (discussed in detail in the chapter on ASC 250). Although ASC 250 requires such changes to be made by retrospective application to all periods presented, it provides an exception if it is not practical to do so.

In periods subsequent to the initial acquisition of the investment, the investor recognizes in net income its share of earnings and losses of an investee in the period in which they are reported by the investee. The investor also adjusts the investment's carrying amount for increases or decreases to the carrying value of the investment. These increases or decreases are recognized in proportion to the common stock held by the investor. (ASC 323-10-35-4)

The adjustment of the carrying amount of the investment is included in net income and is adjusted for:

- Intra-entity profits and losses
- Basis differences, that is, adjustments to amortize differences between cost and equity in net assets
- Investee capital transactions
- Other comprehensive income
  (ASC 323-10-35-5)

A detailed explanation of this exhibit follows.

Intra-entity Gains and Losses In keeping with the one-line consolidation approach, intra-entity profits or losses on assets still remaining with an investor or investee are eliminated, giving effect to any income taxes on the intra-entity transactions, except for any of the following transactions with an investee:

- A transaction accounted for as a deconsolidation of a subsidiary or a derecognition of a group of assets in accordance with ASC 810
- Accounted for as a change in ownership transaction in accordance with ASC 810
- Accounted for as the derecognition of an asset in accordance with ASC 610-20.
  (ASC 323-10-35-7)

In preparing consolidated financial statements, all intercompany (parent-subsidiary) transactions are eliminated. However, when the equity method is used to account for investments, only the profit component of intercompany (investor-investee) transactions is eliminated. (ASC 323-10-35-8) This is because the equity method does not result in the combining of all income statement accounts (such as sales and cost of sales), and therefore will not cause the financial statements to contain redundancies. In contrast, consolidated statements would include redundancies if the gross amounts of all intercompany transactions were not eliminated.

Exhibit—Investor's Procedures When Applying the Equity Method: Overview of Subsequent Accounting

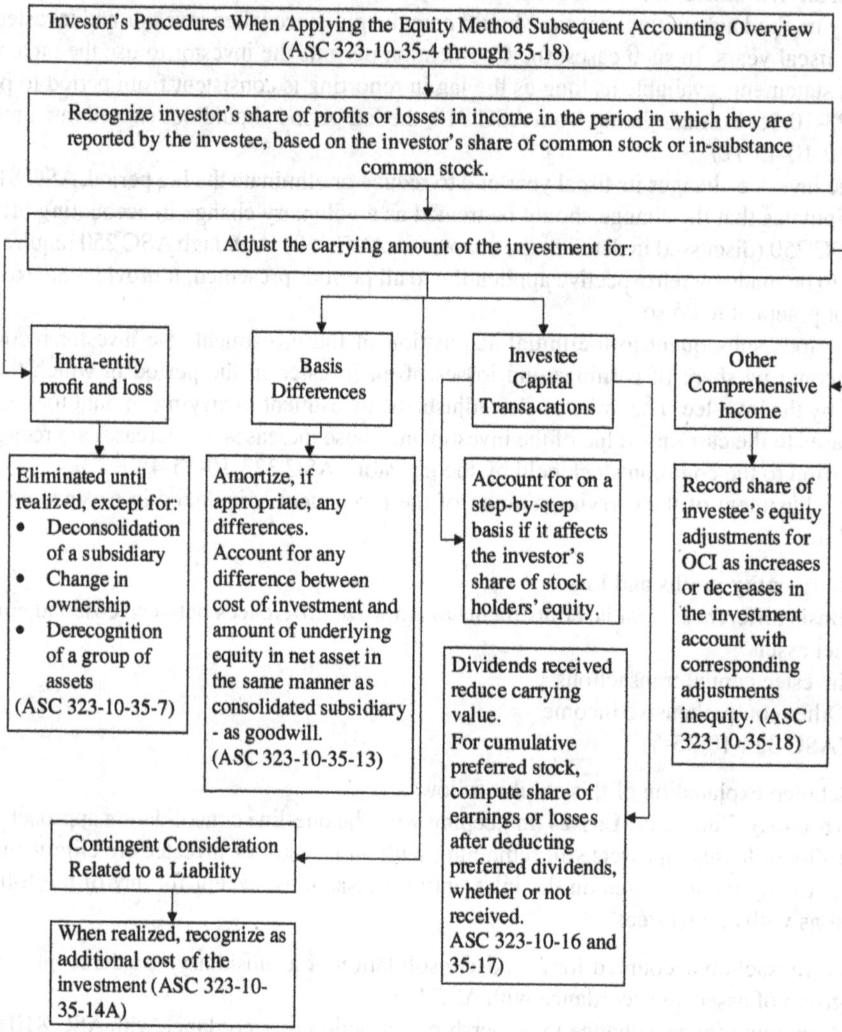

Another distinction between the consolidation and equity method situations pertains to the percentage of intercompany profit to be eliminated. In the case of consolidated statements, the entire intercompany profit is eliminated, regardless of the percentage ownership of the subsidiary. However, only the investor's pro rata share of intercompany profit is eliminated in equity accounting, whether the transaction giving rise to the profit is "downstream" (a sale to the investee) or "upstream" (a sale to the investor). An exception is made when the transaction is not "arm's-length" or if the investee company was created by or for the benefit of the investor. In these cases, 100% profit elimination would be required, unless realized through a sale to a third party before year-end. (ASC 323-10-35-10)

Example of Accounting for Intra-entity Transactions

Continue with the basic facts set forth in an earlier example and also assume that E Company sold inventory that is an output of E Company's ordinary activities to R Corporation in 20X1 in a customer contract that is within the scope of ASC 606. The inventory was sold for $2,000 above E's cost. Of this inventory, 30% remains unsold by R at the end of 20X1. E's net income for 20X1, including the gross profit on the inventory sold to R, is $15,000; E's income tax rate is 34%. R should make the following journal entries for 20X1 (ignoring deferred income taxes):

1. Investment in E Company	6,000	
Equity in E income		6,000
$15,000 × 40%		
2. Equity in E income (amortization of differential)	3,200	
Investment in E Company		3,200
3. Equity in E income	158	
Investment in E Company		*158*
$2,000 × 30% × 66% × 40%		

The amount in the last entry needs further elaboration. Since 30% of the inventory remains unsold, only $600 of the intercompany profit remains unrealized at year-end. This profit, net of income taxes, is $396. R's share of this profit ($158) is included in the first ($6,000) entry recorded. Accordingly, the third entry is needed to adjust or correct the equity in the reported net income of the investee.

Eliminating entries for intercompany profits in fixed assets are similar to those in the examples above. However, intercompany profit is realized only as the assets are depreciated by the purchasing entity. In other words, if an investor buys or sells fixed assets from or to an investee at a price above book value, the gain would only be realized piecemeal over the asset's remaining depreciable life. Accordingly, in the year of sale the pro rata share (based on the investor's percentage ownership interest in the investee, regardless of whether the sale is upstream or downstream) of the unrealized portion of the intercompany profit would have to be eliminated. In each subsequent year during the asset's life, the pro rata share of the gain realized in the period would be added to income from the investee.

Example of Eliminating Intra-entity Profit on Fixed Assets

Assume that Investor Co., which owns 25% of Investee Co., sold to Investee a fixed asset, having a five-year remaining life, at a gain of $100,000. Investor Co. is in the 34% marginal income tax bracket.

The sale occurred at the end of 20X1; Investee Co. will use straight-line depreciation to amortize the asset over the years 20X3 through 20X5.

The entries related to the foregoing are:

20X1		
1. Gain on sale of fixed asset	25,000	
Deferred gain		25,000
To defer the unrealized portion of the gain		
2. Deferred income tax benefit	8,500	
Income tax expense		8,500
Income tax effect of gain deferral		

Alternatively, the 20X1 events could have been reported by this single entry.

Equity in *investee* income	16,500	
Investment in Investee Co.		16,500
20X2 through 20X6 (each year)		
1. Deferred gain	5,000	
Gain on sale of fixed assets		5,000
To amortize deferred gain		
2. Income tax expense	1,700	
Deferred income tax benefit		1,700
Income tax effect of gain realization		

The alternative treatment would be:

Investment in Investee Co.	3,300	
Equity in investee income		3,300

In this example, the income tax currently paid by Investor Co. (34% × $25,000 taxable gain on the transaction) is recorded as a deferred income tax benefit in 20X1 since current income taxes will not be due on the book gain recognized in the years 20X2 through 20X6. Under provisions of ASC 740, deferred income tax assets are recorded to reflect the income tax effects of all future deductible temporary differences. Unless Investor Co. could demonstrate that future taxable amounts arising from existing future taxable temporary differences exist (or, alternatively, that a net operating loss carryback could have been elected), this deferred income tax asset will be offset by an equivalent valuation allowance in Investor Co.'s statement of financial position at year-end 20X1. Thus, the deferred income tax asset might not be recognizable, net of the valuation allowance, for financial reporting purposes unless other future taxable temporary differences not specified in the example generate future taxable income to offset the net deductible effect of the deferred gain.

NOTE: The deferred income tax impact of an item of income for book purposes in excess of tax is the same as a deduction for income tax purposes in excess of book.

Investee Income Items Separately Reportable by the Investor In the examples thus far, the investor has reported its share of investee income, and the adjustments to this income, as a single item described as equity in investee income. However, when the investee has prior period adjustments that are material, the investor reports its share of these separately on its financial statements.

Example of Accounting for Separately Reportable Items

Assume that a prior period adjustment reported in an investee's retained earnings statements is individually considered material from the investor's viewpoint.

Statement of changes in retained earnings

Retained earnings at January 1, 20X1, as originally reported	250,000
Add restatement for prior period adjustment—correction of an error made in 20X0 (net of income taxes of $10,000)	20,000
Retained earnings at January 1, 20X1, restated	$270,000

If an investor owned 30% of the voting common stock of this investee, the investor would make the following journal entries in 20X1:

1. Investment in investee company	24,000	
Equity in investee income		24,000
$80,000 × 30%		
2. Investment in investee company	6,000	
Equity in investee prior period adjustment		6,000
$20,000 × 30%		

The equity in the investee's prior period adjustment should be reported on the investor's statement of changes in retained earnings, which is often presented in a more all-encompassing format with the statement of changes in stockholders' equity.

Basis Differences Since the ultimate income statement effects of applying the equity method of accounting must generally be the same as full consolidation, an adjustment must be made to account for differentials.

Under ASC 323, any premium paid by the investor that cannot be identified as being attributable to appreciated recognized tangible and intangible assets or unrecognized internally developed intangible assets of the investee is goodwill. Goodwill is not amortized unless an entity within the scope of ASC 350-20-15-4 elects the accounting alternative that allows amortization on a straight-line basis for a period not to exceed ten years. (ASC 323-10-35-13) (See the chapter on ASC 350 for more details on this election.)

The following examples present the accounting for equity method investments involving both positive goodwill and negative goodwill.

Example—Equity Method Goodwill: A Complex Case That Ignores Deferred Income Taxes

Foxen Corporation (FC) acquired 40% of Besser, Inc.'s (BI) shares on January 2, 20X1, for $140,000. BI's assets and liabilities at that date had the following book values and fair values:

	Book values	*Fair values*
Cash	$ 10,000	$ 10,000
Accounts receivable (net)	40,000	40,000
Inventories (FIFO cost)	80,000	90,000
Land	50,000	40,000
Plant and equipment (net of accumulated depreciation)	140,000	220,000
Total assets	$ 320,000	$ 400,000
Liabilities	$ (70,000)	$ (70,000)
Net assets (stockholders' equity)	$ 250,000	$ 330,000

The first order of business is the calculation of the differential, as follows:

FC's cost for 40% of BI's common	$ 140,000
Book value of 40% of BI's net assets ($250,000 × 40%)	(100,000)
Total differential	$ 40,000

Next, the $40,000 differential is allocated to those individual assets and liabilities for which fair value differs from book value. In the example, the differential is allocated to inventories, land, and plant and equipment, as follows:

Item	*Book value*	*Fair value*	*Difference debit (credit)*	*40% of difference debit (credit)*
Inventories	$80,000	$90,000	$10,000	$ 4,000
Land	50,000	40,000	(10,000)	(4,000)
Plant and equipment	140,000	220,000	80,000	32,000
Differential allocated				$ 32,000

Assuming that there are no unrecognized identifiable intangibles included in the allocation, the difference between the allocated differential of $32,000 and the total differential of $40,000 is goodwill of $8,000. Goodwill, as shown by the following computation, represents the excess of the cost of the investment over the fair value of the net assets acquired.

FC's cost for 40% of BI's common	$ 140,000
40% of the fair value of BI's net assets ($330,000 × 40%)	$(132,000)
Excess of cost over fair value (goodwill)	$8,000

It is important to note that the allocation of this differential is not recorded formally by either FC or BI. Because the equity method (one-line consolidation) does not involve the recording of individual assets and liabilities of the investee in the financial statements of the investor, FC, the investor does not remove the differential from the investment account and recategorize it in its own respective asset categories. FC leaves the differential of $40,000 in the investment account, as a part of the balance of $140,000 at January 2, 20X1. Accordingly, information pertaining to the allocation of the differential is maintained by the investor, but this information is outside the formal accounting system, presumably on a spreadsheet maintained for this purpose.

After the differential has been allocated, the amortization pattern is developed. To develop the pattern in this example, assume that BI's plant and equipment have ten years of useful life remaining and that BI depreciates its fixed assets on a straight-line basis. FC would prepare the following amortization schedule of BI's assets covering the years 20X1 through 20X3:

			Amortization		
Item	*Differential debit (credit)*	*Remaining useful life*	*20X1*	*20X2*	*20X3*
Inventories (FIFO)	$ 4,000	Sold in 20X1	$ 4,000	$ –	–
Land	(4,000)	Indefinite	–	–	–
Plant and equipment (net)	32,000	10 years	3,200	3,200	3,200
Goodwill	8,000	Not relevant	–	–	–
Totals	$ 40,000		$ 7,200	$ 3,200	$ 3,200

Note that the entire differential allocated to inventories is amortized in 20X3 because the cost flow assumption used by BI is FIFO. If BI had been using LIFO instead of FIFO, no amortization would take place until BI sold some of the inventory included in the LIFO layer that existed at January 2, 20X1. Since this sale could be delayed for many years under LIFO, the differential allocated to LIFO inventories would not be amortized until BI sold more inventory than it manufactured/purchased. Note, also, that the differential allocated to BI's land is not amortized, because land is not a depreciable asset. BI does not elect the private company alternative for amortizing goodwill. The goodwill component of the differential is evaluated along with the investment as a whole as to whether it is other-than-temporarily impaired.

The amortization of the differential is recorded formally in the accounting system of FC. Recording the amortization adjusts the equity in BI's income that FC records based upon BI's income statement. BI's income must be adjusted because it is based upon BI's book values, not upon the cost that FC incurred to acquire its interest in BI. FC makes the following entries in 20X1, assuming that BI reported net income of $30,000 and paid cash dividends of $10,000:

1. Investment in BI	12,000	
Equity in BI income *($30,000 × 40%)*		12,000
To record net income of the investee ($30,000 net income × 40% proportionate share)		
2. Equity in BI income	7,200	
Investment in BI *(See amortization schedule above)*		7,200
To record the amortization of the differential		
3. Cash	4,000	
Investment in BI *($10,000 cash dividend × 40%)*		4,000
To record dividends received by investor ($10,000 × 40%)		

The balance in the investment account on FC's records at the end of 20X1, after giving effect to these entries, is $140,800 ($140,000 + $12,000 – $7,200 – $4,000), and BI's stockholders' equity is $250,000 + net income of $30,000 – dividends of $10,000 = $270,000. FC's investment account balance of $140,800, is not equal to $108,000 (40% of $270,000 BI's equity). However, this difference can easily be reconciled, as follows:

FC's balance in investment account at December 31, 20X1		$140,800
40% of BI's net assets at December 31, 20X1		108,000
Difference at December 31, 20X1		$ 32,800
Differential at January 2, 20X1	$40,000	
Differential amortized during 20X1		
Unamortized differential at December 31, 20X1	(7,200)	
		$ 32,800

FC's share of BI's net income and dividend payments are reflected in BI's net earnings. With the passing years, the balance in FC's investment account approaches the amount representing 40% of the book value of BI's net assets, as the differential is amortized as a component of equity method income or loss. However, since a part of the differential was allocated to land, which is not depreciating, and to goodwill, which is not subject to amortization, the carrying value will most likely never exactly equal the equity in the investee's net assets. If the investee disposes of the land, the investor must also eliminate the associated portion of the differential. If the carrying value of the investment becomes impaired and the impairment is considered other than temporary, the goodwill portion of the differential may also be reduced or eliminated. Thus, under certain conditions the investor's carrying value may subsequently be adjusted to equal the underlying net asset value.

To illustrate how the sale of land would affect equity method procedures, assume that BI sold the land in the year 20X6 for $80,000. Since BI's cost for the land was $50,000, it would report a gain of $30,000, of which $12,000 (= $30,000 × 40%) would be recorded by FC, when it records its 40% share of BI's reported net income, ignoring income taxes. However, from FC's viewpoint, the gain on sale of land should have been $40,000 ($80,000 – $40,000) because the cost of the land from FC's perspective was $40,000 at January 2, 20X3 (since the allocated fair value of the land was below its book value). Therefore, in addition to the $12,000 share of the gain recorded above, FC should record an additional $4,000 gain [($40,000 – $30,000) × 40%] by debiting the investment account and crediting the equity in BI's income account. This $4,000 debit to the investment account will eliminate the $4,000 differential allocated to land on January 2, 20X2, since the original differential was a credit (the fair value of the land was $10,000 less than its book value).

Example—Computation of Negative Goodwill: A Complex Case That Ignores Deferred Income Taxes

The facts in this example are similar to those in the immediately preceding examples, but in this instance the price paid by the investor, Lucky Corp., is less than its proportionate share of the investee's net assets, at fair value. This is analogous to negative goodwill in a business combination, and the accounting for the negative differential between cost and fair value follows the guidance for bargain purchases under ASC 805 on business combinations.

Assume that Lucky Corp. acquired 40% of Compliant Company's shares on January 2, 20X1, for a cash payment of $120,000. Compliant Company's assets and liabilities at that date had the following book and fair values:

	Book values	*Fair values*
Cash	$ 10,000	$ 10,000
Accounts receivable (net)	40,000	40,000
Inventories (FIFO cost)	80,000	90,000
Land	50,000	40,000
Plant and equipment (net of accumulated depreciation)	140,000	220,000
Total assets	$ 320,000	$ 400,000
Liabilities	$ (70,000)	$ (70,000)
Net assets (stockholders' equity)	$ 250,000	$ 330,000

The first step is to compute the differential, which is as follows:

Lucky's cost for 40% of Compliant's common stock	$ 120,000
Book value of 40% of Compliant's net assets ($250,000 × 40%)	(100,000)
Total differential	$ 20,000

Next, the $20,000 is allocated, on a preliminary basis, to those individual assets and liabilities for which fair value differs from book value. In the example, the differential is initially allocated to inventories, land, and plant and equipment, as follows:

Item	*Book value*	*Fair value*	*Difference debit (credit)*	*40% of difference debit (credit)*
Inventories	$ 80,000	$ 90,000	$ 10,000	$ 4,000
Land	50,000	40,000	(10,000)	(4,000)
Plant and equipment	140,000	220,000	80,000	32,000
Differential allocated				$32,000

The difference between the allocated differential of $32,000 and the actual differential of $20,000 is negative goodwill of $12,000. Negative goodwill, as shown by the following computation, represents the excess of the fair value of the net assets acquired over the cost of the investment.

Lucky's cost for 40% of Compliant's common stock	$ 120,000
40% of the fair value of Compliant's net assets ($330,000 × 40%)	(132,000)
Excess of fair value over cost (negative goodwill)	$ 12,000

The investor's handling of negative goodwill should track how this would be dealt with by a parent company preparing consolidated financial statements following a "bargain purchase" business combination.

Contingent Considerations Upon the resolution of a contingent liability recorded under ASC 323-10-25-2A discussed above, when the consideration is issued or becomes issuable:

- Any excess of the fair value of the contingent consideration issued or issuable over the amount previously recognized as a liability should be recognized as an additional cost of the investment.
- Any excess of the amount previously recognized as a liability over the contingent consideration issued or issuable should be applied to reduce the cost of the investment. (ASC 323-10-35-14A)

Investor Accounting for Investee Capital Transactions Investee transactions of a capital nature that affect the investor's share of the investee's stockholders' equity are accounted for on a step-by-basis. (ASC 323-10-35-15) If the investor participates in these transactions on a pro rata basis, its percentage ownership will not change and no special accounting will be necessary. These transactions principally include situations where the investee

- Purchases treasury stock from outside shareholders or
- Sells unissued shares or reissues treasury shares it holds to outside shareholders.

Similar results are obtained when holders of outstanding options or convertible securities acquire investee common shares.

When the investee engages in one of the above capital transactions and the investor's ownership percentage is changed, a gain or loss arises, depending on whether the price paid (for treasury shares acquired) or received (for shares issued) is greater or lesser than the per share carrying value of the investor's interest in the investee. Any gain or loss is recognized in earnings. (ASC 323-10-40-1)

Example of Accounting for an Investee Capital Transaction

Assume R Corp. purchases, on 1/2/X1, 25% (2,000 shares) of E Corp.'s outstanding shares for $80,000. The cost is equal to both the book and fair values of R's interest in E's underlying net assets (i.e., there is no differential to be accounted for). One week later, E Corp. buys 1,000 shares of its stock from other shareholders for $50,000. Since the price paid ($50 per share) exceeded R Corp.'s per share carrying value of its interest, $40, R Corp. has in fact suffered an economic loss by the transaction. Also, its percentage ownership of E Corp. has increased as the number of shares held by third parties has been reduced.

R Corp.'s new interest in E's net assets is:

$$\frac{2{,}000 \text{ shares held by R} \times \text{E Corp net assets}}{7{,}000 \text{ shares outstanding}}$$

$$.2857 \times (\$320{,}000 - \$50{,}000) = \$77{,}143$$

The interest held by R Corp. has thus been diminished by $80,000 – $77,143 = $2,857. Therefore, R Corp. should make the following entry:

Loss on E Corp. purchase of its stock	2,857	
Investment in E Corp.		2,857

R Corp. charges the loss against additional paid-in capital if such amounts have accumulated from past transactions of a similar nature; otherwise the debit is to retained earnings. Had the transaction given rise to a gain it would have been credited to additional paid-in capital only (never to retained earnings) following the rule that transactions in one's own shares cannot produce net income.

Note that the amount of the charge to additional paid-in capital (or retained earnings) in the entry above can be verified as follows: R Corp.'s share of the post-transaction net equity (2/7) times the "excess" price paid ($50 – $40 = $10) times the number of shares purchased = 2/7 × $10 × 1,000 = $2,857.

Other Comprehensive Income The investee may adjust its other comprehensive income for items such as:

- Unrealized gains and losses on available-for-sale securities
- Foreign currency items
- To the extent not yet recognized as components of net periodic benefit cost, pension and other postretirement benefits' prior service costs or credits, gains and losses, and transition assets or obligations

If so, the investor should record its proportionate share of the investee's equity adjustment to its equity. (ASC 323-10-35-18)

Equity Method Losses

Equity investors should report losses up to the carrying amount of the investment, including any additional committed financial support, such as capital contributions, loans, advances, and additional investments. (ASC 323-10-35-19) In general, an equity method investment would not be permitted to have a negative (i.e., credit) balance, since this would imply that it represented a liability. In the case of normal corporate investments, the investor would enjoy limited liability and would not be held liable to the investee's creditors should, for instance, the investee become insolvent. For this reason, excess losses of the investee would not be reflected in the financial statements of the investor. The practice is to discontinue application of the equity method when the investment account reaches a zero balance, with adequate disclosure being made of the fact that further investee losses are not being reflected in the investor's earnings. (ASC 323-10-35-20) Two situations where investors should provide for additional losses are:

1. If imminent return to profitability seems assured. This may occur in cases where, for instance, the investee experiences a nonrecurring loss. (ASC 323-10-35-21) If the investee later returns to profitability, the investor ignores its share of earnings until the previously ignored losses have been fully offset; thereafter, normal application of the equity method is resumed. (ASC 323-10-35-22)

   or

2. Where the investor's losses are not limited to the amount of the original investment because the investor has obligations or other commitments to the investee. (ASC 323-10-35-20) Often the investor has guaranteed or otherwise committed to indemnify creditors or other investors in the investee entity for losses incurred, or to fund continuing operations of the investee. Having placed itself at risk in the case of the investee's insolvency, continued application of the equity method is deemed to be appropriate, since the net credit balance in the investment account (reportable as a liability entitled "losses in excess of investment made in investee") would indeed represent an obligation of the investor.

Exhibit—Investor Procedures When Applying the Equity Method—Overview of Accounting for Equity Method Losses

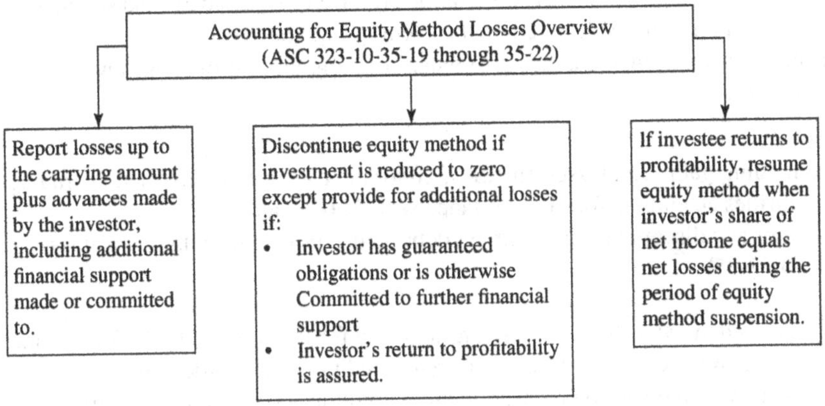

Exhibit—Investor Has Other Investments in the Investee

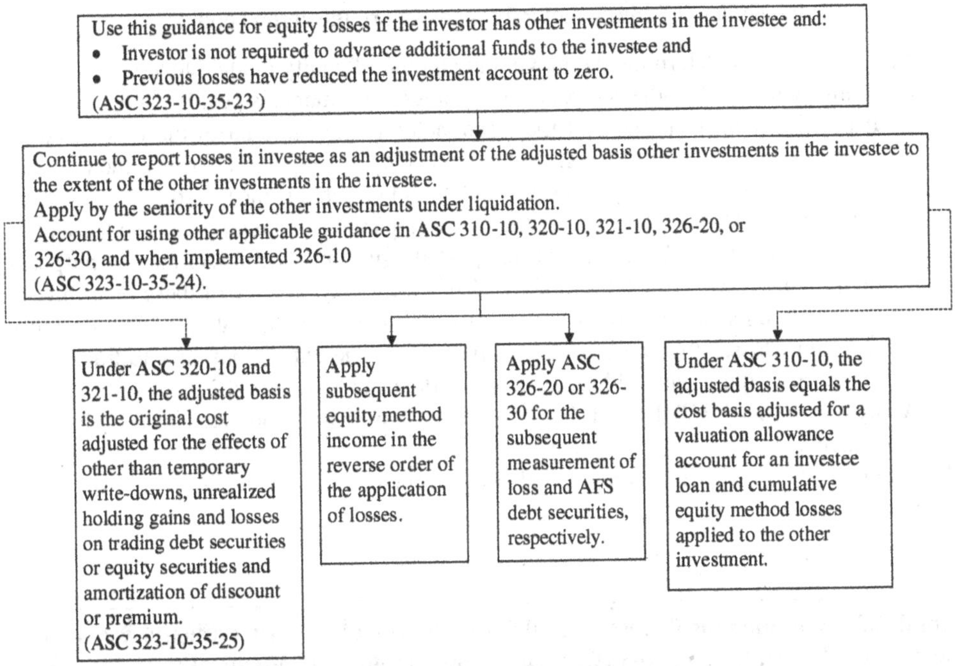

Equity Method Losses When The Investor Has Other Investments in the Investee For this section, assume the investor is not required to advance additional funds and previous losses have reduced the common stock investment account to zero. (ASC 323-10-35-23)

In those situations, the investor continues to report its share of equity method losses to the extent of the adjusted basis of its other investments in the investee. The order of applications follows the seniority of the other investments (priority in liquidation). Then the investor applies

ASCs 310-10, 320-10, 321-10, and (when implemented) 326-20 or 326-30. (ASC 323-10-35-24) This sequence is logical because it tracks the risk of investor loss. Common shareholders' interests are the first to be eliminated, followed by those of the preferred shareholders, and so on, with debt having the highest claim to investee assets in the event of liquidation.

The basis of the other investments is taken to mean the original cost of those investments adjusted for the effects of:

- Write-downs,
- Unrealized holding gains and losses on ASC 320-10 debt securities classified as trading or equity securities accounted for in accordance with 321-10, and
- Amortization of any discount or premium on debt securities or financing receivables. (ASC 323-10-35-25)

The adjusted basis is defined as the cost basis, as adjusted for the ASC 310-10-35 valuation allowance account for an investee loan or the allowance for credit losses recorded under the guidance of ASC 326 (when implemented) on measurement of credit losses for an investor financing receivables and debt security and for the cumulative equity method losses applied to the other investments. Any equity method income subsequently recorded is applied to the adjusted basis of other investments in reverse order. (ASC 323-10-35-25)

To determine the amount of equity method loss to report, the entity should:

1. Apply ASC 323 to determine the maximum amount of equity method losses
2. Determine whether the adjusted basis of the other investments is positive and
   a. If positive, adjust the basis of the investments for the amount of the loss based on seniority. For ASC 320 debt securities and ASC 321 equity securities, the adjusted basis becomes the security's basis from which fair value is measured.
   b. If the adjusted basis reaches zero, the entity stops reporting equity method losses, but continues tracking the amount of unreported equity method losses for the purposes of applying ASC 323-10-35-20 above. The entity may sell one of these other investments when its carrying value exceeds its adjusted basis. In that case, the difference represents losses that were reversed upon sales. The entity continues to track these unreported equity method losses before income can be reported.
3. Apply ASC 310-10, 320-10, 321-10, 326-20, and 326-30 to the adjusted basis of the other investments
4. Apply GAAP to other investments within the scope of the guidance in "3" above. (ASC 323-10-35-26)

Example of Accounting for Excess Loss of Investee When Other Investments Are Also Held in Same Entity, When Proportions of All Investments Are Identical

Assume the following facts: Dardanelles Corporation owns 25% of the common stock of Bosporus Company. Dardanelles also owns 25% of Bosporus's preferred shares, and 25% of its commercial debt. Bosporus has $50,000 of debt and $100,000 of preferred stock outstanding.

As of 1/1/20X1 the carrying (i.e., book) value of Dardanelles' investment in Bosporus common stock was $12,000, after having applied the equity method of accounting in prior periods, per ASC 323. In 20X1, 20X2, and 20X3, Bosporus incurs net losses of $140,000, $50,000, and $30,000, respectively.

As of 1/1/20X1, the carrying (book) values of Dardanelles' investment in Bosporus's preferred stock and commercial debt were $25,000 and $12,500, respectively. Due to its continuing losses, the market or fair value of Dardanelles' outstanding preferred shares and its commercial debt decline over the years 20X1–20X3; Bosporus's portion of these values are as follows:

	Fair value of preferred shares, consistent with ASC 320 or 321	Fair value of commercial debt, consistent with ASC 310-10-35
1/1/20X1	N/A	N/A
12/31/20X1	$20,000	$12,000
12/31/20X2	9,500	8,000
12/31/20X3	2,000	7,000

The following table indicates the adjustments that would be made on the books of Dardanelles to record its share of Bosporus's losses in 20X1–20X3:

	Common stock	Preferred stock		Commercial debt	
Book value	Book value	Book value	Fair value	Book value	Fair value
1/1/20X1	$ 12,000	$ 25,000	N/A	$ 12,500	N/A
20X1 loss (25% × 140,000 = 35,000)	(12,000)		(23,000)	–	
		2,000	$ 20,000	12,500	$ 12,000
Adjust pfd. stk. to FMV and debt to FV		18,000		(500)	
12/31/20X1 values	0	20,000		12,000	
20X1 loss (25% × 50,000 = 12,500)		(2,000)		(10,500)	
		18,000	9,500	1,500	8,000
Adjust pfd. stk. to FMV and debt to FV		(8,500)		–	
12/31/20X2 values	0	9,500		1,500	
20X2 loss (25% × 30,000 = 7,500)		–		(1,500)	
		9,500	2,000	0	7,000
Adjust pfd. stk. to FMV and debt to FV		(7,500)		–	
12/31/20X3 values	$ 0	$ 2,000		$ 0	

Actual journal entries and explanations for the foregoing are given as follows:

12/31/X1	Investee losses	35,000	
	Investment in Bosporus common stock		12,000
	Investment in Bosporus preferred stock		23,000
	To record Dardanelles' share of Bosporus's loss for the year; the excess over the carrying value of the common stock is used to reduce the carrying value of the preferred shares.		
12/31/X1	Investment in Bosporus preferred stock	18,000	
	Unrealized gain on securities available for sale (other comprehensive income)		18,000
	Since the fair value of the preferred shares is $20,000, per ASC 320 the carrying value must be upwardly revalued, and the adjustment is included in other comprehensive income for the year.		
12/31/X1	Loss from impairment of loan	500	12,000
	Investment in Bosporus commercial debt		23,000
	As required by ASC 310-10-35, the impairment of the loan to Bosporus must be recognized by a charge against current period net income.		

12/31/X2	Investee losses	12,500	
	Investment in Bosporus preferred stock		2,000
	Investment in Bosporus commercial debt		10,500
	To record Dardanelles' share of Bosporus's loss for the year; the excess over the remaining carrying value of the preferred stock (without consideration of the ASC 320 adjustment) is used to reduce the carrying value of the commercial debt held.		
12/31/X2	*Unrealized* gain on securities available for sale (other comprehensive income)	8,500	
	Investment in Bosporus preferred stock		8,500
	Since the fair market value of the preferred shares is not $9,500, the adjustment booked in the prior period must be partially reversed, this adjustment is included in other comprehensive income for the year.		
12/31/X3	Investee losses	1,500	
	Investment in Bosporus commercial debt		1,500
	To record Dardanelles' share of Bosporus's loss for the year; the maximum to be recognized is the carrying value of the commercial debt since the carrying value of common and preferred stock investments has already been reduced to zero.		
	Unrealized gain on securities available for sale (other comprehensive income)	7,500	
	Investment in Bosporus preferred stock		7,500
	Since the fair value of the preferred shares is now $2,000, the carrying value must be further reduced, with the adjustment included in other comprehensive income.		

It should be noted in the foregoing example that in year 20X3 there will be $6,000 of unrecognized investee losses, since as of the end of that year the carrying value of all the investor's investments in the investee will have been reduced to zero, except for the fair value of the preferred stock, which is presented pursuant to ASC 321. Also note that the carrying value of the commercial debt is reduced for an impairment in 20X1 because the fair value is lower than the cost basis; in later years the fair value exceeds the cost basis, but under ASC 310-10-35 net upward adjustments would not be permitted.

Investee has other investments in the same entity and proportions of investments vary ASC 323-10-35 addresses only the situation where the investor had the same percentage interests in common stock and all the other equity or debt securities of the investee. However, a further complication can arise when the investor's share in the common stock of the investee is not mirrored in its investment in the other debt or equity securities of the investee that it also holds. While this possibility is discussed in ASC 323, GAAP is not definitive regarding the mechanism by which the investor's share of further losses should be recognized in such situations. What is clear, however, is that merely applying the investor's percentage interest in the investee's common stock to the period's loss would not be appropriate in these cases.

Two approaches are justifiable. The first is to eliminate the carrying value of the common stock, and then the other securities of the investee (including loans made to the investee), in reverse order of seniority, as set forth under ASC 323-10-35. The percentage of the investee's loss to be absorbed against each class of investment other than common stock would be governed by the proportion of that investment held by the investor—and emphatically not by its common stock ownership percentage. (ASC 323-10-55-50) The logic is that, if the investor entity were to be harmed by the investee's further losses (once the common stock investment were reduced to zero carrying value), the harm would derive from being forced to take a reduced settlement in a liquidation of the investee, at which point the percentage ownership in separate classes of stock or in holdings of classes of debt would determine the amount of the investor's losses.

The second acceptable approach also takes into account the investor's varying percentage interests in the different equity and debt holdings. However, rather than being driven by the investee's reported loss for the period, the investor's loss recognition is determined by the period-to-period change in its claim on the net assets of the investee, as measured by book value. (ASC 323-10-55-54) This approach implicitly assumes that fair values upon a hypothetical liquidation of the investee would equal book values—an assumption which is obviously unlikely to be borne out in any actual liquidation scenario. Nonetheless, given the enormous difficulty of applying this measurement technique to the continuously varying fair values of the investee's assets and liabilities, this was deemed to be a necessary compromise.

Thus, both methods of computing the excess investee losses to be recognized by an investor having more than just a common stock interest in the investee depend on the varying levels of those other investment vehicles.

Example of Accounting for Excess Loss of Investee When Other Investments Are Also Held in Same Entity, When Proportions of Investments Vary—First Method: Investee's Reported Loss Used as Basis for Recognition

When the percentage interest in common stock of the investee is not mirrored by the level of ownership in its other securities, the process of recognizing the investor's share of investee losses becomes much more complex. Per ASC 323, there are two acceptable approaches, both of which are illustrated here. The first approach is to recognize the investor's share of investee losses by reducing the various investments held in the investee (common and preferred stock and commercial debt, in this example) by the relevant percentages applicable to each class of investment.

In the following, the same facts as in the preceding example are continued, except that the percentage of ownership in the equity and debt instruments is as follows:

	Percentage ownership by Dardanelles Corporation
Common stock	25%
Preferred stock	50%
Commercial debt	100%

Note that the fair values of the securities held (using the new assumed percentages of ownership of each class) are as follows:

	Fair value of preferred shares, consistent with ASC 320	Fair value of commercial debt, consistent with ASC 310-10-35
1/1/20X1	N/A	N/A
12/31/20X1	$40,000	$48,000
12/31/20X2	19,000	32,000
12/31/20X3	4,000	28,000

Given the foregoing, the period-by-period adjustments are summarized in the following table:

	Common stock	Preferred stock		Commercial debt	
	Book value	Book value	Fair value	Book value	Fair value
1/1/20X1	$ 12,000	$ 50,000	N/A	$ 50,000	N/A
20X1 loss = $140,000	(12,000)				
Eliminate @ 25% ratio					
Reduce preferred @ 50% ratio		($46,000)			
		4,000	$ 40,000		$48,000
Adjust pfd. stk. to FMV and debt to FV		36,000		(2,000)	
12/31/20X1 values	0	40,000		48,000	
20X2 loss = $50,000		(4,000)			
Eliminate preferred @ 50% ratio					
Reduce commercial debt @ 100% ratio				(42,000)	
		36,000	19,000	6,000	32,000
Adjust pfd. stk. to FMV and debt to FV		17,000		–	
12/31/20X2 values	0	19,000		6,000	
20X3 loss = $30,000				(6,000)	
Reduce commercial debt @ 100% ratio					
			4,000	0	7,000
Adjust pfd. stk. to FMV and debt to FV		(15,000)			
12/31/20X3 values	$ 0	$ 4,000		$ 0	

Journal entries and explanations for the adjustments that would be made consistent with the foregoing fact pattern are as follows:

12/31/X1	Investee losses	58,000	
	Investment in Bosporus common stock		12,000
	Investment in Bosporus preferred stock		46,000

To record Dardanelles' share of Bosporus' loss for the year; the excess over the carrying value of the common stock is used to reduce the carrying value of the preferred shares based on Dardanelles' 50% ownership interest in the preferred stock outstanding

	Investment in Bosporus preferred stock	36,000	
	Unrealized gain on securities available for sale (other comprehensive income)	36,000	

Since the fair value of the preferred shares is $40,000, per ASC 320 the carrying value must be upwardly revalued and the adjustment is included in other comprehensive income for the year

	Loss from impairment of loan	2,000	
	Investment in Bosporus commercial debt		2,000

As required by ASC 310-10-35, the impairment of the loan to Bosporus must be recognized by a charge against current period net income

12/31/X2	Investee losses	46,000	
	Investment in Bosporus preferred stock		4,000
	Investment in Bosporus commercial debt		42,000

To record Dardanelles' share of Bosporus' loss for the year; the excess over the remaining carrying value of the preferred stock (without consideration of the ASC 321 adjustment) is used to reduce the carrying value of the commercial debt held

12/31/X2	Unrealized gain on securities available for sale (other comprehensive income)	17,000	
	Investment in Bosporus preferred stock		17,000
A	*Since the fair value of the preferred shares is not $19,000, the adjustment booked in the prior period must be partially reversed; this adjustment is included in other comprehensive income for the year*		
12/31/X3	Investee losses	6,000	
	Investment in Bosporus commercial debt		6,000
	To record Dardanelles' share of Bosporus' loss for the year; the maximum to be recognized is the carrying value of the commercial debt since the carrying value of common and preferred stock investments has already been reduced to zero		
	Unrealized gain on securities available for sale (other comprehensive income)	15,000	
	Investment in Bosporus preferred stock		15,000
	Since the fair value of the preferred shares is now $4,000, the carrying value must be further reduced, with the adjustment included in other comprehensive income		

It should be noted in the foregoing example that the limitation on loss recognition each year is given by reference to the investor's percentage interests in the various classes of equity or debt held. The 20X1 loss is allocated between the common and preferred interests. A $12,000, 25% interest in the common stock equates to a total of $48,000 of common stock ($12,000 ÷ 25%). Therefore, if the full $140,000 loss were first allocated to reduce the book value of the common stock, $48,000 would have been applied to reduce that book value to zero. That would leave $92,000 of loss ($140,000 – $48,000) that remains to be allocated to the preferred interests. $92,000 × the 50% preferred interest of the investor is $48,000. Since the carrying value of the preferred stock investment is greater than this amount, the full loss is recognized by the investor proportional to its interest.

Similarly, the investee loss of $50,000 in 20X2 is first used to eliminate the remaining carrying value (before the ASC 321 adjustment) of the preferred stock investment, at a 50% ratio. The total of the preferred interests is computed by dividing the remaining carrying value of the preferred stock, $4,000, by the 50% interest that it represents. Therefore, the $8,000 of the $50,000 loss would be allocated to the preferred interests, thus leaving $42,000 to allocate to the commercial debt. Since Dardanelles owns all of this debt issue, the limitation on loss recognition would be the lesser of the remaining loss ($42,000) or the carrying value of the debt (before the ASC 310-10-35 adjustment) of $48,000.

Finally, note that in year 20X3 there will be $24,000 of unrecognized investee losses, since as of the end of that year the carrying value of all the investor's investments in the investee will have been reduced to zero (except for the fair value of the preferred stock which is presented pursuant to ASC 320).

Example of Accounting for Excess Loss of Investee When Other Investments Are Also Held in Same Entity, When Proportions of Investments Vary—Second Method: Investee's Reported Change in Net Assets Used as Basis for Recognition

The alternative, equally acceptable approach to investee loss recognition when various equity and debt interests are held in the investee, at varying percentage ownership levels, ignores the investee's reported loss for the period in favor of an indirect approach, making reference to the change in the investor's interest in the investee's reported net assets (net book value). In theory, the results will often be very similar if not identical, but investee capital transactions with other owners (e.g., issuing another series of preferred shares) could impact the loss recognition by the investor under some circumstances. Furthermore, since the investor's cost of its investments in the investee will normally vary from the investee's book value of those investments (e.g., if the investments were acquired in the secondary market), the losses computed by this method may differ from those computed by the first of the two alternative approaches.

To illustrate, again assume all the facts above, including the percentage interests in the immediately preceding example. Also, the condensed statements of financial position of Bosporus Corporation as of the relevant dates are given as follows:

	1/1/X1	12/31/X1	12/31/X2	12/31/X3
Total assets	$270,000	$135,000	$ 90,000	$ 50,000
Commercial debt	50,000	50,000	50,000	50,000
Other liabilities	20,000	25,000	30,000	20,000
Preferred stock	100,000	100,000	100,000	100,000
Common stock + retained earnings	100,000	(40,000)	(90,000)	$(120,000)
Total liabilities and equity	$270,000	$135,000	$ 90,000	$ 50,000

The investor's share of the investee's net assets at these respective dates and the changes to be recognized therein as the investor's share of investee losses for the years 20X1–20X3 are given below.

	1/1/X1	12/31/X1	12/31/X2	12/31/X3
		(At investee's book values)		
Investor's shares of:				
Commercial debt (100%)	$ 50,000	$ 50,000	$ 50,000	$ 30,000
Preferred stock (50%)	50,000	30,000	5,000	0
Common stock + retained earnings (25%)	25,000	0	0	0
Total share of investee's net assets	$ 125,000	$ 80,000	$ 55,000	$ 30,000
Change in share from prior year (investor's share of investee loss for year)		$(45,000)	$(25,000)	$(25,000)

In terms of how the actual investee losses should be recorded by the investor, the standard is not explicit, but there is no reason to depart from the approach illustrated above. Thus, the investment in Bosporus common stock would be eliminated first, then the investment in the preferred stock, and finally the investment in the debt securities. The provisions of ASC 310-10-35, ASC 320, or ASC 321 would have to be adhered to as well, again similar to the illustration above.

One part of the foregoing analysis that may need elaboration is the decision, in 20X3, to absorb all the excess investee losses against the investor's interest in the commercial debt. In many cases the commercial debt will be secured or for other reasons have preference over the other liabilities (which would tend to include accruals, trade payables, etc.). Therefore, in an actual liquidation situation the unsecured creditors would be eliminated before the commercial debtholders. However, the purpose of this computation—determining how much of the investee's losses should be reported by the investor—is not predicated on an actual liquidation but, rather, is based on a going concern assumption and conservatism. Since the investor in this example owns a major position in the common stock, half of the preferred stock, and all of the debt, presumably if the ongoing losses were indicative of imminent demise the investor would have already put the investee into liquidation or taken other dramatic steps. Since this has not occurred, the appropriate computational strategy, it is believed, is to allocate further losses against the investor's remaining interest, which is in the commercial debt. (If actual liquidation were being contemplated, it would be necessary to consider an even greater write-down of the carrying value of this investment.)

Note that the loss recognized each period differs from that under the previous approach, since the allocation is based on the book values of the various interests on the investee's statement of financial position, not the cost basis from the investor's perspective, as detailed below.

	Common stock	*Preferred stock*		*Commercial debt*	
	Book value	*Book value*	*Fair value*	*Book value*	*Fair value*
1/1/20X1	$12,000	$50,000	N/A	$ 50,000	N/A
20X1 change in investor's share of investee's net book value = –45,000	(12,000)				
Eliminate carrying value of common		(33,000)			
Reduce carrying value of preferred					
		17,000	$40,000		$48,000
Adjust pfd. stk. to FMV and debt to FV		23,000		(2,000)	
12/31/20X1 values	0	40,000		48,000	
20X2 change in investor's share of investee's net book value = –25,000					
Reduce carrying value of commercial debt		17,000		(8,000)	
		23,000	19,000	40,000	32,000
Adjust pfd. stk. to FMV and debt to FV			(4,000)		(8,000)
12/31/20X2 values		0	19,000		32,000
20X3 change in investor's share of investee's net book value = –25,000					
Reduce carrying value of commercial debt				(25,000)	32,000
			4,000	7,000	7,000
Adjust pfd. stk. to FMV and debt to FV		(15,000)		–	
12/31/20X3 values	$ 0	$ 4,000		$7,000	

Journal entries and explanations for the adjustments that would be made consistent with the foregoing fact pattern would be similar to those shown earlier in this section and therefore will not be repeated here.

Accounting for subsequent investments in an investee after suspension of equity method loss recognition Recognition of investee losses by the investor is suspended when the investment account is reduced to zero, subject to the further reduction in the carrying value of any other investments (preferred stock, debt, etc.) in that investee, as circumstances warrant. In some cases, after the recognition of investee losses is suspended, the investor will make a further investment in the investee, and the question arises whether recognition of some or all of the previously unrecognized investee losses should immediately be given recognition, up to the amount of the additional investment.

For SEC filers, ASC 323-10-S99 addresses the situation where the increased investment in the equity method investee triggered a need to consolidate (i.e., the 50% ownership threshold was exceeded), and cites the Securities and Exchange Commission (SEC)'s position against further loss recognition. ASC 323-10-35-29 deals with the situation where the increased investment did not cause control to be assumed, but rather where equity method accounting was specified both before and after the further investment is made (e.g., the investor owned 30% of the investee's common stock previously, and then increased the interest to 35%) has been dealt with.

According to ASC 323-10-35-29, recognition of some or all of the previously unrecognized ("suspended") losses is conditioned on whether the new investment represents funding of prior investee losses. To the extent that it does, the previously unrecognized share of prior losses will be given recognition (i.e., reported in the investor's current period net income). Making this determination requires the use of judgment and is fact-specific, but some of the considerations would be as follows:

- Whether the additional investment is acquired from a third party or directly from the investee, since it is unlikely that funding of prior losses occurs unless funds are infused into the investee;
- The fair value of the consideration received in relation to the value of the consideration paid for the additional investment, with an indicated excess of consideration paid over that received being suggestive of a funding of prior losses;
- Whether the additional investment results in an increase in ownership percentage of the investee, with investments being made without a corresponding increase in ownership or other interests (or, alternatively, a pro rata equity investment made by all existing investors) being indicative of the funding of prior losses; and
- The seniority of the additional investment relative to existing equity of the investee, with investment in subordinate instruments being suggestive of the funding of prior losses.

When additional investments are made in an investee that has experienced losses, the corollary issue of whether the investor has committed to further investments may arise. (ASC 323-10-35-30) If such is the case, then yet-unrecognized (suspended) investee losses may also need to be recognized in investor net income currently—in effect, as a loss contingency that is deemed probable of occurrence.

Example of Subsequent Investments in Investee with Losses in Excess of Original Investment

R Corp. invested $500,000 in an investee, E Company, representing a 40% ownership interest. Investee losses caused R Corp. to completely eliminate the carrying value of this investment, and the recognition of R Corp.'s share of a further $200,000 of E Company losses ($200,000 × 40% = $80,000) was suspended. Later, R Corp. invested another $100,000 in E Company. Application of the criteria above led to the conclusion that one-half of its investment was in excess of the value of the consideration received, and thus the entry to record the further investment would be:

Investment in E Company stock	50,000	
Loss on equity method investment in E Company	50,000	
Cash		100,000

If it is determined, however, that R Corp. has "otherwise committed" to further investment in E Company, the investor might have to recognize losses up to the full amount of the suspended losses. The entry might therefore be:

Investment in E Company stock	20,000	
Loss on equity method investment in E Company	80,000	
Cash		100,000

Deferred Income Tax Accounting

The equity method is not a recognized accounting method for federal income tax purposes under the U.S. Internal Revenue Code (IRC). For income tax purposes, the investor's share of the investee's net income is not recognized until it is realized through either the investor's receipt of dividends from the investee or the investor's sale of the investment. Thus, when the investor, under the equity method, recognizes its proportionate share of the net income of the investee as an increase to the carrying value of the investment, a future taxable temporary difference between the carrying value of the equity method investment for financial reporting purposes and the income tax basis of the investment will arise. The temporary difference will give rise to recognition of a deferred income tax liability.

For more information on computing the deferred income tax effects of income recognized by applying the equity method, see the chapter on ASC 740.

Decreases in Investment Value

A series of operating losses or other factors may indicate that losses in an investee are other than temporary. If so, the investor should recognize the decrease in value, even though the decrease is more than what would normally be recognized in applying the equity method. (ASC 323-10-35-31)

An investee may experience a loss that is other than temporary. This may be evidenced by circumstances, such as

- Absence of ability of the investor to recover its carrying value in the investee or
- Inability of the investee to sustain earnings that justify the carrying value.

On the other hand, the following do not necessarily indicate an other-than-temporary loss in value:

- A decline in market value blow the carrying value or
- The existence of operating losses.

If the loss is other than temporary, the investor should recognize it. (ASC 323-10-35-32)

Equity method investors recognize their share of impairments charges recognized by investees and consider the effect on the basis difference. (ASC 323-10-35-32A)

Example of Adjustment of Goodwill for Other-Than-Temporary Impairment of an Equity Method Investment—That Ignores Income Taxes

Building on the facts from the example in the earlier section on basis differences, BI's reported net income in 20X2 and loss in 20X3 are $15,000 and ($12,000), respectively. No dividends are paid by BI after 20X1. FC's carrying value, before considering possible impairment in value, as of year-end 20X2 is computed as follows:

Carrying value of investment, December 31, 20X1	$ 140,800
FC's interest in BI's 20X2 net income ($15,000 × 40%)	6,000
Amortization of differential between fair value and carrying value	(3,200)
Carrying value, December 31, 20X2	143,600
FC's interest in BI's 20X3 net loss ($12,000 × 40%)	(4,800)
Amortization of differential between fair value and carrying value	(3,200)
Carrying value, December 31, 20X3, before considering additional charge for impairment	$ 135,600

If, at December 31, 20X3, FC determines that the fair value of its investment in BI has declined to $130,000, and this decline in value is judged to be other than temporary in nature, then FC must, per ASC 323, recognize a further loss amounting to $5,600 for the year. Notice that this fair value decline is assessed with reference to the fair (presumably, but not necessarily, market) value of the investment in BI. It would not be determined with specific reference to the value of BI's business operations, in the manner that the implied fair value of goodwill is assessed in connection with business combinations accounted for by the presentation of consolidated financial statements, although such a decline in value of the investment would likely be related to the value of BI's operations.

While the ASC is silent on this issue, it is reasonable that any recognized decline in value be assigned first to the implicit goodwill component of the investment account. In this example, since the decline, $5,600, is less than the $8,000 goodwill component of the differential, it will be fully absorbed, and future periods' amortization of the differential assigned to other assets will not be affected. On the other hand, if the value decline had exceeded $8,000, the excess would logically have been allocated to the underlying nonmonetary assets of the investee, such that the remaining differential previously identified with plant and equipment might have been reduced or eliminated, thereby altering future amortization on a prospective basis.

The impact of interperiod income tax allocation in the foregoing example is similar to that demonstrated earlier in the simplified example. Under GAAP goodwill rules, unless goodwill has been reduced for financial reporting purposes due to other-than-temporary impairment of the investment, there will be no book-tax difference and hence no deferred income tax issue to be addressed. The other components of the differential in the foregoing example are all temporary differences, with normal deferred income tax implications.

Changes in Level of Ownership or Degree of Influence

Increases in Level of Ownership or Degree of Influence When an investment that an entity had accounted for by another method initially qualifies for the equity method, entities should:

- Apply the equity method prospectively from the date investments qualify for the equity method.
- Add the carrying values of existing investments to the costs of the additional investments in order to determine the initial cost basis of the equity method investment. Note this bullet is effective upon implementation of ASU 2020-01.
- Immediately before adopting the equity method, remeasure the basis of the investor's previously held interest according to the guidance in ASC 321-10-35-1 or 35-2. If applying ASC 321-10-35-2, the entity remeasures the previously held interest at fair value. (ASC 323-10-35-33)

Decreases in Level of Ownership or Degree of Influence The process of discontinuing the use of the equity method and adopting ASC 320 or ASC 321 as necessitated by a reduction in ownership below the significant influence threshold level, does not require retroactive application. If stock is sold, the investor records gains or losses for the difference between the selling price and the carrying value. Upon implementation of ASU 2020-01, when the equity method is discontinued, the investors should remeasure the remaining investment by applying the guidance in ASC 321-10-35-1 or 35-2. If applying ASC 321-10-35-2, and observing price changes for the same or similar investments, the remaining investments should be measured at fair value immediately after discontinuance of the equity method. (ASC 323-10-35-35 and 35-36) The example and discussion below covers the accounting issues that arise when the investor sells some or all of its equity in the investee or acquires additional equity in the investee.

Example of Accounting for a Discontinuance of the Equity Method

Assume that an investor owns 10,000 shares (30%) of XYZ Company common stock, for which it paid $250,000 ten years ago. On July 1, 20X1, the investor sells 5,000 XYZ shares for $375,000. The balance in the investment in XYZ Company account at January 1, 20X1, was $600,000. Assume that the original differential between cost and book value has been fully amortized. To calculate the gain (loss) upon this sale of 5,000 shares, it is first necessary to adjust the investment account so that it is current as of the date of sale. Assuming that the investee had net income of $100,000 for the six months ended June 30, 20X1, the investor would record the following entries:

1. Investment in XYZ Company	30,000	
Equity in XYZ income		*30,000*
$100,000 × 30%		
Income tax expense	2,040	
Deferred income tax liability		2,040
$30,000 × 20% × 34%		

The gain upon sale can now be computed, as follows:

Proceeds upon sale of 5,000 shares	$ 375,000
Book value of the 5,000 shares ($630,000 × 50%)	315,000
Gain from sale of XYZ common	$ 60,000

Two entries will be needed to reflect the sale: one to record the proceeds, the reduction in the investment account, and the gain (or loss); and the other to record the related income tax effects. Remember that the investor must have computed the deferred tax effects of the undistributed earnings of the investee that it had recorded each year, on the basis that those earnings either would eventually be paid as dividends or would be realized as capital gains. When those dividends are ultimately received or when the investment is disposed of, the previously recorded deferred income tax liability must be reversed.

To illustrate, assume that the investor in this example provided deferred income taxes at an effective rate for dividends (considering the 80% exclusion) of 6.8%. The realized capital gain will be taxed at an assumed 34%. For income tax purposes, this gain is computed as $375,000 – $125,000 = $250,000, yielding an income tax effect of $85,000. For accounting purposes, the deferred income taxes already provided are 6.8% × ($315,000 – $125,000), or $12,920. Accordingly, an additional income tax expense of $72,080 is incurred upon the sale, due to the fact that an additional gain was realized for book purposes ($375,000 – $315,000 = $60,000; income tax at 34% = $20,400) and that the deferred income tax previously provided for at dividend income rates was lower than the real capital gains rate [$190,000 × (34% – 6.8%) = $51, 680 extra income tax due]. The entries are as follows:

1. Cash	375,000	
Investment in XYZ Company		315,000
Gain on sale of XYZ Company stock		60,000
2. Deferred income tax liability	12,920	
Income tax expense	72,080	
Income taxes payable—current		85,000

The gains (losses) from sales of investee stock are reported on the investor's income statement in the "Other income and expense" section, assuming that a multistep income statement is presented.

In this example, the sale of investee stock reduced the percentage owned by the investor to 15%. In such a situation, the investor would discontinue use of the equity method. The balance in the investment account on the date the equity method is suspended ($315,000 in the example) will be accounted for on the basis of fair value, under ASC 321. This accounting principle change does not require the computation of a cumulative effect or any retroactive disclosures in the investor's financial statements. In periods subsequent to this principles change, the investor records cash dividends received from the investment as dividend income and subjects the investment to the appropriate GAAP used to assess "other-than-temporary" impairment. Any dividends received in excess of the investor's share of post-disposal net income of the investee are credited to the investment, rather than to income.

When significant influence or control is lost, the investor should offset its share of the investee's equity adjustments for OCI against the carrying value of the investment. If this results in a carrying value less than zero, the investor should reduce the carrying value of the investment to zero and record the remaining balance in income. (ASC 323-10-35-37 and 35-39)

Presentation and Disclosure

The table below summarizes the presentation of equity method investments. Additional detail is included in the *Disclosure and Presentation Checklist for Commercial Businesses* at www.wiley.com/go/GAAP2021.

Equity Method Investments	
Balance Sheet	*Income Statement*
Recognized at cost.	
Subsequently adjusted for the investor's share of the investee's earnings or losses and decreased by dividends received. Classified as long term.	Recognize revenue to the extent of the entity's share of investee's earnings or losses reported subsequent to the initial date of investment.

CONCEPTS, RULES, AND EXAMPLES—ASC 323-30, *EQUITY INVESTMENTS IN CORPORATE JOINT VENTURES AND NONCORPORATE ENTITIES*

Scope and Scope Exceptions

ASC 323-30 follows the same scope and scope exceptions as ASC 323-10, providing guidance specifically on:

- Partnerships
- Unincorporated joint ventures
- Limited liability companies

Overview

This subtopic includes guidance on investments in partnerships, joint ventures, and limited liability entities that follow the equity method of accounting. The guidance is generally the same as that in ASC 323-10. Exceptions or additions are found in this section.

A wide variety of noncorporate entities and structures are used to:

- Operate businesses,
- Hold investments in real estate or in other entities, or
- Undertake discrete projects as joint ventures.

These include:

- Partnerships, for example, limited partnerships, general partnerships, limited liability partnerships, and
- Limited liability companies (LLC).

Practice questions persistently arise regarding whether directly or by analogy, authoritative GAAP literature that applies to corporate structures is also applicable to investors in noncorporate entities.

By analogy to ASC 323-10, investors with controlling interests in unincorporated entities, such as partnerships and other unincorporated joint ventures, generally should account for their investments using the equity method. (ASC 323-30-25-1)

General Partnerships

There is a rebuttable presumption that a general partner that has a majority voting interest is in control of the partnership. If voting rights are indeterminate under the provisions of the partnership agreement or applicable law, the general partner with a majority of the financial interests in the partnership's profits or losses would be presumed to have control. If this presumption is not overcome, the general partner with voting control or the majority financial interest would consolidate the partnership in its financial statements and the other noncontrolling general partners would use the equity method. (ASC 323, ASC 970-323)

Limited Liability Companies

A limited liability company may maintain a specific ownership account for each investor— similar to a partnership capital account structure. In that case, the investment in the limited liability company is viewed as similar to an investment in a limited partnership for purposes of determining whether a noncontrolling investment in a limited liability company is accounted for using the guidance in ASC 321 or the equity method. (ASC 323-30-35-3)

CONCEPTS, RULES, AND EXAMPLES—ASC 323-740, *QUALIFIED AFFORDABLE HOUSING PROJECT INVESTMENTS*

Scope and Scope Exceptions

ASC 323-740 follows the same scope and scope exceptions as ASC 323-10 and the guidance applies to investments in limited partnerships that operate qualified affordable housing projects.

Overview

ASC 323-740 provides guidance on a specific U.S. tax issue—investments in a Qualified Affordable Housing Project. Created under the Tax Reform Act of 1986, this federal program gives incentives for the utilization of private equity in the development of affordable housing for low-income Americans. The Revenue Reconciliation Act of 1993 retroactively extended and made permanent the affordable housing credit. Corporations eligible for the credits generally purchase an interest in a limited partnership that operates the qualified affordable housing projects. So, the guidance in ASC 323-740 applies to investments in limited partnerships that operate qualified affordable housing projects.

These investments are accounted for using:

- Effective yield method, or
- The guidance in ASC 970-323, *Real Estate General—Investments-Equity Method and Joint Ventures.*

The cost method may be appropriate and the guidance in ASC 323-740-25-3 through 25-5 that are not related to the proportional method may be applied. (ASC 323-740-25-2A)

The Proportional Amortization Method Election

The Codification includes an election available to qualified affordable housing projects. The election allows a "proportional amortization method" that can be used to amortize the investment basis of investments that meet certain conditions. If elected, the method is required for all eligible investments in qualified affordable housing projects and must be applied consistently. It replaces the effective yield method. Under the proportional method, an investor amortizes the costs of its investment, in proportion to the tax credits and other tax benefits it receives, to income tax expense.

To elect the proportional method, all of the following conditions must be met:

- It is probable that the tax credits allocable to the investor will be available.
- The investor does not have the ability to exercise significant influence over the operating and financial policies of the limited liability entity.
- Substantially all of the projected benefits are from tax credits and other tax benefits (for example, tax benefits generated from the operating losses of the investment).
- The investor's projected yield is based solely on the cash flows from the tax credits and other tax benefits is positive.
- The investor is a limited liability investor in the limited liability entity for both legal and tax purposes, and the investor's liability is limited to its capital investment. (ASC 323-740-25-1)

The decision to use the proportional amortization method is an accounting policy decision that must be applied consistently to individual qualifying investments. (ASC 323-740-25-4)

Equity Method

Investors that do not qualify for the proportional amortization presentation must continue to account for their investments under the equity method or cost method, which results in losses recognized in pretax income and tax benefits recognized in income taxes ("gross" presentation of investment results).

Recognition

The investor should recognize a liability for:

- Delayed equity contributions that are unconditional and legally binding
- Equity contributions that are contingent upon a future event when that event becomes probable
  (ASC 323-740-25-3)

An investor should not recognize credits before their inclusion in the investor's tax return. (ASC 323-740-25-5)

Subsequent Measurement

Under the proportional allocation method, investors amortize the initial cost of the investment to recognize an effective yield in proportion to the tax credit and other tax benefits allocated to the investor. (ASC 323-740-35-2) Investors include in earnings any cash received from operations of the limited partnership. (ASC 323-740-35-5)

Presentation

Under the proportional amortization method, the investor recognizes the amortization of the investment in the income statement as a component of income tax expense or benefit. The current portion of the expense or benefit is accounted for under the requirements of ASC 740. (ASC 323-740-45-2)

Other Sources

Investments—Equity Method and Joint Venture—Overall	
See ASC Location—*Wiley GAAP* Chapter	***For information on . . .***
ASC 260-10-55-20	The computation of consolidated earnings per share (EPS) if equity method investees or corporate joint ventures have issued options, warrants, and convertible securities.
ASC 958-810-15-4	The use of the equity method if a not-for-profit entity (NFP) has common stock investments that are 50% or less of the voting stock of for-profit entities.ss
ASC 958-810-15-4	NFPs that choose to report investment portfolios at fair value instead of applying the equity method.
ASC 974-323-25-1	The use of the equity method by a real estate investment trust with an investment in a service corporation.
Equity Method and Joint Venture Investments in Partnerships, Joint Ventures, and Limited Liability Entities	
ASC 310-10-25	Accounting for an acquisition, development, and construction arrangement, see the Acquisition, Development, and Construction Arrangements subsection.
ASC 970-323	An investment in real estate or real estate development projects in a form that otherwise would be within the scope of this subtopic.
ASC 808	Collaborative arrangements.

20 ASC 325 INVESTMENTS—OTHER

PERSPECTIVE AND ISSUES

Technical Alert

This topic is affected by ASU 2016-13. For more information about the ASU, see the chapter on ASC 326.

Investment Topics

The Codification contains several topics dealing with investments, including:

- ASC 320, *Investments—Debt Securities*
- ASC 321, *Investments—Equity Securities*
- ASC 323, *Investments—Equity Method and Joint Ventures*
- ASC 325, *Investments—Other*
- ASC 326, *Financial Instruments—Credit Losses*

Subtopics

ASC 325 provides guidance for investments not within the scope of other Topics: investments in insurance contracts and in securitized financial assets.

ASC 325 contains three subtopics:

- ASC 325-10, *Overall*, which merely identifies the other three topics
- ASC 325-30, *Investments in Insurance Contracts*, which provides guidance on investments, life insurance contracts in general, and life settlement contracts

- ASC 325-40, *Beneficial Interests in Securitized Financial Assets*, which provides guidance on accounting for a transferor's interest in securitized transactions accounted for as sales and purchased beneficial interests

Scope

ASC 325-10 Note: This Subtopic does not contain a scope section.

ASC 325-30 ASC 325-30 applies to all entities and transactions for entities that purchase life insurance where the entity is either the owner or beneficiary of the contract. Life insurance purchased by retirement plans and subject to ASC 960 are not in the scope of ASC 325-30. (ASC 325-30-15-1 through 15-3) The subtopic's guidance on life settlement contracts applies to all entities.

ASC 325-40 ASC 325-40 applies to:

- A transferor's interests in securitization transactions that are accounted for as sales under Topic 860 and
- Purchased beneficial interests in securitized financial assets. (ASC 325-40-15-2)

The guidance applies to beneficial interests that have *all* of the following characteristics:

a. Are either debt securities under Subtopic 320-10 or required to be accounted for like debt securities under that subtopic per ASC 860-20-35-2.
b. Involve securitized financial assets that have contractual cash flows.
c. Do not result in consolidation of the entity issuing the beneficial interest by the holder of the beneficial interests.
d. Are not within the scope of ASC 310-30.[1]
e. Are not beneficial interests in securitized financial assets that have both of the following characteristics:
    - Are of high credit quality.
    - Cannot contractually be prepaid or otherwise settled in a way that the holder would not recover substantially all of its recorded investment.

    (ASC 325-40-15-3)

For guidance on the recognition of interest income on beneficial interest for items with the characteristics in "e" above, entities should refer to the guidance in ASC 320-10. Guidance on other-than-temporary impairment can be found in ASC 320-10-35-17 through 35-34 or when ASU 2016-13 is implemented in ASC 326.[2] (ASC 325-40-15-4)

Note that a beneficial interest in securitized financial assets that is in equity form may meet the definition of a debt security. These beneficial interests would be within the scope of this topic and ASC 320 because ASC 320 requires them to be accounted for as debt securities:

- If the beneficial interests issued in the form of equity:
    - Represent solely a right to receive a stream of future cash flows to be collected under preset terms and conditions, or
    - According to the terms of the special-purpose entity, must be redeemed by the issuing entity or must be redeemable at the option of the investor.

  (ASC 325-40-15-5)

---

[1] This item is superseded upon implementation of ASU 2016-13.

[2] Upon implementation of ASU 2016-13, this sentence changes to: "For guidance on determining the allowance for credit losses on beneficial interests with the characteristics in 'e' above, other than trading debt securities, see ASC 326."

If beneficial interests are issued in the form of equity but do not meet the criteria in ASC 325-40-15-5, those interests should be accounted for under ASC 323-10, ASC 320-10, ASC 810-10, or ASC 321-10. (ASC 325-40-15-6)

ASC 325-40 does not apply to hybrid beneficial interests measured at fair value pursuant to paragraphs 815-15-25-4 through 25-6 for which the transferor does not report interest income as a separate item in its income statements. (ASC 325-40-15-9)

DEFINITIONS OF TERMS

Source: ASC 325. *Glossaries*.

See Appendix A, *Definitions of Terms*, for other terms related to this topic: Beneficial Interests, Debt Security (Def. 1), Financial Asset (Def. 1), Financial Asset (Def. 2), Purchased Financial Assets with Credit Deterioration, Probable, and Publicly Traded Company.

Cash Surrender Value. The amount of cash that may be realized by the owner of a life insurance contract or annuity contract upon discontinuance and surrender of the contract before its maturity. The cash surrender value may be different from the policy account balance due to outstanding loans (including accrued interest) and surrender charges. (Note: The use of this glossary term is not consistent among legal contracts. When determining the applicability of this term, the economic substance of the item shall be taken into consideration.)

Certificates. An insurance entity issues to each individual in a group contract a certificate of insurance for each person insured under the group contract. The certificate is merely a summary of the rights, duties, and benefits available under a group policy. If there is any conflict between the certificate and a group policy, the group policy is the controlling document. (Note: The use of this glossary term is not consistent among legal contracts. When determining the applicability of this term, the economic substance of the item shall be taken into consideration.)

Insurance Policy. The legal agreement between the policyholder and the insurance entity that states the terms of the arrangement. The term insurance policy includes all riders, attachments, side agreements, and other related documents that are either directly or indirectly part of the contractual arrangement. (Note: The use of this glossary term is not consistent among legal contracts. When determining the applicability of this term, the economic substance of the item shall be taken into consideration.)

Life Settlement Contract. A life settlement contract is a contract between the owner of a life insurance policy (the policy owner) and a third-party investor (investor), and has all of the following characteristics:

1. The investor does not have an insurable interest (an interest in the survival of the insured, which is required to support the issuance of an insurance policy).
2. The investor provides consideration to the policy owner of an amount in excess of the current cash surrender value of this life insurance policy.
3. The contract pays the face value of the life insurance policy to an investor when the insured dies.

Policy Account Balance. At any point in time, this is the amount held by the insurance entity on behalf of the policyholder. This balance may be held in a general account, a separate account (a legally segregated account), or a combination of both on the insurance entity's balance sheet. This account includes premiums received from the policyholder, plus any credited income, less any relevant charges (acquisition costs, cost of insurance, and so forth). (Note: The use of this glossary term is not consistent among legal contracts. When determining the applicability of this term, the economic substance of the item shall be taken into consideration.)

Surrender Charge. A contractual fee imposed by the insurance entity when a policyholder surrenders the insurance policy that typically decreases over the life of the policy. The surrender charge represents a recovery of costs incurred by the insurance entity in originating the policy. It may or may not be explicitly called a surrender charge and can be embedded in other agreements besides the insurance contract. (Note: The use of this glossary term is not consistent among legal contracts. When determining the applicability of this term, the economic substance of the item shall be taken into consideration.)

CONCEPTS, RULES, AND EXAMPLES

Presentation and Disclosure

For information on presentation and disclosure related to ASC 325, see www.wiley.com/go/ GAAP2021.

ASC 325-10, *Overall*

ASC 325-10 merely lists the investment topics and the ASC 325-10 Subtopics and other sources. It does not have recognition, subsequent measurement, presentation, or disclosure guidance.

ASC 325-30, *Investments in Insurance Contracts*

Overview ASC 325-30 provides guidance on investments in insurance contracts and is divided between general guidance and guidance for life settlement contracts. See the definition of life settlement contracts in the "Definitions of Terms" section above.

General Guidance Exchange of Mutual Membership Interests for Stock in a Demutualization Entities should measure stock received in a demutualization at fair value. (ASC 325-30-1AA) A gain on exchange of mutual membership interests is recognized in income from continuing operations. (ASC 325-*30-40-1)*

Guidance for Investments in Life Settlement Contracts For a life settlement contract, the investor must elect to account for these investments using either the investment method or the fair value method. (ASC 325-30-25-2) This irrevocable election is made in one of two ways:

1. On an instrument-by-instrument basis supported by documentation prepared concurrently with acquisition of the investment, or
2. Based on a pre-established, documented policy that automatically applies to all such investments.

The Investment Method If the investor elects this method, the investor recognizes the initial investment at the transaction price plus all initial direct external costs. (ASC 325-30-30-1C) Continuing costs (payments of policy premiums and direct external costs, if any) necessary to keep the policy in force are capitalized. (ASC 325-30-35-8) Gain recognition is deferred until the death of the insured. (ASC 325-30-35-9) At that time the investor recognizes in net income (or other applicable performance indicator) the difference between the carrying amount of the investment and the policy proceeds. (ASC 325-30-40-1A)

The investor is required to test the investment for impairment upon the availability of new or updated information that indicates that, upon the death of the insured, the expected proceeds from the insurance policy may not be sufficient for the investor to recover the carrying amount of the investment plus anticipated gross future premiums (undiscounted for the time value of money) and capitalizable external direct costs, if any. Indicators to be considered include, but are not limited to:

- A change in the life expectancy of the insured
- A change in the credit standing of the insurer
  (ASC 325-30-35-10)

As a result of performing an impairment test, if the undiscounted expected cash inflows (the expected proceeds from the policy) are less than the carrying amount of the investment plus the undiscounted anticipated gross future premiums and capitalizable external direct costs, an impairment loss is recognized. The loss is recorded by reducing the carrying value of the investment to its fair value. The fair value computation is to employ current interest rates. (ASC 325-30-35-11) Note that a change in interest rates would not by itself require an impairment test.

The Fair Value Method If the investor elects the fair value method for life settlement contracts, the initial investment is recorded at the transaction price. (ASC 325-30-30-2) Each subsequent reporting period, the investor remeasures the investment at fair value and recognizes changes in fair value in current period net income (or other relevant performance indicators for reporting entities that do not report net income). (ASC 325-30-35-12) Cash outflows for policy premiums and inflows for policy proceeds are included in the same financial statement line item as the changes in fair value are reported.

ASC 325-40, *Beneficial Interests in Securitized Financial Assets*

Overview ASC 325-40 provides guidance on another type of investment. When a reporting entity sells a portion of an asset that it owns, the portion retained becomes an asset separate from the portion sold and separate from the assets obtained in exchange. This is the situation when financial assets such as loans are securitized with certain interests being retained (e.g., a defined portion of the contractual cash flows).

Initial Recognition and Measurement The reporting entity must allocate the previous carrying amount of the assets sold based on the relative fair values of each component at the date of sale or upon implementation of ASU 2016-13, the fair value of the beneficial interest at the date of transfer following the guidance in ASC 860-20-30-1. (ASC 325-40-30-1) In most cases, the initial carrying amount (i.e., the allocated cost) of the retained interest will be different from the fair value of the instrument. Furthermore, cash flows from those instruments may be delayed depending on the contractual provisions of the entire structure (for example, cash may be retained in a trust to fund a cash collateral account).

Upon implementation of ASU 2016-13, entities with purchased financial assets with credit deterioration should follow the guidance in ASC 326-20 for beneficial interests classified as available for sale if

- There is a significant difference between contractual cash flow and expected cash flow at the date of recognition or
- The beneficial interests meet the definition of purchased assets with credit deterioration
  (ASC 325-40-30-1A)

The holder of the beneficial interest must recognize the excess of all cash flows anticipated at the acquisition transaction date over the initial investment. (ASC 325-40-30-2) Upon implementation of ASU 2016-13, for beneficial interests that do not apply the accounting for purchased financial assets with credit deterioration, the entity should measure accretable yield initially at the excess of all cash flows expected to be collected that is attributable to the beneficial interest estimated at the transaction date over the initial investment. If the beneficial interests that do apply the accounting for purchased financial assets with credit deterioration, the entity measures accretable yield initially as the excess of all contractual cash flows attributable to the beneficial interest at the transaction date over the amortized cost basis. (ASC 325-10-30-2)

Subsequent Measurement Accretable Yield

The holder recognizes accretable yield as interest income using the effective yield method. The holder is required to update the estimate of cash flows over the life of the beneficial interest. (ASC 325-40-35-1) The method used for recognizing and measuring the amount of interest income is the same for each classification of beneficial interest. (ASC 325-40-35-2) Note upon implementation of ASU 2016-13, ASC 325-40-35-2 is superseded.

If the estimated cash flows change, but there is still an excess over the carrying amount, the adjustment is accounted for prospectively as a change in estimate with the amount of the periodic accretion adjusted over the remaining life of the beneficial interest. If the fair value of the beneficial interest declines below its carrying amount, the reporting entity should determine if the decline is other than temporary and apply the impairment guidance below on OTTI evaluations. (ASC 325-40-35-4)[3]

Credit Losses[4]

NOTE: For credit losses on beneficial interests held to maturity and available for sale, entities should apply the guidance in ASC 326. (ASC 325-40-6A)

Credit losses should be measured using the present value of expected future cash flows. If the original estimate of present value is less than the current estimate, the change is favorable. Conversely, if the previous estimate is greater than the current one, the change is adverse. (ASC 325-40-35-7)

Entities should look to the guidance on credit losses in ASC 326 and unless that guidance points to a credit loss, changes in an interest rate generally would not result in the recognition of a credit loss. (ASC 325-40-35-9)

Entities should not assume that a credit loss has occurred simply because not all the scheduled payments have been received. So, too, not every decline in fair value is a credit loss. The entity must analyze the situation further and exercise judgment to assess the decline. (ASC 325-40-35-10A)

NOTE: It is inappropriate for management to automatically conclude that, because all of the scheduled payments to date have been received, a security has not incurred an OTTI.[5] *Conversely, it is also inappropriate for management to automatically conclude that every decline in fair value of a security represents OTTI.*[6] *The longer*[7] *and/or the more severe the decline in fair value, the more persuasive the evidence that would be needed to overcome the premise that it is probable that the holder will not collect all of the contractual or estimated cash flows from the security. (ASC 325-40-35-10A)*

If it is not practicable for a holder/transferor to estimate the fair value of the beneficial interest at the securitization date, interest income is recognized using the cost recovery method. (ASC 325-40-35-16)

---

[3] Upon implementation of ASU 2016-13, entities should look to the guidance in ASC 326 for guidance on evaluation of changes in cash flows for beneficial interests classified as held-to-maturity and available for sale. (ASC 325-40-35-4)

[4] The paragraphs below in this section reflect the guidance in ASU 2016-13.

[5] Upon implementation of ASU 2016-13, this language changes to: "It is inappropriate for management to automatically conclude because all of the scheduled payments to date have been received that no credit loss exists."

[6] Upon implementation of ASU 2016-13, this language changes from "represents OTTI" to "represents credit loss."

[7] Upon implementation of ASU 2016-13, "longer" is deleted.

OTTI Evaluations[8] The objective of the other-than-temporary impairment analysis is to determine whether it is probable that the holder will realize some portion of the unrealized loss on an impaired security.

Further analysis and the exercise of judgment are required to assess whether a decline in fair value indicates that it is probable that the holder will not collect all of the contractual or estimated cash flows from the security.

In performing the assessment of OTTI and developing estimates of future cash flows, the holder also should look to the guidance in ASC 320-10-35-33G through 35-33I and consider all information available that is relevant to collectibility, including information about past events, current conditions, and forecasts that are reasonable and supportable. (ASC 325-40-35-10B)[9] This information should generally include:

- The remaining payment terms of the security
- Prepayment speeds
- The issuer's financial condition
- Expected defaults
- The value of the underlying collateral
  (ASC 320-10-35-33G)[10]

Entities should consider:

- Industry analyst reports and forecasts, sector credit ratings, and other relevant market data
- The effect, if applicable, of any credit enhancements on the expected performance of the security, including consideration of the current financial condition of a guarantor of the security
  (ASC 320-10-35-33H)[11]

NOTE: This applies only if the guarantee is not a separate contract. Per ASC 320-10-35-23, the holder should not combine separate contracts (such as a debt security and a guarantee or other credit enhancement) for the purpose of the determination of impairment or the determination of whether the debt security can be contractually prepaid or otherwise settled in a manner that would preclude the holder from recovering substantially all of its cost.

Some or all of the securitized loans that comprise many beneficial interests may be structured with payment streams that are not level over the life of the loan. Thus, the remaining payments expected to be received from the security could differ significantly from those received in prior periods.

This type of structure necessitates consideration by the holder of whether a security backed by loans that are currently performing will continue to perform when the contractual provisions of those loans require increasing payments on the part of the borrowers. In addition, the holder is to consider how the value of any collateral would affect the expected performance of the security. Naturally, if the fair value of the collateral has declined, the holder must assess the effect of the

---

[8] Upon implementation of ASU 2016-13, the OTTI evaluations are deleted.

[9] Upon implementation of ASU 2016-13, this paragraph is deleted.

[10] Ibid.

[11] Ibid.

decline on the ability of the borrower to make the balloon payment since the decline in value may preclude the borrower from obtaining sufficient funds from a potential refinancing of the debt.

Timing of recognition of an OTTI A write-down for other-than-temporary impairment is recognized as a charge to net income in the period in which the decision to sell the beneficial interest is made if management of the entity *both:*

- Holds an available-for-sale beneficial interest whose fair value is less than its amortized cost basis *and*
- Does not expect the fair value to recover prior to an expected sale shortly after the date of the statement of financial position.

(ASC 325-40-35-13)[12]

[12] Ibid.

21 ASC 326 FINANCIAL INSTRUMENTS—CREDIT LOSSES

PERSPECTIVE AND ISSUES

Technical Alert

ASU 2019-10 Guidance regarding effective dates. In November 2019, the FASB issued ASU 2019-10, *Financial Instruments—Credit Losses (Topic 326), Derivatives and Hedging (Topic 815), and Leases (Topic 842: Effective Dates*. The ASU grants private companies, not-for-profit organizations, and certain small public company SEC filers additional time to implement recent FASB standards on current expected credit losses (CECL).

ASU 2019-10 Effective Dates		
Topic	*Public business entities that meet the definition of SEC Filers, except Smaller Reporting Companies (SRCs) as determined by the SEC as of November 15, 2019*	*All Other Entities*
CECL (ASC 326)	Fiscal years beginning after December 15, 2019	Fiscal years beginning after December 15, 2022

ASU 2017-03 See the Technical Alert in the chapter on ASC 250 for information on SEC preadoption disclosures for new standards.

ASU 2016-13 In June 2016, the FASB issued ASU 2016-13, *Financial Instruments—Credit Losses (Topic 326) Measurement of Credit Losses on Financial Instruments*. This ASU makes changes to several topics and adds a new topic—ASC 326. ASU 2016-13 marks a significant change in practice, requiring the immediate recognition of estimated credit losses expected to occur over the remaining life of many financial assets.

Effective date Early adoption is allowed for all entities for fiscal years beginning after December 15, 2018, including interim periods therein. (ASC 326-10-65-1)

Also, please see the information below on ASU 2019-05.

Transition Except where noted in the table below, entities should use a modified-retrospective approach and record a cumulative-effect adjustment to retained earnings as of the beginning of the first reporting period that the entity adopts the guidance. (ASC 326-10-65-1) For example, a calendar-year private company that adopts the standard in 2022 records the cumulative effect adjustment on January 1, 2022. The transition adjustment includes those adjustments made as a result of an entity amending its accounting policy if it adopts the amendments in ASU 2019-04 related to determining when accrued interest receivables are deemed uncollectible and written off. Also, see the information below on ASU 2019-05 for an option to select the fair value option.

Prospective Transition Approach Required	
Circumstance	*Accounting Treatment*
Debt securities for which an OTTI was recognized before the adoption date	If amounts relate to improvements in cash flows expected to be collected, continue to accrete into income over the remaining life of the asset. If cash flows improve because of improvements in credit after the adoption date, record in the income statement in the period received. If cash flows are expected to decrease because of deterioration in credit expectations, record an allowance.
Assets previously accounted for as PCD (purchased financial assets with credit deterioration)	Adjust the amortized cost basis on adoption to reflect the addition of the allowance for credit losses on the transition date. Continue to accrete or amortize, at the effective interest rate at the adoption date, the remaining noncredit discount or premium. Apply the same transition requirements to beneficial interests that previously applied the PCD model or have a significant difference between contractual cash flows and expected cash flows.
(ASC 326-10-65-1)	

ASU 2018-19 In November 2018, the FASB issued *Codification Improvements to Topic 326, Financial Instruments—Credit Losses*. This update changes the effective date for nonpublic entities and clarifies ASC 326's scope related to leases. Those changes are reflected in the effective dates above and in the scope guidance in this chapter. Also, for the fair value option, see the information on ASU 2019-05 below.

ASU 2019-04 In April 2019, the FASB issued ASU 2019-04, *Codification Improvements to Topic 326, Financial Instruments—Credit Losses, Topic 815, Derivatives and Hedging, and Topic 825, Financial Instruments*. The ASU addresses four issues:

- Scope,
- Held-to-maturity disclosures,
- Measurements alternative, and
- Remeasurement of equity securities.

The ASC 326 amendments in ASU 2019-04 are incorporated in this chapter and relate to:

- Accrued interest:
  - Provisions to measure, present, and disclose the allowance for credit losses separately.
  - An accounting policy election to write off accrued interest through interest income, credit loss expense, or a combination of both.
  - An accounting policy election to record no accrued credit loss if accrued interest is remeasured on a timely basis.
- Transfers from HFS (held-to-investment) to HFI (held-for-investment) loans, AFS (available-for-sale) to held-to-maturity (HTM) debt securities:
  - Guidance on how the CECL model should be applied to an HFS loan transferred to HFI or credit-impaired AFS security transferred to HTM.
- Recoveries:
  - Expected recoveries required to be considered when measuring a credit loss.
  - Permits a negative allowance, but only up to the amount previously written off.
- Consideration of prepayment in determining the EIR (effective interest rate):
  - Policy election to adjust the EIR for expected prepayments when using a DCF (discounted cash flow) method.
- Projections of interest rate environments for variable rate financial instruments:
  - Policy election to project future interest rate environments when using a DCF method on variable-rate financial instruments.
  - If above is elected, entity must also elect to adjust the effective interest rate for expected prepayments.
  - Vintage disclosure:
    - Lines of credit that are converted to term loans
- Consider contractual extensions and renewals of a financial asset:
  - Contractual extensions and renewals that are in the original or modified contract at the reporting date and are not unconditionally cancelable by the entity.

ASU 2019-05 In May 2019, the FASB issued ASU 2019-05, *Financial Instruments—Credit Losses (Topic 326) - Targeted Transition Relief.*

Guidance This Update provides an option to irrevocably elect the fair value option for certain financial assets previously measured at amortized cost basis. The FASB expects this amendment to increase comparability because it aligns measurement methodologies for similar financial assets. This option is available to reporting entities within the scope of ASC 326. The new option may be applied on an instrument-by-instrument basis for eligible instruments. Note that this option *does not* apply to held-to-maturity debt securities. An entity that applies the fair value option should then apply the guidance in ASC ASC 825-10. (ASC 326-10-65-1)

Effective Date See the information on effective dates in the technical alert on ASU 2019-10 at the beginning of this chapter.

Transition Entities should adopt the changes using a modified-retrospective basis by means of a cumulative-effect adjustment to the opening balance of retained earnings balance as of the date the entity adopted ASU 2016-13.

ASU 2019-11 In November 2019, the FASB issued ASU 2019-11, *Codification Improvements to Topic 326, Financial Instruments—Credit Losses*. The purpose of the update is to clarify certain aspects of ASC 326.

The guidance is incorporated in this chapter and the effective dates are the same as those for ASU 2016-13 included in the information on ASU 2019-10 at the beginning of this chapter.

Overview

ASC 326 changes the impairment model for most financial assets currently measured at amortized cost and certain other instruments. The model changes from an incurred loss model to an expected loss model, referred to as the current expected credit loss model (CECL).

The incurred loss model was criticized for delaying recognition of losses. The model had a critical shortcoming. It did not allow debt holders to realize expected losses until they met the probable recognition threshold. The CECL model's underlying principle is that a reporting entity holding financial assets is exposed to credit risk throughout the holding period, that is, from origination until settlement or disposal. The CECL model, based on an expected loss approach, should result in entities recognizing losses on a timely basis.

Subtopics

ASC 326 contains three subtopics:

- ASC 326-10, *Overall*, which contains scope, definitions, and effective date information
- ASC 326-20, *Financial Instruments—Credit Losses—Measured at Amortized Cost*, which provides guidance on how entities measure expected credit losses on
  - Financial instruments measured at amortized cost and
  - Leases.
- ASC 326-30, *Financial Instruments—Credit Losses—Available-for-Sale Debt Securities*

Scope and Scope Exceptions

ASC 326-10, *Overall* This guidance applies to all entities.

ASC 326-20, *Financial Instruments—Credit Losses—Measured at Amortized Cost* This subtopic applies to all entities and the following items:

- Financial assets measured at amortized cost, such as financing receivables, HTM debt securities, receivables recorded under ASC 606 and ASC 610, and receivables related to repurchase agreements and securities lending agreements under ASC 860,
- Net investments in leases,
- Off-balance-sheet credit exposures not accounted for as insurance, and
- Reinsurance recoverables from insurance transactions within the scope of ASC 944. (ASC 326-20-15-1 and 15-2)

Exhibit—What's In Scope and What's Not

In Scope	Out of Scope
ASC 326-20	
Loans	Loan receivables held for sale
Loan commitments	Financial assets where the fair value option is elected
Held-to-maturity debt securities	Equity instruments
Trade receivables	Equity method investments
Reinsurance receivables	Derivatives
Financial guarantees	Related party loans to entities under common control
Net investments in leases arising from sales-type and direct financing leases	Receivables arising from operating leases
Purchased credit deteriorated assets recoded at amortized cost	
ASC 326-30	
Available-for-sale debt securities	

The subtopic *does not* apply to:

a. Financial assets measured at fair value through net income,
b. Available-for-sale debt securities (see ASC 326-30),
c. Loans made to participants by defined contribution employee benefit plans,
d. Policy loan receivables of an insurance entity,
e. Promises to give (pledges receivable) of a not-for-profit entity,
f. Loans and receivables between entities under common control, and
g. Receivables resulting from operating leases accounted for under ASC 842. (ASC 326-20-15-3)

ASC 326-30, *Financial Instruments—Credit Losses—Available-for-Sale Debt Securities* The FASB decided that the measurement attribute for AFS debt securities requires a separate credit loss model. This subtopic applies to all entities and debt securities classified as available-for-sale securities, including loans that meet the definition of debt securities and are classified as available-for-sale securities. (ASC 326-30-15-1 and 15-2) Therefore, the credit loss model to use under the new standard depends on the classification of the debt security. This is a change from existing practice.

ASC 326 also requires recording available-for-sale (AFS) debt securities' credit losses through an allowance account.

Comparison of Loss Models	
Extant GAAP—Incurred Loss Model	*New ASC 326—CECL Model*
Delays recognition credit loss until it is *probable* that the loss has been incurred.	Estimates credit losses over the entire contractual term of the instrument from the date of initial recognition, reflecting future events that will lead to a realized loss. Does not include "trigger" to record losses.

Comparison of Loss Models	
Extant GAAP—Incurred Loss Model	*New ASC 326—CECL Model*
Generally, estimated using past events and current conditions.	Also includes expectations for the future.

It is anticipated that entities will recognize losses earlier under the new model.

DEFINITIONS OF TERMS

Source: ASC 326 *Glossaries*. Also see Appendix A, *Definitions of Terms*, for additional terms related to this topic: Amortized Cost Basis, Bargain Purchase Option, Bargain Purchase Renewal, Contract, Debt Security, Effective Interest Rate, Fair Value (Def. 2), Financial Asset, Financing Receivable, Freestanding Contract, Indirectly Related to the Leased Property, Lease, Lease Term, Lessee, Lessor, Market Participants, Noncancelable Lease Term, Not-for-Profit Entity, Orderly Transaction, Penalty, Public Business Entity, Related Parties, Securities and Exchange Commission (SEC) Filer, Security, Standby Letter of Credit, Troubled Debt Restructuring, Underlying Assets

Class of Financing Receivable. Note: The following definition is pending content; effective upon implementation of ASU 2016-13

A group of financing receivables determined on the basis of both of the following:

a. Risk characteristics of the financing receivable
b. An entity's method for monitoring and assessing credit risk

Credit Quality Indicator. Note: The following definition is pending content; effective upon implementation of ASU 2016-13. A statistic about the credit quality of a financial asset.

Freestanding Contract. A freestanding contract is entered into either:

a. Separate and apart from any of the entity's other financial instruments or equity transactions
b. In conjunction with some other transaction and is legally detachable and separately exercisable

Line-of-Credit Arrangement. A line-of-credit or revolving-debt arrangement is an agreement that provides the borrower with the option to make multiple borrowings up to a specified maximum amount, to repay portions of previous borrowings, and to then reborrow under the same contract. Line-of-credit and revolving-debt arrangements may include both amounts drawn by the debtor (a debt instrument) and a commitment by the creditor to make additional amounts available to the debtor under predefined terms (a loan commitment).

Loan. A contractual right to receive money on demand or on fixed or determinable dates that is recognized as an asset in the creditor's statement of financial position. Examples include but are not limited to accounts receivable (with terms exceeding one year) and notes receivable.

Loan Commitment. Note: The following definition is pending content; it is effective upon implementation of ASU 2016-13.

Loan commitments are legally binding commitments to extend credit to a counterparty under certain prespecified terms and conditions. They have fixed expiration dates and may either be fixed-rate or variable-rate. Loan commitments can be either of the following:

a. Revolving (in which the amount of the overall commitment is reestablished upon repayment of previously drawn amounts)
b. Nonrevolving (in which the amount of the overall commitment is not reestablished upon repayment of previously drawn amounts)

Loan commitments can be distributed through syndication arrangements, in which one entity acts as a lead and an agent on behalf of other entities that will each extend credit to a single borrower. Loan commitments generally permit the lender to terminate the arrangement under the terms of covenants negotiated under the agreement.

Portfolio Segment. Note: The following definition is pending content; it is effective upon adoption of ASC 2016-13.

The level at which an entity develops and documents a systematic methodology to determine its allowance for credit losses. See paragraphs 326-20-50-3 and 326-20-55-10.

Purchased Financial Assets with Credit Deterioration. Note: The following definition is pending content; effective upon implementation of ASU 2016-13.

Acquired individual financial assets (or acquired groups of financial assets with similar risk characteristics) that as of the date of acquisition have experienced a more-than-insignificant deterioration in credit quality since origination, as determined by an acquirer's assessment. See paragraph 326-20-55-5 for more information on the meaning of similar risk characteristics for assets measured on an amortized cost basis.

Reinsurance Recoverable. All amounts recoverable from reinsurers for paid and unpaid claims and claim settlement expenses, including estimated amounts receivable for unsettled claims, claims incurred but not reported, or policy benefits.

CONCEPTS, RULES, AND EXAMPLES—ASC 326-10, *OVERALL*

This subtopic contains scope, definitions, and transition guidance. It does not contain recognition, measurement, presentation, or disclosure guidance.

CONCEPTS, RULES, AND EXAMPLES—ASC 326-20, *MEASURED AT AMORTIZED COST*

Estimating Expected Credit Losses

The allowance for credit losses should reflect the portion of the amortized cost basis of a financial asset that the entity does not expect to collect. Entities record the expected credit loss as an allowance deducted from or added to the amortized cost basis of the financial asset. A related credit loss expense is recorded in net income. The allowance account includes:

- Recoveries of amounts previously written off and
- Amounts expected to be written off.

However, these amounts must not exceed amounts previously written off and expected to be written off. The estimate for expected credit losses is updated at each reporting date. (ASC 326-20-30-1)

Exhibit—CECL Model Inputs

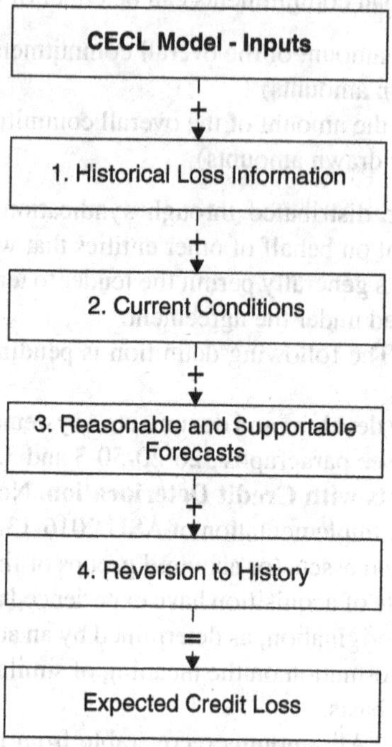

1. **Historical Loss Information.** Entities should measure expected credit losses on a pool basis, that is, aggregate financial assets that have similar risk characteristics, such as:
   - Risk rating,
   - Effective interest rate,
   - Type,
   - Size, and
   - Term.

   A financial asset may only be measured individually if it does not share similar risk characteristics with other financial assets. A financial asset should be included in a pool or on an individual basis, but not both.
   (ASC 326-20-30-2 and 55-5)
2. **Current Conditions.** Entities should adjust the historical data to reflect
   - current asset-specific risk characteristics.
   - differences in economic conditions, including current conditions and reasonable economic forecasts.

   (ASC 326-20-30-7 through 30-11)
3. **Reasonable and Supportable Forecasts.** ASC 326 allows for flexibility in modeling. It does not require a discounted cash flow method and does not prescribe a particular method for measuring the allowance. The entity may use methods such as:
   - Discounted cash flow,
   - Loss-rate,
   - Roll-rate,

- Probability-of-default, or
- Methods that use an aging schedule.

(ASC 326-20-30-3)

While not prescribing a method, ASC 326 does provide guidance on how an entity should calculate the loss based on the method chosen.

Discounted Cash Flow Method If using a discounted cash flow method, the entity should discount using the effective interest rate. The resulting allowance reflects the difference between the amortized cost basis and the present value of the expected cash flows. (ASC 326-30-4 and 30-6)

Amortized cost basis—present value of the expected cash flows allowance In some situations, the effective interest rate varies based on an independent factor, such as an index or rate like LIBOR. In those cases, the effective interest rate (EIR) should be calculated based on the factor as it changes over the life of the asset. The entity is not required to project changes in the factor when estimating expected cash flows. If it does, the entity should adjust the EIR to consider the timing resulting from prepayments as noted below. (ASC 326-20-30-4)

Accounting Policy Election—Effective Interest Rate Use in Discounted Cash Flow Method For each class of financing receivable or major security type, entities may elect to adjust the effective interest rate used to discount expected cash flows to consider the timing of the expected cash flows as a result of prepayments. This accounting policy election is not available if the asset is restructured in a TDR. (ASC 326-20-30-4A)

Other Than Discounted Cash Flow Method If the entity uses a method other than discounted cash flow, the allowance should reflect the entity's estimate of the amortized cost basis of the asset as of the reporting date. So, for example, if the entity uses a loss-rate method, the numerator would include the expected credit loss of the amortized cost basis.

The estimate of credit losses may be developed by measuring components of amortized cost on a combined basis or by separately measuring:

- Amortized cost basis, excluding applicable accrued interest, premiums, discounts, foreign exchange and fair value hedge accounting adjustments.
- Premiums or discount, including net deferred fees and costs, foreign exchange, and fair value hedge accounting adjustment, and
- Applicable accrued interest

(ASC 326-20-30-5)

Estimate Losses over the Contractual Term of the Asset When using one of these methods, the estimates should be made over the contractual term of the financial asset. Prepayments:

- Should be considered a separate input or
- Embedded in the credit loss information.

Prepayments should be factored into the future principal and interest cash flows. The estimate should be made over the period when the commitment is legally binding and the entity is exposed to credit risk. The contractual term should be extended for expected extensions, renewals, and modification unless:

- There is a reasonable expectation at the reporting date that it will execute a TDR with the borrower or
- The extension or renewal options are included in the original or modified contract at the reporting date and are not unconditionally cancelable by the entity.

(ASC 326-20-30-6)

Accounting Policy Election—Accrued Interest Receivable

At the class of financing receivable or the major security-type level, an entity may elect not to measure an allowance for credit losses for accrued interest receivables. This election is allowed as long as the entity writes off the uncollectible accrued interest receivable balance on a timely basis. (ASC 326-20-30-5A)

1. **Reversion to History.** When unable to make reasonable and supportable forecasts, entities should revert to historical loss information. If this approach is used, it should be well documented.

Factors to consider: When making their estimates, entities should consider:

- Internal and external information related to:
  - Past events
  - Current conditions
  - Reasonable and supportable forecasts
- Qualitative factors
- Quantitative factors

Entities should search information that is available without undue cost and effort. In many cases, the internal information may be sufficient and historical losses of assets with similar risk characteristics may provide a basis for assessment. (ASC 326-20-30-7 and 30-8) However, entities should be careful not to rely exclusively on historical loss information and should consider the need to adjust it for differences in risk characteristics of current assets. (ASC 326-20-30-9) The estimate should include a measure of the risk of credit loss, even if remote. If the expectation of nonpayment is zero, entities are not required to measure expected credit losses in a financial asset. (ASC 326- 20-30-10) For example, if an entity invests in U.S. Treasury securities and intends to hold them to maturity, it is reasonable to assume that the long history with no credit losses indicates an expectation of nonpayment if the amortized cost basis is zero. (ASC 326-20-55-50)

Off-Balance-Sheet Credit Exposures Credit losses on off-balance-sheet credit exposure should be reported as a liability and a related credit loss expense. An exception to this is off-balance-sheet credit obligations that can be canceled unconditionally by the issuer. Those are not considered. (ASC 326-20-30-11)

Credit Enhancements Expected credit loss estimates reflect how credit enhancements, exclusive of freestanding credit contracts, mitigate losses on financial assets. Items to consider include:

- Financial condition of the guarantor,
- Guarantor's willingness to pay, and
- Whether subordinated interest may be capable of absorbing the losses.

When making the estimate, entities should not combine financial assets with separate, freestanding contracts. (ASC 326-20-30-12)

Example—CECL Model: Initial Recognition

Assumptions:

- Entity A purchases a portfolio of nonamortizing bonds, classified as held-to-maturity debt securities.
- Because the bonds share similar risk characteristics, they are pooled.

Entity A estimates the following credit losses for the portfolio:

Characteristics		Expected loss rate estimate	
Purchase price	**$150,000**	**Historical loss rate**	**2.25%**
Premiums (discounts)	None	Adjustment for current conditions	.15%
Remaining estimate life	10 years	Adjustment for forecast and reversion	.075%
Coupon	5%	Expected credit loss on date of purchase	2.475%

Accounting entries on initial recognition of the purchase:

Bonds	**$150,000**		
Expense	$3,712.50*	Cash	$150,000
		Allowance	$3,712.50*

* *$150,000 × 2.475%*

Example—CECL Model: Trade Receivables

The Good Life to a Tee manufactures and sells T-shirts, sweatshirts, and mugs with a golfing theme to a broad range of retail stores located in private and public golf clubs. Customers are provided with payment terms of 90 days with a 2% discount if payments are received within 60 days. The following reflects The Good Life's historical credit loss percentages:

Current	0.4%
1–30 days past due	7%
31–60 days past due	25%
61–90 days past due	59%
More than 90 days past due	84%

The Good Life finds that the composition of the trade receivables at the reporting date is consistent with that used to develop the percentages above because the customers' risk characteristics and The Good Life's lending practices have not changed significantly over time. Therefore, The Good Life concludes that the historical credit loss information is a reasonable first step in determining expected credit losses for trade receivables. The Good Life then examines current conditions and concludes that because of the demographics of the golfing population, it should factor in a 10% increase in the loss rate in each aging group. The Good Life developed this estimate based on the aging population in the geographic area it serves and discussions with shop managers.

The Good Life develops the following aging schedule to estimate expected credit losses.

Past-due Status	Amortized Cost Basis	Credit Loss Rate	Expected Credit Loss Estimates
Current	$ 488,625	0.4% × 1.10 = .044%	$21,450
1–30 days past due	11,087	7.7%	854
31–60 days past due	5,234	27.5%	1,439

Past-due Status	Amortized Cost Basis	Credit Loss Rate	Expected Credit Loss Estimates
61–90 days past due	888	59% × 1.10 = 64.9%	1,368
More than 90 days past due	1,563	84% × 1.10 = 92.4%	1,444
	507,397		$26,555

Purchased Financial Assets with Credit Deterioration (PCD) Model PCD assets are purchased financial assets measured at amortized cost basis, with a more-than-insignificant amount of credit deterioration since origination of the asset. Their allowances for credit losses are determined similarly to those for other financial assets. However, upon acquisition, the initial allowance is added to the purchase price (the "gross up" approach) rather than being reported as a credit loss expense. The entity's method for measuring expected credit losses must be consistent with the method the entity uses for originated and purchased noncredit deteriorated assets.

Income for these assets is recognized based on the effective interest rate, but excludes the discount included in the purchase price that is attributable to the assessment of credit losses at the time of acquisition. (ASC 326-20-30-13)

Method for Discounting Expected Credit Losses of PCDs	
Estimate made using discounted cash flow	Discount expected credit losses at the rate that equates to present value of the purchaser's estimate of the asset's future cash flow with purchase price of the asset.
Estimate made using other method	Estimate expected credit losses based on unpaid principal balance of the financial asset.
(ASC 326-20-30-14)	

If an entity uses a method other than the discounted cash flow method to estimate expected credit losses, expected recourses should not include any amounts that result in an acceleration of the nonprofit discount. However, an entity may include increases in expected cash flows after acquisition. (ASC 326-20-30-13A)

If purchased financial assets do not have a more-than-insignificant deterioration in credit quality since origination, entities should account for them consistent with other financial assets. (ASC 326-20-30-15)

Example—PCD Model: Initial Recognition

Assumptions:

- Entity A purchases a loan with more than significant credit deterioration since origination.
- Entity A chooses to use a discounted cash flow method to estimate credit losses.
- The face value of the loan is $150M.
- Purchase price is $105M representing the fair value of cash flows not expected to be collected.
- The loan is discounted $45M.
- The allowance calculated for credit loss, including forward-looking conditions, on day 1 is $28M.
- The remainder of the discount is for noncredit losses.

Accounting entries on initial recognition:

Debit		Credit	
Loan	150M		
		Loan—noncredit discount	22M
		Allowance for credit losses	28.26M (record allowance on PCD)
		Cash	105M (purchase price)

Note that for PCDs, the discount embedded in the purchase price attributable to expected credit losses is not recognized in interest income and not reported as a credit loss expense at acquisition. (ASC 326-20-30-13 and 35-53B)

Subsequently, the $22M noncredit discount is accreted into interest income over the life of the asset. The $28M allowance for credit losses is updated at each reporting period, and changes are reported as a credit loss expense.

Subsequent Measurement

At each reporting date, entities should compare their current estimate of expected credit losses with the estimate recorded. (ASC 326-20-35-1) The amount needed to adjust the allowance for credit losses is reported in net income as a

- Credit loss expense or
- A reversal of a credit loss expense

Generally, an entity would want to use the same estimation method applied consistently over time. (ASC 326-20-35-2)

Off-balance-sheet exposures must be evaluated and reported in the same way. (ASC 326-20-35-3)

Financial Assets Secured by Collateral

Collateral-dependent Financial Assets Foreclosure Is Probable The process for estimating expected credit losses of collateral-dependent assets differs from the CECL's general measurement principles. The Exhibit below diagrams the decision-making process.

When the entity determines that foreclosure of a collateral-dependent financial asset is probable, the entity should measure expected credit losses based on fair value of the collateral at the reporting date. The entity should consider any credit enhancements as discussed earlier in this

Exhibit

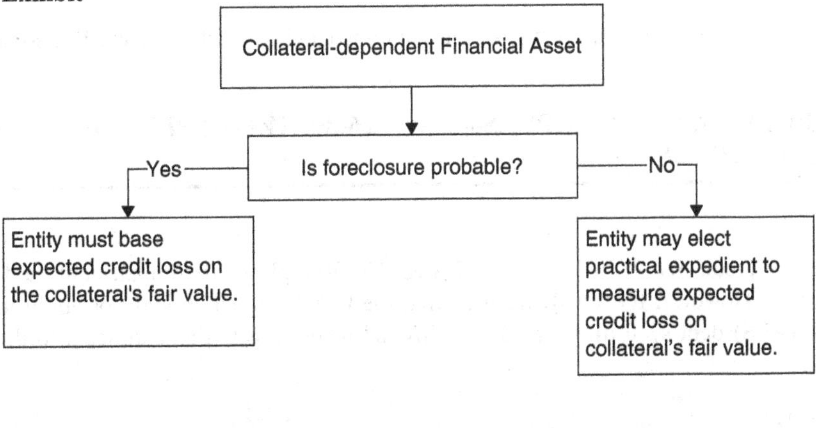

chapter. An allowance that is added *to* the amortized cost basis must not exceed amounts previously written off. (ASC 326-20-35-4)

As a practical expedient, the entity may use the fair value of the collateral at the reporting date. If this expedient is used, the entity should adjust the estimate for estimated costs to sell unless the repayment or satisfaction of the financial asset depends only on the operation of the collateral. If the fair value of the collateral exceeds the amortized cost basis of the financial asset, the entity should adjust the allowance so that the entity presents the net amount to be collected equal to the fair value as long as the allowance added does not exceed a previous write-off. (ASC 326-20-35-5)

Financial Assets Secured by Collateral Maintenance Provisions Some financial assets contractually require borrowers to adjust the amount of the collateral securing the financial asset. If so and if the entity has a reasonable expectation that the borrower will continue to replenish the collateral to meet the contract's requirement, the entity may use, as a practical expedient, a method that compares the amortized cost basis with the fair value of collateral at the reporting date to measure the estimated expected credit losses. In such cases, the entity may determine that the expectation of nonpayment is zero. The entity should estimate the allowance for credit losses as the difference between the fair value of the collateral and the amortized cost basis of the asset, provided that the fair value of the collateral is less than the amortized cost basis. (ASC 326-20-35-6)

Loans Subsequently Identified for Sale If an entity decides to sell loans, the entity should transfer loans to the hold-for-sale classification. Upon transfer, the entity should look to the guidance in ASC 310-10-35-48A for guidance on mortgage loans, ASC 948 for guidance on mortgage loans, and to ASC 326-20-25-8 for guidance on write-offs. (ASC 326-20-35-7)

Write-Offs and Recoveries of Financial Assets Write-offs are deducted from the allowance in the period in which the financial assets are deemed uncollectible. Recoveries should be recorded when received. (ASC 326-20-35-8)

Accounting Policy Election—Accrued Interest Receivable An entity may elect, at the class of financing receivable or the major security type level, to write off accrued interest income. The entity does this by

a. Reversing interest income
b. Recognizing credit lost expired, or
c. Both a and b.
(ASC 326-20-35-8A)

Interest Income on Purchased Financial Assets with Credit Deterioration Refer to the guidance in ASC 310 for guidance on the recognition of interest income on PCDs. (ASC 326-20-35-10)

Presentation and Disclosure

The presentation and disclosure requirements for this subtopic can be found at www.wiley.com/go/GAAP2021.

CONCEPTS, RULES, AND EXAMPLES—ASC 326-30, *AVAILABLE-FOR-SALE DEBT SECURITIES*

Overview

The current expected credit loss (CECL) model in ASC 326-20 replaces the impairment guidance in ASC 310-10. However, the FASB decided that the CECL model should not apply to available-for-sale (AFS) debt securities. The FASB instead made targeted amendments to the

Exhibit—Comparison of Extant Guidance with ASU 2016-13 Guidance

AFS Debt Securities		
Item	**Existing Guidance**	**New ASU 2016-13 Guidance**
Credit losses	Recognize impairment as a write-down, as a reduction of the cost basis of the investment. Record losses only related to credit through earnings.	Recognize an allowance for credit losses. The allowance is limited by the amount that the fair value is less than the amortized cost basis.* Record in period of change as credit loss expense. The amount related to noncredit loss factors is recognized net of taxes in OCI.
Improvements in estimated credit losses	Prospectively recognize as interest income over time.	Recognize in the period of change reversal of credit losses as areduction in the allowance and credit loss expense.
(ASC 326-30-35-2 and 35-3)		

* *The credit loss is limited to fair value because it is assumed that the entity can sell the security at fair value to stop further losses.*

Exhibit—AFS Debt Security—Impairment

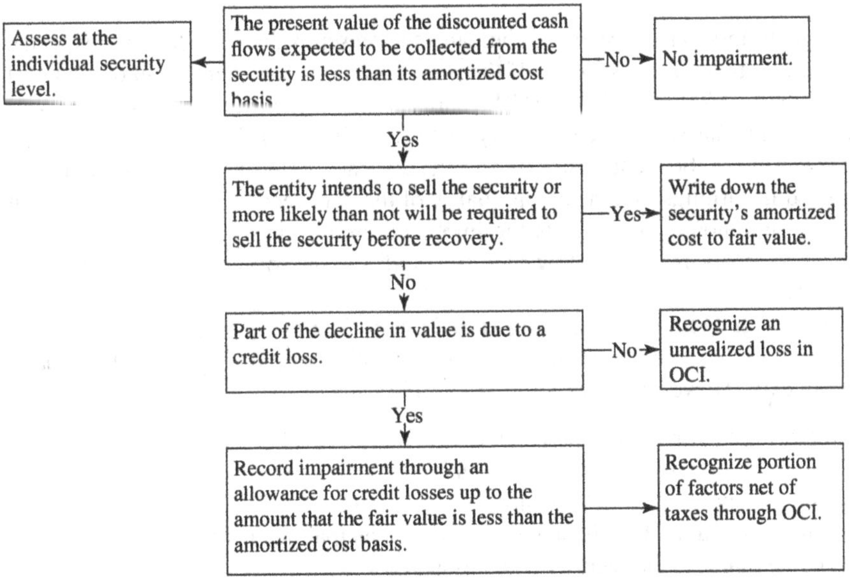

current AFS debt security impairment model and places the new guidance in a new subtopic, ASC 326-30. This will result in entities using different impairment models for AFS debt securities than those that are classified as held to maturity.

In addition to the changes indicated in the exhibit above, the ASU eliminates "other-than-temporary" impairment (OTTI). The new guidance focuses on determining whether unrealized losses are credit losses or whether they are caused by other factors. (ASC 326-30-35-2) Also, when assessing whether a credit loss exists, the entity may not consider recoveries in fair value after the balance sheet date.

Initial Measurement—Determining Whether a Credit Loss Exists

Accrued Interest When identifying and measuring an impairment, an entity may exclude applicable accrued interest fair value and amortized cost basis. In that case, the entity may estimate expected credit losses by:

- Measuring components of the ACB on a combined basis or
- Measuring separately the applicable accrued interest component from other components of ACB.
  (ASC 326-30-30-1A)

Accounting Policy Election—Accrued Interest Receivable At the class of financing receivable or the major security-type level, an entity may elect not to measure an allowance for credit losses for accrued interest receivables. This election is allowed as long as the entity writes off the uncollectible accrued interest receivable balance on a timely basis. (ASC 326-30-30-1B)

Purchased Financial Assets with Credit Deterioration If the indicators of a credit loss described in ASC 326-30-55-1 (see Factors to Consider When Determining Impairment) exist, the purchased AFS debt security is considered a purchased financial asset with credit deterioration. Entities should measure the allowance for credit losses at the individual security level as discussed in ASC 326-30-35-3 through 35-10. (ASC 326-30-30-2)

Subsequent Measurement

To determine if a credit loss exists, the entity compares the present value of cash flows expected with the amortized cost basis of the security. If the present value is less than the amortized cost basis, a credit loss exists. (ASC 326-30-35-1) The entity records the difference in an allowance for credit losses up to the fair value of the security. (ASC 326-30-35-2)

If the fair value of a debt security does not exceed its amortized cost after a credit loss has been recognized in earnings, but the credit quality of the debt security improves, the credit loss is reversed for an amount that reflects the improved credit quality. However, the entity cannot reverse a previously recorded allowance for credit losses to an amount below zero. (ASC 326- 30-35-12)

Factors to Consider When Determining Impairment The entity can no longer use the length of time a security has been in an unrealized loss position as a factor to conclude that a credit loss does not exist. However, it can consider the following:

- The extent to which fair value is less than the amortized cost basis.
- Adverse conditions related to the security, an industry, or geographical area.
- The payment structure of the debt security.
- Failure of the issuer to make scheduled interest or principal payments.
- Changes to the rating of the security by a rating agency.
  (ASC 326-30-55-1)
- Information relevant to the collectibility of the security, such as remaining payment terms, prepayment speeds, financial condition of the issuer, expected defaults, value of collateral
- Industry analyst reports, credit ratings, other relevant market data.
- How other credit enhancements affect the expected performance of the security.
  (ASC 326-30-55-2 through 55-4)

Accounting Policy Elections For each major security type of AFS debt securities, the entity may adjust the EIR used to discount expected cash flows to consider the timing resulting from expected prepayments. (ASC 326-30-35-7A)

An entity may elect a policy to write off accrued interest receivable by

a. Accruing interest income,
b. Recognizing credit loss expense, or
c. Both a. and b.

This option applies to identifying and measuring an impairment when the accrued interest is excluded from the fair value and the amortized cost basis for the AFS debt security. (ASC 326- 30-35-13A)

Presentation and Disclosure

The ASU retains the existing AFS debt security disclosure requirements, but amends them to reflect the use of an allowance for credit losses and the elimination of the OTTI concept. The new guidance requires some new disclosures. Entities will have to disclose a tabular rollforward of the allowance account and to disclose their accounting policy for recognizing write-offs. See www.wiley.com/go/GAAP2021, for detailed information on presentation and disclosure.

22 ASC 330 INVENTORY

PERSPECTIVE AND ISSUES

Subtopic

ASC 330, *Inventory*, consists of one subtopic:

- ASC 330-10, *Overall*, that provides guidance on the accounting and reporting practices on inventory.

ASC 330, *Inventory*, discusses the definition, valuation, and classification of inventory.

Scope

ASC 330 applies to all entities but is not necessarily applicable to:

- Not-for-profit entities
- Regulated utilities
  (ASC 330-10-15-2 and 15-3)

Overview

Issues The accounting for inventories is a major consideration for many entities because of its significance to both the income statement (cost of goods sold) and the statement of financial position (current assets).

The complexity of accounting for inventories arises from factors that include:

- The high volume of activity (or turnover) and the associated challenges of keeping accurate, up-to-date records.
- Choosing from among various cost flow alternatives that are permitted by GAAP.
- Ensuring compliance with complex U.S. income tax laws and regulations when electing to use the last-in, first-out (LIFO) method.
- Monitoring and properly accounting for adjustments necessitated by the decline in inventory value.

Classification There are two types of entities for which the accounting for inventories is relevant:

1. Merchandising
2. Manufacturing

The merchandising entity normally purchases ready-to-use inventory for resale to its customers, and only one inventory account is needed.

Manufacturers, on the other hand, may have raw goods, work-in-process, and finished goods inventory classifications. The manufacturer buys raw materials and processes those raw materials, using labor and equipment, into finished goods that are then sold to its customers. While the production process is progressing, the accounting system accumulates as work in process the costs of the raw materials, salaries, and wages paid to the labor force (and related benefits), depreciation of the machinery, and an allocated portion of the manufacturer's overhead as work-in-process (WIP). Finished goods inventory is the completed product that is on hand awaiting shipment or sale.

In the case of either type of entity, entities are concerned with answering the same basic questions:

- At what point in time should the items be included in inventory (ownership)?
- What costs incurred should be included in the valuation of inventories?
- What cost flow assumption should be used?
- At what value should inventories be reported?

DEFINITIONS OF TERMS

Source: ASC 330-10-20. Also see Appendix A, *Definitions of Terms*, for other definitions relevant to this chapter: Customer, Reseller, and Vendor.

Direct Effects of a Change in Accounting Principle. Those recognized changes in assets or liabilities necessary to effect a change in accounting principle. An example of a direct effect is an adjustment to an inventory balance to effect a change in inventory valuation method. Related changes, such as an effect on deferred income tax assets or liabilities or an impairment adjustment resulting from applying the subsequent measurement guidance in Subtopic 330-10 to the adjusted inventory balance, also are examples of direct effects of a change in accounting principle.

Inventory. The aggregate of those items of tangible personal property that have any of the following characteristics:

- Held for sale in the ordinary course of business
- In the process of production for such sale
- To be currently consumed in the production of goods or services to be available for sale

The term inventory embraces goods awaiting sale (the merchandise of a trading concern and the finished goods of a manufacturer), goods in the course of production (work-in-process), and goods to be consumed directly or indirectly in production (raw materials and supplies). This definition of inventories excludes long-term assets subject to depreciation accounting, or goods that, when put into use, will be so classified. The fact that a depreciable asset is retired from regular use and held for sale does not indicate that the item should be classified as part of the inventory. Raw materials and supplies purchased for production may be used or consumed for the construction of long-term assets or other purposes not related to production, but the fact that inventory items representing a small portion of the total may not be absorbed ultimately in the production process does not require separate classification. By trade practice, operating materials and supplies of certain types of entities such as oil producers are usually treated as inventory.

Market. As used in the phrase lower of cost or market, the term market means current replacement cost (by purchase or by reproduction, as the case may be) provided that it meets both of the following conditions:

- Market shall not exceed the net realizable value.
- Market shall not be less than net realizable value reduced by an allowance for an approximately normal profit margin.

Net Realizable Value. Estimated selling price in the ordinary course of business less reasonably predictable costs of completion, disposal, and transportation.

CONCEPTS, RULES, AND EXAMPLES

Accounting for Inventories

A major objective of accounting for inventories is the matching of appropriate costs to the period in which the related revenues are earned in order to properly compute gross profit, also referred to as gross margin. Inventories are recorded in the accounting records using either a periodic or perpetual system.

Periodic Inventory System In a periodic inventory system, upon acquisition, a purchase account is debited and inventory quantities are determined periodically thereafter by physical count. Cost of goods sold is a residual amount, computed by adding beginning inventory and net purchases (or cost of goods manufactured) and subtracting ending inventory.

Using a periodic inventory system necessitates the taking of physical inventory counts to determine the quantity of inventory on hand at the end of a reporting period. To facilitate accurate annual financial statements, in practice physical counts are performed at least annually.

Perpetual Inventory System A perpetual inventory system keeps a running total of the quantity (and possibly the cost) of inventory on hand by maintaining subsidiary inventory records that reflect all sales and purchases as they occur. When inventory is purchased, inventory (rather than purchases) is debited. When inventory is sold, the cost of goods sold and corresponding reduction of inventory are recorded.

If the entity maintains a perpetual inventory system, it must regularly and systematically verify the accuracy of its perpetual records by physically counting inventories and comparing the quantities on hand with the perpetual records. GAAP does not provide explicit requirements regarding the timing and frequency of physical counts necessary to verify the perpetual records; however, there is an income tax requirement (IRC §471[b][1]) that a taxpayer perform ". . . a physical count of inventories at each location on a regular and consistent basis." The purpose of this requirement is to enable the taxpayer to support any tax deductions taken for inventory shrinkage if it elects not to take a complete physical inventory at all locations on the last day of the fiscal year. The IRS, in its Rev. Proc. 98-29, provided a "retail safe harbor method" that permits retailers to deduct estimated shrinkage where the retailer takes physical inventories at each location at least annually.

Control of Goods

Generally, in order to obtain an accurate measurement of inventory quantity, it is necessary to determine when control passes from seller to buyer. Generally, entities consider inventory is the buyer's when it is released. The exception to this general rule arises from situations when the buyer assumes the significant risks of ownership of the goods prior to taking title and/or physical possession of the goods. Substance over form in this case would dictate that the inventory is an asset of the buyer and not the seller, and that a purchase and sale of the goods should be recognized by the parties irrespective of the party that holds legal title.

The most common error made in this area is to assume that an entity has title only to the goods it physically holds. This may be incorrect because:

- Goods held may not be owned, and
- Goods that are not held may be owned.

Goods in Transit At year-end, any goods in transit from seller to buyer must be included in one of those parties' inventories based on the conditions of the sale. Such goods are included in the inventory of the firm financially responsible for transportation costs.

Issue	Explanation	Accounting Treatment
FOB Shipping Point	"Free on board"—transportation costs are paid by the buyer.	Buyer's when carrier takes possession
FOB Destination Point	"Free on board"—transportation costs are paid by the seller.	Buyer's when carrier delivers the goods to the buyer
FAS	Free alongside— Seller bears expense and risk involved in delivering the goods to the dock next to (alongside) the vessel on which they are to be shipped. Buyer bears the costs of loading and shipment.	Buyer's when carrier, as agent for the buyer, takes possession
CIF	Cost, insurance, and freight— Buyer pays in a lump sum the cost of the goods, insurance costs, and freight charges and delivers goods to buyer's agent and pays loading costs.	Buyer's (both title and risk of loss) when carrier takes possession
C&F	Cost and freight— Buyer pays a lump sum that includes the cost of the goods and all freight charges and delivers goods to buyer's agent and pays loading costs.	Both title and risk of loss pass to the buyer upon delivery of the goods to the carrier
Ex-Ship Delivery	Used in maritime contracts.	At time goods are unloaded, title and risk pass to buyer

Examples of Goods in Transit

The Meridian Vacuum Company is located in Santa Fe, New Mexico, and obtains compressors from a supplier in Hong Kong. The standard delivery terms are free alongside (FAS) a container ship in Hong Kong harbor, so that Meridian takes legal title to the delivery once possession of the goods is taken by the carrier's dockside employees for the purpose of loading the goods on board the ship. When the supplier delivers goods with an invoiced value of $120,000 to the wharf, it e-mails an advance shipping notice (ASN) and invoice to Meridian via an electronic data interchange (EDI) transaction, itemizing the contents of the delivery. Meridian's computer system receives the EDI transmission, notes the FAS terms in the supplier file, and therefore automatically logs it into the company computer system with the following entry:

Inventory	120,000	
Accounts payable		120,000

The goods are assigned an "In Transit" location code in Meridian's perpetual inventory system. When the compressor eventually arrives at Meridian's receiving dock, the receiving staff records a change in inventory location code from "In Transit" to a code designating a physical location within the warehouse.

Meridian's secondary compressor supplier is located in Vancouver, British Columbia, and ships overland using free on board (FOB) Santa Fe terms, so the supplier retains title until the shipment arrives at Meridian's location. This supplier also issues an advance shipping notice by EDI to inform Meridian of the estimated arrival date, but in this case Meridian's computer system notes the FOB Santa Fe terms, and makes no entry to record the transaction until the goods arrive at Meridian's receiving dock.

Other Control Issues

Issue	Explanation	Accounting Treatment
Consignment Goods	Consignor ships goods to the consignee, who acts as the agent of the consignor in trying to sell the goods.	Consignor's
Sales with Buybacks	Entity simultaneously sells and agrees to repurchase inventory to and from a financing entity. The substance is that of a borrowing transaction, not a sale. ASC 470-40 addresses the issues involved with product financing arrangements.	Seller's
Sales with High Rates of Return	The sale is recorded only when six specified conditions are met including the condition that the future amount of returns can be reasonably estimated by the seller. For more information, see the chapter on ASC 605 or, when ASU 2014-09 is implemented, the chapter on ASC 606. The ASC 606 guidance on this subject is codified in ASC 606-10-55-22 through 29.	Buyer's if returns can be estimated
Installment Sales	Buyer receives goods and makes payments over a period of time.	Buyer's if collectibility can be estimated

Example of a Consignment Arrangement

The Portable Handset Company (PHC) ships a consignment of its cordless phones to a retail outlet of the Consignee Corporation. PHC's cost of the consigned goods is $3,700. PHC shifts the inventory cost into a separate inventory account to track the physical location of the goods. The entry follows:

Consignment out inventory	3,700	
Finished goods inventory		3,700

To record shipment of inventory to retail outlet on consignment

A third-party shipping company ships the cordless phone inventory from PHC to Consignee. Upon receipt of an invoice for this $550 shipping expense, PHC charges the cost to consignment inventory with the following entry:

Consignment out inventory	550	
Accounts payable		550

To record the cost of shipping goods from the factory to consignee

Consignee sells half the consigned inventory during the month for $2,750 in credit card payments, and earns a 22% commission on these sales, totaling $605. According to the consignment arrangement, PHC must also reimburse Consignee for the 2% credit card processing fee, which is $55 ($2,750 × 2%). The results of this sale are summarized as follows:

Sales price to Consignee's customer earned on behalf of PHC	$2,750
Less: Amounts due to Consignee in accordance with arrangement	
22% sales commission	(605)
Reimbursement for credit card processing fee	(55)
	(660)
Due to PHC	$2,090

Upon receipt of the monthly sales report from Consignee, PHC records the following entries:

Accounts receivable	2,090	
Cost of goods sold	55	
Commission expense	605	
Sales		2,750

To record the sale made by Consignee acting as agent of PHC, the commission earned by Consignee and the credit card fee reimbursement earned by Consignee in connection with the sale

Costs of goods sold	2,125	
Consignment out inventory		2,125

To transfer the related inventory cost to cost of goods sold, including half the original inventory cost and half the cost of the shipment to consignee [($3,700 + $550 = $4,250) × ½ = $2,125]

Costs Included in Inventory

The primary basis of accounting for inventories is cost. Cost is defined as the sum of the applicable expenditures and charges directly or indirectly incurred in bringing an article to its existing condition and location. (ASC 330-10-30-1) This definition allows for a wide interpretation of the costs to be included in inventory.

Merchandise Inventory The identification of cost for merchandise inventory that is purchased outright is relatively straightforward. The cost of these purchased inventories includes all expenditures incurred in bringing the goods to the point of sale and converting them to a salable condition. These costs include the purchase price, transportation costs (freight-in), insurance while in transit, and handling costs charged by the supplier.

Manufacturing Inventories Inventory cost in a manufacturing enterprise includes both acquisition and production costs. This concept is commonly referred to as *full absorption* or *full costing*. The raw material's costs include all expenditures incurred in acquiring the goods and bringing them to the manufacturing facility, such as, purchase price, transportation costs, insurance while in transit, and handling costs. The WIP and finished goods inventories include direct materials, direct labor, and an appropriately allocated portion of indirect production costs referred to as indirect overhead.

Under full absorption costing, indirect overhead costs—costs that are incidental to and necessary for production—are allocated to goods produced and, to the extent those goods are uncompleted or unsold at the end of a period, are included in ending WIP or finished goods inventory, respectively. Indirect overhead costs include such costs as:

- Depreciation and cost depletion
- Repairs
- Maintenance
- Factory rent and utilities
- Indirect labor
- Normal rework labor, scrap, and spoilage
- Production supervisory wages
- Indirect materials and supplies
- Quality control and inspection
- Small tools not capitalized.

Example of Recording Raw Material Costs

Aruba Bungee Cords, Inc. (ABC) purchases rubber bands, a raw material that it uses in manufacturing its signature product. The company typically receives delivery of all its raw materials and uses them in manufacturing its finished products during the winter, and then sells its stock of finished goods in the spring. The supplier invoice for a January delivery of rubber bands includes the following line items:

Rubber band (1,681 pounds at $3 per pound)	$5,043
Shipping and handling	125
Shipping insurance	48
Subtotal	5,216
Sales tax	193
Total	$5,409

Since ABC is using the rubber bands as raw materials in a product that it resells, it will not pay the sales tax. However, both the shipping and handling charge and the shipping insurance are required for ongoing product acquisition, and so are included in the following entry to record receipt of the goods:

Inventory raw materials	5,216	
Accounts payable		5,216

To record purchase of rubber bands and related costs

On February 1, ABC purchases a $5,000, two-month shipping insurance policy (a type of policy sometimes referred to as "inland marine" coverage) that applies to all incoming supplier deliveries for the remainder of the winter production season. This allows ABC to refuse shipping insurance charges on individual deliveries. Since the policy insures all inbound raw materials deliveries (not just rubber bands), it is too time-consuming to charge the cost of this policy to individual raw material deliveries using specific identification, and accordingly, the controller can estimate a flat charge per delivery based on the number of expected deliveries during the two-month term of the insurance policy as follows:

$5,000 insurance premium ÷ 200 expected deliveries during the policy term = $25 per delivery and then charge each delivery with $25 as follows:

Inventory—raw materials	25	
Prepaid insurance		25

To allocate cost of inland marine coverage to inbound insured raw materials shipments

In this case, however, the controller determined that shipments are expected to occur evenly during the two-month policy period and therefore will simply make a monthly standard journal entry as follows:

Inventory—raw materials	2,500	
Prepaid insurance		2,500

To amortize premium on inland marine policy using the straight-line method

Note that the controller must be careful, under either scenario, to ensure that perpetual inventory records appropriately track unit costs of raw materials to include the cost of shipping insurance. Failure to do so would result in an understatement of the cost of raw materials inventory on hand at the end of any accounting period.

Discounts Purchases can be recorded at their gross amount or net of any allowable discount. If recorded gross, the discounts taken represent a reduction in the purchase cost for purposes of determining cost of goods sold. On the other hand, if they are recorded net, any lost discounts are treated as a financial expense, not as cost of goods sold, and reported as other expenses and losses. The net method is considered to be theoretically preferable because it provides an accurate reporting of inventory costs and the related liability. However, gross method is simpler and, thus, more commonly used. Either method is acceptable under GAAP, provided that it is consistently applied.

Indirect overhead Indirect overhead is comprised of two elements, variable and fixed overhead. Variable overhead is allocated to work-in-process and finished goods based on the actual usage of the production facilities. Fixed overhead, however, is allocated to work-in-process and finished goods based on the normal expected capacity of the enterprise's production facilities. (ASC 330-10-30-3)

Normal production capacity For the purpose of determining normal productive capacity, it is expected that capacity will vary from period to period based on enterprise-specific or industry-specific experience. (ASC 330-10- 30-4) Management must formulate a judgment regarding a reasonable range of normal production levels expected to be achieved under normal operating conditions. The overhead rate is recalculated and decreased in instances when actual production exceeds the normal capacity. (ASC 330-10-30-6) Initially, this may appear to be an inconsistent accounting method; however, the use of this convention ensures that the inventory is not recorded at an amount in excess of its actual cost.

Abnormal expenditures The enterprise may incur unusually large expenses resulting from idle facilities, excessive waste, spoilage, freight, or handling costs. When this situation occurs, the abnormal portion of these expenses should be treated as a period cost and should not be allocated to inventory. (ASC 330-10-30-7)

General, administrative, and selling Most general and administrative and selling expenses are also expensed as incurred, although ASC 606 has modified the guidance on selling expenses. (ASC 330-10-30-8) See the chapter on ASC 606 for additional details.

Interest Generally, interest costs incurred during the production of inventory that an entity routinely manufactures in large quantity on a repetitive basis are not capitalized under ASC 835-20. A complete discussion regarding the capitalization of interest costs is provided in the chapter on ASC 835.

Example of Allocating Fixed Overhead to Units Produced

Brewed Refreshment Plant, Inc. (BRP), located in Washington, D.C., has historically produced between 3,200 and 3,800 barrels of beer annually with its average production approximating 3,500 barrels. This average takes into account its normal number of work shifts and the normal operation of its machinery adjusted for downtime for normal maintenance and recalibration. BRP's average capacity and overhead costs (partial list) are presented below.

(a) Normal expected annual productive capacity		3,500 barrels
Fixed overhead costs (partial list):		
Depreciation of machinery	$600	
Factory rent	800	
Plant superintendent	80	
(b) Total fixed overhead to allocate		$ 1,480
(c) Fixed overhead rate per barrel produced (b ÷ a)		$ 0.4229 per barrel

Scenario 1: The Washington Nationals major-league baseball team outperforms expectations; since BRP's beer is sold at the Nationals' stadium, BRP substantially increases production beyond the normal level expected.

Actual production level	4,500 barrels

If BRP were to apply fixed overhead using the rate based on its normal productive capacity, the calculation would be as follows:

4,500 barrels produced × $0.4229 per barrel = $1,903 of overhead applied

This would result in an over-allocation of $423, the difference between the $1,903 of overhead applied and the $1,480 of overhead actually incurred. This violates the lower of cost or market principle, since the inventory would be valued at an amount that exceeded its actual cost. Therefore, BRP applied ASC 330 and recomputed its fixed overhead rate as follows:

1,480 fixed overhead incurred ÷ Revised production level of 4,500 barrels = $0.3289 per barrel

Scenario 2: The Washington Nationals experience a cold, rainy summer and worse-than-expected attendance. If production lags expectations and BRP only produces 2,500 barrels of beer, the original overhead rate is not revised. The fixed overhead is allocated as follows:

2,500 barrels produced × $0.4229 per barrel = $1,057 of overhead applied

When production levels decline below the original expectation, the fixed overhead rate is not recomputed. The $423 difference between the $1,480 of actual fixed overhead incurred and the $1,057 of overhead applied is accounted for as an expense in the period incurred.

Example of Variable and Fixed Overhead Allocation

The InCase Manufacturing Company (IMC) uses injection molding to create two types of plastic CD cases—regular size and mini—on a seven-day, three-shift production schedule. During the current month, it records the following overhead expenses:

Depreciation of machinery	$232,000	Rent	$36,000
Indirect labor	208,000	Repairs	12,000
Indirect materials	58,000	Small tools	28,000
Maintenance	117,000	Scrap and spoilage	49,000
Production supervisory wages	229,000	Utilities	37,000
Quality control	82,000		

IMC's controller analyzed scrap and spoilage statistics and determined that abnormal losses of $32,000 were incurred due to a bad batch of plastic resin pellets. She adjusted scrap and spoilage expense by charging the cost of those pellets to cost of goods sold during the current period, resulting in a reduced scrap and spoilage expense of $17,000. Also, the rent cost includes a $6,000 lease termination penalty payable to the lessor of a vacant factory. Since this cost is considered an exit or disposal activity under ASC 420, it does not benefit production and is, therefore, charged directly to expense in the current period.

For allocation purposes, IMC's controller elects to group the adjusted overhead expenses into two cost pools.

1. Pool #1—machinery cost pool contains all expenses related to machinery operation, which includes depreciation, indirect labor, indirect materials, maintenance, rent, repairs, small tools, and utilities.
2. Pool #2—production cost pool contains all expenses related to production runs, which includes production supervisory wages, quality control, scrap, and spoilage.

The controller makes three journal entries. The first records period expenses, while the second and third relate to Pool #1 and Pool #2 respectively.

Cost of goods sold expense	38,000	
Scrap and spoilage expense		32,000
Rent expense		6,000

To record excess scrap and unused facilities in the current period

Overhead pool #1—Machinery operation		
Depreciation		232,000
Indirect labor		208,000
Indirect material		58,000
Maintenance		117,000
Rent		30,000
Repairs		12,000
Small tools		28,000
Utilities		37,000
Total		722,000

To record the allocation of costs to the machinery cost pool

Overhead pool #2—Production runs		
Production supervisory wages		229,000
Quality control		82,000
Scrap and spoilage		17,000
Total		328,000

To record the allocation of costs to the production runs cost pool

Allocation of pool #1—costs to production Because the costs in overhead pool #1 are centered on machine usage, the controller elects to use the total operating hours used for the production of each product as the allocation basis for that pool. The accumulated production hours by machine for the past month are as follows:

Machinery type	*Regular CD production hours*	*Mini CD production hours*
50-ton press	0	710
55-ton press	310	290
70-ton press	480	230
85-ton press	690	0
Total hours	1,480	1,230
Percentage of total hours	55%	45%

Allocation of pool #2—costs to production Since the costs in overhead pool #2 are centered on production volume, the controller decides to use the total pounds of plastic resin pellets used for production during the month as the allocation basis for that cost pool. The total plastic resin usage, adjusted for spoilage, was 114,000 pounds of resin for the regular CD cases and 76,000 pounds for the mini CD cases, which is a percentage split of 60% for regular CD cases and 40% for mini CD cases.

With the calculation of allocation bases completed, the split of overhead costs between the two products is:

Overhead pool #1	*Total costs in pool*	*55% regular CD allocation*	*45% mini CD allocation*
	722,000	397,100	324,900
Overhead pool #2	*Total costs in pool*	*60% regular CD allocation*	*40% mini CD allocation*
	328,000	196,800	131,200
Totals		593,900	456,100

Allocating Overhead to Products in Costs of Goods Sold and Finished Goods Inventory Of the case quantities produced, 85% of the regular CD cases and 70% of the mini CD cases were sold during the month, with the remainder being transferred into finished goods inventory. IMC's controller uses these percentages to apportion the cost of allocated overhead between the cost of goods sold and finished goods inventory, as shown in the following entry:

Cost of goods sold—regular CD cases ($593,000 × 85%)	504,815	
Cost of goods sold—mini CD cases ($456,000 × 70%)	319,270	
Finished goods inventory—regular CD cases ($593,000 – 504,815)	89,085	
Finished goods inventory—mini CD cases ($456,100 – 319,270)	136,830	
Overhead pool #1—Machinery operation		722,000
Overhead pool #2—Production runs		328,000

Cost Flow Assumptions

The most common cost flow assumptions used are specified in ASC 330-10-30-9:

- Average
- First-in, first-out (FIFO),
- Last-in, first-out (LIFO), and
- Retail inventory method.

Additionally, there are variations in the application of each of these assumptions, which are commonly used in practice. ASC 330-10-30-9 points out that:

"The major objective in selecting a method should be to choose the one which, under the circumstances, most clearly reflects periodic income."

In selecting which cost flow assumption to adopt as its accounting policy for a particular type of industry, management should consider a variety of factors:

- The industry norm, as this will facilitate intercompany comparison by financial statement users,
- The nature of the industry, and
- The expected economic climate.

The appropriate method in a period of rising prices differs from the method that is appropriate for a period of declining prices. Each of the foregoing assumptions and their relative advantages or disadvantages are discussed next. Examples are provided to enhance understanding of the application.

Specific Identification The theoretical basis for valuing inventories and cost of goods sold requires assigning production and/or acquisition costs to the specific goods to which they relate. This method of inventory valuation is usually referred to as specific identification. It matches costs against actual revenue, and the cost flow matches the physical flow of products. However, specific identification is generally not practical because in most environments the product will generally lose its separate identity as it passes through the production and sales process. Exceptions to this would arise in situations involving small inventory quantities with high unit value and low turnover rate, such as automobiles or heavy machinery. Where it is not practical to use specific identification, it is necessary to make certain assumptions regarding the cost flows associated with inventory. Although these cost flow assumptions are used for accounting purposes, they may or may not reflect the actual physical flow of the inventory.

Average Cost Another method of inventory valuation involves averaging and is commonly referred to as the weighted-average method.

Under this method the cost of goods available for sale (beginning inventory plus net purchases) is divided by the number of units available for sale to obtain a weighted-average cost per unit. Ending inventory and cost of goods sold are then priced at this average cost.

Example of the Weighted-Average Method

Assume the following data:

	Units available	*Units sold*	*Actual unit cost*	*Actual total cost*
Beginning inventory	100	–	$2.10	$210
Sale	–	75	–	–
Purchase	150	–	2.80	420
Sale	–	100	–	–
Purchase	50	–	3.00	150
Total	300	175		$780

The weighted-average cost per unit is $780/300, or $2.60. Ending inventory is 125 units (300 – 175) at $2.60, or $325; cost of goods sold is 175 units at $2.60, or $455.

When the weighted-average assumption is applied using a perpetual inventory system, the average cost is recomputed after each purchase. This process is referred to as a moving average. Cost of goods sold is recorded using the most recent average. This combination is called the moving-average method and is applied below to the same data used in the weighted-average example above.

	Units on hand	*Purchases in dollars*	*Cost of sales in dollars*	*Inventory total cost*	*Inventory moving average unit cost*
Beginning inventory	100	$ –	$ –	$210.00	$2.10
Sale (75 units @ $2.10)	25	–	157.50	52.50	2.10
Purchase (150 units, $420)	175	420.00	–	472.50	2.70
Sale (100 units @ $2.70)	75	–	270.00	202.50	2.70
Purchase (50 units, $150)	125	150.00	–	352.50	2.82

Cost of goods sold is 75 units at $2.10 and 100 units at $2.70, or $427.50.

First-in, First-out (FIFO) The FIFO method of inventory valuation assumes that the first goods purchased are the first goods used (manufacturing) or sold (merchandising), regardless of the actual physical flow. This method is thought to most closely parallel the physical flow of the units in most industries. The strength of this cost flow assumption lies in the inventory amount reported on the statement of financial position. Because the earliest goods purchased are the first ones removed from the inventory account, the remaining balance is composed of items priced at more recent cost. This yields results similar to those obtained under current cost accounting on the statement of financial position. However, the FIFO method does not necessarily reflect the most accurate income figure as older, historical costs are being charged to cost of goods sold and matched against current revenues.

Example of the Basic Principles Involved in the Application of FIFO

	Units available	*Units sold*	*Actual unit cost*	*Actual total cost*
Beginning inventory	100	–	$2.10	$210
Sale	–	75	–	–
Purchase	150	–	2.80	420
Sale	–	100	–	–
Purchase	50	–	3.00	150
Total	300	175		$780

Given this data, the cost of goods sold and ending inventory balance are determined as follows:

	Units	*Unit cost*	*Total cost*
Cost of goods sold	100	$2.10	$210
	75	2.80	210
	175		420
Ending inventory	50	3.00	150
	75	2.80	210
	125		360
Totals	300		$780

Notice that the total of the units in cost of goods sold and ending inventory, as well as the sum of their total costs, is equal to the goods available for sale and their respective total costs.

The FIFO method provides the same results under either the periodic or perpetual inventory tracking system.

Last-in, First-out (LIFO) The LIFO method of inventory valuation assumes that the last goods purchased are the first goods used or sold. This allows the matching of current costs with current revenues and provides the best measure of gross profit. However, unless costs remain relatively unchanged over time, the LIFO method will usually misstate the ending inventory amount on the statement of financial position amount, because LIFO inventory usually includes costs of acquiring or manufacturing inventory that were incurred in earlier periods. LIFO does not usually follow the physical flow of merchandise or materials. However, the matching of physical flow with cost flow is not an objective of accounting for inventories.

LIFO accounting is actually an income tax concept. The rules regarding the application of the LIFO method are found in the U.S. Internal Revenue Code (IRC) §472. U.S. Treasury regulations provide that any taxpayer that maintains inventories may select LIFO application for any or all inventoriable items. This election is made with the taxpayer's income tax return on Form 970 after the close of the first tax year that the taxpayer intends to use (or expand the use of) the LIFO method.

The quantity of ending inventory on hand at the beginning of the year of election is termed the "base layer." This inventory is valued at actual (full absorption) cost, and unit cost for each inventory item is determined by dividing total cost by the quantity on hand. At the end of the initial and subsequent years, increases in the quantity of inventory on hand are referred to as increments, or LIFO layers. These increments are valued individually by applying one of the following costing methods to the quantity of inventory representing a layer:

- The actual cost of the goods most recently purchased or produced.
- The actual cost of the goods purchased or produced in order of acquisition.
- An average unit cost of all goods purchased or produced during the current year.
- A hybrid method that more clearly reflects income (for income tax purposes, this method must meet with the approval of the IRS Commissioner).

Thus, after using the LIFO method for five years, it is possible that an enterprise could have ending inventory consisting of the base layer and five additional layers (or increments) provided that the quantity of ending inventory increased every year.

Example of the Single Goods (Unit) LIFO Approach

Rose Co. is in its first year of operation and elects to use the periodic LIFO method of inventory valuation. The company sells only one product. Rose applies the LIFO method using the order of current year acquisition cost. The following data are given for years 1 through 3:

		Units			*Purchase cost*	
Year 1	*Beginning inventory*	*Purchased*	*Sold*	*Ending inventory*	*Unit cost*	*Total cost*
Purchase		200			$2.00	$400
Sale			100		–	–
Purchase		200			3.00	600
Sale	—	—	150	150		
	—	400	250	150		

	Units					Purchase cost	
Year 2	*Beginning inventory*	*Purchased*	*Sold*	*Ending inventory*		*Unit cost*	*Total cost*
Purchase		300				$3.20	$960
Sale			200			–	–
Purchase		100				3.30	3300
	150	400	200	350			
Year 3							
Purchase		100				$3.50	$360
Sale			200				
Sale			100			–	–
	350	100	300	150			

In year 1 the following occurred:

- The total goods available for sale were 400 units.
- The total sales were 250 units.
- Therefore, the ending inventory was 150 units.

The ending inventory is valued at the earliest current year acquisition cost of $2.00 per unit. Thus, ending inventory is valued at $300 (150 × $2.00).

Another way to look at this is to analyze both cost of goods sold and ending inventory.

Year 1	*Units*	*Unit cost*	*Unit cost*
Cost of goods sold	200	$3.00	$600
	50	2.00	100
	250		$700
Ending inventory	150	2.00	$300

Note that the base-year cost is $2.00 and that the base-year level is 150 units. Therefore, if ending inventory in the subsequent period exceeds 150 units, a new layer (or increment) will be created.

Year 2	*Units*	*Unit cost*	*Total cost*	
Cost of goods sold	100	$3.30	$330	
	100	3.20	320	
	200		$650	
Ending inventory	150	2.00	$300	Base-year layer
	200	3.20	640	Year 2 increment
	350		$940	

If ending inventory exceeds 350 units in the next period, a third layer (increment) will be created.

Year 3	*Units*	*Unit cost*	*Total cost*	
Cost of goods sold	100	$3.50	$350	
	200	3.20	640	
	300		$990	
Ending inventory	150	2.00	$300	Base-year layer

Notice how the decrease (decrement) of 200 units in year 3 eliminated the entire year 2 increment. Thus, any year 4 increase in the quantity of inventory would result in a *new* increment, which would be valued at year 4 prices.

LIFO liquidations In situations where the ending inventory decreases from the level established at the close of the preceding year, the enterprise experiences a decrement or LIFO liquidation. Decrements reduce or eliminate previously established LIFO layers. Once any part of a LIFO layer has been eliminated, it cannot be reinstated after year-end. For example, if in its first year after the election of LIFO an enterprise establishes a LIFO layer (increment) of ten units, then in the next year inventory decreases by four units, leaving the first layer at six units, the enterprise is not permitted in any succeeding year to increase the number of units in the first year layer back up to the original ten units. The quantity in the first layer remains at a maximum of six units subject to further reduction if decrements occur in future years. Any unit increases in future years will create one or more new layers. The effect of LIFO liquidations in periods of rising prices is to transfer, from ending inventory into cost of goods sold, costs that are below the current cost being paid. Thus, the resultant effect of a LIFO liquidation is to increase income for both accounting and income tax purposes. Because of this, LIFO is most commonly used by companies in industries in which levels of inventories are consistently maintained or increased over time.

LIFO liquidations can be either voluntary or involuntary. A voluntary liquidation occurs when an enterprise deliberately lets its inventory levels drop. Voluntary liquidations may be desirable for a number of reasons. Management might consider the current price of purchasing the goods to be too high, a smaller quantity of inventory might be needed for efficient production due to conversion to a "just-in-time" production model, or inventory items may have become obsolete due to new technology or transitions in the enterprise's product lines.

Involuntary LIFO liquidations stem from reasons beyond the control of management, such as a strike, material shortages, shipping delays, etc. Whether voluntary or involuntary, all LIFO liquidations result in a corresponding increase in income in periods of rising prices.

To determine the effect of the liquidation, management must compute the difference between actual cost of sales and what cost of sales would have been had the inventory been reinstated. The Internal Revenue Service has ruled that this hypothetical reinstatement must be computed under the company's normal pricing procedures for valuing its LIFO increments. In the preceding example the effect of the year 3 LIFO liquidation would be computed as follows:

$$\text{Hypothetical inventory reinstatement}: 200\text{ units} @ \$3.50 - \$3.20 = \$60$$

Hypothetically, if there had been an increment instead of a decrement in year 3 and the year 2 inventory layer had remained intact, 200 more units (out of the 300 total units sold in year 3) would have been charged to cost of goods sold at the year 3 price of $3.50 instead of the year 2 price of $3.20. Therefore, the difference between $3.50 and the actual amount charged to cost of sales for these 200 units liquidated ($3.20) measures the effect of the liquidation.

The following is considered acceptable GAAP disclosure in the event of a LIFO liquidation:

> *During 20X3, inventory quantities were reduced below their levels at December 31, 20X2. As a result of this reduction, LIFO inventory costs computed based on lower prior years' acquisition costs were charged to cost of goods sold. If this LIFO liquidation had not occurred and cost of sales had been computed based on the cost of 2013 purchases, cost of goods sold would have increased by approximately $xxx and net income decreased by approximately $xx or $x per share.*

LIFO pools Applying the unit LIFO method requires a substantial amount of recordkeeping. The recordkeeping becomes more burdensome as the number of products increases. For this reason a "pooling" approach is often used to compute LIFO inventories.

Pooling is the process of grouping items that are naturally related and then treating this group as a single unit in determining LIFO cost. Because the ending inventory normally includes many items, decreases in one item can be offset by increases in others, whereas under the unit LIFO approach a decrease in any one item results in a liquidation of all or a portion of a LIFO layer.

Complexity in applying the pooling method arises from the income tax regulations. These regulations require that the opening and closing inventories of each type of good be compared. In order to be considered comparable for this purpose, inventory items must be similar as to character, quality, and price. This qualification has generally been interpreted to mean identical. The effect of this interpretation is to require a separate pool for each item under the unit LIFO method. To provide a simpler, more practical approach to applying LIFO and allow for increased use of LIFO pools, election of the dollar-value LIFO method is permitted.

Identifying pools Three alternatives exist for determining pools under dollar-value LIFO: the natural business unit method, (2) the multiple pooling method, and (3) pools for wholesalers, retailers, jobbers, and the like.

The natural business unit is defined by the existence of separate and distinct processing facilities and operations and the maintenance of separate income (loss) records. The concept of the natural business unit is generally dependent upon the type of product being produced, not the various stages of production for that product. Thus, the pool of a manufacturer can (and will) contain raw materials, WIP, and finished goods. The three examples below, adapted from the U.S. Treasury regulations, illustrate the application of the natural business unit concept.

Example 1—Identifying Pools

A corporation manufactures, in one division, automatic clothes washers and dryers of both commercial and domestic grade as well as electric ranges and dishwashers. The corporation manufactures, in another division, radios and television sets. The manufacturing facilities and processes used in manufacturing the radios and television sets are distinct from those used in manufacturing the automatic clothes washers, etc. Under these circumstances, an enterprise consisting of two business units and two pools would be appropriate: one consisting of all of the LIFO inventories involved with the manufacture of clothes washers and dryers, electric ranges and dishwashers and the other consisting of all the LIFO inventories involved with the production of radios and television sets.

Example 2—Identifying Pools

A taxpayer produces plastics in one of its plants. Substantial amounts of the production are sold as plastics. The remainder of the production is shipped to a second plant of the taxpayer for the production of plastic toys that are sold to customers. The taxpayer operates its plastics plant and toy plant as separate divisions. Because of the different product lines and the separate divisions, the taxpayer has two natural business units.

Example 3—Identifying Pools

A taxpayer is engaged in the manufacture of paper. At one stage of processing, uncoated paper is produced. Substantial amounts of uncoated paper are sold at this stage of processing. The remainder of the uncoated paper is transferred to the taxpayer's finishing mill where coated paper is produced and sold. This taxpayer has only one natural business unit, since coated and uncoated paper are within the same product line.

A pool consists of all items entering into the entire inventory investment of a natural business unit, unless the taxpayer elects to use the multiple-pooling method.

The multiple-pooling method is the grouping of "substantially similar" items. In determining substantially similar items, consideration is given to the processing applied, the interchangeability, the similarity of use, and the customary practice of the industry. While the election of multiple pools will necessitate additional recordkeeping, it may result in a better estimation of gross profit and periodic net income.

According to Reg. §1.472-8(c), inventory items of wholesalers, retailers, jobbers, and distributors are to be assigned to pools by major lines, types, or classes of goods. The natural business unit method may be used with permission of the Commissioner.

All three methods of pooling allow for a change in the components of inventory over time. New items that properly fall within the pool may be added, and old items may disappear from the pool, but neither will necessarily cause a change in the total dollar value of the pool.

Dollar-value LIFO Under the dollar-value LIFO method of inventory valuation, the cost of inventories is computed by expressing base-year costs in terms of total dollars rather than specific prices of specific units. The dollar-value method also provides an expanded interpretation of the use of LIFO pools. Increments and decrements are treated the same as under the unit LIFO approach but are reflected only in terms of a *net* increment or liquidation for the entire pool.

Computing dollar-value LIFO The purpose of the dollar-value LIFO method of valuing inventory is to convert inventory priced at end-of-year prices to that same quantity of inventory priced at base-year (or applicable LIFO layer) prices. The dollar-value method achieves this result through the use of a conversion price index. The inventory computed at current year cost is divided by the appropriate index to arrive at its base-year cost. The main computational focus is on the determination of the conversion price index. There are four types of methods that can be used in the computation of the ending inventory amount of a dollar-value LIFO pool:

1. double-extension,
2. link-chain,
3. indexing, and
4. alternative LIFO for automobile dealers.

Double-extension method This method was originally developed to compute the conversion price index. It involves extending the entire quantity of ending inventory for the current year at both base-year prices and end-of-year prices to arrive at a total dollar value for each, hence the title "double-extension." The dollar total computed at end-of-year prices is then divided by the dollar total computed at base-year prices to arrive at the index, usually referred to as the conversion price index. This index indicates the relationship between the base-year and current prices in terms of a percentage. Each layer (or increment) is valued at its own percentage. Although a representative sample is allowed (meaning that not all of the items need to be double-extended; this is discussed in more detail under indexing), the recordkeeping under this method is very burdensome. The base-year price must be maintained for each inventory item. Depending upon the number of different items included in the inventory of the enterprise, the necessary records may be too detailed to keep past the first year or two.

The following example illustrates the double-extension method of computing the LIFO value of inventory. The example presented is relatively simple and does not attempt to incorporate all of the complexities of LIFO inventory accounting.

Example of the Dollar-Value LIFO Method

Isaacson, Inc. uses the dollar-value method of LIFO inventory valuation and computes its price index using the double-extension method. Isaacson has a single pool that contains two inventory items, A and B. Year 1 is the company's initial year of operations. The following information is given for years 1 through 4:

	Ending inventory	*Ending quantity (units)and current unit price*			
Year	*current prices*	*A*		*B*	
1	$100,000	5,000	$6.00	7,000	$10.00
2	120,300	6,000	6.30	7,500	11.00
3	122,220	5,800	6.40	7,400	11.50
4	133,900	6,200	6.50	7,800	12.00

In year 1 there is no computation of an index; the index is 100%. The LIFO cost is the same as the actual current year cost. This is the base year.

In year 2 the first step is to double-extend the quantity of ending inventory at base-year and current year costs.

Item	*Quantity*	*Base-year cost/unit*	*Extended*	*Current year cost/unit*	*Extended*
A	6,000	$ 6.00	$ 36,000	$ 6.30	$ 37,800
B	7,500	10.00	75,000	11.00	82,500
			$111,000		$120,300*

* *When using the double-extension method and extending all of the inventory items to arrive at the index, this number must equal the ending inventory at current prices. If a sampling method is used (as discussed under indexing), this number divided by your ending inventory at current prices is the percentage sampled.*

Now we can compute the conversion price index, which is:

$$\frac{\text{Ending inventory at current year prices}}{\text{Ending inventory at base-year prices}}$$

$$\text{In this case} = \frac{120{,}300}{111{,}000} = 108.4\%(\text{rounded})$$

Next, compute the year 2 layer at base-year cost by taking the current year-ending inventory at base-year prices (if you only extend a sample of the inventory, this number is arrived at by dividing the ending inventory at current year prices by the conversion price index) of $111,000 and subtracting the base-year cost of $100,000. In year 2 we have an increment (layer) of $11,000 valued at base-year costs.

The year 2 layer of $11,000 at base-year cost must be converted so that the layer is valued at the prices in effect when it came into existence (i.e., at year 2 prices). This is done by multiplying the increment at base-year cost ($11,000) by the rounded conversion price index (1.084). The result is the year 2 layer at LIFO prices.

Base-year layer	$100,000
Year 2 layer ($11,000 × 1.084)	11,924
	$111,924

In year 3 the same basic procedure is followed.

Item	Quantity	Base-year cost/unit	Extended	Current year cost/unit	Extended
A	5,800	$ 6.00	$ 34,800	$ 6.40	$ 37,120
B	7,400	10.00	74,000	11.50	85,100
			$108,800		$122,220

There has been a decrease in the base-year cost of the ending inventory ($111,000 – $108, 800 = $2,200), which is referred to as a decrement. A decrement results in the decrease (or elimination) of previously provided layers. In this situation, the computation of the index is not necessary as there is no LIFO layer that requires a valuation. If a sampling approach has been used, the index is needed to arrive at the ending inventory at base-year cost and thus determine if there has been an increment or decrement.

Now the ending inventory at base-year cost is $108, 800. The base-year cost layer is still intact at $100,000, so the cumulative increment is $8, 800. Since this is less than the $11,000 increment of year 2, no additional increment is established in year 3. The LIFO cost of the inventory is shown below.

Base-year layer	$100,000
Year 2 layer ($8,800 × 1.084)	9,539
	$109,539

The fourth year then follows the same steps.

Items	Quantity	Base-year cost/unit	Extended	Current year cost/unit	Extended
A	6,200	$ 6.00	$ 37,200	$ 6.50	$ 40,300
B	7,800	10.00	78,000	12.00	93,600
			$115,200		$133,900

The conversion price index is 116.2% (133,900/115,200).

A current year increment exists because the ending inventory at base-year prices in year 4 of $115,200 exceeds the year 3 number of $108,800. The current year increment of $6,400 must be valued at year 4 prices. Thus, the LIFO cost of the year 4 inventory is:

Base-year layer	$100,000
Year 2 layer ($8,800 × 1.084)	9,539
Year 4 layer ($6,400 × 1.162)	7,437
	$116,976

It is important to point out that once a layer is reduced or eliminated it is never reinstated (as with the year 2 increment) after year-end.

Link-chain method Since the double-extension method computations are arduous even if only a few items exist in the inventory, consider the complexity that arises when there is a constant change in the inventory mix or when there is a large number of inventory items. The link-chain method of applying dollar-value LIFO was developed to mitigate the effects of this complexity.

Consider the situation where the components of inventory are constantly changing. The regulations require that any new products added to the inventory be recorded at base-year prices. If these are not available, then the earliest cost available after the base year is used. If the item was not in existence in the base year, the taxpayer may reconstruct the base cost, using a reasonable method to determine what the cost would have been if the item had been in existence in the base year. Finally, as a last resort, the current year purchase price can be used. While this does not appear to be a problem on the surface, imagine a base period that is twenty-five to fifty years in the past. The difficulty involved with finding the base-year cost may require using a more current cost, thus eliminating some of the LIFO benefit. Imagine a situation faced by a company in a "high- tech" industry where inventory is continually being replaced by newer, more advanced products. The effect of this rapid change under the double-extension method (because the new products did not exist in the base period) is to use current prices as base-year costs. When inventory has such a rapid turnover, the overall LIFO advantage becomes diluted as current and base-year costs are often identical. This situation necessitated the development of the link-chain method.

The link-chain method was originally developed for (and limited to) those companies that wanted to use LIFO but, because of a substantial change in product lines over time, were unable to reconstruct or maintain the historical records necessary to make accurate use of the double extension method. It is important to note that the double-extension and link-chain methods are not elective alternatives for the same situation. For income tax purposes, the link- chain election requires that substantial changes in product lines be evident over the years, and may not be elected solely because of its ease of application. The double-extension and index methods must be demonstrably impractical in order to elect the link-chain method. However, an enterprise may use different computational techniques for financial reporting and income tax purposes. Therefore, the link-chain method could be used for financial reporting purposes even if a different application is used for income tax purposes. Obviously, the recordkeeping burdens imposed by using different LIFO methods for GAAP and income tax purposes (including the deferred income tax accounting that would be required for the temporary difference between the GAAP and income tax bases of the LIFO inventories) would make this a highly unlikely scenario.

The link-chain method is the process of developing a single cumulative index, which is applied to the ending inventory amount priced using beginning-of-the-year costs. Thus, the index computed at the end of each year is "linked" to the index from all previous years. A separate cumulative index is used for each pool regardless of the variations in the components of these pools over the years. Technological change is accommodated by the method used to calculate each current year's index. The index is calculated by double-extending a representative sample of items in the pool at both beginning-of-year prices and end-of-year prices. This annual index is then applied to (multiplied by) the previous period's cumulative index to arrive at the new current year cumulative index.

An example of the link-chain method is shown below. The end-of-year costs and inventory quantities used are the same as those used in the double-extension example.

Example—Link-Chain Method

Assume the following inventory data for years 1–4 for Dickler Distributors, Inc. Year 1 is assumed to be the initial year of operation for the company. The LIFO method is elected on the first income tax return. Assume that A and B constitute a single pool.

		Cost per unit		*Extension*	
Product	*Ending inventory quantity*	*Beginning of year*	*End of year*	*Beginning*	*End*
Year 1					$ 30,000
A	5,000	N/A	$ 6.00	N/A	70,000
B	7,000	N/A	10.00	N/A	$100,000
Year 2					
A	6,000	$ 6.00	6.30	$ 36,000	$ 37,800
B	7,500	10.00	11.00	75,000	82,500
				$111,000	$120,300
Year 3					
A	5,800	6.30	6.40	$ 36,540	$ 37,120
B	7,400	11.00	11.50	81,400	85,100
				$117,940	$122,220
Year 4					
A	6,200	6.40	6.50	$ 39,680	$ 40,300
B	7,800	11.50	12.00	89,700	93,600
				$129,380	$133,900

The initial year (base year) does not require the computation of an index under any LIFO method. The base-year index will always be 1.00.

Thus, the base-year inventory layer is $100,000 (the end-of-year inventory stated at base-year cost). The second year requires the first index computation. Notice that in year 2 our extended totals are:

Product	*Beginning-of-year prices*	*End-of-year prices*
A	$ 36,000	$ 37,800
B	75,000	82,500
	$111,000	$120,300

The year 2 index is 1.084 (120,300/111,000). This is the same as computed under the double-extension method because the beginning-of-the-year prices reflect the base-year price. This will not always be the case, as sometimes new items may be added to the pool, causing a change in the index. Thus, the cumulative index is the 1.084 current year index multiplied by the preceding year index of 1.00 to arrive at a link-chain index of 1.084.

This index is then used to restate the inventory to base-year cost by dividing the inventory at end-of-year prices by the cumulative index: $120,300/1.084 = $111,000. The determination of the LIFO increment or decrement is then basically the same as the double-extension method. In year 2 the increment (layer) at base-year cost is $11,000 ($111,000 – 100,000). This layer must be valued at the prices effective when the layer was created, or extended at the cumulative index for that year. This results in an ending inventory at LIFO cost of:

	Base-year cost	Index	LIFO cost
Base-year layer	$100,000	1.000	$100,000
Year 2 layer	11,000	1.084	11,924
	$111,000		$111,924

The index for year 3 is computed as follows:

	Beginning-of-year prices	End-of-year prices
A	$ 36,540	$ 37,120
B	81,400	85,100
	$117,940	$122,220
		122,220/117,940 = 1.036

The next step is to determine the cumulative index, which is the product of the preceding year's cumulative index and the current year index, or 1.123 (1.084 × 1.036). The new cumulative index is used to restate the inventory at end-of-year dollars to base-year cost. This is accomplished by dividing the end-of-year inventory by the new cumulative index. Thus, current inventory at base-year cost is $108,833 ($122,220 ÷ 1.123). In this instance we have experienced a decrement (a decrease from the prior year's $111,000). The determination of ending inventory is:

	Base-year cost	Index	LIFO cost
Base-year layer	$100,000	1.000	$100,000
Year 2 layer	8,833	1.084	9,575
Year 3 layer	–	1.123	–
	$108,833		$109,575

Finally, the same steps are performed for the year 4 computation. The current year index is 1.035 (133, 900/129, 380). The new cumulative index is 1.162 (1.035 × 1.123). The base-year cost of the current inventory is $115,232 (133, 900/1.162). Thus, LIFO inventory at the end of year 4 is:

	Base-year cost	Index	LIFO cost
Base-year layer	$100,000	1.000	$100,000
Year 2 layer	8,833	1.084	9,575
Year 3 layer	–	1.123	–
Year 4 layer	6,399	1.162	7,435
	$115,232		$117,010

Notice how even though the numbers used were the same as those used in the double-extension example, the results were different (year 4 inventory under double-extension was $116,976)—however, not by a significant amount. It is much easier to keep track of beginning-of-the-year prices than base-year prices, but perhaps more importantly, it is easier to establish beginning-of-the-year prices for new items than to establish their base-year price. This latter reason is why the link-chain method is so much more desirable than the double-extension method. However, before electing or applying this method, a company must be able to establish a sufficient need as defined in the Treasury regulations.

Indexing methods Indexing methods can basically be broken down into two types: (1) an internal index and (2) an external index.

The internal index is merely a variation of the double-extension method. The regulations allow for the use of a statistically valid representative sample of the inventory to be double-extended. The index computed from the sample is then used to restate the inventory to base-year cost and to value the new layer.

The external index method, referred to in Treasury regulations as the Inventory Price Index Computation (IPIC) Method, involves using indices published by the U.S. Department of Labor's Bureau of Labor Statistics (BLS)[1] and applying them to specified categories of inventory included in the taxpayer's LIFO pools. Taxpayers wanting to change to the IPIC Method from another LIFO method must obtain IRS consent by filing Form 3115, *Application for Change in Accounting Method.*

Alternative LIFO method for automobile dealers A simplified dollar-value method is available for use by retail automobile dealers for valuing inventory of new automobiles and light-duty trucks. The use of this method and its acceptance for income tax purposes is conditioned on the application of several LIFO submethods, definitions, and special rules. The reader is referred to Rev. Proc. 92-79 for a further discussion of this method.

LIFO accounting literature GAAP for the application of LIFO has been based upon income tax rules rather than on financial accounting pronouncements. LIFO is cited in GAAP as an acceptable inventory method, but specific rules regarding its implementation are not provided. The income tax regulations, as discussed below, do provide specific rules for the implementation of LIFO and require financial statement conformity. For this reason, income tax rules have essentially defined the financial accounting treatment of LIFO inventories.

In recognition of the lack of authoritative accounting guidelines in the implementation of LIFO, the American Institute of Certified Public Accountants (AICPA)'s Accounting Standards Division formed a task force on LIFO inventory problems to prepare an Issues Paper on this topic. "Identification and Discussion of Certain Financial Accounting and Reporting Issues Concerning LIFO Inventories," issued in 1984, identifies financial accounting issues resulting from the use of LIFO and includes advisory guidance on resolving them. Issues Papers do not establish authoritative standards of financial accounting, however, the SEC in SAB Topic 5.L, *LIFO Inventory Practices* does mention the Issues Papers. The SEC's staff position on the Issues Papers is:

> *In the absence of existing authoritative literature on LIFO accounting, the staff belies the registrants and their independent accountants should look to the papers for guidance in determining what constitutes acceptable LIFO accounting practices.* (ASC 330- 10-S99-1)

The guidance provided by the task force is described below.[2]

- Specific goods versus dollar-value. Either the specific goods approach or dollar-value approach to LIFO is acceptable for financial reporting. Disclosure of whether the specific goods or dollar-value approach is used is not required.
- Pricing current year purchases. Three approaches to pricing LIFO inventory increments are available under income tax regulations—earliest acquisition price, latest acquisition price, and average acquisition price. The earliest acquisition price approach is the most compatible with financial reporting objectives, but all three are acceptable for financial reporting.
- Quantity to use to determine price. The price used to determine the inventory increment should be based on the cost of the quantity or dollars of the increment rather than on the cost of the quantity or dollars equal to the ending inventory. Disclosure of which approach is used is not required.

[1] For more information see http://www.bls.gov.

[2] The Issues Paper can be found at tinyurl.com/8j3f8t7.

- Disclosure of LIFO reserve or replacement cost. The LIFO reserve or replacement cost and its basis for determination should be disclosed for financial reporting.
- Partial adoption of LIFO. If a company changes to LIFO, it should do so for all of its inventories. Partial adoption should only be allowed if there exists a valid business reason for not fully adopting LIFO. A planned gradual adoption of LIFO over several time periods is considered acceptable if valid business reasons exist (lessening the income statement effect of adoption in any one year is not a valid business reason). Where partial adoption of LIFO has been justified, the extent to which LIFO has been adopted should be disclosed. This can be disclosed by indicating either the portion of the ending inventory priced on LIFO or the portion of cost of sales resulting from LIFO inventories.
- Methods of pooling. An entity should have valid business reasons for establishing its LIFO pools. Additionally, the existence of a separate legal entity that has no economic substance is not reason enough to justify separate pools. Disclosure of details regarding an entity's pooling arrangements is not required.
- New items entering a pool. New items should be added to a pool based on what the items would have cost had they been acquired in the base period (reconstructed cost) rather than based on their current cost. The reconstructed cost should be determined based on the most objective sources available, including published vendor price lists, vendor quotes, and general industry indexes. Where necessary, the use of a substitute base year in making the LIFO computation is acceptable. Disclosure of the way that new items are priced is not required.
- Dollar-value index. The required index can be developed using two possible approaches, the unit cost method or the cost component method. The unit cost method measures changes in the index based on the weighted-average increase or decrease in the unit costs of raw materials, work-in-process, and finished goods inventory. The cost component method, on the other hand, measures changes in the index by the weighted-average increase or decrease in the component costs of material, labor, and overhead that make up ending inventory. Either of these methods is acceptable.
- LIFO liquidations. The effects on income of LIFO inventory liquidations should be disclosed in the notes to the financial statements. A replacement reserve for the liquidation should not be provided. When an involuntary LIFO liquidation occurs, the effect on income of the liquidation should not be deferred.

  When a LIFO liquidation occurs, there are three possible ways to measure its effect on income:

  a. The difference between actual cost of sales and what cost of sales would have been had the inventory been reinstated under the entity's normal pricing procedure.
  b. The difference between actual cost of sales and what cost of sales would have been had the inventory been reinstated at year-end replacement cost.
  c. The amount of the LIFO reserve at the beginning of the year that was credited to income (excluding the increase in the reserve due to current year price changes).

  The first method is considered preferable. Disclosure of the effect of the liquidation should give effect only to pools with decrements (i.e., there should be no netting of pools with decrements against other pools with increments).
- Lower of cost or market. The most reasonable approach to applying the lower of cost or market rules to LIFO inventory is to base the determination on groups of inventory rather than on an item-by-item approach. A pool constitutes a reasonable grouping for

this purpose. An item-by-item approach is permitted by authoritative accounting literature, particularly for obsolete or discontinued items.

For companies with more than one LIFO pool, it is permissible to aggregate the pools in applying the lower of cost or market test if the pools are similar. Where the pools are significantly dissimilar, aggregating the pools is not appropriate.

Previous write-downs to market value of the cost of LIFO inventories should be reversed after a company disposes of the physical units of the inventory for which reserves were provided. The reserves at the end of the year should be based on a new computation of cost or market.

- LIFO conformity and supplemental disclosures. A company may present supplemental non-LIFO disclosures within the historical cost framework. If nondiscretionary variable expenses (i.e., profit sharing based on earnings) would have been different based on the supplemental information, then the company should give effect to such changes. Additionally, the supplemental disclosure should reflect the same type of income tax effects as required by generally accepted accounting principles in the primary financial statements.

  A company may use different LIFO applications for financial reporting than it uses for income tax purposes. Any such differences should be accounted for as temporary differences with the exception of differences in the allocation of cost to inventory in a business combination. Any differences between LIFO applications used for financial reporting and those used for income tax purposes need not be disclosed beyond the requirements of ASC 740.
- Interim reporting and LIFO. The FASB guidance on interim reporting of LIFO inventory is discussed in the chapter on ASC 270.
- Different financial and income tax years. A company with different fiscal year-ends for financial reporting and income tax reporting should make a separate LIFO calculation for financial purposes using its financial reporting year as a discrete period for that calculation.
- Business combinations accounted for by the purchase method. Inventory acquired in a business combination accounted for by the purchase method will be recorded at fair value at the date of the combination. The acquired company may be able to carry over its prior basis for that inventory for income tax purposes, causing a difference between GAAP and income tax basis. An adjustment should be made to the fair value of the inventory only if it is reasonably estimated that it will be liquidated in the future. The adjustment would be for the income tax effect of the difference between income tax and GAAP basis.

  Inventory acquired in such a combination should be considered the LIFO base inventory if the inventory is treated by the company as a separate business unit or a separate LIFO pool. If instead the acquired inventory is combined into an existing pool, then the acquired inventory should be considered as part of the current year's purchases.
- Changes in LIFO applications. A change in a LIFO application is a change in accounting principle. LIFO applications refer to the approach (i.e., dollar value or specific goods), computational technique, or the numbers or contents of the pools.

ASC 810-10-55 provides guidance for intercompany transfers. The focus of this section is the LIFO liquidation effect caused by transferring inventories, which in turn creates intercompany profits. This liquidation can occur when (1) two components of the same taxable entity transfer inventory, for example, when a LIFO method component transfers inventory to a non-LIFO component, or (2) when two separate taxable entities that consolidate transfer inventory, even though both use the LIFO method.

This LIFO liquidation creates profit that must be eliminated along with other intercompany profits.

LIFO income tax rules and restrictions As discussed previously, most of the rules and regulations governing LIFO originate in the IRC and the related regulations, revenue rules, revenue procedures, and judicial decisions. Taxpayers electing to use the LIFO inventory method are subject to myriad rules and restrictions, such as:

- The inventory is to be valued at cost regardless of market value (i.e., application of the lower of cost or market rule is not allowed).
- Changes in the LIFO reserve can potentially cause the taxpayer to be subject to alternative minimum tax (AMT) or increase the amount of AMT.
- Corporations that use the LIFO method whose stockholders subsequently elect to be taxed as an "S" corporation are required to report as income their entire LIFO reserve resulting in a special tax under IRC §1363(d) that is payable in four annual installments. The "S" corporation is, however, permitted to retain LIFO as its inventory accounting method after the election.
- Once elected, the LIFO method must continue to be used consistently in future periods. A taxpayer is permitted, subject to certain restrictions, to revoke its LIFO election in accordance with Rev. Proc. 99-49. After revocation, however, the taxpayer is precluded from reelecting LIFO for a period of five taxable years beginning with the year of the change. For GAAP purposes, a change to or from the LIFO method is accounted for as a change in accounting principle under ASC 250.

A unique rule regarding LIFO inventories is referred to as the LIFO Conformity Rule. (Sec. 472(c)) A taxpayer may not use a different inventory method in reporting income, profit, or loss of the entity for external financial reports. Thus, if LIFO is elected for income tax purposes, it must also be used for accounting purposes.

Treasury regulations permit certain exceptions to this general rule. Among the exceptions allowable under the regulations are the following:

- The use of an inventory method other than LIFO in presenting information reported as a supplement to or explanation of the taxpayer's primary presentation of income in financial reports to outside parties. (Reg. §1.472-2[e][1][i])
- The use of an inventory method other than LIFO to determine the value of the taxpayer's inventory for purposes of reporting the value of such inventory as an asset on the statement of financial position. (Reg. §1.472-2[e][1][ii])
- The use of an inventory method other than LIFO for purposes of determining information reported in internal management reports. (Reg. §1.472-2[e][1][iii])
- The use of an inventory method other than LIFO for financial reports covering a period of less than one taxable year. (Reg. §1.472–2[e][1][iv])
- The use of lower of LIFO cost or market to value inventories for financial statements while using LIFO cost for income tax purposes. (Reg. §1.472-2[e][1][v])
- For inventories acquired by a corporation in exchange for issuing stock to a stockholder that, immediately after the exchange, is considered to have control (a section 351 transaction), the use of the transferor's acquisition dates and costs for GAAP while using redetermined LIFO layers for tax purposes. (Reg. §1.472-2[e][1][vii])
- The inclusion of certain costs (under full absorption) in inventory for income tax purposes, as required by regulations, while not including those same costs in inventory under GAAP (full absorption). (Reg. §1.472-2[e][8][i])

- The use of different methods of establishing pools for GAAP purposes and income tax purposes. (Reg. §1.472-2[e][8][ii])
- The use of different determinations of the time sales or purchases are accrued for GAAP purposes and tax purposes. (Reg. §1.472-2[e][8][xii])
- In the case of a business combination, the use of different methods to allocate basis for GAAP purposes and income tax purposes. (Reg. §1.472-29[e][8][xiii])

Another important consideration in applying the LIFO conformity rule is the law concerning related corporations. In accordance with the Tax Reform Act of 1984, all members of the same group of financially related corporations are treated as a single taxpayer when applying the conformity rule. Previously, taxpayers were able to circumvent the conformity rule by having a subsidiary on LIFO, while the non-LIFO parent presented combined non-LIFO financial statements. This is a violation of the conformity requirement (see. 472(g)).

Comparison of Cost Flow Assumptions Of the three cost flow assumptions, FIFO and LIFO produce the most extreme results, while results from using the weighted-average method generally fall somewhere in between. The selection of one of these methods involves a detailed analysis of the organization's objectives, industry practices, current and expected future economic conditions, and most importantly, the needs of the intended users of the financial statements.

The following table compares the relative effects of using FIFO and LIFO cost assumptions on the statement of financial position and statement of income under differing economic conditions:

Changes in price levels	*Relative effect on statement of financial position*		*Relative effect on statement of income*	
	FIFO	*LIFO*	*FIFO*	*LIFO*
Inflation (i.e., rising prices)	Higher inventory carrying value	Lower inventory carrying value	Lower cost of sales; higher gross profit and net income	Higher cost of sales; lower gross profit and net income
Deflation (i.e., falling prices)	Lower inventory carrying value	Higher inventory carrying value	Higher cost of sales; lower gross profit and net income	Lower cost of sales; higher gross profit and net income

In periods of rising prices, the LIFO method is generally thought to best fulfill the objective of providing the clearest measure of periodic net income. It does not, however, provide an accurate estimate of inventory cost in an inflationary environment. However, this shortcoming can usually be overcome by providing additional disclosures in the notes to the financial statements. In periods of rising prices, a prudent business should use the LIFO method because it will result in a decrease in the current income tax liability when compared to other alternatives. In a deflationary period, the opposite is true.

FIFO is a balance-sheet-oriented costing method. It gives the most accurate estimate of the current cost of inventory during periods of changing prices. In periods of rising prices, the FIFO method will result in higher income taxes than the other alternatives, while in a deflationary period FIFO provides for a lesser income tax burden. However, a major advantage of the FIFO method is that it is not subject to all of the complex regulations and requirements of the income tax code that govern the use of LIFO.

The average methods do not provide an estimate of current cost information on either the statement of financial position or income statement. The average methods are not permitted to be used for income tax purposes and, therefore, their use for financial reporting purposes would necessitate the use of FIFO for income tax reporting purposes since LIFO requires financial statement conformity.

Although price trends and underlying objectives are important to consider in selecting a cost flow assumption, other considerations are the risk of experiencing unintended liquidations of LIFO layers, as well as the effects of the chosen method on cash flow, capital maintenance, collateral requirements, and restrictive covenants imposed by lenders, and so forth.

Other Issues

Inventory Purchases and Sales with the Same Counterparty Some enterprises sell inventory to another party from whom they also acquire inventory in the same line of business. These transactions may be part of a single arrangement or separate arrangements and the inventory purchased or sold may be raw materials, work-in-process, or finished goods. More detailed information can be found in the chapter on ASC 845-10-55-10 through 55-26. (ASC 330-10-30-16)

Inventory Hedges One notable exception to recording inventories at cost is provided by the hedge accounting requirements of ASC 815. If inventory has been designated as the hedged item in a fair value hedge, changes in the fair value of the hedged inventory are recognized on the statement of financial position as they occur, with the offsetting charge or credit recognized currently in net income. Hedging is discussed in detail in the chapter on ASC 815. (ASC 330-10-35-7A)

Valuation Issues

Inventory can lose value for a variety of reasons including damage, spoilage, obsolescence, changes in market prices, and the like. The Codification essentially divides valuation methods into two sections:

1. Lower of cost or net realizable value and
2. Lower of cost or market.

The lower of cost or market (LCM) method is applicable to LIFO and retail methods, and all other methods use the lower of cost or net realizable value method.

The application of LCM is a means of attempting to measure loss of value and recognize the effects in the period in which this occurs.

Lower of Cost or Net Realizable Value

Entities, other than those using the LIFO or retail inventory methods, can use the lower of cost and net realizable value as their inventory impairment model. (ASC 330-10-35-1A) NRV is selling price in the ordinary course of business less reasonably estimable costs of completion, disposal, and transportation. If NRV is less than cost due, for example, to damage, physical deterioration, obsolescence, changes in price level or other cause, entities must recognize the difference as a loss in the period it occurs. (ASC 330-10-35-1B)

Practice Alert: Bear in mind that for raw materials or work in process, entities will still need to consider the costs to complete and sell finished goods, including direct selling costs such as transportation costs and sales commissions.

Lower of Cost or Market (LCM)

NOTE: LCM applies only to inventories using LIFO or retail inventory cost flow methods.

The term "market" means current replacement cost not to exceed a ceiling of net realizable value (selling price in the ordinary course of business less reasonably estimable costs of completion, disposal, and transportation) or be less than a floor of net realizable value adjusted for a normal profit margin.

LCM is not applied in conjunction with the LIFO method of inventory valuation for income tax purposes. However, it is important to note that LCM/LIFO is applied for financial reporting purposes. Such application gives rise to a temporary difference in the carrying value of inventory between financial statements and income tax returns. LCM/LIFO for financial reporting was discussed earlier in this chapter.

LCM may be applied to either the entire inventory or to each individual inventory item. The primary objective for selecting between the alternative methods of applying the LCM rule is to select the one that most clearly reflects periodic income. The rule is most commonly applied to the inventory on an item-by-item basis. The reason for this application is twofold:

1. It is required for income tax purposes unless it involves practical difficulties, and
2. It provides the most conservative valuation of inventories, because decreases in the value of one item are not offset by increases in the value of another.

Example of the Lower of Cost or Market Calculation

The application of these principles is illustrated in this example. Assume the following information for products A, B, C, D, and E:

Item	*Cost*	*Replacement cost*	*Est. selling price*	*Cost to complete*	*Normal profit percentage*	*Normal profit amount*
A	$2.00	$1.80	$ 2.50	$0.50	24%	$0.60
B	4.00	1.60	4.00	0.80	24%	0.96
C	6.00	6.60	10.00	1.00	18%	1.80
D	5.00	4.75	6.00	2.00	20%	1.20
E	1.00	1.05	1.20	0.25	12.5%	0.15

First, determine the market value and then compare this to historical cost. Market value is equal to the replacement cost, but cannot exceed the net realizable value (NRV) nor be below net realizable value less the normal profit percentage.

Market Determination

Item	*Cost*	*Replacement cost*	*NRV (ceiling)*	*NRV less profit (floor)*	*Market*	*LCM*
A	$2.00	$1.80	$2.00	$1.40	$1.80	$1.80
B	4.00	1.60	3.20	2.24	2.24	2.24
C	6.00	6.60	9.00	7.20	7.20	6.00
D	5.00	4.75	4.00	2.80	4.00	4.00
E	1.00	1.05	0.95	0.80	0.95	0.95

NRV (ceiling) equals selling price less costs of completion (e.g., item A: $2.50 – .50 = $2.00). NRV less profit (floor) is self-descriptive (e.g., item A: $2.50 – .50 – .60 = $1.40). Market is replacement cost unless lower than the floor or higher than the ceiling. Note that market must be designated before LCM is determined. Finally, LCM is the lower of cost or market value.

Replacement cost is a valid measure of the future utility of the inventory item, since increases or decreases in the enterprise's purchase price generally foreshadow related increases or decreases in the price at which it is able to sell the item. The ceiling and the floor provide safeguards against the recognition of either excessive profits or excessive losses in future periods in those instances where the selling price and replacement cost do not move in the same direction in a proportional manner. The ceiling avoids the recognition of additional losses in the future when the selling price is falling faster than replacement cost. Without the ceiling constraint, inventories would be carried at an amount in excess of their net realizable value. The floor avoids the recognition of abnormal profits in the future when replacement cost is falling faster than the selling price. Without the floor, inventories would be carried at a value less than their net realizable value minus a normal profit.

The loss from writing inventories down to LCM is generally reflected on the income statement in cost of goods sold. If material, the loss must be separately captioned in the income statement. While GAAP is not explicit as to presentation, it would appear that this adjustment could either be displayed as a separately identified charge within cost of goods sold, or as an administrative expense. The write-down is recorded as a debit to a loss account and a credit either to an inventory or a valuation allowance account.

Retail Inventory Method The retail inventory method is used by retailers to estimate the cost of their ending inventory. The retailer can either take a physical inventory at retail prices or estimate ending retail inventory and then use a computed cost-to-retail ratio to convert the ending inventory priced at retail to its estimated cost. This method eliminates the process of going back to original vendor invoices or other documents in order to determine the original cost for *each* inventoriable item. To apply this method, the retailer must record:

- The total cost of retail value of:
  - Purchased goods
  - Goods available for sale
- Sales for the period

The retail method can be used under any of the three cost flow assumptions discussed earlier: average cost, FIFO, or LIFO.

Cost-to-Retail Calculation The key to applying the retail method is determining the cost-to-retail ratio. The cost-to-retail ratio provides a measure of the relationship between the cost of goods available for sale and the retail price of these same goods. The calculation of this ratio varies depending upon the cost flow assumption selected. This ratio is used to convert the ending retail inventory back to cost.

- FIFO cost—The FIFO method assumes that the ending inventory is made up of the latest purchases. Therefore, beginning inventory is excluded from the computation of the cost-to-retail ratio, and the computation uses the cost of current year net purchases divided by their retail value adjusted for both net markups and net markdowns as will be further explained and illustrated.
- FIFO (LCM)—The computation is basically the same as FIFO cost, except that markdowns are excluded from the computation of the cost-to-retail ratio.
- Average cost—Average cost assumes that ending inventory consists of all goods available for sale. Therefore, the cost-to-retail ratio is computed by dividing the cost of goods

available for sale (Beginning inventory + Net purchases) by the retail value of these goods adjusted for both net markups and net markdowns.

- Average cost (LCM)—Is computed in the same manner as average cost, except that markdowns are excluded from the calculation of the cost-to-retail ratio.

Example of the Retail Inventory Method Assuming FIFO and Average Cost Flows—No Markdowns Exist

A simple example illustrates the computation of the cost-to-retail ratio under both the FIFO cost and average cost methods in a situation where no markups or markdowns exist.

	FIFO cost		*Average cost*	
	Cost	*Retail*	*Cost*	*Retail*
Beginning inventory	$100,000	$ 200,000	$100,000	$ 200,000
Net purchases	500,000 (a)	800,000 (b)	500,000	80,000
Total goods available for sale	$600,000	1,000,000	$600,000 (c)	1,000,000 (d)
Sales at retail		(80,000)		(80,000)
Ending inventory—retail		$ 200,000		$ 200,000
Cost-to-retail ratio	(a) 500,000	= 62.5%	(a) 600,000	= 60%
(b) 800,000	(b) 800,000		(b) 100,000	
Ending inventory—cost				
200,000 × 62.5%				
200,000 × 60%		$ 125,000		$ 120,000

Note that the only difference in the two examples is the numbers used to calculate the cost-to-retail ratio.

Treatment of Markups and Markdowns The lower of cost or market aspect of the retail method is a result of the treatment of net markups and net markdowns. Net markups (markups less markup cancellations) are net increases above the original retail price, which are generally caused by changes in supply and demand. Net markdowns (markdowns less markdown cancellations) are net decreases below the original retail price. An approximation of "lower of cost or market" pricing is achieved by including net markups but excluding net markdowns, from the cost-to-retail ratio.

To understand this approximation, assume a toy is purchased for $6, and the retail price is set at $10. It is later marked down to $8. A cost-to-retail ratio including markdowns would be $6 divided by $8 or 75%, and ending inventory would be valued at $8 times 75%, or $6 (original cost). The logic behind including markdowns in the cost-to-retail ratio is the assumption that these inventories would eventually be marked down and that markdowns are a normal part of business for this enterprise and/or these types of inventories. A cost-to-retail ratio excluding markdowns would be $6 divided by $10 or 60%, and ending inventory would be valued at $8 times 60%, or $4.80 (LCM). The logic behind excluding markdowns from the cost-to-retail ratio is that the enterprise did not expect to mark these inventory items down and that this is not a normal occurrence. The write-down to $4.80 reflects the loss in utility, which is evidenced by the reduced retail price.

The application of the lower of cost or market rule is illustrated for both the FIFO and average cost methods in the example below. Remember, if the markups and markdowns below had been included in the previous example, both would have been included in the cost-to-retail ratio.

Example of the Retail Inventory Method—Lower of Cost or Market Rule: FIFO and Average Cost Methods

	FIFO cost (LCM)		*Average cost (LCM)*	
	Cost	*Retail*	*Cost*	*Retail*
Beginning inventory	$ 100,000	$ 200,000	$ 100,000	$ 200,000
Net purchases	500,000 (a)	800,000 (b)	500,000	800,000
Net markups	–	250,000 (b)	–	250,000
Total goods available for sale	$ 600,000	1,250,000	$ 600,000 (c)	1,250,000 (d)
Net markdowns		(50,000)		(50,000)
Sales at retail		(800,000)		(800,000)
Ending inventory--retail		$ 400,000		$ 400,000
Cost-to-retail ratio	(a) 500,000 / (b) 1,050,000 = 47.6%		(c) 600,000 / (d) 1,250,000 = 48%	
Ending inventory—LCM				
400,000 × 47.6%		$ 190,400		
400,000 × 48%				$ 192,400

Under the FIFO (LCM) method all of the markups are considered attributable to the current period purchases. While this is not necessarily accurate, it provides the most conservative estimate of the ending inventory.

Other Considerations There are a number of additional issues that affect the computation of the cost-to-retail ratio.

- **Purchase discounts.** Purchase discounts affect only the cost column in this computation.
- **Shipping.** Freight-in affects only the cost column in this computation.
- **Sales discounts and adjustment for returns.** The sales figure that is subtracted from the adjusted cost of goods available for sale in the retail column must be gross sales after adjustment for sales returns. Sales discounts are not included in the computation. If sales are recorded gross, then deduct the gross sales figure. If sales are recorded net, then both the recorded sales and sales discount must be deducted to give the same effect as deducting gross sales.
- **Spoilage.** Normal spoilage is generally allowed for in the enterprise's pricing policies, and for this reason it is deducted from the retail column after the calculation of the cost-to-retail ratio. Abnormal spoilage, on the other hand, is deducted from both the cost and retail columns before the cost-to-retail calculation as it could otherwise distort the ratio. It is then generally reported as a separate loss, either within cost of goods sold or administrative expenses. Abnormal spoilage generally arises from a major theft or casualty, while normal spoilage is usually due to shrinkage or breakage. These determinations and their treatments will vary depending upon the enterprise's policies.

When applying the retail inventory method, separate computations are made for any departments that experience significantly higher or lower gross profit margins. Distortions arise in applying the retail method when a department sells goods with gross profit margins that vary in a proportion different from the gross profit margins of goods purchased during the period. In this case, the cost-to-retail percentage would not be representative of the mix of goods in ending inventory. Also, manipulations of income are possible by planning the timing of markups and markdowns.

The retail inventory method is an acceptable method of estimating inventories for income tax purposes. Income tax regulations require valuation at lower of cost or market (except for LIFO) and regular and consistent physical counts of inventory at each location. Entities should consult the current IRS regulations for more information.

LIFO Retail Inventory Method As with other LIFO methods, Treasury regulations are the governing force behind the LIFO retail inventory method. The regulations differentiate between a "variety" store, which is required to use an internally computed index, and a "department" store, which is permitted to use a price index published by the Bureau of Labor Statistics. The computation of an internal index was previously discussed in the dollar-value LIFO section. It involves applying the double-extension method to a representative sample of the ending inventory. Selection of an externally published index is to be in accordance with the Treasury regulations.

The steps used in computing the value of ending inventory under the LIFO retail inventory method are listed below and then applied in an example for illustrative purposes.

- Calculate (or select) the current year conversion price index. Recall that in the base year this index will be 1.00.
- Calculate the value of the ending inventory at both cost and retail. Remember, as with other LIFO methods, income tax regulations do not permit the use of LCM, so both markups and markdowns are included in the computation of the cost-to-retail ratio. However, the beginning inventory is excluded from goods available for sale at cost and at retail.
- Restate the ending inventory at retail to base-year retail. Divide the current ending inventory at retail by the current year index determined in Step 1.
- Layers are then treated as they were for the dollar-value LIFO example presented earlier. If the ending inventory restated to base-year retail exceeds the previous year's amount at base-year retail, a new layer is established.
- The computation of LIFO cost is the last step and requires multiplying each layer at base year retail by the appropriate price index and multiplying this product by the cost-to-retail ratio in order to arrive at the LIFO cost for each layer.

Example of the LIFO Retail Inventory Method

The following example illustrates a two-year period to which the LIFO retail method is applied. The first period represents the first year of operations for the company and is its base year.

Year 1

Step 1—Because this is the base year, there is no need to compute an index, as it will always be 1.00.

Step 2—

	Cost	*Retail*
Beginning inventory	$ –	$ –
Purchases	582,400	988,600
Markups	–	164,400
Markdowns	–	(113,000)
Subtotal	582,400	1,040,000
Total goods available for sale	$582,400	1,040,000
Sales—at retail		840,000

Year 1

Ending year 1 inventory—at retail		$200,000
Cost-to-retail ratio	(a) 582,400 / (b) 1,040,000 = 56%	
Ending inventory at cost $200,000 × 56%	$112,000	

Step 3—Because this is the base year, the restatement to base-year cost is not necessary; however, the computation would be $200,000/1.00 = $200,000.

Steps 4 and 5—The determination of layers is again unnecessary in the base year; however, the computation would take the following format:

	Ending inventory at base-year retail	*Conversion price index*	*Cost-to retail ratio*	*LIFO cost*
Base year ($200,000/1.00)	$200,000	1.00	0.56	$112,000

Year 2

Step 1—We make the assumption that the computation of an internal index yields a result of 1.12 (obtained by double-extending a representative sample).

Step 2—

	Cost	*Retail*
Beginning inventory	$112,000	$ 200,000
Purchases	716,300	1,168,500
Markups	–	87,500
Markdowns	–	(21,000)
Subtotal	$716,300	1,235,000
Total goods available for sale		1,435,000
Sales—at retail		1,171,800
Ending year 2 inventory—at retail		$ 263,200
Cost-to-retail ratio	716,300 / 1,235,000 = 58%	

Step 3—The restatement of ending inventory at current year retail to base-year retail is done using the index computed in Step 1. In this case it is $263,200/1.12 = $235,000.

Steps 4 and 5—There is a LIFO layer in year 2 because the $235,000 inventory at base-year retail exceeds the year 1 amount of $200,000.

The computation of the LIFO cost for each layer is shown below.

	Ending inventory at base-year retail	*Conversion price index*	*Cost-to-retail ratio*	*LIFO cost*
Base year ($200,000/1.00)	$200,000	1.00	0.56	$112,000
Year 2 layer	35,000	1.12	0.58	22,736
	$235,000			
Ending year 2 inventory at LIFO cost				$134,736

The treatment of subsequent increments and decrements is the same for this method as it is for the regular dollar-value method.

Gross Profit Method The gross profit method is used to estimate ending inventory when a physical count is not taken. It can also be used to evaluate the reasonableness of a given inventory amount. The gross profit method is used for interim reporting estimates, for conducting analytical review procedures by independent accountants in audits and review engagements, and for estimating inventory lost in fires or other catastrophes. The method is not acceptable, however, for either income tax or annual financial reporting purposes.

Example—Using the Gross Profit Method to Estimate Ending Inventory

Assume the following data:

Beginning inventory	$ 125,000
Net purchases	450,000
Sales	600,000
Estimated gross profit percentage	32%

Ending inventory is estimated as follows:

Beginning inventory	$ 125,000
Net purchases	450,000
Cost of goods available for sale	575,000
Cost of goods sold [$600,000 – (32% × $600,000)] or (68% × $600,000)	408,000
Estimated ending inventory	$ 167,000

Standard Costs Standard costs are predetermined unit costs used by manufacturing firms for planning and control purposes. Standard costs are often used to develop approximations of GAAP inventories for financial reporting purposes. The use of standard cost approximations in financial reporting is acceptable only if adjustments to the standards are made at reasonable intervals to reflect current conditions and if their use approximates the results that would be obtained by directly applying one of the recognized cost flow assumptions. (ASC 330-10-30-12)

Example of Standard Costing

The Bavarian Clock Company (BCC) uses standard costing to value its FIFO inventory. One of its products is the Men's Chronometer wristwatch, for which the following bill of materials has been constructed:

Part description	*Quantity*	*Cost*
Titanium watch casing	1	$212.25
Leather strap	1	80.60
Scratch resistant crystal bezel	1	120.15
Double timer shock-resistant movement	1	42.80
Multilingual instruction sheet	1	0.80
Ornamental box	1	2.75
Overhead charge	1	28.00
Total		$487.35

The industrial engineering department designed the following labor routing for assembly of the Men's Chronometer and determined the standard process times:

Labor routing description	Quantity/minutes	Labor type	Cost/minute	Cost
Quality review of raw materials received	3.5	Quality assurance	$0.42	$ 1.47
Attach strap to casing	7.5	Watch maker	0.79	5.93
Insert movement in casing	10.8	Watch maker	0.79	8.53
Attach bezel	3.2	Watch maker	0.79	2.53
Final quality review and testing	11.0	Quality assurance	0.42	4.62
Insert into packing case	1.5	Assembler	0.13	.20
Total	37.5			$23.28

Thus, the total standard cost of the Men's Chronometer is $510.63 ($487.35 material and overhead cost + $23.28 labor cost). At the beginning of December, there are 1,087 Men's Chronometers in finished goods inventory, which are recorded at standard cost, resulting in a beginning inventory valuation of $555,054.81 (= $510.63 × 1,087 units).

During December, BCC records actual material costs of $1,915,312.19, actual labor costs of $111,844.40, and actual overhead costs of $124,831.55 related to the Men's Chronometer, which are charged to the inventory account. During the month, BCC manufactures 4,105 Men's Chronometers and ships 4,385, leaving 807 units in finished goods inventory. At a standard cost of $510.63 per unit, this results in a month-end finished goods inventory balance of $412,078.41. The monthly charge to cost of goods sold is calculated as follows:

Beginning inventory at standard cost	$ 555,054.81
+ Actual material costs incurred	1,915,312.19
+ Actual labor costs incurred	111,844.40
+ Actual overhead costs incurred	124,831.55
– Ending inventory at standard cost	(412,078.41)
= Cost of goods sold	$2,294,964.54

At month-end, the purchasing manager conducts his quarterly review of the bill of materials and determines that the cost of the bezel has permanently increased by $4.82, bringing the total standard bezel cost to $124.97 and therefore the total standard cost of the Men's Chronometer to $515.45. This increases the value of the ending inventory by $3,889.74 ($4.82 standard cost increase × 807 units in finished goods inventory), to $415,968.15, while reducing the cost of goods sold to $2,291,074.80. The following entry records the month-end inventory valuation at standard cost:

Cost of goods sold	2,291,074.80	
Finished goods inventory		2,291,074.80

As a cross-check, BCC's controller divides the cost of goods sold by the total number of units shipped, and arrives at an actual unit cost of $522.48, as opposed to the standard costs of $515.45. The variance from the standard cost is $7.03 per unit, or a total of $30,826.55. Upon further investigation, she finds that overnight delivery charges of $1,825 were incurred for a shipment of watch casings, while there was a temporary increase in the cost of the leather strap of $2.83 for a 1,000-unit purchase, resulting in an additional charge of $2,830. She elects to separately track these excess material-related costs with the following entry:

Material price variance	4,655.00	
Cost of goods sold		4,655.00

In addition, the production staff incurred overtime charges of $16,280 during the month. Since overtime is not included in the labor routing standard costs, the controller separately tracks this information with the following entry:

Labor price variance	16,280.00	
Cost of goods sold		16,280.00

Finally, the controller determines that some costs comprising the overhead cost pool exceeded the budgeted overhead cost during the month, resulting in an excess charge of $9,891.55 to the Men's Chronometer cost of goods sold. She separates this expense from the cost of goods sold with the following entry:

Overhead price variance	9,891.55	
Cost of goods sold		9,891.55

Her variance analysis has identified all causes of the $30,826.55 cost overage, as noted in the following table:

Total cost of goods sold	$ 2,291,074.80
Standard cost of goods sold	(2,260,248.25)
Material price variance	(4,655.00)
Labor price variance	(16,280.00)
Overhead price variance	(9,891.55)
= Remaining unresolved variance	–

As explained previously, variances resulting from abnormal costs incurred are considered period costs and, thus, are not allocated to inventory.

Relative Sales Value Relative sales (or net realizable) values are used to assign costs to inventory items purchased or manufactured in groups. This method is applicable to joint products, subdivided assets such as real estate lots, and basket purchases.

For example, products A and B have the same processes performed on them up to the split-off point. The total cost incurred to this point is $80,000. This cost can be assigned to products A and B using their relative sales value at the split-off point. If A could be sold for $60,000 and B for $40,000, the total sales value is $100,000. The cost would be assigned on the basis of each product's relative sales value. Thus, A would be assigned a cost of $48,000 (60,000/100,000 × 80,000) and B a cost of $32,000 (40,000/100,000 × 80,000).

Differences between GAAP and Income Tax Accounting for Inventories

Full Absorption Costing—Income Tax The Tax Reform Act (TRA) of 1986 included provisions referred to as Uniform Capitalization (UNICAP) requiring certain additional indirect costs that are not capitalizable under GAAP to be capitalized rather than expensed for income tax purposes:

- Depreciation and amortization in excess of that reported in financial statements
- Percentage depletion in excess of cost
- Rework labor, scrap, and spoilage costs
- Allocable general and administrative costs related to the production function

For income tax purposes, these costs, as well as the indirect production costs listed above for inventory costing under GAAP, are allocated to the WIP and finished goods inventories. Examples of general and administrative costs that must be allocated include payroll department costs, wages of security guards, and the president's salary. The difference between the GAAP and income tax inventory carrying values is a temporary difference, which requires deferred income tax accounting (discussed in Chapter 24).

Uniform Capitalization Rules—Income Tax versus GAAP TRA 1986 established the UNICAP rules for inventory costs for tax purposes. ASC 330-10-55-4 states that capitalizing a cost for income tax purposes does not, by itself, indicate that it is preferable or even appropriate to capitalize the cost for financial reporting purposes. Although a cost may be required to be capitalized for income tax purposes, management must analyze the individual facts and circumstances based on the nature of its operations and industry practice to determine whether to capitalize the cost for financial reporting purposes.

Inventory Capitalization for Retailers/Wholesalers—Income Tax versus GAAP TRA 1986 applied UNICAP (uniform capitalization) to certain retailers and wholesalers and introduced a requirement that additional costs be capitalized. Inventories of retailers/wholesalers whose average annual gross receipts for the preceding three years are $10 million or less are exempt from applying UNICAP.

The costs that must be capitalized have been divided into two categories. The first category is direct costs and includes the inventory invoice price plus transportation. Also included in direct costs is the cost of labor for purchasing, storing, and handling inventory items. The second category is indirect costs and consists of any costs that directly benefit or are incurred because of the performance of a resale activity. The following types of indirect costs must be capitalized under UNICAP:

- Off-site storage or warehousing
- Purchasing
- Handling, processing, assembly, and repackaging
- Allocable general and administrative costs related to the above three functions

The indirect costs are allocated between inventory and cost of goods sold by using traditional methods (specific identification, standard costing methods, etc.) or one of three simplified methods. Temporary differences require deferred income tax accounting as discussed in the chapter on ASC 740, *Income Taxes*.

Other Inventory Topics

Inventories Valued at Selling Price In exceptional cases, inventories may be reported at sales price less estimated disposal costs. Such treatment is justified when cost is difficult to determine, quoted market prices are available, marketability is assured, and units are interchangeable. Precious metals, certain agricultural products, and meat are examples of inventories valued in this manner. When inventory is valued above cost, revenue is recognized before the time of sale. Naturally, full disclosure in the financial statements is required.

Stripping Costs Incurred during Production in the Mining Industry ASC 930-330-25-1 states that stripping costs incurred during a mine's production phase are to be accounted for as variable production costs and therefore allocated to inventory. The ASC is limited to stripping costs incurred during the period when inventory is being produced (i.e., extracted) and did not address the accounting for these costs when incurred during the preproduction phase of the mine. (d)

23 ASC 340 OTHER ASSETS AND DEFERRED COSTS

PERSPECTIVE AND ISSUES

Subtopics

ASC 340, *Other Assets and Deferred Costs*, contains four subtopics:

- ASC 340-10, *Overall*, which provides guidance on certain deferred costs and prepaid expenses.
- ASC 340-30, *Insurance Contracts That Do Not Transfer Insurance Risk*, which provides guidance on how to apply the deposit method of accounting when it is required for insurance and reinsurance contracts that do not transfer risk.

NOTE: The revenue standard superseded most of ASC 340-20, Other Asset and Deferred Costs and created the new Subtopic ASC 340-40. That subtopic contains new cost capitalization guidance. When initially released, the revenue standard inadvertently superseded the ASC 340-20 guidance on when to recognize a liability. To rectify that oversight, ASU 2016-20 reinstates the guidance on the accrual of advertising costs and moves it to ASC 720-30, Other Expenses-Advertising Costs.

- ASC 340-40, *Contracts with Customers*, provides guidance on costs incurred related to a contract with a customer. It also covers amortization of assets arising from costs to obtain or fulfill a contract, and impairment of assets arising from costs to obtain or fulfill a contract. This Subtopic has been added by ASU 2014-09 and will be effective when ASU 2014-09 becomes effective.

The specific guidance for many other deferred costs is included in various other areas of the Codification.

Scope and Scope Exceptions

ASC 340-10 The guidance in Topic 340 applies to all entities and to all subtopics of ASC 340 unless specifically excepted.

ASC 340-30 The guidance in the subtopic includes the following transactions:

- Short-duration insurance and reinsurance contracts that do not transfer insurance risk as described in paragraph 720-20-25-1 and, for reinsurance contracts, as described in Section 944-20-15.
- Multiple-year insurance and reinsurance contracts that do not transfer insurance risk or for which insurance risk transfer is not determinable.
(ASC 340-30-15-3)

The guidance in ASC 340-30 does not apply to the following transactions and activities:

- Long-duration life and health insurance contracts that do not indemnify against mortality or morbidity risk. These are accounted for as investment contracts under Topic 944.
(ASC 340-30-15-4)

ASC 340-40 ASC 340-40 applies to the following costs of obtaining a contract with a customer within the scope of ASC 606:

- Incremental costs of obtaining a contract with a customer
- Costs of fulfilling a contract with a customer

The guidance on costs incurred in fulfilling a contract does not apply to costs included in:

- ASC 330 on inventory
- ASC 340-10-25-1 through 25-4 on preproduction costs related to long-term supply arrangements
- ASC 350-40 on internal-use software
- ASC 360 on property, plant, and equipment
- ASC 985-20 on cost of software to be sold leased or otherwise marketed
(ASC 340-40-15-3)

DEFINITIONS OF TERMS

Source: ASC 340 *Glossaries*. Also see Appendix A, *Definitions of Terms*, for other terms related to this chapter: Contract, Customers, Not-for-Profit Entity, Performance Obligations, Public Business Entity, Revenue, and Transaction Price.

Assuming Entity. The party that receives a reinsurance premium in a reinsurance transaction. The assuming entity (or reinsurer) accepts an obligation to reimburse a ceding entity under the terms of the reinsurance contract.

Ceding Entity. The party that pays a reinsurance premium in a reinsurance transaction. The ceding entity receives the right to reimbursement from the assuming entity under the terms of the reinsurance contract.

Experience Adjustment. A provision in an insurance or reinsurance contract that modifies the premium, coverage, commission, or a combination of the three, in whole or in part, based on experience under the contract.

Insurance Risk. The risk arising from uncertainties about both underwriting risk and timing risk. Actual or imputed investment returns are not an element of insurance risk. Insurance risk is fortuitous; the possibility of adverse events occurring is outside the control of the insured.

Timing Risk. The risk arising from uncertainties about the timing of the receipt and payments of the net cash flows from premiums, commissions, claims, and claim settlement expenses paid under a contract.

Underwriting Risk. The risk arising from uncertainties about the ultimate amount of net cash flows from premiums, commissions, claims, and claim settlement expenses paid under a contract.

CONCEPTS, RULES, AND EXAMPLES

ASC 340-10, *Overall*

The guidance in ASC 340-10 is limited to a discussion of the nature of prepaid expenses and guidance for preproduction costs related to long-term supply arrangements. Prepaid expenses are amounts paid to secure the use of assets or the receipt of services at a future date or continuously over one or more future periods. Prepaid expenses will not be converted to cash, but they are classified as current assets because, if they were not prepaid, they would have required the use of current assets during the coming year (or operating cycle, if longer).

Prepaid Expenses

Types of Prepaid Expenses Prepaid expenses are amounts paid to secure the use of assets or the receipt of services at a future date or continuously over one or more future periods. Prepaid expenses will not be converted to cash, but they are classified as current assets because, if they were not prepaid, they would have required the use of current assets during the coming year (or operating cycle, if longer). Examples of items that are often prepaid include dues, subscriptions, maintenance agreements, memberships, licenses, rents, and insurance.

Amortization Prepaid expenses are amortized to expense on a ratable basis over the period during which the benefits or services are received. For example, if rent is prepaid for the quarter at the beginning of the quarter, two months of the rent will be included in the prepaid rent account. At the beginning of the second month, the equivalent of one month's rent would be charged to rent expense. At the beginning of the third month, the remaining prepayment would be charged to rent expense.

Example of Prepaid Expenses

The PipeTrak Company starts using geographical information systems (GIS) software to track the locations of the country's pipeline infrastructure under a contract for the Department of Homeland Security. It pays maintenance fees on three types of GIS software, for which the following maintenance periods are covered:

Software name	Maintenance start date	Maintenance duration	Maintenance fee
Culture Data (CD)	February	Annual	$4,800
Map Layering (ML)	April	Semiannual	18,000
Land Grid (LG)	June	Quarterly	6,000

It initially records these fee payments as prepaid expenses. PipeTrak's controller then uses the following amortization table to determine the amount of prepaid expenses to charge to expense each month:

Software	Feb	Mar	Apr	May	Jun	Jul	Aug	Sep	Oct	Nov	Dec
CD	400	400	400	400	400	400	400	400	400	400	400
ML			3,000	3,000	3,000	3,000	3,000	3,000			
LG					2,000	2,000	2,000				
Totals	400	400	3,400	3,400	5,400	5,400	5,400	3,400	400	400	400

In June, for example, PipeTrak records the following entry to charge a portion of its prepaid software maintenance to expense:

Software maintenance expense	5,400	
Prepaid expenses		5,400

Preproduction Costs Related to Long-Term Supply Arrangements

Manufacturers often incur preproduction costs related to products and services they will supply to their customers under long-term arrangements. The supplier may be:

- Contractually guaranteed reimbursement of design and development costs,
- Implicitly guaranteed reimbursement of design and development costs through the pricing of the product or other means, or
- Not guaranteed reimbursement of the design and development costs incurred under the long-term supply arrangement.

ASC 340-10-25 states the following with respect to these costs:

- Costs of design and development of products to be sold under long-term supply arrangements are expensed as incurred. (ASC 340-10-25-1)

- Costs of design and development of molds, dies, and other tools that the supplier will own and that will be used in producing the products under the long-term supply arrangement are capitalized as part of the molds, dies, and other tools (subject to an ASC 360 recoverability assessment when one or more impairment indicators is present). There is an exception, however, for molds, dies, and other tools involving new technology, which are expensed as incurred as research and development costs under ASC 730. (ASC 340-10-25-2)
- If the molds, dies, and other tools described in the bullet point immediately above are *not to be owned* by the supplier, then their costs are expensed as incurred unless the supply arrangement provides the supplier the noncancelable right (as long as the supplier is performing under the terms of the supply arrangement) to use the molds, dies, and other tools during the term of the supply arrangement. (ASC 340-10-25-2)
- If there is a legally enforceable contractual guarantee for reimbursement of design and development costs that would otherwise be expensed under these rules, the costs are recognized as an asset as incurred. Such a guarantee must contain reimbursement provisions that are objectively measurable and verifiable. The ASC provides examples illustrating this provision. (ASC 340-20-25-3)

It is important to note that the above provisions do not apply to assets acquired in a business combination that are used in research and development activities. Instead, such assets are accounted for in accordance with ASC 805, which permits recognition of in-process research and development assets.

ASC 340-30, *Insurance Contracts That Do Not Transfer Insurance Risk*

Overview Insurance risk is comprised of both timing risk and underwriting risk, and one or both of these may not be transferred to the insurer (assuming entity in the case of reinsurance) under certain circumstances. For example, many workers' compensation policies provide for *experience adjustments* which have the effect of keeping the underwriting risk with the insured, rather than transferring it to the insurer; in such instances, deposit accounting would be prescribed.

Deposit method—a revenue recognition method under which premiums are not recognized as revenue and claim costs are not charged to expense until the ultimate premium is reasonably estimable, and recognition of income is postponed until that time. (ASC Master Glossary)

This subtopic offers guidance for applying the deposit method of accounting when it is required for insurance and reinsurance contracts. If insurance risk is not transferred, there are four possible categories for deposit arrangements:

1. Only significant timing risk is transferred
2. Neither significant timing nor underwriting risk is transferred
3. Only significant underwriting risk is transferred
4. The insurance contract has an indeterminate risk.

   (ASC 340-30-05-2)

Transfer of Significant Timing Risk or Neither Significant Timing nor Underwriting Risk For contracts that transfer only significant timing risk or that transfer neither significant timing nor underwriting risk, the entity should recognize at inception a:

- Deposit asset (from the insured's or ceding entity's perspective, respectively, for insurance and reinsurance arrangements), or
- Liability (from the insurer's or assuming entity's perspective, respectively, for insurance and reinsurance arrangements).

The deposit asset or liability should be remeasured at subsequent financial reporting dates by calculating the effective yield on the deposit to reflect actual payments to date and expected future payments. Yield is determined as set forth in ASC 310-20, using the estimated amounts and timings of cash flows. The deposit is adjusted to the amount that would have existed at the statement of financial position date had the new effective yield been applied since inception of the contract. (ASC 340-30-35-1 through 35-3) Thus, expense or income for a period will be determined by first calculating the necessary amount in the related statement of financial position account.

Transfer of Only Significant Underwriting Risk For contracts that transfer only significant underwriting risk, a deposit asset or liability is also established at inception. However, subsequent remeasurement of the deposit does not occur until such time as a loss is incurred that will be reimbursed under the contract. Instead, the deposit is reported at its amortized amount. Once the loss occurs, the deposit should be remeasured by the present value of expected future cash flows arising from the contract, plus the remaining unexpired portion of the coverage. (ASC 340-30-35-6) Changes in the deposit arising from the present value measure are reported:

- In the insured's income statement as an offset against the loss to be reimbursed
- In the insurer's income statement as an incurred loss

(ASC 340-30-45-3)

The reduction due to amortization of the deposit is reported as an adjustment to incurred losses by the insurer. (ASC 340-30-45-4) The discount rate used to compute the present value is the rate on government obligations with similar cash flow characteristics, adjusted for differences in default risk. The default risk is based on the insurer's credit rating. Rates are determined at the loss date(s) and not revised later, absent further losses.

Insurance Contract That Has Indeterminate Risk For insurance contracts with indeterminate risk, the procedures set forth in ASC 944-605 (the open-year method) should be applied. (ASC 340-40-05-8) This involves the segregation, in the statement of financial position, of amounts that have not been adjusted due to lack of sufficient loss or other data. When sufficient information becomes available, the deposit asset or liability is adjusted and reported as an accounting change per ASC 250.

ASC 340-40, *Contracts with Customers*

Overview The exhibit below gives an overview of how costs associated with contracts with customers are treated in Subtopic ASC 340-40.

Exhibit—Costs Associated with Contracts with Customers—Overview

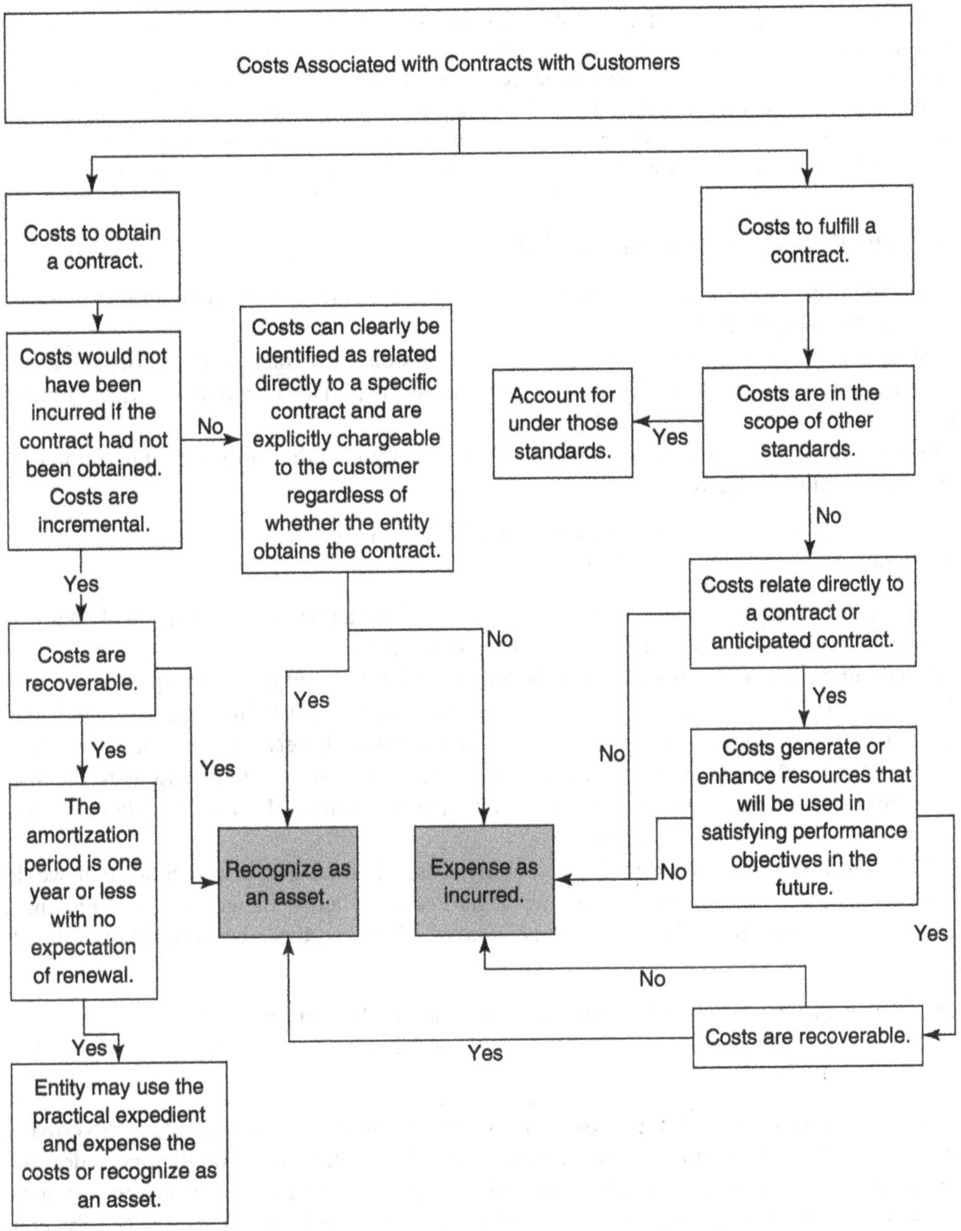

Practice Pointer Applying the guidance on contract costs will likely result in the recognition of more assets than currently. For example, if recoverable, entities will have to capitalize and amortize costs related to sales commissions and start-up costs. Applying the guidance may also require extra effort and changes to internal systems in order to track commissions on contracts. Likewise, entities that capitalize bid costs of trying to obtain a contract will have to analyze whether those costs are incremental to obtaining a contract and generally will have to exclude nonincremental bid costs incurred regardless of whether the contract is obtained. See "Costs That Are Not Incremental" for limited exceptions to this guidance.

Incremental Costs of Obtaining a Contract

Incremental costs are those that an entity would not have incurred if the contract had not been obtained. (ASC 340-40-25-2)

An example of this type of cost is a sales commission. Such incremental costs should be recognized as assets if the entity expects to recover those costs. This is in line with the definition of an asset.[1]

Recoverability Recoverable amounts are an asset, provided the entity's right to reimbursement is unconditional. Recovery may be:

- Direct, through explicit reimbursement under the contract, or
- Indirect through the margin in a contract.

Recoverability of costs is assessed on a contract-by-contract basis or for a group of contracts if the costs in question are associated with a group of contracts.

Determining When Costs Are Incremental Because the capitalization requirements only apply to incremental costs that are incurred to obtain a contract, it is important to understand what is meant by "incremental costs." Entities must distinguish between incremental costs to obtain a contract and other customer-related costs, such as those related to managing a customer relationship or costs incurred to grow sales in an existing contract. Entities and their systems must track these different types of costs.

Costs That Are Not Incremental Generally, costs that are not incremental, that would have been incurred trying to obtain a contract regardless of whether the contract was obtained, for example bid costs, should be expensed as incurred. However, those costs should be capitalized if they:

- Can clearly be identified as related directly to a specific contract, and
- Are explicitly chargeable to the customer regardless of whether a contract is obtained. (ASC 340-40-25-3)

Direct Response Advertising Costs Under legacy standards, direct response advertising costs are capitalized if certain criteria are met. (ASC 340-20-25) ASC 340-40 supersedes that legacy guidance and relocates some of it to industry-specific guidance or insurance contracts. Under ASC 340-40, these costs are not considered incremental and, therefore, are not subject to the capitalization rules and are expensed as incurred.

---

[1] Assets are "probable future economic benefits obtained or controlled by a particular entity as a result of past transactions or events." FASB Statement of Financial Accounting Concepts No. 6, para. 25.

Other Marketing Related Costs Bid, proposal, selling, and marketing costs, including the advertising costs mentioned above, are not incremental. The entity incurs those costs whether or not it obtains the contract.

Fixed salaries for sales personnel, unlike sales commissions mentioned above, are not considered incremental.

Practical Expedient A practical expedient offers relief to entities with short-duration contracts without expectation of renewal. If the amortization period of capitalizable incremental contract costs of obtaining a contract is one year or less, the entity may recognize it as an expense. (ASC 340-40-25-4) When determining the amortization period, the entity should take into account renewals, amendments, and follow-on contracts.

Example—Costs of Obtaining a Contract: Commissions, Bonuses

Mary Mays, a sales representative for InfoTech, sells to MegaCo a one-year subscription to a database information system. Mary earns a 5% commission on the sale. The contract is not expected to be renewed, and InfoTech expects to recover the costs.

The commission is considered an incremental cost to obtain the contract. The commission would not have been incurred if the contract had not been obtained. Because InfoTech expects to recover the cost, under the ASC 340-40, it is allowed to record the commission as an asset and amortize it as revenue is recognized over the year. However, because the amortization period is one year or less and the entity does not expect the contract to be renewed, InfoTech has the option to use the practical expedient and expense the commission as incurred.

Mary's manager also earns a commission on Mary's sales. InfoTech determines that the manager's commission is incremental to obtaining the specific MegaCo contract.

Mary, as a member of the sales team, is also entitled to a bonus based on the "success" of Info-Tech. The bonus is expensed because it is not directly attributable to obtaining a particular contract. Bonuses based on quantitative and qualitative measures, such as profitability, EPS, or performance evaluations, are not directly related to the contract and, therefore, probably do not meet the capitalization criteria.

Example—Costs of Obtaining a Contract: Travel, Due Diligence Costs

Mary incurs travel fees when meeting with the customer. InfoTech does not recognize those fees as assets because they are costs associated with trying to obtain the contract and would have been incurred whether or not the contract was obtained.

Also, in preparation for offering the contract, InfoTech incurs external legal fees related to due diligence. The legal costs are associated with trying to obtain the contracts, and they also would have been incurred even if the contract is not obtained. Therefore, the legal fees are expensed as incurred.

Costs of Fulfilling a Contract

Before transferring goods or services, an entity often incurs costs to fulfill the contract's performance obligations. An entity may also incur such costs in anticipation of obtaining a specifically identified contract. Those costs can be capitalized.

To address how to recognize fulfillment costs, the entity must first determine whether those costs are addressed by other guidance. Cost to fulfill a contract required to be expensed by other standards cannot be capitalized under ASC 340-40. That is, entities should first refer to the out-of-scope guidance listed at the beginning of this chapter and then use ASC 340-40's guidance to determine whether costs need to be capitalized. If the other standards preclude capitalization of a cost, then it cannot be capitalized under ASC 340-40.

Three Criteria for Recognizing Assets for Costs of Fulfilling a Contract Entities are required to recognize assets for costs of fulfilling a contract, if not addressed by other standards, and if all of the following three criteria are met:

1. The costs relate directly to a contract or to an anticipated contract that the entity can specifically identify. An example of this would be costs relating to services to be provided under renewal of an existing contract or costs of designing an asset to be transferred under a specific contract that has not yet been approved.
2. The costs generate or enhance resources of the entity that will be used in satisfying (or in continuing to satisfy) performance obligations in the future.
3. The costs are expected to be recovered. (More information on recoverability can be found earlier in this chapter.)
(ASC 340-10-25-5)

Notice that the criteria above align with the definition of an asset. If all three criteria above are met, the fulfillment costs must be capitalized. They cannot be expensed, and there is no practical expedient.

Categories of Fulfillment Costs Determining which costs should be recognized requires judgment. Some costs are straightforward. Others are not as clear. There may be costs that relate to a contract, but that do not meet the definition of an asset, that is, they do not generate or enhance the resources of the entity or relate to the satisfaction or fulfillment of performance obligations. To help make these distinctions, ASC 340-40 divided contract fulfillment costs into two categories: costs to be capitalized and costs to be expensed as incurred. ASC 340-40 includes specific guidance on each type of contract-related costs. The exhibit below summarizes that guidance and lists both types of contract-related costs—those that should be capitalized and those that should be expensed.

Exhibit—Treatment of Costs of Fulfilling a Contract

Costs Required to Be Capitalized Related Directly to a Contract or Specific Anticipated Contract If Other Criteria Are Met (ASC 340-10-25-7)	Costs Required to Be Expensed as Incurred (ASC 340-10-25-8)
Direct labor (salaries, wages of employees providing services directly to the customer, etc.).	General and administrative costs (unless they are explicitly chargeable to the customers under the contract, in which case an entity shall evaluate those costs in accordance with ASC 340-40-25-7).
Direct materials (for example, supplies used in fulfilling the performance obligations).	Costs of wasted materials, labor, or other resources to fulfill the contract that were not reflected in the price of the contract.
Allocation of costs that relate directly to the contract or to contract activities (for example, costs of contract management and supervision, insurance, and depreciation of tools and equipment used in fulfilling the contract).	Costs that relate to satisfied or partially satisfied performance obligations in the contract (that is, costs that relate to past performance) even if the related revenue has not been recognized.
Costs that are explicitly chargeable to the customer under the contract.	Costs for which an entity cannot distinguish whether the costs relate to unsatisfied performance obligations or to satisfied or partially satisfied performance obligations.
Other costs that are incurred only because an entity entered into the contract (for example, payments to subcontractors).	

Bear in mind that costs must be recoverable in order to be capitalized. (See discussion earlier in this section.)

If a cost cannot be capitalized under other guidance and if an entity cannot determine whether a cost relates to past or future performance, it must be expensed as incurred.

Example—Costs That Create an Asset

Mary May, a sales representative for InfoTech, signed a five-year contract with MegaCo to provide a learning management system (LMS) to train Mega's 100,000 employees. InfoTech expects that Mega will renew the contract for one 5-year period. Mary earns the CU 10,000 sales commission on the deal, which she receives before InfoTech begins work on the contract. Before InfoTech delivers the LMS, it works on the platform that will host the LMS and the technology that will connect the LMS to Mega's employees. InfoTech does not deliver the platform, but it will be used to deliver the training courses to Mega's employees, track results, and provide reports to Mega's human resources team. The costs incurred in setting up the technology and other costs are:

Cost Item	Amount	Recognition
Mary's sales commission	10,000	Recognize an asset under ASC 340-40 because the entity expects to recover the cost.
Consulting with Mega's LMS implementation team to create a statement of work (SOW)	40,000	If the costs meet the three criteria in ASC 340-40 for capitalization, record an asset.
Designing the interface	75,000	If the costs meet the three criteria in ASC 340-40 for capitalization, record an asset.
Hardware	10,000	Account for in accordance with ASC 360, *Property, Plant, and Equipment*, or IAS 16, *Property, Plant and Equipment*.
Software	15,000	Account for in accordance with ASC 350-40, *Intangibles Goodwill and Other Internal-Use Software*, or IAS 38, *Intangible Assets*.
Migration and beta testing the LMS	60,000	Recognize an asset under ASC 340-40 because the costs meet the three criteria for capitalization.
Final deployment of the system	30,000	Recognize an asset under ASC 340-40 because the costs meet the three criteria for capitalization.
Two employees to provide service to MegaCo		The entity concludes that the employees are responsible for providing customer services. However, they do not generate or enhance resources of the entity, therefore, Infotech recognizes payroll expense as incurred.

InfoTech will amortize the assets over a 10-year period, the initial five years plus one five-year renewal period.

Set-Up Costs Some of the costs in the previous example might be considered set-up costs, costs incurred at the beginning of the contract that enable an entity to fulfill a contract. Such costs might include labor, travel, or overhead. If these costs do not fall into the scope of other standards, they should be assessed under ASC 340-40.

Abnormal Costs An entity, like InfoTech in the previous example, may incur learning curve expenses. Such costs are usually anticipated and built into the price of the contract. Those costs should be assessed to see if they meet the criteria for capitalization.

There may be other costs that are not anticipated. These may involve waste, spoiled goods, or unproductive labor costs. These "abnormal costs" should be expensed as incurred.

Amortization of Costs

The costs capitalized in connection with contracts with customers must be amortized. The amortization method selected must result in a systematic basis consistent with the contract's transfer of goods or services to the customer. (ASC 340-10-35-1) For example, if the services are transferred continuously and evenly, then the straight-line method may be appropriate. On the other hand, if, for instance, renewals are anticipated and no additional costs are expected, it may be appropriate for the amortization period to be longer than the initial contract period. Similarly, certain costs, like design costs, may relate to more than one contract and the amortization period could be longer than the term of just one contract. In determining the pattern of transfer, entities should analyze the specific terms of the contract and take into account their experience with the pattern of transfer and the timing of the transfer of control to the customer.

If there is a significant change in the timing of the contract, the entity should update the amortization schedule and account for any change as a change in accounting estimate. (ASC 340-10-35-2)

Example—Costs: Recognition and Amortization

Alarm Systems enters into a contract and installs a security system at Condo Complex. The contract includes five years of monitoring the system for $40 per month. Alarm determines that there is one performance obligation. Alarm incurs $750 to install the system. Alarm recognizes an asset of $750 for installation costs and amortizes it over five years, consistent with the pattern of satisfaction of the performance obligation.

Example—Costs: Amortization—Contract Extension

Use the same set of facts as in the preceding example. In year 3 of the contract, Alarm Systems extends the contract for two years beyond the 5-year initial term. Condo Complex will benefit from the initial set-up costs during the extension period. Alarm Systems amortizes the remaining set-up costs over the now remaining four years of the contract. The costs are adjusted in accordance with other guidance on changes in accounting estimates.

If the extension had been anticipated at the inception of the contract, Alarm Systems would have initially amortized the costs over seven years.

Impairment Loss

Assets must be tested for impairment at the end of each reporting period. Before recognizing an impairment loss related to contract costs, the entity should recognize impairment losses on contract assets in accordance with other guidance, for example:

Sequence of Testing Entities should perform impairment testing in the following order:

- Assets not within the scope of AC 340, ASC 350, or ASC 360 (e.g., investors subject to ASC 330)
- Assets within the scope of ASC 340
- Asset groups and reporting units within the scope of ASC 360 or ASC 350 (ASC 340-40-35-5)

Impairment Unit Entities can make their recoverability assessment contract by contract or for a group of contracts if the costs are associated with a group of contracts. Entities will have to exercise considerable judgment when assessing the amortization pattern for a contract cost asset related to multiple performance obligations that are satisfied over different periods of time.

Objectives of Recoverability Assessment The objective of the recoverability assessment is to consider only the economic benefits in the contract. To do so, the entities must compare the carrying amount with the remaining amount of promised consideration. To calculate an impairment loss for an asset recognized in relation to contracts with customers, an entity uses the formula below.

Exhibit—Calculation of Impairment Loss

Impairment loss	=	Carrying amount of the asset	–	Remaining amount of consideration entity expects to receive	–	Costs that relate directly to providing goods and services and that have not been recognized as expense

(ASC 340-40-35-3)

Practice Pointer The amortization costs may include those related to anticipated contracts that are specifically identifiable. To determine which contracts are specifically identifiable, entities may want to look at past history with similar customers and the market beyond the initial contract term.

The entity should use the principles in ASC 606 for determining the transaction price to determine the amount of consideration. For this purpose, though, the entity should not include the guidance on constraining estimates of variable consideration in ASC 606, but the entity should adjust the amount to reflect the customer's credit risk. When determining the transaction price, ASC 340-40 states than an entity should not anticipate that the contract will be "cancelled, renewed, or modified." However, when determining consideration for impairment purposes, the entity should include contract renewals and extensions. (ASC 340-40-35-4)

An entity should not reverse an impairment loss previously recognized.

Other Sources

See ASC Location—*Wiley GAAP* Chapter	For information on . . .
ASC 340-10-60	
ASC 310-20	Nonrefundable fees and costs associated with lending, committing to lend, or purchasing a group of *loans and for accounting for fees and initial direct costs associated with leasing.*
ASC 350-40	Capitalization of internal and external costs incurred to develop computer software.

See ASC Location—*Wiley GAAP* Chapter	For information on . . .
ASC 410-30	Capitalization of costs incurred to treat asbestos and criteria for environmental contamination treatment costs.
ASC 605-20	Deferral of costs directly related to the acquisition of a contract and costs incurred in anticipation of future construction and certain production-type contract sales.
ASC 720-45	The cost of business process reengineering activities.
ASC 912-20-45	The allocation of general and administrative costs to government contract inventories and cost-reimbursement contracts.
ASC 922-360	The capitalization and subsequent measurement of initial subscriber installation costs.
ASC 928-340	Reporting of an advance royalty to an artist as an asset.
ASC 940-340	Consideration of a membership as an asset by broker dealers and distribution fees by broker dealers.
ASC 940-20	Accounting guidance for underwriting expenses by broker dealers.
ASC 946-20	Accounting for offering costs by investment companies.
ASC 950-350-30	Capitalization guidance for costs incurred to construct a title plant.
ASC 985-20	Accounting for costs of computer software to be sold, leased, or otherwise marketed.

24 ASC 350 INTANGIBLES—GOODWILL AND OTHER

PERSPECTIVE AND ISSUES

Subtopics

ASC 350, *Intangibles—Goodwill and Other*, consists of five subtopics:

- ASC 350-10, *Overall*, which provides an overview of the other subtopics and the overall scope of the topic.
- ASC 350-20, *Goodwill*, which provides guidance on the measurement of goodwill subsequent to acquisition and for the derecognition of goodwill allocated to a reporting unit. It also provides guidance on the accounting alternative for private companies. It also provides presentation and measurement guidance.
- ASC 350-30, *General Intangibles Other Than Goodwill*, which provides guidance on initial accounting and reporting for intangible assets, other than goodwill, acquired individually or with a group of other assets acquired in a transaction that is not a business combination or an acquisition by a not-for-profit entity or are internally generated.
- ASC 350-40, *Internal-Use Software*, which provides guidance on accounting for the costs of software developed or obtained for internal use and hosting arrangements obtained for internal use. ASU 2018-15 adds two Subsections to the Sections in this Subtopic:
    - General and
    - Implementation Costs of a Hosting Arrangement That Is a Service Contract.
- ASC 350-50, *Website Development Costs*, which provides guidance on accounting for costs associated with the development of a website, including costs incurred:
    - In the planning, application development, infrastructure development, and operating stages
    - To develop graphics and content

  (ASC 350-10-05-3)

For guidance on goodwill or intangible assets acquired in a business combination or acquisition by a not-for-profit entity guidance, see ASC 805 or 958-805. (ASC 350-10-05-3A)

Presentation and Disclosure

Presentation and disclosure requirements can be found at www.wiley.com/go/GAAP2021.

Issues

For many entities, especially high-technology, knowledge-based companies, the primary assets are intangible, such as patents and copyrights, and for professional service firms the key assets may be "soft" resources, such as knowledge bases and client relationships. Overall, enterprises for which intangible assets constitute a large and growing component of total assets are a rapidly growing part of the economy.

Intangible assets are defined as both current and noncurrent assets that lack physical substance. Specifically excluded, however, are financial instruments and deferred income tax assets. The value of intangible assets is based on the rights or privileges to which they entitle the reporting entity. Most of the accounting issues associated with intangible assets involve their characteristics, valuation, and amortization. Adequate consideration must be given to the economic substance of the transaction.

According to a recent study, goodwill impairment amounts for public companies doubled in recent years, making it critical for entities to understand the need for and the process of accounting for goodwill and testing it for impairment.[1]

NOTE: For a summary and comparison of accounting and impairment rules for property, plant, and equipment and intangibles, see the "Perspectives and Issues" section of the chapter on ASC 360.

Technical Alert

ASU 2017-04, *Intangibles—Goodwill and Other (Topic 350): Simplifying the Test for Goodwill Impairment* To simplify the accounting for goodwill impairment, in January 2017, the FASB issued ASU 2017-04. The new guidance eliminates the need to determine the fair value of individual assets and liabilities of a reporting unit in order to measure goodwill impairment.

Guidance

Impairment Step 2 eliminated This new guidance simplifies accounting for goodwill impairment by eliminating Step 2 of the current goodwill impairment test. The need to determine the fair value of a reporting unit's assets and liabilities will no longer be needed. Under the new guidance, the existence of impairment and the amount of impairment charges are based on Step 1 in the current guidance. Impairment charges will be based on the excess of a reporting unit's carrying amount over its fair value. The amount of impairment is limited to the reporting unit's goodwill. In addition, entities will no longer be able to recsord a preliminary impairment in the one period and determine the final amount in a later period.

In the table below, assume the following facts:

Fair value of the reporting unit	138
Carrying amount of the reporting unit	150
Fair value of identified assets and liabilities	120
Carrying amount of goodwill	22

	Extant Guidance	ASU 2017-04	Extant Guidance	ASU 2017-04
Step 1	Determine whether the fair value of the reporting unit is less than its carrying amount.		138<150	

[1] http://www.duffandphelps.com/about-us/news/news/duff-phelps-publishes-eighth-annual-us-goodwill-impairment-study/.

	Extant Guidance	ASU 2017-04	Extant Guidance	ASU 2017-04
Step 2	Determine the implied fair value of goodwill: reporting unit's fair value less fair value of assets and liabilities.	Eliminated	138 – 120 = 18	N/A
Impairment amount	Excess of carrying amount less goodwill over the implied fair value	Excess of carrying amount of reporting unit over its fair value.	22 – 18 = 4	150 – 138 = 12

What does not change?

- The timing of goodwill assessments.
- The units of account used in testing.
- Guidance related to completing Step 1.
- Step 0—optional qualitative goodwill assessment.
- Private companies will still have the option to elect the PCC alternative on goodwill.

Tax deductible goodwill In the ASU, FASB tackled another goodwill issue. In some tax jurisdictions goodwill is deductible. In those cases a goodwill impairment charge either increases a deferred tax asset or decreases a tax liability. Such charges result in the reporting units carrying value exceeding its fair value that would require another impairment charge. The new guidance addresses that problem by requiring an entity to calculate the impairment charge and a deferred tax effect using the simultaneous equation method. This method is similar to the measurement of goodwill and related deferred tax assets in a business combination. (ASC 350-20-35-8B)

Reporting units with zero or negative carrying amendment Currently, entities with reporting units with zero or negative carrying amounts must perform a qualitative assessment to determine whether it is necessary to perform the two-step goodwill impairment test. With the deletion of ASC 350-20-35-8A, those entities will not be required to perform the qualitative assessment and will only be expected to pass the simplified impairment test. Entities will be required to identify those units and disclose which reportable segments include those reporting units.

Implementation Entities should apply this update on a prospective basis. This is considered a change in accounting principle, and entities must disclose the nature of and reason for the change in accounting principle upon transition.

Effective Dates[2] The effective dates are as follows:

[2] This section is updated for changes made by ASU 2019-10, *Financial Instruments—Credit Losses (Topic 326), Derivatives and Hedging (Topic 815), and Leases (Topic 842).* The change in effective dates maintains the alignment of the mandatory effective dates of goodwill with those for credit losses.

- For public business entities that are SEC filers, excluding entities eligible to be smaller reporting entities. The one-time determination of whether an entity is eligible to be a smaller reporting company shall be based on an entity's most recent determination as of November 15, 2019.
    - For annual or any interim goodwill impairment tests in fiscal years beginning after December 15, 2019.
- All other entities, including not-for-profit entities
    - For annual or any interim goodwill impairment tests in fiscal years beginning after December 15, 2022.

Early adoption is permitted for interim or annual goodwill impairment tests performed on testing dates after January 1, 2017.

ASU 2018-15, *Intangibles—Goodwill and Other—Internal-Use Software: Subtopic 350-40, Customer's Accounting for Implementation Costs Incurred in a Cloud Computing Arrangement That Is a Service Contract* In August 2018, FASB issued ASU 2018-15. Its goal is to clarify the guidance and align the requirements for customer's accounting for implementation, set-up, and other up-front costs incurred in a cloud computing arrangement (CCA) hosted by the vendor, that is a service contract with those incurred to develop or obtain internal-use software and hosting arrangements that include an internal-use software license. Currently, if a CCA includes a license for internal-use software, then the software license is accounted for under ASC 350-40 and an intangible asset is recognized for the license and a liability is recognized. If a CCA does not include a software license, it is accounted for as a service contract and the fees associated with the hosting element are expensed as incurred. Stakeholders raised questions as to the treatment of costs of implementation activities performed in a CCA that is a service contract.

Guidance The FASB widened the definition of a hosting arrangement to include an arrangement where the customer accesses or uses software but does not take possession of software.

Regarding implementation costs, the ASU requires capitalizing:

- Those costs incurred in a hosted CCA that is a service contract.
- Those costs incurred in developing or obtaining an internal-use software license and hosting arrangements that include an internal-use software license.

The guidance in the latter bullet requires the entity to capitalize or expense costs depending on:

- The nature of the cost and
- The project stage when they occurred.

For further details, see the guidance in the section in this chapter on ASC 350-40 for additional details on capitalizing cost, impairment, and amortization and examples of the accounting treatment of activities during the various project stages.

Implementation The customer in a CCA that is a service contract should follow the internal-use software guidance in ASC 350-40 to determine which costs to capitalize and which costs to expense as incurred. The changes should be applied to all implementation costs incurred after the date of the adoption either:

- Retrospectively or
- Prospectively.

Effective Dates The effective dates are as follows:

- For public business entities that are SEC filers
  - For annual or any interim periods in fiscal years beginning after December 15, 2019.
- All other entities
  - For annual periods in fiscal years beginning after December 15, 2020.
  - For interim periods within annual periods beginning after December 15, 2021.

Early adoption is permitted.

ASC 2019-06, *Intangibles—Goodwill and Other (Topic 350) and Not-for-Profits (Topic 958): Extending the Private Company Accounting Alternatives on Goodwill and Certain Identifiable Assets to Not-for-Profit Entities* In May 2019, the FASB issued ASU 2019-06. This ASU is intended to reduce the cost of accounting for goodwill and for measuring certain identifiable intangible assets for not-for-profit organizations.

Guidance The guidance extends two private company alternatives discussed later in this chapter to not-for-profit entities. Instead of testing goodwill for impairment annually at the reporting unit level, a not-for-profit entity that elects the accounting alternative will be able to:

- Amortize goodwill over ten years or less, on a straight-line basis,
- Test for impairment on a triggering event, and
- Have the option to elect to test for impairment at the entity level.

A not-for-profit entity now has the option to subsume certain customer-related intangible assets and all noncompete agreements into goodwill and subsequently amortize it.

Effective Date The ASU is effective upon issuance.

Implementation If a not-for-profit entity elects the accounting alternative, it should apply the alternative prospectively for existing goodwill and for all new goodwill generated through an acquisition. If the not-for-profit elects the accounting alternative in ASC 805, it should adopt it prospectively upon the occurrence of the first transaction in the scope of the alternative.

Effective Dates The guidance is effective upon issuance.

DEFINITIONS OF TERMS

Source: ASC 350, *Glossary Sections*. See Appendix A, *Definitions of Terms*, for terms relevant to this topic: Acquiree, Acquirer, Acquisition by a Not-for-Profit Entity, Business, Business Combination, Conduit Debt Securities, Contract, Customer, Defensive Intangible Asset, Goodwill, Hosting Arrangement, Intangible Asset Class, Intangible Assets, Leases, Legal Entity, Mutual Entity, Noncontrolling Interest, Nonprofit Activity, Nonpublic Entity, Not-for-Profit Entity, Operating Segment, Preliminary Project State, Private Company, Public Business Entity, Reporting Unit, Residual Value, Securities and Exchange (SEC) Filer, Standalone Price, Useful Life, and Variable Interest Entity.

CONCEPTS, RULES, AND EXAMPLES—ASC 350-10, *OVERALL*

Scope and Scope Exceptions

The guidance in ASC 350 applies to all entities.

All of the subtopics in this topic adopt the following scope limitations of ASC 350-10. The guidance does *not* apply to:

- Accounting at acquisition for goodwill acquired in a business combination (see ASC 805-30) or in an acquisition by a not-for-profit entity (see ASC 958-805).

- Accounting at acquisition for intangible assets other than goodwill acquired in a business combination or in an acquisition by a not-for-profit entity (see ASC 805-20 and ASC 958-805). (ASC 350-10-15-3)

ASC 350-10-15-4 goes on to list Codification locations that are *not* affected by the guidance in ASC 350:

- Research and development costs under Subtopic 730-10
- Extractive activities under Topic 932
- Entertainment and media, including records and music under Topic 928
- Financial services industry under Topic 950
- Entertainment and media, including broadcasters under Topic 920
- Regulatory operations under paragraphs 980-350-35-1 through 35-2
- Software under Topic 985
- Income taxes under Topic 740
- Transfers and servicing under Topic 860

Derecognition. In addition to the Scope section discussed above, ASC 350-10 contains an overview of the other subtopics. It also contains a derecognition section: ASC 350-10-40. The guidance in the derecognition section explains that

- Derecognition of a nonfinancial asset that falls under the scope of ASC 350 should be accounted for under the guidance in ASC 610, unless that asset meets a scope exception in ASC 610. (ASC 350-10-40-1)
- Derecognition of a subsidiary or group of assets that qualifies as a business or not-for-profit activity should be accounted for under the guidance in ASC 810 10. (ASC 350-10- 40-2)

If a nonfinancial asset is transferred under ASC 350-10-40-1 the transfer should meet the requirements in ASC 606-10-25-1. (See the "Five Contract Criteria" section in the chapter on ASC 606.) If the transfer does not meet the requirements, the entity should account for it as follows until it does:

- Continue to report it in the financial statements.
- Report related amortization currently in the income statement.
- Account for impairments according to the guidance in ASC 350-30-35.
(ASC 350-10-40-3)

CONCEPTS, RULES, AND EXAMPLES—ASC 350-20, *GOODWILL*

Scope and Scope Exceptions

All of the ASC 350 subtopics follow the scope guidance in ASC 350-10. In addition, ASC 350-20 applies to:

- Goodwill recognized in a business combination after it has been initially recognized and measured.
- The costs of internally developed goodwill.
- Amounts recognized as goodwill in applying the equity method of accounting and to the excess reorganization value recognized by entities that adopt the fresh-start reporting guidance in ASC 852.
(ASC 350-20-15-2)

The accounting alternative policy election for a private company or not-for-profit entity follows the same scope guidance as above, except it does not apply to the costs of internally developed goodwill. (ASC 350-20-15-4)

Overall

Goodwill is an intangible asset; however, in this subsection "intangible asset" is used to refer to intangible assets other than goodwill. (ASC 350-20-15-3) The guidance in this Section is presented in two Subsections:

a. General and
b. Accounting Alternative.

Goodwill is not considered an identifiable intangible asset, and accordingly, under ASC 350-20, it is accounted for differently from identifiable intangibles. The lack of identifiability is the critical element in the definition of goodwill.

Goodwill is considered to have an indefinite life and, therefore, is not amortized. (See the "Goodwill—Accounting Alternative" section for a different approach to amortization for private companies and not-for-profit entities.) Goodwill is, however, subject to impairment testing. ASU 2017-04 requires impairment testing at the reporting unit level at least annually. (ASC 350-20-35-1) Goodwill is impaired when its *implied* fair value is less than its carrying amount. (AC 350-20-35-2) The fair value of goodwill cannot be measured directly; it can only be "implied," that is, measured as a residual.[3] (Also see the Technical Alert section at the beginning of this chapter for updated information on ASU 2017-04 and tax deductible goodwill.)

Performing the Impairment Test

Step 0 Determine whether it is more likely than not that the fair value of the reporting unit is less than the carrying amount.

To what had been a two-step process, the FASB has inserted what is commonly known as "Step 0." Step 0 gives entities the option of performing a qualitative assessment before performing the extensive calculations of fair value in Step 1. This qualitative assessment is optional and entities may bypass it for any reporting unit in any period and may resume it in any subsequent period. (ASC 350-20-35-3A and 3B)

These are the factors that should be considered in the qualitative assessment:

- Macroeconomic conditions, such as
  - A deterioration in general economic conditions,
  - Limitations on accessing capital,
  - Fluctuations in foreign exchange rates, or
  - Other developments in equity and credit markets

[3] Upon implementation of ASU 2017-04, "implied fair value" in ASC 350-20-35-2 changes to "fair value" and impairment recognition is described as follows: "A goodwill impairment loss is recognized for the amount that the carrying amount of a recording unit, including goodwill, exceeds its fair value, limited to the total amount of goodwill allocated to that reporting unit. However, an entity shall consider the related income tax effect from any tax deductible goodwill, if applicable, in accordance with paragraph 350-20-35-8B."

- Industry and market considerations, such as
    - A deterioration in the environment in the city in which an entity operates,
    - An increased competitive environment,
    - A decline in market-dependent multiples or metrics (consider in both absolute terms and relative to peers),
    - A change in the market for entity's products or services, or
    - A regulatory or political development
- Cost factors, such as increases in raw materials, labor, or other costs that have a negative effect on earnings and cash flows
- Overall financial performance, such as negative or declining cash flows or a decline in actual or planned revenue or earnings compared with actual and projected results of relevant prior periods
- Other relevant entity-specific events, such as changes in management, key personnel, strategy, or customers; contemplation of bankruptcy; or litigation
- Events affecting a reporting unit, such as a change in the composition or carrying amount of its net assets, a more-likely-than-not expectation of selling or disposing all, or a portion, of a reporting unit, or recognition of a goodwill impairment loss in the financial statements of a subsidiary that is a component of a reporting unit
- If applicable, a sustained decrease in share price (consider in both absolute terms and relative to peers).
  (ASC 350-20-35-3C)

These examples are not all-inclusive, and there are other events and circumstances that an entity must consider:

> *. . . an entity shall consider the extent to which each of the adverse events and circumstances identified could affect the comparison of a reporting unit's fair value with its carrying amount. An entity should place more weight on the events and circumstances that most affect a reporting unit's fair value or the carrying amount of its net assets. An entity also should consider positive and mitigating events and circumstances that may affect its determination of whether it is more likely than not that the fair value of a reporting unit is less than its carrying amount. If an entity has a recent fair value calculation for reporting unit, it also should include as a factor in its consideration the difference between the fair value and the carrying amount in reaching its conclusion about whether to perform the first step of the goodwill impairment test.*
> (ASC 350-20-35-3F)

The events and circumstances should be considered in context, and no one event necessarily requires the entity to perform Step 1. (ASC 350-20-35-3G)

If it is *not* more likely than not that the fair value of the reporting unit is less than the carrying amount, further testing is not needed. If it *is* more likely than not that the fair value of the reporting unit is less than the carrying amount, the entity must perform the two-step goodwill impairment test, and the entity proceeds to Step 1. (ASC 350-20-35-3D through 3E)[4]

[4] Upon implementation of ASU 2017-04, "Step 2" is eliminated, but the quantitative test described in "Step 1" is retained. See the Technical Alert on ASU 2017-04 for changes in this step.

Step 1[5] Compare the fair value of the reporting unit as a whole to its carrying amount, including goodwill. (ASC 350-20-35-4)

The following should be considered in determining the reporting unit's fair value:

- If the reporting unit's carrying amount is greater than zero and its fair value exceeds its carrying value, goodwill is not impaired and Step 2 is not required. (ASC 350-20-35-6)
- If the reporting unit has a zero or negative carrying amount, then the entity must proceed to Step 2 if it is more likely than not that a goodwill impairment exists. In making this evaluation, the entity should consider whether there are significant differences between the carrying amount and the estimated fair value of the assets and liabilities, and the existence of significant unrecognized intangible assets. (ASC 350-20-35-6 and 35-8A)
- If the carrying value of the reporting unit exceeds its fair value, the second step of the impairment test is required. (ASC 350-20-35-8)[6]

Note that: For the purpose of goodwill impairment testing, the carrying value of a reporting unit includes deferred income taxes regardless of whether the fair value of the reporting unit will be determined using the assumption it is sold in a taxable or nontaxable transaction. (ASC 350-20-35-7)

Step 2[7] Measure the impairment loss by comparing the implied fair value of reporting unit goodwill with the carrying amount of that goodwill. (ASC 350-20-35-9)[8]

The implied fair value of goodwill is the excess of the fair value of the reporting unit as a whole over the fair values that would be assigned to its assets and liabilities in a purchase business combination. (ASC 350-20-35-2)[9]

Determine whether and by how much goodwill is impaired as follows:

- Estimate the implied fair value of goodwill.
- Compare the implied fair value of goodwill to its carrying amount.
- If the carrying amount of goodwill exceeds its implied fair value, it is impaired and is written down to the implied fair value. The recognized loss cannot exceed the carrying amount of goodwill.

(ASC 350-20-35-9 through 35-11)[10]

[5] Ibid.

[6] Upon implementation of ASU 2017-04, this language changes to: "If the carrying amount of a reporting unit exceeds its fair value, an impairment loss shall be recognized in an amount equal to the excess limited to the total amount of goodwill allocated to that reporting unit. Additionally, an entity shall consider the income tax effect from any tax deductible goodwill or the carrying amount of the reporting unit, if applicable in accordance with paragraph 350-20-35-8B when remeasuring the goodwill impairment loss." (ASC 350-20-35-8)

[7] See the Technical Alert on ASU 2017-04 at the beginning of this chapter. Under the ASU, Step 2 is eliminated.

[8] Upon implementation of ASU 2017-04, this paragraph is superseded.

[9] Upon implementation of ASU 2017-04, "implied fair value" in ASC 350-20-35-2 changes to "fair value."

[10] Upon implementation of ASU 2017-04, these paragraphs are superseded.

Upon recognition of an impairment loss, the adjusted carrying amount of goodwill becomes its new cost basis, and future restoration of the written down amount is prohibited. (ASC 350-20- 35-12 and 35-13)

If the second step of the impairment test is not completed before the financial statements are issued and a loss is probable, the entity should recognize the loss and disclose the fact that it is an estimate. Upon completion of the test, the entity may make an adjustment to that estimated loss in the subsequent period. (ASC 350-20-35-18 and 35-19)[11]

Determining the Implied Fair Value of Goodwill The fair value of a reporting unit is defined in the ASC 350 Glossary as the price that would be received to sell the unit as a whole in an orderly transaction between market participants at the measurement date. The determination of the implied fair value of goodwill is based on the assumption that the fair value of a reporting unit as a whole differs from the fair value of its identifiable net assets. This is the general principle that gives rise to goodwill in the first place. The acquirer assigns additional value to the acquiree based on the acquirer's perceived ability to take advantage of synergies and other benefits that flow from its control over the acquiree. This additional value is evidenced by a purchase price that exceeds the collective fair values of the assets and liabilities to be acquired. (ASC 350-20-35-14 through 35-17)[12]

Deferred Income Taxes For the purpose of computing the implied fair value of a reporting unit's goodwill, assumptions must be made as to the income tax bases of the reporting unit's assets and liabilities in order to compute any relevant deferred income taxes. If the computation of the reporting unit's fair value in Step 1 of the goodwill impairment test assumed that the reporting unit was structured as a taxable transaction, then new income tax bases are used. If not, the existing income tax bases are used. (ASC 350-20-35-20)

Determining the Fair Value of a Reporting Unit

Quoted market prices in active markets are considered the best evidence of fair value of a reporting unit and should be used if available. (ASC 350-20-35-22) However, market capitalization of a publicly traded business unit is computed based on a quoted market price per share that does not consider any advantages that might inure to an acquirer in a situation where control is obtained. For this reason, the market capitalization of a reporting unit with publicly traded stock, may not be representative of its fair value. Presumably, estimating the fair value of a privately held business using earnings multiples derived from publicly traded companies in the same line of business might have the same limitation. (ASC 350-20-35-23)

ASC 350 also prescribes that when a significant portion of a reporting unit is comprised of an acquired entity, the same techniques and assumptions used to determine the purchase price of the acquisition should be used to measure the fair value of the reporting unit unless such techniques and assumptions are not consistent with the objective of measuring fair value. (ASC 350-20-35-24)

If quoted market prices are not available, the estimate of fair value is based on the best information available, including prices for similar assets and liabilities or the results of applying available valuation techniques. Such techniques include expected present value methods, option pricing models, matrix pricing, option-adjusted spread models, and fundamental analysis.

---

[11] Ibid.

[12] Upon implementation of ASU 2017-04, these paragraphs are superseded.

The weight given to evidence gathered in the valuation process must be proportional to the ability to objectively observe it. When an estimate is in the form of a range of either the amount or timing of estimated future cash flows, the likelihood of possible outcomes should be considered (i.e., probability weightings are assigned in order to estimate the most likely outcome).

The measurement techniques and assumptions used to estimate the fair values of the reporting unit's net assets should be consistent with those used to measure the fair value of the reporting unit as a whole. For example, estimates of the amounts and timing of cash flows used to value the significant assets of the reporting unit should be consistent with those assumptions used to estimate such cash flows at the reporting unit level when a cash flow model is used to estimate the reporting unit's fair value as a whole.

For the purposes of determining the fair value of a reporting unit, the relevant facts and circumstances should be carefully evaluated with respect to whether to assume that the reporting unit could be bought or sold in a taxable or nontaxable transaction. (ASC 350-20-35-25) Factors to consider in making the evaluation are:

- The assumptions that marketplace participants would make in estimating fair value
- The feasibility of the assumed structure considering:
  - The ability to sell the reporting unit in a nontaxable transaction, and
  - Any limits on the entity's ability to treat a sale as a nontaxable transaction imposed by income tax laws or regulations, or corporate governance requirements.
- Whether the assumed structure would yield the best economic after-tax return to the (hypothetical) seller for the reporting unit.

(ASC 350-20-35-26 and 35-27)

If a reporting unit is not wholly owned by the reporting entity, the fair value of that reporting unit and the implied fair value of goodwill are determined in the same manner as prescribed by ASC 805.[13] If the reporting unit includes goodwill that is solely attributable to the parent, any impairment loss would be attributed entirely to the parent. If, however, the reporting unit's goodwill is attributable to both the parent and the noncontrolling interest, the impairment loss would need to be allocated to both the parent and the noncontrolling interest in a rational manner. The same logic applies to gain or loss on disposal of all or a portion of a reporting unit. When that reporting unit is disposed of, the gain or loss on disposal is to be attributed to both the parent and to the noncontrolling interest. (ASC 350-20-35-57A and 57B)

Timing of Testing The annual goodwill impairment test may be performed at any time during the fiscal year as long as it is done consistently at the same time each year. Each reporting unit is permitted to establish its own annual testing date. (ASC 350-20-35-28)

ASC 350-20-35-30 indicates that additional impairment tests are required between annual impairment tests if:

1. They are warranted by a change in events and circumstances, *and*
2. It is more likely than not that the fair value of the reporting unit is below its carrying amount.

The factors that indicate impairment testing should be done between annual tests are the same as those that should be considered when performing Step 0. See ASC 350-20-35-3C in the

[13] Upon implementation of ASU 2017-04, this sentence will change to: "If a reporting entity is not wholly owned by the reporting entity, the fair value of the reporting unit as a whole is determined in accordance with the guidance in ASC 350-20-35-22 through 35-24 (see above) including any portion attributed to the noncontrolling interest."

section above on Step 0. (ASC 350-20-35-30) That list is not intended to be all-inclusive. Other indicators may come to the attention of management that would indicate that goodwill impairment testing should be performed between annual tests. Goodwill must also be tested for impairment if a portion of goodwill is allocated to a business to be disposed of.

If goodwill is tested for impairment at the same time as tangible long-lived assets or amortizable intangibles, the other assets are tested/evaluated first and any impairment loss is recognized prior to testing goodwill for impairment. (ASC 350-20-35-31)

Reporting Unit The impairment test for goodwill is performed at the level of the reporting unit. A reporting unit, as detailed in ASC 350-20-35-33 through 46, is an operating segment or one level below an operating segment. In the chapter on ASC 280, the diagram entitled "Alternative Balance Sheet Segmentation" illustrates how different groupings in a business can be characterized as reporting units. The diagram is accompanied by definitions of reporting units, operating segments, and other organizational groupings. The reporting entity may internally refer to reporting units by terms such as business units, operating units, or divisions. The guidance in ASC 280 determines the entity's reporting unit. (ASC 350-20-35-33)

Determination of reporting units is largely dependent on how the business is managed and its structure for reporting and management accountability. An entity may have only one reporting unit, which would, of course, result in the goodwill impairment test being performed at the entity level. This can occur when the entity has acquired a business that it has integrated with its existing business in such a manner that the acquired business is not separately distinguishable as a reporting unit.

On the date an asset is acquired or a liability is assumed, the asset or liability is assigned to a reporting unit if it meets both of the following conditions:

- The asset will be used in or the liability is related to the operations of a reporting unit.
- The asset or liability will be considered in determining the fair value of the reporting unit. (ASC 350-20-35-39)

To perform Step 1 of the impairment test, entities may need to allocate the assets and liabilities of existing businesses and subsidiaries among their reporting units in a reasonable and supportable way. Note that upon implementation of ASU 2017-04, foreign currency translation adjustments should not be allocated from an entity's other comprehensive income to a reporting unit. (ASC 350-20-35-39A)

Provided they meet the criteria above, corporate assets or liabilities that relate to more than one unit should be assigned to the unit. Net assets include assets and liabilities that are recognized as "corporate" items if they, in fact, relate to the operations of the reporting unit. (ASC 350-20-35-40) Examples of corporate items are environmental liabilities associated with land owned by a reporting unit, and pension assets and liabilities attributable to employees of a reporting unit. Executory contracts (e.g., operating leases, contracts for purchase or sale, construction contracts) are considered part of net assets only if the amount reflected in the acquirer's financial statements is based on a fair value measurement subsequent to entering into the contract. To illustrate, if an acquiree had a preexisting operating lease on either favorable or unfavorable terms as compared to its fair value on the date of acquisition, the acquirer would recognize, in its purchase price allocations, an asset or liability for the fair value of the favorable or unfavorable terms, respectively. ASC 350 distinguishes between accounting for this fair value of an otherwise unrecognized executory contract and prepaid rent or rent payable, which generally have carrying values that approximate their fair values.

The methodology used to determine reporting units must be reasonable and supportable and must be applied similarly to how aggregate goodwill is determined in a purchase business combination. (ASC 350-20-35-41 and 35-42)

Example of the Goodwill Impairment Test

Spectral Corporation acquires FarSite Binocular Company for $5,300,000; of this amount, $3,700,000 is assigned to a variety of assets, with the remaining $1,600,000 assigned to goodwill, as noted in the following table:

Purchase price	$ 5,300,000
Accounts receivable	(450,000)
Inventory	(750,000)
Production equipment	(1,000,000)
Acquired formulas and processes	(1,500,000)
= Goodwill	$ 1,600,000

The asset allocation related to acquired formulas and processes is especially critical to the operation, since it refers to the use of a proprietary lens coating system that allows FarSite's binoculars to yield exceptional clarity in low-light conditions. This asset is being depreciated over ten years.

One year after the acquisition date, the FarSite division has recorded annual cash flow of $1,450,000; assuming the same cash flow for the next five years, the present value of the expected cash flows, discounted at the corporate cost of capital of 8%, is roughly $5,789,000. Also, an independent appraisal firm assigns a fair value of $3,600,000 to FarSite's identifiable assets. With this information, the impairment test follows:

FarSite division's fair value	$ 5,789,000
– Fair value of identifiable assets	(3,600,000)
= Implied fair value of goodwill	$ 2,189,000

Though the implied fair value of FarSite's goodwill has increased, Spectral's controller cannot record this increase.

A few months later, Spectral's management learns that a Czech optics company has created a competing optics coating process that is superior to and less expensive than FarSite's process. Since this will likely result in a reduction in FarSite's fair value below its carrying amount, Spectral conducts another impairment test. Management assumes that the forthcoming increase in competition will reduce the expected present value of its cash flows to $3,900,000. In addition, the appraisal firm now reduces its valuation of the acquired formulas and processes asset by $1,200,000. The revised impairment test follows:

FarSite division's fair value	$ 3,900,000
Fair value of identifiable assets	(2,400,000)
= Implied fair value of goodwill	1,500,000
Carrying amount of goodwill	1,600,000
= Impairment loss	$ 100,000

Since the implied fair value of goodwill is $100,000 less than its current carrying amount, Spectral's controller uses the following entry to record reduction in value:

Impairment loss	100,000	
Goodwill		100,000

In addition, Spectral's controller writes down the value of the acquired formulas and processes by the amount recommended by the appraisal firm with the following entry:

Impairment loss	1,200,000	
Accumulated depreciation		1,200,000

A year later, FarSite's research staff discovers an enhancement to its optical coating process that will restore FarSite's competitive position against the Czech firm. However, Spectral's controller cannot increase the carrying cost of the acquired formulas and processes or goodwill to match their newly increased fair value and implied fair value, respectively.

Other Goodwill Considerations Other provisions included in ASC 350 include the following:

- Equity method goodwill continues to be recognized under ASC 323 and is not subject to amortization. This goodwill is not tested for impairment under ASC 350, but rather, is tested under ASC 323. This test considers whether the fair value of the underlying investment has declined and whether that decline is "other than temporary."
- Goodwill of a reporting unit that is fully disposed of is included in the carrying amount of the net assets disposed of in computing the gain or loss on disposal. (ASC 350-20-40-1)
- If a significant portion of a reporting unit is disposed of, the goodwill of that unit is required to be tested for impairment. In performing the impairment test, only the net assets to be retained after the disposal are included in the computation. If, as a result of the test, the carrying amount of goodwill exceeds its implied fair value, the excess carrying amount is allocated to the carrying amount of the net assets disposed of in computing the gain or loss on disposal and, consequently, is not considered an impairment loss. (ASC 350-20-40-2 and 40-3)

Goodwill—Accounting Alternative[14]

Scope Public companies and employee benefit plans within the scope of Topics 960 through 965 on plan accounting are outside the scope of this alternative.

Entities electing this alternative are subject to its related subsequent measurement, derecognition, other presentation, and disclosure requirements. Once an entity elects the alternative, it must apply it to existing goodwill and additional goodwill recognized in the future. (ASC 350- 20-15-5)

Amortization of Goodwill Companies within scope are allowed to amortize goodwill, including equity method goodwill:

- Existing at the beginning of the period of adoption
- Prospectively
- On a straight-line basis over a period of no more than ten years

[14] See the Technical Alerts on ASU 2017-04 and ASU 2019-06 at the beginning of this chapter for important updates on goodwill impairment testing.

A period of less than ten years is allowed if a shorter life is more appropriate. (ASC 350-20-35-63)

Goodwill Impairment

Testing level Entities electing this alternative must make an accounting policy decision to test goodwill for impairment at either the reporting-unit level or the entity level.

Timing of testing Under this alternative impairment model, goodwill should be tested when a triggering event occurs, rather than once a year as required for other entities. A triggering event is one that indicates that the fair value of the reporting unit or the company may be below its carrying value. (ASC 350-20-35-66)

Measurement In addition, for companies electing the alternative, step two of the existing impairment model is eliminated. Once impairment is indicated, no further testing is necessary. The entity measures the amount of goodwill impairment to recognize by determining the fair value of the entity or reporting unit and comparing it to the carrying amount. The impairment loss should not exceed the entity's or reporting unit's carrying amount of goodwill. (ASC 350-20-35-71 through 35-73) Upon implementation of ASU 2017-04, the entity should also consider the income tax effect from any tax deductible goodwill on the carrying amount of the entity or reporting unit when measuring the goodwill impairment loss. Also see the guidance in ASC 350-20-35-73 cited previously. (ASC 350-20-35-73)

Exhibit—Comparison of General Goodwill Impairment Requirements with the Private Company Alternative

General Goodwill Impairment Requirements	Private Company Alternative
Do not amortize goodwill.	Amortize goodwill over 10 years or less on a straight-line basis.
Test for impairment at least annually or more frequently.	Test for impairment upon occurrence of triggering event.
Reporting unit level.	Entity level or reporting unit level.
Two-step test.	One-step test.
Optional qualitative assessment.	Optional qualitative assessment.

CONCEPTS, RULES, AND EXAMPLES—ASC 350-30, *GENERAL INTANGIBLES OTHER THAN GOODWILL*

Scope and Scope Exceptions

All of the ASC 350 subtopics follow the scope guidance in ASC 350-10. In addition, the guidance in ASC 350-30 applies to:

- Intangible assets acquired individually or with a group of other assets
- Intangible assets (other than goodwill) after initial recognition and measurement that an entity recognizes in accordance with the guidance in ASC 805-20 or ASC 985-805
- Internally developed identifiable intangible assets
  (ASC 350-30-15-3)

The guidance does not apply to:

- Capitalized software costs, except as noted above
- Intangible assets recognized for acquired insurance contracts[15]
(ASC 350-30-15-4)

Overall

Intangible assets, other than goodwill, fall into two categories:

1. Those with *finite* useful lives, which are amortized and subject to impairment testing
2. Those with *indefinite* lives, which are not amortized, but are subject to impairment testing

Initial Recognition of Intangible Assets Intangibles acquired individually or with a group of other assets[16] are initially recognized and measured based on their fair values. Fair value, consistent with ASC 820, *Fair Value Measurements,* is determined based on the assumptions that market participants would use in pricing the asset. Even if the reporting entity does not intend to use an intangible asset in a manner that is its highest and best use, the intangible is nevertheless measured at its fair value.

Per 805-20-S99-3, the SEC does not allow an entity to assign a purchase price, rather than fair value, to intangible assets, and then allocate the remainder of the acquisition price to an "indistinguishable" intangible asset.

The aggregate amount assigned to a group of assets acquired in other than a business combination should be allocated to the individual assets acquired based on their relative fair values. Goodwill is prohibited from being recognized in such an asset acquisition. (ASC 350-30-25-2)

Although a reporting entity can purchase intangibles that were developed by others, the Codification has a strict prohibition against capitalizing costs of internally developing, maintaining, or restoring intangibles, including goodwill. (ASC 350-30-25-3) Exceptions to this general rule are software developed for internal use and website development costs. Both are discussed later in this chapter.

Defensive Intangible Assets In connection with a business combination or asset acquisition, management of the acquirer may acquire intangible assets that it does not intend to actively use but, rather, wishes to hold in order to prevent other parties from employing them or obtaining access to them. These intangibles are often referred to as defensive assets, or as "locked-up assets." (ASC 350-30-25-5) Defensive assets exclude intangible assets used in research and development activities, because such assets are subject to different accounting rules under ASC 730-10-25-2c.

To qualify as a defensive intangible asset, the asset must be either:

- Acquired with the intent to not use it, *or*
- Used by the acquirer with the intent to discontinue its use after completion of a transition period.
(ASC 350-30-55-1)

---

15 Upon implementation of ASU 2018-12 for financial statements issued after December 15, 2020 (public entities) and December 15, 2021 (nonpublic entities), this bullet adds: "Disclosures required by ASC 946-805-50-1."

16 See discussion in the chapter on ASC 805, *Business Combinations.*

Upon being characterized as a defensive intangible, the asset is precluded from being considered abandoned upon acquisition, regardless of the fact that it is not being used.

Subsequent to the asset being characterized as a defensive intangible, management may decide to actively employ the asset. If so, it would cease to be considered a defensive intangible asset. (ASC 350-30-55-1B)

At acquisition, defensive intangibles are subject to the same fair value valuation principles as any other acquired intangible asset, including that they be measured considering exit price to marketplace participants that would put them to their highest and best use. In making the measurement, defensive intangibles are accounted for as a separate unit of accounting and are not grouped with other intangibles.

It would be rare for defensive intangible assets to have an indefinite life, since lack of market exposure and competitive and other factors contribute to diminish the fair value of these assets over time. (ASC 350-30-35-5B)

Defensive intangible assets should, in theory, be assigned a useful life representing how (and for how long) the entity expects to consume the expected benefits related to them in the form of direct and indirect cash flows that would result from the prevention of others from realizing any value from them. In practice, however, such estimates would be difficult to make and highly subjective; consequently, the Codification contains what is believed to be a more workable determination of useful life based on management's estimate of the period over which the defensive intangible asset diminishes in fair value. (ASC 350-30-35-5A)

Determining the Useful of Life of Intangible Assets An income approach is commonly used to measure the fair value of an intangible asset. The period of expected cash flows used to measure fair value of the intangible, adjusted for applicable entity-specific factors should be considered by management in determining the useful life of the intangible for amortization purposes.

Under ASC 350-30-35-3, in estimating the useful life of an intangible asset, the reporting entity should consider:

- The entity's expected use of the asset.
- The expected useful life of another asset or asset group to which the useful life of the intangible asset may be related.
- Any provisions contained in applicable law, regulation, or contract that may limit the useful life.
- The entity's own historical experience in renewing or extending similar arrangements if such experience is consistent with the intended use of the intangible asset by the reporting entity, irrespective of whether those similar arrangements contained explicit renewal or extension provisions. In the absence of such historical experience, management should consider the assumptions that market participants would use about the renewal or extension consistent with their highest and best use of the asset, and adjusted for relevant entity-specific factors.
- The effects of obsolescence, demand, competition, and other economic factors such as:
  - Stability of the industry,
  - Known technological advances,
  - Legislative action that results in an uncertain or changing regulatory environment, and
  - Expected changes in distribution channels.
- The level of maintenance expenditures that would be required to obtain the expected future cash flows from the asset.

If no legal, regulatory, contractual, competitive, economic, or other factors limit the useful life of an intangible asset to the reporting entity, the useful life of the asset is considered to be indefinite (which, of course, is not the same as unlimited or infinite). (ASC 350-30-35-4)

Amortization of Intangible Assets Identifiable intangible assets, such as franchise rights, customer lists, trademarks, patents and copyrights, and licenses should be amortized over their expected useful economic life with required impairment reviews of their recoverability when necessitated by changes in facts and circumstances in the same manner as set forth in ASC 360 for tangible long-lived assets.

Residual value ASC 350-30-35-8 also requires consideration of the intangible's residual value (analogous to salvage value for a tangible asset) in determining the amount of the intangible to amortize. Residual value is defined as the value of the intangible to the entity at the end of its (entity-specific) useful life reduced by any estimated disposition costs. The residual value of an amortizable intangible is assumed to be zero unless the intangible will continue to have a useful life to another party after the end of its useful life to its current holder, and one or both of the following criteria are met:

- The current holder has received a third-party commitment to purchase the intangible at the end of its useful life, *or*
- A market for the intangible exists and is expected to continue to exist at the end of the asset's useful life as a means of determining the residual value of the intangible by reference to marketplace transactions.

The entity should evaluate the residual value each reporting period. (ASC 350-30-35-9)

Intangible Assets Subject to Amortization and Impairment Considerations Many intangible assets are based on rights that are conveyed legally by contract, statute, or similar means. For example, governments grant franchises or similar rights to taxi companies, cable companies, and hydroelectric plants; and companies and other private-sector organizations grant franchises to automobile dealers, fast-food outlets, and professional sports teams. Other rights, such as airport landing rights, are granted by contract. Some of those franchises or similar rights are for finite terms, while others are perpetual. Many of those with finite terms are routinely renewed, absent violations of the terms of the agreement, and the costs incurred for renewal are minimal. Many such assets are also transferable, and the prices at which they trade reflect expectations of renewal at minimal cost. However, for others, renewal is not assured, and their renewal may entail substantial cost.

Trademarks, service marks, and trade names may be registered with the government for a period of twenty years and are renewable for additional twenty-year periods as long as the trademark, service mark, or trade name is used continuously. (Brand names, often used synonymously with trademarks, are typically not registered and thus the required attribute of control will be absent.) The U.S. government now grants copyrights for the life of the creator plus fifty years. Patents are granted by the government for a period of seventeen years but may be effectively renewed by adding minor modifications that are patented for additional seventeen-year periods. Such assets also are commonly transferable.

A broadcast license, while nominally subject to expiration in five years, might be indefinitely renewable at little additional cost to the broadcaster. If cash flows can be projected indefinitely, and assuming a market exists for the license, no amortization should be recorded until such time as a finite life is predicted. However, impairment must be tested at least annually to ensure that the asset is carried at no more than its fair value. (ASC 350-30-55-12)

The foregoing examples all addressed identifiable intangibles, which are recognized in the financial statements when purchased separately or in connection with a business combination. There are other intangibles, which are deemed to not be identifiable because they cannot be reliably measured. Technological know-how and an assembled workforce are examples of such intangible assets. Intangibles that cannot be separately identified are considered integral components of goodwill.

Indefinite-Lived Intangible Assets—Not Subject to Amortization Identifiable intangible assets having indefinite useful economic lives supported by clearly identifiable cash flows are not subject to regular periodic amortization. (ASC 350-30-35-15) Instead, the carrying amount of the intangible asset is tested for impairment annually, and again between annual tests if events or circumstances warrant such a test. (ASC 350-30-35-18) An impairment loss is recognized if the carrying amount exceeds the fair value. Furthermore, amortization of the asset commences when evidence suggests that its useful economic life is no longer deemed indefinite. (ASC 350-30-35-18A)

Testing for impairment of indefinite-lived intangible assets The Codification gives entities the option to first assess qualitatively whether it is more likely than not (more than 50 percent) that the asset is impaired. The qualitative assessment test can be performed on some or all of the assets, or the entity can bypass the qualitative test and perform the quantitative test.

If it is not more likely than not that the asset is impaired, the entity does not have to calculate the fair value of the intangible asset and perform the quantitative impairment test. If it is more likely than not that the asset is impaired, the entity must perform the quantitative impairment test and calculate the fair value of an indefinite-lived intangible asset.

If performing the qualitative assessment, the entity needs to identify and consider those events and circumstances that, individually or in the aggregate, most significantly affect an indefinite-lived intangible asset's fair value. Examples of events and circumstances that should be considered include those listed in ASC 350-30-35-18B:

- Cost factors such as increases in raw materials, labor, or other costs that have a negative effect on future expected earnings and cash flows that could affect significant inputs used to determine the fair value of the indefinite-lived intangible asset
- Financial performance such as negative or declining cash flows or a decline in actual or planned revenue or earnings compared with actual and projected results of relevant prior periods that could affect significant inputs used to determine the fair value of the indefinite-lived intangible asset
- Legal, regulatory, contractual, political, business, or other factors, including asset- specific factors that could affect significant inputs used to determine the fair value of the indefinite-lived intangible asset
- Other relevant entity-specific events such as changes in management, key personnel, strategy, or customers; contemplation of bankruptcy; or litigation that could affect significant inputs used to determine the fair value of the indefinite-lived intangible asset
- Industry and market considerations such as a deterioration in the environment in which an entity operates, an increased competitive environment, a decline in market-dependent multiples or metrics (in both absolute terms and relative to peers), or a change in the market for an entity's products or services due to the effects of obsolescence, demand, competition, or other economic factors (such as the stability of the industry, known technological advances, legislative action that results in an uncertain or changing business environment, and expected changes in distribution channels) that could affect significant inputs used to determine the fair value of the indefinite-lived intangible asset

- Macroeconomic conditions such as deterioration in general economic conditions, limitations on accessing capital, fluctuations in foreign exchange rates, or other developments in equity and credit markets that could affect significant inputs used to determine the fair value of the indefinite-lived intangible asset

Any positive and mitigating events and circumstances should also be considered, as well as the difference between the fair value in a recent calculation of an indefinite-lived intangible asset and the then carrying amount, whether there have been changes to the carrying amount of the indefinite-lived intangible asset. (ASC 350-30-35-18C)

Determining the unit of accounting The Codification provides guidance about when it is appropriate to combine into a single "unit of accounting," for impairment testing purposes, separately recorded indefinite-life intangibles, whether acquired or internally developed.

The assets may be combined into a single unit of accounting for impairment testing if they are operated as a single asset and, therefore, are inseparable from one another. The following indicators should help the entity use its judgment when evaluating the individual facts and circumstances and determining whether indefinite-lived intangibles should be combined as a single unit of accounting. (ASC 350-30-35-21 and 35-23):

- The intangibles will be used together to construct or enhance a single asset.
- If the intangibles had been part of the same acquisition, they would have been recorded as a single asset.
- The intangibles, as a group, represent "the highest and best use of the assets" (e.g., they could probably realize a higher sales price if sold together than if they were sold separately). Indicators pointing to this situation are:
  - The unlikelihood that a substantial portion of the assets would be sold separately, or
  - The fact that, should a substantial portion of the intangibles be sold individually, there would be a significant reduction in the fair value of the remaining assets in the group.
- The marketing or branding strategy of the entity treats the assets as being complementary (e.g., a trademark and its related trade name, formulas, recipes, and patented or unpatented technology can all be complementary to an entity's brand name).

The following are indicators that indefinite-lived intangibles are *not* to be combined as a single unit of accounting. (ASC 350-30-35-24):

- Each separate intangible generates independent cash flows.
- In a sale, it would be likely that the intangibles would be sold separately. If the entity had previously sold similar assets separately, this would constitute evidence that combining the assets would not be appropriate.
- The entity is either considering or has already adopted a plan to dispose of one or more of the intangibles separately.
- The intangibles are used exclusively by different asset groups. (See Appendix A.)
- The intangibles have differing useful economic lives.

ASC 350-30-35-26 provides guidance regarding the "unit of accounting" determination.

1. Goodwill and finite-lived intangibles are not permitted to be combined in the "unit of accounting" since they are subject to different impairment rules.
2. If the intangibles collectively constitute a business, they may not be combined into a unit of accounting.

3. If the unit of accounting includes intangibles recorded in the separate financial statements of consolidated subsidiaries, it is possible that the sum of impairment losses recognized in the separate financial statements of the subsidiaries will not equal the consolidated impairment loss.
4. If a unit of accounting is included in a single reporting unit, that same unit of accounting and associated fair value should be used in computing the implied fair value of goodwill for measuring any goodwill impairment loss.[17]

NOTE: Although counterintuitive, the situation in number 4 (above) can occur when:

---

1. At the separate subsidiary level, an intangible asset is impaired since the cash flows from the other intangibles included in the unit of accounting that reside in other subsidiaries cannot be considered in determining impairment, and
2. At the consolidated level, when the intangibles are considered as a single unit of accounting, they are not impaired.

Quantitative Impairment Test for Indefinite-Lived Intangible Asset This test consists simply of comparing the fair value of the asset with its carrying amount. (ASC 350-30-35-19)

CONCEPTS, RULES, AND EXAMPLES—ASC 350-40, *INTERNAL-USE SOFTWARE*

Overview

ASC 350-40 offers guidance on whether the costs of computer software developed for internal use can be capitalized. ASC 350-40 also provides guidance on cloud computing arrangements (CCAs). The Subtopic provides guidance clarifying whether costs relating to CCAs can be capitalized or whether they should be treated as service contracts. ASU 2018-15 requires a customer in a CCA that is a service contract to capitalize implementation costs as though the CCA was an internal-use project.

It is important to note that some costs of internal-use computer software are research and development costs and treated under ASC 730-10. These include:

- Purchased or leased software used in research and development when the software has no alternate use.
- Internally developed internal-use software where:
  - The software is a pilot project or
  - The software is used for a particular research and development project whether or not it has alternate uses.

  (ASC 350-40-15-2)

The Codification provides guidance in ASC 985-20 on the accounting treatment for software to be sold, leased, or otherwise marketed as a separate product or as part of a product or

[17] Upon implementation of ASU 2017-04, bullet number 4 is deleted.

process whether internally developed and produced or purchased. (ASC 350-40-15-5 and ASC 985-20-05-1)

Scope—General Subsections[18]

All of the ASC 350 subtopics follow the scope guidance in ASC 350-10. (ASC 350-10-15-1) In addition, the General Subsections in ASC 350-40 apply to:

- Internal-use software
- The proceeds of computer software developed or obtained for internal use that is marketed
- New internal-use software that replaces previously existing internal-use software
- Computer software that consists of more than one component or module
  (ASC 350-40-15-2)

Software must meet two criteria to be accounted for as internal-use software:

1. The software is acquired, internally developed, or modified *solely* to meet the reporting entity's *internal* needs.
2. During the period in which the software is being developed or modified, there can be *no plan or intent to market* the software externally.
   (ASC 350-40-15-2A)

The guidance in this Subtopic does *not* apply to:

- Software to be sold, leased, or otherwise marketed as a separate product or as part of a product or process, subject to Subtopic 985-20
- Software to be used in research and development, subject to Subtopic 730-10
- Software developed for others under a contractual arrangement, subject to contract accounting standards
- Accounting for costs of reengineering activities, which often are associated with new or upgraded software applications
- Software that a customer obtains access to in a hosting arrangement that does not meet the criteria in paragraph 350-40-15-4A (Upon implementation of ASU 2018-15, this bullet is superseded.)
  (ASC 350-40-15-4)

The guidance in the General Subsections of this Topic applies to internal-use software that a customer obtains access to in a hosting arrangement only if *both* of the following criteria are met:

1. The customer has the contractual right to take possession of the software at any time during the hosting period without significant penalty. Indicators that there is not significant penalty would be the ability to:
   a. Take delivery of the underlying software without significant cost.
   b. Use that software separately without a significant reduction in the value. (ASC 350-40-15-4B)
2. It is feasible for the customer to either run the software on its own hardware or contract with another party unrelated to the vendor to host the software.
   (ASC 350-40-15-4A)

[18] Upon implementation of ASU 2018-15, these Sections are divided into two Subsections: General and Implementation Costs of a Hosting Arrangement That Is a Service Contract.

If both those provisions are *not* met, the hosting arrangement is treated as service contract, and separate accounting for a license is not permitted. (ASC 350-40-15-4C)

Upon implementation of ASU 2018-15, if implementation costs of a hosting arrangement do *not* meet the criteria above, they should be accounted for under the provisions for implementation costs of a hosting arrangement that is a service contract. (ASC 350-40-15-4D)

Examples of computer software developed for internal use The Codification provides examples of when computer software is acquired or developed for internal use. The following is a list of examples illustrating when computer software is developed for internal use:

- A manufacturing entity purchases robots and customizes the software that the robots use to function. The robots are used in a manufacturing process that results in finished goods.
- An entity develops software that helps it improve its cash management, which may allow the entity to earn more revenue.
- An entity purchases or develops software to process payroll, accounts payable, and accounts receivable.
- An entity purchases software related to the installation of an online system used to keep membership data.
- A travel agency purchases a software system to price vacation packages and obtain airfares.
- A bank develops software that allows a customer to withdraw cash, inquire about balances, make loan payments, and execute wire transfers.
- A mortgage loan servicing entity develops or purchases computer software to enhance the speed of services provided to customers.
- A telecommunications entity develops software to run its switches that are necessary for various telephone services such as voice mail and call forwarding.
- An entity is in the process of developing the accounts receivable system. The software specifications meet the entity's internal needs and the entity did not have a marketing plan before or during the development of the software. In addition, the entity has not sold any of its internal-use software in the past. Two years after completion of the project, the entity decided to market the product to recoup some or all of its costs.
- A broker-dealer entity develops a software database and charges for financial information distributed through the database.
- An entity develops software to be used to create components of music videos (for example, the software used to blend and change the faces of models in music videos). The entity then sells the final music videos, which do not contain the software, to another entity.
- An entity purchases software to computerize a manual catalog and then sells the manual catalog to the public.
- A law firm develops an intranet research tool that allows firm members to locate and search the firm's databases for information relevant to their cases. The system provides users with the ability to print cases, search for related topics, and annotate their personal copies of the database.
(ASC 350-40-55-1)

ASC 350-40-55-2 contains these and other examples of software that does *not* qualify as being developed for internal use includes:

- Software sold by a robot manufacturer to purchasers of its products;
- The cost of developing programs for microchips used in automobile electronic systems;
- Software developed for both sale to customers and internal use;

- Computer programs written for use in research and development efforts; and
- Costs of developing software under contract with another entity.

Scope—Implementation Costs of a Hosting Arrangement That Is a Service Contract[19] These subsections follow the General Subsections scope and guidance with the qualification that follows. (ASC 350-40-15-8) The implementation Section provides guidance on when to capitalize costs incurred to implement a hosting arrangement.

Exhibit—Software License in a Hosting Arrangement (ASC 350-40-15-4A and 15-4C)

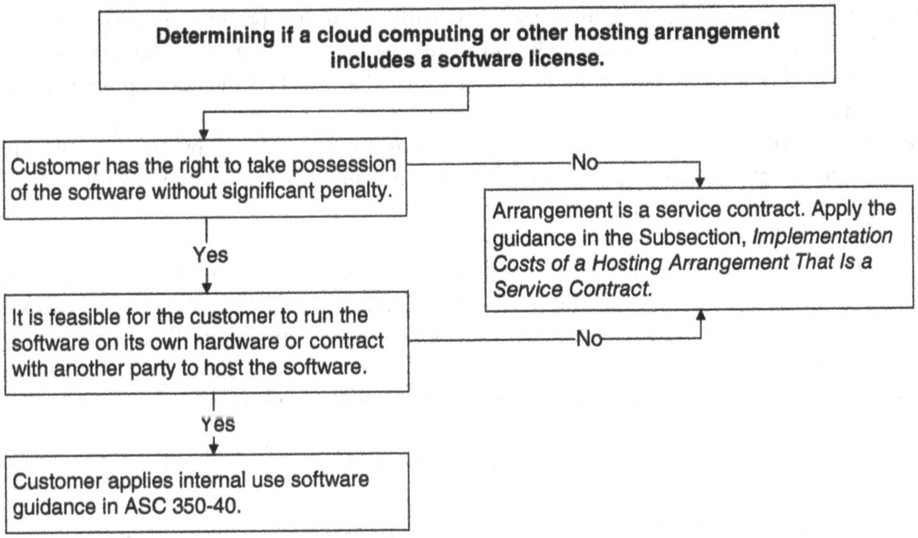

Customer's Accounting for Fees Paid in a Cloud Computing Arrangement In cloud computing arrangements, the customer never takes possession of a physical product. Instead, the software resides on a vendor's or third party's hosting site, which the customer accesses remotely. Customers will essentially use the same criteria as vendors in determining whether the arrangement contains a software license or is solely a service contract. See paragraphs ASC 350-40-15-4A throuh15-4C in the "Scope" section at the beginning of this section.

Recognition and Measurement: General Subsection and Implementation Costs of a Hosting Arrangement That Is a Service Contract Subsection

Cost Recognition—General Subsection[20] To justify capitalization of related costs, it is necessary for management to conclude that it is probable that the project will be completed and that the software will be used as intended. Absent that level of expectation, costs must be expensed currently as research and development costs. Entities that engage in both research and development of software for internal use and for sale to others must carefully identify costs with

[19] This Subsection is effective upon implementation of ASU 2018-15.

[20] Upon implementation of ASU 2018-15 the General Subsection should be applied as though a hosting arrangement that meets the qualifications for a service contract were an internal-use computer software project. (ASC 350-40-25-18 and 30-5)

one or the other activity, since the former is (if all conditions are met) subject to capitalization, while the latter is expensed as research and development costs until technological feasibility is demonstrated, per ASC 985-20.

Software projects can be divided into three phases:

- Preliminary Project Stage
- Application Development Stage
- Post Implementation-Operation Stage

Cost capitalization commences when an entity has completed the conceptual formulation, design, and testing of possible project alternatives, including the process of vendor selection for purchased software, if any. These early-phase costs (referred to as "preliminary project stage" in ASC 350-40) are analogous to research and development costs and must be expensed as incurred. (ASC 350-40-25-1) These cannot be later restored as assets if the development proves to be successful.

Preliminary project stage Internal and external costs are expensed as incurred during this stage. (ASC 350-40-25-1) When a computer software project is in the preliminary project stage, entities will likely do the following:

- Make strategic decisions to allocate resources between alternative projects at a given point in time. For example, should programmers develop a new payroll system or direct their efforts toward correcting existing problems in an operating payroll system?
- Determine the performance requirements (that is, what it is that they need the software to do) and systems requirements for the computer software project it has proposed to undertake.
- Invite vendors to perform demonstrations of how their software will fulfill an entity's needs.
- Explore alternative means of achieving specified performance requirements. For example, should an entity make or buy the software? Should the software run on a mainframe or a client server system?
- Determine that the technology needed to achieve performance requirements exists.
- Select a vendor if an entity chooses to obtain software.
- Select a consultant to assist in the development or installation of the software. (ASC 350-40-20)

Application development stage Certain qualifying costs, both internal and external, incurred during this stage of development of internal-use software are capitalized. (ASC 350-40-25-2)

Capitalization of costs begins when both conditions in ASC 350-40-25-12 are met:

- The conceptual formulation, design, and testing of possible software project alternatives (i.e., the preliminary project stage) have all been completed.
- Management having the relevant authority authorizes and commits to funding the project and believes that it is probable that it will be completed and that the resulting software will be used as intended.

ASC 350-40-30-1 limits capitalizable costs to:

- External direct costs of materials and services consumed in developing or obtaining internal-use computer software:
    - Fees paid to third parties for services provided to develop the software during the application development stage.
    - Costs incurred to obtain computer software from third parties.
    - Travel expenses incurred by employees for work directly associated with developing software.
- Costs of compensation and benefits for employees who are directly associated with and who devote time to the internal-use computer software project to the extent of the time spent directly on the project; and
- Interest cost incurred while developing internal-use computer software, consistent with the provisions of ASC 835-20.

Entities need to maintain records that support the capitalization of qualifying costs.

Post implementation-operation stage Internal and external training costs and maintenance incurred during this stage are expensed. (ASC 350-40-25-6)

Entities should expense as incurred the following types of indirect costs during the application development stage

- Training costs
- Data conversion costs, except for costs to develop or obtain software allowing for access or conversion of old data by new systems
- General and administrative costs
- Overhead costs

License from a third party If an entity licenses internal-use software from a third party and the license is in the scope of ASC 350-40, the license is accounted for as an intangible asset and a liability to the extent that all or a portion of the licensing fees are not paid on or before the acquisition date. (ASC 350-40-25-17) The asset is recognized and measured at cost. Cost includes the present value of the license obligation if the license is paid over time.

Costs expensed General and administrative costs, overhead costs, and training costs are expensed as incurred. (ASC 350-40-30-3) Even though these may be costs associated with the internal development or acquisition of software for internal use, under the Codification those costs relate to the period in which they are incurred. The issue of training costs is particularly important, since internal-use computer software purchased from third parties often includes, as part of the purchase price, training for the software (and often fees for routine maintenance as well). When the amount of training or maintenance fees is not specified in the contract, entities are required to allocate the cost among training, maintenance, and amounts representing the capitalizable cost of computer software. Training costs are recognized as expense as incurred. (ASC 350-40-25-4) Maintenance fees are recognized as expense ratably over the maintenance period.

Multiple-Element Arrangements Entities may enter into a CCA where the customer pays the vendor or another third party to provide services, such as training employees to use the software, maintenance, data conversion, reengineering of hardware and business processes, and rights to future upgrades and enhancements. Current guidance requires these costs to be allocated on objective evidence of the fair value of the elements of the contract. ASU 2018-15 changes this and upon implementation, these costs must be allocated to each element based on the relevant standalone price of the contract for each element. (ASC 350-40-30-4)

Subsequent Measurement—General Subsection

Impairment—General Subsection Impairment of capitalized internal-use software is recognized and measured in accordance with the provisions of ASC 360 in the same manner as tangible long-lived assets and other amortizable intangible assets. Circumstances that might suggest that an impairment has occurred and that would trigger a recoverability evaluation include:

- A realization that the internal-use computer software is not expected to provide substantive service potential;
- A significant change in the extent or manner in which the software is used;
- A significant change has been made or is being anticipated to the software program; or
- The costs of developing or modifying the internal-use computer software significantly exceed the amount originally expected. These conditions are analogous to those generically set forth by ASC 360, *Property, Plant, and Equipment*.
(ASC 350-40-35-1)

In some instances, ongoing software development projects will become troubled before being discontinued. ASC 350-40 indicates that management needs to assess the likelihood of successful completion of projects in progress. When it becomes no longer probable that the computer software being developed will be completed and placed in service, the asset is written down to the lower of the carrying amount or fair value less costs to sell. (ASC 350- 40-35-3) Importantly, it is a rebuttable presumption that any uncompleted software has a zero fair value.

Indicators that the software is no longer expected to be completed and placed in service include:

- A lack of expenditures budgeted or incurred for the project;
- Programming difficulties that cannot be resolved on a timely basis;
- Significant cost overruns;
- Information indicating that the costs of internally developed software will significantly exceed the cost of comparable third-party software or software products, suggesting that management intends to obtain the third-party software instead of completing the internal development effort;
- The introduction of new technologies that increase the likelihood that management will elect to obtain third-party software instead of completing the internal project; and
- A lack of profitability of the business segment or unit to which the software relates or actual or potential discontinuation of the segment.
(ASC 350-40-35-3)

Amortization—General Subsection As with other long-lived assets, the cost of computer software developed or obtained for internal use should be amortized on a straight-line basis unless another systematic and rational manner better represents its use. (ASC 350-40-35-4) The intangible nature of the asset contributes to the difficulty of developing a meaningful estimate, however. Among the factors to be weighed are the effects of obsolescence, new technology, and competition. The entity especially needs to consider if rapid changes are occurring in the development of software products, software operating systems, or computer hardware, and whether it intends to replace any technologically obsolete software or hardware. (ASC 350-40-35-5)

Amortization commences for each module or component of a software project when the software is ready for its intended use, without regard to whether the software is to be placed in service in planned stages that might extend beyond a single reporting period. Computer software is deemed ready for its intended use after substantially all testing has been completed. (ASC 350-40-35-6)

Internal-Use Software Subsequently Marketed In some cases internal-use software is later sold or licensed to third parties, notwithstanding the original intention of management that the software was acquired or developed solely for internal use. In such cases, any proceeds received are to be applied first as a reduction of the carrying amount of the software. (ASC 350-40-35-7) No profit is recognized until the aggregate net proceeds from licenses and amortization have reduced the carrying amount of the software to zero. After the carrying value is fully recovered, any subsequent proceeds are recognized as revenue or gain, depending on whether the contract is with a customer. (ASC 350-40-35-8)

If during the development, management decides to market internal-use software, the entity should follow the guidance in ASC 985-20. (ASC 350-40-35-9)

Example of Software Developed for Internal Use

The Da Vinci Invention Company employs researchers based in countries around the world. The far-flung nature of its operations makes it extremely difficult for the payroll staff to collect timesheets, so the management team authorizes the design of an in-house, web-based timekeeping system. The project team incurs the following costs:

Cost type	Charged to expense	Capitalized
Concept design	$ 2,500	
Evaluation of design alternatives	3,700	
Determination of required technology	8,100	
Final selection of alternatives	1,400	
Software design		$ 28,000
Software coding		42,000
Quality assurance testing		30,000
Data conversion costs	3,900	
Training	14,000	
Overhead allocation	6,900	
General and administrative costs	11,200	
Ongoing maintenance costs	6,000	
Totals	$57,700	$100,000

Thus, the total capitalized cost of this development project is $100,000. The estimated useful life of the timekeeping system is five years. As soon as all testing is completed, Da Vinci's controller begins amortizing using a monthly charge of $1,666.67. The calculation follows:

$$\$100{,}000 \text{ capitalized cost} \div 60 \text{ months} = \$1{,}666.67 \text{ amortization charge}$$

Once operational, management elects to construct another module for the system that issues an e-mail reminder for employees to complete their timesheets. This represents significant added functionality, so the design cost can be capitalized. The following costs are incurred:

Labor type	Labor cost	Payroll taxes	Benefits	Total cost
Software developers	$11,000	$ 842	$1,870	$13,712
Quality assurance testers	7,000	536	1,190	8,726
Totals	$18,000	$1,378	$3,060	$22,438

The full $22,438 amount of these costs can be capitalized. By the time this additional work is completed, the original system has been in operation for one year, thereby reducing the amortization period for the new module to four years. The calculation of the monthly straight-line amortization follows:

$$\$22{,}438 \text{ capitalized cost} \div 48 \text{ months} = \$467:46 \text{ amortization charge}$$

The Da Vinci management then authorizes the development of an additional module that allows employees to enter time data into the system from their cell phones using text messaging. Despite successfully passing through the concept design stage, the development team cannot resolve interface problems on a timely basis. Management elects to shut down the development project, requiring the charge of all $13,000 of programming and testing costs to expense in the current period.

After the system has been operating for two years, a Da Vinci customer sees the timekeeping system in action and begs management to sell it as a stand-alone product. The customer becomes a distributor, and lands three sales in the first year. From these sales Da Vinci receives revenues of $57,000, and incurs the following related expenses:

Expense type	Amount
Distributor commission (25%)	$14,250
Service costs	1,900
Installation costs	4,300
Total	$20,450

Thus, the net proceeds from the software sale are $36,550 ($57,000 revenue less $20,450 related costs). Rather than recording these transactions as revenue and expense, the $36,550 net proceeds are offset against the remaining unamortized balance of the software asset with the following entry:

Revenue	$57,000	
Fixed assets—software		$36,550
Commission expense		14,250
Service expense		1,900
Installation expense		4,300

At this point, the remaining unamortized balance of the timekeeping system is $40,278, which is calculated as follows:

Original capitalized amount	$100,000
+ Additional software module	22,438
24 months' amortization on original capitalized amount	(40,000)
12 months' amortization on additional software module	(5,610)
Net proceeds from software sales	(36,550)
Total unamortized balance	$ 40,278

Immediately thereafter, Da Vinci's management receives a sales call from an application service provider who manages an Internet-based timekeeping system. The terms offered are so good that the company abandons its in-house system at once and switches to the ASP system. As a result of this change, the company writes off the remaining unamortized balance of its timekeeping system with the following entry:

Accumulated depreciation	$45,610	
Loss on asset disposal	40,278	
Fixed assets—software		$85,888

Impairment—Costs of a Hosting Arrangement That Is a Service Contract Subsection Note: The guidance in this section is effective upon implementation of ASU 2018-15.

ASC 360-10-35 requires that assets be grouped at the lowest level for which identifiable cash flows are largely independent of cash flows from other groups. (ASC 360-10-35-23) For example, that guidance applies to the hosting arrangement when the following events or changes occur:

- The arrangement is not expected to provide substantial service potential
- A significant change occurs in the extent or manner of the use or expected use of the hosting arrangement
- A significant change is made or will be made to the hosting arrangement (ASC 350-40-35-11)

The ASC 360-40 impairment guidance is applied to the capitalized implementation costs as if the costs were long-lived assets. On abandonment, the related capitalized implementations costs are also subject to the guidance in ASC 360-10-35. An asset is considered abandoned when it ceases to be used. Each implementation cost should be evaluated separately. (ASC 350-40-35-12)

Amortization—costs of a hosting arrangement that is a service contract subsection Customer entities are required to expense the capitalized implementation costs of a hosting arrangement that is a service contract over the term of the arrangement. The capitalized implementation costs should be amortized on a straight-line basis unless another systematic and rational manner better represents its use. (ASC 350-40-35-13) Periodically, the customer entity should reassess the estimated term of the arrangement. Any change should be accounted for as a change in accounting estimate under ASC 250. (ASC 350-40-35-15)

Under ASU 2018-15, the term includes the noncancelable period of the arrangement plus periods covered by:

- An option to extend the arrangement provided the customer is reasonably certain to exercise the option,
- An option to terminate the arrangement if the customer is reasonably certain not to exercise the termination option, and
- An option to extend or not to terminate the arrangement where exercise of the option is in the control of the vendor.
  (ASC 350-40-35-14)

When considering and reassessing the terms of the hosting arrangement, the entity should weigh the effects of:

- obsolescence,
- new technology,
- competition,
- other economic factors,
- rapid changes, and
- significant implementation costs when the option to extend or terminate becomes exercisable.
  (ASC 350-40-35-16)

Amortization should begin when the module or components are ready for its intended use, regardless of whether the overall CCA has been placed in service. This occurs when all substantial testing is complete. (ASC 350-40-35-17)

CONCEPTS, RULES, AND EXAMPLES—ASC 350-50, *WEBSITE DEVELOPMENT COSTS*

Scope

All of the ASC 350 subtopics follow the scope guidance in ASC 350-10. In addition, the guidance in ASC 350-50 applies to costs incurred to develop a website, but does not apply to the cost of hardware and acquisition of servers and related hardware transactions. (ASC 350-50-15-2 and 15-3)

Capitalization of Costs

The costs of developing a website, including the costs of developing services that are offered to site visitors (e.g., chat rooms, search engines, blogs, social networking, e-mail, calendars, and so forth), are often quite significant. The SEC staff had expressed the opinion that a large portion of those costs should be accounted for in accordance with ASC 350-50, which sets forth certain conditions that must be met before costs may be capitalized.

Here is the accounting treatment for website development costs:

- Costs incurred in the planning stage must be expensed as incurred. (ASC 350-50-25-2)
- The cost of software used to operate a website must be accounted for consistent with ASC 350-40, unless a plan exists to market the software externally, in which case ASC 985-20, *Software-Costs of Software to Be Sold, Leased, or Marketed*, governs, and costs should be expensed until the entity establishes the software's technological feasibility.

- Costs incurred to develop graphics (broadly defined as the "look and feel" of the web page) are included in software costs, and thus accounted for under ASC 350-40 or ASC 985-20. (ASC 350-50-25-4)
- Costs of hosting websites are generally expensed over the benefit period. (ASC 350-50- 25-5)

ASC 350-50-55 includes a detailed list stipulating how a variety of specific costs are to be accounted for under its requirements:

Planning Stage
Develop a business, project plan, or both.
Determine the functionalities.
Identify necessary hardware.
Determine that the technology necessary to achieve the desired functionalities exists.
Explore alternatives for achieving functionalities.
Conceptually formulate and/or identify graphics and content.
Invite vendors to demonstrate how their web applications, hardware, or service will help achieve the website's functionalities.
Select external vendors or consultants.
Identify internal resources for work on the website design and development.
Identify software tools and packages required for development purposes.
Address legal considerations such as privacy, copyright, trademark, and compliance.
Application and Infrastructure Development Stage
Acquire or develop the software tools required for the development work.
Obtain and register an Internet domain name.
Acquire or develop software necessary for general website operations.
Develop or acquire and customize code for web applications.
Develop or acquire and customize database software and software to integrate distributed applications.
Develop HTML web pages or develop templates and write code to automatically create HTML pages.
Purchase the web and application server(s), Internet connection (bandwidth), routers, staging servers, and production servers. Alternatively, these services may be provided by a third party via a hosting arrangement.
Install developed applications on the web server(s).
Create initial hypertext links to other websites or to destinations within the website.
Test the website applications.
Graphics Development Stage
Graphics involve the overall design of the web page (use of borders, background and text colors, fonts, frames, buttons, and so forth) that affect the look and feel of the web page and generally remain consistent regardless of changes made to the content.

Content Development Stage
Content may be created or acquired to populate databases or web pages.
Content may be acquired from unrelated parties or may be internally developed.
Content is text or graphical information on the website, which may include information on the entity, products offered, information sources that the user subscribes to, and so forth.
Content may originate from databases that must be converted to HTML pages or databases that are linked to HTML pages through integration software. Content also may be coded directly into web pages.

Operating Stage
Train employees involved in support of the website.
Register the website with Internet search engines.
Perform user administration activities.
Update site graphics (for updates of graphics related to major enhancements).
Perform regular backups.
Create new links.
Verify that links are functioning properly and update existing links.
Add additional functionalities or features.
Perform routine security reviews of the website and, if applicable, of the third-party host.
Perform usage analysis.

25 ASC 360 PROPERTY, PLANT, AND EQUIPMENT

PERSPECTIVE AND ISSUES

Subtopics

ASC 360, *Property, Plant, and Equipment*, consists of two subtopics:

- ASC 360-10, *Overall*, which is further divided into two subsections:
  - *General*, which provides guidance on accounting and reporting on property, plant, and equipment, including accumulated depreciation
  - *Impairment or disposal of long-lived assets*, which contains guidance for:
    - Recognizing impairment of long-lived assets to be held and used,
    - Long-lived assets to be disposed of by sale, and
    - Disclosures for the implementation and disposals of individually significant components of an entity.
- ASC 360-20, *Real Estate Sales—Sale Leaseback Accounting*. which provides guidance to determine if a sale of real estate has occurred for purposes of applying sale-leaseback accounting. This subtopic is superseded upon adoption of ASU 2016-02, *Leases*.

Overview

Property, plant, and equipment (sometimes referred to as "fixed assets," "tangible long-lived assets," or "plant assets") are tangible property used in a productive capacity that will benefit the reporting entity for a period exceeding one year. They include land, buildings, machinery, furniture, and tools. Items of property, plant, and equipment are used in the ordinary course of business. They are not for resale. Property, plant, and equipment are some of the most significant items in the statement of financial position and usually represent a substantial investment by the entity.

Comparison of Accounting and Impairment Rules The following diagram summarizes and compares the rules affecting the accounting for tangible and intangible long-lived assets.

DEFINITIONS OF TERMS

Source: ASC 360-10-20 and 360-20-20, *Glossaries*, unless otherwise noted. Also see Appendix A, *Definitions of Terms*, for additional terms relevant to this chapter: Business, Component of an Entity, Collections, Cost Recovery Method, Conduit Debt Security, Contract, Customer, Disposal Group, Fair Value, Firm Purchase Commitment, Impairment, Installment Method, Integral Equipment, Lease, Lease Term, Lessee, Lessor, Market Participants, Net Realizable Value, Nonprofit Activity, Nonpublic Entity, Not-for-Profit Entity, Operating Segment, Orderly Transaction,

Exhibit—Summary and Comparison of Accounting and Impairment Rules

Attribute	PP&E, website dev., internal-use software	Amortizable intangibles	Indefinite-lived intangibles	Goodwill[a]
Useful life	Estimated useful life or, for leasehold improvements, the lesser of that life or the term of the lease		Indefinite	Indefinite for public; alternative for private companies of 10-year maximum
Consider residual or salvage value?	Yes	Yes—with either 3rd party commitment or ready market	No	
Capitalize interest if self-constructed?	Yes			
Recoverability evaluation or impairment test?	Recoverability evaluation		Optional qualitative and then quantitative impairment test	Optional Step 0 qualitative assessment and special two-step impairment test
Frequency	When events and circumstances warrant		At least annually; more often if events and circumstances warrant, unless entity has elected alternative, then triggering event.	
Change between amortizable and nonamortizable		Test for impairment, adjust if required		
Subsequent increases recognized?	No			
Level of aggregation for impairment purposes	Asset group or disposal group		Unit of accounting as specified by ASC 350-30-35	Reporting unit

[a] See the chapter on ASC 350 for information on the alternative related to amortization and impairment testing for other than public entities and for a recent update to goodwill accounting.

Penalty, Performance Obligation, Probably, Public Business Entity, Related Parties, Reporting Unit, Revenue, Right-of-Use Asset, Sale-Leaseback Accounting, Security, and Underlying Asset.

Activities. The term activities is to be construed broadly. It encompasses physical construction of the asset. In addition, it includes all the steps required to prepare the asset for its intended use. For example, it includes administrative and technical activities during the preconstruction stage, such as the development of plans or the process of obtaining permits from governmental authorities. It also includes activities undertaken after construction has begun in order to overcome unforeseen obstacles, such as technical problems, labor disputes, or litigation.

Deposit Method. Under the deposit method, the seller does not recognize any profit, does not record notes receivable, continues to report in its financial statements the property and the related existing debt even if it has been assumed by the buyer, and discloses that those items are subject to a sales contract.

Full Accrual Method. A method that recognizes all profit from a real estate sale at the time of sale.

Impairment. Impairment is the condition that exists when the carrying amount of a long-lived asset (asset group) exceeds its fair value.

Reduced-Profit Method. A reduced profit is determined by discounting the receivable from the buyer to the present value of the lowest level of annual payments required by the sales contract over the maximum period, specified in ASC 360-20-40-19 through 360-20-40-20 and excluding requirements to pay lump sums.

OVERALL—ASC 360-10, *PROPERTY, PLANT, AND EQUIPMENT*

Scope and Scope Exceptions

ASC 360-10, *General* The guidance in the ASC 360-10, *General*, subsection applies to all entities.

ASC 360-10, *Impairment of Disposal of Long-Lived Assets* The guidance in the ASC 360-10, *Impairment or Disposal of Long-lived Assets*, subsection applies to:

- Capital leases of lessees or when ASU 2016-02 is implemented, right-of-use assets of lessees,
- Long-lived assets of lessors subject to operating leases,
- Proved oil and gas properties accounted for using the successful-efforts method of accounting, and
- Long-term prepaid assets.
(ASC 360-10-15-4)

The guidance in these subsections does *not* apply to the following transactions and activities:

- Goodwill.
- Intangible assets not being amortized that are to be held and used.
- Servicing assets.
- Financial instruments, including investments in equity securities accounted for under the cost or equity method.
- Deferred policy acquisition costs.
- Deferred tax assets.
- Unproved oil and gas properties that are being accounted for using the successful-efforts method of accounting.
- Oil and gas properties that are accounted for using the full-cost method of accounting as prescribed by the Securities and Exchange Commission (SEC) (see Regulation S-X, Rule 4-10, Financial Accounting and Reporting for Oil and Gas Producing Activities Pursuant to the Federal Securities Laws and the Energy Policy and Conservation Act of 1975).
- Certain other long-lived assets for which the accounting is prescribed elsewhere in the standards. See:
    - ASC 928, *Entertainment—Music*

- ASC 920, *Entertainment—Broadcasters*
- ASC 985-20, *Software*
- ASC 980-360, *Regulated Operations*
  (ASC 360-10-15-5)

Entities holding collections should look to the guidance in ASC 958-360. (ASC 360-10-15-6)

Concepts, Rules, and Examples

Cost Considerations—Initial Acquisition Determination of costs is critical to proper accounting for property, plant, and equipment. Entities use historical cost to value property, plant, and equipment. Upon acquisition, the reporting entity should measure and capitalize all the historical costs necessary to deliver the asset to its intended location and prepare it for its productive use. (ASC 360-10-30-1) This includes interest costs incurred during the period of time necessary to ready the asset for use. (ASC 835-20-05-1) Examples of delivery and asset preparation costs include:

- Sales, use, excise, and other taxes imposed on the purchase
- Import duties
- Finders' fees
- Freight costs and related shipping insurance
- Storage and handling costs
- Installation and setup costs
- Testing and breaking-in costs
- Foundations and other costs related to providing proper support for the asset
- Costs of reconditioning assets that are purchased used in order to prepare them for use

The purchase price, any encumbrances such as tax liens, and all costs to prepare it for use are costs of land. Costs to prepare land for use include demolition of preexisting structures occupying the land, as well as costs related to excavating, grading, or filling the land to ready it for the new structure.

When the asset consists of one or more buildings, capitalized costs include items such as:

- Contract price paid to the general contractor and subcontractors
- Architectural and engineering costs
- Building permits
- Labor and overhead
- Costs of renovating a preexisting purchased building to convert it for use by the buyer

Construction of Tangible Assets for Internal Use All direct costs (labor, materials, payroll, and related benefit costs) of constructing an entity's own tangible fixed assets are capitalized. However, a degree of judgment is involved in allocating costs between indirect costs—a reasonable portion of which are allocable to construction costs—and general and administrative costs, which are treated as period costs.

Prudence suggests that management establish a carefully reasoned policy that is consistently followed and fully disclosed in the notes to the financial statements, to unambiguously inform the user about the methods used and amounts involved.

Interest Cost The principal purposes of capitalizing rather than expensing interest costs are:

- To obtain a more accurate measurement of the costs associated with the investment in the asset

- To achieve a better matching of costs related to the acquisition, construction, and development of productive assets to the future periods that will benefit from the revenues that the assets generate.

Theoretically, all assets that require a time period to get ready for their intended use should include capitalized interest. However, accomplishing this level of capitalization would usually not meet a reasonable cost/benefit test. Accordingly, interest cost is only capitalized as a part of the historical cost of qualifying assets when such interest is considered to be material. For more detailed information on capitalization of interest costs, see the chapter on ASC 835.

Acquisition of an Interest in the Residual Value in Leased Assets An interest in the residual value of a leased asset is recorded as an asset at the date the right is acquired. (ASC 360-10-25-4) The asset is recorded initially at:

- The amount of cash disbursed,
- The fair value of other consideration, and
- The present value of liabilities assumed.
  (ASC 360-10-30-3)

To measure cost, entities may use the fair value of the interest acquired if it is more evident than the fair value of assets or services surrendered or liabilities assumed. (ASC 360-10-30-4)

Accounting for Assets Acquired in a Group It is important to differentiate the acquisition of assets in a group from those acquired in a business combination. If the assets acquired and liabilities assumed constitute a "business," the transaction is a business combination, and it is accounted for under the guidance in ASC 805. Otherwise, it is accounted for as an asset acquisition. For guidance related to assets acquired in a business combination, see the chapter on ASC 805. For the definition of a business, see Appendix A.

When a reporting entity acquires assets and assumes liabilities that do not constitute a business, the transaction is accounted for as an asset acquisition. Assets acquired in an asset acquisition are initially recognized at their cost to the acquirer, including related transaction costs. The costs of assets acquired as a group are allocated to the individual assets acquired or liabilities assumed based on their relative fair values. Goodwill is recognized in a transaction of this nature. (See the chapter on ASC 350 for more information.)

If assets are transferred between entities under common control, the entity receiving the net assets or equity interests initially recognizes the assets and liabilities transferred at their carrying amounts to the transferring entity at the transfer date. There may be a difference between the carrying amount of the assets transferred and the historical cost to the parent company. In that case, the financial statements of the recipient entity should reflect the transferred assets and liabilities at the historical cost of the parent of the entities under common control.

Unit of Accounting GAAP does not provide specific guidance regarding the unit of account to be used by management in capitalizing long-lived assets. Management might choose, with respect to assets it acquires or constructs, to aggregate individually identifiable assets and record them as if they were a single asset, and then depreciate them accordingly. Conversely, management might choose, with respect to longer-lived assets such as buildings or aircraft, to disaggregate the purchase price and separately record and depreciate the asset's major components over each component's own, individually determined estimated useful life. (Note that there may be significant tax advantages to separately accounting for components.)

Absent specific guidance regarding such practices, it is important that the financial statements provide sufficient information on the reporting entity's policies regarding capitalization of property, plant, and equipment and the criteria used by management to determine whether to record specified categories of assets in groups and/or by component. These policies should be followed consistently, once adopted. Future voluntary, postadoption changes in the policies are subject to ASC 250, *Accounting Changes and Error Corrections*.

Other Asset Acquisition Concerns For general guidance on assets acquired:

- In a business combination, see ASC 805-20-25
- In a nonmonetary transaction, see ASC 845-10-30-1 through 30-10
- Under a lease, see ASC 840-30 or ASC 842-20 upon adoption of ASU 2016-02 (ASC 360-10-30-6 through 30-8)

Cost Considerations—Postacquisition Many different terms are used to describe costs that occur subsequent to initial acquisition including, but not limited to, the following:

- Addition
- Alteration
- Betterment
- Improvement
- Maintenance
- Overhaul
- Planned major maintenance
- Rearrangement
- Redevelopment
- Refurbishment
- Rehabilitation
- Renovation
- Repair
- Replacement
- Retooling
- Retrofitting
- Turnaround

Regardless of the terminology used to describe a cost, the proper accounting treatment depends on a careful analysis of whether the cost is expected to provide future benefits to the reporting entity and, if so, the nature of those expected benefits. Costs incurred that bring greater future benefit should generally be capitalized. There are two major categories of such costs:

1. Costs that increase the value of the asset by increasing capacity or operating efficiency
2. Costs that increase the useful life of the asset.

Costs that increase the value of the asset If the cost to improve the capacity or operating efficiency of an asset adds to the value of the existing asset, in effect a new asset has been created that is subject to the same capitalization considerations applied in recognizing the original asset. When the cost is significant, the cost is capitalized and the depreciation for future periods is revised based on the new book value of the asset. As a practical expedient, most reporting entities establish a dollar threshold under which such costs are charged to expense, irrespective of their purpose (e.g., all costs under $1,500 are charged to expense). This is done under the assumption that the costs of capitalizing and depreciating the item exceed the benefits to users of the financial statements. In effect, these items are considered to be immaterial to the financial statements, both individually and in the aggregate.

Costs and their effect on the future service potential of the asset If the cost affects the future service potential of the asset, it is accounted for in one of the following ways, depending on the individual facts and circumstances:

- *Costs that do not extend the overall useful life of the asset.* If a portion of the original asset is being replaced, theoretically, the carrying value, if any, of the corresponding

portion of the asset that is being replaced (cost less accumulated depreciation and less any impairment charges recognized in prior periods) should be removed from the accounting records and recorded as a loss in the period of the replacement. This accounting is seldom used in practice because, in general, accounting records for fixed assets are not maintained in the painstaking detail necessary to determine the carrying value of the individual components that comprise each asset. Instead, most companies capitalize the replacement components under the rationale that the portion of the asset being replaced would have been depreciated sufficiently based on the useful life of the host asset so that at the time of replacement, little or no carrying value would remain to be removed.
- *Costs that extend the overall useful life of the asset.* If, as a result of incurring a cost, the useful life of the asset is extended, depreciation for future periods is revised based on the new estimated remaining useful life.

Reinstallations and rearrangements If, as a result of reinstallation and rearrangement activities, the reporting entity expects to obtain benefits that extend into future years arising from improved production efficiency or reduced production costs, these costs can be capitalized and depreciated. If the activities are not expected to provide those future benefits, the costs are to be recognized as expense as incurred.

Relocation The costs of moving a fixed asset to a new location at which it will operate in the same manner and with the same functionality as it did at its former location does not result in any future benefits, and therefore the costs of dismantlement, packaging/crating, shipping, and reinstallation should be recognized as expenses as incurred.

Repairs and maintenance If a cost does not extend an asset's useful life, increase its productivity, improve its operating efficiency, or add additional production capacity, the cost should be recognized as an expense as incurred.

Depreciation and Depletion—Overview

The costs of property, plant, and equipment are allocated to the periods of their expected useful life through depreciation or depletion. (ASC 360-10-35-4) The method of depreciation chosen is that which results in a systematic and rational allocation of the cost of the asset (less its residual or salvage value) over the asset's expected useful life, the periods over which the entity will benefit. (ASC 360-10-35-4) The entity must determine:

- The depreciable base
- Useful life
- The best method to apportion costs

The Depreciable Base The factors to consider in determining the depreciable base are discussed above.

The Useful Life The estimation of useful life takes a number of factors into consideration, including:

- Technological change,
- Normal deterioration, and
- Actual physical usage.

The depreciation method is selected based on either a function of time (e.g., obsolescence or normal wear and tear) or as a function of actual physical usage. (ASC 360-10-35-8)

Depreciation Methods

Annuity Methods The ASC states that the annuity method of depreciation is not acceptable. (ASC 360-10-35-10)

Income Tax Methods The ASC specifically prohibits use of the IRS's Accelerated Cost Recovery System (ACRS) if a reasonable range of the asset's useful life is not reflected within the years specified by the ACRS. Income tax deductions for depreciation (referred to in income tax law as "cost recovery deductions"), including Section 179 and bonus depreciation deductions, are not in accordance with GAAP because, in general, they are not based on estimated useful lives and do not allocate cost to future periods benefited on a systematic and rational basis. Therefore, differences between financial statement and income tax depreciation result in temporary differences between the carrying values of the long-lived assets for income tax and financial reporting purposes. These temporary differences are taken into account in the calculation of deferred income taxes, as discussed in the chapter on ASC 740. The Codification specifically prohibits use of the years specified by ACRS unless they fall within a reasonable range of the asset's useful life. (ASC 360- 10-35-10)

Income tax depreciation will differ in amount from financial statement depreciation because of differences in treatment of salvage value, recovery methods, recovery periods, and the use of conventions for assets placed in service during the year. The difference between income tax depreciation and financial statement depreciation is reported as a reconciling item (referred to as a "Schedule M-1 or Schedule M-3 adjustment") on a corporation's U.S. federal income tax return.

Exhibit—Types of Depreciation Methods

Depreciation based on a function of time:	• Straight line
	• Accelerated methods
	o Declining balance
	o Double-declining balance
	o Sum-of-the-years' digits
Depreciation based on activity:	Units of production
Other methods	Group or composite methods

Depreciation Methods as a Function of Time Each of the examples below is based on the following facts.

Straight-line method With this method, depreciation expense is recognized evenly over the estimated useful life of the asset. Here is the formula:

a. Compute the straight-line depreciation rate as:

$$\frac{1}{\text{Estimated Useful Life}}$$

b. Multiply the depreciation rate by the cost less estimated salvage value.

Accelerated methods This method recognizes that depreciation expense is higher in the early years of the asset's useful life and lower in the later years. These methods are more appropriate than straight-line if the asset depreciates more quickly or has greater production capacity in the earlier years than it does as it ages. They are also sometimes used on the theory that maintenance and repair costs typically increase as assets age; therefore, in conjunction with accelerated depreciation total ownership costs (depreciation, maintenance, and repairs) will approximate straight-line.

Declining balance Annual depreciation is computed by multiplying the book value at the beginning of the fiscal year by a multiple of the straight-line rate of depreciation as computed above. (ASC 360-10-35-7)

Double-declining balance Double-declining balance (ceases when the book value = the estimated salvage value) 2 × straight-line depreciation rate × book value at the beginning of the year.

The double-declining balance and the sum-of-the-years' digits methods reflect greater expected productivity or revenue-generating power of the asset in the earlier years of the asset's life or with maintenance charges expected to be greater in the later years of the asset's life. (ASC 360-10-35-7) The declining balance methods do not deduct the salvage value from the cost when calculating depreciation.

Partial-Year Depreciation When an asset is either acquired or disposed of during the year, the full-year depreciation calculation is prorated between the accounting periods involved. As an alternative to proration for partial year depreciation, an entity may follow any one of several simplified conventions as long as the method does not make a material difference.

- Record a full year's depreciation in the year of acquisition and none in the year of disposal.
- Record one-half year's depreciation in the year of acquisition and one-half year's depreciation in the year of disposal.

Examples of Depreciation Methods Each of the examples below is based on the following facts.

Michele Corporation purchased a production machine and placed it in service on January 1, 20X1. The machine cost $100,000, has an estimated salvage value of $10,000, and an estimated useful life of five years.

Example of Straight-line Depreciation

a. Straight-line depreciation = 1/5 = 20% per year
b. 20% × ($100,000 – $10,000) = $18,000 annual depreciation

Example of Double-Declining Balance Depreciation

Year	*Net book value, beginning of year*	*Double-declining balance depreciation computed as 2 × SL rate (40% in this case) × beginning NBV*	*Net book value, end of year*
1	$100,000	$40,000	$60,000

Year	*Net book value, beginning of year*	*Double-declining balance depreciation computed as 2 × SL rate (40% in this case) × beginning NBV*	*Net book value, end of year*
2	60,000	24,000	36,000
3	36,000	14,400	21,600
4	21,600	8,640	12,960
5	12,960	2,960	10,000 limited by salvage value
Total		$90,000	

c. Sum-of-the-years' digits (SYD) depreciation. The formula is:

$$(\text{Cost} - \text{Estimated salvage value}) \times \text{Applicable percentage}$$

$$\text{Applicable percentage} = \frac{\text{Number of years of estimated life remaining at the beginning of the year}}{\text{SYD}}$$

$$\text{SYD} = \frac{n(n+1)}{2} \text{ where n = estimated useful life}$$

Example of Sum-of-the-Years' Digits (SYD) Depreciation

$$\text{SYD} = \frac{5(5+1)}{2} = 15$$

This formula yields the sum of each year of the estimated useful life

$1 + 2 + 3 + 4 + 5 = 15$

Year	*Remaining estimated useful life at beginning of year*	*SYD*	*Applicable percentage*	*Annual depreciation*
1	5	5/15	33.33%	$30,000
2	4	4/15	26.67	24,000
3	3	3/15	20.00	18,000
4	2	2/15	13.33	12,000
5	1	1/15	6.67	6,000
Totals	15		100.00%	$90,000

Example of Partial-Year Depreciation

Ginger Corporation, a calendar-year entity, acquired a machine on June 1, 20X2, that cost $40,000 with an estimated useful life of four years and a $2,500 salvage value. The depreciation expense for each full year of the asset's life is calculated as:

	Straight-line	*Double-declining balance*	*Sum-of-years' digits*
Year 1	37,5001 ÷ 4 = 9,375	50% × 40,000 = 20,000	4/10 × 37,500* = 15,000
Year 2	9,375	50% × 20,000 = 10,000	3/10 × 37,500 = 11,250
Year 3	9,375	50% × 10,000 = 5,000	2/10 × 37,500 = 7,500
Year 4	9,375	50% × 5,000 = 2,500	1/10 × 37,500 = 3,750
	37,500	37,500	37,500

* *(40,000 - 2,500)*

Because the first full year of the asset's life does not coincide with the company's fiscal year, the amounts shown above must be prorated as follows:

	Straight-line	*Double-declining balance*	*Sum-of-years' digits*
20X2	7/12 × 9,375 = 5,469	7/12 × 20,000 = 11,677	7/12 × 15,000 = 8,750
20X3	9,375	5/12 × 20,000 = 8,333	5/12 × 15,000 = 6,250
		7/12 × 10,000 = 5,833	7/12 × 11,250 = 6,563
		14,166	12,813
20X4	9,375	5/12 × 10,000 = 4,167	5/12 × 11,250 = 4,687
		7/12 × 5,000 = 2,917	7/12 × 7,500 = 4,375
		7,084	9,062
20X5	9,375	5/12 × 5,000 = 2,083	5/12 × 7,500 = 3,125
		7/12 × 2,500 = 1,458	7/12 × 3,750 = 2,188
		3,541	5,313
20X6	5/12 × 9,375 = 3,096	5/12 × 2,500 = 1,042	5/12 × 3,750 = 1,562
	37,500	37,500	37,500

Depreciation Method Based on Actual Physical Usage Units of production: Depreciation is based upon the number of units produced by the asset in a given year.

$$\text{Depreciation rate} = \frac{\text{Cost less salvage value}}{\text{Estimated number of units to be produced by the asset over its estimated useful life}}$$

$$\text{Units of production depreciation} = \text{Depreciation rate} \times \text{Number of units produced during the current year}$$

Other Depreciation Methods

Group (Composite) Method In addition to the foregoing, group and composite methods are sometimes used. The group method is frequently used if the assets are similar and have close to the same useful lives. A composite is made up of dissimilar assets. These methods average the service lives of multiple assets using a weighted-average of the units and depreciates the group or composite as if it were a single unit.

$$\text{Depreciation rate} = \frac{\text{Sum of the straight-line depreciation of individual assets}}{\text{Total asset cost}}$$

$$\text{Depreciation expense} : \text{Depreciation rate} \times \text{Total group}(\text{composite})\text{cost}$$

Gains and losses are not recognized on the disposal of one of the assets in a group but are netted into accumulated depreciation.

Practice Pointer: The SEC has questioned the use of the composite method in some circumstances, stating that, "a composite (or group) method of depreciation is generally used in specialized industries, such as railroads and utilities, where groups for assets are significant in number, but have relatively small unit values." When choosing to use a composite or group method, management should make sure that the method is appropriate for the assets and allocates the cost of the asset over its estimated useful life in a systematic and rational manner.

Depletion Depletion is the annual charge for the use of natural resources. In order to compute depletion, it is first necessary to establish a depletion base, the amount of the depletable asset. The depletion base includes the following elements:

- *Acquisition costs*—The cost to obtain the property rights through purchase or lease, royalty payments to the property owner
- *Exploration costs*—Typically, these costs are expenses as incurred; however, in certain circumstances in the oil and gas industry, they may be capitalized
- *Development costs*—Intangible development costs such as drilling costs, tunnels, shafts, and wells
- *Restoration costs*—The costs of restoring the property to its natural state after extraction of the natural resources has been completed

The amount of the depletion base, less its estimated salvage value, is charged to depletion expense each period using a depletion rate per unit extracted, or *unit depletion rate* that is computed using the following formula:

$$\frac{1}{\text{Total expected recoverable units}} \times \text{Depletion base} \times \text{Units extracted}$$

The unit depletion rate is revised frequently due to the uncertainties surrounding the recovery of natural resources. The revision is made prospectively; the remaining undepleted cost is allocated over the remaining expected recoverable units.

Example of Depletion

The Cheyenne Oil Company drills a well in the Denver Basin oil field. It expects to incur the following acquisition, development, and restoration costs associated with the well:

Land acquisition	$ 172,000
Land preparation (road and drill pad)	38,000
Well drilling	301,000
Trunk line construction	29,000
Estimated site restoration cost	50,000
Total	$ 590,000

A considerable amount of extraction equipment is also positioned at the well, but since it can be moved among well sites and is therefore not a fixed part of this well, it is depreciated separately.

The entire $590,000 is capitalized. Cheyenne's geologists calculate that the well has proven reserves of 250,000 barrels of crude oil. In the first year of production, the well produces 45,000 barrels of oil. The depletion charge for the first year of operation follows:

$$\frac{1}{250{,}000 \text{ barrels of proven reserves}} \times \$590{,}000 = \$2.36 \text{ per barrel extracted unit depletion rate}$$

$$\$2.36 \text{ per barrel extracted} \times 45{,}000 \text{ barrels extracted} = \$106{,}200 \text{ first-year depletion charge}$$

During the second year of the well's operation, Cheyenne's engineers revise the estimated remaining proven reserves upward by 20,000 barrels from 250,000 barrels to 270,000 barrels, based on improved oil recovery techniques. Also, due to new environmental laws, the estimated site restoration cost increases by $10,000, increasing the depletion base from $590,000 to $600,000. Total production for the second year is 62,000 barrels of oil. The depletion charge for the first year is not retroactively adjusted; instead changes in cost and estimated total production are accounted for prospectively. The depletion calculation for the second year follows:

$$\frac{1}{225{,}000 \text{ barrels of proven reserves remaining}} \times \$493{,}800 \times 62{,}000 \text{ barrels extracted in year 2}$$
$$= \$136{,}069, \text{ which is the depletion charge of } \$2.19 \text{ per barrel extracted}$$

These depletion expenses leave $357,731 of capitalized costs yet to be amortized over remaining proven reserves of 163,000 barrels, representing a future depletion charge of $2.19 per barrel, barring any further future changes in estimates.

Impairment The impairment provisions of ASC 360-10 are generally split between:

- Long-lived assets classified as held and used, and
- Long-lived assets classified as held for sale.

The Codification rules for measuring and recording impairment of assets are not uniform for all assets or for all industries, and preparers should review the applicable industry guidance.

Impairment of Long-Lived Assets to Be Held and Used Impairment losses are only recognized when the carrying amount of the impaired asset (or asset group) is not recoverable and exceeds its fair value. Recoverability is determined by comparing the carrying amount of the asset (or asset group) on the date it is being evaluated for recoverability to the sum of the undiscounted cash flows expected to result from its use and eventual disposition. It is important to note that, as opposed to the measure used in recoverability testing, the impairment loss to be recorded is measured by the amount by which the carrying amount exceeds its fair value. If the carrying value is recoverable from expected future cash flows from its use and disposition, as defined, no impairment loss is recognized. (ASC 360-10-35-17) This can be seen as a multi-step process:

1. Determine when to use the recoverability test—indicators of impairment
2. Test for recoverability
3. Measure impairment
4. Allocate the loss
5. Recognize the new cost basis
6. Report and disclose.

Step 1—Determine when to use the recoverability test—indicators of impairment "Events and circumstances" criteria determine when, if at all, an asset (or asset group) is evaluated for recoverability. Thus, there is no set interval or frequency for recoverability evaluation. The Codification provides a list of examples of events or changes in circumstances that indicate the carrying amount of an asset (asset group) *may* not be recoverable and thus should be evaluated for recoverability. It is important to note that the list of events and circumstances below is not intended to be all-inclusive. Rather, it is intended to provide examples of situations that warrant evaluation of an asset or group of assets for recoverability. These examples also apply to asset groups. See the section that follows for an explanation of asset groups.

- A significant decrease in the market price of a long-lived asset (asset group)
- A significant adverse change in the extent or manner in which a long-lived asset (asset group) is being used or is in its physical condition
- A significant adverse change in legal factors or in the business climate that could affect the value of a long-lived asset (asset group), including an adverse action or assessment by a regulator
- An accumulation of costs significantly in excess of the amount originally expected for the acquisition or construction of a long-lived asset (asset group)
- A current period operating or cash flow loss combined with a history of operating or cash flow losses or a projection or forecast that demonstrates continuing losses associated with the use of a long-lived asset (asset group)
- A current expectation that, more likely than not, a long-lived asset (asset group) will be sold or otherwise disposed of significantly before the end of its previously estimated useful life
(ASC 360-10-35-21)

Financial statement preparers should routinely assess whether the indicators above or other indicators are present.

In conjunction with the recoverability evaluation, it may also be necessary to review the appropriateness of the method of depreciation (amortization) and depreciable life of the asset or group of assets. If as a result of that review the remaining useful life of the asset (group) is revised, the revised useful life is used to develop the cash flow estimates used to evaluate recoverability. Changes to the accounting method (e.g., from straight-line to accelerated depreciation) under ASC 250, however, would be made prospectively after the application of ASC 360. (ASC 360-10-35-22)

Asset group impairment analysis. ASC 360 includes the concept of the *asset group*, defined as the lowest level for which identifiable cash flows are largely independent of the cash flows of other assets and liabilities. (ASC 360-10-35-23)

An asset group could be:

- The whole company
- An operating segment (See Appendix A for a definition.)
- A reporting unit (See Appendix A for a definition.)
- A business
- A part of a business (such as a division or department)

The asset groups referenced below are shown in the diagram entitled "Alternative Balance Sheet Segmentation" in the chapter on ASC 280.

- Asset group (a) in the diagram is a single division of a subsidiary.
- Asset groups (b) and (c) are each separate businesses that comprise another division of the same subsidiary.
- Asset group (d) is an entire subsidiary consisting of a single business.
- Asset group (e) is a product line that is part of a larger business and, after the disposal of disposal group (f), will constitute an entire operating segment.
- Asset groups (g) and (h) are each separate businesses that comprise a subsidiary.

If a long-lived asset cannot be assigned to any asset group because it does not have identifiable cash flows largely independent of other long-lived assets individually or in asset groups, then that asset is evaluated for recoverability by reference to all assets and liabilities of the entity. An example of this might be corporate headquarters. (ASC 360-10-35-24)

Assets and liabilities in a group may be neither long-lived assets nor goodwill. If so, they should be separately identified. Since those assets and liabilities are not subject to the provisions of ASC 360, the guidance applicable to their valuation is applied *before* applying ASC 360 to the group. For example, allowances for uncollectible accounts receivable and inventory obsolescence are recorded as necessary. (ASC 360-10-35-27)

Effect of goodwill on grouping In assessing the composition of asset groups, management must be aware of the interrelationship between ASC 360, *Property, Plant, and Equipment*, and ASC 350, *Intangibles—Goodwill and Other*. Goodwill can only be assigned to an asset group that is being evaluated for recoverability if the asset group is either a reporting unit or includes a reporting unit. (ASC 360-10-35-26)

Step 2—Test for recoverability

Estimates of future cash flows For the purposes of recoverability evaluation, future cash flows are defined as cash inflows less the associated cash outflows directly associated with, and that are expected to arise as a direct result of, the use and eventual disposition of the asset group, excluding interest that is recognized as a period expense when incurred. (ASC 360-10-35-29) The estimate of future cash flows:

- Is based on all available evidence
- Incorporates assumptions that marketplace participants would use in their estimates of fair value when that information is available without undue cost or effort; otherwise, the entity incorporates its own assumptions, including the "highest and best use" of the asset (or group)
- Should be consistent with assumptions used by the entity for comparable periods such as internal budgets and projections, accruals related to incentive compensation plans, or information communicated to others
- Is made for the remaining estimated useful life of the asset (or the primary asset of an asset group) to the entity

---

NOTE: The primary asset is the long-lived asset being depreciated (or intangible asset being amortized) that is the most significant component asset from which the group derives its cash-flow generating capacity. The primary asset cannot be land or nonamortizing intangible assets. (ASC 360-10-35-31) If the primary asset does not have the longest useful life of the long-lived assets in the group, cash flow estimates must assume that the entire group will be sold at the end of the primary asset's useful life. (ASC 360-10-35-31)

- Takes into account future expenditures necessary to complete an asset under development including interest capitalized under ASC 835-20
- Includes future outflows necessary to maintain the existing service potential of all or a component of the asset or group of assets
- Excludes cash flows for future capital expenditures that increase the service potential of a long-lived asset or group of assets
- Is required to take into account the likelihood of possible cash flow outcomes if alternative courses of action are being contemplated, or if ranges of cash flows are estimated to occur under different scenarios
(ASC 360-10-35-30)

NOTE: ASC 360 indicates that, when uncertainties exist with respect to timing and amount of future cash flows, using an expected present value technique is the appropriate way to estimate fair value. (ASC 360-10-35-36)

Recall from previous discussion that the recoverability test is a screening test. Under that test, if the carrying amount of an asset or asset group exceeds the estimated gross, undiscounted cash flows from use and disposition, then the carrying value is deemed not recoverable and an impairment loss must be recognized. (ASC 360-10-35-17)

Step 3—Measure the impairment loss The impairment loss is measured as the excess of the carrying amount over the asset's (or asset group's) fair value.

Impairment loss = Carrying amount – Fair value

Fair value is the price that the reporting entity would receive to sell the asset on the measurement date in an orderly transaction between market participants in the principal (or most advantageous) market for the asset. To measure fair value, management must determine the asset's highest and best use, which may not coincide with the manner in which the reporting entity is currently using it. Fair value measurements are discussed and illustrated in the chapter on ASC 820.

Step 4—Allocate impairment losses If an asset group is found to have sustained an impairment loss, the loss is only applied to reduce the carrying amounts of the long-lived asset or assets in the group. In general, the loss is allocated to the long-lived assets in the group based on their relative carrying values. However, the carrying value of any individual asset in the group that has a fair value that is separately identifiable without "undue cost or effort" must not be reduced below that fair value. (ASC 360- 10-35-28)

Step 5—Recognize the new cost basis After recognition of impairment losses, the adjusted carrying amounts of the impaired long-lived assets constitute their new cost bases. Depreciation (amortization) is recognized prospectively over their remaining estimated useful lives. The adjustment to carrying values to reflect an impairment loss may never be restored.

Step 6—Reporting and disclosure For presentation and disclosure information, see www.wiley.com/go/GAAP2021.

Example of Impairment

(Refer to the diagram under the section entitled "Alternative Balance Sheet Segmentation" in the chapter on ASC 280.)

The Parent Holding Company (PHC) owns and operates seven subsidiaries comprising eleven businesses, primarily engaged in the manufacturing and distribution of food and beverages. All of the businesses are headquartered in the same building that is owned by PHC. Additional facts are as follows:

- Due to general economic conditions and the failure, in 20X4, of several high-tech start-ups in the city in which PHC is headquartered, the local commercial real estate market is depressed. PHC's headquarters building has eight years remaining in its expected useful life and its carrying value is $4,500,000. PHC has substantial excess space in the building, which it does not expect to need in the foreseeable future. PHC management expects the real estate market to remain depressed for the next two years and when the market recovers, it will consider selling the building and either leasing or purchasing a smaller facility in the area.
- Subsidiary 2 operates a South American bottling plant that produces a line of carbonated beverages that is sold exclusively on that continent. A large increase in sugar prices during 20X4 has resulted in lower margins and, due to partial price increases, a 30% decrease in units sold during the year. The plant operates in a building that Subsidiary 2 leases under an operating lease with five years remaining. The primary asset owned by Subsidiary 2 is what it refers to as its "bottling line" which consists of equipment that mixes ingredients, adds carbon dioxide, and fills and caps the bottles. The bottling line has a remaining useful life of four years. The other assets in the asset group have remaining useful lives of seven years. Subsidiary 2 has been profitable for the past three years (20X1–20X3) but is showing a small operating loss for 20X4. Additional information regarding Subsidiary 2 follows:

	Bottling line (primary asset)	*Asset B*	*Asset C*	*Totals*
Net book value	$87,000	$19,000	$17,000	$123,000
Remaining life	4 years	7 years	7 years	

	Bottling line (primary asset)	*Asset B*	*Asset C*	*Totals*
Expected cash inflows, net of outflows				
20X5				4,000
20X6				6,000
20X7				7,000
20X8				8,000
From assumed disposition—end of 20X8				75,000
Total expected net operating cash flows				$100,000

- PHC is in the process of preparing its consolidated financial statements for the year ended December 31, 20X4. Thus far, normal depreciation of PHC and its subsidiaries' fixed assets has been recorded and impairment has not yet been considered.

Analysis

Identify asset groups This has been illustrated in the diagram in the chapter on ASC 280. Note that the headquarters building cannot be assigned to any specific asset group since it does not generate independent cash flows. Therefore, its potential impairment is assessed at the PHC level on a consolidated basis.

Step 1—Determine when to use the recoverability test—impairment indicators Assess each of PHC's asset groups (and on a consolidated basis), as to whether the example events and circumstances provided by ASC 360 or any other events and circumstances indicate that PHC's long-lived assets may be impaired. Based on the decline in the local real estate market, it would be presumed that the market price of the headquarters building has declined, and thus the building should be evaluated for recoverability. Analysis of the situation of Subsidiary 2 is more complex. Two of the factors in ASC 360 warrant consideration. First, it could be argued that the increase in sugar prices constitutes a significant adverse change in the business climate. This might be mitigated if management believed the price increase to be a short-term condition and assuming this belief was supportable by past experience. Second, the current period operating loss should be considered. Since there has not been a history of such losses, the relevance of this factor depends on management's forecast of future results. If Subsidiary 2 were forecast to continue to experience operating losses, this would indicate that the asset group needs to be evaluated for recoverability. For the purposes of this example, we will assume that continuing losses are forecast.

Step 2—Test for recoverability Two recoverability evaluations are required, one for the headquarters building and the other for the asset group represented by Subsidiary 2. Since the headquarters building is not allocable to an asset group, its recoverability is evaluated using consolidated cash flows that include the cash flows of Subsidiary 2. Thus, the recoverability evaluation for Subsidiary 2 is performed first.

Subsidiary 2's recoverability evaluation is performed by reference to the four-year remaining useful life of the bottling line, its primary asset. The cash flows used to evaluate recoverability are required to assume that the asset group will be sold in its entirety at the end of four years.

Comparison of the $100,000 sum of the undiscounted expected cash flows from use and disposition to the carrying amount of $123,000 indicates that the carrying amount of the asset group is not expected to be fully recoverable. Therefore, the asset group is impaired.

The recoverability evaluation for the building is performed using an estimate of expected cash flows, weighted for the probabilities as to whether management will pursue the sale of the facility when the local economy recovers in two years, versus retaining it for the remaining eight years of its expected useful life. In addition, depending on different scenarios of future economic conditions and business performance by PHC's businesses, different levels of cash flows could result both from operations and from disposition. Acknowledging the inherent uncertainties associated with predicting future results and the subjectivity involved in the estimation process, management formulated its best judgment regarding the probabilities of the best, worst, and most-likely scenarios.

Estimate of Future Cash Flows

Course of action	*Use of the asset (consolidated basis)*	*Disposition of the asset*	*Total*	*Probability assessment*	*Probability-weighted possible cash flows*
Sale at the end of 2 years	$100,000	$3,500,000	$3,600,000	20%	$ 720,000
	130,000	4,600,000	4,730,000	60%	2,838,000
	150,000	4,600,000	4,750,000	20%	950,000
				100%	$4,508,000
Sale at the end of 8 years	$410,000	$4,000,000	$4,410,000	20%	$ 882,000
	550,000	4,700,000	5,250,000	60%	3,150,000
	620,000	4,800,000	5,420,000	20%	1,084,000
				100%	$5,116,000

Upon review of the analysis above, management determined that it is 70% probable that it will sell the building at the end of two years. Consequently, the expected cash flows from the use and disposition of the building are as follows:

Course of action	*Probability-weighted possible cash flows*	*Probability assessment for course of action*	*Undiscounted Expected cash flows*
Sale at the end of 2 years	$4,508,000	70%	$3,155,600
Sale at the end of 8 years	5,116,000	30%	1,534,800
		100%	$4,690,400

Comparison of the undiscounted expected cash flows or $4,690,400 per above to the $4,500,000 carrying value of the building at December 31, 20X4, indicates that the carrying value of the building is expected to be fully recoverable, and thus the building is not impaired.

As a result of the above analysis, management may decide upon one of the alternative courses of action. If so, the expected cash flows from that course of action would be used in the recoverability evaluation since it would no longer be necessary to probability-weight the outcomes.

Step 3—Measure impairment, if any Market information regarding the asset group of Subsidiary 2 is not available "without undue cost and effort." Management elects to use the traditional present value of estimated cash flows method to estimate fair value because it believes that uncertainty regarding the timing and amounts of cash flows is minimal (but, if this were not the case, management would use an *expected present value* technique to make this estimate). This estimation method is referred to in ASC 820 as a *discount rate adjustment* technique. Using this technique requires:

- A single set of most-likely cash flows that includes assumptions regarding the likelihood of occurrence or nonoccurrence of events that potentially influence the estimated amounts
- A discount rate approximating a market rate of return based on observable rates of return for comparable assets traded in the same market as the asset or group of assets being measured.

The 8% interest rate used for this illustration is assumed to be a rate commensurate with the risks involved (unlike the risk-free rate sometimes used in applying an expected present value technique). The computation is as follows:

Year	*Net cash flows*	*Present value at 8%*[a]	*Carrying value of asset group*	*Impairment adjustment required*
20X5	$ 4,000	$ 3,704		
20X6	6,000	5,144		
20X7	7,000	5,557		
20X8–Use	8,000	5,880		
20X8–Sale	75,000	55,127		
	$100,000	$75,412	$123,000	$47,588

[a] These present values can be calculated using standardized spreadsheet software; specialized software used to compute time value of money and amortization schedules; the table of factors in Chapter 1 for the present value of a single future amount; or the formula used to derive that table, which is also cited in Chapter 1.

Asset	*Carrying value*	*Pro rata allocation*	*Allocation of impairment loss*	*Tentative adjusted carrying amount*
Bottling line	$ 87,000	71%	$33,660	$53,340
Asset B	19,000	15%	7,351	11,649
Asset C	17,000	14%	6,577	10,423
Total	$123,000	100%	$47,588	$75,412

Step 4—Allocate the loss Note that the adjusted carrying amount is captioned "tentative." This is because Subsidiary 2 was able to obtain a quoted market price of $16,000 for Asset B. ASC 360 specifies that assets are not to be reduced to an amount below their fair value.

Step 5—Recognize the new cost basis To obtain the proper result, the impairment loss requires reallocation among the assets comprising the asset group.

Asset	*Tentative adjusted carrying amount*	*Pro rata reallocation factor*	*Reallocation of excess impairment loss*	*Adjusted carrying amount*
Bottling line	$53,340	84%	$(3,640)	$49,700
Asset C	10,423	16%	(711)	9,712
Subtotal	63,763	100%	(4,351)	
Asset B	11,649		4,351	16,000
Total	$75,412		$ –	$75,412

Step 6—Report and disclose The entry to record impairment in the accounting records of Subsidiary 2 is as follows:

Impairment loss (operating section of income statement)	47,588	
Accumulated depreciation—Machinery and equipment		47,588

To adjust the carrying value of the bottling line and related assets to reflect an impairment loss for 20X4.

Other Impairment Considerations Besides the foregoing, other issues arise as a consequence of applying the impairment rules.

Going concern The example above included an estimate of cash flows at the entity level to assess whether the building was impaired. If the estimate had indicated that the building was impaired, management must consider whether the cash flows estimated for at least the ensuing year will be sufficient for the entity to continue as a going concern. Disclosure in the financial statements of management's plans may be required under ASC 205-30, *Going Concern.*

Significant estimates If, in the example above, the expected cash flows used to assess the recoverability of the building were closer to the building's $4,500,000 carrying value, consideration is given to the applicability of ASC 275, *Risks and Uncertainties*. The assumptions used in the cash flow estimates could be considered significant estimates for which it is reasonably possible changes could occur in the near term (the ensuing year) and, consequently, disclosure would be required.

Treatment of certain site restoration/environmental exit costs ASC 360-10-55 discusses how, for the purpose of performing the recoverability evaluation under ASC 360, to treat the costs of future site restoration or closure (referred to as "environmental exit costs") that may be incurred if the asset is sold, abandoned, or ceases operations. To conform to ASC 360, references to an "asset" are also applicable to an "asset group."

ASC 410-20, *Asset Retirement and Environmental Obligations*, requires asset retirement obligations recognized as liabilities to be included as part of the capitalized cost of the related asset and, to avoid double-counting, the cash settlement of those liabilities to be excluded from the expected future cash flows used to evaluate recoverability under ASC 360. If the asset retirement costs have not yet been recognized under ASC 410-20 because the obligation is being incurred over more than one reporting period during the useful life of the asset, then the cash flows for those unrecognized costs are to be included in the expected future cash flows.

The cash flows for environmental exit costs that are not recorded as liabilities under ASC 410-30 may not occur until the end of the asset's life if the asset ceases to be used or may be delayed indefinitely as long as management retains ownership of the asset and chooses not to sell or abandon it. Consequently, management's intent regarding future actions with respect to the asset is to be taken into account in determining whether to include or exclude these cash flows from the computation of the expected future cash flows used to evaluate recoverability under ASC 360. If management is contemplating alternative courses of action to recover the carrying amount of the asset or if a range is estimated for the amount of possible future cash flows, the likelihood (probability) of these possible outcomes is to be considered in connection with the recoverability evaluation under ASC 360.

ASC 360-10-55 provides examples illustrating situations where cash flows for environmental exit costs not recognized as liabilities under ASC 410-30 are either included in or excluded from the undiscounted expected future cash flows used to evaluate a long-lived asset or group of assets for recoverability under ASC 360.

Deferred income taxes Impairment losses are not deductible for U.S. federal income tax purposes. Consequently, financial statement recognition of these losses will result in differences between the carrying amounts of the impaired assets for financial reporting purposes and income tax purposes. These differences are considered temporary differences and are accounted for under the provisions of ASC 740.

Exhibit—Impairment Process

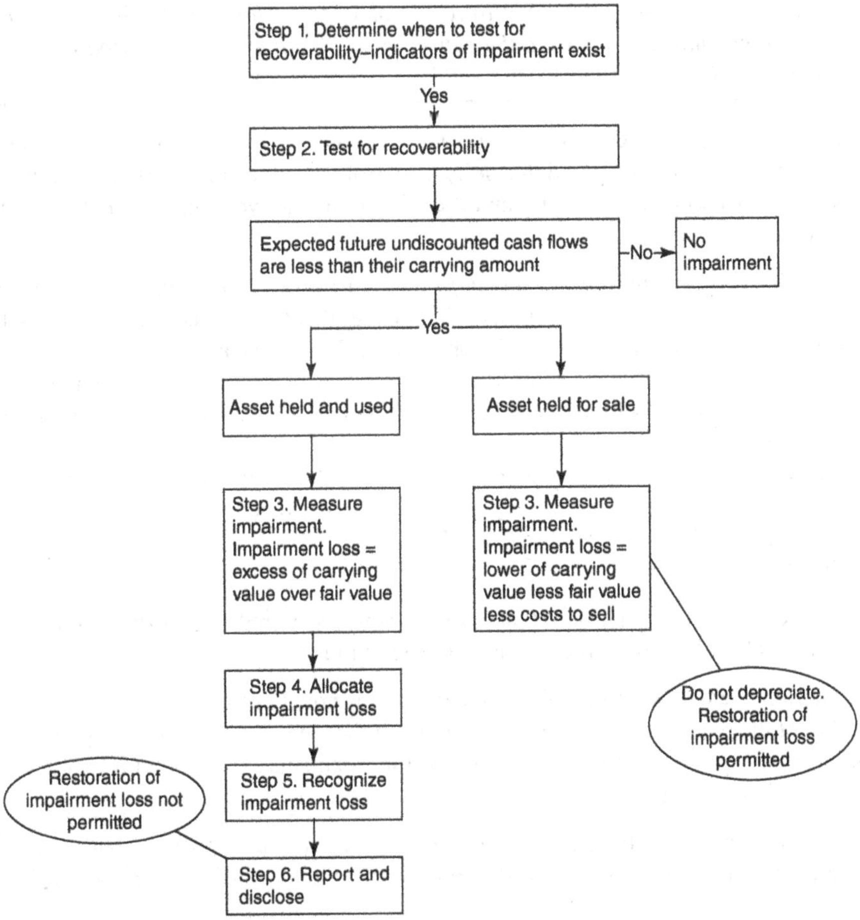

Long-Lived Assets Classified as Held for Sale An asset may be disposed of individually or as part of a disposal group (see Appendix A for a description of disposal group).

The six held-for-sale criteria Long-lived assets (or disposal groups) are classified as held-for-sale in the period in which *all* of the following six criteria are met:

1. Management possesses the necessary authority commits to a plan to sell.
2. The asset (disposal group) is immediately available for sale on an "as is" basis (i.e., in its present condition subject only to usual and customary terms for the sale of such assets).
3. An active program to find a buyer and other actions required to execute the plan to sell the asset (disposal group) have commenced.
4. An assessment of management plans indicates that it is unlikely that significant changes will be made to the plan or that the plan will be withdrawn.
5. Sale is probable, as that term is used in the context of ASC 450-20 (i.e., likely to occur), and transfer of the asset (disposal group) is expected to qualify for recognition as a completed sale within one year.
   (ASC 360-10-45-9)
6. The asset (disposal group) is being actively marketed for sale at a price that is reasonable in relation to its current fair value.
   (ASC 360-10-45-9)

NOTE: Certain exceptions to the one-year requirement are set forth in ASC 360-10-45-11 for events and circumstances beyond the entity's control that extend the period required to complete the sale.

When the criteria are no longer met, the asset is reclassified as held and used. (ASC 360-10-45-10) It is possible that events beyond the entity's control may extend the period required to complete the sale. The Codification provides an exception to the one-year rule in number 5 (on the previous page) if:

- The entity, at the date committed to a plan to sell, reasonably expects that entities other than the buyer, will impose conditions and the transfer that will extend the period to sell and a firm purchase commitment must be obtained within one year.
- The entity has a firm purchase commitment and the buyers impose conditions that will extend the period and the actions needed to meet those conditions have or will be initiated timely and a favorable resolution is expected.
- Circumstances previously considered unlikely arise and the entity has initiated the necessary response, the asset is being actively marketed as a reasonable price, and the criteria above from ASC 360-10-45-9 are met.
  (ASC 360-10-45-11)

For a long-lived asset (disposal group) that has been newly acquired in a business combination to be classified as held for sale at the acquisition date, it must:

- Meet criterion 5 above (subject to the same exceptions noted in 5), *and*
- Any other of the required criteria that are not met at the date of acquisition are judged to be probable of being met within a short period (approximately three months or less) of acquisition. (ASC 360-10-45-12)

If the criteria are met after the date of the statement of financial position but prior to issuance of the entity's financial statements, the long-lived asset continues to be classified as held-and- used at the date of the statement of financial position. (ASC 360-10-45-13) Appropriate subsequent events disclosures would be included in the financial statements in accordance with ASC 855, *Subsequent Events*.

Measuring Expected Disposal Gain or Loss (ASC 360-10-35-43) Long-lived assets (disposal groups) classified as held-for-sale are measured at the lower of their carrying amount or fair value less cost to sell. A loss is recognized for any initial or subsequent write-down to fair value less cost to sell. A gain is recognized for any subsequent increase in fair value less cost to sell, but recognized gains may not exceed the cumulative losses previously recognized. Long-lived assets that are classified as held-for-sale are presented separately on the statement of financial position.

Long-lived assets (disposal groups) being held for sale are not depreciated (amortized) while being presented under the held-for-sale classification. Interest and other expenses related to the liabilities of a held-for-sale disposal group are accrued as incurred.

Cost to sell consists of costs that directly result from the sales transaction that would not have been incurred if no sale were transacted. Cost to sell includes brokerage commissions, legal fees, title transfer fees, and other closing costs that must be incurred prior to transfer of legal title to assets. Prior to measurement of fair value less cost to sell, the entity adjusts the carrying amounts of any assets included in the disposal group not covered by ASC 360 including any goodwill (e.g., establishes appropriate valuation allowances for receivables and inventory, recognizes other-than-temporary impairment of applicable investment securities, etc.). The entity may not accrue, as part of cost to sell, expected future losses associated with operating the long-lived asset (disposal group) while it is classified as held-for-sale.

Costs associated with the disposal, including costs of consolidating or closing facilities, are only recognized when the actual costs are incurred. If the exception to the one-year requirement applies (permitted when there are certain events and circumstances beyond the entity's control), and the sale is expected to occur in more than one year, the cost to sell is discounted to its present value. (ASC 360-10-35-38)

Reclassification—Changes to a Plan to Sell If, at any time after meeting the criteria to be classified as held-for-sale, the asset (disposal group) no longer meets those criteria, the long-lived asset (disposal group) should be reclassified from held-for-sale to held-and-used (ASC 360-10-45-10), measured at the *lower of*:

- Carrying amount prior to classification as held-for-sale, adjusted for any depreciation (amortization) that would have been recognized had the asset (disposal group) continued to be classified as held-and-used, or
- Fair value at the date of the subsequent decision not to sell the asset (disposal group). (ASC 360-10-35-44)

The adjustment required to the carrying amount of an asset (disposal group) being reclassified from held-for-sale to held-and-used is included in income from continuing operations in the period that the decision is made not to sell. (ASC 360-10-45-7) Impairment losses from long-lived assets to be held and used, gains or losses recognized on long-lived assets to be sold, and other costs associated with exit or disposal activities (as defined in ASC 420) should be accounted for consistently. Therefore, if the entity reports income from operations, these amounts are reported in operations unless they qualify as discontinued operations.

Upon removal of an individual asset or liability from a disposal group classified as held-for-sale, the remaining part of the group should be evaluated to determine if it still meets all six of the criteria to be classified as held-for-sale. If all of the criteria are still met, then the remaining assets and liabilities will continue to be measured and accounted for as a group. If not all of the criteria are met, then the remaining long-lived assets are to be measured individually at the lower of their carrying amounts or fair value less cost to sell at that date. (ASC 360-10-35-45) Any assets that will not be sold are reclassified as held-and-used as described above. (ASC 360-10-35-44)

Transfer or Sale of Property, Plant, or Equipment For the derecognition of an asset within the scope of ASC 360, an entity should account for the gains and losses from the derecognition using the guidance in ASC 610-20. This assumes that a scope exception from Subtopic 610-20 does not apply. (ASC 360-10-40-3A)

One example of a scope exception is the derecognition of a nonfinancial asset in a contract with a customer. In that case, the entity should apply the guidance in ASC 606. (ASC 360-10-40-3A) Derecognition of a subsidiary or group of assets that is either a business or nonprofit activity is accounted for under ASC 810. (ASC 360-10-40-3B)

A gain or loss not previously recognized that results from the sale of a long-lived asset is recognized when the asset is derecognized in accordance with applicable topic in the Codification. Examples of these topics are:

- ASC 610 on other income,
- ASC 810 on consolidation, or
- ASC 860 on transfers and servicing.
  (ASC 360-10-40-5)

Example of Long-Lived Assets to Be Disposed of by Sale

Classification as held-for-sale. The Hewitt Candy Company chooses to stop sales of its candy cane product line, and accordingly shifts the $840,000 carrying cost (i.e., book value) of its candy cane twister equipment into a held-for-sale account. After several months of trying to close a sale of the equipment, Hewitt's controller determines that the fair value of the twister equipment is now $855,000. However, after projected sale costs that include commissions, legal fees, and title transfer fees are included, the net fair value is only $825,000. The controller accordingly writes down the equipment cost to $825,000 with the following entry:

Loss on decline of fair value of equipment held-for-sale	15,000	
Equipment held-for-sale		15,000

After another two months, the controller determines that the equipment's fair value, net of estimated disposition costs, has increased to $860,000. Although this represents a gain of $35,000 over the adjusted carrying cost of the equipment, he can only recognize a gain up to the amount of all previously recorded losses, which he does with the following entry:

Equipment held-for-sale	15,000	
Recovery of fair value of equipment held-for-sale		15,000

Reclassification from held-for-sale to held-and-used. Six months after the twister equipment is classified as held-for-sale, Hewitt's management concludes that it will wait for better economic conditions to market and sell the equipment. Hewitt's controller reclassifies the equipment as held-and-used with the following entry:

Equipment held-and-used	840,000	
Equipment held-for-sale		840,000

Prior to its classification as held-for-sale, the equipment had been depreciated on a straight-line basis over a ten-year life span using an original equipment base cost of $1.2 million, so $60,000 would otherwise have been incurred in the six months the equipment was classified as held-for-sale; this would have reduced the equipment's net carrying cost (i.e., book value) from $840,000 to $780,000. Since this is lower than the estimated fair value of $860,000 as of the date when the decision was made to halt sale activities, the controller records the following entry:

Depreciation—equipment	60,000	
Accumulated depreciation—equipment		60,000

Sale of equipment. After four more months, Hewitt receives an unsolicited cash offer of $875,000 for the twister equipment, which it accepts. During these additional four months, the equipment has been depreciated by a further $40,000. Hewitt's controller records the sale with the following entry:

Cash	875,000	
Accumulated depreciation—equipment	460,000	
Equipment held-and-used		1,200,000
Gain on equipment sale		135,000

Long-Lived Assets to Be Disposed of Other Than by Sale

Long-lived assets may be abandoned, exchanged, or distributed to owners in a spin-off. Until the actual disposal occurs, the assets continue to be classified on the statement of financial position as "held and used." (ASC 360-10-45-15)

If the entity commits to a plan to abandon the asset before the end of its previously estimated useful life, the depreciable life is revised in accordance with the rules governing a change in estimate under ASC 250 and depreciation of the asset continues until the end of its shortened useful life. (ASC 360-10-35-47) Abandoned assets are considered disposed of when they cease to be used. Temporary idling of an asset, however, is not considered abandonment. (ASC 360-10-35-49)

At the time an asset is abandoned, its carrying value should be adjusted to its salvage value, if any, but not less than zero (i.e., a liability cannot be recorded upon abandonment). (ASC 360-10-35-48) If an acquired asset meets the criteria to be considered a defensive intangible asset, it is prohibited from being considered abandoned upon its acquisition.

Discontinued Operations Discontinued operations are covered in depth in the chapter on ASC 205, *Presentation of Financial Statements*.

Long-Lived Assets Temporarily Idled The only reference in ASC 360 to the temporary idling of long-lived assets is the provision that prohibits recognizing temporary idling as abandonment. At a minimum, however, if material assets are temporarily idled, the following considerations apply:

- Idling constitutes a "significant adverse change in the extent or manner in which . . ." the asset (or asset group) is being used, which is an indicator requiring a recoverability evaluation under ASC 360.
- The estimates of future cash flows used in performing the recoverability evaluation are to consider, on a probability-weighted basis, the range of outcomes under consideration by management regarding when the asset will be returned to service, sold, or abandoned.
- Idle property and equipment is to be clearly and unambiguously captioned and segregated on the statement of financial position from both the "held-and-used" and "held-for-sale" categories, since it does not qualify for either classification, with appropriate disclosure of the relevant circumstances.
- As part of the ongoing review of the appropriateness of useful lives, the remaining useful life of the idle equipment is to be reassessed.
- Evaluation by management of whether temporary suspension of depreciation or amortization of the asset is warranted until it is returned to service.

CONCEPTS, RULES, AND EXAMPLES—ASC 360-20, *REAL ESTATE SALES*— Sale Leaseback Accounting

Note: Upon implementation of ASU 2016-02, *Leases*, this Subtopic is superseded. See the chapter on ASC 842 for more information.

Scope and Scope Exceptions

Entities must determine under what circumstances a transaction is an in-substance sale of real estate. To make that determination, ASC 360-20 suggests the preparer consider the nature of the entire component being sold, that is

- The land,
- The property improvements, and
- The integral equipment.

Further, when making that determination, entities should not consider whether the operations in which the assets are involved are traditional or nontraditional real estate activities. For example, if a ski resort is sold and the lodge and ski lifts are considered to be affixed to the land (that is, they cannot be removed and used separately without incurring significant cost), then it would appear that the sale is in substance the sale of real estate and that the entire sale transaction would be subject to the provisions of ASC 360-20. For purposes of determining profit recognition involving the sale of underlying land (or the sale of the property improvements or integral equipment subject to a lease of the underlying land), the transactions should not be bifurcated into a real estate component (the sale of the underlying land) and a non-real estate component (the sale of the lodge and lifts). (ASC 360-20-15-2)

In addition, the following assets that are part of a sale-leaseback transaction are included in ASC 360-20 guidance. (Note: See Practice Alert below.)

1. Real estate, including real estate with property improvements or integral equipment. The terms *property improvements* and *integral equipment* as they are used in this Subtopic refer to any physical structure or equipment attached to the real estate that cannot be removed and used separately without incurring significant cost. Examples include an office building, a manufacturing facility, a power plant, and a refinery.
2. Property improvements or integral equipment subject to an existing lease of the underlying land should be accounted for in accordance with paragraphs 360-20-40-56 through 40-59.
3. An investment in the form of a financial asset that is in substance real estate.
4. Timberlands or farms (that is, land with trees or crops attached to it).
   (ASC 360-20-15-3)

ASC 360-20-15 *excludes* the following transactions and activities:

- The sale of only property improvements or integral equipment without a concurrent (or contemplated) sale of the underlying land. However, ASC 360-20 does apply to sales of property improvements or integral equipment with the concurrent lease (whether explicit or implicit in the transaction) of the underlying land to the buyer.
- The sale of the stock or net assets of a subsidiary or a segment of a business if the assets of that subsidiary or that segment contain real estate. If such a transaction is, in substance, the sale of real estate, ASC 360-20 does apply.
- Exchanges of real estate for other real estate. See the accounting for nonmonetary transactions in ASC 845.
- The sale of debt and equity securities accounted for under ASC 320 or ASC 321. See ASC 860 for guidance on sales of such assets.
- Retail land sales.
- Natural assets such as those that have been extracted from the land (for example, oil, gas, coal, and gold). See ASC 932.
  (ASC 360-20-15-10)

Introduction

The substance of a sale of any asset is that the transaction unconditionally transfers the risks and rewards of ownership to the buyer. However, the economic substance of many real estate sales is that the risks and rewards of ownership have *not* been clearly transferred. The turbulent and cyclical environments in the real estate and debt markets have led to the evolution of many complex methods of financing real estate transactions. For example, in some transactions the seller, rather than an independent third party, finances the buyer, while in others, the seller may be required to guarantee a minimum return to the buyer or continue to operate the property for a specified period of time. In many of these complex transactions, the seller still has some association with the property even after the property has been sold. The question that must be answered in these transactions is: At what point does the seller become disassociated enough from the property that profit may be recognized on the transaction?

ASC 976 provides guidance on accounting for retail land sales, that is, sales on a volume basis of lots that are subdivisions of large tracts of land. The purpose of ASC 360-20 is to present the guidelines that need to be considered when analyzing nonretail real estate transactions. ASC 840-40 dealing with sales-type real estate leases and sales-leaseback real estate transactions is covered in the chapter on ASC 840. Also see the chapter on ASC 842.

Criteria for Using Full Accrual Method

Profit from real estate sales is recognized in full, provided the following:

- The profit is determinable (i.e., the collectability of the sales price is reasonably assured or the amount that will not be collectible can be estimated), and
- The earnings process is virtually complete, that is, the seller is not obliged to perform significant activities after the sale to earn the profit.
(ASC 360-20-40-3)

When both of these conditions are satisfied, the method used to recognize profits on real estate sales is referred to as the full accrual method. If both of these conditions are not satisfied, recognition of all or part of the profit is postponed.

For real estate sales, the collectibility of the sales price is reasonably assured when the buyer has demonstrated a commitment to pay. This commitment is supported by a substantial initial investment, along with continuing investments that give the buyer a sufficient stake in the property such that the risk of loss through default motivates the buyer to honor its obligations to the seller. Collectibility of the sales price is also assessed by examining the conditions surrounding the sale (e.g., credit history of the buyer; age, condition, and location of the property; and history of cash flows generated by the property). (ASC 360-20-40-4)

The profit is recognized by the full accrual method when all of the following criteria are met (ASC 360-20-40-5):

1. A sale is consummated.
2. The buyer's initial and continuing investments are adequate to demonstrate a commitment to pay for the property.
3. The seller's receivable is not subject to future subordination.
4. The seller has transferred to the buyer the usual risks and rewards of ownership in a transaction that is in substance a sale, and the seller does not have a substantial continuing involvement in the property.

On sales in which an independent third party provides all of the financing for the buyer, the seller is most concerned that criterion number 1 above is met. For such sales, the sale is usually consummated on the closing date. When the seller finances the buyer, the seller must analyze the economic substance of the agreement to ascertain that criteria 2, 3, and 4 are also met (i.e., whether the transaction clearly transfers the risks and rewards of ownership to the buyer).

Criterion 1—Consummation of a Sale A sale is considered consummated when the following conditions are met (ASC 360-20-40-7):

- The parties are bound by the terms of a contract.
- All consideration has been exchanged.
- Any permanent financing for which the seller is responsible has been arranged.
- All conditions precedent to closing have been performed.

When a seller is constructing office buildings, condominiums, shopping centers, or similar structures, item 4 may be applied to individual units rather than the entire project. These four conditions are usually met on or after closing, not at the point the agreement to sell is signed or at a preclosing meeting. Closing refers to the final steps of the transaction (i.e., when consideration is paid, the mortgage is secured, and the deed is delivered or placed in escrow).

Criterion 2—Adequacy of the Buyer's Initial and Continuing Investment Once the sale is consummated, the next step is to determine whether the buyer's initial investment adequately demonstrates a commitment to pay for the property and the reasonable likelihood that the seller will collect it. This determination is made by comparing the buyer's initial investment to the sales value of the property. ASC 360-20-55-1 and 55-2 specifically detail items that are includable as the initial investment and the minimum percentages that the initial investment must bear to the sales value of the property. To make the determination of whether the initial investment is adequate, the sales value of the property must also be computed.

Computation of sales value The sales value of property in a real estate transaction is computed as follows:

	Stated sales price
+	Proceeds from the issuance of an exercised purchase option
+	Other payments that are, in substance, additional sales proceeds (e.g., management fees, points, prepaid interest, or fees required to be maintained in advance of the sale that will be applied against amounts due to the seller at a later point)
–	A discount that reduces the buyer's note to its present value
–	Net present value of services seller agrees to perform without compensation
–	Excess of net present value of services seller performs over compensation that seller will receive
=	Sales value of property in a real estate transaction

Composition of the Initial Investment Sales transactions are characterized by many different types of payments and commitments made between the seller, buyer, and third parties; however, the buyer's initial investment only includes the following (ASC 360-20-40-10):

- Cash paid to the seller as a down payment
- Buyer's notes given to the seller that are supported by irrevocable letters of credit from independent lending institutions
- Payments by the buyer to third parties that reduce existing indebtedness the seller has on the property
- Other amounts paid by the buyer that are part of the sales value
- Other consideration received by the seller that can be converted to cash without recourse to the seller; for example, other notes of the buyer

ASC 360-20-40-13 specifically states that the following items are not included as initial investment:

- Payments by the buyer to third parties for improvements to the property
- A permanent loan commitment by an independent third party to replace a loan made by the seller
- Funds that have been or will be loaned, refunded, or directly or indirectly provided to the buyer by the seller or loans guaranteed or collateralized by the seller for the buyer

Buyer's initial and continuing involvement The initial and continuing investment requirements for the full accrual method apply unless the seller receives any of the following as the full sales value of the property (ASC 360-20-40-15):

- Cash without any seller contingent liability on any debt on the property incurred or assumed by the buyer,
- The buyer's assumption of the seller's existing nonrecourse debt on the property,
- The buyer's assumption of all recourse debt on the property with the complete release of the seller from those obligations, or
- Any combination of such cash and debt assumption.

If the seller has received full payment for the sale and has no financing risk, the buyer's commitment to pay is not a factor in the seller's recognition of the sale. (ASC 360-20-40-16)

In computing the buyer's initial investment, debt incurred by the buyer that is secured by the property is not considered part of the buyer's initial investment. This is true whether the debt was incurred directly from the seller or other parties or indirectly through assumption. Payments to the seller from the proceeds of such indebtedness are not included as part of the buyer's initial investment. (ASC 360-20-40-17)

If the transaction does not qualify for full accrual accounting and, consequently, is being accounted for using installment, cost recovery, or reduced profit methods, payments made on the debt in the preceding paragraph are not considered to be buyer's cash payments. However, if the profit deferred under the applicable method exceeds the outstanding amount of seller financing and the outstanding amount of buyer's debt secured by the property for which the seller is contingently liable, the seller recognizes the excess in income.

Size of initial investment Once the initial investment is computed, its size must be compared to the sales value of the property. To qualify as an adequate initial investment, the initial investment must be equal to at least a major part of the difference between usual loan limits established by independent lending institutions and the sales value of the property. The minimum initial investment requirements for real estate sales (other than retail land sales) vary depending upon the type of property being sold. (ASC 360-20-40-18) The following table from ASC 360-20-55-2 provides the limits for the various properties:

Type of property	*Minimum initial investment expressed as a percentage of sales value*
Land	
Held for commercial, industrial, or residential development to commence within two years after sale	20
Held for commercial, industrial, or residential development to commence more than two years after sale	25
Commercial and Industrial Property	
Office and industrial buildings, shopping centers, and so forth:	
Properties subject to lease on a long-term lease basis to parties with satisfactory credit rating; cash flow currently sufficient to service all indebtedness	10

Type of property	*Minimum initial investment expressed as a percentage of sales value*
Single-tenancy properties sold to a buyer with a satisfactory credit rating	15
All other	20
Other income-producing properties (hotels, motels, marinas, mobile home parks, and so forth):	
Cash flow currently sufficient to service all indebtedness	15
Start-up situations or current deficiencies in cash flow	25
Multifamily Residential Property	
Primary residence:	
Cash flow currently sufficient to service all indebtedness	10
Start-up situations or current deficiencies in cash flow	15
Secondary or recreational residence:	
Cash flow currently sufficient to service all indebtedness	15
Start-up situations or current deficiencies in cash flow	25
Single-Family Residential Property (including condominium or cooperative housing)	
Primary residence of the buyer	52[a]
Secondary or recreational residence	10[a]

[a] *If collectibility of the remaining portion of the sales price cannot be supported by reliable evidence of collection experience, the minimum initial investment [is to] be at least 60% of the difference between the sales value and the financing available from loans guaranteed by regulatory bodies such as the Federal Housing Administration (FHA) or the Veterans Administration (VA), or from independent, established lending institutions. This 60% test applies when independent first-mortgage financing is not utilized and the seller takes a receivable from the buyer for the difference between the sales value and the initial investment. If independent first mortgage financing is utilized, the adequacy of the initial investment on sales of single-family residential property [is] determined [as described in the next paragraph].*

Lenders' appraisals of specific properties often differ. Therefore, if the buyer has obtained a permanent loan or firm permanent loan commitment for maximum financing of the property from an independent lending institution, the minimum initial investment must be the greater of the following (ASC 360-20-55-1):

- The minimum percentage of the sales value of the property specified in the above table or
- The lesser of:
  - The amount of the sales value of the property in excess of 115% of the amount of a newly placed permanent loan or firm loan commitment from a primary lender that is an independent established lending institution, or
  - 25% of the sales value.

To illustrate the determination of whether an initial investment adequately demonstrates a commitment to pay for property, consider the following example.

Example Determining Adequacy of Initial Investment

Marcus, Inc. exercised a $2,000 option for the purchase of an apartment building from Rubin, Inc. The terms of the sales contract required Marcus to pay $3,000 of delinquent property taxes, pay a $300,000 cash down payment, assume Rubin's recently issued first mortgage of $1,200,000, and give Rubin a second mortgage of $500,000 at a prevailing interest rate.

Step 1—Compute the sales value of the property.

Payment of back taxes to reduce Rubin's liability to local municipality	$3,00
Proceeds from exercised option	2,000
Cash down payment	300,000
First mortgage assumed by Marcus	1,200,000
Second mortgage given to Rubin	500,000
Sales value of the apartment complex	$2,005,000

Step 2—Compute the initial investment.

Cash down payment	$ 300,000
Payment of back taxes to reduce Rubin's liability to local municipality	3,000
Proceeds from exercised option	2,000
	$ 305,000

Step 3—Compute the minimum initial investment required.

a. The minimum percentage of the sales value of the property as specified in the table is 200,500 (= $2,005,000 × 10%).

b. 1. The amount of the sales value of the property in excess of 115% of the recently placed permanent mortgage is $625,000 (sales value of $2,005,000 – $1,380,000 [= 115% of $1,200,000]).

2. 25% of the sales value ($2,005,000) is $501,250.

The lesser of b.1 and b.2 is b.2, $501,250. The greater of a and b is b, $501,250. Therefore, to record this transaction under the full accrual method (assuming all other criteria are met), the minimum initial investment must be equal to or greater than $501,250. Since the actual initial investment is only $305,000, all or part of the recognition of profit from the transaction must be postponed.

Adequacy of the buyer's continuing investments assured The collectibility of the buyer's receivable must be reasonably assured; therefore, for full profit recognition under the full accrual method, the buyer must be contractually required to pay each year on its total debt for the purchase price of the property an amount at least equal to the level annual payment that would be needed to pay that debt (both principal and interest) over a specified period. This period is no more than twenty years for land, and no more than the customary amortization term of a first mortgage loan by an independent lender for other types of real estate. For continuing investment purposes, the contractually required payments must be in a form that is acceptable for an initial investment. If the seller provides funds to the buyer, either directly or indirectly, these funds must be subtracted from the buyer's payments in determining whether the continuing investments are adequate. (ASC 360-20-40-19 and 55-02)

The indebtedness on the property does not have to be reduced proportionately. A lump-sum (balloon) payment will not affect the amortization of the receivable as long as the level annual payments still meet the minimum annual amortization requirement. For example, a land real estate sale may require the buyer to make level annual payments at the end of each of the first five years and then a balloon payment at the end of the sixth year. The continuing investment criterion is met provided the level annual payment required in each of the first five years is greater than or equal to the level annual payment that would be made if the receivable were amortized over the maximum twenty-year (land's specified term) period.

Release provisions An agreement to sell real estate may provide that part or all of the property sold will be released from liens by payment of an amount sufficient to release the debt or by an assignment of the buyer's payments until release. To meet the criteria of an adequate initial investment, the investment must be sufficient both to pay the release on property released and to meet the initial investment requirements on property not released. If not, profit is recognized on each released portion as if it were a separate sale when a sale has been deemed to have taken place. (ASC 360- 20-40-21 through 40-23)

Buyer's initial or continuing investments do not qualify for full accrual method If the sale has been consummated but the buyer's initial investment does not adequately demonstrate a commitment to pay, the transaction is accounted for using:

- The installment method when the seller is reasonably assured of recovering the cost of the property if the buyer defaults.
- The cost recovery or deposit method
  - If the recovery of the cost of the property is not reasonably assured should the buyer default or
  - If the cost has been recovered and the collection of additional amounts is uncertain

  (ASC 360-20-40-31)

Exhibit—Recognition of Profit When Sale Is Not Consummated or Full Accrual Requirements Are Not Met

Circumstances	Accounting Treatment
Sale not consummated	Deposit method
Buyer's initial investment does not meet criteria for recognition of profit by the full accrual method: • Recovery of the property is reasonably assured if buyer defaults • Recover of the property is not reasonably assured if buyer defaults • Cost has already been recovered and collection of additional amounts is uncertain (ASC 360-40-28 through 40-31)	Installment method or cost recovery method Cost recovery or deposit method Cost recovery or deposit method

Criterion 3—Future Subordination The seller's receivable should not be subject to future subordination. Future subordination by a primary lender would permit the lender to obtain a lien on the property, giving the seller only a secondary residual claim. This subordination criterion does not apply if either of the following occur (ASC 360-20-40-25):

- A receivable is subordinate to a first mortgage on the property existing at the time of sale.
- A future loan, including an existing permanent loan commitment, is provided for by the terms of the sale and the proceeds of the loan will be applied first to the payment of the seller's receivable.

If the seller's receivable is subject to future subordination, profit is recognized using the cost recovery method. The cost recovery method is justified because the collectibility of the sales price is not reasonably assured in circumstances when the receivable may be subordinated to amounts due to other creditors.

Criterion 4—Continuing Involvement Sometimes sellers continue to be involved with property for periods of time even though the property has been legally sold. The seller's involvement often takes the form of profit participation, management services, financing, guarantees of return, construction, etc. The seller does not have a substantial continuing involvement with property unless the risks and rewards of ownership have been clearly transferred to the buyer.

If the sale has been consummated and the minimum initial investment criteria have been satisfied but the continuing investment by the buyer does not meet the stated criterion, the seller recognizes profit by the reduced profit method at the time of sale if payments by the buyer each year will at least cover both of the following (ASC 360-20-40-33):

- The interest and principal amortization on the maximum first mortgage loan that could be obtained on the property
- Interest, at an appropriate rate, on the excess of the aggregate actual debt on the property over such a maximum first mortgage loan.

If the payments by the buyer do not cover both of the above, the seller recognizes profit by either the installment or cost recovery method. (ASC 360-20-40-34)

Graduated payment mortgages Graduated payment mortgages for which negative principal amortization is recognized do not meet the continuing investment tests in ASC 360, and thus full profit is not recognized immediately. (ASC 360-20-40-35) Mortgage insurance should not be considered the equivalent of an irrevocable letter of credit in determining whether profit is to be recognized, and the purchase of such insurance is not in itself a demonstration of commitment by the buyer to honor its obligation to pay for the property. The sole exception to this rule is that in an irrevocable financial instrument from an established independent insuring institution, such as FHA (Federal Housing Administration) and VA (Veteran's Affairs), profits may be recognized under the full accrual method. (ASC 360-20-40-12) The seller may consider these to be the equivalent of irrevocable letters of credit.

If the seller has some continuing involvement with the property and does not clearly transfer substantially all of the risks and rewards of ownership, profit is recognized by a method other than the full accrual method. The method chosen is determined by the nature and extent of the seller's continuing involvement. As a general rule, profit is only recognized at the time of sale if the amount of the seller's loss due to the continued involvement with the property is limited by the terms of the sales contract. In this event, the profit recognized at this time is reduced by the maximum possible loss from the continued involvement. (ASC 360-20-40-37)

Profit-sharing, financing, and leasing arrangements In real estate sales, it is often the case that economic substance takes precedence over legal form. Certain transactions, though possibly called sales, are in substance profit-sharing, financing, or leasing arrangements and are accounted for as such. These include situations in which:

- The seller has an obligation to repurchase the property, or the terms of the transaction allow the buyer to compel the seller to repurchase the property or give the seller an option to do so. (ASC 360-20-40-38)

- The seller is a general partner in a limited partnership that acquires an interest in the property sold and holds a receivable from the buyer for a significant part (15% of the maximum first-lien financing) of the sales price. (ASC 360-20-40-40)
- The seller guarantees the return of the buyer's investment or a return on that investment for an extended period of time. (ASC 360-20-40-41)
- The seller is required to initiate or support operations, or continue to operate the property at its own risk for an extended period of time. (ASC 360-20-40-42)

Buy-sell agreements A buy-sell clause is not a prohibited form of continuing involvement precluding partial sales treatment, but only if:

- The buyer can act independently from the seller, or if
- The seller is not compelled to reacquire the other investor's interest in the jointly owned entity.

The decision is judgmental, requiring consideration of numerous factors.

Factors to consider in determining whether the buyer cannot act independently from the seller are:

- The presence of a predetermined buy-sell price,
- The seller has a strategic necessity barring it from relinquishing its ownership rights to the buyer,
- The seller has business arrangements with the jointly owned entity that economically require it to reacquire the real estate to avoid losing economic benefits or escaping negative consequences of the arrangements, or
- Tax implications compelling the seller to acquire the buyer's interest in the entity.

Factors to consider in determining if the buyer can compel the seller to repurchase the property include:

- The buyer is financially unable to acquire the seller's interest,
- The buy-sell clause contains a specified rate of return for either party,
- The buyer has a strategic necessity requiring it to sell its interest to the seller,
- The buyer is legally restricted from acquiring the seller's interest,
- The buyer cannot realize its economic interest by sale to a third party, due to the integration of the real estate into the seller's business, or
- Tax implications compelling the buyer to sell its interest to the seller.

Antispeculation clauses ASC 360-20-40-39 deals with antispeculation clauses sometimes found in land sale agreements, requiring the buyer to develop the land in a specific manner or within a specific period of time and giving the seller the right, but not the obligation, to reacquire the property when the condition is not met. This option does not preclude recognition of a sale if the probability of the buyer not complying is remote.

Options to purchase real estate property Often a buyer will buy an option to purchase land from a seller with the hopeful intention of obtaining a zoning change, building permit, or some other contingency specified in the option agreement. Proceeds from the issue of an option by a property owner (seller) are accounted for by the deposit method. If the option is exercised, the seller includes the option proceeds in the computation of the sales value of the property. If the option is not exercised, the seller recognizes the option proceeds as income at the time the option expires. (ASC 360-20-40-45)

Partial sales of property Per ASC 360-20-40-46, "a sale is a partial sale if the seller retains an equity interest in the property or has an equity interest in the buyer." Profit on a partial sale may be recognized on the date of sale if all of the following occur:

- The buyer is independent of the seller.
- Collection of the sales price is reasonably assured.
- The seller will not be required to support the operations of the property on its related obligations to an extent greater than its proportionate interest.

If the buyer is not independent of the seller, the seller may not be able to recognize any profit that is measured at the date of sale (see the previous Buy-sell agreements section). (ASC 360-20-40-47)

If the seller is not reasonably assured of collecting the sales price, the cost recovery or installment method is used to recognize profit on the partial sale. (ASC 360-20-40-48)

A seller who separately sells individual units in condominium projects or time-sharing interests recognizes profit by the percentage-of-completion method on the sale of individual units or interests if all of the following criteria are met (ASC 360-20-40-50):

- Construction is beyond a preliminary stage (i.e., engineering and design work, execution of construction contracts, site clearance and preparation, excavation, and completion of the building foundation have all been completed).
- The buyer is unable to obtain a refund except for nondelivery of the units or interest.
- Sufficient units have been sold to ensure that the entire property will not revert to being rental property.
- Sales prices are collectible.
- Aggregate sales proceeds and costs can be reasonably estimated.

The deposit method is used to account for these sales up to the point all the criteria are met for recognition of a sale. (ASC 360-20-40-54)

Leases involving real estate (ASC 360-20-40-60) ASC 840-40 dealing with sales-type real estate leases and sale-leaseback real estate transactions is covered in the chapter on ASC 840. Also see the chapter on ASC 842.

Methods of Accounting for Real Estate Sales Other Than Retail Land Sales

Selection of Method The full accrual method of accounting for nonretail sales of real estate is appropriate when all four of the recognition criteria discussed above have been satisfied.

If all of the criteria have not been met, the seller records the transaction by one of the following methods as indicated by ASC 360-20-40-21 through 40-64:

- Deposit
- Cost recovery
- Installment
- Reduced profit
- Percentage-of-completion

The installment method is used if the full accrual method cannot be used due to an inadequate initial investment by the buyer, provided that recovery of cost is reasonably assured if the buyer defaults. (ASC 360-20-40-31)

The cost recovery method or the deposit methods are used if such cost recovery is not assured. The reduced profit method is used when the buyer's initial investment is adequate but the continuing investment is not adequate, and payments by the buyer at least cover the sum of:

- The amortization (principal and interest) on the maximum first mortgage that could be obtained on the property, and
- The interest, at an appropriate rate, on the excess of aggregate debt over the maximum first mortgage.

Full Accrual Method The full accrual method is simply the application of the revenue recognition principle. Profit under the full accrual method is computed by subtracting the cost basis of the property surrendered from the sales value given by the buyer. Also, the computation of profit on the sale includes all costs incurred that are directly related to the sale, such as accounting and legal fees.

If a loss is apparent (e.g., the carrying value of the property exceeds the sum of the deposit, fair value of unrecorded note receivable, and the debt assumed by the buyer), then immediate recognition of the loss is required.

A real estate sale is recognized in full when the profit is determinable and the earnings process is virtually complete. The profit is determinable when the first three recognition criteria listed above have been met. The earnings process is virtually complete when the fourth criterion has been met.

Installment Method Under the installment method (ASC 360-20-55-7), each cash receipt and principal payment by the buyer on debt assumed with recourse to the seller consists of part recovery of cost and part recovery of profit. The apportionment between cost recovery and profit is in the same ratio as total cost and total profit bear to the sales value of the property sold. Therefore, under the installment method, the seller recognizes profit on each payment that the buyer makes to the seller and on each payment the buyer makes to the holder of the primary debt. When a buyer assumes debt that is without recourse to the seller, the seller recognizes profit on each payment made to the seller and on the entire debt assumed by the buyer. The accounting treatment differs because the seller is subject to substantially different levels of risk under the alternative conditions. For debt that is without recourse, the seller recovers a portion, if not all, of the cost of the asset surrendered at the time the buyer assumes the debt.

Example of the Installment Method

Assume Tucker sells to Price a plot of undeveloped land for \$2,000,000. Price will assume, with recourse, Tucker's existing first mortgage of \$1,000,000 and also pay Tucker a \$300,000 cash down payment. Price will pay the balance of \$700,000 by giving Tucker a second mortgage payable in equal installments of principal and interest over a ten-year period. The cost of the land to Tucker was \$1,200,000, and Price will commence development of the land immediately.

1. Computation of sales value:

Cash down payment	$ 300,000
First mortgage	1,000,000
Second mortgage	<u>700,000</u>

Sales value	$2,000,000
2. Computation of the initial investment:	
Cash down payment	$ 300,000
3. Computation of the minimum required initial investment:	
a. $400,000 ($2,000,000 20%)	
b. 1. $850,000 [$2,000,000 – (115% × 1,000,000)]	
2. $500,000 ($2,000,000 × 25%)	

The minimum initial investment is $500,000 since b.2 is less than b.1 and b.2 is greater than a.

The initial investment criterion has not been satisfied because the actual initial investment is less than the minimum initial investment. Therefore, assuming the sale has been consummated and Tucker is reasonably assured of recovering the cost of the land from Price, the installment method is to be used. The gross profit to be recognized over the installment payment period by Tucker is computed as follows:

Sales value	$2,000,000
Cost of land	(1,200,000)
Gross profit	$ 800,000

The gross profit percentage to apply to each payment by Price to Tucker and the primary debt holder is 40% ($800,000/$2,000,000).

If Price also pays $50,000 of principal on the first mortgage and $70,000 of principal on the second mortgage in the year of sale, Tucker would recognize the following profit in the year of sale:

Profit recognized on the down payment ($300,000 × 40%)	
Profit recognized on the principal payments:	$120,000
First mortgage ($50,000 × 40%)	20,000
Second mortgage ($70,000 × 40%)	28,000
Total profit recognized in year of sale	$168,000

Note that Tucker recognizes profit only on the payment applicable to the first mortgage. This is because Tucker may be called upon to satisfy the liability on the first mortgage if Price defaults.

If Tucker's first mortgage was assumed without recourse, Tucker would recognize the following profit in the year of sale:

Profit recognized on the down payment ($300,000 × 40%)	$120,000
Profit recognized on Price's assumption of Tucker's first mortgage without recourse ($1,000,000 × 40%)	400,000
Profit recognized on the principal payment of the second mortgage ($70,000 × 40%)	28,000
Total profit recognized in year of sale	$548,000

The income statement (or related notes) for the period of sale includes the sales value received, the gross profit recognized, the gross profit deferred, and the costs of sale. In future periods when further payments are made to the buyer, the seller realizes gross profit on these payments. This amount is presented as a single line item in the revenue section of the income statement.

If, in the future, the transaction meets the requirements for the full accrual method of recognizing profit, the seller may change to that method and recognize the remaining deferred profit as income at that time.

Cost Recovery Method When the cost recovery method (ASC 360-20-55-13) is used (e.g., when the seller's receivable is subject to subordination or the seller is not reasonably assured of recovering the cost of the property if the buyer defaults), no profit is recognized on the sales transaction until the seller has recovered the cost of the property sold. If the buyer assumes debt that is with recourse to the seller, profit is not recognized by the seller until the cash payments by the buyer, including both principal and interest on debt due the seller and on debt assumed by the buyer, exceed the seller's cost of the property sold. If the buyer assumes debt that is without recourse to the seller, profit may be recognized by the seller when the cash payments by the buyer, including both principal and interest on debt due the seller, exceed the difference between the seller's cost of the property and the nonrecourse debt assumed by the buyer.

For the cost recovery method, principal collections reduce the seller's related receivable, and interest collections on such receivable increase the deferred gross profit on the statement of financial position. (ASC 360-20-55-14)

Example of the Cost Recovery Method

Assume that on January 1, 20X1, Simon, Inc. purchased undeveloped land with a sales value of $365,000 from Davis Co. The sales value is represented by a $15,000 cash down payment, Simon assuming Davis's $200,000 first mortgage (10%, payable in equal annual installments over the next twenty years), and Simon giving Davis a second mortgage of $150,000 (12%, payable in equal annual installments over the next ten years). The sale has been consummated, but the initial investment is below the minimum required amount and Davis is not reasonably assured of recovering the cost of the property if Simon defaults. The cost of the land to Davis was $300,000. The circumstances indicate the cost recovery method is appropriate. The transaction is recorded by Davis as follows:

1/1/X1	Notes receivable	150,000	
	First mortgage payable	200,000	
	Cash	15,000	
	Revenue from sale of land		365,000
	Revenue from sale of land	365,000	
	Land		300,000
	Deferred gross profit		65,000

Case 1—The first mortgage was assumed with recourse to Davis. Immediately after the sale, the unrecovered cost of the land is computed as follows:

Land	$300,000
Less: Cash down payment	(15,000)
Unrecovered cost	$285,000

The note (second mortgage) is reported as follows:

Note receivable	$150,000	
Less: Deferred gross profit	(65,000)	$85,000

At the end of the year Simon pays $26,547.64 ($8,547.64 principal and $18,000.00 interest) on the second mortgage note and $23,491.94 ($3,491.94 principal and $20,000.00 interest) on the first mortgage. At 12/31/X1 the unrecovered cost of the land is computed as follows:

Previous unrecovered cost		$285,000.00	
Less:	Note receivable payment	$ 26,547.64	
	First mortgage payment	23,491.94	(50,039.58)
Unrecovered cost			
$ 234,960.42			

The receivable is reported on the 12/31/X1 statement of financial position as follows:

Note receivable ($150,000 – 8,547.64)	$141,452.36	
Less: Deferred gross profit ($65,000 + 18,000)	83,000.00	$58,452.36

Case 2—The first mortgage is assumed without recourse to Davis. The reporting of the note is the same as Case 1; however, the unrecovered cost of the property is different. Immediately after the sale, the unrecovered cost of the property is computed as follows:

Land		$ 300,000
Less:	Cash down payment	(15,000)
	Nonrecourse debt assumed by Simon	(200,000)
Unrecovered cost		$ 85,000

After Simon makes the payments at the end of the year, the unrecovered cost is computed as follows:

Previous unrecovered cost		$85,000.00
Less:	Notes receivable payment	26,547.64
Unrecovered cost		$58,452.36

For the cost recovery method, the income statement for the year the real estate sale occurs includes the sales value received, the cost of the property given up, and the gross profit deferred.

In future periods, after the cost of the property has been recovered, the income statement includes the gross profit earned as a separate revenue item.

If, after accounting for the sale by the cost recovery method, circumstances indicate that the criteria for the full accrual method are satisfied, the seller may change to the full accrual method and recognize any remaining deferred gross profit in full.

Deposit Method The deposit method is used until the sale is consummated. (ASC 360-20-40-28) When the deposit method (ASC 360-20-55-17) is used (e.g., when the sale is, in substance, the sale of an option and not real estate), the seller does not recognize any profit, does not record a receivable, continues to report in its financial statements the property and the related existing debt even if the debt has been assumed by the buyer, and discloses that those items are subject to a sales contract. The seller also continues to recognize depreciation expense on the property for which the deposits have been received, unless the property has been classified as held for sale (per ASC 360-10). Cash received from the buyer (initial and continuing investments) is reported as a deposit on the contract. However, some amounts of cash may be received that are not subject to refund, such as interest on the unrecorded principal. These amounts are used to offset any carrying charges on the property (e.g., property taxes and interest on the existing debt). If the interest collected on the unrecorded receivable is refundable, the seller records this interest as a deposit before the sale is consummated and then includes it as a part of the initial investment once the sale is consummated. If deposits on retail land sales are eventually recognized as sales, the interest portion of the deposit is separately recognized as interest income. For contracts that are canceled, the nonrefundable amounts are recognized as income and the refundable amounts returned to the depositor at the time of cancellation.

As stated, the seller's statement of financial position continues to present the debt assumed by the buyer (this includes nonrecourse debt) among its other liabilities. However, the seller reports any principal payments on the mortgage debt assumed as additional deposits, while correspondingly reducing the carrying amount of the mortgage debt.

Example of a Deposit Transaction

Elbrus Investments enters into two separate property acquisition transactions with the Buena Vista Land Company.

1. Elbrus pays a $50,000 deposit and promises to pay an additional $800,000 to buy land and a building in an area not yet properly zoned for the facility Elbrus intends to construct. Final acquisition of the property is contingent upon these zoning changes. Buena Vista does not record the receivable, and records the deposit with the following entry:

Cash	50,000	
Customer deposits		50,000

Part of the purchase agreement stipulates that Buena Vista will retain all interest earned on the deposit, and that 10% of the deposit is nonrefundable. Buena Vista earns 5% interest on Elbrus' deposit over a period of four months, resulting in $208 of interest income that is offset against the property tax expenses of the property with the following entry:

Cash	208	
Property tax expense		208

Immediately thereafter, the required zoning changes are turned down, and Elbrus cancels the sales contract. Buena Vista returns the refundable portion of the deposit to Elbrus and records the nonrefundable portion as income with the following entry:

Customer deposits	50,000	
Income from contract cancellation		10,000
Cash		40,000

2. Elbrus pays a $40,000 deposit on land owned and being improved by Buena Vista. Elbrus immediately begins paying $5,000/month under a four-year, 7% loan agreement totaling $212,000 of principal payments, and agrees to pay an additional $350,000 at closing, subject to the land being approved for residential construction. After two months, Buena Vista has earned $167 of refundable interest income on Elbrus' deposit and has been paid $7,689 of refundable principal and $2,311 of refundable interest on the debt. Buena Vista records these events with the following entry:

Cash	10,167	
Customer deposits		10,167

The land is approved for residential construction, triggering sale of the property. Buena Vista's basis in the property is $520,000. Buena Vista uses the following entry to describe completion of the sale:

Cash	350,000	
Note receivable	204,311	
Customer deposits	50,167	
Gain on asset sale		84,478
Land		520,000

Reduced Profit Method The reduced profit method is appropriate when the sale has been consummated and the initial investment is adequate but the continuing investment does not clearly demonstrate the buyer's willing commitment to pay the remaining balance of the receivable. For example, a buyer may purchase land under an agreement in which the seller will finance the sale over a thirty-year period. ASC 976 specifically states twenty years as the maximum amortization period for the purchase of land; therefore, the agreement fails to meet the continuing investment criteria.

Under the reduced profit method (ASC 360-20-55-16), the seller recognizes a portion of the profit at the time of sale with the remaining portion recognized in future periods. The amount of reduced profit recognized at the time of sale is determined by discounting the receivable from the buyer to the present value of the lowest level of annual payments required by the sales contract over the maximum period of time specified for that type of real estate property (twenty years for land and the customary term of a first mortgage loan set by an independent lending institution for other types of real estate). The remaining profit is recognized in the periods that lump-sum or other payments are made.

Example of the Reduced Profit Method

Assume Levinson, Inc. sells a parcel of land to Raemer Co. Levinson receives sales value of \$2,000,000. The land cost \$1,600,000. Raemer gave Levinson the following consideration:

Cash down payment	\$500,000
First mortgage note payable to an independent lending institution (payable in equal installments of principal and 12% interest, \$133,887 payable at the end of each of the next twenty years)	1,000,000
Second mortgage note payable to Levinson (payable in equal installments of principal and 10% interest, \$53,039 payable at the end of each of the next thirty years)	500,000
Total sales value	\$2,000,000

The amortization term of the second mortgage (seller's receivable) exceeds the twenty-year maximum permitted by ASC 976. It is assumed that the payments by the buyer will cover the interest and principal on the maximum first mortgage loan that could be obtained on the property and interest on the excess aggregate debt on the property over such a maximum first mortgage loan; consequently, the reduced profit method is appropriate. It is also assumed that the market interest rate on similar agreements is 14%.

The present value of \$53,039 per year for twenty years at the market rate of 14% is \$351,278 (\$53,039 × 6.623).

The gross profit on the sale (\$400,000) is reduced by the difference between the face amount of the seller's receivable (\$500,000) and the reduced amount (\$351,278) or \$148,722. The profit recognized at the time of sale is the sales value less the cost of the land less the difference between the face amount of the receivable and the reduced amount. Therefore, the reduced profit recognized on the date of sale is computed as follows:

Sales value		\$2,000,000
Less:	Cost of land	(1,600,000)
	Excess	(148,722)
Reduced profit		\$ 251,278

Under the reduced profit method, the seller amortizes its receivable at the market rate, not the rate given on the second mortgage. The receivable's carrying balance is zero after the specified term expires (in this case, twenty years). The remaining profit of \$148,722 is recognized in the years after the specified term expires as the buyer makes payments on the second mortgage (years twenty-one through thirty).

Other Guidance for Accounting for Real Estate Sales Transactions

Integral Equipment Sales of integral equipment are within the scope of ASC 360, and thus the determination of whether equipment is integral is an important one. A determination of whether equipment to be leased is integral is also necessary to enable lessors to determine the proper accounting for sales-type leases. This determination is made based on two factors:

1. The first is the significance of the cost to remove the equipment from its existing location (which would include any costs of repairing the damage done to that location by the act of removal). (ASC 360-20-15-4)

2. The second is the decrease in value of the equipment that results from its removal (which is, at a minimum, the cost to ship and reinstall the equipment at a new site). (ASC 360- 20-15-5)

The nature of the equipment and whether others can use it is considered in determining whether there would be any further diminution in fair value. When the combined total of the cost to remove and any further diminution of fair value exceeds 10% of the fair value of the equipment (installed), the equipment is to be deemed integral equipment, and thus accounted for under the provisions of ASC 360. (ASC 360-20-15-7)

Collateralized Loan Valuation Allowance ASC 310-40-55 deals with the question of whether a valuation allowance previously established for a loan which is collateralized by a long-lived asset should be carried forward after the asset is foreclosed due to loan default. It holds that, when such a loan is foreclosed, any valuation allowance established for the foreclosed loan should not be carried over as a separate element of the cost basis for purposes of accounting for the long-lived assets under ASC 360. Rather, upon foreclosure the lender must measure the long-lived asset received in full satisfaction of a receivable at fair value less cost to sell as prescribed by ASC 310-40. Application of ASC 310-40 results in the identification of a new cost basis for the long-lived asset received in full satisfaction of a receivable.

Foreclosure—Subsequent Recovery of Value ASC 310-40-55 also addresses the limitation on gain recognition when an impaired asset obtained by means of foreclosure later recovers some value. ASC 360-10-35-40 states that "a loss shall be recognized for any initial or subsequent write-down to fair value less cost to sell. A gain shall be recognized for any subsequent increase in fair value less cost to sell, but not in excess of the cumulative loss previously recognized (for a write-down to fair value less cost to sell)." Thus, gain recognition is limited to the cumulative extent that losses have been recognized while the assets were accounted for as long-lived assets under ASC 360. Put differently, ASC 360 does not allow the lender to "look back" to lending impairments measured and recognized under ASC 450 or ASC 310, for purposes of measuring the cumulative loss previously recognized. "Recovery" of losses not recognized is thus not permitted.

Homebuilder Builds Home on Own Lot ASC 970-360-55 addresses the timing of income recognition when a homebuilder enters into a contract to build a home on its own lot, relinquishing title to both the lot and the home at closing. It states that profit recognition is not appropriate until the conditions specified in ASC 360 have been met. Deposit accounting should be used for both the land and building activity until the conditions are met.

Repossessed Real Estate ASC 310-40-40-7 deals with the proper valuation for repossessed real estate which is recorded at the lower of the net receivable due to the seller at foreclosure or the fair value of the property.

Minority Interests in REITs ASC 974-810-30 addresses the proper treatment of minority interests in certain real estate investment trusts. See the chapter on ASC 900s, *Specialized Industries*, for more information.

ADC Loans The matter of appropriate accounting for transfers of investments that are in substance real estate is addressed by ASC 360-20-15-3, which holds that in such circumstances the accounting is to follow ASC 360. Thus, transfers of acquisition, development, and construction loans (ADC loans), which are deemed in substance real estate under ASC 815-15-55-10, are subject to this rule, and transfers of marketable investments in a REIT which are accounted for under ASC 320 are to be accounted for per ASC 860.

Condominium Unit Sales ASC 360-20-40 addresses the applicability of a buyer's continuing investment to an entity's recognition of revenue when selling condominium units. An entity can assess the collectibility of the sales price as per ASC 360 by requiring the buyer to either make additional payments during the construction term at least equal to the level annual payments that would be required to fund principal and interest on a customary mortgage for the remaining purchase price of the property, or increase the minimum initial investment by an equivalent aggregate amount. If these criteria cannot be met, then the seller should record the transaction under the deposit method.

Investments in Real Estate Ventures ASC 970-323 specifies the accounting for investments in real estate ventures. For additional information, see the chapter on ASC 900s.

Real Estate Syndications ASC 970 contains information on real estate syndications. See the chapter on ASC 900s for more information.

26 ASC 405 LIABILITIES

PERSPECTIVE AND ISSUES

Subtopics

ASC 405, *Liabilities*, consists of four subtopics:

- ASC 405-10, *Overall*, which merely points to other areas of the Codification that contain guidance on liabilities
- ASC 405-20, *Extinguishments of Liabilities*, which provides guidance on when an entity should consider a liability settled
- ASC 405-30, *Insurance-Related Assessments*, which provides guidance on items such as assessments for state guaranty funds and workers' compensation second-injury funds
- ASC 405-40, *Obligations Resulting from Joint and Several Liabilities*, which provides guidance on arrangements where the total amount of the obligation is fixed at the reporting date.

Scope and Scope Exceptions

ASC 405-20 ASC 20 applies to:

- All entities with the covered transactions and
- Extinguishments of both financial and nonfinancial liabilities unless addressed by another topic.
  (ASC 405-20-15-2)

ASC 405-30 ASC 405-30 applies to entities:

- Subject to guaranty-forward assessments
- Subject to other insurance-related assessments.
  (ASC 405-30-15-1)

The guidance also applies to assessments mandated by statue or regulatory authority related directly or indirectly to underwriting activities, such as self-insurance. (ASC 405-30-30-15-2)

ASC 405-30 does *not* apply to the following:

- Amounts payable or paid as a result of reinsurance contracts or arrangements that are in substance reinsurance, including assumed reinsurance activities and certain involuntary pools that are covered by Topic 944.
- Assessments of depository institutions related to bank insurance and similar funds.
- The annual fee imposed on health insurers by the Patient Protection and Affordable Care Act as amended by the Health Care and Education Reconciliation Act (the Acts). The accounting for the Acts' fee is addressed in Subtopic 720-50.
  (ASC 405-30-15-3)

ASC 405-30 also does not apply to assessments related to income taxes and premium taxes.

ASC 405-40 ASC 405-40 applies to all entities and obligations such as debt arrangements, other contractual obligations, and settled litigation and judicial rulings. The guidance does *not* apply to obligations accounted for under the following topics:

- ASC 410, Asset Retirement and Environmental Obligations
- ASC 450, Contingencies
- ASC 460, Guarantees
- ASC 715, Compensation—Retirement Benefits
- ASC 740, Income Taxes.
  (ASC 405-40-15-1)

To be within the scope of this subtopic, the total amount of the entity's and its co-obligors' obligation must be fixed at the reporting date. However, the amount the entity expects to pay on behalf of its co-obligors may be uncertain. (ASC 405-40-15-2)

Overview

ASC 405 provides accounting and reporting guidance related to short-term liabilities and certain guidance that may apply broadly to any liability.

The FASB has declared, as a long-term goal, that all financial liabilities should be recognized in the statement of financial position at fair value, rather than at amounts based on their historical cost. The proper calculation of fair value is described in detail in the chapter on ASC 820, *Fair Value Measurements*. Under ASC 825, *Financial Instruments*, an entity has the option to record certain of its current liabilities that meet the definition of financial liabilities (see Appendix A) at their respective fair values, with changes in fair value recognized each period in net income. Liabilities that require the entity to provide goods or services to settle the obligation, instead of cash settlement, are not financial liabilities and thus are not eligible for the fair value measurement election permitted by ASC 825. This option is addressed in detail in the chapter on ASC 825.

Although measurement of liabilities is generally straightforward, some liabilities are difficult to measure because of uncertainties. Uncertainties can impact whether, when, and for how much an obligation will be recognized in the financial statements. Uncertainties include:

- Subsequent events,
- Whether an obligation exists,
- How much of an entity's assets will be needed to settle the obligation, and
- When the settlement will take place.

Most entities continue to measure their current liabilities at their settlement value, which is the amount of cash (or its equivalent amount of other assets) that will be paid to the creditor to liquidate the obligation during the current operating cycle. Accounts payable, dividends payable, salaries payable, and other current obligations are measured at settlement value because they require the entity to pay a determinable amount of cash within a relatively short period of time. If a current liability is near its payment date, there will be only an insignificant risk of changes in fair value because of changes in market conditions or the entity's credit standing, and settlement value and fair value will be essentially the same.

Other current liabilities are measured at the proceeds received when the obligation arose. Liabilities that are measured in this manner generally require the entity to discharge the obligation by providing goods or services rather than by paying cash. Deposits payable, or rents paid in advance on the statement of financial position of a lessor, are examples of current liabilities measured by reference to proceeds received.

DEFINITIONS OF TERMS

Source: ASC 405, *Glossaries*. Also see Appendix, *Definitions of Terms,* for Conduit Debt Security, Nonpublic Entity, and Reinsurance.

In-force Policies. Policies effective before a specified date that have not yet expired or been canceled.

Incurred Losses. Losses paid or unpaid for which the entity has become liable during a period.

Involuntary Pools. A residual market mechanism for insureds who cannot obtain insurance in the voluntary market.

Life, Annuity, and Health Insurance Entities. An entity that may issue annuity, endowment, and accident and health insurance contracts as well as life insurance contracts. Life and health insurance entities may be either stock or mutual entities.

Obligated to Write. A circumstance in which an entity has no discretion to cancel a policy because of legal obligation under state statute, contract terms, or regulatory practice and is required to offer or issue insurance policies for a period in the future.

Premium Tax Offsets. Offsets against premium taxes levied on insurance entities by states.

Premiums Written. The premiums on all policies an entity has issued in a period.

Property and Casualty Insurance Entity. An entity that issues insurance contracts providing protection against either of the following:

a. Damage to or loss of property caused by various perils, such as fire and theft
b. Legal liability resulting from injuries to other persons or damage to their property

Property and liability insurance entities may be either stock or mutual entities.

CONCEPTS, RULES, AND EXAMPLES

ASC 405-10, *Overall*

ASC 405-10 contains no guidance. Its purpose is to point to guidance in other areas of the Codification. ASC 410-10-05-02 points to the following Codification topics, which contain guidance on accounting and reporting on liabilities:

- *Asset Retirement and Environmental Obligations*—ASC 410
- *Exit or Disposal Cost Obligations and Contract Liabilities (added by ASU 2014-09)*—ASC 420
- *Deferred Revenue and Contract Liabilities*—ASC 430
- *Commitments*—ASC 440
- *Contingencies*—ASC 450
- *Guarantees*—ASC 460
- *Debt*—ASC 470
- *Distinguishing Liabilities from Equity*—Topic 480

ASC 405-20, *Extinguishments of Liabilities*

Unless addressed by other guidance, the entity recognizes extinguishment of a liability when:

- The debtor pays the creditor.
- The debtor is legally given relief from the liability.
  (ASC 405-20-40-1)

If the entity becomes a guarantor on the debt, the entity applies the guidance in ASC 460. (ASC 405-20-40-2)

Example of Accounting for the Extinguishment of Debt

1. A 10%, 10-year, $200,000 bond is dated and issued on 1/2/X2 at 98, with the interest payable semiannually.
2. Associated bond issue costs of $14,000 are incurred.
3. Four years later, on 1/2/X6, the entire bond issue is repurchased at 102 (i.e., 102% of face value) and is retired.
4. At 1/2/X6 the unamortized discount using the effective interest rate of 10.325% is $2,858.

Reacquisition price [(102%) × $200,000]		$204,000
Net carrying amount:		
Face value	$200,000	
Unamortized discount	(2,858)	
Unamortized issue costs [14,000 × (6/10)]	(8,400)	188,742
Loss on bond repurchase		$ 15,258

ASC 405-30, *Insurance-Related Assessments*

Entities that self-insure, as well as insurance entities, are subject to assessments related to insurance activities. However, note that the annual fee imposed on health insurers by the Patient Protection and Affordable Care Act is not considered an insurance-related assessment. The accounting for that fee falls under the guidance in ASC 720-50. (ASC 405-30-05-1)

Entities that are subject to assessment recognize liabilities when all of the following conditions are met:

- It is probable, before the financial statements are issued or available to be issued, an assessment will be imposed
- The events obligating the entity to pay has occurred on or before the date of the financial statements
- The entity can reasonably estimate the assessment
  (ASC 405-30-25-1)

It requires issuers to derecognize financial liabilities related to breakage amounts in either of the following two ways:

- If the entity expects to have a related breakage amount, derecognize the liability:
  - In amounts proportionate to the pattern of rights expected to be exercised by the holder of the product
  - To the extent that a significant reversal of the breakage amount will not subsequently occur, or
- If the entity does not expect to be entitled to a breakage amount, the entity derecognizes the liability when the likelihood of the exercise of rights becomes remote.
  (ASC 405-20-40-4)

Entities must reassess their breakage estimates each reporting period. Changes in estimates are accounted for as a change in accounting estimate under the guidance in ASC 250-10-45-17 through 45-20.

ASC 405-40, *Obligations Resulting from Joint and Several Liabilities*

ASC 405-40 requires an entity to measure obligations resulting from joint and several liability arrangements for which the total amount of the obligation within the scope of the guidance is fixed at the reporting date as the sum of:

- The amount the reporting entity agreed to pay on the basis of its arrangement among its obligors, and
- Any additional amount the entity expects to pay on behalf of its co-obligors.
  (ASC 405-40-30-1)

The corresponding entry depends on the particular facts and circumstances. (ASC 405-40-30-2)

27 ASC 410 ASSET RETIREMENT AND ENVIRONMENTAL OBLIGATIONS

PERSPECTIVE AND ISSUES

Overview

An asset retirement obligation (ARO) is a legal obligation:

- Established between two or more parties,
- Imposed by the government, or
- Arisen because of a promissory estoppel.

Activities that may result in an ARO because of legal obligations include:

- Removal of asbestos when the related asset is retired,
- Removal of transmission assets, such as transformers and wires,
- Cleanup of landfill contamination, or
- Removal of lessee's leasehold improvements

Subtopics

ASC 410, *Asset Retirement and Environmental Obligations*, consists of three subtopics. The sole purpose of ASC 410-10 is to explain the difference between the other two subtopics.

Subtopic	*Accounting and Financial Reporting of:*
ASC 410-20, *Asset Retirement Obligations*	• A liability associated with the retirement of a long-lived asset (ARO) and the associated capitalized asset retirement cost (ARC) • The obligation is unavoidable • An environmental remediation liability resulting from the acquisition, construction, or development and/or *normal* operation of a long-lived asset.
ASC 410-30, *Environmental Obligations*	• Environmental remediation liabilities that relate to ◦ Pollution from some past action generally as a result of, • Provisions of the Superfund Act, • The corrective provisions of the Recourse Conservation Recovery Act, or • Analogous state and non-U.S. laws and regulations (ASC 410-30-10-1)
(ASC 410-10-05-2)	

Another way to distinguish AROs from environmental obligations is the timing. If immediate remediation is required, it may be because of the improper operation of an asset, for example, in an oil spill.

The Scope and Scope Exceptions paragraphs provide details of the transactions covered by each subtopic.

Scope and Scope Exceptions

ASC 410-20 ASC 410-20 applies to all entities and the following events and transactions.

a. Legal obligations associated with the retirement of a tangible long-lived asset result from the acquisition, construction or development, and/or the normal operation of a long-lived asset.
b. An environmental liability that results from the normal operation of a long-lived asset and that is associated with the retirement of that asset.
c. A conditional obligation to perform a retirement activity.
d. Obligations of a lessor in connection with leased property meeting the provisions in "a" above. (Upon adoption of ASU 2016-02, this language will change to: Obligations of a lessor in connection with an underlying asset that meet the provisions in "a" above.)
e. The costs associated with the retirement of specified assets that qualifies as historical waste equipment defined by EU Directive 2002/96/EC.
(ASC 410-20-15-1 and 15-2)

It does *not* apply to these transactions:

- Obligations that arise solely from a plan to sell or otherwise dispose of a long-lived asset.
- An environmental remediation liability that results from the improper operation of a long-lived asset.
- Activities necessary to prepare an asset for an alternative use as they are not associated with the retirement of the asset.
- Historical waste held by private households.
- Obligations of a lessee in connection with leased property, whether imposed by a lease agreement or by a party other than the lessor, that meet the definition of either minimum lease payments or contingent rentals in paragraphs. (Upon adoption of ASU 2016-02 on leases, this wording will change to: Obligations of a lessee in connection with an underlying asset, whether imposed by a lease or by a party other than the lessor, that meet the definition of either lease payments or variable lease payments in ASC 842-10.)
- An obligation for asbestos removal resulting from the other-than-normal operation of an asset.
- Costs associated with complying with funding or assurance provisions.
- Obligations associated with maintenance, rather than retirement, of a long-lived asset.
- The cost of a replacement part that is a component of a long-lived asset.
  (ASC 410-20-15-3)

Examples of the Scope of ASC 410-20

Example 1—Leased premises. In accordance with the terms of a lease, the lessee is obligated to remove its specialized machinery from the leased premises prior to vacating those premises, or to compensate the lessor accordingly. The lease imposes a legal obligation on the lessee to remove the asset at the end of the asset's useful life or upon vacating the premises, and therefore this situation would be covered by ASC 410-20.

Example 2—Owned premises. The same machinery described in example 1 is installed in a factory that the entity owns. At the end of the useful life of the machinery, the entity will either incur costs to dismantle and remove the asset or will leave it idle in place. If the entity chooses to do nothing and not remove the equipment, this would adversely affect the fair value of the premises should the entity choose to sell the premises on an "as is" basis. Conceptually, to apply the matching principle in a manner consistent with example 1, the cost of asset retirement should be recognized systematically and rationally over the productive life of the asset and not in the period of retirement. However, in this example, there is no *legal obligation* on the part of the owner of the factory and equipment to retire the asset and, thus, this would *not* be covered by ASC 410-20.

Example 3—Promissory estoppel. Assume the same facts as in example 2. In this example, however, the owner of the property sold to a third party an option to purchase the factory, exercisable at the end of five years. In offering the option to the third party, the owner verbally represented that the factory would be completely vacant at the end of the five-year option period and that all machinery, furniture, and fixtures would be removed from the premises. The property owner would reasonably expect that the purchaser of the option relied to the purchaser's detriment (as evidenced by the financial sacrifice of consideration made in exchange for the option) on the representation that the factory would be vacant. This would trigger promissory estoppel and the owner's obligation would be covered by ASC 410-20.

ASC 410-30 ASC 410-30 applies to all entities. It applies to accounting for environmental remediation liabilities and is written in the context of operations taking place in the United States, however, it is applicable to all the operations of an entity. The guidance should be applied on a site by site basis. (ASC 410-30-15-1 and 15-2)

It does *not* apply to these transactions:

- Environmental contamination incurred in the normal operation of a long-lived asset.
- Pollution control costs with respect to current operations or on accounting for costs of future site restoration or closure that are required upon the cessation of operations or sale of facilities, as such current and future costs and obligations represent a class of accounting issues different from environmental remediation liabilities.
- Environmental remediation actions that are undertaken at the sole discretion of management and that are not induced by the threat, by governments or other parties, of litigation or of assertion of a claim or an assessment.
- Recognizing liabilities of insurance entities for unpaid claims.
- Natural resource damages and toxic torts.
- Asset impairment issues.

(ASC 410-30-15-3)

DEFINITIONS OF TERMS

Source: ASC 410. *Glossaries*. Also see Appendix A, *Definitions of Terms*, for definitions of Commencement Date of the Lease, Contract, Customer, Fair Value (Def. 3), Lease, Lease Payments, Lease Term, Lessee, Lessor, Revenue, Underlying Asset, and Variable Lease Payments. Also see the FASB Codification Master Glossary for the following terms not used in this chapter: Conditional Asset Retirement Obligation, Consent Decree, Hazardous Waste Constituent, Joint and Several Liability, Orphan Share, Orphan Share Potentially Responsible Party, Removal Action, Unknown Potentially Responsible Party, Unproven Potentially Responsible Party.

Accretion Expense. An amount recognized as an expense classified as an operating item in the statement of income resulting from the increase in the carrying amount of the liability associated with the asset retirement obligation.

Asset Retirement Cost. The amount capitalized that increases the carrying amount of the long-lived asset when a liability for an asset retirement obligation is recognized.

Asset Retirement Obligation. An obligation associated with the retirement of a tangible long-lived asset.

Closure. Related to the Resource Conservation and Recovery Act of 1976: the process in which the owner-operator of a hazardous waste management unit discontinues active operation of the unit by treating, removing from the site, or disposing of all on-site hazardous wastes in accordance with an Environmental Protection Agency or state-approved plan. Included, for example, are the processes of emptying, cleaning, and removing or filling underground storage tanks and the capping of a landfill. Closure entails specific financial guarantees and technical tasks that are included in a closure plan and must be implemented.

Corrective Action. Related to the Resource Conservation and Recovery Act of 1976: action to remedy releases from hazardous waste management units, or any other sources of releases at or from a treatment, storage, or disposal facility.

Discount Rate Adjustment Technique. A present value technique that uses a risk-adjusted discount rate and contractual, promised, or most likely cash flows.

Disposal. Related to the Comprehensive Environmental Response, Compensation, and Liability Act of 1980 and the Resource Conservation and Recovery Act of 1976: under the Resource Conservation and Recovery Act of 1976, the discharge, deposit, injection, dumping, spilling, leaking, or placing of any solid waste or hazardous waste into or on any land or water so that such solid waste or hazardous waste or any constituent thereof may enter the environment or be emitted into the air or discharged into any waters, including groundwaters. Similarly under the Comprehensive Environmental Response, Compensation, and Liability Act of 1980 with regard to hazardous substances.

Hazardous Substance. Related to Superfund: the definition of hazardous substance in the Comprehensive Environmental Response, Compensation, and Liability Act of 1980 is broader than the definition of hazardous wastes under the Resource Conservation and Recovery Act of 1976. Under the Comprehensive Environmental Response, Compensation, and Liability Act of 1980, a hazardous substance is any element, compound, mixture, solution, or substance that, when released to the environment, may present substantial danger to the public health or welfare or to the environment. It also includes the following:

- Specifically designated substances
- Toxic pollutants under the Federal Water Pollution Control Act
- Hazardous wastes having the characteristics identified under or listed pursuant to the Resource Conservation and Recovery Act of 1976 (excluding any waste suspended from regulation under the Solid Waste Disposal Act by Congress)
- Hazardous air pollutants under the Clean Air Act
- Any imminently hazardous chemical substance or mixture for which the government has taken action under section 7 of the Toxic Substances Control Act.

Petroleum (including crude oil not otherwise specifically listed or designated as a hazardous substance under any of those laws), natural gas, natural gas liquids, liquefied natural gas, or synthetic gas usable for fuel (or mixtures of natural gas and such synthetic gas) are excluded.

Hazardous Waste. Related to Resource Conservation and Recovery Act of 1976: a waste, or combination of wastes, that because of its quantity, concentration, toxicity, corrosiveness, mutagenicity or inflammability, or physical, chemical, or infectious characteristics may cause, or significantly contribute to, an increase in mortality or an increase in serious irreversible, or incapacitating reversible illness or pose a substantial present or potential hazard to human health or the environment when improperly treated, stored, transported, or disposed of, or otherwise managed. Technically, those wastes that are regulated under the Resource Conservation and Recovery Act of 1976 40 CFR Part 261 are considered to be hazardous wastes.

Legal Obligation. An obligation that a party is required to settle as a result of an existing or enacted law, statute, ordinance, or written or oral contract or by legal construction of a contract under the doctrine of promissory estoppel.

Natural Resources. Under the Comprehensive Environmental Response, Compensation, and Liability Act of 1980, natural resources are defined as land, fish, wildlife, biota, air, water, groundwater, drinking water supplies, and other such resources belonging to, managed or held in trust by, or otherwise controlled by the United States, state or local governments, foreign governments, or Indian tribes.

Participating Potentially Responsible Party. A party to a Superfund site that has acknowledged potential involvement with respect to the site. Active potentially responsible parties may participate in the various administrative, negotiation, monitoring, and remediation activities related to the site. Others may adopt a passive stance and simply monitor the activities and decisions of the more involved potentially responsible parties. This passive stance could result from a variety of factors such as the entity's lack of experience, limited internal resources, or relative involvement at a site. This category of potentially responsible parties (both active and passive) is also referred to as players.

Potentially Responsible Party. Any individual, legal entity, or government—including owners, operators, transporters, or generators—potentially responsible for, or contributing to, the environmental impacts at a Superfund site. The Environmental Protection Agency has the authority to require potentially responsible parties, through administrative and legal actions, to remediate such sites. At early stages of the remediation process, the list of potentially responsible parties may be limited to a handful of entities that either were significant contributors of waste to the site or were easy to identify, for example, because of their proximity to the site or because of labeled material found at the site. As further investigation of the site occurs and as remediation activities take place, additional potentially responsible parties may be identified. Once identified, the additional potentially responsible parties would be reclassified from this category to either the participating potentially responsible party or recalcitrant potentially responsible party category. The total number of parties in this category and their aggregate allocable share of the remediation liability varies by site and cannot be reliably determined before the specific identification of individual potentially responsible parties. For example, some ultimately may be dropped from the potentially responsible party list because no substantive evidence is found to link them to the site. For others, substantive evidence eventually may be found that points to their liability. The presentation of that evidence to the entity would result in a reclassification of the party from this category of potentially responsible parties (sometimes referred to as hiding in the weeds) to either the participating potentially responsible party or recalcitrant potentially responsible party category.

Promissory Estoppel. "The principle that a promise made without consideration may nonetheless be enforced to prevent injustice if the promisor should have reasonably expected the promisee to rely on the promise and if the promisee did actually rely on the promise to his or her detriment." (See *Black's Law Dictionary,* seventh edition.)

Recalcitrant Potentially Responsible Party. A party whose liability with respect to a Superfund site is substantiated by evidence, but that refuses to acknowledge potential involvement with respect to the site. Recalcitrant potentially responsible parties adopt a recalcitrant attitude toward the entire remediation effort even though evidence exists that points to their involvement at a site. Some may adopt this attitude out of ignorance of the law; others may do so in the hope that they will be considered a nuisance and therefore ignored. Typically, parties in this category must be sued in order to collect their allocable share of the remediation liability; however, it may be that it is not economical to bring such suits because the parties' assets are limited. This category of potentially responsible parties is also referred to as nonparticipating potentially responsible parties.

Release. Related to Superfund: any spilling, leaking, pumping, pouring, emitting, emptying, discharging, injecting, escaping, leaching, dumping, or disposing into the environment. Includes the abandonment or discarding of barrels, containers, and other closed receptacles containing any hazardous substance, pollutant, or contaminant. The law provides for several exclusions. Release also means the substantial threat of release.

Remedial Action. Related to Superfund: generally long-term actions taken to do any of the following:

- Investigate, alleviate, or eliminate the effects of a release of a hazardous substance into the environment.
- Investigate, alleviate, or eliminate a threat of the release of an existing hazardous substance that could potentially harm human health or the environment.
- Restore natural resources.

Also refers to corrective action under the Resource Conservation and Recovery Act of 1976.

Remedial Investigation-Feasibility Study. Extensive technical studies conducted by the government or by the potentially responsible parties to investigate the scope of site impacts and determine the remedial alternatives that, consistent with the National Contingency Plan, may be implemented at a Superfund site. Government-funded remedial investigation-feasibility studies do not recommend a specific alternative for implementation. Remedial investigation-feasibility studies conducted by potentially responsible parties usually do recommend and technically support a remedial alternative. A remedial investigation-feasibility study may include a variety of on- and off-site activities, such as monitoring, sampling, and analysis.

Strict Liability. Liability imposed without regard to the liable party's fault.

Unilateral Administrative Order. Order issued unilaterally by the Environmental Protection Agency under section 106(a) of the Comprehensive Environmental Response, Compensation, and Liability Act of 1980 to potentially responsible parties, or to nonpotentially responsible parties such as adjacent landowners, requiring them to take a response action. Unilateral administrative orders contain findings of fact and conclusions of law, and they specify the work to be performed and the Environmental Protection Agency's right to take over the work in the event of noncompliance, inadequate performance, or an emergency. A unilateral administrative order does not allocate conduct required by the order between individual potentially responsible par- ties; however, the Environmental Protection Agency may issue carve-out orders requiring individual potentially responsible parties to perform specific actions. Also referred to as a section 106 order.

ASC 410-20, *ASSET RETIREMENT OBLIGATIONS*

Concepts, Rules, and Examples

ASC 410-20 is designed to bring consistency to the way entities account for asset retirement obligations, that is, to avoid some entities recognizing liabilities as the costs are incurred and others postponing recognition until the asset is retired. ASC 410-20 provides standards for measuring the future cost to retire an asset and recognizing that cost in the financial statements as a liability, and correspondingly, as part of the depreciable cost of the asset.

Asset Retirement Obligations (AROs) Requiring Recognition When an entity acquires, constructs, and operates assets, it often incurs obligations that are unavoidable. Much of the discussion in ASC 410-20 pertains to specialized industry applications such as offshore oil platforms, nuclear power plants, mining operations, landfills, and underground storage tanks. However, the criteria for recognizing an ARO are also intended to apply to situations encountered more frequently in practice, such as in the examples later in this chapter.

Recognition

Upon initial recognition of a liability for an asset retirement obligation, the entity records an increase to the carrying amount of the related long-lived asset and an offsetting liability. (ASC 410-20-25-5) Asset retirement obligations are initially measured at fair value. The ARO may be incurred in one or more of the entity's reporting periods. Each period's incremental liability incurred is recognized as a separate liability and is estimated using these principles based on market and interest rate assumptions existing in the period of recognition. The table below summarizes the accounting treatment and is explained in detail in the information and examples that follow

Circumstance	Accounting Treatment		
	Statement of Financial Position	***Income Statement***	***Statement of Cash Flows***
Initial Recognition in the Period Incurred or When a Reasonable Estimate Can Be Made	Record the ARO liability at fair value of legal obligation. Capitalize the ARC by increasing the carrying amount of the related asset for the same amount as the ARO.	No impact	No impact
Changes in the Liability—Passage of Time	Increase ARO through periodic accretion expense.	Accretion expense recorded as part of operating expenses.	Classify accretion and depreciation expenses as noncash adjustments to net income in operating cash flows.
	Allocate ARC expense using a systematic and rational method over its useful life.	ARC expense recorded as depreciation.	
Subsequent Measurement—Change in Expected Cash Flows: PV Increases	Increase the carrying amount of the related ARC and ARO using the current credit-adjusted risk-free rate.	No effect at time of change, but will affect future amortization and accretion expense.	
Subsequent Measurement—Change in Expected Cash Flows: PV Decreases	Decrease the carrying amount of the related ARC and ARO using the current credit-adjusted risk-free rate that existed at the time the ARO was originally recorded.	No effect at time of change, but will affect future amortization and accretion expense.	
Retirement	Derecognize ARO as costs are incurred	Record a gain or loss for the difference between the recorded ARO and the cost of settling the liability.	Classify cash outflows for settlement of the ARO in operating cash flows. Settlement difference is presented as a noncash adjustment to net income within operating cash flows.
	Derecognize unamortized ARC	Record a loss for any unamortized ARC.	

An ARO is required to be recognized when incurred (or acquired), even if uncertainty exists regarding the timing and/or method of eventually settling the obligation. (ASC 410-20-25-7) In effect, ASC 410-20 distinguishes between a contingency and an uncertainty. If the obligation to perform the retirement activities is unconditional, the fact that uncertainty exists regarding the timing and/or method of retirement does not relieve the reporting entity of the requirement to estimate and record the obligation if, in fact, it is reasonably estimable. The assumptions regarding the probabilities of the various outcomes used in the computation are to take into account that uncertainty. An ARO is considered reasonably estimable if:

- It is evident that the obligation's fair value is included in an asset's acquisition price,
- An active market exists for the transfer of the obligation, or
- Sufficient information is available to enable the use of the CON 7 expected present value technique to estimate the obligation.
  (ASC 410-20-25-6)

Sufficient information is considered to be available to reasonably estimate the obligation if either:

- The settlement date and method of settlement have been specified by others (e.g., the end of a lease term or the end of a statutory period), or
- Information is available to reasonably estimate:
  - The settlement date or range of potential settlement dates
  - The settlement method or potential settlement methods
  - The probabilities of occurrence of the dates and methods in a and b

  (ASC 410-20-25-8)

If management concludes that sufficient information to record the obligation at inception is not available, management is expected to continuously consider whether this remains true in future accounting periods, and to recognize the obligation in the first period when sufficient information becomes available to enable the fair value estimate. (ASC 410-20-25-10)

The information necessary to make these estimates can be based on the reporting entity's own historical experience, industry statistics or customary practices, management's own intent, or estimates of the asset's economic useful life. (ASC 410-20-25-11)

Example of Timing of Recognition

Phyl Corporation owns and operates a chemical company. At its premises, it maintains underground tanks used to store various types of chemicals. The tanks were installed when Phyl Corporation purchased its facilities seven years prior. On February 1, 20X7, the governor of the state signed a law requiring removal of such tanks when they are no longer being used. Since the law imposes a legal obligation on Phyl Corporation, upon enactment, recognition of an asset retirement obligation (ARO) would be required.

Example of Ongoing Additions to the Obligation

Joyce Manufacturing Corporation (JMC) operates a factory. As part of its normal operations it stores production byproducts and uses cleaning solvents on site in a reservoir specifically designed for that purpose. The reservoir and surrounding land, all owned by JMC, are contaminated with these chemicals. On February 1, 20X7, the governor of the state signed a law requiring cleanup and disposal of hazardous waste from an already existing production process upon retirement of the facility. Upon enactment of the law, immediate recognition would be required for the ARO associated with the contamination that had already occurred. In addition, liabilities will continue to be recognized over the remaining life of the facility as additional contamination occurs.

Initial Measurement

Fair value is the price that would be paid to transfer the liability in an orderly transaction between market participants at the measurement date. ASC 410-20-30-1 explains how to determine a reasonable estimate of fair value.

The determination of fair value for an ARO may be difficult, especially if the volume and level of activity for the asset or liability have significantly decreased to the extent where there are few recent transactions or price quotations vary substantially. If so, it may be necessary to use multiple valuation techniques, and select a point within the derived range of values that is most representative of fair value.

Factors to Consider in the Initial ARO Measurement	
Timing	Assumptions and probabilities related to: • When the entity expects to settle the ARO • Uncertainties regarding the timing of the settlement • Differences between the expected settlement date and the asset's useful life.
Amount	Market rate assumptions Cost of third-party resources Amount at which the ARO may be settled
Discount Rate	Credit-adjusted risk-free rate used to discount cash flows. Funding and assurance arrangements used to determine the appropriate rate.

The fair value measurement is not based on the amount that the reporting entity (the obligor) would be required to pay to settle the liability on the measurement date (which would be difficult, if not impossible, to estimate in the absence of a market for the transfer of such obligations). Rather, the measurement assumes that the reporting entity remains the obligor under the ARO and that the obligee has transferred its rights by selling them to a hypothetical market participant on the measurement date. In determining the price it would be willing to pay for the rights associated with the ARO, a third-party market participant would consider the risk of nonperformance of the reporting entity, since that entity will continue to be the obligor after the measurement date. Thus, the fair value measurement of the obligation, under ASC 820, takes into consideration the reporting entity's own risk of nonperformance that includes, but is not limited to, the effect of its own credit standing.

> *Rarely, if ever, would there be an observable rate of interest for a liability that has cash flows similar to an asset retirement obligation being measured. In addition, an asset retirement obligation usually will have uncertainties in both timing and amount. In that circumstance, employing a discount rate adjustment technique, where uncertainty is incorporated into the rate, will be difficult, if not impossible.* (ASC 410-20-30-1)

This lack of observability means that management, in order to estimate the ARO, will be required to use an expected present value technique that uses its own assumptions regarding the necessary adjustment for market risk.

The discount rate to be used in the present value calculations is the *credit-adjusted risk-free rate* that adjusts a risk-free rate of interest for the effects of the entity's own credit standing. The risk-free interest rate is the interest rate on monetary assets with maturity dates or durations that coincide with the period covered by the estimated cash flows associated with the ARO. When the measurement involves cash flows denominated in U.S. dollars, entities should use the yield curve for U.S. Treasury securities. (ASC 810-10-55-5c)

In adjusting the risk-free rate for the entity's credit standing, the entity takes into account the effects on the fair value estimate of all terms, collateral, and existing guarantees. In ASC 820, FASB indicated that it believed, when it issued ASC 410, that it would be more practical for management to reflect an estimate of its own credit standing as an adjustment to the risk-free rate rather than as an adjustment to the expected cash flows. In fact, based on the model FASB chose to account for subsequent upward and downward changes in the ARO, ASC 410 would not be operational unless the adjustment for credit standing was made to the risk-free interest rate. (ASC 410-20-55-15 through 17)

As a practical matter, for companies whose debt is not rated by a bond-rating agency, the adjustment for credit standing may be difficult to establish. For such companies, the incremental borrowing rate used for lease testing may serve as an acceptable approximation of the credit-adjusted risk-free rate.

Initially Applying an Expected Present Value Method ASC 820-10-55 provides two alternative methods for determining expected present value. To apply Method 1, management adjusts the expected cash flows for market risk by incorporating a cash risk premium in them and uses a risk-free interest rate to discount the risk-adjusted expected cash flows. To apply Method 2, management does not adjust the expected cash flows, but instead adjusts the risk-free interest rate by incorporating a risk premium in it.

As discussed later in this section, Method 1 cannot be used to estimate the expected present value of an ARO due to computational difficulties that cannot be overcome. As a result, the following discussion, adapted from ASC 410-20, uses Method 2 to illustrate the estimation of expected present value.

Management begins by estimating a series of cash flows that reflect its marketplace estimates of the cost and timing of performing the required retirement activities. Marketplace amounts are those amounts that would be expended by the entity to hire a third party to perform the work. Explicit assumptions are to be developed and incorporated in the estimates about all of the following matters:

- The costs that a third party would incur in performing the necessary tasks associated with retiring the asset.
- Additional amounts that the third party would include in pricing the work, related to such factors as inflation, overhead, equipment charges, profit margins, anticipated technological advances, and offsetting cash inflows, if any.
- The extent to which the amount of the third party's costs or their timing might differ under various future scenarios and the relative probabilities of those scenarios actually occurring.

- The price that the third party would demand and could expect to receive for bearing the uncertainties and unforeseeable circumstances inherent in the obligation. This is referred to as a *market-risk premium.*

(ASC 410-20-55-17)

If data is available regarding assumptions that marketplace participants would make that contradict management's own assumptions, management must adjust its assumptions accordingly. For example, if the costs of labor in the marketplace exceed those of the entity, the higher marketplace costs should be used in the cash flow estimates. Even if the entity can and will retire the asset using internal resources, the obligation must be computed as if a third party will be retained to perform the work, including provisions for recovery of the contractor's overhead and profit.

For the purposes of measurement in subsequent periods, in the unlikely event that an entity originally determined its ARO based on available market prices rather than using the expected present value method, it would be required to determine the undiscounted cash flows embedded in that market price. This process is analogous to computing the rate of interest implicit in a lease.

Subsequent Measurement of an Asset Retirement Obligation

Depreciation The entity depreciates the combined cost of the asset and the capitalized asset retirement obligation using a systematic and rational allocation method over the period during which the long-lived asset is expected to provide benefits, taking into consideration any expected salvage value. Conceptually, this accounting treatment is an application of the matching principle in that the total investment in the asset, including the cost of its eventual retirement, is charged to expense over the periods benefited. Depending on the pattern and timing of obligating events, an entity could, under these rules, capitalize an amount of asset retirement cost during a period and, in the same period, allocate an equal amount to depreciation expense. (ASC 410-20- 35-2) It is important to note that, for the purpose of capitalizing interest under ASC 835-20, these additions to the carrying amounts of long-lived assets are not considered expenditures.

Changes in the Liability After the initial period of ARO recognition, the liability will change as a result of either

- The passage of time or
- Revisions to the original estimates of either the amounts of estimated cash flows or their timing.

(ASC 410-20-35-3)

Such changes can arise due to the effects of inflation, changes in the probabilities used in the original estimate, changes in interest rates, changes in laws, regulations, statutes, and contracts.

ASC 410-20 does not require detailed cash flow estimates every reporting period, but rather allows the exercise of judgment as to when facts and circumstances indicate that the initial estimate requires updating.

If a change to the liability is deemed necessary, it is recognized by first adjusting its carrying amount for changes due to the passage of time (referred to as *accretion* and discussed in detail below) and then, if applicable, for changes due to revisions in either amounts or timing of estimated cash flows. (ASC 410-20-55-4)

Changes Due to Passage of Time Changes due to the passage of time increase the carrying amount of the liability because there are fewer periods remaining from the initial measurement date until the settlement date; thus, the present value of the discounted future settlement amount increases. These changes are recorded as a period cost called *accretion expense* and classified separately in the operating section of the statement of income (or not-for-profit statement of activities). Accretion is computed using the interest method of allocation that results in periodic accretion expense representing a level effective interest rate applied to the carrying amount of the liability at the beginning of each period. The effective interest rate used to calculate accretion is the credit-adjusted risk-free rate or rates applied when the liability or portion of the liability (as explained below) was initially measured and recognized. Accretion expense is not combined with interest expense, and is not considered interest cost for the purpose of applying the interest capitalization criteria of ASC 835-20. (ASC 410-20-35-5)

Changes in Amounts or Timing of Cash Flows ASC 410-20-35-8 explains how to account for changes in estimates. Changes in the ARO that result from changes in the estimates of the timing or amounts of future cash flows are accounted for differently for increases and decreases.

Expected Present Value Increases If the expected present value increases, the increase gives rise to a new obligation accounted for separately just as the ARO was originally measured but using current market value assumptions, and the current credit-adjusted risk-free rate. Thus, over time, a particular long-lived asset may have multiple layers of obligations associated with it that are based on different assumptions measured at different dates during the asset's useful life. The incremental obligation is recorded by increasing the recorded ARO and the ARC. If multiple layers have been recorded and it is not practical to separately identify the period (or layer) to which subsequent revisions in estimated cash flows relate, management is permitted to use a *weighted-average credit-adjusted risk-free rate* to measure the change in the liability resulting from that revision.

If the increase in carrying amount of the affected long-lived asset resulting from the remeasurement of ARO in a subsequent period impacts only that period, then the increase is fully depreciated in that period. Otherwise, the increase is depreciated in the period of change and future periods as a change in estimate in accordance with ASC 250. Both depreciation and accretion are classified as operating expenses in the statement of income.

Expected Present Value Decreases If, however, the expected present value subsequently decreases, the difference between the remeasured amount and the carrying amount of the liability (after adjustment for inception-to-date accretion) is recorded as a decrease in the ARO and in the corresponding ARC. In this case, the previously recognized layers of liabilities are reduced pro rata so as not to affect the overall effective rate of accretion over the remaining life of the obligation.

The difference in the accretion of the ARO and the depreciation of the ARC may result in an ARO that is greater than the carrying value of the related ARC. If so, the ARO should be reduced to reflect the change. The ARC should be credited, but only until the balance is reduced to zero. Additional credit amounts should be recorded in income.

Funding and Assurance Provisions Factors such as laws, regulations, public policy, the entity's creditworthiness, or the sheer magnitude of the future obligation may cause an entity to be required to provide third parties with assurance that the entity will be able to satisfy its ARO in the future. Such assurance is provided using such instruments as surety bonds, insurance policies, letters of credit, guarantees by other entities, establishment of trust funds, or by custodial arrangements segregating other assets dedicated to satisfying the ARO. Although providing such means of assurance does not satisfy the underlying obligation, the credit-adjusted interest rate used in calculating the expected present value is adjusted for the effect on the entity's credit standing of employing one or more of these techniques. (ASC 410-20-35-9)

Rate-Regulated Entities Many rate-regulated entities (as defined in ASC 980 and discussed in the chapter on ASC 980) follow current specialized accounting that capitalizes costs not otherwise afforded that treatment under GAAP. These entities recover these additional costs in the rates that they charge their customers. These additional capitalized costs may or may not meet the definition of ARO under ASC 410. The differences in the amounts and timing of assets and liabilities between GAAP and regulatory accounting used for rate-making purposes give rise to temporary differences and the resultant deferred income tax accounting.

ASC 410 provides that, if the criteria in ASC 980 are met, the rate-regulated entity is to recognize a regulatory asset or liability for differences in the timing of recognition of the period costs associated with ARO for financial reporting and rate-making purposes. Accounting for the ARO arising from closed or abandoned long-lived assets of rate-regulated entities is covered by ASC 980-360.

Example—Initial Measurement and Recognition

Gerald Corporation constructs and places into service on January 1, 20X1, specialized machinery on premises that it leases under a fifteen-year lease. The machinery cost $1,750,000 and has an estimated useful life of ten years. Gerald Corporation is contractually obligated, under the terms of the lease, to remove the machinery from the premises when it is no longer functional. Gerald is unable to obtain current market-related information regarding the costs of settling the liability at inception and, therefore, chooses to estimate the initial fair value of the ARO using an expected present value technique. The significant assumptions used by Gerald in applying this technique are as follows:

1. Labor costs are based on prevailing wage rates in that geographic area that a contractor would pay to hire qualified workers. Gerald assigns probability assessments to the range of cash flow estimates as follows:

Cash flow estimate	Probability assessment	Expected cash flows for labor costs
$40,000	25%	$10,000
60,000	50	30,000
75,000	25	18750
	100%	$58,750

2. Based on its own experience, which Gerald believes is indicative of local market conditions, Gerald estimates that a contractor will apply a 75% rate to labor costs to charge for overhead and equipment usage and that, based on published industry statistics for the region, a contractor would add a markup of 8% to the combined labor, overhead, and equipment costs.
3. Since the eventual dismantlement and removal will be occurring ten years later, Gerald expects that a contractor would receive a market-risk premium of 5% of the expected cash flows adjusted for inflation. This premium is to compensate the contractor for assuming the risks and uncertainties of contracting now for a project ten years later.
4. The risk-free rate of interest as evidenced by the price of zero-coupon U.S. Treasury instruments that mature in ten years is 4.5%. Gerald adjusts that rate by 2.5% to reflect the effect of its credit

standing as evidenced by its incremental borrowing rate of 7%. Therefore, the credit-adjusted risk-free rate used to compute the expected present value is 7%.

5. Gerald assumes an average rate of inflation of 3.5% over the ten-year period.

The ARO is initially measured as follows as of January 1, 20X1:

	Expected cash flows as of January 1, 20X1
Expected cash flows for labor costs	$ 58,750
Allocated overhead and equipment charges (75% × $58,750)	44,063
Contractor's markup [8% × ($58,750 + $44,063)]	8,225
Expected cash flows before inflation adjustment	111,038
Average annual compounded inflation rate of 3.5% for 10 years (1.03510)	× 1.4106
Expected cash flows adjusted for inflation	156,630
Market-risk premium (5% × $156,630)	7,832
Expected cash flows adjusted for market risk	164,462
Present value using credit-adjusted risk-free rate of 7% for 10 years, compounded annually	$ 83,604

On January 1, 20X1, Gerald would record the initial ARO as follows:

Machinery and equipment	83,604	
ARO liability		83,604

Example—Accounting in Subsequent Periods

Assuming the same facts as above, during the ten-year life of the machinery, Gerald would record entries to recognize accretion and depreciation as follows (assuming no remeasurement of the ARO is required):

Year	Liability balance as of January 1	Annual accretion	Liability balance as of December 31
20X1	$ 83,604	$ 5,852	$ 89,456
20X2	89,456	6,262	95,718
20X3	95,718	6,700	102,418
20X4	102,418	7,169	109,587
20X5	109,587	7,671	117,258
20X6	117,258	8,208	125,466
20X7	125,466	8,783	134,249
20X8	134,249	9,397	143,646
20X9	143,646	10,055	153,701
20Y0	153,701	10,761	164,462

Entries to Record Annual Accretion

The accretion for each year presented in the table is recorded as follows:

Accretion expense (presented on the income statement as part of operating expense)	xx, xxx	
Asset retirement obligation		xx, xxx

Depreciation Computations

Acquisition cost of asset	$ 1,750,000
Capitalized ARO	83,604
Adjusted carrying amount of asset	$ 1,833,604
Estimated salvage value (assumed)	100,000
	$ 1,733,604
Estimated useful life	÷ 10 years
Annual depreciation expense	$ 173,360

Entry to Record Annual Depreciation

Depreciation expense	173,360	
Accumulated depreciation		173,360

Settlement of ARO

On December 31, 20Y0, Gerald uses its internal workforce to dismantle and dispose of the machinery and incurred costs as follows:

Labor	$ 70,000
Internally allocated overhead and equipment charges (75% of labor)	52,500
Total costs incurred	122,500
ARO liability	164,462
Gain on settlement of ARO	$ 41,962

Note that, because Gerald chose to perform the retirement activities using its own workforce, the "market approach" mandated by ASC 410 and ASC 820 does not achieve an even matching of the total costs of acquisition and retirement to the periods benefited. The period of the retirement reflects a gain on settlement that would not have occurred had Gerald hired a contractor to perform the work instead of using its own employees.

Electronic Equipment Waste Obligations ASC 720-40 prescribes the proper treatment of electronic equipment waste obligations. See the chapter on ASC 720 for more information.

ASC 410-30, *ENVIRONMENTAL OBLIGATIONS*

Concepts, Rules, and Examples

Environmental remediation costs, the costs of cleaning up environmental contamination, are generally expensed as incurred as operating expenses. (ASC 410-30-25-16) The exceptions to this general rule that result in capitalizing these costs are as follows:

- If the costs result from legal obligations associated with the eventual retirement of an asset or group of assets they will be capitalized as an ARO, as discussed and illustrated in the previous section of this chapter on ASC 410-20.
- If the costs do not qualify as ARO, but they meet one of the following criteria, they may be capitalized subject to reduction for impairment, if warranted:
  - The costs extend the life, increase the capacity, or improve the safety or efficiency of property owned by the reporting entity.
  - The costs mitigate or prevent future environmental contamination while also improving the property compared with its condition when originally constructed or acquired by the reporting entity.
  - The costs are incurred in preparing for sale a property that is currently held for sale (the application of this criterion must be balanced with the limitation in ASC 360 regarding assets held for sale being carried at the lower of carrying value or fair value less cost to sell).

  (ASC 410-30-25-17)

SEC registrants are required to disclose any significant exposure for asbestos treatment in the management discussion and analysis (MD&A).

Environmental costs associated with the improper operation or use of an asset (e.g., penalties and fines) are specifically excluded from the accounting guidance with respect to ARO and, should they be incurred, under ASC 410-30, they would most likely not qualify to be capitalized under GAAP.

Environmental Remediation Liabilities

Obligations arising from pollution of the environment have become a major cost for businesses. ASC 410-30 sets forth a very detailed description of relevant laws, remediation provisions, and other pertinent information, which is useful to auditors as well as to reporting entities. In terms of accounting guidance, ASC 430-30 contains the principal rules with respect to accounting for environmental obligations (e.g., determining the threshold for accrual of a liability, etc.) and it sets "benchmarks" for liability recognition. The benchmarks for the accrual and evaluation of the estimated liability (i.e., the stages which are deemed to be important to ascertaining the existence and amount of the liability) are:

- The identification and verification of an entity as a potentially responsible party (PRP), since ASC 410-30 stipulates that accrual is to be based on the premise that expected costs will be borne by only the "participating potentially responsible parties" and that the "recalcitrant, unproven and unidentified" PRP will not contribute to costs of remediation
- The receipt of a "unilateral administrative order"
- Participation, as a PRP, in the remedial investigation/feasibility study (RI/FS)

- Completion of the feasibility study
- Issuance of the Record of Decision (RoD)
- The remedial design through operation and maintenance, including postremediation monitoring.

  (ASC 410-30-25-15)

ASC 430-30 explains that the amount of the liability to be accrued is affected by the entity's allocable share of liability for a specific site and by its share of the amounts related to the site that will not be paid by the other PRP or the government. The categories of costs to be included in the accrued liability include incremental direct costs of the remediation effort itself, as well as the costs of compensation and benefits for employees directly involved in the remediation effort. (ASC 410-30-30-10) Costs should be estimated based on existing laws. (ASC 410-30-30-15)

Incremental direct costs include such items as fees paid to outside law firms for work related to the remediation effort, costs relating to completing the RI/FS, fees to outside consulting and engineering firms for site investigations and development of remedial action plans and remedial actions, costs of contractors performing remedial actions, government oversight costs and past costs, the cost of machinery and equipment dedicated to the remedial actions that do not have an alternative use, assessments by a PRP group covering costs incurred by the group in dealing with a site, and the costs of operation and maintenance of the remedial action, including costs of postremediation monitoring required by remedial action plan.

ASC 410-30 states that potential recoveries cannot be offset against the estimated liability, and further notes that any recovery recognized as an asset is to be reflected at fair value, which implies that only the present value of future recoveries can be recorded. It is presumed that the costs are operating in nature and thus cannot normally be included in the "other income and expense" category of the income statement, either. Disclosure of accounting policies regarding recognition of the liability and of any related asset (for recoveries from third parties) is also needed, where pertinent.

28 ASC 420 EXIT OR DISPOSAL COST OBLIGATIONS

PERSPECTIVE AND ISSUES

Subtopic

ASC 420, *Exit or Disposal Cost Activities*, consists of one subtopic:

- ASC 420-10, *Overall*, which provides guidance on the definition, reporting, and disclosure of such costs.

Scope and Scope Exceptions

The guidance in ASC 420 applies to:

- Termination benefits for current employees involuntarily terminated under the terms of a benefit arrangement that is not an ongoing benefit arrangement or individual deferred compensation contract
- Costs related to:
  - A contract that is not a lease
  - Consolidation of facilities or relocation of employees
  - A disposal activity under ASC 205-20
  - An exit activity

  (ASC 420-10-15-3)

ASC 420 applies to all entities. It does *not* apply to:

- Costs associated with the retirement of a long-lived asset covered by ASC 410-20
- Impairment of an unrecognized asset while it is being used (ASC 420-10-15-5)

ASC 420-10-15-4 clarifies that an exit activity includes, but is not limited to:

- A restructuring
- The sale or termination of a line of business
- The closure of business activities in a particular location
- The relocation of business activities
- Changes in management structure
- A fundamental reorganization that affects the nature and focus of operation

DEFINITIONS OF TERMS

Source: ASC 420-10-20. Also see Appendix A, *Definitions of Terms*, for: Acquiree, Acquirer, Acquisition by a Not-for-Profit Entity, Business, Business Combination, Legal Entity, Not-for-Profit Entity, and Variable Interest Entity.

Cease-Use Date. The date the entity ceases using the right conveyed by the contract, for example, the right to use a leased property or to receive future goods or services.

Communication Date. The date the plan of termination for onetime employee termination benefits meets all of the criteria in paragraph 420-10-25-4 and has been communicated to employees.

Legal Notification Period. The notification period that an entity is required to provide to employees in advance of a specified termination event as a result of an existing law, statute, or contract.

One-Time Employee Termination Benefits. Benefits provided to current employees that are involuntarily terminated under the terms of a one-time benefit arrangement.

Restructuring. A program that is planned and controlled by management, and materially changes either the scope of a business undertaken by an entity, or the manner in which that business is conducted, as defined by the International Accounting Standard No. 37 in 2002.

CONCEPTS, RULES, AND EXAMPLES

General

When to Recognize a Liability Except for employee termination benefits discussed below, an entity should recognize exit or disposal costs in the same period it incurs the liability. If the fair value cannot be estimated initially, the cost should be recognized in the first period that it can be estimated. This should be a rare occurrence. (ASC 420-10-25-1)

Subsequent Measurement Entities should measure changes in the initial measurement using the credit-adjusted risk-free rate used for the initial measurement. (ASC 420-10-35-1) The table below summarizes how to account for various changes.

Change	Recognition
Cumulative effect of a change resulting from a revision to the timing or the estimated amount of cash flows.	As an adjustment in the period of change.
Employees that were expected to be terminated within the minimum retention period are retained beyond that period.	Adjust the liability in the period of change.
Changes due to the passage of time.	As an increase in the carrying amount of the liability and as an expense.
(ASC 420-10-35-2 through 35-4)	

Employee Termination Benefits

ASC 420, *Exit or Disposal Cost Obligations*, applies to termination benefits provided to current employees that are involuntarily terminated under the terms of a benefit arrangement that applies to a specified termination event or for a specified future period. Those benefits are referred to as onetime termination benefits. If an entity has a history of providing similar benefits to employees involuntarily terminated in earlier events, the benefits are presumed to be part of an ongoing benefit arrangement (rather than a onetime benefit arrangement) unless there is evidence to the contrary.

A onetime benefit arrangement first exists at the date the plan of termination meets *all* of the following criteria:

- Management approves and commits to the termination plan.
- The termination plan specifies the number of employees to be terminated, their job classifications or functions, and their locations, as well as the expected completion date.
- The termination plan establishes the terms of the benefit arrangement in sufficient detail that employees are able to determine the type and amount of benefits that they will receive if they are involuntarily terminated.
- Actions required to complete the plan indicate that significant changes to the plan are unlikely.
(ASC 460-10-25-4)

Communicating the plan to employees creates a liability at the communication date. (ASC 420-10-25-5)

Timing The timing of recognition of the liability for onetime termination benefits depends on whether the employees are required to render service beyond a minimum retention period. (ASC 420-10-25-6) The minimum retention period is the notification period that an entity is required to provide to employees in advance of a termination event as a result of law, statute, or contract, or in the absence of a legal notification period, the minimum retention period cannot exceed sixty days. (ASC 420-10-25-7)

If employees are entitled to receive the termination benefits regardless of when they leave or if employees will not be retained to render service beyond the minimum retention period, the liability for the termination benefits is recognized and measured at its fair value at the communication date. (ASC 420-10-25-8)

If employees are required to render service until they are terminated in order to receive the termination benefit and will be retained beyond the minimum retention period, the liability for the termination benefits is measured at its fair value at the communication date and recognized ratably over the service period. (ASC 420-10-25-9)

Measurement Exit or disposal costs should be measured at fair value. Often, quoted market values are not available for those costs. A present value technique may be the best option. However, in some situations the use of estimates may not be materially different from present value techniques and those are acceptable if consistent with a fair value measurement objective. (ASC 420-10-30-1 through 3)

Examples of the Determination of the Minimum Retention Period and Recognition

Master Mobile Communications announces that it will close its Donnybrook plant and terminate all 120 employees there. The terms of the plan meet the criteria above. There are three major groups of employees: management, union workers, and nonunion workers. Management is required to stay and render service until the plant's closing, which is four months from now, and each of the twelve management employees will receive $10,000. The union workers' contract states that they must be notified ninety days in advance before they can be terminated. The union workers will be terminated in ninety days. The termination benefit for each of the fifty union employees is one week per every six months of employment. The nonunion workers can leave at any time within the next three months and still collect the termination benefit. Each of the fifty-eight nonunion employees will receive a termination benefit of $1,000 for each year of service. There is no state statute specifying a notification period.

Case 1: Management

Management is required to work until termination, so it is necessary to determine whether the service period is beyond the minimum retention period. There is no state statute specifying a notification period, but the Worker Adjustment and Retraining Act, which applies to entities with over 100 employees, requires a sixty-day notification period for this plant's closing. Thus, the minimum retention period is sixty days. Management must work beyond the minimum retention period, so the $120,000 liability (12 × $10,000) is recognized at $30,000 per month for the next four months. Present value techniques are not necessary to measure the liability because the discount period is so short that the face amount would not differ materially from the fair value.

Case 2: Union employees

The union employees' contract requires a ninety-day notification period, so the minimum retention period for these employees is ninety days. The union workers will be terminated at the end of the ninety-day period, so they will not be required to work beyond the minimum retention period. If the total of the termination benefits for the fifty union employees is $142,500, a liability of $142,500 is recognized at the communication date. Present value techniques are not necessary to measure the liability because the discount period is so short that the face amount would not differ materially from the fair value.

Case 3: Nonunion workers

Nonunion workers are not required to work until the termination date to collect the termination benefit. Therefore, it is not necessary to determine the minimum retention period for these employees. If the fifty-eight nonunion employees have 230 years of service among them, a liability of $230,000 is recognized at the communication date. Present value techniques are not necessary to measure the liability because the discount period is so short that the face amount would not differ materially from the fair value.

Subsequent Measurement If subsequent to the communication date there are changes in either the timing or amount of the expected termination benefit cash flows, the cumulative effect of the change should be computed and reported in the same line item(s) in the income statement in which the costs were initially reported. If present value techniques were used to measure the initial liability, the same credit-adjusted risk-free rate should be used to remeasure the liability.

Changes in the liability due to the passage of time (accretion) are recognized as accretion expense in the income statement. (ASC 420-10-35-4) If employees are not required to provide services or are required to provide services only during the minimum retention period, accretion expense is charged for the passage of time after the communication date. If employees are required to provide services beyond the minimum retention period, accretion expense is charged for the passage of time after the termination date. Accretion expense should not be titled interest expense or be considered interest costs subject to capitalization. (ASC 420-10-45-5)

According to ASC 420-10-55, if newly offered benefits represent a revision to an ongoing arrangement that is not limited to a specified termination event or to a specified future period, the benefits represent an enhancement to an ongoing benefit arrangement.

If a plan of termination changes and employees that were expected to be terminated within the minimum retention period are retained to render service beyond that period, the liability amount should be recomputed as though it had been known at the initial communication date that those employees would be required to render services beyond the minimum retention period. (ASC 420-10-35-3) The cumulative effect of the change is recognized as a change in the liability and reported in the same line item(s) in the income statement in which the costs were initially reported. The remainder of the liability is recognized ratably from the date of change to the termination date.

Plan Includes Voluntary and Involuntary Benefits If a plan of termination includes both voluntary and involuntary termination benefits, a liability for the involuntary benefits is recognized as described above. A liability for the incremental voluntary benefits (the excess of the voluntary benefit amount over the involuntary benefit amount) is recognized in accordance with ASC 712-10-25-1 through 25-3. That is, if the benefits are special termination benefits offered only for a short period of time, the liability is recognized when the employees accept the offer and the amount can be reasonably estimated. If, instead, the voluntary termination benefits are contractual termination benefits (for example, required by a union contract or a pension contract) the liability is recognized when it is probable that employees will be entitled to benefits and the amount can be reasonably estimated.

Contract Termination Costs

In addition to employee termination costs, an entity may incur contract termination costs, relocation costs, plant consolidation costs, and other costs associated with the exit or disposal activity. ASC 420 offers the following guidance for recognition. Note that upon implementation of ASU 2016-02, *Leases,* leases within the scope of ASC 842 are excluded from this guidance. (ASC 420-10-25-11)

Recognition A liability for the costs to terminate a contract before the end of its term is recognized and measured at its fair value when the entity actually terminates the contract in accordance with the contractual term (e.g., by written notice). (ASC 420-10-25-12) A liability for the costs that will continue to be incurred under a contract for its remaining term without economic benefit to the entity is recognized at its cease-use date. (ASC 420-10-25-13)

Measurement If an entity terminates a contract according to the terms of the contract, the entity should record a liability for the termination costs measured at fair value at the time of termination. (ASC 420-10-30-7)

An entity may continue to incur costs without realizing any economic benefit. In that case, the entity should record a liability at its fair value at the cease-use date. (ASC 420-10-30-9)

If the contract is an operating lease, the fair value of the liability should be determined based on the remaining lease rentals, reduced by estimated sublease rentals, even if the entity does not intend to find a sublease. However, remaining operating lease payments should not be reduced to an amount less than zero by the estimated sublease payments. (ASC 420-10-30-8)

Other Associated Costs to Exit an Activity

Recognition Other associated costs are items such as employee relocation costs and costs associated with facility closings or consolidations (ASC 420-10-25-14). A liability for other costs associated with the exit or disposal activity should be recognized when the liability is incurred, which is generally when the goods or services associated with the activity are received. The liability should not be recognized before it is incurred even if the costs are incremental and a direct result of the exit or disposal plan. (ASC 420-10-25-15)

Measurement The liability should be measured at fair value in the period when the liability is incurred. This is usually when goods or services associated with the activity are received. (ASC 420-10-30-10)

Presentation and Disclosure

Presentation and disclosure requirements can be found at www.wiley.com/go/GAAP2021.

29 ASC 430 DEFERRED REVENUE AND CONTRACT LIABILITIES

This Topic only provides a link to deferred revenue *and* contract liabilities. See the chapter on ASC 606 for guidance.

30 ASC 440 COMMITMENTS

PERSPECTIVE AND ISSUES

The FASB codification has three related Topics:

- ASC 440, *Commitments*,
- ASC 450, *Contingencies*, and
- ASC 460, *Guarantees*

Subtopics

ASC 440, *Commitments*, contains only one subtopic:

- ASC 440-10, *Overall*, which provides general guidance on financial accounting and reporting for certain commitments.

The subtopic has two subsections:

1. *General*
2. *Unconditional Purchase Obligations*

The *General* subsection provides guidance for:

- Unused letters of credit,
- Preferred stock dividends in arrears,
- Commitments such as those for plant acquisitions, and
- Obligations to reduce debts, maintain working capital, or restrict dividends. (ASC 440-10-05-2)

The *Unconditional Purchase Obligation* subsection provides guidance for unconditional purchase obligations, such as throughput and take-or-pay contracts. (ASC 440-10-05-3)

Scope and Scope Exceptions

ASC 440 applies to all entities and to all relevant transactions. (ASC 440-10-15-1 through 15-3) However, for guidance on product financing arrangements, the preparer should look to ASC 470-40-15 and repurchase agreements within the scope of ASC 606-10-55-66 through 55-78.

DEFINITIONS OF TERMS

Source: ASC 440-10-20. In addition to the terms listed below, see Appendix A for additional terms related to this topic: Contract, Lease, Lease Payments, Lessee, Lessor, Underlying Asset.

Purchaser's Incremental Borrowing Rate. The rate that, at the inception of an unconditional purchase obligation, the purchaser would have incurred to borrow over a similar term the funds necessary to discharge the obligation.

Take-or-Pay Contract. An agreement between a purchaser and a seller that provides for the purchaser to pay specified amounts periodically in return for products or services. The purchaser must make specified minimum payments even if it does not take delivery of the contracted products or services.

Throughput Contract. An agreement between a shipper (processor) and the owner of a transportation facility (such as an oil or natural gas pipeline or a ship) or a manufacturing facility that provides for the shipper (processor) to pay specified amounts periodically in return for the transportation (processing) of a product. The shipper (processor) is obligated to provide specified minimum quantities to be transported (processed) in each period and is required to make cash payments even if it does not provide the contracted quantities.

Unconditional Purchase Obligation. An obligation to transfer funds in the future for fixed or minimum amounts or quantities of goods or services at fixed or minimum prices (for example, as in take-or-pay contracts or throughput contracts).

CONCEPTS, RULES, AND EXAMPLES

Unconditional Purchase Obligations

An unconditional purchase obligation may be subject to:

- ASC 840 (or ASC 842 upon implementation of ASU 2016-02, *Leases*), or
- ASC 815, or
- Neither.
  (ASC 440-10-25-1)

To determine the appropriate guidance, entities should determine first if an obligation is subject to the guidance on leases. (ASC 440-10-25-2) Then, the entity should apply the guidance in ASC 815 to determine if any portion of the obligation that is not a lease is subject to 815 and whether the lease portion contains an embedded derivative. (ASC 440-10-25-3)

Throughput and take-or-pay contracts are sometimes used to help a supplier pay for new facilities, machines, or other expenditures. (See the Definitions of Terms section above.) They are negotiated as a way of arranging financing for the facilities that will produce the goods or provide the services desired by a purchaser. Some of these contracts are reported on the statement of financial position as an asset and a liability. Others are not reported.

Losses on unconditional purchase obligations for goods or inventory should be recognized under the provisions contained in ASC 330-10-35. (ASC 440-10-25-4)

The disclosure requirements for ASC 440 can be found at www.wiley.com/go/ GAAP2021.

Other Sources

See ASC Location—*Wiley GAAP* Chapter	*For information on . . .*
ASC 310-20	Fees received for a commitment to originate or purchase a loan or group of loans.
ASC 330-10-35-17	Guidance on accrual of net losses on firm purchase commitments for goods for inventory.
ASC 410-30	Postremediation monitoring commitments.
ASC 715	Commitments related to pension plans.
ASC 720-25	For commitments to contribute.
ASC 730-20	Royalty arrangements, purchase provisions, license agreements, and commitments to provide additional funding and other commitments under research and development arrangements.
ASC 815-25	Designating a derivative instrument as a hedge of the exposure to changes in the fair value of an unrecognized firm commitment.
ASC 815-10-15-71	Loan commitments that relate to the origination of mortgage loans that will be held for sale.
ASC 830-20-35-3	Foreign currency commitments.
ASC 840	Commitments under lease agreements.[1]
ASC 840-10-55-7	Nuclear fuel leases structured as take-or-pay contracts.[2]
ASC 860-30	Assets pledged as collateral for secured borrowings.
ASC 948-310-35	Fair value of committed and uncommitted mortgage loans and mortgage-backed securities.
ASC 948-310-35-7	Recognition of loan and commitment fees.
ASC 948-720-25-1	Commitment fees relating to loans held for sale (residential or commercial loan commitment fees).
ASC 954-450-25-4	Prepaid health care services contracts.

[1] Upon implementation of ASU 2016-02, *Leases*, this reference will change to ASC 842.

[2] Upon implementation of ASU 2016-02, *Leases*, this reference will change to ASC 842-10-55-1.

31 ASC 450 CONTINGENCIES

PERSPECTIVE AND ISSUES

Subtopics

ASC 450, *Contingencies*, contains guidance for reporting and disclosure of gain and loss contingencies and has three subtopics:

- ASC 450-10, *Overall*, which, along with ASC 450-20 and 450-30, provides guidance on accounting and disclosures for contingencies.
- ASC 450-20, *Loss Contingencies*, which describes accounting for potential liabilities in circumstances involving uncertainties.
- ASC 450-30, *Gain Contingencies*, which describes accounting and disclosure requirements for gain contingencies.

Scope and Scope Exceptions

ASC 450-10 ASC 450-10 applies to all entities. Not all uncertainties are contingencies. ASC 450-10-55 points out several common estimates that do not fall under the contingency guidance:

- Depreciation
- Estimates used in accruals
- Changes in tax law

ASC 450 guidance does *not* apply to the recognition and initial measurement of:

- Assets or liabilities arising from contingencies that are measured at fair value or
- Assets arising from contingencies measured at an amount other than fair value on the acquisition date in a business combination or
- An acquisition by a not-for-profit entity under the requirements of Subtopic 805-20 or 958-805. (ASC 450-10-15-2A)

ASC 450-20 The following transactions are excluded from the guidance in ASC 450-20 because for them guidance is elsewhere in the Codification:

- Stock issued to employees. (ASC 718)
- Employment-related costs, including deferred compensation contracts. (ASC 710, 712, and 715) However, certain postemployment benefits are included in the scope of this ASC 450-20 by reference in 712-10-25-4 through 25-5.
- Uncertainty in income taxes. (ASC 740-10-25)
- Accounting and reporting by insurance entities. (ASC 944)
  (ASC 450-20-15-2)

ASC 450-30 ASC 450-30 follows the same scope guidance as ASC 450-10.

DEFINITIONS OF TERMS

See Appendix A, *Definitions of Terms*, for terms relevant to this topic: Acquiree, Acquirer, Acquisition by a Not-for-Profit Entity, Acquisition Date, Business, Business Combinations, Commencement Date of the Lease (Commencement Date), Contingency, Contract, Customer, Direct Financing Leases, Finance Lease, Gain Contingency, Lease, Legal Entity, Lessee, Lessor, Loss contingency, Not-for-Profit Entity, Operating Lease, Probably, Reasonably Possible, Reinsurance, Remote, Sales-Type Lease, Transaction Price, Underlying Asset, Variable Interest Rate, and Variable Lease Payments.

CONCEPTS, RULES, AND EXAMPLES

ASC 450-10, *Overall*

ASC 450 defines a contingency as an existing condition, situation, or set of circumstances involving uncertainty as to possible gain or loss and that will result in the acquisition of an asset, the reduction of a liability, the loss or impairment of an asset, or the incurrence of a liability. (ASC 450-10-05-5) The uncertainty will ultimately be resolved when one or more future events occur or fail to occur.

ASC 450-20, *Loss Contingencies*

Overview Loss contingencies are common and include those related to product warranties and litigation.

Recognition Loss contingencies are recognized only if there is an impairment of an asset or the incurrence of a liability as of the date of the statement of financial position. ASC 450-20-25-2 states that a loss must be accrued if *both* of the following conditions are met:

a. It is *probable* that an asset has been impaired or a liability has been incurred at the date of the financial statements.
b. The amount of loss can be *reasonably estimated*.
   (ASC 450-20-25-2)

For example, estimated settlement amounts for ongoing lawsuits are recognized prior to a court's decision if it is probable that the outcome will be unfavorable. Further, difficulty in measuring an obligation is not, by itself, a reason for not recording a liability if the amount can be estimated. For example, warranty obligations are commonly recognized as liabilities even though the number of claims and the amount of each claim are unknown at the time of the sale of the item covered by the warranty. Although future events will eventually resolve the uncertainties (the warranty claims will be paid and the lawsuit will be adjudicated or settled), the liabilities are required to be recognized before all of the uncertainties are resolved so that relevant information is provided on a timely basis.

Levels of Probability ASC defines the different levels of probability as to whether or not future events will confirm the existence of a loss as follows:

- *Probable*—The future event or events are likely to occur.
- *Reasonably possible*—The chance of the future event or events occurring is more than remote but less than likely.
- *Remote*—The chance of the future event or events occurring is slight.
  (ASC 450-20-20)

Professional judgment is required to classify the likelihood of the future events occurring. All relevant information that can be acquired concerning the uncertain set of circumstances needs to be obtained and used to determine the classification. Probable is generally understood as a 75% threshold.

The table below summarizes the three possible outcomes related to loss contingencies.

Material loss contingency is:	**Action**
Probable and reasonably estimable	Accrue a loss
Probable but not reasonably estimable	Disclose the nature of the contingency and the fact that an estimate cannot be made
Possible but not probable	Disclose the nature of the contingency and an estimate of the range of loss or the fact that an estimate cannot be made
Remote	No accrual or disclosure required[1]
(ASC 450-10-25-2 and 50-1 through 50-5)	

Estimating the Loss When estimating the fair value of the loss, it is not necessary that a single amount be identified. A range of amounts is sufficient to indicate that some amount of loss has been incurred and is required to be accrued. (ASC 450-20-25-5) The amount accrued is the amount within the range that appears to be the best estimate. If there is no best estimate, the minimum amount in the range is accrued, since it is probable that the loss will be at least that amount. (ASC 450-20) The maximum amount of loss is required to be disclosed. (ASC 450-20-30-1) If future events indicate that the minimum loss originally accrued is inadequate, an additional loss should be accrued in the period when this fact becomes known. This accrual is a change in estimate, not a prior period adjustment.

Generally, the liability is not discounted. However, if the amount and timing of the payments are fixed or determinable, then discounting may be appropriate under the provisions in ASC 835-30-15-2. For more information, preparers should review the guidance in ASC 450-20-S99-1, SAB Topic 5-1, Question 1 for SEC staff review on this issues.

[1] Note that there is an exception to the no disclosure for remotely possible loss contingencies under ASC 460.

Events Subsequent to Balance Sheet Date It is important for the entity to distinguish between events that provide additional information about circumstances that existed at the balance sheet date and those related to conditions that did not exist at the balance sheet date. In the table, an accrual is not appropriate but disclosures should be conducted. Events that occur after the date of the statement of financial position (i.e., bankruptcy or expropriation) but before issuance of the financial statements that give rise to loss contingencies may require disclosure so that statement users are not misled. The information may relate to an impairment of an asset or liability incurred that did not exist at the date of the statement of financial position, and, therefore, the conditions for accrual are not present. (ASC 450-20-50-9)

Unasserted Claims or Assessments It is not necessary to disclose loss contingencies for an unasserted claim or assessment where there has been no manifestation of an awareness of possible claim or assessment by a potential claimant unless it is deemed probable that a claim will be asserted and a reasonable possibility of an unfavorable outcome exists. (ASC 450-20-50-6) Under the provisions of ASC 450, general or unspecified business risks are not loss contingencies and therefore no accrual is necessary. Disclosure of these business risks may be required under ASC 275. (ASC 450-20-50-8)

Every business risks loss by fire, explosion, government expropriation, or casualties in the ordinary course of business. To the extent those losses are not (or cannot be) insured, the risks are contingencies. Because those events are often random in their occurrence, uncertainty surrounds whether the future event confirming the loss will or will not take place. The passage of time usually resolves the uncertainty. Until the event confirming the loss occurs (or is probable of occurrence) and the amount of the loss can be reasonably estimated, the potential loss is not recognized in financial statements.

Litigation The most difficult area of contingencies is litigation. Accountants must rely on attorneys' assessments concerning the likelihood of such events. Unless the attorney indicates that the risk of loss is remote or slight, or that the loss if it occurs would be immaterial to the company, disclosure in financial statements is necessary and an accrual may also be necessary. In practice, attorneys are loathe to state that the risk of loss is remote, as that term is defined by ASC 450, although the likelihood of obtaining a definitive response to lawyers' letters under AU-C Section 501 is improved if the auditors explicitly cite a materiality threshold. In cases where judgments have been entered against the reporting entity, or where the attorney gives a range of expected losses or other amounts and indicates that an unfavorable outcome is probable, accruals of loss contingencies for at least the minimum point of the range must be made. In determining whether an accrual or disclosure is required, the entity should consider:

- The period in which the underlying cause takes place
- The degree of probability of an unfavorable outcome
- The ability to make a reasonable return of the loss
  (ASC 450-20-55-10)

In most cases, however, an estimate of the contingency is unknown and the contingency is reflected only in footnotes.

Accruals for contingencies, including those arising in connection with litigation, are limited under GAAP to expected losses resulting from events occurring prior to the date of the statement of financial position. (ASC 450-20-25-6) One unresolved issue is whether expected legal costs to be incurred in connection with a loss contingency that is being accrued should be accrued as well. Apparently, GAAP would permit such an accrual, but practice is varied. Preparers may want to refer to the SEC staff reviews. The SEC staff expects consistency and the decision to do so to be disclosed in the financial statements and applied consistently. (ASC 450-20-S99)

ASC 450-30, *Gain Contingencies*

The guidance in ASC 450-30 states simply that a "contingency that might result in a gain usually should not be reflected in the financial statements because to do so might be to recognize revenue before its realization." (ASC 450-30-25-1) However, it also states that entities may consider disclosing a gain contingency as long as the disclosure is adequate and is not misleading. (ASC 450-30-50-1) Preparers should refer to the guidance in ASC 220-30 on business interruption insurance and the ASC 210 Subtopic 20 on offsetting.

Other Sources

The *Contingencies* subtopics do not include all guidance related to contingencies. The following chart, based on information in the ASC Subtopics "60" sections, references other Codification sources of guidance.

See ASC Location—*Wiley GAAP* Chapter	*For information on . . .*
From ASC 450-10, *Overall*	
ASC 270-10-50-6	Contingencies and other uncertainties that could be expected to affect the fairness of presentation of financial data at an interim date.
ASC 340-30	Contingencies associated with insurance and reinsurance contracts that do not transfer insurance risk.
ASC 605-15	Recognition of revenue when uncertainties exist about possible returns.
ASC 605-40-25-4	Cases in which a nonmonetary asset is destroyed or damaged (that is, an involuntary conversion) and the amount of monetary assets to be received is uncertain.
ASC0-606-10-32-5 through 32-15	Estimating and constraining estimates of variable consideration.
ASC 610-30-25-4	Cases in which a nonmonetary asset is destroyed or damaged and the amount of monetary assets to be received is uncertain.
ASC 720-20	Accounting by an insured entity for the contingencies associated with a multiple-year retrospectively rated insurance contract accounted for as insurance.
ASC 740-10-25	Accounting for uncertainty in income taxes.
ASC 805-20-55-50 through 55-51	Recognition of contingent obligations for contractual termination benefits and curtailment losses under employee benefit plans that will be triggered by the consummation of the business combination.
ASC 840-10-25-35	Contingent rentals.[2]
ASC 842-20-55-1 and 55-2	Variable lease payments.

[2] Upon implementation of ASU 2016-02, Leases, this item will change to: For a lessor's accounting for income from variable lease payments, see paragraphs 842-30-25-2 (for sales-type leases), 842-30-25-9 (for direct financing leases), and 842-30-25-11 (for operating leases).

ASC 944-40	Contingencies that arise when an insurance entity or a reinsurance entity issues an insurance contract.
ASC 944-20-15	Contingencies associated with a reinsurance contract between insurance entities (including retrocession).
ASC 944-20	Contingencies associated with multiple-year retrospectively rated contracts.
ASC 985-605 (This paragraph will be superseded upon transition to ASC 606.)	Revenue recognition when uncertainties exist if licensing, selling, leasing, or otherwise marketing computer software.
ASC 450-20, Loss Contingencies	
ASC 275	Disclosure of certain risks and uncertainties that stem from the nature of an entity's operations and from significant concentrations in certain aspects of an entity's operations, many of which are noninsured or underinsured risks.
ASC 310-10-35[3]	Contingencies related to the collectibility of receivables.
ASC 310-10-35[4]	Application of this subtopic to the collectibility of a loan portfolio.
ASC 330-10-35	Inventories that are impaired by damage, deterioration, obsolescence, changes in price levels, or other causes.
ASC 330-10-35	Losses that are expected to arise from firm, uncancelable, and unhedged commitments for the future purchase of inventory.
ASC 405-30	Assessments by state guaranty funds and workers' compensation second-injury funds and other assessments related to insurance activities, including insurance activities of an entity that self-insures.
ASC 410-20	Contingencies associated with the retirement of a tangible long-lived asset that result from the acquisition, construction, or development and/or the normal operation of a long-lived asset.
ASC 410-30	Contingencies related to environmental remediation liabilities that arise from the improper operation of a long-lived asset.
The Product Warranties Subsections of Subtopic 460-10	Contingencies related to product warranties and product defects.
ASC 460	Contingencies related to guarantees of indebtedness of others.
ASC 460	Contingencies related to obligations of commercial banks under financial standby letters of credit.
ASC 326-20	Contingencies related to collectibility of receivables, upon implementation of ASU 2016-13.
ASC 326-20	Contingencies related to a loan portfolio, upon implementation of ASU 2016-13.
ASC 470-60-35	Contingent payments of a troubled debt restructuring.
ASC 715-80-35-2 and 715-80-50-2	Contingencies related to withdrawal from a multiemployer plan.
ASC 720-20-25-1	Contingencies related to an insurance contract or reinsurance contract that does not, despite its form, provide for indemnification of the insured or the ceding company by the insurer or reinsurer against loss or liability.

[3] Upon implementation of ASU 2016-13, this reference changes to ASC 326-20.

[4] Ibid.

ASC 840-10-25-12	Classification effect of a provision in a lease that requires lessee indemnifications for environmental contamination caused by a lessee during its use of the property.
ASC 840-10-25-35	Contingent rent.
ASC 842-10-55-1 and 55-2	Variable lease payments, upon implementation of ASU 2016-02, *Leases*.
ASC 842-10-55-15	Classification effects of a provision in a lease that requires lessee indemnifications for environmental contamination caused by the lessee during its use of the property.
ASC 860-10-40	Contingencies related to agreements to repurchase receivables (or to repurchase the related property) that have been sold or otherwise assigned.
ASC 930-715	Contingencies resulting from the Coal Industry Retiree Health Benefit Act of 1992.

See ASC Location—*Wiley GAAP* Chapter	*For information on . . .*
ASC 450-20, *Loss Contingencies*	
ASC 944-40	Contingencies related to the risk of loss that is assumed by a property and casualty insurance entity or reinsurance entity when it issues an insurance policy covering risk of loss from catastrophes.
ASC 946 320-35-17 to 35-19	Contingencies related to the collectibility of interest receivable, including purchased interest.
ASC 954-450	Contingencies related to malpractice claims.
ASC 450-30, *Gain Contingencies*	
ASC 210-20-45	The determination of whether a receivable resulting from the recognition of a gain contingency may be offset against an existing liability.
ASC 225-30-45	The presentation of business interruption insurance recoveries in the income statement.
ASC 225-30-50	Disclosure of information about business interruption insurance recoveries.
ASC 720-20-25-3	Recognition of insurance recoveries by an entity insured through a purchased retroactive insurance contract (other than for core insurance operations of an insurance entity).
ASC 840-10-50-5	A lessor's accounting for contingent rental income. Upon implementation of ASU 2016-01, *Leases*, this item will change to: For a lessor's accounting for income from variable lease payments, see paragraphs ASC 842-30-25-2 (for sales-type leases), ASC 842-30-25-9 (for direct financing leases) and ASC 842-30-55-11 (for operating leases).
ASC 842-30-25-2, 25-9, and 25-11	Upon implementation of ASU 2016-02, respectively, lessor's accounting for income from variable lease payments, direct financing leases, and operating leases.

32 ASC 460 GUARANTEES

PERSPECTIVE AND ISSUES

Overview

Guarantees embody two separate obligations:

1. The contingent obligation to make future payments under the guarantee in the event of nonperformance by the party whose obligation is guaranteed, and
2. An obligation to be ready to perform, referred to as a standby obligation, during the period that the guarantee is in effect.

As a result of this bifurcation of the obligation, many guarantees are now required to be recognized as liabilities on the statement of financial position.

Subtopic

ASC 460, *Guarantees*, consists of one subtopic:

- ASC 460-10, *Overall*, which provides requirements to be met by a guarantor for certain guarantees issued and outstanding.

ASC 460-10 has two subsections:

1. *General,* which discusses the guarantor's recognition and disclosure of a liability at the inception of a guarantee
2. *Product Warranties*
(ASC 460-10-05-1)

Additional sources of guidance are listed in the "Other Sources" section at the end of this chapter.

Scope and Scope Exceptions

General ASC 460 applies to all entities. (ASC 460-10-15-1) ASC 460 applies to:

a. Guarantee contracts that contingently require the guarantor to make payments to the guaranteed party as described in "b" below based on changes to an underlying related to an asset, a liability, or an equity security of the guaranteed party.
b. Contracts that contingently require a guarantor to make payments based on another entity's failure to perform under an obligating agreement. For example, the provisions apply to a performance standby letter of credit, which obligates the guarantor to make a payment if the specified entity fails to perform its nonfinancial obligation. (ASC 460-10-55-12)
c. The occurrence of a specified event or circumstance in an indemnification agreement that requires the indemnifying party to pay an indemnified party based on changes in underlying related to an asset, a liability, or an equity security of the indemnified party. Examples are an adverse judgment in a lawsuit or the imposition of additional taxes due to either a change in the tax law or an adverse interpretation of the tax law, provided that the guarantor is an entity other than an insurance or reinsurance company. (ASC 460-10-55-13)
d. Indirect guarantee of the indebtedness of others even though the payment may not be based on changes to an underlying related to an asset, liability, or equity security of the guaranteed party.
(ASC 460-10-15-4)

The following are examples of the types of contracts referred to in ASC 460-10-15-4(b) above:

- A financial standby letter of credit
- A market value guarantee on either securities (including the common stock of the guaranteed party) or a nonfinancial asset owned by the guaranteed party
- A guarantee of the market price of the common stock of the guaranteed party
- A guarantee of the collection of the scheduled contractual cash flows from individual financial assets held by a variable interest entity (VIE)
- A guarantee granted to a business or its owners that the revenue received by the business will equal or exceed some stated amount.
(ASC 460-10-55-2, with reference to ASC 460-10-15-4(a))

One common example of this type of situation is where a hospital lures a doctor to open a practice in an underserved community with a guarantee of fee income for an initial period. ASC 460 explicitly states that these types of assurances are guarantees and must be given accounting recognition.

ASC 460 does *not* apply to:

- A guarantee or an indemnification that is excluded from the scope of Topic 450, *Contingencies*, primarily employment-related guarantees
- A lessee's guarantee of the residual value of leased property if the lessee accounts for the lease as a capital lease[1]

[1] Upon implementation of ASU 2016-02, *Leases*, this bullet will read: "A lessee's guarantee of the residual value of the underlying asset at the expiration of the lease term under Topic 8842."

- Contingent rents[2]
- A guarantee contract or an indemnification agreement, accounted for under ASC 944, that is issued by either an insurance or a reinsurance company
- Vendor rebates (by the guarantor) based on either the sales revenues of or the number of units sold by the guaranteed party
- Vendor rebates (by the guarantor) based on the volume of purchases by the buyer (because the underlying relates to an asset of the seller not the buyer who receives the rebate)
- Guarantees that prevent the guarantor from recognizing either the sale of the asset underlying the guarantee or the profits from that sale
- A registration payment arrangement within the scope of ASC 825-20-15, *Financial Instruments, Registration Payment Arrangements*
- A guarantee or an indemnification of an entity's own future performance
- A guarantee accounted for as a credit derivative instrument at fair value under ASC 815-10-50-4 J through 4 L
- A sales incentive program where a manufacturer guarantees to recognize the equipment at a specified time or place.
  (ASC 460-10-15-7)

Product Warranties The guidance in the Product Warranties subsections applies only to product warranties, which include all of the following:

- Product warranties issued by the guarantor, regardless of whether the guarantor is required to make payment in services or cash.
- Separately priced extended warranty or product maintenance contracts and (per ASC 606) "warranties that provide a customer with a service in addition to the assurance that product complies with agreed-upon specifications."
- Warranty obligations that are incurred in connection with the sale of the product, that is, obligations in which the customer does not have the option to purchase the warranty separately and that do not provide the customer with a service in addition to the assurance that the product complies with agreed-upon specifications.
  (ASC 460-10-15-9)

DEFINITIONS OF TERMS

Source: ASC 460-10-20. Also see Appendix A, *Definitions of Terms*, for other terms relevant to this topic: Acquiree, Acquirer, Acquisition by a Not-for-Profit Entity, Business, Business Combination, Commencement Date of the Lease (Commencement Date), Contingency, Contract, Customer, Direct Guarantee of Indebtedness, Fair Value (Def. 3), Gain Contingency, Lease, Lease Payments, Lease Term, Legal Entity, Lessee, Lessor, Loss Contingency, Not-for- Profit Entity, Penalty, Performance Obligation, Probable, Related Parties, Registration Payment Arrangement, Reinsurance, Revenue, Underlying Asset, Variable Interest Entity, Variable Lease Payments, Weather Derivative.

Commercial Letter of Credit. Document issued typically by a financial institution on behalf of its customer (the account party) authorizing a third party (the beneficiary), or in special

[2] Upon implementation of ASU 2016-02, this bullet will change to "A contract that is accounted for as Variable lease payments."

cases the account party, to draw drafts on the institution up to a stipulated amount and with specified terms and conditions; it is a conditional commitment (except if prepaid by the account party) on the part of the institution to provide payment on drafts drawn in accordance with the terms of the document.

Direct Guarantee of Indebtedness. An agreement in which a guarantor states that if the debtor fails to make payment to the creditor when due, the guarantor will pay the creditor. If the debtor defaults, the creditor has a direct claim on the guarantor.

Financial Standby Letter of Credit. An undertaking (typically by a financial institution) to guarantee payment of a specified financial obligation.

Indirect Guarantee of Indebtedness. An agreement that obligates the guarantor to transfer funds to a debtor upon the occurrence of specified events, under conditions whereby:

- After funds are transferred from the guarantor to the debtor, the funds become legally available to creditors through their claims against the debtor.
- Those creditors may enforce the debtor's claims against the guarantor under the agreement.

In contrast with a direct guarantee of indebtedness, if the debtor defaults, the creditor has a direct claim on the guarantor. Examples of indirect guarantees include agreements to advance funds if a debtor's net income, coverage of fixed charges, or working capital falls below a specified minimum.

Indirectly Related to the Leased Property.[3] The provisions or conditions that in substance are guarantees of the lessor's debt or loans to the lessor by the lessee that are related to the leased property but are structured in such a manner that they do not represent a direct guarantee or loan. Examples include a party related to the lessee guaranteeing the lessor's debt on behalf of the lessee, or the lessee financing the lessor's purchase of the leased asset using collateral other than the leased property.

Minimum Revenue Guarantee. A guarantee granted to a business or its owners that the revenue of the business (or a specific portion of the business) for a specified period of time will be at least a specified minimum amount.

Noncancelable Lease Term.[4] That portion of the lease term that is cancelable only under any of the following conditions:

- Upon the occurrence of some remote contingency.
- With the permission of the lessor.
- If the lessee enters into a new lease with the same lessor.
- If the lessee incurs a penalty in such amount that continuation of the lease appears, at inception, reasonably assured.

Performance Standby Letter of Credit. An irrevocable undertaking by a guarantor to make payments in the event a specified third party fails to perform under a nonfinancial contractual obligation.

Warranty. A guarantee for which the underlying is related to the performance (regarding function, not price) of nonfinancial assets that are owned by the guaranteed party. The obligation may be incurred in connection with the sale of goods or services; if so, it may require further performance by the seller after the sale has taken place.

[3] Upon implementation of ASU 2016-02, this term is deleted from ASC 460.
[4] Ibid.

CONCEPTS, RULES, AND EXAMPLES

ASC 460's requirement to recognize an initial liability does *not* apply to the following types of guarantees. However, these guarantees are subject only to ASC 460's disclosure requirements:

- A guarantee that is accounted for as a derivative instrument at fair value under ASC 815.
- A contract that guarantees the functionality of nonfinancial assets that are owned by the guaranteed party (product warranties)
- Contingent consideration in a business combination or an acquisition of a business or nonprofit activity by a not-for-profit entity
- A guarantee that requires the guarantor to issue its own equity shares
- A guarantee by an original lessee that has become secondarily liable under a new lease that relieved the original lessee of the primary obligation under the original lease
- A guarantee issued between parents and their subsidiaries or between corporations under common control
- A parent's guarantee of a subsidiary's debt to a third party (irrespective of whether the parent is a corporation or an individual)
- A subsidiary's guarantee of a parent's debt to a third party or the debt of another subsidiary of the parent.
  (ASC 460-10-25-1)

Guarantees

ASC 460:

- Requires that the fair value of guarantees be recognized as a liability, and
- Establishes the notion that a guarantee actually consists of two distinct components.

These two components have quite different accounting implications:

1. *Noncontingent obligation*. The first of these components is a noncontingent obligation, namely, the obligation to stand ready to perform over the term of the guarantee in the event that the specified triggering events or conditions occur. This stand-ready obligation is unconditional and thus is not considered a contingent obligation.
2. *Contingent obligation*. The second component, which is a contingent obligation, is the obligation to make future payments if those triggering events or conditions occur.
   (ASC 460-10-25-2)

Note that ASC 460 does not require bifurcation nor separate accounting for the contingent and noncontingent assets of the guarantee. Upon implementation of ASC 2016-13, that will be true only for guarantees not within the scope of ASC 326-20. For those within the scope of ASC 326-20, the contingent aspect should be measured and accounted for in addition to and separately from the fair value of the noncontingent aspect. (ASC 460-10-25-2)

Even though it is not probable that payments will be required, a guarantor may recognize a liability for a guarantee. (ASC 460-10-25-3)

Initial Recognition At the inception of a guarantee, the guarantor recognizes a liability for both the noncontingent and contingent obligations at their fair values. (ASC 460-10-25-4) However, in the unusual circumstance that a liability is recognized under ASC 450-20 for the contingent obligation (i.e., because it is deemed probable of occurrence and reasonable of estimation that the guarantor will pay), the liability initially recognized for the noncontingent obligation would only be the portion, if any, of the guarantee's fair value not already recognized to comply with ASC 450-20. (ASC 460-10-25-3)

It is important to stress that this does not mean that the guarantor records the entire face amount of the guarantee; rather, it is the fair value of the stand-ready obligation that is recognized. When a guarantee is issued in a stand-alone, arm's-length transaction with an unrelated party, the fair value of the guarantee (and thus the amount to be recognized as a liability) is the premium received by the guarantor. When a guarantee is issued as part of another transaction (such as the sale or lease of an asset) or as a contribution to an unrelated party, the fair value of the liability is measured by the premium that would be required by the guarantor to issue the same guarantee in a stand-alone, arm's-length transaction with an unrelated party.

In practice, if the likelihood that the guarantor will have to perform is judged to be only "reasonably possible" or "remote," the only amount recorded is the fair value of the noncontingent obligation to stand ready to perform. If, however, the contingency is probable of occurrence and can be reasonably estimated under ASC 450-20, that amount must be recognized and the liability under the guarantee arrangement will be the greater of:

- The fair value computed as explained above, or
- The amount computed in accordance with ASC 450-20's provisions.
  (ASC 460-10-30-3)

Upon implementation of ASU 2016-13, at the inception of a guarantee on financial instruments measured at amortized costs, the guarantor should recognize as liabilities:

- The amount that satisfies the fair value obligation in ASC 460-10-30-2 described above and
- The contingent liability related to the expected credit loss measured according to ASC 326-20
  (ASC 460-10-30-5)

When initially issued, the guidance on computing guarantees where no market information is available made reference to CON 7. In so doing, FASB endorsed the use of the discounted, probability-weighted cash flow method for estimating the stand-ready obligation.

Since, in the author's opinion, in the absence of other, better input data, such as the pricing of insurance to assume the risk of performing on the guarantee, the probability-weighted present value of possible future cash flows could serve as useful input to determining the fair value of guarantees made, the following example is presented.

Example of Estimating the Fair Value of a Guarantee Using CON 7 When Recognition of a Loss Contingency under ASC 450 Would Not Be Otherwise Required

Big Red Company guarantees a $1,000,000 debt of Little Blue Company for the next three years in conjunction with selling equipment to Little Blue. Big Red evaluates its risk of payment as follows:

1. There is no possibility that Big Red will pay during year 1.
2. There is a 15% chance that Big Red will pay during year 2. If it has to pay, there is a 30% chance that it will have to pay $500,000 and a 70% chance that it will have to pay $250,000.
3. There is a 20% chance that Big Red will pay during year 3. If it has to pay, there is a 25% chance that it will have to pay $600,000 and a 75% chance that it will have to pay $300,000.

The expected cash flows are computed as follows:

Year 1 100% chance of paying $0 = $0
Year 2 85% chance of paying $0 and a 15% chance of paying (.30 × $500,000 + .70 × $250,000) = $325,000 = $48,750
Year 3 80% chance of paying $0 and a 20% chance of paying (.25 × $600,000 + .75 × $300,000) = $375,000 = $75,000

The present value of the expected cash flows is computed as the sum of the years' probability-weighted cash flows, here assuming an appropriate discount rate of 8%.

Year 1	$0 × 1 / 1.08	=	$ 0
Year 2	$48,750 × 1 / (1.08)²	=	41,795
Year 3	$75,000 × 1 / (1.08)³	=	59,537
Fair value of the guarantee			$101,332

Based on the foregoing, a liability of $101,332 would be recognized at inception. This would reduce the net selling price of the equipment sold to Little Blue, thereby reducing the profit to be reported on the sale transaction.

Example of Estimating the Fair Value of a Guarantee Using CON 7 When Recognition of a Loss Contingency under ASC 450 Is Also Required

Assume the same basic facts as in the foregoing example, but now also assume that it has been determined that there is a 60% likelihood that the buyer will eventually default and, after legal process, Big Red will have to repay debt amounting to $400,000 at the end of the fifth year. Assume also that a likelihood of 60% is deemed to make this contingent obligation "probable" under ASC 450. The present value of that payment is $272,233, but ASC 450 does not address or seemingly anticipate the application of present value methods. Thus, it would appear that accrual of the full $400,000 expected loss is required, unaffected by expected timing or by the probability (60%, in this example) that it will occur. Since this amount exceeds the amount computed under ASC 460, no additional amount would be recognized in connection with the noncontingent obligation to stand ready to perform.

If, instead of the immediate foregoing facts, the probable repayments were estimated to be $75,000, then the liabilities to be recognized would total $101,322, of which $75,000 would be required to satisfy the provisions of ASC 450, and the incremental amount, $26,332, would be attributed to the noncontingent obligation.

The entry to record the liability depends upon the circumstances under which the guarantee arose. If the guarantee was issued in a standalone transaction for a premium, the offset would be to the asset accepted for the premium's payment (most likely, cash or a receivable). If the guarantee was issued in conjunction with the sale of assets, the proceeds would be allocated between the sale of the asset and the guarantee obligation, so that the profit (loss) on the sale of the asset would be reduced (increased). If the guarantee was issued in conjunction with the formation of a business accounted for under the equity method, the offset would be an increase in the carrying amount of the investment. If the guarantee was issued to an unrelated party for no consideration, an immediate expense would be recognized. If a residual value guarantee was provided by a lessee-guarantor, the offset would be reported as prepaid rent and then amortized over the term of the lease to rent expense. The residual value of equipment by the manufacturer is recognized by the manufacturer as an asset (included in the seller/lessor's net investment in lease).

Subsequent Measurement After initial recognition, the liability is adjusted as the guarantor either is released from risk or is subject to increased risk. If the guarantor is subsequently released from risk, logically that could be recognized in one of three ways:

1. The liability could simply be written off at its expiration or settlement.
2. The liability could be amortized systematically over the guarantee period.
3. The liability might be adjusted to reflect changing fair value, which presumably declines over time as the risk of having to perform decreases.

ASC 460 does not prescribe the accounting for guarantees subsequent to initial recognition, and there is no requirement to reassess the fair value of the guarantee after inception. Fair value should only be used in subsequent accounting for the guarantee if the use of that method can be justified under other authoritative guidance. (ASC 460-10-35-2)

This guidance does not address the recognition and subsequent accounting of the contingent liability related to the contingent loss for the guarantee. That should be accounted for using the guidance in:

- ASC 450-20 unless the guarantee is
  - Accounted for as a derivative under the provisions of ASC 815 or
  - Within the scope of ASC 326-20, when implemented

  (ASC 460-10-35-4)

Disclosure Requirements Disclosures can be found in the *Disclosure and Presentation Checklist for Commercial Businesses* at www.wiley.com/go/GAAP2021.

Product Warranties

Product warranties providing for repair or replacement of defective products may be sold separately or may be included in the sale price of the product. ASC 460-10-25-5 points out that "because of the uncertainty surrounding claims that may be made under warranties, warranty obligation falls within the definition of a contingency" and losses are accrued under the conditions in ASC 450-20-25 are met:

- If it is *probable* that an obligation has been incurred because of a transaction or event that occurred on or before the date of the financial statements, and
- If the amount of the obligation can be *reasonably estimated.*

These conditions may be made for individual elements or groups of items and the particular parties making claims may not be identified at the time of the accrual. (ASC 460-10-25-7)

For more information on extended warranty contracts, product maintenance contracts, and warranties that provide a service in addition to the assurance that the product complied with the specifications, see the chapter on ASC 606. (ASC 460-10-25-8)

Example of Product Warranty Expense

The Churnaway Corporation manufactures clothes washers. It sells $900,000 of washing machines during its most recent month of operations. Based on its historical warranty claims experience, it records an estimated warranty expense of 2% of revenues with the following entry:

Warranty expense	18,000	
Accrued warranty claims		18,000

During the following month, Churnaway incurs $10,000 of actual labor and $4,500 of actual materials expenses to perform repairs required under warranty claims, which it charges to the warranty claims accrual with the following entry:

Accrued warranty claims	14,500	
Labor expense		10,000
Materials expense		4,500

Churnaway also sells three-year extended warranties on its washing machines that begin once the initial one-year manufacturer's warranty expires. During one month, it sells $54,000 of extended warranties, which it records with the following entry:

Cash	54,000	
Unearned warranty revenue		54,000

This liability is unaltered for one year from the purchase date, after which the extended warranty servicing period begins. Churnaway recognizes the warranty revenue on a straight-line basis over the 36 months of the warranty period, using the following entry each month:

Unearned warranty revenue	1,500	
Warranty revenue		1,500

Software vendors/licensors often include, as part of their customary contractual terms, an indemnification clause that indemnifies the licensee against liability and damages (including costs of legal defense) that could arise in the event that a third-party claims patent, copyright, trademark, or trade secret infringement with respect to the licensor's software. The indemnification requires the licensor/guarantor to make a payment to the licensee/guaranteed party based on the occurrence of an infringement claim against the licensor that results in liabilities or damages related to the licensed software being used by the licensee. Under such a scenario, an infringement claim covered by the indemnification could impair the ability of the licensee to use the licensed software if, for example, a court orders an injunction or assesses damages.

The indemnification qualifies for the scope exception in ASC 460-10-25-1(b) (discussed in the "Scope and Scope Exceptions" section at the beginning of this chapter) as a product warranty or other guarantee for which the underlying is related to the performance of a nonfinancial asset (the software) owned (leased) by the guaranteed party since the licensed software cannot function as intended until the seller-licensor cures the alleged infringement defect.

These arrangements are subject to the same disclosure requirements imposed on other warranty obligations.

Other Sources

See ASC Location—*Wiley GAAP* Chapter	For information on . . .
ASC 323-10-35-20	Guaranteed obligations of an investee that is accounted for using the equity method.
ASC 340-10-25-3	Contractual guarantees for reimbursement of design and development costs related to long-term supply arrangements.
ASC 360-20-40-41	A seller's guarantee of a return of the buyer's investment in real estate or a seller's guarantee of a return on that investment for an extended period.[5]

[5] Upon implementation of ASU 2016-02, *Leases*, this item will be superseded by the item below on ASC 842-40.

See ASC Location—*Wiley GAAP* Chapter	For information on . . .
ASC 405-20-40-2	The guarantee obligation that results if a primary debtor becomes secondarily liable upon a release by a creditor.
ASC 480-10-55-23	An entity's guarantee of the value of an asset, liability, or equity security of another entity that may require or permit settlement in the entity's equity shares.
ASC 480-10-55-53 through 55-58	A freestanding put option indexed to a subsidiary's equity shares.
ASC 480-10-55-59 through 55-62	Embedded put options indexed to the stock of a consolidated subsidiary.
ASC 606-10-55-30 through 55-35	Recognition of revenue for a warranty that is identified as a separate performance obligation.
ASC 718-40-25-9	An employer's guarantee of the debt of an employee stock option plan.
ASC 805-30	Guarantees that represent contingent consideration in a business combination.
ASC 810-10-55-25 through 55-26	Guarantees of the value of the assets or liabilities of a variable interest entity (VIE), written put options on the assets of the VIE, or similar obligations.
ASC 815-10-15-77 and 810-10-45-16A	Freestanding derivative instruments indexed to, and potentially settled in, the stock of a consolidated subsidiary.
ASC 815-45	Weather derivatives.
Definition of lease term	The effect on the lease term of a provision or condition that in substance is a guarantee of a lessor's debt or a loan to a lessor by the lessee that is related to the leased property but is structured in such a manner that it does not represent a direct guarantee or loan.[6]
ASC 840-10-25-5	The effects on minimum lease payments of a guarantee by the lessee of the lessor's debt.[7]
ASC 840-10-25-6 and 840-10-55-8 through 55-10	The effects on minimum lease payments of a guarantee by the lessee of the residual value of the leased property at the expiration of the lease term.[8]
ASC 840-10-15-20[9]	A determination of whether a residual value guarantee is subject to the requirements of Topic 815.
ASC 840-10-25-21 through 25-22	Allocation of a residual value or first-loss guarantee to minimum lease payments in leases involving land and building(s).[10]

[6] Upon implementation of ASU 2016-02, "property" will be replaced by "underlying asset."

[7] Upon implementation of ASU 2016-02, this reference will change to ASC 842-10-30-6 and the item will change to: "The effects on lease payments of a guarantee by the lessee of the lessor's debt."

[8] Upon implementation of ASU 2016-02, this reference will change to ASC 842-10-30-5 and 842-10-55-34 through 55-36 and the item will change to: "The effects on lease payments of a guarantee by the lessee of the residual value of the underlying asset at the expiration of the lease term."

[9] Upon implementation of ASU 2016-02, this reference will change to ASC 842-10-15-43.

[10] Upon implementation of ASU 2016-02, this item will be superseded.

See ASC Location—*Wiley GAAP* Chapter	For information on . . .
ASC 840-10-25-42 through 25-43[11]	The classification of a lease that includes a commitment by a lessor to guarantee performance of the leased property in a manner more extensive than a typical product warranty or to effectively protect the lessee from obsolescence of the leased property.
ASC 840-10-55-12 through 55-25[12]	A manufacturer's guarantee of the resale value of equipment to the purchaser.
ASC 840-10-25-13[13]	A lessee's indemnification for environmental contamination.
ASC 840-20-30-1[14]	A guarantee by a lessee of the leased property's residual value in an operating lease transaction.
ASC 840-30-35[15]	A guarantee by a lessee of the leased property's residual value in a capital lease transaction.
ASC 840-40-25-14[16]	The effect of providing an independent third-party guarantee of the lease payments in a sale-leaseback transaction.
ASC 840-40-25-15[17]	Classification of a lease that contains an entity's unsecured guarantee of its own lease payments.
ASC 840-40-25-16[18]	Classification of a lease that contains an unsecured guarantee of the lease payments of one member of a consolidated group by another member of the consolidated group.
ASC 840-40-55-9[19]	An indemnification or guarantee of an owner-lessor against third-party claims relating to construction completion in a sale-leaseback transaction.
ASC 840-40-55-15[20]	An indemnification or guarantee of an owner-lessor against third-party damage claims other than claims caused by or resulting from the lessee's own actions or failures to act while in possession or control of the construction project in a sale-leaseback transaction.
ASC 840-40-55-15[21]	An indemnification or guarantee by the seller-lessee to a party other than the owner-lessor in a sale-leaseback transaction.

[11] Upon implementation of ASU 2016-02, this reference will change to ASC 842-10-55-32 through 55-33, and the item will change to: "A commitment by a lessor to guarantee performance of the underlying asset in a manner more extensive than a typical product warranty or to effectively protect the lessee from obsolescence of the underlying asset."

[12] Upon implementation of ASU 2016-02, this reference will change to ASC 842-30-55-1 through 55-15.

[13] Upon implementation of ASU 2016-02, this reference will change to ASC 842-10-55-15.

[14] Upon implementation of ASU 2016-02, this reference will change to ASC 842-10-30-5 and 842-10-55-34 through 55- 35, and the item will change to: "A guarantee by a lessee of the underlying asset's residual value in a lease transaction."

[15] Upon implementation of ASU 2016-02, this item will be superseded.

[16] Ibid.

[17] Ibid.

[18] Ibid.

[19] Ibid.

[20] Ibid.

[21] Ibid.

See ASC Location—*Wiley GAAP* Chapter	For information on . . .
ASC 840-40-55-26[22]	A guarantee by the seller-lessee of the leased property's residual value in a sale-leaseback transaction.
ASC 842-40	A seller's guarantee of a return of the buyer's investment in real estate of a seller's guarantee of a return on that investment for an extended period.[23]
ASC 860-20-55-20	Transactions that involve the sale of a marketable security to a third-party buyer, with the buyer's having an option to put the security back to the seller at a specified future date or dates for a fixed price.
ASC 860-50-40-7 through 40-9	A sale of mortgage servicing rights with a subservicing agreement in which the seller-subservicer directly or indirectly guarantees a yield to the buyer.
ASC 926-605-25-19 through 25-21[24]	Nonrefundable minimum guarantees contained in certain film licensing arrangements.
ASC 960-325-35-3	Guaranteed investment contracts held by defined benefit pension plans.
ASC 970-470-25-3	An entity's agreement to either make up shortfalls in the annual debt service requirements or guarantee a tax increment financing entity's debt.

[22] Upon implementation of ASU 2016-02, this reference will change to ASU 842-40-55-20 through 21, and the item will change to: "A guarantee by the seller-lessee of the underlying asset's residual value in a sale and leaseback transaction."

[23] This item is effective upon implementation of ASU 2016-02.

[24] Upon implementation of ASU 2016-02, this item will be superseded.

33 ASC 470 DEBT

PERSPECTIVE AND ISSUES

Subtopics

ASC 470, *Debt*, consists of six subtopics:

- ASC 470-10, *Overall*, which provides guidance on classification of obligations, such as:
  - Short-term debt expected to be refinanced on a long-term basis,
  - Due-on-demand loans,
  - Callable debt,
  - Sales of future revenue,
  - Increasing rate debt, debt with covenants,
  - Revolving credit agreements subject to lockbox arrangements and subjective acceleration clauses, and
  - Indexed debt.

  (ASC 470-10-05-5)
- ASC 470-20, *Debt with Conversion and Other Options*, which provides guidance on debt and certain preferred stock with specific conversion features:
  - Debt instruments with detachable warrants,
  - Convertible securities in general,
  - Beneficial conversion features,
  - Interest forfeiture,
  - Induced conversions,
  - Conversion upon issuer's exercise of call option,
  - Convertible instruments issued to nonemployees for goods and services, and
  - Own-share lending arrangements issued in contemplation of convertible debt issuance.
- ASC 470-30, *Participating Mortgage Loans*, which provides guidance on the borrower's accounting for a participating mortgage loan if the lender is entitled to participate in appreciation in the fair value of the mortgaged real estate project or the results of operations of the mortgaged real estate project.
- ASC 470-40, *Product Financing Arrangements*, which provides guidance for determining whether an arrangement involving the sale of inventory is in substance a financing arrangement.
- ASC 470-50, *Modifications and Extinguishments*, which provides guidance on all debt instruments extinguishment, except for debt extinguished in a troubled debt restructuring.
- ASC 470-60, *Troubled Debt Restructurings by Debtors*, which addresses measuring and recognition from the debtor's perspective.

Scope and Scope Exceptions

ASC 470-20 ASC 470-20 is divided into two subsections:

1. General
2. Cash conversion

General subsections The guidance in the General subsections' paragraphs does not apply to those instruments within the scope of the Cash Conversion subsections. The guidance on own-share lending arrangements applies to an equity-classified share-lending arrangement on an entity's own shares when executed in contemplation of a convertible debt offering or other financing. (ASC 470-20-15-2)

It is important to note that the guidance in this subsection should be considered after consideration of the guidance in Subtopic 815-15 on bifurcation of embedded derivatives, as applicable (see paragraph 815-15-55-76A).

Cash conversion subsections The guidance in the Cash Conversion subsections applies only to convertible debt instruments that may be settled in cash (or other assets) upon conversion, unless the embedded conversion option is required to be separately accounted for as a derivative instrument under Subtopic 815-15. (ASC 470-20-15-4)

The Cash Conversion subsections do *not* apply to any of the following instruments:

- A convertible preferred share that is classified in equity or temporary equity.
- A convertible debt instrument that requires or permits settlement in cash (or other assets) upon conversion only in specific circumstances in which the holders of the underlying shares also would receive the same form of consideration in exchange for their shares.
- A convertible debt instrument that requires an issuer's obligation to provide consideration for a fractional share upon conversion to be settled in cash but that does not otherwise require or permit settlement in cash (or other assets) upon conversion.
  (ASC 470-20-15-5)

For purposes of determining whether an instrument is within the scope of the Cash Conversion subsections, a convertible preferred share should be considered a convertible debt instrument if it is:

- A mandatorily redeemable financial instrument *and*
- Classified as a liability under Subtopic 480-10.
  (ASC 470-20-15-6)

ASC 470-30 ASC 470-30 does *not* apply to creditors in participating mortgage loan arrangements and to the following transactions:

- Participating leases
- Debt convertible at the option of the lender into equity ownership of the property
- Participating loans resulting from troubled debt restructurings
  (ASC 470-30-15-2 and 15-3)

ASC 470-40 The guidance in ASC 470-40 applies to product financing arrangements for products that were purchased by another entity on behalf of the sponsor. The arrangement must have the following characteristics:

- The financing arrangement requires the sponsor to purchase the product, a substantially identical product, or processed goods of which the product is a component at specified prices. The specified prices are not subject to change except for fluctuations due to finance and holding costs. This characteristic of predetermined prices also is present if any of the following circumstances exist:

  - The specified prices in the financing arrangement are in the form of resale price guarantees under which the sponsor agrees to make up any difference between the specified price and the resale price for products sold to third parties.
  - The sponsor is not required to purchase the product but has an option to purchase the product, the economic effect of which compels the sponsor to purchase the product; for example, an option arrangement that provides for a significant penalty if the sponsor does not exercise the option to purchase.
  - The sponsor is not required by the agreement to purchase the product but the other entity has an option whereby it can require the sponsor to purchase the product.

- The payments that the other entity will receive on the transaction are established by the financing arrangement, and the amounts to be paid by the sponsor will be adjusted, as necessary, to cover substantially all fluctuations in costs incurred by the other entity in purchasing and holding the product (including interest). This characteristic ordinarily is not present in purchase commitments or contractor-subcontractor relationships.
  (ASC 470-40-15-2)

ASC 470-40 does *not* apply to the following transactions and activities:

- Ordinary purchase commitments in which control of goods or services are retained by the seller (for example, a manufacturer or other supplier) until the goods or services are transferred to a purchaser.
- Typical contractor-subcontractor relationships in which the contractor is not in substance the owner of product held by the subcontractor and the obligation of the contractor is contingent on substantial performance on the part of the subcontractor.
- Long-term unconditional purchase obligations (for example, take-or-pay contracts) specified by Subtopic 440-10. At the time a take-or-pay contract is entered into, which is an unconditional purchase obligation, either the product does not yet exist (for example, electricity) or the product exists in a form unsuitable to the purchaser (for example, unmined coal); the purchaser has a right to receive future product but is not the substantive owner of existing product.
- Unmined or unharvested natural resources and financial instruments.
- Transactions for which sales revenue is recognized currently in accordance with the provisions of ASC 606.
- Typical purchases by a subcontractor on behalf of a contractor. In a typical contractor-subcontractor relationship, the purchase of product by a subcontractor on behalf of a contractor ordinarily leaves a significant portion of the subcontractor's obligation unfulfilled.
  The subcontractor has the risks of ownership of the product until it has met all the terms of a contract. Accordingly, the typical contractor-subcontractor relationship shall not be considered a product financing arrangement.
  (ASC 470-40-15-3)

ASC 470-50 The general guidance for extinguishment of liabilities can be found in the chapter on ASC 405. The guidance in ASC 470-50 applies in part to extinguishments of debt effected by issuance of common or preferred stock that do not represent the exercise of a conversion right contained in the debt. (ASC 470-50-15-2)

ASC 470-50 does *not* apply to the following transactions and activities:

- Conversions of debt into equity securities of the debtor pursuant to conversion privileges provided in the terms of the debt at issuance. Additionally, the guidance in this subtopic does not apply to conversions of convertible debt instruments pursuant to terms that reflect changes made by the debtor to the conversion privileges provided in the debt at issuance (including changes that involve the payment of consideration) for the purpose of inducing conversion. Guidance on conversions of debt instruments (including induced conversions) is contained in paragraphs 470-20-40-13 and 470-20-40-15.
- Extinguishments of debt through a troubled debt restructuring. (See information later in this chapter on Section 470 for guidance on determining whether a modification or exchange of debt instruments is a troubled debt restructuring. If it is determined that the modification or exchange does not result in a troubled debt restructuring, the guidance in ASC 470-50 should be applied.)
- Transactions entered into between a debtor or a debtor's agent and a third party that is not the creditor.
  (ASC 470-50-15-3)

ASC 470-60 The guidance in ASC 470-60 applies to all debtors and all troubled debt restructurings (TDRs) by debtors. (ASC 470-60-15-1 and 15-2) Note that the creditor's accounting for a TDR may differ if the debtor's carrying amount and the creditor's amortized cost basis differ. Also, a debtor may have a TDR under ASC 470-60, but the related creditor may not have a TDR under the tests in ASC 310-40. That is, the tests established by the two topics are not symmetrical. (ASC 470-60-15-3) In this Topic, debt whether a receivable or a payable represents a contractual right to receive money or a contractual obligation to pay money on demand or on fixed or determinable dates that is already included as an asset or a liability in the creditor's or debtor's balance sheet at the time of the restructuring. (ASC 470-60-15-4A) Troubled debt restructurings under ASC 470-60 include situations in which the creditor, for economic or legal reasons related to the debtor's financial difficulties, grants the debtor a concession that would not otherwise be granted. (ASC 470-60-15-5)

The objective of the creditor in a TDR is to protect as much of its investment as possible. To accomplish that a creditor may restructure the terms to alleviate the burden or accept assets or an equity interest in satisfaction of the debt at a value less than the amount of the debt. TDRs include debt that is fully satisfied by foreclosure, repossession, or other transfer of assets or by grant of equity securities. (ASC 470-60-15-6)

If a debtor can obtain funds from other than existing creditors at or near market interest rates for nontroubled debt, the debtor is not involved in a TDR. A debtor in a TDR can only obtain funds at interest rates that are so high that the debtor cannot afford them. (ASC 470-60-15-8)

A TDR may include:

- Transfer from the debtor to the creditor assets to fully or partially satisfy a debt
- Granting of an equity interest
- Modification of terms of a debt, such as through:
  - Reduction of the stated interest rate
  - Extension of the maturity date at a lower interest rate

  - Reduction of the face amount of the debt
  - Reduction of the accrued interest

  (ASC 470-60-15-9)

ASC 470-60 does not apply to debtors in bankruptcy unless the restructuring does not result from a general restatement of the debtor's liabilities in bankruptcy proceedings. That is, ASC 470-60 applies only if the debt restructuring is isolated to the creditor. (ASC 470-60-15-10)

None of the following are considered TDRs under ASC 470-60:

- Lease modifications
- Change in employment-related agreements
- Unless they involve an agreement between debtor and creditor to restructure, neither:
  - Debtor's failure to pay trade accounts according to their terms
  - Creditor delays in taking legal action to collect overdue amounts of interest and principal

  (ASC 470-60-15-11)

In any of the following four situations, a concession granted by the creditor does *not automatically* qualify as a restructuring:

- The fair value of the assets or equity interest accepted by a creditor from a debtor in full satisfaction of its receivable is at least equal to the creditor's amortized cost basis in the receivable.
- The fair value of the assets or equity interest transferred by a debtor to a creditor in full settlement of its payable is at least equal to the carrying value of the payable.
- The creditor reduces the effective interest rate to reflect a decrease in current interest rates or a decrease in the risk, in order to maintain the relationship.
- The debtor, in exchange for old debt, issues new marketable debt with an interest rate that reflects current market rates.

  (ASC 470-60-15-12)

Overview

Debt remains on the books of the debtor until it is extinguished. In many cases, a debt is extinguished at maturity when the required principal and interest payments have been made and the debtor has no further obligation to the creditor. In other cases, the debtor may extinguish the debt before its maturity. For example, if market interest rates are falling, a debtor may choose to issue debt at the new lower rate and use the proceeds to retire older higher-interest-rate debt. A debt is extinguished if either of two conditions is met:

1. The debtor pays the creditor and is relieved of its obligation for the liability.
2. The debtor is legally released from being the primary obligor under the liability, either judicially or by the creditor.

   (ASC 405-20-40-1)

If a debtor experiences financial difficulties before the debt is repaid and for economic or legal reasons related to the debtor's financial difficulties, the creditor grants the debtor concessions that would not otherwise have been granted, the debtor must determine how to recognize the effects of the troubled debt restructuring. (ASC 470-60)

Some debt is issued with terms that allow it to be converted to an equity instrument (common or, less often, preferred stock) at a future date. These issuances can create complex accounting issues. In certain situations, a debtor will modify the conversion privileges after issuance of the debt in order to induce prompt conversion of the debt into equity, in which case the debtor must recognize an expense for this consideration. (ASC 470-20-40-16)

Debt can also be issued with stock warrants, which allow the holder to purchase a stated number of common shares at a certain price within a defined time period. If debt is issued with detachable warrants, the proceeds of issuance are allocated between the two financial instruments. (ASC 470-20-05)

DEFINITIONS OF TERMS

Source: ASC 470. Also see Appendix A, *Definitions of Terms*, for terms relevant to this chapter: Contract, Customer, Debt, Fair Value, Firm Commitment, Lease, Lease Modification, Long-Term Obligation, Operating Cycle, Probable, Public Entity, Reacquisition Price of Debt, Reasonably Possible, Revenue, Time of Restructuring, Troubled Debt Restructuring, Working Capital, and Unconditional Purchase Obligation.

Beneficial Conversion Feature. A nondetachable conversion feature that is in the money at the commitment date.

Callable Obligation. An obligation is callable at a given date if the creditor has the right at that date to demand, or to give notice of its intention to demand, repayment of the obligation owed to it by the debtor.

Carrying Amount. For a receivable, the face amount increased or decreased by applicable accrued interest and applicable unamortized premium, discount, finance charges, or issue costs and also an allowance for uncollectible amounts and other valuation accounts. For a payable, the face amount increased or decreased by applicable accrued interest and applicable unamortized premium, discount, finance charges, or issue costs.

Convertible Security. A security that is convertible into another security based on a conversion rate. For example, convertible preferred stock that is convertible into common stock on a two-for-one basis (two shares of common for each share of preferred).

Lockbox Arrangement. An arrangement with a lender whereby the borrower's customers are required to remit payments directly to the lender and amounts received are applied to reduce the debt outstanding. A lockbox arrangement refers to any situation in which the borrower does not have the ability to avoid using working capital to repay the amounts outstanding. That is, the contractual provisions of a loan arrangement require that, in the ordinary course of business and without another event occurring, the cash receipts of a debtor are used to repay the existing obligation.

Product Financing Arrangement. A product financing arrangement is a transaction in which an entity sells and agrees to repurchase inventory with the repurchase price equal to the original sale price plus carrying and financing costs, or other similar transactions.

Recorded Investment in the Receivable. The recorded investment in the receivable is the face amount increased or decreased by applicable accrued interest and unamortized premium, discount, finance charges, or acquisition costs and may also reflect a previous direct write-down of the investment.

Springing Lockbox Arrangement. Some borrowings outstanding under a revolving credit agreement include both a subjective acceleration clause and a requirement to maintain a springing lockbox arrangement, whereby remittances from the borrower's customers are forwarded to the debtor's general bank account and do not reduce the debt outstanding until and unless the lender exercises the subjective acceleration clause.

Subjective Acceleration Clause. A subjective acceleration clause is a provision in a debt agreement that states that the creditor may accelerate the scheduled maturities of the obligation under conditions that are not objectively determinable (for example, if the debtor fails to maintain satisfactory operations or if a material adverse change occurs).

Substantive Conversion Feature. A conversion feature that is at least reasonably possible of being exercisable in the future absent the issuer's exercise of a call option.

Time of Issuance. The date when agreement as to terms has been reached and announced, even though the agreement is subject to certain further actions, such as directors' or stockholders' approval.

Units-of-Revenue Method. A method of amortizing deferred revenue that arises under certain sales of future revenues. Under this method, amortization for a period is calculated by computing a ratio of the proceeds received from the investor to the total payments expected to be made to the investor over the term of the agreement, and then applying that ratio to the period's cash payment.

Violation of a Provision. The failure to meet a condition in a debt agreement or a breach of a provision in the agreement for which compliance is objectively determinable, whether or not a grace period is allowed or the creditor is required to give notice of its intention to demand repayment.

CONCEPTS, RULES, AND EXAMPLES

ASC 470-10, *Overall*

Debt with Covenants Most commercial debt agreements contain a range of financial covenants. These covenants legally bind the borrower to comply with their requirements as a condition of the lender extending credit. The failure by the borrower to comply with these conditions often provides the lender with the contractual right to accelerate the due date, commonly to declare the full amount of the debt due and payable on demand. Unless a properly worded waiver is obtained by the borrower in such a situation, its statement of financial position would have to reflect the debt, that which would otherwise be classified as long-term, as a current liability. This in turn might create or complicate issues for management with respect to the assessment of whether there is substantial doubt about the ability of the reporting entity to continue as a going concern.

Under these circumstances, management of the borrower/reporting entity considers whether both of the following conditions exist under the specific circumstances:

- A violation of one or more covenants that gives the lender the right to call the debt (declare it payable on demand) has occurred at the statement of financial position date, or would have occurred absent a modification of the loan, and
- It is probable that, at measurement dates occurring during the next 12 months, the borrower will be unable to cure the default (i.e., comply with the covenant). (ASC 470-10-45-1)

If both of these conditions are present, the borrower is required to classify the debt as a current liability; otherwise, it can continue to classify the debt as noncurrent.

Subjective Acceleration Clauses Long-term obligations that contain subjective acceleration clauses are classified as current liabilities if circumstances (such as recurring losses or liquidity problems) indicate that it is probable that the lender will exercise its rights under the clause and demand repayment within one year (or one operating cycle, if longer). If, on the other hand, the likelihood of the acceleration of the due date is remote, the obligation continues to be classified as long-term debt on the statement of financial position. Situations between the probable and remote thresholds (i.e., it is deemed reasonably possible that the lender would demand repayment) require disclosure of the existence of the provision of the agreement. (ASC 470-10-45-2)

Revolving Credit Agreements Borrowings outstanding under a revolving credit agreement sometimes include both a subjective acceleration clause (as discussed above) and a requirement to maintain a lockbox into which the borrower's customers send remittances that are then used to reduce the debt outstanding. These borrowings are short-term obligations and are classified as current liabilities unless the entity has the intent and ability to refinance the revolving credit agreement on a long-term basis (i.e., the conditions in ASC 470-10-45-14, as discussed below, are met). (ASC 470-10-45-5) However, if the lockbox is a springing lockbox, which is a lockbox agreement in which remittances from the borrower's customers are forwarded to its general bank account and do not reduce the debt outstanding unless the lender exercises the subjective acceleration clause, the obligations are still considered to be long term since the remittances do not automatically reduce the debt outstanding if the acceleration clause has not been exercised. ASC (470-10-45-6)

Increasing-Rate Debt Arrangements commonly referred to as "increasing-rate notes" are debt instruments that mature at a defined, near-term date, but which can be continually extended (renewed) by the borrower for a defined longer period of time with predefined increases in the interest rate as extensions are elected. (ASC 470-10-35-1)

The borrower entity estimates the effective outstanding term of the debt after considering its plans, ability, and intent to service the debt. Based upon this estimated term, the borrower's periodic interest rate is determined using the interest method. Thus, a constant yield is computed over the estimated term resulting in the accrual of additional interest during the earlier portions of the term. Debt interest costs are amortized over the estimated outstanding term of the debt using the interest method. Any excess accrued interest resulting from repaying the debt prior to the estimated maturity date is an adjustment of interest expense in the period of repayment. (ASC 470-10-35-2)

The classification of the debt as current or noncurrent is based on the expected source of repayment. Thus, this classification need not be consistent with the period used to determine the periodic interest cost. (ASC 470-10-45-7) For example, the time frame used for the estimated outstanding term of the debt could be a year or less, but because of a planned long-term refinancing agreement the noncurrent classification could be used.

Furthermore, the term-extending provisions of the debt instrument are evaluated to ascertain whether they constitute a derivative financial instrument under ASC 815. (ASC 470-10-35-2) If so, the derivative element of the instrument is, in all likelihood, not considered "clearly and closely related" to the host instrument (the debt), and thus would have to be reported separately at fair value with changes in fair value reported in net income each period.

Due on Demand Loans Obligations that, by their terms, are due on demand or will be due on demand within one year, or one operating cycle if longer, from the statement of financial position date, even if liquidation is not expected to occur within that period, are required to be classified as current liabilities. (ASC 470-10- 45-10)

Demand notes with scheduled repayment terms In some instances, a demand loan will include a repayment schedule calling for scheduled principal reductions. The loan agreement may contain language such as:

> "This term note shall mature in monthly installments as set forth herein, or on demand, whichever is earlier."

"Principal and interest are due on demand, or if demand is not made, in quarterly installments commencing on."

An obligation containing such terms is considered due on demand even though the debt agreement specifies repayment terms. (ASC 470-10-45-9) The creditor, at its sole discretion, can demand full repayment at any time. This situation is distinguished from a subjective acceleration clause, which is addressed separately below.

Callable Debt Even noncurrent debt may be due on demand under certain circumstances. Long-term obligations that contain creditor call provisions should be classified as current liabilities, if as of the statement of financial position date the debtor is in violation of the agreement and either:

- That violation makes the obligation callable, *or*
- Unless cured within a grace period specified in the agreement, that violation will make the obligation callable.

If either of the two conditions above exist, the long-term obligation is required to be classified as a current liability unless either:

- The creditor has waived the right to call the obligation caused by the debtor's violation or the creditor has subsequently lost the right to demand repayment for more than one year (or one operating cycle, if longer) from the statement of financial position date, *or*
- The obligation contains a grace period for remedying the violation, and it is probable that the violation will be cured within the grace period.
(ASC 470-10-45-11)

If either of these situations applies, management is required to disclose the circumstances in the financial statements.

While a complete waiver, effectively a promise by the lender that it will not exercise its rights under the financial covenants for at least one year from the statement of financial position date, makes it possible to continue presenting the debt as noncurrent, great care must be exercised in interpreting the substance of such an agreement. (ASC 470-10-45-11)

In practice, many waivers are not effective and cannot form the basis for continued accounting for the debt as noncurrent. For example, a waiver "as of" the current statement of financial position date provides no real comfort, since the lender is entitled to assert its rights as soon as the very next day. Likewise, a waiver pending (i.e., conditioned on) compliance with the covenants at the next scheduled submission of a borrower's covenant compliance letter (generally quarterly, possibly monthly) offers no assurance that the borrower will successfully meet its obligations, and hence also affords no basis for presentation of the debt as noncurrent.

A loan covenant may require that compliance determinations be made at quarterly or semiannual intervals. A borrower may be in violation of the covenant at the end of its fiscal year and obtain a waiver from the lender, for a period greater than one year, of the lender's right to demand repayment arising from that specific year-end violation. Often, however, the lender will include language in the waiver document that reserves its right to demand repayment should another violation occur at a subsequent measurement date, including those dates that occur during the ensuing year.

Short-Term Obligations Expected to Be Refinanced Short-term obligations that arise in the normal course of business and are due under customary trade terms are classified as current liabilities. Under certain circumstances, however, the reporting entity is permitted to exclude all or a portion of these obligations from current liabilities. To qualify for this treatment, management must have both the intent and ability to refinance the obligation on a long-term basis. Management's intent should be supported by *either* of the following:

- **Post-statement of financial position date issuance of a long-term obligation or equity securities.** After the date of the entity's statement of financial position, but before that statement of financial position is issued, a long-term obligation is incurred or equity securities are issued for the purpose of refinancing the short-term obligations on a long-term basis.
- **Financing agreement.** Before the statement of financial position is issued, the entity has entered into a financing agreement that clearly enables the entity to refinance its short-term obligation on a long-term basis on readily determinable terms that meet *all* of the following requirements:

a. The agreement is noncancelable by the lender (or prospective lender) or investor and will not expire within one year (or one operating cycle, if longer) of the statement of financial position date.
b. The replacement debt will not be callable during that period except for violation of a provision of the financing agreement with which compliance is objectively determinable or measurable.
c. At the date of the statement of financial position, the reporting entity is not in violation of the terms of the financing agreement and there is no information that a violation occurred subsequent to the statement of financial position and before issuance of the financial statements, unless such a violation was waived by the lender.
d. The lender (prospective lender) or investor is expected to be financially capable of honoring the financing agreement.
(ASC 470-10-45-14)

For the purposes of condition b in the list above, the Glossary section for ASC 470-10 defines violation of a provision as:

- A failure of the reporting entity to meet a condition included in the agreement, or
- The violation of a provision such as a restrictive covenant, representation, or warranty.

A violation should not be disregarded for this purpose, even if the agreement contains a grace period to cure it and/or if the lender is required to give the borrower notice. The requirement that compliance be objectively determinable or measurable precludes commitments that include subjective acceleration clauses (discussed below) from being considered qualified financing agreements. (ASC 470-10-45-14)

The above scenario is based on an assumption that the refinancing takes place subsequent to the date of the statement of financial position. However, prior to the date of the statement of financial position, the reporting entity may receive cash proceeds from long-term financing intended to be used to repay a short-term obligation after the date of the statement of financial position. In that case, the cash received is classified on the statement of financial position in noncurrent assets if the short-term obligation to be settled with that cash is classified in noncurrent liabilities.

The amount of short-term debt to be reclassified should not exceed:

- The amount raised by the replacement debt or equity issuance or
- The amount specified in the financing agreement.

If the amount specified in the financing agreement can fluctuate, then the maximum amount of short-term debt that can be reclassified is equal to a reasonable estimate of the minimum amount expected to be available on any date from the due date of the maturing short-term obligation to the end of the succeeding fiscal year. If no estimate can be made of the minimum amount available under the financing agreement, none of the short-term debt can be reclassified as long term. (ASC 470-10-45-19)

If the short-term debt is refinanced by issuing equity instruments, the portion excluded from current liabilities should be classified under noncurrent liabilities. Under no circumstances should the reclassified debt be shown in the equity section of the statement of financial position.

Other agreements may limit the ability of the reporting entity to fully utilize the proceeds of the refinancing agreement. This may happen, for example, if a clause in another debt agreement sets a maximum debt-to-equity ratio. In such a case, only the amount that can be borrowed without violating the limitations expressed in those other agreements can be reclassified as long term. (ASC 470-10-45-18)

If an entity uses current assets after the statement of financial position date to repay a current obligation, and then replaces those current assets by issuing either equity securities or long-term debt before the issuance of the statement of financial position, the currently maturing debt must continue to be classified as a current liability at the date of the statement of financial position. (ASC 470-10-45-15)

Example of Short-Term Obligations to Be Refinanced

Duboe Distribution Co. has obtained $3,500,000 of bridge financing in the form of a construction loan to assist it in completing construction of a new public warehouse. All construction is completed by the date of the statement of financial position, after which Duboe has the following three choices for refinancing the bridge loan:

- Enter into a 30-year fixed-rate mortgage for $3,400,000 at 7% interest, leaving Duboe with a $100,000 shortfall it would have to repay with available cash. Under this scenario, Duboe reports as current debt the $100,000, as well as $31,566, the portion of the mortgage principal due within one year, with the remainder of the mortgage itemized as long-term debt. The presentation follows:

Current liabilities:	
Current portion of construction loan payable	100,000
Current maturities of long-term debt	31,566
Noncurrent liabilities:	
Construction loan payable, to be refinanced on a long-term basis at 7% due in 2X40, net of current portion	3,368,434

- Pay off the bridge loan with Duboe's existing variable-rate line of credit (LOC), which expires in two years. The maximum allowable amount that can be borrowed under the LOC is 80% of Duboe's eligible accounts receivable, defined as those accounts receivable not more than 90 days old. Over the two-year remaining term of the LOC, the lowest level of qualifying accounts receivable is expected to be $2,700,000. Thus, only $2,160,000 (calculation: $2,700,000 × 80%) of the debt would be classified as long term, while $1,340,000 is classified as a short-term obligation. The presentation follows:

Current liabilities:	
Current portion of construction loan payable	1,340,000
Noncurrent liabilities:	
Construction loan payable, to be refinanced on a long-term basis under a variable rate line of credit due in 20XX	2,160,000

- Obtain a 10% loan from Duboe's majority stockholders, with a balloon payment due in five years. Under the terms of this arrangement, the owner is entitled to withdraw up to $1,500,000 of funding at any time, even though $3,500,000 is currently available to Duboe. Under this approach, $1,500,000 is callable, and therefore must be classified as a short-term obligation.
- The remainder is classified as long-term debt. The presentation follows:

Current liabilities:	
Current portion of construction loan payable	1,500,000
Noncurrent liabilities:	
Construction loan payable, to be refinanced on a long-term basis under a five-year, 10% balloon note payable to the majority stockholder, due in 20XX	2,000,000

See Appendix B (ASC 470-10-50-4) for note disclosures for the presentations illustrated under the general terms of the financing agreement, as well as the terms of the new obligation incurred, or expected to be incurred, as a result of the refinancing (www.wiley.com/go/ GAAP2021).

Indexed Debt Occasionally, debt instruments are issued with guaranteed and contingent payments. The contingent payments may be linked to a specific index, like the S&P 500 or the price for a specific commodity. If the right to receive the indexing feature is separable from the debt instrument, the proceeds are allocated between the debt instrument and investor's stated right to receive the contingent payment. (ASC 470-10-25-3 and 25-4)

ASC 470-20, *Debt with Conversion and Other Options*

Convertible Debt—Overall

Purpose Debt is frequently issued with the right or requirement to convert into common stock of the company at the holder's option. Convertible debt is typically used for two reasons:

1. When a specific amount of funds is needed, convertible debt often allows a lesser number of shares to be issued (assuming conversion) than if the funds were raised by directly issuing the shares. Thus, less dilution occurs.
2. The conversion feature allows debt to be issued at a lower interest rate and with fewer restrictive covenants than if the debt was issued without it.

Features Features of convertible debt typically include:

- A conversion price 15–20% greater than the fair value of the stock when the debt is issued;
- Conversion features (price and number of shares), which protect against dilution from stock dividends, splits, etc.; and

- A callable feature at the issuer's option, which is usually exercised once the conversion price is reached (thus forcing conversion or redemption).

Disadvantages Convertible debt has its disadvantages. If the stock price increases significantly after the debt is issued, the issuer would have been better off by simply issuing the stock. Additionally, if the price of the stock does not reach the conversion price, the debt will never be converted (a condition known as overhanging debt).

Commitment Date If an instrument includes both detachable instruments and an embedded beneficial conversion option, the commitment date should be used when determining the relative fair values of all the instruments issued.

This Section is divided into two Subsections: General and Cash Conversion. The items in the General discussion will be examined first.

General Subsection *Debt issued with detachable stock warrants* Warrants are certificates enabling the holder to purchase a stated number of shares of stock at a certain price within a certain time period. They are often issued with bonds to enhance the marketability of the bonds and to lower the bond's interest rate.

When bonds with detachable warrants are issued, the purchase price must be allocated between the debt and the stock warrants based on relative fair values. Amounts allocated to the warrants are recorded as paid-in-capital. The remainder is recorded as debt. Resulting discounts or reduced premiums are accounted for using the guidance in ASC 835. Since two separate instruments are involved, a fair value must be determined for each at time of issuance. However, if one value cannot be determined, the fair value of the other should be deducted from the total value to determine the unknown value. (ASC 470-20-25-2)

Example of Accounting for a Bond with a Detachable Warrant

1. A $1,000 bond with a detachable warrant to buy 10 shares of $10 par common stock at $50 per share is issued for $1,025.
2. Immediately after the issuance the bonds trade at $995 and the warrants at $35.
3. The fair value of the stock is $48.

The relative fair value of the bonds is 96.6% [995/(995 + 35)] and the warrant is 3.4% [35/ (995 + 35)]. Thus, $34.85(3.4% × $1,025) of the issuance price is assigned to the warrants. The journal entry to record the issuance is:

Cash	1,025.00	
Discount on bonds payable	9.85	
Bonds payable		1,000.00
Paid-in capital—warrants (or "Stock options outstanding")		34.85

The discount is the difference between the purchase price assigned to the bond, $990.15 (96.6% × $1,025), and its face value, $1,000. The debt itself is accounted for in the normal fashion.

The entry to record the subsequent future exercise of the warrant would be:

Cash	500.00	
Paid-in capital—warrants	34.85	
Common stock		100.00
Paid-in capital		434.85 (difference)

Assuming the warrants are not exercised, the journal entry is:

Paid-in capital—warrants	34.85	
Paid-in capital—expired warrants		34.85

Debt Issued with Both Conversion Features and Stock Warrants ASC 470-20 states that when a debt instrument includes both detachable instruments such as warrants, and an embedded beneficial conversion option, the proceeds of issuance should first be allocated among the convertible instrument and the other detachable instruments based on their relative fair values. Following this, the ASC 470-20 model should be applied to the amount allocated to the convertible instrument to determine if the embedded conversion option has an intrinsic value. (ASC 470-20-25-5)

Example of Convertible Debt Issued with Stock Warrants

Cellular Communicators issues $1,000,000 of convertible debt with 100,000 detachable warrants. The debt is convertible into $10 par common stock at a price of $50 per share. At the commitment date of this issuance, the common stock is trading at $46 per share. Immediately after the issuance, the bonds trade at 85 and the warrants trade at $2. The issuance proceeds of $1,000,000 are allocated to the two instruments as follows:

$$\$850,000 / (\$850,000 + \$200,000) \times \$1,000,000 = \$809,524 \text{ to the debt}$$

$$\$200,000 / (\$850,000 + \$200,000) \times \$1,000,000 = \$190,476 \text{ to the warrants}$$

The intrinsic value of the conversion feature is next computed as follows:

$$\$1,000,000 / \$50 \text{ per share} = 20,000 \text{ shares to be issued upon conversion}$$

$$\text{The effective conversion price is the bond's allocated proceeds of } \$809,524 \text{ divided by } 20,000 \text{ shares or } \$40.48$$

$$(\$46 \text{ current fair value of the stock} - \$40.48 \text{ effective conversion price}) \times 20,000 \text{ shares} = \$110,476, \text{ which is the implied discount granted on the bonds in connection with the conversion feature.}$$

Cellular Communicators would make the following entry to recognize the issuance of the bonds with warrants at 100:

Cash	1,000,000	
Discount on bonds payable	110,476	
Bonds payable		809,524
Additional paid-in capital		110,476
Paid-in capital—warrants		190,476

A wide range of features may be incorporated into stock purchase warrants and it will often be a challenge to identify the substance of these features, and to then prescribe the proper accounting for each feature. One such example involves warrants that are issued with put options, sometimes called "puttable warrants." Such warrants allow the holder to purchase a fixed number of the issuer's shares at a fixed price (common to all warrants), but also are puttable by the holder at a specified date for a fixed monetary amount that the holder could require the issuer to pay in cash. For example, assume the warrants are issued when the entity's shares are trading at $12, and each warrant permits the purchase of 100 shares at $15 through April 30, 20X3. If not previously exercised, the warrant holders can put each warrant back to the issuer for the equivalent of $14 per share, that is, for 100 × ($14 – $12) = $200 per warrant. The warrant holder is thus assured (given the underlying stock price at inception) of at least $2 per share income, and of course may reap a much larger reward if the share price has risen beyond $15 by the expiration date.

The disclosures for an entity having an outstanding own-share lending program can be found in Appendix B (www.wiley.com/go/GAAP2021).

Convertible Debt without Beneficial Conversion

Recognition When convertible debt is issued and the conversion price is greater than the fair value of the stock on the issuance date, there is no beneficial conversion. No value is apportioned to the conversion feature when recording such an issue. (ASC 470-20-25-12) The debt and its interest are reported as if it were a nonconvertible debt.

Conversion Upon conversion, the stock is valued at the carrying value of the debt. Including any amortized premium or discount. No gain or loss is recognized upon conversion. (ASC 470-20-40-4) The conversion represents the transformation of contingent shareholders into shareholders. It does not represent the culmination of an earnings cycle. The primary weakness of this method is that the total value attributed to the equity security by the investors is not given accounting recognition.

Example of Conversion of Convertible Debt without Beneficial Conversion

Assume that a $1,000 bond with an unamortized discount of $50 and a fair value of $970 is converted into 10 shares of $10 par common stock whose fair value is $97 per share. Conversion is recorded as follows:

Bonds payable	1,000	
Discount on bonds payable		50
Common stock		100
Additional paid-in capital		850

Derecognition When convertible debt is retired, the transaction is handled in the same manner as nonconvertible debt: the difference between the acquisition price and the carrying value of the bond is reported currently as a gain or loss. (ASC 470-20-40-3)

Convertible Securities with Beneficial Conversion Features Reporting entities sometimes issue convertible securities (debt or preferred stock) that are "in the money" at the issuance date (i.e., where it would be economically advantageous to the holders if the securities were converted immediately). That type of conversion feature is called an "embedded beneficial conversion feature." Variations of such securities may be converted at:

- A fixed price,
- A fixed discount to the fair value at date of conversion,
- A variable discount to the fair value at conversion, or
- The conversion price may be dependent upon future events.

In addition, the conversion feature can be exercisable at issuance, at a stated date in the future, or upon the happening of a future event (such as an IPO). ASC 470-20 addresses the assorted accounting issues arising for issuers of such securities (the reporting entity or debtor).

Embedded beneficial conversion features are valued separately at issuance. The feature is recognized as additional paid-in capital by allocating a portion of the proceeds equal to the intrinsic value of the feature. (ASC 470-20-25-5) The intrinsic value is computed at the commitment date as (1) the difference between the conversion price and the fair value of the common stock (or other securities) into which the security is convertible, multiplied by (2) the number of shares into which the security is convertible. (ASC 470-20-30-6)

Accounting Treatment of Beneficial Conversion Features The following are discussed below:

- Instruments having a stated redemption date
- Instruments with a multiple-step conversion feature
- All other instruments

Instruments having a stated redemption date If a convertible instrument has a stated redemption date, the entity accretes the discount from the date of issuance to the stated redemption date, without regard to when the earliest conversion date occurs. (ASC 470-20-35-7A)

Instruments with multiple-step conversion feature If the conversion feature has multiple step discounts and does not have a stated redemption date, the computation of the intrinsic value is made using the conversion terms most beneficial to the investor, the minimum period in which the investor can recognize that return. For example, if the security was convertible at a 10% discount to fair value after three months and then at a 25% discount to fair value after one year, the 25% discount terms would be used to measure the intrinsic value of the feature. Any resulting discount on the convertible debt would be amortized to the earliest date at which the particular discount (25% in this case) could be achieved (one year). However, at any financial statement date, the cumulative amortization recorded must be the greater of:

- The amount computed using the effective interest method of amortization or
- The amount of the benefit the investor would receive if the securities were converted at that date.

If the securities are converted prior to the full amortization of the discount, the unamortized discount is to be included in the amount transferred to equity upon conversion. (ASC 470-20-35-7b)

All other instruments For convertible instruments that do *not* have a stated redemption date and a multiple-step discount, such as perpetual preferred stock or a multiple-step discount, a discount resulting from the accounting for a beneficial conversion option should be amortized from the date of issuance to the earliest conversion date. (ASC 470-20-35-7c.)

Instruments Paid-in-Kind If interest or dividends are paid in kind, the commitment date for the paid-in-kind securities is the commitment date for the original instrument if the payment in kind is not discretionary. (ASC 470-20-30-16) The payment is not discretionary:

- If neither the issuer nor the holder can elect other forms of payment for the interest or dividends, and
- If the original instrument is converted before dividends are declared or interest is accrued, the holder will always receive the number of shares as if all dividends or interest have been paid in kind.
  (ASC 470-20-30-17)

If the payment in kind is discretionary, the commitment date for the paid-in-kind securities is the date that the interest is accrued or the dividends are declared.

Instruments Issued as a Repayment for Nonconvertible Instrument If an issuer issues a convertible instrument as repayment of a nonconvertible instrument, the fair value of the newly issued convertible instrument equals the redemption amount owed at the maturity date of the old debt. This accounting is contingent upon the original debt having reached maturity and the exchange not being a TDR. (ASC 470-20-30-19)

If a convertible instrument is extinguished prior to its maturity date, apply the guidance in ASC 470-50. (ASC 470-20-30-21)

Derecognition If a convertible debt security having a beneficial feature is extinguished prior to conversion, a portion of the reacquisition price of the debt security is allocated to the beneficial conversion feature. That portion is measured as the intrinsic value of the conversion feature at the extinguishment date. Since the beneficial conversion feature was originally recognized as equity, the redemption or cancellation of this feature would give rise not to gain or loss, but rather to an adjustment within stockholders' equity. (ASC 470-20-40-3) For example, if $2,000 of the redemption payment was identified with the beneficial feature to which $1,200 had originally been allocated, the net result would be that the original allocation would be eliminated and an $800 charge would be made against retained earnings (analogous to a loss on a treasury stock transaction). Any residual beyond the allocated cost of redeeming the beneficial conversion feature would be allocated to the retirement of the debt security, and a gain or loss on extinguishment would be reported in current earnings.

Contingent Conversion If the conversion price could change upon the occurrence of a future event, entities should assume that there are no changes to the current circumstances except the passage of time. The most favorable price that would be in effect if nothing were changed at the conversion date is used to measure the intrinsic value of an embedded conversion option. Changes to the conversion terms that are caused by future events not controlled by the issuer are recognized if and when the trigger event occurs. (ASC 470-20-25-20) The value of the contingent beneficial conversion feature should be measured as of the commitment date; but it is not recognized in the financial statements until the contingency is resolved. (ASC 470-20-35-1) This may be combined with a beneficial conversion feature. For example, a debt instrument issued with a conversion feature at 20% below then-fair value, to become effective conditioned on the consummation of a planned refinancing, would be contingently convertible with a beneficial feature. Any contingent beneficial conversion feature should be measured at the commitment date, but not reflected in earnings until the contingent condition has been met. (ASC 470-20-35-3)

If there is no intrinsic value to a conversion right at issuance, but the conversion price resets after the commitment date and, upon reset, the conversion price is greater than the fair value of the underlying stock, the beneficial conversion amount is recognized when the reset occurs. The beneficial conversion amount is measured by the number of shares that will be issued upon conversion, multiplied by the decrease in price between the original conversion price and the reset price. (ASC 470-20-35-4)

The definition of "conventional contingently convertible debt instrument" is later addressed by ASC 815-40-25. The issue arises because of one of the requirements under ASC 815—namely, that embedded derivatives be bifurcated and accounted for separately under certain conditions, but with an exception for accounting for conversion privileges by issuers of certain convertible securities. Thus, instruments that provide holders the right to convert at a fixed ratio (or equivalent cash value, at the issuer's discretion), for which option exercise is based on either the passage of time or a contingent event, are deemed "conventional."

ASC 815-15 also states that, when a previously bifurcated conversion option in a convertible debt instrument no longer meets the bifurcation criteria in ASC 815, one should reclassify the fair value of the liability for the conversion option to shareholders' equity. If a debt discount was recognized when the conversion option was bifurcated, then it should continue to be amortized.

Example 1: Intrinsic Value of a Conversion Feature—Fixed Dollar Terms

Software Solutions issues $1,000,000 of convertible debt, which is convertible into $10 par common stock at a price of $50 per share. The fair value of the common stock on the commitment date of the issue is $60. The intrinsic value of the conversion feature is computed as follows:

$$\$1,000,000 / \$50 \text{ per share} = 20,000 \text{ shares to be issued upon conversion}$$

$$(\$60 \text{ fair value} - \$50 \text{ conversion price}) 20,000 \text{ shares} = \$200,000 \text{ intrinsic value}$$

Software Solutions would make the following entry to recognize the issuance of the bonds at 100:

Cash	1,000,000	
Discount on bonds payable	200,000	
Bonds payable		1,000,000
Additional paid-in capital		200,000

If the price at which the bond is convertible to stock changes over the life of the bond, the intrinsic value should be computed using the terms that are most beneficial to the holder. The most favorable conversion price that would be in effect, assuming that there are no changes to the current circumstances except for the passing of time, should be used to measure the intrinsic value.

Example 2: Intrinsic Value of a Conversion Feature—Variable Terms

American National Biotech issues $1,000,000 of convertible debt, convertible into $10 par common stock at a price 15% below the commitment date fair value for years 1 and 2, 20% below the commitment date fair value for years 3 to 5, and 25% below the commitment date fair value for years 6 to maturity. The fair value of the common stock on the commitment date of the issue is $50. The intrinsic value of the conversion feature is computed as follows:

The most beneficial price is the 25% discount available in year 6 to maturity

That price would be $37.50 ($50 × .75)

$1,000,000 / $37.50 per share = 26,667 shares to be issued upon conversion

($50 fair value – $37.50 conversion price) × 26,667 shares = $333,337 intrinsic value

American National Biotech would make the following entry to recognize the issuance of the bonds at 100:

Cash	1,000,000	
Discount on bonds payable	333,337	
Bonds payable		1,000,000
Additional paid-in capital		333,337

In some cases, the conversion price will be dependent on a future event, or the bond becomes convertible only upon the occurrence of a future event. In those cases, the contingent beneficial conversion feature should be measured at the commitment date but not recognized in earnings until the contingency is resolved.

Example 3: Intrinsic Value of a Conversion Feature—Contingent Price Terms

Major Manufacturing Co. issues $1,000,000 of convertible debt, which is convertible into $10 par common stock at a discount of 20% off of the conversion date fair value. The fair value of the common stock on the commitment date of the issue is $50. The intrinsic value of the conversion feature is computed as follows:

Because the conversion percentage is fixed, the intrinsic value is always $250,000.

Market price at conversion	$ 40	$50	$60	$70
Conversion price	$32	$40	$48	$56
Number of shares issued	31,250	25,000	20,833	17,857
Discount	$8	$10	$12	$14
Intrinsic value	$250,000	$250,000	$250,000	$250,000

Major Manufacturing Co. would make the following entry to recognize the issuance of bonds at

Cash	1,000,000	
Discount on bonds payable	250,000	
Bonds payable		1,000,000
Additional paid-in capital		250,000

Example 4: Intrinsic Value of a Conversion Feature—Contingent Conversion

Shoemaker Co. issues $1,000,000 of convertible debt, which is convertible into $10 par common stock at a discount of 25% below the commitment date fair value. The fair value of the common stock on the commitment date of the issue is $60, so the conversion price is $45. The debt is convertible only upon an initial public offering. The intrinsic value of the conversion feature is computed as follows:

$$\$1,000,000 / \$45 \text{ per share} = 22,222 \text{ shares to be issued upon conversion}$$

$$(\$60 \text{ fair value} - \$45 \text{ conversion price}) \times 22,222 \text{ shares} = \$333,330 \text{ intrinsic value}$$

Shoemaker Co. would not allocate any portion of the proceeds to the conversion feature at issuance. It would make the following entry to recognize the issuance of the bonds at 100:

Cash	1,000,000	
Bonds payable		1,000,000

Upon the occurrence of an initial public offering, Shoemaker would make the following entry:

Discount on bonds payable	333,330	
Additional paid-in capital		333,330

Example 5: Intrinsic Value of a Conversion Feature—Contingent Conversion with Variable Terms

Food Franchisers issues $1,000,000 of convertible debt, which is convertible into $10 par common stock at a price of $50. The fair value of the common stock on the commitment date of the issue is $60. The debt is convertible only upon an initial public offering. If the stock's fair value is at least 20% higher than the IPO price one year after the IPO, the conversion price will be 70% of the then fair value. The intrinsic value of the contingent conversion feature at issuance is computed as follows:

$$\$1,000,000 / \$50 \text{ per share} = 20,000 \text{ shares to be issued upon conversion}$$

$$(\$60 \text{ fair value} - \$50 \text{ conversion price}) \times 20,000 \text{ shares} = \$200,000 \text{ intrinsic value}$$

The intrinsic value of the contingent conversion price change is also computed at the commitment date using the assumptions that the IPO price will be the same as the current market price and that the stock price one year after the IPO is 20% higher, as follows:

$$\text{Contingent conversion price} = \$60 \times 120\% \times 70\% = \$50.40$$

$$\$1{,}000{,}000 / \$50.40 \text{ per share} = 19{,}841 \text{ shares to be issued upon conversion}$$

$$(\$72 \text{ fair value} - \$50.40 \text{ conversion price}) \times 19{,}841 \text{ shares} = \$428{,}565 \text{ intrinsic value}$$

Food Franchisers would not allocate any portion of the proceeds to the conversion feature at issuance. It would make the following entry to recognize the issuance of the bonds at 100:

Cash	1,000,000	
Bonds payable		1,000,000

Upon the occurrence of an initial public offering at $55, Food Franchisers would make the following entry:

Discount on bonds payable	250,000	
Additional paid-in capital		250,000

If the stock price increased to $66 ($55 × 120%), Food Franchisers would make the following entry for the difference between the two intrinsic values:

Discount on bonds payable	178,565
Additional paid-in capital	178,565

If a bond with an embedded beneficial conversion feature is extinguished prior to conversion, a portion of the reacquisition price is allocated to the repurchase of the conversion feature. That portion is the intrinsic value of the conversion feature at the extinguishment date, which would be recorded as a decrease in additional paid-in capital. That accounting may result in a reduction in additional paid-in capital that is larger than the amount originally recorded in paid-in capital at issuance. However, no portion of the reacquisition price should be allocated to the conversion feature if that feature had no intrinsic value at the issuance date.

Example of Extinguishment of Debt with an Embedded Conversion Feature

Software Solutions (Example 1, above) repurchases $500,000 face of its debt at 140. At the date of issuance, the following entry had been made relating to the debt that is later extinguished.

Cash	500,000	
Discount on bonds payable	100,000	
Bonds payable		500,000
Additional paid-in capital		100,000

At the date of the repurchase, the fair value of the stock is $85, and the unamortized discount on the debt was $20,000. The intrinsic value of the conversion feature at the date of the repurchase is computed as follows:

$$\$500,000 / \$50 \text{ per share} = 10,000 \text{ shares to be issued upon conversion}$$

$$(\$85 \text{ fair value} - \$50 \text{ conversion price}) \times 10,000 \text{ shares} = \$350,000 \text{ intrinsic value}$$

Software Solutions would make the following entry to recognize the retirement of the bonds:

Bonds payable	500,000	
Additional paid-in capital	350,000	
Discount on bonds payable		20,000
Gain on extinguishment of debt		130,000
Cash		700,000

Questions have arisen regarding the accounting for the settlement of this instrument partially in cash (the recognized liability) and partially in stock (the unrecognized equity instrument). ASC 470-20-40-12 states that only the cash payment should be considered in computing gain or loss on settlement of the recognized liability. Shares transferred to the holder to settle the excess conversion spread represented by the embedded equity instrument are not considered part of the settlement of the debt component of the instrument.

Contingent Conversion Rights Triggered by Issuer Call In some instances a debt instrument may include a contingent conversion privilege that becomes exercisable if the issuer attempts to call the debt before maturity, even if the stated contingency (e.g., the underlying stock price hitting some predefined threshold value) has not occurred, at which time the holders may elect to surrender the debt for cash (perhaps with a call premium, if the indenture contains such a provision) or to convert at a defined ratio for stock. If the debt remains outstanding until scheduled redemption, there will be no opportunity to convert. (Another variant exists where the debt has a contingent conversion feature at inception, e.g., where the debt becomes convertible if some other event, such as a refinancing, occurs, as well as if the issuer attempts to call the debt.)

ASC 470-20-40-5 states that no gain or loss should result from the creation of a conversion opportunity caused by the issuer's exercise of its call option, if the debt as originally issued contained a substantive conversion feature. In such circumstances, conversion of the debt to equity—assuming the existence of substantive rights in the original debt issuance—would be accounted for as a book value swap. On the other hand, if the conversion feature had not been substantive, the conversion triggered by the exercise by the issuer of its call option would be accounted for as a debt extinguishment, with the fair value of the equity being issued used to define the cost of the extinguishment. This would create a gain or loss to be recognized in virtually all situations.

ASC 470-20-40-7 defines a *substantive* conversion feature as a conversion feature that was, when the debt instrument was first issued, at least *reasonably possible* of being exercisable in the future, absent the issuer's exercise of a call option—where *reasonably possible* has the same meaning as under ASC 450. In practical terms, evaluation of whether the original conversion feature had been substantive, in the context of the facts and circumstances at the date of issuance, might include consideration of the interest yield of the contingently convertible debt compared to equivalent rates then required for debt lacking that feature, the likelihood of the occurrence of the defined contingent event, and the relative value of the conversion feature versus the related debt instrument.

Discount Accretion and Amortization For convertible debt securities, a discount on the debt may result from the allocation of a portion of the proceeds to the conversion feature. For convertible instruments that have a stated redemption date, a discount resulting from recording a beneficial conversion option shall be required to be amortized from the date of issuance to the stated redemption date of the convertible instrument, regardless of when the earliest conversion date occurs. (ASC 470-20-35-7a)

Interest Forfeiture If terms of the convertible debt instrument provide that any accrued but unpaid interest at the date of conversion is forfeited by the former debt holder, the accrued interest (net of income tax) from the last payment date to the conversion date should be charged to interest expense and credited to capital as a part of the cost basis of the securities issued. (ASC 470-20-40-11)

Induced Conversion of Debt A special situation exists in which the conversion privileges of convertible debt are modified after issuance. These modifications may take the form of reduced conversion prices or additional consideration paid to the convertible debt holder. The debtor offers these modifications or "sweeteners" to induce prompt conversion of the outstanding debt.

ASC 470-20-40 specifies the accounting method used in these situations and only applies when the convertible debt is converted into equity securities. Upon conversion, the debtor must recognize an expense for the excess of the fair value of all the securities and other consideration given over the fair value of the securities specified in the original conversion terms.

Determining applicability of ASC 470-20 ASC 470-20 specifies the accounting for "sweeteners" used to induce the conversion of convertible debt. Traditionally, this involves enhancements offered by the debtor to encourage conversions, often motivated by the desire to bring an end to interest payments on the convertible debt. ASC 470-20-40-13 addresses the related circumstance of conversions when the enhanced terms are proposed or requested by the creditors/debtholders. In some instances, only the requesting parties are granted the sweetened terms. Thus, ASC 470-20 applies to all conversions of convertible debts that:

1. Occur pursuant to changed conversion privileges that are exercisable only for a limited period of time, and
2. Include the issuance of all of the equity securities issuable pursuant to conversion privileges included in the terms of the debt at issuance for each debt instrument that is converted, regardless of the party that initiates the offer or whether the offer relates to all debtholders.

(ASC 470-20-40-13)

Example of Induced Conversion Expense

1. January 1, 20X1, XYZ Company issued ten 8% convertible bonds at $1,000 par value without a discount or premium, maturing December 31, 20Y1.
2. The bonds are initially convertible into no par common stock of XYZ at a conversion price of $25.
3. On July 1, 20X5, the convertible bonds have a fair value of $600 each.

4. To induce the convertible bondholders to quickly convert their bonds, XYZ reduces the conversion price to $20 for bondholders who convert before July 21, 20X5 (within twenty days).
5. The fair value of XYZ Company's common stock on the date of conversion is $15 per share.

The fair value of the incremental consideration paid by XYZ upon conversion is calculated for each bond converted before July 21, 20X5.

Value of securities issued to debtholders:		
Face amount	$1,000	per bond
÷ New conversion price	÷$ 20	per share
Number of common shares issued upon conversion	50	shares
× Price per common share	×$ 15	per share
Value of securities issued	$ 750	(a)
Face amount	$1,000	per bond
÷ Original conversion price	÷$ 25	per share
Number of common shares issuable pursuant to original conversion privilege	40	shares
× Price per share	×$ 15	per share
Value of securities issuable pursuant to the original conversion privileges	$ 600	(b)
Value of securities issued	$ 750	(a)
Value of securities issuable pursuant to original conversion privileges	600	(b)
Fair value of incremental consideration	$ 150	
The entry to record the debt conversion for each bond is:		
Convertible debt	1,000	
Debt conversion expense	150	
Common stock—no par		1,150

Convertible Instrument as Part of a Share-Based Payment Transaction to a Nonemployee for Goods or Services A convertible instrument may be granted as part of a share-based payment transaction to a nonemployee for goods or services, and that instrument may contain a nondetachable conversion option. To determine the fair value, the entity should first apply ASC 718 on stock compensation. (ASC 470-20-30-22) The measurement date under ASC 470-20 should then be used to measure the intrinsic value of the conversion option rather than the commitment date. The proceeds from issuing the instrument for purposes of determining whether a beneficial conversion option exists is the fair value of the instrument or the fair value of the goods and services received, whichever is more reliably measured. The fair value of the convertible instrument can be measured by applying ASC 718. (For details, see the chapter on ASC 505.) Once the convertible instrument is issued, distributions paid or payable are financing costs rather than adjustments of the cost of the goods or services received. (ASC 470-20-25-18 and ASC 470-20-30-22 through 30-26)

If a purchaser of a convertible instrument that contains an embedded beneficial conversion option provides goods or services to the issuer under a separate contract, the contracts should be considered separately unless the separately stated pricing is not equal to fair value. If not equal to fair value, the terms of the respective transactions should be adjusted. The convertible instrument should be recognized at its fair value with a corresponding increase or decrease to the purchase price of the goods or services.

Own-Share Lending Arrangements Related to a Convertible Debt Issuance An entity may enter into a share-lending arrangement with an investment bank, whereby it lends shares to the bank to facilitate investors' ability to hedge the conversion option in the entity's convertible debt issuance. The entity issues the share in exchange for a nominal loan processing fee; the investment bank returns the shares upon the maturity or conversion of the convertible debt.

In a share-lending arrangement, the entity issuing shares measures them at their fair value and recognizes them as a debt issuance cost, which offsets the additional paid-in capital account. (ASC 470-20-25-20A) If it subsequently becomes probable that the counterparty will default, then the entity recognizes an expense equaling the fair value of any unreturned shares on that date, minus the fair value of probable share recoveries, which offsets the additional paid-in capital account. The entity continues to remeasure the fair value of unreturned shares until the consideration payable by the counterparty becomes fixed. (ASC 470-20-25-20A)

Cash Conversion Subsections

Convertible bonds with issuer option to settle for cash upon conversion The guidance in ASC 470-50 related to cash conversions of convertible debt should only be considered after considering the guidance in ASC 815-15 on bifurcation of embedded derivatives. (Also see the "Scope" section at the beginning of this chapter.)

Fair value option The fair value option is not available for convertible debt instruments within the scope of the cash conversion section (ASC 470-20-25-21)

Initial measurement—liability and equity For instruments addressed by ASC 470, initial measurement of the carrying amount of the liability component is determined by measuring the fair value of a similar liability (including any embedded features other than the conversion option) that does not have an associated equity component. (ASC 470-20-30-27) The carrying amount of the equity component represented by the embedded conversion option is then computed by deducting the fair value of the liability component from the initial proceeds ascribed to the convertible debt instrument as a whole. (ASC 470-20-30-28) Embedded features that are determined to be nonsubstantive at the issuance date should not affect the initial measurement of the liability component. (ASC 470-20-30-29)

Determining whether an embedded feature is nonsubstantive In this context, an embedded feature other than the conversion option (including an embedded prepayment option) is considered nonsubstantive if, at issuance, the issuer concludes that it is probable that the embedded feature will not be exercised. (ASC 470-20-30-30) If the allocation to the liability component using this methodology results in a difference in basis versus that reported for tax purposes, then deferred tax accounting must also be applied.

Subsequent measurement The debt must be reported in subsequent periods at amortized cost. (ASC 470-20-35-12) The variance between the convertible debt's face value and the amount of proceeds that are allocated to the debt instrument, net of the amount allocated to the conversion feature, must be treated as a discount to be accreted using the effective yield method as additional interest expense. The accretion period is based on the expected term of a similar instrument lacking the conversion feature. (ASC 470-20-35-13) The expected life is not subject to reassessment in later periods, unless there is a modification to the terms of the instrument. (ASC 470-20-35-16) The equity component is not reassessed either, unless it ceases to meet the criteria in ASC 815-40. In that case the difference between the amount previously recognized in equity and the fair value of the conversion option at the date of the reclassification as a liability at fair value is accounted for as an adjustment to stockholders' equity. (ASC 470-20-35-17 through 35-19)

Derecognition Upon derecognition, an entity should account for convertible obligations that can be settled in whole or in part for cash, as follows:

- The proceeds transferred to affect the extinguishment of the liability and the reacquisition of the associated conversion feature should be allocated first to the extinguishment of the liability component equal to the fair value of that component immediately prior to extinguishment.
- Recognize in the statement of financial performance as a gain or loss on debt extinguishment any difference between the consideration attributed to the liability component and the sum of: (1) the net carrying amount of the liability component, and (2) any unamortized debt issuance costs.
- Assign any remaining settlement consideration to the reacquisition of the equity component, with recognition of that amount as a reduction of stockholders' equity.
- Any costs incurred (e.g., banker fees) should be allocated pro rata to the debt and equity in proportion to the allocation of consideration transferred at settlement, and accounted for as debt extinguishment costs and equity reacquisition costs, respectively.
  (ASC 470-20-40-19 and 40-20)

Modification If an instrument within the scope of the guidance above is modified such that the conversion option no longer requires or permits cash settlement upon conversion, it is necessary to account for the components of the instrument separately, unless the original instrument is required to be derecognized under ASC 470-50. If an instrument is modified or exchanged in a manner that requires derecognition of the original instrument under ASC 470-50 and the new instrument is a convertible debt instrument that may not be settled in cash upon conversion, the new instrument would be subject to ASC 470-50. (ASC 470-20-40-24)

On the other hand, if a convertible debt instrument is not at first subject to this guidance, but is later modified so as to become subject to it, then ASC 470-50 should be applied to ascertain whether the original instrument should be derecognized. If not, the issuer should apply the guidance prospectively from the date of the modification. In such a circumstance, the liability component should be measured at its fair value as of the modification date, with the carrying amount of the equity component represented by the embedded conversion option to be determined by deducting the fair value of the liability component from the overall carrying amount of the convertible debt instrument as a whole. At the modification date, a portion of any unamortized debt issuance costs incurred previously should be reclassified and accounted for as equity issuance costs based on the proportion of the overall carrying amount of the convertible debt instrument that is allocated to the equity component. (ASC 470-20-40-25)

Induced conversion If the terms of an instrument are revised to induce early conversion (e.g., by offering a more favorable conversion ratio or paying other additional consideration in the event of conversion before a specified date), then the entity recognizes a loss equal to the fair value of all securities and other consideration transferred in the transaction in excess of the fair value of consideration issuable in accordance with the *original* conversion terms. The derecognition treatment described above is then to be applied using the fair value of the consideration that was issuable in accordance with the original conversion terms. However, derecognition transactions in which the holder does not exercise the embedded conversion option are not affected. (ASC 470-20-40-26)

ASC 470-30, *Participating Mortgage Loans*

Accounting by Participating Mortgage Loan Borrowers Certain mortgage loan agreements provide, generally in exchange for a lower interest rate, that the lender shares in price appreciation of the property securing the loan. Other arrangements provide that the lender receives a share of the earnings or cash flows from the commercial real estate for which the loan was made. ASC 470-30 establishes the borrower's accounting for a participating mortgage loan if the lender participates in increases in the fair value of the mortgaged real estate project, the results of operations of that mortgaged real estate project, or both. It requires that certain disclosures be made in the financial statements. In addition, the Codification requires the following:

- At origination, if the lender is entitled to participate in appreciation in the market value of the mortgaged real estate project, the borrower should determine the fair value of the participation feature and should recognize a participation liability for that amount. A corresponding debit should then be recorded to a debt-discount account. (ASC 470-30-30-1) The debt discount should be amortized by the interest method, using the effective interest rate. (ASC 470-30-35-5) The net result should include the expected cost of the participating feature in the periodic interest cost associated with the loan.
- At the end of each reporting period, the balance of the participation liability should be adjusted if necessary, so that the liability equals the current fair value of the participation feature at that point in time. The corresponding debit or credit should be adjusted to the related debt-discount account. The revised discount should then be amortized prospectively. (ASC 470-30-35-34 and 35-34A)

ASC 470-40, *Product Financing Arrangements*

A product financing arrangement is a transaction in which an entity (referred to as the "sponsor") simultaneously sells and agrees to repurchase inventory to and from a financing entity. The repurchase price is contractually fixed at an amount equal to the original sales price plus the financing entity's carrying and financing costs. The purpose of the transaction is to enable the sponsor enterprise to arrange financing of its original purchase of the inventory. The various steps involved in the transaction are illustrated by the diagram.

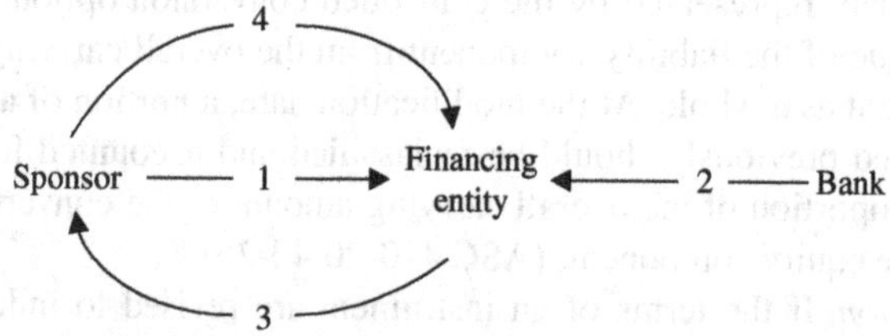

- In the initial transaction, the sponsor "sells" inventoriable items to the financing entity in return for the remittance of the sales price and at the same time agrees to repurchase the inventory at a specified price (usually the sales price plus carrying and financing costs) over a specified period of time.

- The financing entity borrows from a bank (or other financial institution) using the newly purchased inventory as collateral.
- The financing entity remits the proceeds of its borrowing to the sponsor and the sponsor presumably uses these funds to pay off the debt (accounts payable) incurred for the original purchase.
- The sponsor then, over a period of time as funds become available, repurchases the inventory from the financing entity for the specified price plus carrying and financing costs.

The substance of this transaction is that of a borrowing transaction, not a sale. That is, the transaction is, in substance, no different from the sponsor directly obtaining third-party financing to purchase inventory. ASC 470-40 specifies that the proper accounting by the sponsor is to record a liability in the amount of the selling price when the funds are received from the financing entity in exchange for the initial transfer of the inventory. The sponsor proceeds to accrue carrying and financing costs in accordance with its normal accounting policies. These accruals are eliminated and the liability satisfied when the sponsor repurchases the inventory. The inventory is not removed from the statement of financial position of the sponsor and a sale is not recorded. Thus, although legal title has passed to the financing entity, for purposes of measuring and valuing inventory, the inventory is considered to be owned by the sponsor. (Per ASC 606-10-55-403: Control of the entity has not passed to the buyer.)

Example of a Product Financing Arrangement

The Medieval Illumination Company (MIC) has borrowed the maximum amount it has available under its short-term line of credit. MIC obtains additional financing by selling $280,000 of its candle inventory to a third-party financing entity. The third party obtains a bank loan at 6% interest to pay for its purchase of the candle inventory, while charging MIC 8% interest and $1,500 per month to store the candle inventory at a public storage facility. As MIC obtains candle orders, it purchases inventory back from the third party, which in turn authorizes the public warehouse to drop ship the orders directly to MIC's customers at a cost of $35 per order. Since this is a product financing arrangement, MIC cannot remove the candle inventory from its accounting records or record revenue from sale of its inventory to the third party. Instead, the following entry records the initial financing arrangement:

Cash	280,000	
Short-term debt		280,000

After one month, MIC records accrued interest of $1,867 ($280,000 × 8% interest × 1/12 year) on the loan, as well as the monthly storage fee of $1,500, as shown in the following entry:

Interest expense	1,867	
Storage expense	1,500	
Accrued interest		1,867
Accounts payable		1,500

On the first day of the succeeding month, MIC receives a prepaid customer order for $3,800. The margin on the order is 40% and, therefore, the related inventory cost is $2,280. MIC pays the third party $2,280 to buy back the required inventory as well as $35 to the public storage facility to ship the order to the customer, and records the following entries:

Short-term debt	2,280	
Cash		2,280

To repurchase inventory from the third-party financing entity

Cash	3,800	
Sales		3,800

To record the sale to the customer

Cost of goods sold	2,280	
Inventory		2,280

To record the cost of the sale to the customer

Freight out	35	
Accounts payable		35

To record the cost of fulfilling the order

ASC 470-40 identifies variations of the terms of the above arrangement that also meet the criteria for being accounted for as product financing arrangements:

1. The third-party financing entity purchases the inventory directly from the sponsor's supplier (instead of from the sponsor) with a simultaneous agreement to sell the inventory to the sponsor.
2. The sponsor enters into an agreement with a third-party financing entity to control the disposition of product that has been purchased by the third party either from the sponsor or from the sponsor's supplier.

ASC 470-50 and ASC 470-60—Overview: Modifications, Extinguishments, and Troubled Debt Restructurings

The next two sections on ASC 470-50 and ASC 470-60 examine the accounting for debt modifications and exchanges. These transactions generally require analysis to determine the substance of the transactions. However, two scenarios are fairly straightforward:

1. If an entity repays a debt using funds received from a contemporaneous issuance of new debt to a different lender, it is accounted for as debt extinguishment of the original debt.
2. The sale of a debt instrument by one lender to another without involvement of the debtor is not a modification and does not require any changes in accounting on the part of the debtor. (ASC 470-50-40-7)

The following exhibit gives an overview of the analysis process. The discussions that follow detail the requirements depicted.

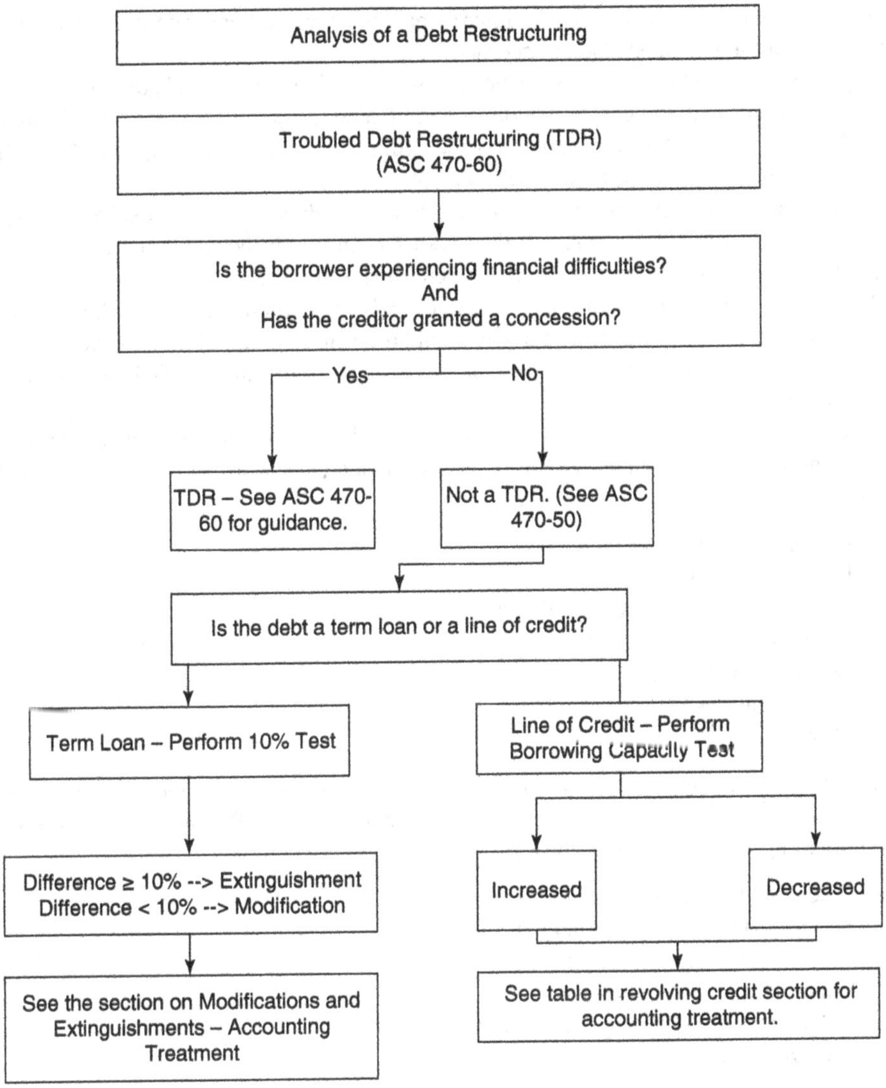

ASC 470-50, Modifications and Extinguishments

The general guidance for the extinguishment of liabilities can be found in ASC 405-20. (ASC 470-50-40-1) See the chapter on ASC 405 for more information.

Gain or Loss on Debt Extinguishment The difference between the net carrying value and the price paid to acquire the debt instruments should be recorded as a gain or loss in current income. If the acquisition price is greater than the carrying value, a loss exists. A gain is generated if the acquisition price is less than the carrying value. These gains or losses are recognized in the period in which the extinguishment takes place. (ASC 470-50-40-2)

The unamortized premium or discount and issue costs should be amortized to the acquisition date and recorded prior to the determination of the gain or loss. If the extinguishment of debt does not occur on the interest date, the interest payable accruing between the last interest date and the acquisition date must also be recorded.

If the fair value option has been elected, the net carrying value equals the fair value. When the debt is extinguished, the entity includes in net income the cumulative amount of gain or loss included in other comprehensive income for the extinguishment debt that resulted from changes in the instrument-specific credit risk. (ASC 470-50-40-2A)

Modifications and Exchanges If a modification of a debt issue or an exchange of cash for another debt issuance is not a troubled debt restructuring with the same creditor, the debtor's accounting is based on whether an analysis determines that the modifications are substantial. (ASC 470-50-40-6) Based on the results of the analysis, extinguishment of the original debt could be found to have occurred and carry financial reporting ramifications. An exchange of debt instruments with substantially different terms is a debt extinguishment and should be accounted for in accordance with ASC 405-20.

Cash flows can be affected by changes in principal amounts, interest rates, maturity, or by fees exchanged between the parties. Substantial change can also result from changes in the following provisions:

- Recourse or nonrecourse features
- Priority of the obligation
- Collateralized or noncollateralized features
- Debt covenants and/or waivers
- The guarantor
- Option features
  (ASC 470-50-40-3)

The 10% Test An exchange or modification is considered substantial when the present value of cash flows under the new debt instrument is at least 10% different from the present value of the remaining cash flows under the terms of the original instrument.

1. Calculate the change in cash flows:
   Present value of the original debt cash flows
   <u>Less: Present value of new debt cash flows</u>
   Equals: Change in cash flows
2. Calculate the percentage change in cash flows:
   <u>Change in cash flows</u>
   Present value of the original debt cash flows
3. Evaluate the difference:

   Difference ≥ 10% Extinguishment
   Difference < 10% Modification

In making the calculation for the 10% test, the entity should consider:

- *Cash flows*. The cash flows of the new debt instrument include:
  - All cash flows specified by the terms of the new debt instrument:
    - Plus, amounts paid by the debtor to the creditor,
    - Less amounts received by the debtor from the creditor as part of the exchange or modification.
- *Floating interest rate*. For the purpose of the 10% test, the effective interest rate of the original debt instrument is used as the discount rate. If the original debt instrument or

the new debt instrument has a floating interest rate, the entity should use the variable rate in effect at the date of the exchange or modification to calculate the cash flows of the variable-rate instrument.

- *Callable or puttable instrument.* The entity should perform separate cash flow analyses assuming exercise and nonexercise of the call or put. Whichever cash flow assumption generates the smaller change would be the basis for determining whether the 10 percent threshold is met.
- *Contingent payment terms or unusual interest rate terms.* The entity should use its judgment to determine the appropriate cash flows.
- *Discount rate for present value of cash flows.* The discount rate is the effective interest rate, for accounting purposes, of the original debt instrument.
- If within a year of the current transaction the debt has been exchanged or modified without being deemed to be substantially different, then the debt terms that existed a year ago shall be used to determine whether the current exchange or modification is substantially different.
- *The change in the fair value of an embedded conversion option resulting from an exchange of debt instruments or a modification in the terms of an existing debt instrument.* This should not be included in the 10% cash flow test. A separate test should be performed that compares the change in the fair value of the embedded conversion option to the carrying amount of the original debt instrument immediately before the modification.
(ASC 470-50-40-12)

Even if the 10% test is not met, debt extinguishment accounting should be used in the following situations.

- The change in the fair value of the embedded conversion option is at least 10% of the carrying value of the original debt instrument just prior to the debt being modified or exchanged, or
- The debt instrument modification or exchange adds or eliminates a substantive conversion option.
(ASC 470-50-40-10)

Subsequent Accounting—Modifications and Exchanges If Extinguishment Accounting Is Applied Assuming the 10% test is met and the debt instruments are deemed to be substantially different, the new investment should be initially recorded at fair value and that amount should be compared to the carrying value of the old debt to determine debt extinguishment gain or loss to be recognized, as well as the effective rate of the new instrument. (ASC 470-50-40-13)

Subsequent Accounting—Modifications and Exchanges If Extinguishment Accounting Is *Not* Applied Assuming the 10% test is *not* met and the debt instruments are not deemed to be substantially different, a modification has occurred. The new effective interest is determined based on the carrying amount of the original instrument and the revised cash flows. (ASC 470-50-40-14) This results in an increase in the fair value of an embedded conversion option, reducing the debt and increasing additional paid-in capital.

The modification of a convertible debt instrument affects subsequent recognition of interest expense for the associated debt instrument for changes in the fair value of the embedded conversion option. The change in the fair value of an embedded conversion option is the difference between the fair value of the embedded conversion option immediately before and after the modification. The value exchanged by the holder for the modification of the conversion option should be recognized as a discount (or premium) with a corresponding increase (or decrease) in additional paid-in capital.

Issuers should not recognize a beneficial conversion feature or reassess an existing beneficial conversion feature at the date of the modification of a convertible debt instrument. (ASC 470-50-40-16)

A decrease in the fair value of the conversion option is not recognized. (ASC 470-50-40-15)

Fees between Debtor and Creditor Fees paid by the debtor to the creditor or received by the debtor from the creditor should be included in determining debt extinguishment gain or loss. Fees paid by the debtor to the creditor or received by the debtor from the creditor should be amortized as an adjustment to interest expense over the remaining term of the modified debt instrument using the interest method. See the discussion below on revolving debt agreements or lines of credit for associated fees. (ASC 470-50-40-17)

Third-Party Costs Any costs incurred with third parties should be amortized using the interest method in a manner similar to that used for debt issue costs. Additionally, any costs incurred with third parties should be expensed as incurred. (ASC 470-50-40-18) See discussion below on revolving debt agreements or lines of credit for associated fees.

Revolving Debt Agreements or Lines of Credit Accounting for modifications of revolving credit facilities differs from modification of term loans. To determine the proper accounting the debtor must use the borrowing capacity test. That is, the borrower must evaluate whether the lender's borrowing capacity has increased or decreased. The table below summarizes the appropriate accounting depending on the outcome of the test.

Borrowing Capacity	**Unamortized Fees**	**New Creditor or Third-Party Fees**
Increases or stays the same	Amortized over new term	Amortized over new term
Decreases	Expense proportion decreased	Amortized over new term
	Remainder amortized over new term	
(ASC 470-50-40-21)		

Note: Entities should refer to ASC 470-50-40-17 and 40-18 for guidance on fees between the debtor and creditor or third-party costs unrelated to exchanges or modifications of a line-of-credit or revolving debt arrangement that results in a new line-of-credit or revolving debt arrangement.

ASC 470-60, *Troubled Debt Restructurings by Debtors*

Note: For this Subtopic, it is particularly important to consider the scope and scope exceptions information at the beginning of this chapter.

A troubled debt restructuring can occur in one of two ways:

- A settlement of the debt at less than the carrying amount
- A continuation of the debt with a modification of terms

As explained in ASC 470-60-55-5, no single characteristic or factor, taken alone, is determinative of whether a modification of terms or an exchange of a debt instrument is a TDR under ASC 470-60. Thus, making this determination requires the exercise of judgment. ASC 470-60-55-5 poses two questions to assist in making a determination of whether ASC 470-60 applies in a particular instance:

- Is the debtor experiencing financial difficulty?
- Has the creditor granted a concession it would not otherwise consider?

Both of these questions must be answered in the affirmative for ASC 470-60 to be applicable.

Is the Debtor Experiencing Financial Difficulty? If the debtor's creditworthiness has deteriorated since the debt was originally issued, the debtor should evaluate whether it is experiencing financial difficulties. The following factors are indicators that this may be the case:

- The debtor is in default on some of its debt, or it is probable that the debtor will be in payment default on any of its debt in the foreseeable future without the restructuring modification.
- The debtor has declared, or is in the process of declaring bankruptcy.
- There is doubt as to whether the debtor is a going concern.
- The debtor's securities have been or are likely to be delisted.
- The debtor forecasts that its entity-specific cash flows are insufficient to service the debt through its maturity in accordance with its terms.
- The debtor cannot obtain resources at the current market rates for nontroubled debtors except through existing creditors.
  (ASC 470-60-55-8)

If both of the following factors are present, it would be concluded that the debtor is not experiencing financial difficulty:

- The creditors agree to restructure the old debt solely to reflect either: (1) a decrease in the current interest rates for the debtor, or (2) an increase in the debtor's creditworthiness.
- The debtor is currently servicing the old debt and can obtain funds to repay the old debt at the current market rate for a nontroubled debtor.
  (ASC 470-60-55-9)

Has the Creditor Granted a Concession? The creditor has granted a concession when a restructuring results in its expectation that it will not collect all amounts due. If so, and if the payment of principal is mostly dependent on the value of collateral, the creditor should consider the current value of the collateral in deciding whether the principal will be paid.

If the creditor restructures a debt in exchange for additional collateral or guarantees, the creditor has granted a concession when the amount of these additional items is not adequate compensation for other terms of the restructuring.

If the debtor does not have access to funds at a market rate, then the creditor should consider the restructuring to be at a below-market rate; this is an indicator that the creditor has granted a concession. It may also be a concession when the interest rate in the restructuring agreement has increased, if the new rate is below the market interest rate for new debt having similar risk characteristics. If so, the creditor should consider all aspects of the restructuring agreement to determine whether it has granted a concession.

It is *not* a concession when a restructuring only results in a delay in payment that is insignificant. However, if the debt has been previously restructured, the creditor should consider the cumulative effect of the past restructurings when determining whether a delay in payment resulting from the most recent restructuring is insignificant.

Recognition

Unit of accounting At times a debtor may negotiate with creditors as a group, but sign individual debt instruments with each creditor. For ASC 470-60 purposes, each payable, whether negotiated separately or jointly, is accounted for separately. (ASC 470-60-15-4)

Measurement If the debt is settled by the exchange of assets, a gain is recognized in the period of transfer for the difference between the carrying amount of the debt (defined as the face amount of the debt increased or decreased by applicable accrued interest and applicable unamortized premium, discount, or issue costs) and the consideration given to extinguish the debt. (ASC 470-60-35-3) A two-step process is used:

1. Any noncash assets used to settle the debt are revalued at fair value and the associated ordinary gain or loss is recognized, and
2. The debt restructuring gain is determined and recognized. The gain or loss is evaluated under the "unusual and infrequent" criteria of ASC 225-20. If stock is issued to settle the liability, the stock is recorded at its fair value.
(ASC 470-60-35-4)

Example 1: Settlement of Debt by Exchange of Assets

Assume the debtor company transfers land having a book value of $70,000 and a fair value of $80,000 in full settlement of its note payable. The note has a remaining life of five years, a principal balance of $90,000, and related accrued interest of $10,000 is recorded. The following entries are required to record the settlement:

Debtor		
Land	10,000	
Gain on transfer of assets		10,000
Note payable	90,000	
Interest payable	10,000	
Land		80,000
Gain on settlement of debt		20,000

If the debt is continued with a modification of terms, it is necessary to compare the total future cash flows of the restructured debt (both principal and stated interest) with the carrying value of the original debt. If the total amount of future cash payments is greater than the carrying value, no adjustment is made to the carrying value of the debt. However, a new lower effective interest rate must be computed. This rate makes the present value of the total future cash payments equal to the present carrying value of debt and is used to determine interest expense in future periods. The effective interest method must be used to compute the expense. If the total future cash payments of the restructured debt are less than the present carrying value, the current debt should be reduced to the amount of the future cash flows and a gain should be recognized. No interest expense would be recognized in subsequent periods, since only the principal is being repaid.

According to ASC 470-60, a troubled debt restructuring that involves only a modification of terms is accounted for *prospectively*. Thus, there is no change in the carrying value of the liability unless the carrying amount of the original debt exceeds the total future cash payments specified by the new agreement.

If the restructuring consists of part settlement and part modification of payments, the part settlement is accounted for first and then the modification of payments.

Future undiscounted cash flows of the new debt are:	Effect on gain recognition and interest expense	New fees paid to lender	New fees paid to third parties
Less than the net carrying value of the original debt	Record a gain for the difference. Adjust the carrying value to future undiscounted cash flows. Record no interest expense going forward because only the principal is being repaid.	Reduces the recorded gain	Expense
Greater than the net carrying value of the original debt	Record no gain. Use new, lower effective interest rate.	Capitalize and amortize	Expense

Example 2: Restructuring with Gain/Loss Recognized (Payments Are Less Than Carrying Value)

Assume that the note has a principal balance of $90,000, accrued interest of $10,000, an interest rate of 5%, and a remaining life of five years. The interest rate is reduced to 4%, the principal is reduced to $72,500, and the accrued interest at date of restructure is forgiven.

Future cash flows (after restructuring):

Principal	$ 72,500
Interest (5 years × $72,500 × 4%)	14,500
Total cash to be paid	$ 87,000

Amount prior to restructure

($90,000 principal + $10,000 accrued interest)	(100,000)
Debtor's gain	$ 13,000

The following entries need to be recorded by the debtor to reflect the terms of the agreement:

Beginning of Year 1

Interest payable	10,000	
Note payable	3,000	
Gain on restructure of debt		13,000

End of Years 1–5

Note payable	2,900	
Cash		2,900

Note: \$14,500 ÷ 5 yrs. = \$2,900; no interest expense is recorded in this case.

End of Year 5

Note payable	72,500	
Cash		72,500

Example 3: Restructuring with No Gain/Loss Recognized (Payments Exceed Carrying Value)

Modify Example 2 as follows: Assume the \$100,000 owed is reduced to a principal balance of \$95,000. The interest rate of 5% is reduced to 4%.

Future cash flows (after restructuring):

Principal	\$ 95,000
Interest (5 years × \$95,000 × 4%)	19,000
Total cash to be received	\$ 114,000

Amount prior to restructure:

(\$90,000 principal + \$10,000 accrued interest)	(100,000)
Interest expense/revenue over 5 years	\$ 14,000

In this example, a new effective interest rate must be computed such that the present value of the future payments equals \$100,000. A trial and error approach is used to calculate the effective interest rate that discounts the \$95,000 principal and the \$3,800 annual interest payments to \$100,000, the amount owed prior to restructuring.

Trial and Error Calculation

	(n = 5, i = 2.5%)	(n = 5, i = 3%)
PV of ordinary annuity	4.64583	4.57971
PV of 1	.88385	.86261

$$2.5\% : (.88385 \times \$95{,}000) + (4.64583 \times \$3{,}800) = \$101{,}620$$

$$3\% : (.86261 \times \$95{,}000) + (4.57971 \times \$3{,}800) = \$99{,}351$$

Interpolation:

Interpolation:

$$\left[\frac{101{,}602 - 100{,}000}{101{,}620 - 99{,}351}\right] \times (3\% - 2.5\%) = .357\%$$

New effective rate = 2.5% + .357% = 2.857%

Interest amortization schedule:

Year	Cash	Interest at effective rate	Reduction in carrying value	Carrying amount
			$100,000	
1	$ 3,800*	$2,857**	$ 943***	99,057
2	3,800	2,830	970	98,087
3	3,800	2,802	998	97,089
4	3,800	2,774	1,026	96,063
5****	3,800	2,737	1,063	95,000
	$19,000			

* $3,800 = $95,000 × .04
** $2,857 = $100,000 × 2.857%
*** $943 = $3,800 – $2,857
**** Row 5 is rounded by $5 to arrive at $95,000.

The following entries are made by the debtor to recognize the cash payments in the subsequent periods:

End of Year 1		
Note payable ($3,800 – $2,857)	943	
Interest expense ($100,000 × .02857)	2,857	
Cash		3,800
End of Year 5		
Note payable	95,000	
Cash		95,000

When the total future cash payments may exceed the carrying amount of the liability, no gain or loss is recognized on the books of the debtor unless the maximum future cash payments are less than the carrying amount of the debt. For example, if the debtor is required to make interest payments at a higher rate if its financial condition improves before the maturity of the debt, the debtor should assume that the larger payments would have to be made. The contingent payments would be included in the total future cash payments for comparison with the carrying amount of the debt. If the future cash payments exceed the carrying amount, a new effective interest rate should be determined. The new rate should be the rate that equates the present value of the future cash payments with the carrying amount of the liability. Interest expense and principal reduction are then recognized as the future cash payments are made.

Example 4: Contingent Payments

Modify Example 2 as follows: The new agreement states that if financial condition at maturity improves as specified, an additional principal payment of $15,000 is required and additional 1% of interest must be paid in arrears for Years 4 and 5.

Future cash payments:	
Required principal per agreement	$ 72,500
Required interest per agreement (5 years × $72,500 × 4%)	14,500
Contingent principal payment	15,000
Contingent interest payments (2 years × 72,500 × 1%)	1,450
	$ 103,450
Amount prior to restructure ($90,000 + $10,000)	(100,000)
	$ 3,450

When computing the new effective interest rate, only as many contingent payments as are needed to make the future cash payments exceed the carrying value are included in the calculation. Thus, the contingent principal payment would be included, but the contingent interest would not. The contingent interest payments would be recognized using the same criteria as are used in ASC 450; that is, the payments are recognized when they are both probable and reasonably estimable.

34 ASC 480 DISTINGUISHING LIABILITIES FROM EQUITY

PERSPECTIVE AND ISSUES

Subtopic

ASC 480, *Distinguishing Liabilities from Equity* Topic, contains one subtopic:

- ASC 480-10, *Overall*, which provides guidance on how an issuer classifies and measures financial instruments with characteristics of both liabilities and equity.

Scope and Scope Exceptions

ASC 480

- Applies to all entities and to any freestanding financial instrument, including financial instruments that:
  - Comprise more than one option or forward contract.
  - Have characteristics of both a liability and equity and, in some circumstances, also has characteristics of an asset, including those composed of more than one option or forward contract embodying obligations that require or that may require settlement by transfer of assets.
- Does *not* address an instrument that has only characteristics of an asset.
  (ASC 480-15-2 and 15-3)

ASC 480 does *not* apply to:

1. A feature embedded in a financial instrument that is not a derivative instrument in its entirety. (ASC 480-10-15-5)
2. Mandatorily redeemable financial instruments that are:
   - Issued by nonpublic entities that are not SEC registrants and
   - Mandatorily redeemable but not on fixed dates or not for amounts that are fixed or determined by reference to an interest rate index, currency index, or other external index.
   - Even if it is a nonpublic entity, SEC registrants are not eligible for the scope exception. (ASC 480-10-15-7A and 15-7B)
3. An obligation under share-based compensation arrangements if that obligation is accounted for under ASC 718. (ASC 480-10-15-8)
4. SEC registrants with mandatorily redeemable noncontrolling interests are subject to the scope exception in ASC 480-10-15-7F. However, those entities must still adhere to the disclosure requirements in ASC 480-10-50-1 through 50-3. (ASC 480-10-15-7F)
5. Registration payment arrangements in the scope of ASC 825-20. (ASC 480-10-15-8A)

ASC 480 does *not* apply to mandatorily redeemable noncontrolling interests as follows:

- The classification and measurement provisions do not apply to mandatorily redeemable noncontrolling interests that would not have to be classified as liabilities by the subsidiary, under the only upon liquidation exception in paragraphs 480-10-25-4 and 480-10-25-6, but would be classified as liabilities by the parent in consolidated financial statements.
- The measurement provisions do not apply to other mandatorily redeemable noncontrolling interests that were issued before November 5, 2003, both for the parent in consolidated financial statements and for the subsidiary that issued the instruments that result in the mandatorily redeemable noncontrolling interest. For those instruments, the measurement guidance for redeemable shares and noncontrolling interests in other predecessor literature continues to apply.
  (ASC 480-10-15-7E)

Entities should look to the guidance in ASC 805 for recognition and initial measure of consideration issued in a business combination. However, if a financial instrument in the scope of ASC 480 is issued as consideration, it should be classified under the guidelines in this Topic. (ASC 480-10-15-9 and 15-10)

Overview

Standard setters struggled with the proper reporting for hybrid instruments— instruments having characteristics of both liabilities and equity. ASC 480 addresses the needs to:

- Establish criteria for classification of certain instruments (e.g., mandatorily redeemable stock) that nominally are equity and have key characteristics of debt, but which will significantly impact corporate statements of financial position if a "substance over form" approach is strictly enforced; and
- Develop the methodology for disaggregating the constituent parts of compound instruments so that they may be accounted for as debt and as equity, respectively.

DEFINITIONS OF TERMS

Source: ASC 480-20. See Appendix A, *Definitions of Terms*, for additional terms related to this Topic: Call Option, Employee Stock Ownership Plan, Equity Shares, Fair Value, Financial Instrument, Freestanding Financial Instrument, Mandatorily Redeemable Financial Instruments, Market Participants, Noncontrolling Interest, Nonpublic Entity, Orderly Transaction, Parent, Put Option, Registration Payment Arrangement, Securities and Exchange Commission Registrant, Subsidiary, and Warrant

Issuer. The entity that issued a financial instrument or may be required under the terms of a financial instrument to issue its equity shares.

Issuer's Equity Shares. The equity shares of any entity whose financial statements are included in the consolidated financial statements.

Monetary Value. What the fair value of the cash, shares, or other instruments that a financial instrument obligates the issuer to convey to the holder would be at the settlement date under specified market conditions.

Net Cash Settlement. A form of settling a financial instrument under which the entity with a loss delivers to the entity with a gain cash equal to the gain.

Net Share Settlement. A form of settling a financial instrument under which the entity with a loss delivers to the entity with a gain shares of stock with a current fair value equal to the gain.

Obligation. A conditional or unconditional duty or responsibility to transfer assets or to issue equity shares. Because Topic 480 relates only to financial instruments and not to contracts to provide services and other types of contracts, but includes duties or responsibilities to issue equity shares, this definition of obligation differs from the definition found in FASB Concepts Statement No. 6, Elements of Financial Statements, and is applicable only for items in the scope of that topic.

Physical Settlement. A form of settling a financial instrument under which both of the following conditions are met:

- The party designated in the contract as the buyer delivers the full stated amount of cash or other financial instruments to the seller.
- The seller delivers the full stated number of shares of stock or other financial instruments or nonfinancial instruments to the buyer.

Shares. Shares includes various forms of ownership that may not take the legal form of securities (for example, partnership interests), as well as other interests, including those that are liabilities in substance but not in form. (Business entities have interest holders that are commonly known by specialized names, such as stockholders, partners, and proprietors, and by more general names, such as investors, but all are encompassed by the descriptive term owners. Equity of business entities is, thus, commonly known by several names, such as owners' equity, stockholders' equity, ownership, equity capital, partners' capital, and proprietorship. Some entities [for example, mutual organizations] do not have stockholders, partners, or proprietors in the usual sense of those terms but do have participants whose interests are essentially ownership interests, residual interests, or both.)

Transfer (Def. 1). The term transfer is used in a broad sense consistent with its use in FASB Concepts Statement No. 6, Elements of Financial Statements (such as in paragraph 137), rather than in the narrow sense in which it is used in Subtopic 860-10.

Variable-Rate Forward Contracts. Variable-rate forward contracts are commonly used to effect equity forward transactions. The contract price on those forward contracts is not fixed at inception but varies based on changes in a specified index (for example, three-month U.S. London Interbank Offered Rate [LIBOR]) during the life of the contract.

CONCEPTS, RULES, AND EXAMPLES

Initial Recognition and Measurement

The Codification emphasizes that to prevent the objectives of ASC 480 from being circumvented by the insertion of nonsubstantive or minimal features into financial instruments, these features should be disregarded in applying ASC 480's classification provisions. (ASC 480-10-25-1) Note that when analyzing an embedded feature as though it were a separate instrument, entities should not apply ASC 480-10-25-4 through 25-14, but should look to other guidance. (ASC 480-10-25-2)

Mandatorily Redeemable Financial Instruments A mandatory redemption clause requires common or preferred stock to be redeemed (retired) at a specific date or upon occurrence of an event which is uncertain as to timing, although ultimately certain to occur (for example, the death of the holder). (ASC 480-10-20) The obligation to transfer assets must be unconditional—that is, there is no specified event that is outside the control of the issuer that will release the issuer from its obligation. Thus, callable preferred shares, which are redeemable at the issuer's option, and convertible preferred shares, which are redeemable at the holder's option, are not mandatorily redeemable shares.

Mandatory redemption features are not uncommon in practice. For example, closely held corporations have "buy-sell" agreements to redeem the shares of retiring or deceased owners at formula prices, often book value.

Mandatorily redeemable financial instruments are reported as liabilities. The only exception is for shares that are required to be redeemed only upon the liquidation or termination of the issuer, since the fundamental "going concern assumption" underlying GAAP financial statements means that such an eventuality is not given recognition (ASC 480-10-25-4)

In determining if an instrument is mandatorily redeemable, the entity should consider all terms. The following, however, do not affect the classification of a mandatorily redeemable financial instrument as a liability:

- A term extension option
- A provision that defers redemption until a specified liquidity level is reached
- A similar provision that may delay or accelerate the timing of a mandatory redemption (ASC 480-10-25-6)

If shares have a conditional redemption feature, which requires the issuer to redeem the shares by transferring its assets upon an event not certain to occur, the shares become mandatorily redeemable—and, therefore, become a liability—if that event occurs, the event becomes certain to occur, or the condition is otherwise resolved. (ASC 480-10-25-5) The fair value of the shares is reclassified as a liability, and equity is reduced by that amount, recognizing no gain or loss. (ASC 480-10-30-2) An assessment must be made each reporting period to ascertain whether the triggering event has yet occurred. If it has, the conditionally mandatorily redeemable stock must be reclassified to liabilities. (ASC 480-10-25-7)

Guidance offers two examples. First, if shares are to become mandatorily redeemable upon a change in control of the issuing corporation, these remain classified within equity until that event occurs, if ever. When it does occur, the equity is reclassified to liabilities, measured at the fair value at that date, with no gain or loss recognized. Any disparity between the carrying value of the equity and the amount transferred to liabilities would therefore remain in equity as additional paid-in capital or as a reduction to paid-in capital or to retained earnings. (ASC 480-10-55-10)

Another example of conditional mandatory redemption would occur when preferred stock is issued with a mandatory redemption at a certain date, say ten years hence, conditioned on the failure of the preferred stockholders to exercise the right to convert to common stock before another defined date, say five years from issuance. For the first five years, the preferred stock would be displayed as equity, since the mandatory redemption feature has yet to become activated. If the shareholders elect to exchange the preferred stock to common stock, the usual accounting for such conversions would apply. If the five-year period elapses and the preferred shares are not exchanged, the mandatory redemption provision becomes effective, and the preferred stock is to be reclassified to liabilities, measured at fair value. (ASC 480-10-55-11)

Mandatorily redeemable financial instruments are initially recognized at fair value. (ASC 480-30-1)

Obligations to Repurchase Shares Obligations to repurchase the issuer's equity shares by transferring assets include financial instruments, other than outstanding shares, that, at inception:

- Require or may require the issuers to settle the obligations by transferring assets.
- Embody obligations to repurchase the issuers' equity shares, or are indexed to the price of its own shares.
  (ASC 480-10-25-8)

These contracts should be reported as liabilities (or rarely, as assets, if the fair value of the contract is favorable to the issuer). (ASC 480-10-25-8) Examples of that type of financial instrument are written put options on the option writer's (issuer's) equity shares, and forward contracts to repurchase an issuer's own equity shares if those instruments require physical or net cash settlement. (ASC 480-10-25-10)

Forward contracts that require physical settlement by repurchase of a fixed number of the issuer's equity shares in exchange for cash are measured initially at the fair value of the shares, as adjusted for any consideration or unstated rights or privileges. (ASC 480-10-30-3) Equity is reduced by this same amount. (ASC 480-10-30-5) Fair value in this context may be determined by reference to the amount of cash that would be paid under the conditions specified in the contract if the shares were repurchased immediately. Alternatively, the settlement amount can be discounted at the rate implicit at inception after taking into account any consideration or unstated rights or privileges that may have affected the terms of the transaction. (ASC 480-10-30-4)

Obligations to Issue a Variable Number of Shares If an entity enters into a contract that requires it or permits it at the entity's discretion to issue a variable number of shares upon settlement, that contract is recognized as a liability if at inception the monetary value of the obligation is based solely or predominantly on one of the following criteria:

- A fixed monetary amount known at inception (e.g., a $100,000 payable can be settled by issuing shares worth $100,000 at the then-current market value).
- An amount that varies based on something other than the fair value of the issuer's equity shares (for example, a financial instrument indexed to the Dow that can be settled by issuing shares worth the index-adjusted amount at the then-current market value).
- Variations inversely related to changes in the fair value of the entity's equity shares (i.e., a written put option that could be net share settled).
  (ASC 480-10-25-14)

Subsequent Measurement

Certain Physically Settled Forward Purchase Contracts and Mandatorily Redeemable Financial Instruments Subsequent measurement can be effected by either:

- Accretion (which is feasible only if the amount to be paid and the settlement date are both fixed), or
- By determining the amount of cash that would be paid under the conditions specified in the contract if settlement occurred at the reporting date (useful when either the amount to be paid or the settlement date vary based on defined conditions and terms).
  (ASC 480-10-35-3)

In either case, the change from the amount reported in the prior period is interest expense. If accretion is appropriate, the instruments should be measured subsequently at the present value of the amount to be paid at settlement, accruing interest cost using the rate implicit at inception.

Example of Mandatorily Redeemable Stock (Ref.: ASC 480-10-55-10 and 25-7)

A major shareholder of the Atlantic Corporation swaps the company two tracts of prime real estate (Tract A and Tract B) in exchange for 10,000 shares and 5,000 shares, respectively, of $1 par value preferred stock. Each block of stock is mandatorily redeemable within one year if Atlantic ever sells the related tract of real estate. -Tract A has a fair value of $400,000 and Tract B has a fair value of $200,000 on the initial transaction date. Since the shares are only conditionally redeemable at this time, Atlantic records a credit to equity accounts with the following entry:

Land	600,000	
Preferred stock		15,000
Additional paid-in capital		585,000

Five years later, Atlantic sells Tract A for $550,000, which is the fair value of the land. Because the status of the shares has now changed to mandatorily redeemable, Atlantic reclassifies the related 10,000 shares as a liability, measured at their fair value on the reclassification date. Since the fair value has increased by $150,000, Atlantic shifts an additional $150,000 from the additional paid-in capital account to the liability account. It uses the following entry to do so:

Preferred stock	10,000	
Additional paid-in capital	540,000	
Liabilities—shares subject to mandatory redemption		550,000

Two years later, Atlantic sells Tract B for $125,000, which is the fair value of the land. The status of these shares has also now changed to mandatorily redeemable, so Atlantic reclassifies the related 5,000 shares as a liability, measured at their fair value on the reclassification date. Since the fair value has decreased by $75,000, Atlantic retains $75,000 in the additional paid-in capital account. It uses the following entry to do so:

Preferred stock	5,000	
Additional paid-in capital	120,000	
Liabilities—shares subject to mandatory redemption		125,000

Note that when redemption value is based on a notion of fair value, defined in the underlying agreement, the initial recognition of the difference between this computed amount and the corresponding book value will almost inevitably result in a surplus or deficit. In other words, the promised redemption amounts, measured at transition and again at the date of each statement of financial position, will not equal the book value of the equity which is subject to redemption. This discrepancy must be reflected in stockholders' equity, even though the redeemable equity is reclassified to a liability. In effect, the redemption arrangement will result in either a residual in equity (assuming that a redemption was to fully occur at the date of the statement of financial position) or a deficit, because the agreement provides that redeeming shareholders are entitled to more or less than their respective pro rata shares of the book value of their equity claims. If the redemption price of mandatorily redeemable shares is greater than the book value of those shares, the company should report the excess as a deficit (equity), even though the mandatorily redeemable shares are reported as a liability.

Common shares that are mandatorily redeemable are not included in the denominator when computing basic or diluted earnings per share. If any amounts, including contractual (accumulated) dividends, attributable to shares that are to be redeemed or repurchased have not been recognized as interest expense, those amounts are deducted in computing income available to common shareholders (the numerator of the calculation), consistently with the "two-class" method set forth in ASC 260. The redemption requirements for mandatorily redeemable shares for each of the next five years are required to be disclosed in the notes to the financial statements.

ASC 480-10-S99 addresses concerns raised by the SEC regarding the financial statement classification and measurement of securities subject to mandatory redemption requirements or whose redemption is outside the control of the issuer. Questions also arose regarding disclosures needed to comply with SEC requirements.

These rules require securities with redemption features that are not solely within the control of the issuer to be classified outside of permanent equity. The SEC staff believes that all of the events that could trigger redemption should be evaluated separately and that the possibility that *any* triggering event that is not *solely* within the control of the issuer could occur—without regard to probability—would require the security to be classified outside of permanent equity. Determining whether an equity security is redeemable at the option of the holder or upon the occurrence of an event that is solely within the control of the issuer can be complex. Accordingly, all of the individual facts and circumstances should be considered in determining how an equity security should be classified.

ASC 480-10-S99 offers several examples of complex fact patterns to help registrants in determining whether classification as a liability or as equity would be appropriate.

For example, if a preferred security has a redemption provision stating that it may be called by the issuer upon an affirmative vote by the majority of its board of directors, but the preferred security holders control a majority of the votes of the board of directors through direct representation on the board of directors or through other rights, the preferred security is effectively redeemable at the option of the holder and its classification in temporary equity is required. Thus, in assessing such situations, any provision that requires approval by the board of directors cannot be assumed to be within the control of the reporting entity itself. All of the relevant facts and circumstances would have to be considered. (ASC 480-10-S99-1.7)

As another example, if a security with a deemed liquidation clause that provides that the security becomes redeemable if the stockholders of the reporting entity (those immediately prior to a merger or consolidation) hold, immediately after such merger or consolidation, stock representing less than a majority of the voting power of the outstanding stock of the surviving corporation, this would not be permanent equity. A purchaser could acquire a majority of the voting power of the outstanding stock, without company approval, thereby triggering redemption. (ASC 480-10-S99-1.8)

Securities with provisions that allow the holders to be paid upon occurrence of events that are solely within the issuer's control should thus always be classified outside of permanent equity. Such events include:

- The failure to have a registration statement declared effective by the SEC by a designated date
- The failure to maintain compliance with debt covenants
- The failure to achieve specified earnings targets
- A reduction in the issuer's credit rating

(ASC 480-10-S99-1.9)

ASC 480-10-S99 notes that if a reporting entity issues preferred shares that are conditionally redeemable (e.g., at the holder's option or upon the occurrence of an uncertain event not solely within the company's control), the shares are not within the scope of ASC 480 because there is no unconditional obligation to redeem the shares by transferring assets at a specified or determinable date or upon an event certain to occur. (ASC 480-10-S99-1.2) If the uncertain event occurs, the condition is resolved, or the event becomes certain to occur, then the shares become mandatorily redeemable and would require reclassification to a liability. Under SEC rules, however, these shares cannot be included in permanent equity, and thus would be displayed as a "mezzanine" equity category. Mezzanine capital is an SEC reporting concept that has no analog under GAAP rules.

ASC 480 requires that the issuer measure that liability initially at fair value and reduce equity by the amount of that initial measure, recognizing no gain or loss. ASC 480-10-S99 observes that this reclassification of shares to a liability is akin to the redemption of such shares by issuance of debt. Similar to the accounting for the redemption of preferred shares, to the extent that the fair value of the liability differs from the carrying amount of the preferred shares, upon reclassification that difference should be deducted from or added to net earnings available to common shareholders in the calculation of earnings per share.

Contingent Consideration in a Business Combination If contingent consideration in a business combination is classified initially as a liability under the guidance in ASC 480, that consideration should be measured subsequently at fair value in accordance with the guidance in ASC 805-30. (ASC 480-10-35-4A)

All Other Financial Instruments All other financial instruments are recognized at fair value at the date of issuance and at every measurement date afterwards. (ASC 480-10-30-7) The changes in the fair value are recognized in earnings unless this subtopic or another specifies otherwise. (ASC 480-10-35-5)

Freestanding Instrument Involving Multiple Components That May Be Settled in a Variable Number of Shares If a freestanding instrument is composed of more than one option or forward contract and one of those contracts embodies an obligation to repurchase the issuer's shares that require or may require settlement by a transfer of assets, the financial instrument is a liability. In addition, if a freestanding instrument composed of more than one option or forward contract includes an obligation to issue shares, the various component obligations must be analyzed to determine if any of them would be obligations under ASC 480. If one or more would be obligations under this standard, then judgment must be used to determine if the monetary value of the obligations that would be liabilities is collectively predominant over the other component liabilities. If so, the instrument is a liability. If not, the instrument is outside the scope of ASC 480. (ASC 480-10-55-42 and 55-43) Following is a list of examples of these types of financial instruments:

- Puttable warrant
- Warrant for shares that can be put by the holder immediately after exercise
- Warrant that allows the holder to exercise the warrant or put the warrant back to the issuer on the exercise date for a variable number of shares with a fixed monetary value
- Forward contract in which the number of shares to be issued depends on the issuer's share price on the settlement date
- Warrant with a "liquidity make-whole" put to issue additional shares to the holder if the sales price of the shares when later sold is less than the share price when the warrant is exercised
- Warrant that allows the holder to exercise the warrant or, if a contingent event does not occur, put the warrant back to the issuer on the exercise date for a variable number of shares with a fixed monetary value
  (ASC 480-10-55-45 through 55-52)

Put options ASC 480-10-55 provides examples of put options that are subject to only cash payment and also of those that could be settled by an issuance of stock. The former case is straightforward: the instrument must be classified as a liability if the share price at the reporting date is such that a cash payment would be demanded by the holders of the puttable warrants. If the share price at that date is such that exercise of the warrant would be elected over exercise of the put option, then the warrant would be included in equity, not in liabilities. In other words, classification would depend on current stock price and could change from period to period, although ASC 480-10-55 is not explicit on this point.

Other put arrangements call for settlement in shares. That is, if advantageous to do so, the warrant holders exercise the warrants and acquire shares, but if the strike price has not been attained at expiration date, the put is exercised and the reporting entity would have to settle, but instead of paying cash it would issue shares having an aggregate value equal to the put amount. Thus, at inception, the number of shares that the puttable warrant obligates the reporting entity to issue can vary, and the instrument must be examined under the provisions of ASC 480 that deal with obligations to issue a variable number of shares. The facts and circumstances must be considered in judging whether the *monetary value* of the obligation to issue a number of shares that varies is predominantly based on a fixed monetary amount known at inception; if so, it is a liability under ASC 480.

Put warrant A detachable put warrant can either be put back to the debt issuer for cash or can be exercised to acquire common stock. These instruments should be accounted for in the same manner as a mezzanine security. The proceeds applicable to the put warrant ordinarily are to be classified as equity and should be presented between the liability and equity sections in accordance with SEC ASR 268. (ASC 480-10-S99)

In the case of a warrant with a put price substantially higher than the value assigned to the warrant at issuance, however, the proceeds should be classified as a liability since it is likely that the warrant will be put back to the company.

Warrant Yet another variation illustrated by ASC 480-10-55 is the warrant for the purchase of shares, where the shares are puttable. The holder can exercise the warrant and then immediately force the issuer to repurchase the shares issued. The price at which the shares could be put would be defined in the warrant, and the likelihood that the put option would be exercised would vary with the market value of the shares. Obviously, if the shares acquired by exercise of the warrant had a greater market value than the put price, the put would not be invoked. Accordingly, whether these warrants would be classified as equity or liability would depend on the market value of the underlying shares, and this could change from the date of one statement of financial position to that of the next. However, if the shares to be issued upon warrant exercise were to have a mandatory redemption feature, then the warrants would be reportable as liabilities in any case.

ASC 480-10-55 offers several other examples, illustrating more complex features that may be found in stock purchase warrants which, depending on circumstances, might necessitate classification as liabilities in the statement of financial position.

ASC 480 does not apply to or affect the timing of recognition of financial instruments issued as contingent consideration in a business combination, nor the measurement guidance for contingent consideration, as set forth in ASC 805. It also does not affect accounting for stock-based compensation or ESOP plans. (ASC 718)

Presentation and Disclosure Presentation and disclosure requirements can be found in Appendix B at www.wiley.com/go/GAAP2021.

Application of ASC 480

Example—Obligations That Require Net Share Settlement: Monetary Value Changes in the Same Direction as the Fair Value of the Issuer's Equity Shares

Tyler Corp. grants 10,000 stock appreciation rights that entitle the holder to receive a number of equity shares to be determined based on the change in the fair value of Tyler's equity shares. At the date of the grant, the fair value of Tyler's equity shares is $25 per share. Subsequently, the fair value of Tyler's equity shares increases to $28 per share. Tyler is thus required to issue shares worth $30,000 [($28 – $25) × 10,000], or 1,072 shares.

This financial instrument contains an obligation to issue a number of equity shares with a value equal to the appreciation of 10,000 equity shares. The number of shares to be issued, therefore, is not fixed. Classification will depend on whether the monetary value changes in the same direction as changes in the fair value of the equity shares. In this example, the monetary value changes in the same direction as changes in the fair value of the equity shares.

The increase in fair value of the equity shares from $25 to $28 resulted in an increase in the monetary value of the obligation from $0 to $30,000. If the fair value of the equity shares increases further, for example to $30 per share, the monetary value of the obligation increases as well to $50,000 [($30 – $25) × 10,000]. If the fair value of the equity shares then decreases, for example from $30 to $27, the monetary value of the obligation decreases to $20,000 [($27 – $25) × 10,000]. Because the monetary value of the obligation changes in the same direction as the change in fair value of the issuer's equity shares, this obligation does not qualify as a liability and the equity classification is prescribed.

Example—Obligations That Require Net Share Settlement: Monetary Value Changes in Opposite Direction as the Fair Value of the Issuer's Equity Shares (Ref.: ASC 480-10-55-26 and 25-14(c))

Harrison Corp. issues equity shares to Middleboro Co. for $5 million (1 million shares at $5 each). Simultaneously, Harrison enters into a financial instrument with Middleboro, under the terms of which, if the per share value of Harrison' shares is greater than $5 on a specified date, Middleboro will transfer shares of Harrison with a value of [(share price – $5) × 1,000,000] to Harrison. If the per share is less than $5 on a specified date, Harrison transfers shares of its own equity with a value of [($5 – share price) × 1,000,000] to Middleboro.

The 1,000,000 shares issued to Middleboro do not embody an obligation. They also do not convey to the issuer the right to receive cash or another financial instrument from the holder, or to exchange other financial instruments on potentially favorable terms with the holder. Therefore, the equity classification criteria are met and the component is classified as equity.

The financial instrument issued to Middleboro contains an obligation to issue a variable number of equity shares if the fair value of Harrison's equity shares is less than $5 on a certain date. As a result, the classification will depend upon

a. whether the monetary value is equal to the change in fair value of a fixed number of equity shares, and
b. whether the changes are in the same direction as the fair value of the equity shares.

The first criterion is met because the monetary value of the obligation is equal to the appreciation of a fixed number (1,000,000) of the issuer's equity shares. However, the second criterion is not met because the monetary value of the obligation changes in a direction opposite to the changes in the fair value of the issuer's equity shares. If the fair value of the equity shares increases, the monetary value of the obligation decreases (and may in fact be reduced to zero or result in a receivable from the counterparty). If the fair value of the equity shares decreases, the monetary value of the obligation increases. Because the monetary value of the obligation does not change in the same direction as the fair value of the equity shares, criterion b above is not met; therefore, the obligation is classified as a liability and *not* as equity.

Example—Written Put Options That Require Physical Settlement (Ref.: ASC 480-10-55-27)

Carlyle Corp. writes a put option that allows a holder, Yetta Co., to put 200 shares of Carlyle stock to Carlyle for $33 per share on a specified date. The put option requires physical settlement (delivery of the shares and payment therefore). Because the put option requires Carlyle to transfer assets (cash) to settle the obligation, the component is classified as a liability under ASC 480-10-25-14.

Example—Forward Purchase Contract That Requires Physical or Net Cash Settlement (Ref.: ASC 480-10-55-14 and 25-8 through 25-12)

In a fact pattern slightly at variance with the preceding example, Carlyle Corp. enters into a freestanding forward purchase arrangement with Yetta Co., under which Yetta is to transfer 200 shares of Carlyle stock to Carlyle for $33 per share on a specified date. The forward purchase agreement requires physical settlement (delivery of the shares and payment therefore). Because the forward purchase arrangement requires Carlyle to transfer assets (cash) to settle the obligation, the component is classified as a liability. The same result would hold if the contract called for a net cash settlement. While a put option (the preceding example) requires that the liability be initially recorded, and subsequently remeasured, at fair value, the forward purchase arrangement is to be recorded at fair value, and then accreted to the present value of the forward purchase price at the date of each statement of financial position, using the implicit interest rate given by the initial fair value.

Example—Written Put Options That Require Net Share Settlement

Dragoon Corp. writes a put option that allows the holder, Zitti Corp., to put 200 shares of Dragoon stock to Dragoon for $44 a share on a specified date. The put requires net share settlement (i.e., shares having a value equal to the spread between the option price and fair value must be delivered in settlement). Assume the fair value of the shares at the date the put is issued is $44. The monetary value of the obligation at that time is therefore zero.

Subsequently, the fair value of Dragoon's equity shares decreases to $36 and the put option is exercised. At this point, the monetary value of the obligation is $1,600 [200 shares × ($44 – $36)]. Dragoon would be required to issue about 45 shares ($1,600 divided by $36). The monetary value of the obligation increased because of a decrease in the fair value of Dragoon's equity shares. Because changes in the monetary value of the obligation are not in the same direction as changes in the fair value of Dragoon's equity shares, the component is not classified as equity, but rather as a liability. The contract is measured initially and subsequently at fair value, with changes in fair value recognized in current earnings.

Example—Unconditional Obligation That Must Be Either Redeemed for Cash or Settled by Issuing Shares (ASC 480-10-55-27 and 28 and 25-14)

If the reporting entity issues financial instruments that do not require the transfer of assets to settle the obligation but, instead, unconditionally require the issuer to settle the obligation either by transferring assets or by issuing a variable number of its equity shares, this may or may not create a liability. Because such instruments do not require the issuer to settle by transfer of assets, they are not automatically classified as liabilities under ASC 480. However, those instruments may still be classified as liabilities, if other stipulated conditions are met.

Assume that Zylog Corp. issues one million shares of cumulative preferred stock for cash equal to the stock's liquidation preference of $25 per share. Under the terms, Zylog is required either to redeem the shares on the third anniversary of the issuance, for the issuance price plus any accrued but unpaid dividends, either in cash or by issuing sufficient shares of its common stock to be worth $25 per share. This does not represent an unconditional obligation to transfer assets, and therefore the preferred stock is not a mandatorily redeemable financial instrument as that term is defined in ASC 480. However, the stock is still a liability, because the preferred shares represent an unconditional obligation that the issuer may settle by issuing a variable number of its equity shares with monetary value that is fixed and known at inception. Because the preferred shares are liabilities, payments to holders are reported as interest cost, and accrued but not-yet-paid payments are part of the liability for the shares.

Example of Mandatorily Redeemable Preferred Shares

On June 1, 20X1, Verde Corporation issues 1,000 shares of mandatorily redeemable 5% preferred stock with a par value $100 for $110,330. The shares are redeemable at $150 on May 31, 20X8. At issuance, Verde Corporation recognizes a liability of $110,330.

The effective interest rate is 8.5%. Verde would recognize the following annual interest expense and liability amounts:

	Cash paid	Interest at 8.5% annually	Change in liability	Ending liability
06/01/X3				110,330
05/31/X4	5,000	9,378	4,378	114,708
05/31/X5	5,000	9,750	4,750	119,458
05/31/X6	5,000	10,154	5,154	124,612
05/31/X7	5,000	10,592	5,592	130,204
05/31/X8	5,000	11,067	6,068	136,271
05/31/X9	5,000	11,583	6,583	142,854
05/31/X0	155,000	12,146	(142,854)	0

The entry to record the first "dividend" payment would be

Interest expense	9,378	
Liability		4,378
Cash		5,000

Example of Shares That Are Mandatorily Redeemable at the Death of the Holder (ASC 480-10-55-64)

Mike and Ike are equal shareholders in M&I's Auto Repair, Inc. Upon the death of either shareholder, the corporation will redeem shares of the deceased for half of the book value of the corporation. The following information would be disclosed in the notes to the financial statements:

All of the corporation's shares are subject to mandatory redemption upon death of the shareholders, and are thus reported as a liability. The liability amount consists of:

Common stock—$100 par value, 1,000 shares authorized, issued, and outstanding	$100,000
Undistributed earnings attributable to those shares	50,000
Accumulated other comprehensive income	(2,000)
Total liability	$148,000

Example of a Contract with a Fixed Monetary Amount Known at Inception (ASC 480-10-55-21 and 25-14a)

Numero Uno Corp. purchases equipment worth $100,000 and agrees to pay $110,000 at the end of one year or, at its option, to issue shares worth $112,000. The contract is recognized as a liability at issuance of $100,000. Subsequent to issuance the liability is remeasured at the fair value of the contract, which would be the accreted value of the cash payment amount ($110,000).

Example of a Written Put Option on a Fixed Number of Shares

Numero Dos Corp. writes a put allowing the purchaser to sell 100 shares of Numero Dos common stock at $20 per share in six months. The purchaser pays Numero Dos $300 for the right to put the 100 shares. Numero Dos's common stock is currently trading at $23. Numero Dos reports a liability of $300. The liability is subsequently remeasured at the fair value of the put option.

Example of a Put Warrant

Caspian Corporation issues 100 bonds with detachable put warrants, each of which allows holders, after two years have elapsed, to purchase one share of Caspian's $1 par value common stock from the company for $20 per share, and which are puttable for a cash payment of $5. Caspian apportions $5 of the bond sale price to the warrants. Caspian's share price on the issuance date is $23. At this price, warrant holders can purchase shares from Caspian for $20 and resell them for $23, yielding a net gain of $3. Since this is less than the $5 to be gained from the put feature of the warrants, this is classified as a liability, and is recorded as such with the following entry (the remaining entries for the issuance of the bond are not given here):

Cash	500	
Liabilities—puttable warrants		500

After two years, Caspian's stock price has declined to $20, so the warrant stock purchase feature clearly has no value. Instead, a warrant holder puts 30 warrants back to the company, which requires a cash payment of $5 for each warrant, and results in the following entry:

Liabilities—puttable warrants	150	
Cash		150

Caspian's stock price then increases to $30, which allows warrant holders to achieve a $10 gain if they acquire shares with their warrants for $20. Accordingly, another warrant holder acquires shares with 50 warrants, resulting in the following entry:

Cash	1,000	
Liabilities—puttable warrants	250	
Common stock		50
Additional paid-in capital		1,200

In a separate bond issuance, Caspian again issues put warrants under the same terms, but now its stock price is $35 at the time of bond issuance, making the warrant feature more likely to be exercised than the put feature. Accordingly, Caspian records the proceeds in equity with the following entry (again, the remaining entries recording the bond issuance are omitted):

Cash	500	
Additional paid-in capital—warrants		500

Investors use all 100 warrants to acquire shares at the $20 exercise price. The entry follows:

Cash	2,000	
Paid-in capital—warrants	500	
Common stock		100
Additional paid-in capital		2,400

The original classification should not be changed because of subsequent economic changes in the value of the put. The value assigned to the put warrant at issuance, however, should be adjusted to its highest redemption price, starting with the date of issuance until the earliest date of the warrants. Changes in the redemption price before the earliest put dates are changes in accounting estimates and changes after the earliest put dates should be recognized in income. If the put is classified as equity, the adjustment should be reported as a charge to retained earnings, and if the put is classified as a liability the adjustment is reported as interest expense.

Regardless of how the put is classified on the statement of financial position, the primary and fully diluted EPS should be calculated on both an equity basis (warrants will be exercised) and on a debt basis (put will be exercised) and the more dilutive of the two methods should be used.

Example of a Forward Contract with a Variable Settlement Date

Numero Tres Corp. enters into a contract to purchase 200 shares of its subsidiary at $25 in two years. However, if the holder of the shares dies before the settlement date, Numero Tres agrees to purchase the shares at the present value of $25 at the settlement date computed using the then-current prime rate. The shares are currently trading at $22. The liability to repurchase shares is initially reported at $4,400. At each subsequent measurement date, Numero Tres would adjust the liability to the present value of $25 at settlement date using the discount rate implicit in the contract, unless the holder of the shares had died. If the holder of the shares had died, Numero Tres would adjust the liability to the present value of $25 at settlement date using the then-current prime rate. For example, if one year from issuance date the holder is still alive, the liability would be adjusted to $4,690 using the 6.6% rate implicit in the agreement. The adjustment amount of $290 would be charged to interest expense. If instead the holder had died and the prime rate was 5%, the liability would be adjusted to $4,762 ($5,000/1.05) and the adjustment of $362 would be charged to interest expense.

35 ASC 505 EQUITY

PERSPECTIVE AND ISSUES

Subtopics

ASC 505 consists of five subtopics:

- ASC 505-10, *Overall*, provides guidance on issues not addressed in the other ASC 505 subtopics
- ASC 505-20, *Stock Dividends and Stock Splits*, provides guidance for the recipient and the issuer
- ASC 505-30, *Treasury Stock*, provides guidance on an entity's repurchase of its own shares of outstanding common stock and the subsequent retirement of those shares
- ASC 505-60, *Spin-offs and Reverse Spin-offs*, provides guidance on the distribution of nonmonetary assets in spin-off transactions

Scope and Scope Exceptions

Guidance in ASC 505 generally applies to all entities unless more specific guidance is provided in other topics. (ASC 505-10-15-1) Specific exceptions follow.

ASC 505-20 applies to corporations and their stock dividends and stock splits, except it does *not* apply to distribution or issuance to shareholders of:

- Shares of another corporation held as an investment,
- Shares of a different class,
- Rights to subscribe for additional shares, and
- Shares of the same class where each shareholder is given an election to receive cash or shares with both of the following characteristics:
  - The shareholder can elect to receive the entire distribution in cash or shares of equivalent value and
  - There is a potential limitation on the total amount of cash that all shareholders can elect to receive in the aggregate.

(ASC 505-20-15-1 through 3A)

ASC 505-30 applies to transactions involving the repurchase of an entity's own outstanding common stock and to the subsequent constructed or actual retirement of those shares. If other topics provide more specific guidance, then that guidance should be followed. (ASC 505-30-15-2)

ASC 505-60 does *not* apply to nonmonetary assets that do not constitute a business. (ASC 505-60-15-3)

Overview

CON 6 defines equity as the residual interest in the assets of an entity after deducting its liabilities. Stockholders' equity is comprised of all capital contributed to the entity plus its accumulated earnings less any distributions that have been made. There are three major categories within the equity section:

1. Paid-in capital. Paid-in capital represents equity contributed by owners.
2. Retained earnings. Retained earnings represents the sum of all earnings less those not retained in the business (i.e., what has been paid out as dividends).

3. Other comprehensive income. Other comprehensive income represents revenues, expenses, gains, and losses, which are included in comprehensive income because they are not yet realized, but have been excluded from net income under applicable GAAP rules (e.g., accumulated translation gains or losses).

Comprehensive income is the change in equity (net assets) of a business entity from nonowner sources.

Depending on the laws of the jurisdiction of incorporation, distributions to shareholders may be subject to various limitations, such as to the amount of retained (accounting basis) earnings.

A major objective of the accounting for equity is the adequate disclosure of the sources from which the capital was derived. For this reason, a number of different paid-in capital accounts may be presented in the statement of financial position. The rights of each class of shareholder must be disclosed. Where shares are reserved for future issuance, such as under the terms of stock option plans, this fact must also be made known.

DEFINITIONS OF TERMS

Source: ASC 505, *Glossary* sections. Also see Appendix A, *Definitions of Terms*, for additional terms relevant to this chapter: Business; Component of an Entity; Customer; Down Round Feature; Equity Restructuring; Fair Value (Def. 2); Financial Instrument; Issued, Issuance, or Issuing of an Equity Instrument; Market Participants; Operating Segment; Orderly Transaction; Registration Payment Arrangements; Related Parties; Reporting Unit; Security; Standard Antidilution Provisions; and Stock Dividend.

Bankruptcy Code. A federal statute, enacted October 1, 1979, as title 11 of the United States Code by the Bankruptcy Reform Act of 1978, that applies to all cases filed on or after its enactment and that provides the basis for the current federal bankruptcy system.

Claim. As defined by Section 101(4) of the Bankruptcy Code, a right to payment, regardless of whether the right is reduced to judgment, liquidated, unliquidated, fixed, contingent, matured, unmatured, disputed, undisputed, legal, secured, or unsecured, or a right to an equitable remedy for breach of performance if such breach results in a right to payment, regardless of whether the right is reduced to a fixed, contingent, matured, unmatured, disputed, undisputed, secured, or unsecured right.

Market Condition. A condition affecting the exercise price, exercisability, or other pertinent factors used in determining the fair value of an award under a share-based payment arrangement that relates to the achievement of either of the following:

- A specified price of the issuer's shares or a specified amount of intrinsic value indexed solely to the issuer's shares.
- A specified price of the issuer's shares in terms of a similar (or index of similar) equity security (securities). The term similar as used in this definition refers to an equity security of another entity that has the same type of residual rights. For example, common stock of one entity generally would be similar to the common stock of another entity for this purpose.

Participation Rights. Contractual rights of security holders to receive dividends or returns from the security issuer's profits, cash flows, or returns on investments.

Preferred Stock. A security that has preferential rights compared to common stock.

Reverse Spin-off. A spin-off of a subsidiary to an entity's shareholders in which the legal form of the transaction does not match its substance such that the new legal spun-off entity (the spinnee) will be the continuing entity.

Spin-off. The transfer of assets that constitute a business by an entity (the spinnor) into a new legal spun-off entity (the spinnee), followed by a distribution of the shares of the spinnee to its shareholders, without the surrender by the shareholders of any stock of the spinnor.

Stock Split. An issuance by a corporation of its own common shares to its common shareholders without consideration and under conditions indicating that such action is prompted mainly by a desire to increase the number of outstanding shares for the purpose of effecting a reduction in their unit market price and, thereby, of obtaining wider distribution and improved marketability of the shares. Sometimes called a stock split-up.

CONCEPTS, RULES, AND EXAMPLES

Legal Capital and Capital Stock

Legal capital typically refers to that portion of the stockholders' investment in a corporation that is permanent in nature and represents assets that will continue to be available for the satisfaction of creditor's claims. Traditionally, legal capital was comprised of the aggregate par or stated value of common and preferred shares issued. In recent years, however, many states have eliminated the requirement that corporate shares have a designated par or stated value. States that have adopted provisions of the Model Business Corporation Act[1] have eliminated the distinction between par value and the amount contributed in excess of par. In more than thirty states, the Model Act is the basis for business corporation statutes.

The specific requirements regarding the preservation of legal capital are a function of the business corporation laws in the state in which a particular entity is incorporated. Accordingly, any action by the corporation that could affect the amount of legal capital (e.g., the payment of dividends in excess of retained earnings) must be considered in the context of the relevant laws of the state where the company is chartered.

Ownership interest in a corporation is made up of common and, optionally, preferred shares. The common shares represent the residual risk-taking ownership of the corporation after the satisfaction of all claims of creditors and senior classes of equity.

Preferred Stock Preferred shareholders are owners who have certain rights superior to those of common shareholders. Preferences as to earnings exist when the preferred shareholders have a stipulated dividend rate (expressed either as a dollar amount or as a percentage of the preferred stock's par or stated value). Preferences as to assets exist when the preferred shares have a stipulated liquidation value. If a corporation were to liquidate, these preferred holders would be paid a specific amount before the common shareholders would have a right to participate in any of the proceeds.

In practice, preferred shares are more likely to have preferences as to earnings than as to assets. Although unusual, preferred shares may have both preferential rights. Preferred shares may also have the following optional features:

- Participation in earnings beyond the stipulated dividend rate;
- The cumulative feature, ensuring that dividends in arrears, if any, will be fully satisfied before the common shareholders participate in any earnings distribution; and
- Convertibility or callability by the corporation.

[1] The Model Business Corporation Act is a model created by the American Bar Association's Committee on Corporate Law and first published in 1950. It has since been extensively revised and is adopted in various forms in the majority of states.

Preferences must be disclosed adequately in the financial statements, either on the face of the statement of financial position or in the notes thereto.

In exchange for the preferences, the preferred shareholders' other rights or privileges are often limited. For instance, the right to vote may be restricted to common shareholders. The most important right denied to the preferred shareholders, however, is the right to participate without limitation in the earnings of the corporation. Thus, if the corporation has exceedingly large earnings for a particular period, most of these earnings would accrue to the benefit of the common shareholders. This statement is true even if the preferred stock is participating (a fairly uncommon feature) because participating preferred stock usually has some upper limitation placed upon the extent of participation.

Occasionally, several classes of stock will be categorized as common (e.g., Class A common, Class B common, etc.). Since there can be only one class of shares that represents the true residual risk-taking ownership in a corporation, it is clear that the other classes, even though described as common shareholders, must in fact have some preferential status. Typically, these preferences relate to voting rights. An example of this situation arises when a formerly closely held corporation sells shares to the public but gives the publicly held shares a disproportionately small capacity to exercise influence over the entity, thereby keeping control in the hands of the former majority owners even as they are reduced to the status of minority owners. The rights and responsibilities of each class of shareholder, even if described as common, must be fully disclosed in the financial statements.

Convertible Preferred Stock

The treatment of convertible preferred stock at its issuance is no different than that of nonconvertible preferred. When it is converted, the book value approach is used to account for the conversion. Use of the market value approach would entail a gain or loss for which there is no theoretical justification, since the total amount of contributed capital does not change when the stock is converted. When the preferred stock is converted, the "Preferred stock" and related "Additional paid-in capital—preferred stock" accounts are debited for their original values when purchased, and "Common stock" and "Additional paid-in capital—common stock" (if an excess over par or stated value exists) are credited. If the book value of the preferred stock is less than the total par value of the common stock being issued, retained earnings are charged for the difference. This charge is supported by the rationale that the preferred shareholders are offered an additional return to facilitate their conversion to common stock. Many states require that this excess instead reduces additional paid-in capital from other sources.

Example of Convertible Preferred Stock

Caspian Corporation issues 10,000 shares of $1 par value convertible preferred stock, and receives $1.25 per share. It records the initial sale with the following entry:

Cash	12,500	
Convertible preferred stock		10,000
Additional paid-in capital—preferred stock		2,500

The terms of the convertible preferred stock allow Caspian's shareholders to convert one share of preferred for one share of common stock at any time. The preferred shareholders convert all of their shares to Caspian common stock, which has a par value of $2. This requires the following entry:

Convertible preferred stock	10,000	
Additional paid-in capital—preferred stock	2,500	
Retained earnings	7,500	
Common stock		20,000

Issuance of Shares The accounting for the sale of shares by a corporation depends upon whether the stock has a par or stated value. If there is a par or stated value, the amount of the proceeds representing the aggregate par or stated value is credited to the common or preferred stock account. The aggregate par or stated value is generally defined as legal capital not subject to distribution to shareholders. Proceeds in excess of par or stated value are credited to an additional paid-in capital account. The additional paid-in capital represents the amount in excess of the legal capital that may, under certain defined conditions, be distributed to shareholders.

A corporation selling stock below par value credits the capital stock account for the par value and debits an offsetting discount account for the difference between par value and the amount actually received. If the discount is on original issue capital stock, it serves to notify the actual and potential creditors of the contingent liability of those investors. As a practical matter, corporations avoid this problem by reducing par values to an arbitrarily low amount. This reduction in par eliminates the chance that shares would be sold for amounts below par.

Where the Model Business Corporation Act has been adopted or where corporation laws have been conformed to the guidelines of that Act, there is often no distinction made between par value and amounts in excess of par. In those jurisdictions, the entire proceeds from the sale of stock may be credited to the common stock account without distinction between the stock and the additional paid-in capital accounts. The following example illustrates these concepts.

Example—Treatment of Par and No-Par Stock in a Stock Sale

Facts: A corporation sells 100,000 shares of $5 par common stock for $8 per share cash.

Cash	800,000	
Common stock		500,000
Additional paid-in capital		300,000

Facts: A corporation in a state where the Model Business Corporation Act has been adopted sells 100,000 shares of no-par common stock for $8 per share cash.

Cash	800,000	
Common stock		800,000

Preferred stock will often be assigned a par value because in many cases the preferential dividend rate is defined as a percentage of par value (e.g., 10%, $25 par value preferred stock will have a required annual dividend of $2.50).

Shares Issued to Employees for Services For information on share-based compensation for employees, see the chapters on ASC 718 for guidance on share-based payment transactions with employees and ASC 323 for guidance on accounting for share-based compensation for employees or nonemployees of an equity method investee that provides goods or services to the investee that are used in the investee's operations. (ASC 505-10-25-3)

Stock Subscriptions

Occasionally, particularly in the case of a newly organized corporation, a contract is entered into between the corporation and prospective investors, whereby the investors agree to purchase specified numbers of shares to be paid for over some installment period. These stock subscriptions are not the same as actual stock issuances and the accounting differs.

The amount of stock subscriptions receivable by a corporation is occasionally accounted for as an asset on the statement of financial position and is categorized as current or noncurrent in accordance with the terms of payment. However, in accordance with SEC requirements, entities are required to use a contra equity account approach. Since subscribed shares do not have the rights and responsibilities of actual outstanding stock, the credit is made to a stock subscribed account instead of to the capital stock accounts.

ASC 505-10-45-2 states that a contribution to a company's equity made in the form of a note receivable should generally not be reported as an asset except on the very limited circumstances when there is substantial evidence of both the ability and intent to pay in a reasonably short period of time. Public companies may want to refer to ASC 210-10-S99-1, paragraphs 27 through 29. The ASC notes that the most widespread practice is to report these notes as a reduction of equity. However, if the cash is received prior to the issuance of the financial statements, the note may be reported as an asset. For more on subsequent events, see the chapter on ASC 855.

If the common stock has par or stated value, the common stock subscribed account is credited for the aggregate par or stated value of the shares subscribed. The excess over this amount is credited to additional paid-in capital. No distinction is made between additional paid-in capital relating to shares already issued and shares subscribed for. This treatment follows from the distinction between legal capital and additional paid-in capital. Where there is no par or stated value, the entire amount of the common stock subscribed is credited to the stock subscribed account.

As the amount due from the prospective shareholders is collected, the stock subscriptions receivable account is credited and the proceeds are debited to the cash account. Actual issuance of the shares, however, must await the complete payment of the stock subscription. Accordingly, the debit to common stock subscribed is not made until the subscribed shares are fully paid for and the stock is issued.

The following examples illustrate these concepts.

Examples of Stock Subscription Transactions

1. 10,000 shares of $50 par preferred are subscribed at a price of $65 each; a 10% down payment is received.

Cash	65,000	
Stock subscriptions receivable	585,000	
Preferred stock subscribed		500,000
Additional paid-in capital		150,000

2. 2,000 shares of no-par common shares are subscribed at a price of $85 each, with one-half received in cash.

Cash	85,000	
Stock subscriptions receivable	85,000	
Common stock subscribed		170,000

3. All preferred subscriptions are paid and subscribed preferred shares are issued, and one-half of the remaining common subscriptions are collected in full.

Cash [$585,000 + ($85,000 × .50)]	627,500	
Stock subscriptions receivable		627,500
Preferred stock subscribed	500,000	
Preferred stock		500,000

4. The remaining common subscriptions are collected in full.

Cash ($85,000 × .50)	42,500	
Stock subscriptions receivable		42,500
Common stock subscribed	170,000	
Common stock		170,000

When a subscriber defaults on an obligation under a stock subscription agreement, the accounting will follow the provisions of the state in which the corporation is chartered. In some jurisdictions, the subscriber is entitled to a proportionate number of shares based upon the amount already paid on the subscriptions, sometimes reduced by the cost incurred by the corporation in selling the remaining defaulted shares to other stockholders. In other jurisdictions, the subscriber forfeits the entire investment upon default. In this case, the amount already received is credited to an additional paid-in capital account that describes its source.

Additional Paid-In Capital

Additional paid-in capital represents all capital contributed to a corporation other than that defined as par, stated value, no-par stock, or donated capital. Additional paid-in capital can arise from proceeds received from the sale of common and preferred shares in excess of their par or stated values. It can also arise from transactions related to the following:

- Sale of shares previously issued and subsequently reacquired by the corporation (treasury stock)
- Retirement of previously outstanding shares
- Payment of stock dividends in a manner that justifies the dividend being recorded at the market value of the shares distributed
- Lapse of stock purchase warrants or the forfeiture of stock subscriptions, if these result in the retaining by the corporation of any partial proceeds received prior to forfeiture
- Warrants that are detachable from bonds

- Conversion of convertible bonds
- Other "gains" on the entity's own stock, such as that which results from certain stock option plans

When the amounts are material, the sources of additional paid-in capital should be described in the financial statements.

Examples of Additional Paid-In Capital Transactions

ABC Company issues 2,000 shares of common stock having a par value of $1, of a total price of $8,000. The following entry records the transaction:

Cash	8,000	
Common stock		2,000
Additional paid-in capital		6,000

ABC Company buys back 2,000 shares of its own common stock for $10,000 and then sells these shares to investors for $15,000. The following entries record the buyback and sale transactions, respectively, assuming the use of the cost method of accounting for treasury stock:

Treasury stock	10,000	
Cash		10,000
Cash	15,000	
Treasury stock		10,000
Additional paid-in capital		5,000

ABC Company buys back 2,000 shares of its own $1 par value common stock (which it had originally sold for $8,000) for $9,000 and retires the stock, which it records with the following entry:

Common stock	2,000	
Additional paid-in capital	6,000	
Retained earnings	1,000	
Cash		9,000

ABC Company issues a small stock dividend of 5,000 common shares at the market price of $8 per share. Each share has a par value of $1. The following entry records the transaction:

Retained earnings	40,000	
Common stock		5,000
Additional paid-in capital		35,000

ABC Company previously has recorded $1,000 of stock options outstanding as part of a compensation agreement. The options expire a year later, resulting in the following entry:

Stock options outstanding	1,000	
Additional paid-in capital		1,000

ABC Company sells 2,000 of par $1,000 bonds, as well a 2,000 attached warrants having a market value of $15 each. Pro rata apportionment of the $2,000,000 cash received between the bonds and warrants results in the following entry:

Cash	2,000,000	
Discount on bonds payable	29,557	
Bonds payable		2,000,000
Additional paid-in capital—warrants		29,557

ABC's bondholders convert a $1,000 bond with an unamortized premium of $40 and a market value of $1,016 into 127 shares of $1 par common stock whose market value is $8 per share. This results in the following entry:

Bonds payable	1,000	
Premium on bonds payable	40	
Common stock		913
Additional paid-in capital		127

When the amounts are material, the sources of additional paid-in capital should be described in the financial statements.

Donated Capital

Donated capital can result from an outright gift to the corporation (e.g., a major shareholder donates land or other assets to the company in a nonreciprocal transfer) or may result when services are provided to the corporation.

Donations should be reflected in the income statement, which means that, after the fiscal period has ended and the books have been closed, the effect of donations will be incorporated in the reporting entity's retained earnings. See the chapter on ASC 845, *Nonmonetary Transactions,* for more information.

Retained Earnings

Legal capital, additional paid-in capital, and donated capital collectively represent the contributed capital of the corporation. The other major source of capital is retained earnings, which represents the accumulated amount of earnings of the corporation from the date of inception (or from the date of reorganization) less the cumulative amount of distributions made to shareholders and other charges to retained earnings (e.g., from treasury stock transactions). The distributions to shareholders generally take the form of dividend payments but may take other forms as well, such as the reacquisition of shares for amounts in excess of the original issuance proceeds. The key events impacting retained earnings are:

- Dividends
- Certain treasury stock resales at amounts below acquisition cost
- Certain stock retirements at amounts in excess of book value
- Prior period adjustments
- Recapitalizations and reorganizations

Examples of Retained Earnings Transactions

Merrimack Corporation declares a dividend of $84,000, which it records with the following entry:

Retained earnings	84,000	
Dividends payable		84,000

Merrimack acquires 3,000 shares of its own $1 par value common stock for $15,000, and then resells it for $12,000. The following entries record the buyback and sale transactions respectively, assuming the use of the cost method of accounting for treasury stock:

Treasury stock	15,000	
Cash		15,000
Cash	12,000	
Retained earnings	3,000	
Treasury stock		15,000

Merrimack buys back 12,000 shares of its own $1 par value common stock (which it had originally sold for $60,000) for $70,000 and retires the stock, which it records with the following entry:

Common stock	12,000	
Additional paid-in capital	48,000	
Retained earnings	10,000	
Cash		70,000

Merrimack's accountant makes a mathematical mistake in calculating depreciation, requiring a prior period reduction of $30,000 to the accumulated depreciation account, and corresponding increases in its income tax payable and retained earnings accounts. Merrimack's income tax rate is 35%. It records this transaction with the following entry:

Accumulated depreciation	30,000	
Income taxes payable		10,500
Retained earnings		19,500

Retained earnings are also affected by action taken by the corporation's board of directors. Appropriation serves disclosure purposes and restricts dividend payments, but does nothing to provide any resources for the satisfaction of the contingent loss or other underlying purpose for which the appropriation has been made. Any appropriation made from retained earnings must eventually be returned to the retained earnings account. It is not permissible to charge losses against the appropriation account nor is it to credit any realized gain to that account. The use of appropriated retained earnings has diminished significantly over the years.

If a series of operating losses have been incurred or distributions to shareholders in excess of accumulated earnings have been made, and if there is a debit balance in retained earnings, the account is generally referred to as accumulated deficit.

ASC 505-20, *Stock Dividends and Stock Splits*

Dividends Dividends are the pro rata distribution of earnings to the owners of the corporation. The amount and the allocation between the preferred and common shareholders is a function of:

- the stipulated preferential dividend rate;
- the presence or absence of:
  - a participation feature,
  - a cumulative feature, and
  - arrearages on the preferred stock; and
- the wishes of the board of directors. Dividends, even preferred stock dividends, where a cumulative feature exists, do not accrue.

Dividends only become a liability of the corporation when declared by the board of directors.

Traditionally, corporations were not allowed to declare dividends in excess of the amount of retained earnings. Alternatively, a corporation could pay dividends out of retained earnings and additional paid-in capital but could not exceed the total of these categories (i.e., they could not impair legal capital by the payment of dividends). States that have adopted the Model Business Corporation Act grant more latitude to the directors. Corporations can now, in certain jurisdictions, declare and pay dividends in excess of the book amount of retained earnings if the directors conclude that, after the payment of such dividends, the fair value of the corporation's net assets will still be a positive amount. Thus, directors can declare dividends out of unrealized appreciation that, in certain industries, can be a significant source of dividends beyond the realized and recognized accumulated earnings of the corporation. This action, however, represents a major departure from traditional practice and demands both careful consideration and adequate disclosure.

Three important dividend dates are:

1. The declaration date, when a legal liability is incurred by the corporation
2. The record date, the point in time when a determination is made as to which specific registered stockholders will receive dividends and in what amounts
3. The payment date, to the date when the distribution of the dividend takes place. These concepts are illustrated in the following example:

Example of Dividends

On May 1, 20X1, the directors of River Corp. declared a $.75 per share quarterly dividend on River Corp.'s 650,000 outstanding common shares. The dividend is payable May 25 to holders of record May 15.

May 1	Retained earnings (or dividends)	487,500	
	Dividends payable		487,500
May 15	No entry		
May 25	Dividends payable	487,500	
	Cash		487,500

If a dividends account is used, it is closed to retained earnings at year-end.

Occasionally, what appear to be disproportionate dividend distributions are paid to some, but not all, of the owners of closely held corporations. Such transactions need to be carefully analyzed. In some cases these may actually represent compensation paid to the recipients. In other instances, these may be a true dividend paid to all shareholders on a pro rata basis, to which certain shareholders have waived their rights. If the former, the distribution should not be accounted for as a dividend. It should be accounted for as compensation or some other expense category and included on the income statement. If the latter, the dividend should be "grossed up" to reflect payment on a proportional basis to all the shareholders, with an offsetting capital contribution to the company recognized as having been effectively made by those to whom payments were not made.

Dividends may be made in the form of cash, property, or scrip:

- *Cash dividends* are either a given dollar amount per share or a percentage of par or stated value.
- *Property dividends* consist of the distribution of any assets other than cash (e.g., inventory or equipment).
- *Scrip dividends* are promissory notes due at some time in the future, sometimes bearing interest until final payment is made.

Property Dividends If property dividends are declared, the paying corporation may incur a gain or loss. Since the dividend should be reflected at the fair value of the assets distributed, the difference between fair value and book value is recorded at the time the dividend is declared and charged or credited to a loss or gain account.

Scrip Dividends If a corporation declares a dividend payable in scrip that is interest bearing, the interest is accrued over time as a periodic expense. The interest is not a part of the dividend itself.

Liquidating Dividends Liquidating dividends are not distributions of earnings, but rather a return of capital to the investing shareholders. A liquidating dividend is normally recorded by the declarer through charging additional paid-in capital rather than retained earnings. The exact accounting for a liquidating dividend is affected by the laws of the states where the business is incorporated.

Stock Dividends Stock dividends represent neither an actual distribution of the assets of the corporation nor a promise to distribute those assets. For this reason, a stock dividend is not considered a legal liability or a taxable transaction.

Despite the recognition that a stock dividend is not a distribution of earnings, the accounting treatment of relatively insignificant stock dividends (generally less than 20% to 25% of the outstanding shares prior to declaration) is consistent with it being a real dividend. (ASC 505-20-25-3) Accordingly, retained earnings are debited for the fair market value of the shares to be paid as a dividend, and the capital stock and additional paid-in capital accounts are credited for the appropriate amounts based upon the par or stated value of the shares, if any. A stock dividend declared but not yet paid is classified as such in the stockholders' equity section of the statement of financial position. Because a stock dividend never reduces assets, it cannot be a liability.

The selection of 20% to 25% as the threshold for recognizing a stock dividend as an earnings distribution is arbitrary, but it is based somewhat on the empirical evidence that small stock dividends tend not to result in a reduced market price per share for outstanding shares. The aggregate value of the outstanding shares should not change, but the greater number of shares outstanding after the stock dividend should necessitate a lower per share price. As noted, however, the declaration of small stock dividends tends not to have this impact, and this phenomenon supports the accounting treatment.

Stock Splits When stock dividends are larger in magnitude, it is observed that per-share market value declines after the declaration of the dividend. (ASC 505-20-25-2) In such situations, it would not be valid to treat the stock dividend as an earnings distribution. Rather, logic suggests that it should be accounted for as a split. The precise treatment depends upon the legal requirements of the state of incorporation and upon whether the existing par value or stated value is reduced concurrent with the stock split.

If the par value is not reduced for a large stock dividend and if state law requires that earnings be capitalized in an amount equal to the aggregate of the par value of the stock dividend declared, the event should be described as a stock split effected in the form of a dividend, with a charge to retained earnings and a credit to the common stock account for the aggregate par or stated value. (ASC 505-20-25-3) When the par or stated value is reduced in recognition of the split and state laws do not require treatment as a dividend, there is no formal entry to record the split but merely a notation that the number of shares outstanding has increased and the per share par or stated value has decreased accordingly. (ASC 505-20-25-6) It should be noted that many companies account for stock splits as if they were a large stock dividend. By doing this, par value per share remains unchanged. The concepts of small versus large stock dividends are illustrated in the following examples.

Example of Small Stock Dividend

Assume that stockholders' equity for the Wasatch Corp. on November 1, 20X1, is as follows.

Common stock, $1 par, 100,000 shares outstanding	$ 100,000
Paid-in capital in excess of par	1,100,000
Retained earnings	750,000

Small stock dividend: On November 10, 20X1, the directors of Wasatch Corp. declared a 15% stock dividend, or a dividend of 1.5 shares of common stock for every 10 shares held. Before the stock dividend, the stock is selling for $23 per share. After the 15% stock dividend, each original share worth $23 will become 1.15 shares, each with a value of $20 ($23/1.15). The stock dividend is to be recorded at the market value of the new shares issued, or $300,000 (15,000 new shares at the post-dividend price of $20). The entries to record the declaration of the dividend and the issuance of stock (on November by Wasatch Corp. are as follows:

Nov. 10	Retained earnings	300,000	
	Stock dividends distributable		15,000
	Paid-in capital in excess of par		285,000
Nov. 30	Stock dividends distributable	15,000	
	Common stock, $1 par		15,000

Large stock dividend: Because the focus of the Committee on Accounting Procedure was on small stock dividends, the accounting requirements for governing large stock dividends are less specific than those for small stock dividends. In practice, ASC 505-20-30-3 results in the par or stated value of the newly issued shares being transferred to the capital stock account from either retained earnings or paid-in capital in excess of par.

Example of Large Stock Dividend

On November 10, 20X1, Wasatch Corp. declares a 50% large stock dividend, a dividend of one share for every two held. Legal requirements call for the transfer to capital stock of an amount equal to the par value of the shares issued. Entries for the declaration on November 10 and the issuance of 50,000 new shares (100,000 × .50) on November 30 are as follows:

Nov. 10	Retained earnings	50,000	
	Stock dividends distributable		50,000
	Or		
	Paid-in capital in excess of par	50,000	
	Stock dividends distributable		50,000
Nov. 30	Stock dividends distributable	50,000	
	Common stock, $1 par		50,000

Distributions to Shareholders Having Cash and Stock Components If a corporation makes a distribution to shareholders that allows them to elect to receive their distribution in either cash or shares of an equivalent value, and there is a limitation on the total amount of cash that shareholders can receive, then the stock portion of the distribution is considered a share issuance, not a stock dividend.

ASC 505-30, *Treasury Stock*

Entities often buy back shares in their own stock. There are several reasons for this; among them:

- To increase earnings per share are return an equity
- To provide stock for share-based payments
- To defeat takeover attempts
- To eliminate outside ownership

After buying back shares, entities may retire them or account for them as treasury stock.

Treasury stock consists of a corporation's own stock that has been issued, subsequently reacquired by the firm, and not yet reissued or canceled. Treasury stock does not reduce the number of shares issued but does reduce the number of shares outstanding, as well as total stockholders' equity. These shares are not eligible to receive cash dividends. Reacquired stock that is awaiting delivery to satisfy a liability created by the firm's compensation plan or reacquired stock held in a profit-sharing trust is still considered outstanding and would not be considered treasury stock. In such cases, the stock would be presented as an asset with the accompanying footnote disclosure. Accounting for excesses and deficiencies on treasury stock transactions is governed by ASC 505-30-30.

Three approaches exist for the treatment of treasury stock:

1. Cost,
2. Par value, and
3. Constructive retirement.

Cost Method Under the cost method, the gross cost of the shares reacquired is debited to a contra equity account (treasury stock) for the cost of the reacquisition. The treasury stock account is reported as a deduction from total paid-in capital and retained earnings. The equity accounts that were credited for the original share issuance (common stock, paid-in capital in excess of par, etc.) remain intact. When the treasury shares are reissued, proceeds in excess of cost are credited to a paid-in capital account. When proceeds are below cost, any deficiency is charged to retained earnings (unless paid-in capital from previous treasury share transactions exists, in which case the deficiency is charged to that account, with any excess charged to retained earnings). If many treasury stock purchases are made, a cost flow assumption (e.g., first-in, first-out (FIFO) or specific identification) should be adopted to compute excesses and deficiencies upon subsequent share reissuances. The advantage of the cost method is that it avoids identifying and accounting for amounts related to the original issuance of the shares and is, therefore, the simpler, more frequently used method.

The cost method is most consistent with the one-transaction concept. This concept takes the view that the classification of stockholders' equity should not be affected simply because the corporation was the middle "person" in an exchange of shares from one stockholder to another. In substance, there is only a transfer of shares between two stockholders. Since the original balances in the equity accounts are left undisturbed, the cost method is most acceptable when the firm acquires its stock for reasons other than its retirement, or when its ultimate disposition has not yet been decided.

Par Value Method Under the par value method, the treasury stock account is charged only for the aggregate par (or stated) value of the shares reacquired. Other paid-in capital accounts (excess over par value, etc.) are reported as a deduction in proportion to the amounts recognized upon the original issuance of the shares. The treasury share acquisition is treated almost as a retirement. However, the common (or preferred) stock account continues at the original amount, thereby preserving the distinction between an actual retirement and a treasury share transaction.

When the treasury shares accounted for by the par value method are subsequently resold, the excess of the sale price over par value is credited to paid-in capital. A reissuance for a price below par value does not create a contingent liability for the purchaser. It is only the original purchaser who risks this obligation to the entity's creditors.

Share Retirement Method The constructive retirement method is similar to the par value method, except that the aggregate par (or stated) value of the reacquired shares is charged to the stock account rather than to the treasury stock account. This method is superior when:

- it is management's intention not to reissue the shares within a reasonable time period or
- the state of incorporation defines reacquired shares as having been retired.

In the latter case, the constructive retirement method is probably the only method of accounting for treasury shares that is not inconsistent with the state Business Corporation Act, even if the state law does not necessarily dictate such accounting. Certain states require that treasury stock be accounted for by this method.

The two-transaction concept is most consistent with the par value and constructive retirement methods. First, the reacquisition of the firm's shares is viewed as constituting a contraction of its capital structure. Second, the reissuance of the shares is the same as issuing new shares. There is little difference between the purchase and subsequent reissuance of treasury shares and the acquisition and retirement of previously issued shares and the issuance of new shares.

Treasury shares originally accounted for by the cost method can subsequently be restated to conform to the constructive retirement method. If shares were acquired with the intention that they would be reissued and it is later determined that such reissuance is unlikely (due, for example, to the expiration of stock options without their exercise), then it is proper to restate the transaction.

Example of Accounting for Treasury Stock

1. 100 shares ($50 par value) that were originally sold for $60 per share are later reacquired for $70 each.
2. All 100 shares are subsequently resold for a total of $7,500. To record the acquisition, the entry is:

Cost method			**Par value method**			**Constructive retirement method**		
Treasury stock	7,000		Treasury stock	5,000		Common stock	5,000	
Cash		7,000	Additional paid-in capital—common stock	1,000		Additional paid-in capital—common stock	1,000	
			Retained earnings	1,000		Retained earnings	1,000	
			Cash		7,000	Cash		7,000

To record the resale, the entry is:

Cost method			**Par value method**			**Constructive retirement method**		
Cash	7,500		Cash	7,500		Cash	7,500	
Treasury stock		7,000	Treasury stock		5,000	Common stock		5,000
Additional paid-in capital—treasury stock		500	Additional paid-in capital—common stock		2,500	Additional paid-in capital—common stock		2.500

If the shares had been resold for $6,500, the entry is:

Cost method			**Par value method**			**Share retirement method**		
Cash	6,500		Cash	6,500		Cash	6,500	
Retained earnings*	500		Treasury stock		5,000	Common stock		5,000
Treasury stock		7,000	Additional paid-in capital—common stock		1,500	Additional paid-in capital—common stock		1,500

* *"Additional paid-in capital—treasury stock" or "Additional paid-in capital—retired stock" of that issue would be debited first to the extent it exists.*

Alternatively, under the par or constructive retirement methods, any portion of or the entire deficiency on the treasury stock acquisition may be debited to retained earnings without allocation to paid-in capital. Any excesses will always be credited to an "Additional paid-in capital—retired stock" account. (ASC 505-30-30-6)

The laws of some states govern the circumstances under which a corporation may acquire treasury stock and may prescribe the accounting for the stock. For example, a charge to retained earnings may be required in an amount equal to the treasury stock's total cost. In such cases, the accounting per the state law prevails. Also, some states (including those that have adopted the Model Business Corporation Act) define excess purchase cost of reacquired (i.e., treasury) shares as being "distributions" to shareholders that are no different in nature than dividends. In such cases, the financial statement presentation should adequately disclose the substance of these transactions (e.g., by presenting both dividends and excess reacquisition costs together in the retained earnings statement).

When a firm decides to formally retire the treasury stock, the journal entry is dependent on the method used to account for the stock.

Example of the Cost and Par Value Methods

Using the original sale and reacquisition data from the illustration above, the following entries would be made if the cost and par value methods, respectively, were employed:

Cost method			**Par value method**		
Common stock	5,000		Common stock	5,000	
Additional paid-in capital—common stock	1,000		Treasury stock		5,000
Retained earnings	1,000				
Treasury stock		7,000			

If the constructive retirement method was used to record the treasury stock purchase, no additional entry would be necessary upon the formal retirement of the shares.

After the entry is made, the pro rata portion of all paid-in capital existing for that issue (i.e., capital stock and additional paid-in capital) will have been eliminated. If stock is purchased for immediate retirement (i.e., not put into the treasury) the entry to record the retirement is the same as that made under the constructive retirement method.

In some circumstances, shares held by current stockholders may be donated back to the reporting entity, possibly to facilitate a resale to new owners who will infuse needed capital into the business. In accounting for donated treasury stock, the intentions of management regarding these reacquired shares is key; if these are to simply be retired, the common stock account should be debited for the par or stated value (if par or stated value stock) or the original proceeds received (if no-par, no-stated-value stock). The current fair value of the shares should be credited to the "donated capital" account, and the difference should be debited or credited to a suitably titled paid-in capital account, such as "additional paid-in capital from share donations."

If the donated shares are to be sold (the normal scenario), variations on the par and cost methods of treasury stock accounting can be employed, with "donated capital" being debited and credited, respectively, when shares are received and later reissued, instead of the "treasury stock" account employed in the above illustrations. Note, however, that if the cost method is used, the debit to the donated capital account should be for the fair value of the shares, not the cost (a seeming contradiction). If the constructive retirement method is utilized instead, only a memorandum entry will be recorded when the shares are received; when reissued, the entire proceeds should be credited to "donated capital."

Other Treasury Stock Issues

Takeover Defense as Cost of Treasury Stock In certain instances an entity may incur costs to defend against an unwelcome or hostile attempted takeover. In some cases, in fact, putative acquirers will threaten a takeover struggle in order to extract so-called *greenmail* from the target entity, often effected through a buyback of shares held by the acquirer at a premium over market value. ASC 505-30-30-3 states that the excess purchase price of treasury shares should not be attributed to the shares, but rather should be attributed to the other elements of the transaction and accounted for according to their substance, which could include the receipt of stated or unstated rights, privileges, or agreements. The SEC's position is that such excess is anything over the quoted market price of the treasury shares.

Accelerated Share Repurchase Programs Accelerated share repurchase programs are combinations of transactions that permit an entity to purchase a targeted number of shares immediately, with the final purchase price determined by an average market price over fixed periods of time. Such programs are intended to combine the immediate share retirement benefits (boosting earnings per share, etc.) of tender offers with the market impacts and pricing benefits of disciplined open market stock repurchase programs. (ASC 505-30-25-5)

The ASC states that an entity should account for an accelerated share repurchase program as two separate transactions:

1. As shares of common stock acquired in a treasury stock transaction recorded on the acquisition date, and
2. As a forward contract indexed to its own common stock.
   (ASC 505-30-25-6)

An entity would classify the forward contract in the above example as an equity instrument because the entity will receive cash when the contract is in a gain position but pay cash or stock when the contract is in a loss position. Changes in the fair value of the forward contract would not be recorded, and the settlement of the forward contract would be recorded in equity.

The treasury stock transaction would result in an immediate reduction of the outstanding shares used to calculate the weighted-average common shares outstanding for both basic and diluted (EPS). The effect of the forward contract on diluted EPS would be calculated in accordance with ASC 260.

Own-Share Lending Arrangements Related to Convertible Debt Financing An entity may enter into a share-lending arrangement with an investment bank that is related to a convertible debt offering. (ASC 470-20-05) See the chapter on ASC 470 for more information.

Other Equity Accounts A principle of GAAP financial reporting is that all items of income, expense, gain, or loss (other than transactions with owners) should flow through the income statement. In fact, however, a number of important exceptions have been made, including:

- Translation gains or losses (ASC 830),
- Certain adjustments for minimum pension obligations (ASC 715), and
- Unrealized gains and losses on available-for-sale portfolios of debt or equity investments. (ASC 320)

Hedging gains and losses qualifying under ASC 815 are also deferred for income measurement purposes. ASC 220 established the concept of comprehensive income. Comprehensive income must be reported either in a combined statement with the income statement or as a standalone statement.

Refer to the chapter on ASC 220 for more information.

ASC 505-60, *Spin-offs and Reverse Spin-offs*

Spin-offs One method that is used as a means of reorganizing an entity's operations is through the use of a spin-off. This can involve the transfer of assets that constitute a business, by their holder referred to as the spinnor, into a new legal entity (spinnee), the shares of which are distributed to the spinnor's shareholders. The distribution is nonreciprocal in that the shareholders of the spinnor are not required to surrender any of their stock in the spinnor in exchange for the shares of the spinnee. (ASC 505-60-05-2)

Besides facilitating a reorganization of the reporting entity, a spin-off may also qualify as a nontaxable reorganization with the distribution not being treated as a taxable gain by the spinnor or its shareholders. In addition, if the spinnee stock is subsequently sold by the shareholders, they avoid the effect of the double taxation that would occur if the company sold the company directly and distributed the net proceeds to the stockholders in a taxable cash dividend. (ASC 505-60-05-3)

The accounting rules governing spin-offs and reverse spin-offs are found in ASC 505-60 and ASC 845-10-30.

Further, in accordance with ASC 845-10-30-10, a pro rata distribution to owners of an entity of shares of a subsidiary or other investee entity that has been or is being consolidated or accounted for under the equity method should be considered the equivalent of a spin-off. The distribution of shares of a wholly owned or consolidated subsidiary that constitutes a business to an entity's shareholders is recorded based on the carrying value of the subsidiary. Irrespective of whether the spun-off operations are to be sold immediately following the spin-off, management is not to account for the transaction as a sale of the spinnee followed by a distribution of the proceeds. (ASC 505-60-25-2)

Reverse Spin-offs Under certain circumstances, a spun-off subsidiary/spinnee will function as the continuing entity post-spin-off. When the spin-off of a subsidiary is structured in such a way that the legal form of the transaction does not represent its economic substance, this will be accounted for as a reverse spin-off whereby the legal spinnee is treated as if it were the spinnor for financial reporting purposes. (ASC 505-60-05-4)

The determination of whether reverse spin-off accounting is appropriate is a matter of professional judgment that depends on a careful analysis of all relevant facts and circumstances. The guidance provides indicators to be considered in determining whether a spin-off should be accounted for as a reverse spin-off. No one indicator is to be considered presumptive or determinative:

- *The relative sizes of the legal spinnor and the legal spinnee.* If all other factors are equal, in a reverse spin-off, the legal spinnee/accounting spinnor is larger than the legal spinnor/accounting spinnee. This comparison is to be based on assets, revenues, and earnings of the two entities with no established bright lines that should be applied.
- *The relative fair value of the legal spinnor and the legal spinnee.* All other factors being equal, in a reverse spin-off, the fair value of the legal spinnee/accounting spinnor is greater than the fair value of the legal spinnor/accounting spinnee.
- *Retention of the majority of senior management.* All other factors being equal, in a reverse spin-off, the legal spinnee retains the senior management of the formerly consolidated entity. Senior management is generally understood to include the chairman of the board of directors, chief executive officer, chief operating officer, chief financial officer, the divisional heads that report directly to them, or the executive committee, if applicable.
- *Length of holding period.* All other factors being equal, in a reverse spin-off, the legal spinnee is held for a longer period than the legal spinnor. A proposed or approved plan of sale for one of the separate entities concurrent with the spin-off transaction may assist in the identification of the entity to be sold as the spinnee for accounting purposes.
(ASC 505-60-25-8)

The guidance contains a rebuttable presumption that a spin-off should be accounted for based on its legal form. When the indicators are mixed, significant judgment is required to determine if the rebuttable presumption has been overcome. The determination of the accounting spinnor and spinnee, respectively, has significant implications. In a spin-off, the net book value of the spinnee is treated, in effect, as a dividend distribution to the shareholders of the spinnor. Since the net book value of these entities will differ from each other, the amount of the reduction to retained earnings of the surviving reporting entity (the accounting spinnor) will be affected by this determination. ASC 505-60 offers several examples of fact patterns that support spin-off or reverse spin-off determinations.

Finally, the accounting for a reverse spin-off is further complicated by the fact that the determination of the accounting spinnor and spinnee significantly affects the reporting of discontinued operations in accordance with ASC 360. The accounting spinnee is reported as a discontinued operation by the accounting spinnor if the spinnee is a component of an entity and meets the conditions for such reporting contained in ASC 360.

Disclosure Requirements

See the *Disclosure and Presentation Checklist for Commercial Businesses* at www.wiley.com/go/GAAP2021, for detailed information on disclosures.

Other Sources

See ASC Location—*Wiley GAAP* Chapter	*For information on . . .*
	From ASC 505-10, *Overall*
ASC 220-10-45-1 through 45-17	The required presentation and disclosure related to other comprehensive income.
ASC 470-20	The measurement and recognition as equity of beneficial conversion features of convertible debt and certain preferred stock.
ASC 470-20	The need to allocate proceeds from the sale of debt with stock purchase warrants to the debt and the warrants.
ASC 480	Whether a specific financial instrument shall be classified as equity or outside of the equity classification.
ASC 805-20	Accounting for a registration payment arrangement.
ASC 810-10-45-5	The treatment of shares of a parent held by its subsidiary in the consolidated balance sheet.
ASC 810-10-40-1 through 40-2A	The accounting for the purchase (early extinguishment) of a wholly owned subsidiary's mandatorily redeemable preferred stock.
ASC 815	The potential classification of an embedded derivative as an equity instrument.
ASC 825-20	The accounting for a registration payment arrangement.
	ASC 505-30, *Treasury Stock*
ASC 225-20	The income statement classification requirements applicable to the costs incurred by an entity to defend itself against a takeover attempt or the cost attributed to a standstill agreement.
ASC 260	The determination of the effect of a treasury stock transaction and the effect of a forward contract that may be settled in stock or cash on the computation of earnings per share.
	ASC 505-60, *Spin-offs and Reverse Spin-offs*
ASC 718	Compensation-related consequences of exchanges of share options or other equity instruments or changes to their terms in conjunction with an equity restructuring.

36 ASC 605 REVENUE RECOGNITION

CONCEPTS, RULES, AND EXAMPLES

Subtopics

With the implementation of ASU 2014-09, *Revenue Recognition,* there is no revenue recognition guidance in ASC 605. The topic does provide guidance on losses. ASC 605, *Revenue Recognition*, contains two subtopics:

- ASC 605-20, *Revenue Recognition—Provision for Losses on Separately-Priced Extended Warranty and Product Maintenance Contracts*, which provides guidance on separately priced extended warranty and product maintenance contracts.
- ASC 605-35, *Revenue Recognition—Provision for Losses on Construction-Type and Production-Type Contracts*, which provides guidance on the accounting for a provision for losses on a contract for which a customer provides specifications for the production of facilities or the provision of related services.
(ASC 605-10-05-02)

The following industry Subtopics contain revenue guidance:

- ASC 905-605, *Agriculture—Revenue Recognition*
- ASC 944-605, *Financial Services—Revenue Recognition*
- ASC 954-605, *Health Care Entities—Revenue Recognition*
- ASC 958-605, *Not-for-Profit Entities—Revenue Recognition*
- ASC 980-605, *Regulated Operations—Revenue Recognition*
(ASC 605-10-05-03)

Scope

The guidance in ASC 605-20 applies to:

- Separately extended warranty contracts and
- Product maintenance contracts
  (ASC 605-20-15-2)

The guidance does not apply to:

- Guarantees accounted for as derivatives under ASC 815-10-15
- Product warranties, except the items listed above in ASC 605-20-15-2
- Guarantees required to be accounted for as financial guarantee insurance contracts under the guidance in ASC 944 on insurance.
  (ASC 605-20-15-3)

DEFINITIONS OF TERMS

Source: ASC 605, *Glossaries*, unless otherwise noted. Also see Appendix A, *Definitions of Terms*, for additional terms relevant to this chapter: Contract, Contract Liability, Customer, Revenue

Extended Warranty. An agreement to provide warranty protection in addition to the scope of coverage of the manufacturer's original warranty, if any, or to extend the period of coverage provided by the manufacturer's original warranty.

Product Maintenance Contracts. An agreement to perform certain agreed-upon services to maintain a product for a specified period of time. The terms of the contract may take different forms, such as an agreement to periodically perform a particular service a specified number of times over a specified period of time, or an agreement to perform a particular service as the need arises over the term of the contract.

Separately Priced Contracts. An agreement under which the customer has the option to purchase an extended warranty or a product maintenance contract for an expressly stated amount separate from the price of product.

ASC 605-20, REVENUE RECOGNITION—PROVISION FOR LOSSES ON SEPARATELY PRICED EXTENDED WARRANTY AND PRODUCT MAINTENANCE CONTRACTS

Recognition of Loss

Separately Priced Extended Warranty. Extended warranties provide additional protection beyond that of the manufacturer's original warranty, lengthen the period of coverage specified in the manufacturer's original warranty, or both. Similarly, a product maintenance contract is an agreement for services to maintain a product for a certain length of time. The contract price of the contracts is not included in the original price of the product caused by the contracts. (ASC 605-20-25-1)

Losses on these contracts are recognized immediately if the sum of the expected costs of providing services under the contracts and any asset recognized for the incremental cost of obtaining a contract exceeds the total unearned revenue (contract liability). To determine if a loss exists, the contracts should be grouped in a consistent manner. In contracts within the scope of

ASC 606, the loss should be changed to expense any recognized asset for the incremental costs of obtaining a contract determined under the guidance in ASC 340-40-25-1 through 25-4. If the loss is greater than the recognized asset for the incremental costs of obtaining a contract, the entity should recognize the excess.

ASC 605-35, *CONSTRUCTION-TYPE AND PRODUCTION-TYPE CONTRACTS*

Contract Losses

Where losses are anticipated, they are recognized in the period in which they become evident. (ASC 605-35-25-45)

To determine the amount the entity expects to receive from a contract, the entity should:

- Refer to the principles in ASC 606-10-32-2 through 32-27 to determine the transaction price. In this calculation, entities should ignore ASC 606-10-32-11 through 32-13 on contraining estimates of variable consideration.
- Allocate the transaction price using the guidance in ASC 606-10-32-28 through 41. Adjust that amount to reflect the customer's credit risk. (ASC 605-35-25-46A)

Exhibit Title—Steps to Determine Amount Entity Expects to Receive from a Contract

Determine transaction price
↓
Allocate the price
↓
Adjust for customer's credit risk

Losses on cost-type contracts should be recognized using the contractor's normal cost accounting methods to determine cost overruns. Costs for performance penalties should be included in the loss. (ASC 605-35-48)

Costs included in the calculation of estimated losses should include all the types allocable to a contract under ASC 340-40-25-5 through 25-8. Entities should also consider:

- Variable consideration
- Nonembursable costs on cost-plus contracts
- Change orders that meet the guidance for contract modifications in ASC 606-10-25-10 through 25-13

Combining Contracts

For the purpose of determining the need for a loss provision, a group of contracts may be combined if they meet the criteria in ASC 606-10-25-9. The contracts may include more than one performance obligation. (ASC 605-35-25-7 and 25-10)

37 ASC 606 REVENUE FROM CONTRACTS WITH CUSTOMERS

PERSPECTIVE AND ISSUES

Technical Alert

ASU 2019-08 In November 2019, the FASB issued Accounting Standards Update 2019-08, *Compensation—Stock Compensation (Topic 718) and Revenue from Contracts with Customers (Topic 606) Codification Improvements—Share-Based Consideration Payable to a Customer.* The purpose of the ASU is to provide guidance on measuring share-based payment awards granted to a customer. Relevant changes are included in this chapter. For more information on the ASU, see the chapter on ASC 718.

ASU 2020-05 In June 2020, the FASB issued ASU 2020-05, *Revenue from Contracts with Customers (Topic 606) and Leases (Topic 842): Effective Dates for Certain Entities*. For entities that have not yet issued or made available to be issued financial statements reflecting the adoption of ASC 606, the ASU offers an option to extend the effective date of ASC 606. For those entities that choose the option, the effective date of ASC 606 will be for annual reporting periods beginning after December 15, 2019 and interim reporting periods within annual reporting periods beginning after December 15, 202. Early application is still applicable.

What Is Revenue?

Revenue Influx or other enhancement of assets of an entity or settlements of liabilities (or a combination of both) from delivering or producing goods, rendering services, or other activities that constitute the entity's ongoing major or central operations. (ASC 606-10-20)

Revenue versus Gains The FASB distinguishes revenues from gains. Gains are defined in Statement of Financial Accounting Concept 6 (CON 6), Elements of Financial Statements, as:

> *Increases in equity (net assets) from peripheral or incidental transactions of an entity and from all other transactions and other events and circumstances affecting the entity except those that result from revenues or investments by owners.*

Exhibit—Distinguishing between Revenue and Gains in GAAP

Revenues	Gains
Result from an entity's central operations.	Result from incidental or peripheral activities of the entity.
Are usually earned.	Result from nonreciprocal transactions (such as winning a lawsuit or receiving a gift) or other economic events for which there is no earnings process.
Are reported gross.	Are reported net.

Revenues are commonly distinguished in GAAP from gains for the three reasons listed in the chart below.

Development of Revenue Guidance

Revenue recognition guidance was initially found in:

- CON 5, which specifies that an entity should recognize revenue when realized or realizable and earned, and
- CON 6, which defines revenues as inflows or other enhancements of assets and/or settlements of liabilities from delivering goods or services as a result of the entity's ongoing major or central operations.

GAAP related to revenue developed piecemeal, with specific, often industry-related requirements, but it also had broad concepts. In some cases, the guidance resulted in different accounting for economically similar transactions. Industry guidance often addressed narrow issues and was not built on a common framework. This led to economically similar transactions accounted for differently. Even though there were two hundred separate pieces of guidance, there were still transactions which there was no guidance, in particular, for service transactions.

The Revenue Recognition Project

Driven by the need to achieve simplification and consistency, the FASB and the IASB (the Boards) began a joint project in 2002. The resulting, basically converged, revenue standard, codified in ASC 340-40, 606, and 610, is principles-based, eliminating the existing transaction- and industry-specific guidance. This move away from prescriptive guidance and bright lines increases the need for professional judgment, which in turn increases the need for expanded disclosures. To compensate for the lack of rules, the ASC 606 provides extensive application guidance.

Scope

The scope of ASC 606 is wide. It affects all public companies, nonpublic companies, and nonprofit organizations and applies to contracts with customers.

Scope Exceptions The following are outside the scope of ASC 606:

- Lease contracts in the scope of ASC 840, *Leases*, and ASC 842, *Leases*, when implemented
- Contracts issued within the scope of ASC Topic 944, *Financial Services—Insurance*.
- Financial instruments and other contractual rights or obligations in the scope of:

  - ASC 310, *Receivables*
  - ASC 320, *Investments—Debt Securities*
  - ASC 321, *Investments in Equity Securities (when implemented)*
  - ASC 323, *Investments—Equity-Method and Joint Ventures*
  - ASC 325, *Investments—Other*
  - ASC 405, *Liabilities*
  - ASC 470, *Debt*
  - ASC 815, *Derivatives and Hedging*
  - ASC 825, *Financial Instruments*
  - ASC 860, *Transfers and Servicing*
- Guarantees other than product or service warranties, in the scope of ASC 460, *Guarantees* (Entities should look to ASC 815 for guidance on guarantees accounted for as derivatives.)
- Nonmonetary exchanges between entities in the same line of business to facilitate sales to customers or potential customers.
  (ASC 606-10-15-2)

Revenue from transactions or events that do not arise from contracts with customers is not in the scope of ASC 606, such as:

- Dividends
- Non-exchange transactions, like donations or contribution
- Changes in regulatory assets and liabilities arising from alternative revenue programs for rate-regulated activities in the scope of ASC 930, *Regulated Operations*
  (ASC 606-10-15-3)

The guidance included in ASC 340-40 applies only if the costs are incurred related to a contract under ASC 606. (ASC 606-10-15-5) The guidance in topic ASC 610 specifies ASC 606s for income that is not in the scope of ASC 606, including gains and losses from the derecognition of nonfinancial assets and from gains and losses on involuntary conversions.

Contracts Partially in Scope If a contract is partially within the scope of ASC 606 and partially within the scope of other guidance, the entity should apply the other guidance first. That is, if the other standard specifies how to separate or initially measure parts of the contract, then the entity should apply those requirements first. The remaining portion is accounted for under the requirements of the new Standard. If the other standard does not have applicable separate and/or initial measurement guidance, the entity should apply the revenue standard to separate and/or initially measure the contract. (ASC 606-10-15-4)

Sale or Transfer of Nonfinancial Assets Transactions that are not part of the entity's ordinary activities, such as the sale of property, plant, and equipment, nonetheless fall under certain aspects of ASC 606. An entity involved in such activities applies the guidance related to transfer of control and measurement of the transaction price to evaluate the timing and amount of the gain or loss. Entities should also apply the guidance in ASC 606 to determine whether the parties are committed to perform under the contract and, therefore, whether a contract exists.

Objective of ASC 606

The objective of ASC 606 is:

. . . to establish the principles that an entity shall apply to report useful information to users of financial statements about the nature, amount, timing, and uncertainty of revenue and cash flows arising from a contract with a customer. (ASC 606-10-10-1)

ASC 606 provides principles to help entities meet this objective when measuring and reporting on revenue.

Core Principle and the Five Steps of the Revenue Recognition Model

ASC 606 takes an asset and liability approach and articulates a core principle on which the new guidance is based.

Core Principle

. . . recognize revenue to depict the transfer of promised goods or services to customers in an amount that reflects the consideration to which the entity expects to be entitled in exchange for those goods or services. (FASB ASC 606-10-05-3 et al.)

This core principle reflects the asset and liability approach that underlies ASC 606. This approach recognizes revenue based on changes in assets and liabilities. The Boards believe this is consistent with the conceptual framework approach to recognition and brings more consistency to the measurement compared with the "earned and realized" criteria in previous standards.

Example: Application of the Core Principle through the Five Steps

Assume that on May 1, 20X1, ACME enters into a contract to sell 50 desktop computers to XYZ Company for CU 50,000 with delivery promised on July 15, 20X1. On July 31, 20X1, ACME completes a performance obligation by delivering all the computers and makes the following entries:

	Debit		Credit
Accounts Receivable CU	50,000	Revenue	50,000
Cost of Goods Sold CU	30,000	Inventory	30,000

On August 15, 20X1, the customer makes the payment and ACME makes the following entry:

	Debit		Credit
Cash	CU 50,000	Accounts Receivable	50,000

Under ASC 606, entities account for assets and liabilities arising from customer contracts. Entities must carefully analyze their contracts for

- terms,
- measurements, and
- promises.

Five Steps Achieve the core principle, entities should follow these five steps:

1. Identify the contract with customer. (ASC 606-10-25-1 through 25-13)
2. Identify performance obligations (promises) in the contract. (ASC 606-10-25-1 through 25-13)
3. Determine the transaction price. (ASC 606-10-32-2 through 32-27)
4. Allocate the transaction price. (ASC 606-10-32-28 through 25-41)
5. Recognize revenue when or as the entity satisfies a performance obligation by transferring promised goods or services to a customer. (ASC 606-10-25-23 through 25-30)

Exhibit Overview and Application of the Five Steps in the Revenue Recognition Project

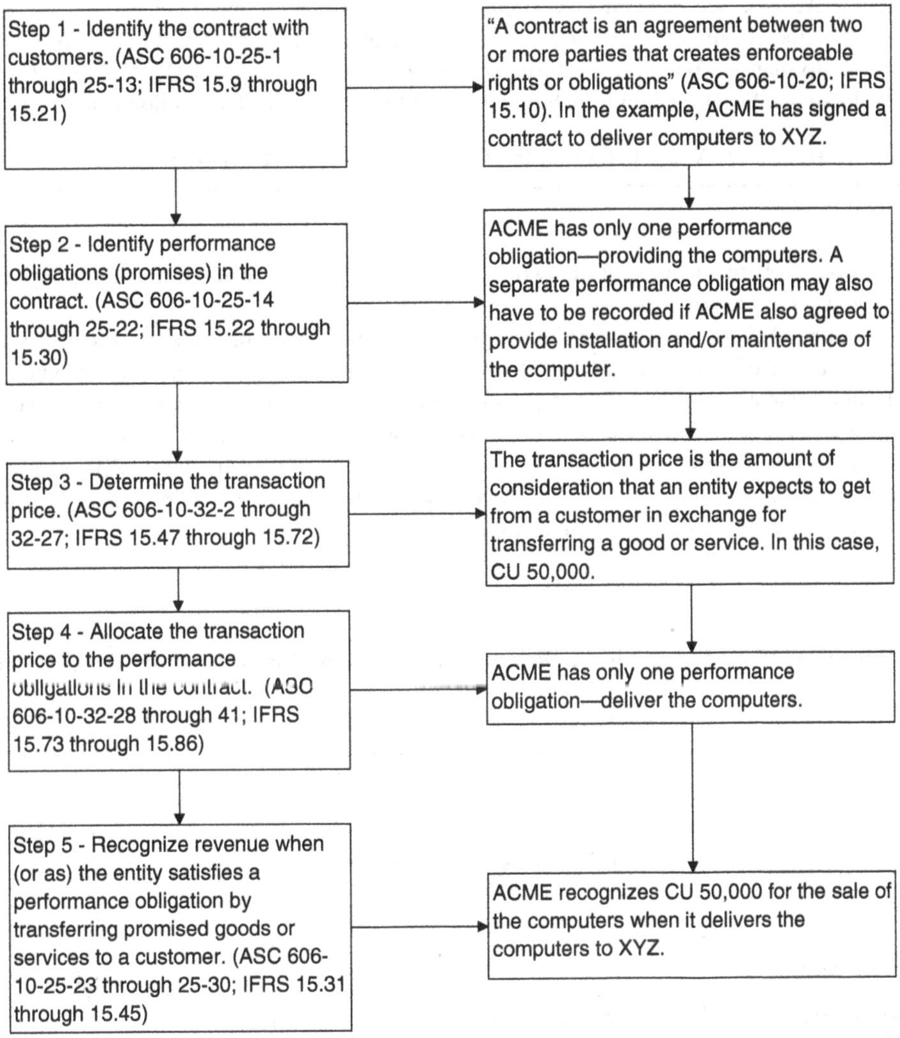

In reviewing a transaction, each of the five steps above may not be needed, and they may not always be applied sequentially. Be aware that ASC 606 is not organized by these five steps, but the Boards believe the steps offer a methodology for entities to use when deciding the appropriate accounting for a transaction. Although the model is based on an assets and liabilities or control approach as opposed to the risk and rewards approach under previous standards, risk and rewards are a factor when determining control for point in time revenue recognition.

Each of the steps encompasses new concepts, and entities should carefully analyze their contracts with customers as they transition to the new guidance.

DEFINITIONS OF TERMS

Source: ASC 606. See Appendix A, *Definitions of Terms*, for terms relevant to this chapter: Award, Contract, Contract Asset, Contract Liability, Customer, Grant Date, Lease, Not-for-Profit Entity, Performance Condition, Performance Objective, Probable (2nd Def.), Public Business Entity, Revenue, Service Condition, Standalone Selling Price, and Transaction Price.

STEP 1: IDENTIFY THE CONTRACT WITH THE CUSTOMER

Overview

Contract Agreement between two or more parties that creates enforceable rights and obligations. (ASC 606-10-20)

To apply ASC 606, entities should first determine whether a contract is specifically excluded from the guidance in ASC 606 under the scope exceptions detailed earlier in this chapter. After determining that a contract is not specifically excluded, entities must identify the contracts that meet the criteria in Step 1 of the revenue recognition model. If the entity determines a contract does not meet the criteria for Step 1, the contract does not exist for purposes of ASC 606 and the entity does not apply Steps 2 through 5. A contract as articulated in ASC 606 must exist before an entity can recognize revenue from a customer.

Exhibit: Overview of Step 1 of the Revenue Recognition Model—Identify the Contracts

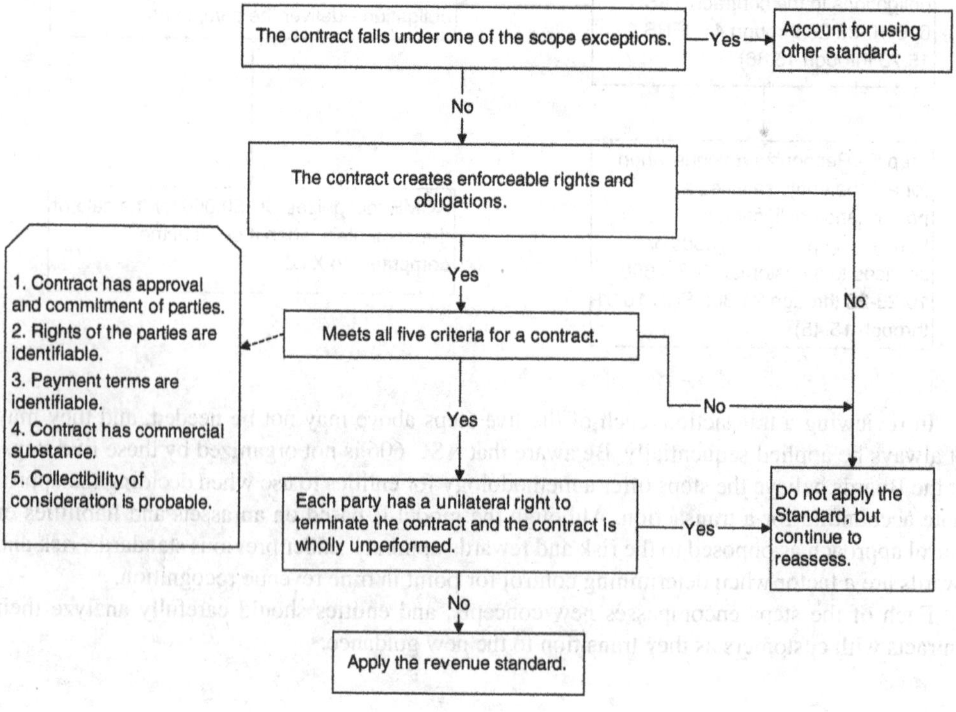

Assessing Whether Contracts Are within the Scope of ASC 606

To be within the scope of the revenue standard, and in accordance with the definition of contracts in ASC 606, the agreement must not fall under one of the scope exceptions and must:

- Create enforceable rights and obligations, and
- Meet the five criteria listed in ASC 606.

Enforceable Rights and Obligations The enforceability of the contract:

- Is a matter of law
- Varies across legal jurisdictions, industries, and entities
- May vary within an entity
- May depend on the class of customer or nature of goods or services.

Determining whether an arrangement has created enforceable rights is a matter of law and evaluating the legal enforceability of the contract can be particularly challenging. This is particularly true if multiple jurisdictions are involved. Entities also need to consider whether, in order to comply with jurisdictional or trade regulation, a written contract is required. Significant judgment may be involved for some cases and qualified legal counsel may need to be consulted.

The FASB clarified that even though the contract must be legally enforceable to be within the scope of the guidance, the performance obligations within the contract may not be legally enforceable, but may be based on the reasonable expectations of the customer.

The Five Contract Criteria ASC 606 lists five criteria that are assessed at contract inception and that must be met for agreements to be considered contracts subject to the guidance of ASC 606. A contract exists if:

1. The contract has approval and commitment of the parties
2. Rights of the parties are identifiable
3. Payment terms are identifiable
4. The contract has commercial substance
5. Collectibility of *substantially all of the consideration* is probable
   (ASC 606-10-25-1)

The five criteria are essentially a financial accounting definition of a contract. The entity needs to exercise judgment when applying the criteria. The entity must also be aware that the parties may enter into amendments or side agreements that change the substance of the contract. So, it is important to understand the entire contract, including the amendments and side agreements. A contract that has enforceable rights and obligations between two or more parties is within the scope of the revenue standard when *all* five of the above criteria are met.

The assessment of the fifth criterion, collectibility, must reflect the customer's *ability and intent* to pay. This criterion acts as a collectibility threshold. A more detailed discussion of the collectibility threshold can be found below.

The Contract Has Approval and Commitment of the Parties The approval of the parties can be

a. written,
b. oral, or
c. implied by the entity's customary business practice.

This criterion is included because if not approved, a contract may not be legally enforceable. ASC 606 focuses on the enforceability of the contract rather than its form (oral, written, or implied). An entity may take into consideration its past business practices when assessing this criterion. For example, an entity that has a practice of performing based on oral agreements may determine that those oral agreements meet the requirement. If an oral agreement meets the requirement, an entity may need to account for the contract as soon as performance begins rather than wait for a signed agreement.

Example: Oral Contract

Scan Safe provides virus scanning services over the Internet. A customer calls to sign up for the service and provides the sales representative with credit card authorization. The customer agrees to the terms, and the service begins immediately. The oral agreement that Scan Safe and the customer have entered into is legally enforceable in its jurisdiction. The agreement meets the criteria for a contract with a customer, and the agreement falls under the guidance in ASC 606.

Example: Product Delivered, but No Written Contract Exists

Office Supplier usually delivers products based on a written contract. However, a regular customer had a flood that destroyed furniture and computers. Because of the customer's urgent need, Office Supplier provides replacement products without a written contract. To determine whether an enforceable contract exists even though Office Supplier has deviated from its usual business practice and has no written agreement, Office Supplier must determine if it has legally enforceable rights and the oral agreement meets all five of the criteria to be a contract.

Automatic Renewal. Some contracts may automatically renew. Entities should applyASC 606 to the period for which the parties have enforceable rights and obligations.

Example: Contract Extension

LMS provides web hosting services to Publishing Company. The written contract calls for Publishing Company to pay CU 1,500 per month for the services. The contract expires on June 30, 20X1, and contains no provision for automatic extensions. There are no performance issues and no expected changes in performance requirements. While the entities negotiate new payment terms, LMS continues to provide the hosting services for July and August and Publishing Company continues to pay CU 1,500 per month. The entities sign a new contract on August 27, 20X1, that requires Publishing Company to pay CU 2,000 per month.

In this case, a contract appears to exist because LMS performed and Publishing Company paid for the service under the terms of the previous contract. LMS should analyze the contract for legal enforceability and recognize revenue accordingly.

Commitment to Perform It is not necessary for the parties to be committed to fulfilling all of their rights and obligations, but there must be sufficient evidence that the parties are substantially committed.

Termination Clauses and Wholly Unperformed Contracts When determining the parties' commitment to perform under a contract, termination clauses are a key element to consider. Termination clauses are an indicator of both parties' commitment to perform under the contract. The contract *does not exist*, for the purposes of the revenue standard, if

- each party has a unilateral right to terminate, and
- the contract is wholly unperformed without compensating the other party.

However, the contract does exist for the purposes of the revenue standard if only one party has the right to terminate the contract without penalty. If both parties have a unilateral right to terminate the agreement, then the agreement should be treated as a month-to-month contract. Where a substantive termination clause exists, the contract term is the stated contract term or, if earlier, the date when the termination payment is no longer due.

A contract is considered *wholly unperformed* if the entity has

- not satisfied any part of its performance obligation,
- not transferred any of the promised goods or services to the customer, and
- the customer has not paid, or is obligated to pay, any other consideration under the contract. (ASC 606-10-25-4)

Example: Meeting the Termination Criteria

Office Supplier enters into an agreement with Business Center to supply furniture and computers for an office complex under development in an economically disadvantaged country. Business Center agrees to pay an advance deposit. Office Supplier determines that the agreement does not meet the collectibility criteria. Office Supplier determines that it has fulfilled its performance obligations and Business Center has paid the consideration it was obligated to pay under the contract. The contract does not meet the wholly unperformed criteria for a terminated contract, therefore, the contract has not been terminated.

Rights of the Parties Are Identifiable This criterion is relatively straightforward and is necessary in order to assess when the entity has transferred control of the goods or services. If the rights of each party cannot be identified, revenue cannot be recognized.

Payment Terms Are Identifiable This criterion is necessary to determine the transaction price. It does not mean that the transaction price has to be fixed or explicitly stated. There must be an enforceable right to payment and sufficient information to estimate the transaction price. For more on determining the transaction price, see Chapter 3.

The Contract Has Commercial Substance Designed to prevent entities from artificially inflating revenue by transferring goods back and forth, this criterion requires the entity to demonstrate a substantive business purpose for the transaction. Commercial substance means that the contract is expected to change the risk, timing, or amount of the entity's future cash flows. No changes in cash flow likely indicate there is no commercial substance. This criterion also applies to noncash transactions. A noncash transaction may have commercial substance because it might result in reduced cash outflows in the future.

Collectibility Threshold

To be considered a contract with a customer under ASC 606, it must be probable that the entity will collect the consideration to which it is entitled. In addition, under legacy guidance, collectibility is evaluated when revenue is recognized, whereas in the revenue standard, collectibility is assessed when determining whether a contract exists. The Codification considers the customer's credit risk an important part of determining whether a contract is valid. It is not an indicator of whether revenue is recognized but an indicator of whether the customer is able to meet its obligation. (ASC 606-10-25-1(e))

The Codification defines probable as "likely to occur." This is generally interpreted as a 75 to 80% probability. The collectibility threshold is similar to that in ASC 985-605, *Software: Revenue Recognition*. The threshold is slightly higher than that in SEC SAB Topic 13, which is "reasonably assured."

Assessing Collectibility To be accounted for under ASC 606, a contract must have commercial substance. To have commercial substance, the consideration must be collectible. So, the underlying objective of the collectibility assessment is to determine if there is a substantive transaction.

Collectibility is a "gating" question designed to prevent entities from applying ASC 606 to problematic contracts and recognizing revenue and an impairment loss at the same time.

Judgment Collectibility is partly a forward-looking assessment and requires the entity to look at all the factors and circumstances including the entity's customary business practices and knowledge of the customer.

Timing of assessment Collectibility must be evaluated, like the other criteria, at contract inception, but also must be re-evaluated when significant facts and circumstances change.

Collectibility = intent and ability to pay Collectibility refers only to the company's credit risk—the customer's intent and ability to pay—and in making the collectability assessment not to any other uncertainty or risk. Credit risk is the risk that the entity will not be able to collect the contract consideration to which it is entitled from the customer.

Consider only transaction price Entities should be aware that collectibility relates to the *transaction* price, a term introduced in the revenue standard, not the *contract* price. The transaction price is the amount the entity expects to be entitled to. The transaction price is not adjusted for credit risk. The entity may have to consider transaction price in Step 3 before making a conclusion regarding Step 1's collectibility threshold.

Entities should take into account factors that might mitigate credit risk such as:

- Payment terms, like up-front payments, or
- The ability to stop transferring goods or services.

A factor that should not be considered is the ability of the entity to repossess an asset. (ASC 606-10-55-3c)

Variable consideration in the transaction price The revenue standard requires an entity to consider whether the price is variable because if so the entity may wind up offering a price concession. The collectibility assessment is made after taking into account any price concessions that may be made to the customer. The transaction price may be less than the stated contract price if the entity intends to offer a price concession.

Basis of assessment may be less than total consideration The assessment is not necessarily based on the entire amount of consideration for the entire duration of the contract. For example, the entry may have the ability and expectation to stop transferring goods or services if the customer stops paying consideration when due. In another example, if an entity expects to receive only partial payment for performance, the contract may still meet the contract criteria. The expected shortfall is similar to a price concession. The entity must exercise its judgment to determine if the partial payment is:

- An implied price concession
- An impairment loss
- A contract lacking commercial substance

When this occurs, the entity must exercise significant judgment to determine the proper accounting.

Example: Assessing Collectibility—Implied Price Concession

ACME enters into a contract to sell 1,000 desks to a customer for CU 200,000. The customer is based in a geographic area suffering significant economic difficulty. This is a new customer and a new region for ACME. ACME expects that it will not be able to collect the full contract amount. However, because it wants to establish a customer base in the region, ACME enters into the contract expecting to accept a lower amount of consideration. With the implied price concession, ACME expects to be entitled to CU 160,000. Considering the customer's intent and ability to pay, and the region's economic difficulty, ACME concludes that it is probable that it will collect the CU 160,000.

Example: Assessing Collectibility—Meeting the Collectibility Threshold

Truman Construction, a real estate developer, enters into a contract to sell Pearl River, Inc. a commercial building in the downtown area. The consideration is CU 1,000,000 broken down as follows:

- CU 50,000 nonrefundable fee paid at the contract inception, and
- CU 950,000 financed long term by Truman Construction.

The financing is provided on a nonrecourse basis. This means that if Pearl River defaults on the debt, Truman can repossess the property and keep the deposit, but cannot seek further compensation. Pearl River intends to open an Asian fusion restaurant in the facility. Pearl River has business experience from its previous import–export endeavor, but this is its first venture into the highly competitive restaurant industry. Truman evaluates the facts and circumstances of the agreement. It determines that the factors below put the entity's intent and ability to pay substantially all of the consideration in doubt and, therefore, the agreement does not meet the collectibility threshold:

- The debt will be repaid by proceeds from the risky restaurant venture.
- Pearl River has no other assets or income to repay the debt.
- Pearl River's liability under the terms of the loan is limited because the loan is nonrecourse.

Truman does not recognize the receivable from the real estate asset. Because the contract does not meet the collectibility threshold, the contract does not meet the criteria for a contract and is out of scope of ASC 606. So, initially Truman

- monitors the situation to determine if, and when, the contract does meet the contract criteria, and
- looks to the guidance in ASC 606-10-25-7 through 25-8; IFRS 15.15–16 to determine the accounting for the nonrefundable deposit.

Contract Recognition

The Exhibit below summarizes the qualifications of contracts that fall under the guidance in ASC 606 and those that do not.

Exhibit—Contracts In and Out of Scope

Apply ASC 606 if the contract creates enforceable rights and obligations and:	Do not apply ASC 606 to a contract if:
1. The contract has approval and commitment of the parties. 2. The rights of the parties are identifiable. 3. Payment terms are identifiable. 4. The contract has commercial substance. 5. Collectibility of consideration is probable. (ASC 606-10=32-17)	Each party has unilateral right to terminate contract *and* The contract is wholly unperformed.

A contract that meets the qualifications for recognition under ASC 606:

- Gives the entity the right to receive consideration, and
- Creates obligations for the entity to deliver goods and services

This combination of rights and obligations gives rise to net assets or net liabilities. These assets and liabilities are not recognized until one or both parties perform. Entities must monitor contracts for when performance has begun. Once performance has begun, a contract that is enforceable and meets the five contract criteria exists for purposes of the revenue standard. Even if a contract has not been signed, entities may determine that a contract exists and may need to account for a contract as soon as performance begins rather than delay revenue recognition for an executed contract. In some cases, timing of revenue recognition may differ from that under legacy standards.

If a contract does not meet the five criteria listed previously and the performance is not complete, the entity recognizes a liability for any nonrefundable amounts received. (ASC 606-10-25-8) This can be contrasted with current standards where revenue may be recognized in the amount of cash received. The section on Step 5 has a detailed discussion of recognizing revenue, contract assets, and contract liabilities.

Arrangements Where Contract Criteria Are Not Met

If the entity receives consideration from the customer, but the contract fails Step 1, the entity should apply what is sometimes referred to as the alternate recognition model and recognize the consideration received only when *one* of the following occurs:

a. The entity has no remaining obligations to transfer goods or services to the customers, and all or substantially all of the consideration promised by the customer has been received by the entity and is nonrefundable,
b. The contract has been terminated, and the consideration received from the customer is nonrefundable, or
c. The entity has transferred control of the goods or services to which the consideration that has been received relates, the entity has stopped transferring goods and services to the customer and has no obligation to transfer additional goods or services, and the consideration received from the customer is nonrefundable.
(ASC 606-10-25-7)

If an arrangement does not meet the contract criteria in the revenue standard, consideration received should be accounted for as a liability until:

- "a," "b," or "c" above occur, or
- The arrangement meets the contract criteria.

The liability is measured at the amount of consideration received from the customer. The liability represents the entity's obligations to:

- Transfer goods or services in the future, or
- Refund the consideration received.
(ASC 606-10-25-8)

Reassessment When an arrangement has been assessed and is considered a contract under the revenue standard, the entity is not required to reassess the contract unless there is an indication of a significant change. A significant change might be, for example, a significant deterioration in the customer's ability to pay. (ASC 606-10-25-5) In that case, the entity needs to assess whether it is probable the customer will pay the consideration for the remaining goods or services. In contrast, if the arrangement is not initially considered a contract and if there is an indication that there has been a significant change in facts and circumstances, the entity should reassess to determine whether the criteria are met subsequently. (ASC 606-10-25-6) The entity applies the provisions of ASC 606 from the date the criteria are met.

Only the rights and obligations that have *not* transferred are reassessed. Therefore, a reassessment will not result in any reversal of revenue, receivables, or assets already recognized. Those assets are assessed for impairment under the relevant financial instruments standard. The entity does not recognize any additional revenue from the agreement.

TRG members have acknowledged the assessment of whether significant changes have occurred that require a reassessment of collectibility or even a determination that a contract no longer exists underASC 606 will be situation specific and require judgment.

The Portfolio Approach and Combining Contracts

The revenue standard includes:

- A practical expedient for combining groups of contracts, and
- A requirement to combine contacts.

A Practical Expedient An entity normally applies the revenue standard to individual contracts. However, in certain circumstances, an entity may use a practical expedient and apply the revenue standard to a group of contracts. This expedient allows for the portfolio approach—applying the revenue standard to a group of contracts or performance obligations under these conditions:

- The contracts must have similar characteristics, *and*
- The entity must reasonably expect that the effects of applying the guidance to a portfolio would not differ materially from applying it to individual contracts or performance obligations.
  (ASC 606-10-10-4)

Combination of Contracts Required ASC 606 *requires* a combination of contracts under certain circumstances. Entities have to assess existing contracts to determine whether combination is required and should also be mindful of the combination requirement when writing new contracts. The decision to combine contracts is made at the inception of the contracts.

The entity needs to assess whether the substance of the contract is that the pricing or economics of the contracts are interdependent. ASC 606 offers guidance to help make that judgment. The contracts should be accounted for as a single contract when the contracts are entered into at or near the same time with the same customers or parties related to the customer and if *any* of the following conditions are met:

a. The entity negotiates the contracts as a package with a single commercial objective.
b. The amount of consideration to be paid in the contract depends on the price or performance of the other contract.
c. The goods or services promised in the contracts (or some goods or services promised in the contracts) constitute a single performance obligation.
   (ASC 606-10-25-9)

The entity should apply the guidance on identifying performance obligations when assessing "c." (See information later in this chapter.)

The fact that multiple contracts are negotiated at the same time is not sufficient evidence to demonstrate that the contracts represent a single arrangement. (ASU 2014-09 BC73)

Tip: The entity needs to exercise significant judgment in determining what constitutes "at or near the same time." If the time period between execution of the contracts is short, contracts may meet the "at or near the same time" condition. Also, subsequent promises not considered at contract inception are generally accounted for as contract modifications.

If the criteria are met, contracts between the same customer or related parties of the customer should be combined. Related parties are those defined in the guidance, ASC 850, *Related Parties Disclosures*. See the chapter on ASC 850 for a list of related parties.

Assessing Collectability of a Portfolio of Contracts An issue was raised with the TRG regarding how to deal with situations in a portfolio of homogeneous contracts where some customers will pay amounts owed, but the entity has historical experience indicating that some customers will not pay the full consideration. In that case, the entity should record revenue, but separately evaluate the contract asset or receivable for impairment. The entity will have to exercise judgment regarding whether to record a bad debt expense or reduce revenue for an anticipated price concession.

Identifying the Customer

Customer: A party that has contracted with an entity to obtain goods or services that are an output of the entity's ordinary activities in exchange for consideration. (ASC 606-10-20)

Collaborative Arrangements A collaborative arrangement is not in ASC 606 unless the collaboration meets the definition of a customer. In most cases, the identification of the customer is straightforward. However, the FASB decided not to offer additional application guidance and, therefore, a collaborative arrangement requires more careful analysis of the facts and circumstances. For example, an arrangement with a counterparty where both parties share the risks and benefits will most likely not result in a counterparty meeting the definition of customer, and, therefore, the arrangement will not fall under the revenue standard. (ASC 606-10-15-3) On the other hand, an arrangement where the entity is selling a good or service, even if the arrangement is labeled a collaboration, will likely fall under the scope of the revenue standard.

It is also possible that portions of the contract will be a collaboration, while other portions will be a contract with a customer. The latter portion will be in the scope of the revenue standard. After a thorough analysis of the agreement, the entity should decide whether to apply the revenue standard and/or other guidance, such as ASC 808, *Collaborative Arrangements*.

Example: Collaborative Arrangement

A company in the biotech industry enters into an agreement with a company in the pharmaceutical industry to share equally in the revenue from work on the development of a specific new drug. If the companies agree to simply work together, this collaborative arrangement is not in the scope of the revenue standard because there is no customer. If, on the contrary, the biotech company is selling its compound to the pharmaceutical company, then the arrangement is likely in the scope of ASC 606.

Arrangements with Multiple Parties There are cases where multiple parties are involved in the transaction. For example, pharmaceutical companies provide products to customers and parts of the fees are paid by an insurer and the remaining fees are paid by the customer. Or, manufacturers issue coupons directly to the consumer and reimburse the retailer for the coupons.

The entity must also determine if it is the principal or agent in the transaction. This matters because the principal recognizes the revenue for the gross amount, and the agent recognizes the transaction at net—the amount that the entity expects to retain after paying the other party for goods or services provided. Principal versus agent guidance is discussed later in this chapter.

STEP 2: IDENTIFYING THE PERFORMANCE OBLIGATIONS

Performance Obligation A promise in a contract with a customer to transfer to the customer either:

1. A good or service (or a bundle of goods and services) that is distinct
2. A series of goods or services that are substantially the same and that have the same pattern of transfer to the customer
   (ASC 606-10-20)

Overview

The purpose of identifying the performance obligations in a contract is to establish the unit of account to which the transaction price should be allocated. The accounting unit affects when and how revenue should be recognized. Because the revenue recognition model is an allocated transaction price model, identifying a meaningful unit of account is critical. Once the performance obligations are identified, the entity can then assess whether they are immaterial.

ASC 606 uses the term "performance obligation" to distinguish obligations to provide goods or services to a customer from other obligations. Although it is a new term, "performance obligation" is similar to the notions of deliverables, components, or elements of a contract in legacy guidance. In the definition above, ASC 606 essentially provides two categories of performance obligations:

1. A distinct good or service, and
2. A series of goods or services with the same pattern of transfer.

This chapter examines both.

To apply Step 2 of the revenue standard, at the inception of the contract, the entity should assess the contract and:

- Identify all promised goods or services or bundle of goods or services, and then
- Identify the contract's performance obligations.

The purpose of the first part of the assessment is to identify the promises in the contract, taking note of terms and customary business practices. The entity must identify all promises, even if they seem inconsequential or perfunctory. An entity is not required to assess whether promised goods or services are performance obligations if they are immaterial in the context of the contract. (ASC 606-10-25-16A) Materiality should be assessed in the context of the arrangement as a whole, and the quantitative and qualitative nature of the promised goods or services should be considered.

In the second part of the assessment, the entity determines which of those promises are performance obligations that should be accounted for separately. Some contracts contain single performance obligations and are relatively straightforward. Multiple elements in a contract may present more challenges.

Exhibit: Overview of Step 2—Identifying the Performance Obligation

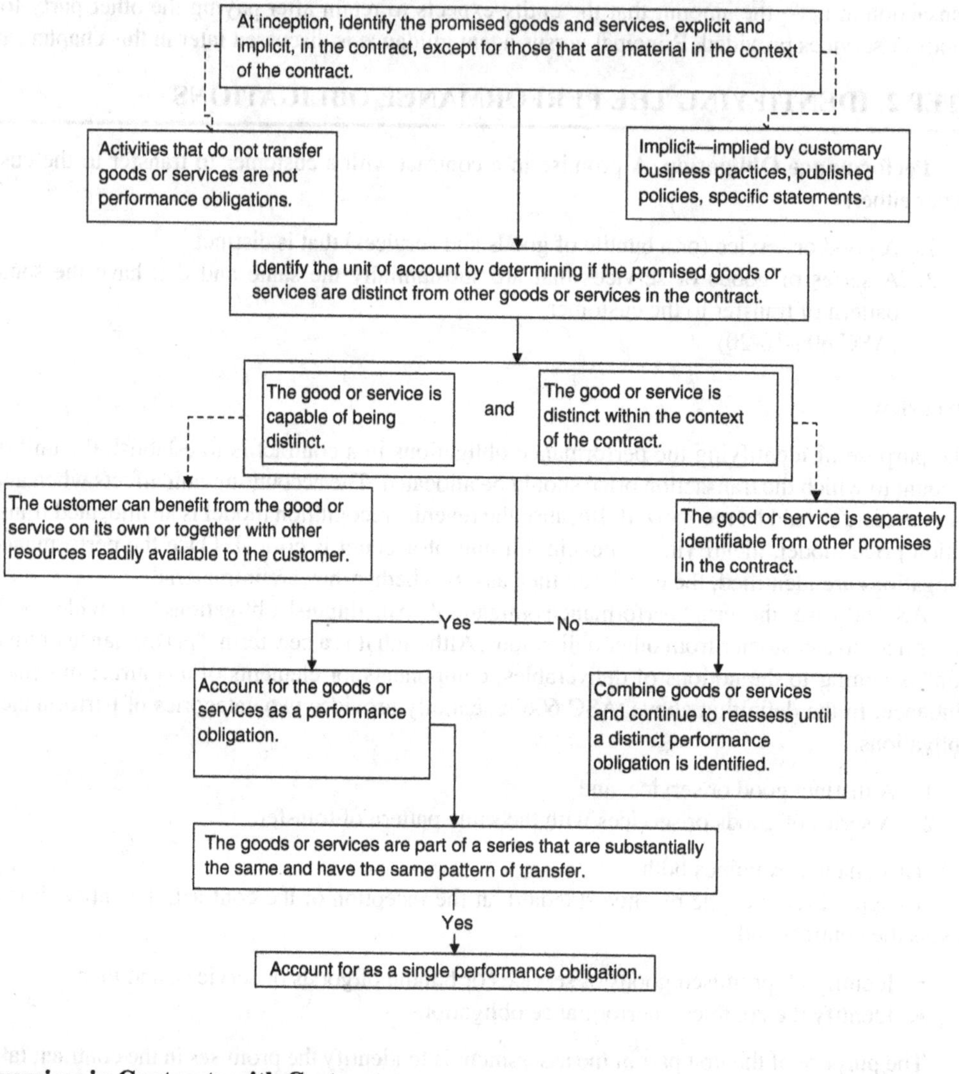

Promises in Contracts with Customers

When identifying the promises in a contact, the entity must identify not only the explicit promises, but also the implicit promises and those activities associated with the contracts that do not meet the criteria for performance obligations.

Promises to provide goods or services are performance obligations even if they are satisfied by another party.

Implicit Promises In addition to promised goods or services explicitly detailed in the contract, a contract may include implicit promises for goods or services. Promises are normally specified, but may include those implied by, for example:

- Customary business practices of a particular industry,
- An entity's published policies, and
- Specific statements.

These implicit promises may create a reasonable expectation on the part of the customer that the entity will transfer a good or service. (ASC 606-10-25-16) It is important, therefore, to understand the entity's customary business practices, marketing materials, and representations made during contract negotiations. The entity must determine if the customer has a valid or reasonable expectation that the entity will provide a good or service.

Constructive performance obligation As noted in the section on Step 1, the customer's expectation may arise from a constructive performance obligation outside of a written contract. So, in evaluating whether a reasonable expectation exists, the entity must consider industry norms, past business practice, etc. Examples of constructive performance obligations are, for instance, customer loyalty points, free handsets provided by telecommunication companies, or free maintenance with the purchase of a car. These kinds of implied promises may not be enforceable by law, and the entity itself may consider them marketing incentives or incidental to the goods or services for which the customer is paying. However, the customer may see them as part of the negotiated exchange. The FASB decided that they are goods or services for which the customer pays and that the entity should include them in performance obligations for the purpose of recognizing revenue under ASC 606. (ASU 2014-09.BC 87-88) That said, some incentives do not represent performance obligations if they are provided independently.

Goods to Be Provided in the Future The FASB also concluded that goods or services to be provided in the future give rise to performance obligations. In some industries it is common practice to provide services to the customer's customer. For example, an automotive manufacturer may promise to provide service to a vehicle sold by a dealer. This type of promise is a performance obligation if it can be identified in the contract with the customer, either explicitly or implicitly.

Example: Implied Performance Obligation

WPS, a manufacturer of project management software, enters into a contract with Big Box Office Supply Company to sell 250 units of its project management software. Big Box intends to resell the software to its end customers—small business owners. WPS has historically offered free online support directly to the end user. WPS and Big Box expect that this support will continue. The online support meets the definition of a performance obligation when WPS transfers control of the products to Big Box. Because WPS and Big Box are not related parties, the contracts will not be combined. Therefore, WPS accounts for the online support as a separate performance obligation.

Activities Not Included as Performance Obligations Only promises that transfer goods or services to the customer can be performance obligations. An entity may need to undertake set-up activities to fulfill performance obligations. If those activities transfer goods or services to the customer, they are part of the performance obligations. However, activities that do not transfer goods or services, like administrative tasks, are not promised goods or services in the contract with the customer. (ASC 606-10-25-17) Some organizations may have a significant number of performance obligations, especially, for example, if "free" items are included and they have to be recognized underASC 606.

Example: Activities Not Included as Performance Obligations

Main Street Sports sells annual memberships. The process includes sale of the membership, enrolling the customers, and activating the customer's gym membership card. Selling the membership, enrolling a customer, and activating the service are considered administrative tasks and are not performance obligations.

What Is a Promised Good or Service? ASC 606 offers some clarity by providing examples of promised goods or services. Bear in mind this is not an exhaustive list. Promised goods or services may include:

- Sale of goods produced by an entity
- Resale of goods purchased by an entity
- Resale of rights to goods or services purchased by an entity
- A contractually agreed-upon task for a customer
- Standing ready to provide goods or services
- Arranging for another party to transfer goods or services to a customer
- Rights to goods or services to be provided in the future that a customer can resell or provide to its customer
- Licenses
- Constructing, manufacturing, or developing an asset on behalf of a customer
- Options to purchase additional goods or services.
  (ASC 606-10-25-18)

Shipping and Handling Services Shipping and handling services performed prior to the customer obtaining control of the goods are not promises to the customer. They are activities to fulfill the promise. (ASC 606-10-25-18A) However, ASC 606 gives the entity the choice to account for shipping and handling services performed after the customer takes control as a fulfillment cost. Entities electing this practical expedient must disclose it in accordance with ASC 606's disclosure requirements. Be aware this is an election and not a requirement. (ASC 606-10-25-18A and 18B)

Determining Whether a Good or Service Is Distinct

After the entity identifies a contract's promises, where there are multiple promises in a contract, the entity must determine which are separate performance obligations. That is, the entity must identify the separate units of account. Performance obligations are the accounting unit for applying the revenue standard.

This is a key decision because:

- Determining the unit of account dictates how and when revenue is recognized, and
- The key determinant when identifying a separate performance obligation is whether a good or service or bundle is distinct.

To determine whether an entity has to account for multiple performance obligations, the entity must assess whether the good or service is distinct, that is, separately identifiable, from other promises in the contract. A good or service is distinct if it meets both these criteria:

1. Capable of being distinct. The customer can benefit from the good or service on its own or together with other resources that are readily available to the customer, and
2. Distinct within the context of the contract. The entity's promise to transfer the good or service to the customer is separately identifiable from other promises in the contract. (ASC 606-10-05-4B)

In some cases, even though a good or service is capable of being distinct, accounting for it as a separate performance obligation might not reflect the entity's performance in that contract. Therefore, the entity uses a two-part process for determining whether a promised good or service or bundle of goods or services is distinct:

1. Assess at the level of the good or service, that is, is the good or service inherently capable of being distinct and
2. Assess in the context of the contract, that is, is the promise to transfer goods or services separately identifiable from other promises in the contract?
(ASC 606-10-25-19)

Criterion number 1 is similar to the stand-alone value criterion in previous GAAP, but criterion number 2 is a new concept. If *both* these criteria are met, the individual units of accounts must be separated. ASC 606 includes indicators to help the entity determine whether the distinct criterion is met. These are discussed below.

Criterion 1: Good or Service Is Capable of Being Distinct A good or service is capable of being distinct if the customer can benefit from it on its own or together with other resources readily available to the customer. (ASC 606-10-25-19a)

Customer can benefit from a performance obligation. A good or service is capable of being distinct if the customer can benefit from it. What does it mean to "benefit from a good or service"? To benefit, the customer must be able to:

- Use,
- Consume,
- Sell for an amount greater than scrap value, or
- Otherwise generate economic benefit.

The ability to sell the good or service at scrap value would not necessarily support a conclusion that the good or service is capable of being distinct.

The assessment of whether the customer can benefit from the good or service on its own is based on the characteristics of the goods or services themselves, rather than how the customer might use them. The benefit may come from one good or service on its own or in conjunction with other readily available resources. A readily available resource is:

- A good or service that is sold separately by the entity or by another entity, or
- A resource that the customer has already obtained either from the entity or through other transactions or events.

One indication that the customer can benefit from the goods or services is that the entity regularly sells it separately. (ASC 606-10-25-20)

Example: Capable of Being Distinct

Builder enters into a contract to remodel a kitchen. Builder will supply the design, demolition services, cabinets, flooring, and other materials, in addition to the plumbing and electrical work. Builder regularly sells these goods and services individually.

Builder must identify the performance obligations in the contract. Because Builder sells the items individually and the homeowner could benefit from them on their own or together with other readily available services, the promised goods and services are capable of being distinct.

However, the goods and services are not distinct within the context of the contract because they are not separately identifiable. Builder provides significant integration services when remodeling the homeowner's kitchen.

In order to assess whether to combine goods or services and account for them as one performance obligation, the entity must understand what the customer expects to receive. For instance, a contract may promise to deliver multiple goods, but the customer may be buying the finished good that those items create.

Criterion 2: Distinct within the Context of the Contract After an entity has determined a good or service is capable of being distinct, the second step in the assessment of whether the performance obligations are distinct is to determine if they are distinct within the context of the contract.

The concept of distinct within the context of the contract is based on the idea of "separable risks," which the Boards explain as follows:

> *. . . the individual goods or services in a bundle would not be distinct if the risk that an entity assumes to fulfill its obligation to transfer one of those promised goods or services to the customer is a risk that is inseparable from the risk relating to the transfer of the other promised goods or services in the bundle.* (ASU 2014-09 BC103)

Because the notion of separable risks is not a practical criterion, ASC 606 requires the entity to determine if the good or service is separately identifiable or distinct within the context of the contract.

The objective when assessing whether an entity's promise to transfer goods or services to the customer are separately identifiable is to determine whether the nature of the entity's overall promise in the contract is to transfer each of those goods or services or whether the promise is to transfer a combined item or items to which the promised goods or services are inputs. (ASC 606-10-25-21)

Separately identifiable indicators The objective when assessing whether an entity's promise to transfer goods or services to the customer are separately identifiable is to determine whether the nature of the entity's overall promise in the contract is to transfer each of those goods or services or whether the promise is to transfer a combined item (or items to which the promised goods or services are inputs).ASC 606 provides indicators rather than criteria to help determine when goods or services are distinct within the context of the contract. Providing guideposts rather than hard and fast rules allows the entity to exercise its judgment to reflect the underlying economic substance of the transaction. Some indicators that a good or service are not separately identifiable are:

- The entity *provides a significant integration service*. That is, the entity is providing the good or service as an input for the combined output specified by the customer.
- One or more of the goods or services *significantly modifies or customizes* or is significantly modified or customized by one or more of the other good or service promised in the contract. The software industry illustrates this indicator.
- The good or service is *highly dependent on, or highly interrelated with*, other goods or services promised in the contract. In other words, each of the goods or services is significantly affected by one or more of the other goods or services in the contract.
(ASC 606-10-25-21)

Example: Significant Integration Service

If an entity contracts to construct a building, all the goods or services involved in the construction are probably capable of being distinct, but would likely not be considered distinct within the context of the contract. That is, the customer could benefit from each on its own. For instance, many of the materials used in the construction might be delivered before actual construction begins. However, the entity would likely take the position that the materials are an input to building the house and there is a significant level of integration required to transform the materials into the building. Therefore, the materials and the construction services are a single performance obligation. It would be impractical to account for each item of construction separately, and to do so would not faithfully represent the promise in the contract or result in a useful reflection of the entity's performance.

Many long-term construction and service contracts will be identified as single performance obligations because they tend to include significant integration services. For instance, a house painter will likely consider the paint as an input to produce the painted house. The service is a significant integration service and, therefore, the paint and the painting services are a single performance obligation.

Promised Good or Service Is Not Distinct Once an entity determines that a promised good or service is not distinct, it must combine it with other promises in the contract until it identifies a bundle of goods or services that is distinct. The result may be that all the promises in a contract are accounted for as a single purchase obligation.

Example: Significant Customization

An entity contracts to sell a software system. The customer is not a typical consumer-driven business. It is a membership organization that produces publications and sells them to its members at a discount and at full price to the general public. During the purchasing process, the customer wants to interact differently with its members than it does with nonmembers. It also wants to maintain detailed information on its members' purchases. Because of its unique needs, the customer requires the entity to perform extensive customization of the software. The sale includes

- the software license
- help desk support for three years
- any available software updates, including the resources to integrate the customized elements.

Element	Step 1—Capable of Being Distinct?	Step 2—Distinct in the Context of the Contract?
Software license and customization	Can be used without help desk support and upgrades. Is capable of being distinct.	The software is significantly customized. Within the context of the contract, the promise to transfer the software license is not separately identifiable, distinct, from the customization. The software license and the customization are not distinct from each other. However, the software is separately identifiable from the other goods and services in the contract. The customer's ability to use and benefit from the software is not affected by the help desk support or the updates. Product is distinct.
Help desk support	Help desk support services are sold separately. Services are capable of being distinct.	Support is separately identifiable from other goods and services in the contract. Services are distinct from the other promises in the contract.
Any available software update and any needed customization	The updates are not available separately, but the customer can benefit from them with other resources readily available (the software license and services previously delivered). Services are capable of being distinct.	Upgrades are separately identifiable from other goods and services in the contract. They do not significantly modify or customize the software, and the software is not highly dependent or integrated with the upgrade. The software remains functional without the upgrades. The updates do not significantly affect the customer's ability to use and benefit from the software. Services are distinct.

The entity concludes that the contract includes three performance obligations:

- the software and its customization;
- the help desk support, which is distinct because the customer can benefit from it on its own;
- the software updates and resources for customization that are readily available to the customer.

All these are distinct within the context of the contract and, applying the indicators, are separately identifiable performance obligations.

It is expected that ASC 606 may lead to entities identifying more performance obligations than under previous guidance. For example, free products or services or service-type warranties might be separate performance obligations under the guidance in ASC 606.

Example: Highly Independent or Highly Interrelated

Fabricator agrees to design a new type of wine bottle opener for Inventor and to produce ten prototypes. The specifications provided by Inventor include untested functionality. As part of the contract, Fabricator will be required to test the product and revise the design while making and testing the prototypes, modifying the prototypes as necessary. As the design changes during the production process, Fabricator expects that all prototypes will need to be reworked. The customer cannot purchase either the design service or the manufacturing service. Because of the iterative process used, the two services are highly dependent and highly related to each other. Within the context of the contract, the two services are not separately identifiable.

Example: Multiple Performance Obligations

Mobile Telephone enters into a contract with a customer to deliver a cell phone and 24 months of voice and data services. The cell phone cannot be used on another telecom company's network. However, certain functions can be used outside the network: playing music and accessing calendars, contacts, emails, and the Internet.

In addition, customers have sold the cell phone to third-party resellers for a portion of the original purchase price. Mobile Telephone also sells the voice and data services to customers through renewals and to customers who purchased the handset at a retailer.

At first glance, it might appear that the cell phone and services are one performance obligation. However, after further analysis, Mobile Telephone concludes that the cell phone and services are two separate performance obligations. The cell phone is

- capable of being distinct because the customer can benefit from the phone on its own by selling it for more than scrap value, and it has functionality that the customer can benefit from without Mobile Telephone's network with the readily available resource of the cell phone either on its own or with services sold separately by Mobile Telephone *and*
- distinct within the context of the contract because the phone and the wireless services are not inputs to a single asset, indicating that Mobile Telephone is not providing significant integration services, the products of the phone and services separately indicating that they are not highly dependent on or interrelated with each other.

Series of Distinct Goods or Services That Are Substantially the Same and Have the Same Pattern of Transfer

There are two ways an entity may determine that two or more goods or services are a single performance obligation. The first is if the entity determines the goods or services are not distinct from each other. The second involves the goods or services that meet the criteria for being distinct, but may still be a single performance obligation. (Refer to the definition of performance obligation at the beginning of this chapter.)

The Series Provision The second category of performance obligations requires the entity to assess whether the performance obligations are a series of distinct goods or services that are "substantially the same or have the same pattern of transfer to the customer." Without this part of the definition, some entities would face significant operational challenges. For example, services provided on an hourly or daily basis, like a cleaning service, might meet the criteria for a single performance obligation and the entity would be faced with accounting separately for numerous repetitive services. The series provision is a concept that is introduced by ASC 606 and does not exist in the legacy standards. This series provision guidance is intended to simplify the application of the revenue recognition model and promote consistency.

To have the same pattern of transfer, both of the following criteria must be met:

- Each distinct good or service in the series that the entity promises to transfer consecutively represents a performance obligation satisfied over time if it were accounted for separately.
- The entity uses the same method of progress to measure the transfer of each distinct good or service in the same series to the customer.
  (ASC 606-10-25-15)

If the criteria are met, the series of goods or services must be treated as a single performance obligation, the so-called "series requirement." The accounting treatment may vary for this application when accounting for contract modifications, variable consideration, and changes in transaction price.

Exhibit—Series of Distinct Goods or Services—Criteria for Same Pattern of Transfer

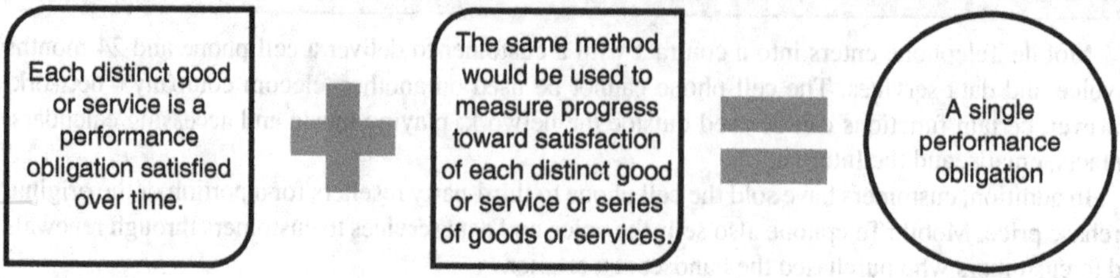

The box on the left in the exhibit is similar to the principles in legacy GAAP (ASC 605-10-25-13) for multiple element arrangements. The second is a new requirement, and for some entities, this may result in a change in practice.

Example: Series of Distinct Goods or Services Treated as a Single Performance Obligation

File Manufacturer signs a contract with Office Suites to deliver 500 customized filing cabinets over time. If Office Suites terminates the contract for convenience, the contract requires Office Suites to pay File Manufacturer for any finished or in-process cabinets, including a reasonable margin.

Each of the cabinets is distinct because each can be used on its own, and each is separately identifiable from the others because it does not affect, modify, or customize another.

Although each cabinet is distinct, File Manufacturer accounts for 500 units as a single performance obligation because

- each cabinet transfers to Office Suites over time, and
- File Manufacturer uses the same method to measure progress toward completion.

STEP 3: DETERMINE THE TRANSACTION PRICE

Overview

Transaction Price *The amount of consideration to which an entity expects to be entitled in exchange for transferring promised goods or services to a customer, excluding amounts collected on behalf of third parties (for example, some sales taxes).* (ASC 606-10-20)

Step 3 of the revenue recognition model requires entities to consider the terms of the contract and the entity's customary business practices to determine the transaction price. Transaction price is a new term. Entities will have to understand the term conceptually and in practice compared with the extant term "contract values." The transaction price only includes amounts to which the entity has rights and does not include:

- Amounts collected on behalf of another, such as sales taxes, and
- Estimates of options on and future change orders for additional goods and services.

Determining the transaction price is critical because it is the amount ultimately recognized as revenue. The objective of the guidance in Step 3 is to predict at the end of the reporting period the total amount of consideration to which the entity is entitled.

The transaction price should be determined at the inception of the contract. As with other steps of the revenue recognition model, when determining the transaction price, the entity should look more widely than the contract terms and examine the entity's customary business practices, published policies, and specific statements. Also, the entity should assume that the terms of the contract will be fulfilled, that is, the goods or services will be transferred as promised and that the contract will not be canceled, renewed, or modified. (ASC 606-10-32-4)

Exhibit—Determining the Transaction Price

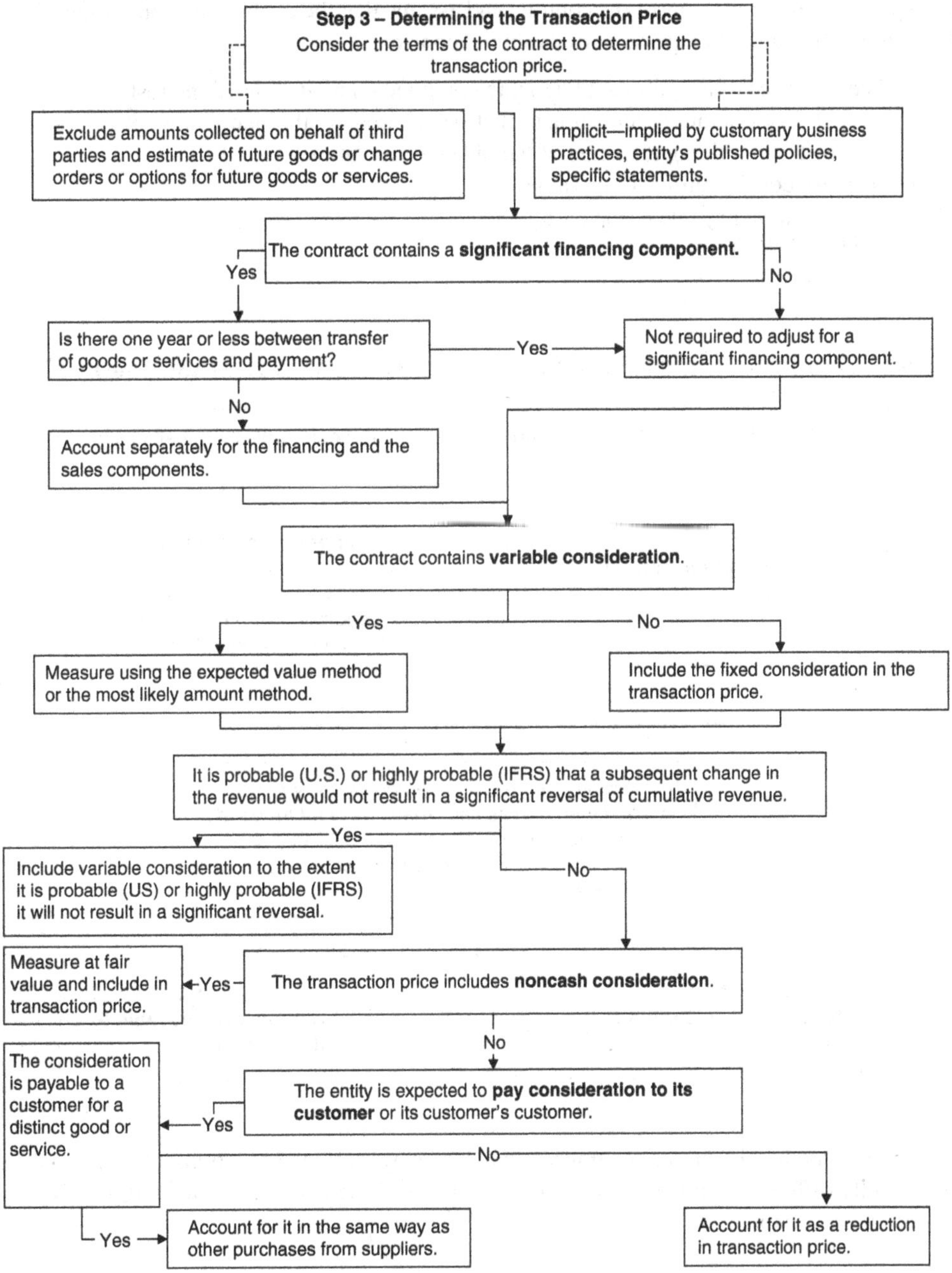

A contract may include fixed amounts, variable amounts, or both. Determining transaction price can be straightforward or complex. For example, sales to a customer in a retail store are relatively simple. In other situations, for example where noncash consideration is included or the consideration varies depending on circumstances, determination of the transaction price can be more complex.

The transaction price excludes amounts collected on behalf of third parties and estimates of future goods or change orders or options for future goods or services. Entities should consider the explicit and implicit terms of the contract and assume that the contract will be fulfilled. When determining the transaction price, entities should consider:

- The existence of a significant financing component and its related interest.
- Variable consideration, an estimate that better predicts the likely amount of consideration, and constraining elements of variable consideration.
- Noncash consideration at fair value.
- Consideration payable to the customer.
  (ASC 606-10-32-3)

Exhibit—Factors to Consider When Determining Transaction Price (ASC 606-10-32-3)

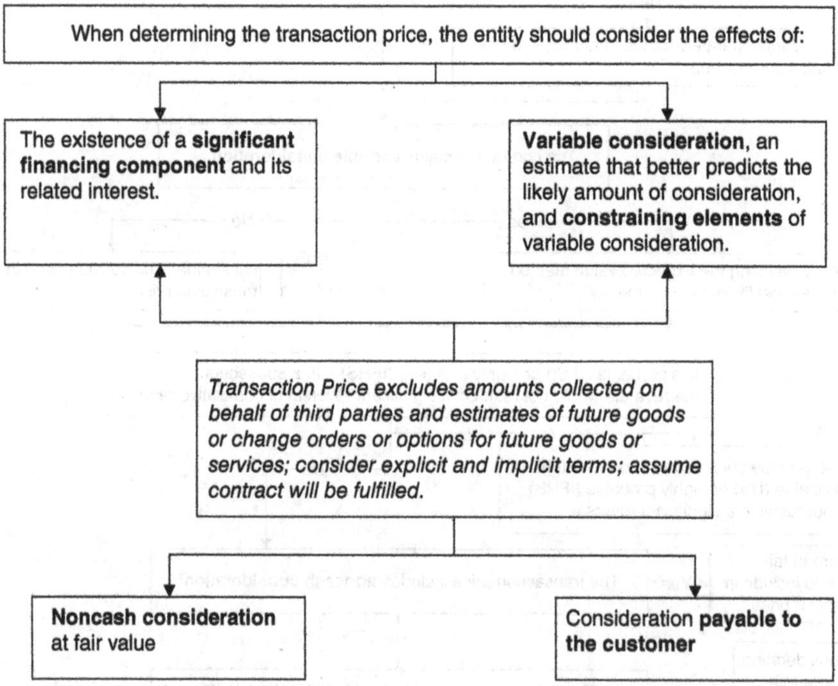

The factors that determine the transaction price may well lead to a transaction price that is significantly different than the contractual price. Each of the above elements will be discussed in depth in this chapter.

Significant Financing Component

Under some arrangements, there is a difference in timing—the timing of the payment does not match the timing of the transfer of goods or services. It is not uncommon for an entity to enter into a contract that includes, either explicitly or implicitly, payments over time.

Through the agreed-upon payment terms, the timing may provide the customer or the entity with a significant financing benefit. If the customer pays in advance, the entity has received financing from the customer. If the entity transfers the goods or services in advance of payment, the entity has provided financing to the customer. If one of these is the case, the entity must then examine the facts and circumstances to determine if a significant financing component exists that must be accounted for. See the section that follows for more detail.

Exhibit—Timing of Payment Does Not Match Timing of Transfer of Goods or Services

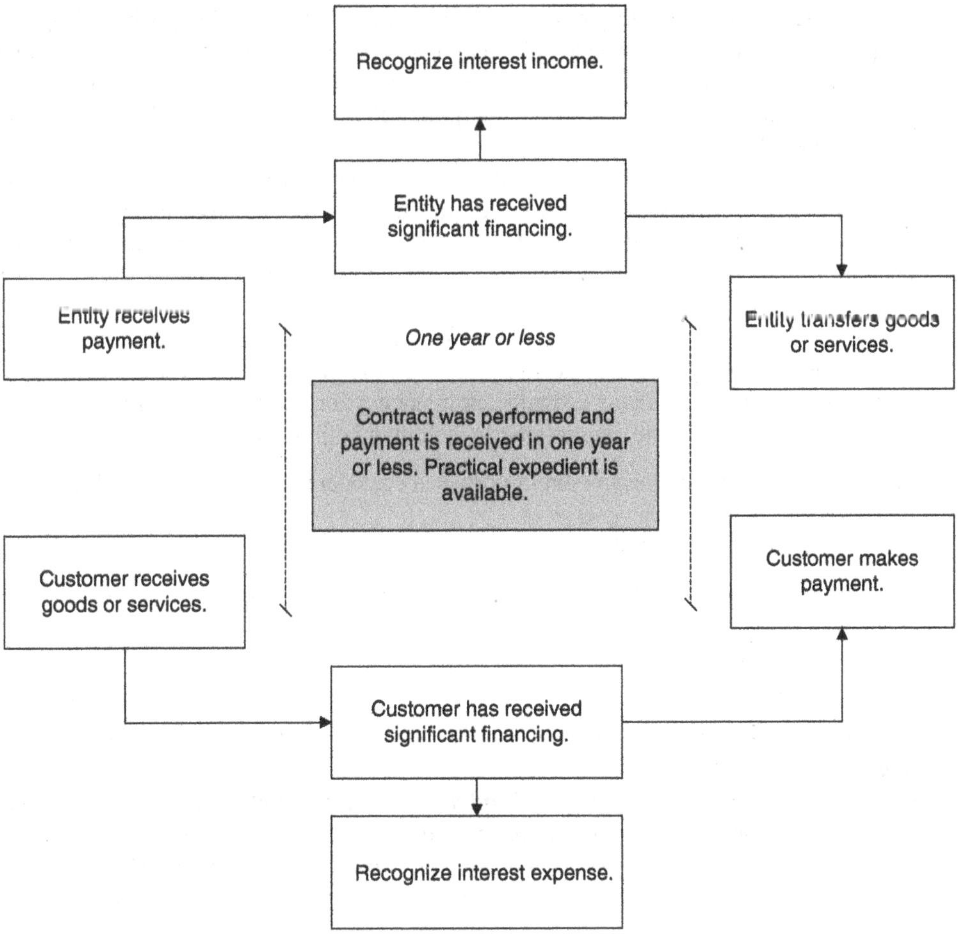

Practical Expedient ASC 606 includes a practical expedient for significant financing components. The amount of consideration does not have to be adjusted if, at contract inception, the entity expects that there will be one year or less between:

- Transfer of goods or services, and
- Payment.

(ASC-606-10-32-18)

When assessing whether the practical expedient can be applied, the entity must focus on the timing of the two events (transfer and payment) rather than the length of the contract. If an entity chooses to apply the practical expedient, it should apply it consistently to similar contracts under similar circumstances.

Determining Whether There Is a Financing Component Conceptually, ASC 606 recognizes that a contract with a financing component has two transactions—a sale and a financing. If a contract has a significant financing component, the entity should account for the financing component and adjust the transaction price. (ASC 606-10-32-15) Determining what a "significant" component is may require considerable judgment. Companies that have contracts with a significant financing component may have operational challenges connected to measuring and tracking the time value of money. However, the practical expedient explained earlier should provide some relief.

The consideration recorded should reflect the price the customer would have paid if the customer paid cash when (or as) the goods or services transferred to the customer, that is, the objective is to reflect the cash selling price. ASC 606 factors in the effects of a significant financing component because excluding it could result in two economically similar transactions recording substantially different revenue amounts.

The determination of whether a contract contains a significant financing component occurs at the contract level, not the contract portfolio level or the performance obligation level. In assessing whether a contract contains a significant financing component, the entity should take into consideration all the facts and circumstances, including both of the following:

1. The difference between the amount of promised consideration and the cash selling price upon transfer of the goods or services.
2. The combined effects of both of the following:
    - The expected length of time between the transfer of goods or services and when the customer pays.
    - The prevailing interest rates in the relevant market.

(ASC 606-10-32-16)

And, as with other assessments in the model, it is necessary to look at implicit and explicit contract terms.

Significant Financing Component—Contra Indicative Factors A time difference between payment of consideration and transfer of goods and services to the customer does not always mean there is a significant financing component. If *any* of the factors listed in the exhibit below exist, a contract with a customer would *not* have a significant financing component.

Exhibit—Significant Financing Component—Contra Indicative Factors

Contra Indicative Factors	Examples
The customer paid in advance, and the timing of the transfer of goods and services is in the hands of the customer.	Customer loyalty points usable in the future, prepaid phone cards, gift cards.
A substantial amount of the consideration promised by the customer is variable, and the timing of that consideration varies on the basis of the occurrence or nonoccurrence of a future event not substantially within the control of the customer or entity.	Sales-based royalty.
The timing difference between the promised consideration and the cash selling price are justified for reasons not related to financing and the difference between those amounts is proportional to the reason for the difference.	Payment terms might provide the customer with protection if the other party fails to adequately complete some or all of its obligations under the contract, for example, retention payments in construction contracts.
(ASC 606-10-32-17)	

Determining the Discount Rate for a Significant Financing Component The entity should use the discount rate that would be reflected in a separate financing transaction between the entity and its customers at the time of the inception of the contract. (ASC 606-10-32-19) That rate should reflect:

- Inflation,
- The credit risk of the financing party,
- The credit characteristics of the party receiving the financing, and
- Any collateral or security provided, including assets transferred in the contract.

The entity needs to have access to enough information to determine the discount rate.

The rate may be determined by identifying the interest rate that discounts the nominal amount of the promised consideration to the cash the customer would pay when (or as) the goods or services transfer to the customer. If the contract contains an explicit rate, the entity should consider whether that rate reflects the market rate. In some cases, the contract may contain a low rate as a marketing incentive. If the contract does not reflect the market rate, the entity should impute a more representative rate. The rate determined at the inception of the contract is the rate used throughout the terms of the contact. (ASC 606-10-32-19)

Customer's credit risk Generally, under ASC 606, the transaction price is not adjusted for customer's credit risk, that is, the risk that a customer will not pay the entity. However, there is an exception when the contract includes a significant financing component. The *only* time the transaction price is adjusted for credit risk is if there is a significant financing component. Note that the discount rate is not adjusted *after* contract inception for changes in interest rates or other circumstances, including a change in the customer's credit risk.

Based on the facts and circumstances, management needs to decide whether billing adjustments are:

- A modification of the transaction price that reduces revenue, or
- A credit adjustment, write-off of an uncollectible amount that impairs a contract asset, or receivable and is assessed under ASC 310, *Receivables*.

Implied price concession If the customer's credit risk is known at the inception of the contract, the entity must determine if there is an implied price concession. If so, it is not included in the estimated transaction price. This may be difficult to determine: has the entity offered an implied price concession or has the entity chosen the risk of the customer defaulting? ASC 606 does not provide detailed application guidance to help distinguish between price concessions (reduction of revenue) and customer credit risk (bad debt expense). Entities will have to exercise significant judgment and will need to have clear policies in place. (Also see the section in this chapter on "Variable Consideration.")

Impairment If a customer's credit risk is impaired resulting in an impairment of a contract asset or receivable, the entity should measure the impairment based on the guidance in ASC 310.

Presentation of a Significant Financing Component The entity should separate the loan component from the revenue component. Interest income or expense resulting from a financing should be presented separately from the revenue component. Once a performance obligation is satisfied, the entity recognizes the present value of the consideration as revenue. The financing component (interest income or expense) is recognized over the financing period. The income or expense is recognized only to the extent that a contract asset, receivable, or contract liability, such as deferred revenue, is recognized for the customer contract. When accounting for the financing component, the entity should look to the relevant guidance on the effective interest method in ASC 835-30, *Interest—Imputation of Interest:*

- Subsequent measurement guidance in ASC 835-30-45-1A through 45-3
- Application of the interest method in ASC 835-30-55-2 and 55-3
  (ASC 606-10-32-20)

Variable Consideration

Variable consideration in contracts is common, and the guidance applies to a wide variety of fact patterns. The entity must examine the explicit and implicit terms of the contract to identify variable consideration. Variability in the consideration could affect:

- Whether the entity is entitled to the consideration. An example of this is a requirement to meet a deadline for a performance bonus.
- The specific amount of consideration. This might come into play when the quantity of customer purchases is tied to a volume discount.

Types and Sources of Variable Consideration Variable consideration comes in two types:

1. Pricing adjustments for transactions that have already been completed, for instance, refunds, and
2. Incentive and performance-based fees, for example, licenses and royalties.

Exhibit—Sources of Variable Consideration

Common Examples of Consideration That Cause Variable Consideration		
Discounts	Rebates	Refunds
Credits	Price concessions	Incentives
Performance bonuses	Penalties	Returns
Market-based fees	Money-back guarantees	Service-level agreements
Liquidating damages	Price protection plans	Price matching plans
(ASC 606-10-32-6)		

Under legacy guidance, some of these items caused entities to delay revenue recognition. Under the revenue model in ASC 606, entities will now have to estimate their effect because the model focuses on when control transfers. Even if a contract has a stated fixed price, the consideration may still be variable. This happens when the consideration is contingent on the occurrence or nonoccurrence of an event.

Exception If a contract is for a license of intellectual property for which the consideration is based on the customer's subsequent sales or usage, the entity should *not* recognize revenue for uncertain amounts.

Determining If Variable Consideration Exists Variable consideration may be explicitly stated in the contract or may be variable if either of the following exists:

- The customer has a valid expectation arising from an entity's customary business practices, published policies, or specific statements that the entity will accept an amount of consideration that is less than the price stated in the contract. That is, it is expected that the entity will offer a price concession. Depending on the jurisdiction, industry, or customer, this offer may be referred to as a discount, rebate, refund, or credit.
- Other facts and circumstances indicate that the entity's intention, when entering into the contract with the customer, is to offer a price concession to the customer.
(ASC 606-10-32-7)

Estimating Total Variable Consideration If the contract's consideration includes a variable amount, the entity must go through a process to determine the effect of that variability on the transaction price. It must:

- Determine the method for estimating the consideration
- Measure the consideration
- Determine if the variable consideration should be constrained
- Account for subsequent changes in transaction price

Determine the method for estimating variable consideration To determine the amount of variable consideration to include in the transaction price, the entity must first estimate the amount by using one of two methods. This is not a free policy choice. There are two methods, and the entity is required to choose the method it expects to better predict the amount of variable consideration under the specific facts and circumstances and must apply that method consistently for similar contracts. The two methods that the entity must choose from are:

1. The expected value method, and
2. The most likely amount method.

Exhibit—The Two Methods for Estimating Variable Consideration

The Expected Value Method: The sum of probability weighted amounts within a range of possible consideration amounts.	This method may be most predictive when the entity has a large number of contracts with similar characteristics. This method reflects all the uncertainties—the probability of receiving greater amounts and lesser amounts. However, it may not always be the best predictor.
The Most Likely Amount Method: Identifies the single most likely amount in the range of possible consideration amounts.	This method may be appropriate when the contract has only two or a small number of possible outcomes because the expected value method might not result in one of the possible outcomes. This method would be appropriate, for example, when a performance bonus is either met or not, that is, it is binary.
(ASC 606-10-32-8)	

Measuring the variable consideration. Whichever method an entity chooses to estimate the consideration, it should be applied consistently throughout the contract when estimating the effects and uncertainty of an amount of variable consideration. All reasonably available information should be considered, including historical, current, and forecast data. The entity would normally use the same information it used during the proposal process and when it set prices. Note that the entity does not need to use every outcome in its analysis. A few discrete outcomes may provide a valid estimate. (ASC 606-10-32-9)

Refund Liability If an entity receives consideration from the customer and expects to refund some or all of that consideration, the entity must recognize a refund liability. The liability is measured at the amount of consideration received (or receivable) for which the entity does not expect to be entitled. The refund liability should be updated at the end of each reporting period for changes in circumstances. (ASC 606-10-32-10) See information later in this chapter on rights of return.

Tip: Manufacturers and retailers, not otherwise significantly affected by ASC 606, need to assess whether new policies and procedures are needed for returns.

Constraining Estimates of Variable Consideration Because revenue is a critical metric, it is important to include estimates of consideration that are robust and give useful information. Some estimates of variable consideration are too uncertain and should not be included in the transaction price. After estimating the amount of variable consideration, the entity then should apply the following constraint focused on the probability of a significant reversal of cumulative revenue recognized:

> *The entity should include some or all of the variable consideration in the transaction price to the extent that it is probable that a subsequent change in the estimate would not result in a significant reversal of cumulative revenue recognized.* (ASC 606-10-32-11)

The constraint of variable consideration addresses concerns about premature recognition of revenue, that is, recognizing revenue based in the future before there is sufficient certainty that the amount will be realized. Focusing on the potential for significant reversals of revenue helps lower the risk that revenue will be overstated. Revenue that would not reverse significantly in a subsequent period is more predictive of future revenues.

Application to fixed fees The significance of the reversal is assessed compared to the cumulative amount of revenue recognized. So, in its analysis, the entity should consider not only variable consideration but factor in fixed consideration as well. The constraint applies to contracts with a fixed price if it is uncertain whether the entity will be entitled to all the consideration even after the performance obligation is satisfied. An example of this is a legal service provided for a fixed fee that is only payable if the customer wins the case. The revenue might still be recognized before the court rules if the entity considers it probable that the fee is not subject to significant reversal of cumulative revenue recognized.

Assessing probability of a reversal "Significant" is relative to the amount of total revenue in the contract (total variable and fixed consideration), not just the possible variable consideration. Determining the probability of a reversal of revenue requires considerable judgment, and it is good practice for the entity to document its basis of conclusion. It may be particularly difficult to assess the probability under certain situations. These include:

- Payments contingent on regulatory approval, for example, of a new drug
- Long-term commodity supply arrangements dependent on market prices at a future delivery date
- Contingency fees based on the outcome of litigation or the settlement of claims with government agencies

To assess the probability of a reversal, the entity takes into account two elements:

1. The likelihood of a reversal, and
2. The magnitude of a reversal.

Indicators that significant revenue reversal will occur ASC 606 includes indicators to help assess whether it is probable that a significant reversal of cumulative revenue recognized will occur. The presence of one of these indicators does not necessarily mean that the constraint applies, but might be an indicator that could increase the likelihood or the magnitude of a revenue reversal. Note that these are factors to consider rather than criteria.

Exhibit—Factors That Increase the Likelihood or Magnitude of a Significant Reversal

- The high susceptibility to factors outside the entity's influence. Such factors might be:
  - The volatility of the market,
  - Third-party judgment or actions,
  - Weather conditions, or
  - The promised goods' high risk of obsolescence.
- The uncertainty will not be resolved for a long period of time.
- The entity's experience with similar contracts is limited or that experience has low predictive value.
- With similar contracts under similar circumstances, the entity has a history of offering a broad range of price concessions or changing the payment terms or conditions.
- The contract has a large number and broad range of possible consideration amounts.

(ASC 606-10-32-12

When making the assessment, the entity should evaluate, among others, the factors in the preceding exhibit.

Reassessing the Transaction Price for Variable Consideration The estimated transaction price should be reassessed and updated at the end of each reporting period until the underlying uncertainty is resolved. Included in this update is an assessment of whether an estimate of variable consideration is constrained. Changes in the estimate are treated the same way as any other changes in the transaction price. These updates will then represent faithfully at the end of the reporting period the circumstances present at that time and a change in circumstance during that period. (ASC 606-10-32-14) (See Step 5 in this chapter for more information about updating changes in transaction price.)

Sales-Based or Usage-Based Royalty Exception to Variable Constraint Guidance A narrow exception to the guidance on constraints in variable consideration involves sales-based or usage-based royalty consideration promised in exchange for a license of intellectual property only. For those types of consideration the entity should recognize only when (or as) the later of the following events occur:

- The subsequent sale or usage occurs.
- The performance obligation to which some or all of the sales-based or usage-based royalty allocated has been satisfied (or partially satisfied).
(ASC 606-10-55-65)

The royalty in its entirety should be either within or not within the scope of the royalties exception. The royalties exception applies when the license of intellectual property is the predominant item to which the royalty relates. Determining when a license is the predominant item requires judgment on the part of the entity. In making this judgment, the entity may want to consider the value the customer places on the license in comparison with the other goods or services in the bundle. (ASC 606-10-55-65A-B)

Noncash Consideration

To determine the transaction price at contract inception, any noncash consideration promised by the customer should be measured at fair value of the noncash consideration. Entities should look to determine fair value of the consideration first. This is the opposite of legacy guidance where entities first look at what was given up. If fair value cannot be reasonably estimated, the entity should measure the consideration indirectly by reference to the stand-alone selling price of the goods or services promised to the customer. (ASC 606-10-32-21 and 32-22)

The fair value of a noncash contribution may vary because of:

- The occurrence or nonoccurrence of a future event, or
- The form of the consideration, for example, a change in the price of stock the entity is entitled to receive.

If the fair value varies because of a reason other than the form of the consideration, the entity should apply the guidance on constraining estimates of variable consideration. (ASC 606-10-32-23) ASC 606 includes information about how to apply the constraint in situations where consideration varies because of both the form of consideration and for reasons other than the form of consideration. The guidance on constraining the estimate of variable consideration applies to variability resulting from reasons other than the form of consideration. Changes in the fair value after contract inception because of the form of the consideration are not included in the transaction price. Therefore, the variable consideration guidance would not apply, for example, to variability related to changes in stock price when consideration is in the form of equity instruments.

In some cases the entity may receive goods or services, like materials, equipment, or labor, from the customer in order to facilitate delivery of the promised goods or services. In that case, the entity should assess whether it has control of those goods or services. If it does have control, the entity should account for them as noncash consideration received from the customer. (ASC 606-10-32-24)

Consideration Payable to the Customer

Customer contracts may include provisions where the entity is expected to pay consideration to its customers or its customer's customers. Consideration payable to a customer includes:

- Cash amounts the entity pays or expects to pay to the customer
- Cash amounts the entity pays or expects to pay to other parties that purchase the entity's goods or services from the customer
- Credit, coupons, vouchers, or other items that can be applied against amounts owed.
- Equity instruments, classified as liabilities or equity, granted in conjunction with selling goods or services, such as shares, share options, or other equity instruments.
(ASC 606-10-32-25)

Measurement—Cash Amounts Unless consideration payable to a customer is for distinct goods or services received in return, it should be accounted for as a reduction of the transaction price. "Distinct" in this context is consistent with the guidance in Step 2. If the amount is variable, the entity should estimate the amount in accordance with the guidance on variable consideration. (ASC 610-10-32-25)

If consideration payable to the customer is for a distinct good or service, the entity should account for it in the same way it accounts for other purchases from suppliers. If consideration payable to the customer is not for a distinct good or service, the consideration should be treated as a reduction in transaction price. The consideration payable to the customer may be greater than the fair value of the good or service received. In that case, to depict revenue faithfully, the entity should account for the excess as a reduction of the transaction price. If the fair value of the goods or services is not reasonably estimable, the entity should account for all the consideration payable to the customer as a reduction of the transaction price. (ASC 610-10-32-25)

Equity instruments that an entity grants for selling goods or services should be measured and classified under the guidance in ASC 718 on stock compensation. The instruments are measured at the grant date. Changes in the measurement of the equity instrument after the grant date due to form of the consideration are not included in the transaction price and should be reflected elsewhere in the grantor's income statement. (ASC 606-10-32-25A)

Recognition For recognition of consideration payable to a customer accounted for as a reduction in transaction price, ASC 606 provides the following guidance:

> *. . . the entity shall recognize the reduction when (or as) the later of either of the following events occurs:*
>
> - The entity recognizes revenue for the transfer of the related goods or services to the customer.
> - The entity pays or promises to pay the consideration (even if payment is conditional on a future event). That promise may be implied by the entity's customary business practices.
> (ASC 606-10-32-27)

The TRG brought to the FASB an issue related to variable consideration payable to a customer and the timing of recognition. Some stakeholders questioned whether the guidance above is inconsistent with that on variable consideration, which might be interpreted to require earlier recognition under some circumstances. The staff view that the board members deemed reasonable was that entities should consider both areas of guidance and record the reduction in revenue at the earlier of when it would be required under the variable consideration guidance as a change in transaction price and the consideration is payable to a customer—when a promise is made or implied.

STEP 4: ALLOCATE THE TRANSACTION PRICE

Overview

In Step 4, the entity allocates the transaction price to each of the performance obligations (units of account). This is usually done in proportion to the stand-alone selling price, that is, on a relative stand-alone selling price basis. With some exceptions, discounts are allocated proportionately to the separate performance obligations.

This objective of Step 4 is key to understanding the related guidance.

> *The objective when allocating the transaction price is for an entity to allocate the transaction price to each performance obligation (or distinct good or service) in an amount that depicts the amount of consideration to which the entity expects to be entitled in exchange for transferring the promised goods or services to the customer.* (ASC 606-10-32-28)

This step is actually a two-part process:

1. **Determine the Stand-Alone Selling Price.** In some situations, the stand-alone selling price may not be observable. For example, the entity may not sell the good or service separately. If a stand-alone selling price is not observable, the entity must estimate it. (ASC 606-10-30-31)
2. **Allocate the Transaction Price to the Performance Obligations.** The transaction price must be allocated proportionately to each performance obligation on a relative stand-alone selling price basis with some limited exceptions. However, when specific criteria are met, there are exceptions to the relative stand-alone selling price basis, and those exceptions relate to one or more (but less than all) performance obligations involving:
    - Discounts, and
    - Variable consideration.

ASC 606 specifies the situations where the discounts or variable consideration should be allocated to a specific part of the contract rather than to all the performance obligations. These exceptions are discussed later in this chapter.

Determining Stand-Alone Selling Price

> *Stand-Alone Selling Price: The price at which an entity would sell a promised good or service separately to a customer.* (ASC 606-10-20)

The stand-alone selling price is determined at contract inception and is *not updated* for changes in selling prices between contract inception and when the performance under the contract is complete. If the entity enters into a *new* contract for the same good or service, it would reassess the stand-alone selling price and use the changed price for the new arrangement. A new contract may occur:

- When the entity enters into a new arrangement in the future, or
- As a result of a contract modification.

If the contract is modified and the modification is not treated as a separate contract, the entity updates the estimate of the stand-alone selling price at the time of the modification. (See the section later in this chapter on "Changes in Transaction Price" and the section on "Contract Modifications.")

Unlike the stand-alone selling price, the transaction price may be updated. It must be reassessed, and if necessary updated, at the end of each reporting period. Resulting changes to the transaction price should be allocated on the same basis as at contract inception.

Stand-Alone Selling Price Directly Observable The best evidence of the stand-alone selling price is the *observable* price charged by the entity when the entity sells those goods or services separately in similar circumstances to similar customers. However, goods or services are not always sold separately. If the stand-alone selling price is not directly observable, the entity must estimate it.

Tip: The contract price or the list price might be the stand-alone price; however, the entity should not presume that is the case. (ASC 606-10-32-32) As in other steps in the process, the entity should consider customary business practices when determining the stand-alone selling price. For instance, the entity may regularly provide discounts to customers and those should be considered.

Estimating a Stand-Alone Selling Price That Is Not Directly Observable If the product or service is not sold separately, the entity must use another method to determine the stand-alone selling price. ASC 606 does not allow for postponement of revenue recognition because of a lack of reliable evidence. If the stand-alone selling price is not directly observable, it must be estimated. When estimating the stand-alone selling price, entities need to exercise judgment. Some entities may have robust procedures in place to estimate prices; others may need to put procedures in place. In estimating the stand-alone selling prices, the entity should *maximize the use of observable inputs* and consider all reasonably available and relevant information, including:

- Reasonably available data points, such as:
  - Stand-alone prices,
  - Manufacturing costs,
  - Margins,
  - Price listings, and
  - Third-party pricing,
- Market conditions, such as:
  - Demand,
  - Competition,
  - Constraints, and
  - Trends,

- Entity-specific factors, such as:
  - Pricing strategies,
  - Objectives,
  - Market share, and
- Information about the customer or class of customer, such as:
  - Geographical distribution,
  - Type, and
  - Distribution channels.

The entity must apply estimation methods *consistently* for similar circumstances. ASC 606 does not prescribe or preclude any one method. It indicates that the method used to estimate the stand-alone selling prices should result in an estimate that represents faithfully the price an entity would charge for the goods or services if they were sold separately. ASC 606 does describe three estimation methods, and they are listed in the exhibit below. (ASC 606-10-32-33)

Exhibit—Estimation Methods

Estimation Method	Description
Adjusted Market Assessment Approach	The entity evaluates the market in which it sells goods or services and estimates the price that a customer in the market would be willing to pay.
Expected Cost Plus a Margin Approach	The entity builds up a stand-alone selling price using costs and an appropriate margin.
Residual Approach	The entity estimates the stand-alone selling price by deducting from the total transaction price the sum of the observable stand-alone selling prices of other goods or services promised in the contract. (See below for restrictions on the use of the residual approach.)
(ASC 606-10-32-34)	

Other approaches may be appropriate as long as the objective of those approaches is to identify the amount the entity would charge if selling the underlying goods or services on their own.

The Residual Approach The use of this approach is restricted. Entities may use this approach *only* if the stand-alone selling price is *uncertain* or *highly variable.*

- Uncertain. A stand-alone selling price is highly uncertain if the entity has not yet established a price for the good or service and the good or service has not previously been sold on a stand-alone basis.
- Highly variable. A stand-alone selling price is highly variable if the entity sells the same good or service to different customers, at or near the same time, for a broad range of amounts.

  [ASC 606-10-32-34(c)]

The use of the residual approach is intentionally limited. The entity should not use the residual approach in cases where, for example,

- There is no remaining transaction price to allocate to the remaining performance obligations or
- The allocated amount is not within a range of the entity's observable selling prices for the good or service.

The entity should be wary if applying the residual approach results in consideration of zero or very little consideration. Such an outcome may not be reasonable unless other GAAP applies, for instance, in cases where the obligation is partially out of scope of ASC 606.

Some arrangements may include a discount that specifically relates to only certain performance obligations that are typically sold together as a bundle. In those cases, when using the residual approach, the discount must be allocated to those performance obligations before deducting the stand-alone selling price from the total transaction price. (ASC 606-10-32-38)

In arrangements where price can be highly variable because there is little incremental cost in order for the entity to provide the goods or services, the residual approach may be the most reliable approach to determine the stand-alone selling price. This may be especially relevant to intellectual property and other intangible assets. In addition, determining stand-alone selling prices for intangible property, including intellectual property, can be especially challenging because those items may often be sold as part of a widely priced bundle. For example, an entity may license software using a wide price band. Using the residual approach allows entities to bring in elements of the arrangement where prices are more reliable and to use the remainder to price the intangibles.

If the residual approach is used, the entity should be comfortable that the residual approach results in a faithful representation of the stand-alone selling price.

Example: Estimating the Stand-Alone Selling Price Using the Residual Approach

Computer Solutions enters into a contract with a customer to provide three separate performance obligations: computers, services, and a license for newly developed software. The total transaction price is CU 30,000. Computer Solutions regularly sells the computers for CU 10,000 and the services for CU 12,000. The license has not been sold previously, there is no established price, and there is no comparable product sold by competitors. The computers, services, and license are not regularly sold at a discount.

Computer Solutions meets the requirements to use the residual approach to estimate the stand-alone selling price for the license because the stand-alone selling price is uncertain—a price has not been established and it has not been sold previously. Computer Solutions also determines that another method would not be appropriate.

Calculation of stand-alone selling price using the residual approach:

Total transaction price:	CU 30,000	
Less: Computers	<10,000>	Directly observable price
Servicing	<12,000>	Directly observable price
License	CU 8,000	Residual price

Combination of Methods Entities may use the residual approach if more than one good or service in the contract has a highly variable or uncertain stand-alone selling price. However, in this situation, an entity may have to use a combination of methods to estimate the selling prices. To use a combination of methods, entities should use this process:

1. Apply the residual approach to estimate the aggregate of the stand-alone selling price for all the goods or services with highly variable or uncertain selling prices.
2. Use another technique to estimate the stand-alone selling price of each promised good or service with highly variable or uncertain selling prices.

If the entity uses a combination of methods, it needs to evaluate whether allocating the transaction price at those estimated stand-alone selling prices is consistent with ASC 606's allocation objectives and the guidance on estimating stand-alone selling prices. (ASC 606-10-32-35)

Allocating the Transaction Price

If there is one performance obligation in a contract, there are usually no issues with allocation. However, it is not unusual for a contract to have more than one performance obligation. Performance obligations may include multiple goods, initial services, and ongoing services. In cases with more than one performance obligation, the entity must allocate, at contract inception, the transaction price to the performance obligations so that revenue is recognized at the right time for the proper amount.

The allocation is based on the fair value of each performance obligation. The best indicator of the fair value of the performance obligation is the observable, stand-alone selling price of the underlying good or service, sold in similar circumstances to similar customers. The transaction price, generally, should be allocated in proportion to the stand-alone selling prices. (ASC 606-10-30-31)

Allocating the transaction price on the relative stand-alone selling price basis is the default method to achieve the objectives of Step 4. It has the advantages of bringing rigor and discipline to the process and should enhance impartiality, but it is not an allocation principle.

Allocation of a Discount If an entity sells a bundle of goods or services for an amount less than the total of the stand-alone selling prices of the individual goods or services, the entity should treat the difference as a discount. The entity generally allocates the discount proportionally based on relative stand-alone selling prices. There is significant judgment involved in allocating a discount, and entities will need to have robust policies in place. For instance, the entity will need to have a policy that defines "regularly sells." (ASC 606-10-32-36)

Exception to proportional allocation of a discount Generally, proportional allocation of a discount achieves the objective of Step 4 and reflects the economic substance of the transaction. However, there is an exception to proportional allocation of a discount. The entity may have observable evidence that the discount relates specifically to only some, but not all, performance obligations in the contracts. In that case, the entity should allocate the discounts to those performance obligations causing the discount if *all* of the following criteria are met:

a. The entity regularly sells each distinct good or service (or each bundle of distinct goods or services) in the contract on a stand-alone selling basis.
b. The entity also regularly sells, on a stand-alone basis, a bundle (or bundles) some of those distinct goods or services at a discount to the stand-alone selling prices of the goods or services in each bundle.
c. The discount attributable to each bundle of goods or services in (b) is substantially the same as the discount in the contracts, and an analysis of the goods or services in each bundle provides observable evidence of the performance obligation (or performance obligations) to which the entire discount in the contract belongs.

(ASC 606-10-32-37)

The criteria above are fairly restrictive, and the exception may not be common. As mentioned earlier in this chapter in the section on the "Residual Approach," if the entity meets the above criteria for allocating the discount entirely to one or more performance obligations in the contract, the entity must allocate the discount *before* using the residual approach to estimate the stand-alone selling price of a remaining performance obligation. (ASC 606-10-32-38)

Allocation of Variable Consideration As discussed earlier, some contracts contain consideration that is variable based on achievement of certain thresholds or goals being met, such as on-time completion of a project. Variable consideration is measured using one of two methods—probability weighted or most likely amount—and is subject to constraint. Variable consideration adds a layer of complexity to allocating the transaction price and may be subject to change over time.

Variable consideration—exception to proportional allocation ASC 606 provides that the entity allocates total transaction consideration to the performance obligations based on the stand-alone selling price of those performance obligations. There are some situations where proportional allocation to all transactions does not represent the economic substance of the transaction and so its use may not be appropriate. For example, the contract may call for an entity to produce two products at different times with a bonus contingent on and related to the timely delivery of only the second product. In another instance, the entity may be obligated to provide two products at different times, with a fixed amount for the first product that represents the product's stand-alone selling price and a variable amount contingent on the delivery of the second product. The variable amount might be excluded because of the requirements for constraining estimates of the transaction price. Therefore, it might be inappropriate to attribute the fixed consideration to both products.

To accommodate such situations, ASC 606 provides another exception to proportional allocation of the selling price. The first, discussed previously, relates to discounts; the second exception relates to variable consideration. Variable consideration in the contract may be attributable to the entire contract or to a specific part of the contract. The variable consideration may be attributable to a specific part of the contract, for example, in cases where the variable consideration relates to:

- One or more, but not all, of the performance obligations, as in the case of a bonus contingent on the entity transferring a good or service in a specified timeframe.
- One or more, but not all, of the distinct goods or services of a single performance obligation, as in the case of consideration increasing based on the consumer price index in the second year of a two-year contract.
  (ASC 606-10-32-39)

This exception may be applied to:

- A single performance obligation,
- A combination of performance obligations, or
- Distinct goods or services that make up part of a performance obligation.

Note that a relative stand-alone selling price allocation is not required to meet the allocation objective when it relates to the allocation of variable consideration to a specific part of a contract, such as a distinct good or service or a series.

Applying the variable consideration Exception to a single performance obligation The entity is required to allocate a variable amount entirely to a single performance obligation or to distinct goods or services that form part of a single performance obligation *only* when *both* of the following criteria are met:

a. The variable consideration specifically relates to the entity's efforts to satisfy the performance obligation or transfer the distinct good or service.
b. The allocation is consistent with the overall objective for allocating the transaction price. (ASC 606-10-32-40)

This fact pattern may be commonly found in long-term service contracts that include a bonus.

Series not accounted for as a single performance obligation In other instances, the variable consideration may *not* be allocated entirely to a performance obligation or to a distinct good or service that forms part of a single performance obligation. At times variable consideration might be attributable to some, but not all, performance obligations. If that is the case, to reflect the economic substance of the transaction, the entity should allocate the remaining amount of the transaction price based on the allocation requirements for stand-alone selling prices and allocation of a discount discussed earlier in this chapter.

Interaction between the two allocation exceptions—variable discount A discount may meet the definition of variable consideration if it is variable in amount or contingent on the occurrence or nonoccurrence of future events. The question becomes which exception would apply—the variable consideration exception or the discount exception. Responding to this issue, the TRG generally agreed that the entity should first determine whether the variable discount meets the variable consideration exception. If not, the entity then considers whether it meets the discount exception.[1]

Recognition

The amount the entity allocates to an unsatisfied performance obligation should be recognized in the period in which the transaction changes as:

- Revenue, or
- Reduction in revenue.

Changes in the Transaction Price

As uncertainties are resolved or new information becomes available, the entity should revise the amount of consideration it expects to receive. Revising the expectation gives the financial statement users better information than ignoring changes and retaining original estimates, especially for long-term contracts. Transaction prices, including variable consideration and the related constraints, are updated at each reporting date. The update may result in changes in the transaction price after inception of the contract. Changes in the transaction price may be related to:

- Contract modifications, or
- Changes in one or more of the factors used in estimating the transaction price, such as the resolution of uncertain events.

Except for changes resulting from modifications where the modification is treated as the end of the existing contract and the start of a new contract, entities should recognize a change in the transaction price by allocating it to performance obligations on the same basis as at contract

[1] IFRS.org; March 2015 Meeting—Summary of Issues Discussed and Next Steps, July 13, 2015, http://www.ifrs.org/Meetings/MeetingDocs/Other%20Meeting/2015/June/RTRG-34-March-Meeting-Summary.pdf.

inception. This should ensure that the changes in the estimate of variable consideration are allocated to the performance obligations to which that variable consideration relates. These changes should be recognized in the period in which they change. Changes in transaction price related to contract modification are discussed in detail later in this chapter. Note that the treatment of changes in stand-alone selling prices differs from changes in transaction price. Entities should not reallocate the transaction price for changes in the stand-alone selling prices. That is, the entity should use the same proportionality of the transaction price as at contract inception and *not reallocate* the transaction price to reflect changes in stand-alone selling prices after contract inception.

Change in Transaction Price Not Related to Modification The change in transaction price should be recognized as revenue or as a reduction in revenue in the period in which the change takes place. (ASC 606-10-32-43) The cumulative recognized revenue will then represent faithfully the revenue the entity would have recognized at the end of the subsequent reporting period as though the entity had that information at contract inception.

Variable consideration exception There is an exception to this allocation approach. The exception occurs when the changes in transaction price:

- Are shown to be related to one or more, but less than all, performance obligations or distinct goods or services in a series of distinct goods or services that are appropriately accounted for as a single performance obligation, and
- Meet the requirements for variable consideration to be allocated entirely to a performance obligation or to a distinct performance obligation that forms part of a single performance obligation.
  (ASC 606-10-32-44)

Where the exception applies, the entity should allocate the change in transaction price entirely to one or more, but not to all, performance obligations or a series that meets the requirements to be treated as a single performance obligation. The allocated adjustment amount should be reflected as an increase or decrease to revenue in the period of adjustment.

Subsequent Information Related to Variable Consideration In cases where information related to variable consideration comes to the entity's attention between the end of the reporting period and the release of the financial statements, the entity should follow the guidance in Topic 855, *Subsequent Events*.

STEP 5: RECOGNIZE REVENUE WHEN (OR AS) THE ENTITY SATISFIES A PERFORMANCE OBLIGATION

An entity shall recognize revenue when (or as) the entity satisfies a performance obligation by transferring a promised good or service (that is, an asset) to a customer. An asset is transferred when (or as) the customer obtains control of the asset. (ASC 606-10-25-23)

Overview

Step 5 addresses when to recognize revenue. At this point in the process, entities have determined the transaction price, allocated it, and are ready to record revenue.

According to ASC 606, revenue is recognized when control is transferred. So, the critical question is: When is control transferred? A performance obligation is satisfied when the customer obtains control of the good or service (asset). To implement Step 5, the entity must determine at contract inception whether it will satisfy its performance obligation over time or at a point in time. This key part of the model requires the entity first to determine if the obligation is satisfied over time. If not, it is, by default, satisfied at a point in time. (ASC 610-10- 25-24) This decision is also important because whether an entity transfers an asset over time also affects whether the sale meets the series requirement discussed earlier in this chapter and consequently, the allocation of variable consideration, change in transaction price, and contract modification.

Control of an Asset

ASC 606 applies a single model, based on control, to allow entities to determine when revenue should be recognized. (ASC 610-10-25-25) The concept of control is not only applicable to goods, but services as well. At some point, goods and services are assets when they are received or used. Services are an asset as they are consumed, even if only briefly, and even though they may not be recognized as an asset. The asset can be tangible or intangible. Transfer of control aligns with the FASB's definition of an asset, which includes the use of control to determine recognition of an asset. Assets are "probable future economic benefits obtained or controlled by a particular entity as a result of past transactions or events." (FASB Statement of Financial Accounting Concepts No. 6, para. 25.)

Determining whether the customer obtains control may require judgment. To have control of an asset, entities must have the ability to:

- Direct the use of the asset, and
- Obtain substantially all of the remaining benefits of the asset.

Direct the Use of an Asset A customer may have the future right to direct the use of an asset. However, the customer must have actually obtained that right for control to have transferred. Transfer of control may occur during production or afterwards. Directing the use of an asset means the customer has the right to:

- Deploy the asset,
- Allow another entity to deploy it, or
- Prevent other companies from having control of the asset.

Benefits of the Asset Conceptually, the benefits of the asset are the potential cash flows—either inflows or savings in outflows. These benefits can be obtained directly or indirectly by, for example:

- Using the asset to:
  - Produce goods
  - Provide services
  - Enhance the value of the assets
  - Settle liabilities
  - Reduce expenses
- Selling the asset
- Exchanging the asset
- Pledging the asset
- Holding the asset.

Other Considerations When evaluating control, the entity must consider the effect of any agreement to repurchase the assets. (ASC 610-10-25-26) Repurchase agreements are explored in detail later in this chapter.

Note that, unlike other aspects of ASC 606, Step 5 does not have a practical expedient for contracts with a duration of less than a year. The entity has to analyze all contracts to determine if the obligation is satisfied over time or at a point in time.

Performance Obligations Satisfied Over Time

As ASC 606 developed, constituents, especially in the construction industry, were concerned that it might be difficult to determine when control transferred. The construction industry constituents were concerned that they would have to change to the completed contract method and that would not be a faithful depiction of the underlying economics. Therefore, the guidance includes criteria that focus on timing for assessing when performance obligations are satisfied over time.

A performance obligation is satisfied over time if *any one* of the following three criteria is met (ASC 606-10-25-27):

1. The customer simultaneously receives and consumes the benefits as the entity performs. Examples of this include a one-year gym membership or a recurring service, like a cleaning service or a monthly payroll processing service. In those cases, the entity transfers the benefit of the services to the customer as the entity performs. An indication that the customer receives and consumes the benefits is if another entity would not need to substantially reperform the work completed to date.
2. The entity creates or enhances an asset that the customer controls as the asset is created or enhanced. Examples that fit this criterion might be a work-in-process asset that passes to the customer's control as the entity manufactures goods or a building under construction on the customer's land. It is common in government contracts for the customer (the governmental entity) to control work in process or other outputs. On the other hand, a commercial contract may not give control of a work in process to a customer.
3. This criterion consists of two parts:
   - The asset created by the entity does not have an alternative use to the entity, and
   - The entity has an enforceable right to payment for performance completed to date.

For example, a plane built to the customer's specifications where the entity has a right to payment may fit this criterion.

Criterion 1—Customer Simultaneously Receives and Consumes the Benefit as the Entity Performs The FASB created this criterion to clarify that for pure service contracts, services are transferred over time even if the services are received and consumed at the same time. They specified that this criterion does not apply to an asset that is not consumed completely as the asset is received. (ASU 2014-09 BC 125-128)

Contractual or practical limitations that prevent an entity from transferring the remaining obligations to another entity are not part of this assessment. However, the entity should consider the implications of possible termination of the agreement.

Bear in mind that not all service contracts fit this criterion, particularly those that create a work-in-process asset. The criterion does not apply when the entity's performance is not immediately consumed by the customer. For example, an entity may have a contract to provide a professional opinion. During the course of the engagement the entity creates a work in process. These circumstances do not fit Criterion 1. For those cases, the entity must consider Criteria 2 and 3.

Customer simultaneously receives and benefits from a commodity Subsequent to the issuance of ASC 606, constituents raised an issue regarding the factors that an entity should consider when determining whether an entity simultaneously receives and consumes the benefits of a commodity, such as electricity, natural gas, heating oil, and so forth. As with other assessments, the TRG members and FASB and IASB staff believe that an entity, as with any agreement, should consider all facts and circumstances including:

- Inherent characteristics, for example, whether the commodity can be stored,
- Contract terms, for example, whether it is a continuous supply contract or a contract to meet immediate demands, and
- Information about infrastructure or other delivery mechanisms.

Depending on the entity's assessment of the facts and circumstances of the contract and whether the contract indicates that the customer will simultaneously receive and consume benefits, revenue related to the sale of a commodity may or may not be recognized over time.

Reperforming the work The customer receives and consumes the benefits if another entity would not need to substantially reperform the work completed to date. The assessment of benefit can be subjective. The fact that reperformance is not necessary is an objective basis for determining whether the customer receives a benefit. In determining whether another entity would need to substantially reperform the work completed to date, the vendor is required to:

- Disregard any contractual or practical barriers to the transfer of the remaining performance obligations to another entity, and
- Presume that any replacement vendor would not benefit from an asset that it currently controls (such as work-in-process balance).

Criterion 2—Entity's Performance Creates an Asset That the Customer Controls as the Asset Is Created or Enhanced The customer's control of an asset as it is being created or enhanced indicates that the customer is getting the benefits of the asset. Thus, the entity's performance transfers the assets to a customer over time. This criterion is consistent with the rationale for using the percentage-of-completion method in previous standards. In effect, the entity agrees to a continuous sale of assets as it performs.

Criterion 3—Entity's Performance Does Not Create an Alternative Use, but Entity Has an Enforceable Right to Payment for Performance Completed In some situations, applying the first two criteria might be challenging, and it might be unclear whether the asset is controlled by the customer. So, the FASB developed Criterion 3 for entities that create assets with no alternative use, but where the entity has the right to payment. This criterion might be useful for goods or services that are specific to a customer.

Criterion 3 may be the criterion most relevant to long-term contracts accounted for under the percentage-of-completion method, although ASC 606 does not use that term. Instead, ASC 606 looks to the terms of the contract. Thus, a reporting entity may not be able to use the same measure of progress as under the percentage-of-completion method. The criterion also puts even greater importance on the way a contract is drafted.

In applying this criterion, entities should consider contractual restriction and practical limitations, but not possible termination.

Alternative use What is meant in Criterion 3 by "alternative use"? An alternative use might be selling the asset to another customer. An asset is considered *not* to have an alternative use if there are:

- Contractual restrictions preventing the entity from readily directing the asset to another use during the creation or enhancement of the asset, or
- Practical limitations to readily directing the completed asset to another use. (ASC 610-10-25-28)

Contractual restrictions A contract may restrict the entity from readily directing the asset for another use, such as sale to a different customer, while creating or enhancing the asset. Another type of restriction might be where the entity has to deliver the first 100 items of an otherwise standard item to the customer. The contractual restriction has to be substantive—and customer's right to the promised asset enforceable. The restriction is not substantive if the asset is interchangeable with other assets and could be transferred to another customer without breach of contract or significant incremental costs. The possibility of the customer terminating the contract is not relevant to the consideration of whether the entity could redirect the asset for another use.

Practical limitations Practical limitations, such as incurring significant cost to repurpose the asset or the asset having specifications unique to the customer, preclude the entity from readily directing the completed asset for another use. Entities should consider the characteristics of the asset that will transfer. Customization might be a factor in assessing alternative use, but it is not determinative. Some goods, for example real estate, might be standardized, but not have an alternative use because the entity is legally obligated to transfer the asset to the customer.

The alternative use assessment requires judgment and is made at contract inception and is not updated unless the parties agree to a contract modification that substantially alters the performance obligation.

Right to payment for performance completed to date Alternative use is necessary, but it is not enough to demonstrate control. An entity must also have an enforceable right to payment for performance completed to date. The second part of Criterion 3 is the "enforceable right to payment for performance completed to date." The entity may have a contract to construct an asset with no alternative use, constructing at the direction of the customer. If the entity is also entitled to payment completed to date at all times during the term of the contract and if the contract is terminated for reasons other than nonperformance, Criterion 3 is met. (ASC 606-10-25-29) As with many aspects of ASC 606, readers must be judicious in carefully considering the terms of the contract. Factors to consider when assessing whether a right to payment exists include:

- Amount of payment
- Payment terms
- Payment schedule
- Contractual terms
- Legislative or legal precedent.

The amount of payment To protect itself from the risk that the customer will terminate the contract and leave the entity with an asset of little or no value, the contract will often provide some compensation. Requirement to pay for performance suggests that the customer has obtained the benefits from the entity's performance. This payment does not need to be a fixed amount, but the amount:

- At a minimum must compensate the entity for performance to date at any point if the contract is terminated for reasons other than failure to perform.
- Should reflect the selling price of the items transferred to date covering the entity's cost plus a reasonable profit margin.

The margin does not have to equal the margin the entity would have gotten if the contract was fulfilled. It should reflect the extent of the entity's effort or a reasonable return on the entity's capital costs if the contract's margin is higher than the return the entity usually generates. In calculating a net amount that covers costs incurred and a reasonable profit, deposits and other up-front payments should be considered. (ASC 606-10-55-11)

If the entity is only entitled to reimbursement of costs, then the entity does not have a right to payment for the work to date.

Payment terms The FASB believes that a customer's obligation to pay for performance indicates that the customer obtained benefit from the performance. The right to payment does not have to be a present unconditional right, but the entity must have an enforceable right to demand or retain payment. For example, the payment may only be required at specified intervals or upon completion. The entity must assess whether it has the right to demand or retain payment if the customer cancels the contract for other than nonperformance. Even if the contract does not explicitly give the entity the right to payment, the entity would also have a right to payment if the customer does not have an explicit right to cancel the contract, but the contract entitles the entity to fulfill the contract and demand payment if the customer tries to terminate the contract.

Payment schedule A right to payment for performance to date in a contract is not the same as a payment schedule that specifies milestone or progress payments. A payment schedule may be based on milestones not related to performance.

A right to payment for performance schedule gives the entity a contractual right to demand payment if the customer terminates the contract prior to completion. These terms may not always align with the entity's rights to payment for performance obligation completed to date. For example, the contract might specify that consideration is refundable for reasons other than failure to perform.

Contractual terms A customer may terminate a contract without having the right to terminate at that point in time, for example, if the customer has failed to fulfill its obligations under the contract. In such cases, law or legal precedent may allow the entity to fulfill its performance obligation and require the entity to pay the appropriate consideration. The entity could also have an enforceable right to payment in a case where the customer might not have the right to terminate the contract or might have the right to terminate only at specified times.

Legislative or legal precedent and customary practices In making the right to payment assessment, the entity should look at legal precedents and customary business practices. The entity may have the right to payment even if the right is not specified in the contract. On the other hand, relevant legal precedent for similar contracts may indicate that entity has no right to payment. Because the entity has a customary business practice of not enforcing a right to payment, the right to payment may be unenforceable.

Performance Obligations Satisfied at a Point in Time

By default, if the performance obligation is not satisfied over time, it is satisfied at a point in time. How does the entity determine the point in time?

Determining the Point in Time at Which a Performance Obligation Is Satisfied To determine the point in time, the entity must consider when control has transferred and the customer has control of the assets. (Control is discussed earlier in this chapter. Remember, control is determined from the customer's perspective.) Also, ASC 606 provides indicators (not conditions that must be met) that help the entity assess when the customer has the ability to direct the use of the asset, tangible or intangible, and obtains the benefits from the asset. Indicators of control include when the customer has:

- Present obligation to pay
- Legal title
- Physical possession

- Risks and rewards of ownership
- Accepted the asset

Not all of the indicators need to be met. These indicators are not hierarchical, and there is no suggestion that certain indicators should be weighted more heavily than others. (ASC 606-10-25-30) Below is more information about the indicators.

The entity has a present right to payment This may indicate that the customer has the ability to direct the use of, and obtain substantially all of, the remaining benefits from an asset.

The entity has transferred legal title to the asset The entity with legal title typically can direct the use of the asset and receive the benefits from an asset, such as selling or exchanging the asset or secure or settle debt. If the entity retains legal control only to protect against the customer's failure to pay, those rights would not mean that the customer does not have control of the asset.

The entity has transferred physical possession Physical possession does not always mean more control. For example, in a consignment arrangement or under a repurchase agreement, the entity may have control. On the other hand, in some bill-and-hold arrangements where the entity has physical possession, the customer controls the assets.

The customer has the significant risks and rewards of ownership In considering the risks and rewards, the entity should exclude any risks that give rise to a separate performance obligation. For example, an entity may have transferred a computer to a customer, but has not performed an additional performance obligation to perform maintenance services. Notice that although ASC 606 is a control-based model rather than the legacy risk and rewards model, the FASB did include risks and rewards as one of the factors to consider.

The customer has accepted the asset Some contracts contain an acceptance clause that protects the customer, enabling the customer to force corrective actions for items that do not meet the contract's requirements. In some cases, the clause may be a mere formality. The entity must exercise judgment to determine if control has transferred. In making the assessment, the entity should look at its history of customer acceptance. The acceptance clause may be significant if the product is unique or there is no product history. An acceptance clause that includes a trial before payment does not indicate control. This, however, is different from a right of return as discussed later in this chapter.

Measuring Progress Toward Complete Satisfaction of a Performance Obligation

For each performance obligation satisfied over time:

> *... the objective when measuring progress is to depict an entity's performance in transferring control of goods or services promised to a customer (that is satisfaction of an entity's performance obligation).* (ASC 606-10-25-31)

Once the entity determines that a performance obligation is satisfied over time, it measures progress toward completion to determine the amount and timing of revenue recognition.

The entity must apply a single method of measuring progress for each performance obligation that best reflects the transfer of control, that is, a measure that is consistent with the objective of depicting its performance. The entity should apply the method consistently to enhance comparability of revenue in different reporting periods. The entity must apply that method consistently to "similar performance obligations in similar circumstances," and the entity must be able to apply that method reliably. (ASC 606-10-25-32)

Adjusting the measure of progress Circumstances, like changes in costs, can affect the measure of progress. The progress toward completion must be measured at the end of each reporting period. (ASC 606-10-25-35) If the measure of progress changes, the resulting changes should be accounted for as changes in accounting estimate per FASB ASC 250-10.

Practical Expedient If an entity has a right to consideration for an amount that corresponds directly to the value transferred to the customer of the entity's performance obligation completed to date, the entity may, as a practical expedient, recognize revenue for the amount the entity has a right to invoice. (ASC 606-10-55-18) A common example of this is a service contract where the entity bills a fixed amount for each block of time provided. Assessing whether an entity's right to consideration corresponds directly with the value to the customer requires judgment.

The TRG[2] examined a question regarding situations where an entity may change the price per unit transferred to the customer over the term of the contract. TRG members generally agreed that the resolution depends on the facts and circumstances of the arrangement. The TRG further opined that in contracts with changes in rates, it is possible to meet the practical expedient requirement as long as the rate changes reasonably represent the changes in value to the customer. For example, an IT support services contract where the level of service decreases as the level of effort decreases might qualify. The TRG gave another example: A contract to purchase electricity at prices that change each year based on the forward market price of electricity would qualify for the practical expedient if the rates per unit reflect the value of the provision of those units to the customer. Note of caution to SEC reporters: The SEC observer at the TRG meeting noted that entities need to have strong supporting evidence that variable prices represent the value to the customer.

In assessing whether the practical expedient can be applied, entities should also evaluate significant up-front payments or retrospective adjustments to determine if they have a right to invoice for each incremental good or service that corresponds directly to the value to the customer. In addition, entities should be aware that the presence of an agreed-upon customer payment schedule does not mean that the amount an entity has the right to invoice corresponds directly with the value to the customer of the entity's performance completed to date. In addition, the existence of specific contract minimums or volume discounts does not necessarily preclude use of the practical expedients if those clauses are nonsubstantive.

Methods for Measuring Progress To determine the best method, the entity should look at the nature of the promised goods and services and the nature of the entity's performance. ASC 606s do not prescribe any particular methods, but do present two broad methods to consider. Progress measures may be input or output methods.

Output methods are:

- Based on the value to the customer of the goods or services transferred,
- The results of the efforts expended, and
- Directly measure the value to the customer relative to the total goods or services provided.

"Value to the customer" is an objective measure of the entity's performance. As seen below by the types of output method, value to the customer is not assessed on market prices or standalone selling prices.

Input methods use the entity's efforts, or inputs, devoted to satisfying performance obligation.

Two common methods are the cost-to-cost method (input) and units of delivery method (output).

---

[2] IASB, July 2015 Meeting—Summary of Issues Discussed and Next Steps.

Output methods Output methods include:

- Surveys of work performed to date
- Appraisals of results achieved
- Contract milestones reached
- Time elapsed
- Units produced
- Units delivered

ASC 606 does not list all possible methods. Entities need to exercise judgment when choosing an output method. The entity should consider whether the method faithfully depicts progress toward complete satisfaction of the performance obligation. For example, an entity may choose to base its assessment on units delivered. However, if the entity has produced a material amount of work in process or finished goods that belong to the customer, those units are ignored and the method may result in units delivered or units produced that are not included in the measurement. The units-delivered method would then distort the entity's performance by not recognizing revenue for assets controlled by the customer but created before delivery or before production is complete. The units-delivered or units-produced methods would be acceptable if the value of any work in process or units produced but not delivered at the end of the period is immaterial to the contract or to the financial statements as a whole. (ASC 606-10-25-33)

The units-of-delivery and units-of-production methods may not be appropriate where the contract includes design and production services. Each item transferred may not have an equal value to the customer. Items produced earlier in the process will probably have a higher value. However, in the case of a long-term manufacturing contract, for standard items that individually transfer an equal amount of value to the customer, a units-of-delivery method might be appropriate.

Likewise, the contract milestone measure is not appropriate if material amounts of goods or services transferred between milestones would be excluded, even though the next milestone has not been met.

It is clear from the discussion above that the entity must be careful in its selection of measurement method. ASC 606 emphasizes the need for an entity to consider the contract's facts and circumstances and select the best method to depict performance and transfer of control. For example, an output measure may be the most faithful depiction of an entity's performance. However, it may be difficult to directly observe the outputs used to measure, and it may be costly to gather the output information, and in some circumstances, an entity may need to use an input method.

Input methods Inputs are measured relative to total inputs expected to be used. Inputs may include:

- Resources consumed
- Labor hours expended
- Costs incurred
- Timing elapsed
- Machine hours

Input methods that use costs incurred may not be proportionate to the entity's progress. For example, if the performance obligation includes goods or services, the customer may control the goods before the services are provided.

A challenge with input methods is connecting the input to the transfer of control of goods or services to the customer, that is, making a direct relationship between inputs and the transfer of control. There may not be a direct relationship between inputs and the transfer of goods or services. Only those inputs that depict the entity's performance toward fulfilling the performance obligation should be used. Other inputs should be excluded. Judgment is needed in making these determinations. The entity may need to adjust the measure of progress and to exclude from the end inputs:

- Costs incurred that do not contribute to the entity's progress in satisfying the obligation, for example, set-up costs. (Such costs may need to be capitalized as fulfillment costs. See information later in this chapter on contract costs.)
- Costs that are not proportionate to the entity's progress.

In the latter case, to achieve a faithful representation, the entity may recognize revenue to the extent of cost of goods incurred. This may be done at contract inception, if the entity expects all of the following conditions would be met:

- The good is not distinct.
- The customer is expected to obtain control significantly before receiving services related to the goods.
- The cost of the transferred good is significant relative to the total expected cost to completely satisfy the performance obligation.
- The entity procures the good from the third party and is not significantly involved in designing and manufacturing the good, but the entity is acting as a principal. (ASC 606-10-55-21)

Uninstalled materials Because of diversity in practice, ASC 606 includes guidance related to uninstalled materials. To ensure that the input method faithfully measures progress toward completion of a performance obligation, ASC 606 clarifies the adjustment for uninstalled materials. If a customer obtains control of goods before they are installed, the entity should not continue to carry them as inventory. It would not be appropriate for the entity to include the uninstalled goods in a cost-to-cost calculation. That could overstate the entity's performance, and, therefore, revenue. The entity should recognize revenue for the transferred goods, but only for the cost of those goods. The goods should be excluded from the cost-to-cost calculation. This adjustment should generally apply to goods that have a relatively significant cost and only if the entity is essentially providing a procurement service to the customer.

Cost-to-cost method As mentioned previously, one common input method is the cost-to-cost method. Costs included in the cost-to-cost method might be:

- Direct labor
- Direct materials
- Subcontractor costs
- Those allocation costs, directly related to contract activities, that depict the transfer of control to the customer
- Cost chargeable to the customer under the contract
- Costs incurred solely because of the contract

Direct labor and direct materials are relatively straightforward to identify and associate with a contract. It may be more difficult to decide whether other costs contribute to the transfer of control to the customer. For example, the following generally would not depict progress toward satisfying a performance obligation:

- General and administrative expenses not related to the contract, unless the terms call for reimbursement
- Selling and marketing costs
- Research and development costs not specific to the contract
- Depreciation of idle plant and equipment
- Wasted materials, unless budgeted when negotiating the contract
- Abnormal costs, again unless budgeted when negotiating the contract

ASC 606 does not provide guidance on how to identify unexpected costs. Entities must, therefore, exercise judgment to distinguish normal wasted materials or inefficiencies from those that do not dictate progress toward completion.

Inability to Estimate Progress It may be possible that an entity cannot reasonably estimate its progress toward completion of a performance obligation, for example, if it does not have reliable information or is in the early stages of the contract. In that case, the entity may recognize revenue as the work is performed, but only to the extent of cost incurred if the entity expects to recover costs. However, no profit can be recognized. Once the entity is able to make a reasonable estimate of performance, it should make a cumulative catch-up adjustment for any revenue not previously recognized. This adjustment should be made in the period of the change in the estimate. (ASC 606-10-25-36 and 25-37)

Measuring Progress Toward Satisfaction of a Stand-Ready Obligation The promise in a stand-ready obligation is the assurance that the customer will have access, not delivery, to a good or service. If the stand-ready obligation is satisfied over time, a time-based measure of progress, like a straight line, may be appropriate. Often, this might be the case for unspecified upgrade rights. However, entities should examine the contract and not automatically default to a straight-line attribution model. For example, straight-line attribution would not be appropriate if the benefits are not spread evenly over the life of the contract. An example of this is a contract with a snow removal provision that obviously provides more benefit in winter.

Determining the Measure of Progress for a Combined Performance Obligation For a performance obligation consisting of two or more goods or services that is satisfied over time, an entity must select a measure of progress that faithfully depicts the economics of the transfer. Such a determination may be difficult and require significant judgment. Entities should not merely default to an approach, like final deliverable, where revenue would be recognized over the performance period of the last promised goods or services. When choosing a method, entities should consider the reason why the goods or services were bundled in the first place. If a good or service was bundled because it was not capable of being distinct, it may not provide value on its own, and the entity may not want to consider that good or service when determining the pattern of transfer. If a measure of progress does not faithfully depict the economics of the transfer, the entity should consider whether there may actually be more than one performance obligation.

OTHER ISSUES

Right of Return

Rights of return affect the transaction price by creating variability in the transaction price. It is not uncommon for an entity to transfer control of a product while granting to the customer the right to return the product for reasons such as defective product or dissatisfaction with the product. The refund might include:

- A full or partial refund
- A credit that can be applied against amounts owed or which will be owed in the future to the vendor
- Another product in exchange

ASC 606 does not apply to exchanges for another product of the same type, quality, condition, and price. The guidance for warranties applies to returns of faulty goods or replacements.

At the time of initial sale, when revenue is deferred for the amount of the anticipated return, the entity recognizes a refund liability and a return asset. The asset is measured at the carrying amount of the inventory less expected cost to recover the goods. If the realizable value of the item expected to be returned is expected to be less than the cost of the related inventory, the entity makes an adjustment to cost of goods sold. The realizable value includes:

- Any adjustment, for example, costs of recovering the item, and
- Any potential decrease in value.

At the end of the reporting period, the entity reassesses the measurement and adjusts for any changes in expected level of returns and decreases in the value of the returned products.

In summary, the entity should recognize all of the following for the transfer of products with right of return and the services subject to refund:

- Revenue in the amount of consideration to which the entity expects to be entitled,
- A refund liability, and
- A return asset and corresponding adjustment to cost of sales for its right of return products from customers upon settling the refund liability.

The entity applies the revenue recognition constraint and does not recognize the revenue until the constraint no longer applies, which could be at the end of the return period. (ASC 606-10-55-25 through 27)

In some cases, the entity may charge the customer a restocking fee to compensate for repackaging, shipping, or reselling the item at a lower price. At the March 2015 TRG meeting, TRG members generally agreed that those costs should be recorded as a reduction of the amount of the return asset when or as control of the good transfers.[3]

To recap, rights of return are not considered a performance obligation in the revenue model. They are a form of variable consideration. Entities must estimate rights of return using the guidance on estimating variable consideration and apply the variable constraint. Once the entity determines it has rights of return amounts, it records a liability (balance sheet) and net revenue (income statement) amount. In the revenue model, all variable consideration must be included in the top line revenue number. In addition, the entity must record a returned asset outside of inventory and a contra amount against cost of sales. To measure the returned asset, the entity looks at the value of the inventory previously held and reduces it by the expected costs to recover that inventory. The entity also must test the returned asset for impairment, not as part of inventory, but as its own separate asset. This test must be done periodically, and estimates must be updated at each reporting period.

[3] TRG Agenda Paper 34, March 2015 Meeting Summary of Issues Discussed and Next Steps, dated July 13, 2015.

Warranties

Overview As any consumer knows, there are different types of warranties. Some warranties may simply provide assurance that the product will function as expected in accordance with certain specifications—assurance-type warranties. Other warranties provide customers with additional protection—service-type warranties. The type of warranty and the benefits provided by the warranty dictate the accounting treatment. So, the entity must first assess the nature of the warranty.

Warranties can be:

- Explicit—written in the contract, or
- Implicit as a result of customary business practices or law.

Warranties can also be standard or extended.

Assessing the Warranty A warranty purchased separately is a separate performance obligation. Revenue allocated to the warranty is recognized over the warranty period. A warranty not sold separately may still be a performance obligation. Entities have to assess the terms of the warranty and determine under which category below the warranty falls:

- Category 1. These warranties, called assurance-type warranties, provide assurance that the product will function. A warranty that only covers the compliance of the product with agreed-upon specifications is termed "an assurance warranty." These warranties obligate the entity to repair or replace the product and are accounted for under the guidance in ASC 460, *Guarantees*.
- Category 2. These warranties, called service-type warranties, provide a service in addition to product assurance. For example, this category of warranty offers additional protection against wear and tear or against certain types of damage. The additional service is accounted for as a separate performance obligation.

When assessing whether the warranty, in addition to product assurance, provides a service that should be accounted for as a separate performance obligation, an entity should consider factors such as:

- Whether the warranty is required by law—If the entity is required by law to provide a warranty, the existence of the law indicates that the promised warranty is not a performance obligation because such requirements typically exist to protect customers from the risk of purchasing defective products.
- The length of the warranty coverage—The longer the coverage period, the more likely it is that the promised warranty is a performance obligation because it is more likely to provide a service in addition to the assurance that the product complies with agreed-upon specifications.
- The nature of the tasks that the entity promises to perform—If it is necessary for an entity to perform specific tasks to provide the assurance that the product complies with agreed-upon specifications (for example, a return shipping service for defective products), then those tasks likely do not give rise to a performance obligation. (ASC 606-10-55-33)

Warranty is a performance obligation If a warranty is determined to be a performance obligation, the entity applies Step 4 of the revenue recognition model and allocates a portion of the transaction price to the warranty. The entity will have to exercise judgment to determine the appropriate pattern of revenue recognition. For example, an entity may determine it is appropriate to recognize revenue on a straight-line basis over the term of the warranty, or based on historical fact patterns, the entity may recognize revenue in the latter part of the term.

Contract includes both types of warranties Some contracts may include both an assurance-type and a service-type warranty. If the entity cannot reasonably account for the service element separately from the assurance amount, it should account for the assurance and service elements as a single performance obligation. Revenue is allocated to the combined warranty and recognized over the warranty period. The guidance does not make clear how the entity should interpret the "reasonably account" threshold.

Principal versus Agent

Overview More than one party may be involved in providing goods or services to a customer. In those situations, ASC 606 requires the entity to determine whether for each specified good or service it is a principal or an agent, whether the nature of its promise is a performance obligation:

- To provide the specified goods or services (principal), or
- To arrange for another party to provide them (agent).

Exhibit—Principal versus Agent

	Performance obligation to:	Report:
Principal	Provide the specified goods or services.	Gross, when or as the performance obligation is satisfied, for the consideration received from the customer.
Agent	Arrange for the specified goods or services to be provided by the other party.	Net for the fee the entity expects. (ASC 606-10-55-37B)
(ASC 606-10-55-37B and 55-38)		

As with other issues in ASC 606, whether an entity is a principal or an agent depends on control. Before assessing control, the entity must identify the unit of account, that is, the specified good or service being provided to the customer. An entity may be a principal for one or more specified goods or services in a contract and an agent for others in the same contract. The entity must also determine the nature of each specified good or service:

- A good
- A service
- A right to a good or service from the other party that it then combines with other goods or services to provide a specified good or service to the customer (ASC 606-10-55-37A)

The entity must determine whether it has control of the goods or services before they are transferred. If the entity has control before transfer to the customer, it is the principal. ASC 606 includes indicators to support the assessment of whether an entity controls the specified good or service before it is transferred. These include but are not limited to:

- The entity is primarily responsible for fulfilling the promise to provide the specified good or service.
- The entity has inventory risk before or after the goods have been transferred.
- The entity has discretion in establishing prices for the specified goods or services. (ASC 606-10-55-39)

These indicators are meant to support the entity's assessment. They should be considered in context and not be used as a checklist. The relevance of individual indicators to the control evaluation may vary from contract to contract.

Control of inventory is an indicator that one entity is the principal. Having substantive inventory risk may indicate the entity is the principal. An entity may fulfill the performance obligation or it may engage another party to do so.

If control of the specified goods or services is unclear, the entity should recognize revenue net.

Customer Options to Purchase Additional Goods or Services

Some contracts give customers the option to purchase additional goods or services. These options may include:

- Sales incentives
- Customer awards
- Contract renewal options
- Other discounts on future goods or services

These options may be offered at a discount or for free. These options are separate performance obligations if they provide a *material right* to the customer. A right is material if it results in a discount that the customer would not receive if not for entering into the contract, that is, it must be incremental to the discounts typically given for the good or service, to that class of customer, in that geographical area. (ASC 606-10-55-42) This provision acknowledges that customers are implicitly paying for the option as part of the transaction—the old accounting theory that there is no such thing as a free lunch.

Assessing Whether the Customer Has a Material Right When assessing whether a customer has a material right, the entity should consider quantitative and qualitative factors. Qualitative factors might be:

- What a new customer would pay for the same service
- The availability and pricing of competitors' alternatives
- Whether the average customer life indicates the fee is an incentive to stay beyond the stated contract term

In addition, entities should consider not only the current transaction, but also accumulations in programs, such as loyalty programs.

Some contracts restrict customers from selling a good or service and that raised an issue with the FASB. The entity might conclude that the customer cannot benefit from a good or service because it cannot resell the good or service for more than scrap value. On the other hand, the entity might conclude that the customer can benefit from the good together with other readily available resources. The FASB concluded that the assessment should be based on whether the customer could benefit from the good or service on its own rather than how the customer may actually use the good or service. Therefore, in making the assessment, the entity should disregard any contractual limitations.

However, if the option price reflects the stand-alone selling price, the entity is deemed to have made a marketing offer. (ASC 606-10-55-43)

Entities must carefully assess contract terms to distinguish between options and marketing offers.

Recognition Revenue is recognized when future goods and services are transferred or when the option expires. The transaction price is allocated to the performance obligations (including the option based on relative stand-alone selling prices). The estimate of the stand-alone selling price of an option reflects the discount a customer receives when exercising the option, adjusted for the discount a customer receives without exercising the option and the likelihood the option will be executed.

Practical Alternative Estimating the stand-alone selling price may be difficult because the option may not be sold separately. ASC 606 provides a practical alternative. Instead of estimating the stand-alone selling price of the option, the entity can use the practical alternative and evaluate the transaction assuming the option will be exercised. The transaction price is determined by including any consideration estimated to be received from the optional goods and services. The transaction price is then allocated to all goods and services, including those under option. The alternative can be applied if the additional goods or service meet both of the following conditions:

1. They are similar to the original goods and services in the contract, and
2. They were provided in accordance with the original contract's terms.
   (ASC 606-10-55-45)

Customer's Unexercised Rights (Breakage)

Breakage Are Rights Unexercised by the Customer Under some arrangements, a customer may make a nonrefundable prepayment. For that prepayment, the customer has a right to a good or service in the future, and the entity stands ready to deliver goods or services in the future. However, the customer may not actually exercise those rights. The most common examples of this situation are gift cards or vouchers. These unexercised rights are known as breakage.

Recognition Upon receipt of the customer's advance payment, the entity records a contract liability for the amount of the payment. When the contract performance obligations are satisfied, the entity recognizes revenue. A portion of the payment may relate to contractual rights that the entity does not expect the customer to exercise. The timing of revenue recognition related to breakage depends on whether the entity expects to be entitled to a breakage amount. To determine whether it expects to be entitled to a breakage amount, the entity should look to the guidance on constraining amounts of variable consideration found earlier in this chapter. The entity should recognize revenue for breakage proportionately as other balances are redeemed.

The assessment of estimated breakage should be updated at each reporting period. Any changes should be accounted for by adjusting the contract liability.

Practice Pointer: Prepaid stored-value products contain stored monetary value that can be redeemed for goods, services, or cash, e.g., gift cards. The Codification requires entities that record financial liabilities related to prepaid stored-value products to follow the breakage model in ASC 606. This aligns the breakage model for financial and nonfinancial liabilities.

Unclaimed Property (Escheat) Laws Legal rights related to unexercised rights vary by jurisdiction. Entities may be required to remit payment related to unexercised rights to a governmental entity. These requirements may fall under unclaimed property or "escheat" laws. If the entity must remit unclaimed property to a governmental entity, the entity should not recognize breakage as revenue. In these situations, it is important for the entity to understand its legal rights and obligations.

Nonrefundable Up-Front Fees

Overview In some industries, it is common to charge an up-front fee. An up-front fee relates to an activity that the entity must undertake to fulfill the contract. The activity occurs at or near inception of the contract, and the up-front fee is an advance payment for future goods or services. Examples of up-front fees are:

- Joining, for example, a gym membership,
- Activation, for example, a cell phone,
- Other initial set-up fees.

Recognition Upon receipt of the fee, the entity should not recognize revenue, even if the fee is nonrefundable, if it does not relate to the performance obligation. Up-front fees are allocated to the transaction price and should be recognized as revenue when the related goods or services are provided. If there is an option to renew the contract and the option provides a material right, the entity should extend the revenue recognition period beyond the initial contract. (ASC 606-10-55-51)

Practical Alternative If it is determined that the up-front fee should be accounted for as an advance payment for future goods or services, the entity may make use of the practical alternative mentioned in the previous section of this chapter on "Customer Options to Purchase Additional Goods or Services." (ASC 606-10-55-45)

Set-Up Costs Some nonrefundable fees are intended to compensate an entity for costs incurred at the beginning of the contract. These costs may be, for example, for the hiring of additional personnel, systems set-up, or moving assets to the service site. These efforts usually do not satisfy performance obligations because goods or services are not transferred to the customer. The fees are advance payment for future goods or services. The underlying costs should not be factored into the measure of progress used for performance obligations satisfied over time if they do not depict the transfer of services to the customer. Some set-up costs might not meet the criteria for capitalization as fulfillment costs.

Renewal Options In some situations, for instance, a gym membership, a customer does not have to pay an additional up-front fee when the contract is renewed. Thus, the renewal option may give the customer a material right.

If a material right is not provided, the fee would be recognized over the contract term.[4] If a material right is provided, it is a performance obligation and the entity should allocate part of the transaction price to the material right. The entity has the option to apply the practical alternative for contract renewal if the criteria are met.

As with other aspects of ASC 606, the entity has to exercise judgment when determining the amount to allocate to a material right. To make its assessment, the entity should look at historical data, expected renewal rates, marketing analysis, customer input, industry data, etc.

---

[4] Ibid.

Licenses

Because of its challenging nature, the guidance in ASC 606 on licenses was one of the last items finalized. Experts had different views of the underlying economics of licensing issues, and those issues did not end with the release of ASC 606 in May 2014.

Sale of Intellectual Property An agreement that calls for the transfer of control of all the worldwide rights, exclusively, in perpetuity, for all possible applications of the intellectual property (IP) may be considered a sale rather than a license. If the use of the IP is limited by, for instance, geographic area, term, or type of application or substantial rights, then the transfer is probably a license. If the agreement represents a sale, the transaction is treated as a sale subject to the five-step model, including the guidance on variable constraint and the recognition constraint to any sale- or usage-based royalties.

Licenses of Intellectual Property A license arrangement establishes a customer's right to an entity's intellectual property and the entity's obligations to provide these rights. With the prevalence of technology in every business, accounting for IP licenses has become more critical than ever. In addition to the software industry, IP licenses are common in other industries, such as:

- Entertainment and media
- Pharmaceuticals
- Retail and consumer
- Franchise.

Licenses may involve patents, trademarks, and copyrights. Licenses can:

- Be term-based or perpetual
- Be exclusive or nonexclusive
- Carry fixed to variable terms
- Require up-front payments or over time installments.

Assessing Whether a License Is Distinct As with other performance obligations, entities should assess if a license represents a distinct performance obligation, including whether the customer can benefit from the license on its own or together with other readily available resources and whether the license is separately identifiable from other goods or services in the contract. Assessing whether a license is distinct may require significant judgment. (For more on determining whether a performance obligation is distinct, see the discussion earlier in this chapter.) The guidance in this section only relates to distinct licenses. Licenses that are not distinct include those that:

- Form a component of a tangible good and that is integral to the functionality of the item.
- The customer can benefit from only in conjunction with a related service. (ASC 606-10-55-56)

If a license is not distinct, entities should account for the license and other goods and services as single performance obligation and look to the guidance in Step 5 to determine if the revenue should be recognized over time or at a point in time.

Nature of the Entity's Promise Before identifying when the customer takes control of an asset, it is necessary to identify the nature of the entity's promise. Therefore, when accounting for a performance obligation that includes a license and other goods or services, the entity should consider the nature of its promise in granting a license. (ASC 606-10-55-57) ASC 606 classifies all distinct licenses of intellectual property into two categories:

1. *A right to access* the entity's intellectual property throughout the license period (or its remaining economic life, if shorter)
2. *A right to use* the entity's intellectual property as it exists at the point in time at which the license is granted.
   (Emphasis added.)
   (ASC 606-10-55-58)

When assessing whether a license is a right to use IP or a right to access IP or when identifying the promises in a contract, the entity does not consider restrictions of time, geography, or use of the license and guarantees provided by the licensor that it has a valid patent to the industry IP and that it will maintain and defend the patent. Those attributes define the scope of the customer's rights and not whether the entity satisfies its performance obligation at a point in time or over time. (ASC 606-10-55-64)

Exhibit—Comparison of Right to Access and Right to Use

	Right to Access	**Right to Use**
Description	The customer simultaneously receives and consumes the benefit of the IP license as the entity performs. The entity undertakes activities that significantly affect the IP (required indirectly by the contract or the customer's reasonable expectation based on business practices, published policies, or specific statements). Those activities affect, positively or negatively, the customer. Those activities do not result in transfer of goods or services.	The license does not meet the criteria for a right to access license.
Examples	Brand, team, or trade names, logos, franchise rights.	Software, biological compounds, drug formulas, and completed media content (films, TV shows, music).
Recognition	Recognize over time, with an appropriate method, because the customer simultaneously receives and consumes the benefit of the IP.	Recognize at a point in time because the customer has control: It can direct the use of and benefit from the license at the point in time at which the license transfers.
(ASC 606-10-55-58A and 58B)		

The entity should assess whether the IP is expected to change during the term of the license. A customer does not meet the criteria for control if the IP is expected to change. If the entity is expected to be involved in the IP and undertake activities that significantly affect the licensed IP, this may be an indication the IP is expected to change.

To determine if a customer could expect the entity to undertake activities that significantly affect the IP, the entity should consider:

- Customary business practices, published policies, or specific statements
- Shared economic interest, such as a sales-based royalty.

To determine whether a license is a right to use or a right to access IP, the FASB provides clarified guidance about the nature of the license. The FASB's approach looks to the nature of the IP and focuses on whether activities undertaken by the entity significantly affect the IP. Utility relates to the IP's ability to provide value or benefits. Entities must determine if the license is either functional or symbolic and that category determines whether the license is a right to access or a right to use. For both types of IP, the entity cannot recognize revenue before the beginning of the period in which the customer is able to use and benefit from the license.

Exhibit—Categories of Distinct Licenses of Intellectual Property: FASB's Alternative Approach

	Symbolic IP	**Functional IP**
Description	This IP does not have significant stand-alone functionality. It represents something else. The lack of stand-alone functionality indicates that substantially all of the utility is derived from the entity's past or ongoing activities of the entity. It is assumed that the entity will continue to support and maintain the IP.	Customer derives a substantial portion of its benefit from stand-alone functionality. The licensor's ongoing activities do not significantly affect the utility of the IP.
Examples	Brand, team or trade names, logos, franchise rights	Software, biological compounds, drug formulas, and completed media content (films, TV shows, music).
Recognition	Over the license period using a measure of progress that reflects the licensor's pattern of performance.	At a point in time* when control of the IP transfers to the customer, that is, when the IP is available for the customer's use and benefit. (*Unless the functionality of IP is expected to substantively change the form or functionality as a result of activities performed by the entity that are not separate performance obligations and the customer would be required or compelled to use the latest version of the IP. This would indicate that the customer has a right to access the IP. In such cases, the activities significantly affect the customer's ability to benefit from the IP and revenue would be recognized over time.)

Symbolic license With a symbolic license, the IP may change over the course of time. This can occur because of the entity's continuing involvement with activities that affect its IP. Even if the right is unchanged, the benefit or value to the customer may be affected by the licensor's activities during the license period. With symbolic IP, the entity fulfills its obligation over time, as the entity:

- Grants the customer rights to use and benefit from the entity's intellectual property by making it available for the customer's use
- Supports or maintains the intellectual property.
(ASC 606-10-55-60)

The customer has an expectation that the entity will undertake positive activities to maintain the value of the IP and avoid actions that would reduce the value of the IP.

Functional license A functional IP license generally grants the customer the right to use the IP at a point of time. However, if both of the following criteria are met, the license grants a right to access the IP:

1. The functionality of the intellectual property to which the customer has rights is expected to substantively change during the license period as a result of activities of the entity that do not transfer a good or service to the customer, and
2. The customer is contractually or practically required to use the updated IP resulting from criterion "1."
(ASC 606-10-55-62)

The IP's utility may be significantly affected when:

- The expected activities are expected to change the form or the functionality of the IP, or
- The value for the customer of the IP is substantially derived from or dependent on the expected activities of the entity.

Examples of these might be when the ability to perform a function or the value of a logo changes.

Sales- or Usage-Based Royalties For related information on sales- and usage-based royalties, see the section on Step 3.

Recognition Revenue from a license of IP that is a right to access should be recognized over time. The entity should use a recognition method that reflects its progress towards completion of the performance obligation. Revenue from a license of IP that is a right to use should be recognized at a point in time. Once the entity determines that the revenue from the license should be recognized over time or at a point in time, the entity should apply the guidance in Step 5 to determine the point in time or to select the appropriate method to measure the revenue over time.

In any case, revenue cannot be recognized from an IP license before:

- The entity has made available a copy of the IP to the customer, *and*
- The license period has begun.
(ASC 610-10-55-58C)

Repurchase Agreements

A repurchase agreement is a contract in which an entity sells an asset and also promises or has the option (either in the same contract or another contract) to repurchase the asset. (ASC 606-10-55-66)

The repurchased asset may be:

- The asset that was originally sold to the customer,
- An asset that is substantially the same as that asset, or
- Another asset of which the asset that was originally sold is a component.

Agreements come in three forms:

1. A forward—the entity has an obligation to repurchase the asset.
2. A call option—the entity has a right to repurchase the asset.
3. A put option—the customer has the option to require the entity to repurchase the asset at a price that is lower than the original selling price.
(ASC 606-10-55-67)

A Forward or Call Option When the entity has an obligation (forward option) or right (call option) to repurchase the asset, the customer may have physical possession, but is limited in its ability to:

- Direct the use of the asset, and
- Obtain substantially all of the remaining benefits from the asset.

Therefore, the conditions as discussed in Step 5 for the customer to have control of the asset are not present, and the customer is deemed not to have control of the asset. The accounting treatment depends on the repurchase amount required. The entity should account for the contract as:

- A lease if the entity can or must repurchase the asset for a lower amount than the original selling price unless the contract is part of a sale-leaseback transaction. If a sale-leaseback transaction, the entity should account for the contract as a financing transaction and not as a sale-leaseback in accordance with ASC 840-40.
- A financing arrangement if the entity can or must repurchase the asset for an amount equal to or more than the original selling price of the asset.
(ASC 606-10-55-68)

Recognition When assessing the repurchase price, the entity should consider the time value of money. If the contract is accounted for as a financing arrangement, the entity should continue to recognize the asset, but the entity also recognizes a financial liability for any consideration received. Interest and processing and holding costs, if applicable, are recognized for the difference between the consideration received and the amount of consideration to be paid to the customer. The entity derecognizes the asset and recognizes revenue if the option is not exercised. (ASC 606-10-55-69 through 55-71)

Put Options A put option gives the customer the right to require the entity to repurchase the asset. If the repurchase price is lower than the original selling price of the asset, the entity must evaluate at contract inception whether the customer has a significant economic incentive to exercise the option. The entity makes that judgment by considering the relationship of the repurchase price to the expected market value of the asset and the amount of time until the right expires.

If the entity concludes that the customer has a significant economic interest and anticipates that the option will be exercised, the option is accounted for as a lease, unless the agreement is part of a sale and leaseback transaction. (ASC 606-10-55-72) If not, the entity accounts for it as a sale with a right of return.

If the repurchase price is greater than or equal to the original selling price and is more than the expected market value of the asset, the entity accounts for the contract as a financing arrangement. The time value of money should be considered when comparing the repurchase price with the selling price. If the option expires unexercised, the entity derecognizes the liability and recognizes revenue.

Consignment Arrangements

A consignment arrangement occurs when an entity ships goods to a distributor, but retains control of the goods until a predetermined event occurs. Because control has not passed, the entity does not recognize revenue upon shipment or delivery to the consignee. ASC 606 includes the following indicators to evaluate whether a consignment arrangement exists:

- The product is controlled by the entity until a specified event occurs, such as the sale of the product to a customer of the dealer, or until a specified period expires.
- The entity is able to require return of the products or transfer the product to a third party (such as another dealer).
- The dealer does not have an unconditional obligation to pay for the product (although it might be required to pay a deposit).
  (ASC 606-10-55-80)

ASC 606 provides these indicators, but the entity is not limited to just them. Once control transfers, the entity recognizes revenue.

Practice Pointer: A distributor may have physical control of the goods, but if the entity has enforceable rights to require return of the goods, the distributor may not have control.

Bill-and-Hold Arrangements

Bill-and-hold situations arise when:

- The entity bills the customer for goods that are ready for shipment, but
- The entity does not ship the goods until a later date.

In these cases, the entity must determine if the customer has control of the goods. These arrangements may sometimes be used to manipulate revenue. ASC 606 provides four criteria, all of which an entity must meet in order to decide that control has passed to the customer:

1. The reason for the bill-and-hold is substantive. For example, a customer may request that an entity hold a shipment because of a lack of warehouse space or because the customer does not yet need the goods in its production process.
2. The product must be identified in some way as belonging to the customer.
3. The product must be ready for physical transfer upon request from the customer.
4. The entity cannot have the ability to use the product or to direct it to another customer. The goods cannot be used to fulfill orders for other contracts. Doing so may indicate the goods are not controlled by the customer.
   (ASC 606-10-55-83)

The entity needs to consider whether it meets those criteria and if it is providing custodial services. If the entity is providing custodial services, part of the transaction price should be allocated to that performance obligation.

Contract Modifications

A contract modification is a change in the scope or price (or both) of a contract that is approved by the parties to the contract. (ASC 606-10-25-10)

Parties to an arrangement frequently modify the scope or price or both of an ongoing contract. Such a change is sometimes called a change order, a variation, or an amendment.

Technical Alert: For an entity with a significant volume of contract modifications occurring over a long period of time, ASC 606's guidance for accounting for modified contracts at times could be costly and complex. Subsequent to release of ASC 606, the FASB clarified the guidance related to implementing contract modifications and provided for a practical expedient related to:

- Accounting for a modification that occurred before transition to ASC 606

For contracts modified before transition to ASC 606, the practical expedient allows an entity to determine and allocate the transaction price on the basis of all satisfied and unsatisfied performance obligation as of the beginning of the earliest period presented. The entity may aggregate the effect of the modifications. This practical expedient relieves entities from having to separately evaluate the effects of each contract modification. Entities should note that the expedient, if used, must be applied consistently to similar types of contracts. (ASC 606-10-65-1f.4)

Approval A contract modification must be approved by the parties. Like the original contract, the modification should be approved:

- In writing,
- Orally, or
- Implied by customary business practice.

Practice Pointer: Entities must exercise judgment when assessing whether a change is a modification or should have been anticipated at the outset because of the entity's customary business practice.

Until the modification is approved, the entity should continue to apply the guidance to the existing contract. (ASC 606-10-25-10)

Disputes A modification may exist even if the parties have a dispute as to scope or price. The revenue standard focuses more on enforceability of the contract than on finalization of the modification. If the change in scope has been agreed to, but the price is not settled, the entity should estimate the change to the price in accordance with the guidance on estimating variable consideration and constraining estimates of variable consideration. (ASC 606-10-25-11)

Recognition Recognition of contract modifications can be complex and requires careful analysis. The following sections explain the recognition process in detail.

When a modification occurs, entities must determine:

- If the modification has created a new contract and performance obligations, or
- If the existing contract has been modified.

If the entity determines that an existing, ongoing contract has been modified, then it must further analyze the modification to determine if the modification should be accounted for as:

1. A separate contract,
2. Effectively, a termination of the contract and execution of a new contract resulting in a prospective treatment,

3. Part of the original contract, which could result in a catch-up adjustment, or
4. A combination of 2 and 3 above.

The accounting treatment depends on what was changed. Under ASC 606, to faithfully depict the rights and obligations of a contract modification, entities must account for modifications on a:

- Prospective basis—when the additional goods or services are distinct, or
- Cumulative catch-up basis—when the additional goods or services are not distinct.

Contract Modification Represents a Separate Contract The concept underlying accounting for a modification as a separate contract is that there is no substantive economic difference under the given set of circumstances between a new contract and a modification. Therefore, the entity must analyze the agreement and account for the modification as a separate contract if:

- The scope of the contract increases because of the addition of *distinct* promised goods or services, *and*
- The price of the contract increases by an amount of consideration that reflects the entity's stand-alone selling prices of the additional promised goods or services and any appropriate adjustment to that price to reflect the circumstances of the particular contract.
  (ASC 606-10-25-12)

Further, to be distinct, two criteria must be met:

1. The customer could benefit from the goods or services.
2. The promise to transfer a good or service is separately identifiable from other promises in the contract.
   (ASC 606-10-25-19)

(See earlier in this chapter for further information on determining whether performance obligations are "distinct.")

When these criteria are met, there is no economic difference between an entity entering into a separate contract for the additional goods or services and an entity modifying an existing contract.

Note that only modifications that *add* distinct goods or services can be treated as separate contracts. Modifications that reduce the amount of good or service or change the scope, by their nature, cannot be considered separate contracts. They would be modifications of the original contract.

If the entity determines that the modification should be accounted for as a separate contract, the next step is to assess the agreement using the five contract criteria detailed earlier in this chapter. If the contract meets the criteria, the company should account for the change prospectively, accounting for the change in the current period and in any future period affected. Previously reported results are not changed.

Contract Modification Does Not Represent a Separate Contract If the new goods or services are not distinct or not priced at the proper stand-alone selling price according to the criteria above, the changes are not treated as a separate contract. They are considered changes to the original contract, and the entity must then determine how to account for the remaining goods or services. That accounting depends on whether or not each of the remaining goods or services is distinct from the goods or services transferred on or before the date of the modification. ASC 606 describes three possible scenarios and the accounting under each:

- Scenario 1—Remaining goods or services are distinct.
- Scenario 2—Remaining goods or services are not distinct.
- Scenario 3—Remaining goods or services are a combination of distinct and not distinct goods or services.

Account for the remaining goods or services, that is, for the goods or services not transferred as an adjustment to the existing contract, as follows.

Scenario 1—remaining goods or services are distinct The remaining goods or services are distinct from the goods or services transferred on or before the date of the contract modification, but the consideration for those goods or services does not reflect the stand-alone selling price.

This type of modification is accounted for in the same way as a modification considered a new contract. In this scenario, the modification is negotiated after the original contract and is based on new facts and circumstances. Entity should account for these changes using a cumulative catch-up basis would be complex and might not reflect the economic substance of the modification. Account for this type of modification prospectively as if it were effectively a termination of the existing contract and the creation of a new contract.

The amount of consideration already recognized under the contract is not adjusted. The amount of consideration allocated to the remaining performance obligations is the sum of:

- Consideration promised by the customer under the original terms of the contract and included in the estimate of the transaction price and that has not yet been recognized as revenue. This amount includes amounts already received from customers and creates contract assets or receivables.
- The consideration promised as part of the contract modification.
(ASC 606-10-25-13a)

Series of distinct goods or services The Scenario 1 accounting treatment also applies to situations where the entity determines that after the modification it has the same single performance obligation as before but that performance obligation represents a series of distinct goods or services. This situation typically may be found in energy contacts, mobile phone airtime services, or service contracts.

Scenario 2—remaining goods or services are not distinct The remaining goods or services are not distinct and, therefore, form part of a single performance obligation that is partially satisfied at the contract modification date.

Account for the modification as if it were a part of the existing contract:

a. Retrospectively through a cumulative catch-up adjustment.
b. Recognize the modification as an increase or decrease in revenue at the contract modification date, measured at the effect that the modification has on the transaction price and on the entity's measure of progress toward satisfaction of the performance obligation.
(ASC 606-10-25-13b)

However, as explained above, modifications of contracts with a single performance obligation that is actually a series of distinct goods or services are accounted for prospectively, not by using a cumulative catch-up adjustment.

Scenario 3—remaining goods or services are a combination of distinct and not distinct goods or services The remaining goods or services are a combination of (a) and (b), that is, a combination of distinct and not distinct goods or services.

In this scenario, a change in the contract is treated as a combination of the first and second scenarios: a modification of the existing contract and the creation of a new contract. So, the entity does not adjust the accounting for completed performance obligations that are distinct from the modified goods or services, but adjusts revenue previously recognized for the effect of the modification on the transaction price allocated to performance obligations that are not distinct and the measure of progress. Account for the effects of the modification on the unsatisfied performance obligations following the guidelines above for (a) goods and services that are distinct and (b) goods and services that are not distinct. (ASC 606-10-25-13c)

Practice Pointer: The amount of consideration allocated to the remaining performance obligation includes amounts received but not yet recognized and amounts the customer has promised to pay that had not yet been recognized. There are situations where the entity may have recognized promised considerations but not yet received those amounts. Those amounts create a contract asset or receivables. Those amounts have to be deducted from the consideration allocated to the remaining performance obligation. Otherwise, the entity would recognize revenue twice.

Change in Transaction Price Resulting from Modification If a change in transaction price occurs as a *result* of a contract modification, ASC 606 takes an approach that is consistent with other modifications. That is, a contract modification that only affects the transaction price is accounted for like other contract modifications:

- Prospectively if the remaining goods or services are distinct.
- As a cumulative catch-up adjustment if the remaining goods or services are not distinct.

A change in transaction price may occur *after* a modification, but before fulfillment of performance obligations is completed. In that case, ASC 606 provides the following guidance.

- If the modification is accounted for as if it were a termination of the existing contract and the creation of a new contract, the entity allocates the change in the transaction price to the performance obligations identified in the contract before the modification if and to the extent that the change in transaction price is attributable to an amount of variable consideration promised before the modification.
- If the modification was not accounted for as a separate contract, the entity allocates the change in the transaction price to the performance obligations in the modified contract. These are the performance obligations that were not fully satisfied at the date of the modification.
  (ASC 606-10-32-45)

For more information on changes in transaction price, see the section on transaction prices earlier in this chapter.

Disclosures Required by ASC 606

ASC 606 requires entities to disclose both quantitative and qualitative information that enables users of financial statements to understand the nature, amount, timing, and uncertainty of revenue and cash flows arising from contracts with customers. The additional disclosures are partially driven by the judgment related to estimates required in ASC 606. The requirements are comprehensive and include quantitative and qualitative information. ASC 606 includes some exceptions for disclosure by nonpublic entities. More information on disclosures can be found at www.wiley.com/go/GAAP2021.

38 ASC 610 OTHER INCOME

PERSPECTIVE AND ISSUES

Subtopics

ASC 610, *Other Income*, contains three subtopics:

1. ASC 610-10, *Overall*, which defines the scope of guidance on revenue recognized that is *not* in the scope of:
   - ASC 606, in other words, that is not from a contract with a customer,
   - Other topics, such as ASC 840 or 842 on leases and ASC 944 on insurance, or
   - Other revenue or income guidance.
2. ASC 610-20, *Gains and Losses from the Derecognition of Nonfinancial Assets*, applies to derecognition of nonfinancial assets with the scope of ASC 350 on intangibles and ASC 360 on property, plant, and equipment that is not in the scope of ASC 606. Nonfinancial assets are, for example, real estate, intangible assets, property, plant, and equipment.
3. ASC 610-30, *Gains and Losses on Involuntary Conversions*, applies to events and transactions in which nonmonetary assets are involuntarily converted to monetary assets that are then reinvested to other nonmonetary assets.

Scope and Scope Exceptions

ASC 610-10, *Overall* ASC 610-10 applies to all entities. (ASC 610-10-15-2)

ASC 610-20, *Gains and Losses from the Derecognition of Financial Assets* ASC 610-20 applies to all entities and the gain or loss recognized upon:

- The derecognition of nonfinancial assets and in substance nonfinancial assets.

For purposes of ASC 610, nonfinancial assets include intangible assets, land, buildings, material, and supplies that may have a zero carrying value. (ASC 610-20-15-1 and 15-2) These are further described below.

The term "in substance nonfinancial asset" is described in ASC 610-20-15-5 through 15-8. The Codification gives the example of a legal entity that holds only nonfinancial assets, for example, real estate, and points the reader to the Scope section for further guidance.

ASC 610-20 applies to a transfer of an ownership interest or a variable interest in a consolidated subsidiary, not a business or nonprofit activity, only if all of+ the assets in the subsidiary are nonfinancial assets or in substance nonfinancial assets. (ASC 610-20-15-3)

The guidance does not apply to the derecognition of:

- A transfer of a nonfinancial asset, including an in substance nonfinancial asset, in a contract with a customer
- A transfer of a subsidiary or group of assets that constitutes a business or nonprofit activity, except for an in substance nonfinancial asset
- Real estate or non-real estate sales-leaseback transactions, which are covered under ASC 360-20, 840-40, or 842-40 (the last upon implementation of ASU 2016-02)
- Conveyance of oil and gas mineral rights under ASC 932-360
- A transaction entirely accounted for under ASC 860
- A transfer of nonfinancial assets that comprise part of the consideration in a business combination under the guidance in ASC 805
- Transfer of nonfinancial assets to another entity in exchange for a noncontrolling ownership interest in that entity under ASC 845-10-30
- A nonmonetary exchange within the scope of ASC 845
- A lease contract
- An exchange of takeoff or landing slots under ASC 908-350
- A contribution of cash and other assets within ASC 720-25 and contributions within the scope of 958-605
- A transfer of an investment in a venture accounted for proportionally as described in ASC 810-10-45-11
- A transfer of nonfinancial or in substance nonfinancial assets between entities under common control
  (ASC 610-20-15-4)

In substance nonfinancial assets An in substance nonfinancial asset is a financial asset promised to a counterparty in a contract if substantially all of the fair value of the assets is concentrated in nonfinancial assets. In that case, then *all* of the financial assets are in substance nonfinancial assets. When evaluating a contract, if the contract includes the transfer of ownership interests in one or more consolidated subsidiaries that is not a business, the entity should consider the underlying assets in those subsidiaries. (ASC 610-20-15-5)

When a contract includes the transfer of ownership interests in one or more consolidated subsidiaries that is not a business and substantially all of the fair value of the assets promised to a counterparty in the contract is *not* concentrated in nonfinancial assets, an entity should evaluate whether substantially all of the fair value of the assets promised to the counterparty is concentrated in nonfinancial assets. If so, then the financial assets in that subsidiary are in substance nonfinancial assets. (ASC 610-20-15-6)

In making the determination whether substantially all of the fair value of the assets is concentrated in nonfinancial assets, the entity should exclude cash or cash equivalents promised to the counterparty and disregard any liabilities assumed or relieved by the counterparty. (ASC 610-20-15-7)

If all of the assets promised to a counterparty in an individual consolidated subsidiary within a contract are not nonfinancial assets and/or in substance nonfinancial assets, an entity should apply the guidance in paragraph 810-10-40-3A(c) or 810-10-45-21A(b)(2) to determine the guidance applicable to that subsidiary.. (ASC 610-20-15-8)

Contracts partially within the scope of other Topics. If the counterparty's promises are not all nonfinancial assets or in substance nonfinancial assets, the contract may fall only partially within the scope of ASC 610. In that case, the entity should apply the guidance in ASC 606-10-15-4 to determine how to measure the contract's elements. (ASC 610-20-15-9)

ASC 610-30, *Gains and Losses on Involuntary Conversions* ASC 610-30 applies to all entities and to events and transactions in which nonmonetary assets are involuntarily converted to monetary assets that are then reinvested in other nonmonetary assets.

DEFINITIONS OF TERMS

Source: ASC 610, *Glossaries.* See Appendix A, *Definitions of Terms*, for terms relevant to this chapter: Business, Contract, Customer, Disposal Group, Nonprofit Activity, Performance Obligation, Revenue, and Transaction Price.

In Substance Nonfinancial Asset. Paragraphs ASC 610-20-15-5 through 15-8 define an in substance nonfinancial asset.

CONCEPTS, RULES, AND EXAMPLES

ASC 610-10, *Overall*

This subtopic establishes the pervasive scope of ASC 610 and provides a glossary. It does not include measurement, presentation, or other guidance.

ASC 610-20, *Gains and Losses from the Derecognition of Financial Assets*

Recognition If an entity has a gain or loss from the transfer of nonfinancial or in substance nonfinancial assets within the scope of ASC 610, it must determine whether to apply the guidance in ASC 810 or ASC 606. (ASC 10-20-25-1) The graphic below illustrates the decision-making process.

Initial Measurement

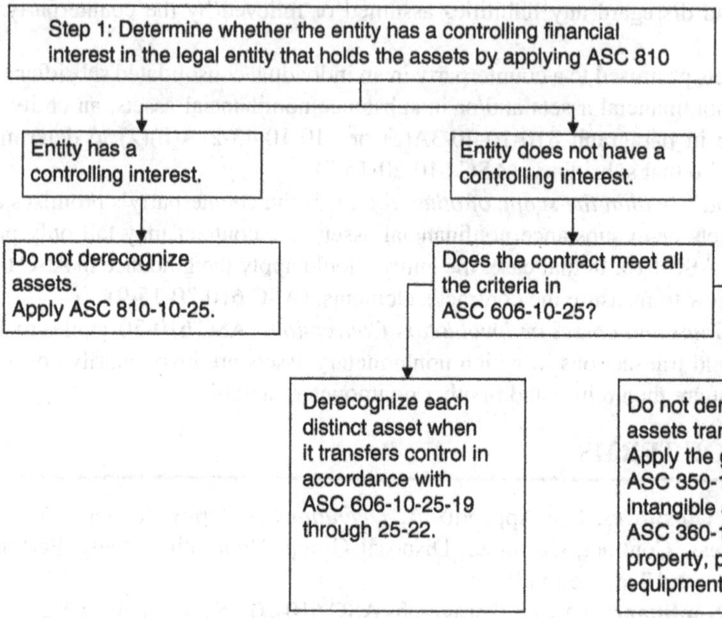

Measurement If the derecognition criteria above are met, the selling entity should recognize a gain or loss equal to the difference between the consideration received and the carrying amount of the asset sold. (ASC 610-20-32-2) The consideration received is the transaction price determined under the guidance in ASC 606-10-32. (ASC 610-20-32-3) If a noncontrolling interest is received by the seller or retained in a partial sale, that noncontrolling interest received is noncash consideration measured at fair value under ASC 606. (ASC 610-20-32-4)

ASC 610-30, *Gains and Losses on Involuntary Conversions*

This subtopic applies to gains and losses on involuntary conversions. It provides guidance when nonmonetary assets are destroyed, stolen, condemned, or otherwise lost and the entity receives monetary assets such as insurance proceeds. The guidance makes clear that this type of transaction is a monetary transaction that results in a gain or loss.

Recognition, Measurement, and Presentation The cost of nonmonetary assets acquired is measured by the consideration paid, not affected by previous transactions. (ASC 610-30-30-1) The gain or loss recognized is classified under the provisions in ASC 225-20. (ASC 610-30-45-1)

If a nonmonetary asset is destroyed or damaged in one period and the amount of monetary assets to be received will not be determinable until a later period, gain or loss is recognized per the guidance in ASC 450. (ASC 610-30-25-4)

39 ASC 705 COST OF SALES AND SERVICES

PERSPECTIVE AND ISSUES

Subtopics

ASC 705 contains two subtopics:

- ASC 705-10, *Overall*, which merely links to guidance in other Codification topics on costs of sales and services.
- ASC 705-20, *Accounting for Consideration Received from a Vendor*.

DEFINITIONS OF TERMS

See Appendix A, *Definitions of Terms*, for terms related to this topic: Cash Consideration, Contract, Customer, Probable, Reseller, Revenue, Standalone Selling Price, and Vendor.

CONCEPTS, RULES, AND EXAMPLES

ASC 705-10, *Overall*

This Subtopic consists solely of links to other Subtopics. This is because the asset liability model requires that the applicable guidance be included in other topics:

Topic	*Codification Location*	*Guidance*
Inventory	ASC 330-10-35-1A through 35-11	Adjustments affecting cost of sales and services
	ASC 330-10-30-1 through 30-13	Adjustments affecting cost of sales and services resulting from establishing the cost basis and the use of inventory pricing methods
	ASC 606-10-32-10 and 606-10-55-22 through 55-29	Accounting for a sale with a right of return

Topic	*Codification Location*	*Guidance*
Other Assets and Deferred Costs—Contracts with Customers	ASC 340-40	Costs related to a contract with a customer within the scope of ASC 606: • Incremental costs of obtaining a contract with a customer • Costs incurred in fulfilling a contract with a customer that are not within the scope of another topic
Property, Plant, and Equipment—Impairment or Disposal of Long-Lived Assets	ASC 360-10-35-38 through 35-40	The costs to sell long-lived assets classified as held for sale for purposes of measuring the expected disposal costs
(ASC 710-10-25-2 through 25-5)		

ASC 705-20, *Accounting for Consideration Received from a Vendor*

In some arrangements, an entity may receive consideration from a vendor. The consideration may be in the form of cash, credit, coupons, etc. This consideration should be accounted for by reducing the purchase price of goods or services acquired from the vendor, except if it is received:

- In exchange for a distinct good or service transferred to the vendor. In this case, the consideration should be accounted for in the same manner as other revenue from contracts with customers. The entity must look to the standalone selling price of the good or service transferred. If the amount of consideration received from the vendor is greater than the standalone selling price, the excess should be accounted for as a reduction of the purchase price of any goods purchased from the vendor. (ASC 705-20-25-02)
- As a reimbursement of costs incurred to sell the vendor's products. The consideration should represent a reduction of these costs and be specific, identifiable, and incremental. If the amount of the reimbursement is greater than the cost, the excess should be accounted for as a reduction of cost of sales. (ASC 705-20-25-03)
- As consideration for sales incentives offered to customers by manufacturers. These may be in the form of coupons or rebates offered to the end buyer by the manufacturer. (ASC 705-20-25-04)

In order to exercise the last exception, the sales incentives must meet *all* of the following criteria:

- The consumer can use the incentive at any reseller.
- The vendor reimburses the reseller directly based on the face amount of the incentive.
- The time of the reseller's reimbursement is determined only by the terms of the customer's incentive.
- The reseller is an agent of the vendor in the incentive transaction between vendor and customer.

(ASC 705-20-25-07)

If an entity meets these criteria, it should account for the transaction based on the guidance for revenues from contract with customers. If the criteria are not met, the incentive is a reduction of the purchase price of goods or services acquired from the vendor. (ASC 705-20-25-08)

The entity's ability to estimate the amount of future rebates or refunds may be hampered by the following:

- The rebate or refund relates to purchases that will occur over a relatively long period.
- The entity has no historical experience with similar products.
- The entity is not able to apply historical experience because circumstances have changed.
- In the past, the entity had to make significant adjustments to expected cash rebates or refunds.
- The product is susceptible to technological obsolescence, changes in demand, or other significant external factors.
  (ASC 705-20-25-11)

A change in estimate is recognized using cumulative catch-up adjustment.

40 ASC 710 COMPENSATION—GENERAL

PERSPECTIVE AND ISSUES

Subtopics

ASC 710, *Compensation—General,* contains one subtopic:

- ASC 710-10, *Overall,* which is divided into two subsections:
  - *General*, which provides guidance on compensated absences, deferred compensation, and lump-sum payments under union contract
  - *Deferred Compensation—Rabbi Trusts*

Scope and Scope Exceptions

ASC 710 applies to all entities, but it does *not* apply to the following transactions:

- Benefits paid to active employees other than compensated absences.
- Benefits paid at retirement or provided through a pension or postretirement benefit plan including special or contractual termination benefits payable upon termination from a pension or other postretirement plan are covered by Subtopics 715-30 and 715-60.
- Individual deferred compensation contracts that are addressed by Subtopics 715-30 and 715-60, if those contracts, taken together, are equivalent to a defined benefit pension plan or a defined benefit other postretirement benefit plan, respectively.
- Special or contractual termination benefits that are not payable from a pension or other postretirement plan are covered by Topic 712.
- Stock compensation plans that are addressed by Topic 718.
- Other postemployment benefits (see Topic 712) that do not meet the conditions in paragraph 710-10-25-1 and are accounted for in accordance with Topic 450.
(ASC 710-10-15-5)

In addition, the *Deferred Compensation—Rabbi Trusts* subsection does not address the accounting for stock appreciation rights even if they are funded through a rabbi trust. (ASC 710- 10-15-8)

DEFINITIONS OF TERMS

Compensated Absences. Employee absences, such as vacation, illness, and holidays, for which it is expected that employees will be paid.

Full Eligibility Date. The date at which an employee has rendered all of the service necessary to have earned the right to receive all of the benefits expected to be received by that employee (including any beneficiaries and dependents expected to receive benefits). Determination of the full eligibility date is affected by plan terms that provide incremental benefits expected to be received by or on behalf of an employee for additional years of service, unless those incremental benefits are trivial. Determination of the full eligibility date is not affected by plan terms that define when benefit payments commence or by an employee's current marital or dependency status.

Rabbi Trusts. Rabbi trusts are grantor trusts generally set up to fund compensation for a select group of management or highly paid executives. To qualify as a rabbi trust for income tax purposes, the terms of the trust agreement must explicitly state that the assets of the trust are available to satisfy the claims of general creditors in the event of bankruptcy of the employer.

Sabbatical Leave. A benefit in the form of a compensated absence whereby the employee is entitled to paid time off after working for an entity for a specified period of time. During the sabbatical, the individual continues to be a compensated employee and is not required to perform any duties for the entity.

CONCEPTS, RULES, AND EXAMPLES

Compensated Absences

Compensated absences refers to paid vacation, paid holidays, paid sick leave, and other paid leaves of absence. ASC 710 requires an employer to accrue a liability for employee's compensation for future absences if all of the following conditions are met:

1. The employee's right to receive compensation for future absences is attributable to employee services already rendered.
2. The right vests or accumulates.
3. Payment of the compensation is probable.
4. The amount of the payment can be reasonably estimated.

(ASC 710-10-25-1)

Vesting If an employer is required to compensate an employee for unused vacation, holidays, or sick days even if employment is terminated, then the employee's right to this compensation is said to vest. Accrual of a liability for nonvesting rights depends on whether the unused rights either expire at the end of the year in which they are earned (often referred to as a "use it or lose it" policy) or accumulate and are carried forward to succeeding years. If the rights expire, a liability for future absences is not accrued at year-end because the benefits to be paid in subsequent years would not be attributable to employee services rendered in prior years. If all or a portion of the unused rights accumulate and increase the benefits otherwise available in subsequent years, a liability is accrued at year-end to the extent that it is probable that employees will be paid in subsequent years for the increased benefits attributable to the accumulated rights and the amount can be reasonably estimated. (ASC 710-10-25-2)

Sick Pay ASC 710-10-25-7 allows an exception for employee paid sick days that accumulate but do not vest. No accrued liability is required for sick days that only accumulate. However, an employer is permitted to accrue these benefits if the four conditions (noted above) for compensated absences are met. FASB believed that these amounts are rarely material and the low reliability of estimates of future illness coupled with the high cost of developing these estimates indicates that accrual is not necessary. The required accounting should be determined by the employer's actual administration of sick pay benefits. If the employer routinely lets employees take time off when they are not ill and allows that time to be charged as sick pay, then an accrual is required. (ASC 710-10-25-6)

Other Types of Paid Time Off Pay for other employee leaves of absence that represent time off for past services (jury duty, personal days) are considered compensation subject to accrual. Pay for employee leaves of absence that will provide future benefits and that are not attributable to past services rendered are not subject to accrual.

ASC 710-10-25-4 and 25-5 govern the accounting for sabbatical leaves or other similar benefit arrangements that require the completion of a minimum service period, and for which the benefit does not increase with additional years of service. Under these arrangements, the individual continues to be a compensated employee and is not required to perform duties for the entity during their absence. Assuming the four conditions noted above are met, the compensation cost associated with a sabbatical or other similar arrangement must be ratably accrued over the presabbatical periods of service.

Bonus Payments

Bonus payments may require estimation since the amount of the bonus may be affected by:

- The entity's net income for the year,
- The income taxes currently payable, or
- Other factors.

Estimation may be challenging if bonus payments are accrued on a monthly basis for purposes of interim financial reporting but are determinable only annually by using a formula whose values are uncertain until shortly before payment.

Deferred Compensation Contracts

If the aggregate deferred compensation contracts with individual employees are equivalent to a pension plan, the contracts are accounted for under the guidance in ASC 715-30. All other deferred compensation contracts are accounted for according to ASC 710.

According to ASC 710, the amount to be accrued should not be less than the present value of the estimated payments to be made. This estimated amount is accrued in a systematic and rational manner. When elements of both current and future employment are present, only the portion attributable to the current services is accrued. (ASC 710-10-25-9) All requirements of the contract, such as continued employment for a specified period, availability for consulting services, and agreements not to compete after retirement, need to be met in order for the employee to receive future payments. Finally, the total amount is amortized to expense over the period from the date the contract is signed to the point when the employee is fully eligible to receive the deferred payments.

One benefit that may be found in a deferred compensation contract is for periodic payments to employees or their beneficiaries for life, with provisions for a minimum lump-sum settlement in the event of early death of one or all of the beneficiaries. The estimated amount to be accrued is based on the life expectancy of each individual concerned or on the estimated cost of an annuity contract, not on the minimum amount payable in the event of early death. (ASC 710-10-25-11)

Example of a Deferred Compensation Contract

The Clear Eye Corporation enters into a deferred compensation contract with its president, Dr. Smith. Under the terms of the agreement, Clear Eye will pay Dr. Smith an amount equal to twice his annual salary in a lump sum on the date of his mandatory retirement from Clear Eye, which is four years in the future. His salary is currently $120,000. In addition, Clear Eye will pay Dr. Smith an annual pension of $45,000 beginning on his mandatory retirement date, or a minimum $200,000 lump-sum payment in the event of his early death. However, these payments are contingent upon his working the remaining four years prior to his mandatory retirement. The actuarial present value of a lifetime annuity of $45,000 that begins at Dr. Smith's expected retirement date is $392,000.

Clear Eye makes the following entry each year to record its annual expense under the lump-sum payment agreement, which is based on a lump-sum payment of $240,000:

Deferred compensation expense	60,000	
Deferred compensation liability		60,000

After two years, Dr. Smith receives a pay raise to $140,000, which increases the amount of his guaranteed lump-sum payment to $280,000. Since Clear Eye has thus far recognized a deferred compensation expense of $120,000, it must now increase its annual expense recognition to $80,000 in order to recognize additional expense totaling $160,000 over the remaining two years prior to the payment date.

Clear Eye makes the following entry to record the actual cash payment to Dr. Smith:

Deferred compensation liability	280,000	
Cash		280,000

Clear Eye must also record the $392,000 present value of the lifetime annuity over the remaining four years of Dr. Smith's employment rather than the smaller $200,000 early death payment, which it does with the following annual entry:

Deferred compensation expense	98,000	
Deferred compensation liability		98,000

Note that all of the foregoing entries assume that Clear Eye Corporation chooses to record the full (i.e., nondiscounted) amount of the estimated future liability pro rata each year. It would also have been acceptable under ASC 710 to record the discounted present value amounts. In that case, while the charge for deferred compensation would have been lower in the earlier years, the accrued amounts would have to be further accreted to reflect interest on the obligation, so the overall charge over the four-year accrual for the lump-sum payment would have still equaled $280,000. The charge for the lifetime annuity over the four years until the payments commence would have been less than the estimated $392,000 obligation, since the amount recorded as of the inception of the annuity (i.e., retirement date) would be the present value of the future estimated payments.

Lump-Sum Payments under Union Contracts

When signing a new union contract, the union may agree to lump-sum cash payments instead of pay increases. Sometimes these provisions eliminate base pay raises that would otherwise be required during the contract period. In these contracts, there is usually no requirement for the employee to reimburse the entity upon leaving the company. There is also an expectation that the employee would be replaced by another union worker at the same pay rate, but without additional lump-sum payments. (ASC 710-10-25-12)

Only when it is clear that the lump-sum payment will benefit a future period in the form of a lower base pay rate, may it be deferred and amortized. (ASC 710-10-25-13)

Deferred Compensation—Rabbi Trusts

The chart below gives an overview of the guidance for rabbi trusts.

Trust	*Description (ASC 710-10-25-15)*	*Accounting (ASC 710-25-16 through 25-18)*
Plan A	Does not permit diversification. Must be settled by delivery of a fixed number of shares of employer stock.	Classify stock held by trust in equity, similar to treasury stock.
Plan B	Does not permit diversification. May be settled by delivery of cash or shares of employer stock.	Classify employee stock in equity in a manner similar to treasury stock. Classify deferred compensation obligation as a liability.
Plan C	Permits diversification, however, the employee has not diversified.	Same as Plan B.
Plan D	Permits diversification, and the employee has diversified.	Assets accounted for in accordance with GAAP for the particular assets. Classify deferred compensation as a liability. Upon acquisition, debt securities may be classified as trading.

41 ASC 712 COMPENSATION—NONRETIREMENT POST-EMPLOYMENT BENEFITS

PERSPECTIVE AND ISSUES

Subtopic

ASC 712, Compensation—Nonretirement Postemployment Benefits, contains one subtopic:

- ASC 712-10, *Overall*, which provides guidance and links to other topics containing guidance on nonretirement postemployment benefits.

Overview

ASC 712 provides guidance for employers that provide benefits for former or inactive employees after the employees' termination. These benefits may include counseling, pay continuation, continuation of health care benefits, etc. The FASB sees these as benefits provided in exchange for service.

DEFINITIONS OF TERMS

Inactive Employees. Employees who are not currently rendering service to the employer and who have not been terminated. They include those who have been laid off and those on disability leave, regardless of whether they are expected to return to active status.

Nonretirement Postemployment Benefits. All types of benefits, other than those provided through a pension or other postretirement plan (see Subtopics 715-30 and 715-60), provided to former or inactive employees, their beneficiaries, and covered dependents.

Other Postemployment Benefits. Benefits, other than special or contractual termination benefits, that are provided by an employer to former or inactive employees after employment but before retirement including benefits provided to beneficiaries and covered dependents.

Special Termination Benefits. Benefits that are offered for a short period of time in exchange for employees' voluntary termination of service.

Termination Benefits. Benefits provided by an employer to employees in connection with their termination of employment. They may be either special termination benefits offered only for a short period of time or contractual benefits required by the terms of a plan only if a specified event, such as a plant closing, occurs.

CONCEPTS, RULES, AND EXAMPLES

Initial Measurement and Recognition

ASC 712 applies the criteria set forth by ASC 710, *Compensation—General*, to accrue an obligation for postemployment benefits other than pensions if:

- Services have been performed by employees,
- Employees' rights accumulate or vest,
- Payment is probable, and
- The amount is reasonably estimable.

If these benefits do not vest or accumulate, ASC 450, *Contingencies*, applies. If neither ASC 710 nor ASC 450 is applicable because the amount is not reasonably estimable, this fact must be disclosed. (ASC 712-10-25-4 and 25-5)

Subsequent Measurement

To the extent they apply, entities may refer to ASC 715-30 and 715-60 for guidance in measuring their postemployment benefit obligations.

Other Sources

See ASC Location—*Wiley GAAP* Chapter	*For information on . . .*
ASC 715-10-25	Recognition of liabilities for contractual termination benefits or changing benefit plan assumptions in anticipation of a business combination
ASC 810-10-15-12(a)	Prohibiting the consolidation of an employee benefit plan subject to the provisions of ASC 712

42 ASC 715 COMPENSATION—RETIREMENT BENEFITS

PERSPECTIVE AND ISSUES

Subtopics

ASC 715, *Compensation-Retirement Benefits*, contains six subtopics:

- ASC 715-10, *Overall*, sets the objectives and the scope for ASC 715
- ASC 715-20, *Defined Benefit Plans—General*, provides guidance on the presentation and disclosure requirements for single-employer defined benefit pension and other postretirement plans (ASC 715-20-05-1)
- ASC 715-30, *Defined Benefit Plans—Pension*, provides accounting guidance related to single-employer defined benefit pension plans
- ASC 715-60, *Defined Benefit Plans—Other Postretirement*, provides guidance on single-employer defined benefit plans other than postretirement benefit plans
- ASC 715-70, *Defined Contribution Plans*, provides guidance on defined contribution plans
- ASC 715-80, *Multiemployer Plans*, provides guidance on multiemployer plans as opposed to multiple employer plans.
  (ASC 715-10-05-2)

Overview

When an entity provides benefits that can be estimated in advance to its retired employees and their beneficiaries, the arrangement is a pension plan or a postretirement plan. These plans include unfunded, insured, trust fund, defined contribution and defined benefit plans, and deferred compensation contracts, if equivalent. Separate deferred profit sharing plans and pension payments to selected employees on a case-by-case basis are *not* considered pension or postretirement plans.

The typical plan is written and the amount of benefits can be determined by reference to the associated documents. The plan and its provisions can also be implied, however, from unwritten but established past practices.

The accounting for such arrangements is complex. In large part the complexity stems from a variety of "smoothing" features that necessitate the use of various accruals and deferrals, and the reporting of certain elements within other comprehensive income. Presentation of benefit plan expense and related items involves lengthy and complex notes.

Although the Codification is generally based on an asset and liability model, the foundation content of ASC 715 is based on an expense recognition model. Expense recognition models focus on remeasurement. Therefore, much of the guidance in ASC 715 is found in the subsequent measurement sections. (ASC 715-10-05-3)

DEFINITIONS OF TERMS

Source: ASC 715 *Glossaries*. See also Appendix A, *Definitions of Terms*, for additional terms related to this chapter: Asset Group, Benefits, Cash Equivalents, Conduit Debt Security, Defined Benefit Plan, Defined Contribution Plan, Expected Return on Plan Assets, Multi-Employer Plan, Net Periodic Pension Cost, Nonpublic Entity, Not-for-Profit Entity, Operating Segment, Participant, Pension Benefits, Plan Assets, Publicly Traded Entity, Related Parties, Reporting Unit, Security, Sponsor.

Accumulated Benefit Obligation. The actuarial present value of benefits (whether vested or nonvested) attributed, generally by the pension benefit formula, to employee service rendered before a specified date and based on employee service and compensation (if applicable) before that date. The accumulated benefit obligation differs from the projected benefit obligation in that it includes no assumption about future compensation levels. For plans with flat-benefit or non-pay-related pension benefit formulas, the accumulated benefit obligation and the projected benefit obligation are the same.

Accumulated Postretirement Benefit Obligation. The actuarial present value as of a particular date of all future benefits attributed to an employee's service rendered to that date assuming the plan continues in effect and that all assumptions about future events are fulfilled. The accumulated postretirement benefit obligation generally reflects a ratable allocation of expected future benefits to employee service already rendered in the attribution period. Before an employee's full eligibility date, the accumulated postretirement benefit obligation as of a particular date for an employee is the portion of the expected postretirement benefit obligation attributed to that employee's service rendered to that date; on and after the full eligibility date, the accumulated and expected postretirement benefit obligations for an employee are the same.

Active Plan Participant. Any active employee who has rendered service during the credited service period and is expected to receive benefits, including benefits to or for any beneficiaries and covered dependents, under the postretirement benefit plan. See Plan Participant.

Actual Return on Plan Assets (Component of Net Periodic Pension Cost). For a funded plan, the actual return on plan assets is determined as the difference between the fair value of plan assets at the end of the period and the fair value at the beginning of the period, adjusted for contributions and payments of benefits during the period.

Actual Return on Plan Assets (Component of Net Periodic Postretirement Benefit Cost). The change in the fair value of the plan's assets for a period including the decrease due to expenses incurred during the period (such as income tax expense incurred by the fund, if applicable), adjusted for contributions and benefit payments during the period. For a funded plan, the actual return on plan assets shall be determined based on the fair value of plan assets (see paragraph 715-60-35-107) at the beginning and end of the period, adjusted for contributions and benefit payments. If the fund holding the plan assets is a taxable entity, the actual return on plan assets shall reflect the tax expense or benefit for the period determined in accordance with (GAAP). Otherwise, no provision for taxes shall be included in the actual return on plan assets.

Actuarial Present Value. The value, as of a specified date, of an amount or series of amounts payable or receivable thereafter, with each amount adjusted to reflect the time value of money (through discounts for interest) and the probability of payment (by means of decrements for events such as death, disability, withdrawal, or retirement) between the specified date and the expected date of payment.

Amortization. (Def. 1) The process of reducing a recognized liability systematically by recognizing gains or by reducing a recognized asset systematically by recognizing losses. In accounting for pension benefits or other postretirement benefits, amortization also means the systematic recognition in net periodic pension cost or other postretirement benefit cost over several periods of amounts previously recognized in other comprehensive income, that is, gains or losses, prior service cost or credits, and any transition obligation or asset.

Annuity Contract. A contract in which an insurance entity unconditionally undertakes a legal obligation to provide specified pension benefits to specific individuals in return for a fixed consideration or premium. An annuity contract is irrevocable and involves the transfer of significant risk from the employer to the insurance entity. Annuity contracts are also called allocated contracts.

Assumed per Capita Claims Cost (by Age). The annual per capita cost, for periods after the measurement date, of providing the postretirement health care benefits covered by the plan from the earliest age at which an individual could begin to receive benefits under the plan through the remainder of the individual's life or the covered period, if shorter. To determine the assumed per capita claims cost, the per capita claims cost by age based on historical claims costs is adjusted for assumed health care cost trend rates. The resulting assumed per capita claims cost by age reflects expected future costs and is applied with the plan demographics to determine the amount and timing of future gross eligible charges. See Gross Eligible Charges and Per Capita Claims Cost (by Age).

Assumptions. Estimates of the occurrence of future events affecting pension costs and other postretirement benefit costs (as applicable), such as turnover, retirement age, mortality, withdrawal, disablement, dependency status, per capita claims costs by age, health care cost trend rates, levels of Medicare and other health care providers' reimbursements, changes in compensation and national pension benefits, and discount rates to reflect the time value of money.

Attribution. The process of assigning pension or other postretirement benefits or costs to periods of employee service.

Attribution Period. The period of an employee's service to which the expected postretirement benefit obligation for that employee is assigned. The beginning of the attribution period is the employee's date of hire unless the plan's benefit formula grants credit only for service from a later date, in which case the beginning of the attribution period is generally the beginning of that credited service period. The end of the attribution period is the full eligibility date. Within the attribution period, an equal amount of the expected postretirement benefit obligation is attributed to each year of service unless the plan's benefit formula attributes a disproportionate share of the expected postretirement benefit obligation to employees' early years of service. In that case, benefits are attributed in accordance with the plan's benefit formula. See Credited Service Period.

Benefit Approach. A group of basic approaches to attributing pension benefits or costs to periods of employee service.

Approaches in this group assign a distinct unit of benefit to each year of credited service. The actuarial present value of that unit of benefit is computed separately and determines the cost assigned to that year. The accumulated benefits approach, benefit-compensation approach, and benefit-years-of-service approach are benefit approaches.

Benefit-Years-of-Service Approach. One of three benefit approaches. Under this approach, an equal portion of the total estimated benefit is attributed to each year of service. The actuarial present value of the benefits is derived after the benefits are attributed to the periods.

Captive Insurer. An insurance entity that does business primarily with related entities.

Career-Average-Pay Formula. A benefit formula that bases benefits on the employee's compensation over the entire period of service with the employer. A career-average-pay plan is a plan with such a formula.

Cash Balance Plan. A plan with the following characteristics:

1. A defined principal-crediting rate as a percentage of salary
2. A defined, noncontingent interest-crediting rate that entitles participants to future interest credits at a stated, fixed rate until retirement.

A cash balance plan communicates to employees a pension benefit in the form of a current account balance that is a function of current and past salary-based principal credits and future interest credits thereon at a stated rate based on those principal credits.

In a cash balance plan, individual account balances are determined by reference to a hypothetical account rather than specific assets, and the benefit is dependent on the employer's promised interest-crediting rate, not the actual return on plan assets. The employer's financial obligation to the plan is not satisfied by making prescribed principal and interest credit contributions—whether in cash or as a hypothetical contribution to participants' accounts—for the period; rather, the employer must fund, over time, amounts that can accumulate to the actuarial present value of the benefit due at the time of distribution to each participant pursuant to the plan's terms. The employer's contributions to a cash balance plan trust and the earnings on the invested plan assets may be unrelated to the principal and interest credits to participants' hypothetical accounts.

A cash balance plan is a defined benefit plan.

Collateral Split-Dollar Life Insurance. A split-dollar life insurance arrangement in which the employee (or the employee's estate or a trust controlled by the employee, referred to as the employee) owns and controls the insurance policy.

Component of an Entity. A component of an entity comprises operations and cash flows that can be clearly distinguished, operationally and for financial reporting purposes, from the rest of the entity. A component of an entity may be a reportable segment or an operating segment, a reporting unit, a subsidiary, or an asset group.

Contributory Plan. A plan under which retirees or active employees contribute part of the cost. In some contributory plans, retirees or active employees wishing to be covered must contribute; in other contributory plans, participants' contributions result in increased benefits.

Cost-Sharing (Provisions of the Plan). The provisions of the postretirement benefit plan that describe how the costs of the covered benefits are to be shared between the employer and the plan participants. Cost-sharing provisions describe retired and active plan participants' contributions toward their postretirement health care benefits, deductibles, coinsurance, out-of-pocket limitations on participant costs, caps on employer costs, and so forth.

Credited Service Period. Employee service period for which benefits are earned pursuant to the terms of the plan. The beginning of the credited service period may be the date of hire or a later date. For example, a plan may provide benefits only for service rendered after a specified age. Service beyond the end of the credited service period does not earn any additional benefits under the plan. See Attribution Period.

Curtailment (of a Postretirement Benefit Plan). An event that significantly reduces the expected years of future service of active plan participants or eliminates the accrual of defined benefits for some or all of the future services of a significant number of active plan participants.

Dependency Status. The status of a current or former employee having dependents (for example, a spouse or other relatives) who are expected to receive benefits under a postretirement benefit plan that provides dependent coverage.

Discount Rate. A rate or rates used to reflect the time value of money. Discount rates are used in determining the present value as of the measurement date of future cash flows currently expected to be required to satisfy the pension obligation or other postretirement benefit obligation. See Actuarial Present Value.

Expected Long-Term Rate of Return on Plan Assets. An assumption about the rate of return on plan assets reflecting the average rate of earnings expected on existing plan assets and expected contributions to the plan during the period.

Expected Postretirement Benefit Obligation. The actuarial present value as of a particular date of the postretirement benefits expected to be paid by the employer's plan to or for each employee, the employee's beneficiaries, and any covered dependents pursuant to the terms of the plan.

Explicit Approach to Assumptions. An approach under which each significant assumption used reflects the best estimate of the plan's future experience solely with respect to that assumption. See Implicit Approach to Assumptions.

Full Eligibility (for Benefits). The status of an employee having reached the employee's full eligibility date. Full eligibility for benefits is achieved by meeting specified age, service, or age and service requirements of the postretirement benefit plan. See Full Eligibility Date.

Full Eligibility Date. The date at which an employee has rendered all of the service necessary to have earned the right to receive all of the benefits expected to be received by that employee (including any beneficiaries and dependents expected to receive benefits). Determination of the full eligibility date is affected by plan terms that provide incremental benefits expected to be received by or on behalf of an employee for additional years of service, unless those incremental benefits are trivial. Determination of the full eligibility date is not affected by plan terms that define when benefit payments commence or by an employee's current marital or dependency status.

Fully Eligible Plan Participants. Collectively, that group of former employees (including retirees) and active employees who have rendered service to or beyond their full eligibility date and who are expected to receive benefits under the plan, including benefits to their beneficiaries and covered dependents.

Fund. Used as a verb, to pay over to a funding agency (as to fund future pension benefits or to fund pension cost). Used as a noun, assets accumulated in the hands of a funding agency for the purpose of meeting pension benefits when they become due.

Gain or Loss. A change in the value of either the benefit obligation (projected benefit obligation for pension plans or accumulated postretirement benefit obligation for other postretirement benefit plans) or the plan assets resulting from experience different from that assumed or from a change in an actuarial assumption, or the consequence of a decision to temporarily deviate from the other postretirement benefit substantive plan. Gains or losses that are not recognized in net periodic pension cost or net periodic postretirement benefit cost when they arise are recognized in other comprehensive income. Those gains or losses are subsequently recognized as a component of net periodic pension cost or net periodic postretirement benefit cost based on the recognition and amortization provisions of Subtopic 715-30 or Subtopic 715-60.

Gain or Loss (Component of Net Periodic Pension Cost). The sum of the difference between the actual return on plan assets and the expected return on plan assets and the amortization of the net gain or loss recognized in accumulated other comprehensive income. The gain or loss component is the net effect of delayed recognition of gains and losses in determining net periodic pension cost (the net change in the gain or loss) in accumulated other comprehensive income except that it does not include changes in the projected benefit obligation occurring during the period and deferred for later recognition in net periodic pension cost.

Gain or Loss (Component of Net Periodic Postretirement Benefit Cost). The sum of all of the following:

- The difference between the actual return on plan assets and the expected return on plan assets
- Any gain or loss immediately recognized or the amortization of the net gain or loss recognized in accumulated other comprehensive income
- Any amount immediately recognized as a gain or loss pursuant to a decision to temporarily deviate from the substantive plan

The gain or loss component is generally the net effect of delayed recognition in determining net periodic postretirement benefit cost of gains and losses (the net change in the net gain or loss recognized in accumulated other comprehensive income) except that it does not include changes in the accumulated postretirement benefit obligation occurring during the period and deferred for later recognition in net periodic postretirement benefit cost.

Gross Eligible Charges. The cost of providing the postretirement health care benefits covered by the plan to a plan participant, before adjusting for expected reimbursements from Medicare and other providers of health care benefits and for the effects of the cost-sharing provisions of the plan.

Health Care Cost Trend Rate. An assumption about the annual rates of change in the cost of health care benefits currently provided by the postretirement benefit plan, due to factors other than changes in the composition of the plan population by age and dependency status, for each year from the measurement date until the end of the period in which benefits are expected to be paid. The health care cost trend rates implicitly consider estimates of health care inflation, changes in health care utilization or delivery patterns, technological advances, and changes in the health status of the plan participants. Differing types of services, such as hospital care and dental care, may have different trend rates.

Implicit Approach to Assumptions. An approach under which two or more assumptions do not individually represent the best estimate of the plan's future experience with respect to those assumptions. Instead, the aggregate effect of their combined use is presumed to be approximately the same as that produced by an explicit approach. See Explicit Approach to Assumptions.

Incurred Claims Cost (by Age). The cost of providing the postretirement health care benefits covered by the plan to a plan participant, after adjusting for reimbursements from Medicare and other providers of health care benefits and for deductibles, coinsurance provisions, and other specific claims costs borne by the retiree. See Net Incurred Claims Cost (By Age).

Insurance Contract. A contract in which an insurance entity unconditionally undertakes a legal obligation to provide specified benefits to specific individuals in return for a fixed consideration or premium. An insurance contract is irrevocable and involves the transfer of significant risk from the employer (or the plan) to the insurance entity.

Interest Cost (Component of Net Periodic Pension Cost). The amount recognized in a period determined as the increase in the projected benefit obligation due to the passage of time.

Interest Cost (Component of Net Periodic Postretirement Benefit Cost). The increase in the accumulated postretirement benefit obligation to recognize the effects of the passage of time.

Loss. See Gain or Loss.

Market-Related Value of Plan Assets. A balance used to calculate the expected return on plan assets. The market-related value of plan assets is either fair value or a calculated value that recognizes changes in fair value in a systematic and rational manner over not more than five years. Different ways of calculating market-related value may be used for different classes of assets (for example, an employer might use fair value for bonds and a five-year-moving-average value for equities), but the manner of determining market-related value is required to be applied consistently from year to year for each asset class. For a method to meet the criteria of being systematic and rational, it must reflect only the changes in the fair value of plan assets between various dates.

Medicare Reimbursement Rates. The health care cost reimbursements expected to be received by retirees through Medicare as mandated by currently enacted legislation. Medicare reimbursement rates vary by the type of benefits provided.

Mortality. The relative incidence of death in a given time or place.

Mortality Rate. The proportion of the number of deaths in a specified group to the number living at the beginning of the period in which the deaths occur. Actuaries use mortality tables, which show death rates for each age, in estimating the amount of pension benefits that will become payable.

Net Incurred Claims Cost (by Age). The employer's share of the cost of providing the postretirement health care benefits covered by the plan to a plan participant; incurred claims cost net of retiree contributions. See Incurred Claims Cost (by Age).

Nonparticipating Annuity Contract. An annuity contract that does not provide for the purchaser to participate in the investment performance or in other experience of the insurance entity.

Nonparticipating Insurance Contract. An insurance contract that does not provide for the purchaser to participate in the investment performance or in other experience of the insurance entity. See Insurance Contract.

Participating Annuity Contract. An annuity contract that provides for the purchaser to participate in the investment performance and possibly other experience (for example, mortality experience) of the insurance entity. Under a participating annuity contract, the insurance entity ordinarily pays dividends to the purchaser.

Participation Right. A purchaser's right under a participating insurance contract to receive future dividends or retroactive rate credits from the insurance entity.

Pay-Related Plan. A plan that has a benefit formula that bases benefits or benefit coverage on compensation, such as a final-pay or career-average-pay plan.

Pension Benefit Formula. The basis for determining payments to which participants may be entitled under a pension plan. Pension benefit formulas usually refer to the employee's service or compensation or both. Sometimes referred to as a plan's benefit formula or benefit formula.

Pension Fund. The assets of a pension plan held by a funding agency.

Per Capita Claims Cost (by Age). The current cost of providing postretirement health care benefits for one year at each age from the youngest age to the oldest age at which plan participants are expected to receive benefits under the plan. See Assumed per Capita Claims Cost (By Age).

Plan. An arrangement that is mutually understood by an employer and its employees, whereby an employer undertakes to provide its employees with benefits after they retire in exchange for their services over a specified period of time, upon attaining a specified age while in service, or a combination of both. A plan may be written or it may be implied by a well-defined, although perhaps unwritten, practice of paying postretirement benefits or from oral representations made to current or former employees. See Substantive Plan.

Plan Amendment. A change in the existing terms of a plan or the initiation of a new plan. A plan amendment may increase benefits (a positive plan amendment), or reduce or eliminate benefits (a negative plan amendment), including those benefits attributed to years of service already rendered.

Plan Curtailment. An event that significantly reduces the expected years of future service of present employees or eliminates for a significant number of employees the accrual of defined benefits for some or all of their future services.

Plan Demographics. The characteristics of the plan population including geographical distribution, age, sex, and marital status.

Plan Participant. Any employee or former employee who has rendered service in the credited service period and is expected to receive employer-provided benefits under the postretirement benefit plan, including benefits to or for any beneficiaries and covered dependents. See Active Plan Participant.

Plan Suspension. An event in which the pension plan is frozen and no further benefits accrue. Future service may continue to be the basis for vesting of nonvested benefits existing at the date of suspension. The plan may still hold assets, pay benefits already accrued, and receive additional employer contributions for any unfunded benefits. Employees may or may not continue working for the employer.

Plan Termination. An event in which the pension plan or postretirement benefit plan ceases to exist and all benefits are settled by the purchase of insurance contracts (for example, annuities) or by other means. The plan may or may not be replaced by another plan. A plan termination with a replacement plan may or may not be in substance a plan termination for accounting purposes.

Plan's Benefit Formula. See Pension Benefit Formula.

Postretirement Benefit Plan. See Plan.

Postretirement Benefits. All forms of benefits, other than retirement income, provided by an employer to retirees. Those benefits may be defined in terms of specified benefits, such as health care, tuition assistance, or legal services, that are provided to retirees as the need for those benefits arises, such as certain health care benefits, or they may be defined in terms of monetary amounts that become payable on the occurrence of a specified event, such as life insurance benefits.

Postretirement Health Care Benefits. A form of postretirement benefit provided by an employer to retirees for defined health care services or coverage of defined health care costs, such as hospital and medical coverage, dental benefits, and eye care.

Prior Service Cost. The cost of retroactive benefits granted in a plan amendment. Retroactive benefits are benefits granted in a plan amendment (or initiation) that are attributed by the benefit formula to employee services rendered in periods before the amendment.

Probable. The future event or events are likely to occur.

Projected Benefit Obligation. The actuarial present value as of a date of all benefits attributed by the pension benefit formula to employee service rendered before that date. The projected benefit obligation is measured using assumptions as to future compensation levels if the pension benefit formula is based on those future compensation levels (pay-related, final-pay, final-average-pay, or career-average-pay plans).

Retirees. Collectively, that group of plan participants that includes retired employees, their beneficiaries, and covered dependents.

Service Cost (Component of Net Periodic Pension Cost). A component of net periodic pension cost recognized in a period determined as the actuarial present value of benefits attributed by the pension benefit formula to services rendered by employees during that period. The service cost component is a portion of the projected benefit obligation and is unaffected by the funded status of the plan.

Service Cost (Component of Net Periodic Postretirement Benefit Cost). The actuarial present value of benefits attributed to services rendered by employees during the period (the portion of the expected postretirement benefit obligation attributed to service in the period). The service cost component is the same for an unfunded plan, a plan with minimal funding, and a well-funded plan.

Settlement of a Pension or Postretirement Benefit Obligation. A transaction that is an irrevocable action, relieves the employer (or the plan) of primary responsibility for a pension or postretirement benefit obligation, and eliminates significant risks related to the obligation and the assets used to effect the settlement.

Single-Employer Plan. A pension plan or other postretirement benefit plan that is maintained by one employer. The term also may be used to describe a plan that is maintained by related parties such as a parent and its subsidiaries.

Substantive Plan. The terms of the postretirement benefit plan as understood by an employer that provides postretirement benefits and the employees who render services in exchange for those benefits. The substantive plan is the basis for the accounting for that exchange transaction. In some situations an employer's cost-sharing policy, as evidenced by past practice or by communication of intended changes to a plan's cost-sharing provisions, or a past practice of regular increases in certain monetary benefits, may indicate that the substantive plan differs from the extant written plan.

Termination Benefits. Benefits provided by an employer to employees in connection with their termination of employment. They may be either special termination benefits offered only for a short period of time or contractual benefits required by the terms of a plan only if a specified event, such as a plant closing, occurs.

Termination Indemnities. Arrangements, usually or more frequently encountered outside the United States, that are also referred to as termination allowances or severance indemnities. Termination indemnities are amounts payable to eligible employees upon termination of employment. Eligibility may be determined by law, by local custom, by the employer's policy, or by contract with the employer. Plans may or may not be in writing. Termination indemnities are normally, but not exclusively, associated with preretirement severance of employment. They are usually payable as a lump sum, or occasionally in a few payments over a short period of time.

Transition Asset. The amount, as of the date Subtopic 715-60 was initially applied, of the fair value of plan assets plus any recognized accrued postretirement benefit cost or less any recognized prepaid postretirement benefit cost in excess of the accumulated postretirement benefit obligation.

Transition Obligation. The amount, as of the date Subtopic 715-60 was initially applied, of the accumulated postretirement benefit obligation in excess of the fair value of plan assets plus any recognized accrued postretirement benefit cost or less any recognized prepaid postretirement benefit cost.

Turnover. Termination of employment for a reason other than death or retirement.

Unfunded Accumulated Postretirement Benefit Obligation. The accumulated postretirement benefit obligation in excess of the fair value of plan assets.

Unfunded Projected Benefit Obligation. The excess of the projected benefit obligation over plan assets.

Vested Benefit Obligation. The actuarial present value of vested benefits.

Vested Benefits. Benefits for which the employee's right to receive a present or future pension benefit is no longer contingent on remaining in the service of the employer. (Other conditions, such as inadequacy of the pension fund, may prevent the employee from receiving the vested benefit.) Under graded vesting, the initial vested right may be to receive in the future a stated percentage of a pension based on the number of years of accumulated credited service; thereafter, the percentage may increase with the number of years of service or of age until the right to receive the entire benefit has vested.

Scope and Scope Exceptions

ASC 715 applies to all entities and many types of compensation arrangements including:

- Any arrangement that is in substance a postretirement benefit plan (regardless of its form or means or timing of funding),
- Written and unwritten plans,

- Deferred compensation contracts with individuals which taken together are the equivalent of a plan, and
- Health and other welfare benefits for employees on disability retirement.
  (ASC 715-10-15-3)

The guidance also applies to:

- Settlement of all or part of an employer's pension or other postretirement benefit obligation,
- Curtailment of a pension or other postretirement benefit plan, and
- Employers that provide pension or other postretirement benefits as part of a termination benefit not addressed in other Subtopics.
  (ASC 715-10-15-4)

ASC 715 does *not* apply to:

- Contracts with "selected employees under individual contracts with specific terms determined on an individual-by-individual basis" and
- Postemployment benefits paid after employment, but before retirement, like layoff benefits.
  (ASC 715-10-15-5)

The ASC also provides guidance on the accounting treatment of contributions to the plan and significant events requiring a remeasurement occurring during the interim period between the month-end measurement date and the fiscal year-end.

ASC 715-60 follows the scope guidance in ASC 715-10 with some qualifications. (ASC 715-60-15-1) It applies to single-employer plans. (ASC 715-60-15-6) It does not apply to:

- Pension or life insurance benefits provided through a pension plan. That guidance can be found in ASC 715-30.
- Disability benefits paid to former or inactive employees on disability retirement. That guidance is found in ASC 712.
- Disability benefits paid pursuant to a pension plan. See ASC 715-30 for guidance on those plans.
- COBRA benefits
  (ASC 715-60-15-6)

ASC 715-60 applies to Medicare, Prescription Drug, and Modernization Act that are single employer plans. (ASC 715-60-15-11) The Subtopic does not address:

- Situations where the expected subsidy exceeds the employer's share of the cost on which the subsidy is based
- Multiemployer health and welfare benefit plans
  (ASC 715-60-15-12)

ASC 715-60 applies to:

- Settlement of all or a part of an employee's APBO or curtailment of a postretirement benefit plan
- Termination benefits not otherwise addressed by ASC 420, 710, 712, 715-30
  (ASC 715-60-15-15 and 15-18)

The guidance does not apply to a split-dollar life insurance arrangement that provides a specified benefit to an employee that is limited to the employee's active service period with an employer. (ASC 715-60-15-21)

ASC 715-10, *DEFINED BENEFIT PLANS—OVERALL*

ASC 715-10 sets the objectives and scope for ASC 715. See the section above for scope and scope exceptions.

ASC 715-20, *DEFINED BENEFITS PLANS—GENERAL*

Concepts, Rules, and Examples

Scope ASC 715-20 follows the scope guidance in ASC 715-10 and applies to all single-employer defined benefit pension or other post-retirement benefit plans.

Overview ASC 715-20, *Compensation—Retirement Benefits, Defined Benefits Plans, General*, provides disclosure and presentation guidance for defined benefit pension and other retirement benefit plans. The disclosure and presentation requirements for ASC 715-20 and all subtopics can be found in the *Disclosure and Presentation Checklist for Commercial Businesses* at www.wiley.com/go/GAAP2021 (password: Flood).

ASC 715-30, *DEFINED BENEFIT PLANS—PENSION*

Concepts, Rules, and Examples

Scope ASC 715-30 follows the same scope and scope exceptions as ASC 715-10 with the exceptions noted below. (ASC 715-30-15-1)

ASC 715-30 applies to defined benefit plans, including:

- Cash balance plans
- Termination benefits provided in the event of a voluntary or involuntary severance if the arrangement is in substance a termination
  (ASC 715-30-15-3)

This subtopic does not apply to:

- Life insurance benefits provided outside a pension plan or
- Other postretirement health and welfare benefits. For health care benefits provided through a pension plan, look to the guidance in ASC 715-60.
  (ASC 715-30-15-4)

For plans with characteristics of defined benefit and defined contribution plans, entities should look to the guidance in ASC 715-70-15-2. (ASC 715-30-15-4A)

Overview ASC 715-30 specifies the accrual basis of accounting for pension costs. It includes three primary characteristics:

1. Delayed recognition. Changes are not recognized immediately but are subsequently recognized in a gradual and systematic way.
2. Reporting net cost. Various expense and income items are aggregated and reported as one net amount.

3. Offsetting assets and liabilities. Assets and liabilities are sometimes shown net. Fundamentally, pension accounting includes:
   - Measurement of net periodic pension costs and benefit obligations,
   - Assumptions, and
   - Measurement of plan assets.
   (ASC 715-30-05-6)

ASC 715-30 focuses directly on the terms of the plan to assist in the recognition of compensation cost over the service period of the employees. The full amount of under- and overfunding of pension plans is reported in the statement of financial position.

The principal emphasis of ASC 715-30 is the present value of the pension obligation and the fair value of plan assets. The main accounting issues revolve around the amount of expense to recognize on the income statement and the liability to be accrued on the statement of financial position. Because of the substantial use of smoothing, the periodic expense to be recognized under GAAP is a modified version of the actual economic consequence of the employer's commitment to pay future benefits. Theoretically, over the full-time horizon, which is measured in decades, all the expense should be recognized in results of operations.

ASC 715-30 also establishes standards to be followed by sponsors of defined benefit pension plans when:

- Obligations are settled,
- Plans are curtailed,
- Benefits are terminated,
- Events require adjustment, or
- Amounts previously recognized in AOCI should be recognized in earnings.
  (ASC 715-30-05-9)

Pension Fund Although some companies manage their own plans, contributions are usually made to an independent trustee. These contributions are used by the trustee to invest in plan assets of various types, for example, treasury bonds and bills, certificates of deposit, annuities, marketable securities, corporate bonds, etc. The plan assets are expected to generate a return generally in the form of interest, dividends, and appreciation in asset value. The return on the plan assets and the proceeds from their liquidation provide the trustee with cash to pay the benefits to which the employees are entitled. These benefits, in turn, are defined by the plan's benefit formula.

Pension Benefit Formula The benefit formula, which is the basis for determining payments to plan participants, incorporates many factors including employee compensation, employee service longevity, employee age, and the like, and is considered to provide the best indication of pension obligations and costs. (ASC 715-30-20) It is used as the basis for determining the pension cost recognized in the financial statements each fiscal year.

Benefit Obligations

Vested benefit obligations are those that participants are entitled to receive even if they render no additional service to the entity. Most plans require a minimum number of years of service before a participant is vested. The vested benefit obligation is calculated using only current salary levels.

Pension plans may or may not be sensitive to future salary progression. Plans where the benefit formula is based on future compensation are called a pay-related, final-pay, or career-average-pay plan. These plans measure benefits based on service performed to date but also factor in assumptions as to future compensation increases, staff turnover rates, etc. Other plans where the formula is not based on future pay are referred to as non-pay-related or flat benefit plans.

The obligation, in present value terms, for future pension payments that include the effects of future compensation adjustments is referred to as the *projected* benefit obligation (PBO). (ASC 715-30-35-1A) The obligation computed *without* regard to future salary progression is called the *accumulated* benefit obligation (ABO). For those plans that do not depend on salary progression, the accumulated and the projected benefit obligations are the same. (ASC 715-30-35-2)

Exhibit

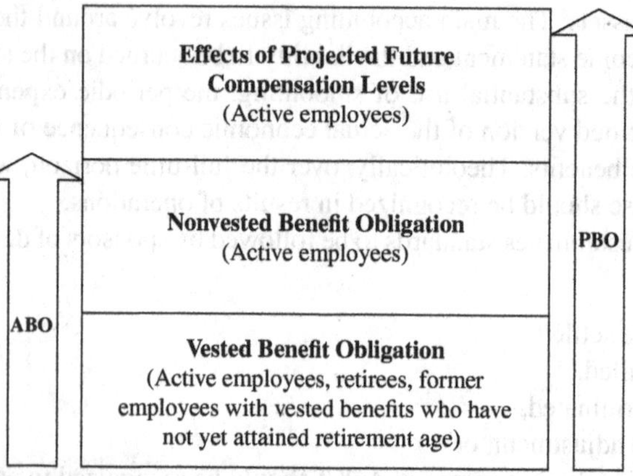

To calculate the net periodic pension cost, the ABO and the PBO must both be computed. Both of these obligation amounts are actuarially determined using the actuarial present value of benefits earned that are attributable to services rendered by the employee to the date of the computation. Under the provisions of most pension plans, the PBO provides a more relevant measure of the estimated cost of the benefits to be paid upon retirement. This is because many plans' benefit formulas normally result in increases in future pension benefits based on increases in the employee's compensation. The ABO and the vested benefit obligation provide information about the employer's obligation if the plan was discontinued. The FASB believes that the PBO is a more reliable measure of the obligation and reflects a going concern assumption.

The Codification mandates the benefits/years of service actuarial approach, which determines pension expense based on the plan's benefit formula.

Example

	January 1, 20X3
Accumulated benefit obligation	$(1,500)
Progression of salary and wages	(400)
Projected benefit obligation	$(1,900)

The expected progression of salary and wages is added to the accumulated benefit obligation to arrive at the projected benefit obligation. These amounts are provided by the actuary in a pension plan report.

Computation of the amounts to be presented on the statement of financial position requires the determination of plan assets. Plan assets include:

Contributions made by the employer that sponsors the pension plan (sponsor)

plus the net earnings on the plan's investments (dividends, interest, and asset appreciation),
less asset depreciation,
less benefits paid to retired participants.

Assumptions

When measuring the pension cost obligation:

- Estimates or assumptions must be made concerning future events and
- An attribution method approach must be selected to attribute costs to individual years of service
  (ASC 715-30-35-29)

Each significant assumption should reflect the best estimate with respect to that particular assumption. Absent evidence to the contrary, the underlying assumption should be that the plan will continue. Actuarial assumptions must include:

- the time value of money
- the probability of payment

It is not acceptable to determine that the aggregate assumptions are reasonable if any of the individual assumptions are unreasonable. (ASC 715-30-35-42)

Discount Rate The discount rate used in the calculation of service costs is the rate at which benefits could be settled. Examples include:

- those rates in current annuity contracts,
- those published by the Pension Benefit Guaranty Corporation (PBGC), and
- those that reflect returns on high-quality, fixed-income investments.
  (ASC 730-30-35-43)

Expected Long-Term Rate of Return The expected long-term rate of return used to calculate the expected return on plan assets is the average rate of return expected to be earned on invested funds to provide for pension benefits included in the PBO. Present rates of return and expected future reinvestment rates of return are considered in arriving at the rate to be used. (ASC 715-30-35-47)

Net Periodic Pension Cost

The following discussion employs a component-by-component analysis, providing a series of examples that cumulatively build to the comprehensive summary of net periodic pension costs and the sample pension disclosures that follow. Key amounts are cross-referenced between examples using parenthesized lowercase letters [(a), (b), etc.]. In accordance with accounting convention, obligations and increases in obligations are presented in parentheses.

A pension plan creates long-term obligations. It is assumed that a company will continue to provide retirement benefits well into the future. The accounting for the plan's costs is reflected in the financial statements.

Smoothing All pension costs incurred are recognized as expenses, but under the smoothing approach taken by ASC 715-30 and ASC 715-60, recognition of some elements of pension and postretirement benefit expense may be partially deferred until later periods.

Because pension obligations are long-term liabilities, some current period effects should not be fully recognized in earnings as incurred. Short-term fluctuations in interest rates, market prices of plan investments, and other factors could, if recognized as incurred, cause material swings in the net periodic pension cost and net income reported in the financial statements of the employer/sponsor. Such fluctuations would quite likely be offset by reversals in subsequent periods—for example, market declines in one period would be followed by market upward movements in later periods. This possibility has traditionally been cited to justify the use of smoothing techniques in order to recognize certain of these changes in a systematic and rational manner (e.g., by amortization) instead of recognizing them immediately.

Components of Net Periodic Pension Cost The benefits earned and costs recognized over the employees' service periods are computed by reference to the pension plan's benefit formula. Net periodic pension cost consists of the sum of the five components in the exhibit below. (ASC 715-30-35-4)

Exhibit—Five Components of Net Periodic Pension Cost

Component	Description	Effect on Pension Expense
1. Service cost	Expense from the increase in the PBO resulting from employee services rendered during the current year.	Increases
2. Interest cost on the liability, the PBO	Expense related to the PBO resulting from the discounted pension liability.	Increases
3. Actual return on plan assets	Adjustment for interest and dividends that the funds accumulated and increases and decreases in the fair value of the fund's assets.	Generally increases
4. Amortization of any prior service cost included in AOCI	Allocation of prior service cost of providing retroactive benefits.	Generally increases
5. Gain or loss	Results from the difference between actual obligations different from assumptions, a change in assumptions, a change in the value of either PBO or plan asset.	Decreases or increases

1. *Service cost.* Service cost is the actuarial present value of benefits attributed to services rendered by employees during the current period. (ASC 730-30-35-6) To measure the service cost, an attribution method is used and assumptions are made. (ASC 715-30-35-6) The plan's benefit formula is the key to attributing benefits to employee service periods. In most cases, this attribution is straightforward. If the benefit formula is ambiguous, the accounting for pension service costs must be based on the substantive plan. In some cases, this means that if an employer has committed to make future amendments to provide benefits greater than those written in the plan, that commitment is the basis for the accounting. (ASC 730-30-35-34) The relevant facts regarding that implicit commitment should be disclosed.

The service cost component is the only component eligible in the Codification to be capitalized as part of inventory costs or other assets. (ASC 715-30-35-7A)

Vesting To provide incentives for employees to continue their employment with the entity over time, plan participants' rights to receive present or future pension benefits are often conditioned on continued employment with the employer/plan sponsor for a specified period. As the conditions are satisfied, the employee is said to "vest" in that portion of the future benefits that become unconditional.

Vesting schedules can result in a disproportionate share of plan benefits being attributed to later years of employment, an in-substance delayed vesting of benefits. In this situation, instead of applying the benefit formula, proportions or ratios are used to attribute projected benefits to years of service in a manner that more equitably reflects the substance of timing of earning of the employee benefits. (ASC 730-30-35-38a) Normally, the actuary accomplishes this by attributing plan benefits to completed years of service by multiplying total benefits by the following ratio:

$$\frac{\text{Number of years of service completed by the employee}}{\text{Number of years of service required to be completed for full vesting}}$$

Certain types of benefits are not includable in vested benefits (e.g., death or disability benefit) and, thus, require a different allocation formula to attribute them to years of service. (ASC 730-30-35-38b) If the plan's benefit formula does not specify how to relate the benefit to years of service, the following formula is used by the actuary to attribute the benefits to years of service:

$$\frac{\text{Number of completed years of service}}{\text{Total projected years of service}}$$

Future compensation Future compensation is considered in the calculation of the service cost component to the extent specified by the benefit formula. (ASC 730-30-35-31) To the degree considered in the benefit formula, future compensation includes changes due to:

- Advancement,
- Longevity,
- Inflation, etc.

Indirect effects, such as predictable bonuses based on compensation levels and automatic increases specified by the plan, also need to be considered. The effect of retroactive amendments is included in the calculation when the employer has contractually agreed to them.

Service costs attributed to the period increase both the ABO and PBO, since they result in additional benefits to be payable in the future.

Example: PBO—Service Cost

	January 1, 20X3	*20X3 Service cost*
Accumulated benefit obligation	$(1,500)	$ (90)
Progression of salary and wages	(400)	(24)
Projected benefit obligation	$(1,900)	$(114) (a)*

* *Component of net periodic pension cost.*

The current period service cost component is found in the actuarial report.

2. *Interest on the liability—the PBO.* Because the employer sponsor defers paying the liability, the PBO is a discounted amount. It represents the discounted actuarial present value, at the date of the valuation, of all benefits attributed under the plan's formula to employee service rendered prior to that date. (ASC 715-30-35-8) Each year, when the actuary calculates the end- of-year PBO, it is one year closer to the year in which the benefits attributed in prior years will be paid to participants. Consequently, the present value of those previously attributed benefits will have increased to take into account the time value of money. This annual increase is computed by multiplying the assumed settlement discount rate times the PBO at the beginning of the year. It increases net periodic pension cost and the PBO.

Since this "interest" cost is accounted for as part of pension cost, it is not treated as interest for the purposes of computing capitalized interest under ASC 835-20. (ASC 715-30-35-9)

Example: PBO—Service Cost and Interest Cost

	January 1, 20X3	*20X3 Service cost*	*20X3 Interest cost*
Accumulated benefit obligation	$ (1,500)	$ (90)	$ (120)
Progression of salary and wages	(400)	(24)	(32)
Projected benefit obligation	$ (1,900)	$ (114) (a)*	$ (152) (b)*

* *Component of net periodic pension cost.*

The interest cost component is calculated by multiplying the start of the year obligation balances by an assumed for this example 8% settlement rate. This amount is found in the actuarial report.

Benefits paid to retirees are deducted from the above to arrive at the end-of-the-year statement of financial position amounts of the accumulated benefit obligation and the projected benefit obligation.

Example: PBO—Benefits Paid

	January 1, 20X3	*20X3 Service cost*	*20X3 Interest cost*	*20X3 Benefits paid*	*December 31, 20X3*
Accumulated benefit obligation	$ (1,500)	$ (90)	$(120)	$160	$(1,550)
Progression of salary and wages	(400)	(24)	(32)	—	(456)
Projected benefit obligation	$ (1,900)	$ (114) (a)	$(152) (b)	$160	$(2,006)

Benefits of $160 were paid to retirees during the current year. This amount is found in the report of the pension plan trustee.

3. *Actual return on plan assets.* This component of net periodic benefit cost is the difference between the fair value of the plan assets at the end of the period and the fair value of the

plan assets at the beginning of the period adjusted for contributions and payments during the period. (ASC 715-30-20)

$$\text{Actual Return} = \text{Plan Assets Ending Balance} - \text{Plan Assets Beginning Balance} - (\text{Contributions} - \text{Benefits Paid})$$

The actual return on plan assets of $158, cash deposited with the trustee of $145, and benefits paid ($160) are amounts found in the report of the pension plan trustee. These items increase the plan assets to $1,519 at the end of the year. The actual return on plan assets is adjusted, however, to the expected long-term rate (9% assumed) of return on plan assets ($1,376 × 9% = $124). The difference ($158 – $124 = $34) is a return on asset adjustment and is deferred as a gain (loss). The return on asset adjustment is a component of net periodic pension cost and is discussed in detail in the following section.

Example: Calculation of Actual Return on Plan Assets

20X3 Actual return on plan assets		*Ending balance December 31, 20X3*		*Beginning balance January 1, 20X3*		*20X3 Sponsor funding*		*20X3 Benefits paid*
$ 158(c)*	=	$1,519	–	$1,376	–	[$145	–	$(160)]

* *Component of net periodic pension cost.*

Measurements of defined benefit plan assets and obligations must (with limited exceptions) be as of the date of the statement of financial position of the respective reporting entity.

4. *Amortization of any prior service cost included in AOCI.* Prior service costs are incurred when the sponsor adopts plan amendments that increase plan benefits attributable to services rendered by plan participants in the past. (ASC 715-30-35-10) These costs are accounted for as a change to other comprehensive income. Prior service costs are measured at the amendment date by the increase in the projected benefit obligation. The remaining service period of every active employee expected to receive benefits is estimated, and an equal amount of prior service cost is assigned to each future period. (ASC 715-30-35-11) This is called the years-of-service amortization method.

Example of the Years-of-Service Amortization Method

The ABC Company amends its pension plan, granting $40,000 of prior service costs to its 100 employees. The employees are expected to retire in accordance with the following schedule:

Group	*Number of employees*	*Expected year of retirement*
A	10	20X4
B	15	20X5
C	20	20X6
D	20	20X7
E	35	20X8
	100	

The calculation of the service years to be recognized from this group is as follows:

	Service years					
Year	*A*	*B*	*C*	*D*	*E*	*Total*
20X4	10	15	20	20	35	100
20X5		15	20	20	35	90
20X6			20	20	35	75
20X7				20	35	55
20X8					35	35
	10	30	60	80	175	355

Consequently, there are 355 service years over which the $40,000 prior service cost can be spread, which equates to $112.68 per service year. The following table shows the annual amortization expense based on the standard charge of $112.68 per service year.

Year	Total service years	×	Cost per service year	=	Annual amortization
20X3	100		$112.68		$11,268
20X4	90		112.68		10,141
20X5	75		112.68		8,451
20X6	55		112.68		6,197
20X7	35		112.68		3,943
	355				$40,000

The example above illustrates the years-of-service amortization method. Consistent use of an accelerated amortization method is also acceptable and must be disclosed if used. (ASC 715- 30-35-13)

If most of the plan's participants are inactive, remaining life expectancy is used as a basis for amortization instead of estimated remaining service period. If economic benefits will be realized by plan participants over a shorter period than the remaining service period, amortization of costs is accelerated to recognize the costs in the periods that the participants benefit. If an amendment *reduces* the projected benefit obligation, unrecognized prior service costs are reduced to the extent that they exist and any excess is amortized in the manner described above for benefit increases. (ASC 715-30-35-14)

Example—Amortization of Unrecognized Service Cost

	January 1, 20X3	*20X3 Amortization*	*December 31, 20X3*
Unrecognized prior service cost	$320	$(27) (e)*	$293

* *Component of net periodic pension cost.*

Unrecognized prior service cost ($320) is amortized over the years of average remaining service (twelve years assumed) at the amendment date with a result rounded to $27. The straight-line method was used. These amounts are found in the actuarial report.

While the vast preponderance of changes to plans increase benefits with credit for prior service, there may be plan amendments that reduce benefits, also with reference to past service.

In such instances, under ASC 715, the decreases to the projected benefit obligation are given immediate recognition. The reduction in benefits should be recognized as a credit (referred to as a prior service credit) to other comprehensive income, which is to be used to offset any remaining prior service cost included in accumulated other comprehensive income (i.e., from previous plan amendments increasing benefits). Any remaining prior service credit should be amortized as a component of net periodic pension cost on the same basis as the cost of a benefit increase.

Thus, under requirements established by ASC 715, changes in prior service costs (and in certain other components affecting pension and other postretirement benefit costs) arising in a given reporting period, but not included in current period pension or other benefit costs (e.g., due to the above-described amortization requirements), are fully reported in other comprehensive income. (ASC 715-30-35-17)

5. *Gains or losses*. Gains or losses result from:

- Changes in plan actuarial assumptions,
- Changes in the value of plan assets, and
- Changes in the value of the projected benefit obligation.
  (ASC 715-30-35-18)

This Subtopic generally does not distinguish between gains or losses due to the experience assumed and actuarial assumptions. Gains and losses include realized and unrealized amounts.

Even though these gains or losses are economic events that impact the sponsor's obligations under the plan, immediately upon their occurrence, their immediate recognition in the sponsor's results of operations in the period they occurred is not required. (ASC 715-30-35-19) Immediate recognition of gains and losses as a component of net periodic pension cost is permitted. If gains or losses are recognized immediately, the method should be applied consistently and applied to all gains and losses on plan assets and obligations. (ASC 715-30-35-20)

To provide "smoothing" of the effects of what are viewed as short-term fluctuations, the net gain or loss may be amortized. If gains and losses are not recognized immediately as a component of net periodic cost, they should be recognized in other comprehensive income as they occur, thus affecting statement of financial position display in full, even as the expense recognition is deferred and amortized. (ASC 715-30-35-21)

Plan asset gains or losses result from both realized and unrealized amounts. They represent periodic differences between the actual return on assets and the expected return. (ASC 715-30-35-22)

The expected return is generated by multiplying the expected long-term rate of return by the market-related value of plan assets. (ASC 705-30-20) Market-related value is a concept unique to pension accounting. It results from the previously discussed actuarial smoothing techniques under ASC 715-30. Market-related value is either:

- The fair value of the plan assets or
- A calculated value that recognizes, in a systematic and rational manner, changes in fair value over not more than five years.
  (ASC 715-30-20)

Consistently applied means from year to year for each asset class (i.e., bonds, equities), since different classes of assets may have their market-related value calculated in a different manner (i.e., fair value in one case, moving average in another case). Thus, the market-related value may be fair value, but it also may be other than fair value if all or a portion of it results from calculation. Plan asset gains or losses include both

- Changes in the market-related value of assets (regardless of definition) from one period to another—recognized and amortized—and
- Any changes that are not yet reflected in market-related value (i.e., the difference between the actual fair values of assets and the calculated market-related values)—recognized over time through the calculated market-related values.

(ASC 715-30-35-22)

Amortization—10% corridor Regardless of the income smoothing techniques used, if the unrecognized net gain or loss exceeds a "corridor" of 10% of the greater of the beginning balances of the market-related value of plan assets or the projected benefit obligation, a minimum amount of amortization is required. The excess over 10% is divided by the average remaining service period of active employees and included as a component of net pension costs. Average remaining life expectancies of inactive employees may be used if that is a better measure due to the demographics of the plan participants.

An accelerated method of amortization of unrecognized net gain or loss is acceptable if it is applied consistently to both gains and losses, and if the method is disclosed in the notes to the financial statements. In all cases, at least the minimum amount discussed above must be amortized. (ASC 715-30-35-24) ASC 715-30 sets forth a methodology for the deferred recognition of the income statement effects of actuarial changes pertaining to plan assets and obligations.

Example—Gain or Loss Exceeds 10% Corridor

	January 1, 20X3	20X3 Return on asset adjustment	20X3 Amortization	December 31, 20X3
Unrecognized actuarial gain (loss)	$ (210)	$ 34 (d)*	$2 (d)*	$ (174)

* *Components of net periodic pension cost.*

The return on asset adjustment of $34 is the difference between the actual return of $158 and the expected return of $124 on plan assets. The actuarial loss at the start of the year ($210 assumed) is amortized if it exceeds a "corridor" of the larger of 10% of the projected benefit obligation at the beginning of the period ($1,900 × 10% = $190) or 10% of the fair value of plan assets ($1,376 × 10% = $138). In this example, $20 ($210 – $190) is amortized by dividing the years of average remaining service (twelve years assumed), with a result rounded to $2. The straight-line method is used, and it is assumed that market-related value is the same as fair value.

Net periodic pension costs—gain or loss Net periodic pension costs include only the expected return on plan assets. Any difference between actual and expected returns is deferred through the gain or loss component of net pension cost. If actual return is greater than expected return, net pension cost is increased to adjust the actual return to the lower expected return. If expected return is greater than actual return, the adjustment results in a decrease to net pension cost to adjust the actual return to the higher expected return. If the unrecognized net gain or loss is large enough, it is amortized. Conceptually, the expected return represents the best estimate of long-term performance of the plan's investments. In any given year, however, an unusual short- term result may occur given the volatility of financial markets. (ASC 715-30-35-26 and 35-27)

To summarize, net periodic pension cost includes a gain or loss component consisting of both of the following, if applicable:

- As a minimum, the portion of the unrecognized net gain or loss from previous periods that exceeds the greater of 10% of the beginning balances of the market-related value of plan assets *or* the PBO, usually amortized over the average remaining service period of active employees expected to receive benefits.
- The difference between the expected return and the actual return on plan assets. (ASC 715-30-35-26)

Example—Summary of Net Periodic Pension Cost

The components that were identified in the above examples are summed as follows to determine the amount defined as net periodic pension cost:

		20X3
Service cost	(a)	$114
Interest cost	(b)	152
Actual return on plan assets	(c)	(158)
Gain (loss)	(d)	36
Amortization of any prior service cost or credit	(e)	27
Total net periodic pension cost		$171

The calculation of net periodic pension cost may also include, if any, amortization of net transition asset or obligation that exists at the date of initial application of ASC 715-30 that remains in accumulated other comprehensive income. (ASC 715-30-35-4)

One possible source of confusion is the actual return on plan assets ($158) and the unrecognized gain of $36 that net to $122. The actual return on plan assets reduces pension cost because, to the extent that plan assets generate earnings, those earnings help the plan sponsor subsidize the cost of providing the benefits. Thus, the plan sponsor will not have to fund benefits as they become due, to the extent that plan earnings provide the plan with cash to pay those benefits. This reduction, however, is adjusted by increasing pension cost by the difference between actual and expected return of $34 and the amortization of the excess actuarial loss of $2, for a total of $36. The net result is to include the expected return of $124 ($158 – $34) less the amortization of the excess of $2 for a total of $122 ($158 – $36). In recognizing the components of net periodic pension costs, the entity must disclose this expected return of $124 and the loss of $2.

The prior service cost is included in accumulated other comprehensive income, and then amortized to pension cost. The amortization of gain or loss (which pertains to actuarially driven changes to the projected benefit obligation, as well as to asset valuation adjustments not recognized in current income) is associated with an item incorporated in accumulated other comprehensive income.

Exhibit—Reconciliation of Beginning and Ending ABO, PBO, and Plan Assets

The following table summarizes the 20X3 activity affecting ABO, PBO, and plan assets and reconciles the beginning and ending balances per the actuarial report:

	Accumulated benefit obligation	*Progression of salaries and wages*	*Projected benefit obligation*	*Fair value of plan assets**
Balance, January 1, 20X3	$ (1,500)	$ (400)	$ (1,900)	$ 1,376
Service cost	(90)	(24)	(114) (a)	
Interest cost	(120)	(32)	(152) (b)	
Benefits paid to retired participants	160		160	(160)
Actual return on plan assets				158 (c)
Sponsor's contributions				145
Balance, December 31, 20X3	$ (1,550)	$ (456)	$ (2,006)	$ 1,519

* *Assumed to be the same as market-related value for this illustration.*

Disclosure is required regarding the portfolio assets maintained to pay future pension and other postretirement benefits. This information should be presented in tabular format.

Employer's Liabilities and Assets under ASC 715-30

The full amount (measured by projected or accumulated benefit obligations, for pensions and other postretirement benefits, respectively) of over- or underfunding is recognized in the statement of financial position recognition, with the offsetting entry being to other comprehensive income. (ASC 715-30-25-1)

Fair value is determined as of the financial statement date. The amount is that which would result from negotiations between a willing buyer and seller not in a liquidation sale. Fair value is measured in preferred order by market price, selling price of similar investments, or discounted cash flows at a rate indicative of the risk involved.

Additional ASC 715-30 Guidance

Cash Balance Plans Some employers have terminated classic defined benefit pension plans and replaced them with "cash balance" plans. The scope of ASC 715-30-15 includes plans that are characterized by defined principal-crediting rates as percentages of salary, and offer defined, noncontingent interest-crediting rates that entitle participants to future interest credits at stated, fixed rates until retirement. (ASC 715-30-15-3) The standard states that "cash balance" plans with the foregoing attributes should be deemed defined benefit plans. (ASC 715-30-20) This is true because an employer's contributions to a cash balance plan trust and the earnings on the invested plan assets may be unrelated to the principal and interest credits to participants' hypothetical accounts.

The benefit promise in the cash balance arrangement is not pay related and, accordingly, use of a projected unit credit method is neither required nor appropriate for purposes of measuring the benefit obligation and annual cost of benefits earned. The appropriate cost attribution approach, therefore, is the traditional unit credit method. (Also see the "Definitions of Terms" section.)

Reporting Funded Status When There Is More Than One Plan When the reporting entity has more than one plan, it is not acceptable to display one single net amount of over- or underfunding. Rather, all overfunded plans must be separately aggregated, as must underfunded plans. (ASC 715-30-25-2) The amount of overfunding is included in noncurrent assets, with no portion of the overfunding permitted to be displayed as a current asset. On the other hand, total underfunding is allocated between current and noncurrent liabilities, with the current portion computed (on a plan-by-plan basis) as the sum of the actuarial present value of benefits included in the benefit obligation payable over the ensuing twelve months, to the extent that it exceeds the fair value of plan assets.

In the highly unlikely event an employer has the right to use the assets of an overfunded plan to pay the obligations of another, underfunded plan, it would be acceptable to offset the overfunding asset and the underfunding liability.

To illustrate, if the reporting entity has three postretirement benefit plans, one of which is overfunded and two of which are underfunded, the amount of overfunding must be included in noncurrent assets. The amount of underfunding of the two other plans must be reported in liabilities, but a portion of this total might have to be included in current liabilities. This is illustrated in the following table:

	Overfunded plan	Underfunded plan #1	Underfunded plan #2	Statement of financial position totals
FV of plan assets	$400,000		$700,000	$20,000
PV of benefit obligation (total)	340,000		874,000	240,000
next twelve months)	28,000		32,000	31,000
Overfunding asset (noncurrent)	60,000			$60,000
Underfunding liability (noncurrent)		174,000	209,000	383,000
Underfunding liability (current)			11,000	11,000

In the table above, note that the overfunded plan results in the reporting of a noncurrent asset, and this is not mitigated by the simultaneous existence of underfunded plans. Also note that underfunded plan #1 has sufficient assets to satisfy the amounts due within one year, and therefore the sponsoring entity's statement of financial position will not report any current liability with respect to this plan. However, plan #2, which is also underfunded, has benefit payments due over the twelve months following the statement of financial position date that exceed the amount of plan assets, and thus the sponsor will have to provide additional funding in the current period. That amount must be reported as a current liability. Finally, observe that the noncurrent obligations pertaining to both underfunded plans are combined into a single statement of financial position amount.

Reporting Funded Status and Benefit Plans Transactions and Events in Comprehensive Income An employer must recognize all transactions and events affecting the overfunded or underfunded status of a defined benefit postretirement plan in comprehensive income (or changes in unrestricted net assets, if the entity is a not-for-profit organization) in the year in which they occur.

The reporting entity must recognize as a component of other comprehensive income the gains or losses and prior service costs or credits arising during that reporting period that are not recognized as components of net periodic benefit cost of the period pursuant to ASC 715-30 and ASC 715-60. For example, if a plan amendment is adopted that credits employees with prior service, this is not reflected immediately in benefit costs, but rather is subject to amortization (i.e., it is recognized as part of pension or other postretirement benefit plan cost over an extended period of time). These requirements make it necessary to record in other comprehensive income, in the year the amendment is effected, the full amount of the prior service cost less what is recognized in pension cost in that period. (ASC 715-30-35-11)

The effect of recording this debit in comprehensive income is balanced by recording an additional underfunding liability. Also, in accordance with ASC 740, this is treated as a temporary difference, since the liability has a different basis (carrying value) for financial reporting purposes than it does for tax purposes. The deferred tax asset (in the normal circumstances) or liability will be recorded. The deferred tax effects, in turn, will be allocated to other financial statement components, including comprehensive income. (ASC 715-30-25-3)

Example

If Varga Corp., which is in the 30% tax bracket, grants its workers an amendment to a defined benefit pension plan that increases its obligation by $60,000, to be reflected in pension expense over fifteen years (i.e., amortized at $4,000 per year), under ASC 715 the following entry would be made (assuming the amendment is granted at year-end, and thus amortization will begin in the next period):

Accumulated other comprehensive income	42,000	
Deferred tax asset	18,000	
Pension liability		60,000

As noted earlier, the elements that will be reported in accumulated other comprehensive income, until taken into benefit expense as required under ASC 715-30 or ASC 715-60, include:

- gains and losses (i.e., those due to differences between expected and actual returns on plan assets, and those arising from actuarially determined adjustments), and
- prior service cost or credits from plan amendments.

For new amounts (e.g., actuarial adjustment in the current period), there will be an entry similar to the above, whereby accumulated other comprehensive income is adjusted to reflect the full amount of the item, as well as the (offsetting) deferred tax effect thereof.

In subsequent periods, there will be opposite direction adjustments to the amount provided in other comprehensive income, as amortization occurs. For example, if the prior service cost recognized by Varga Corp. above is to be amortized based on average remaining service lives of current employees and the amount so determined for 20X2, the first period after the amendment, is $5,000, the following entry would be recorded:

Pension cost	5,000	
Deferred tax asset		1,500
Accumulated other comprehensive income		3,500

For each annual statement of income presented, these amounts should be recognized in accumulated other comprehensive income, showing *separately* the amounts ascribed to net gain or loss and net prior service cost or credit. Those amounts are separated into amounts arising during the period and reclassification adjustments of other comprehensive income as a result of being recognized as components of net periodic benefit cost for the period. (ASC 715-30- 35-63A)

Measurement Date for Year-End Financial Statements ASC 715 requires that valuations be as of the date of the statement of financial position.

An exception is allowed in the instance of plans sponsored by consolidated subsidiaries or equity-method investees. (ASC 715-30-35-62) This is a practical concession, but given that under U.S. GAAP subsidiaries and investees are permitted to report financial results using year-ends different than the parent's or investor's, the exception is a reasonable and logical one. In those situations, the determinations of the fair values of plan assets and obligations must be as of the subsidiaries' or investees' respective dates of the statements of financial position. (ASC 715-30-35-63)

For an employer whose fiscal year-end does not coincide with a calendar month end, the employer has a practical expedient to measure defined benefit retirement obligations and related plan assets as of the month-end closest to its fiscal year-end. (ASC 715-30-35-63A)

Measurement Date for Interim Financial Statements Publicly held entities must report quarterly, and private companies may choose to issue interim financial statements that are represented as being in accordance with GAAP. ASC 715 does not impose a requirement to evaluate plan assets and obligations more frequently than on an annual basis. Therefore, unless there has been an interim revaluation conducted—for example, because a plan amendment was adopted, or there had been a settlement or curtailment of a plan—the funded status as of the most recent year-end should be used in interim period reporting, with certain adjustments. The adjustments to be made are for subsequent accruals of service cost, interest, and return on plan assets included in current earnings (excluding, however, any amortization of amounts first recognized in other comprehensive income), subsequent contributions to the plan, and subsequent benefit payments from the plan. (ASC 715-30-35-65) However, if there had been a revaluation subsequent to the prior year-end, the most recent valuation data would be used, again updated as just described, for any postvaluation accruals, contributions, and benefit payments.

Other Pension Considerations

Annuity and Insurance Contracts Benefits of annuity contracts and other insurance contracts that are equivalent in substance are excluded from plan assets and from the accumulated and projected benefit obligations if:

- They are valid and irrevocable,
- They transfer significant risks to an unrelated insurance company (not a captive insurer), and
- There is no reasonable doubt as to their payment.

Most other contracts are not considered annuities for ASC 715-30 purposes. If a plan's benefit formula specifies coverage by annuity contracts without participation rights, the service component of net pension costs is the cost of those contracts. In the case of an annuity contract with participation rights, the cost of the participation right is recognized as an asset and measured annually at its fair value. If fair value is inestimable, the cost is systematically amortized and carried at amortized cost (not to exceed net realizable value). Benefits provided by the formula beyond those provided by annuities are accounted for in the usual ASC 715-30 manner. All other insurance contracts are considered investments and are usually measured at cash surrender value, conversion value, contract value, or some equivalent.

In certain circumstances, annuity benefits are paid by employers after the insurer fails to make required payments. According to ASC 715-30-35-91, a loss is recognized by an employer at the time the employer assumes the benefit obligation payments to retirees for an insolvent insurance company that held these pension obligations. The loss recognized is the lesser of any gain recognized in the original contract with the insurance company or the amount of benefit obligation payments assumed by the company. Any additional loss not recognized is accounted for as a plan amendment in accordance with ASC 715-30.

Non-U.S. Pension Arrangements The terms and conditions that define the amount of benefits and the nature of the obligation determine the substance of a non-U.S. pension arrangement. If they are, in substance, similar to pension plans, ASC 715-30 applies.

Settlements and Curtailments of Plans

ASC 715-30-35 contains a subsection on the accounting to be followed by obligors when all or part of defined benefit pension plans have been settled or curtailed. It establishes employer accounting procedures for benefits offered when employment is terminated. A curtailment and a settlement can occur separately or together. (ASC 715-30-35-74)

Settlements Settlements include both the purchase of annuity contracts without participation rights and lump-sum cash payments. The following three criteria must all be met in order to constitute a pension obligation settlement:

1. It must be irrevocable.
2. It must relieve the obligor of primary responsibility for the obligation.
3. It must eliminate significant risks associated with the obligation and the assets used to effect it.
   (ASC 715-30-20)

Transactions that do not meet these three criteria do not qualify for treatment as a settlement under ASC 715-30. For example, an obligor could invest in a portfolio of high-quality fixed-income securities that would provide cash flows of interest and return-of-principal payments on dates that approximate the dates on which settlement payments are expected to become due. This would not meet the above criteria, however, because the employer is still primarily liable for the pension obligation and the investment is not irrevocable. Such a defeasance strategy does not constitute a settlement.

Recognition of settlements If the entire projected benefit obligation is settled, any ASC 715-30 unrecognized net gain (loss) is immediately recognized. A pro rata portion is recognized in the case of partial settlement. If the obligation is settled by purchasing annuities with participation rights, the cost of the right of participation is deducted from the gain (but not from the loss) before recognition. (ASC 715-30-35-79)

If the cost of all settlements is greater than the sum of the service cost and interest components of net periodic pension cost, the entity must recognize the gain or loss in earnings. If the total of the interest cost and service cost components of the ASC 715-30 periodic pension cost is greater than or equal to the settlement costs during a given year, the recognition of the above gain (loss) is not required, but is permitted. However, a consistent policy must be followed in this regard. (ASC 715-30-35-82) The settlement cost is generally the cash paid, or the cost of annuities without participation rights purchased, or the cost of annuities with participation rights reduced by the cost of the right of participation.

Example of a Settlement

To use information from the previous baseline example, the company's pension plan settles the $1,150 vested benefit portion of its projected benefit obligation by using plan assets to purchase an annuity contract without participation rights for $1,150. As a result of this settlement, nonvested benefits and the effects of projected future compensation levels remain in the plan. Also, a pro rata amount of the unrecognized net actuarial loss on assets, unrecognized prior service cost, and unamortized net asset at ASC 715-30 adoption are recognized due to settlement. Because the projected benefit obligation is reduced from $1,550 to $400, a drop of 74%, the pro rata amount used for recognition purposes is 74%. These changes are noted in the following table:

	Before settlement	*Effect of settlement*	*After settlement*
Assets and obligations:			
Vested benefit obligation	$(1,150)	$1,150	$0
Nonvested benefits	(400)	–	(400)
Accumulated benefit obligation	(1,550)	1,150	(400)
Effects of projected future compensation levels	(456)	–	(456)
Projected benefit obligation	(2,006)	1,150	(856)
Plan assets at fair value	1,519	(1,150)	369
Items not yet recognized in earnings:			
Funded status	(487)	0	(487)
Unrecognized net actuarial loss on assets	174	(129)	45
Unrecognized prior service cost	293	(217)	76
Unamortized net asset at ASC 715-30 adoption	(3)	(2)	(1)
Prepaid (accrued) benefit cost	$ (23)	$ (344)	$(367)

The entry used by the company to record this transaction does not include the purchase of the annuity contract since the pension plan acquires the contract with existing funds. The recognition of the pro rata amount of the unrecognized net actuarial loss on assets, unrecognized prior service cost, and unamortized net asset at ASC 715-30 adoption is recorded with the following entry:

Loss from settlement of pension obligation	344	
Accrued/prepaid pension cost		344

The maximum gain or loss subject to recognition in earnings when an obligation is settled is the net gain or loss that is remaining in accumulated other comprehensive income. The maximum gain or loss, first determined at the date of settlement, is fully reported in earnings only if the entire projected benefit obligation is settled; if it is only partially settled, only a pro rata portion of the maximum gain or loss can be recognized.

Annuity contracts in settlement transactions Under an annuity contract settlement, an unrelated insurance company unconditionally accepts an obligation to provide the required benefits. The following criteria must be met for this type of settlement:

- It must be irrevocable.
- It must involve a transfer of material risk to the insurance company.

There can be no reasonable doubt as to the ability of the insurance company to meet its contractual obligation. (ASC 715-30-35-86) The substance of any annuity contract with participation rights must relieve the employer of most of the risks and rewards or it does not meet the criteria. (ASC 715-30-35-87)

Curtailments Curtailments include early discontinuance of employee services or cessation or suspension of a plan. Additional benefits may not be earned, although future service time may be counted towards vesting. A curtailment must meet the following criteria:

- It must materially diminish present employees' future service, or
- It must stop or materially diminish the accumulation of benefits by a significant number of employees.

  (ASC 715-30-20)

Recognition of Curtailments A curtailment results in the elimination of future years of service. To the extent that prior service costs are included in accumulated other comprehensive income, and this is associated with service years no longer expected to be rendered, this must be recognized currently as a loss. This would occur if prior service cost is being amortized over a term that no longer accurately reflects expected future service by the post-curtailment workforce. Prior service cost, in this context, includes that resulting from plan amendments. (ASC 715-30-35-92) The pro rata portions of any unrecognized cost of retroactive plan amendments are immediately recognized as a loss.

If curtailment results in a decrease in the projected benefit obligation, a gain is indicated. An increase in the projected benefit obligation (excluding termination benefits) indicates a loss. This indicated gain (loss) is then netted against the loss from unrecognized prior service cost recognized in accordance with the preceding paragraph. (ASC 715-30-35-93) The net result is the curtailment gain or curtailment loss. A gain is recognized upon actual employee termination or plan suspension. A loss is recognized when both the curtailment is probable and the effects are reasonably estimable. (ASC 715-30-35-94)

Example of a Curtailment

To use information from the previous baseline example, the company shuts down one of its factories, which terminated the employment of a number of its staff. The terminated employees have nonvested benefits of $120 and projected benefit obligation of $261. As a result of this curtailment, 19% of the projected benefit obligation has been eliminated ($381 PBO reduction resulting from the curtailment, divided by the beginning $2,006 PBO). Accordingly, 19% of the unrecognized prior service cost and unamortized net asset at ASC 715-30 adoption are recognized due to the curtailment. In addition, the total projected benefit reduction of $381 is first netted against the unrecognized net actuarial loss on assets of $174, leaving $207 to be recognized as a gain. These changes are noted in the following table:

	Before curtailment	*Effect of curtailment*	*After curtailment*
Assets and obligations:			
Vested benefit obligation	$ (1,150)		$ (1,150)
Nonvested benefits	(400)	$120	(280)
Accumulated benefit obligation	(1,550)	120	(1,430)
Effects of projected future compensation levels	(456)	261	(195)

	Before curtailment	*Effect of curtailment*	*After curtailment*
Projected benefit obligation	(2,006)	381	(1,625)
Plan assets at fair value	1,519	0	1,519
Items not yet recognized in earnings:			
Funded status	(487)	381	(106)
Unrecognized net actuarial loss on assets	174	(174)	0
Unrecognized prior service cost	293	(56)	237
Prepaid (accrued) benefit cost	$ (20)	$151	$ 131

The company records the recognition of the pro rata amount of the unrecognized prior service cost and unamortized net asset at ASC 715-30 adoption with the following entry, which is offset against the net gain of $207 resulting from the reduction in the planned benefit obligation:

Accrued/prepaid pension cost	151	
Gain from curtailment of pension obligation		151

Termination Benefits Termination benefits may be categorized as special termination benefits for contractual termination benefits.

- Special short time period benefits require that a loss and a liability be recognized when the offer is accepted and the amount can be reasonably estimated.
- Contractual termination benefits require that a loss and a liability be recognized when it is probable that employees will receive the benefits and the amount can be reasonably estimated.
  (ASC 715-30-25-10)

The cost of these benefits is the cash paid at termination and the present value of future payments. (ASC 715-30-25-11) Termination benefits and curtailments can occur together.

Example of Termination Benefits

Again using the information from the previous baseline example, the company offers a onetime early retirement bonus payment, which is in addition to existing pension benefits. As a result of the offer, the company directly pays $200 in termination benefits. As a result of the employee retirements, the liability associated with projected future compensation levels drops by $60, while the pro rata portion of the unrecognized prior service cost associated with the retiring employees is $39. These changes are noted in the following table:

	Before termination benefit	*Effect of termination benefit*	*After termination benefit*
Assets and obligations:			
Vested benefit obligation	$(1,150)		$(1,150)
Nonvested benefits	(400)		(400)
Accumulated benefit obligation	(1,550)		(1,550)
Effects of projected future compensation levels	(456)	$60	(396)
Projected benefit obligation	(2,006)	$60	(1,946)
Plan assets at fair value	1,519	0	1,519

	Before termination benefit	Effect of termination benefit	After termination benefit
Items not yet recognized in earnings:			
Funded status	(487)	(427)	
Unrecognized net actuarial loss on assets	174	(60)	114
Unrecognized prior service cost	293	(39)	254
Unamortized net asset at ASC 715-30 adoption	(3)	–	(3)
			$ (62)
Prepaid (accrued) benefit cost	$ (23)	(39)	
Cost of termination benefits		200	
		$(239)	
Total loss on terminations			

The company nets the $60 gain on reduction of projected future compensation levels against the existing unrecognized net actuarial loss on assets. It then records the $39 loss caused by the increased amortization of the unrecognized prior service cost and the $200 cost of the termination benefits with the following entry:

Loss on employee terminations	239	
Accrued/prepaid pension cost		39
Cash		200

Component Disposal Gains or losses, as calculated above, that result because of a disposal of a component of the entity are recognized according to the provisions of ASC 360.

ASC 715-60, *Defined Benefits Plans—Other Postretirement*

ASC 715-60 contains the guidance for employers' accounting for other (than pension) postretirement employee benefits (commonly called OPEB). This guidance prescribes a single method for measuring and recognizing an employer's (APBO). It applies to all forms of postretirement benefits, although the most material such benefit is usually postretirement health care coverage. (ASC 715-60-05-6) It uses the fundamental framework established by ASC 715-30. To the extent that the promised benefits are similar, the accounting provisions are similar. Only when there is a compelling reason is the accounting different. (ASC 715-60-05-7)

The guidance considers OPEB to be a form of deferred compensation and requires accrual accounting. The terms of the individual contract govern the accrual of the employer's obligation for deferred compensation and the cost is attributed to employee service periods until full eligibility to receive benefits is attained. The employer's obligation for OPEB is fully accrued when the employee attains full eligibility for all expected benefits.

Funded status is determined by the difference between the fair value of plan assets and the accumulated benefit obligation. (ASC 715-60-35-5)

ASC 715-60 requires accrual accounting and adopts the three primary characteristics of pension accounting as follows:

1. Delayed recognition (changes are not recognized immediately but are subsequently recognized in a gradual and systematic way)
2. Reporting net cost (aggregates of various items are reported as one net amount)
3. Offsetting assets and liabilities (assets and liabilities are sometimes shown net)

ASC 715-60 distinguishes between the substantive plan and the written plan. Although generally the same, the substantive plan (the one understood as evidenced by past practice or by communication of intended changes) is the basis for the accounting if it differs from the written plan.

ASC 715-60 focuses on accounting for a single-employer plan that defines the postretirement benefits to be provided. A defined benefit postretirement plan defines benefits in terms of the provision for:

- Monetary amounts, or
- Benefit coverage.

Postretirement benefits can include tuition assistance, legal services, day care, housing subsidies, health insurance coverage (probably the most significant), and other benefits. The amount of benefits usually depends on a benefit formula. OPEB may be provided to current employees, former employees, beneficiaries, and covered dependents. The guidance applies to:

- Settlement of the APBO, and
- Curtailment of a plan as part of a special termination benefit offer.

The guidance also applies to deferred compensation contracts with individuals. Taken together, these contracts are equivalent to an OPEB plan. ASC 715-60 does not apply to benefits provided through a pension plan. If part of a larger plan with active employees, the OPEB is segregated and accounted for in accordance with this standard. If not materially different, estimates, averages, and computational shortcuts may be used.

The basic tenet of ASC 715-60 is that accrual accounting is better than cash basis accounting. Recognition and measurement of the obligation to provide OPEB is required in order to provide relevant information to financial statement users. Although funding and cash flow information is incorporated into the statement, the overall liability is the primary focus.

The guidance attempts, in accordance with the terms of the substantive plan, to account for the exchange transaction that takes place between the employer, who is ultimately responsible for providing OPEB, and the employee who provides services, in part at least, to obtain the OPEB. ASC 715-60 accounting requires that the liability for OPEB be fully accrued when the employee is fully eligible for all of the expected benefits. The fact that the employee may continue to work beyond this date is not relevant, since the employee has already provided the services required to earn the OPEB.

OPEB are considered to be deferred compensation earned in an exchange transaction during the time periods that the employee provides services. The expected cost generally is attributed in equal amounts (unless the plan attributes a disproportionate share of benefits to early years) over the periods from the employee's hiring date (unless credit for the service is only granted from a later plan eligibility or entry date) to the date that the employee attains full eligibility for all benefits expected to be received. This accrual is followed even if the employee provides service beyond the date of full eligibility.

Accounting for Postretirement Benefits The expected postretirement benefit obligation (EPBO) is the actuarial present value (APV) as of a specific date of the benefits expected to be paid to the employee, beneficiaries, and covered dependents. Measurement of the EPBO is based on the following:

- Expected amount and timing of future benefits.
- Expected future costs.

- Extent of cost sharing (contributions, deductibles, coinsurance provisions, etc.) between employer, employee, and others (i.e., the government). The APV of employee contributions reduces the APV of the EPBO. Obligations to return employee contributions, plus interest if applicable, are recognized as a component of EPBO.
(ASC 715-60-35-2)

The EPBO includes an assumed salary progression for a pay-related plan. Future compensation levels represent the best estimate after considering the individual employees involved, general price levels, seniority, productivity, promotions, indirect effects, and the like.

The APBO is the APV as of a specific date of all future benefits attributable to service by an employee to that date. It represents the portion of the EPBO earned to date. After full eligibility is attained, the APBO equals the EPBO.

The APBO also includes an assumed salary progression for a pay-related plan. Thus, this term is more comparable to the projected benefit obligation (PBO) under ASC 715-30. The accumulated benefit obligation in ASC 715-30 has no counterpart in ASC 715-60.

Net periodic postretirement benefit costs include the following components:

- Service cost
- Interest cost—Interest on the APBO
- Actual return on plan assets
- Gain or loss
- Amortization of unrecognized prior service cost
(ASC 715-60-35-9)

Note that return on plan assets is included in the periodic expense determination, consistent with accounting for defined benefit pension plans. However, in virtually all cases, OPEB plans are unfunded, and thus there will be no asset return. If a trust has been established to fund these benefits, it does not necessarily have to be "bankruptcy proof," or insulated completely from the claims of general creditors, to qualify as plan assets in accordance with ASC 715-60-55. On the other hand, assets held in a trust that explicitly makes them available to the general creditors in bankruptcy do not qualify as plan assets under ASC 715-60. The funded status of other postretirement defined benefit plans must be formally reported in the statement of financial position, as described above.

Service costs and interest costs are defined and measured in the same manner by both ASC 715-60 and ASC 715-30. However, under ASC 715-60, interest increases the APBO while under ASC 715-30, interest increases the PBO.

Under ASC 715-60, a single method is required to be followed in measuring and recognizing the net periodic cost and the liability involved. That method attributes the EPBO to employee service rendered to the full eligibility date.

Assumptions ASC 715-60 requires the use of explicit assumptions using the best estimates available of the plan's future experience, solely with regard to the individual assumption under consideration. Plan continuity is to be presumed, unless there is evidence to the contrary. Principal actuarial assumptions include:

- Discount rates,
- Retirement age,
- Participation rates (contributory plans),
- Salary progression (pay-related plans), and
- Probability of payment (turnover, dependency status, mortality).
(ASC 715-60-35-73a-e)

Present value factors for health care OPEB include:

- Cost trend rates,
- Medicare reimbursement rates, and
- Per capita claims cost by age.
  (ASC 715-60-35-73f)

Current interest rates, as of the measurement date, are used for discount rates in present value calculations. Examples include high-quality, fixed-income investments with similar amounts and timing and interest rates at which the postretirement benefit obligations could be settled. The EPBO, APBO, service cost, and interest cost components use assumed discount rates. (ASC 715-60-35-79)

The expected long-term rate of return on plan assets is an assumption about the average rate of return expected on contributions during the period and on existing plan assets. Current returns on plan assets and reinvestment returns are considered in arriving at the rate to be used. Related income taxes, if applicable, reduce the rate. Expected return on plan assets and the fair value of plan assets use this rate in their calculation. (ASC 715-60-35-84) Since the Employee Retirement Security Act of 1974 (ERISA) does not require OPEB plans to be funded via the separate trust vehicles used for pension plans, OPEB plans are often unfunded. Thus, there are no "plan assets." Instead, the sponsor pays benefits directly, as they become due, from general corporate assets.

Example

A sample illustration of the basic accounting for OPEB as established by ASC 715-60 follows. Kinetic Corporation established a new OPEB plan as of January 1, 20X5. Although the plan was new, it retroactively credited employees for their years of service to Kinetic prior to the establishment of the plan.

All employees had been hired at age 30 and become fully eligible for benefits at age 60. The plan is unfunded and, thus, there are no plan assets. The first calculation is the determination of the unrecognized transition obligation (UTO).

Kinetic Corporation December 31, 20X4

Employee	*Age*	*Years of service*	*Total years when fully eligible*	*Expected retirement age*	*Remaining service to retirement*	*EPBO*	*APBO*
A	35	5	30	60	25	$ 14,000	$ 2,333
B	40	10	30	60	20	22,000	7,333
C	45	15	30	60	15	30,000	15,000
D	50	20	30	60	10	38,000	25,333
E	55	25	30	65	10	46,000	38,333
F	60	30	30	65	5	54,000	54,000
G	65	RET	–		–	46,000	46,000
H	70	RET	–		–	38,000	38,000
					85	$288,000	$226,332

Explanations

1. EPBO is usually determined by an actuary, although it can be calculated if complete data are available.
2. APBO is calculated using the EPBO. Specifically, it is EPBO × (Years of service/Total years when fully eligible).
3. The UTO is the APBO at 12/31/X1, since there are no plan assets to be deducted. The $226,332 can be amortized over the average remaining service to retirement of 14.17 (85/6) years or an optional period of 20 years, if longer. Kinetic selected the 20-year period of amortization.
4. Note that Employee F has attained full eligibility for benefits and yet plans to continue working.
5. Note that the above 20X4 table is used in the calculation of the 20X5 components of OPEB cost that follows.

After the establishment of the UTO, the next step is to determine the benefit cost for the year ended December 31, 20X5. This calculation follows the framework established by ASC 715-30. The discount rate is assumed to be 10%.

Kinetic Corporation
OPEB Cost December 31, 20X5

1. Service cost	$ 5,500
2. Interest cost	22,633
3. Actual return on plan assets	–
4. Gain or loss	–
5. Amortization of unrecognized prior service cost	–
6. Amortization of UTO	11,317
Total OPEB cost	$39,450

Explanations

1. Service cost calculation uses only employees not yet fully eligible for benefits.

Employee	*[a] 12/31/X1 EPBO*	*[b] Total years when fully eligible*	*[a ÷ b] Service cost*
A	$14,000	30	$ 467
B	22,000	30	733
C	30,000	30	1,000
D	38,000	30	1,267
E	46,000	30	1,533
			$5,000
	Interest for 20X0	($5,000 × 10%)	500
	Total service cost		$5,500

2. Interest cost is the 12/31/X4 APBO of $226,332 × 10% = $22,633.
3. There are no plan assets so there is no return.
4. There is no gain (loss) since there are no changes yet.
5. There is no unrecognized prior service cost initially.
6. Amortization of UTO is the 12/31/X4 UTO of $226,332/20-year optional election = $11,317.

After calculation of the 20X5 benefit cost, the next step is to project the EPBO and APBO for December 31, 20X5. Assuming no changes, it is based on the December 31, 20X4, actuarial measurement and it is calculated as shown earlier in the determination of the UTO.

Kinetic Corporation
December 31, 20X5

Employee	Age	Years of service	Total years when fully eligible	EPBO	APBO
A	36	6	30	$ 15,400	$ 3,080
B	41	11	30	24,200	8,873
C	46	16	30	33,000	17,600
D	51	21	30	41,800	29,260
E	56	26	30	50,600	43,853
F	61	31	–	59,400	59,400
G	66	RET		44,620	44,620
H	71	RET		36,860	36,860
				$305,880	$243,546

Changes in experience or assumptions will result in gains or losses. The gain (loss) is measured by the difference resulting in the APBO or the plan assets from that projected. However, except for the effects of a decision to temporarily deviate from the substantive plan, these gains or losses have no impact in the year of occurrence. They are deferred and amortized as in ASC 715-30. Amortization of unrecognized net gain (loss) is included as a component of net postretirement cost for a year if, as of the beginning of the year, it exceeds 10% of the greater of the APBO or the market-related value of plan assets. The minimum amortization is the excess divided by the remaining average service period of active plan participants. A systematic method of amortization that amortizes a greater amount, is applied consistently to both gains and losses, and is disclosed may also be used. If gains or losses are recognized immediately, special rules of offsetting may be required.

Effect of the Prescription Drug Benefit on OPEB Computations The Medicare Prescription Drug, Improvement, and Modernization Act Subsections provide guidance on accounting for the effects of the ACT. (ASC 715-60-05-8) Under ASC 715-60, the effects of the Act on current period measurements of postretirement benefit costs and the APBO must be accounted for, if defined criteria are met.

The guidance regarding accounting for the subsidiary set forth in ASC 715-60 applies only to sponsors of a single-employer defined benefit postretirement health care plan for which

1. the employers have concluded that prescription drug benefits available under the plan to some or all participants for some or all future years are "actuarially equivalent" to Medicare Part D and thus qualify for the subsidy under the Act, and
2. the expected subsidiaries will offset or reduce the employers' shares of the cost of the underlying postretirement prescription drug coverage on which the subsidies are based. (ASC 715-60-15-11)

ASC 715-60 also provides guidance for disclosures about the effects of the subsidy for employers that sponsor postretirement health care benefit plans that provide prescription drug coverage but for which the employers have not yet been able to determine actuarial equivalency.

The central question raised has been whether a subsidy is substantively similar to other Medicare benefits that existed when ASC 715-60 was issued—and therefore to be accounted for as a reduction of the APBO and net periodic postretirement benefit cost—or whether the subsidy represents a payment to the employer that is determined by reference to its plan's benefit payments but is not, in and of itself, a direct reduction of postretirement benefit costs. A secondary issue pertains to the timing of accounting recognition of the subsidy.

FASB concluded that the former interpretation is the correct one. That is, measures of the APBO and net periodic postretirement benefit cost on or after the date of enactment are to reflect the effects of the Act. When an employer initially accounts for the subsidy, its effect on the APBO is to be accounted for as an actuarial experience gain. Additionally, the subsidy reduces service cost when it is recognized as a component of net periodic postretirement benefit cost. If the estimated expected subsidy changes, the effect is to be treated as an actuarial experience gain or loss.

Plan amendments will also affect the reporting of OPEB cost and the APBO. If prescription drug benefits currently available under an existing plan are deemed not actuarially equivalent as of the date of enactment of the Act, but the plan is later amended to provide actuarially equivalent benefits, the direct effect of the amendment on the APBO and the effect on the APBO from any resulting subsidy to which the employer is expected to be entitled as a result of the amendment are to be combined, and deemed to be an actuarial experience gain if it reduces APBO. On the other hand, if the combined effect increases the APBO, it is deemed to be prior service cost that is to be accounted for consistent with ASC 715-60.

Additionally, according to ASC 715-60, if a plan that provides prescription drug benefits that previously were deemed actuarially equivalent under the Act is subsequently amended to reduce its prescription drug coverage such that the coverage is not considered actuarially equivalent, any actuarial experience gain related to the subsidy previously recognized is unaffected. The combined net effect on the APBO of (1) the subsequent plan amendment that reduces benefits under the plan and thus disqualifies the benefits as actuarially equivalent, and (2) the elimination of the subsidy is to be accounted for as prior service cost (credit) as of the date the amendment is adopted.

In the periods in which the subsidy affects the employer's accounting for the plan, this will have no effect on any plan-related temporary difference accounted for under ASC 740, because the subsidy is exempt from federal taxation.

There may be a time lag before the employer is able to determine whether the benefits provided by its plan are actuarially equivalent. During the interim period, it is required to disclose: the existence of the Act and the fact that measures of the APBO or net periodic postretirement benefit cost do not reflect any amount associated with the subsidy because the employer is unable to conclude whether the benefits provided by the plan are actuarially equivalent to Medicare Part D under the Act.

In interim and annual financial statements for the first period in which an employer includes the effects of the subsidy in measuring the APBO and the first period in which an employer includes the effects of the subsidy in measuring net periodic postretirement benefit cost, it is required to disclose the following:

- The reduction in the APBO for the subsidy related to benefits attributed to past service.
- The effect of the subsidy on the measurement of net periodic postretirement benefit cost for the current period. That effect includes (1) any amortization of the actuarial experience gain in (a) as a component of the net amortization called for by ASC 715-60, (2) the reduction in current period service cost due to the subsidy, and (3) the resulting reduction in interest cost on the APBO as a result of the subsidy.
- Any other disclosures required by ASC 715-20, specifically disclosure of an explanation of any significant change in the benefit obligation or plan assets not otherwise apparent in the other disclosures required by that standard.

When ASC 715-60 is initially adopted, a remeasurement of the plan's assets and APBO, including the effects of the subsidy, if applicable, as well as the other effects of the Act, is to be made as of the earlier of (1) the plan's measurement date that normally would have followed enactment of the Act, or (2) the end of the employer's interim or annual period that includes the date of the Act's enactment. Alternatively, employers are permitted, but not required, to perform that remeasurement as of the date of enactment. The measurement of the APBO is to be based on the plan provisions in place on the measurement date (i.e., later amendments are not to be anticipated in the computation).

Deferred Compensation Contracts

If the aggregate deferred compensation contracts with individual employees are equivalent to a pension plan, the contracts are accounted for according to ASC 715-30 and ASC 715-60. All other deferred compensation contracts are accounted for according to ASC 710.

ASC 715-60 states that the terms of the individual contract will govern the accrual of the employee's obligation for deferred compensation and the cost is to be attributed over the employee service period until full eligibility is attained.

ASC 715-70, *Defined Contribution Plans*

In the typical defined contribution plan, the contribution is either discretionary or derived from a formula, and that amount is the expense the sponsor should report in its financial statements for the year. Benefits are generally paid from the pool of accumulated contributions and are limited to the plan assets available to pay them. If, however, the defined contribution plan has defined benefits, the provision is calculated as required under ASC 715-30.

ASC 715-80, *Multiemployer Pension Plans*

A multiemployer plan is one to which two or more unrelated employers contribute, often pursuant to collectively bargained, union-sponsored agreements. For essentially practical reasons, the Codification requires that the contribution for the period be recognized as net pension cost and that any contributions due and unpaid be recognized as a liability. Thus, most of the complexities arising from smoothing are avoided in accounting for sponsors participating in multiemployer plans. Assets of all the employers sponsoring this type of plan are usually commingled and not segregated or restricted. A Board of Trustees usually administers these plans. If there is a withdrawal of an employer from this type of plan and if an obligation to make up any funding deficiency is either probable or reasonably possible, ASC 450 applies.

Some plans are, in substance, a pooling or aggregation of single-employer plans and are ordinarily without collective-bargaining agreements. Contributions are usually based on a specified benefit formula. These plans are not considered multiemployer, and the accounting is based on each employer's respective interest in the plan.

The existence of an executed agreement does not require recognition by an employer of a liability beyond currently due and unpaid contributions. (ASC 715-80-55-2)

Presentation and Disclosure

Disclosure requirements for postretirement plans are, of necessity, voluminous and complex. Detailed disclosure requirements can be found at www.wiley.com/go/GAAP2021.

Other Sources

See ASC Location—*Wiley GAAP* Chapter	*For information on . . .*
	ASC 715-10-60
ASC 710	Deferred compensation contracts that are accounted for individually on an accrual basis in accordance with the terms of the underlying contract.
	ASC 715-30-60
ASC 220-10	The required display and reporting in comprehensive income of information about gains or losses associated with pension or other postretirement benefits, prior service costs or credits associated with pension or other postretirement benefits, and transition assets or obligations associated with pension or other postretirement benefits.
ASC 330-10	The capitalization of net periodic pension cost or net periodic pension income as part of the cost of inventory or other assets. Upon implementation of ASC 2017-07, this language will change to: The capitalization of the service cost component of net periodic pension cost as part of the cost of inventory.
ASC 420-10	The required accounting associated with one-time termination benefits provided to current employees that are involuntarily terminated under the terms of a one-time benefit arrangement.
ASC 420-10	Whether additional termination benefits should be considered one-time termination benefits and accounted for under Subtopic 420-10 or be considered an enhancement to an ongoing benefit arrangement and, therefore, subject to the provisions of either this Topic or Subtopic 712-10.
ASC 805-20	The required pension-related accounting for issues arising in connection with a business combination, including plans to terminate certain employees, the measurement of projected benefit obligations, and the assignment of the purchase price to individual assets acquired and liabilities assumed.
ASC 810-10	Whether to consolidate an employee benefit plan.
ASC 845-10	The requirements related to gain or loss recognition for the spinoff of pension- related assets or obligations transferred in a spinoff of nonmonetary assets to owners of an entity.
ASC 958-715	The required accounting by a not-for-profit employer for the gains or losses and the prior service costs or credits that would be recognized in other comprehensive income under the guidance in the General Subsections of this Subtopic.
ASC 980-715	Treatment by rate-regulated entities of the possible difference between net periodic pension cost as defined in the General Subsections of this Subtopic and amounts of pension cost considered for rate-making purposes.

ASC 715-60	
ASC 805-20-25-25	The accounting when an employer is acquired in a business combination and that employer sponsors a single-employer defined benefit postretirement plan.
ASC 805-20-55-50 through 55-51	Plans to terminate certain employees if a business combination is probable.
ASC 810-10-15-12	Consolidation guidance on employee benefit plans.
ASC 930-715	The United Mine Workers of America Combined Benefit Fund.
ASC 980-715	Rate-regulated entities, and the actions of regulators that may change the timing of recognition of net periodic postretirement benefit cost.
ASC 980-715	A continuing other postretirement plan of a rate-regulated entity.

43 ASC 718 COMPENSATION—STOCK COMPENSATION

PERSPECTIVE AND ISSUES

Technical Alert ASU 2019-07, *Compensation—Stock Compensation (Topic 718) and Revenue from Contracts with Customers (Topic 606) Codification: Improvements—Share-Based Consideration Payable to a Customer*

In November 2019, the FASB issued Accounting Standards Update 2019-08, *Compensation—Stock Compensation (Topic 718) and Revenue from Contracts with Customers (Topic 606) Codification Improvements—Share-Based Consideration Payable to a Customer.* The purpose of the ASU is to provide guidance on measuring share-based payment awards granted to a customer.

Guidance ASU 2019-08 clarifies the guidance in ASU 2018-07 by requiring entities to measure and classify share payment awards granted to a customer by applying the guidance in Topic 718. The amount recorded as a reduction of the transaction price must be measured on the basis of the grant-date fair value of the share-based payment award in accordance with Topic 718. See Appendix A for the definition of "grant date." The classification and subsequent measurement of the award follow the guidance in Topic 718 unless the share-based payment award is subsequently modified and the grantee is no longer a customer.

Effective Dates The effective dates are as follows:

- For entities that have not yet adopted the amendments in ASU 2018-07—
  - for public business entities, in fiscal years beginning after December 15, 2019, and interim periods within those fiscal years, and
  - for other than public business entities, in fiscal years beginning after December 15, 2019, and interim periods within fiscal years beginning after December 15, 2020.
- For entities that have adopted the amendments in ASU 2018-07—
  - for all entities, in fiscal years beginning after December 15, 2019, and interim periods within those fiscal years.

Early adoption is permitted, but not before the entity adopts the amendments in ASU 2018-07.

Transition An entity may adopt the amendments in ASU 2019-08 either in the same fiscal year that it adopts the amendments in ASU 2018-07 or in a fiscal year after the fiscal year that the entity adopts the amendments in ASU 2018-07 as follows:

- If an entity adopts the amendments in ASU 2019-08 in the same fiscal year that it adopts the amendments in ASU 2018-07, the entity should apply the amendments in ASU 2019-08 through a cumulative-effect adjustment to the opening balance of retained earnings at the beginning of the fiscal year in which it adopted the amendments in ASU 2018-07.
- If an entity adopts the amendments in ASU 2019-08 in a fiscal year after the fiscal year that the entity adopts the amendments in ASU 2018-07, the entity should apply the amendments in ASU 2019-08 through a cumulative-effect adjustment to the opening balance of retained earnings at the beginning of either:
  - The fiscal year in which it adopted the amendments in ASU 2018- 07.
  - The fiscal year in which it adopts the amendments in ASU 2019-08.

Subtopics

ASC 718, *Compensation-Stock Compensation*, provides guidance for employee and nonemployee share-based payments and contains five subtopics:

- ASC 718-10, *Overall*, contains the high-level objectives and general guidance for the topic

- ASC 718-20, *Awards Classified as Equity*, deals with share-based payments classified as equity
- ASC 718-30, *Awards Classified as Liabilities*, deals with share-based payments classified as liabilities
- ASC 718-40, *Employee Stock Ownership Plans*, contains the following subsections:
  - General
  - Leveraged employee stock ownership plans
  - Nonleveraged employee stock ownership plans
- ASC 718-50, *Employee Share Purchase Plans*, contains guidance for compensatory and noncompensatory plans
  (ASC 718-10-05-1 and 15-2)

Note that ASC 718-20 and ASC 718-30 are interrelated with ASC 718-10. Generally, guidance that relates to both equity and liability instruments is included in ASC 718-10, while guidance specific to equity or liability instruments is in their respective Subtopics. (ASC 718-10-05-3)

Scope and Scope Exceptions

ASC 718 applies to all entities. It also applies to all share-based payment transactions where the entity acquires goods or services to be used or consumed in the grantor's own operations or provides consideration payable to a customer by issuing or offering to issue equity instruments or incurring liabilities to an employee or nonemployee that meet these conditions:

- The amounts are based in whole or in part on the price of the entity's shares or equity instruments
- The awards require or may require settlement by issuing the entity's equity instruments.
  (ASC 718-10-15-3)

Entities should look to ASC 323-10-25-3 through 25-5 for guidance on share-based compensation granted by an investor to the employees, or nonemployees of an equity method investee that provide goods or services to the investor that are used or consumed by the investee's operations. (ASC 718-10-15-3A)

If the purpose of awarding the shares is other than compensation, ASC 718 does not apply. (ASC 718-10-15-4)

ASC 718 does not apply to transactions involving share-based payment awards granted to a lender or an investor that provides financing to the issuer. (ASC 718-10-15-5)

If share-based payment awards are granted to a customer, as opposed to an employee, the awards should be:

- Measured and classified under the guidance in ASC 718
- Accounted for as a reduction of the transaction price and, therefore, of revenue, unless the consideration is in exchange for a distinct good or service. In that case, the entity should apply the guidance in ASC 606.
  (ASC 718-10-15-5A)

For guidance on whether share-based payment awards issued in a business combination are part of a considerate transfer, see ASC 805-30-30-9. (ASC 718-10-15-6)

The guidance in ASC 718-20 applies to share-based payment awards that are classified in equity, and ASC 718-30 applies to share-based payment awards that are classified as liabilities. (ASC 718-20-15-3 and ASC 718-30-15-2)

Overview

The economic substance of share-based payment arrangements is to provide compensation for goods or services as they are received, resulting in costs that should be reported by the entity using the fair value method of accounting. (ASC 718-10-10-1) ASC 718 requires fair value accounting for all share-based payment plans, except for equity instruments held by Employer Stock Ownership Plans (ESOPs). (ASC 718-10-10-2)

DEFINITIONS OF TERMS

Source: ASC 718-20. See Appendix A, *Definitions of Terms*, for other terms relevant to this topic: Call Option; Cash Consideration; Contract, Employee; Stock Ownership Plan (ESOP); Fair Value; Freestanding Financial Instrument; Grant Date; Issued, Issuing, or Issuance of an Equity Instrument; Nonpublic Entity; Option; Performance Condition; Probable; Public Entity; Purchased Call Option; Related Party; Securities and Exchange Commission; and Service Condition.

Allocated Shares. Allocated shares are shares in an employee stock ownership plan trust that have been assigned to individual participant accounts based on a known formula. Internal Revenue Service (IRS) rules require allocations to be nondiscriminatory generally based on compensation, length of service, or a combination of both. For any particular participant such shares may be vested, unvested, or partially vested.

Award. The collective noun for multiple instruments with the same terms and conditions granted at the same time either to a single grantee or to a group of grantees. An award may specify multiple vesting dates, referred to as graded vesting, and different parts of an award may have different expected terms. References to an award also apply to a portion of an award.

Broker-Assisted Cashless Exercise. The simultaneous exercise by a grantee of a share option and sale of the shares through a broker (commonly referred to as a broker-assisted exercise). Generally, under this method of exercise:

a. The grantee authorizes the exercise of an option and the immediate sale of the option shares in the open market.
b. On the same day, the entity notifies the broker of the sale order.
c. The broker executes the sale and notifies the entity of the sales price.
d. The entity determines the minimum statutory tax-withholding requirements.
e. By the settlement day (generally three days later), the entity delivers the stock certificates to the broker.
f. On the settlement day, the broker makes payment to the entity for the exercise price and the minimum statutory withholding taxes and remits the balance of the net sales proceeds to the grantee.

Calculated Value. A measure of the value of a share option or similar instrument determined by substituting the historical volatility of an appropriate industry sector index for the expected volatility of a nonpublic entity's share price in an option-pricing model.

Closed-Form Model. A valuation model that uses an equation to produce an estimated fair value. The Black-Scholes-Merton formula is a closed-form model. In the context of option valuation, both closed-form models and lattice models are based on risk-neutral valuation and a contingent claims framework. The payoff of a contingent claim, and thus its value, depends on the value(s) of one or more other assets. The contingent claims framework is a valuation methodology that explicitly recognizes that dependency and values the contingent claim as a function of the value of the underlying asset(s). One application of that methodology is risk-neutral valuation in which the contingent claim can be replicated by a combination of the underlying asset and a risk-free bond. If that replication is possible, the value of the contingent claim can be determined without estimating the expected returns on the underlying asset. The Black-Scholes-Merton formula is a special case of that replication.

Derived Service Period. A service period for an award with a market condition that is inferred from the application of certain valuation techniques used to estimate fair value. For example, the derived service period for an award of share options that the employee can exercise only if the share price increases by 25% at any time during a five-year period can be inferred from certain valuation techniques. In a lattice model, that derived service period represents the duration of the median of the distribution of share price paths on which the market condition is satisfied. That median is the middle share price path (the midpoint of the distribution of paths) on which the market condition is satisfied. The duration is the period of time from the service inception date to the expected date of satisfaction (as inferred from the valuation technique). If the derived service period is three years, the estimated requisite service period is three years, and all compensation cost would be recognized over that period, unless the market condition was satisfied at an earlier date. Compensation cost would not be recognized beyond three years even if after the grant date the entity determines that it is not probable that the market condition will be satisfied within that period. Further, an award of fully vested, deep out-of-the-money share options has a derived service period that must be determined from the valuation techniques used to estimate fair value. (See Explicit Service Period, Implicit Service Period, and Requisite Service Period.)

Direct Loan. A direct loan is a loan made by a lender other than the employer to the employee stock ownership plan. Such loans often include some formal guarantee or commitment by the employer.

Equity Restructuring. A nonreciprocal transaction between an entity and its shareholders that causes the per-share fair value of the shares underlying an option or similar award to change, such as a stock dividend, stock split, spinoff, rights offering, or recapitalization through a large, nonrecurring cash dividend.

Excess Tax Benefit. The realized tax benefit related to the amount (caused by changes in the fair value of the entity's shares after the measurement date for financial reporting) of deductible compensation cost reported on an employer's tax return for equity instruments in excess of the compensation cost for those instruments recognized for financial reporting purposes.

Explicit Service Period. A service period that is explicitly stated in the terms of a share-based payment award. For example, an award that vests after three years of continuous employee service from a given date (usually the grant date) has an explicit service period of three years. See Derived Service Period, Implicit Service Period, and Requisite Service Period.

Implicit Service Period. A service period that is not explicitly stated in the terms of a share-based payment award but that may be inferred from an analysis of those terms and other facts and circumstances. For instance, if an award of share options vests upon the completion of a new product design, which is deemed probable in 18 months, the implicit service period is 18 months. See Derived Service Period, Explicit Service Period, and Requisite Service Period.

Intrinsic Value. The amount by which the fair value of the underlying stock exceeds the exercise price of an option. For example, an option with an exercise price of $20 on a stock whose current market price is $25 has an intrinsic value of $5. (A nonvested share may be described as an option on that share with an exercise price of zero. Thus, the fair value of a share is the same as the intrinsic value of such an option on that share.)

Lattice Model. A model that produces an estimated fair value based on the assumed changes in prices of a financial instrument over successive periods of time. The binomial model is an example of a lattice model. In each time period, the model assumes that at least two price movements are possible. The lattice represents the evolution of the value of either a financial instrument or a market variable for the purpose of valuing a financial instrument. In this context, a lattice model is based on a risk-neutral valuation and a contingent claims framework. See Closed-form Model for an explanation of the terms *risk-neutral valuation* and *contingent claims framework*.

Market Condition. A condition affecting the exercise price, exercisability, or other pertinent factors used in determining the fair value of an award under a share-based payment arrangement that relates to the achievement of either of the following:

- A specified price of the issuer's shares or a specified amount of intrinsic value indexed solely to the issuer's shares
- A specified price of the issuer's shares in terms of a similar (or index of similar) equity security (securities). The term "similar," as used in this definition, refers to an equity security of another entity that has the same type of residual rights. For example, common stock of one entity generally would be similar to the common stock of another entity for this purpose.

Measurement Date. The date at which the equity share price and other pertinent factors, such as expected volatility, that enter into measurement of the total recognized amount of compensation cost for an award of share-based payment fixed.

Modification. A change in the terms or conditions of a share-based payment award.

Nonvested Shares. Shares that an entity has not yet issued because the agreed upon consideration, such as the delivery of specified goods or services, and any other conditions necessary to earn the right to benefit from the instruments, has not yet been satisfied. Nonvested shares cannot be sold. The restriction on sale of nonvested shares is due to the forfeitability of the shares if specified events occur (or do not occur).

Reload Feature and Reload Option. A reload feature provides for automatic grants of additional options whenever a grantee exercises previously granted options using the entity's shares, rather than cash, to satisfy the exercise price. At the time of exercise using shares, the grantee is automatically granted a new option, called a reload option, for the shares used to exercise the previous option.

Restricted Share. A share for which sale is contractually or governmentally prohibited for a specified period of time. Most grants of shares to grantees are better termed nonvested shares because the limitation on sale stems solely from the forfeitability of the shares before grantees have satisfied the necessary service or performance, or other condition(s) necessary to earn the rights to the shares. Restricted shares issued for consideration other than for goods or employee services, on the other hand, are fully paid for immediately. For those shares, there is no period analogous to an employee's requisite service period or a nonemployee's vesting period during which the issuer is unilaterally obligated to issue shares when the purchaser pays for those shares, but the purchaser is not obligated to buy the shares. The term restricted shares refers only to fully vested and outstanding shares whose sale is contractually or governmentally prohibited for a specified period of time. Vested equity instruments that are transferable to a grantee's immediate family members or to a trust that benefits only those family members are restricted if the transferred instruments retain the same prohibition on sale to third parties. See Nonvested Shares.

Replacement Award. An award of share-based compensation that is granted (or offered to grant) concurrently with the cancellation of another award.

Requisite Service Period. The period or periods during which an employee is required to provide service in exchange for an award under a share-based payment arrangement. The service that an employee is required to render during that period is referred to as the requisite service. The requisite service period for an award that has only a service condition is presumed to be the vesting period, unless there is clear evidence to the contrary. If an award requires future service for vesting, the entity cannot define a prior period as the requisite service period. Requisite service periods may be explicit, implicit, or derived, depending on the terms of the share-based payment award.

Restriction. A contractual or governmental provision that prohibits sale (or substantive sale by using derivatives or other means to effectively terminate the risk of future changes in the share price) of an equity instrument for a specified period of time.

Service Inception Date. The date at which the employee's requisite service period or the nonemployee's vesting period begins. The service inception date usually is the grant date, but the service inception date may differ from the grant date (see Example 6 [see ASC 718-10-55-107] for an illustration of this term to an employee award).

Settlement of an Award. An action or event that irrevocably extinguishes the issuing entity's obligation under a share-based payment award. Transactions and events that constitute settlements include the following:

- Exercise of a share option or lapse of an option at the end of its contractual term
- Vesting of shares
- Forfeiture of shares or share options due to failure to satisfy a vesting condition
- An entity's repurchase of instruments in exchange for assets or for fully vested and transferable equity instruments

The vesting of a share option is not a settlement because the entity remains obligated to issue shares upon exercise of the option.

Share-Based Payment Arrangement. An arrangement under which either of the following conditions is met:

- One or more suppliers of goods or services (including employees) receive awards of equity shares, equity share options, or other equity instruments
- The entity incurs liabilities to suppliers that meet either of the following conditions:
  - The amounts based, at least in part, on the price of the entity's shares or other equity instruments. (The phrase at least in part is used because an award may be indexed to both the price of the entity's shares and something other than either the price of the entity's shares or a market, performance, or service condition.)
  - The awards require or may require settlement by issuance of the entity's shares.

The term shares includes various forms of ownership interest that may not take the legal form of securities (for example, partnership interests), as well as other interests, including those that are liabilities in substance but not in form. Equity shares refers only to shares that are accounted for as equity. Also called *share-based compensation arrangements*.

Share-Based Payment Transaction. A transaction under a share-based payment arrangement, including a transaction in which an entity acquires goods or services because related parties or other holders of economic interest in that entity awards a share-based payment to an employee or other supplier of goods or services for the entity's benefit. Also called *share-based compensation transactions.*

Share Option. A contract that gives the holder the right, but not the obligation, either to purchase (to call) or to sell (to put) a certain number of shares at a predetermined price for a specified period of time.

Share Unit. A contract under which the holder has the right to convert each unit into a specified number of shares of the issuing entity.

Short-Term Inducement. An offer by the entity that would result in modification of an award to which an award holder may subscribe for a limited period of time.

Tandem Award. An award with two or more components in which exercise of one part cancels the other(s).

Terms of a Share-Based Payment Award. The contractual provisions that determine the nature and scope of a share-based payment award. For example, the exercise price of share options is one of the terms of an award of share options. As indicated in ASC 718-10-25-5, the written terms of a share-based payment award and its related arrangement, if any, usually provide the best evidence of its terms. However, an entity's past practice or other factors may indicate that some aspects of the substantive terms differ from the written terms. The substantive terms of a share-based payment award as those terms are mutually understood by the entity and a party (either an employee or a nonemployee) who receives the award, provide the basis for determining the rights conveyed to a party and the obligations imposed on the issuer, regardless of how the award and related arrangement, if any, are structured. See ASC 718-10-30-5.

Time Value. The portion of the fair value of an option that exceeds its intrinsic value. For example, a call option with an exercise price of $20 on a stock whose current market price is $25 has intrinsic value of $5. If the fair value of that option is $7, the time value of the option is $2 ($7 – $5).

Vest. To earn the rights to. A share-based payment award becomes vested at the date that the grantee's right to receive or retain shares, other instruments, or cash under the award is no longer contingent on satisfaction of either a service condition or a performance condition. Market conditions are not vesting conditions.

The stated vesting provisions of an award often establish the employee's requisite service period or the nonemployee's vesting period, and an award that has reached the end of the applicable period is vested. However, as indicated in the definition of requisite service period, and equally applicable to a nonemployee's vesting period, the stated vesting period may differ from those periods in certain circumstances. Thus, the more precise (but cumbersome) terms would be options, shares, or awards for which the requisite good has been delivered or service has been rendered and the end of the employee's requisite service period or the nonemployee's vesting period.

Volatility. A measure of the amount by which a financial variable such as a share price has fluctuated (historical volatility) or is expected to fluctuate (expected volatility) during a period. Volatility also may be defined as a probability-weighted measure of the dispersion of returns about the mean. The volatility of a share price is the standard deviation of the continuously compounded rates of return on the share over a specified period. That is the same as the standard deviation of the differences in the natural logarithms of the stock prices plus dividends, if any, over the period. The higher the volatility, the more the returns on the shares can be expected to vary—up or down. Volatility is typically expressed in annualized terms.

CONCEPTS, RULES, AND EXAMPLES

Recognition

Recognition Principle The entity recognizes the goods acquired or services received when obtained or received. The entity also recognizes a corresponding charge to equity or liabilities. (ASC 718-10-25-2)

The grant date is used to fix the value of equity-based awards. This is because recognizing subsequent changes in compensation based on post-grant-date changes to the value of the underlying equity would be equivalent to recognizing changes in the value of the entity's own equity shares in earnings, which is prohibited under the Codification. The grant date is when the parties have fixed the terms of their arrangement. This provides a meaningful measure of the cost to be incurred by the entity. This differs from the situation with equity-based compensation classified as a liability, where awards are settled for assets (e.g., cash from stock appreciation rights). In that scenario, the entity is obligated to distribute assets, so the relevant measure of compensation cost, ultimately, is the amount of assets disbursed.

ASC 718 sets forth criteria for determining that a share-based payment award has been granted. One of the criteria is a mutual understanding by the grantor and grantee of the key terms and conditions of a share-based payment award. (ASC 718-10-55-81) However, the "mutual" aspect may not occur until sometime after the formal grant, when actual communications between grantor and grantee are held, sometimes not until, for example, a regularly scheduled performance review which might not occur for weeks or months thereafter. To address these practical concerns, guidance provides that, assuming all other criteria in the grant date definition (see the definition in Appendix A) have been met, a mutual understanding of the key terms and conditions of an award to an individual grantee is presumed to exist at the date the award is approved in accordance with the relevant corporate governance requirements (that is, by the board or management with the relevant authority), if both the following conditions are met:

1. The award is a unilateral grant and, therefore, the recipient does not have the ability to negotiate the key terms and conditions of the award with the grantor, and
2. It is expected that the key terms and conditions of the award will be communicated to an individual recipient within a relatively short time period from the date of approval. (ASC 718-10-25-5)

In some circumstances, the cost of services may be capitalized initially and later expensed. For example, an entity may capitalize the cost of services for constructing an asset or acquiring inventory. When that asset is consumed or disposed of, the entity recognizes it in the income statement. (ASC 718-10-25-2A)

Likewise, share-based payments to nonemployees made in exchange for goods or services may span several financial reporting periods. The entity must exercise judgment to determine the nonemployee's vesting period, that is, the period over which to recognize the costs. (ASC 718-10-25-2B) Entities are required to record an asset or expense in the same period and manner as though the grantor had paid cash. A share-based payment award granted to a customer is accounted for as a reduction of the transaction in price, unless the payment is in exchange for goods or services. If so, and the amount of consideration is greater than the fair value of the good or service received, the entity accounts for the excess as a reduction of the transaction price. If the fair value cannot be estimated, all the consideration payable to the customer is accounted for as a reduction in the transaction price. (ASC 718-10-25-2C and 606-10-32-26)

Classifying Awards as Liabilities or Equity Determining whether a share-based payment should be categorized as a liability requires close attention to the guidance of ASC 718. In turn, ASC 718 points to the classification criteria of ASC 480 to determine whether a freestanding financial instrument granted to a grantee is a liability or equity. (ASC 718-10-25-7)

Note that a share that is mandatorily or optionally redeemable upon the occurrence of a defined contingency, such as an initial public offering by the grantor entity, would not make this share-based payment a liability, unless the contingency were deemed probable of occurrence within a reasonable period of time. For example, if the entity had begun the regulatory approval and registration process, this might trigger liability classification. (ASC 718-10-25-8)

A puttable share (giving the grantee the right to demand that the issuer redeem for cash equal to its fair value) or a callable share awarded to an employee as compensation should be classified as a liability if either:

a. The repurchase feature permits the grantee to avoid bearing the risks and rewards normally associated with equity share ownership for a reasonable period of time from the date the good is delivered or service is rendered and the share is issued, *or*
b. It is probable that the grantor would prevent the grantee from bearing those risks and rewards for a reasonable period of time from the date the share is issued. A period of six months or more is considered a reasonable period of time.
(ASC 718-10-25-9)

Note that a share that is mandatorily or optionally redeemable upon the occurrence of a defined contingency, such as an initial public offering by the grantor entity, would not make this share-based payment a liability, unless the contingency were deemed probable of occurrence within a reasonable period of time. For example, if the entity had begun the regulatory approval and registration process, this might trigger liability classification. (ASC 718-10-25-9a)

ASC 718 stipulates logically that options or similar instruments on shares should be categorized as liabilities if:

- The underlying shares are classified as liabilities or
- The reporting entity can be required to transfer cash or other assets under any circumstances in order to settle the option.
(ASC 718-10-25-11)

Stock appreciation rights (SARs) are a popular means of providing share-based compensation awards to employees. Essentially, these bonus arrangements pay employees the amount by which the share price at a defined date (say, three years hence) exceeds what it was at the measurement date. Depending on the plan, the award may be payable in the entity's shares, in cash, or in either at the option of the grantee. If the optionee has the right to demand cash or the SAR is payable in cash only, the grantor entity recognizes a liability for the accrued compensation.

If an SEC registrant grants an option to a grantee that, upon exercise, would be settled by issuing a mandatorily redeemable share, the option must be classified as a liability. This is because the share would be classified as a liability. (ASC 718-10-25-12)

An award may be indexed to a factor beyond the entity's share price. If that additional factor is not a market, performance, or service condition, the award is classified as a liability. In such a case, the additional factor is reflected in estimating the fair value of the award. (ASC 718-10-25-13) An example of such a circumstance is an award of options whose exercise price is indexed to the market price of the commodity (e.g., wheat or gold). Another example is a share award that will vest based on the appreciation in the price of that commodity. Such an award is indexed to both the value of that commodity and the issuing entity's shares. If an award is so indexed, the relevant factors (expected commodity price change) should be included in the fair value estimate of the award. ASC 718 states that the award would be classified as a liability even if the entity granting the share-based payment instrument were a producer of the commodity whose price changes are part or all of the conditions that affect an award's vesting conditions or fair value.

If an entity awards equity share options to a grantee of its foreign operation and the award provides a fixed exercise price denominated in the foreign operation's functional currency or the denomination of the employee's pay, that award does not contain a market, performance, or service condition. If it otherwise qualifies as equity, it is not required to be classified as a liability. (ASC 718-10-25-14) If the exercise price of an award is denominated in the currency of a market in which a substantial portion of the entity's shares trades, the award does not contain a market, performance, or service condition. (ASC 718-10-25-14A)

The accounting for an award should reflective the substance of the terms of the award. The written terms usually provide the best evidence of the terms of an award. An entity's past practices also may indicate the substance of an award. If an entity has the choice of settling an award and has a substantive liability, the entity should also consider whether:

- It has the ability to deliver the shares.
- It is required to pay cash if a contingent event occurs. (ASC 718-10-25-15)

If an award permits grantees to effect a broker-assisted cashless exercise of at least part of an award of share options through a broker, a liability classification does not result if both the following criteria are met:

- The cashless exercise requires a valid exercise of the share options.
- The grantee is the legal owner of the shares subject to the option.
  (ASC 718-10-25-16)

If a broker is a related party of the entity, selling the shares in the open market for three days is generally sufficient for the award to qualify as equity. (ASC 718-10-25-17) Likewise, a provision for direct or indirect repurchase of shares issued upon exercise of options or the vesting of nonvested shares, with payment due employees withheld to meet the employer's withholding requirements, does not in and of itself result in liability classification of instruments otherwise classified as equity. However, if the amount of the withholding at the discretion of the employer is over the maximum tax rates in the employee's jurisdiction, the entire award should be classified as a liability. (ASC 718-10-25-18)

Market Performance and Service Conditions If an award has a performance condition, entities estimate the compensation costs based on whether or not it is probable the performance obligation will be achieved:

- If it is probable, it is recognized in the period it becomes probable.
- If it is not probable, no accrual is made.
  (ASC 718-10-25-20)

If an award is based on satisfaction of one or more market performance or service conditions, the grantor should not recognize compensation cost if the good is not delivered or the service is not rendered. (ASC 718-10-25-21)

Effect of Employer Payroll Taxes A liability for employee payroll taxes on stock compensation should be recognized and measured on the date of the event triggering the measurement and payment of the tax to the taxing authority (which would generally be the exercise date). (ASC 718-10-25-22) Payroll taxes should be presented as operating expenses on the statement of operations. (718-10-25-23)

Initial Measurement

Entities should use fair value to measure a share-based payment transaction. (ASC 718-10-30-2)

- The cost of goods obtained or services received should be measured on the fair value of equity issued or the liabilities settled. (ASC 718-10-30-3)
- The compensation cost is net of any amount the grantee pays for the instrument. (ASC 718-10-30-3)
- A share-based payment award granted to a customer is accounted for as a reduction of the transaction in price, unless the payment is in exchange for goods or services. If so, and the amount of consideration is greater than the fair value of the good or service received, the entity accounts for the excess as a reduction of the transaction price. If the fair value cannot be estimated, all the consideration payable to the customer is accounted for as a reduction in the transaction price.

Note that: For public entities, the measurement objective at grant date for awards classified as liabilities is the same as above. However, the measurement date for liabilities is the settlement date. (ASC 718-30-30-1)

As discussed below, there are circumstances where a nonpublic entity may replace fair value measurement with the:

- Intrinsic value method, which equals the market price less the exercise price at grant date or
- Calculated value method, which substitutes the historical volatility of an appropriate industry sector index for the expected volatility of a nonpublic entity's share price in an option pricing model.
  (ASC 718-10-30-4)

Ideally, equity share options should be valued using the observable market price. (ASC 718-10-30-7) However, few employee stock compensation awards are publicly traded and have observable market prices. (ASC 718-10-30-8) If market prices are not available, equity share option awards are valued using a model, such as the binomial model or the Black-Scholes- Merton formula. (ASC 718-10-30-9) These models take into account the volatility of the underlying stock, the expected life of the options, risk-free rate during the option life, and expected dividends during the option life.

Factors That Affect the Fair Value at Grant Date The treatment of restrictions and conditions in equity awards depend on whether those restrictions and conditions continue in effect after the requisite service period or the nonemployee's vesting period. (ASC 718-10-30-10) Restrictions and conditions include:

- Vesting versus Nontransferability
- Forfeitability
- Performance or service conditions
- Market conditions
- Market performance or service conditions that affect factors other than vesting or exercisability

- Nonvested or restricted shares
- When estimating the fair value of a nonemployee award, the entity may elect to use the contractual term on an award-by-award basis. (ASC 718-10-30-10A)
- If a nonpublic entity opts to measure a nonemployee award to estimate its expected term and applies the practical expedient in ASC 718-10-30-20A, it must apply the practical expedient to all nonemployee awards meeting the conditions in ASC 718-10-30-20B. A nonpublic entity may choose to use the contractual term on an award-by-award basis as described above. (ASC 718-10-30-10B)

The table below summarizes the effect on fair value estimation at grant date of restrictions or conditions.

Restriction or Condition	**Effect on Fair Value Estimate at Grant Date**	**Comment**
Nontransferability	Considered in estimating fair value at grant date.	For equity share options, taken into account in estimating fair value by reflecting the effects of employee's expected exercise and postemployment termination behavior.
Forfeitability	Not reflected.	Taken into account by recognizing compensation cost only for awards for which grantees deliver the goods or render the service.
Performance or service conditions	No compensation cost reflected for instruments that employees forfeit because condition is not satisfied.	This applies to instruments for which the requisite service is not rendered.
Market conditions	Reflected in grant date fair value.	Compensation cost recognized provided the good is delivered or the service is rendered regardless of when, if ever, the condition is satisfied.
Market, performance, or service conditions that affect factors other than vesting or exercisability	Considered.	Fair value estimated for each possible outcome. The final measure is based on the amount estimated at grant date that the company actually satisfied.
Nonvested shares	Measure as if they were vested and exercised at the grant date.	Restricted shares in ASC 718 are those whose sale is contractually or governmentally prohibited for a specified period of time.
Restricted shares	Measure at fair value—same amount for which a restricted share would be issued to third parties.	ASC 718 differentiates between nonvested and restricted shares.
(ASC 718-10-30-10 through 30-19)		

Valuation Models In the absence of an observable market price for an award, reporting entities must use a valuation technique that is:

- Applied consistently with ASC 718's fair value measurement objectives
- Based on established financial economic theory principles and is generally applied in that field
- Reflects all substantive characteristics of the equity or liability instrument, unless the Codification specifically excludes them, for example, vesting
(ASC 718-10-55-11)

While ASC 718 does not dictate a valuation model, FASB points out that the binomial or other so-called *lattice* models meet the requirements of ASC 718-10-55-16 and is preferred. The binomial model is favored over the closed-form model like the Black-Scholes-Merton formula, because the lattice model accommodates more potential post-vesting behaviors than the closed-form models.

Binomial or other lattice models value options by constructing lattices or trees that represent different possible stock prices at different future points in time. The value of the option is determined at each node or branch of the tree. To determine these values, companies need to develop information about expected volatility, dividends, and risk-free rates that will apply at each of the possible branches or nodes of the model. In addition, information about employee post-vesting behavior is needed to determine likely exercise dates. Note that under ASC 718 it is necessary to use expected volatility of share prices.

Assumptions for use in an option pricing model The valuation model should take into account the following factors, at a minimum:

- Exercise price of the option.
- Expected term of the option, taking into account several things including the contractual term of the option, vesting requirements, and post vesting employee termination behaviors. (The SEC states in 718-10-S99 that a registrant cannot use an expected term that is shorter than the vesting period.)
- Current price of the underlying share.
- Expected volatility of the price of the underlying share. (According to the SEC in 718-10-S99-1, a registrant may consider historical volatility in determining expected volatility, which in turn should take into consideration historical volatility over a period generally commensurate with the expected or contractual option term, as well as regular intervals for price observations. A registrant can also ignore a period of historical volatility if it can support a conclusion that the period is not relevant to estimating expected volatility due to nonrecurring historical events. The SEC would also not object to the use of an industry sector index to determine the expected volatility of its share price.)
- Expected dividends on the underlying share.
- Risk-free interest rate(s) for the expected term of the option.
(ASC 718-10-55-21)

In practice, there are likely to be ranges of reasonable estimates for expected volatility, dividends, and option term. The closed-form models, of which Black-Scholes (now Black-Scholes-Merton) is the most widely regarded, are predicated on a set of deterministic assumptions that remain invariant over the full term of the option. In the real world, this condition is almost always not met. For this reason, current thinking is that a lattice model, of which the binomial model is an example, would be preferred. Lattice models explicitly identify nodes, such as the anniversaries of the grant date, at each of which new parameter values can be specified (e.g., expected dividends can be independently defined each period).

Nonpublic Entity—Calculated Value for Nonemployee Awards Because a nonpublic entity may not practically estimate the expected volatility of its share price, it may not be able to reasonably estimate the fair value of its share price and, therefore, the fair value of its nonemployee awards. In those circumstances, a nonpublic entity should account for nonemployee *equity* share options and similar instruments using a basis calculated using the historical volatility of an appropriate industry section instead of the calculated value discussed below. Use of the calculated value should be consistent with employee share-based payment transactions. (ASC 718-10-30-19A)

Nonpublic Entities—Calculated Value Method Stocks or options issued as part of an employee stock compensation plan should be measured at fair value. Because nonpublic companies do not trade shares on an exchange, it may be difficult for those companies to estimate the value of the underlying stock, and, thus, its volatility. For those cases, ASC 718 provides a measurement alternative. To measure equity- or liability-classified awards, nonpublic companies may choose to use either

- Fair values or
- Calculated values.

If the entity estimates based on a calculated value, it calculates the value using the historical volatility of the appropriate industry sector index instead of the expected volatility of the entity's share price. (ASC 718-10-30-20) If a nonpublic reporting entity chooses to use the calculated value alternative, the calculated value of an equity-classified award must be remeasured each reporting period. (ASC 718-10-55-52) However, if a company uses fair value, no remeasurement is required, which could reduce fluctuations in reported earnings. If nonpublic companies choose the fair value approach, they will not later be able to return to the use of calculated value, because fair value is deemed preferable for purposes of applying ASC 250 (accounting changes).

Nonpublic Entity—Practical Expedient for Intrinsic or Calculated Value for Liability-Classified Awards Nonpublic entities must make a policy decision as to whether to measure all of their liability-classified awards at fair value or at intrinsic value. If a nonpublic entity is not able to reasonably estimate fair value, it can choose to value its liability-classified awards at calculated value or at intrinsic value. However, for awards determined to be consideration payable to a customer, a nonpublic entity should initially and subsequently measure the award at fair value according to the guidance in ASC 606-10-32-25. (ASC 718-30-30-2)

In addition, an entity may make a one-time election to change its liability-classified awards to intrinsic value, even if it is already accounting for liability awards at fair value under ASC 718. (ASC 718-30-30-2A)

Nonpublic Entity—Practical Expedient for Expected Term In the absence of observable market prices to determine fair value, an entity must use a valuation technique that factors in the term of the award. The Codification offers nonpublic companies a practical expedient for estimating the term. To be eligible for the expedient, the award must meet specified criteria, including being granted-at-the money and not having a market-based vesting condition. A share option or similar award must also have the following characteristics:

- If the grantee no longer provides goods or terminates service after vesting or ceases to be a customer, the employee has only a limited time to exercise the award—typically 30–90 days.

- The grantee can only exercise the award; he or she cannot sell or hedge the award.
- The award does not include a market condition.

(ASC 718-10-30-20B)

The exhibit below summarizes the practical expedient, which is based on the type of vesting provision.

Exhibit—Nonpublic Entities—Practical Expedient for Expected Term

Type of Vesting Provision	Probability, at measurement date, of performance condition being met.	Practical expedient for expected term
Only dependent on a service condition	Not applicable	Midpoint between the employee's requisite service period or the nonemployee/s vesting period and the contractual term of the award
Dependent on service and performance conditions	Probable	Midpoint between the employee's requisite service period or the nonemployee/s vesting period and the contractual term
	Not probable	The contractual term if the service period is implied The midpoint between the employee's requisite service period or the nonemployee/s vesting period and the contractual term if the requisite service period explicit
(ASC 718-10-30-20A)		

Difficulty in Estimation In rare cases, an entity may not be able to measure fair value at the grant date because of the complexity of the terms of equity share options or other equity instruments. (ASC 718-10-30-21) In these cases, an entity may use intrinsic value. (ASC 718-10-30-22)

Reload Feature and Reload Option A reload feature provides for automatic grants of additional options whenever an employee exercises previously granted options using the entity's shares, rather than cash, to satisfy the exercise price. At the time of exercise using shares, the employee is automatically granted a new option, called a reload option, for the shares used to exercise the previous option. (ASC 718-10-20)

Each award of an equity instrument is measured separately based on its terms, conditions, and features including reload features. (ASC 728-10-30-23)

Example of Reload Options

Mr. Jones has 6,000 shares of ABC Company's $1 par value common stock, as well as options to purchase an additional 8,000 shares at an exercise price of $12. It will cost Jones $96,000 to exercise the options. The current market price of ABC stock is $16, so he trades in his existing 6,000 shares, which have a market value of $96,000, to purchase 8,000 shares with his options. The option plan has a reload feature, so ABC issues 6,000 replacement options (matching the number of shares traded in), for which the exercise price is set at the current market value of $16. ABC records the stock sale with the following entry:

Treasury stock	96,000	
Common stock		8,000
Additional paid-in capital		88,000

Jones elects to exercise his options when the market value of ABC Company's stock reaches $24. At an exercise price of $16, it will again cost Jones $96,000 to purchase shares. At the current market price of $24, Jones can trade in 4,000 of his existing shares to acquire new shares. However, he chooses to trade in only 3,000 shares and pay for the remaining options with cash. ABC records the stock sale with the following entry:

Cash	24,000	
Treasury stock	72,000	
Common stock		6,000
Additional paid-in capital		90,000

The reload feature still applies, but now ABC only issues 3,000 replacement options, which matches the number of shares Jones traded in to acquire new shares. The new options are assigned at an exercise price of $24, to match the market value on the grant date.

Contingent Features That May Affect the Valuation Model Contingent features that could cause either a loss of equity shares earned or a reduction of realized gains from sale of equity instruments earned, such as a *clawback feature* (ASC 718-10-30-24) (for example, where an employee who terminates the employment relationship and begins to work for a competitor is required to transfer to the issuing enterprise shares granted and earned under a share-based payment arrangement would be factors affecting the valuation model.

Market, Performance Conditions, and Service Conditions Some option arrangements provide grants of share options with a performance or service condition that affects vesting. These types of plans permit employees to vest in differing numbers of options depending on the increase in market value of one of the company's products (or other condition) over a vesting period. These performance conditions can include factors such as market share increases, passing clinical trials, and other performance goals. Vesting can be based on a service condition, performance condition, or a combination of both. These conditions are not reflected in the estimate of fair value.

In addition to performance conditions, market conditions may also affect the option arrangements. These would include such things as indexing share prices to an industry group and the exercise price of options tied to this index. Therefore, the exercise price could go up or down depending on how the index performs. A market condition is not considered a vesting condition and a market condition is reflected in the estimate of fair value at grant date. (ASC 718-10-30-21)

Arrangements exist for share units to have both performance and market conditions. These are accounted for in the same way as other options. The difficulty is in determining the fair values, as there are more factors contributing to uncertainty. These factors can, however, be modeled

Performance target could be achieved after the requisite service period Compensation cost is recognized based on the actual number of awards that are expected to vest based on the performance target. For awards where the terms provide that a performance target could be achieved after the requisite service period or a nonemployee's vesting period, guidance provides that:

- A performance target that affects vesting and that could be achieved after the requisite service period should be treated as a performance condition.
- A reporting entity should apply the guidance in ASC 718 as it relates to awards with performance conditions that affect vesting to account for such awards.
- The performance condition should not be reflected when estimating fair value at the grant date.
- Compensation cost should be recognized in the period in which it becomes probable that the performance target will be achieved.
- The amount recognized should represent compensation costs attributable to the periods for which the requisite service or goods have already been provided.
- Estimates are used to make accruals each period, and adjustments are made based on current estimates of expected future vesting until the actual number of awards that vest are known.
- If an award is forfeited before completion of the employee's requisite service or the nonemployee's vesting period, entities that have a policy to account for forfeitures when they occur should reverse compensation cost previously recognized in the period the award is forfeited.

(ASC 718-10-30-28)

Subsequent Measurement of Compensation

Compensation Costs for Awards Classified as Equity Where it is not possible to reasonably estimate the fair value of an equity instrument at the grant date, the entity must remeasure the instrument at each reporting date through the date of exercise or other settlement. Compensation cost for each period consists of the change in the instrument's value or a portion of the change. The portion depends on the percentage of employee requisite service rendered or the amount of cash that would have been paid for goods or services instead of a nonemployee award. If an entity subsequently finds that it is reasonable to estimate the fair value, it still must continue to use the intrinsic value method. (ASC 718-20-35-1)

The cost of share-based employee compensation that is classified as equity is recognized over the requisite service period. The corresponding credit is made to equity, usually additional-paid-in capital. The requisite service period is the period an employee is required to provide service in order to earn the award. It is often the same as the vesting period. (ASC 718-10-35-2)

The total amount of compensation cost at the end of the requisite service period is based on the number of instruments for which the requisite service is rendered. If the share option expires unexercised and the requisite service has been rendered, the compensation cost is not reversed. To determine the amount of compensation cost to recognize in each period, an entity must elect an accounting policy for all employee share-based payment awards to:

- Estimate the number of forfeitures in compensation cost. The initial accrual of compensation cost is based on the estimated number of instruments for which the requisite service is expected to be rendered. The estimate is revised if subsequent information indicates a different number of actual instruments is likely. Entities should recognize the cumulative effect on current and prior periods in compensation cost in the period of change.

- When they occur, recognize the effect of forfeiture in compensation cost and reverse previously recognized compensation cost in the period in which the award is forfeited. (ASC 718-10-35-3)

Compensation Costs for Awards Classified as Liabilities The fair value of liabilities incurred is estimated at each reporting date from grant date through settlement date. (ASC 718-30-35-1)

Prior to vesting, the cumulative compensation costs would equal the proportionate amount of the award earned to date, and thus the periodic compensation cost would reflect both the passage of time (service period) and change in the fair value or intrinsic value (for nonpublic entities that elect the intrinsic value method) of the ultimate award. Subsequent to the employee's requisite service period or the nonemployee's vesting period, any further change in fair value or intrinsic value of a liability issued in exchange for goods or services is compensation cost in the period when the changes occur and recorded as a charge against earnings and an offsetting charge to liabilities. If there is a difference between the amounts for which a liability award issued in exchange for goods or services is settled and its fair value at the settlement date, the entity should record an adjustment of compensation cost. (ASC 718-30-35-2)

Public entities Public entities measure a liability award at the award's fair value. Compensation cost is based on the change in the fair value of the instrument. If the requisite period has not been completed, the cost is calculated based on the percentage of the requisite service rendered for an employee award or the percentage that would have been recognized had the grantor paid cash for the goods or services instead of paying with a nonemployee award. (ASC 718-30-35-3)

Nonpublic entities Regardless of the method selected for initial measurement, a nonpublic entity remeasures a liability-based award each reporting period until settlement date. A nonpublic entity should subsequently measure an award for consideration payable to a customer as a reduction of the transaction in price, unless the payment is in exchange for a good or service. If it is in exchange for a good or service and the amount of consideration is greater than the fair value of the good or service received, the entity accounts for the excess as a reduction of the transaction price. If the fair value cannot be estimated, all the consideration payable to the customer is accounted for as a reduction in the transaction price. (ASC 718- 30-35-4 and 606-10-32-25)

Valuation for Graded-Vesting Employee Awards Companies that grant awards with graded, that is with multiple, vesting dates elect whether to recognize the awards on a straight-line basis as if it were

- One award, or
- Several separate awards.

At a minimum, the compensation cost at any period must be equal to the portion of the grant-date value of the award that is vested. (ASC 718-10-35-8)

Awards Subject to Other Guidance Freestanding financial instruments issued to grantees in exchange for goods or services received or to be received are subject to the recognition and measurement provisions of ASC 718 throughout the life of the instruments, unless their terms are modified when the nonemployee vests in the award and is no longer providing goods or services or a grantee is no longer an employee. For instruments originally issued as employee compensation and then modified, and where that modification to the terms of the instrument is made *solely* to reflect an equity restructuring that occurs when the holders are no longer employees, no change in the recognition or the measurement (due to a change in classification) of those instruments will result if a grantee:

- Vests in the award and is no longer providing goods or services
- Vests in the award and is no longer a customer
- Is no longer an employee
(ASC 718-10-35-10)

A modification in the context of ASC 718-10-35-10 does not include a change to the terms of the award if the change is made solely to an equity restructuring provided that both of these criteria are met:

- The fair value of the award (or the ratio of intrinsic value to the exercise price of the award is preserved—i.e., the holder is made whole) has not increased, or the antidilution provision is not added to the terms of the award in contemplation of an equity restructuring; *and*
- All holders of the same class of equity instruments are treated in the same manner.
(ASC 718-10-35-10A)

Other modifications of the instrument (that is, any modification that fails to meet the dual tests above) that take place when the grantee vests in the award and is no longer providing goods or services, is no longer a customer, or is no longer an employee, are subject to modification accounting guidance in ASC 718-10-35-14. Following modification, the accounting must follow other applicable GAAP. (ASC 718-10- 35-11) An entity may modify or settle a fully vested, freestanding financial instrument after it becomes subject to ASC 480 or other Codification Topics. If so, the entity accounts for the modification settlement under the ASC 718 guidance. The exception to this accounting treatment is if the modification or settlement applies equally to all financial instruments of the same class. This exception applies whether the grantee is or was an employee or a vendor. (ASC 718-10-35-14)

Modifications of Awards Modifications of awards can occur because of

- repricing,
- extending the life, or
- changing the vesting condition.

Modifications of liability awards Modifications of liability awards are accounted for as an exchange of the original award for a new award. Because liability awards are always remeasured at each reporting date, no special guidance for a modification is needed as long as the award remains a liability award after the modification. (ASC 718-30-35-5)

Modifications of Awards of Equity Instruments

Except as described in ASC 718-20-35-2a, cancellations of existing awards and concurrent replacement with new ones are accounted for as modifications. (ASC 718-20-35-8) An entity should account for the effects of a modification as described below unless the value, (fair, calculated, or intrinsic), the vesting conditions, and the classification of the modified award is the same as those elements of the original award before the original award is modified. If the modification does not affect any of the inputs to the valuation model used by the entity, the entity is not required to estimate the value immediately before and after the modification. (ASC 718-20-35-2A)

In practice, modifications will rarely result in recognized compensation costs less than the fair value of the award at the grant date, but this could conceivably result if the original service or performance vesting conditions were not expected to be satisfied at the modification date.

Changes not requiring modification accounting The FASB in its background for conclusions in ASU 2017-09 BC 11 provided examples of changes to an award that generally do not require modification accounting include the following:

- Changes that are administrative in nature, such as a change to the company name, company address, or plan name
- Changes in an award's net settlement provisions related to tax withholdings that do not affect the classification of the award.

Changes requiring modification accounting The Codification provides examples of changes to an award that generally do require modification accounting, adding that these need to be evaluated in light of the guidance in ASC 718-20-35-2A below, include the following:

- Repricing of share options that results in a change in value of those share options
- Changes in a service condition
- Changes in a performance condition or a market condition
- Changes in an award that result in a reclassification of the award (equity to liability or vice versa)
- Adding an involuntary termination provision in anticipation of a sale of a business unit that accelerates vesting of the award.

Modifications of terms or conditions ASC 718 requires that modification of the terms or conditions of an equity award should be treated as an exchange of the original award for a new award, unless they meet the requirements of ASC 718-20-35-2A above. In substance, the event is accounted for as if the entity repurchases the original instrument by issuing a new instrument of equal or greater value, incurring additional compensation cost for any incremental value. (ASC 718-20-35-3)

Incremental compensation cost related to modification of terms or conditions Incremental compensation cost of equity awards that do not meet the equity awards criteria above from ASC 718- 20-30-2A is measured as the excess, if any, of the fair value of the modified award—determined in accordance with the provisions of ASC 718—over the fair value of the original award immediately before its terms are modified. These measures should be based on the share price and other pertinent factors at the modification date. Any effect of the modification on the number of instruments expected to vest should also be reflected in determining incremental compensation cost. The estimate at the modification date of the portion of the award expected to vest may also be subsequently adjusted, if necessary, as estimates or experience may dictate prior to final settlement. (ASC 718-20-35-3a)

The total recognized compensation cost for an equity award will at least equal the fair value of the award at the grant date, except for those instances when, at the date of the modification, the performance or service conditions of the original award are not expected to be satisfied. Accordingly, the total compensation cost measured at the date of a modification will be:

- The portion of the grant-date fair value of the original award for which the promised good is expected to be delivered or the service is expected to be rendered (or has already been rendered) at that date, plus
- The incremental cost resulting from the modification.
  (ASC 718-20-35-3b)

The change in compensation cost for an equity award measured at intrinsic value (if elected for nonpublicly held companies) is to be measured by comparing the intrinsic value of the modified award, if any, with the intrinsic value of the original award, if any, immediately before the modification. (ASC 718-20-35-3c)

At the date of the modification, if the entity has a policy to account for forfeiture when they occur, the entity should assess whether it expects the performance or services condition of the original award to be satisfied. Subsequently, for the modified award, the entity should apply its forfeiture accounting policy when the forfeitures occur. (ASC 781-20-35-3A)

Equity-to-Liability Modification In some cases, an option or similar instrument is initially classified as equity, but subsequently the contingent cash settlement event becomes probable of occurring. The instrument should then be classified as a liability. This change should be accounted for as a change from an equity to a liability award. On the date the contingent event becomes *probable* of occurring, the entity should recognize a share-based liability. The liability is equal to the portion of the award attributed to past service (reflecting any provision for acceleration of vesting) multiplied by the award's fair value on that date. The entity accounts for any differences as follows:

- To the extent the liability equals or is less than the amount previously recognized in equity, that is, the amount transferred from equity to the liability the entity debits equity for the difference.
- To the extent that the liability exceeds the amount previously recognized in equity, the excess is recognized as additional compensation cost in that period.

The total recognized compensation cost for an award with a contingent cash settlement feature must at least equal the fair value of the award at the grant date. (ASC 718-10-35-15)

Liability-to-Equity Modification If a modification results in what had been a liability award becoming an equity award, the amount of the fair value (or implicit value, if such were elected as a measurement method by a nonpublic company), the amount becomes "fixed" as of the modification date, and this will differ from the amount that would have been recognized had the award been classified as equity at inception.

Example of a Liability-to-Equity Modification

Assume that a cash payment stock appreciation rights (SAR) plan is created, with these features: 10,000 SARs granted, with three-year term, 3% forfeiture per year expectation. The share-based compensation liability is (9,127 × $10 ÷ 3 =) $30,423, based on reporting date fair value measurement. On January 1 of the second year, the company modifies the SAR by replacing the cash-settlement feature with a net-share settlement feature, which converts the award from a liability award to an equity award, because there is no longer an obligation to settle for cash, or an obligation classified as a liability per ASC 480. For the equity award, fair value is to be measured at grant date only. Per ASC 718, when no other terms are altered by the modification, the fair value at the modification date is used to measure the amount of the total compensation to be awarded in equity instruments.

The journal entry to reclassify the liability to equity would be:

Share-based compensation SAR liability	30,423	
Additional paid-in capital—SAR		30,423

Since no further remeasurement would be permitted, additional compensation cost of $30,423 per year will be recorded at the end of the second and third years, with credits to the additional paid-in capital account. In this example, total compensation cost was greater because the effective measurement date was the end of the first year, but it could also have happened that compensation cost was reduced for the same reason.

Example of an Equity-to-Liability Modification

Assume that a SAR plan, payable in shares, is created, with features similar to the example above (10,000 SARs granted, with three-year term, 3% forfeiture per year expectation). Using a valuation model, the amount of compensation is determined to be $40,000 in total, computed at grant date. At the end of the first year, compensation expense and additional paid-in capital of $13,333 is recorded, based on completion of one of the three years' required service. At that date the fair value of the SARs amounts to $45,000. If the plan is amended at the start of the second year to offer grantees the right to a cash payout, the equity must be reclassified to liability and the value must be remeasured at each reporting date. At the time of modification, since the fair value exceeds what had been accrued, additional compensation cost must be recognized. The entry would be:

Additional paid-in capital—SAR	13,333	
Compensation cost	1,667	
Share-based compensation—SAR liability		15,000

On the other hand, if the fair value of the liability for the SAR at the modification date had been only $30,000, the difference between the amount accrued in the first year and the modified value would have been left in the additional paid-in capital account. The entry follows:

Additional paid-in capital—SAR	10,000	
Share-based compensation—SAR liability		10,000

Modification as a result of an acquisition A share-based payment award may also be modified as a result of an acquisition. ASC 805 describes the accounting for several instances where an acquirer exchanges its share-based payment awards for rewards held by the employees of an acquiree. See the chapter on ASC 805 for more information on business combinations.

If equity instruments are exchanged because of an equity restructuring or business combination, a modification has occurred, and the entity should apply the guidance in ASC 718-20-35-2A to determine how to account for the effects of those transactions. (ASC 718-20-35-6)

Change in Model If a reporting entity changes from the BSM model to a binomial model, the change is deemed a change in accounting estimate, not a change in accounting principle. A change from a binomial model back to a less desirable BSM model is to be discouraged, but apparently not prohibited if use of BSM or a similar closed-form model is supportable. The presumption is that moving from a binomial model to the BSM model would not be well received. (ASC 718-10-55-27)

Change in the Issuer's Credit Risk A change in the issuer's credit risk may affect the value of the option include changes in the issuer's credit risk, if the value of the awards contains cash settlement features (i.e., if they are liability instruments). Entities need to consider these risks and may have to adjust the fair value of the awards with cash payoffs. (ASC 718-10-55-46)

Option Fair Value Calculations Before presenting specific examples of accounting for stock options, simple examples of calculating the fair value of options using both the Black-Scholes-Merton and the binomial/lattice methods are provided. First, an example of the Black-Scholes-Merton closed-form model is provided.

Black-Scholes-Merton actually computes the theoretical value of a so-called *European* call option, where exercise can occur only on the expiration date. *American* options, which include most employee stock options, can be exercised at any time until expiration. The value of an American-style option on dividend paying stocks is generally greater than a European-style option, since preexercise the holder does not have a right to receive dividends that are paid on the stock. (For nondividend-paying stocks, the value of American and European options will tend to converge.) Black-Scholes-Merton ignores dividends, but this is readily dealt with, as shown below, by deducting from the computed option value the present value of expected dividend stream over the option holding period.

Black-Scholes-Merton also is predicated on constant volatility over the option term, which available evidence suggests may not be a wholly accurate description of stock price behavior. On the other hand, the reporting entity would find it very difficult, if not impossible, to compute differing volatilities for each node in the lattice model described later in this section, lacking a factual basis for presuming that volatility would increase or decrease in specific future periods.

The Black-Scholes-Merton model:

$$C = SN(d_1) - Ke^{(-rt)}N(d_2)$$

$$\ln(S/K) + (r + s^2/2)_t$$

C = theoretical call premium
S = current stock price
t = time until option expiration
K = option striking price
r = risk-free interest rate
N = cumulative standard normal distribution
e = exponential term (2.7183)

$$d_1 = \frac{\ln(S/K) + (r + s^2/2)^t}{s\sqrt{t}}$$

$$d_2 = d_1 - s$$

s = standard deviation of stock returns
ln = natural logarithm

The Black-Scholes-Merton valuation is illustrated with the following assumed facts; note that dividends are ignored in the initial calculation, but will be addressed once the theoretical value is computed. Also note that volatility is defined in terms of the variability of the entity's stock price, measured by the standard deviation of prices over, say, the past three years, which is used as a surrogate for expected volatility over the next twelve months.

Example—Determining the Fair Value of Options Using the Black-Scholes-Merton Model

Black-Scholes-Merton is a closed-form model, meaning that it solves for an option price from an equation. It computes a theoretical call price based on five parameters—the current stock price, the option exercise price, the expected volatility of the stock price, the time until option expiration, and the short-term risk-free interest rate. Of these, expected volatility is the most difficult to ascertain. Volatility is generally computed as the standard deviation of recent historical returns on the stock. In the following example, the stock is currently selling at $40 and the standard deviation of prices (daily closing prices can be used, among other possible choices) over the past several years was $6.50, yielding an estimated volatility of $6.50/$40 = 16.25%.

Assume the following facts:

S = $40
t = 2 years
K = $45
r = 3% annual rate
s = standard deviation of percentage returns = 16.25% (based on $6.50 standard deviation of stock price compared to current $40 price)

From the foregoing data, all of which is known information (the volatility, s, is computed or assumed, as discussed above), the factors $d1$ and $d2$ can be computed. The cumulative standard normal variates (N) of these values must then be determined (using a table or formula), following which the Black-Scholes-Merton option value is calculated, *before the effect of dividends*. In this example, the computed amounts are:

$$N(d_1) = 0.2758$$
$$N(d_2) = 0.2048$$

With these assumptions the value of the stock options is approximately $2.35. This is derived from the Black-Scholes-Merton as follows:

$$\begin{aligned} C &= SN(d_1) - Ke^{(-rt)}N(d_2) \\ &= 40(.2758) - 45(.942)(.2048) \\ &= 11.032 - 8.679 \\ &= 2.35 \end{aligned}$$

The foregone two-year stream of dividends, which in this example are projected to be $0.50 annually, have a present value of $0.96. Therefore, the net value of this option is $1.39 ($2.35 – .96).

Example—Determining the Fair Value of Options Using the Binomial/Lattice Model

In contrast to the Black-Scholes-Merton, the binomial/lattice model is an open form, inductive model. It allows for multiple (theoretically, unlimited) branches of possible outcomes on a "tree" of possible price movements and induces the option's price. As compared to the Black-Scholes-Merton approach, this relaxes the constraint on exercise timing. It can be assumed that exercise occurs at any point in the option period, and past experience may guide the reporting entity to make certain such assumptions (e.g., that one-half the options will be exercised when the market price of the stock reaches 150% of the strike price, etc.). It also allows for varying dividends from period to period.

It is assumed that the common (Cox, Ross, and Rubinstein) binomial model will be used in practice. To keep this preliminary example relatively simple in order to focus on the concepts involved, a single-step binomial model is provided here for illustrative purposes. Assume an option is granted on a $20 stock that will expire in one year. The option exercise price equals the stock price of $20. Also, assume there is a 50% chance that the price will jump 20% over the year and a 50% chance the stock will drop 20%, and that no other outcomes are possible. The risk-free interest rate is 4%. With these assumptions there are three basic calculations:

1. Plot the two possible future stock prices.
2. Translate these stock prices into future options values.
3. Discount these future values into a single present value.

In this case, the option will only have value if the stock price increases, and otherwise the option would expire worthless and unexercised. In this simplistic example, there is only a 50% chance of the option having a value of $3.84, and therefore the option is worth $1.92 at grant date.

The foregoing was a simplistic single-period, two-outcome model. A more complicated and realistic binomial model extends this single-period model into a randomized walk of many steps or intervals. In theory, the time to expiration can be broken into a large number of ever-smaller time intervals, such as months, weeks, or days. The advantage is that the parameter values (volatility, etc.) can then be varied with greater precision from one period to the next (assuming, of course, that there is a factual basis upon which to base these estimates). Calculating the binomial model, then, involves the same three calculation steps. First, the possible future stock prices are determined for each branch, using the volatility input and time to expiration (which grows shorter with each successive node in the model). This permits computation of terminal values for each branch of the tree. Second, future stock prices are translated into option values at each node of the tree. Third, these future option values are discounted and added to produce a single present value of the option, taking into account the probabilities of each series of price moves in the model.

Example—Multiperiod Option Valuation Using Binomial Model

Consider the following example of a two-period binomial model. Again, certain simplifying assumptions will be made so that a manual calculation can be illustrated (in general, computer programs will be necessary to compute option values). Eager Corp. grants 10,000 options to its employees at a time when the market price of shares is $40. The options expire in two years; expected dividends on the stock will be $0.50 per year; and the risk-free rate is currently 3%, which is not expected to change over the two-year horizon. The option exercise price is $43.

The entity's past experience suggests that, after one year (of the two-year term) elapses, if the market price of the stock exceeds the option exercise price, one-half of the options will be exercised by the holders. The other holders will wait another year to decide. If at the end of the second year—without regard to what the stock value was at the end of the first year—the market value exceeds the exercise price, all the remaining options will be exercised. The workforce has been unusually stable and it is not anticipated that option holders will cease employment before the end the option period.

The stock price moves randomly from period to period. Based on recent experience, it is anticipated that in each period the stock may increase by $5, stay the same, or decrease by $5, with equal probability, versus the price at the period year-end. Thus, since the price is $40 at grant date, one year hence it might be $45, $40, or $35. The price at the end of the second year will follow the same pattern, based on the price when the first year ends.

Logically, holders will exercise their options rather than see them expire, as long as there is gain to be realized. Since dividends are not paid on options, holders have a motive to exercise earlier than the expiration date, which explains why historically one-half the options are exercised after one year elapses, as long as the market price exceeds the exercise price at that date, even though the exercising holders risk future market declines.

The binomial model formulation requires that each sequence of events and actions be explicated. This gives rise to the commonly seen decision tree representation. In this simple example, following the grant of the options, one of three possible events occurs: (1) the stock price rises $5 over the next year, (2) it remains constant, or (3) it falls by $5. Since these outcomes have equal *a priori* probabilities, $p = 1/3$ is assigned to each outcome of this first year event. If the price does rise, one half the option holders will exercise at the end of the first year, to reap the economic gain and capture the second year's dividend. The other holders will forego this immediate gain and wait to see what the stock price does in the second year before making an exercise decision.

If the stock price in the first year either remains flat or falls by $5, no option holders are expected to exercise. However, there remains the opportunity to exercise after the second year elapses, if the stock price recovers. Of course, holding the options for the second year means that no dividends will be received.

The cost of the options granted by Eager Corp., measured by fair value using the binomial model approach, is computed by the sum of the probability-weighted outcomes, discounted to present value using the risk-free rate. In this example, the rate is expected to remain at 3% per year throughout the option period, but it could be independently specified for each period—another advantage the binomial model has over the more rigid Black-Scholes-Merton. The sum of these present value computations measures the cost of compensation incorporated in the option grant, regardless of what pattern of exercise ultimately is revealed, since at the grant date, using the available information about stock price volatility, expected dividends, exercise behavior and the risk-free rate, this best measures the value of what was promised to the employees.

The following graphic offers a visual representation of the model, although in practice it is not necessary to prepare such a document. The actual calculations can be made by computer program, but to illustrate the application of the binomial model, the computation will be presented explicitly here. There are four possible scenarios under which, in this example, holders will exercise the options, and thus the options will have value. All other scenarios (combinations of stock price movements over the two-year horizon) will cause the holders to allow the options to expire unexercised.

First, if the stock price goes to $45 in the first year, one-half of the holders will exercise at that point, paying the exercise price of $43 per share. This results in a gain of $2 ($45 – $43) per share. However, having waited until the first year-end, they lost the opportunity to receive the $0.50 per share dividend, so the net economic gain is only $1.50 ($2.00 – $0.50) per share. As this occurs after one year, the present value is only $\$1.50 \times 1.03^{-1} = \$1.46$ per share. When this is weighted by the probability of this outcome obtaining (given that the stock price rise to $45 in the first year has only a 1/3 probability of happening, and given further that only one-half the option holders would elect to exercise under such conditions), the actual expected value of this outcome is [(1/3)(1/2)($1.46)] = $0.24. More formally,

$$\left[(1/3)(1/2)(\$2.00-\$0.50)\right]\times 1.03^{-1} = \$0.2427$$

The second potentially favorable outcome to holders would be if the stock price rises to $45 the first year and then either rises another $5 the second year or holds steady at $45 during the second year. In either event, the option holders who did not exercise after the first year's stock price rise will all exercise at the end of the second year, before the options expire. If the price goes to $50 the second year, the holders will reap a gross gain of $7 ($50 – $43) per share; if it remains constant at $45, the gross gain is only $2 per share. In either case, dividends in both the first and second years will have been foregone. To calculate the compensation cost associated with these branches of the model, the first-year dividend lost must be discounted for one year, and the gross gain and second-year dividend must be discounted for two years. Also, the probabilities of the entire sequence of events must be used, taking into account the likelihood of the first year's stock price rise, the proclivity of holders to wait for a second year to elapse, and the likelihood of a second-year price rise or price stability. These computations are shown below.

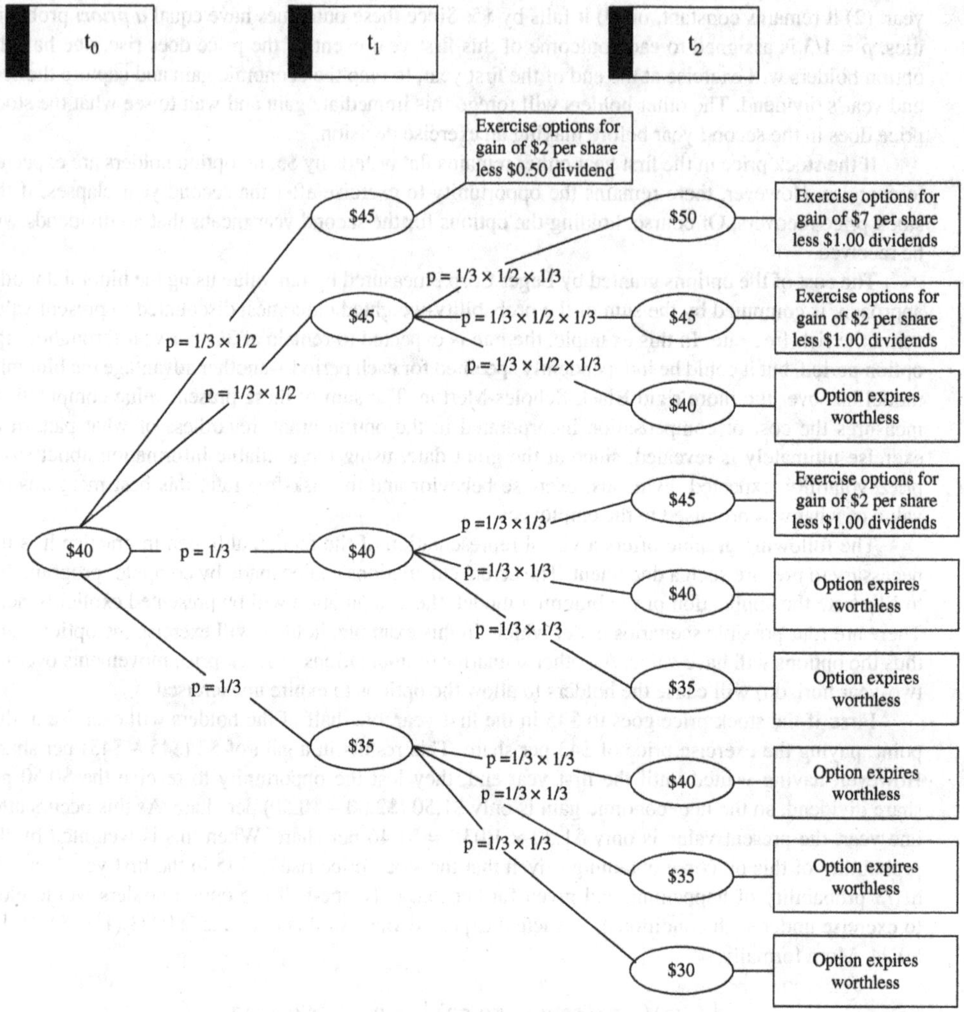

For the outcome if the stock price rises again:

$$[(1/3)(1/2)(1/3)]\{[(\$7.00)\times 1.03^{-2}]-[\$0.50)\times 1.03^{-1}]-[\$0.50\times 1.03^{-2}]\}$$
$$=[0.05544]\{6.59-\$0.48-\$0.47\}=\$0.31276$$

For the outcome if the stock price remains stable:

$$[(1/3)(1/2)(1/3)]\{[(\$2.00)\times 1.03^{-2}]-[(\$0.50)\times 1.03^{-1}]-[(\$0.50)\times 1.03^{-2}]\}$$
$$=[0.05544]\{1.88-\$0.48-\$0.47\}=\$0.05147$$

The final, favorable outcome for holders would occur if the stock price holds constant at $40 the first year but rises to $45 the second year, making exercise the right decision. Note that none of the holders would exercise after the first year given that the price, $40, was below exercise price. The calculation for this sequence of events is as follows:

$$[(1/3)(1/3)]\{[(\$2.00)\times 1.03^{-2}]-[(\$0.50)\times 1.03^{-1}]-[(\$0.50)\times 1.03^{-2}]\}$$
$$=[0.1111]\{1.88-\$0.48-\$0.47\}=\$0.10295$$

Summing these values yields $0.709879 ($0.2427 + $0.31276 + $0.05147 + $0.10295), which is the expected value per option granted. When this per-unit value is then multiplied by the number of options granted (10,000), the total compensation cost to be recognized, $7,098.79, is derived. This would be attributed over the required service period, which is illustrated later in this section. (In the facts of this example, no vesting requirements were specified; in such cases, the employees would not have to provide future service in order to earn the right to the options, and the entire cost would be recognized upon grant.)

A big advantage of the binomial model is that it can value an option that is exercisable before the end of its term (an American-style option). This is the style that employee share-based compensation arrangements normally take. FASB prefers the binomial model, because it can incorporate the unique features of employee stock options. Two key features that FASB recommends that companies incorporate into the binomial model are vesting restrictions and early exercise. Doing so, however, requires that the reporting entity had previous experience with employee behaviors (e.g., gained with past employee option programs) that would provide it with a basis for making estimates of future behavior. In some instances, there will be no obvious bases upon which such assumptions can be developed.

The binomial model permits the specification of more assumptions than does the Black-Scholes-Merton, which has generated the perception that the binomial will more readily be manipulated so as to result in lower option values, and hence lower compensation costs, than the Black-Scholes-Merton. But this is not necessarily the case: switching from Black-Scholes-Merton to the binomial model can increase, maintain, or decrease the option's value. Having the ability to specify additional parameters, however, probably does give management greater flexibility and, accordingly, will present additional challenges for the auditors who must attest to the financial statement effects of management's specification of these variables.

To calculate option values using either the Black-Scholes-Merton or binomial models without the aid of computer software would be very difficult, but hardly impossible. Fortunately, reasonably priced software is widely available to perform these calculations. What managers must do is determine the assumptions that should be used to create an unbiased, representative value of the options. Following are specific examples of accounting for share-based compensation as required under ASC 718.

NOTE: All examples ignore deferred tax effects for simplicity.

Example—Accounting for Stock Options for a Publicly Held Entity

Options are granted to corporate officers to purchase 10,000 shares of $1 par stock at a price of $50 per share, which is equal to the current market price. The options may not be exercised until three years from the grant date (that is, they vest in three years). ASC 718 provides that public companies must use the fair value method to measure compensation cost associated with share-based equity programs. This means that it will be necessary to determine the expected volatility of the share price over the service period. Assume that either a lattice model or Black-Scholes-Merton has been used and that the fair value per option has been determined to be $7. Past experience suggests that forfeitures will be 4% per year, so that compensation cost under ASC 718 will be based on the net number of shares expected to vest, given as (.96 × .96 × .96 =) .885. Total share-based compensation will be ($7 × .885 × 10,000 =) $61,932. The annual entries would be:

Compensation cost	20,644	
Additional paid-in capital		20,644

If all the options are subsequently exercised, the derived proceeds of the stock issuance will be $566,000. The entry would be:

Cash	500,000 (option price)	
Additional paid-in capital	61,932	
Common stock		10,000 (par)
Additional paid-in capital		551,932 (excess)

Example—Accounting for Stock Options for a Nonpublic Entity That Is Not an SEC Registrant and Elects the Calculated Value Method

Options are granted to corporate officers to purchase 10,000 shares of $1 par stock at a price of $50 per share, which is the current market price. The options may not be exercised until three years from the grant date (that is, they vest in three years). ASC 718 provides that nonpublic companies may use a surrogate measure of fair value, called calculated fair value, when it is not possible to determine the expected volatility of the share price over the service period. Essentially, this requires that a relevant industry sector-specific index be identified for use in place of the volatility factor in the normal Black-Scholes-Merton or lattice models.

In this case, the reporting entity identifies such an index and proceeds to compute a value of $6.60 per option. The total compensation cost thereby calculated, $66,000, is accrued over the three-year period ratably. The annual entries would be:

Compensation cost	22,000	
Additional paid-in capital		22,000

If all the options are subsequently exercised, the derived proceeds of the stock issuance will be $566,000. The entry would be:

Cash	500,000 (option price)	
Additional paid-in capital	66,000	
Common stock		10,000 (par)
Additional paid-in capital		556,000 (excess)

Example—Accounting for Stock Options for a Nonpublic Entity That Is Not an SEC Registrant and Elects the Intrinsic Value Method

As discussed above, nonpublic companies are permitted to elect the intrinsic value method of accounting for the cost of share-based compensation plans. Using this method, the intrinsic value must be measured at each reporting date, and used to accrue compensation cost for the period.

Assume again that options are granted to corporate officers to purchase 10,000 shares of $1 par stock at a price of $50 per share, which is the current market price. The options may not be exercised until three years from the grant date. These options have no intrinsic value ($50 – $50 = 0) at the grant date. The intrinsic value method and fair value method require the same measurement date (grant date) for shares and similar instruments whose fair value does not differ from their intrinsic value (and instruments with no time value). This example assumes there is no forfeiture before vesting occurs. Because of the company's decision to use the intrinsic value method, its share options are recognized at intrinsic value at each reporting date through the date of settlement, and the periodic adjustment in intrinsic value, prorated over the service period, is included in compensation cost for that period. Consequently, the compensation cost recognized each year of the three-year requisite service period will vary based on changes in the share option's intrinsic value. For example, assume that at the end of the first year, stock is valued at $55 per share, resulting in a ($55 – $50) $5 intrinsic value per share—thus, a total value of $50,000 for the award. In the first year, the compensation cost would be 1/3 of $50,000. This entry would be:

Compensation cost	16,667	
Additional paid-in capital		16,667

Assume now that at the end of the second year the stock is valued at $53 per share, and thus the intrinsic value is ($53 – $50 =) $3 per share option, for an intrinsic value of the award of $30,000 at that date. The intrinsic value of the award has declined by ($50,000 – $30,000 =) $20,000. Because services for two of the three years of service have now been rendered, the company must recognize *cumulative* compensation cost for two-thirds of the intrinsic value of the award, or ($30,000 × 2/3 =) $20,000. Because the company already recognized $16,667 in the first year, only $3,333 in further compensation cost is to be recognized in the second:

Compensation cost	3,333	
Additional paid-in capital		3,333

Note that, depending on the change in intrinsic value from the prior reporting date, the current period could be credited with *negative* compensation expense. To illustrate, assume instead that at the end of the second year, the stock is valued at $52 per share, for an intrinsic value of $20,000. Since two years of the three-year service period have elapsed, the cumulative compensation cost to be recognized is ($20,000 × 2/3 =) $13,333. Because the company already recognized $16,667 in the first year, *negative* $3,333 compensation cost is to be recognized in the second year:

Additional paid-in capital	3,333	
Compensation cost		3,333

Example of Fair Value Accounting for Stock Options with Cliff Vesting—Measurement and Grant Date the Same

Options are granted to corporate officers to purchase 10,000 shares of $1 par stock at a price of $50 per share, which is also the market price on the grant date. The options may not be exercised until three years from the grant date, and only if the employees remain employed through that date. The company has no reason to expect that any of the options will be forfeited by the employees to whom they are granted (i.e., after the completion of the service period). The company uses the following assumptions to apply the binomial model:

Share options granted	10,000
Employees granted options	100
Expected forfeitures per year	3.0%
Share price at the grant date	$50
Exercise price	$50
Par value per share	$1
Number of years to vest	3 years
Contractual term (CT) of options	10 years
Risk-free interest rate over CT	2 to 5%
Expected volatility over CT	40 to 700%
Expected dividend yield	1.0%
Suboptimal exercise factor	2

Given these assumptions needed to construct a binomial model to value the options, a fair value estimate of approximately $6 per option is determined (details not presented). It is estimated that 3% of employees will turn over each year during the service period. The number of share options expected to vest is estimated at the grant date of (10,000 × .97 × .97 × .97 =) $9,127. The estimated fair value of the award on the grant date would be (9,127 × $6 =) $54,762. The entry to record the compensation cost [($54,762 ÷ 3) = $18,254] in each of the three years is:

Compensation cost	18,254	
Additional paid-in capital		18,254

If in the first year the actual forfeiture rate is 6% instead of the 3% expected rate, and management determines that the forfeiture rate should change to 6%, then in the second year an adjustment would be needed. The revised estimate of the number of options expected to vest is (10,000 × .94 × .94 × .94 =) 8,306. The revised cumulative compensation cost would be (8,306 × $6 =) $49,836. The cumulative adjustment to reflect adjustment of the forfeiture rate is the difference between two-thirds of the revised cost of the award and the cost already recognized in the first year. The related entries and computations are:

Revised total compensation cost	$49,836
Revised cumulative cost as of the end of year 1	$16,112
Cost already recognized in year 1	$18,254
Adjustment to cost at the end of year 1	$(2,142)

The related journal entries are:

Compensation cost	2,142	
Additional paid-in capital		2,142

Entries in years 2 and 3

Compensation cost	16,112	
Additional paid-in capital		16,112

At the end of the third year, the company would examine actual forfeitures and make any necessary adjustments to reflect compensation cost for the number of shares actually vested. Assuming vesting equals expected, the journal entry at exercise of the options would be:

Cash	500,000 (option price)	
Additional paid-in capital	49,836	
Common stock		10,000 (par)
Additional paid-in capital		539,836 (excess)

The difference between the market price of the shares and the exercise price at the date of exercise is deductible for tax purposes because the share options do not qualify as incentive stock options. The realized tax benefits result in a credit to income taxes payable and a reduction in the deferred tax asset.

The statement of cash flows requires that the cash flow benefit that results from the tax benefit be classified as a cash inflow from operating activities and a cash outflow from operating activities.

Example of Accounting for Stock Options with Graded Vesting—Measurement and Grant Date the Same

In a shift from the position espoused in the exposure draft, ASC 718 requires each reporting entity to make a policy decision about whether to recognize compensation cost for an award with only service conditions that has a graded vesting schedule either (1) on a straight-line basis over the requisite service period for each separately vesting portion of the award as if the award was, in-substance, multiple awards, or (2) on a straight-line basis over the requisite service period for the entire award (that is, over the requisite service period of the last separately vesting portion of the award). However, ASC 718 requires that the amount of compensation cost recognized at any date must at least equal the portion of the grant-date value of the award that is vested at that date.

For this example, assume the basic facts from the prior example, but now the 10,000 options vest according to a graded schedule of 25% for the first and second years of service and 50% for the third year. Using the 3% annual employee turnover forfeiture rate, 300 options are expected to never vest, leaving 9,700 options expected to vest at 25% of the award—or 2,425 options vested. In the second year, it is anticipated that another 3% will be forfeited, leaving 9,409 to vest at 25% of the award—or 2,352 options vested. In the final year another 3% are forfeited and vesting occurs at 50% of the remaining—or 4,563 vested options. (Data upon which value per option amounts are derived are not presented in this example.)

Year	*Vested option*	*Value per option*	*Compensation cost*
1	2,425	$5.00	$12,125
2	2,352	$5.50	12,936
3	4,563	$6.00	27,378
	9,340		$52,439

The value of the option is determined separately for different vesting periods after which exercise might occur. Thus, the compensation cost associated with the options is less in the earlier years, as reflected in the table above. Compensation cost is recognized over the periods of requisite service during which each group of share options is earned. In the first year, therefore, compensation cost is [$12,125 + ($12,936 ÷ 2) + ($27,378 ÷ 3) =] $27,719. The journal entry for the first year would be:

Compensation cost	27,719	
Additional paid-in capital		27,719

If the entity is publicly held, measurement at fair value is required, with revaluation at each reporting date through final settlement. For nonpublicly held entities, an election must be made to use fair value or intrinsic value—but again, in either case, remeasurement at each reporting date until final settlement is required.

Example of Accounting for SARs—Share-Based Liabilities[1]

The company grants SARs with the same terms and conditions used in the examples above. Each SAR entitles the holder to receive an amount in cash equal to the increase in value of one share of company stock over $50. Using the same assumptions and option-pricing model, the fair value of the share options is computed to be $6 per SAR (details not presented). The awards cliff-vest at the end of three years. The forfeitures are expected to be 3% a year: thus, SARs expected to vest are (10,000 × × .97 × .97 =) 9,127, and the fair value of the award at the beginning of the first year is (9,127 × $6 =) $54,762. It is assumed that expected and actual forfeitures are the same. The share-based compensation liability at the end of the first year is ($54,762 ÷ 3 =) $18,254. The journal entry for the first year is:

Compensation cost	18,254	
Share-based compensation SAR liability		18,254

Under ASC 718, compensation arising in connection with share-based liabilities must be valued at fair value at each reporting date. At the end of the second year, the estimated fair value is assumed to be $10 per SAR. Therefore, the award's fair value is (9,270 × $10 =) $91,270, and the corresponding liability at that date is ($91,270 × 2/3 =) $60,847 because service has now been provided for two of the three years required. Compensation cost recognized for the award in the second year is ($60,847 – $18,254 =) $42,593. The journal entry for the second year is:

Compensation cost	42,593	
Share-based compensation SAR liability		42,593

[1] This example describes employee awards. However, the principles, except for compensation cost attribution are the same for nonemployee awards. Compensation cost for nonemployee awards is recognized as if the entity had paid cash. Valuation amounts may also be different if the entity elects to use the contractual term as the expected term of share options when valuing nonemployee share-based transactions. (ASC 718-10-55-116A)

At the end of the third year, the estimated fair value is assumed to be $9 per SAR. Therefore, the award's fair value is (9,270 × $9 =) $83,430 and the corresponding liability at that date is the same because the award is fully vested. Compensation cost for the third year is ($83,430 – $42,593 – $18,254 =) $22,583. The journal entry for the third year is:

Compensation cost	22,583	
Share-based compensation SAR liability		22,583

Common Stock SARs If the SARs were to be redeemed (only) in common stock of the entity, "Stock rights outstanding" (a paid-in capital account) would replace the liability account in the above entries. Fair value would be assessed at the grant date (measurement date), and then not altered over the time to final settlement, consistent with how other equity compensation awards are measured under ASC 718.

Tandem Plans Often stock option plans and SARs are joined in tandem plans, under the terms of which the exercise of one automatically cancels the other. In the absence of evidence to the contrary, however, the presumption is that the SAR, not the options, will be exercised. If the SAR-portion of the tandem plan is such that classification as a liability is required, as described above, then remeasurement through the settlement date is required. Tandem plans with phantom shares or share options are similar to the plan above, but the employee's choice of which component to exercise depends on the relative value of the components when the award is exercised.

Other ASC 718 Matters

The most common share-based compensation arrangements have been presented. Other more complicated awards have been developed. Some of these are presented below. For a further discussion with examples refer to ASC 718.

Some Other Types of Share-Based Compensation Awards Covered in ASC 718 Other share awards that ASC 718 addresses are outlined below:

- *Share award with a clawback feature.* These are restrictions on the employee's subsequent employment with a direct competitor, that if violated, cause the ex-employee to return the value of the share award to the company.
- *Escrowed share arrangements.* The SEC has stated in ASC 718-10-S99-2 that it considers the release of shares from an escrowed share arrangement based on performance-related criteria to be compensation. The SEC goes on to articulate circumstances where an entity could overcome this presumption.

ASC 718-40, *Employee Stock Ownership Plans*

There has been a steady increase in the number of corporations that are entirely or partially employee-owned under terms of ESOPs. The accounting for ESOP is governed by ASC 718-40.

Depending on what motivated the creation of the ESOP (e.g., estate planning by the controlling shareholder, expanding the capital base of the entity, rewarding and motivating the work force), the sponsor's shares may be contributed to the plan in annual installments in a block of shares from the sponsor, or shares from an existing shareholder may be purchased by the plan.

ESOPs are defined contribution plans in which shares of the sponsoring entity are awarded to employees as additional compensation. Briefly, ESOPs are created by a sponsoring corporation which either funds the plan directly (unleveraged ESOP) or, more commonly, facilitates the borrowing of money either directly from an outside lender (directly leveraged ESOP) or from the employer, which in turn will borrow from an outside lender (indirectly leveraged ESOP).

Borrowings from outside lenders may or may not be guaranteed by the sponsor. However, since effectively the only source of funds for debt repayment is future contributions by the sponsor, the Codification requires that the ESOP's debt be considered debt of the sponsor even absent a guarantee.

When recording the direct or indirect borrowings by the ESOP as debt in the sponsor's statement of financial position, a debit to a contra equity account, not to an asset, is also reported. The credit would be to cash. (ASC 718-40-25-4) This is necessary since the borrowings represent a commitment (morally if not always legally) to make future contributions to the plan and this is certainly not a claim to resources. Significantly, this results in a "double hit" to the sponsor's statement of financial position (i.e., the recording of a liability and the reduction of net stockholders' equity), which is often an unanticipated and unpleasant surprise to plan sponsors. This contra equity account is referred to as "unearned ESOP shares" in accordance with provisions of ASC 718-40. If the sponsor itself lends funds to the ESOP without a "mirror loan" from an outside lender, this loan should not be reported in the employer's statement of financial position as debt, although the debit should still be reported as a contra equity account.

As the ESOP services the debt, using contributions made by the sponsor and/or dividends received on sponsor shares held by the plan, it reflects the reduction of the obligation by reducing both the debt and the contra equity account on its statement of financial position. Simultaneously, income and thus retained earnings will be impacted as the contributions to the plan are reported in the sponsor's current statement of earnings. Thus, the "double hit" is eliminated, but net worth continues to reflect the economic fact that compensation costs have been incurred.

The interest cost component of debt service must be separated from the remaining compensation expense. (ASC 718-40-25-9) That is, the sponsor's income statement should reflect the true character of the expenses being incurred, rather than aggregating the entire amount into a category which might have been denoted as "ESOP contribution."

In a leveraged ESOP, shares held serve as collateral for the debt and are not allocated to employees until the debt is retired. In general, shares must be allocated by the end of the year in which the debt is repaid. However, to satisfy the tax laws, the allocation of shares may take place at a faster pace than the retirement of the principal portion of the debt.

The cost of ESOP shares allocated is measured based upon the fair value on the release date for purposes of reporting compensation expense in the sponsor's income statements. This is in contradistinction to the actual historical cost of the shares to the plan.

Furthermore, dividends paid on unallocated shares (i.e., shares held by the ESOP) are not treated as dividends, but rather must be reported in the sponsor's income statement as compensation cost and/or as interest expense. (ASC 718-40-25-16) Of less significance to nonpublic companies is the fact that under the new rules only common shares released and committed to be released are treated as being outstanding, with the resultant need to be considered in calculating both basic and diluted EPS.

Example of Accounting for ESOP Transactions

Assume that Intrepid Corp. establishes an ESOP, which then borrows $500,000 from Second Interstate Bank. The ESOP then purchases 50,000 shares of Intrepid no-par shares from the company; none of these shares are allocated to individual participants. The entries would be:

Cash	500,000	
Bank loan payable		500,000
Unearned ESOP shares (contra equity)	500,000	
Common stock		500,000

The ESOP then borrows an additional $250,000 from the sponsor, Intrepid, and uses the cash to purchase a further 25,000 shares, all of which are allocated to participants:

Compensation	250,000	
Common stock		250,000

Intrepid Corp. contributes $50,000 to the plan, which the plan uses to service its bank debt, consisting of $40,000 principal reduction and $10,000 interest cost. The debt reduction causes 4,000 shares to be allocated to participants at a time when the average market value had been $12 per share:

Interest expense	10,000	
Bank loan payable	40,000	
Cash		50,000
Compensation	48,000	
Additional paid-in capital		8,000
Unearned ESOP shares		40,000

Dividends of $.10 per share are declared (only the ESOP shares are represented in the following entry, but dividends are paid equally on all outstanding shares):

Retained earnings (on 29,000 shares)	2,900	
Compensation (on 46,000 shares)	4,600	
Dividends payable		7,500

Note that in all the foregoing illustrations the effect of income taxes is ignored. Since the difference between the cost and fair values of shares committed to be released is analogous to differences in the expense recognized for tax and accounting purposes with regard to stock options, the same treatment should be applied. That is, the tax effect should be reported directly in stockholders' equity, rather than in earnings.

ASC 718-50, *Employee Share Purchase Plans*

Employee share purchase plans are not compensatory if their terms are no more favorable than those available to all holders of the same class of shares and if all employees that meet limited employment qualifications may participate in the plan on an equitable basis. (ASC 718- 50-25-1)

ASC 718-740, *Income Taxes*

Generally, it is inevitable that both the timing and the amounts of compensation expense related to share-based compensation will differ from the amounts and timing of compensation costs recorded in the financial statements. To the extent that these are timing differences, deferred tax accounting is appropriate. The cumulative amount of compensation cost that will result in a tax deduction should be considered a deductible temporary difference. This applies both for instruments classified as equity and for those categorized as liabilities. Any compensation cost recognized in the financial statements for instruments that will not result in a tax deduction should not be considered to result in a deductible temporary difference under ASC 740. (ASC 718-740-25-2 and 25-4)

In general, the fair value of stock-based compensation, which is computed at grant date and recognized over the vesting period as compensation cost in the financial statements, will not be tax deductible currently, giving rise to deferred tax benefits measured grantee's with reference to the book compensation expense recognized. Ultimately, when the options vest and are exercised, the company is able to deduct the intrinsic value, measured by the spread between fair value on exercise date and exercise price. To the extent this exceeds or is less than the fair value of the stock-based compensation recognized as GAAP-basis expense, the tax effect is recognized as a tax expense or benefit in the income statement in the period in which the amount of the deduction is determined, usually when the award is exercised or expires in the case of share options or vests in the case of nonvested stock awards. (ASC 718-740-35-2)

Disclosure Requirements for ASC 718

For a company to achieve the objectives of ASC 718, the information needed to achieve disclosure objectives can be found at www.wiley.com/go/GAAP2021.

Other Sources

See ASC Location—*Wiley GAAP* Chapter	*For information on . . .*
	From ASC 718-10, *Overall*
ASC 505-10-25-3	An investor providing stock compensation on behalf of an investee.
ASC 805-20-55-50 through 51	Accounting for contractual termination benefits and curtailment losses under employee benefit plans that will be triggered by the consummation of a business combination.
ASC 815-40-15-15a	Equity-linked financial instruments issued to investors for purposes of establishing a market-based measure of the grant-date fair value of employee stock options.
ASC 815-10-55-46 through 55-48	Stock options in an unrelated entity given to employees.
	ASC 718-40, *Employee Stock Ownership Plans*
ASC 718-740-25-6 and 718-740-45-5	Determining the accounting for the effect of income tax factors on employee stock ownership plans.

44 ASC 720 OTHER EXPENSES

PERSPECTIVE AND ISSUES

Subtopics

ASC 720, *Other Expenses*, contains nine subtopics and there is no relationship between the Subtopics:

- ASC 720-10, *Overall*, which merely lists the other subtopics
- ASC 720-15, *Start-Up Costs*
- ASC 720-20, *Insurance Costs*
- ASC 720-25, *Contributions Made*
- ASC 720-30, *Real and Personal Property Taxes*
- ASC 720-35, *Advertising Costs*
- ASC 720-40, *Electronic Equipment Waste Obligations*
- ASC 720-45, *Business and Technology Reengineering*
- ASC 720-50, *Fees Paid to the Federal Government by Pharmaceutical Manufacturers and Health Insurers*

Scope and Scope Exceptions

ASC 720-15, *Start-Up Costs* ASC 720-15 applies to all nongovernmental entities. (ASC 720-15-15-1)

Start-up activities are based on the nature of the activity and not a time period. They include activities relating to organizing a new entity, and they may be called preoperating costs, preopening costs, and organization costs. (ASC 720-15-15-2 and 3)

The Subtopic lists the following specific activities that are *not* considered start-up costs and should be accounted for in accordance with other existing authoritative literature:

- Ongoing customer acquisition costs, such as policy acquisition costs (see Subtopic 944-30)
- Loan origination costs (see Subtopic 310-20)
- Activities related to routine, ongoing efforts to refine, enrich, or otherwise improve upon the qualities of an existing product, service, process, or facility
- Activities related to mergers or acquisitions
- Business process reengineering and information technology transformation costs addressed in Subtopic 720-45
- Costs of acquiring or constructing long-lived assets and getting them ready for their intended uses (however, the costs of using long-lived assets that are allocated to start-up activities [for example, depreciation of computers] are within the scope of this subtopic)
- Costs of acquiring or producing inventory
- Costs of acquiring intangible assets (however, the costs of using intangible assets that are allocated to start-up activities (for example, amortization of a purchased patent) are within the scope of this subtopic)
- Costs related to internally developed assets (for example, internal-use computer software costs) (however, the costs of using those assets that are allocated to start-up activities are within the scope of this subtopic)
- Research and development costs that are within the scope of Section 730-10-15
- Regulatory costs that are within the scope of Section 980-10-15
- Costs of fundraising incurred by NFPs
- Costs of raising capital
- Costs of advertising
- Learning or start-up costs incurred in connection with existing contracts or in anticipation of future contracts for the same goods or services
- Costs incurred in connection with acquiring a contract

(ASC 720-15-15-4)

ASC 720-20, *Insurance Costs* ASC 720-20 applies to all entities. (ASC 720-20-15-2) The Subtopic contains Subsections with scope guidance as detailed below.

Retroactive Contracts This Subsection applies to the following transactions:

- Those that meet the indemnification against loss or liability conditions of ASC 720-20-25-1
- Those that provide indemnification against loss or liability incurred related to a past event.

(ASC 720-20-15-5)

The guidance in this subsection does not apply to:

- Activities that legally extinguish the entity's liability
- Reinsurance transactions

(ASC 720-20-15-6)

Claims-Made Contracts The Subsection does not apply to reinsurance transactions. (ASC 715-20-15-8)

Multiple-Year Retrospectively Rated Contracts The Subsection does not apply to a retrospectively rated insurance contract that is not a multiple-year contract or one that could be cancelled by either party without further obligations. (ASC 720-20-15-10)

ASC 720-25, *Contributions Made* ASC 720-25 applies to all entities. Not-for-profit entities should look to ASC 958-720 for additional guidance. (ASC 720-25-15-1) This Subtopic applies to contributions of cash and other assets, including promises to give made by resource providers, but it does not apply to items specified in ASC 958-605-15-6 as listed in the chapter in this volume on ASC 900s. (ASC 720-25-15-2 and 15-3)

ASC 720-30, *Real and Personal Property Taxes* This Subtopic applies to all entities. (ASC 720-30-15-1)

ASC 720-35, *Advertising Costs* ASC 720-35 applies to all entities and to all advertising transactions and activities, except it does *not* apply to the following transactions:

- Direct-response advertising costs of an insurance entity (for guidance, see ASC 944-30).
- Advertising costs in interim periods (for guidance, see ASC 270-10-45-7).
- Costs of advertising conducted for others under contractual arrangements.
- Indirect costs that are specifically reimbursable under the terms of a contract.
- Fundraising by not-for-profit organizations (NFPs) (however, ASC 720-35 does apply to advertising activities of NFPs).
- Customer acquisition activities, other than advertising.
- The costs of premiums, contest prizes, gifts, and similar promotions, as well as discounts or rebates, including those resulting from the redemption of coupons. (Other costs of coupons and similar items, such as costs of newspaper advertising space, are considered advertising costs.)
  (ASC 720-35-15-3)

ASC 720-35 may or may not apply to activities, such as product endorsements and sponsorships of events, which may be performed pursuant to executory contracts. Generally, executory contract costs are recognized as performance under the contract is received. If the costs are advertising costs, then this Subtopic applies. (ASC 720-35-15-4)

ASC 720-40, *Electronic Equipment Waste Obligations* ASC 720-40 applies to all entities affected by Directive 2002/96 adopted by the European Union. (ASC 720-40-15-1) The guidance does not apply to:

- Historical costs from commercial users addressed in ASC 410-20 and
- New waste as defined in the Directive
  (ASC 720-40-15-2)

ASC 720-45, *Business and Technology Reengineering* This Subtopic does not provide guidance for:

- Internal-use software costs (see ASC 350-40)
- The acquisition of property and equipment
  (ASC 720-45-15-2)

ASC 720-50, *Fees Paid to the Federal Government by Pharmaceutical Manufacturers and Health Insurers* This Subsection applies to all pharmaceutical and health insurers subject to the annual fee described later in this chapter. (ASC 720-50-15-1)

DEFINITIONS OF TERMS

Source: ASC 720, *Glossaries*. See Appendix A, *Definitions of Terms*, for other terms relevant to this Topic: Conditional Contribution, Contract, Contribution, Customer, Donor-Imposed Condition, Not-for-Profit Entity, Promise to Give, Reinsurance, Revenue.

Incurred but Not Reported. Losses incurred by the insured entity that have not yet been reported to the insurance entity.

Inherent Contribution. A contribution that results if an entity voluntarily transfers assets (or net assets) or performs services for another entity in exchange for either no assets or for assets of substantially lower value and unstated rights or privileges of a commensurate value are not involved.

Start-Up Activities. Defined broadly as those one-time activities related to any of the following:

- Opening a new facility
- Introducing a new product or service
- Conducting business in a new territory
- Conducting business with an entirely new class of customer (for example, a manufacturer who does all of their business with retailers attempts to sell merchandise directly to the public) or beneficiary
- Initiating a new process in an existing facility
- Commencing some new operation

Unconditional Promise to Give. A promise to give that depends only on passage of time or demand by the promisee for performance.

CONCEPTS, RULES, AND EXAMPLES

ASC 720-10, *Overall*

ASC 720-10 provides no guidance. It merely lists all the subtopics in Topic 720.

ASC 720-15, *Start-Up Costs*

ASC 720-15 provides guidance on financial reporting of start-up costs, including organization costs, and requires such costs to be expensed as incurred. (ASC 720-15-25-1) In addition to items mentioned in the Scope section of this chapter, other costs outside the scope are: store advertising, coupon giveaways within the scope of ASC 605 or ASC 606 when implemented, uniforms, furniture, cash registers, obtaining licenses, deferred financing costs, costs related to construction activities, such as security, property taxes, insurance, and utilities. (ASC 720-15-55-7)

ASC 720-20, *Insurance Costs*

ASC 720-20 provides guidance on:

- Retroactive contracts
- Claims-made contracts
- Multiple-year retrospectively rated contracts.

Guidance for each of the above is in a separate subsection. (ASC 720-20-05-1)

The premium paid minus the amount of the premium retained by the insurer is accounted for as a deposit by the insured. This is only to "the extent that an insurance contract or reinsurance contract does not, despite its form, provide for indemnification of the insured or the ceding entity by the insurer or reinsurer against loss or liability." (ASC 720-20-25-1)

Retroactive Contracts Amounts paid for retroactive insurance should be expensed when paid with a receivable established for expected recoveries. (ASC 720-20-25-3) If the amount paid for the insurance is less than the receivable, the entity should record a deferred gain. (ASC 720-20-25-4)

Claims-Made Contracts Retroactive and prospective provisions should be accounted for separately. If that is not practicable, the policy should be accounted for as a retrospective contract. (ASC 720-25-25-7 and 25-8)

Multiple-Year Retrospectively Rated Contracts For these contracts, the entity should recognize:

- A liability for the consideration the insured must pay
- An asset for any consideration the insurer must pay to the insured
  (ASC 720-20-25-15)

ASC 720-25, *Contributions Made*

Contributions made are expenses in the period when the contribution is made with the offsetting credit recorded as a decrease in assets or an increase in liabilities. Unconditional promises to give are recognized as payables and contribution expenses. ASC 958- 605-25 contains guidance on conditional contributions. (ASC 720-25-25-1) Entities should recognize a gain or loss if a transferred asset's fair value differs from its carrying amount as listed in the chapter in this volume on ASC 900s. (ASC 720-25-25-2)

ASC 720-30, *Real and Personal Property Taxes*

Accrued real estate and personal property taxes represent the unpaid portion of an entity's obligation to a state, county, or other taxing authority that arises from the ownership of real or personal property, respectively. The most acceptable method of accounting for property taxes is a monthly accrual of property tax expense during the fiscal period of the taxing authority for which the taxes are levied. (ASC 720-30-25-7) The fiscal period of the taxing authority is the fiscal period that includes the assessment or lien date.

Example of Accrued Real Estate Taxes

Rohlfs Corporation is a calendar-year corporation that owns real estate in a state that operates on a June 30 fiscal year. In this state, real estate taxes are assessed and become a lien against real property on July 1. These taxes, however, are payable in arrears in two installments due on April 1 and August 1 of the next calendar year. Real estate taxes assessed were $18,000 and $22,000 for the years ended

6/30/20X2 and 6/30/20X3, respectively. Rohlfs computes its accrued real estate taxes at December 31, 20X1, as follows:

		Investment due					
Fiscal year-end of tax jurisdiction	*Assessment date/lien date*	*April 1*	*August 1*	*Annual assessment*	*20X2 Expense*	*Portion of expense paid in 20X2*	*Accrued real estate dates tax at 12/31/X2*
6/30/20X2	7/1/20X1	20X2	20X2	$18,000	$ 9,000	$9,000	$-
6/30/20X3	7/1/20X2	20X3	20X3	22,000	11,000	–	11,000
					$20,000	$9,000	$11,000

Proof of the accrual computation is as follows:

$$\text{Annual assessment—year-end } 6/30/X3 \text{ of } \$22,000 \div 12$$
$$= \$1,833/\text{month} \times 6 \text{ months } \$11,000$$

ASC 720-35, *Advertising Costs*

Except for the expenses detailed below in ASC 720-35-25-1A, the guidance offers two alternatives to accounting for the costs of advertising within the scope of the subtopic:

- Expensed as incurred
- Expensed the first time the advertising takes place, for example, the first time a television commercial airs or the first time a magazine appears for their intended purposes.

Whichever alternative an entity chooses, it must apply it consistently to similar kinds of advertising. If the entity defers the costs, it must have the expectation that the advertising will occur. (ASC 720-35-25-1)

Advertising expenditures are sometimes made subsequent to the recognition of revenue (such as in "cooperative advertising" arrangements with customers). In order to achieve proper matching, these costs are estimated, accrued, and charged to expense when the related revenues are recognized. (ASC 720-35-25-1A)

Materials, such as sales brochures and catalogues, are accounted for as prepaid supplies until they are used. At that time, they are accounted for as advertising costs. (ASC 720-35-25-3)

ASC 720-35 has a separate guidance on communication advertising—television, airtime, and print advertising space. Costs associated with communication advertising are reported as advertising expense when the item or service has been received. (ASC 720-35-25-5)

Depreciation or amortization costs of a tangible asset used for advertising may be a cost of advertising. (ASC 720-35-35-1)

ASC 720-40, *Electronic Equipment Waste Obligations*

ASC 720-40 contains "guidance on accounting for historical electronic equipment waste held by private households for obligations associated with Directive 2002/96/EC on Waste Electrical and Electronic Equipment adopted by the European Union." (ASC 720-40-05-01)

The Directive distinguishes between new and historical waste:

- New waste—put on the market after August 13, 2005
- Historical waste—put on the market on or before August 13, 2005

Only historical waste is dealt with by the Directive. (ASC 720-40-05-3) The Directive also distinguishes between waste from private households and commercial users. (ASC 720-45-05-4)

According to the Directive, producers in the markets should finance historical waste by private households. The obligation is not recognized before the beginning of a measurement period. (ASC 720-40-25-1) Producers bear the cost proportionally based on their share of the market as determine by each EU member country. (ASC 720-40-25-2) As the entity receives actual market share and program cost, it should adjust the liability. (ASC 720-40-35-1)

ASC 720-45, *Business and Technology Reengineering*

ASC 720-45 states that the cost of business process reengineering activities should be expensed as incurred. This includes internal efforts or third-party activities. (ASC 720-45-25-1)

These third-party costs should be expensed as incurred:

- Preparation of request for proposal
- Business current state assessment
- Business process reengineering
- Restructuring the workforce
  (ASC 720-45-25-2)

ASC 720-50, *Fees Paid to the Federal Government by Pharmaceutical Manufacturers and Health Insurers*

ASC 720-50 provides guidance on certain provisions of the Patient Protection and Affordable Care Act, as amended by the Health Care and Education Reconciliation Act. Those Acts require pharmaceutical manufacturers and health insurers to pay annual fees. (ASC 720-50-05-1 and 05-2)

The liability should be "estimated and recorded in full upon the first qualifying sale for pharmaceutical manufacturers or once the entity provides qualifying health insurance for health insurers in the applicable calendar year in which the fee is payable with a corresponding deferred cost that is amortized to expense using a straight-line method of allocation unless another method better allocates the fee over the calendar year that it is payable." (ASC 720-50-25-1)

45 ASC 730 RESEARCH AND DEVELOPMENT

PERSPECTIVE AND ISSUES

Subtopics

ASC 730, *Research and Development*, contains two subtopics:

- ASC 730-10, *Overall*, which provides guidance on the activities, elements, costs, accounting, and disclosures for research and development
- ASC 730-20, *Research and Development Arrangements*, which provides guidance on arrangements used to finance research and development

Scope and Scope Exception

ASC 730 applies to all entities and to "activities aimed at developing or significantly improving a product or service (referred to as product) or a process or technique (referred to as process) whether the product or process is intended for sale or use." (ASC 710-30-15-3)

ASC 730 does *not* apply to:

- The costs of research and development activities conducted for others under a contractual arrangement
- Indirect costs
- Activities that are unique to entities in the extractive industries
- A process for use in an entity's selling or administrative activities
- Routine alterations to existing products and processes
- Market research
- Research and development assets acquired in an acquisition by not-for-profit entity or business combination
- Internally developed computer software and costs incurred to purchase or use computer software unless it is intended for use with R&D activities

(ASC 730-10-15-4 and 5)

Note the following is effective upon implementation of ASU 2014-09, *Revenue from Contracts with Customers*: ASC 730-20 applies to arrangements for software development fully or partially funded by a party other than the vendor developing the software, and where technological feasibility has not been established. If the technological feasibility has been established before the arrangement is entered into, the guidance in ASC 730-20 does not apply to funded software arrangements. Neither does it apply to government research and development. (ASC 730-20-15-1A and 15-4)

Overview

ASC 730 addresses the proper accounting and reporting for research and development costs. It identifies:

- Those activities that should be identified as research and development,
- The elements of costs that should be identified with research and development activities, and the accounting for these costs, and
- The financial statement disclosures related to them.
(ASC 730-10-05-1)

The central issue in regard to research and development costs is that the future benefits related to these expenditures are uncertain. Given this uncertainty, it is generally difficult to justify classifying them as an asset. Generally, entities should charge them to expense as incurred. (ASC 730-10-05-2 and 05-3)

DEFINITIONS OF TERMS

Source: ASC 710-10-20 and ASC 710-20-20. Also see Appendix A, *Definitions of Terms*, for other terms relevant to this topic: Acquiree, Acquier, Acquisition by a Not-for-Profit Entity, Business, Business Combination, Legal Entity, Not-for-Profit Entity, Probably, Related Parties, and Variable Interest Entity.

Research and Development. Research is planned search or critical investigation aimed at discovery of new knowledge with the hope that such knowledge will be useful in developing a new product or service (referred to as product) or a new process or technique (referred to as process) or in bringing about a significant improvement to an existing product or process.

Development is the translation of research findings or other knowledge into a plan or design for a new product or process or for a significant improvement to an existing product or process whether intended for sale or use. It includes the conceptual formulation, design, and testing of product alternatives, construction of prototypes, and operation of pilot plants.

Sponsor. An entity that capitalizes a research and development arrangement.

CONCEPTS, RULES, AND EXAMPLES

ASC 730-10, *Research and Development—Overall*

There are three ways in which R&D costs are incurred by a business:

1. Purchase of R&D from other entities
2. Conducting R&D for others under a contractual arrangement
3. Conducting R&D activities for the benefit of the reporting entity

The accounting treatment relative to R&D depends upon the nature of the cost. R&D costs incurred in the ordinary course of operations consist of materials, equipment, facilities, personnel, and indirect costs that can be attributed to research or development activities. These costs are expensed in the period in which they are incurred unless they have alternative future uses. Examples of such R&D costs with alternative future uses include:

- Laboratory research to discover new knowledge
- Searching for applications of new research findings or other knowledge
- Formulation and design of product alternatives
- Testing for product alternatives
- Modification of products or processes
- Design, construction, and testing preproduction prototypes and models
- Design of tools, dies, etc. for new technology
- Pilot plants not capable of commercial production
- Engineering activity until the product is ready for manufacture
- Design and development tools used to facilitate research and development or components of a product or process that are undergoing research and development activities
  (ASC 730-10-55-1)

Examples of costs that are *not* considered R&D include:

- Engineering during an early phase of commercial production
- Quality control for commercial production
- Troubleshooting during a commercial production breakdown
- Routine, ongoing efforts to improve products
- Adaptation of existing capacity for a specific customer or other requirements
- Seasonal design changes to products
- Routine design of tools, dies, etc.
- Design, construction, startup, etc. of equipment except that used solely for R&D
- Legal work related to patents or litigation
  (ASC 730-10-55-2)

Example of Research and Development

The TravelBins Corporation is developing a hard-shell plastic ski case on wheels. It assigns two staff to the design of the case, as well as a product design consultant, and also contracts with a Portuguese firm to develop suitable molds for the main case and ancillary parts. The company works its way through 17 product development and production activities before it is satisfied that the new ski case is ready for general distribution. The following matrix shows where costs are charged as various steps are completed:

Step No.	Activity	Charge to R&D expense	Charge to production overhead	Move to inventory	Capitalize
1	Cost of product design consultant	xxx			
2	Salaries related to design of the ski case	xxx			

Step No.	Activity	Charge to R&D expense	Charge to production overhead	Move to inventory	Capitalize
3	Purchase of design computers and rapid prototyping machines				xxx
4	Allocation of indirect development costs	xxx			
5	Cost of preliminary test molds	xxx			
6	Cost of building in which test facility is housed				xxx
7	Cost of resin pellets acquired for test runs			xxx	
8	Scrapped cases from test runs	xxx			
9	Good-quality cases from test runs			xxx	
10	Cost of independent stress test firm	xxx			
11	Patent filing cost				xxx
12	Cost to defend patent				xxx
13	Cost of final mold				xxx
14	Machine set-up time		xxx		
15	Quality control during commercial production		xxx		
16	Routine mold adjustments		xxx		
17	Production engineering to reduce scrap rate		xxx		

The costs of design computers and building are capitalized, since they can be used independently from the product development process. The cost of the final mold is capitalized and amortized over the life of the mold, while patent costs are capitalized and amortized over the life of the product (which may extend past the life of the first mold). The cost of the plastic resin and good-quality ski cases can be transferred to inventory for use in regular production and for sale to customers, respectively.

ASC 730-20, *Research and Development Arrangements*

In many cases, entities will pay other parties to perform R&D activities on their behalf. Substance over form must be used in evaluating these arrangements. A financial reporting result cannot be obtained indirectly if it would not have been permitted if accomplished directly. Thus, if costs are incurred to engage others to perform R&D activities that, in substance, could have been performed by the reporting entity itself, those costs must be expensed as incurred.

An alternative arrangement may consist of a business entering into a limited partnership where the limited partners provide funding and the business conducts the research under a contract with the partnership. Under such an arrangement, the partnership may retain legal ownership of the results of the research. The business may have an option to buy back the results of the research upon payment of a stipulated amount to the partnership.

On the other hand, if the payment is to acquire intangibles for use in R&D activities, and these assets have other uses, then the expenditure is capitalized and accounted for in accordance with ASC 350.

When R&D costs are incurred as a result of contractual arrangements, the nature of the agreement dictates the accounting treatment of the costs involved. The key determinant is the transfer of the risk associated with the R&D expenditures. Risk is not transferred to the other parties if there is a commitment by the business to repay the other parties. Examples of commitments to repay are:

- The entity guarantees repayment regardless of the outcome
- The other parties can require the entity to purchase their interests
- The other parties receive debt or equity securities issued by the entity upon completion of the project, irrespective of the outcome.
  (ASC 730-20-25-4)

If the business receives funds from another party to perform R&D and is obligated to repay those funds regardless of the outcome, a liability must be recorded and the R&D costs expensed as incurred. To conclude that a liability does not exist, the transfer of the financial risk must be substantive and genuine.

Nonrefundable Advance Payments Related to Future R&D Activities

Entities conducting R&D activities may make payments in advance for goods or services to be used in R&D activities. Often, these payment arrangements involve a specific R&D project and the R&D activities to be performed generally have no alternative future use at the time the arrangements are entered into. All or a portion of the advance payment may be nonrefundable to the entity con- ducting the R&D activities. For example, if the R&D project does not advance to a stage where the goods or services that were paid for in advance are necessary, the entity conducting the R&D activities will not recover its advance payments.

Nonrefundable advance payments are deferred and capitalized. (ASC 730-20-25-13) As the related goods are delivered and services performed, the capitalized amounts are to be recognized as expense. (ASC 730-20-35-1) On a continuous basis, management should evaluate whether it expects the goods to be delivered or services rendered and to charge the capitalized advance payments to expense when there no longer is an expectation of future benefits.

This is limited to nonrefundable advance payments for goods to be used or services to be rendered in future R&D activities pursuant to an executory contractual arrangement where the goods or services have no alternative future use.

Other Sources

See ASC Location—*Wiley GAAP* Chapter	*For information on . . .*
ASC 730-10	
ASC 350-40	The costs of internal-use computer software.
ASC 350-50	Website development costs.
ASC 985-20-25-1	Costs incurred to establish the technological feasibility of a computer software product to be sold, leased, or otherwise marketed.
ASC 985-605-25-86 through 25-87	A funded software development arrangement.

See ASC Location—*Wiley GAAP* Chapter	*For information on . . .*
Upon implementation of ASU 2014-09: ASC 730-25-15-1A and 958-20-25-12	A funded software development arrangement.
ASC 730-20	
ASC 450-20	Related to loss contingencies.
ASC 810-30	Whether and how a sponsor should consolidate a research and development arrangement.

46 ASC 740 INCOME TAXES

PERSPECTIVE AND ISSUES

Technical Alert

In December 2019, the FASB issued ASU 2019-12, *Simplifying the Accounting for Income Taxes*. The ASU is part of the FASB's simplification initiative and is intended to simplify accounting for income taxes.

Guidance The ASU simplifies the accounting for income taxes by removing the following exceptions:

- Exception to the incremental approach for intraperiod tax allocation when there is a loss from continuing operations and income or gain from other items
- Exception to the requirement to recognize a deferred tax liability for equity method investments when a foreign subsidiary becomes an equity method investment
- Exception to the ability not to recognize a deferred tax liability for a foreign subsidiary when a foreign equity method investment becomes a subsidiary
- Exception to the general methodology for calculating income taxes in an interim when a year-to-date loss exceeds the anticipated loss for the year

The ASU is also designed to improve financial statement preparers-application of income tax–related guidance and simplify GAAP for:

- Franchise taxes that are partially based on income
- Transactions with a government that result in a step-up in the tax basis of goodwill
- Separate financial statements of legal entities that are not subject to tax
- Enacted changes in tax laws in interim periods

Subtopics

ASC 740, *Income Taxes*, consists of three subtopics:

- ASC 740-10, *Overall*, which provides most of the guidance on accounting and reporting for income taxes
- ASC 740-20, *Intraperiod Tax Allocation*, which provides guidance on the process of allocating income tax benefits or expenses to different components of comprehensive income and shareholders' equity. This includes allocating income tax expense or benefit to:
  - Continuing aspects
  - Discontinued operations
  - Other comprehensive income
  - Items charged or credited directly to shareholder's equity
- ASC 740-30, *Other Considerations or Special Areas,* which provides guidance for specific limited exceptions, identified in ASC 740-10, related to investments in subsidiaries and corporate joint ventures arising from undistributed earnings or other causes

Incremental guidance may also be found in other topics, for example: Investments—Equity Method and Joint Ventures, Compensation—Stock Compensation, Business Combinations, Foreign Currency Matters, Reorganizations, Entertainment—Casinos, Extractive Activities—Oil and Gas, Financial Services—Depository and Lending, Financial Services—Insurance, Health Care Entities, Real Estate—Common Interest Realty Associations, and Regulated Operations. (ASC 740-10-05-4)

Scope and Scope Exceptions

The guidance in ASC 740-10 relating to uncertainty in income taxes includes any entity potentially subject to income taxes, including:

- Nonprofit organizations
- Flow-through entities (e.g., partnerships, limited liability companies, and S corporations)
- Entities whose income tax liabilities are subject to 100% credit for dividends paid such as real estate investment trusts (REITs) and registered investment companies. (ASC 740-10-15-2AA)

ASC 740-10 does not apply directly or by analogy to:

- Other taxes,
- Franchise taxes or similar taxes to the extent based on capital or a non-income-based amount and there is no portion of the tax based on income.

The following guidance is added to ASC 740-10-15-4 by ASU 2019-12. (See Technical Alert at the beginning of this chapter.) If a franchise tax is partially based on income, deferred tax assets and liabilities should be recognized and accounted for under the guidance in ASC 740. The effect of potentially paying a non-income-based tax in future years when evaluating the realizability of its deferred tax assets. The amount of current tax expense equal to the amount that is based on income is accounted for under the guidance in this Topic. Any incremental amount incurred is accounted for as a non-income-based tax.

- A withholding tax for the benefit of the recipients of a dividend (ASC 740-10-15-4)

The guidance in ASC 740-20 applies to basis differences arising from investments in subsidiaries and corporate joint ventures. The basic differences arise from exceptions to the general requirements in ASC 740-10 for the comprehensive recognition of deferred income taxes on temporary differences. (ASC 740-20-15-2 and 15-3)

Overview

Accounting Theory—A Balance Sheet Approach When reporting income taxes, accounting theory has prioritized the statement of financial position. To compute deferred income taxes consistent with this balance sheet orientation requires use of the "liability method." This essentially ascertains, as of each date for which a statement of financial position is presented, the amount of future income tax benefits or obligations that are associated with the reporting entity's assets and liabilities existing at that time. Any adjustments necessary to increase or decrease deferred income taxes to the computed balance, plus or minus the amount of income taxes owed currently, determine the periodic income tax expense or benefit to be reported in the income statement. Put another way, income tax expense is the residual result of several other computations oriented to measurement in the statement of financial position.

There are two main objectives to accounting for income taxes:

1. Recognize the taxes payable or refundable on tax returns for the current year as a tax liability or asset.
2. Recognize a deferred tax liability or asset for the estimated future tax effects attributable to temporary differences and carryforwards.

ASC 740 provides guidance for:

- Recognizing and measuring the tax position taken in a tax return that affects amounts in financial statements. (See Definitions of Terms for an explanation of "tax positions.")
- Individual tax positions that do not meet the recognition thresholds required for the benefit of a tax position to be recognized in the financial statements. (ASC 740-10-05-6)

Temporary differences, differences between the tax basis for an asset or liability, result in taxable or deductible amounts in future years. Thus, these differences are often referred to as:

- Taxable temporary differences if they will result in taxable amounts in the future or
- Deductible temporary differences if they will result in deductible amounts in the future. (ASC 740-10-05-7 and 05-8)

DEFINITIONS OF TERMS

Source: ASC 740, *Glossaries*. See Appendix A, *Definitions of Terms*, for other definitions related to this topic: Acquisition by a Not-for-Profit Entity, Business, Business Combination, Commencement Date of the Lease, Component of an Entity, Conduit Debt Securities, Consolidation, Contract, Contract Assets, Corporate Joint Venture, Customer, Debt Security, Inventory, Lease, Lessee, Lessor, Leveraged Lease, Merger of Not-for-Profit Entities, Noncontrolling Interests, Nonpublic Entity, Not-for-Profit Entity, Parent, Public Business Entity, Public Entity, Revenue, Subsidiary, and Underlying Asset.

Alternative Minimum Tax. A tax that results from the use of an alternate determination of a corporation's federal income tax liability under provisions of the U.S. Internal Revenue Code.

Carrybacks. Deductions or credits that cannot be utilized on the tax return during a year that may be carried back to reduce taxable income or taxes payable in a prior year. An operating loss carryback is an excess of tax deductions over gross income in a year; a tax credit carryback is the amount by which tax credits available for utilization exceed statutory limitations. Different tax jurisdictions have different rules about whether excess deductions or credits may be carried back and the length of the carryback period.

Carryforwards. Deductions or credits that cannot be utilized on the tax return during a year that may be carried forward to reduce taxable income or taxes payable in a future year. An operating loss carryforward is an excess of tax deductions over gross income in a year; a tax credit carryforward is the amount by which tax credits available for utilization exceed statutory limitations. Different tax jurisdictions have different rules about whether excess deductions or credits may be carried forward and the length of the carryforward period. The terms carryforward, operating loss carryforward, and tax credit carryforward refer to the amounts of those items, if any, reported in the tax return for the current year.

Consolidated Financial Statements. The financial statements of a consolidated group of entities that include a parent and all its subsidiaries presented as those of a single economic entity.

Current Tax Expense (or Benefit). The amount of income taxes paid or payable (or refundable) for a year as determined by applying the provisions of the enacted tax law to the taxable income or excess of deductions over revenues for that year.

Deductible Temporary Difference. Temporary differences that result in deductible amounts in future years when the related asset or liability is recovered or settled, respectively.

Deferred Tax Asset. The deferred tax consequences attributable to deductible temporary differences and carryforwards. A deferred tax asset is measured using the applicable enacted tax rate and provisions of the enacted tax law. A deferred tax asset is reduced by a valuation allowance if, based on the weight of evidence available, it is more likely than not that some portion or all of a deferred tax asset will not be realized.

Deferred Tax Consequences. The future effects on income taxes as measured by the applicable enacted tax rate and provisions of the enacted tax law resulting from temporary differences and carryforwards at the end of the current year.

Deferred Tax Expense (or Benefit). The change during the year in an entity's deferred tax liabilities and assets. For deferred tax liabilities and assets acquired in a purchase business combination during the year, it is the change since the combination date. Income tax expense (or benefit) for the year is allocated among continuing operations, discontinued operations, and items charged or credited directly to shareholders' equity.

Deferred Tax Liability. The deferred tax consequences attributable to taxable temporary differences. A deferred tax liability is measured using the applicable enacted tax rate and provisions of the enacted tax law.

Gains and Losses Included in Comprehensive Income but Excluded from Net Income. Gains and losses included in comprehensive income but excluded from net income include certain changes in fair values of investments in marketable equity securities classified as noncurrent assets, certain changes in fair values of investments in industries having specialized accounting practices for marketable securities, adjustments related to pension liabilities or assets recognized within other comprehensive income, and foreign currency translation adjustments. Future changes to generally accepted accounting principles (GAAP) may change what is included in this category.

Income Taxes. Domestic and foreign federal (national), state, and local (including franchise) tax based on income.

Tax Position. A position in a previously filed tax return or a position expected to be taken in a future tax return that is reflected in measuring current or deferred income tax assets and liabilities for interim or annual periods. A tax position can result in a permanent reduction of income taxes payable, a deferral of income taxes otherwise currently payable to future years, or a change in the expected realizability of deferred tax assets. The term tax position also encompasses, but is not limited to:

- A decision not to file a tax return
- An allocation or a shift of income between jurisdictions
- The characterization of income or a decision to exclude reporting taxable income in a tax return
- A decision to classify a transaction, entity, or other position in a tax return as tax exempt
- An entity's status, including its status as a pass-through entity or a tax-exempt not-for-profit entity

Taxable Income. The excess of taxable revenue over tax deductible expenses and exemptions for the year as defined by the governmental taxing authority.

Taxable Temporary Differences. Temporary differences that result in taxable amounts in future years when the related asset is recovered or the related liability is settled.

Tax-Planning Strategy. An action (including elections for tax purposes) that meets certain criteria (see paragraph 740-10-30-19) and that would be implemented to realize a tax benefit for an operating loss or tax credit carryforward before it expires. Tax-planning strategies are considered when assessing the need for and amount of a valuation allowance for deferred tax assets.

Temporary Difference. A difference between the tax basis of an asset or liability computed pursuant to the requirements in Subtopic 740-10 for tax positions, and its reported amount in the financial statements that will result in taxable or deductible amounts in future years when the reported amount of the asset or liability is recovered or settled, respectively. Paragraph 740-10-25-20 cites examples of temporary differences. Some temporary differences cannot be identified with a particular asset or liability for financial reporting (see paragraphs 740-10-05-10 and 740-10-25-24 through 25-25), but those temporary differences do meet both of the following conditions:

- Will result from events that have been recognized in the financial statements
- Will result in taxable or deductible amounts in future years based on provisions of the tax law

Some events recognized in financial statements do not have tax consequences. Certain revenues are exempt from taxation and certain expenses are not deductible. Events that do not have tax consequences do not give rise to temporary differences.

Tentative Minimum Tax. An intermediate calculation used in the determination of a corporation's federal income tax liability under the alternative minimum tax system in the United States.

Unrecognized Tax Benefits. The difference between a tax position taken or expected to be taken in a tax return and the benefit recognized and measured pursuant to Subtopic 740-10.

Unrelated Business Income. Income earned from a regularly carried-on trade or business that is not substantially related to the charitable, educational, or other purpose that is the basis of an organization's exemption from income taxes. This income subjects the otherwise tax-exempt organization to an entity-level unrelated business income tax (UBIT).

Valuation Allowance. The contra asset that is to be reflected to the extent that, in management's judgment, it is "more likely than not" that the deferred income tax asset will not be realized.

CONCEPTS, RULES, AND EXAMPLES

Recognition

ASC 740 requires that all deferred income tax assets are given full recognition, whether arising from deductible temporary differences or from net operating loss or tax credit carryforwards. (ASC 740-10-25-2)

The only exceptions to applying the basic principles are:

- Where a deferred tax liability is not recognized for the following types of temporary differences unless it becomes apparent that they will reverse in the foreseeable future.
  - An essentially permanent difference in an excess of the amount for financial reporting over the tax basis of an investment for the foreign subsidiary or a foreign corporate joint venture
  - An essentially permanent difference in underestimated earnings of a domestic subsidiary or corporate joint venture that was in fiscal years beginning on or before December 15, 1992
  - For qualified thrift lenders, bad debt reserves for tax purposes that arose in tax years beginning before December 31, 1987
  - Policyholders of stock life insurance that arose in fiscal years beginning on or before December 15, 1992
- Upon implementation of ASC 842, the pattern of recognition of after-tax income for leveraged leases or the allocation of the purchase price in a purchase business combination of acquired leveraged leases.
- A prohibition on recognition of
  - A deferred tax liability related to goodwill where amortization is not deductible for tax purposes
  - A deferred tax asset for the difference between the tax basis of inventory in the buyer's tax

  (ASC 740 10-25-3)

Under ASC 740 it is necessary to assess whether the deferred income tax asset is realizable. Testing for realization is accomplished by means of a "more-likely-than-not" criterion that indicates whether an allowance is needed to offset some or all of the recorded deferred income tax asset. (ASC 740-10-25-5) While the determination of the amount of the allowance may make use of the scheduling of future expected reversals, other methods may also be employed.

Basic Recognition Threshold The process of filing income tax returns requires management, in consultation with its tax advisors, to make judgments regarding how it will apply intricate and often ambiguous laws, regulations, administrative rulings, and court precedents. These judgements are called tax positions. If and when the income tax returns are audited by the taxing authority, sometimes years after they are filed, these judgments may be questioned or disallowed in their entirety or in part. As a result, management must make assumptions regarding the likelihood of success in defending its judgments in the event of audit in determining the accounting entries necessary to accurately reflect income taxes currently payable and/or refundable.

The primary driver behind the perceived need for guidance on tax positions is the notion that, in general, irrespective of the method being used to recognize and measure these assets and/ or liabilities, management of reporting entities historically has not used a high degree of rigor in their determination. Consequently, especially in the case of public companies, where earnings per share are viewed as an important measure of performance, the estimation of the allowance for income taxes payable was sometimes viewed as a management tool to either improve reported earnings by reducing the allowance or to build up excess liabilities (sometimes referred to as "cookie-jar reserves") that, when needed in future periods, could be reduced in order to achieve the desired result of greater earnings.

ASC 740-10 uses a two-step approach to recognition and measurement. The entity must evaluate each tax position as to whether, based on the position's technical merits, it is "more likely than not" that the position would be sustained upon examination by the taxing authority. The term "more likely than not," consistent with its use in ASC 740-10, means that there is a probability of more than 50% that the tax position would be sustained upon examination. A judgment of more likely than not represents a positive assertion by management that the reporting entity is entitled to the economic benefits provided by the tax position it is taking. (ASC 740-10- 25-6) The term "upon examination" includes resolution of appeals or litigation processes, if any, necessary to settle the matter.

In making its evaluation, the entity is required to assume that the tax position will be examined by the taxing authority and that the taxing authority will be provided with all relevant facts and will have full knowledge of all relevant information. Thus, the entity is prohibited from asserting that a position will be sustained because of a low likelihood that the reporting entity's income tax returns will be examined. (ASC 740-10-25-7A)

This threshold establishes a requirement for whether to give *any* accounting recognition to the income tax effects of questionable tax positions being taken. Failing to meet this threshold test means that, for example, an income tax deduction being claimed would not be accompanied by recognition of a reduction of income tax expense in a GAAP-basis financial statement, and thus that an income tax liability would be required to be reported for the entire tax benefit claimed on the income tax return, notwithstanding management's assertion that a deduction claimed on its income tax return was valid.

In considering the technical merits of its tax positions, management must consider the applicability of the various sources of tax authority (enacted legislation, legislative intent, regulations, rulings, and case law) to the facts and circumstances. The entity may also take into account, if applicable, any administrative practices and precedents that are widely understood with respect to the manner that the taxing authority deals specifically with the reporting entity or other similar taxpayers. (ASC 740-10-25-7b)

Positions must be evaluated independently of each other without offset or aggregation. (ASC 740-10-25-7c) A "unit of account" approach can be taken in this evaluation if it is based on the manner in which the entity prepares and supports its income tax return and is consistent with the approach that the taxing authority would reasonably be expected to use in conducting an examination.

For tax positions taken by management that do not meet the initial recognition criterion, the benefit becomes recognizable in the first interim period that the position meets any one of the following three conditions:

1. The more-likely-than-not threshold is met by the reporting date.
2. The tax position is effectively settled through examination, negotiation, or litigation.
3. The statute of limitations for the relevant taxing authority to examine and challenge the tax position has expired.

(ASC 740-10-25-8)

Determining whether a tax position is effectively settled (condition 2 above) upon examination by a tax authority requires judgment and must be made on a position-by-position basis. (ASC 740-10-25-9)

In determining whether the condition of "effective settlement" has occurred, ASC 740 provides that management should evaluate whether all of the following conditions have been met:

- The taxing authority has completed its examination procedures, including all levels of appeal and administrative reviews that are required by that authority for the specific tax position.
- Management does not intend to appeal or litigate any aspect of the position included in the completed examination.
- The possibility of the taxing authority examining or reexamining any aspect of the tax position is remote, considering:
  - The authority's policy on reopening closed examinations,
  - The specific facts and circumstances of the tax position, and
  - The authority has full knowledge of all relevant information that might cause it to reopen an examination that had been previously closed.

(ASC 740-10-25-10)

When a taxing authority conducts an examination of a tax year, it may not choose to examine a particular tax position taken by management. Nevertheless, upon completion of the examination and all levels of appeal and review, management is permitted to consider that position effectively settled for that tax year. (ASC 740-10-25-11) Management is not permitted, however, to consider that tax position or a tax position similar to it to be settled for any other open periods that were not subject to examination, nor is management permitted to use the "effectively settled" criteria for a tax position as a basis for changing its assessment of the technical merits of any tax position taken in other periods. (ASC 740-10-25-12)

Temporary Differences

Deferred income taxes are provided for temporary differences, but not for permanent differences. Thus, it is important to be able to distinguish between the two. While many typical business transactions are accounted for identically for income tax and financial reporting purposes, there are many others subject to different income tax and accounting treatments, often leading to their being reported in different periods in financial statements than they are reported on income tax returns.

The concept of temporary differences includes all differences between the income tax basis and the financial reporting carrying value of assets and liabilities, if the reversal of those differences will result in taxable or deductible amounts in future years. (ASC 740-10-25-19)

Major Categories of Temporary Differences The major categories or sources of temporary differences are shown in the following table.

Source	Comments/Examples
Revenues or gains recognized for financial reporting purposes before being recognized for income tax purposes.	Revenue accounted for by the installment method for income tax purposes, but fully reflected in current GAAP income, for example a receivable from an installment sale. These are future taxable temporary differences because future periods' taxable income will exceed GAAP income as the differences reverse; thus they give rise to deferred income tax liabilities.
Revenues or gains recognized for income tax purposes prior to recognition in the financial statements.	Certain taxable revenue received in advance, such as prepaid rental income or subscription revenue not recognized in the financial statements until later periods. These are future deductible temporary differences, because the costs of future performance will be deductible in the future years when incurred without being reduced by the amount of revenue deferred for GAAP purposes. Consequently, the income tax benefit to be realized in future years from deducting those future costs is a deferred income tax asset.
Expenses or losses deductible for income tax purposes prior to recognition in the financial statements.	Accelerated depreciation methods or shorter statutory useful lives used for income tax purposes, while straight-line depreciation or longer useful economic lives are used for financial reporting; amortization of goodwill and nonamortizable intangible assets over a 15-year life for income tax purposes while not amortizing them for financial reporting purposes unless they are impaired. Upon reversal in the future, the effect would be to increase taxable income without a corresponding increase in GAAP income. Therefore, these items are future taxable temporary differences, and give rise to deferred income tax liabilities.
Expenses or losses recognized in the financial statements prior to becoming deductible for income tax purposes.	Certain estimated expenses, such as warranty costs, as well as such contingent losses as accruals of litigation expenses, are not tax deductible until the obligation becomes fixed. In those future periods, those expenses will give rise to deductions on the reporting entity's income tax return. Thus, these are future deductible temporary differences that give rise to deferred income tax assets.
(ASC 740-10-25-20)	

Other Sources of Temporary Differences In addition to the familiar and well-understood categories in the table above, temporary differences include a number of other categories that also involve differences between the income tax and financial reporting bases of assets or liabilities.

Source	Comments/Examples
Reductions in tax-deductible asset bases arising in connection with tax credits.	For example, a tax credit may reduce the asset basis for tax depreciation, but is still fully depreciable for financial reporting purposes. Accordingly, this type of election is accounted for as a future taxable temporary difference, which gives rise to a deferred income tax liability.

Source	Comments/Examples
Investment tax credits accounted for by the deferral method.	Investment tax credits are accounted for as a reduction of the cost of the related asset. Amounts received when the asset is recognized in the future will be less than the tax basis of the asset and the difference will be tax deductible when the asset is recovered.
Increases in the income tax bases of assets resulting from the indexing of asset costs for the effects of inflation where the local currency is the functional currency.	The tax laws of certain jurisdictions might require adjustment of the tax basis of assets for the effects of inflation giving rise to tax differences upon recovery of the assets.
Business combinations and combinations accounted for by not-for-profit entities.	Under certain circumstances, the amounts assignable to assets or liabilities acquired in business combinations will differ from their income tax bases. Such differences may be either taxable or deductible in the future and, accordingly, may give rise to deferred income tax liabilities or assets. These differences are explicitly recognized by the reporting of deferred income taxes in the consolidated financial statements of the acquiring entity.
Intra-entity transfers of an asset other than inventory.	There may be a difference between the tax basis of an asset in the buyer's tax jurisdiction and the carrying value of the asset reported in the consolidated financial statements as the result of an intra-entity transfer of an asset other than inventory from one tax-paying component to another tax-paying component of the same consolidated group. That difference will result in taxable or deductible amounts when the asset is recovered.
Life insurance, such as key person insurance where the entity is the beneficiary.	Since proceeds of life insurance are not subject to income tax under present law, the excess of cash surrender values over the sum of premiums paid is not a temporary difference, if the intention is to hold the policy until death benefits are received. On the other hand, if the entity intends to cash in (surrender) the policy at some point prior to the death of the insured (i.e., it is holding the insurance contract as an investment), this is a taxable event and the excess surrender value is a temporary difference.
Accounting for investments.	Use of the equity method for financial reporting while using the cost method for income tax purposes.
Accrued contingent liabilities.	Not deductible for income tax purposes until the liability becomes fixed and determinable.
Cash basis versus accrual basis.	Use of the cash method of accounting for income tax purposes and the accrual method for financial reporting.

Source	Comments/Examples
Charitable contributions that exceed the statutory deductibility limitation.	These can be carried over to future years for income tax purposes.
Deferred compensation.	Under GAAP, the present value of deferred compensation agreements must be accrued and charged to expense over the employee's remaining employment period, but for income tax purposes these costs are not deductible until actually paid.
Depreciation.	A temporary difference will occur unless the modified ACRS method is used for financial reporting over estimated useful lives that are the same as the IRS-prescribed recovery periods. This is only permissible for GAAP if the recovery periods are substantially identical to the estimated useful lives.
Estimated costs (e.g., warranty expense).	Estimates or provisions of this nature are not included in the determination of taxable income until the period in which the costs are actually incurred.
Goodwill.	For U.S. federal income tax purposes, amortization over fifteen years is mandatory. Amortization of goodwill is permitted under GAAP if the entity elects the accounting alternative for goodwill amortization, but periodic write-downs for impairment may occur, with any remainder of goodwill being expensed when the reporting unit to which it pertains is ultimately disposed of.
Income received in advance (e.g., prepaid rent).	Income of this nature is includable in taxable income in the period in which it is received, while for financial reporting purposes, it is considered a liability until the revenue is earned.
Installment sale method.	Use of the installment sale method for income tax purposes generally results in a temporary difference because that method is generally not permitted to be used in accordance with GAAP.
Long-term contracts.	A temporary difference will arise if different methods are used for GAAP and income tax purposes.
Mandatory change from the cash method to the accrual method.	Generally one-fourth of this adjustment is recognized for income tax purposes each year.
Net capital loss.	C corporation capital losses are recognized currently for financial reporting purposes but are carried forward to be offset against future capital gains for income tax purposes.
Organization costs.	GAAP requires organization costs to be treated as expenses as incurred. For income tax purposes, organization costs are recorded as assets and amortized over a 60-month period. Also see the following section, "Permanent Differences." (ASC 740-10-25-25)
Uniform cost capitalization (UNICAP).	Income tax accounting rules require manufacturers and certain wholesalers to capitalize as inventory costs certain costs that, under GAAP, are considered administrative costs that are not allocable to inventory.

Source	Comments/Examples
Share-based compensation arrangements.	Differences between the accounting rules and the income tax laws can result in situations where the cumulative amount of compensation cost recognized for financial reporting purposes will differ from the cumulative amount of compensation deductions recognized for income tax purposes. Also see the discussion in the chapter on ASC 718.
(ASC 740-10-25-20)	

Other Common Temporary Differences

Temporary differences arising from convertible debt with a beneficial conversion feature Issuers of debt securities sometimes structure the instruments to include a nondetachable conversion feature. If the terms of the conversion feature are "in-the-money" at the date of issuance, the feature is referred to as a "beneficial conversion feature." Beneficial conversion features are accounted for separately from the host instrument under ASC 470-20.

For financial statement purposes, the beneficial conversion feature effectively creates two separate instruments:

- A debt instrument
- An equity instrument

The liability is presumed to be settled at its carrying amount.

The separate accounting results in an allocation to additional paid-in capital of a portion of the proceeds received from issuance of the instrument that represents the intrinsic value of the conversion feature calculated at the commitment date, as defined. The convertible security is recorded at its par value (assuming there is no discount or premium on issuance). A discount is recognized to offset the portion of the instrument that is allocated to additional paid-in capital. The discount is accreted from the issuance date to the stated redemption date of the convertible instrument or through the earliest conversion date if the instrument does not include a stated redemption date.

For U.S. income tax purposes, the proceeds are recorded entirely as debt and represent the income tax basis of the debt security, thus creating a temporary difference between the basis of the debt for financial reporting and income tax reporting purposes.

The income tax effect associated with this temporary difference is to be recorded as an adjustment to additional paid-in capital. It would not be reported, as are most other such income tax effects, as a deferred income tax asset or liability in the statement of financial position. (ASC 740-10-55-51)

Temporary differences arising from tax credits related to undistributed earnings Some taxing jurisdictions have differing income tax rates that are applied to taxable income based on whether that income is distributed to investors or retained in the business. For example, Germany taxes undistributed profits at a 45% rate and distributed profits at a 30% rate. When previously undistributed profits are distributed, the taxpayer earns an income tax credit for the differential between the two rates. Accounting for the income tax credit in the separate financial statements of the reporting entity paying the dividend is a reduction of income tax expense in the period that the credit is included in its income tax return. During the period of time that the earnings remain undistributed, the rate applied to the temporary difference in computing deferred income taxes is the rate applicable to the undistributed profits (45% in this example). (ASC 740-10-25-41)

Temporary differences arising from taxes for short year–flow-through entities S corporations and partnerships are permitted to elect tax fiscal years other than a calendar year. (IRC §444) If the election is made, however, the electing entity is required to make a payment to the Internal Revenue Service in an amount that approximates the income tax that the stockholders (or partners) would have paid on the income for the period between the fiscal year-end elected and the end of the calendar year. This payment, which is not a tax, is recomputed and adjusted annually and is fully refundable to the electing entity in the future upon liquidation, conversion to a calendar tax year-end, or a decline in its taxable income to zero. This "required payment" should be accounted for as an asset, analogous to a deposit. (ASC 740-10-55-70 and 55-71)

Permanent Differences

Permanent differences are book-tax differences in asset or liability bases that will never reverse and, therefore, affect income taxes currently payable but do not give rise to deferred income taxes.

Common permanent differences are listed in the table below and include:

Source	Examples/Comments
Club dues	Generally, dues assessed by business, social, athletic, luncheon, sporting, airline, and hotel clubs are not deductible for federal income tax purposes unless they are included as an employer's W-2 compensation.
Meals and entertainment	A percentage of business meals and entertainment costs may not be deductible for federal income tax purposes.
Officer's life insurance premiums and proceeds	Premiums paid for an officer's life insurance policy under which the company is the beneficiary are not deductible for income tax purposes, nor are any death proceeds taxable. (ASC 740-10-25-30)
Penalties and fines	Any penalty or fine arising as a result of violation of the law is not allowed as an income tax deduction. This includes a wide range of items including parking tickets, environmental fines, and penalties assessed by the U.S. Internal Revenue Service.
Tax-to-tax differences	Excess of the parent entity's tax basis of the stock of the acquired entity over the tax basis for net assets of the acquired entity. (ASC 740-10-25-31)
Wages and salaries eligible for jobs credit	The portion of wages and salaries used in computing the jobs credit is not allowed as a deduction for income tax purposes.

Treatment of Net Operating Loss Carryforwards All temporary differences and carryforwards have been conferred identical status, and their income tax effects are given full recognition on the statement of financial position. (ASC 740-10-25-2) Specifically, the income tax effects of net operating loss carryforwards are equivalent to the income tax effects of future deductible temporary differences. (ASC 740-10-25-16) The deferred income tax effects of net operating losses are computed and recorded, but as is the case for all other deferred income tax assets, the need for a valuation allowance must also be assessed (as discussed below). The income tax effects of income tax credit carryforwards (e.g., general business credits, alternative minimum tax credits) are used to increase deferred income tax assets dollar-for-dollar versus being treated in the same manner as future deductible temporary differences, as illustrated in the following example.

Example—Net Operating Loss Carryforwards and Income Tax Credit Carryforwards

Casey Corporation has the following future deductible temporary differences and available carryforwards at December 31, 20X1:

Inventory costs capitalized under Internal Revenue Code §263A	$40,000
Allowance for uncollectible accounts receivable	20,000
Net operating loss carryforward	18,000
General business credit carryforward	14,000

Casey's computation of deferred income taxes at December 31, 20X2, is as follows:

Capitalized inventory costs	$40,000
Allowance for uncollectible accounts receivable	20,000
Net operating loss carryforward	18,000
	78,000
Assumed income tax rate	× 34%
	26,520
General business credit carryforward	14,000
Deferred income tax asset	$40,520

Note the net operating loss is multiplied by the income tax rate to compute its effect on the deferred income tax asset since it is available to reduce future years' *taxable income*. In contrast, the general business credit carryforward is not multiplied by the *income tax* rate since it is available to be used to offset future years' income tax.

ASC 740 provides that the income tax benefits of net operating loss carrybacks and carryforwards, with limited exceptions (discussed below), should be reported in the same manner as the source of either income or loss in the current year. As used in the Codification, the phrase "in the same manner" refers to the classification of the income tax benefit in the income statement (i.e., as income taxes on income from continuing operations, discontinued operations, etc.) or as the income tax effect of gains included in other comprehensive income but excluded from net income on the income statement. The income tax benefits are not reported in the same manner as the source of the net operating loss carryforward or income taxes paid in a prior year, or as the source of the expected future taxable income that will permit the realization of the carryforward.

For example, if the income tax benefit of a loss that arose in a prior year in connection with a discontinued operation is first given recognition in the current year, the benefit would be allocated to income taxes on income from continuing operations if the benefit offsets income taxes on income from continuing operations in the current year. The expression "first given recognition" means that the net deferred income tax asset, after deducting the valuation allowance, reflects the income tax effect of the loss carryforward for the first time. (ASC 740-10-55-38)

The gross deferred income tax asset will always reflect all future deductible temporary differences and net operating loss carryforwards in the periods they arise. Thus, first given recognition means that the valuation allowance is eliminated for the first time. If it offsets income taxes on income from discontinued operations in the current year, then the benefits would be reported in discontinued operations. As another example, the tax benefit arising from the entity's loss from continuing operations in the current year would be allocated to continuing operations, regardless of whether it might be realized as a carryback against income taxes paid on discontinued operations in prior years. The income tax benefit would also be allocated to continuing operations in cases where it is anticipated that the benefit will be realized through the reduction of income taxes to be due on gains from discontinued operations in future years. (See the "Intra-period Income Tax Allocation" section later in this chapter.)

Thus, the general rule is that the reporting of income tax effects of net operating losses is driven by the source of the tax benefits in the current period.

Certain Income Tax Benefits Allocable to Stockholders' Equity The second exception to the aforementioned general rule is that certain income tax benefits allocable to stockholders' equity should not be reflected in the income statement. Specifically, income tax benefits arising in connection with contributed capital, employee stock options, dividends paid on unallocated ESOP shares, or temporary differences existing at the date of a quasi-reorganization are reported as accumulated other comprehensive income in the stockholders' equity section of the statement of financial position and are not included in the income statement.

Certain transactions among stockholders that occur outside the company can affect the status of deferred income taxes. The most commonly encountered of these is the change in ownership of more than 50% of the company's stock, which limits or eliminates the company's ability to utilize net operating loss carryforwards, and accordingly requires the reversal of deferred income tax assets previously recognized under ASC 740. Changes in deferred income taxes caused by transactions among stockholders should be included in current period income tax expense in the income statement, since these are analogous to changes in expectations resulting from other external events (e.g., changes in enacted income tax rates). However, the income tax effects of changes in the income tax bases of assets or liabilities caused by transactions among stockholders would be included in equity, not in the income statement, although subsequent period changes in the valuation account, if any, would be reflected in income. (ASC 740-20-45)

Interest and Penalties If a tax position taken by the reporting entity fails the "more-likely-than-not" recognition test, the presumption is that the position would not be sustained and that the entire tax benefit and associated interest (and penalties, if applicable) should be recognized as a liability on the statement of financial position. Since interest is a period cost for the use of borrowed funds, it must be accrued until the taxing authorities reject the tax position and formally impose the demand for back taxes and interest, or the statute of limitations for the position lapses.

If the relevant taxing jurisdiction requires interest to be paid on income tax underpayments, the reporting entity should recognize interest expense in the first period that interest would begin to accrue under that jurisdiction's relevant tax law. (ASC 740-10-25-56) Interest should be computed using the following formula:

Amount of tax position claimed (expected to be claimed) on income tax return
– Amount of tax position recognized in the financial statements
= Amount of tax position claimed not recognized in the financial statements
× Jurisdiction's applicable statutory interest rate
× Period of time from date that interest first became accruable to reporting date
= Accrued interest on tax positions taken but not recognized in the financial statements

If upon disallowance on examination, a position would subject the taxpayer to penalty, the reporting entity recognizes an expense for that penalty in the period it claims or expects to claim the position in its income tax return. That is, the penalty must be accrued as the tax position becomes formalized in a tax filing. (ASC 740-10-25-57) An exception is permitted if the positions taken that would be subject to penalty are under the minimum threshold that the jurisdiction uses to assess the penalty. If management later changes its assessment of whether the minimum threshold has been exceeded in a subsequent period, the penalty is to be recognized as an expense in that period.

Initial Measurement

Scheduling the Reversal Years of Temporary Differences There is no need to forecast (or "schedule") the future years in which temporary differences are expected to reverse except in the most exceptional circumstances. To eliminate the burden, it was necessary to endorse the use of the expected average (i.e., effective) income tax rate to measure the deferred income tax assets and liabilities and to forego a more precise measure of marginal tax effects. The effects of future changes in the tax law rates are not anticipated. (ASC 740-10-30-2)

If a tax position meets the initial recognition threshold, it is then measured to determine the amount to recognize in the financial statements. The following considerations apply to the measurement process:

- Consider if the position is based on clear and unambiguous tax law. If so, and management has a high level of confidence in the technical merits of the position, the position qualifies as a "highly certain tax position" and, consequently, the full benefit would be recognized in the financial statements. The measurement of the maximum amount of income tax benefit that is more than 50% likely to be realized is 100% of the benefit claimed. (ASC 740-10-30-7)

NOTE: Management may deem the ***amount*** *of a tax position to be highly certain of being sustained but may not be highly certain as to the* ***timing*** *of the benefit. For example, in deciding whether to record a cost as an expense of the period in which it is incurred or to capitalize it, management may be highly certain that the cost will be deductible in some period but not be highly certain as to whether the proper period to deduct it is in the current period or ratably over multiple future periods. Under these circumstances, management would be required to measure the maximum amount that it believed was more than 50% likely to be sustained in the period that the cost is incurred.* (ASC 740-10-55-111)

- If it is not highly certain that the full benefit of a position would be sustained in the year claimed, then the amount to be recognized for the tax position is measured as management's *best estimate* of the *maximum* benefit that is more than 50% likely to be realized upon effective settlement with a taxing authority possessing full knowledge of all relevant information. Management should consider the amounts and probabilities of various settlement outcomes based on the facts, circumstances, and information available at the date of the statement of financial position. As stated above, management must assume that the taxing authority will conduct an examination and may not consider the likelihood of this not occurring in this measurement process.

As explained above, measurement of an uncertain tax position under ASC 740-10 can be a fairly complex process. It requires that management consider the amounts and probabilities of various effective settlement outcomes. The amount of the income tax benefit to be given financial statement recognition is the largest (i.e., most favorable) estimated outcome that is more than 50% probable, as illustrated in the following example.

Example of the Two-Step Initial Recognition and Measurement Process

Menkin Manufacturing planned to claim a $10,000 credit for increasing research activities (R&D credit) on its 20X2 corporate income tax return. In consultation with its tax advisor, management believes that a portion of the credit is at risk because of ambiguity regarding the technical merits of the decision to classify certain costs as qualifying to be included in the computation of the credit.

Management does believe, however, that it is "more likely than not" that the reporting entity will qualify for all or a portion of the R&D credit, and thus recognition will have to be limited to only a portion of the amount it will be claiming on its income tax return.

Since the credit meets the more-likely-than-not threshold for initial recognition, management must measure the amount to be recognized. It has estimated the range of possible outcomes (i.e., of credit allowed) and related likelihoods as follows:

Estimated outcome	*Probability of occurrence*	*Cumulative probability of occurrence*
$10,000	5%	5%
8,500	35%	40%
7,500	25%	65%
7,000	20%	85%
6,500	10%	95%
6,000	5%	100%

The largest outcome above that has a more than 50% cumulative probability of being realized is $7,500, which management has estimated as having a cumulative probability of 65%. Therefore, management would recognize only $7,500 of this tax position in the reporting entity's financial statements. This would result in Menkin Manufacturing reflecting a liability for unrecognized income tax benefits in the amount of $2,500 on its statement of financial position as of December 31, 20X2.

Note, in the foregoing example, that while the income tax return will claim an R&D credit for the full $10,000, GAAP-basis financial statements will only reflect a credit of $7,500, and thus will report an accrued tax liability of $2,500 pertaining to the credit taken but not likely to be allowed upon examination. ASC 740 complies with the GAAP imperative of reporting the entity's assets and liabilities on an appropriate measurement basis. GAAP financial reporting, in other words, is not a tool to be used by management to avoid recording the accounting consequences of the tactical decisions it makes regarding the tax positions it takes.

The following diagram illustrates the application of the recognition and measurement criteria:

Probability of Position Being Sustained upon Examination

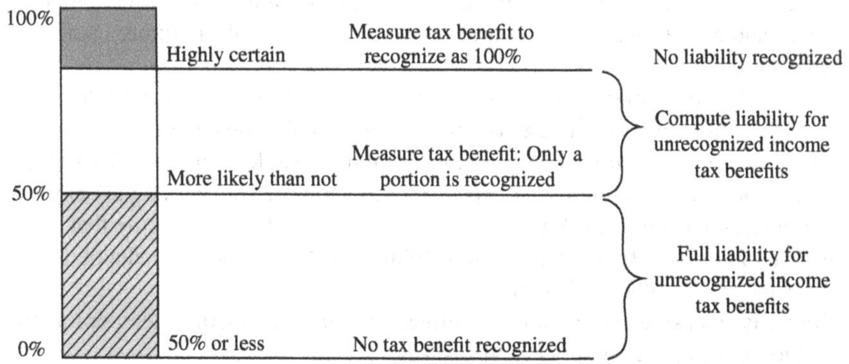

Determining the Appropriate Income Tax Rate The objective is to measure deferred taxes using the enacted tax rate expected to apply to taxable income in the period when the deferred tax liability or asset is expected to be recovered or settled. (ASC 740-10-30-8)

Assume C corporations with taxable income between $335,000 and $10,000,000 are taxed at an expected income tax rate equal to the 34% marginal rate and the effect of the surtax exemption has fully phased out at that level, effectively resulting in a flat tax. Thus, the computation of deferred federal income taxes for these entities is accomplished simply by applying the 34% top marginal rate to all temporary differences and net operating loss carryforwards outstanding at the date of the statement of financial position. This technique is applied to future taxable temporary differences (producing deferred income tax liabilities), and to future deductible temporary differences and net operating loss carryforwards (giving rise to deferred income tax assets). The deferred income tax assets computed must still be evaluated for realizability. Some, or all, of the projected income tax benefits may fail the "more-likely-than-not" test and consequently may need to be offset by a valuation allowance.

On the other hand, reporting entities that have historically been taxed at an effective federal income tax rate lower than the top marginal rate compute their federal deferred income tax assets and liabilities by using their expected future effective income tax rates. Consistent with the goal of simplifying the process of calculating deferred income taxes, reporting entities are permitted to apply a single, long-term expected income tax rate, without attempting to differentiate among the years when temporary difference reversals are expected to occur. In any event, the inherent imprecision of forecasting future income levels and the patterns of temporary difference reversals make it unlikely that a more sophisticated computational effort would produce better financial statements. Therefore, absent such factors as the phasing in of new income tax rates, it is not necessary to consider whether the reporting entity's effective income tax rate will vary from year to year.

The effective income tax rate convention obviates the need to predict the impact of the alternative minimum tax (AMT) on future years. In determining an entity's deferred income taxes, the number of computations may be as few as one.

Computing Deferred Income Taxes To compute the gross deferred income tax provision (i.e., before addressing the possible need for a valuation allowance):

- Identify all temporary differences existing as of the reporting date. This process is simplified if the reporting entity maintains both GAAP and income tax statements of financial position for comparison purposes.
- Segregate the temporary differences into future taxable differences and future deductible differences. This step is necessary because a valuation allowance may be required to be provided to offset the income tax effects of the future deductible temporary differences and carryforwards, but not the income tax effects of the future taxable temporary differences.
- Accumulate information about available net operating loss and tax credit carryforwards as well as their expiration dates or other types of limitations, if any.
- Measure the income tax effect of aggregate future taxable temporary differences by separately applying the appropriate expected income tax rates (federal plus any state, local, and foreign rates that are applicable under the circumstances). Ensure that consideration is given in making these computations to the federal income tax deductibility of income taxes payable to other jurisdictions.
- Similarly, measure the income tax effects of future deductible temporary differences, including net operating loss carryforwards.
  (ASC 740-10-30-5)

Separate computations must be made for each taxing jurisdiction. In many cases, this level of complexity is not needed and a single, combined effective income tax rate can be used. However, in assessing the need for valuation allowances, it is necessary to consider the entity's ability to absorb deferred income tax benefits against income tax liabilities. In as much as benefits from one tax jurisdiction will not reduce income taxes payable to another tax jurisdiction, separate calculations will be needed in these situations. Also, for purposes of presentation in the statement of financial position (discussed below), offsetting of deferred income tax assets and liabilities is only permissible within the same jurisdiction. (ASC 740-10-45-6)

Separate computations are made for each taxpaying component of the primary reporting entity. If a parent company and its subsidiaries are consolidated for financial reporting purposes but file separate income tax returns, the reporting entity comprises a number of components, and the income tax benefits of any one will be unavailable to reduce the income tax obligations of the others.

The principles set forth above are illustrated by the following example.

Example—Computation of Deferred Income Tax Liability and Asset: Basic Example

Assume that Humfeld Company has a total of \$28,000 of future taxable temporary differences and a total of \$8,000 of future deductible temporary differences. There are no available operating loss or tax credit carryforwards. Taxable income is \$230,000 and the income tax rate is a flat (i.e., not graduated) 34% for the current year and not anticipated to change in the future. Also assume that there were no deferred income tax liabilities or assets in prior years.

Current income tax expense and income taxes currently payable are computed as taxable income times the current rate (\$230,000 × 34% = \$78,200). The deferred income tax asset is computed as \$2,720, representing 34% of future deductible temporary differences of \$8,000. The deferred income tax liability of \$9,520 is calculated as 34% of future taxable temporary differences of \$28,000. The deferred income tax expense of \$6,800 is the net of the deferred income tax liability of \$9,520 and the deferred income tax asset of \$2,720.

The journal entry to record the required amounts is:

Current income tax expense	78,200	
Deferred income tax asset	2,720	
Income tax expense—deferred	6,800	
Deferred income tax liability		9,520
Income taxes currently payable		78,200

In 20X1, Humfeld Company has taxable income of \$411,000, aggregate future taxable and future deductible temporary differences are \$75,000 and \$36,000, respectively, and the income tax rate remains a flat 34%.

Current income tax expense and income taxes currently payable are each \$139,740 (\$411,000 × 34%).

Deferred amounts are calculated as follows:

	Deferred tax liability	*Deferred tax asset*	*Income tax expense—deferred*
Required balance at 12/31/X2			
\$75,000 × 34%	\$25,500		-
\$36,000 × 34%		\$12,240	-
Balances at 12/31/X1	9,520	2,720	-
Adjustment required	\$15,980	\$ 9,520	\$6,460

The journal entry to record the deferred amounts is:

Deferred income tax asset	9,520	
Income tax expense–deferred	6,460	
Deferred income tax liability		15,980

Because the increase in the liability in 20X2 is larger (by $6,460) than the increase in the asset for that year, the result is a deferred income tax expense for 20X2.

Applicability to Business Combinations ASC 805 clarifies that an acquirer should apply its provisions to income tax positions taken by the acquiree prior to the date of the business combination. Thus, the provisions of ASC 740-10 apply to the determination of the income tax bases used to compute deferred income tax assets and liabilities as well as amounts of income taxes currently payable to or refundable from taxing authorities. For more information, see the chapter on ASC 805.

Establishing a Valuation Allowance for Deferred Income Tax Assets All deferred income tax assets must be given full recognition, subject to the possible provision of an allowance when it is determined that an asset is not expected to be realized. This includes the need for a valuation allowance for a deferred tax asset related to an available-for-sale security. (ASC 740-10-30-16) This approach conveys the greatest amount of useful information to the users of the financial statements.

A valuation allowance is to be provided for that fraction of the computed year-end balances of the deferred income tax assets for which it has been determined that it is more likely than not that the reported asset amount will not be realized. As used in this context, "more likely than not" represents a probability of just over 50%. Since it is widely agreed that the term probable, as used in ASC 450, denotes a much higher probability (perhaps 85% to 90%), the threshold for reflecting an impairment of deferred income tax assets is much lower than the threshold for other assets (i.e., in most cases, the likelihood of a valuation allowance being required is greater than, say, the likelihood that a long-lived asset is impaired).

Example—Establishment of a Valuation Allowance

Assume that Couch Corporation has a future deductible temporary difference of $60,000 at December 31, 20X2. The tax rate is a flat 34%. Based on available evidence, management of Couch Corporation concludes that it is more likely than not that all sources will not result in future taxable income sufficient to realize an income tax benefit of more than $15,000 (25% of the future deductible temporary difference). Also assume that there were no deferred income tax assets in previous years and that prior years' taxable income was inconsequential.

At 12/31/X2 Couch Corporation records a deferred income tax asset in the amount of $20,400 ($60,000×34%) and a valuation allowance of $15,300 (34% of the $45,000 difference between the $60,000 of future deductible temporary differences and the $15,000 of future taxable income expected to absorb the future tax deduction arising from the reversal of the temporary difference).

The journal entry at 12/31/X2 is:

Deferred income tax asset	20,400	
Valuation allowance		15,300
Income tax benefit–deferred		5,100

The deferred income tax benefit of $5,100 represents that portion of the deferred income tax asset (25%) that, more likely than not, is realizable

Assume that at the end of 20X3, Couch Corporation's future deductible temporary difference has decreased to $50,000 and that Couch now has a net operating loss carryforward of $42,000. The total of the net operating loss carryforward ($42,000) plus the amount of the future deductible temporary difference ($50,000) is $92,000. A deferred income tax asset of $31,280 ($92,000 × 34%) is recognized at the end of 20X3. Also assume that management of Couch Corporation concludes that it is more likely than not that $25,000 of the tax asset will not be realized. Thus, a valuation allowance in that amount is required, and the balance in the allowance account of $15,300 must be increased by $9,700 ($25,000 – $15,300).

The journal entry at 12/31/X3 is:

Deferred income tax asset	10,880	
Valuation allowance		9,700
Income tax benefit—deferred		1,180

The deferred income tax asset is debited $10,880 to increase it from $20,400 at the end of 20X2 to its required balance of $31,280 at the end of 20X3. The deferred income tax benefit of $1,180 represents the net of the $10,880 increase in the deferred income tax asset and the $9,700 increase in the valuation allowance.

While the meaning of the "more-likely-than-not" criterion is clear (more than 50%), the practical difficulty of assessing whether or not this subjective threshold test is met in a given situation remains. A number of positive and negative factors need to be evaluated in reaching a conclusion as to the necessity of a valuation allowance. Positive factors (those suggesting that an allowance is not necessary) include:

- Evidence of sufficient future taxable income to realize the benefit of the deferred income tax asset
- Evidence of sufficient future taxable income arising from the reversals of existing future taxable temporary differences (deferred income tax liabilities) to realize the benefit of the deferred income tax asset
- Evidence of sufficient taxable income in prior year(s) available for realization of a net operating loss carryback under existing statutory limitations
- Evidence of the existence of prudent, feasible tax planning strategies under management control that, if implemented, would permit the realization of the deferred income tax asset
- Existing contracts or firm sales that will produce more than enough taxable income to realize the deferred tax asset
- An excess of appreciated asset values over their tax bases, in an amount sufficient to realize the deferred income tax asset
- A strong earnings history exclusive of the loss creating the deferred tax asset, along with evidence that the loss is an aberration
  (ASC 740-10-30-22 and 740-10-55-37 through 55-39)

While the foregoing may suggest that the reporting entity will be able to realize the benefits of the future deductible temporary differences outstanding as of the date of the statement of financial position, certain negative factors must also be considered in determining whether a valuation allowance needs to be established against deferred income tax assets. These factors include:

- If unfavorably resolved, circumstances that would negatively affect future profits on a continuing basis.
- A history of operating losses, or of net operating loss or tax credit carryforwards that have expired unused.

- Losses that are anticipated in the near future years, despite a history of profitable operations.
- Carryback or carryforward period so brief that tax benefit realization would limit realization of a tax benefit if a single deductible temporary difference is expected to reverse in a single profit on a continuing basis in future years or the entity operates in a cyclical business.

(ASC 740-10-30-21)

Thus, the process of evaluating whether a valuation allowance is needed involves the weighing of both positive and negative factors to determine whether, based on the preponderance of available evidence, it is more likely than not that the deferred income tax assets will be realized.

Example of Applying the More-Likely-Than-Not Criterion to a Deferred Income Tax Asset

Assume the following facts:

- Foy Corporation reports on a calendar year, and it commenced operations and began applying ASC 740 in 20W6.
- As of December 31, 20X2, it has future taxable temporary differences of $85,000 relating to income earned on equity-method investments; future deductible temporary differences of $12,000 relating to deferred compensation arrangements; a net operating loss carryforward (which arose in 20W9) of $40,000; and a capital loss carryforward of $10,000 (which arose in 20X2).
- Foy's expected effective income tax rate for future years is 34% for both ordinary income and net long-term capital gains. Capital losses cannot be offset against ordinary income.

The first steps are to compute the deferred income tax asset and/or liability without consideration of the possible need for a valuation allowance.

Deferred income tax liability:	
Future taxable temporary difference (equity-method investment)	$85,000
Effective tax rate	× 34%
Required balance	$28,900
Deferred income tax asset:	
Future deductible temporary differences and carryforwards:	
Deferred compensation	$12,000
Net operating loss carryforward	40,000
	52,000
Effective tax rate	× 34%
Required balance (a)	$17,680
Capital loss	$10,000
Effective tax rate	× 34%
Required balance (b)	$ 3,400
Total deferred income tax asset: (a) + (b)	
Ordinary	$17,680
Capital	3,400
Total required balance	$21,080

The next step is to consider the need for a valuation allowance to partially or completely offset the deferred income tax asset, based on a "more-likely-than-not" assessment of the asset's realizability. Foy management must evaluate both positive and negative evidence to determine the need for a valuation allowance, if any. Assume that management identifies the following factors that may affect this need:

- Before the net operating loss deduction, Foy reported taxable income of $5,000 in 20X2. Management believes that taxable income in future years, apart from net operating loss deductions, should continue at approximately the same level experienced in 20X2.
- The future taxable temporary differences are not expected to reverse in the foreseeable future as the equity method investee is not expected to incur losses or pay dividends to Foy.
- The capital loss arose in connection with a securities transaction of a type that is unlikely to recur. The company does not generally engage in activities that have the potential to result in capital gains or losses.
- Management estimates that certain productive assets have a fair value exceeding their respective income tax bases by about $30,000. The entire gain, if realized for income tax purposes, would result in recapture of depreciation previously taken. Since the current plans call for a substantial upgrading of the company's plant assets, management feels it could easily accelerate those actions in order to realize taxable gains, should it be desirable to do so for income tax planning purposes.

Based on the foregoing information, Foy Corporation management concludes that a $3,400 valuation allowance is required. The reasoning is as follows:

- There will be some taxable operating income generated in future years ($5,000 annually, based on the earnings experienced in 20X2), which will absorb a modest portion of the reversal of the deductible temporary difference ($12,000) and net operating loss carryforward ($40,000) existing at year-end 20X2.
- More importantly, the feasible tax planning strategy of accelerating the taxable gain relating to appreciated assets ($30,000) would certainly be sufficient, in conjunction with operating income over several years, to permit Foy to fully realize the income tax benefits of the future deductible temporary difference and net operating loss carryover.
- However, since capital losses can only be carried forward for five years, are only usable to offset future capital gains, and Foy management is unable to project future realization of capital gains, it is more likely than not that the associated tax benefit accrued ($3,400) will not be realized, and thus a valuation allowance must be recorded.

Based on this analysis, an allowance for unrealizable deferred income tax benefits in the amount of $3,400 is established by a charge against the current (20X2) income tax provision.

Among the foregoing positive and negative factors to be considered, perhaps the most difficult to fully grasp is that of available income tax planning strategies. Also see ASC 740-10-30-7 for information about tax strategies. (ASC 740-10-30-20) Since ASC 740 requires that all available evidence be assessed to determine the need for a valuation allowance, the matter of the cost of implementing those strategies is irrelevant. In fact, there is no limitation regarding strategies that may involve significant costs of implementation, although in computing the amount of valuation allowance needed, any costs of implementation must be netted against the benefits to be derived.

For example, if a gross deferred income tax asset of $50,000 is recorded, and certain strategies have been identified by management that would protect realization of the future deductible item associated with the computed income tax benefit at an implementation cost of $10,000, then the net amount of income tax benefit, which is more likely than not to be realizable, would not be $50,000. Rather, it may be only $43,400, which is the gross benefit less the after-tax cost of implementation, assuming a 34% tax rate {$50,000 – [$10,000 × (1 – .34)]}. Accordingly, a valuation allowance of $6,600 is established in this example.

Example—Impact of a Qualifying Tax Strategy

Assume that Kruse Company has a $180,000 net operating loss carryforward as of 12/31/X2, scheduled to expire at the end of the following year. Future taxable temporary differences of $240,000 exist that are expected to reverse in approximately equal amounts of $80,000 in 20X3, 20X4, and 20X5. Kruse Company estimates that taxable income for 20X3 (exclusive of the reversal of existing temporary differences and the operating loss carryforward) will be $20,000. Kruse Company expects to implement a qualifying income tax planning strategy that will accelerate the total of $240,000 of taxable temporary differences to 20X3. Expenses to implement the strategy are estimated to approximate $30,000. The tax rate is 34%.

In the absence of the income tax planning strategy, $100,000 of the net operating loss carryforward could be realized in 20X3 based on estimated taxable income of $20,000 plus $80,000 of the reversal of future taxable temporary differences. Thus, $80,000 would expire unused at the end of 20X3 and the net amount of the deferred income tax asset at 12/31/X2 would be recognized as $34,000, computed as $61,200 ($180,000 × 34%) minus the valuation allowance of $27,200 ($80,000 × 34%).

However, by implementing the income tax planning strategy, the deferred income tax asset is calculated as follows:

Taxable income for 20X3:	
Expected amount without reversal of taxable temporary differences	$ 20,000
Reversal of taxable temporary differences due to tax-planning strategy, net of costs	210,000
	230,000
Net operating loss to be carried forward	(180,000)
Net operating loss expiring unused at 12/31/X3	$ –

The gross deferred income tax asset thus can be recorded at the full benefit amount of $61,200 ($180,000 × 34%). However, a valuation allowance is required for $19,800, representing the net-of-tax effect of the $30,000 in anticipated expenses related to implementation of the strategy. The net deferred income tax asset at 12/31/X1 is $41,400 ($61,200 – $19,800). Kruse Company will also recognize a deferred income tax liability of $81,600 at the end of 20X2 (34% of the taxable temporary differences of $240,000).

The adequacy of the valuation allowance must be assessed at the date of each statement of financial position. Adjustments to the amount of the valuation allowance are recorded by a charge against, or a credit to, current earnings, via the current period income tax expense or benefit. Thus, even if the gross amount of future deductible temporary differences has remained constant during a year, income tax expense for that year might be increased or decreased as a consequence of reassessing the adequacy of the valuation allowance at year-end. It is important that these two computational steps be separately addressed:

- First, the computation of the gross deferred income tax assets (the product of the expected effective income tax rate and the total amount of future deductible temporary differences) must be made.
- Second, the amount of the valuation allowance to be provided to offset the deferred income tax asset must be assessed (using the criteria set forth above).

Although changes in both the deferred income tax asset and valuation allowance affect current period income tax expense, the processes of measuring these two amounts are distinct. Furthermore, ASC 740 requires disclosure of both the gross deferred income tax asset (and also the gross deferred income tax liability) and the change in the valuation allowance for the year. These disclosure requirements underline the need to separately measure these items without offsetting.

Changes in a Valuation Allowance for an Acquired Entity's Deferred Income Tax Asset ASC 805 has specific requirements for the acquirer to recognize changes in a valuation allowance for an acquiree's deferred income tax asset. (ASC 740-10-45-20) Also see the chapter on ASC 805 for more detail.

Subsequent Recognition of New Information Affecting Measurement of Tax Positions

Judgments regarding initial recognition and measurement should not be changed based on a reevaluation or reinterpretation of information that was available or should have been available in previous reporting periods. Only if new information becomes available can a new judgment be made. Management's new judgment is to consider the facts, circumstances, and information available at that time. Final certainty is not necessary for this purpose; that is, the position does not have to be subject to final settlement, court ruling, or full resolution to be remeasured. (ASC 740-10-35-2)

Tax positions recognized in previous periods that no longer meet the more-likely-than-not criterion should be reversed ("derecognized," in FASB terminology) in the first period in which that criterion is no longer met. Importantly, it is not permitted that this be accomplished through the use of a valuation account or allowance to offset the recorded benefit; rather, it must be recorded as a direct reversal of the previously recorded benefit. (ASC 740-10-40-2)

The accounting to record a change in judgment depends on whether the amount subject to change had been previously recognized in a prior annual period or in a prior interim period of the same fiscal year.

The effects of changes in tax positions taken in prior annual periods (including related interest and penalties, if any) are to be recognized as a "discrete item" in earnings in the period of change. Although the term "discrete item" is not defined or explained, the intent is for the change to be reported and disclosed in the same manner as the effects of a change in the enacted tax rate. (ASC 740-10-40-4) This entails charging or crediting income from continuing operations for the period of change. Presumably, this would not require a separate line item on the face of the income statement (which would give disproportionate attention to the item), but would require separate disclosure in the notes to the financial statements as a significant component of income tax expense attributable to continuing operations, as specified in ASC 740.

Changes occurring in interim periods are accounted for differently. A change in judgment that applies to a tax position taken in a previous interim period of the current fiscal year is considered an integral part of the annual reporting period. Consequently, the effects of the change are recognized prospectively, through an adjustment to the estimated annual effective tax rate, in accordance with ASC 270 and ASC 740-270-35-6.

Tax Law Changes

General Rules The balance-sheet-oriented measurement approach of ASC 740 makes it necessary to reevaluate the deferred income tax asset and liability balances at each year-end. If changes to income tax rates or other provisions of the income tax law (e.g., deductibility of items) are enacted, the effect of these changes must be recognized so that the deferred income tax assets and liabilities are fairly presented on the statement of financial position. (ASC 740-10-35-4) Any offsetting adjustments are made through the current period's income tax expense or benefit on the income statement; that is, current income tax expense or benefit reflects the income tax effect of current transactions and the revision of previously provided income tax effects for transactions which have yet to reverse.

When income tax rates are revised, this may impact not only the unreversed effects of items that were originally reported in the continuing operations section of the income statement, but also the unreversed effects of items first presented as discontinued operations or in other income statement captions. Furthermore, the impact of changes in income tax rates on the accumulated balance of deferred income tax assets or liabilities that arose through charges or credits to other comprehensive income (under ASC 220) is included in income tax expense associated with continuing operations.

For example, if an entity has unrealized gains on holding available-for-sale securities at a time when relevant income tax rates (presumably, the capital gains rates) are lowered, the reduction in the deferred income tax liability associated with these unrealized gains will reduce current period income tax expense associated with continuing operations, despite the fact that the income tax provision was originally reported in other comprehensive income (not net income) and in the equity section of the statement of financial position as accumulated other comprehensive income.

Entities are permitted to reclassify from accumulated other comprehensive income to actual earnings stranded tax effects from the Tax Cuts and Jobs Act. This provision does not affect other changes in tax law. (ASC 220-10-45-12A)

Enactment Occurring During an Interim Period When income tax law changes occur during an interim reporting period, the effects are reported in the interim period in which enactment occurs. (ASC 740-10-45-15) The effects of the changes are included in continuing operations, whatever the source of the temporary differences being impacted. For example, if in the first fiscal quarter of a year an entity accrued a loss relating to discontinued operations, which is not tax deductible until realized, the income tax effect would be shown in the discontinued operations section of the income statement for that quarter. If income tax rates are changed in the third quarter of the same year, the deferred income tax asset recognized in connection with the loss from discontinued operations would then need to be adjusted upward or downward, based on the difference between the newly enacted income tax rates and the previously effective income tax rates. The income statement effect of this adjustment is included with income tax expense pertaining to income from continuing operations in the third quarter.

Leveraged Leases When a change in the income tax law is enacted, all components of a leveraged lease must be recalculated from the inception of the lease based upon the revised after-tax cash flows resulting from the change. For more guidance on the income tax aspects of leases, see the chapter on ASC 840.

Reporting the Effect of Tax Status Changes

The reporting of changes in an entity's income tax status is entirely analogous to the reporting of newly enacted income tax rate changes. Such adjustments typically arise from a change from (or to) taxable status to (or from) "flow through" or nontaxable status. When a previously taxable C corporation elects to become a flow-through entity (an S corporation), the stockholders become personally liable for income taxes on the company's earnings. This liability occurs whether the earnings are distributed to them or not, similar to the taxation of partnerships and limited liability companies.

When the income tax status change becomes effective, the effect of any consequent adjustments to deferred income tax assets and liabilities is reported in current income tax expense. This is always included in the income tax provision relating to continuing operations. (ASC 740-10-45-19)

Under ASC 740, deferred income taxes are eliminated by reversal through current period income tax expense. Thus, if an entity with a net deferred income tax liability elects S corporation status, it will report an income tax benefit in the continuing operations section of its current income statement.

Similarly, if an S corporation elects to convert to a C corporation, the effect is to assume a net income tax benefit or obligation for unreversed temporary differences existing at the date the change becomes effective. Accordingly, the financial statements for the period in which the change becomes effective will include the effects of the event in current income tax expense. For example, if the entity has unreversed future taxable temporary differences at the date its income tax status change became effective, it reports income tax expense for that period. Conversely, if it had unreversed future deductible temporary differences, a deferred income tax asset (subject to the effects of any valuation allowance necessitated by applying the more-likely-than-not criterion) would be recorded, with a corresponding credit to the current period's income tax expense or benefit in the income statement. Any entity eliminating an existing deferred income tax asset or liability, or recording an initial deferred income tax asset or liability, must fully explain the nature of the events that transpired to cause this adjustment. This is disclosed in the notes to the financial statements for the reporting period.

S corporation elections may be made prospectively at any time during the year preceding the tax year in which the election is intended to be effective and retroactively up to the 16th day of the 3rd month of the tax year in which the election is intended to be effective. The IRS normally informs the electing corporation of whether or not its election has been accepted within 60 days of filing. In practice, however, the IRS seldom denies a timely filed election, and such elections are considered essentially automatic. Consequently, if a reporting entity files an election before the end of its current fiscal year to be effective at the start of the following year, it is logical that the income tax effects would be reported in current year income. For example, an election by a C corporation to become an S corporation that is filed in December 20X1, to be effective at the beginning of the company's next fiscal year, January 1, 20X1, would give rise to the elimination of the deferred income tax assets and liabilities at the date of filing, the effect of which would be reported in the 20X2 financial statements. No deferred income tax assets or liabilities would appear on the December 31, 20X1, statement of financial position, and income tax expense or benefit for 20X2 would include the effects of the reversals of deferred income tax assets and liabilities that had been previously recognized.

There are two situations that could result in an S corporation continuing to recognize deferred income taxes. The first situation arises when the S corporation operates in one or more states that impose state income taxes on the S corporation in an amount that is material to the financial statements. In this situation, the S corporation should compute and recognize deferred state income tax assets and liabilities in the same manner that a C corporation recognizes them for federal income taxes.

The second situation is referred to as "built-in gains tax." Under current income tax law, a C corporation electing to become an S corporation may have built-in gains, which could result in a future corporate income tax liability, under defined circumstances. In such cases the reporting entity, even though it has become an S corporation, will continue to report a deferred income tax liability related to this built-in gain.

Reporting the Effect of Accounting Changes for Income Tax Purposes

Occasionally an entity will initiate or be required to adopt changes in accounting that affect income tax reporting, but which will not impact financial statement reporting. Past examples have included the change to the direct write-off method of bad debt recognition (mandated by a change in the income tax law, while the GAAP requirement to recognize an allowance for uncollectible accounts receivable continued in effect for financial reporting); and the adoption of uniform capitalization for valuing inventory for income tax purposes, while continuing to currently expense certain administrative costs not inventoriable under GAAP for financial reporting. Generally, these mandated changes involve two distinct types of temporary differences.

The first of these changes is the onetime, catch-up adjustment which either immediately or over a prescribed time period impacts the income tax basis of the asset or liability in question (net receivables or inventory, in the examples above), and which then reverses as these assets or liabilities are later realized or settled and are eliminated from the statement of financial position. The second change is the ongoing differential in the amount of newly acquired assets or incurred liabilities recognized for income tax and financial reporting purposes; these differences also eventually reverse, when the inventory is ultimately sold or the receivables are ultimately collected. This second type of change is the normal temporary difference that has already been discussed. It is the first type of change that differs from those previously discussed in this chapter, and that will now be illustrated.

Example of Adjustment for Prospective Catch-Up Adjustment Due to Change in Tax Accounting

Blakey Corporation has, at December 31, 20X1, accrued interest of $80,000 on its long-term debt. Also assume that expected future taxes will be at a 34% rate and that, effective January 1, 20X2, the income tax law is revised to eliminate deductions for accrued but unpaid interest with existing accruals to be taken into income ratably over four years (referred to in tax vernacular as "a four-year spread"). A statement of financial position of Blakey Corporation prepared on January 1, 20X2, would report:

- A deferred income tax *asset* in the amount of $27,200 (i.e., $80,000 × 34%, which is the income tax effect of future deductions that Blakey will be entitled to take over the succeeding four years for the amount of interest that had been accrued and unpaid at the effective date of the tax law change, taken when specific receivables are written off and bad debts are incurred for income tax purposes);
- A current income tax liability of $6,800 (one-fourth of the income tax obligation); and a noncurrent income tax liability of $20,400 (three-fourths of the tax income obligation).

The deferred income tax asset is *not* deemed to be identified with the liability, accrued interest (if it were, it would all be reported as a current asset), but rather with the future specific tax benefits expected to be realized from recognizing 25% of the accrual as a deduction in each of the next four years. Accordingly, the deferred income tax asset is categorized as current and noncurrent according to Blakey Corporation's best estimate of the timing of those future income tax benefits.

Deferred Income Tax Effects of Changes in the Fair Value of Debt and Equity Securities

Unrealized gains or losses on holdings of marketable securities are not recognized for income tax purposes until realized through a sale. Thus, the gains or losses that are included in the financial statements (either in the income statement or in other comprehensive income) are temporary differences under ASC 740-10-25-18, et seq. The income tax effects of all temporary differences are recognized in the financial statements as deferred income tax assets or deferred income tax liabilities, with an additional requirement that an allowance be provided for deferred income tax assets that more likely than not will not be realized. Accordingly, adjustments to the carrying value of debt or equity investments for changes in fair value will give rise to deferred income taxes, as will any recognition of "other-than-temporary" declines in the value of debt securities being held to maturity.

For gains or losses recognized in connection with holdings of investments classified as trading, since the fair value changes are recognized in net income currently, the deferred income tax effects of those changes will also be presented in the income statement.

Example of Deferred Income Taxes on Investments in Debt Securities

Odessa Corp. purchased Zeta Company bonds for the purpose of short-term speculation, at a cost of $100,000. At year-end, the bonds had a fair value of $75,000. Odessa has a 40% effective income tax rate. The entries to record the fair value adjustment and the related income tax effect are:

Loss on holding of trading securities	25,000	
Investment in debt securities—trading portfolios		25,000
Deferred income tax benefit	10,000	
Provision for income taxes		10,000

On the other hand, if the investment in Zeta Company bonds had been classified (at the date of acquisition, or subsequently if the intentions had been revised) as available-for-sale, the adjustment to fair value would have been reported in other comprehensive income, and not included in net income. Accordingly, the income tax effect of the adjustment would also have been included in other comprehensive income. The entries would have been as follows:

Unrealized loss on securities—available-for-sale	25,000	
Investment in debt securities—available-for-sale (OCI)		25,000
Deferred income tax benefit	10,000	
Unrealized loss on securities—available-for-sale (OCI)		10,000

Finally, if the investment in Zeta Company bonds had been made with the intention and ability to hold to maturity, recognition of the decline in value would have depended upon whether it was judged to be temporary or other than temporary in nature. If the former, no recognition would be given to the decline, and hence there would be no deferred income tax effect either. If deemed to be other than temporary, the investment would need to be written down, with the loss included in net income. Accordingly, the income tax effect would also be reported in the income statement. The entries would be as follows:

Loss on decline of securities—held-to-maturity	25,000	
Investment in debt securities—held-to-maturity		25,000
Deferred income tax benefit	10,000	
Provision for income taxes		10,000

An other-than-temporary decline in value in debt securities available for sale would also have been recognized in net income (not merely in other comprehensive income), and accordingly the income tax effect of that loss would have been reported in net income.

As with all other transactions or events giving rise to deferred income tax assets, an evaluation must be made as to whether the entity would be more likely than not to ultimately realize the income tax benefit so recorded. To the extent that it was concluded that some or all of the deferred income tax asset would not be realized, an allowance would be recorded, with the offset being either to the current income tax provision (if the income tax effect of the timing difference was reported in net income) or to OCI (if the income tax effect had been reported there).

Deferred income taxes will also be recorded in connection with unrealized gains recognized due to changes in the fair value of debt or equity investments. Deferred income tax liabilities will be reported in the statement of financial position, and the corresponding income tax provision will be reported in the income statement (for fair value gains arising from holdings of securities in the trading portfolio) or in other comprehensive income (for fair value changes relative to available-for-sale investments).

A number of specialized issues arising in connection with short-term (or other) investments are addressed in the following paragraphs.

Tax Allocation for Business Investments There are two basic methods for accounting for investments in the common stock of other corporations:

1. the fair value method as set forth in ASC 320 and ASC 321 when implemented, and
2. the equity method, as prescribed by ASC 323.

The cost method is not appropriate, except for the rare situation when fair value information is absolutely unavailable. If the cost method is used, however, there will be no deferred income tax consequence, since this conforms to the method prescribed for income tax reporting.

Under both the cost and fair value methods, ordinary income is recognized as dividends received by the investor, and capital gains (losses) are recognized upon the disposal of the investment. For income tax purposes, no provision is made during the holding period for the allocable undistributed earnings of the investee. There is no deferred income tax computation necessary when using the cost method, because there is no temporary difference.

Under the equity method, the investment is recorded at cost and subsequently increased by the allocable portion of the investee's net income. The investor's share of the investee's net income is then included in the investor's pretax accounting income. Dividend payments are not included in pretax accounting income but instead are considered to be a reduction in the carrying amount of the investment. For income tax purposes, however, dividends received are the only revenue realized by the investor. As a result, the investor must recognize deferred income tax expense on the undistributed net income of the investee that will be taxed in the future. The current effective GAAP in this area consists of ASC 740-30 and ASC 740-10.

Summary of Temporary Differences of Investees and Subsidiaries

Level of Ownership Interest	0% — <20%	50%	>80%	100%
Accounting				
Income recognition	Fair value method	Equity method		
Deferred income tax on undistributed earnings	No temporary difference	Temporary difference		No temporary difference
Income tax				
Dividends recognized	30% of dividends received (70% deduction)	20% of dividends received (80% deduction)		None (100% deduction)

Asset Acquisitions Outside of a Business Combination

ASC 740-10-25 provides that in situations where an acquiring entity makes an asset acquisition:

- When management recognizes a reduction in the reporting entity's valuation allowance that directly results from the asset acquisition, the reduction should not enter into the accounting for the asset acquisition. The acquiring entity should reduce the valuation allowance and either recognize the reduction:
  - As an income tax benefit, or
  - As a credit to contributed capital if related to items such as employee stock options, dividends on unallocated ESOP shares, or certain quasi-reorganizations.
- Any income tax uncertainties existing at the date of acquisition should be accounted for in accordance with ASC 740-10-45-23.
  (Also see 805-740-30-3)

ASC 740-20, *Intraperiod Income Tax Allocation*

ASC 740-10 deals with most requirements of interperiod income tax allocation (i.e., deferred income tax accounting). ASC 740-20 provides guidance on the allocation of intraperiod income tax expenses or benefits for a period to:

- Continuing operations
- Discontinued operations
- Other comprehensive income
- Items charged or credited directly to shareholders' equity
  (ASC 740-20-05-2)

The general principle is that the income statement presentation of the effects of income taxes should be the same as items to which the income taxes relate. A "with and without" approach is prescribed as the mechanism by which the marginal, or incremental income tax effects of items other than those arising from continuing operations are to be measured.

ASC 740-20 prescribes an incremental calculation of income tax expense to be allocated to classifications other than continuing operations. However, rather than applying successive allocations on the "with and without" basis to determine income tax expense or benefit applicable to each succeeding income statement caption, the income tax effects of all items other than continuing operations are allocated pro rata. That is, once income tax expense or benefit allocable to continuing operations is determined, the residual income tax expense or benefit is apportioned to all the other classifications (discontinued operations, et al.) in the ratios that those other items bear, on a pretax basis, to the total of all such items. (ASC 740-20-45-14) Furthermore, income tax expense or benefit on income from continuing operations includes not only income taxes on the income earned from continuing operations, as expected, but also the following items:

- The impact of changes in income tax laws and rates.
- The impact of changes in the entity's taxable status.
- Changes in estimates about the realization of deferred tax assets in future years.
- The income tax effects of tax-deductible dividends paid to stockholders.
  (ASC 740-20-45-8)

Under ASC 740, stockholders' equity is charged or credited directly with the initial income tax effects of items that are reported in stockholders' equity without being presented on the income statement. These items include the following:

- Corrections of the effects of accounting errors of previous periods.
- Gains and losses that are defined under GAAP as being part of comprehensive income but are not reported in the income statement, such as foreign currency translation adjustments under ASC 830, and the fair value adjustments applicable to available-for-sale portfolios of debt and marketable equity securities held as investments. As per ASC 220, the income tax effects of these types of items will be reported in the same financial statement where other comprehensive income items are reported. These items may be reported either in a stand-alone statement of comprehensive income, or a combined statement of income and other comprehensive income, or in an expanded version of the statement of changes in stockholders' equity.
- Taxable or deductible increases or decreases in contributed capital, such as offering costs reported under GAAP as reductions of the proceeds of a capital stock offering, but which are either immediately deductible or amortizable for income tax purposes.
- Increases in the income tax bases of assets and liabilities caused by shareholder transactions. Note: In subsequent periods, changes in the valuation allowance are included in the income statement.
- Deductible temporary differences and net operating loss and tax credit carryforwards that existed at the date of a quasi-reorganization.
  (ASC 740-20-45-11)

The effects of income tax rate or other income tax law changes on items for which the income tax effects were originally reported directly in stockholders' equity are reported in continuing operations, if they occur in any period after the original event.

Comprehensive Example of the Intraperiod Income Tax Allocation Process

Assume $50,000 in future deductible temporary differences at 12/31/X2; these differences remain unchanged during the current year, 20X3.

	20X3
Income from continuing operations	$ 400,000
Loss from discontinued operations	(120,000)
Correction of error: understatement of depreciation in 20X2	(20,000)
Income tax credits	5,000

Income tax rates are: 15% on the first $100,000 of taxable income; 20% on the next $100,000; 25% on the next $100,000; 30% thereafter.

Expected future effective income tax rates were 20% at December 31, 20X2, but are judged to be 28% at December 31, 20X3.

Retained earnings at December 31, 20X2, were $650,000. Intraperiod tax allocation proceeds as follows:

Step 1—Income tax on total taxable income of $320,000 ($460,000 – $120,000 – $20,000) is $61,000 computed as follows:

Taxable income	*Income tax rate*	*Income tax*
$100,000	15%	$15,000
100,000	20%	20,000

Taxable income	*Income tax rate*	*Income tax*	
100,000	25%	25,000	
20,000	30%	6,000	
$320,000		$66,000	Income tax before credits
		(5,000)	Tax credit
		$61,000	Income tax payable

Step 2—Income tax on income from continuing operations of $400,000 is $85,000, net of tax credit computed as follows.

Taxable income	*Income tax rate*	*Income tax*	
$100,000	15%	$ 15,000	
100,000	20%	20,000	
100,000	25%	25,000	
160,000	30%	30,000	
$460,000		$108,000	Income tax before credits
		(5,000)	Tax credit
		$103,000	Income tax payable

Step 3—The $42,000 difference is allocated pro rata to discontinued operations, unusual gain, and correction of the error in prior year depreciation as follows:

	Gross amount before tax	*Relative %*	*Allocation of difference*
Discontinued operations	$(120,000)	150%	$36,000
Error correction	(20,000)	25%	6,000
	$ (80,000)	100%	$42.000

Step 4—The adjustment of the deferred income tax asset, amounting to a $4,000 increase due to an effective tax rate estimate change [$50,000 × (.28 – .20)], is allocated to continuing operations, regardless of the source of the temporary difference.

A summary combined statement of income and retained earnings for 20X3 is presented below:

Income from continuing operations, before income taxes		$460,000
Income taxes on income from continuing operations:		
Current	$108,000	
Deferred	(4,000)	
Tax credits	(5,000)	99,000
Income from continuing operations, net		361,000
Loss from discontinued operations, net of income tax benefit of $36,000		(84,000)
Net income		277,000
Retained earnings, January 1, 20X3, as originally reported		650,000
Correction of accounting error, net of income tax effects of $6,000		(14,000)
Retained earnings, January 1, 20X3, as restated		636,000
Retained earnings, December 31, 20X3		$913,000

This example does not include items that will, under the provisions of ASC 220, be reported in other comprehensive income.

ASC 740-30, *Other Consideration or Special Areas*

Undistributed Earnings of a Subsidiary These accounting requirements are set forth in ASC 740-30. While the timing of distribution of a subsidiary's net income to its parent may be uncertain, it will eventually occur, whether by means of dividends, or via the disposal of the entity and realization of capital gains. Accordingly, deferred income taxes must be provided, but the amount will be dependent upon the anticipated means of realization, which of course may change over time. (ASC 740-30-25-3)

The magnitude of the income tax effects to be provided depends upon specific application of the income tax laws and management intent. (ASC 740-30-05-5) If the law provides a mechanism under which the parent can recover its investment tax-free, deferred income taxes are not provided. For example, under §332 of the IRC, a parent corporation can liquidate an 80%-or-more-owned subsidiary without recognizing gain or loss for income tax purposes. Also, under IRC §368, a parent can effect a statutory merger or consolidation with its 80%-or-more- owned subsidiary, under which no taxable gain or loss would be recognized.

In other cases, the minimization or avoidance of income taxes can be achieved only if the parent company owns a stipulated share of the subsidiary's stock. A parent owning less than this threshold level of its subsidiary may express its intent to utilize a tax planning strategy to acquire the necessary additional shares to realize this benefit. In evaluating this strategy, the cost of acquiring the additional shares must be considered, and the benefits to be recognized (i.e., a reduced deferred income tax liability) must be offset by the cost of implementing the strategy as discussed earlier in this chapter.

A distinction exists in the application of ASC 740-30 between differences in income tax and financial reporting basis that are considered "inside basis differences" versus "outside basis differences," and this is clarified by ASC 830-740-25. Certain countries' income tax laws allow periodic revaluation of long-lived assets to reflect the effects of inflation with the offsetting credit recorded as equity for income tax purposes. Because this is an internal adjustment that does not result from a transaction with third parties, the additional basis is referred to as "inside basis." ASC 830-740-25 indicates that the ASC 740-30 indefinite reversal criteria only apply to "outside basis differences," and not to "inside basis differences" arising in connection with ownership of foreign subsidiaries. Therefore, a deferred income tax liability is to be provided on the amount of the increased inside basis.

Certain foreign countries tax corporate income at rates that differ depending on whether the income is distributed as dividends or retained by the corporation. Upon subsequent distribution of the accumulated earnings, the taxpayer receives a tax credit or refund for the difference between the two rates. In the consolidated financial statements of a parent company, the future income tax credit and the deferred income tax effects related to dividends that will be paid in the future are recognized based on the distributed rate if the parent provided for deferred income taxes because it did not invoke the indefinite reversal criteria of ASC 740-30. If the parent did not provide for deferred income taxes as a result of applying the ASC 740-30 criterion, the undistributed rate should be used. (ASC 740-10-25) The treatment of the tax credit in the separate financial statements of the foreign company is discussed later in this chapter in the section titled "Separate Financial Statements of Subsidiaries or Investees."

Undistributed Earnings of an Investee When an entity has an equity method investee, it is presumed to be able to exercise significant influence, but lack control. Because the ability to indefinitely postpone income taxes on the investee's net income would be absent in such a case, in contrast to the parent-subsidiary situation above, GAAP requires full interperiod income tax allocation for the effects of undistributed investee net income. (ASC 740-30-25-15) The facts and circumstances involved in each situation, however, will be the final determinant of whether this temporary difference is assumed to be a future dividend or a capital gain for purposes of computing the deferred income tax effect.

Example of Income Tax Effects from Investee Company

To illustrate the application of these concepts, assume Investor Company owns 30% of the outstanding common stock of Investee Company and 70% of the outstanding common stock of Subsidiary Company. Additional data for Subsidiary and Investee companies for the year 20X1 are as follows:

	Investee Company	Subsidiary Company
Net income	$50,000	$100,000
Dividends paid	20,000	60,000

The following sections illustrate how the foregoing data are used to recognize the income tax effects of the stated events.

The pretax accounting income of Investor Company will include its equity in Investee Company net income equal to $15,000 ($50,000×30%). Investor's taxable income, on the other hand, will include dividend income of $6,000 ($20,000×30%), reduced by a deduction of 80% of the $6,000, or $4,800. This 80% dividends-received deduction is a permanent difference between pretax accounting income and taxable income and is allowed for dividends received from domestic corporations in which the taxpaying corporation's ownership is less than 80% but at least 20%. A lower dividends-received deduction of 70% is permitted when the ownership is less than 20%, and a 100% deduction is provided for dividends received from domestic corporations in which the ownership is 80% to 100%.

In this example, a temporary difference results from Investor's equity ($9,000) in Investee's undistributed income of $30,000 (= $50,000 net income less $20,000 dividends). The amount of the deferred income tax credit in 20X1 depends upon the expectations of Investor Company regarding the manner in which the $9,000 of undistributed income will be realized. If the expectation of receipt is via dividends, then the temporary difference is 20% (the net taxable portion, after the dividends-received deduction) of $9,000, or $1,800, and the deferred income tax liability associated with this temporary difference in 20X2 is the expected effective income tax rate times $1,800. However, if the expectation is that receipt will be through future sale of the investment, then the temporary difference is the full $9,000 and the deferred income tax liability is the current corporate capital gains rate times the $9,000.

The entries below illustrate these alternatives. An assumed tax rate of 34% is used for ordinary income, while a rate of 20% is used for capital gains. It is also assumed that there are no pre-20X2 temporary differences to consider. Note that the amounts in the entries below relate only to Investee Company's incremental impact upon Investor Company's income tax assets and liabilities.

	Expectations for undistributed income			
	Dividends		Capital gains	
Income tax expense	1,020		2,208	
Deferred income tax liability		612[b]		1,800[b]
Income taxes payable		408[a]		408[a]

[a]*Computation of income taxes payable*:

[b]*Dividend income—30% × ($20,000)*	*$ 6,000*
Less 80% dividends-received deduction	*(4,800)*
Amount included in Investor's taxable income	*$ 1,200*
Tax liability—34% × ($1,200)	*$ 408*

	Expectations for undistributed income	
	Dividends	*Capital gains*
[b]Computation of deferred income tax liability (dividend assumption):		
Temporary difference:		
Investor's share of undistributed income—30% × ($50,000 – $20,000 = $30,000)		*$ 9,000*
Less 80% dividends-received deduction		*(7,200)*
Temporary difference		*$ 1,800*
[a]Deferred income tax liability—34% × ($1,800)		*$ 612*
[c]Computation of deferred income tax liability (capital gain assumption):		
Temporary difference:		
Investor's share of undistributed income— same as above		*$ 9,000*
Deferred income tax liability—20% × ($9,000)		*$ 1,800*

Example of Income Tax Effects from a Subsidiary

The pretax accounting income of Investor Company will also include equity in Subsidiary income of $70,000 (70% × $100,000). This $70,000 will be included in consolidated pretax income in Investor's consolidated financial statements. For income tax purposes, Investor and Subsidiary cannot file a consolidated income tax return because the minimum level of control (i.e., 80%) is not present. Consequently, the taxable income of Investor will include dividend income of $42,000 (70% × $60,000), and there will be an 80% dividends-received deduction of $33,600. The temporary difference discussed in ASC 740-30 results from Investor's 70% equity ($28,000) in Subsidiary's undistributed earnings of $40,000. The amount of the deferred income tax liability in 20X1 depends upon the expectations of Investor Company as to the manner in which this $28,000 of undistributed income will be received. The same expectations can exist as previously discussed for Investor's equity in Investee's undistributed earnings (i.e., through future dividend distributions or capital gains).

The entries below illustrate these alternatives. A marginal tax rate of 34% is assumed for dividend income, and a rate of 20% applies to capital gains. It is also assumed that there are no pre-20X2 temporary differences to consider. The amounts in the entries below relate only to Subsidiary Company's incremental impact upon Investor Company's income tax assets and liabilities.

	Expectations for undistributed income			
	Capital gains		*Capital gains*	
Income tax expense	4,760		8,456	
Deferred income tax liability		1,904		5,600
Income taxes payable		2,856[a]		2,856[a]
[a]Computation of income taxes payable:				
Dividend income—70% × ($60,000)				*$ 42,000*
Less 80% dividends-received deduction				*(33,600)*
Amount included in Investor's taxable income				*$ 8,400*
Tax liability—34% × ($8,400)				*$ 2,856[b]*
Computation of deferred income tax liability (dividend assumption):				
Temporary difference:				*$ 28,000*
Investor's share of undistributed income— 70% × ($40,000)				*(22,400)*
Less 80% dividend-received deduction (22,400)				*$ 5,600*

	Expectations for undistributed income	
	Capital gains	*Capital gains*
Deferred income tax liability—34% × ($5,600)		*$ 1,904*
[c]*Computation of deferred income tax liability (capital gain assumption):*		
Temporary difference:		
Investor's share of undistributed income—70% × ($40,000)		*$ 28,000*
Deferred income tax liability—20% × ($28,000)		*$ 5,600*

If a company owns 80% or more of the voting stock of a subsidiary and consolidates the subsidiary for both financial reporting and income tax purposes, then no temporary differences exist between consolidated pretax income and taxable income. If, in the circumstances noted above, consolidated financial statements are prepared but a consolidated income tax return is not, IRC §243 allows the Investor to take a 100% dividends-received deduction. Accordingly, the temporary difference between consolidated pretax income and taxable income is zero if the Investor assumes the undistributed income will be realized in dividends.

ASC 740-270, *Accounting for Income Taxes in Interim Periods*

Basic Rules The appropriate perspective for interim period reporting is to view the interim period as an integral part of the year, rather than as a discrete period. This objective is usually achieved by projecting income for the full annual period, computing the income tax thereon, and applying the "effective rate" to the interim period income or loss, with quarterly (or monthly) revisions to the expected annual results and the income tax effects thereof, as necessary.

As discussed in more detail below, this subtopic addresses:

- Recognizing the income tax benefits of interim losses based on expected net income of later interim or annual periods,
- Reporting the benefits of net operating loss carryforwards in interim periods, and
- Reporting the effects of income tax law changes in interim periods.

The computation of interim period income tax expense should be consistent with the asset and liability method used in the computation of the annual income tax expense.

The term "ordinary income" as used in ASC 740-270 is not used in the same way as in the income tax law to distinguish capital gains, for example, from operating income and deductions. The ASC 740-270 definition of "ordinary income" is, formulaically:

Pretax income or loss from continuing operations

+ /– Discontinued operations

+ /– Cumulative effects of changes in accounting principle

+ /– Significant unusual or infrequently occurring items

"Ordinary income" is used as the denominator in calculating an effective income tax rate to be used to compute income tax expense currently payable for the interim period. (ASC 740-270-25-2) Note that pretax income is *not* adjusted for the effects of permanent or temporary differences.

Below is a relatively simple example that illustrates these basic principles.

Basic Example of Interim Period Accounting for Income Taxes

Boffa, Inc. estimates that pretax accounting income for the full fiscal year ending June 30, 20X2, will be $400,000. Boffa does not expect to have any of the items that would adjust its "ordinary income" as defined above either at year-end or during any of its interim quarters. The company expects that it will incur $60,000 of meals and entertainment expenses, of which 50% are nondeductible under the current tax law; the annual premium on an officer's life insurance policy is $12,000; and dividend income (from a less than 20% ownership interest) is expected to be $100,000. The company recognized income of $75,000 in the first quarter of the year. The deferred income tax liability arises solely in connection with property and equipment temporary differences; these differences totaled $150,000 at the beginning of the year and are projected to equal $280,000 at year-end after taking into account expected acquisitions and disposals for the remainder of the fiscal year. The graduated statutory income tax rate schedule is provided below. Boffa management used a future expected effective income tax rate of 34% to compute the beginning deferred income tax liability and does not anticipate changing that percentage at the end of the fiscal year. The change in the future taxable temporary difference during the first quarter is $30,000.

Boffa must first calculate its estimated effective income tax rate for the year. This rate is computed using all of the tax planning alternatives available to the company (e.g., tax credits, foreign rates, capital gains rates, etc.).

Estimated annual pretax accounting income (and "ordinary income" as defined in ASC 740-270)		$ 400,000
Permanent differences:		
Add: Nondeductible officers' life insurance premium	$12,000	
Nondeductible meals and entertainment	30,000	42,000
		442,000
Less: Dividends-received deduction ($100,000 × 70%)		(70,000)
		372,000
Less: Change in future taxable temporary difference		(130,000)
Estimated taxable income for the year		$ 242,000
Annual current tax on estimated taxable income (see below)		$ 70,530
Effective income tax rate for *current* income tax expense (computed as a percentage of "ordinary income") $70,530/400,000		17.6%

Tax rate schedule

At least	*Not more than*	*Rate*	*Taxable income*	*Tax*
$–	$50,000	15%	$50,000	$ 7,500
50,000	75,000	25%	25,000	6,250
75,000	–	34%	167,000	56,780
				$70,530

Computation of the first quarter current income tax expense:

"Ordinary income" for first quarter	$75,000
Estimated annual effective income tax rate per above	× 17.6%
	$13,200

This amount can be "proven" as follows:

Annualized current tax computed above	$70,530
Portion of annual tax attributable to first quarter	
First quarter pretax income as a % of forecast $75,000/$400,000	× 18.75%
Result, materially the same as above	$13,224

Computation of the first quarter deferred income tax expense (same method as year-end).

	Future taxable temporary difference	*Effective tax rate estimated for reversal(s)*	*Computed deferred tax liability*
Property and equipment			
End of first quarter	$180,000	34%	$61,200
Beginning of fiscal year	150,000	34%	51,000
First quarter deferred income tax expense			$10,200

Recap of first quarter income tax expense.

Current	$13,200
Deferred	10,200
Total	$23,400

Finally, the entry necessary to record the income tax expense at the end of the first quarter is as follows:

Income tax expense	23,400	
Income taxes payable—current		13,200
Deferred income tax liability		10,200

In the second quarter, Boffa, Inc. revises its estimate of income for the full fiscal year. It now anticipates only $210,000 of pretax accounting income ("ordinary income"), including only $75,000 of dividend income, because of dramatic changes in the national economy. Other permanent differences are still expected to total $42,000.

Estimated annual pretax accounting income (and "ordinary income" as defined in ASC 740-270)		$ 210,000
Permanent differences:		
Add: Nondeductible officers' life insurance premium	$12,000	
Nondeductible meals and entertainment	30,000	42,000
		252,000
Less: Dividends-received deduction ($75,000 × 70%)		(52,500)
		199,500
Less: Change in future taxable temporary difference		(130,000)
Estimated taxable income for the year		$ 69,500
Annual current tax on estimated taxable income (see below)		$ 12,375
Effective income tax rate for *current* income tax expense (computed as a percentage of "ordinary income" $12,375/$210,000)		5.2%

Tax rate schedule

At least	Not more than	Rate	Taxable income	Tax
$ –	$ 50,000	15%	$50,000	$ 7,500
50,000	75,000	25%	19,500	4,875
			$69,500	$12,375

The actual "ordinary income" for the second quarter was $22,000, and the change in the temporary difference was only an additional $10,000. Income tax expense for the second quarter is computed as follows:

Computation of year-to-date and second quarter current income tax expense (benefit)

"Ordinary income" for the half year ($75,000 + $22,000)	$97,000
Estimated annual effective income tax rate per above	× 5.2%
Year-to-date current income tax expense	$ 5,044
Less: Expense recognized in first quarter	13,200
Current income tax (benefit) for second quarter	$ (8,156)

Computation of year-to-date and second quarter deferred income tax expense (benefit)

	Future taxable temporary difference	Effective tax rate estimated for reversal year(s)	Computed deferred tax liability
Property and equipment			
End of second quarter	$190,000	34%	$64,600
Beginning of fiscal year	150,000	34%	51,000
Year-to-date deferred income tax expense			13,600
Less: Expense recognized in first quarter			10,200
Deferred income tax expense for second quarter			$ 3,400

Recap of second quarter income expense (benefit)

Current	$(8,156)
Deferred	3,400
Total	$ (4,756)

Under ASC 270, and also under the general principle that changes in estimate are reported prospectively (as stipulated by ASC 250), the results of prior quarters are not restated for changes in the estimated effective annual tax rate. Given the current and deferred income tax expense that was recognized in the first quarter, shown above, the following entry is required to record the income taxes as of the end of the second quarter:

Income taxes payable—current	8,156	
Income tax expense (benefit)		4,756
Deferred income tax liability		3,400

The foregoing illustrates the basic problems encountered in applying GAAP to interim reporting. In the following paragraphs, we discuss some of the items requiring modifications to the approach described in the previous example.

Net Operating Losses in Interim Periods ASC 740-270 provides the appropriate accounting when losses are incurred in interim periods or when net operating loss carryforward benefits are realized during an interim reporting period.

Carryforward from prior years The interim accounting for the utilization of a net operating loss carryforward is reflected in one of two ways.

1. If the income tax benefit of the net operating loss is expected to be realized as a result of current year "ordinary income," that income tax benefit is included as an adjustment to the effective annual tax rate computation illustrated above.
2. If the income tax benefit of the net operating loss is not expected to be realized as described in item 1, the benefit is allocated first to reduce year-to-date income tax expense from continuing operations to zero with any excess allocated to other sources of income that would provide the means to utilize the net operating loss (e.g., discontinued operations, etc.).
(ASC 740-270-25-4)

When a valuation allowance is reduced or eliminated because of a revised judgment, the previously unrecognized income tax benefit is included in the income tax expense or benefit of the interim period in which the judgment is revised. An increase in the valuation allowance resulting from a revised judgment would cause a catch-up adjustment to be included in the current interim period's income tax expense from continuing operations. In either situation, the effect of the change in judgment is *not* prorated to future interim periods by means of the effective tax rate estimate. (ASC 740-270-25-7)

Example of Interim-Period Valuation Allowance Adjustments Due to Revised Judgment

Camino Corporation has a previously unrecognized $50,000 net operating loss carryforward—that is, Camino had previously established a full valuation allowance for the deferred income tax asset arising from the net operating loss and thus had not previously recognized any deferred income tax benefit associated with the net operating loss; a flat 40% tax rate for current and future periods is assumed. Income for the full year (before net operating loss) is projected to be $80,000. Consequently, the management of Camino has revised its judgment as to the future realizability of the net operating loss. In the first quarter Camino will report a pretax loss of $10,000:

Projected annual income	$80,000
× Tax rate	40%
Projected tax liability	$32,000

Accordingly, in the income statement for the first fiscal quarter, the pretax operating loss of $10,000 will give rise to an income tax benefit of $10,000 × 40% = $4,000.

In addition, an income tax benefit of $20,000 ($50,000 net operating loss × 40%) is recognized, and is included in the current quarter's income tax benefit relating to continuing operations. Thus, the total income tax benefit for the first fiscal quarter will be $24,000 ($4,000 + $20,000).

If Camino's second quarter results in pretax operating income of $30,000, and the expectation for the full year remains unchanged (i.e., operating income of $80,000), the second quarter income tax expense is $12,000 ($30,000 × 40%).

The income tax provision for the fiscal first half-year will be a benefit of $12,000, as follows:

Cumulative pretax income through second quarter ($30,000 – $10,000)	$ 20,000
× Effective rate	40%
Income tax provision before recognition of net operating loss carryforward benefit	8,000
Benefit of net operating loss carryforward first recognized in first quarter	(20,000)
Total year-to-date tax provision (benefit)	$(12,000)
Consisting of:	
First quarter (benefit)	$(24,000)
Second quarter expense	12,000
Year-to-date benefit, per above	$(12,000)

The foregoing example assumes that during the first quarter Camino's judgment changed as to the full realizability of the previously unrecognized benefit of the $50,000 loss carryforward. Were this not the case, however, the benefit would have been recognized only as actual tax liabilities were incurred (through current period income) in amounts sufficient to offset the net operating loss benefit.

Example of Recognizing Net Operating Loss Carryforward Benefit as Actual Liabilities Are Incurred

To illustrate this latter situation, assume the same facts about net income for the first two quarters, and assume now that Camino's judgment about the realizability of the prior period net operating loss does not change. Tax provisions for the first quarter and first half are as follows:

	First quarter	*First half-year*
Pretax income (loss)	$(10,000)	$20,000
× Effective rate	40%	40%
Tax provision before recognition of net operating loss carryforward benefit	$ (4,000)	$ 8,000
Benefit of net operating loss carryforward recognized	–	(8,000)
Tax provision (benefit)	$ (4,000)	–

Notice that recognition of an income tax benefit of $4,000 in the first quarter is based on the expectation of at least a breakeven full year's results. That is, the benefit of the first quarter's loss was deemed more likely than not. Otherwise, no income tax benefit would have been reported in the first quarter.

Estimated loss for the year When the full year is expected to be profitable, it is irrelevant that one or more interim periods result in a loss, and the expected effective rate for the full year is used to record interim period income tax expense and benefits, as illustrated above. However, when the full year is expected to produce a loss, the computation of the effective annual income tax benefit rate must logically take into account the extent to which a net deferred income tax asset (i.e., the asset less any related valuation allowance) will be recognized at year-end. For the first set of examples, below, assume that the realization of income tax benefits related to net operating loss carryforwards is not entirely more likely than not. That is, the full benefits will be recognized as deferred income tax assets, but those assets will be offset partially or completely by the valuation allowance.

For each of the following examples we will assume that the Gibby Corporation is anticipating a loss of $150,000 for the fiscal year. The company's general ledger currently reflects a deferred income tax liability of $30,000; all of the liability will reverse during the fifteen-year carryforward period. Assume future income taxes will be at a 40% rate.

Example 1 NOL Carryback

Assume that the company can carry back the entire $150,000 net operating loss to the preceding three years. The income tax potentially refundable by the carryback would (remember this is only an estimate until year-end) amount to $48,000 (an assumed amount). The effective rate is then 32% ($48,000/150,000).

	Ordinary income (loss)		*Tax (benefit) expense*		
Reporting period	*Reporting period*	*Year-to-date*	*Year-to-date*	*Less previously provided*	*Reporting period*
1st qtr.	$ (50,000)	$ (50,000)	$(16,000)	$ –	$(16,000)
2nd qtr.	20,000	(30,000)	(9,600)	(16,000)	6,400
3rd qtr.	(70,000)	(100,000)	(32,000)	(9,600)	(22,400)
4th qtr.	(50,000)	(150,000)	(48,000)	(32,000)	(16,400)
Fiscal year	$(150,000)				$(48,000)

Note that both the income tax expense (2nd quarter) and benefit are computed using the estimated annual effective rate. This rate is applied to the year-to-date numbers just as in the previous examples, with any adjustment being made and realized in the current reporting period. This treatment is appropriate because the accrual of income tax benefits in the first, third, and fourth quarters is consistent with the effective rate estimated at the beginning of the year, in contrast to those circumstances in which a change in estimate is made in a quarter relating to the realizability of income tax benefits not previously provided (or benefits for which full or partial valuation allowances were required).

Example 2 NOL Carryback

In this case assume that Gibby Corporation can carry back only $50,000 of the loss and that the remainder must be carried forward. Realization of future taxable income to fully utilize the net operating loss is not deemed to be more likely than not. The estimated carryback of $50,000 would generate an income tax refund of $12,000 (again assumed). The company is assumed to be in the 40% tax bracket (a flat rate is used to simplify the example). Although the benefit of the net operating loss carryforward is recognized, a valuation allowance must be provided to the extent that it is more likely than not that the benefit will not be realized. In this example, management has concluded that only 25% of the gross benefit will be realized in future years. Accordingly, a valuation allowance of $30,000 must be established, leaving a net of $10,000 as an estimated realizable income tax benefit related to the carryforward of the projected loss.

$$\$150{,}000\text{ loss} - \$50{,}000\text{ carried back} = \$100{,}000\text{ net operating loss} \times 40\%\text{ tax rate} =$$
$$\$40{,}000\text{ benefit} \times 75\%\text{ portion deemed unrealizable} = \$30{,}000\text{ valuation allowance}$$

Considered in conjunction with the carryback refund of $12,000, the company will obtain a $22,000 income tax benefit relating to the projected current year loss, for an effective income tax benefit rate of 14.7%. The calculation of the estimated annual effective rate is as follows:

Expected annual net loss			$150,000
Tax benefit from net operating loss carryback		$12,000	
Tax benefit of net operating loss carryforward ($100,000 × 40%)	$ 40,000		
Valuation allowance	(30,000)	10,000	
Total recognized benefit			$ 22,000
Estimated annual effective rate ($22,000 ÷ $150,000)			14.7%

	Ordinary income (loss)		Tax (benefit) expense			
			Year-to-date			
Reporting period	Reporting period	Year-to-date	Computed	Limited to	Less previously provided	Reporting period
1st qtr.	$ 10,000	$ 10,000	$ 1,470	$–	$–	$ 1,470
2nd qtr.	(80,000)	(70,000)	(10,290)	–	1,470	(11,760)
3rd qtr.	(100,000)	(170,000)	(24,990)	(22,000)	(10,290)	(11,710)
4th qtr.	20,000	(150,000)	(22,000)	–	(22,000)	–
Fiscal year	$(150,000)					$(22,000)

In the foregoing, the income tax expense (benefit) is computed by multiplying the year-to-date income or loss by the estimated annual effective rate, and then subtracting the amount of tax expense or benefit already provided in prior interim periods. It makes no difference if the current period indicates an income or a loss, assuming of course that the full-year estimated results are not being revised. However, if the cumulative loss for the interim periods to date exceeds the projected loss for the full year upon which the effective income tax benefit rate had been based, then no further tax benefits can be recorded, as is illustrated above in the benefit for the third quarter.

The foregoing examples cover most of the situations encountered in practice. The reader is referred to ASC 740-270-55 for additional examples.

Operating loss occurring during an interim period An instance may occur in which the company expects net income for the year and incurs a net loss during one of the reporting periods. In this situation, the estimated annual effective rate, which was calculated based upon the expected net income figure, is applied to the year-to-date income or loss to arrive at year-to-date income tax expense. The amount previously provided is subtracted from the year-to-date expense to arrive at the expense for the current reporting period. If the current period operations resulted in a loss, then the period will reflect an income tax benefit.

Income Tax Provision Applicable to Interim Period Nonoperating Items

Unusual or infrequent items Discontinued operations should be shown net of their related income tax effects. Unusual or infrequently occurring items are separately disclosed as a component of pretax income, and the income tax expense or benefit is included in the income tax expense from continuing operations. Presenting these items net of tax is strictly prohibited.

The interim treatment accorded these items does not differ from the fiscal year-end reporting required by GAAP. However, according to ASC 270, these items should not be included in the computation of the estimated effective annual income tax rate. These items should be recognized in the interim period in which they occur rather than being prorated equally throughout the year. Examples of the treatment prescribed by the opinion follow later in this section.

Recognition of the income tax effects of a loss due to any of the aforementioned situations is permitted if the benefits are expected to be realized during the year, or if they will be recognizable as a deferred income tax asset at year-end under the provisions of ASC 740-10. This guidance also applies to a tax benefit from an employee share-based payment award when the deduction for the award for tax purposes exceeds the amount of the cumulative cost of the award recognized for financial reporting purposes. (ASC 740-270-25-12)

If a situation arises where realization is not more likely than not in the period of occurrence but becomes assured in a subsequent period in the same fiscal year, the previously unrecognized income tax benefit is reported in income from continuing operations until it reduces the income tax expense to zero, with any excess reported in those other categories of income (e.g., discontinued operations) which provided a means of realization of the tax benefit.

The following examples illustrate the treatment required for reporting unusual or infrequently occurring items. Again, these items should not be used in calculating the estimated annual tax rate. For income statement presentation, the income tax expense or benefit relating to unusual or infrequently occurring items should be included with ordinary income from continuing operations.

The following data apply to the next two examples:

- Irwin Industries expects fiscal year ending June 30, 20X2, income to be $96,000 and net permanent differences to reduce taxable income by $25,500.
- Irwin Industries also incurred a $30,000 unusual or infrequent loss in the second quarter of the year.

Example 1 Unusual or Infrequent Items

In this case, assume that the loss can be carried back to prior periods and, therefore, the realization of any income tax benefit is assured. Based on the information given earlier, the estimated annual effective income tax rate can be calculated as follows:

Expected pretax accounting income	$ 96,000
Anticipated permanent differences	(25,000)
Expected taxable income	$ 70,000

Example—Income Tax Calculation "Excluding" Unusual or Infrequent Item

$50,000	×	.15 =	$ 7,500
20,500	×	.25 =	5,125
$70,500			$12,625

Effective annual rate $= 13.15\% (\$12{,}625 \div 96{,}000)$

No adjustment in the estimated annual effective rate is required when the unusual or infrequent item occurs. The income tax (benefit) applicable to the item is computed using the estimated fiscal year ordinary income and an analysis of the incremental impact of the unusual or infrequent item. The method illustrated below is applicable when the company anticipates operating income for the year. When a loss is anticipated but realization of benefits of net operating loss carryforwards is not more likely than not, the company computes its estimated annual effective rate based on the amount of tax to be refunded from prior years. The income tax (benefit) applicable to the unusual or infrequent item is then the decrease (increase) in the refund to be received.

Computation of the income tax applicable to the unusual or infrequent item is as follows:

Estimated pretax accounting income	$ 96,000
Permanent differences	(25,500)
Unusual or infrequent item	(30,000)
Expected taxable income	$ 40,500

Example—Income Tax Calculation "Including" Unusual or Infrequent Item

$40,500 × .15 = $ 6,075

Income tax "excluding" unusual or infrequent item	$12,625
Income tax "including" unusual or infrequent item	6,075
Income tax benefit applicable to unusual or infrequent item	$ 6,550

			Income tax (benefit) applicable to				
			Ordinary income (loss)		*Unusual or infrequent item*		
Reporting period	*Ordinary income (loss)*	*Unusual or infrequent item*	*Reporting period*	*Year-to-date*	*Year-to-date*	*Previously provided*	*Reporting period*
1st qtr.	$ 10,000	$ –	$ 1,315	$ 1,315	$ –	$ –	–
2nd qtr.	(20,000)	(30,000)	(2,630)	(1,315)	(6,550)	–	(6,550)
3rd qtr.	40,000	–	5,260	3,945	(6,550)	(6,550)	–
4th qtr.	66,000	–	8,680	12,625	(6,550)	(6,550)	–
Fiscal year	$ 96,000	$(30,000)	$12,625				$ (6,550)

Example 2 Unusual or Infrequent Items

Again, assume that Irwin Industries estimates net income of $96,000 for the year with permanent differences of $25,500 which reduce taxable income. The unusual loss of $30,000 cannot be carried back and the ability to carry it forward is not more likely than not. Because no net deferred income tax assets exist, the only way that the loss can be deemed to be realizable is to the extent that current year ordinary income offsets the effect of the loss. As a result, realization of the loss is assured only as, and to the extent that, there is ordinary income for the year.

			Income tax (benefit) applicable to				
			Ordinary income (loss)		*Unusual or infrequent item*		
Reporting period	*Ordinary income (loss)*	*Unusual or infrequent item*	*Reporting period*	*Year-to-date*	*Year-to-date*	*Previously provided*	*Reporting period*
1st qtr.	$ 10,000	$ –	$ 1,315	$ 1,315	$ –	$ –	$ –
2nd qtr.	20,000	(30,000)	2,630	3,288	(3,288)	–	(3,288)

3rd qtr.	(10,000)	–	(1,315)	1,973	(1,973)[a]	(3,288)	1,315
4th qtr.	81,000	–	10,652	$12,625	(6,550)[a]	(1,973)	(4,577)
Fiscal year	$ 96,000	$(30,000)	12,625				$ (6,550)

a The recognition of the income tax benefit to be realized relative to the unusual or infrequent item is limited to the lesser of the total income tax benefit applicable to the item or the amount available to be realized. Because realization is based upon the amount of income tax applicable to ordinary income during the period, the year-to-date figures for the income tax benefit fluctuate as the year-to-date income tax expense relative to ordinary income fluctuates. Note that at no point does the amount of the income tax benefit exceed what was calculated above as being applicable to the unusual or infrequent item.

Discontinued operations in interim periods Discontinued operations, according to ASC 270, are disclosed in the same way as significant, unusual items. (ASC 740-270-45-3) Therefore, the computations described for unusual or infrequent items will also apply to the income (loss) from the discontinued operation of the entity, including any provisions for operating gains (losses) subsequent to the measurement date.

If the decision to dispose of operations occurs in any interim period other than the first interim period, the operating income (loss) applicable to the discontinued operation has already been used in computing the estimated annual effective tax rate. Therefore, a recomputation of the total tax is not required. However, the total tax should be divided into two components:

1. That tax applicable to ordinary income (loss)
2. That tax applicable to the income (loss) from the discontinued operation.

This division is accomplished as follows: a revised estimated annual effective rate is calculated for the income (loss) from ordinary operations. This recomputation is then applied to the ordinary income (loss) from the preceding periods. The total income tax applicable to the discontinued operation is then composed of two items:

1. The difference between the total income tax originally computed and the income tax recomputed on remaining ordinary income
2. The income tax computed on unusual, infrequent items as described above. (ASC 740-270-45-8)

Example—Discontinued Operations in Interim Periods

Rochelle Corporation anticipates net income of $150,000 during the fiscal year. The net permanent differences for the year will be $10,000. The company also anticipates income tax credits of $10,000 during the fiscal year. For purposes of this example, we will assume a flat statutory rate of 50%. The estimated annual effective rate is then calculated as follows:

Estimated pretax income	$150,000
Net permanent differences	(10,000)
Taxable income	140,000
Statutory rate	50%
Income tax	70,000
Anticipated credits	(10,000)
Total estimated income tax	$ 60,000
Estimated effective rate ($60,000 (÷ 150,000)	40%

The first two quarters of operations were as follows:

Ordinary income (loss)			*Tax expense*		
Reporting period	*Reporting period*	*Year-to-date*	*Year-to-date*	*Less previously provided*	*Reporting period*
1st qtr.	$30,000	$30,000	$12,000	$ –	$12,000
2nd qtr.	25,000	55,000	22,000	12,000	10,000

In the third quarter, Rochelle made the decision to dispose of Division X. During the third quarter, the company earned a total of $60,000. Upon reclassification of Division X's property and equipment to "held-for-sale" on its statement of financial position, the company expects to incur a onetime charge to income of $75,000 and estimates that current year divisional operating losses subsequent to the disposal decision will be $20,000, all of which will be incurred in the third quarter. The company estimates revised ordinary income in the fourth quarter to be $35,000. The two components of pretax accounting income (discontinued operations and revised ordinary income) are shown below.

		Division X	
Reporting period	*Revised ordinary income*	*Loss from operations*	*Asset reclassification*
1st qtr.	$ 40,000	$(10,000)	$–
2nd qtr.	40,000	(15,000)	–
3rd qtr.	80,000	(20,000)	(75,000)
4th qtr.	35,000		–
Fiscal year	$195,000	$(45,000)	$(75,000)

Rochelle must now recompute the estimated annual income tax rate. Assume that all the permanent differences are related to the revised continuing operations. However, $3,300 of the tax credits were applicable to machinery used in Division X. Because of the discontinuance of operations, the credit on this machinery would not be allowed. Any recapture of prior period credits must be used as a reduction in the income tax benefit from either operations or the loss on disposal. Assume that the company must recapture $2,000 of the $3,300 investment tax credit that is related to Division X.

The recomputed estimated annual rate for continuing operations is as follows:

Estimated (revised) ordinary income	$195,000
Less net permanent differences	(10,000)
	$185,000
Tax at statutory rate of 50%	$ 92,500
Less anticipated credits from continuing operations	(6,700)
Tax provision	$85,800
Estimated annual effective tax rate ($85,800 ÷ 195,000)	44%

The next step is to then apply the revised rate to the quarterly income from continuing operations as illustrated below.

Ordinary income				*Tax provision*		
Reporting period	*Reporting period*	*Year-to-date*	*Estimated annual effective rate*	*Year-to-date*	*Less previously provided*	*Reporting period*
1st qtr.	$ 40,000	$ 40,000	44%	$17,600	$ –	$17,600

Ordinary income				*Tax provision*		
Reporting period	*Reporting period*	*Year-to-date*	*Estimated annual effective rate*	*Year-to-date*	*Less previously provided*	*Reporting period*
2nd qtr.	40,000	80,000	44%	35,200	17,600	17,600
3rd qtr.	80,000	160,000	44%	70,400	35,200	35,200
4th qtr.	35,000	195,000	44%	85,800	70,400	15,400
Fiscal year	$195,000					$85,800

The tax benefit applicable to the operating loss from discontinued operations and the loss from the asset reclassification and remeasurement must now be calculated. The first two quarters are calculated on a differential basis as shown below.

	Tax applicable to ordinary income		
Reporting period	*Previously reported*	*Recomputed (above)*	*Tax (benefit) expense applicable to Division X*
1st qtr.	$12,000	$17,600	$ (5,600)
2nd qtr.	10,000	17,600	(7,600)
			$(13,200)

The only calculation remaining applies to the third quarter tax benefit pertaining to the operating loss and the loss on reclassification of the assets of the discontinued operation. The calculation of this amount is made based on the revised estimate of annual ordinary income both including and excluding the effects of the Division X losses. This is shown below:

	Loss from operations of Division X	*Asset reclassification*
Estimated annual income from continuing operations	$195,000	$195,000
Net permanent differences	(10,000)	(10,000)
Loss from Division X operations	(45,000)	–
Provision for loss on reclassification of Division X Assets	–	(75,000)
Total	$140,000	$110,000
Tax at the statutory rate of 50%	$ 70,000	$ 55,000
Anticipated credits (from continuing operations)	(6,700)	(6,700)
Recapture of previously recognized tax credits as a result of disposal	–	2,000
Taxes after effect of Division X losses	63,300	50,300
Taxes computed on estimated income before the effect of Division X losses	85,000	85,800
Tax benefit applicable to Division X	(22,500)	(35,500)
Amounts allocable to quarters one and two ($5,600 + $7,600)	(13,200)	–
Tax benefit to be recognized in the third quarter	$ (9,300)	$ (35,500)

The quarterly tax provisions can be summarized as follows:

	Pretax income (loss)			Tax (benefit) applicable to		
Reporting period	*Continuing operations*	*Operations of Division X*	*Loss on asset reclassification*	*Continuing operations*	*Operations of Division X*	*Loss on asset reclassification*
1st qtr.	$ 40,000	$(10,000)	$ -	$17,60	$ (5,600)	$ –
2nd qtr.	40,000	(15,000)	–	17,600	(7,600)	–
3rd qtr.	80,000	(20,000)	(75,000)	35,200	(9,300)	(35,500)
4th qtr.	35,000	–	–	15,400	–	–
Fiscal year	$195,000	$(45,000)	$(75,000)	$85,800	$(22,500)	$(35,500)

The following income statement shows the proper financial statement presentation of these discontinued operations. The notes to the statement indicate which items are to be included in the calculation of the annual estimated rate.

Income Statement (ASC 740-270-55-52)

Net sales*		$xxxx
Other income*		xxx
		xxxx
Costs and expenses		
Cost of sales*	$xxxx	
Selling, general, and administrative expenses*	xxx	
Interest expense*	xx	
Other deductions*	xx	
Unusual items*	xxx	
Infrequently occurring items*	xxx	xxxx
Income (loss) from continuing operations before income taxes and other items listed below		xxxx
Provision for income taxes (benefit)**		xxx
Income (loss) from continuing operations before items listed below		xxxx
Discontinued operations:		
Income (loss) from operations of discontinued Division X (less applicable income taxes of $xxxx)	xxxx	
Income (loss) on reclassification of assets of Division X to held-for-sale, (less applicable taxes of $xxxx)	xxxx	xxxx
Income (loss) before unusual items and cumulative effect of a change in accounting principle		xxxx
Unusual items (less applicable income taxes of $xxxx)		xxxx
Cumulative effect on prior years of a change in accounting principle (less applicable income taxes of $xxxx)***		xxxx
Net income (loss)		$xxxx

* *Components of ordinary income (loss).*

** *Consists of total income taxes (benefit) applicable to ordinary income (loss), unusual items, and infrequently occurring items.*

*** *This amount is shown net of income taxes. Although the income taxes are generally disclosed (as illustrated), this is not required.*

Presentation and Disclosures

The *Disclosure and Presentation Checklist for Commercial Businesses*, found at www.wiley.com/go/GAAP2021, has a list of the interim and year-end presentation and disclosure requirement for this topic.

Other Sources

See ASC Location—*Wiley GAAP* Chapter	For information on . . .
ASC 715-30	Accounting treatment of the difference between net periodic pension income and the amount deductible for tax purposes.
ASC 718-740	Accounting for income taxes related to stock compensation.
ASC 805-740	Accounting for income taxes related to business combinations.
ASC 840-30 ASC 842-30 (when implemented)	Leases.
ASC 852	Accounting for income taxes related to reorganizations.
ASC 920-740	Tax consequences of bad debt reserves of savings and loans and other qualified thrift lenders that arose in tax years beginning after December 31, 1987.

47 ASC 805 BUSINESS COMBINATIONS

PERSPECTIVE AND ISSUES

Subtopics

ASC 805, *Business Combinations*, consists of six subtopics:

- ASC 805-10, *Overall*, which provides guidance on transactions accounted for under the acquisition method
- ASC 852-20, *Identifiable Assets and Liabilities, and Any Noncontrolling Interest*, which deals with specific aspects of the acquisition method
- ASC 805-30, *Goodwill or Gain from Bargain Purchase, Including Consideration Transferred*, which, like ASC 805-20, deals with specific aspects of the acquisition method
- ASC 805-40, *Reverse Acquisitions*, which provides guidance on business combinations that are reverse acquisitions
- ASC 805-50, *Related Issues*, which offers guidance on two items that are similar, but not the same, as a business combination: acquisition of assets and transactions between entities under common control
- ASC 805-740, *Income Taxes*, which provides "incremental guidance" on business combinations and on acquisitions by a not-for-profit entity

Scope and Scope Exceptions

Transactions or other events that meet the definition of a business combination or an acquisition by a not-for-profit entity are subject to ASC 805. (ASC 801-10-15-3) Excluded from the scope of ASC 805, however, are:

- Formation of a joint venture.
- Acquisition of an asset or group of assets that does not represent a business or a nonprofit activity.
- Combinations between entities, businesses, or nonprofit activities under common control.
- An acquisition by a not-for-profit entity for which the acquisition date is before December 15, 2009, or a merger of not-for-profit entities (NFPs).
- An event in which an NFP obtains control of a not-for-profit entity but does not consolidate that entity, as permitted or required by ASC 958-810-25-4.
- If an NFP that obtained control in an event in which consolidation was permitted but not required decides in a subsequent annual reporting period to begin consolidating a controlled entity that it initially chose not to consolidate.
- Financial assets and liabilities of a consolidated VIE that is a collateralized financing entity within the scope of 815-10.
(ASC 805-10-15-4)

Overview

Historically, one of the most daunting problems facing accountants has been how to account for the acquisition of one enterprise by another, or other combination of two or more formerly unrelated entities, into one new enterprise.

U.S. GAAP requires the acquisition method of accounting for business combinations. The acquisition method requires that the actual cost of the acquisition be recognized, including any excess over the amounts allocable to the fair value of identifiable net assets, commonly known as goodwill.

The major accounting issues in business combinations and in the preparation and presentation of consolidated or combined financial statements are:

- The proper accounting basis for the assets and liabilities of the combining entities
- The accounting for goodwill or negative goodwill (the gain from a bargain purchase)

The accounting for the assets and liabilities of entities acquired in a business combination is largely dependent on the fair values assigned to them at the transaction date. ASC 820, *Fair Value Measurements*, provides a framework for measuring fair value and important guidance when assigning values as part of a business combination. In essence, it favors valuations determined on the open market, but allows other methodologies if open market valuation is not practicable.

Techniques for Structuring Business Combinations A business combination can be structured in a number of different ways that satisfy the acquirer's strategic, operational, legal, tax, and risk management objectives. Some of the more frequently used structures are:

- One or more businesses become subsidiaries of the acquirer. As subsidiaries, they continue to operate as legal entities.
- The net assets of one or more businesses are legally merged into the acquirer. In this case, the acquiree entity ceases to exist (in legal vernacular, this is referred to as a *statutory merger* and normally the transaction is subject to approval by a majority of the outstanding voting shares of the acquiree).
- The owners of the acquiree transfer their equity interests to the acquirer entity or to the owners of the acquirer entity in exchange for equity interests in the acquirer.
- All of the combining entities transfer their net assets (or their owners transfer their equity interests into a new entity formed for the purpose of the transaction). This is sometimes referred to as a *roll-up* or put-together transaction.
- A former owner or group of former owners of one of the combining entities obtains control of the combined entities collectively.
- An acquirer might hold a noncontrolling equity interest in an entity and subsequently purchase additional equity interests sufficient to give it control over the investee. These transactions are referred to as *step acquisitions* or business combinations achieved in stages.
- A business owner organizes a partnership, S corporation, or LLC to hold real estate. The real estate is the principal location of the commonly owned business and that business entity leases the real estate from the separate entity.

DEFINITIONS OF TERMS

Source: ASC 805. For more definitions related to this topic, see Appendix A, *Definitions of Terms*: Acquiree, Acquirer, Acquisition by a Not-for-Profit Entity, Beneficial Interests, Business, Business Combination, Change in Accounting Principle, Conduit Debt Security, Contract, Contract Asset, Defensive Intangible Asset, Direct Financing Lease, Dropdown, Equity Interests, Fair Value, Financial Asset, Financial Statements Are Available to Be Issued, Financial Statements Are Issued, Goodwill, Intangible Asset, Lease, Lease Liability, Lease Payments, Lease Receivable, Lease Term, Lessee, Lessor, Market Participants, Net Investment in the Lease,

Legal Entity, Noncontrolling Interest, Nonprofit Activity, Not-for-Profit Entity, Operating Lease, Private Company, Public Business Entity, Public Entity, Pushdown Accounting, Related Parties, Reorganization, Requisite Service Period, Right-of-Use Asset, Sales-Type Lease, Securities and Exchange Commission (SEC) Filer, Sublease, Underlying Asset, Unguaranteed Residual Asset, and Variable Interest Entity.

Acquisition Date. The date on which control of the acquiree is obtained by the acquirer.

Collateralized Financing Entity. A variable interest entity that holds financial assets, issues beneficial interests in those financial assets, and has no more than nominal equity. The beneficial interests have contractual recourse only to the related assets of the collateralized financing entity and are classified as financial liabilities. A collateralized financing entity may hold nonfinancial assets temporarily as a result of default by the debtor on the underlying debt instruments held as assets by the collateralized financing entity or in an effort to restructure the debt instruments held as assets by the collateralized financing entity. A collateralized financing entity also may hold other financial assets and financial liabilities that are incidental to the operations of the collateralized financing entity and have carrying values that approximate fair value (for example, cash, broker receivables, or broker payables).

Contingency. An existing condition, situation, or set of circumstances involving uncertainty as to possible gain (gain contingency) or loss (loss contingency) to an entity that will ultimately be resolved when one or more future events occur or fail to occur.

Contingent Consideration. Usually an obligation of the acquirer to transfer additional assets or equity interests to the former owners of an acquiree as part of the exchange for control of the acquiree if specified future events occur or conditions are met. However, contingent consideration also may give the acquirer the right to the return of previously transferred consideration if specified conditions are met.

Contingent consideration might also arise when the terms of the business combination provide a requirement that the acquiree's former owners return previously transferred assets or equity interests to the acquirer under certain specified conditions.

Control. The same as the meaning of controlling financial interest in paragraph 810-10-15-8: For legal entities other than limited partnerships, the usual condition for a controlling financial interest is ownership of a majority voting interest, and, therefore, as a general rule ownership by one reporting entity, directly or indirectly, of more than 50 percent of the outstanding voting shares of another entity is a condition pointing toward consolidation. The power to control may also exist with a lesser percentage of ownership, for example, by contract, lease, agreement with other stockholders, or by court decree.

Control of a Not-for-Profit Entity. See Control.

Equity Interests. Used broadly to mean ownership interests of investor-owned entities; owner, member, or participant interests of mutual entities; and owner or member interest in the net assets of not-for-profit entities.

Identifiable Asset. Assets (not including financial assets) that lack physical substance. (The term intangible assets is used to refer to intangible assets other than goodwill.)

Merger of Not-for-Profit Entities. A transaction or other event in which the governing bodies of two or more not-for-profit entities cede control of those entities to create a new not-for-profit entity.

Nonfinancial Asset. An asset that is not a financial asset. Nonfinancial assets include land, buildings, use of facilities or utilities, materials and supplies, intangible assets, or services.

Owners. Used broadly to include holders of ownership interests (equity interests) in investor-owned mutual entities, or not-for-profit entities. Owners include shareholders, partners, proprietors, or members, or participants of mutual entities. Owners also include owner and member interests in the net assets of not-for-profit entities.

Reverse Acquisition. An acquisition in which the entity that issues securities (the legal acquirer) is identified as the acquiree for financial accounting purposes, based on application of the guidance in ASC 805-10-55-11 through 55-15. The entity whose equity interests are acquired (the legal acquiree) must be the acquirer for accounting purposes in order for the transaction to be considered a reverse acquisition.

CONCEPTS, RULES, AND EXAMPLES

Transactions and Events Accounted for as Business Combinations

A business combination results from the occurrence of a transaction or other event that results in an acquirer obtaining control of one or more businesses. This can occur in many different ways that include the following examples individually or, in some cases, in combination:

- Transfer of cash, cash equivalents, or other assets, including the transfer of assets of another business of the acquirer
- Incurring liabilities
- Issuance of equity instruments
- By providing more than one type of consideration

By contract alone without the transfer of consideration, such as when:

- An acquiree business repurchases enough of its own shares to cause one of its existing investors (the acquirer) to obtain control over it.
- There is a lapse of minority veto rights that had previously prevented the acquirer from controlling an acquiree in which it held a majority voting interest.
- An acquirer and acquiree contractually agree to combine their businesses without a transfer of consideration between them.
(ASC 805-10-55-2)

Qualifying as a Business

Clarifying the Definition of a Business Many stakeholders have been concerned that the Codification's definition of a business resulted in transactions that were in substance asset acquisitions being accounted for as businesses. This primarily resulted from a broad interpretation of the provision that if market participants could replace the missing inputs and processes necessary to create an output, the acquisition was a business. In response to stakeholder concerns, the FASB updated the Codification by clarifying the definition of a business. The Codification presents an upfront, initial screen and a framework for financial reporters to use when determining whether a set of assets and activities is a business.

Determining whether a transaction is an asset acquisition or a business combination is important because of the significant differences in accounting for each, some of which are highlighted below.

	Accounting Treatment	
Item	**Business Combination**	**Asset Acquisition**
Goodwill	Recognized for consideration in excess of fair value of assets and liabilities	No goodwill recognized

	Accounting Treatment	
Item	**Business Combination**	**Asset Acquisition**
In-process research and development	Generally recognized and measured at fair value	Expensed at acquisition date if there is no alternative use
Assumed contingencies	Generally recognized and measured at fair value	Expensed at acquisition date if there is no alternative use
Transaction cost	Expense as incurred	Generally capitalized

The definition of a business also affects:

- Accounting for disposals
- Identification of reporting units for goodwill purposes
- Consolidations
- Segment changes
- Foreign currency transactions
- Assessment of VIEs, etc.

Exhibit—Overview of the Process to Determine Whether a Transaction Is an Asset Acquisition or a Business

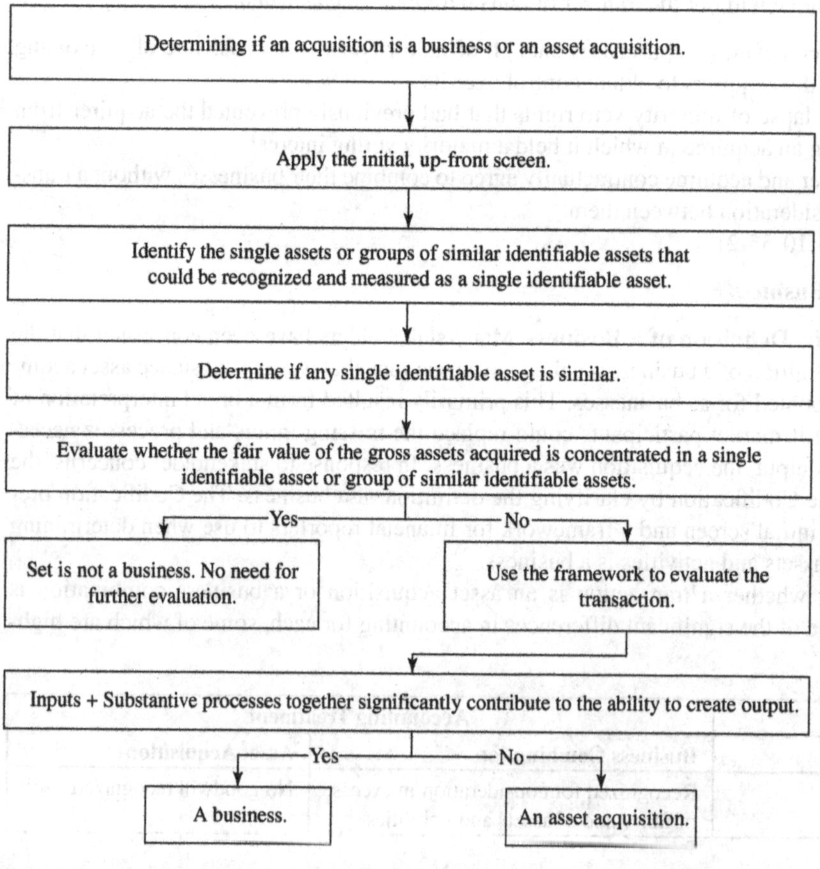

The elements of a business. "A business is an integrated set of assets and activities that is capable of being conducted and managed for the purpose of providing a return in the form of dividends, lower cost or other economic benefits directly to investors or other owners, members or participants." (ASC 805-10-55-3A)

A business typically has:

- Inputs.
- Processes applied to those inputs. Documentation of processes is not required. The ASU clarifies that a process can be provided by the intellectual capacity of an organized workforce with the necessary skills and experience to use inputs to create outputs. For example, consulting firm employees may be capable of using the intellectual capacity to generate a product that can be sold to customers.
- Outputs that are used to generate a return to investors. However, outputs are not required for a set to be a business under both the extant and the new guidance. The new guidance defines an output as the result of inputs and processes applied to those inputs that provide:
    - Goods or services to customers,
    - Investment income (such as dividends or interest), or
    - Other revenues.

  (ASC 805-10-55-4)

The description of outputs narrows the previous definition and focuses on revenue-generating activities, aligning the definition more closely with that in the new revenue guidance in ASC 606.

Missing elements A set that does not generate revenue could still contain outputs. For example, a set could provide goods or services that are used internally and do not generate revenue. The goods or services provided, in such a case, would be considered outputs.

The overall evaluation of whether a set is a business is performed from the perspective of a market participant. That is, how a seller operated the set or how the buyer intends to operate the set does not affect the analysis.

A business must include, at a minimum, an input and a substantive process that together significantly contribute to the ability to create outputs. (ASC 805-10-55-5) Therefore, a business need not include all the inputs and processes that the seller used in operating the set. Judgment is required to evaluate when an input and substantive process together significantly contribute to the ability to create outputs.

The upfront screen—single or similar asset threshold The use of this screen should reduce the number of transactions that need further evaluation. An entity should apply an initial screen and evaluate whether substantially all of the fair value of the gross assets acquired is concentrated in a single identifiable asset or a group of similar identifiable assets. If so, the set is not a business, and the entity does not need to evaluate further. (ASC 805-10-55-5A) The guidance does not define "substantially all," but that phrase is used in other areas of the Codification and is commonly interpreted as 90% or more. That is not a bright line and entities should exercise judgment. The initial screening test may be performed quantitatively or qualitatively. Following is further explanation of the elements in the screen.

Gross assets acquired Gross assets acquired include any consideration transferred (plus the fair value of any noncontrolling interest and previously held interest, if any) in excess of the fair value of the net identifiable assets acquired (e.g., goodwill in a business combination). In determining consideration transferred for the purpose of applying the threshold, entities must include all forms of consideration (e.g., cash, contingent consideration) that would be recognized in a business combination. Consideration transferred would not be affected by elements that are part of a separate transaction (e.g., equity awards that represent compensation for future services). Any liabilities assumed are excluded.

Excluded from gross assets acquired are:

- Cash and cash equivalents,
- Deferred tax assets, and
- Any goodwill that would be created in a business combination from the recognition of deferred tax liabilities.
(ASC 805-10-55-5A)

Single identifiable asset Before applying the screen, the entity must identify the assets or groups of assets that could be recognized and measured as a single identifiable asset in an ASC 805 business combination. A single identifiable asset may include more than one asset. For instance, the ASU offers the example of a trademark asset that includes the related trade name, formulas, recipes, and technological expertise. The ASU also specifically requires entities to combine the following assets that would not be combined into a single identifiable asset in a business combination:

- Two tangible assets, such as land and a building, that are attached and cannot be used separately without incurring significant cost or significant diminution in utility or fair value to either asset (or an intangible asset representing the right to use a tangible asset that cannot be used separately from the tangible asset such as leased land and a building)
- In-place lease intangibles, including favorable and unfavorable intangible assets or liabilities (i.e., an off-market component), and the related leased assets
(ASC 805-10-55-5B)

Similar assets In evaluating whether the screen's threshold is met, an entity also must determine whether any single identifiable assets identified by applying the guidance described in the section above are similar. When evaluating whether assets are similar, an entity should use judgment and consider the nature of each single identifiable asset and the risks associated with managing and creating outputs from the assets. While the guidance provides a framework for evaluating whether assets are similar, the guidance states that the following assets *cannot* be considered similar:

- A tangible asset and an intangible asset
- Identifiable intangible assets in different major intangible asset classes (e.g., customer-related intangibles, trademarks, and in-process research and development)
- A financial asset and a nonfinancial asset
- Different major classes of financial assets, for example accounts receivable and marketable securities
- Different major classes of tangible assets, for example, inventory, manufacturing equipment, automobiles
- Identifiable assets within the same major asset class that have significantly different risk characteristics
(ASC 805-10-55-5C)

Conclusion If the screen is met, the acquisition is not a business and no further evaluation is necessary.

The framework If the screen is not met, the Codification offers a framework to evaluate whether a set has the required input and substantive processes required to be considered a business. There are stringent requirements for a set with no outputs to be considered a business. Entities cannot presume that a set contains a process if the set generates revenues before and after the transaction. Entities must perform additional analysis to determine whether the set contains a substantive process. The criteria to use in the analysis depend on whether the set has outputs.

Criteria to use if outputs are not present In situations when there are no outputs, an acquired process is considered substantive only if the set includes employees with the necessary skills, knowledge, or experience to perform an acquired process that is critical to the ability to develop or convert an acquired input or inputs into outputs. (ASC 805-10-55-5D) Entities must consider the facts and circumstances to determine whether employees perform or are capable of performing a substantive process. An entity cannot consider an organized workforce provided by an outsourced workforce in its assessment of whether the set includes a substantive process, unless an employee oversees the outsourced workforce. If a set without outputs includes both employees and an outsourced workforce, entities will have to apply judgment to determine whether the employees are an organized workforce that provides a substantive process.

Entities also must evaluate the nature of inputs included in a set that is not generating outputs. An input is "any economic resource that creates, or has the ability to contribute to the creation of, outputs when one or more processes are applied to it." (ASC 805-10-55-4(a)) A set might include elements that do not create or have the ability to contribute to the creation of outputs.

Criteria to use if outputs are present An acquired process (or group of processes) is considered substantive when the set has outputs and includes any of the following:

- Employees that form an organized workforce or an acquired contract that provides access to an organized workforce that has the necessary skills, knowledge, or experience to perform an acquired process (or group of processes) that, when applied to an acquired input, is critical to the ability to continue producing outputs
- An acquired process (or group of processes) that, when applied to an acquired input, significantly contributes to the ability to continue producing outputs and cannot be replaced without significant cost, effort, or delay in the ability to continue producing outputs
- An acquired process (or group of processes) that, when applied to an acquired input, significantly contributes to the ability to continue producing outputs and is considered unique or scarce
(ASC 805-10-55-5E)

Assumed contractual arrangements that are part of the set and provide for the continuation of revenue cannot provide a substantive process. The Board made this determination to emphasize that a set is not a business solely because there is a continuation of revenues. (ASC 805-10-55-5F)

The elements of a business vary by industry and the entity's stage of development. For example, a new business may have fewer inputs than a mature business and may have only one output. Most businesses have liabilities, but this is not required to meet the definition of a business. Likewise, some transferred sets of assets may have liabilities, but are not a business. (ASC 805-10-55-6)

Presence of goodwill The existence of more than an insignificant amount of goodwill *may* indicate that a process included in the set is substantive. (ASC 805-10-55-9)

Example—Scenario 1

The ASU provides an example to aid in applying the guidance.

Facts. ABC Company acquires, renovates, leases, sells, and manages real estate. ABC acquires a portfolio of 10 single-family homes that each have in-place leases. The only elements included in the set are the 10 single-family homes and the 10 in-place leases. Each single-family home includes the land, building, and property improvements. Each home has a different floor plan, square footage, lot, and interior design. No employees or other assets are acquired.

Analysis. ABC initially considers the upfront screen and concludes that the land, building, property improvements, and in-place leases at each property are a single asset. The building and property improvements are attached to the land and cannot be removed without incurring significant cost. Additionally, the in-place lease is an intangible asset that should be combined with the related real estate and considered a single asset. The 10 single assets are similar. The nature of the assets (all single-family homes) are similar and the risks associated with managing and creating the outputs are not significantly different because the types of homes, class of customers, and risks in the real estate market are not significantly different.

Conclusion. ABC concludes that substantially all of the fair value of the gross assets acquired is concentrated in the group of similar identifiable assets and the set is not a business.

Example—Scenario 2

Facts. Assume the same facts as above except that ABC also acquires an office park with six 10-story office buildings leased to maximum occupancy, all of which have significant fair value. The set:

- Includes the employees responsible for leasing, tenant management, and managing and supervising all operational processes, and
- Has continuing revenues in the form of the in-place leases revenue and, therefore, has outputs.

Analysis. ABC must consider whether the set includes both an input and a substantive process that together significantly contribute to the ability to create outputs.

ABC determines that the criterion is met because the set includes an organized workforce that performs processes that when applied to the acquired inputs in the set (the land, building, and in-place leases) are critical to the ability to continue producing outputs.

Conclusion. ABC concludes that the leasing, tenant management, and supervision of the operational processes are critical to the creation of outputs. Because it includes both an input and a substantive process, the set is considered a business.

Accounting for Business Combinations under the Acquisition Method

The acquirer accounts for a business combination using the *acquisition method*. (ASC 805-10-25-1) This term represents an expansion of the now-outdated term, "purchase method." The change in terminology was made to emphasize that a business combination can occur even when a purchase transaction is not involved.

The following steps are required to apply the acquisition method:

1. Identify the acquirer.
2. Determine the acquisition date.
3. Identify the assets and liabilities, if any, requiring separate accounting because they result from transactions that are not part of the business combination, and account for them in accordance with their nature and the applicable GAAP.
4. Identify assets and liabilities that require acquisition date classification or designation decisions to facilitate application of GAAP in postcombination financial statements and

make those classifications or designations based on (a) contractual terms, (b) economic conditions, (c) acquirer operating or accounting policies, and (d) other pertinent conditions existing at the acquisition date.
5. Recognize and measure the identifiable tangible and intangible assets acquired and liabilities assumed.
6. Recognize and measure any noncontrolling interest in the acquiree.
7. Measure the consideration transferred.
8. Recognize and measure goodwill or, if the business combination results in a bargain purchase, recognize a gain.
(ASC 805-10-05-4)

Step 1—Identify the Acquirer ASC 805 strongly emphasizes the concept that every business combination has an acquirer. In the "basis for conclusions" that accompanies FASB 141 (R) (the original source of ASC 805), FASB asserted that:

> *. . . "true mergers" or "mergers of equals" in which none of the combining entities obtain control of the others are so rare as to be virtually nonexistent . . .*

The determination of the acquirer is based on application of the provisions of ASC 810 regarding the party that possesses a controlling financial interest in another entity, except when a VIE is acquired. In general, ASC 810 provides that direct or indirect ownership of a majority of the outstanding voting interests in another entity ". . . is a condition pointing toward consolidation." However, this is not an absolute rule to be applied in all cases. In fact, ASC 810 explicitly provides that majority owned entities are not to be consolidated if the majority owner does not hold a controlling financial interest in the entity. Exceptions to the general majority ownership rule include, but are not limited to, the following situations:

- An entity that is in legal reorganization or bankruptcy.
- An entity subject to uncertainties due to government-imposed restrictions, such as foreign exchange restrictions or controls, whose severity casts doubt on the majority interest owner's ability to control the entity.
- Is a broker dealer within the scope of ASC 940 and control is likely to be temporary.
- If the power of the majority voting interest shareholder is restricted by rights given to the noncontrolling shareholder (noncontrolling rights) and are so restrictive that it is questionable whether control exists with majority owners.
- Control exists through other than majority ownership of voting interest.
- If the acquiree is a variable interest entity (VIE), the primary beneficiary of the VIE is always considered to be the acquirer.
(ASC 810-10-15-10)

If applying the guidance in ASC 810 does not clearly indicate the party that is the acquirer, ASC 805-10-55-10 through 15 provides factors to consider in making that determination under different facts and circumstances:

- *Relative size*—Generally, the acquirer is the entity whose relative size is significantly larger than that of the other entity or entities. Size can be compared by using measures such as assets, revenues, or net income. (ASC 805-10-55-13)

- *Initiator of the transaction*—When more than two entities are involved, another factor to consider (beside relative size) is which of the entities initiated the transaction. (ASC 805-10-55-14)
- *Roll-ups or put-together transactions*—When a new entity is formed to issue equity interests to effect a business combination, one of the preexisting entities is to be identified as the acquirer. If, instead, a newly formed entity transfers cash or other assets, or incurs liabilities as consideration to effect a business combination, that new entity may be considered to be the acquirer. (ASC 805-10-55-15)
- *Nonequity consideration*—In business combinations accomplished primarily by the transfer of cash or other assets, or by incurring liabilities, the entity that transfers the cash or other assets, or incurs the liabilities is usually the acquirer. (ASC 805-10-55-11)
- *Exchange of equity interests*—In business combinations accomplished primarily by the exchange of equity interests, the entity that issues its equity interests is generally considered to be the acquirer. One notable exception that occurs frequently in practice is sometimes referred to as a reverse acquisition, discussed in detail later in this chapter. In a reverse acquisition, the entity issuing equity interests is legally the acquirer, but for accounting purposes is considered the acquiree. There are, however, other factors that should be considered in identifying the acquirer when equity interests are exchanged. These include:
    - *Relative voting rights in the combined entity after the business combination*—Generally, the acquirer is the entity whose owners, as a group, retain or obtain the largest portion of the voting rights in the consolidated entity. This determination must take into consideration the existence of any unusual or special voting arrangements as well as any options, warrants, or convertible securities.
    - *The existence of a large minority voting interest in the combined entity in the event no other owner or organized group of owners possesses a significant voting interest*—Generally, the acquirer is the entity whose owner or organized group of owners holds the largest minority voting interest in the combined entity.
    - *The composition of the governing body of the combined entity*—Generally, the acquirer is the entity whose owners have the ability to elect, appoint, or remove a majority of members of the governing body of the combined entity.
    - *The composition of the senior management of the combined entity*—Generally the acquirer is the entity whose former management dominates the management of the combined entity.
    - *Terms of the equity exchange*—Generally, the acquirer is the entity that pays a premium over the precombination fair value of the equity interests of the other entity or entities.

  (ASC 805-10-55-12)

Step 2—Determine the Acquisition Date By definition, the acquisition date is the date on which the acquirer obtains control of the acquiree. As discussed in the chapter on ASC 810, this concept of control (or, more precisely, controlling financial interest) is not always evidenced by voting ownership. Thus, control can be obtained contractually by an acquirer absent that party holding any voting ownership interests.

The general rule is that the acquisition date is the date on which the acquirer legally transfers consideration, acquires the assets, and assumes the liabilities of the acquiree. This date, in a relatively straightforward transaction, is referred to as the *closing date*. Not all transactions are that straightforward, however. All pertinent facts and circumstances should be considered in determining the acquisition date. The parties to a business combination might, for example, execute a contract that entitles the acquirer to the rights and obligates the acquirer with respect to the obligations of the acquiree prior to the actual date of the closing. Thus, in evaluating economic substance over legal form, the acquirer will have contractually acquired the target on the date it executed the contract. (ASC 805-10-25-7)

Guidance on the measurement period, which is relevant to the steps that follow, is described and illustrated below.

Measurement period More frequently than not, management of the acquirer does not obtain all of the relevant information needed to complete the acquisition-date measurements in time for the issuance of the first set of interim or annual financial statements subsequent to the business combination. If the initial accounting for the business combination has not been completed by that time, the acquirer should report provisional amounts in the consolidated financial statements for any items for which the accounting is incomplete. ASC 805 provides for a "measurement period" of a reasonable time not to exceed one year.

In a business combination achieved in stages, the acquirer remeasures its previously held equity interest in the acquiree at its acquisition-date fair value and recognizes the resulting gain or loss in earnings. If in prior periods, the acquirer recognized amounts with respect to its previously held equity method investment in other comprehensive income, the amount that was recognized in other comprehensive income is reclassified and included in the calculation of gain or loss as of the acquisition date. (ASC 805-10-25-10)

During the measurement period, any adjustments to the provisional amounts recognized at the acquisition date should be adjusted to reflect new information that management obtains regarding facts and circumstances existing as of the acquisition date that, if known, would have affected the measurement of the asset recognized. (ASC 805-10-25-13 and 25-14) Any adjustments to provisional amounts should have a corresponding adjustment to goodwill. (ASC 805-10-25-17) Information that has a bearing on this determination must not relate to postacquisition events or circumstances. The information is to be analyzed to determine whether, if it had been known at the acquisition date, it would have affected the measurement of the amounts recognized as of that date. (ASC 805-10-25-18)

In evaluating whether new information obtained meets the criteria for adjusting provisional amounts, management of the acquirer must consider all relevant factors. Relevant factors include:

- The timing of the receipt of the additional information, *and*
- Whether management of the acquirer can identify a reason that a change is warranted to the provisional amounts.
  (ASC 805-10-30-2)

Obviously, information received shortly after the acquisition date has a higher likelihood of relevance to acquisition-date circumstances than information received months later. (ASC 805- 10-30-3)

Example of Consideration of New Information Obtained during the Measurement Period

Krupp Industries, Inc. (KI) acquired Miller Motor Works Corp. (MMW) on January 2, 20X2. In the first quarter 20X2 consolidated financial statements of Krupp Industries and Subsidiary, it assigned a provisional fair value of $40 million to an asset group consisting of a factory and related machinery that manufactures engines used in large trucks and sport utility vehicles (SUVs).

As of the acquisition date, the average cost of gasoline in the markets served by the customers of MMW was $4.30 per gallon. For the first four months subsequent to the acquisition, the per-gallon price of gasoline was relatively stable and only fluctuated slightly up or down on any given day. Upon further analysis, management was able to determine that during that four-month period, the production levels of the asset group and related order backlog did not vary substantially from the acquisition date.

In May 20X2, however, due to an accident on May 3, 20X2, at a large U.S. refinery, the average cost per gallon skyrocketed to more than $6.00 a gallon. As a result of this huge spike in the price of fuel, MMW's largest customers either canceled orders or sharply curtailed the number of engines they had previously ordered.

Scenario 1: On April 15, 20X2, management of KI signed a sales agreement with Joshua International (JI) to sell the asset group for $30 million. Given the fact that management was unable to identify any changes that occurred during the measurement period that would have accounted for a change in the acquisition-date fair value of the asset group, management determines that it will adjust the provisional fair value assigned to the asset group to $30 million.

Scenario 2: On May 15, 20X2, management of KI signed a sales agreement with Joshua International (JI) to sell the asset group for $30 million. Given the intervening events that affected the price of fuel and the demand for MMW's products, management determines that the $10 million decline in the fair value of the asset group from the provisional fair value it was originally assigned resulted from those intervening changes and, consequently, does not adjust the provisional fair value assigned to the asset group at the acquisition date.

In addition to adjustments to provisional amounts recognized, the acquirer may determine during the measurement period that it omitted recognition of additional assets or liabilities that existed at the acquisition date. During the measurement period, any such assets or liabilities identified are also to be recognized and measured as if the accounting had been complete at the acquisition date. (ASC 805-10-25-14)

In determining adjustments to the provisional amounts assigned to assets and liabilities, management should be alert for interrelationships between recognized assets and liabilities. For example, new information that management obtains that results in an adjustment to the provisional amount assigned to a liability for which the acquiree carries insurance could also result in an adjustment, in whole or in part, to a provisional amount recognized as an asset representing the claim receivable from the insurance carrier. (ASC 805-10-25-16) In addition, changes in provisional amounts assigned to assets and liabilities frequently will also affect temporary differences between the items' income tax basis and GAAP carrying amount, which in turn will affect the computation of deferred income assets and liabilities.

Adjustments to the provisional amounts that are made during the measurement period are recognized with a corresponding adjustment to goodwill. This will result in adjustments as needed, including to depreciation, amortization, or other effects on net income or other comprehensive income related to the adjustments. (ASC 805-10-25-17)

The measurement period ends on the *earlier* of:

- The date management of the acquirer receives the information it seeks regarding facts and circumstances as they existed at the acquisition date or learns that it will be unable to obtain any additional information, *or*
- One year after the acquisition date.

After the end of the measurement period, the only revisions that are permitted to be made to the initial acquisition date accounting for the business combination are restatements for corrections of prior period errors in accordance with ASC 250, *Accounting Changes and Error Corrections*. (ASC 805-10-25-19)

Step 3—Identify Assets and Liabilities Requiring Separate Accounting

Recognition principle and conditions ASC 805 provides a basic recognition principle that, as of the *acquisition date*, the acquirer should recognize, separately from goodwill:

- The identifiable assets acquired (whether tangible or intangible),
- The liabilities assumed, and,
- If applicable, any noncontrolling interest (previously referred to as "minority interest") in the acquiree.
  (ASC 805-20-25-1)

Frequently, in a business combination, the acquirer's plans include the future exit of one or more of the activities of the acquiree or the termination or relocation of employees of the acquiree. Since these exit activities are discretionary on the part of the acquirer and the acquirer is not obligated to incur the associated costs, the costs do not meet the definition of a liability and are not recognized at the acquisition date. Rather, the costs will be recognized in post combination financial statements in accordance with ASC 420. (ASC 805-20-25-2)

ASC 805 elaborates on the basic principle above by providing that recognition is subject to the following conditions:

- At the acquisition date, the identifiable assets acquired and liabilities assumed must meet the definitions of assets and liabilities as set forth in CON 6.[1] (ASC 805-20-25-2).
- The assets and liabilities recognized must be part of the exchange transaction between the acquirer and the acquiree (or the acquiree's former owners) and not part of a separate transaction or transactions. (ASC 805-20-25-3)

In applying the recognition principle to a business combination, the acquirer may recognize assets and liabilities that had not been recognized by the acquiree in its precombination financial statements. ASC 805 permits recognition of acquired intangibles (e.g., patents, customer lists) that would not be granted recognition if they were internally developed. (ASC 805-20-25-4)

Determining what is part of the business combination transaction Preexisting relationships and arrangements often exist between the acquirer and acquire prior to beginning negotiations to enter into a business combination. Furthermore, while conducting the negotiations, the parties may enter into separate business arrangements. In either case, the acquirer is responsible for identifying amounts that are not part of the exchange for the acquiree. Recognition under the acquisition method is only given to the consideration transferred for the acquiree and the assets acquired and liabilities assumed in exchange for that consideration. Other transactions outside the scope of the business combination should be recognized by applying other relevant GAAP. (ASC 805-10-25-20)

The acquirer must analyze the business combination transaction and other transactions with the acquiree and its former owners to identify the components that comprise the transaction in which the acquirer obtained control over the acquiree. This distinction is important to ensure that each component is accounted for according to its economic substance, irrespective of its legal form.

The imposition of this condition is based on an observation that, upon becoming involved in negotiations for a business combination, the parties may exhibit characteristics of related parties. In so doing, they may be willing to execute agreements designed *primarily* for the benefit of the

---

[1] Assets are defined as "probable future economic benefits obtained or controlled by a particular entity as a result of past transactions or events." (CON 6, para. 25) Liabilities are defined as "probable future sacrifices of economic benefits arising from present obligations of a particular entity to transfer assets or provide services to other entities in the future as a result of past transactions or events." (CON 6, para. 35)

acquirer of the combined entity that might be designed to achieve a desired financial reporting outcome after the business combination has been consummated. (ASC 805-10-25-21) Thus, the imposition of this condition should curb such practices.

In analyzing a transaction to determine inclusion or exclusion from a business combination, consideration should be given to which of the parties will reap its benefits. If a precombination transaction is entered into by the acquirer, or on behalf of the acquirer, or *primarily* to benefit the acquirer (or to benefit the to-be-combined entity as a whole) rather than for the benefit of the acquiree or its former owners, the transaction most likely would be considered to be a "separate transaction" outside the boundaries of the business combination and for which the acquisition method would not apply.

The acquirer should consider the following factors, which the FASB indicates "are neither mutually exclusive nor individually conclusive," in determining whether a transaction is a part of the exchange transaction or recognized separately:

- *Purpose of the transaction*—Typically, there are many parties involved in the management, ownership, operation, and financing of the various entities involved in a business combination transaction. Of course, there are the acquirer and acquiree entities, but there are also owners, directors, management, and various parties acting as agents representing their respective interests. Understanding the motivations of the parties in entering into a particular transaction potentially provides insight into whether or not the transaction is a part of the business combination or a separate transaction.
- *Initiator of the transaction*—Identifying the party that initiated the transaction may provide insight into whether or not it should be recognized separately from the business combination. The FASB believes that if the transaction was initiated by the acquirer, it would be less likely to be part of the business combination and, conversely, if it were initiated by the acquiree or its former owners, it would be more likely to be part of the business combination.
- *Timing of the transaction*—Examining the timing of the transaction may provide insight into whether, for example, the transaction was executed in contemplation of the future business combination in order to provide benefits to the acquirer or the postcombination entity. The FASB believes that transactions that take place during the negotiation of the terms of a business combination may be entered into in contemplation of the eventual combination for the purpose of providing future economic benefits *primarily* to the acquirer of the to-be-combined entity and, therefore, should be accounted for separately. (ASC 805-10-55-18)

ASC 805 provides the following presumption after analyzing the economic benefits of a precombination transaction:

Primarily for the benefit of:	*Transaction is likely to be:*
Acquirer or combined entity	Separate transaction
Acquiree or its former owners	Part of the business combination

ASC 805 provides three examples of separate transactions that *are not* to be included in applying the acquisition method, each of which will be discussed in further detail:

- Reimbursement to the acquiree or its former owners for paying the acquirer's acquisition-related costs,

- A settlement of a preexisting relationship between acquirer and acquiree, and
- Compensation to employees or former owners of the acquiree for future services. (ASC 805-10-25-21)

Settlements of preexisting relationships between acquirer and acquire Prior to pursuing a business combination, business may have been transacted between the parties. The nature of the transactions may have been contractual, such as the purchase of goods and/or services, or the licensing of intellectual property. On the other hand, the parties may have had an adversarial relationship whereby they were plaintiff and defendant in pending litigation. (ASC 805-10-25-20 and 55-20) If, in effect, a business combination settles such a preexisting relationship, the acquirer recognizes a gain or loss measured in the following manner:

1. If the relationship is noncontractual (e.g., litigation), measure at fair value
2. If the relationship is contractual, measure at the lesser of:
   a. The amount by which, from the acquirer's perspective, the contract is favorable or unfavorable, or
   b. The amount of any settlement provisions stated in the contract that are available to the counterparty for which the contract is unfavorable.

If 2b is less than 2a, the difference is included as part of the accounting for the business combination. In determining whether a contract is favorable or unfavorable to a party, the terms of the contract are compared to current market terms. It is important to note that a contract can be unfavorable to the acquirer and yet not result in a loss. (ASC 805-10-55-21)

The amount of the gain or loss measured as a result of settling a preexisting relationship will, of course, depend on whether the acquirer had previously recognized related assets or liabilities with respect to that relationship. (ASC 805-10-55-22)

Example of Settlement of Preexisting Contractual Supplier Relationship—Contract Unfavorable to Acquirer

Meyer Corporation (MC) and Henning, Inc. (HI) are parties to a 3-year supply contract that contains the following provisions:

- MC is required to annually purchase 3,000 flat-panel displays from HI at a fixed price of $400 per unit for an aggregate purchase price of $1,200,000 for each of the three years.
- MC is required to pay HI the annual $1,200,000 irrespective of whether it takes delivery of all 3,000 units and the required payment is nonrefundable.
- The contract contains a penalty provision that would permit MC to cancel it at the end of the second year for a lump sum payment of $500,000.
- In each of the first two years of the contract, MC took delivery of the full 3,000 units.

At December 31, 20X1, the supply contract was unfavorable to MC because MC would be able to purchase flat-panel displays with similar specifications and of similar quality from another supplier for $350 per unit. Therefore, MC accrued a loss of $150,000 (3,000 units remaining under the firm purchase commitment × $50 loss per unit).

On January 1, 20X2, MC acquires HI for $30 million, which reflects the fair value of HI based on what other marketplace participants would be willing to pay. On the acquisition date, the $30 million fair value of HI includes $750,000 related to the contract with MC that consists of:

Identifiable intangibles[2]	$600,000	Representing the remaining year of the contract, at prevailing market prices
Favorable pricing	$150,000	Representing the portion of the contract price that is favorable to HI and unfavorable to MC
	$750,000	

HI has no other identifiable assets or liabilities related to the supply contract with MC. MC would compute its gain or loss on settlement of this preexisting relationship as follows:

1. Amount of unfavorability to acquirer (MC) at acquisition date	$150,000
2. Lump-sum settlement amount available to MC	500,000
3. Lesser of 1 or 2	150,000
4. Amount by which 1 exceeds 2	N/A

Since MC had already recognized an unrealized loss on the firm purchase commitment as of December 31, 20X1, upon its acquisition of HI, its loss of $150,000 from recognizing the lesser of items 1 and 2 in the preceding list would be offset by the elimination of the liability for the unrealized loss on the firm purchase commitment in the same amount of $150,000. Thus, under these circumstances, MC would have neither a gain nor a loss on the settlement of its preexisting relationship with HI. The entries to record these events are not considered part of the business combination accounting. It is important to note that, from the perspective of MC, when it applies the acquisition method to record the business combination, it will characterize the $600,000 "at market" component of the contract as part of goodwill and not as identifiable intangibles. This is the case because of the obvious fallacy of MC recognizing customer-relationship intangible assets that represent a relationship with itself.

Example of Settlement of Preexisting Contractual Supplier Relationship—Contract Favorable to Acquirer

Using the same facts as the MC/HI example above, assume that, instead of the contract being unfavorable to the acquirer MC, it was unfavorable to HI in the amount of $150,000 and that there was a cancellation provision in the contract that would permit HI to pay a penalty after year two of $100,000 to cancel the remainder of the contract.

On the acquisition date, the $30 million fair value of HI under this scenario would include $450,000 related to the contract with MC that consists of:

• Amount of favorability to acquirer (MC) at acquisition date	$150,000
• Lump-sum settlement amount available to HI	100,000
• Lesser of 1 or 2	100,000
• Amount by which 1 exceeds 2	50,000

[2] In computing the valuation of HI, these amounts would represent such identifiable customer-related intangible assets as customer contract, related customer relationship, production backlog, and the like.

Under these changed assumptions, MC would not have incurred or recorded an unrealized loss on the firm purchase commitment with HI since the contract terms were favorable to MC. The determination of MC's gain or loss would be as follows:

• Amount of favorability to acquirer (MC) at acquisition date	$150,000
• Lump-sum settlement amount available to HI	100,000
• Lesser of 1 or 2	100,000
• Amount by which 1 exceeds 2	50,000

Under this scenario, unless HI believed that the market would change in the near term, it would be economically advantageous, absent a business combination, for HI to settle the remaining contract at the acquisition date by paying the $100,000 penalty because HI would be able to sell the remaining 3,000 units covered by the contract for an aggregate price of $150,000 more than it was committed to sell those units to MC.

At the acquisition date, MC would record a gain of $100,000 to settle its preexisting relationship with HI. The entry to record the gain is not considered part of the business combination accounting.

In addition, however, since item 2 is less than item 1, the $50,000 difference is included in the accounting for the business combination, since economically, postcombination, the combined entity will not benefit from that portion of the acquisition date favorability of the contract.

As was the case in the first example, the portion of the purchase price allocated to the contract in the business combination accounting would be accounted for as goodwill for the same reason.

Acquisition-related costs Acquisition-related costs are charged to expense of the period in which the costs are incurred and the related services received. Examples of these costs include:

Accounting fees	Internal acquisitions department
Advisory fees	Legal fees
Consulting fees	Other professional fees
Finder's fees	Valuation fees

(ASC 805-10-25-23)

ASC 805 makes an exception to the general rule with respect to costs to register and issue equity or debt securities. These costs should be recognized in accordance with other applicable GAAP. (ASC 805-10-25-23)

Contingent payments to employees or former owners of the acquirer The acquirer assesses whether arrangements to make contingent payments to employees or selling owners of the acquiree represent contingent consideration that is part of the business combination transaction or represent separate transactions to be excluded from the application of the acquisition method to the business combination. In general, the acquirer considers:

- The reasons why the terms of the acquisition include the payment provision,
- The party that initiated the arrangement, and
- When (at what stage of the negotiations) the arrangement was entered into by the parties.
  (ASC 805-10-55-24)

When those considerations do not provide clarity regarding whether the transaction is separate from the business combination, the acquirer considers the following indicators:

- *Postcombination employment*—Consideration should be given to the terms under which the selling owners will be providing services as key employees of the combined entity. The terms may be evidenced by a formal employment contract, by provisions included in the acquisition documents, or by other documents. If the arrangement provides that the contingent payments are automatically forfeited upon termination of employment, the consideration is to be characterized as compensation for postcombination services. If, instead, the contingent payments are not affected by termination of employment, this would be an indicator that the contingent payments represent additional consideration that is part of the business combination transaction and not compensation for services.

- *Duration of postcombination employment*—If the employee is contractually bound to remain employed for a period that equals or exceeds the period during which the contingent payments are due, this may be an indicator that the contingent payments represent compensation for services.
- *Amount of compensation*—If the amount of the employee's compensation that is not contingent is considered to be reasonable in relation to other key employees of the combined entity, this may indicate that the contingent amounts represent additional consideration and not compensation for services.
- *Differential between amounts paid to employees and selling owners who do not become employees of the combined entity*—If, on a per-share basis, the contingent payments due to former owners of the acquiree that did not become employees are lower than the contingent payments due to the former owners that did become employees of the combined entity, this may indicate that the incremental amounts paid to the employees are compensation.
- *Extent of ownership*—The relative ownership percentages (e.g., number of shares, units, percentage of membership interest) owned by the selling owners who remain employees of the combined entity serve as an indicator of how to characterize the substance of the contingent consideration. If, for example, the former owners of substantially all of the ownership interests in the acquiree are continuing to serve as key employees of the combined entity, this may be an indicator that the contingent payment arrangement is substantively a profit-sharing vehicle designed with the intent of providing compensation for services to be performed postcombination. Conversely, if the former owners that remained employed by the combined entity collectively owned only a nominal ownership interest in the acquiree and all of the former owners received the same amount of contingent basis on a per-share basis, this may be an indicator that the contingent payments represent additional consideration. In considering the applicability of this indicator, care must be exercised to closely examine the effects, if any, of transactions, ownership interests, and employment relationships, precombination and postcombination, with respect to parties related to the selling owners of the acquiree.
- *Relationship of contingent arrangements to the valuation approach used*—The payment terms negotiated in many business combinations provide that the amount of the acquisition date transfer of consideration from acquirer to acquiree (or the acquiree's former owners) is computed near the lower end of a range of valuation estimates the acquirer used in valuing the acquiree. Furthermore, the formula for determining future contingent payments is derived from or related to that valuation approach. When this is the case, it may be an indicator that the contingent payments represent additional

consideration. Conversely, if the formula for determining future contingent payments more closely resembles prior profit-sharing arrangements, this may be an indicator that the substance of the contingent payment arrangement is to provide compensation for services.

- *Formula prescribed for determining contingent consideration*—Analyzing the formula to be used to determine the contingent consideration may provide insight into the substance of the arrangement. Contingent payments that are determined on the basis of a multiple of earnings may be indicative of being, in substance, contingent consideration that is part of the business combination transaction. Alternatively, contingent consideration that is determined as a prespecified percentage of earnings would be more suggestive of a routine profit-sharing arrangement for the purposes of providing additional compensation to employees for postcombination services rendered.
- *Other considerations*—Given the complexity of a business combination transaction and the sheer volume of legal documents necessary to affect it, the financial statement preparer is charged with the daunting, but unavoidable task of performing a comprehensive review of the terms of all of the associated agreements. These can take the form of noncompete agreements, consulting agreements, leases, guarantees, indemnifications, and, of course, the formal agreement to combine the businesses. Particular attention should be paid to the applicable income tax treatment afforded to the contingent payments. The income tax treatment of these payments may be an indicator that tax avoidance was a primary motivator in characterizing them in the manner that they are structured. An acquirer might, for example, simultaneous to a business combination, execute a property lease with one of the key owners of the acquiree. If the lease payments were below market, some or all of the contingent payments to that key owner/lessor under the provisions of the other legal agreements might, in substance, be making up the shortfall in the lease and thus should be recharacterized as lease payments and accounted for separately from the business combination in the combined entity's postcombination financial statements. If this were not the case, and the lease payments were reflective of the market, this would be an indicator pointing to a greater likelihood that the contingent payment arrangements actually did represent contingent consideration associated with the business combination transaction. (ASC 805-10-55-25)

Step 4—Classify or Designate Identifiable Assets Acquired and Liabilities Assumed

Recognition principle As of the acquisition date, the acquirer shall recognize, separately from goodwill, the identifiable assets acquired, the liabilities assumed, and any noncontrolling interest in the acquiree. Recognition of identifiable assets acquired and liabilities assumed is subject to the guidance in ASC 805-20-25-2 through 25-3. However, an entity (the acquirer) within the scope of ASC 805-20-15-2 may elect to apply the accounting alternative for the recognition of identifiable intangible assets acquired in a business combination as described in ASC 805-20-25-29 through 25-33. (ASC 805-20-25-1)

To facilitate the combined entity's future application of GAAP in its post combination financial statements, management is required to make decisions on the acquisition date relative to the classification or designation of certain items. These decisions are based on contractual terms, economic and other conditions, and the acquirer's operating and accounting policies as they exist *on the acquisition date*. (ASC 805-20-25-6) Examples include, but are not limited to, the following:

- Classification of investments in certain securities as trading, available for sale, or held to maturity under ASC 320, *Investments—Debt and Equity Securities*[3]
- Designation of a derivative instrument as a hedging instrument under the provisions of ASC 815, *Derivatives and Hedging*
- Assessment of whether an embedded derivative should be separated from the host contract under ASC 815.

(ASC 805-20-25-7)

In applying Step 4, specific exceptions are provided for lease contracts and insurance contracts. (ASC 805-20-25-8) Generally, these contracts are classified by reference to the contractual terms and other factors that were applicable *at their inception* rather than at the acquisition date. If, however, the contracts were modified subsequent to inception and those modifications would change their classification at that date, then the accounting for the contracts is determined by the modification date facts and circumstances. Under these circumstances, the modification date could be the same as the acquisition date.

Step 5—Recognize and Measure the Identifiable Tangible and Intangible Assets Acquired and Liabilities Assumed

Measurement principle In general, the acquirer measures the identifiable tangible and intangible assets acquired, liabilities assumed, and, if applicable, noncontrolling interest at fair value on the acquisition date. (ASC 805-20-30-1) The following guidance is followed in applying the recognition and measurement principles (subject to certain specified exceptions).

Private Company Alternative for Accounting for Identifiable Intangible Assets in a Business Combination If an entity adopts this alternative, it should no longer recognize and measure (and instead subsume into goodwill):

- Customer-related intangible assets unless they are capable of being sold or licensed independently from the other assets of the business, and
- Noncompetition agreements.

The alternative use is designed to reduce the costs and complexity of measuring these assets by decreasing the number of intangible assets that need to be recognized separately without diminishing decision-useful information for users of private company financials.

Adopting this alternative will result in a higher goodwill balance at acquisition. An entity that elects the accounting alternative must adopt the private company alternative to amortize goodwill. (ASC 805-20-15-4) See the chapter on ASC 350, *Intangibles—Goodwill and Other*. However, an entity that elects the accounting alternative is not required to adopt the amendments in this topic.

Entities must decide whether or not to apply the accounting alternative upon the occurrence of the first transaction within the scope of this accounting alternative in fiscal years beginning after December 15, 2015. The elective adoption is effective for the fiscal year's first in-scope adoption annual financial reporting and all interim and annual periods thereafter. If the first in-scope transaction occurs in fiscal years beginning after December 15, 2016, the elective adoption

[3] Also see, the Technical Alerts in the chapter on ASC 320 for information on changes to structure of investment guidance.

is effective in the interim period that includes the date of that first in-scope transaction and subsequent interim and annual periods thereafter.

Operating Leases Regardless of whether the acquiree is the lessee or lessor, the acquirer evaluates, as of the acquisition date, each of the acquiree's operating leases to determine whether its terms are favorable or unfavorable compared to the market terms of leases of identical or similar items. Under extant guidance:[4]

- If the lease terms are favorable, the acquirer recognizes an intangible asset;
- If the lease terms are unfavorable, the acquirer recognizes a liability. (ASC 805-20-25-12)

Even when the lease is considered to be at market terms, there nevertheless may be an identifiable intangible associated with it. This would be the case if market participants would be willing to pay to obtain it (i.e., to obtain the rights and privileges associated with it). Examples of this situation are leases for favorably positioned airport gates, and prime retail space in an economically favorable location. If, from the perspective of marketplace participants, acquiring the lease would entitle them to future economic benefits that qualify as identifiable intangible assets (discussed later in this chapter), the acquirer would recognize, separately from goodwill, the associated identifiable intangible asset.

Operating Lease Assets Owned by an Acquiree/Lessor The fair value of assets owned by the acquiree that are subject to operating leases with the acquiree being the lessor are measured separately from the underlying lease to which they are subject. (ASC 805-20-25-13)[5]

Assets with Uncertain Cash Flows Since fair value measurements take into account the effects of uncertainty regarding the amounts and timing of future cash flows, the acquirer does not recognize a separate valuation allowance for assets subject to such uncertainties. (805-30-30-4)

Assets the Acquirer Plans to Idle or to Use in a Manner That Is Not Their Highest and Best Use The measurement of the identifiable assets acquired at fair value should be made in accordance with the requirements of ASC 820. One of those requirements is that the measurement is to assume the highest and best use of the asset by market participants. In applying this requirement to assets that are acquired in a business combination, this assumption is to be used even if it differs from the manner in which the acquiree was using the assets or the manner in which the acquirer intends to use the assets. Thus, even if the acquirer intends to protect its competitive position or for other business reasons to idle an acquired asset or use it in a manner that is not its highest and best use, the acquirer is still required to initially measure the fair value of that asset using the assumption of its highest and best use and to continue to use that assumption for the purposes of subsequently testing the asset for impairment. (ASC 805-20-30-6)

Identifiable Intangibles Are Recognized Separately from Goodwill ASC 350 addresses the accounting for all intangibles and how to distinguish between separately identifiable intangibles having finite lives, those having indefinite lives, and goodwill, which is unique in being

---

[4] Upon implementation of ASU 2016-02 on leases, this guidance makes a distinction as to whether the acquiree is a lessor or a lessee. If the acquiree is a lessor, the acquirer recognizes:

- An intangible asset if the terms of an operating lease are favorable relative to market terms, and a liability if the terms are unfavorable relative to market terms. If the acquiree is a lessee, the acquirer adjusts the measurement of the acquired right-of-use asset for any favorable or unfavorable terms. (ASC 805-20-25-12) In those circumstances, the acquirer measures:
- The lease liability at the present value of the remaining lease payments, as if the acquired lease were a new lease of the acquirer at the acquisition date the right-of-use asset at the same amount as the lease liability as adjusted to reflect favorable or unfavorable terms of the lease when compared with market terms. (ASC 802-20-30-24)

[5] Paragraph superseded by ASU 2016-02 upon implementation.

"unidentifiable" and having an indeterminate life. In a business acquisition, any acquired identifiable intangible asset (e.g., patents, customer lists, etc.) must be recognized separately from goodwill when it meets *either* of the following two criteria:

1. *Separability criterion*—The intangible asset is capable of being separated or divided from the entity that holds it, and sold, transferred, licensed, rented, or exchanged, regardess of the acquirer's intent to do so. An intangible asset meets this criterion even if its transfer would not be alone, but instead would be accompanied or bundled with a related contract, other identifiable asset, or a liability.
2. *Legal/contractual criterion*—The intangible asset results from contractual or other legal rights. An intangible asset meets this criterion even if the rights are not transferable or separable from the acquiree or from other rights and obligations of the acquiree. (ASC 805-20-55-2)

ASC 805-20-55 contains a listing of intangible assets that FASB believes have characteristics that meet one of these two criteria (legal/contractual or separability). A logical approach in practice would be for the acquirer to first consider whether the intangibles specifically included on the FASB list are applicable to the particular acquiree and then to consider whether there may be other unlisted intangibles included in the acquisition that meet one or both of the criteria for separate recognition.

ASC 805-20-55-13 organizes groups of identifiable intangibles into categories related to or based on:

- Marketing
- Customers or clients
- Artistic works
- Contractual
- Technology

Some of the items listed could fall into more than one of the categories. All intangible assets acquired—whether singly, in groups, or as part of a business combination—are initially recognized and measured based on their respective fair values. Under the provisions of ASC 350, serious effort must be directed to identifying the various intangibles acquired, thus minimizing the amount of goodwill to be recognized.

Examples of identifiable intangibles included in each of the categories are as follows:

Marketing-related intangible assets.

- **Newspaper mastheads.** The unique appearance of the title page of a newspaper or other periodical.
- **Trademarks, service marks, trade names, collective marks, certification marks.** A *trademark* represents the right to use a name, word, logo, or symbol that differentiates a product from products of other entities. A *service mark* is the equivalent of a trademark for a service offering instead of a product. A *collective mark* is used to identify products or services offered by members affiliated with each other. A *certification mark* is used to designate a particular attribute of a product or service such as its geographic source (e.g., Colombian coffee or Florida orange juice) or the standards under which it was produced (e.g., ISO 9000 Certified).
- **Trade dress.** The overall appearance and image (unique color, shape, or package design) of a product.

- **Internet domain names.** The unique name that identifies an address on the Internet. Domain names must be registered with an Internet registry and are renewable.
- **Noncompetition Agreements.** Rights to assurances that companies or individuals will refrain from conducting similar businesses or selling to specific customers for an agreed-upon period of time.
  (ASC 820-20-55-14 through 55-19)

Customer-related intangible assets.

- **Customer lists.** Names, contact information, order histories, and other information about a company's customers that a third party, such as a competitor or a telemarketing firm, would want to use in its own business.
- **Customer contracts and related customer relationships.** When a company's relationships with its customers arise primarily through contracts and are of value to buyers who can "step into the shoes" of the sellers and assume their remaining rights and duties under the contracts, and which hold the promise that the customers will place future orders with the entity or relationships between entities and their customers for which:
  - The entities have information about the customers and have regular contacts with the customers, and
  - The customers have the ability to make direct contact with the entity.
- **Noncontractual customer relationships.** Customer relationships that arise through means such as regular contacts by sales or service representatives, the value of which are derived from the prospect of the customers placing future orders with the entity.
- **Order or production backlogs.** Unfilled sales orders for goods and services in amounts that exceed the quantity of finished goods and work-in-process on hand for filling the orders.
  (ASC 820-20-55-20 through 55-28)

Artistic-related intangible assets.

- Plays, operas, ballets
- Books, magazines, newspapers, and other literary works
- Musical works such as compositions, song lyrics, and advertising jingles
- Photographs, drawings, and clip art
- Audiovisual material including motion pictures, music videos, television programs
  (ASC 820-20-55-29)

Contract-based intangible assets.

- **License, royalty, standstill agreements.** License agreements represent the right, on the part of the licensee, to access or use property that is owned by the licensor for a specified period of time at an agreed-upon price. A royalty agreement entitles its holder to a contractually agreed-upon portion of the income earned from the sale or license of a work covered by patent or copyright. A standstill agreement conveys assurances that a company or individual will refrain from engaging in certain activities for specified periods of time.
- **Advertising contracts.** A contract with a newspaper, broadcaster, or Internet site to provide specified advertising services to the acquiree.
- **Lease agreements.** Irrespective of whether the acquiree is the lessee or lessor. [6]

[6] Upon implementation of ASU 2016-02 on leases, this becomes "Operating lease agreements of a lessor."

- **Construction permits.** Rights to build a specified structure at a specified location.
- **Construction contracts.** Rights to become the contractor responsible for completing a construction project and benefit from the profits it produces, subject to the remaining obligations associated with performance (including any past-due payments to suppliers and/or subcontractors).
- **Management, service, or supply contracts.** Rights to manage a construction project for a fee, procure specified services at a specified fee, or purchase specified products at contractually agreed-upon prices.
- **Broadcast rights.** Legal permission to transmit electronic signals using specified band-width in the radio frequency spectrum, granted by the operation of communication laws.
- **Franchise rights.** Legal rights to engage in a trade-named business, to sell a trademarked good, or to sell a service-marked service in a particular geographic area.
- **Operating rights.** Permits to operate in a certain manner, such as those granted to a carrier to transport specified commodities.
- **Use rights.** Permits to use specified land, property, or air space in a particular manner, such as the right to cut timber, expel emissions, or to land airplanes at specified gates at an airport.
- **Servicing contracts.** The contractual right to service a loan. Servicing entails activities such as collecting principal and interest payments from the borrower, maintaining escrow accounts, paying taxes and insurance premiums when due, and pursuing collection of delinquent payments.
- **Employment contract.** The right to succeed the acquiree as the employer under a formal contract to obtain an employee's services in exchange for fulfilling the employer's remaining duties, such as payment of salaries and benefits, as specified by the contract.
  (ASC 820-20-55-38 through 55-45)

Technology-based intangible assets.

- **Patented technology.** Computer software source code, program specifications, procedures, and associated documentation that are legally protected by patent.
- **Computer software and mask works.** Software permanently stored on a read-only memory chip as a series of stencils or integrated circuitry. Mask works may be provided statutory protection in some countries.
- **Unpatented technology.** Access to knowledge about the proprietary processes and work-flows followed by the acquiree to accomplish desired business results.
- **Databases.** Databases are collections of information generally stored digitally in an organized manner. A database can be protected by copyright (e.g., the database contained on the CD-ROM version of this publication). Many databases, however, represent information accumulated as a natural by-product of a company conducting its normal operating activities. Examples of these databases are plentiful and include title plants, scientific data, and credit histories. Title plants represent historical records with respect to real estate parcels in a specified geographic location.
- **Trade secrets.** Trade secrets are proprietary, confidential information, such as a formula, process, or recipe.
  (ASC 805-20-55-39 through 55-45)

One commonly cited intangible asset deliberately omitted by the FASB from its list of identifiable intangibles is an *assembled workforce*. FASB decided that the replacement cost technique that is often used to measure the fair value of an assembled workforce is not a representationally faithful measure of the fair value of the intellectual capital acquired. It was thus decided that an exception to the recognition criteria would be made, and that the fair value of an acquired assembled workforce would remain part of goodwill. (ASC 805-20-55-6)

Subsequent measurement The acquiring entity, after initial measurement, should subsequently account for the acquired assets and liabilities assumed and equity issued in accordance with other relevant GAAP.

Useful economic life Reliably measurable identifiable intangible assets, with the exception of those meeting the criteria for nonamortization (explained below), must be amortized over their respective useful economic lives. Useful economic life is the period over which the asset is expected to contribute (whether directly or indirectly) to cash flows into the entity. Factors to be considered in estimating the useful economic life of an intangible asset to an enterprise can be found in the chapter on ASC 350 in the section on "Determining the useful life of intangible assets."

Residual value Typically, the entire fair value assigned to an intangible asset will be subject to amortization, although in some instances a residual value may be determined, which reduces the asset's amortizable basis. More information on residual value can be found in the chapter on ASC 350 in the section on "Residual value."

Research and development assets ASC 350-30 provides guidance on subsequently measuring and accounting for assets acquired in a business combination, including those used in research and development activities. (ASC 805-20-35-5)

Exceptions to the recognition and/or measurement principles ASC 805 provides certain exceptions to its general principles for recognizing assets acquired and liabilities assumed at their acquisition date fair values. These can be summarized as follows:

Nature of exception	*Recognition*	*Measurement*
1. Assets held for sale		X
2. Contingent assets and liabilities of the acquiree	X	X
3. Indemnification assets	X	X
4. Reacquired rights		X
5. Employee benefits	X	X
6. Share-based payment awards		X
7. Income taxes	X	X
8. Leases[7]		X
9. Purchased financial assets with credit deterioration[8]	X	
(ASC 805-20-30-12)		

1. **Assets held for sale.** (ASC 805-20-30-22) Assets classified as held for sale individually or as part of a disposal group should be measured at acquisition date fair value less cost to sell consistent with ASC 360.

[7] The guidance on the exception for leases is effective upon implementation of ASU 2016-02, Leases. See the chapter on ASC 842 for more information regarding implementation dates.

[8] The guidance on the exception for purchased financial assets with credit deterioration is effective upon implementation of ASU 2016-13, Financial Instruments—Credit Losses (Topic 326) Measurement of Credit Losses on Financial Instruments. See the chapter on ASC 326 for more information regarding implementation dates.

2. **Contingent assets and liabilities of the acquire.** (ASC805-20-30-23) A gain or loss contingency is defined as an existing, unresolved condition, situation, or set of circumstances that will eventually be resolved by the occurrence or nonoccurrence of one or more future events. A potential gain or loss to the reporting entity can result from the contingency's resolution. For assets arising from contingencies that meet the recognition criteria in ASC 805-20-25-20, entities should recognize and initially measure them by applying the guidance in ASC 450, particularly ASC 450-20-25-2.
3. **Indemnification assets.** (ASC 805-20-30-18 and 30-19) Indemnification provisions are usually included in the voluminous closing documents necessary to effect a business combination. Indemnifications are contractual terms designed to fully or partially protect the acquirer from the potential adverse effects of an unfavorable future resolution of a contingency or uncertainty that exists at the acquisition date. Frequently the indemnification is structured to protect the acquirer by limiting the maximum amount of postcombination loss that the acquirer would bear in the event of an adverse outcome. A contractual indemnification provision results in the acquirer obtaining, as a part of the acquisition, an indemnification asset and simultaneously assuming a contingent liability of the acquiree.

   Recognition and initial measurement. ASC 805 requires the acquirer to recognize and measure the indemnification asset using the same measurement basis it uses to measure the indemnified obligation.

   In measuring an indemnification asset, management is to take into account any uncertainty in the amounts or timing of expected future cash flows. If the asset is measured at acquisition-date fair value, those effects are included in the measure of fair value and, therefore, a separate valuation allowance is not recognized. (ASC 805-30-30-18)

   Some indemnifications relate to assets or liabilities that are exceptions to the recognition or measurement principles. Indemnifications may, for example, be *related* to contingencies that do not meet the previously discussed criteria for recognition in the acquisition-date financial statements. Other indemnifications may be related to uncertain income tax positions that are measured, under ASC 740, as the maximum amount that is estimated to be more likely than not of being sustained upon examination by the relevant taxing jurisdiction. In cases such as these, the indemnification asset should be recognized and measured using assumptions consistent with those used to measure the item being indemnified. Since uncertainty with respect to the collectibility of the indemnification asset is not directly included in its measurement, collectibility is considered separately and, to the extent necessary, reflected in a valuation allowance to reduce the carrying amount of the indemnification asset. (ASC 805-30-30-19)

   Subsequent measurement. At each reporting date subsequent to the acquisition date, the acquirer should measure an indemnification asset recognized as part of the business combination using the same basis as the indemnified item, subject to any limitations imposed contractually on the amount of the indemnification. If an indemnification asset is not subsequently measured at fair value (because to do so would be inconsistent with the basis used to measure the indemnified item), management should assess the collectibility of the asset and, to the extent necessary, a valuation allowance should be established or adjusted. (ASC 805-30-35-4)

Derecognition. An indemnification asset is derecognized only when the asset is collected, the rights to receive the asset are sold, or the acquirer otherwise loses its right to receive it. (ASC 805-30-40-3)

4. **Reacquired rights.** (ASC 805-20-30-20) An acquirer and acquiree may have engaged in preacquisition business transactions such as leases, licenses, or franchises that resulted in the acquiree paying consideration to the acquirer to use tangible and/or intangible assets of the acquirer in the acquiree's business.

   Recognition and initial measurement. Upon consummation of the business combination, the acquirer may reacquire a previously granted right. Upon reacquisition, the acquirer is to account for the right as an identifiable, amortizable intangible asset separate from goodwill as found in ASC 805-20-25-14.

   Subsequent measurement. Reacquired rights recognized at the acquisition date are amortized, postcombination, on the basis of the remaining, unexpired term of the related contract. The remaining contractual term is to be used for this purpose even if market participants would consider potential future contract renewals in determining the fair value of the contract. Should the acquirer subsequently sell the reacquired right to a third party, the carrying amount of the intangible asset is to be included in the determination of gain or loss on the sale. (ASC 805-20-35-2)

5. **Employee benefits**. (ASC 805-20-30-14 through 30-17 and 30-21) Liabilities (and assets, if applicable), associated with acquiree employee benefit arrangements are recognized and measured under other GAAP, as applicable.

Types of benefits	Applicable GAAP
Deferred compensation contracts including postretirement benefit aspects of split-dollar life insurance arrangements	ASC 710-10-25, ASC 715-60
Compensated absences and sabbatical leaves	ASC 710-10-15, ASC 710-10-25
Pensions, plan curtailments, and termination benefits	ASC 715-30, ASC 715-20
Postretirement benefits other than pensions, including postretirement benefit aspects of split-dollar life insurance arrangements	ASC 715-60, ASC 715-20
Nonretirement postemployment benefits (benefits provided to inactive or former employees, their beneficiaries, and covered dependents after employment but before retirement) including, but not limited to: • Salary continuation • Supplemental unemployment benefits • Severance benefits • Disability-related benefits including workers' compensation • Job training and counseling (e.g., outplacement) • Continuation of benefits such as health care and life insurance	ASC 712
One-time termination benefits	ASC 420

In researching the application of these pronouncements, it is important to consider the effect on them of ASC 805. For example:

a. ASC 715-30 and ASC 715-60 clarify that:
   1. The acquirer should recognize, as part of the business combination, an asset or liability that represents the funded status of a single-employer defined benefit pension plan and/or a single-employer defined benefit postretirement plan. In determining the funded status, the acquirer is to disregard the effects of expected plan amendments, terminations, or curtailments that it has no obligation to make at the acquisition date.
   2. The projected benefit obligation assumed for a single-employer defined benefit pension plan or the accumulated postretirement benefit obligation assumed for a single-employer defined benefit postretirement plan are to reflect any other necessary changes in assumptions based on an assessment by the acquirer of relevant future events.
   3. If the acquiree participates in a multiemployer-defined benefit pension or postretirement plan, and at the acquisition date it is probable that the acquirer will withdraw from that plan, the acquirer is to recognize a withdrawal liability as of the acquisition date under ASC 450.

b. ASC 420's scope covers exit activities associated with entities that are acquired in a business combination.

   1. *Acquirer share-based payment awards exchanged for acquiree awards held by its employees.* In connection with a business combination, the acquirer often awards share-based payments to the employees of the acquiree in exchange for the employees' acquire awards. Obviously, there are many valid business reasons for the exchange, not the least of which is ensuring smooth transition and integration as well as retention of valued employees.

6. **Share-based payment awards.** The discussion that follows uses concepts and terminology from ASC 718, *Compensation—Stock Compensation.*

   1. *Acquirer not obligated to exchange.* Accounting for the replacement awards under ASC 805 is dependent on whether the acquirer is obligated to replace the acquiree awards. The acquirer is obligated to replace the acquiree awards if the acquiree or its employees can enforce replacement through rights obtained from the terms of the acquisition agreement, the acquiree awards, or applicable laws or regulations.

If the acquirer is not obligated to replace the acquiree awards, all of the fair-value-based measure (FVBM)[9] of the replacement awards is recognized as compensation cost in the post-combination financial statements.

[9] Although the accompanying guidance uses the term "fair-value-based measure" to refer to the measurement of share-based awards, the guidance also applies to awards of both the acquirer and acquiree that are measured using either the calculated value method or intrinsic value method.

Example of Acquirer Replacing Acquiree Awards without the Obligation to Do So

New Parent, Inc. (NP) acquired New Subsidiary, Inc. (NS) on January 1, 20X1. Because of the business combination, the share-based payment awards that had been previously granted by NS to its employees expired on the acquisition date.

Although NP was not obligated, legally or contractually, to replace the expired awards, its Board of Directors approved a grant of NP awards designed so that the employees of NS would not be financially disadvantaged by the acquisition transaction.

Since the replacement awards were voluntary on the part of NP, the FVBM of the replacement award is attributed wholly to the postcombination consolidated financial statements of NP and Subsidiary.

Acquirer obligated to replace acquiree awards If the acquirer is obligated to replace the awards of the acquiree, either all or a portion of the FVBM of the replacement awards is included in measuring the consideration transferred by the acquirer in the business combination. To the extent a portion of the replacement awards is not allocated to consideration transferred, it is accounted for as compensation for postcombination services in the acquirer's consolidated financial statements.

For the purposes of illustrating the allocation computations, the following conventions and abbreviations are used:

$FVBM_{RA}$	Acquisition date fair-value-based measure of acquirer replacement award
$FVBM_{AA}$	Acquisition date fair-value-based measure of acquiree award that is being replaced by the acquirer
RSP_{AA}	Original requisite service period[10] of acquiree awards at their grant date
RSP_{RA}	Requisite service period of the acquirer replacement awards at acquisition date
$CRSP_{AA}$	Portion of requisite service period completed at the acquisition date by employees under the acquiree awards
TSP	Total service period—the service period already satisfied by the employees at the acquisition date under the acquiree awards plus the requisite service period, if any, required by the acquirer replacement awards
PRE	Portion of $FVBM_{RA}$ attributable to precombination services performed by the employees of the acquiree
PCC	Postcombination compensation cost

$$TSP = CRSP_{AA} + RSP_{RA}$$

The following steps are followed to determine the portion of the FVBM of the replacement award to be included as part of the consideration transferred by the acquirer:

1. Compute both $FVBM_{RA}$ and $FVBM_{AA}$ by following the provisions of ASC 718.
2. Compute the portion of the replacement award that is attributable to precombination services rendered by the acquiree's employees as follows:

   a. If $RSP_{AA} > TSP$, then: $PRE = FVBM_{AA}$
   b. If $RSP_{AA} \leq TSP$, then: $PRE = FVBM_{AA}$

[10] The term "requisite service period" includes explicit, implicit, and derived service periods during which employees are required to provide services in exchange for the award. These terms are explained in ASC 718.

3. Compute the portion of the nonvested replacement award attributable to postcombination service as follows: $PCC = FVBM_{RA} - PRE$

This amount is to be recognized as compensation cost in the postcombination financial statements since, at the acquisition date, the requisite service conditions had not been met.

The following examples are adapted from the implementation guidance for ASC 805.

Example of Acquirer Replacement Awards Requiring No Postcombination Services Exchanges for Fully Vested Acquiree Awards Where the Employees Have Rendered All Required Services by the Acquisition Date

New Parent, Inc. (NP) acquired New Subsidiary, Inc. (NS) on January 1, 20X1. In accordance with the acquisition agreement, NP agreed to replace share-based awards that had previously been issued by NS. Details are as follows:

	a. Acquiree Awards	*b. Acquirer Awards*
1. Acquisition date FVBM of awards	$FVBM_{AA} = \$100$	$FVBM_{RA} = \$110$
2. Original requisite service period of acquiree awards at their grant date	$RSP_{AA} = 4$ years	
3. Portion of 2a completed by the acquisition date by employees of the acquire	$CRSP_{AA} = 4$ years	–
4. Requisite service period of acquirer replacement awards at the acquisition date	–	$RSP_{RA} = 0$
5. Total service period (3a + 4b)	–	TSP = 4 years
6. The greater of the total service period (5b) or the original requisite service period of the acquire awards (2a)	–	4 years

Since the acquiree's employees had completed all of the services required under the prior awards, applying the formula yields a result that attributes 100% of the fair value of the acquiree award that is being replaced to precombination services rendered:

$$PRE = \left(\frac{3a}{6b}\right)$$

$$PRE = \$100\left(\frac{4\ years}{4\ years}\right)$$

$$PRE = \$100$$

The $100 result, attributed to precombination services, is included by the acquirer in its computation of the consideration transferred in exchange for control of the acquiree.

The final step in the computation is to account for the difference between the acquisition date fair values of the replacement awards and the acquiree awards as follows:

Fair value of replacement awards—$FVBM_{RA}$	$110
Allocated to consideration per above	100
Additional compensation cost recognized immediately in postcombination financial statements	$ 10

This result illustrates the basic principle in ASC 805 that any excess of $FVBM_{RA}$ over the $FVBM_{AA}$ is to be attributed to postcombination services and recognized as compensation cost in the postcombination financial statements.

Example of Acquirer Replacement Awards Requiring Performance of Postcombination Services Exchanged for Acquiree Awards for Which All Requisite Services Had Been Rendered by the Acquiree's Employees as of the Acquisition Date

The acquisition agreement referred to in the previous example governing the NP acquisition of NS that occurred on January 1, 20X1, contained the following provisions regarding exchange of outstanding NS awards at acquisition date for NP replacement awards:

	a. Acquiree Awards	*b. Acquirer Awards*
1. Acquisition date FVBM of awards	$FVBM_{AA}$ = $100	$FVBM_{RA}$ = $100
2. Original requisite service period of acquiree awards at their grant date	RSP_{AA} = 4 years	–
3. Portion of 2a completed by the acquisition date by employees of the acquiree (the acquiree employees in this example had actually completed a total of 7 years of services by the acquisition date)	$CRSP_{AA}$ = 4 years	–
4. Requisite service period of acquirer replacement awards at the acquisition date	–	RSP_{RA} = 1 year
5. Total service period (3a + 4b)	–	TSP = 5 years
6. The greater of the total service period (5b) or the original requisite service period of the acquiree awards (2a)	–	5 years

Even though the acquiree's employees had completed all of the requisite service required by the acquiree's awards three years prior to the acquisition, the imposition of an additional year of required service by the acquirer's replacement awards results in an allocation between precombination compensation cost and postcombination compensation cost as follows:

$$PRE = 1a\left(\frac{3a}{6b}\right)$$

$$PRE = \$100\left(\frac{4\ years}{4\ years}\right)$$

$$PRE = \$80$$

The $80 result, attributed to precombination services, is included by the acquirer in its computation of the consideration transferred in exchange for control of the acquirer.

The $20 difference between the $100 fair value of the replacement awards and the $80 allocated to precombination services (and included in consideration transferred) is accounted for as compensation cost in the postcombination consolidated financial statements of NP and Subsidiary under the provisions of ASC 718.

Example of Acquirer Replacement Awards Requiring Performance of Postcombination Services Exchanged for Acquiree Awards with Remaining Unsatisfied Requisite Service Period as of the Acquisition Date

The acquisition agreement referred to in the previous examples governing the NP acquisition of NS that occurred on January 1, 20X1, contained the following provisions regarding exchange of outstanding NS awards at acquisition date for NP replacement awards:

	a. Acquiree Awards	*b. Acquirer Awards*
1. Acquisition date FVBM of awards	$FVBM_{AA}$ = \$100	$FVBM_{RA}$ = \$100
2. Original requisite service period of acquiree awards at their grant date	RSP_{AA} = 4 years	–
3. Portion of 2a completed by the acquisition date by employees of the acquire	$CRSP_{AA}$ = 2 years	–
4. Requisite service period of acquirer replacement awards at the acquisition date	–	RSP_{RA} = 1 year
5. Total service period (3a + 4b)	–	TSP = 3 years
6. The greater of the total service period (5b) or the original requisite service period of the acquiree awards (2a)	–	4 years

The portion of the FVBM of the replacement awards attributable to precombination services already rendered by the acquiree employees is computed as follows:

$$PRE = la\left(\frac{3a}{6b}\right)$$

$$PRE = \$100\left(\frac{2\ years}{4\ years}\right)$$

$$PRE = \$50$$

Based on the computation above, at the acquisition date, NP, the acquirer, includes \$50 as consideration transferred to obtain control of NS, the acquiree. The remaining \$50 is attributed to postcombination services and, accordingly, recognized as compensation cost in the consolidated postcombination financial statements of NP and Subsidiary.

Example of Acquirer Replacement Awards That Do Not Require Postcombination Services Exchanged for Acquiree Awards for Which the Acquiree's Employees Had Not Yet Completed All of the Requisite Services by the Acquisition Date

The acquisition agreement referred to in the previous examples governing the NP acquisition of NS that occurred on January 1, 20X1, contained the following provisions regarding exchange of outstanding NS awards at acquisition date for NP replacement awards:

	a. Acquiree Awards	*b. Acquirer Awards*
1. Acquisition date fair-value-based measure of awards	$FVBM_{AA}$ = \$100	$FVBM_{RA}$ = \$100
2. Original requisite service period of acquiree awards at their grant date	RSP_{AA} = 4 years	–

	a. Acquiree Awards	*b. Acquirer Awards*
3. Portion of 2a completed by the acquisition date by employees of the acquire	$CRSP_{AA}$ = 2 years	–
4. Requisite service period of acquirer replacement awards at the acquisition date	–	$RSP_{RA} = 0$
5. Total service period (3a + 4b)	–	TSP = 2 years
6. The greater of the total service period (5b) or the original requisite service period of the acquiree awards (2a)	4 years	

Under this scenario, the terms of the awards previously granted by NS, the acquiree, did not contain a change-in-control provision that would have fully vested them upon the acquisition by NP. If this had been the case, the outcome would be the same as the example above where neither the acquiree awards nor the replacement rewards required the completion of any service on the part of the acquiree's employees.

Since, at the acquisition date, the acquiree employees had completed only two out of the four years of required services and the replacement awards do not extend the duration of services required postcombination, the total service period (TSP) in 5b is the two years already completed by the acquiree's employees under their original awards in 3a ($CRSP_{AA}$).

The portion of the FVBM of the replacement awards attributable to precombination services already rendered by the acquiree employees is computed as follows:

$$PRE = la\left(\frac{3a}{6b}\right)$$

$$PRE = \$100\left(\frac{2\ years}{4\ years}\right)$$

$$PRE = \$50$$

Consequently, $50 of the FVBM of the replacement awards is attributable to precombination services already performed by the acquiree employees and is, therefore, included in computing the consideration transferred in exchange for obtaining control of the acquiree.

The remaining $50 of the FVBM of the replacement awards is attributable to postcombination service. However, since the acquiree's employees are not required to provide any postcombination services under the terms of the replacement awards, the entire $50 is immediately recognized by NP, the acquirer, in its postcombination consolidated financial statements.

Although not illustrated in the preceding examples, ASC 805 requires the acquirer to estimate the number of its replacement awards for which the requisite service is expected to occur. To the extent that service is not expected to occur due to employees terminating prior to meeting the replacement award's requisite service requirements, the portion of the FVBM of the replacement awards included in consideration transferred in the business combination is reduced accordingly.

If the replacement award is subject to a graded vesting schedule, the acquirer is to recognize the related compensation cost in accordance with its policy election for other awards in accordance with ASC 718-10-35. Compensation cost is either:

1. Recognized using the *graded vesting attribution method* that separates the award into tranches according to the year in which they vest and treats each tranche as if it had been a separate award, or
2. Recognized using a straight-line attribution method over the graded vesting period.

If option (2) is elected, compensation cost at any date must equal at least the amount attributable to options that actually vested on or before that date.

Finally, it is important to note that the same requirements for apportioning the replacement award between precombination and postcombination service apply to replacement awards that are classified as equity or as liabilities. All post-acquisition-date changes in the FVBM of liability awards (and their related income tax effects) are recognized in the acquirer's postcombination financial statements in the periods in which the changes occur.

7. **Income taxes.** The basic principle that applies to income tax accounting in a business combination (carried forward without change by ASC 805) is that the acquirer should recognize, as of the acquisition date, deferred income tax assets or liabilities for the future effects of temporary differences and carryforwards of the acquiree that either:

    a. Exist on the acquisition date, *or*
    b. Are generated by the acquisition itself.

ASC 805 also clarifies ASC 740's applicability to business combinations as follows:

a. In computing the acquisition date amount of currently payable or refundable income taxes from a particular taxing jurisdiction, management is to apply the recognition and measurement provisions of ASC 740 to evaluate the amounts to record relative to prior income tax positions taken by the acquiree.
b. As a result of management's evaluation of prior tax positions and the amounts recognized in item 1, management is to adjust the income tax bases used in computing the deferred income tax assets and liabilities associated with the business combination at the acquisition date.
c. New information regarding the facts and circumstances that existed at the acquisition date that comes to the attention of management regarding those income tax positions is treated as follows:

    If the information results in a change during the measurement period, the adjustment is made to goodwill. If goodwill is reduced to zero, any remaining portion of the adjustment is recorded as a bargain purchase gain.

    If the information results in a post-measurement-period change, the change is accounted for in the same manner as any other ASC 740 changes.

Valuation allowances To the extent applicable, deferred income tax assets should be reduced by a valuation allowance for the portion of the asset not deemed MLTN to be realized.

On the acquisition date, any benefits of future deductible temporary differences or *net operating loss carryforwards* (NOLs) of an acquired entity are to be recognized if the acquirer is permitted to utilize those benefits on a consolidated income tax return under the existing income tax law. The income tax benefits will be recorded gross with an offsetting valuation allowance if it is more likely than not that the deferred income tax asset will not be realized by the reporting entity (for example, if it is estimated that there will not be sufficient future taxable income to utilize the NOL prior to its expiration).

Some jurisdictions restrict the future use of income tax benefits of the acquiree and only permit those benefits to be applied to subsequent taxable income generated by the acquiree even though the entities are permitted to file a consolidated income tax return. When this is the case, or when the acquiree is expected to file a separate income tax return, management of the consolidated reporting entity is to assess the need for a valuation allowance for those benefits based only on the acquiree's separate past and expected future taxable income.

As a result of the acquisition and the permissibility of filing a consolidated income tax return in a particular jurisdiction, the acquirer may be able to use future taxable income generated by the acquiree to obtain the tax benefits of its own NOLs for which the acquirer had previously recognized a valuation allowance. If, based on the weight of available evidence, management of the acquirer concludes that its previously recognized valuation allowance can be reduced or eliminated, the adjustment is not considered part of the accounting for the business combination. Instead, the benefit is recognized as a component of income tax expense in the period of the acquisition.

Post-acquisition-date changes in a valuation allowance with respect to an acquiree's deferred income tax asset are to be recognized as follows:

a. If the change in judgment occurs during the measurement period (as defined in ASC 805) that is not to exceed one year from the acquisition date, and results from new information bearing on facts and circumstances that existed at the acquisition date, the change is to be recognized as an adjustment to goodwill. Should the adjustment reduce goodwill to zero, the acquirer is to recognize any further reduction in the valuation allowance as a gain from a bargain purchase.
b. If the change in judgment occurs subsequent to the measurement period, it is reported as an increase or decrease in income tax expense or benefit of the period in which the judgment changed. Exceptions to this treatment are provided for changes attributable to dividends on unallocated shares of an employee stock ownership plan (ESOP), employee stock options, and certain quasi reorganizations. Accounting for these exceptions results in adjustments directly to contributed capital rather than to income tax expense.

Goodwill and income taxes To the extent that goodwill amortization is nondeductible in any applicable taxing jurisdiction, the nondeductible goodwill does not represent a temporary difference between GAAP and tax and consequently does not give rise to deferred income taxes.

U.S. federal income tax law permits the amortization of goodwill and other specified acquired intangibles over a statutory 15-year period (IRC § 197). The method of determining the amount of goodwill to recognize for income tax purposes, however, differs from the method prescribed by ASC 805 for financial reporting purposes. Further complicating matters, other taxing jurisdictions to which the reporting entity is subject may not recognize goodwill amortization as deductible. This can result in onerous recordkeeping of book/tax differences in the carrying amounts of goodwill in each of the major jurisdictions in which the reporting entity is taxed.

When goodwill amortization is tax deductible in a particular jurisdiction, it does result in a temporary difference between the income tax basis and GAAP carrying amount of the goodwill. (ASC 805-740-25-9) GAAP goodwill is only written off if it becomes partially or fully impaired whereas tax goodwill is subject to periodic amortization until its income tax basis is reduced to zero.

Since goodwill represents a residual amount after considering all identifiable assets acquired and liabilities assumed in the business combination, any deferred income tax asset associated with goodwill would necessarily have to be computed in order to determine the residual. Thus, FASB prescribed the use of a simultaneous equation method to compute goodwill net of the deferred income tax asset associated with it. To operationalize this requirement, ASC 805-740-25-9 describes and illustrates it.

8. **Leases.** Upon implementation of ASU 2016-02, if the acquirer is a lessee, the acquirer measures the lease liability as the present value of the remaining lease payments as if the lease were a new lease. The right-of-use asset is measured at the same amount as the lease liability, adjusted to reflect favorable or unfavorable terms compared with market conditions.
9. **Purchased financial assets with credit deterioration.** Upon implementation of ASU 2016-13, the acquirer should recognize these assets in accordance with ASC 326-20-55-57 through 55-78.

Step 6—Recognize and Measure Any Noncontrolling Interest in the Acquiree The term *noncontrolling interest* refers to the portion of the acquiree, if any, that is not controlled by the parent.

ASC 805 requires the noncontrolling interest in the acquiree to be measured at fair value on the basis of a quoted price in an active market at the acquisition date. If the acquirer is not acquiring all of the shares in the acquiree and there is an active market for the remaining out- standing shares in the acquiree, the acquirer may be able to use the market price to measure the fair value of the noncontrolling interest. Otherwise, the acquirer would measure fair value using other valuation techniques. (ASC 805-20-30-7)

In applying the appropriate valuation technique to determine the fair value of the noncontrolling interest, it is likely that there will be a difference in the fair value per share of that interest and the fair value per share of the controlling interest. This difference arises from what has been referred to as a "minority interest discount" applicable to the noncontrolling shares. Obviously, an investor would be unwilling to pay the same amount per share for equity shares in an entity that did not convey control of that entity than it would pay for shares that did convey control. (ASC 805-20-30-8)

Example of Fair Value of Noncontrolling Interest Adjusted for Noncontrolling Interest Discount

Shirley Corporation (SC) is considering acquiring an 80% interest in Jake Industries Inc. (JI), a privately held corporation. SC engages a valuation specialist to determine the fair value of JI whose shares do not trade in an active market.

The specialist's findings with respect to JI as a whole were as follows:

Aggregate fair value of JI	$ 15 million
Number of outstanding shares	375,000
Aggregate fair value per share	$ 40

In valuing the noncontrolling interest, however, the specialist made the following additional assumptions:

Aggregate fair value per share	$ 40
Estimated noncontrolling interest discount per share	10
Estimated fair value per share of noncontrolling interest	$ 30
Fair value of noncontrolling interest	
Fair value per noncontrolling share	$ 30
# of noncontrolling shares outstanding	x 75,000
	$ 2,250,000

It is important to note from this analysis that, from the perspective of the acquirer, the computation of the acquisition-date fair value of the noncontrolling interest in the acquiree is not computed by simply multiplying the same fair value per share that the acquirer used to value the entity by the percentage voting interest retained collectively by the noncontrolling stockholders. Such a simplistic calculation would have yielded a different result:

$15 million aggregate fair value × 20% noncontrolling shares = $3 million

If this method had been used, the noncontrolling interest would be overvalued by $750,000 (the difference between $3 million and $2,250,000).

Step 7—Measure the Consideration Transferred In general, consideration transferred by the acquiree is measured at its acquisition-date fair value. Examples of consideration that could be transferred include

- Cash,
- Other assets,
- A business,
- A subsidiary of the acquirer,
- Contingent consideration,
- Common or preferred equity instruments,
- Options, and
- Warrants.

The aggregate consideration transferred is the sum of the following elements measured at the acquisition date:

- The fair value of the assets transferred by the acquirer,
- The fair value of the liabilities incurred by the acquirer to the former owners of the acquiree, and
- The fair value of the equity interests issued by the acquirer subject to the measurement exception discussed earlier in this chapter for the portion, if applicable, of acquirer share-based awards exchanged for awards held by employees of the acquiree that is included in consideration transferred.

To the extent the acquirer transfers consideration in the form of assets or liabilities with carrying amounts that differ from their fair values at the acquisition date, the acquirer is to remeasure them at fair value and recognize a gain or loss on the acquisition date. If, however, the transferred assets or liabilities remain within the consolidated entity postcombination with the acquirer retaining control of them, no gain or loss is recognized, and the assets or liabilities are measured at their carrying amounts to the acquirer immediately prior to the acquisition date.

This situation can occur, for example, when the acquirer transfers assets or liabilities to the entity being acquired rather than to its former owners. (ASC 805-30-30-8)

The structure of the transaction may involve the exchange of equity interests between the acquirer and either the acquiree or the acquiree's former owners. If the acquisition-date fair value of the acquiree's equity interests is more reliably measurable than the equity interests of the acquirer, the fair value of the acquiree's equity interests is used to measure the consideration transferred.

Contingent consideration Contingent consideration arrangements in connection with business combinations can be structured in many different ways and can result in the recognition of either assets or liabilities under ASC 805. In either case, the acquirer should include contingent assets and liabilities as part of the consideration transferred, measured at acquisition-date fair value.

If the contingent consideration includes a future payment obligation, that obligation is to be classified as either a liability or equity under the provisions of:

- ASC 480,
- ASC 815-40, or
- Other applicable GAAP.
  (ASC 805-30-25-6)

The acquirer should carefully consider information obtained subsequent to the acquisition-date measurement of contingent consideration. Additional information obtained during the measurement period that relates to the facts and circumstances that existed at the acquisition date result in measurement period adjustments to the recognized amount of contingent consideration and a corresponding adjustment to goodwill or gain from bargain purchase. Changes that result from events occurring after the acquisition date, such as meeting a specified earnings target, reaching a specified share price, or reaching an agreed-upon milestone on a research and development project, do not constitute measurement period adjustments. Changes in the fair value of contingent consideration that do not result from measurement period adjustments are to be accounted for as follows:

- If the contingent consideration is classified as equity, it is not to be remeasured and subsequent settlement of the contingency is to be reflected within equity.
- If the contingent consideration is classified as an asset or liability, it is to be remeasured at fair value at each reporting date until resolution of the contingency. Changes in the fair value between reporting dates are to be recognized in net income unless the arrangement is a hedging instrument for which ASC 815, as amended by ASC 805, requires the changes to be initially recognized in other comprehensive income.

Step 8—Recognize and Measure Goodwill or Gain on a Bargain Purchase The last step in applying the acquisition method is the measurement of goodwill or a gain from a bargain purchase. Goodwill represents an intangible that is not specifically identifiable. It results from situations when the amount the acquirer is willing to pay to obtain its controlling interest exceeds the aggregate recognized values of the net assets acquired, measured following the principles of ASC 805. Goodwill's elusive nature as an unidentifiable, residual asset means that it cannot be measured directly but rather can only be measured by reference to the other amounts measured as a part of the business combination:

$$(CT + NI + PE) - NA = GW \text{ or } (NG) \text{ where :}$$

GW	=	Goodwill
NG	=	Negative goodwill
NI	=	Noncontrolling interest in the acquiree, if any, measured at fair value
CT	=	Consideration transferred, generally measured at acquisition-date fair value
PE	=	Fair value of the acquirer's previously held interest in the acquiree if the acquisition was achieved in stages
NA	=	Net assets acquired at the acquisition date—consisting of the identifiable assets acquired and liabilities assumed, measured as described in this chapter

Thus, when application of the formula yields an excess of the consideration transferred, noncontrolling interest, and fair value of previously held interests over the net assets acquired, the acquirer has paid a premium for the acquisition and that premium is characterized as goodwill.

When the opposite is true, that is, when the formula yields a negative result, sometimes referred to as *negative goodwill*, the acquirer has, in fact, obtained a bargain purchase, as the value the acquirer obtained in the exchange exceeded the fair value of what it surrendered.

In a business combination in which no consideration is transferred, the acquirer should use one or more valuation techniques to measure the acquisition-date fair value of its interest in the acquiree and substitute that measurement in the formula for CT, the consideration transferred. The techniques selected require the availability of sufficient data to properly apply them and are to be appropriate for the circumstances. If more than one technique is used, management of the acquirer is to evaluate the results of applying the techniques including the extent of data available and how relevant and reliable the inputs (assumptions) used are. Guidance on the use of valuation techniques is provided in ASC 820.

Bargain purchases If the computation above results in negative goodwill, this constitutes a *bargain purchase*. Under ASC 805, a bargain purchase is recognized in net income as an acquisition-date gain. The gain is not characterized as an extraordinary gain. Rather, it is considered part of income from continuing operations. (ASC 805-30-25-2)

Required reassessment in a bargain purchase Given the complexity of the computations involved, FASB prescribes a verification protocol for management to follow if the computation preliminarily results in a bargain purchase. If the computation initially yields a bargain purchase, management of the acquirer should perform the following procedures before recognizing a gain on the bargain purchase:

- Perform a completeness review of the identifiable tangible and intangible assets acquired and liabilities assumed to reassess whether all such items have been correctly identified. If any omissions are found, recognize the assets and liabilities that had been omitted.
- Perform a review of the procedures used to measure all of the following items. The objective of the review is to ensure that the acquisition-date measurements appropriately considered all available information available at the acquisition date:
  - Identifiable assets acquired
  - Liabilities assumed
  - Consideration transferred
  - Noncontrolling interest in the acquiree, if applicable
  - Acquirer's previously held equity interest in the acquiree for a business combination achieved in stages.

(ASC 805-30-30-4 through 30-6)

Business Combinations Achieved in Stages (Step Acquisitions) A step acquisition is a business combination in which the acquirer held an equity interest in the acquiree prior to the acquisition date on which it obtained control. (ASC 805-10-25-9)

ASC 805 requires the acquirer to remeasure its previous holdings of the acquiree's equity at acquisition date fair value. Any gain or loss on remeasurement is recognized in earnings on that date. If the acquirer had previously recognized changes in the carrying amount of the acquiree's equity in other comprehensive income (e.g., because the investment was classified as available for sale), that amount should be reclassified and included in the computation of the acquisition date gain or loss from remeasurement. (ASC 805-10-25-10)

Example of a Step Acquisition

On 12/31/20X1, Finestone Corporation (FC) owned 5% of the 30,000 outstanding voting com- mon shares of Kitzes Industries (KI). On FC's 12/31/20X statement of financial position, it classified its investment in KI as available-for-sale. On 3/31/20X2, FC acquired additional equity shares in KI sufficient to provide FC with a controlling interest in KI and, thus, became KI's par- ent company.

The following table summarizes FC's initial holdings in KI, the subsequent increase in those holdings, and the computation of the gain on remeasurement at the acquisition date of 3/31/20X2:

			Per share		Aggregate investment		
Dart	*# of Shares*	*Percent interest*	*Cost*	*Fair Value*	*Cost*	*Fair Value*	*Unrealized appreciation included in accumulated other comprehensive*
12/31/20X1	1,500	5%	$10	$16	$ 15,000	$ 24,000	$9,000
3/31/20X2	21,000	70%	20	20	420,000	420,000	
	22,500	75%					

Computation of gain (loss) on remeasurement at acquisition date:

Fair value per share on 4/1/20X2	$ 20
Number of preacquisition shares	× 1,500
Aggregate fair value of preacquisition shares on 4/1/20X2	30,000
Carrying amount of preacquisition shares on 4/1/20X2	24,000
Appreciation attributable to the 1st quarter of 20X2	6,000
Pre-2012 appreciation reclassified from accumulated OCI	9,000
Gain on remeasurement of KI stock on 3/31/20X2	$15,000

ASC 805-40, *Reverse Acquisitions*

Introduction A reverse acquisition is a stock transaction that occurs when one entity (the legal acquirer) issues so many of its shares to the former owners of another entity (the legal acquiree) that those former owners become the majority owners of the resultant consolidated enterprise. As a result of the transaction, the legal and accounting treatments will differ, with the legal acquiree being treated as the acquirer for financial reporting purposes. (ASC 805-40-20) While often the legal acquirer will adopt the acquiree's name, thus alerting users of the financial statements to the nature of the organizational change, this does not necessarily occur, and, in any event, it is critical that the financial statements contain sufficient disclosure so that users are not misled. This is particularly important in the periods immediately following the transaction, and especially when comparative financial statements are presented that include periods prior to the acquisition, since comparability will be affected.

Structure of the Transaction A typical reverse acquisition (see diagram on page 939) involves a public company and a nonpublic operating company. The objective is for the nonpublic entity to "go public" without the usual time-consuming and expensive registration process involved in a formal initial public offering (IPO). However, reverse acquisitions are not limited to such situations, and such transactions have occurred involving two public or two nonpublic companies.

It had become popular for private companies to use this technique by locating a *public shell* (a publicly held company that is dormant or inactive) to serve as the legal acquirer/accounting acquiree. The staff of the SEC Division of Corporate Finance provided the following interpretive guidance in March 2001 that effectively ended the use of reverse acquisition accounting when a public shell is involved:

> *The merger of a private operating company into a nonoperating public shell corporation with nominal net assets typically results in the owners and management of the private company having actual or effective operating control of the combined company after the transaction, with shareholders of the former public shell continuing only as passive investors. These transactions are considered by the staff to be capital transactions in substance, rather than business combinations. That is, the transaction is equivalent to the issuance of stock by the private company for the net monetary assets of the shell corporation, accompanied by a recapitalization. The accounting is identical to that resulting from a reverse acquisition, except that no goodwill or other intangible should be recorded.*[11]

In addition to the foregoing SEC guidance, ASC 805-40-25-1 imposes a requirement that the legal acquirer meet the definition of a business. Thus, the use of a public shell entity would not give rise to goodwill and should be accounted for as described in the SEC guidance.

The reverse acquisition is effected when the shareholders of the legal acquiree obtain control of the postacquisition consolidated enterprise, and most commonly this results from a stock-for-stock exchange. The public entity issues shares of newly registered common stock (the legal acquirer) to the shareholders of the nonpublic company in exchange for their ownership interests.

Based on the application of ASC 805-10-55-11 through 55-15, and as a result of the change in control effected by the exchange of stock, the legal acquiree entity is identified as the accounting acquirer of the legal acquirer/accounting acquiree.

Continuation of the Business of the Legal Acquiree Following a reverse acquisition, just as in any business combination, consolidated financial statements must be presented. Although the financial statements will be identified as being those of the legal acquirer (which will be the legal owner of the legal acquiree), in substance these will be a continuation of the financial

---

[11] "Frequently Requested Accounting and Financial Reporting Interpretations and Guidance"; Accounting staff members of the Division of Corporation Finance, U.S. SEC; Washington, D.C.; March 31, 2001; www.sec.gov/divisions/.

statements of the legal subsidiary/GAAP acquirer, with the assets, liabilities, revenues, and expenses of the legal acquirer being consolidated effective with the acquisition date. Put another way, the consolidated entity will be presented as a continuation of the business of the legal subsidiary, notwithstanding the formal structure of the transaction or the name of the successor enterprise.

Comparative financial statements for earlier periods, if presented, should be consistent, meaning that in order for them to be comparable to the postacquisition financial statements, these would also need to represent the financial statements of the legal acquiree. Since in some instances the acquiree's name is different than that shown in the heading, care must be taken to fully communicate with the readers. The fact that the prior period's financial information, identified as being that of the legal parent, is really that of the legal acquiree is obviously extremely pertinent to a reader's understanding of the financial statements.

If the legal parent/accounting subsidiary does not change its name to that of the accounting parent, it is essential that the financial statement titles be captioned in a way that clearly communicates the substance of the transaction to the readers. For example, the statements may be headed "ABC Company, Inc.—Successor to XYZ Corporation."

Structure of Typical Reverse Acquisition

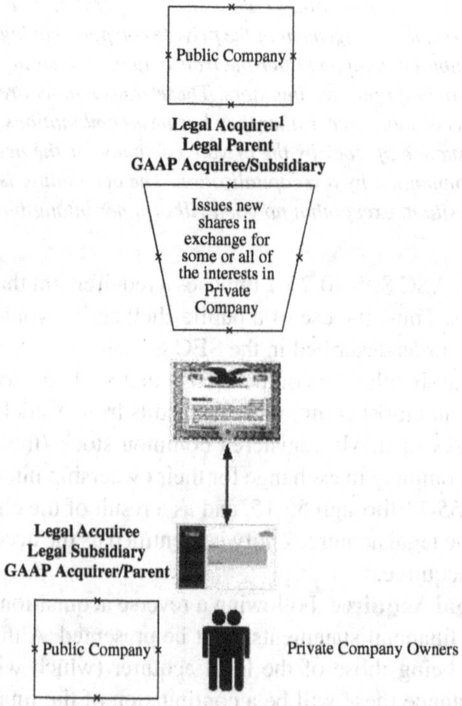

[1] The legal name of the public company/legal acquirer is used in the consolidated financial statements; however, disclosure is included that the entity is a continuation of the business of the legal acquiree/subsidiary.

Equity Structure Adjustments One adjustment to the financial statements is unique to a reverse acquisition. Management must retroactively adjust the capital of the legal acquiree/GAAP acquirer to reflect the legal capital of the legal acquirer/GAAP acquiree. The adjustment is necessary in order for the consolidated statement of financial position to reflect the capital of the legal parent/GAAP subsidiary. Information presented for comparative purposes in the consolidated financial statements should also be retroactively adjusted to reflect the legal parent's legal capital. (ASC 805-40-45-1)

Consolidation Procedures The consolidated financial statements present the continuation of the financial statements of the legal subsidiary with the exception of its capital structure. Thus, those postcombination consolidated financial statements reflect the items detailed in ASC 805-40-45-2. (www.wiley.com/go/GAAP2021)

ASC 805-50, *Related Issues—Pushdown Accounting*

Under new basis (or *pushdown*) accounting, when an acquirer obtains control of an acquiree, an acquirer has the option of adjusting the amounts allocated to various assets and liabilities to reflect the arm's-length valuation reflected in a significant transaction, such as the sale of a majority interest in the entity. (ASC 805-50-25-4) For example, the sale of 90% of the shares of a company by one shareholder to an investor—which under the entity concept would not alter the by the company itself—would, under new basis accounting, be "pushed down" to the entity. The logic is that, as under accounting for business combinations, the most objective gauge of "cost" is that arising from a recent arm's-length transaction.

Applying Pushdown Accounting

Pushdown accounting can be applied retrospectively as a change in accounting policy. Once applied, pushdown accounting cannot be undone. In addition, the SEC rescinded SAS Topic 5.J. Topic 5.J included the staff views on applying pushdown accounting. All entities, including public, will now apply the guidance in ASC 805-50.

Pushdown accounting is optional for an entity each time an acquirer obtains control of the entity. The acquirer must still apply business combination accounting.

Entities should weigh the costs/benefits and the needs of the financial statement users when deciding whether or not to apply pushdown accounting. Some private entities may opt to apply pushdown accounting in order to eliminate separate bases of accounting between parent and subsidiary or to report the fair value, rather than the historical basis, of assets and liabilities. Other private entities may choose not to use pushdown accounting to avoid dragging down earnings as a result of the stepped-up value associated with acquisition accounting.

Example of Pushdown Accounting

Assume that Pullup Corp. acquires, in an open market arm's-length transaction, 90% of the common stock of Pushdown Co. for $464.61 million. At that time, Pushdown Co.'s net book value was $274.78 million (for the entire company). Book and fair values of selected assets and liabilities of Pushdown Co. as of the transaction date are summarized as follows ($000,000 omitted):

	Book value			
	100% of entity	*90% interest*	*Fair value of 90% interest*	*Excess of FV over book*
Assets				
Receivables	$ 24.6	$ 22.14	$ 29.75	$ 7.61
Inventory	21.9	19.71	24.80	5.09
Property, plant, & equipment, net	434.2	390.78	488.20	97.42
All others	223.4	201.06	201.06	0.00
Additional goodwill*			120.00	120.00
Total assets	$704.1	$633.69	$863.81	$230.12
Liabilities				
Bonds payable	104.9	94.41	88.65	5.76
All other liabilities	325.0	292.50	310.55	18.05
Total liabilities	429.9	386.91	399.20	12.29
Equity				
Preferred stock	40.0	36.00	36.00	0.00
Common stock	87.4	78.66	78.66	0.00
Revaluation surplus			217.83	217.83
Retained earnings	146.8	132.12	132.12	0.00
Total equity	274.2	246.88	464.61	217.83
Liabilities + equity	$704.1	$633.69	$863.81	$230.12

* *Net premium paid over book value by arm's-length of "almost all" common stock*

Assuming that "new basis" accounting is deemed to be acceptable and meaningful, since Pushdown Co. must continue to issue separate financial statements to its creditors and holders of its preferred stock, and also assuming that a revaluation of the share of ownership that did not change hands (i.e., the 10% noncontrolling interest in this example) should not be revalued based on the majority transaction, the entries by the subsidiary (Pushdown Co.) for purposes only of preparing standalone financial statements would be as follows:

Accounts receivable	7,610,000	
Inventory	5,090,000	
Plant, property, and equipment (net)	97,420,000	
Goodwill	120,000,000	
Discount on bonds payable	5,760,000	
Other liabilities		18,050,000
Paid-in capital from revaluation		217,830,000

The foregoing entry would only be made for purposes of preparing separate financial statements of Pushdown Co. If consolidated financial statements of Pullup Corp. are also presented, essentially the same result will be obtained. The additional paid-in capital account would be eliminated against the parent's investment account, however, since in the context of the consolidated financial statements this would be a cash transaction rather than a mere accounting revaluation.

The foregoing example obviously ignored the tax effects of the transaction. Since the step-ups in carrying value would not, in all likelihood, alter the corresponding tax bases of the assets and liabilities, deferred income tax effects would also require recognition. This would be done following the procedures set forth at ASC 740. See the chapter on ASC 740 for additional information.

48 ASC 808 COLLABORATIVE ARRANGEMENTS

PERSPECTIVE AND ISSUES

Technical Alert

In November 2018, the FASB issued ASU 2018-18, *Collaborative Arrangements (Topic 808)—Clarifying the Intersection between Topic 808 and Topic 606*. The ASU provides guidance on how to assess whether certain transactions between collaborative arrangement participants should be accounted for under ASC 606.

Guidance The new guidance provides more comparability in the presentation of revenue by allowing organizations to only present units of account in collaborative arrangements that are within the scope of ASC 606 together with the revenue accounted for under ASC 606. The new guidance affects the scope section of ASC 808. Those changes can be found in the Scope section below. Changes to the presentation and disclosure section can be found in the disclosure checklist in Appendix B.

Effective Date The ASU is affective

- For public companies:
  - Fiscal years beginning after December 15, 2019, and interim periods within those fiscal years
- For all other organizations;
  - Fiscal years beginning after December 15, 2020, and interim periods within fiscal years beginning after December 15, 2020

Early adoption is permitted.

Transition The changes should be applied retrospectively to the date of initial application of ASC 606. Entities are permitted to apply the amendments retrospectively to all contracts or only to contracts that are not completed at the date of initial application of ASC 606. The entity should disclose its elections. An entity may also elect to apply the practical expedient of the contract modifications allowed under ASC 606 for entities using modified retrospective transitions.

Subtopic

ASC 808-10, *Collaborative Arrangements*, contains one subtopic:

- ASC 808-10, *Overall,* which defines collaborative arrangements and gives reporting requirements.

Scope

Transactions and Events ASC 808-10 applies to all collaborative arrangements, except for those addressed in other topics. Specifically *excluded* from ASC 808 are arrangements for which the accounting treatment is addressed by other authoritative literature. (ASC 808-10-15-3)

A collaborative arrangement is not *primarily* conducted through a separate legal entity created for it. If a part of the arrangement is conducted through a legal entity, that part is accounted for under ASC 810, *Consolidations,* ASC 323-20 on *Investments—Equity Method and Joint Ventures,* or other relevant accounting literature. A collaborative arrangement may involve various types of activities conducted or supervised by the participants. In some collaborative arrangements, a legal entity may be used for certain specified activities or in certain geographic jurisdictions due, for example, to legal restrictions imposed by the jurisdiction. (ASC 808-10-15-4)

It is important to note that ASC 808 does not address recognition or measurement of collaborative arrangements, including guidance regarding matters such as:

- Determining the appropriate units of accounting
- Determining the appropriate recognition requirements for a given unit of accounting
- The timing of when recognition criteria are considered to have been met (ASC 808-10- 15-5)

Upon implementation of ASU 2018-18, the following scope requirements are effective:

- A collaborative arrangement within the scope of ASC 808 may be partially within the scope of other Codifications Topics including ASC 606. (ASC 808-10-15-5A)
- An entity may have a collaborative arrangement that is partially within the scope of ASC 606 under the following circumstance. If a unit of account, that is a promised good or service, that is distinct within the collaborative arrangement under the guidance in ASC 606 is with a customer, the entity should apply ASC 606 to a unit of account in the scope of ASC 606. Any position of a distinct bundle of goods or services that is not with a customer is not within the scope of ASC 606. (ASC 808-10-15-15B)
- If a collaborative arrangement is wholly or partially outside the scope of other Topics, the unit of account recognition and measurement should be based on an analogy to authoritative accounting literature. If there is no appropriate analogy, a reasonable, rational, and consistently applied accounting policy election should be used. (ASC 808-10-15-5C)

What Constitutes a Collaborative Arrangement? A collaborative arrangement involves a joint operating activity. The activity upon which the participants collaborate is referred to as an endeavor. The subject of a joint operating arrangement is characterized as a collaborative arrangement within the scope of ASC 808 if:

- The collaborative arrangement involves two or more parties.
- The parties are:

- Active participants in the endeavor, and
- Exposed to significant risks and rewards that depend on the endeavor's commercial success.

(ASC 808-10-20)

Criteria for Collaborative Arrangements The description of collaborative arrangements included above lists two criteria:

1. Active involvement by participants
2. Exposure to risks and rewards
   (ASC 808-10-20)

Active involvement In evaluating whether a participant is active with respect to an endeavor, management should consider the arrangement's specific facts and circumstances. Examples of involvement that could constitute active participation include, but are not limited to:

- Directing and executing the activities of the endeavor
- Participating on a steering committee or other oversight or governance body
- Possessing a legal or contractual right to the intellectual property that underlies the endeavor
  (ASC 808-10-15-8)

Solely providing financial resources to an endeavor would not constitute an active level of involvement for the purposes of ASC 808. (ASC 808-10-15-9)

Significant risks and rewards Management of a participant should exercise its best judgment in evaluating whether the participant is exposed to significant risks and entitled to significant rewards. Consideration should be given to the terms and conditions of the arrangement and the facts and circumstances surrounding it. (ASC 808-10-15-10)

Examples of terms and conditions of an arrangement that may indicate that a participant is not exposed to significant risks or entitled to significant rewards include the following:

- Market rates are paid for services provided by the participant
- Ability of a participant to exit the arrangement without cause and recover all or most of its cumulative economic participation through the exit date
- Limits on the rewards that a participant is entitled to receive
- Allocation of initial profits from the endeavor to only one participant
  (ASC 808-10-15-11)

Other factors to consider are:

- The stage of the endeavor's life cycle at which the participant is commencing its involvement
- Management's expectations regarding the duration and extent of its financial participation in relation to the total expected duration and total expected value of the endeavor
  (ASC 808-10-15-12)

Frequently, a collaborative arrangement will involve the license of intellectual property with the participants to the arrangement exchanging consideration with respect to the license at the arrangement's inception. The existence of terms of this nature is not necessarily indicative of the participants not being exposed to significant risks or entitled to significant rewards. (ASC 808- 10-15-13)

Timing and Assessment of Involvement A participant may become involved in a collaborative arrangement at any time during the life cycle of the endeavor. From the perspective of a participant, determination of whether an endeavor is a collaborative arrangement should be made at the inception of the arrangement or when the participant initially becomes involved in the arrangement based on the facts and circumstances existing at that time. A participant should reevaluate whether the arrangement continues to qualify as a collaborative arrangement any time there is a change in a participant's role in the arrangement or a change in a participant's exposure to risks or entitlement to rewards from the arrangement. (ASC 808-10-15-6)

Examples of Joint Operating Activities Collaborative arrangements are used to conduct many different types of business activities including but not limited to research, development, branding, promotion, sales, marketing, order processing, package design, manufacturing, and distribution. Examples include:

- Two or more parties may agree to collaborate on joint operation of a facility, such as a hospital or long-term care nursing facility.
- Two professional services firms (e.g., architects, engineers, consultants) may choose to jointly submit a proposal to obtain a new engagement that neither would have the capacity and/or capability to perform on its own.
- A movie studio may collaborate with another studio because it wants to produce a film starring an actor who is under contract with another studio, or two studios may wish to spread the cost (and, of course, the risk) of producing a film.
- Frequently, in the pharmaceutical industry, two companies engage in a joint operating activity to research, develop, market, manufacture, and/or distribute a drug candidate, including the process of obtaining all necessary regulatory approvals in one or more geographic markets.
  (ASC 808-10-15-7)

The participants' roles and responsibilities vary between arrangements but can be structured where certain responsibilities are shared between the participants and other responsibilities are solely the responsibility of one of the participants.

Overview

A collaborative arrangement (sometimes referred to in practice as "line-item" joint ventures or "virtual" joint ventures) is a contractual agreement between two or more parties (participants) to jointly conduct business activities for their mutual benefit without the formation of a separate entity in which to conduct the activities.

Determining the proper accounting treatment for the various activities included in these endeavors is the subject of ASC 808, *Collaborative Arrangements*.

DEFINITIONS OF TERMS

Source: ASC 808-10-20. Also see Appendix A, *Definitions of Terms*, for additional terms related to this topic: Customer, Contract, Public Business Entity, and Revenue.

Collaborative Arrangement. A contractual agreement that involves a joint operating activity. These arrangements involve two (or more) parties that meet both of the following requirements:

- They are active participants in the activity.
- They are exposed to significant risks and rewards dependent on the commercial success of the activity.

Endeavor. The activity upon which participants in a collaborative arrangement collaborate. For example, in a biotechnology or pharmaceutical environment the endeavor may be the development and commercialization of a drug candidate. In the entertainment industry, it may be production and distribution of a motion picture.

CONCEPTS, RULES, AND EXAMPLES

Presentation and Disclosure

A participant in a collaborative arrangement recognizes revenue earned and costs incurred in transactions with third parties (parties that are not participants to the collaborative arrangement) in its income statement based on whether the participant is serving as a principal or an agent in the transaction as determined under ASC 606-10-55-36 through 55-40. For details on disclosure and presentation requirements see Appendix B, *Disclosure and Presentation Checklist for Commercial Businesses* (www.wiley.com/go/GAAP2021).

Determining the Applicability of ASC 808

Following is an example of a collaborative arrangement that describes the arrangement and how to determine if it meets the requirements for applying ASC 808.

Example of a Collaborative Arrangement[1]

Leonard Sporting Goods Company (LSG) and Maureen Metals LLC (MML) contractually agree to co-develop a new set of golf clubs using a special alloy and what they believe to be a revolutionary design. The terms of their Joint Development Agreement (JDA) are as follows:

LSG responsibilities

- Conducting all necessary research and development activities associated with the design of the club faces and shafts
- Developing the branding strategy, and designing the logo and product packaging
- Engaging a contract manufacturer and performing or supervising all manufacturing, warehousing, logistics, and order processing functions
- Carrying necessary inventories and insuring them against casualty loss
- Establishing prices, and performing all invoicing, credit checks, and collection activities.

MML responsibilities

- Conducting all necessary research and development on the development of the experimental alloy
- Handling all press relations and conducting the advertising campaign

[1] The evaluations in this example are not intended to illustrate the appropriate revenue recognition requirements for any of the transactions described or the appropriateness of conclusions reached on determining whether and how authoritative accounting literature applies directly or by analogy. Rather, those conclusions have been assumed as facts in this example. This example reflects the guidance in ASU 2018-08. See the Technical Alert at the beginning of this chapter for more information on ASU 2018-08.

- Filing of all patents associated with the product, its design, and materials
- Marketing the product in its home state and six surrounding states; sales orders originating in those states are to be forwarded to LSG for processing, and shipment, with LSG responsible for performing all of the activities specified above. In the specified states, MML has limited discretion regarding the pricing of the product.

Other provisions of the JDA include:

- All costs and operating profits are to be split by the participants 50%/50%.
- The participants will co-own the intellectual property arising out of the project.
- Due to legal considerations in the Grand Duchy of Leslie, all sales in that jurisdiction are required to be made by a legal entity duly established within its borders. Consequently, when orders are placed for shipment to the Duchy, LSG sells the golf clubs to Duchy Golf Sales Co. (DGS), a corporation chartered in the Duchy to enable DGS to then transact with the sporting goods retailer located in the Duchy. DGS is owned 50% each by LSG and MML, who each invested $10,000 upon its incorporation on January 2, 20X1.
- On a quarterly basis each participant is to provide the other participant a full accounting for its activities with respect to the endeavor, and whichever participant has advanced a net amount in excess of its proportionate share of the operating results is entitled to receive an "equalization payment" from the other participant.

The following summarizes the transactions associated with the endeavor for calendar year 20X1, including the final activities necessary to commence production of the product and deliver it to sporting goods stores in time for the 20X1 holiday selling season.

(000s omitted)	*Total endeavor results (excluding JV)*	*50% of endeavor results*	*Joint venture DGS*
Sales	$9,200	$4,600	$500
Cost of sales	5,000	2,500	300
Gross profit	4,200	2,100	200
Operating expenses			
Advertising and promotion	500	250	
Bad debts	200	100	
Branding, package, and logo design	300	150	
Legal and patent filing fees	600	300	50
Research and development			
Alloy and metallurgy	200	100	
Club faces and shafts	300	150	
Shipping and delivery	600	300	20
Total operating expenses	2,700	1,350	70
Income from operations	$1,500		$130
× share of operating results allocable to each participant	× 50%		
	$ 750	$ 750	

The annual "equalization" payment was computed as follows, based on the transactions reported by the participants:

(000s omitted)	*Initially recorded in the accounting records of* *LSG*	*MML*
Sales	$9,200	$–
Cost of sales	5,000	–
Gross profit	4,200	–
Operating expenses		
Advertising and promotion	–	500
Bad debts	200	–
Branding, package, and logo design	300	–
Legal and patent filing fees	–	600
Research and development		
Alloy and metallurgy	–	200
Club faces and shafts	300	–
Shipping and delivery	600	–
Total operating expenses	1,400	1,300
Income (loss) from operations prior to equalization	2,800	(1,300)
Share of operating results per agreement	750	750
Equalization payment (receivable) payable	$2,050	$(2,050)

Analysis

- *Determine applicability of ASC 808.* The endeavor involves two parties that are both actively involved and that share equally in both risks and rewards. The existence of the separate entity (DGS) does not disqualify the arrangement, since the joint operating activities are not *primarily* conducted through the separate entity. Thus, from the perspective of the participants, the arrangement is considered a collaborative arrangement within the scope of ASC 808 for the year ended December 31, 20X1.
- *Determine the accounting for the transactions in the separate legal entity.* DGS has no parent company that controls it via ownership as a voting interest entity or via other financial control as a variable interest entity (VIE). Thus, under ASC 323, each participant is to record its investment in DGS and apply the equity method to account for its investment in the joint venture as follows:

1/2/20X1		
Investment in DGS	10,000	
Cash		10,000
To record initial investment in Duchy Golf Sales Co. joint venture		
12/31/20X1		
Investment in DGS	65	
Equity in earnings of investee (income statement)		65
To record 50% interest in the earnings of the joint venture for the year		

- Apply ASC 606-10-32-25 through 27 to determine which of the participants is principal and which is agent. Analysis under the provisions of ASC 606-10-32-25 through 27 yields the following results:

	Indicator (G = Gross; N = Net)	**LSG**	**MML**
a.	Is primary obligor	G	N
b.	Has authority, within reasonable limits, to establish price	G	N*
c.	Involved in determining specifications of product or service	G	N
d.	Changes the product or performs part of the service	G	N
e.	Has discretion in selection of suppliers	G	N
f.	Exposed to inventory risks		
	1. General risk before order placed; upon customer return	G	N
	2. Specific risk after order placed or during shipping	G	N
g.	Exposure to credit risk	G	G
h.	Earnings fixed vs. variable	G	G

* In six states, MML has limited discretion with respect to sales price.

Under ASC 606-10-32-25 through 27, the party that is the primary obligor is a strong indicator of the party that serves as principal to the transactions. In addition, all of the other indicators point towards LSG being the principal. This is irrespective of the fact that MML does have limited authority in certain markets to negotiate price. Even in those limited states, LSG serves as the principal to the transaction. Both participants bear credit risk equally and are not limited to a percentage commission since they share equally in the commercial success of the endeavor, thus the applicability of indicators g and h is neutral between the parties. Based on the analysis of the above factors, management of both participants concluded that LSG is the principal to the transactions associated with the collaborative arrangement and MML functions as an agent.

Note that, in this fact situation, LSG is the principal for all sales other than those made through the joint venture. In some collaborative arrangements, this will not be the case and management will be required to analyze differing sales arrangements to determine separately for each type of arrangement, the party that is the principal. As can be discerned from the analysis above, this involves the exercise of judgment in light of the specific facts and circumstances.

- Determine the applicable GAAP for the transactions and elect an appropriate accounting policy to be disclosed and followed consistently. Management of LSG and MML summarized the various activities, revenues, and expenses associated with the arrangement as follows:

		Functional classification					*Ongoing, major central operations?*	
Natural classification	*Participation with primary responsibility under JDA*	*Directly earned or incurred as principal in transactions with third-party customers*	*Design and development of product, co-owned intellectual property*	*Development of co-owned marketing-related intangibles*	*Marketing*	*LSG*	*MML*
Sales to sporting goods stores	LSG	x				x	
R&D laboratory services; licensing	N/A						x
Advertising and promotion of product	MML				x	x	
Branding, logo, package design	LSG			x		x	
Credit, collections, bad debts	LSG	x				x	
Filing for patents	MML		x			x	x
Manufacturing, delivery, fulfillment	LSG	x				x	
R&D—Clubs	LSG		x			x	
R&D—Metals	MML		x			x	x

Based on the foregoing analysis, LSG's management determines that since it is the principal under ASC 606-10-32-25 through 27, LSG is required to present in its income statement, 100% of the sales, and cost of sales, and other related operating expenses that it incurred in connection with the endeavor. It is unable to find any authoritative GAAP, including ASC 606 because MML is not a customer, that directly or by analogy would address how to account for the equalization payments it is required to make or entitled to receive. LSG concluded that MML is not a customer because MML has not contracted with LSG to obtain goods or services that are an output of LSG's ordinary activities in exchange for consideration. It analyzes the components of the payment and reflects them in LSG's income statement as follows:

Components of Equalization Payment to MML

Presented as additional cost of sales; in effect the sharing of its gross profit with MML results in LSG realizing a reduced margin on its sales of these codeveloped products

a. MML share of gross profit	$2,100

Reimbursements to MML for LSG share of expenses:

These functions were performed under the JDA by MML; LSG elects to present these as operating expenses; none of the advertising expenses were capitalizable as direct response advertising or required to be deferred prior to the first time the advertising takes place under LSG's accounting policies it adopted under ASC 720-35, Advertising Costs.

b. Advertising and promotion	250
c. Legal and patent filing fees	300

LSG records the reimbursement to MML for the metallurgical research and development as additional research and development expense analogous with outsourced contract R&D, since its laboratory did not have the experience or capability to perform such research.

d. Research and development alloy and metallurgy	100

Reimbursement from MML for MML share expenses

LSG elects to present these reimbursements as reductions of its recorded expenses retaining their character; it believes its arrangement with MML to share half of the endeavor's results provides it the benefit of reduced costs and that the benefits it receives from the equalization payment should be characterized in its income statement as reductions of the expenses it would otherwise have borne on its own without MML's participation.

e. Bad debts	(100)
f. Branding, package, and logo design	(150)
g. Research and development—club faces and shafts	(150)
h. Shipping and delivery	(300)
Net equalization payment	$2,050

Leonard Sporting Goods Company
Statement of Income
Ignoring income taxes and other transactions (000s omitted)
Year ended 12/31/20X1

	Prior to application of ASC 808		*Effects of equalization payment*	*Adjusted income statement*
Sales	$9,200			$9,200
Cost of sales				
Sales to third parties	5,000			5,000
Reimbursement to MML as agent		a	$2,100	2,100
Total cost of sales	5,000		2,100	7,100
Gross profit	4,200		(2,100)	2,100
Operating expenses				
Advertising and promotion	–	b	250	250
Bad debts	200	e	(100)	100
Branding, package, and logo design	300	f	(150)	150
Legal and patent filing fees	–	c	300	300
Research and development				
Alloy and metallurgy	–	d	100	100
Club faces and shafts	300	g	(150)	150

Leonard Sporting Goods Company
Statement of Income
Ignoring income taxes and other transactions (000s omitted)
Year ended 12/31/20X1

	Prior to application of ASC 808		*Effects of equalization payment*	*Adjusted income statement*
Shipping and delivery	600	h	(300)	300
Total operating expenses	1,400		(50)	1,350
Income (loss) from operations	2,800		(2,050)	750
Equity interest in income of investee	65			65
Pretax income	$2,865		$(2,050)	$ 815

MML's management analyzed the facts and circumstances associated with the collaborative arrangement. As a research laboratory, performing research and development activities for other entities under contractual arrangements is part of MML's ongoing major and central operations.[2] MML management reached the conclusion that, since LSG is the principal in the transactions with third parties, MML, as an agent, should not recognize revenue or the related cost of that revenue at their gross amounts, nor should it present expenses in the operating expense category in its income statement that are related to these transactions that it considers peripheral. Following this line of reasoning management classifies the activity related to the arrangement as follows:

Maureen Metals LLC
Statement of Income
Ignoring income taxes and other transactions (000s omitted)
Year ended December 31, 20X1

Revenues from collaborative arrangement			
MML revenue from collaborative arrangement			$2,100
Cost of goods sold net of reimbursements			
Advertising and promotion	$500	$(250)	250
Bad debts			100
Branding, package, and logo design			150
Shipping and delivery			300
			800
Net revenues from collaborative arrangement			1,300
Intellectual property design and development			
Legal and patent filing fees	$600	$(300)	300
Research and development expenses			
Metallurgical	200	(100)	100
Club faces and shafts			150
			550
Income from operations			750
Equity interest in income of investee			65
Net profit (pretax)			$ 815

---

[2] The phrase "ongoing, major or central operations" is used in CON 5 to differentiate activities from those that are incidental or peripheral to the reporting entity. Frequently, financial results from incidental or peripheral activities are presented in "other income and expense" if they are unusual or infrequent in nature, whereas the results from ongoing, major, or central operations are shown as components of operating income and expense.

Note MML concludes that the research and development services it provided to LSG represent a distinct service provided to LSG as a customer. LSG is a customer because LSG contracted with MML to develop the intellectual property and protecting it by filing for patents are part of its ongoing, major, or central operations and that this was done in exchange for consideration. Thus, those expenses are not considered directly related to its earnings as agent from the transactions occurring after the product was fully developed and shipments commenced. Although the details are presented for illustrative purposes, the net revenues from the collaborative arrangement could be shown as the first line in the income statement, and MML management could elect to voluntarily disclose the details in the notes to the financial statements to better inform the reader regarding the nature and results of the activities associated with the collaborative arrangement.

49 ASC 810 CONSOLIDATIONS

PERSPECTIVE AND ISSUES

Technical Alert

In October 2018, the FASB issued ASU 2018-17, *Consolidation (Topic 810) Targeted Improvements to Related Party Guidance for Variable Interest Entities.*

The FASB issued the ASU in response to stakeholders' observations that ASC 810 could be improved by:

1. Applying the variable interest entity (VIE) guidance to private companies under common control
2. Considering indirect interests held through related parties under common control for determining whether fees paid to decision makers and service providers are variable interests.

Guidance

The private company accounting alternative The ASU allows a private company to elect not to apply VIE guidance to legal entities under common control (including common control leasing arrangements) if both the parent and the legal entity being evaluated for consolidation are not public business entities. The accounting alternative provides an accounting policy election that a private company will apply to all current and future legal entities under common control that meet the criteria for applying this alternative. Therefore, the alternative cannot be applied to select common control arrangements that meet the criteria for applying this accounting alternative. If the alternative is elected, a private company should continue to apply other consolidation guidance, particularly the voting interest entity guidance, unless another scope exception applies.

Under the accounting alternative, a private company should provide detailed disclosures about its involvement with and exposure to the legal entity under common control.

In effect, the amendments in the ASU expand the private company alternative provided by ASU 2014-07, discussed later in this chapter, not to apply the VIE guidance to qualifying common control leasing arrangements. Because the private company accounting alternative in the ASU applies to all common control arrangements that meet specific criteria and not just leasing arrangements, the amendments in ASU 2014-07 are superseded by the amendments in this Update.

Decision-making fees Indirect interests held through related parties in common control arrangements should be considered on a *proportional* basis for determining whether fees paid to decision makers and service providers are variable interests. This is consistent with how indirect interests held through related parties under common control are considered for determining whether a reporting entity must consolidate a VIE. For example, if a decision maker or service provider owns a 20 percent interest in a related party and that related party owns a 40 percent interest in the legal entity being evaluated, the decision maker's or service provider's indirect interest in the VIE held through the related party under common control should be considered the equivalent of an 8 percent direct interest for determining whether its fees are variable interests.

This change should mean that fewer decision-making fees are variable interests. It should also reduce the risk that decision makers with insignificant direct and indirect interests could be considered to be the primary beneficiary of a VIE.

Effective Dates The ASU is effective as follows.

- For entities other than private companies,
  - for fiscal years beginning after December 15, 2019, and interim periods within those fiscal years.

- For a private company
  - for fiscal years beginning after December 15, 2020, and interim periods within fiscal years beginning after December 15, 2021.

Early adoption is permitted.

Transition All entities are required to apply the amendments in this Update retrospectively with a cumulative-effect adjustment to retained earnings at the beginning of the earliest period presented

Subtopics

ASC 810, *Consolidations*, consists of two subtopics:

- ASC 810-10, *Overall*, which has three subsections:
  - General
  - Variable Interest Entities, which explains how to identify VIEs and when the reporting entity should consolidate the entity
  - Consolidation of Entities Controlled by Contract, which provides guidance for entities that are not VIEs but are controlled by contract, including physician practices and physician practice management entities.
- ASC 810-30, *Research and Development Arrangements*, which provides direction on whether and how those arrangements should be consolidated.

Scope and Scope Exceptions

All *legal* entities are included in the scope of ASC 810. The application to not-for-profit entities is subject to additional guidance in ASC 958-810. (ASC 810-10-15-4 and 15-5) Scope exceptions for ASC 810-10 follow the subsections and breakdown as follows:

- General, applying to all subtopics under ASC 810-10,
- Specific, applying to VIEs, and
- Consolidation of entities controlled by contracts that are not VIEs

Applying the Scope Guidance If a reporting entity is within the scope of the VIE Subsections, that entity should apply the VIE guidance first. If not, then the reporting entity should determine whether it has a direct or indirect controlling financial interest. (ASC 810-10-15-3) For legal entities other than limited partnerships, this is defined as more than 50%. There are circumstances where an entity may hold a majority voting interest, but may not have a controlling interest, that is, the power to control the operations or assets of the investee. This is called a noncontrolling majority interest and may happen through a contract, lease, agreement with other stockholders, or court decrees. For limited partnerships, the usual condition for a controlling financial interest is ownership by one limited partner of more than 50% of the limited partnership's kick-out rights through voting interests. Control may also exist by contract, lease, agreement with partners, or by court decrees. (ASC 810- 10-15-8 and 15-8A)

Also see information below on VIEs within scope according to ASC 810-10-15-14.

If the reporting entity has a contractual management relationship that is not a VIE, the reporting entity should use the guidance in the 810-10 Subsections, *Consolidations of Entities Controlled by Contract*, to determine if the arrangement is a controlling financial interest. (ASC 810-10-15-3(c))

Exhibit—Determining Scope and Scope Exceptions (ASC 810-10-15-3)

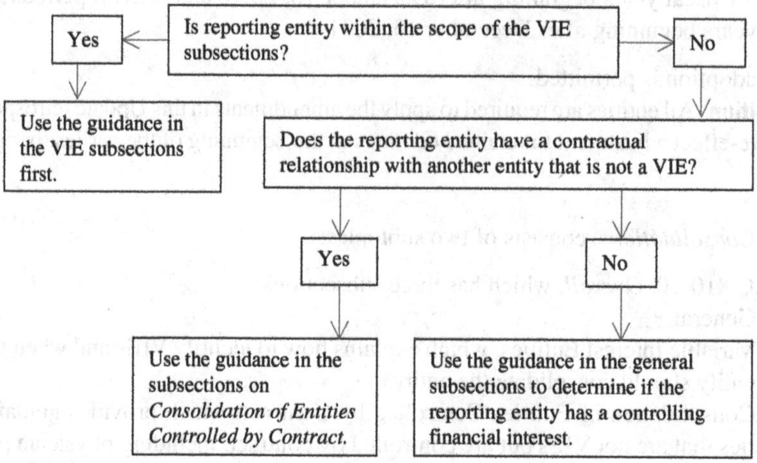

General Scope Exceptions A reporting entity with an explicit or implicit interest in a legal entity that is in the scope of the VIE Subsection follows the guidance in this Topic's VIE Subsections. (ASC 810-10-15-9) For entities that are not in the scope of the VIE subsection, a reporting entity should consolidate all entities in which the parent has a controlling financial interest, *except*:

- If the subsidiary:
  - Is in a legal reorganization
  - Is in bankruptcy
  - Operates under "foreign exchange restrictions, controls, or other governmentally imposed uncertainties, so severe that they cast significant doubt on the parent's ability to control the subsidiary"
  - Is a broker dealer within the scope of ASC 940 and control is likely to be temporary
- If the power of the majority voting interest shareholder or limited partner with majority of kick-out rights through voting interest is restricted by rights given to the noncontrolling shareholder or limited partners (noncontrolling rights) and are so restrictive that it is questionable whether control exists with majority owners.
- If control exists other than through ownership of a majority voting interest or a majority of kick-out rights through voting interests.
(ASC 810-10-15-10)

The guidance in ASC 810 does not apply to:

- An employee benefit plan subject to ASC 712, *Nonretirement Postemployment Benefits*, or to ASC 715, *Retirement Benefits*.
- An investment company within the scope of Topic 946 that is not an investment company, except if the investment company has an investment in an operating entity that provides services to the investment company. (ASC 946-810-45-3)
- A governmental organization.
- A financing entity established by a governmental organization, unless the financing entity meets both of the following conditions:
  - It is not a governmental organization, and

  - It is used by a business entity in a manner similar to a VIE to attempt to circumvent VIE accounting rules.
- Money market funds registered with the SEC pursuant to Rule 2a-7 of the Investment Company Act of 1940, that is, registered money market funds and those legal entities that are similar in purpose and design.
- Similar unregistered money market funds.
  (ASC 810-10-15-12)

Variable Interest Entities within Scope VIEs follow the same scope and scope exceptions as in the general subsection, except as specified below. (ASC 810-10-15-13) The VIE model applies when the reporting entity has a variable interest in a legal entity. Any legal entity that, by design,[1] possesses one of the following characteristics is subject to consolidation under the VIE guidance:

- The entity is thinly capitalized. The total equity investment at risk is not sufficient to permit the entity to finance its activities without additional subordinated financial support from either the existing equity holders or other parties. Normally, the equity provided by shareholders is sufficient to support operations. For this purpose, the total equity investment at risk:
  - Includes only equity investments in the entity that participate significantly in profits and losses even if those investments do not carry voting rights.
  - Does not include equity interests that the entity issued in exchange for subordinated interests in other variable interest entities.
  - Does not include amounts provided to the equity investor directly or indirectly by the entity or by other parties involved with the entity (for example, by fees, charitable contributions, or other payments), unless the provider is a parent, subsidiary, or affiliate of the investor that is required to be included in the same set of consolidated financial statements as the investor.
  - Does not include amounts financed for the equity investor (for example, by loans or guarantees of loans) directly by the entity or by other parties involved with the entity, unless that party is a parent, subsidiary, or affiliate of the investor that is required to be included in the same set of consolidated financial statements as the investor.
- Equity holders lack the ability to direct the activities. For other than limited partnerships, that significantly affect the entity's economic performance, the investors do not have that ability through voting rights or similar rights if no owners hold voting rights or similar rights (such as those of a common stockholder in a corporation or a general partner in a partnership). Limited partners lack power if a simple majority is not able to exercise substantive kick-out rights or participating rights over the general partner.
- Reporting entity lacks the obligation to absorb the expected losses of the entity. Conventionally, the investors are exposed to the risks of ownership. The investor or investors do not have that obligation if they are directly or indirectly protected from absorbing the expected losses or are guaranteed a return by the entity itself or by other parties with whom the entity is involved.

---

[1] "By design" in this context applies to legal entities that meet the conditions in ASC 810-10-15-14 because of their structure.

- Reporting entity lacks the right to receive expected residual returns of the entity. Conventionally, the investors enjoy the benefit of ownership. The investors do not have that right if their benefits are limited to a specified maximum amount by the entity's governing documents or arrangements with other variable interest holders or with the entity.
- The entity was established with nonsubstantive voting interest. The guidance contains what can be thought of as an anti-abuse clause. This is designed to prevent an entity from structuring in a way that allows the sponsor to avoid consolidation under the VIE mode. This provision includes two conditions, both of which must be met:
  - The distribution of economic benefits generated by the entity is proportional to equity ownership and voting rights.
  - Substantially all of the entity's activities either involve or are conducted on behalf of a party that has disproportionally low voting rights relative to economic interest.

(ASC 810-10-15-14)

Variable Interest Entities Scope Exceptions As is clear from the above, a VIE differs from a voting interest entity because the VIE is structured in a way that voting rights are ineffective in determining which party has a controlling interest. In a VIE, control of an entity is achieved through arrangements that do not involve voting equity. The following are excluded from the scope of the subtopics and sections of ASC 810-10 governing variable interest entities (VIEs):

- Not-for-profit entities unless the entity was organized to avoid VIE status. It is important to note, however, that a not-for-profit organization can be a related party for the purpose of determining the primary beneficiary (parent) of a VIE by applying ASC paragraphs 810-10-25-42 through 44.
- Separate accounts of life insurance entities.
- An entity created prior to December 31, 2003, for which, after expending "exhaustive efforts," management of the variable interest holder is unable to obtain information needed to determine whether the entity is a VIE, determine whether the holder is the primary beneficiary, or make the required accounting entries required to consolidate the VIE.
- Entities that meet the definition of a business do not have to be evaluated by a variable interest holder to determine whether they are VIEs unless one or more of the following conditions exists:
  - The variable interest holder and/or its related parties/de facto agents[2] (de facto agents are discussed later in this chapter) participated significantly in the design or redesign of the entity. This factor is not considered when the entity is an operating joint venture jointly controlled by the variable interest holder, and either one or more independent parties, or a franchisee.
  - The design of the entity results in substantially all of its activities either involving or being conducted on behalf of the reporting entity and its related parties.
  - Based on the relative fair values of interests in the entity, the variable interest holder and its related parties provide more than half of its total equity, subordinated debt, and other forms of subordinated financial support.

---

[2] For this purpose, the term "de facto agent" would exclude a party with an agreement that it cannot sell, transfer, or encumber its interests in the entity without the prior approval of the variable interest holder when that right could constrain the other party's ability to manage the economic risks or realize the economic rewards from its interests in a VIE through the sale, transfer, or encumbrance of those interests.

- The entity's activities relate primarily to one or both of the following:
  - Single-lessee leases
  - Securitizations or other forms of asset-backed financings

(ASC 810-10-15-17)

The above requirements for scope exceptions for businesses can be difficult to meet.

Private company alternative for common control arrangements A private company may elect not to apply VIE guidance to a lessor under common control when criteria "a" through "c" are met and in some situations "d" is not:

a. The private company lessee (the reporting entity) and the lessor legal entity are under common control,
b. The private company lessee has a leasing arrangement with the lessor legal entity,
c. Substantially all of the activity between the private company lessee and the lessor legal entity is related to the leasing activities (including supporting leasing activities) between those two entities, and
d. If the private company lessee explicitly guarantees or provides collateral for any obligation of the lessor legal entity related to the asset leased by the private company, then the principal amount of the obligation at inception of such guarantee or collateral arrangement does not exceed the value of the asset leased by the private company from the lessor legal entity.
(ASC 810-10-15-17AB)[3]

Instead of consolidating, the private company would make certain disclosures about the lessor and the leasing arrangement. If elected, the accounting alternative should be applied to all leasing arrangements meeting the above conditions. If the conditions for applying the accounting alternative cease to be met, the private company should apply the VIE subsection guidance prospectively at the date of change. The alternative should be applied retrospectively to all periods presented. (ASC 810-10-15-17B through 17C)[4]

A reporting entity that is a private company is not required to evaluate a legal entity if *all* of the following criteria are met:

a. The reporting entity and the legal entity are under common control.
b. The reporting entity and the legal entity are not under common control of a public business entity.
c. The legal entity under common control is not a public business entity.
d. The reporting entity does not directly or indirectly have a controlling financial interest in the legal entity when considering the General Subsections of this Topic. The Variable Interest Entities Subsections shall not be applied when making this determination.

If a private company elects to apply this accounting alternative, it must apply this alternative to all legal entities if the criteria above are met. A reporting entity that elects the accounting alternative and, thus, does not apply the guidance in the Variable Interest Entities Subsections, shall continue to apply other accounting guidance (including guidance in the General Subsections of this Subtopic) unless another scope exception from this Topic applies. (ASC 810-10-15AD)[5]

---

[3] This paragraph is superseded upon implementation of ASU 2018-17.

[4] Ibid.

[5] This paragraph is effective upon implementation of ASU 2018-17.

For the purpose of applying paragraph 810-10-15-17AD(a) above to determine whether the private company reporting entity and the legal entity are under common control of a parent, the private company should consider only the parent's direct and indirect voting interest in the private company and the legal entity. That is, the guidance in the General Subsections of this Topic shall be considered when applying ASC 810-10-15-17AD(a). The guidance in the VIE Subsections should not be applied for making this determination. (ASC 810-10-15-17AE)[6]

If any of the criteria in ASC 810-10-15-17AD cease to be met, a private company should apply the guidance in the VIE Subsections at the date of change on a prospective basis, except for situations in which a reporting entity becomes a public business entity. When a reporting entity becomes a public business entity, it must apply the guidance in the VIE Subsections in accordance with ASC 250 on accounting changes and error corrections. (ASC 810-10-15-17AF)[7]

Collateralized Financing Entity—Alternative Approach—Scope Criteria An entity may measure the financial assets and financial liabilities of a qualifying collateralized financial entity (CFE) using either the fair value of the financial assets or the financial liabilities, whichever is more observable. (ASC 810-10-30-11)

Entities that elect this option are relieved from independently measuring the fair value of the financial assets and financial liabilities. Entities that do not elect the alternative must attribute any differences in the fair value to the controlling interest holder in the consolidated income statement.

An entity may use the alternative if it meets both of the following conditions:

a. All of the financial assets and the financial liabilities of the collateralized financing entity are measured at fair value in the consolidated financial statements under other applicable Topics, other than financial assets and financial liabilities that are incidental to the operations of the collateralized financing entity and have carrying values that approximate fair value (for example, cash, broker receivables, or broker payables).
b. The changes in the fair values of those financial assets and financial liabilities are reflected in earnings.
(ASC 810-10-15-17D)

This guidance is applied using:

- A modified retrospective approach by recording a cumulative-effect adjustment to equity as of the beginning of the annual period of adoption or
- A retrospective approach by applying the changes retrospectively to all relevant prior periods beginning with the annual period of initial adoption.

ASC 810-30, *Research and Development Arrangements* ASC 810-30 is limited to those research and development arrangements in which all of the funds for the research and development activities are provided by the sponsor of the research and development arrangement. It does not apply to either:

- Transactions in which the funds are provided by third parties, which would generally be within the scope of Subtopic 730-20.
- Legal entities required to be consolidated under the guidance on variable interest entities.
(ASC 810-30-15-3)

---

[6] Ibid.

[7] Ibid.

Overview

The requirement to consolidate financial statements over which a reporting entity has control is a long-standing tenet of GAAP. There is a presumption that consolidated financial statements are more meaningful and are necessary for a fair presentation. Historically, the assessment of whether or not to consolidate was based on the voting interest the reporting entity held in the investee—the voting interest model.

Over the years, managers and their advisors devised many new and creative types of ownership structures, financing arrangements, financial instruments, and business relationships. Perhaps no such type of financial arrangement or structure has received the same level of negative publicity as the special purpose entity (SPE). An SPE is narrowly defined as a trust or other legal vehicle to which a transferor transfers a portfolio of financial assets, such as mortgage loans, commercial loans, credit card debt, automobile loans, and other groups of homogeneous borrowings.

Commonly, SPEs have been organized as trusts or partnerships (flow-through entities, to avoid double corporate income taxation), and the outside equity participant was ultimately defined as having as little as 3% of the total assets of the SPE at risk. No authoritative GAAP ever established this 3% threshold, but nevertheless it evolved somewhat by default and had been subject to varying interpretations under different sets of conditions.

In a process called a *securitization*, the SPE typically issues and sells securities that represent beneficial interests in the cash flows from the portfolio. The proceeds the SPE receives from the sale of these securities are used to purchase the portfolio from the transferor. The cash flows received by the SPE from the dividends, interest, redemptions, principal repayments, and/or realized gains on the financial assets are used to pay a return to the investors in the SPE's securities. By transferring packages of such loans to an SPE, these assets can be legally isolated and made "bankruptcy proof" (and thus made more valuable as collateral for other borrowings); various types of debt instruments can thus be used, providing the sponsor with fresh resources to fund future lending activities.

Exhibit—Special Purpose Entity—Securitization Process

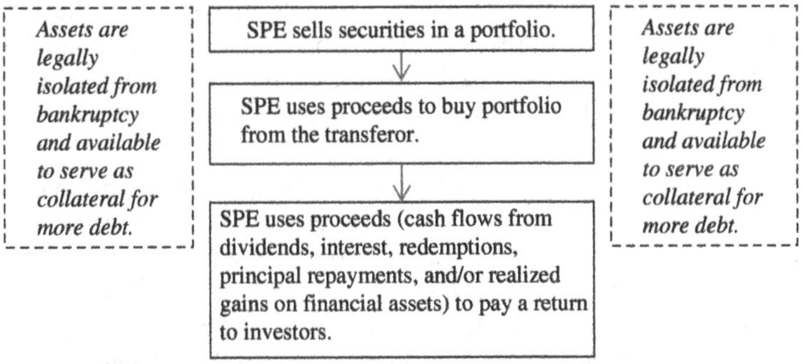

Enron created SPEs to hide debt, avoid taxes, reward management, and otherwise conceal its true financial condition. These entities appeared to be separate legal entities which posed little risk or reward. This was not true, and the risk and rewards of ownership rested with Enron. Enron and other entities exploited GAAP's bright-line, 50% criterion for control.

The increasing use of special purpose entities structured in certain ways created accounting challenges and led to abuses, culminating in the Enron scandal. The FASB recognized the need to expand the existing consolidations model to take into account financial arrangements where parties other than the holders of a majority of the voting interests exercise financial control over another entity. In 2003, the FASB added to consolidation guidance the variable interest model.

The FASB decided not to refer to entities within the scope of the eventual guidance as SPEs. This decision underscores the fact that the type of entity to which the guidance applies is more broadly defined than entities that qualify as SPEs involved in securitization transactions or even SPEs that hold nonfinancial assets. The FASB coined the term *variable interest entity* (VIE) to designate an entity that is financially controlled by one or more parties that do not hold a majority voting interest. A party that possesses the majority of this financial control, if there is one, is referred to as the VIE's *primary beneficiary*. The codification definition of "parent" includes a VIE's primary beneficiary, and the definition of "subsidiary" includes a VIE that is consolidated by its primary beneficiary.

Over the years, the FASB continued to refine the VIE model. The 2003 guidance instituted a risk and reward VIE model to determine the primary beneficiary. With changes made in ASU 2009-17, the model shifted from the original quantitative risk and reward model to a more qualitative "power and economics" model. Under the VIE model, the assessment of control differs from the voting interest model because control of a VIE can be achieved by other than ownership of shares. A controlling financial interest of a VIE requires:

- The power to direct the activities that most significantly impact the VIE's economic performance
- The obligation to absorb losses that could be significant to the VIE or the right to receive benefits from the VIE that could be potentially significant to the VIE.
  (ASC 810-10-05-8A)

DEFINITIONS OF TERMS

Source: ASC 810. See Appendix A, *Definitions of Terms*, for other terms relevant to this chapter: Acquiree, Acquirer, Acquisition by a Not-for-Profit Entity, Beneficial Interest, Business, Business Combination, Cash Equivalents, Combined Financial Statements, Component of an Entity, Contract, Customer, Debt Security, Direct Financing Lease, Equity Security, Fair Value, Financial Asset, Finance Lease, Lease, Inventory, Lease Payments, Lessee, Lessor, Nonfinancial Asset, Nonprofit Activity, Non-reciprocal Transfer, Operating Lease, Operating Segment, Ordinary Course of Business, Owners, Private Company, Public Business Entity, Readily Determinable Fair Value, Reinsurance, Related Parties, Revenue, Sales-type Lease, Security, Underlying Asset, With Cause, Without Cause.

Acquisition, Development, and Construction Arrangements. Acquisition, development, or construction arrangements, in which a lender, usually a financial institution, participates in expected residual profit from the sale or refinancing of property.

Collateralized Financing Entity. A variable interest entity that holds financial assets, issues beneficial interests in those financial assets, and has no more than nominal equity. The beneficial interests have contractual recourse only to the related assets of the collateralized financing entity and are classified as financial liabilities. A collateralized financing entity may hold nonfinancial assets temporarily as a result of default by the debtor on the underlying debt instruments held as assets by the collateralized financing entity or in an effort to restructure the debt instruments held as assets by the collateralized financing entity. A collateralized financing entity also may hold other financial assets and financial liabilities that are incidental to the operations of the collateralized financing entity and have carrying values that approximate fair value (for example, cash, broker receivables, or broker payables).

Consolidated Financial Statements. The financial statements of a consolidated group of entities that include a parent and all its subsidiaries presented as those of a single economic entity.

Consolidated Group. A parent and all its subsidiaries.

Decision Maker. An entity or entities with the power to direct the activities of another legal entity that most significantly impact the legal entity's economic performance.

Decision-making Authority. The power to direct the activities of a legal entity that most significantly impact the entity's economic performance.

Equity Interests. Used broadly to mean ownership interests of investor-owned entities; owner, member, or participant interests of mutual entities; and owner or member interests in the net assets of not-for-profit entities.

Expected Losses. A legal entity that has no history of net losses and expects to continue to be profitable in the foreseeable future can be a variable interest entity (VIE). A legal entity that expects to be profitable will have expected losses. A VIE's expected losses are the expected negative variability in the fair value of its net assets exclusive of variable interests and not the anticipated amount or variability of the net income or loss.

Expected Losses and Expected Residual Returns. Expected losses and expected residual returns refer to amounts derived from expected cash flows as described in FASB Concepts Statement No. 7, *Using Cash Flow Information and Present Value in Accounting Measurements*. However, expected losses and expected residual returns refer to amounts discounted and otherwise adjusted for market factors and assumptions rather than to undiscounted cash flow estimates. The definitions of expected losses and expected residual returns specify which amounts are to be considered in determining expected losses and expected residual returns of a variable interest entity (VIE).

Expected Residual Returns. A variable interest entity's (VIE's) expected residual returns are the expected positive variability in the fair value of its net assets exclusive of variable interests.

Expected Variability. Expected variability is the sum of the absolute values of the expected residual return and the expected loss. Expected variability in the fair value of net assets includes expected variability resulting from the operating results of the legal entity.

Kick-Out Rights (VIE Definition). The ability to remove the entity with the power to direct the activities of a VIE that most significantly impact the VIE's economic performance or to dissolve (liquidate) the VIE without cause.

Kick-Out Rights (VIE Definition). The rights underlying the limited partner's or partners' ability to dissolve (liquidate) the limited partnership or otherwise remove the general partners without cause.

Noncontrolling Interest. The portion of equity (net assets) in a subsidiary not attributable, directly or indirectly, to a parent. A noncontrolling interest is sometimes called a minority interest.

Participating Rights (VIE Definition). The ability to block or participate in the actions through which an entity exercises the power to direct the activities of a VIE that most significantly impact the VIE's economic performance. Participating rights do not require the holders of such rights to have the ability to initiate actions.

Participating Rights (Voting Interest Definition). Participating rights allow the limited partners or non-controlling shareholders to block or participate in certain significant financial and operating decisions of the limited partnership or corporation that are made in the ordinary course of business. Participating rights do not require the holders of such rights to have the ability to initiate actions.

Primary Beneficiary. An entity that consolidates a variable interest entity (VIE). See paragraphs 810-10-25-38 through 25-38J for guidance on determining the primary beneficiary.

Protective Rights (VIE Definition). Rights designed to protect the interests of the party holding those rights without giving that party a controlling financial interest in the entity to which they relate. For example, they include any of the following:

- Approval or veto rights granted to other parties that do not affect the activities that most significantly impact the entity's economic performance. Protective rights often apply to fundamental changes in the activities of an entity or apply only in exceptional circumstances. Examples include both of the following:
    - A lender might have rights that protect the lender from the risk that the entity will change its activities to the detriment of the lender, such as selling important assets or undertaking activities that change the credit risk of the entity.
    - Other interests might have the right to approve a capital expenditure greater than a particular amount or the right to approve the issuance of equity or debt instruments.
- The ability to remove the reporting entity that has a controlling financial interest in the entity in circumstances such as bankruptcy or on breach of contract by that reporting entity.
- Limitations on the operating activities of an entity. For example, a franchise agreement for which the entity is the franchisee might restrict certain activities of the entity but may not give the franchisor a controlling financial interest in the franchisee. Such rights may only protect the brand of the franchisor.

Protective Rights (VIE Definition). Rights that are only protective in nature and that do not allow the limited partners or noncontrolling shareholders to participate in significant financial and operating decisions of the limited partnership or corporation that are made in the ordinary course of business.

Sponsor. An entity that capitalizes a research and development arrangement.

Subordinated Financial Support. Variable interests that will absorb some or all of a variable interest entity's (VIE's) expected losses.

Variable Interests. The investments or other interests that will absorb portions of a variable interest entity's (VIE's) expected losses or receive portions of the entity's expected residual returns are called variable interests. Variable interests in a VIE are contractual, ownership, or other pecuniary interests in a VIE that change with changes in the fair value of the VIE's net assets exclusive of variable interests. Equity interests with or without voting rights are considered variable interests if the legal entity is a VIE and to the extent that the investment is at risk as described in paragraph 810-10-15-14. Paragraph 810-10-25-55 explains how to determine whether a variable interest in specified assets of a legal entity is a variable interest in the entity. Paragraphs 810-10-55-16 through 55-41 describe various types of variable interests and explain in general how they may affect the determination of the primary beneficiary of a VIE. (ASC 810-10-20)

CONSOLIDATION MODELS—INTRODUCTION AND BACKGROUND

ASC 810 provides the primary authority for determining when presentation of consolidated financial statements is required. Consolidation is only required for legal entities within the scope of ASC 810. The rationale underlying ASC 810 is that when one enterprise directly or indirectly holds a controlling financial interest in one or more other enterprises, consolidated financial statements are more informative to users. There are two models for assessing whether a reporting entity has a controlling interest in the entity being evaluated for consolidation:

1. The voting interest model
2. The variable interest entity model

The first step in determining which accounting model applies and which, if any, reporting entity must consolidate an entity is to determine if a VIE scope exception applies. Then the reporting entity must determine whether the entity under consideration for consolidation is a variable interest entity or a voting interest entity.

Exhibit—Steps to Determine Which Consolidation Model Applies to a Legal Entity

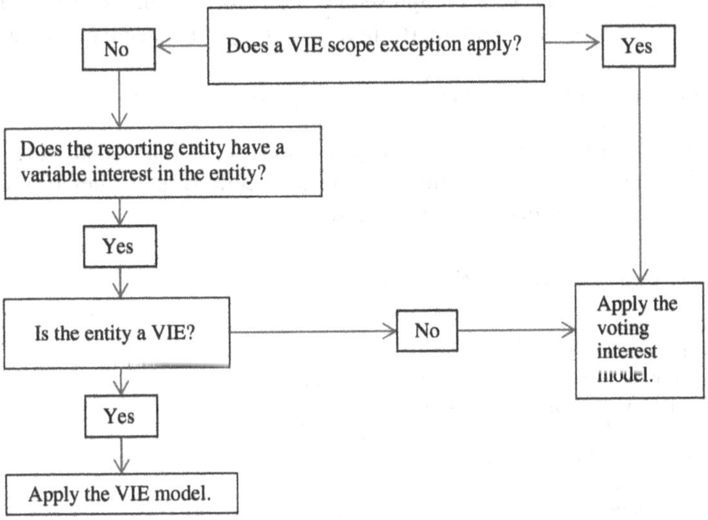

THE VIE MODEL

The VIE model identifies the party that has a controlling financial interest, and, therefore, whether or not the entity should be consolidated and by which reporting entity.

Does a VIE Scope Exception Apply?

The reporting entity first determines if any of the VIE scope exceptions apply. See the "Scope and Scope Exceptions" section at the beginning of this chapter for additional guidance.

Does the Reporting Entity Have a Variable Interest in the Entity?

A variable interest is an investment or other interest that will absorb portions of a VIE's expected losses or receive portions of the entity's expected residual returns. Variable interests in a VIE change with changes in the fair value of the VIE's net assets, exclusive of variable interest.

Is the Reporting Entity a VIE?

The definition of variable interest dictates that the financial statement preparer must determine whether a particular item either absorbs expected losses or receives expected residual returns (collectively referred to as expected variability) or both. Only those interests that absorb changes in the fair value of an entity's net assets are considered variable interests. Changes in cash flows drive the success or failure of the entity. Thus, the cash flows create the variability in the entity. For example, ABC Equity Investment absorbs some or all of the fair value changes of VIE's assets—its variability. ABC will receive a lower return on investment if VIE generates poor cash flows. The cash flows absorb some of the entity's negative variability.

A variable interest is commonly found in:

- Equity or debt investments in a VIE,
- Financing provided to a VIE through such vehicles as guarantees or derivatives,
- A monetary arrangement with a VIE, perhaps through management or service contracts or leases, or
- Implicit relationships, particularly if a related party is involved.

ASC 810-10-55-16 through 55-41, *Identifying Variable Interests*, provides examples of potential variable interests. Each of the items below is potentially an explicit or implicit variable interest in an entity or in specified assets of an entity.

Exhibit—Examples of Potential Variable Interests

1. At-risk equity investments in a VIE
2. Investments in subordinated debt instruments issued by a VIE
3. Investments in subordinated beneficial interests issued by a VIE
4. Guarantees of the value of VIE assets or liabilities
5. Written put options on the assets of a VIE or similar obligations that protect senior interests from suffering losses
6. Forward contracts to sell assets owned by the entity at a fixed price
7. Stand-alone or embedded derivative instruments, including total return swaps and similar arrangements
8. Contracts or agreements for fees to be paid to a decision maker. (These are generally deemed to absorb variability unless the relationship between the entity and the decision maker meets specified criteria to be considered an employee/employer relationship or a "hired service provider" relationship, in which case the arrangement would not be deemed to create a variable interest. In this case, the fees would be included in computations of expected variability.)
9. Other service contracts with nondecision makers
10. Operating leases that include residual value guarantees and/or lessee option to purchase the leased property at a specified price
11. Variable interests of one VIE in another VIE
12. Interests retained by a transferor of financial assets to a VIE

All of these examples potentially qualify as variable interests. However, they may vary widely in the extent of their variability, and that has a direct effect on the determination of the primary beneficiary. (Note that an interest can qualify as a variable interest but the entity in which the interest is held may not qualify as a VIE.) The identification of a variable interest can be challenging. The financial statement preparer identifies variable interests by thoroughly analyzing the assets, liabilities, and contractual arrangements of an entity.

Analyzing an Entity's Design The Codification requires an analysis of an entity's design to determine the variability the entity was designed to create and distribute to the holders of the interest. This determination affects:

- Which interests are variable interests
- Whether the entity is a VIE
- Which party, if any, is the primary beneficiary
(ASC 810-10-25-21)

This "by design" assessment is applied in two steps:

1. Analyze the nature of the risks in the legal entity, including credit, interest rate, foreign currency exchange, commodity price, equity price, and operations risk. (ASC 810-10-25-22 and 25-24)
2. Determine the purpose for which the legal entity was created and the variabilities the legal entity is designed to create and pass along to interest holders. The role—to absorb or receive the legal entity's variability—of the contract or arrangement in the design of the legal entity determines whether the interest *creates* variability or *absorbs* variability. Generally, the assets and operations of the entity create variability and, therefore, are not variable interests. On the other hand, liabilities and equities absorb the variability and, therefore, are variable interests. (ASC 810-10-25-22 and 26)

The analyst should review:

- The activities of the legal entity,
- Contract terms,
- The nature of the legal entity's interests issued,
- How those interests were negotiated or marketed to investors, and
- Which parties had significant participation in the design or redesign of the legal entity.
(ASC 810-10-25-25)

Using the guidance, a qualitative analysis of the legal entity's design will often be sufficient to determine the variability to consider. (ASC 810-10-25-29)

Quantitative analysis of expected losses, expected residual returns, and expected variability The current VIE model can be seen as a "power and "economics" model. However, there are some provisions in the current guidance that reference the earlier expected losses and expected residual returns model, and so it is useful to understand those concepts. Expected losses and expected returns are derived from expected cash flows as explained in CON 7, *Using Cash Flow Information and Present Value in Accounting Measurement* It is important to note that expected losses and expected residual returns are not GAAP losses and income. They are statistical measures of the variability (or risk) inherent in the fair value of the entity.

This quantitative approach to analyzing the expected losses, expected residual returns, and expected variability is not required and should not be the only factor considered when determining whether the entity has the obligation to absorb significant losses or the right to receive significant benefits:

$$\text{Expected losses} + \text{Expected residual returns} = \text{Expected variability}$$

Estimating expected future cash flows The absorbing/receiving of variability of the entity's cash flows is the sole determinant of whether an interest is a variable interest. In analyzing specific situations, the degree of variability can differ widely for each item. It is the role of the item to absorb or receive variability that distinguishes it as a variable interest. The role, in turn, often depends on the design of the legal entity. Therefore, it is critical for the financial statement preparer to understand the purpose and design of the entity being evaluated.

When estimating an entity's expected future cash flows in accordance with CON 7 a range of probability-weighted expected outcomes is used. Mathematically, this is simply a weighted-average calculation. The following example illustrates the mathematical concept of expected variability:

Example of Expected Variability of Cash Flows

Mided Mining Company is computing the probability-weighted expected future cash flows from operating and disposing of a tunnel boring machine that has a remaining estimated useful life of three years. This estimate was necessitated by ASC 360, which requires an evaluation, when certain events or circumstances occur, of whether the future cash flows associated with the use and disposal of long-lived assets are sufficient to recover their carrying value over their estimated remaining depreciable lives. Because of uncertainty regarding the amounts and timing of the cash flows, Mided's management used the CON 7 probability-weighted expected cash flow model with the following results:

	20X1	*20X2*	*20X3*	*3-year outcome*	*Probability of occurrence*	*Probability-weighted expected outcome*
Expected outcome 1	$3,500	$3,200	$2,700	$ 9,400	20%	$ 1,880
Expected outcome 2	4,000	3,900	3,700	11,600	45%	5,220
Expected outcome 3	4,300	4,100	4,000	12,400	30%	3,720
Expected outcome 4	4,400	4,700	–	9,100	5%	455
					100%	
Probability-weighted expected cash flows (weighted-average)						$11,275

The $11,275 weighted-average, undiscounted, is compared to the carrying value of the tunnel boring machine to determine whether or not the carrying value is fully recoverable. The weighted-average consists of four different outcomes, each with its own estimated probability of occurrence. Since these amounts represent management's best estimates, management deems it possible that, at the end of the three-year period, any one of these outcomes could actually occur. When management considers the individual probability of occurrence for each of the four outcomes estimated above, the analysis yields the following results:

	[1] 3-year outcome	*[2]* Probability weighted expected outcome	*[3]* [1] – [2] variation	*[4]* Probability of occurrence	*[5]* [3] × [4] probability weighted variation	*Positive variation*	*Negative variation*
Expected outcome 1	$ 9,400	$11,275	$(1,875)	20%	$(375)	$ –	$(375)
Expected outcome 2	11,600	11,275	325	45%	146	146	–
Expected outcome 3	12,400	11,275	1,125	30%	338	338	–
Expected outcome 4	9,100	11,275	(2,175)	5%	(109)	–	(109)
				100%		$484	$(484)

Careful examination of the above analysis yields the following conclusions:

- Variations naturally occur between expected outcomes and actual outcomes.
- Because the expected outcome is calculated as an average, some of the amounts used to compute it will be higher than the average and some will be lower than the average.

- When the individual variations are computed and each is multiplied by its probability of occurrence, the absolute value of the sum of the positive variations will exactly equal the absolute value of the sum of the negative variations.
- When these two absolute values are summed ($484 + $484 = $968 in the example above), the result, the total variability in both directions, is called the expected variability of the cash flows.
- The higher the expected variability of a set of cash flow estimates, the higher the level of risk and uncertainty associated with the estimate.

Initial Determination of VIE Status Whether or not an entity qualifies as a VIE is initially deter- mined on the date the reporting entity becomes involved with the legal entity. Involvement includes:

- Ownership,
- Contractual interest, or
- Other pecuniary interests.

This determination is based on the circumstances existing at that date, taking into account future changes that are required in existing governing documents and contractual arrangements. (ASC 810-10-25-37)

Is the Reporting Entity the Primary Beneficiary?

Once the reporting entity has determined that:

- A VIE scope exception does not apply, and
- The reporting entity has a variable interest in the legal entity (ASC 810-10-55-16),

then the reporting entity applies the VIE model to determine if it is the primary beneficiary and, therefore, must consolidate the variable entity. (ASC 810-10-25-38)

Exhibit—Overview of the VIE Model

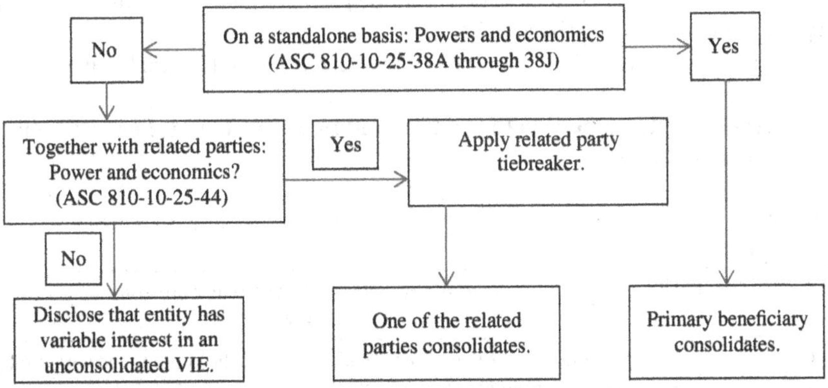

How to Determine If an Interest Holder Is the Primary Beneficiary Once it is determined that the reporting entity has a variable interest in a VIE, the reporting entity must determine whether it has a *controlling* financial interest. This assessment includes:

- The characteristics of the reporting entity's variable interests
- Other involvement, including related parties or de facto agents
- The involvement of other interest holders
- The VIE's purpose and design

The reporting entity is a primary beneficiary and must consolidate when it has:

- The *power* to direct the activities that most significantly affect the economic performance of the entity, *and*
- The *obligation* to absorb losses or the right to receive benefits of the entity that could be potentially significant to the entity.
(ASC 810-10-25-38A)

The primary beneficiary must consolidate the VIE regardless of the extent of ownership (or lack of it) by that entity. More than one entity may have the obligation to absorb losses or the right to receive benefits, but only one reporting entity will have the *power* to direct those activities of the VIE that most significantly affect the VIE's performance and, therefore, be the primary beneficiary. (ASC 810-10-25-38A) Only one enterprise should be identified as the primary beneficiary, with the determining factor being the power to direct those activities of the VIE most significantly impacting its economic performance. It is possible that no primary beneficiary can be identified.

Shared power ASC 810 includes the concept of shared power when evaluating a primary beneficiary: Power is shared:

- if two or more unrelated parties together have the power to direct the activities of a VIE that most significantly impact the VIE's economic performance, and
- if decisions about those activities require the consent of each of the parties.

If power is shared with other unrelated parties and no one party has the power to direct activities that most significantly impact the VIE's economic performance, then the reporting entity is *not* the primary beneficiary. (ASC 810-10-25-38D)

Fees paid to decision maker In some arrangements, a legal entity may outsource all or some decision making over the entity's activities through a contractual arrangement. The fees received by those decision makers or service providers may represent variable interests. Decision makers or service providers may include oil and gas operators, real estate property managers, asset managers, and so forth. The decision maker or service provider must assess the fee arrangement to determine if it qualifies as a variable interest.

If a decision maker meets all three of the criteria below, it is not a variable interest.

Exhibit—Criteria to Determine Whether a Fee Paid to a Decision Maker or Service Provider Is a Variable Interest

ASC 810-10-25-55-37 paragraph:	The fees paid to a decision maker or service provider is a variable interest if:
A	The fees are compensation for services provided and are commensurate with level of effort required to provide those services.
C	The decision maker or service provider does not hold other economic interests in the VIE that individually, or in the aggregate, would absorb more than an insignificant amount of the VIE's expected losses or receive more than an insignificant amount of the VIE's expected residual returns.
D	The service arrangement includes only terms, conditions, or amounts that are customarily present in arrangements for similar services negotiated at arm's length.

In evaluating the criterion to consider the level of other economic interests held by the decision maker, certain related-party interests need to be considered in assessing that criterion. (ASC

810- 10-55-37C above) A decision maker or service provider limits the extent to which related-party interests are included in Criterion C above and should consider only its direct interest plus its proportional share of the related party's or de facto agent's interests, unless the decision maker and related party are under common control. In that case, the decision maker should consider the related party's entire interest.

Related-Party Considerations in Determining the Primary Beneficiary For the purpose of a variable interest holder determining whether it is the primary beneficiary of a VIE, the definition of related parties is expanded from the definition set forth in ASC 850, *Related-Party Disclosures*, to include additional parties that act as "de facto agents" or "de facto principals" of the variable interest holder. Under the VIE model, the identification of related parties and de facto agents is an important step in evaluating which party should consolidate the entity. A de facto agency relationship does not exist if both the reporting entity and the party have the right of prior approval and those rights are agreed to by willing, independent parties who mutually agree on the terms.

A decision maker who is required to evaluate whether it is the primary beneficiary of a VIE considers only its *proportionate* indirect interest in the VIE held through a common control party. (ASC 810-10-25-42)

The following table lists the related parties as described in ASC 850 as well as additional related parties designated for this purpose in ASC 810-10-25-42 and 43:

Related parties	*De facto principals/agents*
• Affiliates of the entity. • Entities for which investments in their equity securities would be required, absent the election of the fair value option under the *Fair Value Option Subsection* of Section 825 10-15, to be accounted for by the equity method by the investing entity. • Trusts for the benefit of employees, such as pension and profit-sharing trusts that are managed by or under the trusteeship of management. • Principal owners of the entity and members of their immediate families. • Management of the entity and members of their immediate families. • Other parties with which the entity may deal if one party controls or can significantly influence the management or operating policies of the other to an extent that one of the transacting parties might be prevented from fully pursuing its own separate interests. • Other parties that can significantly influence the management or operating policies of the transacting parties or that have an ownership interest in one of the transacting parties and can significantly influence the other to an extent that one or more of the transacting parties might be prevented from fully pursuing its own separate interests.	• Parties that cannot finance their operations without subordinated financial support from the variable interest holder (e.g., another VIE of which the variable interest holder is the primary beneficiary). • Parties that received their interest in the VIE as a contribution or loan from the variable interest holder. • Officers and employees of the variable interest holder. • Members of the governing board of the variable interest holder. • Parties that have agreements not to sell, transfer, or encumber their interests in the VIE as collateral without the prior approval of the variable interest holder where that prior approval right constrains that party's ability to manage the economic risks or realize the economic rewards from its interests. • Parties with a close business relationship to the variable interest holder such as the relationship of a professional service provider to one of its significant clients. (ASC 810-10-25-43)

The related-party attribution rules require consolidation of many of the currently popular SPE structures, unless the VIE is well capitalized and such subordinated support vehicles as loan guarantees are dispensed with.

Related-Party Tie Breaker The related-party tiebreaker test helps identify which related party in a group is the primary beneficiary. If two or more related parties (including the de facto principals/agents specified above) hold variable interests in the same VIE, and the aggregate variable interests held by those parties would, if held by a single party, identify that party as the primary beneficiary, then the member of the related-party group that is most closely associated with the VIE is the primary beneficiary and is required to consolidate the VIE as a subsidiary in its financial statements. In determining which party is most closely associated with the VIE, all relevant facts and circumstances are considered, including:

- Whether there is a principal/agent relationship between parties within the related-party group
- The relationship of the activities of the VIE to each of the parties in the related-party group
- The significance of the VIE's activities to each of the parties in the related-party group
- The extent of a party's exposure to the expected losses of the VIE
- The design of the VIE
  (ASC 810-10-25-44)

Sufficiency of Equity Investment at Risk ASC 810-10-25-45 through 25-47. provides a 10% equity threshold test, which in practice may be confusing and unworkable. The guidance indicates that an at-risk equity investment of less than 10% of the entity's total assets is presumptively not considered sufficient to permit the entity to finance its activities without obtaining additional subordinated financial support. The guidance then goes on to say that the presumption of insufficiency can be overcome by either quantitative analysis, qualitative analysis, or both. Financial statement preparers must be careful not to mistakenly rely on the 10% presumption to conclude that an entity with less than 10% at-risk equity is a VIE, when in fact, further analysis would contradict that conclusion. Conversely, it is also possible that an entity can require at-risk equity of more than 10% in order to sufficiently finance its activities. The financial statement preparer also cannot rely on meeting or exceeding the 10% threshold as conclusive proof that the entity is sufficiently capitalized to avoid being characterized as a VIE.

Existing unconsolidated variable interest entities must be consolidated by their primary beneficiaries if the entities do not effectively disperse risks among the parties involved. Variable interest entities that effectively disperse risks will not be consolidated unless a single party holds an interest or combination of interests that effectively recombines risks that were previously dispersed.

Implicit variable interests One of the most misunderstood aspects of this area of the literature is referred to as an implicit variable interest. The Codification attempts to clarify this matter in ASC 810-10-25-49 through 54.

A party that did not explicitly issue a direct guarantee of another party's obligation may, nevertheless, be held to be an implicit guarantor of that obligation and thus, hold a variable interest in the party whose debt is implicitly guaranteed.

Example of Application of ASC 810 to Related-Party Leases

The most commonly encountered potential VIE situations that occur in practice involve related-party leases. Business owners often organize a partnership or LLC (for this discussion, assume an LLC) to own property that is leased to a business with the same or similar ownership. The transaction is structured in this manner for a number of reasons that include avoidance of double taxation of the gain on the eventual sale of the property and legal protection of the building from creditors of the operating business in the event of business bankruptcy.

In attempting to avoid lessee capitalization, the lease is often structured with a short initial term (e.g., three years), with the lessee having successive options to renew the lease at similar terms. The building is pledged as collateral under a mortgage with a third-party lender. The lessor entity is thinly capitalized (i.e., it has very little owner-invested equity). Consequently, the lender, besides holding a mortgage on the building as collateral, has further protected its interests by obtaining a loan guarantee from the lessee, an assignment of rents, and a personal guarantee of the owner.

These relationships are illustrated in the following diagram:

Exhibit—Criteria to Determine Whether a Fee Paid to a Decision Maker or Service Provider Is a Variable Interest

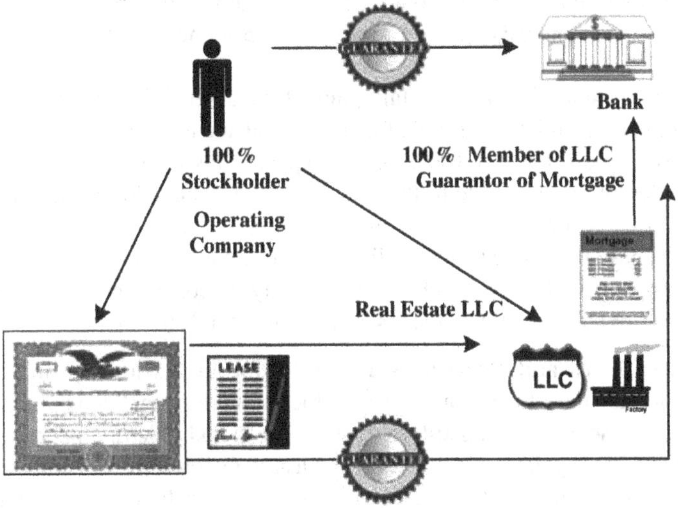

Analysis of Example under ASC 810

Following the decision diagrams and using the related-party/de facto principal and agent rules included in ASC 810:

- The lessee holds a variable interest in the lessor in the form of the guarantee of the lessor's mortgage debt.
- The lessor entity is not "scoped out" of ASC 810.
- The lessor entity is a business. It has inputs (owned fixed assets), processes for managing its investment, and outputs relative to access to the lessee.
- The following "further evaluation factors" apply:
  - The lessee/variable interest holder and its related parties participated significantly in the design of the lessor.

    - The design of the lessor LLC results in all of its activities involving and being conducted on behalf of the lessee/variable interest holder.
    - The lessee/variable interest holder and its related parties provided 100% of the subordinated financial support for the lessor entity.
    - The lessor entity's activities relate to a single-lessee lease.
- The lessee/evaluator and its related-party owner were involved in the design of the lessor entity.
- The lessee's variable interest is assumed to be *significant* for the purpose of this analysis. ASC 810 does not provide guidance on making this determination.
- The lessee's variable interest is in the leased asset.
- The fair value of the leased asset represents 100% of the total fair value of the lessor's assets and thus is deemed to be an interest in the lessor as a whole versus an interest in just the specified assets of the lessor.
- The at-risk equity holder of the lessor does not meet the second criterion for being considered to hold a controlling financial interest (i.e., the variable interest holder/lessee could potentially absorb expected losses of the lessor should the lessee be called upon by the lender to perform under the guarantee of the lessor's indebtedness). Note that, in this case, the other two criteria for controlling financial interest are met.
- As a result of the analysis up to this point, it can be concluded that the lessor is a variable interest entity.
- No silos exist, since 100% of the fair value of the assets is leased to the single lessee.
- Application of the related-party/de facto principal and agent rules to the variable interests in the lessor indicates that 100% of the expected losses and expected residual returns from the lessor are allocable to the members of the related-party group (the lessee and the related-party owner of both). Thus, collectively, the lessee and its 100% stockholder are the primary beneficiary of the VIE/lessor. The party most closely associated with the leased property is the lessee who, consequently, is considered the primary beneficiary that is required to consolidate the lessor in its financial statements.

Other Lease Terms and Provisions The following discussion examines the effect that certain changes to the above facts would have on the foregoing conclusions.

Existence or Absence of Guarantees Even if the stockholder/member's guarantee of the mortgage is not required by the lender and only the lessee guaranteed the debt, the analysis above would be identical. Due to the fact that the lessee/variable interest holder is exposed to the expected losses of the lessor under the terms of the guarantee, the lessor/LLC's sole member (and at-risk equity holder) is not the only party that potentially would absorb expected losses of the lessor.

Conversely, when this guidance was originally issued, many observers initially believed if the lessee was not required by the lender to guarantee the mortgage, and the only guarantee was that of the stockholder/member, that the absence of an explicit variable interest held by the lessee would preclude the conclusion that the lessor was a VIE. This situation illustrates one of the most misunderstood provisions of ASC 810—referred to as an *implicit variable interest*—which the FASB staff attempts to clarify in ASC 810-10-25-49 through 25-54.

Even though the lessee did not directly guarantee the debt of the lessor, consideration must be given to the likely scenarios if the lessor/LLC should be close to a default on the mortgage payments. Realistically, what is the likelihood that the sole stockholder/sole member would perform under his or her personal guarantee obligation rather than directing the lessee to pay additional rent sufficient to enable the LLC to keep its mortgage payments current?

Clearly, it would not make economic sense for the sole stockholder/member to perform personally under the guarantee, as this would, in substance, result in the stockholder/member making a loan or capital contribution to an otherwise insolvent LLC. Instead, it would logically follow that the best course of action would be for the lessee to pay rent in amounts adequate to fund the LLC's mortgage payments so that the lessee would continue to have use of the leased premises without concern over whether the bank will foreclose on and sell the property to a third party. If the lessee were having difficulty funding the rent payments, its owner would probably authorize it to borrow money or sell assets in order to enable it to do so before its owner used personal funds to perform under the guarantee.

After analyzing this situation, with appropriate attention to the substance rather than simply its form, it can be seen that the lessee is the holder of an implicit variable interest in the lessor in the form of an implicit guarantee of the lessor's mortgage debt.

The remainder of the analysis would be identical to what was presented earlier. Due to the fact that the lessee/variable interest holder is exposed to the expected losses of the lessor under the terms of the implicit guarantee, the lessor/LLC's sole member (and at-risk equity holder) is not the only party that potentially would absorb expected losses of the lessor.

Finally, consider the situation where neither the lessee nor the owner is required to guarantee the debt. A prudent lender would probably not waive both guarantees unless the lessor was sufficiently capitalized by the owner's at-risk equity. That is, there is a presumption that the lessor in such an instance is not a VIE. Under this scenario, the lessee would perform the quantitative analysis required to estimate expected losses and estimated residual returns to determine whether the lessor is a VIE and, if it is, whether it is the primary beneficiary.

Other Lease-Related Contractual Arrangements Leases are often accompanied by other contractual arrangements between the lessee and lessor. Such contractual arrangements can include management, marketing, brokerage, and other types of service agreements. These agreements must be carefully analyzed, as ASC 810 provides restrictive rules that often result in such agreements being characterized as variable interests.

All parties affected by these transactions should seek expert professional advice prior to either structuring a new transaction or modifying an existing transaction. For example, adverse income tax consequences could result from the transfer of property from one form of ownership to another.

Variable Interests in "Silos" A party may hold a variable interest in specific assets of a VIE (for example, a guarantee or a subordinated residual interest). In computing expected losses and expected residual returns, a holder of a variable interest in specified assets of a VIE must determine if the interest it holds qualifies as an interest in the VIE itself. The variable interest is considered an interest in the VIE itself if either:

1. The fair value of the specific assets is more than half of the total fair value of the VIE's assets, or
2. The interest holder has another significant variable interest in the entity as a whole.

If the interests are deemed to be interests in the VIE itself, the expected losses and expected residual returns associated with the variable interest in the specified assets are treated as being associated with the VIE. (ASC 810-10-25-55)

Measurement

Initial Measurement with Common Control If the primary beneficiary of a VIE and the VIE itself are under common control, the primary beneficiary (parent) initially measures the assets, liabilities, and noncontrolling interests of the newly consolidated reporting entity at their carrying amounts in the accounting records of the entity that controls the VIE. (ASC 810-10-30-1)

Initial Measurement Absent Common Control The rules governing the initial measurement of the assets and liabilities of a newly consolidated VIE conform closely to the rules governing other business combinations. The following table summarizes the rules.

Accounting by a Primary Beneficiary (Parent) for Initial Consolidation of a Variable Interest Entity

Recognition or measurement issue	Accounting treatment
1. Measurement date	Acquisition date, which is the date the acquirer/primary beneficiary obtains control of the acquiree/VIE. (ASC 805-10-25-6)
2. Measurement amount for assets, liabilities, and noncontrolling interests	The initial consolidation of a VIE that is a business is a business combination and should be accounted for as discussed previously in this chapter.
3. Measurement exception for enterprises under common control	Carrying value (net book value or NBV) in the accounting records of the enterprise that controls the VIE with no "step-up."
4. Assets and liabilities transferred to the VIE by the PB at, after, or shortly before the date of initial consolidation where the VIE *is not a business*	The assets and liabilities are measured at the same amounts in which the assets and liabilities would have been measured if they had not been transferred. No gain or loss is recognized on account of the transfer.
5. Assets and liabilities transferred to the VIE by the PB at, after, or shortly before the date of initial consolidation where the VIE *is a business*	If the VIE is a business, it should follow ASC 805-10-25-20 et seq., Determining What Is Part of the Business Combination Transaction, to assess the substance of such transfers and whether they are to be considered part of the business combination.
6. Recognition and measurement of goodwill	If the VIE is a business, goodwill is recognized and measured identical to the manner described for other business combinations. If the VIE is not a business, goodwill is not to be recognized and, instead, is recognized as a loss in the period of initial consolidation. That loss, however, is not to be characterized as extraordinary.
7. Recognition of negative goodwill	Irrespective of whether the VIE is a business, negative goodwill is not used to reduce the carrying values of any of the acquired assets or liabilities; rather it is recognized and measured identically with the manner described for business combinations as a gain on bargain purchase with a prohibition against characterizing the gain as extraordinary.

After initial measurement, the assets, liabilities, and noncontrolling interests of a consolidated variable interest entity are accounted for as if the entity were consolidated based on majority voting interests.

Example of Consolidation of a VIE—Consolidation Worksheet and Journal Entries

This example uses a structured related-party lease to illustrate application of the consolidation provisions of ASC 810-10-30.

Arielle Aromatics Ltd. (AAL) is a manufacturer of aromatherapy products that is 100% owned by Arielle Stone. AAL's headquarters and manufacturing plant are leased pursuant to an operating lease with an S Corporation, Myles' Management, Inc. (MMI), owned by Arielle's brother, Myles.

AAL's headquarters building and the land on which it is built are the only assets owned by MMI. They have been pledged as collateral for a mortgage loan that is guaranteed by a corporate guarantee of AAL and a personal guarantee of Arielle.

MMI has been determined to be a variable interest entity (VIE) and AAL its primary beneficiary. The following is the consolidating worksheet at December 31, 20X1:

Arielle Aromatics Ltd. and Subsidiary
Consolidating Worksheet
Year Ending December 31, 20X1

(000 omitted)			*Adjustments and Eliminations*			
	AAL	*MMI*	*Debit*	*Credit*	*Noncont. interest*	*Consolidated*
Statement of income:						
Revenues						
Sales	$6,400					$6,400
Rental income		(a) $1,200	$1,200			–
Cost of sales	3,800					3,800
Gross profit	2,600	1,200	1,200			2,600
Depreciation	100	230				330
Rent expense	1,200			(a) $1,200		–
Interest expense	200	400				600
Other expenses	300	–				300
Total operating expenses and interest	1,800	630		1,200		1,230
Income before noncontrolling interest share	800	570	1,200	1,200		1,370
Noncontrolling interest share of income					$570	(570)
Net income	$ $00	$ 570	$1,200	$1,200	$570	$ 800
Statement of retained earnings:						
Retained earnings, beginning						
AAL	$ 1,200					$ 1,200
MMI		$ –				–
Add net income (from above)	800	570	$1,200	$ 1,200	$570	800
Deduct dividends paid	(100)	(500)			(500)	(100)
Retained earnings, ending	$ 1,900	$ 70	$1,200	$ 1,200	$ 70	$ 1,900

(000 omitted)			*Adjustments and Eliminations*			
	AAL	*MMI*	*Debit*	*Credit*	*Noncont. interest*	*Consolidated*
Statement of financial position:						
Cash	$ 2,100					$ 2,100
Accounts receivable, trade (net)	7,500					7,500
Rentals receivable		$ 100	(b)	$ 100		–
Inventories	1,100					1,100
Land				1,000		1,000
Depreciable property and equipment	1,200	7,000				8,200
Accumulated depreciation	(300)	(230)				(530)
Total assets	$11,600	$7,870		100		$19,370
Notes and mortgages payable	$ 5,000	$6,900				$11,900
Accounts payable, trade	4,400					4,400
Rent payable	100		(b) $ 100			
Total liabilities	9,500	6,900	100			–
Common stock	200	900			900	200
Retained earnings (from above)	1,900	70	1,200	1,200	$970	1,900
Noncontrolling interest					970	970
Total stockholders' equity	2,100	970	1,200	1,200		3,070
Total liabilities and stockholders' equity	$11,600	$7,870	$1,300	$1,200		$19,370

The consolidating entries posted to the December 31, 2011, worksheet are as follows:

a. Rental income	1,200	
Rental expense		1,200
To eliminate intercompany rental income and rental expense at December 31, 2011		
b. Rental payable	100	
Rentals receivable		100
To eliminate intercompany rent receivable and rent payable at December 31, 2011		

The consolidation process is relatively straightforward. The effects of the related-party lease, the rental income and expense, and intercompany receivable and payable are eliminated so that, on a consolidated basis, the financial statements reflect the building, mortgage debt, depreciation, and interest expense.

The only difference between this consolidation of a VIE and a conventional consolidation of a voting interest entity in accordance with ASC 810-10-45 is the noncontrolling interest allocation. ASC 810-10-45-18 specifies that the elimination of intraentity profit or loss is not affected by the existence of a noncontrolling interest and that the elimination may be allocated between the parent (the controlling interest) and the noncontrolling interests.

In this example, however, the controlling interest holder, AAL, has no legal claim on the profit of MMI, since MMI's profit or loss is legally allocable to its equity owner. If this example had been a conventional consolidation of a voting interest entity, the effect of eliminating the rental income from MMI would be a remaining MMI loss of $630, computed as follows:

MMI net income	$ 570
Effect of elimination of rental income	(1,200)
MMI net loss after elimination of intercompany rental income	$ (630)

ASC 810-10-35-3 provides a special rule that the effect of eliminating fees or other sources of income or expense between the primary beneficiary and the consolidated VIE is to be attributed solely to the primary beneficiary and not to the noncontrolling interest computed as follows and illustrated above:

Net loss of VIE	$ (630)
Adjustment to allocate rental expense to primary beneficiary	1,200
Adjusted VIE net income allocable to noncontrolling interest	$ 570

The net income allocation to the noncontrolling interest shown above is reduced by the dividends paid to the noncontrolling interest as follows:

Adjusted VIE net income allocable to noncontrolling interest	$ 570
Dividend paid to noncontrolling interest	(500)
Noncontrolling interest retained earnings	70
Noncontrolling interest common stock	900
Total noncontrolling interest	$ 970

The results of the consolidation can be summarized as:

Primary beneficiary rent expense	$1,200
VIE	
Depreciation	230
Interest	400
	630
Net effect, allocable to noncontrolling interest	$ 570

Consolidated net income of $800 is the same as the primary beneficiary's net income since the entire $570 of VIE net income is allocated to the noncontrolling interest. The results, however, can have a profound effect on the way that the financial statements portray the leverage of the primary beneficiary to users, which might be the difference between AAL meeting or violating its loan covenants.

Debt to equity ratio	
Primary beneficiary	4.5:1
Consolidated	5.3:1

Certain practical matters require consideration in the case of consolidating VIEs.

1. *VIE without GAAP financial statements.* Many VIEs structured as shown in this example had not previously prepared financial statements. Prior to consolidating the VIE with the primary beneficiary, the VIE's accounting records must be adjusted to eliminate any differences between GAAP and he basis on which the VIE reports for income tax purposes.
2. *Lack of prior independent CPA involvement with VIE.* VIEs that had not been subject to financial reporting in the past obviously had not needed to engage an independent CPA to perform a compilation, review, or audit engagement. Upon consolidation, the consolidated financial statements, including the VIE's (subsidiary's) financial position and results of operations, will be subject to the same level of service as the financial statements of the primary beneficiary (parent).
3. *Interaction with ASC 460-10. ASC 460-10, Guarantor's Accounting and Disclosure Requirements for Guarantees, Including Indirect Guarantees of Indebtedness of Others,* requires guarantors to recognize a liability at inception for the obligations embodied in the guarantee. In the example above, the guarantee of the VIE's mortgage by the

primary beneficiary would be exempt from the initial recognition and measurement provision of ASC 460-10 because the guarantee is analogous to a parent guarantee of its subsidiary's debt to a third party, which is specifically exempted from the recognition and measurement provisions of ASC 460-10. However, the guarantee is not exempt from the disclosure requirements of ASC 460-10 and ASC 450-10.

4. *General-purpose financial statements*. In the example, AAL is the "parent" company. It would be precluded by ASC 810-10-45-11 from issuing separate, general-purpose financial statements that exclude MMI, since this would be a GAAP departure; however, nothing precludes MMI from issuing separate subsidiary-only financial statements.

Example of an Implicit Variable Interest

Consider the situation where the principal shareholder of a company personally guarantees a mortgage on the premises that the company occupies and leases from a related LLC whose sole member is the lessee's principal shareholder. Normally, the rent payments due under the related-party lease are structured to provide sufficient cash flow to the lessor to enable it to meet its debt service obligations under the mortgage. If the lessee were to become delinquent under its rent obligations to the lessor, the lessor would not have sufficient cash flow to enable it to make the payments due under its mortgage, which would cause a loan delinquency or default.

Should this occur, the following scenarios could occur:

1. The lender could repossess the property and sell it to pay off the loan,
2. The lender could enforce the guarantee and compel the shareholder to pay off the loan on behalf of the lessor or, at least to make the delinquent payments on behalf of the lessor to cure the default, or
3. The lessee could sell off assets or borrow money from its stockholder or a third party to enable it to pay its delinquent rent, thereby enabling the lessor to make its delinquent mortgage payments.

Scenario 1 would not be a desirable outcome, as the lessor would lose title to its property and the lessee, in default on its rent, could end up without the premises in which it operates its business since, upon sale of the property, the successor owner would potentially terminate the lease for nonpayment.

Under scenario 2 if the shareholder were to pay the delinquent mortgage payment on behalf of the lessor, the transactions would be recorded as follows:

Lessor Accounting Records

Rent receivable	xxx	
Rental income		xxx
To record delinquent rent due from lessee		
Mortgage payable	xxx	
Loan payable—member		xxx
To record mortgage payment made on behalf of LLC by its member as a loan		

Lessee Accounting Records

Rent expense	xxx	
Rent payable		xxx
To record delinquent rent due to lessor		

Scenario 3 would be recorded as follows (assuming that the lessee obtains additional funds from its principal shareholder):

Lessee Accounting Records

Cash	xxx	
Loan payable—shareholder		xxx
To record loan from shareholder		
Rent payable	xxx	
Cash		xxx
To record rent payment		

Lessor Accounting Records

Cash	xxx	
Rental income		xxx
To record rent received from lessee		
Mortgage interest	xxx	
Mortgage payable	xxx	
Cash		xxx
To record mortgage payment		

The outcomes of scenarios 2 and 3 are very similar. Under scenario 2, the shareholder/member will have a loan receivable from the thinly capitalized LLC that depends solely on the delinquent corporation for its cash flow. In scenario 2, the lessee will have to raise cash in an amount sufficient to fund the LLC's repayment of its loan to the shareholder/member and keep the mortgage current. Since the LLC is dependent upon the lessee for its cash flow, the lessee has implicitly incurred an obligation to fund the LLC's loan repayment to the shareholder/member. It is, of course, in the best interest of the lessee to fund this, since it entitles the lessee to continue to benefit from the use of the leased property and, contractually, the lessee is already obligated to pay the delinquent rent.

Under scenario 3, the shareholder/member will have a loan receivable from a lessee that is experiencing difficulty in meeting its rent obligations. The lessee will have substituted a presumably interest-bearing loan payable to its shareholder for a noninterest-bearing rent payable obligation to the LLC and will, as in scenario 2, be obligated to raise cash sufficient to repay its shareholder and fund its rent obligations under the lease. In effect, the lessee will have used its available credit that it could have used for other operating purposes to help provide financial support to the LLC that would otherwise have insufficient capital to be self-sustaining. Again, implicitly, the lessee is functioning as a guarantor of the LLC's mortgage indebtedness by its willingness to provide the cash flow necessary for the LLC to meet its obligations.

Based on the foregoing analysis, in substance the lessee is the holder of an implicit variable interest in the lessor in the form of an implicit guarantee of the lessor's mortgage debt. Due to the fact that the implicit guarantee exposes the lessee/variable interest holder to the expected losses of the lessor, the lessor/LLC's sole member (and at-risk equity holder) is not the only party that potentially would absorb expected losses of the lessor. The application of ASC 810 is, of course, not limited to related-party arrangements. The following is an example of the quantitative analysis (versus the qualitative analysis illustrated in the related-party example above) that might be necessary in an arm's-length leasing arrangement.

Example—Arm's-Length Leases: Computing Expected Losses and Expected Residual Returns

Lawrence Lessor, LLC (referred to herein as "the Entity" since it is the entity that the variable interest holders will be evaluating as to whether it is a VIE) is a limited liability company organized specifically for the purpose of building, owning, and operating a single-lessee retail discount warehouse club store on land that it has recently acquired. The store is the only asset owned by the Entity. The 148,000 square foot store will be occupied by Clubco, a nationally known chain that is unrelated to Lawrence Lessor.

The Entity's voting owners (the LLC members) wish only to invest a minimal amount of equity in the Entity and, consequently, the mortgage lender insisted on obtaining a third-party guarantee of the mortgage which Lawrence obtained from an unrelated third party and for which Lawrence paid a premium.

The terms of the lease with the retailer are as follows (assumed to be an operating lease):

Description of space	148,000 square foot retail discount warehouse club store
Lessee	Clubco Stores, Inc.
Initial lease term	Three years
Lease commencement date	1/1/20X1
Annual base rent	$600,000
Contingent rent	1% of annual sales over $30 million
Purchase options	$9 million—not a bargain purchase option in accordance with ASC 840
Residual guarantee	Lessee guarantees to lessor that residual value of the building at the end of the lease term will be at least equal to the $7,500,000 fair value of the store land and building at inception or it will pay the lessor the difference
Executory costs	All real estate taxes, maintenance, insurance, and common area expenses are to be borne by the lessee

The construction has been completed, the occupancy permits issued, and the construction financing settled with the proceeds of a 25-year, 6% mortgage loan on December 1, 20X1. The mortgage loan is guaranteed by an unrelated third-party guarantor. The store is opening and commencing business on January 1, 20X2.

Mortgage details are as follows:

Summary Amortization Schedule for Mortgage

25-year, 6% mortgage, original principal amount of $7,275,750

Year	*Payments*	*Interest*	*Principal*	*Balance*
Original loan				$7,275,750
20X2	$ 562,533	$ 433,022	$129,511	7,146,239
20X3	562,533	425,034	137,499	7,008,740
20X4	562,533	416,553	145,980	6,862,760
	$1,687,599	$1,274,609	$412,990	

The Entity's recorded aggregate carrying amount of $7,500,000 for the land and building represents the fair value at lease inception with the land's fair value representing 10%, or $750,000.

The rental terms for the store are considered to be at market rates. If the terms were not at market rates, additional expected variability would be assigned to the lease (in addition to the expected variability resulting from the purchase option and residual value guarantee).

Expected cash flows are discounted to their present value using an assumed 3% interest rate representing the interest rate available on risk-free investments. To simplify the example, cash flows are assumed to occur at the end of each annual period for the purpose of discounting them to present value. A copy of the statement of financial position from the Entity's annual partnership return at lease inception is as follows:

Schedule L **Statement of Financial Position per Books**

	Beginning of tax year		*End of tax year*	
Assets	(a)	(b)	(c)	(d)
1. Cash				1,000
2. a. Trade notes and accounts receivable				
b. Less allowance for bad debts				
3. Inventories				
4. U.S. government obligations				
5. Tax-exempt securities				
6. Other current assets (*attach schedule*)				
7. Mortgage and real estate loans				
8. Other investments (*attach schedule*)				
9. a. Buildings and other depreciable assets			6,750,000	
b. Less accumulated depreciation				6,750,000
10. a. Depletable assets				
b. Less accumulated depletion				
11. Land (net of any amortization)				750,000
12. a. Intangible assets (amortizable only)				
b. Less accumulated amortization				
13. Other assets (*attach schedule*)				
14. Total assets				7,501,000
Liabilities and Capital				
15. Accounts payable				
16. Mortgages, notes, bonds payable in less than 1 year				
17. Other current liabilities (*attach schedule*)				
18. All nonrecourse loans				7,275,750
19. Mortgages, notes, bonds payable in 1 year or more				
20. Other liabilities (*attach schedule*)				
21. Partners' capital accounts				225,250
22. Total liabilities and capital				7,501,000

Analysis by Clubco

1. Clubco holds a variable interest in Lawrence Lessor ("the Entity") in the form of the lease. Expected variability results from the purchase option and the residual value guarantee.
2. The Entity is not scoped out of ASC 810.
3. The Entity is a business.
4. Further evaluation factor applies for a single-lessee lease.

5. Clubco was not involved in the design of the Entity.
6. For illustrative purposes, assume that the purchase option is significant to Clubco.
7. Clubco holds a variable interest in the leased store (the specified assets) in the form of the lease containing a purchase option and residual value guarantee.
8. The fair value of the building leased by Clubco is 100% of the fair value of the Entity's assets. Therefore, Clubco is deemed to hold a variable interest in the Entity as a whole.
9. In applying the test to determine if the members of the LLC/Entity have a controlling financial interest (distinguished from a controlling voting interest, which they clearly have), the following results are determined:
   a. The LLC members are the sole voting interest holders and, therefore, meet the voting test.
   b. The LLC members are *not* the only parties that absorb expected losses of the lessor due to the existence of the residual value guarantee provision in the lease that potentially could result in Clubco bearing a portion of the expected losses.
   c. The LLC members are also *not* the only parties entitled to receive the expected residual returns from the property due to the existence of the purchase option provision in the lease that potentially could result in Clubco receiving a portion of the expected residual urns.
10. As a consequence of the analysis up to this point, Clubco can conclude that its variable interest is in a lessor that is a VIE.
11. Since Clubco leases 100% of the fair value of the assets held by the Entity, there are no silos included therein.
12. To determine whether or not it is the primary beneficiary of the VIE/lessor, Clubco must determine whether it either will bear the majority of the expected losses, or receive the majority of the expected residual returns. One form this calculation might take is illustrated below.

Computation of expected cash flow possibilities for the lease term

	20X2					
Probability	*5%*	*15%*	*30%*	*35%*	*10%*	*5%*
Assumptions						
Annual store sales	$25,000,000	$30,000,000	$40,000,000	$50,000,000	$55,000,000	$60,000,000
Percentage rent base	$30,000,000	$30,000,000	$30,000,000	$30,000,000	$30,000,000	$30,000,000
Percentage rent rate	1%	1%	1%	1%	1%	1%
Possible cash flow outcomes						
Rent—Base	$ 600,000	$ 600,000	$ 600,000	$ 600,000	$ 600,000	$ 600,000
Rent—Percentage	-	-	100,000	200,000	250,000	300,000
Total rental income	600,000	600,000	700,000	800,000	850,000	900,000
Mortgage payments	562,533	562,533	562,533	562,533	562,533	562,533
Possible net cash flow	$ 37,467	$37,467	$ 137,467	$ 237,467	$ 287,467	$ 337,467
Present value, discounted at 3%	$ 36,376	$ 36,376	$ 133,463	$ 230,550	$ 279,094	$ 327,638

	20X3					
Probability	*5%*	*15%*	*30%*	*35%*	*10%*	*5%*
Assumptions						
Estimated percentage change in sales	-2.00%	0.00%	2.00%	2.50%	3.00%	4.00%
Annual store sales	$24,500,000	$30,000,000	$40,800,000	$51,250,000	$56,650,000	$62,400,000
Percentage rent base	$30,000,000	$30,000,000	$30,000,000	$30,000,000	$30,000,000	$30,000,000
Percentage rent rate	1%	1%	1%	1%	1%	1%

Possible cash flow outcomes						
Rent—Base	$ 600,000	$ 600,000	$ 600,000	$ 600,000	$ 600,000	$ 600,000
Rent—Percentage	–	–	108,000	212,500	266,500	324,000
Total rental income	600,000	600,000	708,000	812,500	866,500	924,000
Mortgage payments	562,533	562,533	562,533	562,533	562,533	562,533
Possible net cash flow	$ 37,467	$ 37,436	$ 145,467	$ 249,967	$303,967	$ 361,467
Present value, discounted at 3%	$ 35,316	$ 35,316	$ 137,117	$ 235,618	$286,518	$ 340,717

	20X4					
Probability	*5%*	*15%*	*30%*	*35%*	*10%*	*5%*
Estimated percentage change in sales	–1.00%	0.00%	2.50%	3.50%	3.75%	5.00%
Annual store sales	$24,255,000	$30,000,000	$41,820,000	$53,043,750	$58,774,375	$65,520,000
Percentage rent base	$30,000,000	$30,000,000	$30,000,000	$30,000,000	$30,000,000	$30,000,000
Percentage rent rate	1%	1%	1%	1%	1%	1%

	20X4					
Probability	*5%*	*15%*	*30%*	*35%*	*10%*	*5%*
Possible cash flow outcomes						
Rent—Base	$ 600,000	$ 600,000	$ 600,000	$ 600,000	$ 600,000	$ 600,000
Rent—Percentage	–	–	118,200	230,438	287,744	355,200
Total rental income	600,000	600,000	718,200	830,438	887,744	955,200
Mortgage payments	562,533	562,533	562,533	562,533	562,533	562,533
Possible net cash flow, operations	37,467	37,467	155,667	267,905	325,211	392,667
Estimated residual amount	7,000,000	8,000,000	9,000,000	10,000,000	12,000,000	13,000,000
Mortgage repayment	6,862,760	6,862,760	6,862,760	6,862,760	6,862,760	6,862,760
Possible net sales proceeds	137,240	1,137,240	2,137,240	3,137,240	5,137,240	6,137,240
Possible net cash flow	$ 174,707	$1,174,707	$2,292,907	$3,405,144	$5,462,451	$6,529,907
Present value, discounted at 3%	$ 159,881	$1,075,023	$2,098,334	$3,116,189	$4,998,916	$5,975,790
3-year totals of present value of possible cash flows discounted at 3%	$ 231,573	$1,146,715	$2,368,914	$3,582,357	$5,564,528	$6,644,145

Note that, in the forecast for 20X4, the effects of the purchase option and residual value guarantee are ignored. They are considered later in the analysis of which variable interest holders participate in expected losses and expected residual returns.

13. Calculation of probability-weighted discounted expected cash flows.

Scenario	**Present value of possible cash flows**	**Estimated probability**	**Discounted probability-weighted expected cash flows**
1	$ 231,573	5%	$11,579
2	1,146,715	15%	172,007
3	2,368,914	30%	710,674
4	3,582,357	35%	1,253,825
5	5,564,528	10%	556,453
6	6,644,145	5%	332,207
		100%	$3,036,745

This computation uses the expected cash flow methodology prescribed by CON 7, which is also used in estimation of fair value for the purposes of impairment testing of goodwill and tangible long-lived assets, and in computing asset retirement obligations.

14. Calculations of expected losses and expected residual returns (and the related expected variability).

Scenario	*Present value of possible cash flows*	*Discounted/ probability-weighted expected cash flows*	*Variance from expected outcome*	*Estimated probability*	*Expected losses*	*Expected residual returns*
1	$ 231,573	$3,036,745	$(2,805,172)	5%	$(140,259)	
2	1,146,715	3,036,745	(1,890,030)	15%	(283,505)	
3	2,368,914	3,036,745	(667,831)	30%	(200,349)	
4	3,582,357	3,036,745	545,612	35%		$190,965
5	5,564,528	3,036,745	2,527,783	10%		252,778
6	6,644,145	3,036,745	3,607,400	5%		180,370
				100%	$(624,113)	$624,113

ASC 810 requires consideration of the "expected variability" inherent in the estimate of probability-weighted expected cash flows; in this case $3,036,745. This amount represents a weighted-average of the various expected outcomes multiplied by their respective probabilities. As is always the case when averaging numbers, the sums of the positive and negative differences between each value included in the average and the average itself are always equal. This explains why the expected losses and expected residual returns each equal $624,113. Therefore, the expected variability in both directions is the sum of the two absolute values (i.e., $624,113 + $624,113 = $1,248,226).

Another important point to note is that the terms "expected losses" and "expected residual returns" are not associated with traditional GAAP income or cash flow measures. The entity illustrated above has positive expected cash flows under all six scenarios for all three years. Notwithstanding that fact, the computation shows that it will experience expected losses and expected residual returns—variations from expectation, positive or negative, that could occur as a result of operations or of changes in the fair value of the property. This will always be the case, irrespective of how profitable an entity is or how much cash flow it generates.

15. For each scenario, the facts are analyzed to determine which of the variable interest holders will bear the expected losses. There were no silos included in the VIE; therefore, only a single primary beneficiary determination is required. The results of the analysis are aggregated as follows:

	Expected losses
Scenario 1	$(140,259)
Scenario 2	(283,505)
Scenario 3	(200,349)
	$(624,113)

Scenario	*Estimated residual value of store*	*Expected losses*	*Clubco*	*3rd-party guarantor*	*At-risk equity holders of entity*	*Mortgage lender*	*Notes*
							$7.5 MM guarantee
1	7,000,000	$(140,259)	$(140,259)				$7 MM residual
2	8,000,000	(283,505)			$(283,505)		
3	9,000,000	(200,349)			(200,349)		
Excess of share of losses over equity		______	______	(258,604)	(258,604)		
		$(624,113)	$(140,259)	(258,604)	$(225,250)	$ –	
		100%	22%	42%	36%	0%	

Total equity at risk is $225,250, which would not be sufficient for the entity to absorb the expected losses of $624,113 without receiving additional subordinated financial support. Consequently, the Entity (Lawrence Lessor, LLC) by definition is a VIE.

Note that, based on the analysis of the expected losses, no variable interest holder will absorb a majority (>50%) of the Entity's losses. Consequently, the expected residual returns need to be analyzed.

Scenario	Estimated residual value of store	Expected residual returns	Clubco	At-risk equity holders of entity	Guarantor	Notes
4	$10,000,000	$190,965	$190,965			Exercise of $9MM option
5	12,000,000	252,778	252,778			Exercise of $9MM option
6	13,000,000	180,370	180,370			Exercise of $9MM option
		$624,113	$624,113			
		100%	100%			

16. Since 100% of the expected residual returns will be received by Clubco, it is the primary beneficiary, the party that is required to consolidate Lawrence Lessor, LLC in its financial statements.

If the interests are not deemed to be interests in the VIE itself, the interests in the specified assets are treated as a separate VIE (referred to as a *silo*) if the expected cash flows from the specified assets (and any associated credit enhancements, if applicable) are essentially the sole source of payment for specified liabilities or specified other interests. Under this scenario, expected losses and expected residual returns associated with the silo assets are accounted for separately to the extent that the interest holder either absorbs the VIE's expected losses or is entitled to receive its expected residual returns. Any excess of expected losses or expected residual returns not borne by (received by) the variable interest holder is considered attributable to the entity as a whole.

If one interest holder is required to consolidate a silo of a VIE, other VIE interest holders must exclude the silo from the remaining VIE.

Reconsideration of VIE Status Once an initial determination is made as to whether an entity is a variable interest entity (as opposed to a voting interest entity), that initial determination need not be reconsidered unless one or more of the following circumstances occurs:

- A change is made to the VIE's governing documents or contractual arrangements that results in changes in either the characteristics or sufficiency of the at-risk equity investment in the VIE.
- As a result of a return of some or all of the equity investment to the equity investors, other interests become exposed to the VIE's expected losses.
- There is an increase in the VIE's expected losses that results from the entity engaging in activities or acquiring assets that were not anticipated at either the inception of the entity or a later reconsideration date.
- There is a decrease in the VIE's expected losses due to the entity modifying or curtailing its activities.
- Additional at-risk equity is invested in the VIE.
- The equity investors, as a group, lose the power to direct the activities of the VIE that most significantly impact its economic performance.

(ASC 810-10-35-4)

VOTING INTEREST MODEL

Voting interest entity is not defined explicitly in ASC 810. By default it means an entity that is not a variable interest entity. ASC 810 stipulates that the usual condition that best evidences which party holds a controlling financial interest is the party that holds a majority voting interest. Voting rights are the key driver in determining which party should consolidate the entity. Kick-out rights through voting interest are analogous to a shareholder's voting rights in a corporation. (ASC 810-10-25-1A) The voting interest model generally assumes the percentage of ownership determines the level of influence that the reporting entity has over an investee. Determination of whether the presumption of control of an investee with a majority voting interest or a limited partner with a majority of kick-out rights through voting interests is overcome is a "facts and circumstances" assessment to be made in each unique situation. For example, depending on which decisions are required to be put to a full vote of the partnership (as opposed to being reserved for the general partner), the limited partners may be found to have substantive participating rights. Another important factor weighing on this determination is the relationships among limited and general partners (using ASC 850 related-party criteria). (ASC 810-10-25-5)

The exhibit below outlines the presumptive control based on voting interest. (Also, see the "Scope and Scope Exceptions" section at the beginning of this chapter for exceptions to the majority control presumption.)

Exhibit—Voting Interest Model

Percentage of Ownership:	0 →50	→50	→100
Presumptive Level of Influence:	Little or none	Significant	Control
Valuation/Reporting Method:	Fair value method	Equity method	Consolidation

Under the equity method, investments are shown as a single line in the statement of financial position and a single line item in the income statement. This is sometimes referred to as a one-line consolidation. In consolidated financial statements, details of all entities are reported in full.

Because of their unique design and purpose, the Codification offers specific guidance for limited partnerships and similar entities, like limited liability companies governed by a managing member, regarding voting rights. Kick-out rights are considered analogous to the voting rights held by a corporation's shareholders. To demonstrate that a limited partnership is a voting entity, the partners or members must have:

- Kick-out rights
- Participating rights
  (ASC 810-10-15-14)

The assessment of noncontrolling rights is made when a majority voting interest or a majority of kick-out rights through voting interests is obtained. The assessment is made again if there is a significant change to the terms or the exercisability of the noncontrolling shareholder's or limited partner's rights. (ASC 810-10-25-6)

Protective Rights Limited partners' rights (whether granted by contract or by law) that would allow the limited partners to block selected limited partnership actions would be considered protective rights. The presence of protective rights does not serve to overcome the presumption of control by the general partner(s). (ASC 810-10-15-20)

Among the actions illustrating protective (not participating) rights are:

- Amendments to the articles of incorporation or partnership agreements
- Pricing on transactions between the owner of a majority interest or limited partner with a majority kick-out right through voting interests and the investee and related self-dealing transactions
- Liquidation of the investee or a decision to cause the investee to enter bankruptcy or other receivership
- Acquisitions and dispositions of assets that are not expected to be undertaken in the ordinary course of business (note that noncontrolling rights relating to acquisitions and dispositions expected to be made in the ordinary course of business are participating rights)
- Issuance or repurchase of equity interests
  (ASC 810-10-25-10)

Substantive Participating Rights Substantive participating rights, on the other hand, do overcome the presumption of general partner control. Such rights could include:

- Selecting, terminating, and setting the compensation of management responsible for implementing the limited partnership's policies and procedures
- Establishing operating and capital decisions of the limited partnership, including budgets, in the ordinary course of business
  (ASC 810-10-25-11)

Kick-Out Rights

If the limited partners have the *substantive ability* to dissolve (liquidate) the limited partnership or otherwise remove the general partners without cause—which is referred to as "kick- out rights"—then the general partners are deemed to lack control over the partnership. In such cases, consolidated financial reporting would not be appropriate, but equity method accounting would almost inevitably be warranted. To qualify, the kick-out rights must be exercisable by a single limited partner or a simple majority (or fewer) of limited partners. Thus, if a supermajority of limited partner votes is required to remove the general partner(s), this would not constitute a substantive ability to dissolve the partnership and would not thwart control by the general partner(s).

For limited partnerships, there is a range of possible qualifying requirements to exercise kick-out rights that could lead to the conclusion that nominal kick-out rights are ineffective in precluding the general partner(s) from exercising control. The Codification offers a series of illustrative examples to help the preparer interpret this guidance and should be consulted to benchmark any real-world set of circumstances. Examples of barriers to the exercise of kick-out rights include:

- Conditions that make it unlikely the rights will be exercisable (e.g., conditions that narrowly limit the timing of the exercise)
- Financial penalties or operational barriers associated with dissolving (liquidating) the limited partnership or replacing the general partners that would act as a significant disincentive for dissolution (liquidation) or removal
- The absence of an adequate number of qualified replacements for the general partners or the lack of adequate compensation to attract a qualified replacement

- The absence of an explicit, reasonable mechanism in the partnership's governing documents or in the applicable laws or regulations, by which the limited partners holding the rights can call for and conduct a vote to exercise those rights
- The inability of the limited partners holding the rights to obtain the information necessary to exercise them
 (ASC 810-10-25-14A)

A limited partner's unilateral right to withdraw is pointedly not equivalent to a kick-out right. However, if the partnership is contractually or statutorily bound to dissolve upon the withdrawal of one partner, that would equate to a potential kick-out right. (ASC 810-10-25-14B)

Deconsolidation of a Subsidiary

Changes in the Parent's Ownership Interest in a Subsidiary Subsequent to a business combination, the parent may increase or decrease its ownership percentage in the acquiree/ subsidiary, which may or may not affect whether the parent continues to control the subsidiary.

Changes Not Affecting Control The treatment of changes not affecting control are detailed in the *Disclosure and Presentation Checklist for Commercial Businesses* at www.wiley.com/go/GAAP2021; references to ASC 810-10-45-22 through 45-24.

Changes Resulting in Loss of Control If a parent company ceases to have a controlling financial interest in a subsidiary, the parent is required to deconsolidate the subsidiary as of the date on which its control ceased. Examples of situations that can result in a parent being required to deconsolidate a subsidiary include:

- Sale by the parent of all or a portion of its ownership interest in the subsidiary resulting in the parent no longer holding a controlling financial interest,
- Expiration of a contract that granted control of the subsidiary to the parent,
- Issuance by the subsidiary of stock that reduces the ownership interest of the parent to a level not representing a controlling financial interest,
- Loss of control of the subsidiary by the parent because the subsidiary becomes subject to control by a governmental body, court, administrator, or regulator.

If a parent effects a deconsolidation of a subsidiary through a nonreciprocal transfer to owners, such as through a spin-off transaction, the transaction is accounted for under ASC 845-10. Otherwise, the parent is to account for the deconsolidation by recognizing, in net income, a gain or loss attributable to the parent. (ASC 810-10-40-5) The gain or loss is measured as follows, where:

FVCR = Fair value of consideration received, if any
FVNIR = Fair value of any noncontrolling investment retained by the former parent at the deconsolidation date
CVNI = Carrying value of the noncontrolling interest in the former subsidiary on the deconsolidation date, including any accumulated other comprehensive income attributable to the noncontrolling interest
CVAL = Carrying value of the former subsidiaries assets and liabilities at the deconsolidation date.

(FVCR + FVNIR + CVNI) – CVAL = Deconsolidation Gain (Loss)

Should the parent's loss of controlling financial interest occur through two or more transactions, management of the former parent should consider whether the transactions should be accounted for as a single transaction. In evaluating whether to combine the transactions, management of the former parent should consider all of the terms and conditions of the transactions as well as their economic impact. The presence of one or more of the following indicators may lead to management concluding that it should account for multiple transactions as a single transaction:

- The transactions are entered into simultaneously or in contemplation of one another,
- The transactions, when considered in tandem, are in substance a single transaction designed to achieve an overall commercial objective,
- The occurrence of one transaction depends on the occurrence of at least one other transaction,
- One transaction, when considered on its own merits, does not make economic sense, but when considered together with the other transaction or transactions would be considered economically justifiable.
  (ASC 810-10-40-6)

Obviously, this determination requires the exercise of sound judgment and attention to economic substance over legal form.

ASC 810-30, *Research and Development Arrangements*

Sponsored Research and Development Activities To illustrate the guidance in this section, ASC 810-30-55 discusses the accounting for a transaction in which a sponsor creates a wholly owned subsidiary with cash and rights to certain technology originally developed by the sponsor, and receives from the newly created subsidiary two classes of stock. The sponsor then distributes one of the classes of stock (e.g., Class to its stockholders. This class of stock has voting rights. Under a purchase option, the sponsor has the right, for a specified period of time, to repurchase all the Class A stock distributed to the stockholders for an exercise price approximating the fair value of the Class A shares. The class retained by the sponsor (e.g., Class B) conveys essentially no financial interest to the sponsor and has no voting rights other than certain blocking rights. The certificate of incorporation prohibits the subsidiary from changing its capital structure, from selling any significant portion of its assets, and from liquidating or merging during the term when the purchase option is outstanding.

The sponsor and the subsidiary enter into a development contract that requires the subsidiary to spend all the cash contributed by the sponsor for research and development activities mutually agreed upon with the sponsor. The subsidiary has no employees other than its CEO. The subsidiary contracts with the sponsor to perform, on behalf of the sponsor, all of the research and development activities under the development contract.

The sponsor accounts for the research and development contract as follows:

- The sponsor reclassifies the cash contributed to the subsidiary as restricted cash when the Class A shares are distributed to its stockholders.
- The distribution of the Class A shares by the sponsor to its stockholders is accounted for as a dividend based on the fair value of the shares distributed.
- In the financial statements of the sponsor, the Class A shares are presented similar to a minority interest.
- The sponsor recognizes research and development expense as the research and development activities are conducted.
- The research and development expense recognized by the sponsor is not allocated to the Class A shares in determining net income or in calculating earnings per share.

- If the Class A purchase option is exercised, the sponsor accounts for the purchase as the acquisition of a minority interest.
- If the Class A purchase option is not exercised by its expiration date, the sponsor reclassifies the Class A stock to additional paid-in capital as an adjustment of the original dividend.

The effect of the above guidance is quite similar to what would be achieved by consolidating the subsidiary.

Other Sources

See ASC Location—*Wiley GAAP* Chapter	***For information on . . .***
ASC 480-10-55-53 through 55-58	Derivative transactions in subsidiary stock with noncontrolling interest.
ASC 740-10-25-39 through 25-41	Deferred taxes on dividends of foreign operations.
ASC 830-30-45-10	The elimination of intraentity profits with foreign entities.
ASC 840-30-45-4 (This is superseded upon implementation of ASC 2016-02)	Leases sold by a manufacturer to a leasing subsidiary.
ASC 842-30-45-3 (Upon implementation of ASC 2016-02)	Leases sold by a manufacturer to a leasing subsidiary.
ASC 860-10-55-13	Transfers of ownership interest in a subsidiary with financial assets.

50 ASC 815 DERIVATIVES AND HEDGING

PERSPECTIVE AND ISSUES

Technical Alert

ASU 2019-10

Guidance regarding effective dates In November 2019, the FASB issued ASU 2019-10, *Financial Instruments—Credit Losses (Topic 326), Derivatives and Hedging (Topic 815), and Leases (Topic 842: Effective Dates*. The ASU grants private companies, not-for-profit organizations, and certain small public company SEC filers additional time to implement recent FASB standards on current expected credit losses (CECL).

ASU 2019-10: Effective Dates		
Topic	**Public business entities that meet the definition of SEC Filers, except Smaller Reporting Companies (SRCs) as determined by the SEC as of November 15, 2019**	**All Other Entities**
Derivatives—ASU 2017-12	Fiscal years beginning after December 15, 2019	Fiscal years beginning after December 15, 2021

ASU 2019-04 In April 2019, the FASB issued ASU 2019-04, *Codification Improvements to Topic 326, Financial Instruments—Credit Losses, Topic 815, Derivatives and Hedging, and Topic 825, Financial Instruments.*

Issue 3A: Partial-Term Fair Value Hedges of Interest Rate Risk

The amendments clarify that an entity may measure the change in fair value of a hedged item using an assumed term only for changes attributable to interest rate risk. They also clarify that an entity may measure the change in the fair value of the hedged item attributable to interest rate risk using an assumed term when the hedged item is designated in a hedge of both interest rate risk and foreign exchange risk. In that instance, the change in carrying value of the hedged item attributable to foreign exchange risk must continue to be measured based on changes in the spot exchange rate in accordance with paragraph 815-25-35-18. In addition, the amendments clarify that one or more separately designated partial-term fair value hedging relationships of a single financial instrument can be outstanding at the same time, and for forward-starting partial-term fair value hedges, the issuance of the hedged item is assumed to occur on the date in which the first hedged cash flow begins to accrue.

Issue 3B: Amortization of Fair Value Hedge Basis Adjustments

The amendments clarify that an entity may, but is not required to, begin to amortize a fair value hedge basis adjustment before the fair value hedging relationship is discontinued. They also clarify that if an entity elects to amortize the basis adjustment during an outstanding partial-term hedge, that basis adjustment should be fully amortized by the hedged item's assumed maturity date in accordance with ASC 815-25-35-13B.

Issue 3C: Disclosure of Fair Value Hedge Basis Adjustments

The amendments clarify that available-for-sale debt securities should be disclosed at their amortized cost and that fair value hedge basis adjustments related to foreign exchange risk should be excluded from the disclosures required by paragraph 815-10-50-4EE.

Issue 3D: Consideration of the Hedged Contractually Specified Interest Rate under the Hypothetical Derivative Method

The amendment clarifies that an entity should consider the contractually specified interest rate being hedged when applying the hypothetical derivative method.

Issue 3E: Scope for Not-for-Profit Entities

The amendments clarify that a not-for-profit entity that does not separately report earnings may not elect the amortization approach for amounts excluded from the assessment of effectiveness for fair value hedging relationships. The amendments also update the cross-references in ASC 815-10-15-1 to further clarify the scope of ASC 815 for entities that do not report earnings separately.

Issue 3F: Hedge Accounting Provisions Applicable to Certain Private Companies and Not-for-Profit Entities

The amendments clarify that a private company that is not a financial institution as described in paragraph 942-320-50-1 should document the analysis supporting a last-of-layer hedge designation concurrently with hedge inception. The amendments also clarify that not-for-profit entities (except for not-for-profit entities that have issued, or are a conduit bond obligor for, securities that are traded, listed, or quoted on an exchange or an over-the-counter market) qualify for the same subsequent quarterly hedge effectiveness assessment timing relief for which certain private companies qualify in accordance with ASC 815-20-25-142.

Issue 3G: Application of a First-Payments-Received Cash Flow Hedging Technique to Overall Cash Flows on a Group of Variable Interest Payments

The amendments clarify that the application of the first-payments-received cash flow hedging technique to changes in overall cash flows on a group of variable interest payments continues to be permitted.

Issue 3H: Update 2017-12 Transition Guidance

The amendment to paragraph 815-20-65-3(e)(1) clarifies that transition adjustments to amend the measurement methodology of the hedged item in a fair value hedge of interest rate risk should be made as of the date of initial application of Update 2017-12. The date of initial application differs from the date of adoption if an entity adopts the amendments in Update 2017-12 in an interim period. The amendments also clarify the following:

1. An entity may rebalance its fair value hedging relationships of interest rate risk when it modifies the measurement methodology used for the hedged item from total contractual coupon cash flows to the benchmark rate component of the contractual coupon cash flows by any combination of increasing or decreasing the designated notional of the hedging instrument or increasing or decreasing the designated proportion of the hedged item. However, the entity may not add new hedged items or hedging instruments to the hedging relationship.
2. An entity may transition from a quantitative method of hedge effectiveness assessment to a method comparing the hedging relationship's critical terms in accordance with paragraphs 815-20-25-84 through 25-85 or paragraphs 815-20-25-129 through 25-129A without dedesignating the existing hedging relationship if the guidance in those paragraphs is met.
3. A debt security reclassified from held-to-maturity to available-for-sale in accordance with paragraph 815-20-65-3(e)(7):
   a. Does not call into question an entity's assertion to hold to maturity those debt securities that continue to be classified as held-to-maturity
   b. Is not required to be designated in a last-of-layer hedging relationship
   c. May be sold by an entity after reclassification.

ASU 2017-12 In August 2017, the FASB issued ASU 2017-12, *Derivatives and Hedging (Topic 815) Targeted Improvements to Accounting for Hedging Activities.*

Guidance The amendments in this Update better align an entity's risk management activities and financial reporting for hedging relationships through changes to

- the designation and measurement guidance for qualifying hedging relationships and
- the presentation of hedge results.

The guidance aligns risk management activities and financial reporting in the following areas:

- Risk Component Hedging
- Accounting for the Hedged Item in Fair Value Hedges of Interest Rate Risk
- Recognition and Presentation of the Effects of Hedging Instruments
- Amounts Excluded from the Assessment of Hedge Effectiveness

Risk Component Hedging To address limitations on how an entity can designate the hedged risk in certain cash flow and fail value hedging relationships, the Update permits hedge accounting for risk components in hedging relationships involving nonfinancial risk and interest rate risk as follows:

1. For a cash flow hedge of a forecasted purchase or sale of a nonfinancial asset, an entity could designate as the hedged risk the variability in cash flows attributable to changes in a contractually specified component stated in the contract. The amendments remove the requirement in current GAAP that only the overall variability in cash flows or variability related to foreign currency risk could be designated as the hedged risk in a cash flow hedge of a nonfinancial asset.
2. For a cash flow hedge of interest rate risk of a variable-rate financial instrument, an entity could designate as the hedged risk the variability in cash flows attributable to the con-

tractually specified interest rate. By eliminating the concept of benchmark interest rates for hedges of variable-rate instruments in current GAAP, the amendments remove the requirement to designate only the overall variability in cash flows as the hedged risk in a cash flow hedge of a variable-rate instrument indexed to a nonbenchmark interest rate.

3. For a fair value hedge of interest rate risk, the amendments add the Securities Industry and Financial Markets Association (SIFMA) Municipal Swap Rate as an eligible benchmark interest rate in the United States in addition to those already permitted under current GAAP (the U.S. Treasury Rate, the London Interbank Offered Rate [LIBOR] Swap Rate, and the Fed Funds Effective Swap Rate [or Overnight Index Swap Rate]). This allows an entity that issues or invests in fixed-rate tax-exempt financial instruments to designate as the hedged risk changes in fair value attributable to interest rate risk related to the SIFMA Municipal Swap Rate rather than overall changes in fair value.

Accounting for the Hedged Item in Fair Value Hedges of Interest Rate Risk To resolve issues with conflicts between an entity's risk management strategies and how an entity can account for hedges involving interest rate risk, the ASU changes the guidance for designating fair value hedges of interest rate risk and for measuring the change in fair value of the hedged item in fair value hedges of interest rate risk. Specifically, the amendments:

1. Permit an entity to measure the change in fair value of the hedged item on the basis of the benchmark rate component of the contractual coupon cash flows determined at hedge inception, rather than on the full contractual coupon cash flows as required by current GAAP.
2. Permit an entity to measure the hedged item in a partial-term fair value hedge of interest rate risk by assuming the hedged item has a term that reflects only the designated cash flows being hedged. Current GAAP does not allow this methodology when calculating the change in the fair value of the hedged item attributable to interest rate risk.
3. For prepayable financial instruments, permit an entity to consider only how changes in the benchmark interest rate affect a decision to settle a debt instrument before its scheduled maturity in calculating the change in the fair value of the hedged item attributable to interest rate risk.
4. For a closed portfolio of prepayable financial assets or one or more beneficial interests secured by a portfolio of prepayable financial instruments, permit an entity to designate an amount that is not expected to be affected by prepayments, defaults, and other events affecting the timing and amount of cash flows (the "last-of-layer" method). Under this designation, prepayment risk is not incorporated into the measurement of the hedged item.

Recognition and Presentation of the Effects of Hedging Instruments The Board determined that achieving the objective of better portraying the economic results of an entity's risk management activities in its financial statements can be accomplished only through a combination of changes to the designation and measurement guidance for qualifying hedging relationships and the method of presenting hedge results. To better portray in the financial statements the economic results of the entity's risk management activities, the ASU aligns the recognition and presentation of the effects of the hedging instrument and the hedged item in the financial statements to increase the understandability of the results of an entity's intended hedging strategies.

The ASU requires an entity to present the earnings effect of the hedging instrument in the same income statement line item in which the earnings effect of the hedged item is reported. This presentation enables users of financial statements to better understand the results and costs of an entity's hedging program. Also, relative to current GAAP, this approach simplifies the financial statement reporting for qualifying hedging relationships. Current GAAP provides special hedge accounting only for the portion of the hedge deemed to be "highly effective" and requires an entity to separately reflect the amount by which the hedging instrument does not offset the hedged item, which is referred to as the "ineffective" amount. However, the concept and reporting of hedge ineffectiveness were difficult for financial statement users to understand and, at times, for preparers to explain. Thus, the Board decided on an approach that no longer separately measures and reports hedge ineffectiveness. To accomplish that objective, the amendments in this Update require the following recognition and presentation guidance for qualifying hedges:

1. For fair value hedges, the entire change in the fair value of the hedging instrument included in the assessment of hedge effectiveness is presented in the same income statement line that is used to present the earnings effect of the hedged item. The timing of recognition of the change in fair value of a hedging instrument included in the assessment of hedge effectiveness is the same as under current GAAP, but the presentation of hedge results could change because current GAAP does not specify a required presentation of the change in fair value of the hedging instrument.
2. For cash flow and net investment hedges, the entire change in the fair value of the hedging instrument included in the assessment of hedge effectiveness is recorded in other comprehensive income (for cash flow hedges) or in the currency translation adjustment section of other comprehensive income (for net investment hedges). Those amounts are reclassified to earnings in the same income statement line item that is used to present the earnings effect of the hedged item when the hedged item affects earnings. The timing of recognition of the change in fair value of a hedging instrument could change relative to current GAAP because hedge ineffectiveness no longer is recognized currently in earnings. The presentation of hedge results also could change because current GAAP does not specify a required presentation of the change in fair value of the hedging instrument in the income statement.

Amounts Excluded from the Assessment of Hedge Effectiveness Current GAAP permits an entity to exclude option premiums and forward points from the assessment of hedge effectiveness. The amendments in this Update continue to allow an entity to exclude those components of a hedging instrument's change in fair value from the assessment of hedge effectiveness. Additionally, the amendments permit an entity to exclude the portion of the change in fair value of a currency swap that is attributable to a cross-currency basis spread from the assessment of hedge effectiveness.

For all types of hedges, if an entity excludes certain portions of a hedging instrument's change in fair value from the assessment of hedge effectiveness (excluded component), the amendments permit an entity to recognize in earnings the initial value of the excluded component using a systematic and rational method over the life of the hedging instrument. If an entity elects this method, any difference between the change in fair value of the excluded component and amounts recognized under the systematic and rational method is recognized in other comprehensive income, whereas for net investment hedges, the difference is recognized in the cumulative translation adjustment section of other comprehensive income. An entity also may elect to recognize all fair value changes in an excluded component currently in earnings, consistent with current GAAP.

For fair value and cash flow hedges, an entity should present amounts related to excluded components that are recognized in earnings in the same income statement line item that is used to present the earnings effect of the hedged item. For net investment hedges, the amendments do not specify a required presentation for excluded components.

Other Simplifications of Hedge Accounting Guidance The ASU also includes certain targeted improvements to ease the application of current guidance related to the assessment of hedge effectiveness. Current GAAP contains specific requirements for initial and ongoing quantitative hedge effectiveness testing and strict requirements for specialized effectiveness testing methods that allow an entity to forgo quantitative hedge effectiveness assessments for qualifying relationships (for example, "shortcut" method and "critical terms match" method). The amendments change effectiveness testing as follows:

1. In instances in which initial quantitative testing is required, an entity may perform subsequent assessments of hedge effectiveness qualitatively. An entity that makes this election is required to verify and document on a quarterly basis that the facts and circumstances related to the hedging relationship have not changed such that the entity can assert qualitatively that the hedging relationship was and continues to be highly effective. An entity may elect to perform qualitative assessments on a hedge-by-hedge basis.
2. For purposes of assessing whether the qualifying criteria for the critical terms match method are met for a group of forecasted transactions, an entity may assume that the hedging derivative matures at the same time as the forecasted transactions if both the derivative maturity and the forecasted transactions occur within the same 31-day period or fiscal month.
3. Entities will be able to perform the initial prospective quantitative assessment of hedge effectiveness at any time after hedge designation, but no later than the first quarterly effectiveness testing date, using data applicable as of the date of hedge inception.
4. To provide additional relief on the timing of hedge documentation, private companies that are not financial institutions and not-for-profit entities (except for not-for-profit entities that have issued, or are a conduit bond obligor for, securities that are traded, listed, or quoted on an exchange or an over-the-counter market) may select the method of assessing hedge effectiveness, and perform the initial quantitative effectiveness assessment and all quarterly hedge effectiveness assessments before the date on which the next interim (if applicable) or annual financial statements are available to be issued. This incremental relief does not affect the simplified hedge accounting approach for private companies.
5. If an entity that applies the shortcut method determines that use of that method was not or no longer is appropriate, the entity may apply a long-haul method for assessing hedge effectiveness as long as the hedge is highly effective and the entity documents at inception which long-haul methodology it will use.

Disclosures The ASU modifies disclosures required in current GAAP. Those modifications include a tabular disclosure related to the effect on the income statement of fair value and cash flow hedges and eliminate the requirement to disclose the ineffective portion of the change in fair value of hedging instruments. The amendments also require new tabular disclosures related to cumulative basis adjustments for fair value hedges.

Effective Dates The changes are effective as follows:

- For public business entities,
  - the amendments in this Update are effective for fiscal years beginning after December 15, 2018, and interim periods within those fiscal years.
- For all other entities, the effective date was extended by ASU 2019-10. The new dates are:
  - the amendments are effective for fiscal years beginning after December 15, 2020, and interim periods within fiscal years beginning after December 15, 2021.

Early application is permitted in any interim period after issuance of the Update.

All transition requirements and elections should be applied to hedging relationships existing (that is, hedging relationships in which the hedging instrument has not expired, been sold, terminated, or exercised or the entity has not removed the designation of the hedging relationship) on the date of adoption. The effect of adoption should be reflected as of the beginning of the fiscal year of adoption (that is, the initial application date).

Transition For cash flow and net investment hedges existing at the date of adoption, an entity should apply a cumulative-effect adjustment related to eliminating the separate measurement of ineffectiveness to accumulated other comprehensive income with a corresponding adjustment to the opening balance of retained earnings as of the beginning of the fiscal year that an entity adopts the amendments in the ASU. The amended presentation and disclosure guidance is required only prospectively.

Transition If an entity elects to apply the proposed guidance in items 1–3 above, it would:

- Apply the guidance prospectively.
- Disclose the nature of and reason for electing the guidance in each interim financial statement of the fiscal year of change and the annual financial statement of the period of the change in accordance with Topic 250, Accounting Changes and Error Corrections.
- Cease applying the guidance as of January 1, 2023.

Subtopics

ASC 815, *Derivatives*, contains eight subtopics:

- ASC 815-10, *Overall*, which contains two subsections:
  - General
  - Certain Contracts on Debt and Equity Securities
- ASC 815-15, *Embedded Derivatives*
- ASC 815-20, *Hedging—General*
- ASC 815-25, *Fair Value Hedges*
- ASC 815-30, *Cash Flow Hedges*
- ASC 815-35, *Net Investment Hedges*
- ASC 815-40, *Contracts in Entity's Own Equity*
- ASC 815-45, *Weather Derivatives*

ASC 815-40 and ASC 815-45 address guidance on accounting for contracts that have characteristics of derivative instruments but that are not accounted for as derivative instruments under ASC 815. The other subtopics provide guidance on accounting for derivative instruments and hedging activities. ASC 815-10 focuses on whether a contract meets the definition of a derivative instrument. (ASC 815-10-05-2)

Scope—ASC 815-10

ASC 815 applies to all entities and to all derivative instruments, but contains extensive scope exceptions. Some of those exceptions relate to items that fall under other guidance; other exceptions are aimed at simplifying the guidance. If an entity, such as a not-for-profit or a defined benefit pension plan, does not report earnings as a separate option, the application of this subtopic to those entities can be found in ASC 815-10-35-3, 815-20-15-1, 815-25-35-19, and 815-30-15-3. (ASC 815-10-15-1)

Scope Exceptions The following instruments are *not* included in the ASC 815 guidance, provided they meet the specific exception criterion in ASC 815-10-15-14 through 15-42.

- Regular-way security trades
- Normal purchases and normal sales
- Certain insurance contracts and market risk benefits
- Certain financial guarantee contracts
- Certain contracts that are not traded on an exchange
- Derivative instruments that impede sales accounting
- Policyholders' investments in life insurance accounted for under ASC 325-30. This exclusion does not affect the accounting by the issuer of the life insurance contract. (ASC 815-10-15-67)
- Certain investment contracts accounted for under either ASC 960-325-35-1 or 35-3. This exclusion applies only to the party accounting for the contract under ASC 960. (ASC 815-10-15-68)
- Certain loan commitments
- Certain interest-only strips and principal-only strips
- Certain contracts involving an entity's own equity
- Leases
- Residual value guarantees subject to the requirements on ASC 840 or ASC 842 when implemented. (ASC 815-10-15-80)
- Registration payment arrangements within the scope of ASC 825-20.
- Certain fixed-odds wagering contracts for entities operating as a casino and for the casino operations of other entities, these contracts are in the scope of ASC 606 (815-10-15-82A) (ASC 815-10-15-13)

The following information expands on the list above and references the scope exceptions:

Regular-way security trades Delivery of a security readily convertible to cash within the time period generally established by marketplace regulations or conventions where the trade takes place rather than by the usual procedure of an individual enterprise. Contracts for the delivery of securities that are not readily convertible to cash are not subject to ASC 815's provisions because net settlement would not be possible.

For example, most trades of equity securities in the United States require settlement in three business days. If an individual contract requires settlement in more than three business days (even if this is normal for a particular entity), this exception would not apply, unless the reporting entity is required, or has a continuing policy, to account for such transactions on a trade-date basis. (ASC 815-10-15-15) This exception also applies to when-issued and to-be-announced securities (except for those contracts accounted for on a trade-date basis), if there is no other way to purchase or sell them and if the trade will settle within the shortest period permitted.

Based on the foregoing, the following may be excluded:

- forward purchases or sales of to-be-announced securities, and
- when-issued, as-issued, or if-issued securities. (ASC 815- 10-15-17)

Note: Counterparties may reach different conclusions as to whether the contracts are derivative instruments. Asymmetrical results are acceptable (i.e., the exception may apply to one party but not the other). (ASC 815-10-15-24)

Normal purchases and normal sales Contracts for purchase or sale of something, other than derivative instruments or financial instruments, that will be delivered in quantities expected to be used or sold over a reasonable time period in the normal course of business. (ASC 815-10-15-22) Terms must be consistent with normal transactions and quantities must be reasonable in relation to needs. (ASC 815-10-15-27) To make that judgment, all relevant factors are to be considered. (ASC 815-10-15-28) An example would include contracts similar to binding purchase orders. However, take or pay contracts that require little or no initial net investment, and that have products readily convertible to cash that do not qualify as normal purchases, would be derivative instruments, and not exceptions. (See 815-20-25-7)

The purpose of the "normal purchases and normal sales" definition is to exclude certain routine types of transactions from the required accounting as derivative instruments. This exemption includes certain contracts that contain net settlement or market mechanisms if it is judged probable, at the inception and throughout the duration of such contracts, that they will not in fact settle net and will instead result in physical delivery. Notwithstanding this more broadly based exemption from the accounting requirements of ASC 815, certain contracts will not qualify for exemption in any case. These include:

- Contracts the price of which are based on an underlying that is not clearly and closely related to the assets being sold or purchased (ASC 815-10-15-30), and
- Contracts requiring cash settlement for any gains or losses or otherwise settled net on a periodic basis. (ASC 815-10-15-35)

The use of locational marginal pricing for certain contracts for the purchase or sale of electricity on a forward basis utilizing a nodal energy market does not, by itself, cause the contract to fail the physical delivery criterion of the normal purchases and normal sales elective scope exception in ASC 815. (ASC 815-10-15-36A) Documentary evidence is required to support the use of the expanded exemption from the ASC 815 provisions. (ASC 815-10-15-37)

On the other hand, a contract that meets the normal purchases and sales exceptions may qualify as a fair value or cash flow hedge if the requirements of ASC 815-20 are met. (ASC 815- 20-25-7)

Power purchase or sales agreements (whether forwards, options, or some combination thereof) pertaining to delivery of electricity qualify for this exception only if a series of conditions are met. The contracts cannot permit net settlement, but must require physical delivery, and must be capacity contracts, as differentiated from ordinary option contracts. For the seller, the quantities deliverable under the contracts must be quantities normally to be sold; for the buyer, quantities must be those to be used or sold in the normal course of business, and the buyer must be an entity which is contractually obligated to maintain sufficient capacity to meet the needs of its customers. Certain additional requirements, and further exceptions, are set forth by ASC 815-10-15-45.

Certain insurance contracts Contracts where the holder is only compensated when an insurable event (other than price or rate change) takes place and:

- The value of the holder's asset or liability is adversely changed, or
- The holder incurs a liability.

For example, contracts generally not considered to be derivative instruments include traditional life insurance and traditional property and casualty insurance policies. (ASC 815-10-15- 53)

Most traditional insurance contracts will not be derivative instruments. Some, however, can include embedded derivatives that must be accounted for separately. For example, embedded derivatives may be found in indexed annuity contracts, variable life and annuity contracts, and property and casualty contracts involving changes in currency rates. (ASC 815-10-15-54)

Certain financial guarantee contracts Contracts that call for payments only to reimburse for a loss from debtor failure to pay when due. However, a credit-indexed contract requiring payment for changes in credit ratings (an underlying) would not be an exception. (ASC 815-10- 15-58)

Certain contracts that are not exchange traded Contracts with underlyings based on one of the following:

- Climatic, geological, or other physical variable: for example, inches of rain or heating-degree days;
- Value or price involving a nonfinancial asset not readily converted to cash;
- Fair value of a nonfinancial liability that does not require delivery of an asset that is readily converted to cash; or
- Specified volumes of revenue of one of the parties: examples are royalty agreements or contingent rentals based on related sales.
  (ASC 815-10-15-59)

In the case of a mixture of underlyings, some of which are exceptions, the predominant characteristic of the combined variable of the contract is the determinant. If there is a high correlation with the behavior of the excepted variables above, it is an exception, and if there is a high correlation with the nonexcepted variables, it is a derivative instrument. (ASC 815-10-15-60)

Derivatives that serve as impediments to sales accounting A derivative instrument that affects the accounting for the transfer of an asset. For example, a call option on transferred assets under ASC 860 would prevent accounting for the transfer as a sale. This exemption is necessary, because recognizing the call as a derivative instrument would result in double counting. (ASC 815-10-15-63)

In addition to the preceding, the following are not considered derivative instruments:

1. Certain contracts involving an entity's own equity issued or held that are both:
   - Indexed to the enterprise's own stock, and
   - Classified in shareholders' equity.

   Derivative instruments are assets or liabilities. Items properly accounted for in shareholders' equity are thus excluded from the definition of derivatives. Contracts that can or must be settled through issuance of an equity instrument but that are indexed in part or in full to something other than the enterprise's own stock are considered derivative instruments if they qualify and they are to be classified as assets or liabilities.
2. Contracts issued in connection with stock-based compensation arrangements as addressed in ASC 718.
3. Any of the following
   a. A contract between an acquirer and a seller to enter into a business combination
   b. A contract to enter into an acquisition by a not-for-profit entity
   c. A contract between one or more NFPs to enter into a merger of not-for-profit entities
4. Forward contracts that require settlement by the reporting entity's delivery of cash in exchange for a fixed number of its equity shares discounted for under ASC 480-10-30-3 through 30-5, 480-10-35-3 and 480-10-45-3.
   (ASC 815-10-15-74)

Note that for purposes of evaluating whether a financial instrument meets this exception, a down round feature is excluded from the consideration of whether the instrument is indexed to the entity's own stock. (ASC 815-10-15-75A)

The exceptions for the above three issued contracts are not applicable to the counterparties. (ASC 815-10-15-75)

Scope—ASC 815-15

The guidance in its entirety in 815-15 applies to all entities, but only to contracts that do not meet the definition of a derivative instrument. (ASC 815-15-15-1 and 15-2)

Scope Exceptions The guidance in ASC 815-15, *Embedded Derivatives*, does not apply to:

- Normal purchases and normal sales contracts
- Unsettled foreign currency transactions
- Plain-vanilla servicing rights
- Features involving certain aspects of credit risk
- Features involving certain currencies

(ASC 815-15-15-3)

Under ASC 815-15, unsettled foreign currency transactions are not considered to certain embedded foreign currency derivatives if the transactions:

- Are monetary items
- Have their principal payments, interest payments, or both denominated in a foreign currency, and
- Are subject to the requirement in ASC 830-20 to recognize any foreign currency gain or loss in earnings.

(ASC 815-15-15-5)

The proscription in ASC 815-15-15-5 also applies to available for sale or trading debt securities that have cash flows denominated in a foreign currency. (ASC 815-15-15-6)

Scope—ASC 815-20

The guidance in ASC 815-20-15-1 applies to all entities except for:

- Entities that do not report entities separately cannot use cash flow hedge accounting under ASC 815-30 on cash flow hedges.
- Entities that do not report earnings separately cannot elect the amortization approach for amounts excluded from the assessment of effectiveness under fair value hedge accounting under the guidance in ASC 815-20-25-83A and 35-1a.

Scope—ASC 815-25

ASC 815-25 follows the scope and scope exceptions listed above.

Scope—ASC 815-30

ASC 815-30 follows the same scope and scope exceptions as those in ASC 815-20 above with the following exceptions:

- ASC 815-30 does not apply to entities that do not report earnings.
- This Topic does not offer guidance on how a not-for-profit should determine the components of an operating measure.

(ASC 815-30-15-1 through 15-3)

Scope—ASC 815-35

ASC 815-35 follows the same scope and scope exceptions in ASC 815-20 above.

Scope—ASC 815-40

ASC 815-40 applies to all entities and to freestanding contracts that are indexed to and potentially settled in an entity's own stock. (ASC 815-40-15-1 and 15-2)

Scope Exceptions ASC 815-40 does not apply to:

a. Either the derivative instrument component or the financial instrument if the derivative instrument component is embedded in and not detachable from the financial instrument
b. Contracts that are issued to compensate grantees in a share-based payment arrangement
c. A written put option and a purchased call option embedded in the shares of a noncontrolling interest of a consolidated subsidiary if the arrangement is accounted for as a financing under the guidance beginning in paragraph 480-10-55-53
d. Financial instruments that are within the scope of ASC 480.
(ASC 815-40-15-3)

ASC 815-40-15-13a above does not negate the applicability of this ASC 815-40 in analyzing the embedded feature under paragraphs 815-15-25-1(c) and 815-15-25-14 as though it were a freestanding instrument. (ASC 815-40-15-4)

Evaluating Whether an Instrument Is Considered Indexed to an Entity's Own Stock The guidance in ASC 815-40-15-5 through 15-8 applies to any freestanding financial instrument or embedded feature[1] that has all the characteristics of a derivative instrument. That guidance applies for the purpose of determining whether that instrument or embedded feature qualifies for the first part of the scope exception in ASC 815-10-15-74(a). That guidance does not address the second part of the scope exception in ASC 815-10-15-74(a). The guidance also applies to any freestanding financial instrument that is potentially settled in an entity's own stock, regardless of whether the instrument has all the characteristics of a derivative instrument for purposes of determining whether the instrument is within the scope of ASC 815-40. (ASC 815-40-15-5)

The guidance in ASC 815-40-15-5A through 15-8 does not apply to share-based payment awards within the scope of ASC 718 for purposes of determining whether instruments are classified as liability awards or equity awards. Equity-linked financial instruments issued to investors for purposes of establishing a market-based measure of the grant-date fair value of employee stock options are not within the scope of ASC 718. The guidance in ASC 815-40-15-5A through 15-8 applies to such market-based share-based payment stock option valuation instruments for purposes of making the determinations regarding the scope exception in ASC 815-10-15-74a. (ASC 815-40-15-5A)

The guidance in paragraphs 815-40-15-5 through 15-8 shall be applied to the appropriate unit of accounting, as determined under other applicable U.S. generally accepted accounting principles.

---

[1] In this section, unless otherwise indicated, the assumption is that "financial instrument" means "financial instrument or embedded feature."

Another factor in determining whether an instrument is considered indexed to its own stock is if the subsidiary is a substantive entity:

- If it is, freestanding financial instruments (and embedded features) for which the payoff to the counterparty is based, in whole or in part, on the stock of a consolidated subsidiary considered indexed to the entity's own stock in the consolidated financial statements of the parent
- If it is not, the instrument or embedded feature should not be considered indexed to the entity's own stock.

If the subsidiary is considered to be a substantive entity, the guidance beginning in paragraph 815-40-15-5 should be applied to determine whether the freestanding financial instrument (or an embedded feature) is indexed to the entity's own stock and should be considered in conjunction with other applicable GAAP (for example, this Subtopic) in determining the classification of the freestanding financial instrument in the financial statements of the entity. The guidance in this paragraph applies to those instruments (and embedded features) in the consolidated financial statements of the parent, whether the instrument was entered into by the parent or the subsidiary. The guidance in this paragraph does not affect the accounting for instruments (or embedded features) that would not otherwise qualify for the scope exception in paragraph 815-10-15-74(a), that is, contracts issued or held by that reporting entity that are both:

- Indexed to its own stock and
- Classified in stockholders' equity in its statement of financial position (ASC 815-40-15-5C)

When classifying a financial instrument with a down round feature, the feature is excluded from the consideration of whether the instrument is indexed to the entity's own stock for the purposes of applying paragraphs 815-40-15-7C through 15-7I (Step 2 below).

The guidance in this paragraph applies to both the issuer and the holder of the instrument. Outstanding instruments within the scope of the guidance in paragraphs 815-40-15-5 through 15-8 should always be considered issued for accounting purposes, except lock-up options should not be considered issued for accounting purposes unless and until the options become exercisable. (ASC 815-40-15D)

An entity should evaluate whether an equity-linked financial instrument (or embedded feature), as discussed in paragraphs 815-40-15-5 through 15-8, is considered indexed to its own stock within the meaning of this Subtopic and paragraph 815-10-15-74(a) using the following two-step approach: (ASC 815-40-15-7)

1. Evaluate contingent exercise provisions.
2. Evaluate settlement provisions.

Evaluation of Contingent Exercise Provisions (Step 1) An exercise contingency should not preclude an instrument (or embedded feature) from being considered indexed to an entity's own stock provided that it is not based on either:

- An observable market, other than the market for the issuer's stock (if applicable) or
- An observable index, other than an index calculated or measured solely by reference to the issuer's own operations (for example, sales revenue of the issuer; earnings before interest, taxes, depreciation, and amortization of the issuer; net income of the issuer; or total equity of the issuer).

If this Step 1 evaluation does not preclude an instrument from being considered indexed to the entity's own stock, the entity should proceed to Step 2 in ASC 815-40-15-7C. (ASC 815-40-15-7A)

If an instrument's strike price or the number of shares used to calculate the settlement amount would be adjusted upon the occurrence of an exercise contingency, the exercise contingency shall be evaluated under Step 1 and the potential adjustment to the instrument's settlement amount should be evaluated under Step 2 detailed below. (ASC 815-40-15-7B)

Evaluation of Settlement Provisions (Step 2) An instrument (or embedded feature) shall be considered indexed to an entity's own stock if its settlement amount will equal the difference between:

- The fair value of a fixed number of the entity's equity shares
- A fixed monetary amount or a fixed amount of a debt instrument issued by the entity (ASC 815-40-15-7C)

An instrument's strike price or the number of shares used to calculate the settlement amount are not considered fixed if its terms provide for any potential adjustment, regardless of the probability of such adjustment or whether such adjustments are in the entity's control. If the instrument's strike price or the number of shares used to calculate the settlement amount are not fixed, the instrument shall still be considered indexed to an entity's own stock if the only variables that could affect the settlement amount would be inputs to the fair value of a fixed-for-fixed forward or option on equity shares.

The settlement amount of a fixed-for-fixed forward or option on equity shares is equal to the difference between the price of a fixed number of equity shares and a fixed strike price. The fair value inputs of a fixed-for-fixed forward or option on equity shares may include the entity's stock price and additional variables, including all of the following:

- Strike price of the instrument
- Term of the instrument
- Expected dividends or other dilutive activities
- Stock borrow cost
- Interest rates
- Stock price volatility
- The entity's credit spread
- The ability to maintain a standard hedge position in the underlying shares.

Determinations and adjustments related to the settlement amount, including the determination of the ability to maintain a standard hedge position, should be commercially reasonable. (ASC 815-40-15-7E)

An instrument should not be considered indexed to the entity's own stock if its settlement amount is affected by variables that are extraneous to the pricing of a fixed-for-fixed option or forward contract on equity shares. An instrument is not considered indexed to the entity's own stock if either:

- The instrument's settlement calculation incorporates variables other than those used to determine the fair value of a fixed-for-fixed forward or option on equity shares.
- The instrument contains a feature (such as a leverage factor) that increases exposure to the additional variables listed in the preceding paragraph in a manner that is inconsistent with a fixed-for-fixed forward or option on equity shares. (ASC 815-40-15-7F)

Standard pricing models for equity-linked financial instruments contain certain implicit assumptions. One such assumption is that the stock price exposure inherent in those instruments can be hedged by entering into an offsetting position in the underlying equity shares. For purposes of applying Step 2, fair value inputs include adjustments to neutralize the effects of events that can cause stock price fluctuations, such as a merger agreement. (ASC 815-40-15-7G)

For purposes of applying Step 2, modifications that benefit the counterparty and give an entity the ability to unilaterally modify the terms of the instrument at any time, do not affect the determination of whether an instrument is considered indexed to an entity's own stock. (ASC 815-40-15-7H)

Strike Price Denominated in a Foreign Currency The issuer of an equity-linked financial instrument incurs an exposure to changes in currency exchange rates if the instrument's strike price is denominated in a currency other than the functional currency of the issuer. An equity-linked financial instrument (or embedded feature) shall not be considered indexed to the entity's own stock if the strike price is denominated in a currency other than the issuer's functional currency (including a conversion option embedded in a convertible debt instrument that is denominated in a currency other than the issuer's functional currency). The determination of whether an equity-linked financial instrument is indexed to an entity's own stock is not affected by the currency (or currencies) in which the underlying shares trade. (ASC 815-40-15-7I)

Instruments Classified as Liabilities on Assets Instruments that do not meet the criteria to be considered indexed to an entity's own stock should be classified as a liability or an asset. (ASC 815-40-15-8A)

Distinguishing Liabilities from Equity ASC 480 does not apply to a feature embedded in a financial instrument that is not a derivative instrument in its entirety. Therefore, entities should apply this Subtopic when evaluating those embedded features under ASC 815-15. (ASC 815-40-15-17)

Overview

The financial engineering efforts common in recent decades resulted in the creation of a wide range of derivatives, from easily understood interest rate swaps (exchanging variable- or floating- rate debt for fixed-rate debt) and interest rate caps (limiting exposure to rising interest rates) to such complicated "exotics" as structured notes, inverse floaters, and interest-only strips. At one time, most of these were not given formal statement of financial position recognition, resulting in great accounting risk, that is, risk of loss in excess of amounts reported in the financial statements. The Codification includes extensive guidance on accounting for and reporting on derivatives and hedges.

ASC 815 requires that entities recognize derivative instruments, including certain derivatives embedded in other contracts, as assets or liabilities on the statement of financial position, measured at fair value. Entities may designate a derivative as:

- A fair value hedge
- A cash flow hedge
- A foreign currency exposure of:
  - An unrecognized firm commitment—a foreign currency fair value hedge
  - Available-for-sale debt security—a foreign currency fair value hedge
  - A forecasted transaction—a foreign currency cash flow hedge
  - A net investment in foreign operations

To be designated as a hedge, the instrument must meet specific requirements. (ASC 815- 10-05-4)

In terms of gain or loss recognition on a hedged instrument, the entity generally recognizes:

- Changes in the fair value of the hedged asset or liability that are attributable to the hedged risk and
- Earnings of the hedged forecasted transaction.
  (ASC 815-10-05-6)

Derivatives literature is exceedingly complex, which is largely a consequence of the rules establishing special accounting for hedging. Limited accounting relief for certain types of hedging activities may be provided by applying the simplified hedge accounting approach in ASC 825-20-25-133 through 25-138, *Financial Instruments: Fair Value Option*, and the "private company alternative" discussed later in this chapter.

Basic Principles of ASC 815 ASC 815 lists four principles or cornerstones that underlie its guidance:

1. Derivative instruments represent rights or obligations that meet the definitions of assets or liabilities and should be reported in financial statements as assets or liabilities.
2. Fair value is the most relevant measure for financial instruments and the only relevant measure for derivative instruments. Derivative instruments should be measured at fair value, and adjustments to the carrying amount of hedged items should reflect changes in their fair value (that is, gains or losses) that are attributable to the risk being hedged and that arise while the hedge is in effect.
3. Only items that are assets or liabilities should be reported as such in financial statements.
4. Special accounting for items designated as being hedged should be provided only for qualifying items. One aspect of qualification should be an assessment of the expectation of effective offsetting changes in fair values or cash flows during the term of the hedge for the risk being hedged. Gains and losses from hedges should be reported differently based on the type of hedge.
   (ASC 815-10-10-1)

DEFINITIONS OF TERMS

Source: ASC 815 and FASB Codification Master Glossary. Also see Appendix A, *Definitions of Terms*, for additional terms relevant to this topic: Acquiree, Acquirer, Acquisition by a Not-for-Profit Entity, Business, Business Combination, Call Option, Combination, Comprehensive Income, Credit Derivative, Credit Risk, Derivative Instruments, Down Round Feature Equity Restructuring, Fair Value, Financial Instrument, Financial Liability, Financial Statements Are Available to Be Issued, Firm Commitment, Interest Rate Risk, Loan Commitments, Market Participants, Market Risk Benefit, Merger of Not-for-Profit Entities, Net Income, Noncontrolling Interest, Not-for-Profit Entity, Orderly Transaction, Other Comprehensive Income, Probable (Def. 2), Public Business Entity, Put Option, Registration Payment Arrangements, Securities Industry and Financial Markets Association (SIFMA) Municipal Swap Rate, Spot Rate, Standard Antidilution Provision, Time Value, Trading, Transaction, Unconditional Purchase Obligation, Underlying, Underlying Asset, Variable Lease Payments.

Asymmetrical Default Provision. A nonperformance penalty provision that requires the defaulting party to compensate the nondefaulting party for any loss incurred but does not allow the defaulting party to receive the effect of favorable price changes.

Benchmark Interest Rate. A widely recognized and quoted rate in an active financial market that is broadly indicative of the overall level of interest rates attributable to high-credit-quality obligors in that market. It is a rate that is widely used in a given financial market as an underlying basis for determining the interest rates of individual financial instruments and commonly referenced in interest-rate-related transactions.

In theory, the benchmark interest rate should be a risk-free rate (that is, has no risk of default). In some markets, government borrowing rates may serve as a benchmark. In other markets, the benchmark interest rate may be an interbank offered rate.

Bid-Ask Spread. A bid-ask spread is the difference between the highest price a buyer will pay to acquire an instrument and the lowest price at which any investor will sell an instrument.

Capacity Contract. An agreement by an owner of capacity to sell the right to that capacity to another party so that it can satisfy its obligations. For example, in the electric industry, capacity (sometimes referred to as installed capacity) is the capability to deliver electric power to the electric transmission system of an operating control area.

Cash Flow Hedge. A hedge of the exposure to variability in the cash flows of a recognized asset or liability, or of a forecasted transaction, that is attributable to a particular risk.

Contractually Specified Component. An index or price explicitly referenced in an agreement to purchase or sell a nonfinancial asset other than an index or price calculated or measured solely by reference to an entity's own operations.

Control Area. A control area requires entities that serve load within the control area to demonstrate ownership or contractual rights to capacity sufficient to serve that load at time of peak demand and to provide a reserve margin to protect the integrity of the system against potential generating unit outages in the control area. A control area is a portion of the electric grid that schedules, dispatches, and controls generating resources to serve area load (ultimate users of electricity) and coordinates scheduling of the flow of electric power over the transmission system to neighboring control areas.

Derivative Instruments. In ASC 815-10-15-83, derivative instruments are defined by their three distinguishing characteristics, which are:

1. One or more underlyings and one or more notional amounts (or payment provisions or both);
2. No initial net investment or a smaller net investment than required for contracts expected to have a similar response to market changes; and
3. Terms that require or permit
   a. Net settlement
   b. Net settlement by means outside the contract
   c. Delivery of an asset that results in a position substantially the same as net settlement

ASC 815 defines derivative instruments by reference to specific characteristics, rather than in terms of classes or categories of financial instruments. These distinctive features are believed to distinguish the fundamental nature of derivative instruments such as options and futures.

Embedded Credit Derivative. An embedded derivative that is also a credit derivative.

Embedded Derivative. Implicit or explicit terms that affect some or all of the cash flows or the value of other exchanges required by a contract in a manner similar to a derivative instrument.

Exercise Contingency. A provision that entitles the entity (or the counterparty) to exercise an equity-linked financial instrument (or embedded feature) based on changes in an underlying, including the occurrence (or nonoccurrence) of a specified event. Provisions that accelerate the timing of the entity's (or the counterparty's) ability to exercise an instrument and provisions that extend the length of time that an instrument is exercisable are examples of exercise contingencies.

Expected Cash Flow. The probability-weighted average (that is, mean of the distribution) of possible future cash flows.

Face Amount. See Notional Amount.

Fair Value Hedge. A hedge of the exposure to changes in the fair value of a recognized asset or liability, or of an unrecognized firm commitment, that are attributable to a particular risk.

Fed Funds Effective Swap Rate. The fixed rate on a U.S. dollar, constant-notional interest rate swap that has its variable-rate leg referenced to the Fed Funds effective rate with no additional spread over the Fed Funds effective rate on that variable-rate leg. That fixed rate is the derived rate that would result in the swap having a zero fair value at inception because the present value of fixed cash flows, based on that rate, equates to the present value of the variable cash flows.

Forecasted Transaction. A transaction that is expected to occur for which there is no firm commitment. Because no transaction or event has yet occurred and the transaction or event when it occurs will be at the prevailing market price, a forecasted transaction does not give an entity any present rights to future benefits or a present obligation for future sacrifices.

Foreign Exchange Risk. The risk of changes in a hedged item's fair value of functional-currency-equivalent cash flows attributable to changes in the related foreign currency exchange rates.

Hybrid Instrument. A contract that embodies both an embedded derivative and a host contract.

Interest Rate Risk. The risk of changes in a hedged item's fair value or cash flows attributable to changes in the designated benchmark interest rate.

Internal Derivative. A foreign currency derivative instrument that has been entered into with another member of a consolidated group (such as a treasury center).

Intrinsic Value. The amount by which the fair value of the underlying stock exceeds the exercise price of an option. For example, an option with an exercise price of $20 on a stock whose current market price is $25 has an intrinsic value of $5. (A nonvested share may be described as an option on that share with an exercise price of zero. Thus, the fair value of a share is the same as the intrinsic value of such an option on that share.)

London Interbank Offered Rate (LIBOR) Swap Rate. The fixed rate on a single-currency, constant-notional interest rate swap that has its variable-rate leg referenced to the London Interbank Offered Rate (LIBOR) with no additional spread over LIBOR on that variable-rate leg. That fixed rate is the derived rate that would result in the swap having a zero fair value at inception because the present value of fixed cash flows, based on that rate, equate to the present value of the variable cash flows.

Make Whole Provision. A contractual option that gives a debtor (that is, an issuer) the right to pay off debt before maturity at a significant premium over the fair value of the debt at the date of settlement.

Mandatorily Redeemable Financial Instrument. Any of various financial instruments issued in the form of shares that embody an unconditional obligation requiring the issuer to redeem the instrument by transferring its assets at a specified or determinable date (or dates) or upon an event that is certain to occur.

Market Value Annuity. An annuity that provides for a return of principal plus a fixed rate of return (that is, book value) if held to maturity or, alternatively, a market-adjusted annuity purchases.

Net Cash Settlement. The party with a loss delivers to the party with a gain a cash payment equal to the gain, and no shares are exchanged.

Net Share Settlements. The party with a loss delivers to the party with a gain shares with a current fair value equal to the gain. The portion of equity (net assets) in a subsidiary not attributable, directly or indirectly, to a parent. A noncontrolling interest is sometimes called a minority interest.

New Basis Event. See Remeasurement.

Nonperformance Risk. The risk that an entity will not fulfill an obligation. Nonperformance risk includes, but may not be limited to, the reporting entity's own credit risk.

Notional Amount. A number of currency units, shares, bushels, pounds, or other units specified in a derivative instrument. Sometimes other names are used. For example, the notional amount is called a face amount in some contracts.

Payment Provision. A payment provision specifies a fixed or determinable settlement to be made if the underlying behaves in a specified manner.

Payout Phase. The period during which the contract holder is receiving periodic payments from an annuity, also referred to as the annuitization phase.

Periodic Ratchet Design. The period during which the contract holder is receiving periodic payments from an annuity, also referred to as the annuitization phase.

Physical Settlement. The party designated in the contract as the buyer delivers the full stated amount of cash to the seller, and the seller delivers the full stated number of shares to the buyer.

Prepayable. Able to be settled by either party before its scheduled maturity.

Private Company. An entity other than a public business entity, a not-for-profit entity, or an employee benefit plan within the scope of Topics 960 through 965 on plan accounting.

Readily Convertible to Cash. Assets that are readily convertible to cash have both of the following:

1. Interchangeable (fungible) units
2. Quoted prices available in an active market that can rapidly absorb the quantity held by the entity without significantly affecting the price

(Based on paragraph 83(a) of FASB Concepts Statement No. 5, Recognition and Measurement in Financial Statements of Business Enterprises.)

Recorded Investment. The amount of the investment in a loan, which is not net of a valuation allowance, but which does reflect any direct write-down of the investment.

Regular-Way Security Trades. Regular-way security trades are contracts that provide for delivery of a security within the period of time (after the trade date) generally established by regulations or conventions in the marketplace or exchange in which the transaction is being executed.

Remeasurement Event. A remeasurement (new basis) event is an event identified in other authoritative accounting literature, other than the measurement of an impairment under Topic 321 or credit loss under Topic 326, that requires a financial instrument to be remeasured to its fair value at the time of the event but does not require that financial instrument to be reported at fair value continually with the change in fair value recognized in earnings. Examples of remeasurement events are business combinations and significant modifications of debt as discussed in paragraph 470-50-40-6.

Secured Overnight Financing Rate (SOFR) Overnight Index Swap Rate. The fixed rate on a U.S. dollar, constant-notional interest rate swap that has its variable-rate leg referenced to the Secured Overnight Financing Rate (SOFR) (an overnight rate) with no additional spread over SOFR on that variable rate leg. That fund rate is the derived rate that would result in the swap having a zero fair value at inception because the present value of fixed cash flows, based on this rate, equates to the present value of the variable cash flows.

Take-or-Pay Contract. Under a take-or-pay contract, an entity agrees to pay a specified price for a specified quantity of a product whether or not it takes delivery.

Trading. An activity involving securities sold in the near term and held for only a short period of time. The term trading contemplates a holding period generally measured in hours and days rather than months or years. See ASC 948-310-40-1 for clarification of the term trading for a mortgage banking entity.

Trading Purposes. The determination of what constitutes trading purposes is based on the intent of the issuer or holder and shall be consistent with the definition of trading in ASC 320-10- 25-1(A).

Zero-Coupon Method. A swap valuation method that involves computing and summing the present value of each future net settlement that would be required by the contract terms if future spot interest rates match the forward rates implied by the current yield curve. The discount rates used are the spot interest rates implied by the current yield curve for hypothetical zero coupon bonds due on the date of each future net settlement on the swap.

CONCEPTS, RULES, AND EXAMPLES

ASC 815-10, *Derivatives and Hedging,* Overall Financial Instruments[2]

Derivative Financial Instruments Derivative financial instruments are financial instruments whose fair value correlates to a specified benchmark, such as stock prices, interest rates, mortgage rates, currency rates, commodity prices, or some other agreed-upon reference. These are called "underlyings." That is, they derive their value from the underlyings. The two basic forms of derivatives are:

1. Option contracts and
2. Forward contracts.

They can be either publicly or privately traded. Forward contracts have symmetrical gain and loss characteristics—that is, they provide exposure to both losses and gains from market movements, although generally there is no initial premium to be paid. Forward contracts are usually settled on or near the delivery date by paying or receiving cash, rather than by physical delivery. On the other hand, option contracts have asymmetrical loss functions: They provide little or no exposure to losses (beyond the premium paid) from unfavorable market movements, but can provide large benefits from favorable market movements. Both forwards and options have legitimate roles to play in hedging programs, if properly understood and carefully managed.

[2] Some of the items subject to the guidance in ASC 815-10 are financial instruments. For additional guidance on financial instruments, including the fair value option, see the chapter on ASC 825.

Typical derivative financial instruments *include:*

1. Option contracts
2. Interest rate caps
3. Fixed-rate loan commitments
4. Note issuance facilities
5. Letters of credit
6. Forward contracts
7. Forward interest rate agreements
8. Interest rate collars
9. Futures
10. Swaps
11. Instruments with similar characteristics.

Examples of Derivatives A financial instrument may give an entity the *contractual right* or obligation to exchange other financial instruments on *potentially* favorable or unfavorable terms. An example of this type of financial instrument would be a call option to purchase a specific U.S. Treasury note for $100,000 in six months. The option *holder* has a contractual right, but not obligation, to exchange the financial instrument on potentially favorable terms. Six months later, if the fair value of the note exceeds $100,000, the holder will exercise the option because the terms are favorable (the option is now "in the money"). The *writer* of the call option has a contractual obligation to exchange financial instruments on potentially unfavorable terms if the holder exercises the option. The writer is normally compensated for accepting this obligation by being paid a premium, which it keeps whether or not the option is exercised.

A put option to sell a Treasury note has similar effects, although the change in fair values making it worthwhile to exercise the option will be a decline, rather than an increase. The holder of the put option, as with the call option, effectively has an unlimited profit potential and no risk of loss (the only sunk cost is the premium paid), whereas the writer of the option has unlimited risk of loss and only a fixed amount of income.

Options are derivative financial instruments because their value is derived from the value of the underlying. A bank's commitment to lend $100,000 to a customer at a fixed rate of 10% any time during the next six months at the customer's option is also a derivative financial instrument, since its value would vary as market interest rates change. It is an option, with the potential borrower being the holder and the bank being the writer (the parties are collectively referred to as the "counterparties").

An interest rate swap is a series of forward contracts to exchange, for example, fixed cash payments for variable cash receipts. The cash receipts are computed by multiplying a specified floating-rate market index by a notional amount of principal. An interest rate swap is both a contractual right and a contractual obligation of both counterparties.

Managing Risk As with other financial instruments, derivatives can be acquired either for investment purposes or for speculation. For enterprises which are not in the business of speculation, however, the typical purpose of derivative financial instrument is to manage risk, such as that associated with stock price movements, interest rate variations, currency fluctuations, and commodity price volatility. The parties involved tend to be brokerage firms, financial institutions, insurance companies, and large corporations, although any two or more entities of any size can hold or issue derivatives. Even small companies often engage in hedging, most commonly for risk arising from importing and exporting denominated in foreign currencies.

Derivative financial instruments are contracts which are intended to protect or hedge one or more of the parties from adverse movement in the underlying base, which can be a financial instrument position held by the entity or a commitment to acquire the same at some future date, among others. These protections or hedges are rarely perfect and sometimes the hedge, once established, is later modified, even indirectly—such as by disposing of the underlying position while retaining the former hedge—so that the derivative financial instrument becomes in effect a speculative position. The derivative financial instruments themselves can become risky and, if leveraged, small adverse price or interest rate variations can produce significant losses.

Subsequent Measurement Derivative instruments are measured subsequently at fair value. (ASC 815-10-35-1) The accounting for changes in fair value depends on whether the instrument is a designated hedge. If it is part of a hedging relationship, see the information in this chapter related to ASC 815-20, including the alternative approach for private companies discussed later in this chapter. If a derivative is not designated as a hedging instrument, any gain or loss on the change in fair value is recognized in earnings in the current period. (ASC 815-10-35-2)

Certain Contracts on Debt and Equity Securities Forward contracts and purchased options are measured according to their initial classification as outlined in the chart below.

Exhibit—Accounting Treatment—Forward Contracts and Purchased Options

Subsequent Accounting for Forward Contracts and Purchased Options on Securities				
	Debt Securities			**Equity Securities**
Event	Held to Maturity[3]	Available-for-Sale[4]	Trading	
Changes in fair value.	Recognize other than temporary declines in earnings. Otherwise, do not recognize.	Recognize other than temporary declines in earnings. Otherwise, a part of separate component of shareholders' equity per ASC 320.	Recognize in earnings as they occur.	Recognize in earnings as they occur.

[3] Upon implementation of ASU 2016-13, changes in the fair value of held-to-maturity forward contracts or purchased options are not recognized. However, credit losses on the underlying securities in a forward contract are recorded through an allowance account and measured at amortized cost. If the credit losses are on the underlying securities in a purchased option, they are recorded in an allowance account, but the losses are limited to the amount of the option premium.

[4] Upon implementation of ASU 2016-13, changes in fair value continue to be recognized as a separate component of shareholders' equity as they occur. However, credit losses on the underlying security in a forward contract are recorded in an allowance account and measured according to the guidance in ASC 326-30. If the credit losses are on the underlying securities in a purchased option, they are recorded in an allowance account, but the losses are limited to the amount of the option premium.

Subsequent Accounting for Forward Contracts and Purchased Options on Securities				
	Debt Securities			Equity Securities
Securities purchased under a forward contract.	Forward contract price at settlement date.	Recognize at fair value at settlement date.	Fair value at settlement date.	Fair value at settlement date.
Securities purchased by exercising an option.	The strike price plus any remaining carrying amount for the option premium at the exercise date.	Option strike price plus fair value of the option at the exercise date.	Fair value at settlement date.	Fair value at settlement date.
Option expires worthless and the same debt security is purchased in the market.	Market price plus any carrying amount for the option premium.	Market price plus any carrying amount for the option premium.		
Entity does not take delivery under the forward contract and purchases the same securities in the market.	If the option expires worthless, entity's intent to hold other debt securities to maturity would be called into question.			
	(ASC 815-10-35-5)			(ASC 815-10-35-6)

Derecognition Derecognition of derivatives is accounted for as follows:

- Liabilities—in accordance with ASC 405-20-40-1
- Assets—in accordance with ASC 860-10-40
  (ASC 815-10-40-1)

ASC 815-15, *Embedded Derivatives*

Recognition. Embedded derivative instruments are defined as explicit or implicit terms affecting:

- The cash flows, or
- The value of other exchanges required by contract in a way similar to a derivative instrument.
  (ASC 815-15-20)

Separate instrument criteria An embedded derivative instrument must be separated from the host contract and accounted for separately as a derivative instrument by both parties if, and only if, *all* three following criteria are met:

1. Risks and economic characteristics are not clearly and closely related to those of the host contract;

2. The hybrid instrument is not required to be measured at fair value under GAAP with changes reported in earnings; and
3. A separate instrument with the same terms as the embedded derivative instrument, according to the guidance in ASC 815-10-15, would be accounted for as a derivative instrument. For this condition, the initial net investment of the hybrid instrument is not the same as that for the embedded derivative instrument.

These three conditions for the separate accounting for embedded derivatives are explained in the following paragraphs. (ASC 815-15-25-1)

Fair value election for hybrid financial instruments ASC 815-15-25 permits, through an irrevocable election, fair value initial measurement and subsequent measurement for any hybrid financial instrument that contains an embedded derivative that otherwise would require bifurcation under ASC 815. Changes to fair value are recognized in earnings and if ASC 825-10-45-5 is applicable, in other comprehensive income. (ASC 815-15-25-4)

If an embedded instrument requires separation (because the close correlation criterion noted above is not met) from its host, but it cannot be reliably identified and measured, the entire contract must be measured at fair value. Upon recognition of a hybrid instrument that would otherwise require separation into a derivative and a host, the reporting entity may elect irrevocably to measure, on an instrument-by-instrument basis, the entire hybrid instrument at fair value. Such an election must be supported either by concurrent documentation or by a preexisting documented policy supporting automatic election.

This fair value election is also available for remeasurement for an event recognized under GAAP, except for the recording of a credit lock under ASC 326 or measurement of an important loss through earnings under ASC 321. Examples of remeasurement events are:

- Business combinations
- A significant modification of debt
  (ASC 815-15-25-5)

Interests in securitized financial assets According to ASC 815, the holder of an interest in securitized financial assets (other than holders of strips or related claims to cash flows) must determine whether the interest is a freestanding derivative or contains an embedded derivative that would be required to be separated from the host contract and accounted for separately. (ASC 815-15-25-11) That determination is based on an analysis of the contractual terms of the interest in securitized financial assets. This, in turn, requires understanding the nature and amount of assets, liabilities, and other financial instruments that constitute the complete securitization transaction. (ASC 815-15-25-12) It is expected that the holder of an interest in securitized financial assets will obtain sufficient information about the payoff structure and the payment priority of the interest to make a determination about whether an embedded derivative exists. (ASC 815-15-25-13)

A reporting entity is not allowed to circumvent the recognition and measurement requirements of ASC 815 by embedding a derivative instrument in another contract. If these embedded derivative instruments would otherwise be subject to ASC 815, they are included in its scope.

Interest-rate related underlyings If the underlying is an interest rate or interest rate index that changes the net interest payments of an interest-bearing contract, it is considered clearly and closely related unless one of the following conditions exist:

- The hybrid instrument can be settled contractually in a manner that permits any possibility whatsoever that the investor would not recover substantially all of the initial recorded investment.

- The embedded derivative instrument could under any possibility whatsoever:
  - At least double the investor's initial rate of return (ROR) on the host contract, and
  - Also result in an ROR at least twice the market return for a similar contract (same host contract terms and same debtor credit quality).

  (ASC 815-15-25-26)

The date acquired (or incurred) is the assessment date for the existence of the above conditions. Thus, the issuer and an acquirer in a secondary market could account for the instrument differently because of different points in time.

Call and put options on debt investments As mentioned previously, one of the criteria for embedded derivatives to be separated from the host contract and accounted for separately as derivatives is known as the "clearly and closely related" criterion. The purpose of the guidance is to clarify that an assessment of whether an embedded contingent put or call option is clearly and closely related to the debt host requires only an analysis of the four-step decision sequence in ASC 815-15-25-42:

Step 1: Is the amount paid upon settlement (the payoff) adjusted based on changes in an index? If yes, continue to Step 2. If no, continue to Step 3.

Step 2: Is the payoff indexed to an underlying other than interest rates or credit risk? If yes, then that embedded feature is not clearly and closely related to the debt host contract and further analysis under Steps 3 and 4 is not required. If no, then that embedded feature should be analyzed further under Steps 3 and 4.

Step 3: Does the debt involve a substantial premium or discount? If yes, continue to Step If no, further analysis of the contract under paragraph 815-15-25-26 (see above) is required, if applicable.

Step 4: Does a contingently exercisable option accelerate the repayment of the contractual principal amount? If yes, the option is not clearly and closely related to the debt instrument. If not contingently exercisable, further analysis of the contract under paragraph 815-15-25-26 is required, if applicable.

Examples of Embedded Instruments That Are Separately Accounted For

Assuming that the host contract is a debt instrument, the following are considered not to be clearly and closely related and would normally have to be separated out as embedded derivatives:

- Interest rate indexes, floors, caps, and collars not meeting the criteria for exclusion (see number 2 in the next set of examples) (ASC 815-15-25-26);
- Leveraged inflation-indexed interest payments or rentals (ASC 815-15-25-21 and 25-49);
- Under certain conditions, certain securitized interests in prepayable financial assets (ASC 815-15-25-33);
- Embedded call options if the right to accelerate repayment of the debt can only be exercised by the debtor. (ASC 815-15-25-37);
- Term-extending options where there is no reset of interest rates (ASC 815-15-25-44);
- Equity-indexed interest payments (ASC 815-15-25-49);
- Commodity-indexed interest or principal payments (ASC 815-15-25-48);
- Call (put) options that do not accelerate the repayment of principal or a debt instrument, but rather require a cash settlement equal to the price of the option at the date of exercise, are

not considered clearly and closely related to the debt instrument in which it is embedded (ASC 815-15-25-41); and

- A convertible preferred stock conversion option if the terms of the preferred stock (not the conversion option) are more similar to debt (a cumulative fixed rate with a mandatory redemption feature) than to equity (cumulative, participating, perpetual).

Examples of Embedded Instruments That Are Not Separately Accounted For

Assuming that the host contract is a debt instrument, the following are considered to be clearly and closely related and would not normally have to be separated out as embedded derivative instruments:

- Interest rate indexes (see below)
- Interest rate floors, caps, and collars, if at issuance:
  - The cap is at or above the current market price (or rate), and/or
  - The floor is at or below the current market price (or rate)(ASC 815-15-25-26)
- Nonleveraged inflation-indexed interest payments or rentals (ASC 815-15-25-50)
- Credit-sensitive payments (interest rate resets for debtor creditworthiness) (ASC 815-15-25-46)
- "Plain-vanilla" servicing rights not containing a separate embedded derivative instrument
- Term-extending options if the interest rate is concurrently reset to approximately the current market rate for the extended term and the host contract had no initial significant discount (ASC 815-15-25-44)

- Contingent rentals based on a variable interest rate (ASC 815-15-25-22)

Based on the foregoing, calls and puts embedded in equity instruments are normally accounted for as follows:

- Investor—Both the call and the put are embedded derivative instruments.
- Issuer—Only the put could be an embedded derivative instrument. The put and the call would not be embedded derivative instruments if they are both:
  - Indexed to the issuing entity's own stock, and
  - Classified in shareholders' equity.

Embedded Derivative Instrument Separated from Host

Recognition If the embedded derivative instrument cannot be reliably identified and measured separately, the contract cannot be designated as a hedging instrument, and the entire contract must be measured at fair value with the gain or loss recognized in income. (ASC 815-15-25-53)

If an embedded derivative instrument is separated from the host, the accounting is as follows:

- The embedded derivative instrument is accounted for based on ASC 815, and
- The host contract is accounted for based on GAAP for that instrument, without the embedded derivative instrument. (ASC 815-15-25-54)

Initial Measurement Both of the following should be measured initially at fair value:

- A hybrid financial instrument required to be separated into a host contract and a derivative instrument that an entity elects to irrevocably measure at fair value
- An entire hybrid instrument where the entity cannot identify and measure the embedded derivative

(ASC 815-15-30-1)

Fair value measurements will often differ because they exclude transaction costs, which are included in many historical cost-based accounting entries, for example, the fair value of stock just purchased on an exchange is lower than cost. ASC 815 holds that any difference at inception of a recognized hybrid financial instrument for which the fair value election is applied and the transaction price is *not* to be included in current earnings (and thus is retained in the asset carrying amount) unless estimated fair value has been determined:

- From a quoted price in an active market,
- From comparison to other observable current market transactions, or
- Using a valuation technique that incorporates observable market data.

Subsequent Measurement

The changes in fair value are reported currently in earnings. (ASC 815-15-35-1)

ASC 815-20, *Hedging—General*

Overview While ASC 815 requires that all derivatives be reported at fair value in the statement of financial position, the changes in fair value are reported in different ways depending on the nature and effectiveness of the hedging activities to which they are related, if held for hedging purposes. (ASC 815-20-35-1) ASC 815 identifies changes in the fair values of derivatives as being the result of:

- Effective hedging,
- Ineffective hedging, or
- Unrelated to hedging.

Furthermore, the hedging itself can be related to the fair value of an existing asset or liability or of a firm commitment, the cash flow associated with forecasted transactions, or foreign currency exposures.

- **Fair value hedges.** Hedges of the changes in fair value can be associated with a recognized asset or liability or of an unrecognized firm commitment. (ASC 815-15-20) In a fair value hedge, gains and losses of both the derivative instrument (DI) and the hedged item are recognized currently in earnings. In the case of a perfectly effective hedge, these gains and losses will fully offset each period, but more typically this result will not be achieved. There will thus be a residual charge or credit to earnings each period that the hedge position is in place.
- **Cash flow hedges.** Cash flow hedges, on the other hand, pertain to forecasted transactions. The highly effective portions of these hedges are initially reported in other comprehensive income and are reclassified into earnings only later, when the forecasted transactions affect earnings. Any ineffective portions of the hedges are reported currently in earnings. (ASC 815-30-35-3)
- **Foreign currency hedges.** In addition to hedging foreign currency risk with fair value and cash flow hedges, an entity may use a hedge of a net investment in a foreign investment. (ASC 815-20-25-28) Hedges of the foreign currency exposure of a net investment in a foreign operation also qualify for special accounting treatment. In a foreign currency net investment hedge, the gain or loss is reported in other comprehensive income as part of the cumulative translation adjustment. (ASC 815-35-35-1) In the case of foreign currency hedges of unrecognized firm commitments, the gain or loss is reported the same way as a fair value hedge. A gain or loss on a foreign currency hedge that is

associated with an available-for-sale security will also be reported the same way as a fair value hedge. Finally, a gain or loss arising from a hedge relating to a foreign currency-denominated forecasted transaction is reported in the same way as a cash flow hedge.

Hedge portions that are not effective are reported in earnings immediately. A nonderivative financial instrument cannot generally be designated as a hedge. One exception, however, occurs under certain circumstances when that instrument is denominated in a foreign currency. (See the section on Foreign Currency Hedges later in this chapter.) Not-for-profit enterprises cannot use hedge accounting for forecasted transactions.

Prepayment risk for a financial asset cannot be hedged, but an option component of a prepayable instrument can be designated as the hedged item in a fair value hedge. Embedded derivatives have to be considered also in designating hedges. For instance, in a hedge of interest rates, the effect of an embedded prepayment option must be considered in the designation of the hedge. (ASC 815-20-25-6)

Private Company Alternative

ASC 815 allows for a simplified hedging accounting approach for private companies. This alternative applies to private companies, except for financial institutions.

The alternative allows private companies to apply a simplified hedge accounting method to hedging relationships. Certain criteria must be met and the relationships must involve receive-variable, pay-fixed, interest rate swap. This approach assumes no hedge ineffectiveness in a cash flow hedging relationship. (ASC 815-20-25-134) This alternative approach results in an income statement impact similar to what could have occurred had the company simply entered into a fixed-rate borrowing. This approach also allows private companies to measure the hedging interest rate swap at its settlement value, rather than at fair value, and gives private companies more time to put hedge documentation in place. (ASC 815-10-35-1A)

Hedges—Designation and Documentation Designation and documentation of a hedge at inception is required. (ASC 815-20-25-3)

Documentation The following must be documented for fair value hedges, cash flow hedges, and net investment hedges:

- The hedging relationship
- The entity's risk management objective and strategy for undertaking the hedge, including identification of all of the following:
  - The hedging instrument.
  - The hedged item or transaction.
- The nature of the risk being hedged.
- The method to retrospectively and prospectively assess the hedging instrument's effectiveness in offsetting the exposure to changes in the hedged item's fair value (if a fair value hedge) or hedged transaction's variability in cash flows (if a cash flow hedge) attributable to the hedged risk.
- If the entity is hedging foreign currency risk on an after-tax basis, that the assessment of effectiveness, including the calculation of ineffectiveness, will be on an after-tax basis. (ASC 815-20-25-3(b))

For a fair value hedge of a firm commitment, the entity also must document a reasonable method for recognizing in earnings the asset or liability representing the gain or loss on the hedged firm commitment. If the entity has a hedging relationship designated under the last-of-layer method, the documentation should include an analysis to support that the hedged item is expected to be outstanding at its maturity rate. (ASC 815-20-25-3(c))

For a cash flow hedge of a forecasted transaction, the entity also must document all relevant details, including all of the following:

- The date or period when the forecasted transaction is expected to occur.
- The specific nature of any asset or liability involved
- Either:
  - The expected currency amount for hedges of foreign currency exchange risk
  - The quantity of the forecasted transaction for hedges of other risks
- If a forecasted sale or purchase is being hedged for price risk, the hedged transaction should not be specified in either:
  - Solely in terms of expected currency amounts or
  - As a percentage of sales or purchases during a period.
- The current price of a forecasted transaction must be identified to satisfy the criterion for offsetting cash flows.
- The hedged forecasted transaction should be described with sufficient specificity so that when a transaction occurs, it is clear whether that transaction is or is not the hedged transaction.
- Identification of the contractually specified component in a forecasted purchase or sale in a nonfinancial asset.
- Identification of the contractually specified interest rate of the hedged risk is the variability in cash flows attributable to changes in a contractually specified interest rate for forecasted interest receipts or payments on a variable-rate financial asset or liability. (ASC 815-20-25-3(d))

Benchmark Interest Rate In each financial market, generally only the most widely used and quoted rates may be considered benchmark interest rates. In the United States, the following are considered to be benchmark interest rates.

- Interest rates on direct Treasury obligations of the U.S. government,
- The London Interbank Offered Rate (LIBOR) swap rate,
- The Fed Funds Effective Rate Overnight Index Swap Rate,
- The Securities Industry and Financial Markets Association (SIFMA) Municipal Swap Rate, and
- The Secured Overnight Financing Rate (SOFR) Overnight Index Swap Rate (ASC 815-20-25-6A)

Fair Value Hedges of Interest Rate Risk in Which the Hedged Item Can Be Settled before Its Scheduled Maturity If a hedged item is a prepayable instrument, an entity may designate a fair value hedge of interest rate risk. When doing so, the entity may consider only how changes in the benchmark interest rate affect the decision to settle the hedged item before its scheduled maturity. The entity is not required to consider other factors that would affect this decision when assessing hedge effectiveness. (ASC 815-20-25-6B)

Designation-Eligibility of Hedged Items and Transactions The method used for assessing the effective and ineffective portions of a hedge must be:

- Defined at the time of designation,
- Used throughout the hedge period, and
- Be consistent with the approach used by the entity for managing risk.

Similar hedges should usually be assessed for effectiveness in a similar manner unless a different method can be justified. If an improved method is identified and is to be applied prospectively to an existing hedge, that hedge must be discontinued. The new method can then be designated and a new hedge relationship can be established.

The effect of all excluded factors and ineffective amounts are included in earnings. For example, if an option contract hedge is assessed for effectiveness based on changes in the option's intrinsic value, the change due to the time value of the contract would be excluded from the effectiveness assessment, and that amount would be included in earnings. As another example, differences in key terms between the hedged item and the hedging instrument such as notional amounts, maturities, quantities, location, or delivery dates would cause ineffectiveness and that amount would be included in earnings.

Hedge effectiveness does not require perfect effectiveness (which is almost never attainable in practice), but the guidance is not explicit regarding the degree of effectiveness that must be attained to justify the use of special hedge accounting. (ASC 815-20-25-40) Should a hedge fail to meet a minimum threshold of effectiveness, should it be redesignated, and hedge accounting ceases. Strategic risk hedges do not meet qualifying criteria. (ASC 815-20-55-40) Thus, hedge accounting is limited to relationships involving derivative instruments and certain foreign currency-denominated instruments that are designated as hedges and meet the qualifying criteria.

Hedging Criteria Applicable to Fair Value Hedges Only To qualify as a fair value hedge, both the hedged items and the designated hedging instruments must meet all of the following criteria:

- At the hedge's inception, the items specified in the documentation section must be documented.
- The hedging relationship is expected to be highly effective in producing offsetting fair value changes throughout the hedge period. This relationship must be assessed at least every three months and each time financial statements or earnings are reported.
- If hedging with a written option, the combination must provide as much potential for gains from positive fair value changes as potential for losses from negative fair value changes. If a net premium is received, a combination of options is considered a written option. The combination of a written option and some other non-option derivative is also considered a written option.

According to ASC 815, an asset or liability will be eligible for designation as a hedged item in a fair value hedge if the hedged item:

- Is specifically identified as all or a specific portion of a recognized asset or liability, or an unrecognized firm commitment;
- Is single item (or portfolio of similar items) that must be specifically identified as hedging all or a specific portion.
    - If similar items are aggregated and hedged, each item has to share the risk exposure that is being hedged (i.e., each individual item must respond in a generally proportionate manner to the change in fair value).
    - A specific portion must be one of the following:
        - A percentage of the total asset, liability, or portfolio;
        - One or more selected contractual cash flows: for instance, the present value of the interest payments due in any consecutive two years of a four-year debt instrument.

ASC 815-25-35-13B offers guidance on the measurement of the hedged item in hedges of interest rate risk.
    - An embedded put, call, cap, or floor that does not qualify as an embedded derivative in an existing asset or liability; or
    - Residual value in a lessor's net investment in a sales-type or direct financing lease.
- Is exposed to fair value changes that are attributable to the hedged risk such that earnings would be affected; and
- Is not either remeasured at fair value for financial reporting purposes, or an equity-method investment, or an equity method or minority interest in a consolidated subsidiary, a firm commitment related to the foregoing, or an equity instrument issued by the entity.
- Is not a held-to-maturity debt security (or similar portfolio), the hedged risk is for fair value changes due to credit risk and/or foreign exchange rates.
- Is a nonfinancial asset or liability (other than a recognized loan servicing right or a nonfinancial firm commitment with financial components), the designated hedged risk is the fair value change of the total hedged item (at its actual location, if applicable); ASC 815 stipulates that the price of a major ingredient cannot be used, and the price of a similar item at a different location cannot be used without adjustment.
- Is a financial asset or liability, a recognized loan servicing right or a nonfinancial firm commitment with financial components, the designated hedge risk is the risk of changes in fair value from fair value changes in:
    - The total hedged item;
    - Market interest rates;
    - Related foreign currency rates;
    - The obligor's creditworthiness; or
    - Two or more of the above (other than the total hedged item)

  (ASC 815-20-25-12)

Hedging Criteria Applicable to a Cash Flow Hedge Only A nonderivative instrument cannot be designated as a hedging instrument for a cash flow hedge. To qualify as a cash flow hedge, both the hedged items and the designated hedging instruments must meet the documentation requirements specified earlier in this chapter. In addition, to be eligible for designation as a cash flow hedge, a forecasted transaction must meet all of the following criteria:

- The single transaction (or group of individual transactions) must be specifically identified. If individual transactions are grouped and hedged, each has to share the same risk exposure that is being hedged (i.e., each individual transaction must respond in a proportionate manner to the change in cash flow). Thus, a forecasted sale and a forecasted purchase cannot both be included in the same group of transactions.
- The occurrence is probable.
- It is a transaction with an external party (unless a foreign currency cash flow hedge) and it has an exposure to cash flow changes that could affect earnings.
- The transaction will not be remeasured subsequently under GAAP with changes in fair value reported in earnings; for example, foreign currency–denominated items would be

excluded for this reason. Forecasted sales on credit and forecasted accrual of royalties on probable future sales are not considered the forecasted acquisition of a receivable. Also, if related to a recognized asset or liability, the asset or liability is not remeasured under GAAP with changes in fair value resulting from the hedged risk reported in earnings.

- If the item is not a held-to-maturity debt security (or similar portfolio) the hedged risk is for cash flow changes due to credit or foreign exchange risk.
- It does not involve:
    - A business combination;
    - A parent company's interest in consolidated subsidiaries;
    - A minority interest;
    - An equity-method investment; or
    - An entity-issued equity interest classified in stockholders' equity.
- If it involves a purchase or sale of a nonfinancial asset, the hedged risk is:
    - The change in the functional-currency-equivalent cash flows resulting from changes in the related foreign currency rates; or
    - The change in cash flows relating to the total hedged purchase or sales price (at its actual location, if applicable); for example, the price of a similar item at a different location cannot be used.
- If it involves a purchase or sale of a financial asset or liability or the variable cash flow of an existing financial asset or liability, the hedged risk is the risk of changes in cash flow of:
    - Tahe total hedged item;
    - Contractually specified interest rate;
    - Changes in the benchmark interest rate;
    - Related foreign currency rates;
    - Obligor's creditworthiness or default; or
    - Two or more of the above, other than (the total hedged item)

  (ASC 815-20-25-15)

Assessing hedge ineffectiveness in a hedge with an interest rate swap The assumption of no ineffectiveness in a hedge between an interest-bearing financial instrument and an interest rate swap can be assumed if all of the following conditions are met for both:

- The principal amount and the notional amount of the swap match;
- The fair value of the swap is zero at origin;
- The net settlements under the swap are computed the same way on each settlement date;
- The financial instrument is not prepayable before its scheduled maturity date or the assumed maturity date if the hedged item is measured under the guidance in ASC 815-25-35-13B; and
- The terms are typical for those instruments and do not invalidate the assumption of effectiveness.

  (ASC 815-20-25-104)

The variable rate on the instrument is not required to exactly match the variable rate on the swap. The fixed and variable rates on the swap can be changed by the same amount.

Summary of Accounting for Hedges

	Type of hedge—ASC 815		
Attribute	**Fair value**	**Cash flow**	**Foreign currency (FC)**
Types of hedging instruments permitted	Derivatives	Derivatives	Derivatives or nonderivatives depending on the type of hedge
Statement of financial position valuation of hedging instrument	At fair value	At fair value	At fair value
Recognition of gain or loss on changes in value of hedging instrument*	Currently in earnings	Currently as a component of other comprehensive income (OCI) and reclassified to earnings in future period(s) that forecasted transaction affects earnings	**FC-denominated firm commitment** Currently in earnings, same as a fair value hedge **Available-for-sale debt security** Currently in earnings **Forecasted FC transaction** OCI and reclassified into earnings in the same period that the hedged forecasted transaction affects earnings
			Net investment in a foreign operation
			OCI as part of the cumulative translation adjustment to the extent it is effective as a hedge
Recognition of gain or loss on changes in the fair value of the hedged item	Currently in earnings	Not applicable; these hedges are not associated with recognized assets or liabilities	FC-denominated firm commitment Currently in earnings Available-for-sale debt security Currently in earnings
			Forecasted FC transaction
			Not applicable; same as cash flow hedge
(ASC 815-20-35-1)			

* *Note: If an entity excludes a portion of the hedging instrument from the assessment of hedge effectiveness, the initial value of the excluded component is recognized in earnings using a systematic and rational method over the life of the hedging instrument. Any difference between the change in fair value of the excluded component and amounts recognized in earnings under that systematic and rational method is recognized in other comprehensive income. For net investment hedges, any difference in the fair value is reported in the cumulative translation adjustment section of OCI. An entity may opt to recognize the excluded component of the gain or loss currently in earnings.*

Discontinuing Hedge Accounting An entity should discontinue hedge accounting if

- Any of the hedge criteria is no longer met,
- The derivative instrument is sold, terminated, or exercised, or
- The entity removes the hedge designation.

Derivative contract novations A novation may occur for many reasons, including:

- Regulatory or legal rule changes,
- Financial institution mergers,
- Intercompany transactions,
- Desire to reduce credit risk,
- Financial institutions voluntarily exiting a particular derivative business, or
- Financial institutions voluntarily exiting a customer relationship.

The Codification makes clear that the fact of a change in counterparty to a derivative contract does not in and of itself require the dedesignation of a hedging relationship. The entity does have to evaluate whether it is probable that the counterparty will perform under the contract as part of its ongoing effectiveness assessment for hedge accounting and should consider counterparty credit risk, which is consistent with existing GAAP. Therefore, a novation may result in the dedesignation of the hedging relationship. (ASC 815-20-55-56A; 815-25-40-1A; 815-30-40-1A)

Items not qualified as hedges Besides those hedged items and transactions that fail to meet the specified eligibility criteria, none of the following should be designated as a hedged item:

For both fair value hedges and cash flow hedges:

- An investment accounted for by the equity method in accordance with the requirements of ASC 323 or ASC 321
- A noncontrolling interest in one or more consolidated subsidiaries
- Transactions with stockholders as stockholders,
- Intra-entity transactions (except for foreign-currency-denominated forecasted intra-entity transactions) between entities included in consolidated financial statements
- The price of stock expected to be issued pursuant to a stock option plan for which recognized compensation expense is not based on changes in stock prices after the date of grant.

For fair value hedges only:

- If the entire asset or liability is an instrument with variable cash flows, an implicit fixed-to-variable swap (or similar instrument) perceived to be embedded in a host con- tract with fixed cash flows
- For a held-to-maturity debt security, the risk of changes in its fair value attributable to interest rate risk
- An asset or liability that is remeasured with the changes in fair value attributable to the hedged risk reported currently in earnings
- An equity investment in a consolidated subsidiary
- A firm commitment either to enter into a business combination or to acquire or dispose of a subsidiary, a noncontrolling interest, or an equity method investee

- An equity instrument issued by the entity and classified in stockholders' equity in the statement of financial position
- A component of an embedded derivative in a hybrid instrument.

For cash flow hedges only:

- If variable cash flows of the forecasted transaction relate to a debt security that is classified as held-to-maturity under ASC 320, the risk of changes in its cash flows attributable to interest rate risk
- In a cash flow hedge of a variable-rate financial asset or liability, either existing or forecasted, the risk of changes in its cash flows attributable to changes in the specifically identified benchmark interest rate if the cash flows of the hedged transaction are explicitly based on a different index.[5]
(ASC 815-20-25-43)

ASC 815-25, *Fair Value Hedges*

The change in the fair value of an entire financial asset or liability for a period is computed as the fair value at the end of the period, adjusted to exclude changes in fair value from

- Payments received or made (partial recoveries or settlements), and
- The passage of time, minus the fair value at the beginning of the period.

Example—Gains and Losses on Fair Value Hedges

An available-for-sale equity security carrying amount is adjusted by the amount resulting from the hedged risk, a fair value hedge.

Hedged item:	Available-for-sale equity security
Hedging instrument:	Put option
Underlying:	Price of the security
Notional amount:	100 shares of the security

On July 1, 20X1, Company XYZ purchased 100 shares of Widgetworks at a cost of $15 per share and classified it as an available-for-sale security. On October 1, 20X1, Company XYZ purchased for $350 an at-the-money put on Widgetworks with an exercise price of $25 and an expiration date of April 20X2. This put purchase locks in a profit of $650 ($1,000 spread in market price less $350 cost of the put), if the price stays at $25 or goes lower, but allows continued profitability if the price of the Widgetworks stock continues to go up. Company XYZ specifies that only the intrinsic value of the option is to be used to measure effectiveness. Thus, the time value decreases in the fair value of the put will be charged against the income of the period. Company XYZ then documents the hedge's strategy, objectives, hedging relationships, and method of measuring effectiveness. The following table shows the fair value of the hedged item and the hedging instrument.

---

[5] This item is superseded upon implementation of ASU 2017-12.

Case 1					
Hedged Item	***10/1/X1***	***12/31/X1***	***3/31/X2***	***4/17/X3***	
Widgetworks share price	$ 25	$ 22	$ 20	$ 20	
Number of shares	100	100	100	100	
Total	$2,500	$2,200	$2,000	$2,000	
Hedging Instrument					
Put option (100 shares)					
Intrinsic value	$ 0	$ 300	$ 500	$ 500	
Time value	350	215	53	0	
Total	$ 350	$ 515	$ 553	$ 500	
Intrinsic Value Gain (Loss) on Put	$ 0	$ 0	$ 300	$ 200	$ 0

Entries: Income Tax Effects and Transaction Costs Are Ignored

7/1/X1	Purchase:	Available-for-sale security	1,500	
		Cash		1,500
9/30/X1	End of Quarter:	Valuation allowance—available-for-sale security	1,000	
		Other comprehensive income		1,000
10/1/X1	Put Purchase:	Put option	350	
		Cash		350
Case 1	End of Year:			
12/31/X1		Put option	300	
		Hedge gain (intrinsic value gain)		300
		Hedge loss	135	
		Put option (time value loss)		135
		Hedge loss	300	
		Valuation allowance—available-for-sale security (fair value loss)		300

Partial Statement of Financial Position
Effect of Hedging Relationships
December 31, 20X1
Dr (Cr)

Cash	$(1,850)
Available-for-sale equity securities	1,200
Plus: Valuation allowance	1,000
Put option	515
Other comprehensive income	(1,000)
Retained earnings	135

Entries

3/31/X2	End of Quarter:	Put option	200	
		Hedge gain (intrinsic value changes)		200
		Hedge loss	162	
		Put option (time value loss)		162
		Hedge loss	200	
		Available-for-sale security (fair value loss)	200	
4/17/X2	Put Expires:	Put option	0	
		Hedge gain (intrinsic value changes)		0
		Hedge loss	53	
		Put option (time value changes)		53
		Hedge loss	0	
		Available-for-sale security (fair value changes)	0	

Partial Statement of Financial Position
Effect of Hedging Relationships
April 17, 20X2 (Expiration of Put)

	Dr (Cr)
Cash	$(1,850)
Available-for-sale equity securities	1,500
Plus: Valuation allowance	500
Put option	500
Other comprehensive income	(1,000)
Retained earnings	350

At or before expiration, an in-the-money put must be sold or exercised. Assuming that it is sold, the entry would be:

Cash	500	
Put option		500

On the other hand, if the put is exercised, the entry would be

Cash (exercise price)	2,500	
Other comprehensive income	1,000	
Available-for-sale equity security		1,500
Valuation allowance		500
Put option		500
Gain on sale		1,000

The net effect on retained earnings of the hedge and sale is a net gain of $650 ($1,000 – $350).

Case 2

	10/1/X1	12/31/X1	3/31/X2	4/17/X2
Hedged Item				
Widgetworks share price	$ 25	$ 28	$ 30	$ 31
Number of shares	100	100	100	100
Total	$ 2,500	$ 2,800	$ 3,000	$ 3,100
Hedging Instrument				
Put option (100 shares)				
Intrinsic value	$ 0	0	$ 0	$ 0
Time value	350	100	25	0
Total	$ 350	$ 100	$ 25	$ 0
Intrinsic Value Gain (Loss) on Put	$ 0	$ 0	$ 0	$ 0

Entries: Income Tax Effects and Transaction Costs Are Ignored

7/1/X1	Purchase:	Available-for-sale security	1,500	
		Cash		1,500
9/30/X1	End of Quarter:	Valuation allowance—available-for-sale security	1,000	
		Other comprehensive income		1,000
10/1/X1	Put Purchase:	Put option	350	
		Cash		350
12/31/X1	End of Year:	Put option	0	
		Hedge gain (intrinsic value gain)		0
		Hedge loss	250	
		Put option (time value loss)		250
		Valuation allowance—available-for-sale security	300	
		Hedge gain (fair value gain)		300

Partial Statement of Financial Position
Effect of Hedging Relationships
December 31, 20X1
Dr (Cr)

Cash	$(1,850)
Available-for-sale equity securities	1,500
Plus: Valuation allowance	1,300
Put option	100
Other comprehensive income	(1,000)
Retained earnings	(50)

Entries

3/31/X2	End of Quarter:	Put option	0	
		Hedge gain (intrinsic value change)		0
		Hedge loss	75	
		Put option (time value loss)		75
		Valuation allowance—available-for-sale security	200	
		Hedge gain (fair value gain)		200
4/17/X2	Put Expires:	Put option	0	
		Hedge gain (intrinsic value change)		0
		Hedge loss	25	
		Put option (time value change)		25
		Valuation allowance—available-for-sale security	100	
		Hedge gain (fair value change)		100

Effect of Hedging Relationships
April 17, 20X2 (Expiration of Put)
Dr (Cr)

Cash	$(1,850)
Available-for-sale securities	1,500
Plus: Valuation allowance	1,600
Put option	0
Other comprehensive income	(1,000)
Retained earnings	(250)

The put expired unexercised and Company XYZ must decide whether to sell the security. If it continues to hold, normal ASC 320 accounting would apply. If it continues to hold and a new put is purchased, the above example would be applicable again with the present position as a starting point. If the security is sold, the entry would be:

Cash (fair value)	3,100	
Other comprehensive income	1,000	
Available-for-sale equity security		1,500
Valuation allowance		1,600
Gain on sale		1,000

Assuming Perfect Hedge Effectiveness—the Shortcut Method for Interest Rate Swaps To relieve entities from ongoing assessment of the effectiveness of interest rate swaps, ASC 815 permits a "shortcut method" to assume perfect effectiveness and compute fair value adjustments. (ASC 815-20-25-102) This shortcut is limited to a fair value or cash flow hedge of a benchmark interest-rate hedge relationships involving a recognized interest-bearing asset or liability and an interest rate swap that meets specific conditions.

Although there are specific conditions applicable to the hedge type (fair value or cash flow), in general, the assumption of perfect effectiveness in a hedging relationship between an interest-bearing financial instrument and an interest rate swap (or a compound hedging instrument composed of an interest rate swap and a mirror-image call or put option) can be made if all of the following conditions are met:

For Both Fair Value and Cash Flow Hedges The following criteria apply to both fair value and cash flow hedges:

- The principal amount of the interest-bearing asset or liability matches the notional amount of the swap.
- The fair value of the swap is zero at inception, if the hedging instrument is solely an interest rate swap. If the hedging instrument is a compound derivative containing the swap and a mirror-image call or put, the premium for the option must be paid or received in the same manner as the premium on the option embedded in the hedged item, and further conditions must be met depending on whether the premium on the option element of the hedged item was paid upon inception or over the life of the instrument.
- The net settlements under the swap are computed the same way on each settlement date.
- The financial instrument is not prepayable, but this criterion does not apply to an interest-bearing asset or liability that is prepayable only due to an embedded call option when the hedging instrument is a compound derivative composed of a swap and a mirror-image call option.
- For any other terms in the interest-bearing financial instruments or interest-rate swaps:
  - The terms are typical of those instruments
  - The terms do not invalidate the assumption of perfect effectiveness

  (ASC 815-20-25-104)

Fair Value Hedges Only For a fair value hedge, the swap must also meet all of these conditions:

- The terms are typical for those instruments and do not invalidate the assumption of effectiveness.
- The expiration date of the interest-rate swap and the maturity date of the interest-bearing asset or liability match, or the assumed maturity date if the hedged item is measured under the guidance in ASC 815-25-35-13B.
- No floor or cap on the variable interest rate of the swap exists.
- For hedges of portfolios
- The notional amount of the interest rate swap matches the aggregate notional amount of the hedged item
- The criteria for the shortcut method are met with respect to the interest rate swap and individual assets or liabilities in the portfolio
- The interval (three to six months or less) between repricings is frequent enough to assume the variable rate is a market rate.

  (ASC 815-20-25-105)

Cash Flow Hedges Only The following criteria apply only to cash flow hedges:

- The index base for the variable leg of the interest rate swap is based matches the contractually specified interest rate;
- All variable rate interest payments or receipts on the instrument during the swap term are designated as hedged and none beyond that term;

- No floor or cap on the variable rate of the swap exists unless the variable rate instrument has one. If the instrument does, the swap must have a comparable (not necessarily equal) one;
- Repricing dates match.
  (ASC 815-30-25-106)

The fixed rate on the hedged item is not required to exactly match the fixed rate on the swap. The fixed and variable rates on the swap can be changed by the same amount. As an example, a swap payment based on LIBOR and a swap receipt based on a fixed rate of 5% can be changed to a payment based on LIBOR plus 1% and a receipt based on 6%. (ASC 815-20- 25-106)

Steps in the Shortcut Method The steps in the shortcut method are as follows:

1. Determine the difference between the fixed rate to be received on the swap and the fixed rate to be paid on the bonds.
2. Combine that difference with the variable rate to be paid on the swap.
3. Compute and recognize interest expense using that combined rate and the fixed-rate liability's principal amount. (Amortization of any purchase premium or discount on the liability also must be considered, although that complication is not incorporated in this example.)
4. Determine the fair value of the interest rate swap.
5. Adjust the carrying amount of the swap to its fair value and adjust the carrying amount

For fair value hedges, an assumption of perfect effectiveness is invalidated when the interest rate index embodied in the variable leg of the interest rate swap is different from the benchmark interest rate being hedged. In situations in which the interest rate index embodied in the variable leg of the swap has greater credit risk than that embodied in the benchmark interest rate, the effect of the change in the swap's credit sector spread over that in the benchmark interest rate would represent hedge ineffectiveness because it relates to an unhedged risk (credit risk) rather than to the hedged risk (interest rate risk). (ASC 815-20-25-102)

In situations in which the interest rate index embodied in the variable leg of the swap has less credit risk than that embodied in the benchmark interest rate, the effect of the change in a certain portion of the hedged item's spread over the swap interest rate would also represent hedge ineffectiveness. For an entity to comply with an assumption of no ineffectiveness, the index on which the variable leg of the swap is based must match the benchmark interest rate designated as the interest rate risk being hedged for the hedging relationship.

Discontinuance of a Fair Value Hedge The accounting for a fair value hedge should not continue if any of the events below occur:

- The criteria are no longer met;
- The derivative instruments expire or are sold, terminated, or exercised; or
- The designation is removed.

If the fair value hedge is discontinued, a new hedging relationship may be designated with a different hedging instrument and/or a different hedged item, as long as the criteria established in ASC 815 are met. (ASC 815-30-40-3)

Ineffectiveness of a Fair Value Hedge Unless the shortcut method is applicable, the reporting entity must assess the hedge's effectiveness at the inception of the hedge and at least every three months thereafter. (ASC 815-20-25-79) In addition, ASC 815 requires that at the inception of the hedge the method to be used to assess hedge effectiveness must be identified. To comply, the reporting entity should decide which changes in the derivative's fair value will be considered in assessing the effectiveness of the hedge, and the method to be used to assess hedge effectiveness. Regarding the former, some derivative instruments (options) have two components: intrinsic value and time value. The intrinsic value of a call option is the excess, if any, of the market price over the strike or exercise price; the intrinsic value of an option recognizes that the price of the underlying item may move above the strike price (for a call) or below the strike price (for a put) during the exercise period. The enterprise elects to measure effectiveness either including or excluding time value; it must do so consistently once the designation is made.

Hedge effectiveness must be assessed in two different ways—in *prospective* considerations and in *retrospective* evaluations. ASC 815 provides flexibility in selecting the method the entity will use in assessing hedge effectiveness, but an entity should assess effectiveness for similar hedges in a similar manner and that the use of different methods for similar hedges should be justified.

Prospectively, the entity must, at both inception and on an ongoing basis, be able to justify an expectation that the relationship will be highly effective in achieving offsetting changes in fair value over future periods. That expectation can be based upon regression or other statistical analysis of past changes in fair values or on other relevant information. Retrospectively, the entity must, at least quarterly, determine whether the hedging relationship has been highly effective in having achieved offsetting changes in fair value through the date of periodic assessment. That assessment can also be based upon regression or other statistical analysis of past changes in fair values, as well as on other relevant information. If at inception the entity elects to use the same regression analysis approach for both prospective and retrospective effectiveness evaluations, then during the term of that hedging relationship those regression analysis calculations should generally incorporate the same number of data points. As an alternative to using regression or other statistical analysis, an entity could use the dollar-offset method to perform the retrospective evaluations of assessing hedge effectiveness.

Impairment Considerations for Hedging and Hedged Items All assets or liabilities designated as fair value hedges are subject to the normal GAAP requirements for impairment assessment and, as needed, accounting adjustment. Those requirements should be applied, however, only after the carrying amounts have been adjusted for the period's hedge accounting. Since the hedging instrument is a separate asset or liability, its fair value is not considered in applying the impairment criteria to the hedged item. (ASC 815-25-35-10)

Example of Applying Fair Value Measurements in Times of Market Inactivity or Stress

Magna Financial holds as an investment a tranche of AA-rated mortgage-backed securities (MBS) that are collateralized by unguaranteed nonconforming residential mortgage loans. The fair value of this financial asset had heretofore been determined based on either (1) quoted prices in active markets for similar MBS (which constituted Level 2 inputs), or (2) quoted prices in inactive markets representing current transactions for the same or similar MBS not requiring significant adjustments (which were also Level 2 inputs).

As of year-end 20X1, the MBS market has grown inactive (as evidenced at first by a widening of the bid-ask spread, and subsequently by a decline in transaction volume). At the date of the statement of financial position, Magna Financial concludes that the markets for identical and similar MBS tranches are inactive. This determination was made by considering that (1) few transactions for the same MBS or similar tranches were presently observable, and (2) the few observable prices for such transactions exhibited substantial variations. Accordingly, valuation information available for Magna Financial's AA-rated MBS tranche was classified within Level 3 of the fair value hierarchy.

Magna Financial determined that use of a present value technique that would maximize the use of observable inputs (and would thus minimize the use of unobservable inputs) would be at least as representative of fair value as the market approach applied at earlier measurement dates. Specifically, Magna Financial decides to employ the "discount rate adjustment technique," under which the adjustment for risk inherent in the asset's contractual cash flows will be incorporated into the discount rate itself.

In determining the interest rate to be applied to the contractually obligated future cash flows as of year-end 20X1, Magna Financial takes into account (1) a 16% implied rate of return on the last date on which the market for an identical MBS was deemed active, and (2) the subsequent 1.5% (150 basis point) widening of credit spreads and the subsequent 4% (400 basis point) increase in liquidity risk premiums. Furthermore, Magna Financial will consider all available market information that could be obtained without due cost and effort, which in the present fact situation will include (1) previous quoted prices in markets for identical or similar MBS, (2) reports issued by analysts and rating agencies, (3) movements in relevant indexes, such as those gauging interest rates and credit risks, (4) data pertaining to the performance of the underlying mortgage loans (including delinquency and foreclosure rates, loss experience, and prepayment speeds), and (5) two indicative (but nonbinding) broker quotes based on proprietary pricing models using Level 3 inputs, which implied rates of return of 20% and 24%, respectively.

Based on the foregoing facts, Magna Financial will be required to select an appropriate interest rate to apply in discounting the contractual cash flows of the MBS for the purpose of estimating fair value for this portfolio at year-end 20X1. Under the circumstances, Magna Financial determined that a 23% rate was to be used, as that was the result of evaluating and weighing the respective indications of the appropriate rate of the MBS tranche's return within a range of 21.5%–25.5%. The low end of the range is computed as follows:

16.0% = Implied rate of return as of the last date on which the market for identical MBS was active
1.5% = Subsequent widening of credit spreads (150 basis points)
4.0% = Subsequent increase in risk premiums (400 basis points)
21.5% = Low end of the range

The high end of the range is based on two nonbinding broker quotes that imply an average 25.5% rate of return (i.e., the average of the implied rates of 23% and 28%). Magna Financial believes that the range is reasonable and the 23% rate reflects the best estimate of the assumptions that would be made by market participants of the fair value at the measurement date and takes into account:

- Nonperformance risk (consisting of both default and collateral value risks), and
- Liquidity risk (determined by the compensation a market participant would expect to receive for acquiring an asset that is difficult to sell under current market conditions).

In this instance, Magna Financial assigned slightly greater weight to its own estimate of fair value (the low end of the range, 21.5%) because:

- Broker quotes were nonbinding and based on models using significant unobservable inputs, and
- The entity was able to use market inputs relating to the performance of the underlying mortgage loans.

ASC 815-30, *Cash Flow Hedges*

The second major subset of hedging arrangements relates to uncertain future cash flows, as contrasted with hedged items engendering uncertain fair values. A derivative instrument may be designated as a hedge to the exposure of fluctuating expected future cash flows produced by a particular risk. The exposure may be connected with an existing asset or liability or with a forecasted transaction.

The Shortcut Method for Interest Rate Swaps Refer to the section in this chapter on ASC 815-20 for information on using the short cut method.

Example of Using Options to Hedge Future Purchase of Inventory

Friendly Chemicals Corp. uses petroleum as a feedstock from which it produces a range of chemicals for sale to producers of synthetic fabrics and other consumer goods. It is concerned about the rising price of oil and decides to hedge a major purchase it plans to make in mid-20X1. Oil futures and options are traded on the New York Mercantile exchange and other markets; Friendly decides to use options rather than futures because it is only interested in protecting itself from a price increase; if prices decline, it wishes to reap that benefit rather than suffer the loss which would result from holding a futures contract in a declining market environment.

At December 31, 20X1, Friendly projects a need for 10 million barrels of crude oil of a defined grade to be purchased by mid-20X2; this will suffice for production through mid-20X3. The current world price for this grade of crude is $164.50 per barrel, but prices have been rising recently. Management desires to limit its crude oil costs to no higher than $165.75 per barrel, and accordingly purchases, at a cost of $2 million, an option to purchase up to 10 million barrels at a cost of $165.55 per barrel (which, when added to the option premium, would make the total cost $165.75 per barrel if the full 10 million barrels are acquired), at any time through December 20X2.

Management has studied the behavior of option prices and has concluded that changes in option prices that relate to time value are not correlated to price changes and hence are ineffective in hedging price changes. On the other hand, changes in option prices that pertain to pricing changes (intrinsic value changes) are highly effective as hedging vehicles. The table below reports the value of these options, analyzed in terms of time value and intrinsic value, over the period from December 2012 through December 20X2.

	Price of oil/	*Fair value of option relating to date*	
Date	*barrel*	*Time value**	*Intrinsic value*
December 31, 20X1	$ 164.50	$ 2,000,000	$ 0
January 31, 20X2	164.90	1,900,000	0
February 28, 20X2	165.30	1,800,000	0
March 31, 20X2	165.80	1,700,000	2,500,000
April 30, 20X2	166.00	1,600,000	4,500,000
May 31, 20X2	165.85	1,500,000	3,000,000
June 30, 20X2**	166.00	700,000	2,250,000
July 31, 20X2	165.60	650,000	250,000
August 31, 20X2	165.50	600,000	0
September 30, 20X2	165.75	550,000	1,000,000
October 31, 20X2	165.80	500,000	1,250,000
November 30, 20X2	165.85	450,000	1,500,000
December 31, 20X2***	165.90	400,000	1,750,000

* *This example does not address how the time value of options would be computed in practice.*
** *Options for 5 million barrels exercised; remainder held until end of December, then sold.*
*** *Values cited are immediately prior to sale of remaining options.*

******

At the end of June 20X2, Friendly Chemicals exercises options for 5 million barrels, paying $165.55 per barrel for oil selling on the world markets for $166.00 each. It holds the remaining options until December, when it sells these for an aggregate price of $2.1 million, a slight discount to the nominal fair value at that date.

The inventory acquired in mid-20X2 is processed and included in goods available for sale. Sales of these goods, in terms of the 5 million barrels of crude oil that were consumed in their production, are as follows:

Date	*Equivalent barrels sold in month*	*Equivalent barrels on hand at month end*
June 30, 20X2	300,000	4,700,000
July 31, 20X2	250,000	4,450,000
August 31, 20X2	400,000	4,050,000
September 30, 20X2	350,000	3,700,000
October 31, 20X2	550,000	3,150,000
November 30, 20X2	500,000	2,650,000
December 31, 20X2	650,000	2,000,000

Based on the foregoing facts, the journal entries prepared on a monthly basis (for illustrative purposes) for the period December 20X1 through December 20X2 are as follows:

December 31, 20X1

Option contract	2,000,000	
Cash		2,000,000

To record purchase premium on option contract for up to 10 million barrels of oil at price of $165.55 per barrel

January 31, 20X2

Loss on hedging transaction	100,000	
Option contract		100,000

To record change in time value of option contract—charge premium to income since this represents payment for time value of money, which expires ratably over two-year term and does not qualify for hedge accounting treatment

Option contract	0	
Other comprehensive income		0

To reflect change in intrinsic value of option contracts (no value at this date)

February 28, 20X2

Loss on hedging transaction	100,000	
Option contract		100,000

To record change in time value of option contract—charge premium to income since this represents payment for time value of money, which expires ratably over two-year term and does not qualify for hedge accounting treatment

Option contract	0	
Other comprehensive income		0

To reflect change in intrinsic value of option contracts (no value at this date)

March 31, 20X2

Loss on hedging transaction	100,000	
Option contract		100,000

To record change in time value of option contract—charge premium to income since this represents payment for time value of money, which expires ratably over two-year term and does not qualify for hedge accounting treatment

Option contract	2,500,000	
Other comprehensive income		2,500,000

To reflect change in intrinsic value of option contracts

April 30, 20X2

Loss on hedging transaction	100,000	
Option contract		100,000

To record change in time value of option contract—charge premium to income since this represents payment for time value of money, which expires ratably over two-year term and does not qualify for hedge accounting treatment

Option contract	2,000,000	
Other comprehensive income		2,000,000

To reflect change in intrinsic value of option contracts (further increase in value)

May 31, 20X2

Loss on hedging transaction	100,000	
Option contract		100,000

To record change in time value of option contract—charge premium to income since this represents payment for time value of money, which expires ratably over two-year term and does not qualify for hedge accounting treatment

Other comprehensive income	1,500,000	
Option contract		1,500,000

To reflect change in intrinsic value of option contracts (decline in value)

June 30, 20X2

Loss on hedging transaction	800,000	
Option contract		800,000

To record change in time value of option contract—charge premium to income since this represents payment for time value of money, which expires ratably over two-year term and does not qualify for hedge accounting treatment; since one-half the options were exercised in June, the remaining unexpensed time value of that portion is also entirely written off at this time

Option contract	1,500,000	
Other comprehensive income		1,500,000

To reflect change in intrinsic value of option contracts (further increase in value) before accounting for exercise of options on 5 million barrels

June 30 intrinsic value of options before exercise	4,500,000
Allocation to oil purchased at $165.55	2,250,000
Remaining intrinsic value of option	2,250,000

The allocation to exercised options will be maintained in other comprehensive income until transferred to cost of goods sold as a contra cost, as the 5 million barrels are sold, at the rate of 45¢ per equivalent barrel ($166.00 – $165.55).

Inventory	827,750,000	
Cash (or accounts payable)		827,750,000

To record purchase of 5 million barrels of oil at option price of $165.55/barrel

Inventory	2,250,000	
Option contract		2,250,000

To increase the recorded value of the inventory to include the fair value of options given up (exercised) in acquiring the oil (taken together, the cash purchase price and the fair value of options surrendered add to $166 per barrel, the world market price at date of purchase)

Cost of goods sold	49,800,000	
Inventory		49,800,000

To record cost of goods sold (300,000 barrels at $166) before amortizing deferred hedging gain in other comprehensive income

Other comprehensive income	135,000	
Cost of goods sold		135,000

To amortize deferred hedging gain at rate of 45¢ per barrel sold

July 31, 20X2

Loss on hedging transaction	50,000	
Option contract		50,000

To record change in time value of option contract—charge premium to income since this represents payment for time value of money, which expires ratably over two-year term, and does not qualify for hedge accounting treatment

Other comprehensive income	2,000,000	
Option contract		2,000,000

To reflect change in intrinsic value of remaining option contracts (decline in value)

Cost of goods sold	41,500,000	
Inventory		41,500,000

To record cost of goods sold (250,000 barrels at $166) before amortizing deferred hedging gain in other comprehensive income

Other comprehensive income	112,500	
Cost of goods sold		112,500

To amortize deferred hedging gain at rate of 45¢ per barrel sold

August 31, 20X2

Loss on hedging transaction	50,000	
Option contract		50,000

To record change in time value of option contract—charge premium to income since this represents payment for time value of money, which expires ratably over two-year term, and does not qualify for hedge accounting treatment

Other comprehensive income	250,000	
Option contract		250,000

To reflect change in intrinsic value of remaining option contracts (decline in value to zero)

Cost of goods sold	66,400,000	
Inventory		66,400,000

To record cost of goods sold (400,000 barrels at $166) before amortizing deferred hedging gain in other comprehensive income

Other comprehensive income	180,000	
Cost of goods sold		180,000

To amortize deferred hedging gain at rate of 45¢ per barrel sold

September 30, 20X2

Loss on hedging transaction	50,000	
Option contract		50,000

To record change in time value of option contract—charge premium to income since this represents payment for time value of money, which expires ratably over two-year term, and does not qualify for hedge accounting treatment

Option contract	1,000,000	
Other comprehensive income		1,000,000

To reflect change in intrinsic value of remaining option contracts (increase in value)

Cost of goods sold	58,100,000	
Inventory		58,100,000

To record cost of goods sold (350,000 barrels at $166) before amortizing deferred hedging gain in other comprehensive income

Other comprehensive income	157,500	
Cost of goods sold		157,500

To amortize deferred hedging gain at rate of 45¢ per barrel sold

October 31, 20X2

Loss on hedging transaction	50,000	
Option contract		50,000

To record change in time value of option contract—charge premium to income since this represents payment for time value of money, which expires ratably over two-year term, and does not qualify for hedge accounting treatment

Option contract	250,000	
Other comprehensive income		250,000

To reflect change in intrinsic value of remaining option contracts (further increase in value)

Cost of goods sold	91,300,000	
Inventory		91,300,000

To record cost of goods sold (550,000 barrels at $166) before amortizing deferred hedging gain in other comprehensive income

Other comprehensive income	247,500	
Cost of goods sold		247,500

To amortize deferred hedging gain at rate of 45¢ per barrel sold

November 30, 20X2

Loss on hedging transaction	50,000	
Option contract		50,000

To record change in time value of option contract—charge premium to income since this represents payment for time value of money, which expires ratably over two-year term, and does not qualify for hedge accounting treatment

Option contract	250,000	
Other comprehensive income		250,000

To reflect change in intrinsic value of remaining option contracts (further increase in value)

Cost of goods sold	83,000,000	
Inventory		83,000,000

To record cost of goods sold (500,000 barrels at $166) before amortizing deferred hedging gain in other comprehensive income

Other comprehensive income	225,000	
Cost of goods sold		225,000

To amortize deferred hedging gain at rate of 45¢ per barrel sold

December 31, 20X2

Loss on hedging transaction	50,000	
Option contract		50,000

To record change in time value of option contract—charge premium to income since this represents payment for time value of money, which expires ratably over two-year term, and does not qualify for hedge accounting treatment

Option contract	250,000	
Other comprehensive income		250,000

To reflect change in intrinsic value of remaining option contracts (further increase in value) before sale of options

Cost of goods sold	107,900,000	
Inventory		107,900,000

To record cost of goods sold (650,000 barrels at $166) before amortizing deferred hedging gain in other comprehensive income

Other comprehensive income	292,500	
Cost of goods sold		292,500

To amortize deferred hedging gain at rate of 45¢ per barrel sold

Cash	2,100,000	
Loss on sale of options	50,000	
Option contract		2,150,000
Other comprehensive income	1,750,000	
Gain on sale of options		1,750,000

To record sale of remaining option contracts; the cash price was $50,000 lower than carrying value of asset sold (options having unexpired time value of $400,000 plus intrinsic value of $1,750,000), but transfer of other comprehensive income to income recognizes formerly deferred gain; since no further inventory purchases are planned in connection with this hedging activity, the unrealized gain is taken into income

Note that at December 31, 20X2, other comprehensive income has a remaining credit balance of $900,000, which represents the deferred gain pertaining to the 2 million equivalent barrels of oil in inventory. As this is sold, the other comprehensive income will be transferred to cost of goods sold as a reduction of cost of sales.

Discontinuance of a Cash Flow Hedge The accounting for a cash flow hedge should not continue if any of the events below occur:

- The criteria in ASC 815-30-25 are no longer met;
- The derivative instrument expires or is sold, terminated, or exercised; or
- The designation is removed by the entity.
  (ASC 815-30-40-1)

Note that a change in the counterparty in and of itself is not considered a termination of the derivative instrument. (ASC 815-30-40-1A)

The net gain or loss in accumulated other comprehensive income should remain there until it is properly reclassified when the hedged transaction affects earnings. If it is probable that the original forecasted transactions will not occur, the net gain or loss in accumulated other comprehensive income should immediately be reclassified into earnings. (ASC 815-30-40-2)

If the cash flow hedge is discontinued, a new hedging relationship may be designated with a different hedging instrument and/or a different hedged item, as long as the criteria established in ASC 815 are met. (ASC 815-30-40-3)

Ineffectiveness of a Cash Flow Hedge In assessing the effectiveness of a cash flow hedge, the time value of money generally will need to be considered, if significant in the circumstances. Doing so becomes especially important if the hedging instrument involves periodic cash settlements. For example, a *tailing strategy* with futures contracts is a situation in which an entity likely would reflect the time value of money. When employing such a strategy, the entity adjusts the size or contract amount of futures contracts used in a hedge so that earnings (or expense) from reinvestment (or funding) of daily settlement gains (or losses) on the futures do not distort the results of the hedge. To assess offset of expected cash flows when a tailing strategy has been used, an entity could reflect the time value of money, possibly comparing the present value of the hedged forecasted cash flow with the results of the hedging instrument.

Impairment or Credit Loss of a Cash Flow Hedge All assets or liabilities designated as cash flow hedges are subject to normal GAAP requirements for assessing impairment or credit losses. Those requirements should be applied, however, after hedge accounting has been applied for the period. Since the hedging instrument is a separate asset or liability, its expected cash flow or fair value is not considered in applying the impairment or credit criteria to the hedged item. If an impairment or credit loss or recovery on a hedged forecasting asset or liability is recognized, any offsetting amount should be immediately reclassified from accumulated other comprehensive income into earnings. (ASC 815-30-35-42 and 43)

Expanded Application of Interest Rate Hedging ASC 815 also permits the use of hedge accounting where the interest rate being hedged is the "benchmark interest rate." As used in the standard, this rate will be either the risk-free rate (i.e., that applicable to direct Treasury borrowings—UST), the LIBOR swap rate, the Fed Funds Effective Swap Rate (Overnight Index Swap Rate) and the Securities Industry and Financial Markets Association (SIFMA) Municipal Swap Rate. LIBOR-based swaps are the most commonly employed interest rate hedging vehicles. (ASC 815-20-25-6A)

With respect to the separation of interest rate risk and credit risk, the risk of changes in credit sector spread and any credit spread attributable to a specific borrower should be encompassed in credit risk rather than interest rate risk. Under such an approach, an entity would be permitted to designate the risk of changes in the risk-free rate as the hedged risk, and any spread above that rate would be deemed to reflect credit risk.

ASC 815 requires that all contractual cash flows be used in determining the changes in fair value of the hedged item when benchmark interest rates are being employed. In other words, cash flows pertaining to the portion of interest payments which is related to the entity's credit risk (the risk premium over the benchmark rate) cannot be excluded from the computation. (ASC 815-25-35-13)

The accounting for an interest rate hedge using a benchmark rate is very similar to the example below in this chapter. However, the variable rate used, rather than reflecting the credit riskiness of the party doing the hedging, would instead be the benchmark rate (e.g., the rate on Treasury five-year notes). Since changes in the benchmark rate might not exactly track the changes in the underlying instrument (due to changes in the "credit spread," which are a reflection of changes in the underlying party's perceived credit risk), the hedge will likely be imperfect, such that a net gain or loss will be reflected in periodic earnings.

Reclassifications to Earnings In the period that the hedged forecasted transaction affects earnings, amounts in accumulated other comprehensive income that are included in the assessment of effectiveness should be reclassified into earnings. (ASC 815-30-35-38) If the transaction results in an asset or liability, amounts in accumulated other comprehensive income that are included in the assessment of effectiveness should be reclassified into earnings when the asset or liability affects earnings through cost of sales, depreciation, interest expense, and the like. (ASC 815-30- 35-39) Any time that a net loss on the combined derivative instrument and the hedged transaction is expected, the amount that is not expected to be recovered should immediately be reclassified into earnings. (ASC 815-30-35-40)

Example of a "Plain Vanilla" Interest Rate Swap

On July 1, 20X1, Abbott Corp. borrows $5 million with a fixed maturity (no prepayment option) of June 30, 20X5, carrying interest at prime + 1/2%. Interest only is due semiannually. At the same date, it enters into a "plain vanilla"–type swap arrangement, calling for fixed payments at 8% and receipt of prime + 1/2%, on a notional amount of $5 million. At that date prime is 7.5%, and there is no premium due on the swap arrangement.

This swap qualifies as a cash flow hedge under ASC 815, and it is appropriate to assume no ineffectiveness, since the criteria set forth in that standard are all met.

NOTE: The criteria for using the shortcut method are in the previous section on the shortcut method for interest rate swaps.

Accordingly, as rates change over the term of the debt and of the swap arrangement, changes in the value of the swap are reflected in other comprehensive income, and the swap will appear on the statement of financial position as an asset or liability at fair value. As the maturity of the debt approaches, the value of the swap will converge on zero. Periodic interest expense in the income statement will be at the effective rate of 8%.

Assume that the prime rate over the four-year term of the loan, as of each interest payment date, is as follows, along with the fair value of the remaining term of the interest rate swap at those dates:

Date	Prime rate (%)	Fair value of swap*
December 31, 20X1	6.5	$-150,051
June 30, 20X2	6.0	−196,580
December 31, 20X2	6.5	−111,296
June 30, 20X3	7.0	- 45,374
December 31, 20X3	7.5	0
June 30, 20X4	8.0	23,576
December 31, 20X4	8.5	24,038
June 30, 20X5	8.0	0

* *Fair values are determined as the present values of future cash flows resulting from expected interest rate differentials, based on the current prime rate, discounted at 8%.*

Regarding the fair values presented in the foregoing table, it should be assumed that the fair values are precisely equal to the present value, at each valuation date (assumed to be the interest payment dates), of the differential future cash flows resulting from utilization of the swap. Future variable interest rates (prime + 1/2%) are assumed to be the same as the existing rates at each valuation date (i.e., there is no basis for any expectation of rate changes, and therefore the best estimate is that the current rate will persist over time). The discount rate, 8%, is assumed to be constant over time.

Thus, for example, the fair value of the swap at December 31, 20X1, would be the present value of an annuity of seven payments (the number of remaining semiannual interest payments due) of $25,000 each (pay 8%, receive 7%, based on then-existing prime rate of 6.5%) to be made to the swap counterparty, discounted at an annual rate of 8% (using 4% for the semiannual discounting, which is a slight simplification). This computation yields a present value of a stream of seven $25,000 payments to the swap counterparty amounting to $150,051 at December 31, 20X1, which is a liability to be reported by the entity at that date. The offset is a debit to other comprehensive income, since the hedge is (presumably) judged to be 100% effective in this case. Semiannual accounting entries will be as follows:

December 31, 20X1

Interest expense	175,000	
Accrued interest (or cash)		175,000

To accrue or pay semiannual interest on the debt at the variable rate of prime + 1/2% (7.0%)

Interest expense	25,000	
Accrued interest (or cash)		25,000

To record net settlement on swap arrangement (8.0 – 7.0%)

Other comprehensive income	150,051	
Swap contract		150,051

To record the fair value of the swap contract as of this date (a net liability because fixed rate payable to counterparty of 8% exceeds floating rate receivable from counterparty of 7%)

June 30, 20X2

Interest expense	162,500	
Accrued interest (or cash)		162,500

To accrue or pay semiannual interest on the debt at the variable rate of prime + 1/2% (6.5%)

Interest expense	37,500	
Accrued interest (or cash)		37,500

To record net settlement on swap arrangement (8.0 – 6.5%)

Other comprehensive income	46,529	
Swap contract		46,529

To record the fair value of the swap contract as of this date (increase in obligation because of further decline in prime rate)

December 31, 20X2

Interest expense	175,000	
Accrued interest (or cash)		175,000

To accrue or pay semiannual interest on the debt at the variable rate of prime + 1/2% (7.0%)

Interest expense	25,000	
Accrued interest (or cash)		25,000

To record net settlement on swap arrangement (8.0 – 7.0%)

Other comprehensive income	150,051	
Swap contract		150,051

To record the fair value of the swap contract as of this date (decrease in obligation due to increase in prime rate)

June 30, 20X3

Interest expense	187,500	
Accrued interest (or cash)		187,500

To accrue or pay semiannual interest on the debt at the variable rate of prime + 1/2% (7.5%)

Interest expense	12,500	
Accrued interest (or cash)		12,500

To record net settlement on swap arrangement (8.0 – 7.5%)

Swap contract	65,922	
Other comprehensive income		65,922

To record the fair value of the swap contract as of this date (decrease in obligation due to further increase in prime rate)

December 31, 20X3

Interest expense	200,000	
Accrued interest (or cash)		200,000

To accrue or pay semiannual interest on the debt at the variable rate of prime + 1/2% (8.0%)

Interest expense	0	
Accrued interest (or cash)		0

To record net settlement on swap arrangement (8.0 – 8.0%)

Swap contract	45,374	
Other comprehensive income		45,374

To record the fair value of the swap contract as of this date (further increase in prime rate to the original rate of inception of the hedge eliminates fair value of the derivative)

June 30, 20X4

Interest expense	212,500	
Accrued interest (or cash)		212,500

To accrue or pay semiannual interest on the debt at the variable rate of prime + 1/2% (8.5%)

Receivable from counterparty (or cash)	12,500	
Interest expense		12,500

To record net settlement on swap arrangement (8.0 – 8.5%), counterparty remits settlement

Swap contract	23,576	
Other comprehensive income		23,576

To record the fair value of the swap contract as of this date (increase in prime rate creates net asset position for derivative)

December 31, 20X4

Interest expense	225,000	
Accrued interest (or cash)		225,000

To accrue or pay semiannual interest on the debt at the variable rate of prime + 1/2% (9.0%)

Receivable from counterparty (or cash)	25,000	
Interest expense		25,000

To record net settlement on swap arrangement (8.0 – 9.0%), counterparty remits settlement

Swap contract	462	
Other comprehensive income		462

To record the fair value of the swap contract as of this date (increase in asset value due to further rise in prime rate)

June 30, 20X5 (Maturity)

Interest expense	212,500	
Accrued interest (or cash)		212,500

To accrue or pay semiannual interest on the debt at the variable rate of prime + 1/2% (8.5%)

Receivable from counterparty (or cash)	12,500	
Interest expense		12,500
Other comprehensive income	24,038	
Swap contract		24,038

To record the fair value of the swap contract as of this date (value declines to zero as expiration date approaches)

Example of an Option on an Interest Rate Swap

The facts of this example are a variation on the previous example. Abbott Corp. anticipates as of June 30, 20X1, that as of June 30, 20X3, it will become a borrower of $5 million with a fixed maturity four years hence (June 30, 20X7). Based on its current credit rating, it expects to be able to borrow at prime + 1/2%. As of June 30, 20X1, it is able to purchase, for a single payment of $25,000, a "swaption" (an option on an interest rate swap), calling for fixed pay at 8% and variable receipt at prime + 1/2%, on a notional amount of $5 million, for a term of four years. The option will expire in two years. At June 30, 20X1, prime is 7.5%.

NOTE: The interest rate behavior in this example differs somewhat from the prior example, to better illustrate the "one-sidedness" of options, versus the obligation under a swap arrangement or other futures and forwards.

It will be assumed that the time value of the swaption expires ratably over the two years.

This swaption qualifies as a cash flow hedge under ASC 815. However, while the change in fair value of the contract is an effective hedge of the cash flow variability of the prospective debt issuance, the premium paid is a reflection of the time value of money and is thus to be expensed ratably over the period that the swaption is outstanding.

The table below gives the prime rate at semiannual intervals including the two-year period prior to the debt issuance, plus the four years during which the forecasted debt (and the swap, if the option is exercised) will be outstanding, as well as the fair value of the swaption (and later, the swap itself) at these points in time.

Date	Prime rate (%)	Fair value of swaption/swap*
December 31, 20X1	7.5	$0
June 30, 20X2	8.0	77,925
December 31, 20X2	6.5	0
June 30, 20X3	7.0	–84,159
December 31, 20X3	7.5	0
June 30, 20X4	8.0	65,527
December 31, 20X4	8.5	111,296
June 30, 20X5	8.0	45,374
December 31, 20X5	8.0	34,689
June 30, 20X6	7.5	0
December 31, 20X6	7.5	0
June 30, 20X7	7.0	0

* *Fair value is determined as the present value of future expected interest rate differentials, based on the current prime rate, discounted at 8%. An "out of the money" swaption is valued at zero, since the option does not have to be exercised. Since the option is exercised on June 30, 2014, the value at that date is recorded, although negative.*

The value of the swaption contract is only recorded (unless and until exercised, of course, at which point it becomes a contractually binding swap) if it is positive, since if "out of the money" the holder would forego exercise in most instances and thus there is no liability by the holder to be reported. (This example is an illustration of the opposite, however, as despite having a negative value, the option holder determines that exercise is advisable.) At June 30, 20X2, for example, the swaption is an asset, since the reference variable rate (prime + 1/2% or 8.5%) is greater than the fixed swap rate of 8%, and thus the expectation is that the option will be exercised at expiration. This would, if present rates hold steady, which is the naïve assumption, result in a series of eight semiannual payments from the swap counterparty in the amount of $12,500.

Discounting this at a nominal 8%, the present value as of the debt origination date (to be June 30, 20X3) would be $84,159, which, when further discounted to June 30, 20X2, yields a fair value of $77,925.

Note that the following period (December 31, 20X2) prime drops to such an extent that the value of the swaption evaporates entirely (actually goes negative, which will not be reported since the holder is under no obligation to exercise it), and the carrying value is therefore eliminated. At expiration, the holder does (for this example) exercise, notwithstanding a negative fair value, and from that point forward the fair value of the swap will be reported, whether positive (an asset) or negative (a liability).

As noted above, assume that, at the option expiration date, despite the fact that prime + 1/2% is below the fixed pay rate on the swap, the management of Abbott Corp. is convinced that rates will climb over the four-year term of the loan, and thus exercises the swaption at that date. Accounting journal entries over the six years are as follows:

June 30, 20X1

Swaption contract	25,000	
Cash		25,000

To record purchase premium on swaption contract

December 31, 20X1

Loss on hedging transaction	6,250	
Swaption contract		6,250

To record change in time value of swaption contract—charge premium to income since this represents payment for time value of money, which expires ratably over two-year term

June 30, 20X2

Swaption contract	77,925	
Other comprehensive income		77,925

To record the fair value of the swaption contract as of this date

Loss on hedging transaction	6,250	
Swaption contract		6,250

To record change in time value of swaption contract—charge premium to income since this represents payment for time value of money, which expires ratably over two-year term

December 31, 20X2

Other comprehensive income	77,925	
Swaption contract		77,925

To record the change in fair value of the swaption contract as of this date; since contract is "out of the money," it is not written down below zero (i.e., a net liability is not reported)

Loss on hedging transaction	6,250	
Swaption contract		6,250

To record change in time value of swaption contract—charge premium to income since this represents payment for time value of money, which expires ratably over two-year term

June 30, 20X3

Other comprehensive	84,159	
Swap contract		84,159

To record the fair value of the swap contract as of this date—a net liability is reported since swap option was exercised

Loss on hedging transaction	6,250	
Swaption contract		6,250

To record change in time value of swaption contract—charge premium to income since this represents payment for time value of money, which expires ratably over two-year term

December 31, 20X3

Interest expense	200,000	
Accrued interest (or cash)		200,000

To accrue or pay interest on the debt at the variable rate of prime + 1/2% (8.0%)

Interest expense	0	
Accrued interest (or cash)		0

To record net settlement on swap arrangement (8.0 – 8.0%)

Swap contract	84,159	
Other comprehensive income		84,159

To record the change in the fair value of the swap contract as of this date

June 30, 20X4

Interest expense	212,500	
Accrued interest (or cash)		212,500

To accrue or pay interest on the debt at the variable rate of prime + 1/2% (8.5%)

Receivable from counterparty (or cash)	12,500	
Interest expense		12,500

To record net settlement on swap arrangement (8.0 – 8.5%)

Swap contract	65,527	
Other comprehensive income		65,527

To record the fair value of the swap contract as of this date

December 31, 20X4

Interest expense	225,000	
Accrued interest (or cash)		225,000

To accrue or pay interest on the debt at the variable rate of prime + 1/2% (9.0%)

Receivable from counterparty (or cash)	25,000	
Interest expense		25,000

To record net settlement on swap arrangement (8.0 – 9.0%)

Swap contract	45,769	
Other comprehensive income		45,769

To record the fair value of the swap contract as of this date

June 30, 20X5

Interest expense	212,500	
Accrued interest (or cash)		212,500

To accrue or pay interest on the debt at the variable rate of prime + 1/2% (8.5%)

Receivable from counterparty (or cash)	12,500	
Interest expense		12,500

To record net settlement on swap arrangement (8.0 – 8.5%)

Other comprehensive income	65,922	
Swap contract		65,922

To record the change in fair value of the swap contract as of this date (declining prime rate causes swap to lose value)

December 31, 20X5

Interest expense	212,500	
Accrued interest (or cash)		212,500

To accrue or pay interest on the debt at the variable rate of prime + 1/2% (8.5%)

Receivable from counterparty (or cash)	12,500	
Interest expense		12,500

To record net settlement on swap arrangement (8.0 – 8.5%)

Other comprehensive income	10,685	
Swap contract		10,685

To record the fair value of the swap contract as of this date (decline is due to passage of time, as the prime rate expectations have not changed from the earlier period)

June 30, 20X6

Interest expense	200,000	
Accrued interest (or cash)		200,000

To accrue or pay interest on the debt at the variable rate of prime + 1/2% (8.0%)

Receivable from counterparty (or cash)	0	
Interest expense		0

To record net settlement on swap arrangement (8.0 – 8.0%)

Other comprehensive income	34,689	
Swap contract		34,689

To record the decline in the fair value of the swap contract to zero as of this date

December 31, 20X6

Interest expense	200,000	
Accrued interest (or cash)		200,000

To accrue or pay interest on the debt at the variable rate of prime + 1/2% (8.0%)

Receivable from counterparty (or cash)	0	
Interest expense		0

To record net settlement on swap arrangement (8.0 – 8.0%)

Swap contract	0	
Other comprehensive income		0

No change to the zero fair value of the swap contract as of this date

June 30, 20X7 (Maturity)

Interest expense	187,500	
Accrued interest (or cash)		187,500

To accrue or pay interest on the debt at the variable rate of prime + 1/2% (7.5%)

Interest expense	12,500	
Accrued interest (or cash)		12,500

To record net settlement on swap arrangement (8.0 – 7.5%)

Other comprehensive income	0	
Swap contract		0

No change to the zero fair value of the swap contract, which expires as of this date

Foreign Currency Hedges

Unlike ASC 830, ASC 815 allows hedges of forecasted foreign currency transactions, including some intercompany transactions. Hedging foreign currency intercompany cash flows with foreign currency options is a common practice. ASC 815 allows entities to use other derivative instruments (forward contracts, etc.), on the grounds that the accounting for all derivative instruments should be the same.

Designated hedging instruments and hedged items qualify for fair value hedge accounting or cash flow hedge accounting only if all of the criteria in ASC 815 for fair value hedge accounting and cash flow hedge accounting are met. Fair value hedges may be used for all recognized foreign currency-denominated asset or liability hedging situations, and cash flow hedges may be used for recognized foreign currency-denominated asset or liability hedging situations in which all of the variability in the functional currency-equivalent cash flows is eliminated by the effect of the hedge. (ASC 815-20-25-15) Remeasurement of the foreign currency-denominated assets and liabilities is based on the guidance in ASC 830-20-35-1, which requires remeasurement based on spot exchange rates, regardless of whether a fair value hedging relationship or a cash flow hedging relationship exists.

Hedged Items and Transactions Involving Foreign Exchange Risk

ASC 815 provides complex hedging rules that permit the reporting entity to elect to obtain special accounting treatment relative to foreign currency risks with respect to the following items:

- Recognized foreign-currency-denominated assets or liabilities
- A forecasted functional-currency-equivalent cash flow associated with a recognized asset or liability
- Unrecognized firm commitments
- Foreign-currency-denominated forecasted transaction
- Net investment in a foreign operation.
  (ASC 815-25-25-26)

Measuring Hedge Effectiveness Periodically, each hedge must be evaluated for effectiveness, using the preestablished criteria, and the gains or losses associated with hedge ineffectiveness must be reported currently in earnings and not deferred to future periods. In the instance of foreign currency hedges, ASC 815 states that reporting entities must exclude from their assessments of hedge effectiveness the portions of the fair value of forward contracts attributable to spot-forward differences (i.e., differences between the spot exchange rate and the forward exchange rate).

In practice, this means that reporting entities engaging in foreign currency hedging will recognize changes in the below-described portion of the derivative's fair value in earnings, in the same manner that changes representing hedge ineffectiveness are reported, but these are not considered to represent ineffectiveness. These entities must estimate the cash flows on forecasted transactions based on the current spot exchange rate, appropriately discounted for time value. Effectiveness is then assessed by comparing the changes in fair values of the forward contracts attributable to changes in the dollar spot price of the pertinent foreign currency to the changes in the present values of the forecasted cash flows based on the current spot exchange rate(s).

Example of Hedge Effectiveness Measurement

On October 1, 20X2, Braveheart Co. (a U.S. entity) orders from its European supplier, Gemutlichkeit GmbH, a machine that is to be delivered and paid for on March 31, 20X3. The price, denominated in euros, is €4,000,000. Although Braveheart will not make the payment until the planned delivery date, it has immediately entered into a firm commitment to make this purchase and to pay €4,000,000 upon delivery. This creates a euro liability exposure to foreign exchange risk; thus, if the euro appreciates over the intervening six months, the dollar cost of the equipment will increase.

To reduce or eliminate this uncertainty, Braveheart desires to lock in the purchase cost in euros by entering into a six-month forward contract to purchase euros on the date when the purchase order is issued to and accepted by Gemutlichkeit. The spot rate on October 1, 20X2, is $1.40 per euro and the forward rate for March 31, 20X3, settlement is $1.44 per euro. Braveheart enters into a forward contract on October 1, 20X2, with the First Intergalactic Bank to pay U.S. $5,760,000 in exchange for the receipt of €4,000,000 on March 31, 20X3, which can then be used to pay Gemutlichkeit. No premium is received or paid at the inception of this forward contract.

Hedging Foreign Currency Exposures

Hedges of foreign currency (FC) exposures (where FC is not the reporting entity's currency) functional

	A	B	C
Types of items that may qualify to be hedged	*Fair value hedges* A1. Recognized assets or liabilities A2. Available-for-sale debt securities A3. Available-for-sale equity securities A4. UFC	*Cash flow hedges* B1. Forecasted cash flow from recognized assets or liabilities B2. Forecasted external transactions B3. Forecasted intercompany transactions B4. UFC	C. Hedges of a net investment in a foreign operation
Risk being hedged	Changes in fair value of the hedged item that result from changes in the exchange rate (ER) of the FC in which it is denominated (which, by definition, is not the functional currency of the reporting entity)	The FC exposure to variability in the "equivalent functional currency cash flows" associated with the hedged item	Exposure of the net investment to changes in the exchange rate applicable to the functional currency of the investee
Type of instruments that qualify for use as hedging instruments	A1, A2, A3—Required to be derivatives A$ can be a derivative instrument or nonderivative financial instrument	Required to be derivatives	Can be a derivative instrument or a nonderivative financial instrument; nonderivative financial instruments, to be designated, cannot be subject to GAAP that requires that they be presented at FV since that accounting treatment would not result in foreign currency transaction gains or losses under ASC 830
Summary of accounting treatment	General Rule: When the ER changes, recognize in current earnings: (1) changes in fair value of hedged item caused by the hedged risk, (2) gain or loss on changes in fair value of the designated hedging instrument, and (3) hedge ineffectiveness, if any AFS securities: Change in fair value of the security attributable to FC risk is reported in earnings; other changes in fair value of the security, not attributable to the hedged risk, continue to be reported in other comprehensive income	General Rule: The gain or loss on a derivative designated as a cash flow hedge is reported currently in earnings. In the period or periods during which a hedged forecasted transaction affects earnings, amounts in AOCI are reclassified to earnings Additional complex accounting provisions are provided by ASC 815-30	To the extent of hedge effectiveness, gains or losses on the hedging derivative instrument (or FC transaction gains or losses on the hedging nonderivative instrument) are accounted for in the same manner as an FC translation adjustment (i.e., reported as other comprehensive income and as a change in accumulated other comprehensive income). The hedged net investment is accounted for consistent with ASC 830 as described in this chapter; any hedge ineffectiveness is reflected as a transaction gain or loss in earnings of the period in which it arises

Applicable conditions, criteria limitations, or exceptions	**Fair value hedges** a. Fair value hedges are required to meet the requirements of ASC 815-20 with respect to such matters as timely hedge designation, tests of hedge effectiveness at inception and on an ongoing basis. b. A3—(i) The AFS equity security cannot be traded on an exchange or market where transactions are denominated in the investor's functional currency, and (ii) dividends and all other cash flows associated with holding or selling the security must be denominated in the same foreign currency. c. A2, A4—The hedged transaction must be denominated in an FC other than the hedging unit's functional currency, and if consolidated financial statements, the party to the hedging instrument must be either (i) the operating unit with the FC exposure or (ii) another member of the consolidated group (subject to certain specified restrictions and meeting certain conditions) with the same functional currency as that operating unit. d. FC derivatives entered into with another member of the consolidated group can be designated as hedging instruments in all fair value hedge transaction types (A1–A4) only if that member has entered into an offsetting contract with an unrelated third party to hedge the exposure it acquired from issuing the derivative instrument to the affiliate that initiated the hedge. **Cash flow hedges and hedges of net investments in foreign operations** e. Cash flow hedges must meet the requirements of ASC 815-20 f. Cash flow hedges of forecasted transactions must additionally meet the requirements of ASC 815-20-25 g. Cash flow hedges of forecasted transactions (B1) and hedges of net investments in foreign operations (C) must also meet the criteria in item d of this list.		
Eligibility for ASC 825-10-25 Fair Value Option (FVO)	A4—Limited eligibility when the UFC involves only financial instruments	Not eligible	Not eligible

The transaction is a firm commitment consistent with the requirements of ASC 815, and fair value hedge accounting is used in accounting for the forward contract.

Assume the relevant time value of money is measured at 1/2% per month (a nominal 6% annual rate). The spot rate for euros at December 31, 20X2, is $1.45, and at March 31, 20X3, it is $1.48. The forward rate as of December 31 for March 31 settlement is $1.46.

Entries to reflect the foregoing scenario are as follows:

10/1/X2	*No entries, since neither the forward contract nor the firm commitment have value on this date*		
12/31/X2	Forward currency contract	78,818	
	Gain on forward contract		78,818

To record present value (at 1/2% monthly rate) of change in value of forward contract [= change in forward rate (1.46 - 1.44) × €4,000,000 = $80,000 to be received in three months, discounted at 6% per annum]

	Loss on firm purchase commitment	197,044	
	Firm commitment obligation		197,044

To record present value (at 1/2% monthly rate) of change in amount of firm commitment [= change in spot rate (1.45 - 1.40) × €4,000,000 = $200,000 to be paid in three months, discounted at 6% per annum]

	Gain on forward contract	78,818	
	Loss on firm purchase commitment		197,044 a
	P&L summary (then to retained earnings)	118,226	

To close the gain and loss accounts to net income and thus to retained earnings

3/31/X3	Forward currency contract	81,182	
	Gain on forward contract		81,182

To record change in value of forward contract {[= (1.48 - 1.44) × €4,000,000 = $160,000] – gain previously recognized ($78,818)}

	Loss on firm commitment	122,956	
	Firm commitment obligation		122,956

To record change in amount of firm commitment {[= (1.48 - 1.40) × €4,000,000] less loss previously recognized ($197,044)}

3/31/X3	Firm commitment obligation	320,000	
	Machinery and equipment	5,600,000	
	Cash		5,920,000

To record purchase of machinery based on spot exchange rate as of date of contractual commitment (1.40) and close out the firm commitment obligation (representing effect of change in spot rate during commitment period)

	Cash	160,000	
	Forward contract		160,000

To record collection of cash on net settlement of forward contract [= (1.48 - 1.44) × €4,000,000]

	Gain on forward contract	81,182	
	P&L summary (then to retained earnings)	41,774	
	Loss on firm purchase commitment		122,956

To close the gain and loss accounts to net income and thus to retained earnings

Observe that in the foregoing example the gain on the forward contract did not precisely offset the loss incurred from the firm commitment. Since a hedge of an unrecognized foreign currency denominated firm commitment is accounted for as a fair value hedge (ASC 815-25- 25-37), with gains and losses on hedging positions and on the hedged item both being recorded in current earnings, it may appear that the matter of hedge effectiveness is of academic interest only. However, according to ASC 815, even if both components (that is, the net gain or loss representing hedge ineffectiveness, and the amount charged to earnings that was excluded from the measurement of ineffectiveness) are reported in current period earnings, the distinction between them is still of importance.

With respect to fair value hedges of firm purchase commitments denominated in a foreign currency, ASC 815 directs that "the change in value of the contract related to the changes in the differences between the spot price and the forward or futures price would be excluded from the assessment of hedge effectiveness." As applied to the foregoing example, therefore, the net credit to income in 20X2 ($118,226) can be further analyzed into two constituent elements: the amount arising from the change in the difference between the spot price and the forward price, and the amount resulting from hedge ineffectiveness.

The former item, not attributed to ineffectiveness, arose because the spread between spot and forward price at hedge inception, (1.44 – 1.40 =) .04, fell to (1.46 – 1.45 =) .01 by December 31, for an impact amounting to (.04 – .01 =) .03 × €4,000,000 = $120,000, which, reduced to present value terms, equaled $118,227. The net credit to earnings in December 2012, ($78,818 + 118,226 =) $197,044, relates to the spread between the spot and forward rates on December 31 and is identifiable with hedge ineffectiveness.

Forward Exchange Contracts

Foreign currency transaction gains and losses on assets and liabilities that are denominated in a currency other than the functional currency can be hedged if a U.S. entity enters into a forward exchange contract. The following example shows how a forward exchange contract can be used as a hedge, first against a firm commitment and then, following delivery date, as a hedge against a recognized liability.

A general rule for estimating the fair value of forward exchange rates under ASC 815 is to use the changes in the forward exchange rates, and discount those estimated future cash flows to a present-value basis. An entity will need to consider the time value of money if significant in the circumstances for these contracts. The following example does not apply discounting of the future cash flows from the forward contracts in order to focus on the relationships between the forward contract and the foreign currency denominated payable.

Example of a Forward Exchange Contract

Durango, Inc. enters into a firm commitment with Dempsey Ing., Inc. of Germany, on October 1, 20X2, to purchase a computerized robotic system for €6,000,000. The system will be delivered on March 1, 20X3, with payment due sixty days after delivery (April 30, 20X3). Durango, Inc. decides to hedge this foreign currency firm commitment and enters into a forward exchange contract on the firm commitment date to receive €6,000,000 on the payment date. The applicable exchange rates are shown in the table below.

Date	Spot rates	Forward rates for April 30, 20X3
October 1, 20X2	€1 = $1.55	€1 = $1.57
December 31, 20X2	€1 = $1.58	€1 = $1.589
March 1, 20X3	€1 = $1.58	€1 = $1.585
April 30, 20X3	€1 = $1.60	

The example on the following pages separately presents both the forward contract receivable and the dollars payable liability in order to show all aspects of the forward contract. For financial reporting purposes, most companies present just the net fair value of the forward contract that would be the difference between the current value of the forward contract receivable and the dollars payable liability. Note that the foreign currency hedges in the illustration are not perfectly effective. However, for this example, the degree of ineffectiveness is not deemed to be sufficient to trigger income statement recognition per ASC 815.

The transactions that reflect the forward exchange contract, the firm commitment and the acquisition of the asset, and retirement of the related liability appear at the end of this section. The net fair value of the forward contract is shown below each set of entries for the forward exchange contract.

In the case of using a forward exchange contract to speculate in a specific foreign currency, the general rule to estimate the fair value of the forward contract is to use the forward exchange rate for the remainder of the term of the forward contract.

Foreign Currency Net Investment Hedge Either a derivative instrument or a nonderivative financial instrument (which can result in a foreign currency transaction gain or loss under ASC 830) can be designated as a hedge of a foreign currency exposure of a net investment in a foreign operation. The gain or loss from the designated instrument to the extent that it is effective is reported as a translation adjustment. The hedged net investment is accounted for under ASC 830.

Example of a Foreign Currency Net Investment Hedge

Auburn Corporation has invested $15 million in a subsidiary in Germany, for which the euro is the functional currency. The initial exchange rate is €1.2:$1, so the initial investment is worth €18,000,000. Auburn issues a debt instrument for €12 million and designates it as a hedge of the German investment. Auburn's strategy is that any change in the fair value of the loan attributable to foreign exchange risk should offset any translation gain or loss on 2/3 of Auburn's German investment. At the end of the year, the exchange rate changes to €0.8:$1. Auburn uses the following calculation to determine the translation gain on its net investment:

$$€18{,}000{,}000 / \$0.8 = \$22{,}500{,}000 \text{ less } €18{,}000{,}000 / \$1.2 = \$15{,}000{,}000 = \$7{,}500{,}000$$

Auburn uses the following calculation to determine the translation loss on its euro-denominated debt:

$$€12{,}000{,}000 / \$0.8 = \$15{,}000{,}000 \text{ less } €12{,}000{,}000 / \$1.2 = \$10{,}000{,}000 = \$5{,}000{,}000$$

Auburn creates the following entries to record changes in the value of the translation gain on its investment and translation loss in its debt, respectively:

Investment in subsidiary	7,500,000	
Cumulative translation adjustment (equity)		7,500,000
Cumulative translation adjustment (equity)	5,000,000	
Euro-denominated debt		5,000,000

The net effect of these translation adjustments is a net increase in Auburn's investment of $2,500,000. In the following year, the exchange rates do not change, and Auburn sells its subsidiary for $17.5 million. Auburn's tax rate is 30%. Its reported annual gains and losses follow:

Forward contract entries			*Hedge against firm commitment entries*		
(1) 10/1/X2 (forward rate for 4/30/X3 €1 = $1.57)					
Forward contract receivable	9,420,000				
Dollars payable		9,420,000			

This entry recognizes the existence of the forward exchange contract using the gross method. Under the net method, this entry would not appear at all, since the fair value of the forward contract is zero when the contract is initiated. The amount is calculated using the 10/1/X2 forward rate for 4/30/X3 (€6,000,000 × $1.57 = $9,420,000).

Net fair value of the forward contract = $0

Note that the net fair value of the forward exchange contact on 10/1/X2 is zero because there is an exact amount offset of the forward contract receivable of $9,420,000 with the dollars payable liability of $9,420,000. Many companies present only the net fair value of the forward contract on their balance sheets, and, therefore, they would have no net amount reported for the forward contract at its inception.

(2) 12/31/X2 (forward rate for 4/30/X3 €1= $1.589)			(3) 12/31/X2		
Forward contract receivable	114,000		Loss on hedge activity	114,000	
Gain on hedge activity		114,000	Firm commitment		114,000

The dollar values for this entry reflect, among other things, the change in the forward rate from 10/1/X2 to 12/31/X2. However, the actual amount recorded as gain or loss (gain in this case) is determined by all market factors.

Net increase in fair value of the forward contract = (1.589 – 1.57 = .019 × €6,000,000 = $114,000)

The increase in the net fair value of the forward exchange contract on 12/31/X0 is $114,000 for the difference between the $7,134,000 ($7,020,000 plus $114,000) in the forward contract receivable and the $7,020,000 for the dollars payable liability. Many companies present only the net fair value on their balance sheet, in this case as an asset. And this $114,000 is the amount that would be discounted to present value, if interest is significant, to recognize the time value of the future cash flow from the forward contract.

The dollar values for this entry are identical to those in entry (2), reflecting the fact that the hedge is highly effective (100%) and also the fact that the market recognizes the same factors in this transaction as for entry (2). This entry reflects the first use of the firm commitment account, a temporary liability account pending the receipt of the asset against which the firm commitment has been hedged.

(4) 3/1/X3 (forward rate for 4/30/X3 €1 = $1.585)			(5) 3/1/X3		
Loss on hedge activity	24,000		Firm commitment	24,000	
Forward contract receivable		24,000	Gain on hedge activity		24,000

These entries again will be driven by market factors, and they are calculated the same way as entries (2) and (3) above. Note that the decline in the forward rate from 12/31/X1 to 3/1/X2 resulted in a loss against the forward contract receivable and a gain against the firm commitment [1.585 – 1.589 = (.004) × €6,000,000 = ($24,000)].

Net fair value of the forward contract = $90,000

The net fair value of the forward exchange contract on 3/1/X1 is $90,000 for the difference between the $9,510,000 ($9,420,000 plus $114,000 minus $24,000) in the forward contract receivable and the $9,420,000 for the dollars payable liability. Another way of computing the net fair value is to determine the change in the forward contract rate from the initial date of the contract, 10/1/X2, which is $1.585 – $1.57 = $.015 × €6,000,000 = $90,000. Also note that the amount in the firm commitment temporary liability account is equal to the net fair value of the forward contract on the date the equipment is received.

(7) 4/30/X3 (spot rate €1 = $1.60)

Forward contract receivable	90,000	
Gain on forward contract		90,000

The gain or loss (gain in this case) on the forward contract is calculated using the change in the forward to the spot rate from 3/1/X3 to 4/30/X3 [€6,000,000 × ($1.60 – $1.585) = $90,000].

Net fair value of the forward contract= $180,000

The net fair value of the forward exchange contract on 4/30/X2 is $180,000 for the difference between the $9,600,000 ($9,510,000 plus $90,000) in the forward contract receivable and the $9,420,000 for the dollars payable liability. The net fair value of the forward contract at its terminal date of 4/30/X3 is based on the difference between the contract forward rate of €1 = $1.57 and the spot rate on 4/30/X3 of €1 = $1.60. The forward contract receivable has reached its maturity and the contract is completed on this date at the forward rate of €1 = $1.57 as contracted on 10/1/X2. If the entity recognizes an interest factor in the forward contract over the life of the contract, then interest is recognized at this time on the forward contract, but no separate accrual of interest is required for the accounts payable in euros.

(9) 4/30/X3

Dollars payable	9,420,000	
Cash		9,420,000
Foreign currency units (€)	9,600,000	
Forward contract receivable		9,600,000

This entry reflects the settlement of the forward contract at the 10/1/X2 contracted forward rate (€6,000,000 × $1.17 = $7,020,000) and the receipt of foreign currency units valued at the spot rate (€6,000,000 × $1.20 = $7,200,000).

(6) 3/1/X3 (spot rate €1 = $1.58)

Equipment	9,390,000	
Firm commitment	90,000	
Accounts payable (€)		9,480,000

This entry records the receipt of the equipment, the elimination of the temporary liability account (firm commitment), and the recognition of the payable, calculated using the spot rate on the date of receipt (€6,000,000 × $1.58 = $9,480,000).

(8) 4/30/X3

Transaction loss	120,000	
Accounts payable (€)		120,000

The transaction loss related to the accounts payable re flects only the change in the spot rates and ignores the accrual of interest [€6,000,000 × ($1.60 – $1.58) = $120,000].

(10) 4/30/X3

Accounts payable (€)	9,600,000	
Foreign currency units (€)		9,600,000

This entry reflects the use of the foreign currency units to retire the account payable.

	Year 1	Year 2
Net income:		
Gain on sale of investment in ABC Company		$2,500,000
Income tax expense		(750,000)
Net gain realized in net income		1,750,000
Other comprehensive income:		
Foreign currency translation adjustment, net of tax	$1,750,000	
Reclassification adjustment, net of tax		$(1,750,000)
Other comprehensive income net gain/(loss)	$1,750,000	(1,750,000)

Foreign Currency Unrecognized Firm Commitment Hedge Either a derivative instrument or a nonderivative financial instrument (which can result in a foreign currency transaction gain or loss under ASC 830) can be designated as a fair value hedge of an unrecognized firm commitment (or a specific portion) attributable to foreign currency. If the criteria are met, this hedging relationship is accounted for as a fair value hedge. (ASC 815-20-25-58)

Foreign Currency Available-for-Sale Security Hedge Only a derivative instrument can be designated as a fair value hedge of an available-for-sale debt security (or a specific portion) attributable to foreign currency. If the criteria are met, this hedging relationship is accounted for as a fair value hedge. (ASC 815-20-25-28)

If the available-for-sale equity security qualifies as a foreign currency hedge, the change in fair value from foreign exchange risk is reported in earnings and not in other comprehensive income.

Any gain or loss on a designated nonderivative hedging instrument from foreign currency risk is determined under ASC 830 (as the increase or decrease in functional currency cash flows produced by the change in spot exchange rates) and is reported in earnings along with the change in the carrying amount of the hedged firm commitment.

Foreign Currency-Denominated Forecasted Transaction Only a derivative instrument can be designated as a cash flow hedge of a foreign currency-denominated forecasted transaction. The parties to this transaction can either be external or intercompany. To qualify for hedge accounting, all of the following criteria must be met:

- For consolidated financial statements either:
  - An operating unit with foreign currency exposure is a party to the derivative instrument or
  - Another member of the consolidated group that has the same functional currency as that operating unit is a party to the hedging instrument and there is no intervening subsidiary with a different functional currency.
- The transaction is denominated in a currency that is not the functional currency. (ASC 815-20-25-30)
  - All of the criteria for a cash flow hedge are met (with the possible exception of allowing a qualifying intercompany transaction); and
  - If a group of individual transactions is involved, both an inflow and an outflow of foreign currency cannot be included in the same group.
  (ASC 815-20-25-39)

If the foregoing criteria are met, this hedging relationship is accounted for as a cash flow hedge.

Using Certain Intercompany Derivatives as Hedging Instruments in Cash Flow Hedges of Foreign Currency Risk in the Consolidated Financial Statements ASC 815 permits the use of intercompany derivatives as the hedging instruments in cash flow hedges of foreign currency risk in the consolidated financial statements, if those intercompany derivatives are offset by unrelated third-party contracts on a net basis. The Codification defines an "internal derivative" as a foreign currency derivative contract that has been entered into with another member of a consolidated group and that can be a hedging instrument in a foreign currency cash flow hedge of a forecasted borrowing, purchase, or sale or an unrecognized firm commitment in the consolidated financial statements only if the following two conditions are satisfied.

- First, from the perspective of the member of the consolidated group using the derivative as a hedging instrument, specific criteria for foreign currency cash flow hedge accounting are satisfied.
- Second, the members of the consolidated group who are not using the derivative as a hedging instrument must either:
  - Enter into a derivative contract with an unrelated third party to offset the exposure that results from that internal derivative, or
  - If certain defined conditions are met, enter into derivative contracts with unrelated third parties that would offset, on a net basis for each foreign currency, the foreign exchange risk arising from multiple internal derivative contracts.

  (ASC 815-20-25-61)

Other Guidance on Accounting for Financial Instruments ASC 932-330-55 is directed at the accounting for derivative contracts held for trading purposes and contracts involved in energy trading and risk management activities. It concluded that energy contracts should not be marked to fair value. It determined, as well, that the common practice of carrying energy physical inventories at fair value had no basis under GAAP. Furthermore, net presentation of gains and losses derived from derivatives is required under ASC 815, even if physical settlement occurs, if the derivatives are held for trading purposes (as that term is defined in ASC 320). It was also decided that a derivative held for trading purposes may be designated as a hedging instrument, if the ASC 815 criteria are all met, on a prospective basis (i.e., from date of the consensus), notwithstanding the ASC 815 prohibition on designation of derivative instruments held for trading as "hedges."

Organizations That Do Not Report Earnings

Not-for-profits or other organizations not reporting earnings recognize gains or losses on nonhedging derivative instruments and hedging instruments as a change in net assets. Changes in the carrying amount of the hedged items are also recognized as a change in net assets.

Organizations that do not report earnings cannot use cash flow hedges. (ASC 815-30-15-2) If the hedging instrument is a foreign currency net investment hedge, it is accounted for in the same manner as described above.

ASC 815-40, *Contracts in Entity's Own Equity*

Accounting for Contracts Held or Issued by the Reporting Entity That Are Indexed to Its Own Stock ASC 815-10-15 provides that the reporting entity is not to consider contracts issued or held by that reporting entity that are both:

- Indexed to its own stock, and
- Classified in stockholders' equity in its statement of financial position to be derivative instruments for purposes of ASC 815.

  (ASC 815-10-15-74)

The first part of this particular exemption (i.e., indexed to the entity's own stock) applies to any freestanding financial instrument or embedded feature that has all the characteristics of a derivative in ASC 815-10-15, for purposes of determining whether that instrument or embedded feature qualifies for the first part of the scope exception in ASC 815-10-15-74. It also applies to any freestanding financial instrument that is potentially settled in an entity's own stock, regardless of whether the instrument has all the characteristics of a derivative in ASC 815-10-15, for purposes of determining whether the instrument is within the scope of ASC 815-40.

An evaluation be made of whether an equity-linked financial instrument (or embedded feature), using the following two-step approach:

1. Evaluate the instrument's contingent exercise provisions, if any;
2. Evaluate the instrument's settlement provisions.
(ASC 815-40-15-7)

An exercise contingency would not preclude an instrument (or embedded feature) from being considered indexed to an entity's own stock provided that it is not based on

- An observable market, other than the market for the issuer's stock (if applicable), or
- An observable index, other than an index calculated or measured solely by reference to the issuer's own operations (e.g., sales revenue of the issuer, EBITDA of the issuer, net income of the issuer, or total equity of the issuer).
(ASC 815-40-15-7A)

If the evaluation of Step 1 does not preclude an instrument from being considered indexed to the entity's own stock, the analysis would proceed to Step 2. An *exercise contingency* is a provision that entitles the entity, or counterparty, to exercise an equity-linked financial instrument (or embedded feature) based on changes in an underlying, including the occurrence (or nonoccurrence) of a specified event. Provisions that accelerate the timing of the entity's, or counterparty's, ability to exercise an instrument, and provisions that extend the length of time that an instrument is exercisable, are examples of exercise contingencies.

An instrument (or embedded feature) would be considered indexed to an entity's own stock if its settlement amount will equal the difference between the fair value of a fixed number of the entity's shares and a fixed monetary amount or a fixed amount of a debt instrument issued by the entity. (ASC 815-40-15-7C)

An equity-linked financial instrument (or embedded feature) would not be considered indexed to the entity's own stock if the strike price is denominated in a currency other than the issuer's functional currency (including a conversion option embedded in a convertible debt instrument that is denominated in a currency other than the issuer's functional currency). (ASC 815-40-15-7I)

Freestanding financial instruments (and embedded features) for which the payoff to the counterparty is based, in whole or in part, on the stock of a consolidated subsidiary are not precluded from being considered indexed to the entity's own stock in the consolidated financial statements of the parent if the subsidiary is a substantive entity. (ASC 815-40-15-5C)

A number of examples of the application of this guidance are provided in the topic. For example, warrants that become exercisable upon an initial public offering (IPO), at a fixed price, would meet the criteria for being deemed indexed to the entity's stock, measured by the difference between fair value and the fixed exercise price. On the other hand, if conditioned on the change in some external index (such as the Dow Industrials) over some defined period, the warrants would not be deemed linked to the entity's stock.

Guidance in ASC 815-40 is summarized as follows:

- *Recognition.* Initial statement of financial position classification is to be guided by the principle that contracts that require net cash settlements are assets or liabilities, and those that require settlement in shares are equity instruments. (ASC 815-40-25-1) If the reporting entity has the choice of settlement modes, settlement in shares is to be assumed; if the counterparty has the option, net cash settlement is presumed. (ASC 815-40-25-2) An exception occurs if the two settlement alternatives are not of equal value, in which case the economic substance should govern. (ASC 815-40-25-3)
- *Initial measurement.* Initial measurement should be at fair value. (ASC 815-40-30-1)
- *Subsequent measurement.* Contracts classed as equity are accounted for in permanent equity, with value changes being ignored, unless settlement expectations change. (ASC 815-40-35-2) For publicly held companies, under defined circumstances, guidance is provided by analogy from Accounting Series Release (ASR) 268. All other contracts would be classified as assets or liabilities, to be measured continuously at fair value. (ASC 815-40-35-4) If settlement in shares ultimately occurs, already recognized gains or losses are left in earnings, not reclassified or reversed.
- *Contract reclassification.* Events may necessitate reclassification of contracts from assets/liabilities to equity. If a contract first classed as equity is later reclassified to assets/liabilities, any value change to the date of reclassification will be included in equity, not earnings. Thereafter, value changes will be reported in earnings. (ASC 815-40-35-9) If partial net share settlement is permitted, the portion that can be so settled remains in equity. Appropriate disclosure under ASC 235 may be required, if more than one contract exists and different methods are applied to them.
- *Equity classification criteria.* All the following conditions must be satisfied in order to classify a contract in equity:
  - The contract permits settlement in unregistered shares (the assumption being that the issuer cannot effectively control the conditions for registration, making cash settlement likely unless unregistered shares can be delivered);
  - There are sufficient authorized, unissued shares to settle the contact, after considering all other outstanding commitments;
  - The contract contains an explicit limit on the number of shares to be issued;
  - There are no required cash payments to the counterparty based on the issuer's failure to make timely SEC filings;
  - There are no "make whole" provisions to compensate the holder after he sells the shares issued in the market at a price below some defined threshold value;
  - A change in control provision requires that net cash settlement is accompanied by similar requirements for counterparties and existing shareholders; (ASC 815-40-55-3)
  - There are no provisions that indicate that the counterparties have rights greater than those of the actual shareholders; and
  - There is no requirement for any collateral posting for any reason. (ASC 815-40-25-10)
- *Hedge accounting applicability.* Contracts that are subject to this consensus cannot qualify for hedge accounting.
- *Multiple settlement alternatives.* Contracts offering multiple settlement alternatives that require the company to receive cash when the contract is in a gain position but pay either stock or cash at the company's option when in a loss position should be accounted for as equity. Also, such contracts requiring payment of cash when in a loss position but receipt

of either cash or stock at the company's option when in a gain position must be accounted for as assets/liabilities. (ASC 815-40-25-37 and 25-38)

ASC 815-45, *Weather Derivatives*

ASC 815-45 applies to all weather derivatives that are not exchange-traded, and, therefore, not subject to the requirements of ASC 815-10. (ASC 815-45-15-2)

ASC 815-45 states that an entity that enters into a nonexchange-traded forward-based weather derivative in connection with nontrading activities is to account for the contract by applying an "intrinsic value method." The intrinsic value method computes an amount based on the difference between the expected results from an upfront allocation of the cumulative strike and the actual results during a period, multiplied by the contract price (for example, dollars per heating degree day). The use of external statistical sources, such as the National Weather Service, is necessary in applying this technique. (ASC 815-45-30-3 and 35-1 and 35-2)

Furthermore, an entity that purchases a nonexchange-traded option-based weather derivative in connection with nontrading activities is to amortize to expense the premium paid (or due) and apply the intrinsic value method to measure the contract at the date of each interim statement of financial position. The premium asset is to be amortized in a rational and systematic manner. (ASC 815-45-35-4)

Also, all entities that sell or write a nonexchange-traded option-based weather derivative are to initially recognize the premium as a liability and recognize any subsequent changes in fair value currently in earnings (the premium would not be amortized). (ASC 815-45-35-5)

In addition, a purchased or written weather derivative may contain an "embedded" premium or discount when the contract terms are not consistent with current market terms. In those circumstances, the premium or discount is to be quantified, removed from the calculated benchmark strike, and accounted for as noted above. (ASC 815-45-30-3A)

Finally, all weather derivative contracts entered into under trading or speculative activities are to be accounted for at their fair value, with subsequent changes in fair value reported currently in earnings.

Presentation and Disclosure

Extensive information on presentation and disclosure for ASC 815 can be found at www.wiley.com/go/GAAP2021.

51 ASC 820 FAIR VALUE MEASUREMENTS

PERSPECTIVE AND ISSUES

Subtopic

ASC 820 contains one subtopic:

- ASC 820-10, *Overall*, which defines fair value, describes a framework for measuring fair value, and details required disclosures.

Scope and Scope Exceptions

ASC 820 does not require fair value measurements in addition to those required by other topics in the Codification.

Scope In pursuing an incremental approach, ASC 820 contains scope exceptions for certain, highly complex specialized applications. It does *not* apply to:

- Accounting principles for share-based payments in all ASC 718 Subtopics, except for transactions covered in ASC 718-40, which are within the scope of ASC 820

- Measurements that are similar to fair value but that are not intended to measure fair value, including:
  - Measurements models that are based on standalone selling price
  - Inventory
- Recognition and measurement of revenue from contracts with customers
- Recognition and measurement of gains and losses upon the derecognition of nonfinancial assets
  (ASC 820-10-15-2)

In addition to the scope exceptions listed above, ASC 820 retains the practicability exceptions included in GAAP that applies when, in management's judgment, it is not practical to estimate fair value. In such instances, management is required to inform the reader in an explanatory note to the financial statements that it is unable to estimate fair value and the reasons that such an estimate cannot be made. (ASC 820-10-15-3)

The practicability exception applies to certain measurements made in connection with the following matters:

GAAP measurement category	**Primary GAAP**
Asset retirement obligations	ASC 410-20 and 440-10-50 and 440-10-55
Business combinations, for specific items where other measures are allowed	ASC 805-20-30-10
Financial assets or financial liabilities of a consolidated VIE when these items are measured using the measurement alternative	ASC 810-10-30-10 through 30-30 and 810-10-35-6 through 35-8.
Guarantees, the use of an entry price at initial recognition	ASC 460
Nonmonetary transactions	ASC 845, 605-20-25, and 605-20-50
Participation rights	ASC 715-30 and 715-60
Restructuring obligations	ASC 420
Where the fair value cannot be reasonably estimated, such as noncash consideration	ASC 606-10-32-21 through 32-24
(ASC 820-10-15-3)	

Overview

ASC 820, *Fair Value Measurement*. ASC 820 provides:

- A unified definition of fair value,
- Related guidance on measurement, and
- Enhanced disclosure requirements to inform financial statement users about:
  - The fair value measurements included in the financial statements,
  - The methods and assumptions used to estimate them, and
  - The degree of observability of the inputs used in management's estimation process.

Practice alert If a reporting entity measures an investment's fair value using the net asset value per share (or an equivalent) practical expedient, the Codification provides those reporting entities with an option to measure the fair value of certain investments using net asset value instead of fair value. Thus, the Codification eliminates the requirement to classify the investment measured using the practical expedient within the fair value hierarchy based on whether the investment is:

- Redeemable with the investee at net asset value on the measurement date,
- Never redeemable with the investee at net asset value, or
- Redeemable with the investee at net asset value at a future date.

DEFINITIONS OF TERMS

Source: ASC 820-10-20. Also see Appendix A, *Definitions of Terms*, for additional terms relevant to this chapter: Acquiree, Acquirer, Acquisition by a Not-for-Profit Entity, Benchmark Interest Rate, Beneficial Interests, Business, Conduit Debt Security, Contract, Credit Risk, Customer, Discount Rate Adjustment Technique, Expected Cash Flow, Fair Value, Financial Asset (2nd def.), Financial Instrument, Financial Liability, Financial Statements Are Available to Be Issued, Interest Rate Risk, Legal Entity, Liability Issued with an Inseparable Third-Party Credit Enhancement, Management, Market Participants, Most Advantageous Market, Net Asset Value Per Share, Nonperformance Risk, Nonpublic Entity, Not-for-Profit Entity, Orderly Transaction, Principal Market, Public Business Entity, Readily Determinable Fair Value, Related Parties, Revenue, Standalone Selling Price, Unit of Account, and Variable Interest Entity.

Active Market. A market in which transactions for the asset or liability occur with sufficient frequency and volume to provide pricing information on an ongoing basis.

Brokered Market. A market in which brokers attempt to match buyers with sellers, but do not stand ready to trade for their own account.

Cost Approach. A valuation approach that reflects the amount that currently would be required to replace the service capacity of an asset, often called current replacement cost.

Currency Risk. The risk that the fair value or future cash flows of a financial instrument will fluctuate because of changes in foreign exchange rates.

Dealer Market. A market in which dealers stand ready to trade (either buy or sell for their own account), thereby providing liquidity by using their capital to hold an inventory of the items for which they make a market. Typically, bid and ask prices (representing the price at which the dealer is willing to buy and the price at which the dealer is willing to sell, respectively) are more readily available than closing prices. Over-the-counter markets (for which prices are publicly reported by the National Association of Securities Dealers Automated Quotations systems or by OTC Markets Group Inc.) are dealer markets. For example, the market for U.S. Treasury securities is a dealer market. Dealer markets also exist for some other assets and liabilities, including other financial instruments, commodities, and physical assets (for example, used equipment).

Entry Price. The price paid to acquire an asset, or received to assume a liability in an exchange transaction.

Exchange Market. A market in which closing prices are both readily available and generally representative of fair value (such as the New York Stock Exchange).

Exit Price. The price that would be received to sell an asset or paid to transfer a liability.

Highest and Best Use. The use of a nonfinancial asset by market participants that would maximize the value of the asset or the group of assets and liabilities (for example, a business) within which the asset would be used.

Income Approach. Valuation approaches that convert future amounts (for example, cash flows or income and expenses) to a single current (that is, discounted) amount. The fair value measurement is determined on the basis of the value indicated by current market expectations about those future amounts.

Inputs. The assumptions that market participants would use when pricing the asset or liability, including assumptions about risk, such as the following:

- The risk inherent in a particular valuation technique used to measure fair value (such as a pricing model)
- The risk inherent in the inputs to the valuation technique.

Inputs may be observable or unobservable.

Level 1 Inputs. Quoted prices (unadjusted) in active markets for identical assets or liabilities that the reporting entity can access at the measurement date.

Level 2 Inputs. Inputs other than quoted prices included within Level 1 that are observable for the asset or liability, either directly or indirectly.

Level 3 Inputs. Unobservable inputs for the asset or liability.

Market Approach. A valuation approach that uses prices and other relevant information generated by market transactions involving identical or comparable (that is, similar) assets, liabilities, or a group of assets and liabilities, such as a business.

Market Risk. The risk that the fair value or future cash flows of a financial instrument will fluctuate because of changes in market prices. Market risk comprises the following:

- Interest rate risk
- Currency risk
- Other price risk

Market-Corroborated Inputs. Inputs that are derived principally from or corroborated by observable market data by correlation or other means.

Observable Inputs. Inputs that are developed using market data, such as publicly available information about actual events or transactions, and that reflect the assumptions that market participants would use when pricing the asset or liability.

Other Price Risk. The risk that the fair value of future cash flows of a financial instrument will fluctuate because of changes in market prices (other than those arising from interest rate risk or currency risk), whether those changes are caused by factors specific to the individual financial instrument or its issuer or by factors affecting all similar financial instruments traded in the market.

Present Value. A tool used to link future amounts (cash flows or values) to a present amount using a discount rate (an application of the income approach). Present value techniques differ in how they adjust for risk and in the type of cash flows they use.

Principal-to-Principal Market. A market in which transactions, both originations and resales, are negotiated independently with no intermediary. Little information about those transactions may be made available publicly.

Risk Premium. Compensation sought by risk-averse market participants for bearing the uncertainty inherent in the cash flows of an asset or a liability. Also referred to as a *risk adjustment*.

Systematic Risk. The common risk shared by an asset or a liability with the other items in a diversified portfolio. Portfolio theory holds that in a market in equilibrium, market participants will be compensated only for bearing the systematic risk inherent in the cash flows. (In markets that are inefficient or out of equilibrium, other forms of return or compensation might be available.) Also referred to as *nondiversifiable risk.*

Transaction Costs. The costs to sell an asset or transfer a liability in the principal (or most advantageous) market for the asset or liability that are directly attributable to the disposal of the asset or transfer of the liability and meet both of the following criteria:

1. They result directly from and are essential to that transaction.
2. They would not have been incurred by the entity had the decision to sell the asset or transfer the liability not been made (similar to costs to sell, as defined in ASC 360-10-35-38).

Transportation Costs. The costs that would be incurred to transport an asset from its current location to its principal (or most advantageous) market.

Unobservable Inputs. Inputs for which market data are not available and that are developed using the best information available about the assumptions that market participants would use when pricing the asset or liability.

Unsystematic Risk. The risk specific to a particular asset or liability. Also referred to as *diversifiable risk.*

CONCEPTS, RULES, AND EXAMPLES

Definition of Fair Value

The term fair value rather than market value emphasizes that, even in the absence of active primary markets for an asset or liability, the asset or liability can be valued by reference to prices and rates from secondary markets. Over time, this concept has been expanded further to include the application of various fair value estimation models, such as the discounted probability-weighted expected cash flow model first introduced in CON 7.

Measurement Principles and Methodologies

ASC 820 contains a fair value measurement framework, which is used at both initial and subsequent measurement.

Initial Recognition When the reporting entity first acquires an asset or incurs (or assumes) a liability in an exchange transaction, the transaction price is an entry price, the price paid to acquire the asset and the price received to assume the liability. Fair value measurements are based not on entry prices, but rather on exit prices—the price that would be received to sell the asset or paid to transfer the liability. While entry and exit prices differ conceptually, in many cases they may be identical and can be considered to represent fair value of the asset or liability at initial recognition. (ASC 820-10-30-2) This is not always the case, however, and in assessing fair value at initial recognition, management should consider transaction-specific factors and factors specific to the assets and/or liabilities that are being initially recognized. Examples of situations where transaction price might not represent fair value at initial recognition include:

- Related-party transactions, unless the entity has evidence that the transaction was entered into at market terms.
- Transactions taking place under duress or the seller is forced to accept the price, such as when the seller is experiencing financial difficulties.
- Different units of account that apply to the transaction price and the assets/liabilities being measured. This can occur, for example, where the transaction price includes other elements besides the assets/liabilities that are being measured such as unstated rights and

privileges that are subject to separate measurement or when the transaction price includes transaction costs (see discussion below).
- The exchange transaction takes place in a market different from the principal or most advantageous market in which the reporting entity would sell the asset or transfer the liability. An example of this situation is when the reporting entity is a securities dealer that enters into transactions with customers in the retail market, but the principal market for the exit transaction is with other dealers in the dealer market.
(ASC 820-10-30-3A)

If another ASC topic requires or permits fair value measurement initially and the transaction price differs from fair value, the resulting gain or loss is recognized in earnings, unless otherwise specified. (ASC 820-10-30-6)

Subsequent Measurement

Transaction costs Transaction costs are the incremental direct costs that would be incurred to sell an asset or transfer a liability. While, as previously discussed, transaction costs are considered in determining the market that is most advantageous, they are not used to adjust the fair value measurement of the asset or liability being measured. The FASB excluded them from the measurement because they are not characteristic of an asset or liability being measured. (ASC 820-10-35-9B)

Transportation costs If an attribute of the asset or liability being measured is its location, the price determined in the principal or most advantageous market is to be adjusted for the costs that would be incurred by the reporting entity to transport it to or from that market. (ASC 820-10-35-9C) *The measurement process.* It is helpful to break down the measurement process under ASC 820 into a series of steps. Although not necessarily performed in a linear manner, the following procedures and decisions need to be applied and made, in order to value an asset or liability at fair value under ASC 820. The process will be discussed in greater detail:

1. *Identify the item to be valued and the unit of account.* Specifically identify the asset or liability, including the unit of account to be used for the measurement. (ASC 820-10-35-2B through 2E)
2. *Determine the principal or most advantageous market and the relevant market participants.* From the reporting entity's perspective, determine the principal market in which it would sell the asset or transfer the liability. In the absence of a principal market, consider the most advantageous market for the asset or the liability. Once the principal or most advantageous market is identified, determine the characteristics of the market participants. It is not necessary that specifically named individuals or enterprises be identified for this purpose. (ASC 820-10-35-5A through 35-6C)
3. *Select the valuation premise to be used for asset measurements.* If the item being measured is an asset, determine the valuation premise to be used by evaluating whether marketplace participants would judge the highest and best use of the nonfinancial asset on a stand-alone basis or in combination with other assets as a group or with other assets and liabilities. Note that the highest and best use and valuation premise concepts only apply to measuring of nonfinancial assets. (ASC 820-10-35-10A through 10D)
4. *Consider the risk assumptions applicable to liability measurements.* If the item being measured is a liability, identify the key assumptions that market participants would make regarding nonperformance risk including, but not limited to, the reporting entity's own credit risk (credit standing).

5. *Identify available inputs.* Identify the key assumptions that market participants would use in pricing the asset or liability, including assumptions about risk. In identifying these assumptions, referred to as "inputs" by ASC 820, maximize the inputs that are relevant and observable (i.e., that are based on market data available from sources independent of the reporting entity). In so doing, assess the availability of relevant, reliable market data for each input that significantly affects the valuation, and identify the level of the fair value input hierarchy in which it is to be categorized. (ASC 820-10-35-16B through 16BB)
6. *Select the appropriate valuation approach(es).* Based on the nature of the asset or liability being valued, and the types and reliability of inputs available, determine the appropriate valuation approach or combination of approaches to use in valuing the asset or liability. The three broad categories of approaches are the market approach, the income approach, and the cost approach. (ASC 820-10-35-24A)
7. *Make the measurement.* Measure the asset or liability.
8. *Determine amounts to be recognized and information to be disclosed.* Determine the amounts and information to be recorded, classified, and disclosed in interim and annual financial statements.

The flowchart that follows outlines the steps in the process.

Applying the Fair Value Measurement Framework

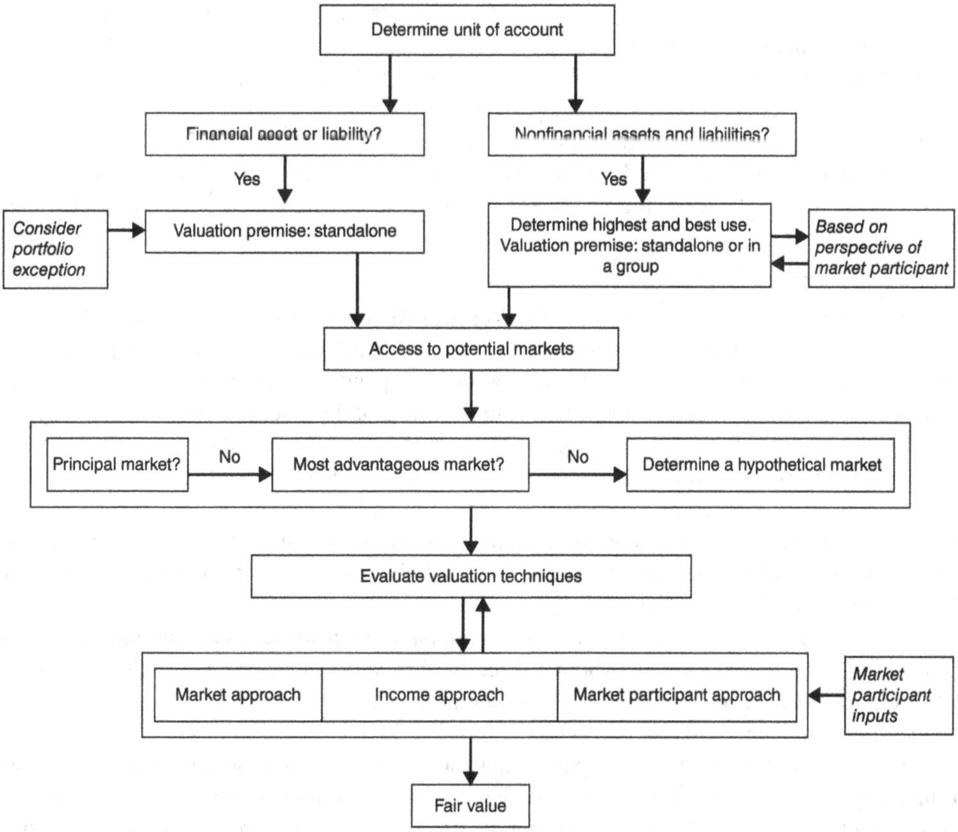

Item Identification and Unit of Account In general, the same unit of account at which the asset or liability is aggregated or disaggregated by applying other applicable GAAP pronouncements is used for fair value measurement purposes. (ASC 820-10-35-36B) ASC 820-10-35-44 prohibits adjustment to the valuation for a "blockage factor" if the fair value is measured using a quoted price on an active market. A blockage factor is an adjustment made to a valuation that takes into account the fact that the investor holds a large quantity (block) of shares relative to the market trading volume in those shares. The prohibition applies even if the quantity held by the reporting entity exceeds the market's normal trading volume—and that, if the reporting entity were, hypothetically, to place an order to sell its entire position in a single transaction, that transaction could affect the quoted price.

There is an exception for financial assets, financial liabilities, and nonfinancial items accounted for as derivatives under ASC 815, or combinations of those items entered into with a particular counterparty. If certain criteria are met, the entity can measure the fair value of net position in a manner that is consistent with how market participants would price the net position. (ASU 820-10-35-18D) To use the exception, all the following conditions must be met. The company:

- Manages the group of financial assets, financial liabilities, nonfinancial items accounted for as derivatives in accordance with ASC 815, or of those items on the basis of the reporting entity's net exposure to a particular market risk (or risks) or to the credit risk of a particular counterparty in accordance with the reporting entity's documented risk management or investment strategy.
- Provides information on that basis about the group of financial assets and financial liabilities to the reporting entity's management.
- Is required or has elected to measure those financial assets, financial liabilities, nonfinancial items accounted for as derivatives in accordance with ASC 815, or of those items at fair value in the statement of financial position at the end of each reporting period.
  (ASU 820-10-35-18E)

Principal or Most Advantageous Market and Market Participants ASC 820 requires the person performing the valuation to maximize the use of relevant assumptions (inputs) that are observable from market data obtained from sources independent of the reporting entity. In making a fair value measurement, management is to assume that the asset or liability is exchanged in an orderly transaction between market participants at the measurement date.

To characterize the exchange as orderly, it is assumed that the asset or liability will have been exposed to the market for a sufficient period of time prior to the measurement date to enable marketing activities to occur that are usual and customary with respect to transactions involving such assets or liabilities. It is also to be assumed that the transaction is not a forced transaction (e.g., a forced liquidation or distress sale).

ASC 820 also specifies that if there is a principal market for an asset, the measure of fair value is the price in that market (whether directly observable or determined indirectly using a valuation approach), even if the price in a different market is potentially more advantageous at the measurement date. (ASU 820-10-35-6)

Management identifies the principal market for the asset or liability, if such a market exists. If the entity has access to more than one market, the principal market is the market in which the reporting entity would sell the asset or transfer the liability that has the greatest volume and activity level for the asset or liability. The greater volume of activity ensures that the measurement is based on multiple transactions potentially between multiple counterparties, and is thus more representative of fair value than if the measurement were based on less extensive data.

Note that the determination of the principal market is made from the perspective of the reporting entity. Thus, different reporting entities engaging in different specialized industries, or with access to different markets, might not have the same principal market for an identical asset or liability. Inputs from the principal market are to be used irrespective of whether the price is directly observable or determined through the use of a valuation approach.

If there is no principal market for an asset or liability from the perspective of the reporting entity, then management uses the most advantageous market for the measurement. (ASC 820-10-35-5) In determining the most advantageous market, management considers transaction costs. However, once the most advantageous market had been identified, transaction costs are not used to adjust the market price used for the purposes of the fair value measurement.

ASC 820 provides a typology of markets that potentially exist for assets or liabilities. (See the "Definitions of Terms" section at the beginning of this chapter for descriptions of each of these markets.)

- Active market
- Dealer market
- Brokered market
- Principal-to-principal market

Market participants in the principal or most advantageous market are buyers and sellers that:

- Are unrelated third parties
- Have the ability to enter into a transaction for the asset or liability
- Have the motivation to voluntarily enter into a transaction for the asset or liability without being forced to do so under duress
- Are knowledgeable about the asset or liability since they would possess a reasonable understanding of the asset or liability and the terms of the transaction based on all available information including information obtainable through the performance of usual and customary due diligence procedures

The person determining the measurement is not required to identify specific individuals or enterprises that would potentially be market participants. Instead, it is important to identify the distinguishing characteristics of participants in the particular market by considering factors specific to the asset or liability being measured, the market identified, and the participants in that market with whom the reporting entity would enter into a transaction for the asset or liability.

Measurement Considerations When Markets Become Illiquid or Less Liquid Questions have arisen regarding whether transactions occurring in less liquid markets with less frequent trades might cause those market transactions to be considered forced or distress sales, thus rendering valuations made using those prices not indicative of the actual fair value of the securities.

Under ASC 820, orderly transactions are occurring in the marketplace for an asset or liability when knowledgeable buyers and sellers independent of the reporting entity are willing and able to transact and are motivated to transact without being forced to do so. If orderly transactions are occurring in a manner that is usual and customary for the asset or liability, then the transactions are not to be characterized as forced or distress sales. Just because transaction volume in a market drops significantly from prior periods does not necessarily mean that the market is no longer active.

Determining Whether There Has Been a Significant Decrease in Level of Activity Management is to consider the volume and level of activity in the market compared with normal market activity for the asset or liability (or similar assets or liabilities) being measured. In making that comparison, the following indicators of declining activity may point to a decrease that is considered significant. The indicators include, but are not limited to the following (which are not to be considered of equal significance or relevance, when evaluating the weight of evidence):

- Few recent transactions
- Price quotations based on information that is not current
- Price quotations vary substantially over time or among market makers (e.g., in some brokered markets)
- Indexes that were previously highly correlated with the fair values of the asset or liability have become demonstrably uncorrelated with recent indications of fair value for that asset or liability
- There has been a significant increase in implied liquidity risk premiums, yields, or performance indicators (such as delinquency rates or loss severities) for observed transactions or quoted prices when compared with management's estimate of expected cash flows, taking into consideration all available market data about credit and other nonperformance risk for the asset or liability being measured
- There is a wide bid-ask spread or a significant increase in that spread
- There is a significant decline or absence of a market for new issuances (that is, a primary market) for the asset or liability (or similar assets or liabilities)
- Little information is publicly released (e.g., in a principal-to-principal market) (ASC 820-10-35-54C)

Management evaluates the relevance and significance of these indicators as well as whether other indicators might be present to determine whether, based on the weight of the evidence, there has been a significant decrease in the volume and level of activity for the asset or liability.

If management concludes that a significant decrease has occurred, it must perform further analysis of the transactions or quoted prices in that market in order to determine whether it is necessary to significantly adjust the quoted prices to estimate fair value in accordance with ASC 820. It is important to note that, for the purpose of estimating fair value, management's own intention to hold an asset or liability is not relevant. Fair value is a market-based measurement, not an entity-specific measurement. (ASC 820-10-35-54D)

Other unrelated circumstances might also necessitate significant adjustments to quoted prices, such as when a price for a similar asset requires a significant adjustment in order to compensate for characteristics or attributes of the comparable asset that are different from those of the asset whose fair value is being measured, or when a quoted price may not be sufficiently close to the measurement date.

FASB stresses that, even if there has been a significant decrease in the market volume and level of activity for the item being measured, it is inappropriate, based solely on that judgment, to conclude that all transactions occurring in that market are not orderly transactions. Factors to consider in judging whether a transaction might not be orderly include, but are not limited to:

- Insufficient time period of exposure to the market prior to the measurement date to allow for usual or customary marketing activities for transactions involving assets or liabilities *under the current market conditions*.
- The marketing exposure period was sufficient, but the seller only marketed the item being measured to a single market participant.

- The seller is in or near bankruptcy or receivership (in other words, the seller is "distressed"), or the seller is being compelled to sell in order to meet legal or regulatory requirements (in other words, the sale is "forced").
- The transaction price is an outlier when compared with recently occurring transactions for the same or similar item.
  (ASC 820-10-35-54I)

Management considers the weight of the evidence in determining whether a particular market transaction is orderly. In making that determination, management is to consider the following guidance:

- *Transactions considered orderly.* If the weight of the evidence indicates a transaction is *orderly*, management considers that transaction price when estimating fair value or market risk premiums. The weight to be placed on that transaction price versus other indications of fair value is dependent on the specific facts and circumstances such as:
  - The volume of shares (or units) included in the transaction,
  - The extent of comparability between the items included in the transaction and the asset or liability being measured, and
  - How close the transaction was to the measurement date.
- *Transactions considered not orderly.* If the weight of the evidence indicates a transaction is not orderly, management is to place little, if any, weight on that transaction price as compared to other indications of fair value when estimating fair value or market risk premiums.
- *Insufficient information to determine whether or not transactions are orderly.* If management lacks sufficient information to conclude whether or not a transaction is orderly, the transaction price is to be considered when estimating fair value or market risk premiums. However, that transaction may not be the sole or even the primary basis for estimating fair value or market risk premiums. Management is to place less weight on transactions of this nature, where sufficient information is not available to conclude whether the transaction is orderly when compared with other transactions that are known to be orderly. (ASC 820-10-35-54 J)

In making the determinations above, management is not required to make all possible efforts to obtain relevant information; however, management is not to ignore information available without undue cost and effort. Obviously, management would be prevented from asserting that it lacks sufficient information with respect to whether a transaction is orderly when the reporting entity was a party to that transaction. (ASC 820-10-35-54 J)

Irrespective of what valuation approach or combination of approaches is used to measure fair value, the measurement should include appropriate risk adjustments. According to ASC 820-10-55-8, risk-averse market participants seek compensation for bearing the uncertainties inherent in the estimated future cash flows associated with an asset or liability. This compensation is referred to as a risk premium or market risk premium and it reflects the amount that the market participant would demand in order to obtain adequate compensation for that market participant's perception of the risks associated with either the amounts or timing of the estimated future cash flows. Absent such an adjustment, a measurement would not faithfully represent fair value. While determination of the appropriate risk premium may be difficult, the degree of difficulty alone is an insufficient rationale for management excluding a risk adjustment from its fair value measurement. The risk premium adjustment, however, is to reflect an orderly transaction between market participants at the measurement date *under current market conditions.*

Quoted prices obtained from third-party pricing services or brokers may be used as inputs in the fair value measurement if management had determined that those quoted prices were determined by the third party in accordance with the principles of ASC 820, which in practical terms means that management will need to inquire of the information provider as to, among other things, the origin of the quote, the methodology followed to compute it, the types of inputs used and their sources, the level of activity in the market for market-based quotes, the age of the data used (its proximity to the measurement date), and other information relevant in the circumstances.

When there has been a significant decrease in the volume and level of activity for the asset or liability, management is to evaluate whether those quoted prices are based on current information that reflects orderly transactions (mark-to-market) or are based on application of a valuation approach reflecting market participant assumptions, including assumptions about risk premiums (mark-to-model). Management is to place less weight on quotes that are not based on the results of actual market transactions than on other indications of fair value. The type of quote is also to be considered, for example, whether the quote represents a binding offer or an indicative price, with a binding offer to be given greater weight than an indicative price.

Selection of the Valuation Premise for Asset Measurements The measurement of the fair value of a nonfinancial asset is to assume the highest and best use of that asset from the perspective of market participants. (ASC 820-10-35-10A) Generally, the highest and best use is the way that market participants would be expected to deploy the asset (or a group of assets within which they would use the asset) that would maximize the value of the asset (or group). This highest and best use assumption might differ from the way that the reporting entity is currently using the asset or group of assets or its future plans for using it (them).

At the measurement date, the highest and best use must be:

- Physically possible (given the physical characteristics of the asset),
- Legally permissible (taking into account any legal restrictions), and
- Financially feasible (based on income or cash flows).
  (ASC 820-10-35-10B)

Determination of the highest and best use of the nonfinancial asset will establish which of the two valuation premises to use in measuring the asset's fair value, the in-use valuation premise, or the in-exchange valuation premise. (ASC 820-10-35-10E)

Strategic Buyers and Financial Buyers ASC 820 differentiates between two broad categories of market participants that would potentially buy an asset or group of assets.

1. *Strategic buyers* are market participants whose acquisition objectives are to use the asset or group of assets (the "target") to enhance the performance of their existing business by achieving benefits such as additional capacity, improved technology, managerial, marketing, or technical expertise, access to new markets, improved market share, or enhanced market positioning. Thus, a strategic buyer views the purchase as a component of a broader business plan and, as a result, a strategic buyer may be willing to pay a premium to consummate the acquisition and may, in fact, be the only type of buyer available with an interest in acquiring the target. Ideally, from the standpoint of the seller, more than one strategic buyer would be interested in the acquisition which would create a bidding situation that further increases the selling price.
2. *Financial buyers* are market participants who seek to acquire the target based on its merits as a stand-alone investment. A financial buyer is interested in a return on its investment over a shorter time horizon, often three to five years, after which time their objective

would typically be to sell the target. An attractive target is one that offers high growth potential in a short period of time resulting in a selling price substantially higher than the original acquisition price. Therefore, even at acquisition, a financial buyer is concerned with a viable exit strategy. A financial buyer, unlike a strategic buyer, typically does not possess a high level of industry or managerial expertise in the target's industry.
(ASC 820-10-55-27 and 55-28)

The Combination Valuation Premise This premise assumes that the maximum fair value to market participants is the price that would be received by the reporting entity (seller) assuming the asset would be used by the buyer with other assets as a group and further, that the other assets in the group would be available to potential buyers. The target might continue to be used as presently installed or may be configured in a different manner by the buyer. The assumptions regarding the level of aggregation (or disaggregation) of the asset and other associated assets may be different than the level used in applying other accounting pronouncements. Thus, in considering highest and best use and the resulting level of aggregation, the evaluator is not constrained by how the asset may be assigned by the reporting entity to a reportable or operating segment under ASC 820, a business, reporting unit, asset group, or disposal group. (ASC 820-10-35-10E) The assumptions regarding the highest and best use of the target should normally be consistent for all of the assets included in the group within which it would be used. (ASC 820-10-35-11A) Generally, the market participants whose highest and best use of an asset or group of assets would be in combination are characterized as strategic buyers, as previously described.

The stand-alone valuation premise This premise assumes that the maximum fair value to market participants is the price that would be received by the reporting entity (seller) assuming the asset would be sold principally on a stand-alone basis. (ASC 820-10-35-10E)

Transaction costs Transaction costs are the incremental direct costs that would be incurred to sell an asset or transfer a liability. While, as previously discussed, transaction costs are considered in determining the market that is most advantageous, they are not used to adjust the fair value measurement of the asset or liability being measured. FASB excluded them from the measurement because they are not characteristic of an asset or liability being measured. (ASC 820-10-35-9B)

Transportation costs If an attribute of the asset or liability being measured is its location, the price determined in the principal or most advantageous market is to be adjusted for the costs that would be incurred by the reporting entity to transport it to or from that market. (ASC 820-10-35-9C)

Risk Assumptions When Valuing a Liability Many accountants, analysts, and others find the concept of computing fair value of liabilities and recognizing changes in fair value as they occur to be counterintuitive. Consider the case when a reporting entity's own credit standing declines (universally acknowledged as a "bad thing"). A fair value measurement that incorporates the effect of this decline in credit rating would result in a decline in the fair value of the liability and a resultant increase in stockholders' equity (a "good thing"). The justification provided in ASC 820 (and by referencing CON 7) is that:

A change in credit standing represents a change in the relative positions of the two classes of claimants (shareholders and creditors) to an entity's assets. If the credit standing diminishes, the fair value of creditors' claims diminishes. The amount of shareholders' residual claims to the entity's assets may appear to increase but that increase is probably offset by losses that may have occasioned the decline in credit standing. Because shareholders usually cannot be called on to pay a corporation's liabilities, the amount of their residual claims approaches, and is limited by zero. Thus a change in the position of borrowers necessarily alters the position of shareholders, and vice versa. (CON 7, Paragraph 82)

The Hypothetical Transaction and Operational Difficulties Experienced in Practice Under ASC 820, fair value measurements of liabilities assume that a hypothetical transfer to a market participant occurs on the measurement date. In measuring the fair value of a liability, the evaluator assumes that the reporting entity's obligation to its creditor (i.e., the counterparty to the obligation) will continue at and after the measurement date (i.e., the obligation will not be repaid or settled prior to its contractual maturity). (ASC 820-10-35-16) This being the case, this hypothetical transfer price would most likely represent the price that the current creditor (holder of the debt instrument) could obtain from a marketplace participant willing to purchase the debt instrument in a transaction involving the original creditor assigning its rights to the purchaser. In effect, the hypothetical market participant that purchased the instrument would be in the same position as the current creditor with respect to expected future cash flows (or expected future performance, if the liability is not settleable in cash) from the reporting entity. (ASC 820-10-35-16BB)

The evaluator further assumes that the nonperformance risk related to the obligation would remain outstanding and the transferee would fulfill the obligation. Nonperformance risk is the risk that an entity will not fulfill its obligation. (ASC 820-10-35-17) It is an all-encompassing concept that includes the reporting entity's own credit standing but also includes other risks associated with the nonfulfillment of the obligation. For example, a liability to deliver goods and/or perform services may bear nonperformance risk associated with the ability of the debtor to fulfill the obligation in accordance with the timing and specifications of the contract. Further, nonperformance risk increases or decreases as a result of changes in the fair value of credit enhancements associated with the liability (e.g., collateral, credit insurance, and/or guarantees).

Liabilities with Inseparable Third-Party Credit Enhancements Creditors often impose a requirement that, in connection with granting credit to a debtor, the debtor obtain a guarantee of the indebtedness from a creditworthy third party. Under such an arrangement, should the debtor default on its obligation, the third-party guarantor would become obligated to repay the obligation on behalf of the defaulting debtor and, of course, the debtor would be obligated to repay the guarantor for having satisfied the debt on its behalf.

In connection with a bond issuance, for example, the guarantee is generally purchased by the issuer (debtor) and the issuer then combines (bundles) the guarantee (also referred to as a "credit enhancement") with the bonds and issues the combined securities to investors. (ASC 820-10-35-18A) By packaging a bond with a related credit enhancement, the issuer increases the likelihood that the bond will be successfully marketed as well as reduces the effective interest rate paid on the bond by obtaining higher issuance proceeds than it would otherwise receive absent the bundled credit enhancement.

Scope exceptions The following guidance does *not* apply to:

- Credit enhancements provided:
  - By a government or government agency (such as deposit insurance provided by the U.S. Federal Deposit Insurance Corporation [FDIC])
  - Between reporting entities within a consolidated or combined group
  - Between entities under common control
- The holder of the issuer's credit-enhanced liability

Measurement—Credit Enhancements In accordance with ASC 820-10-35-18a, the issuer is not to include the effect of the credit enhancement in its fair value measurement of the liability. Thus, in determining the fair value of the liability, the issuer would consider its own credit standing and would not consider the credit standing of the third-party guarantor that provided the credit enhancement. Consequently, the unit of accounting to be used in the fair value measurement of a liability with an inseparable credit enhancement is the liability itself, absent the credit enhancement.

In the event that the guarantor is required to make payments to the creditor under the guarantee, it would result in a transfer of the issuer's obligation to repay the original creditor to the guarantor with the issuer then obligated to repay the guarantor. Should this occur, the obligation of the issuer to the guarantor would be an unguaranteed liability. Thus, the fair value of that transferred, unguaranteed obligation only considers the credit standing of the issuer.

Upon issuance of the credit-enhanced debt, the issuer is to allocate the proceeds it receives between the liability issued and the premium for the credit enhancement.

Inputs For the purpose of fair value measurements, inputs are the assumptions that market participants would use in pricing an asset or liability, including assumptions regarding risk. An input is either observable or unobservable. Observable inputs are either directly observable or indirectly observable. ASC 820 requires the evaluator to maximize the use of relevant observable inputs and minimize the use of unobservable inputs.

An observable input is based on market data obtainable from sources independent of the reporting entity. For an input to be considered relevant, it must be considered determinative of fair value. Even if there has been a significant decrease in the volume and level of market activity for an asset or liability, it is not to be automatically assumed that the market is inactive or that individual transactions in that market are disorderly (that is, are forced or liquidation sales made under duress).

An unobservable input reflects assumptions made by management of the reporting entity with respect to assumptions it believes market participants would use to price an asset or liability based on the best information available under the circumstances.

ASC 820 provides a fair value input hierarchy (see diagram below) to serve as a framework for classifying inputs based on the extent to which they are based on observable data.

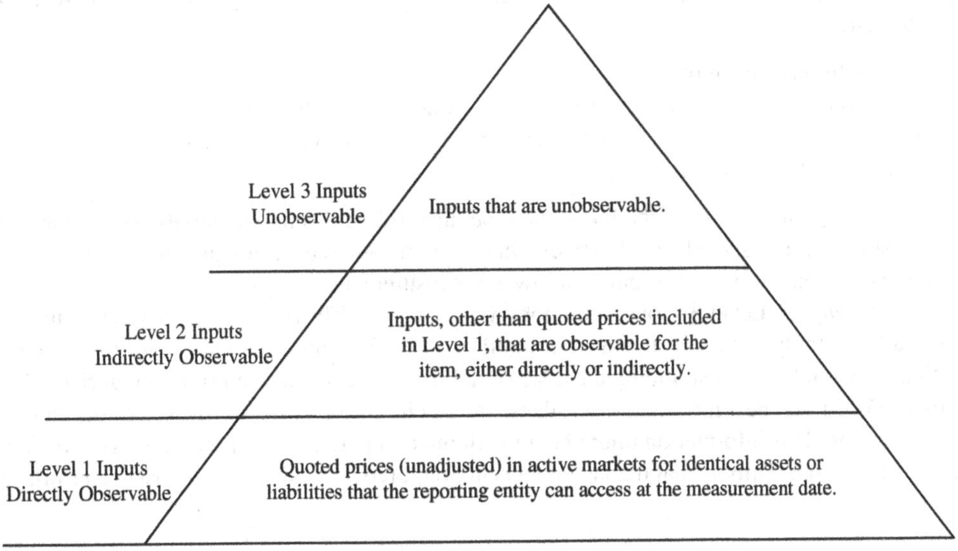

Level 1 inputs Level 1 inputs are considered the most reliable evidence of fair value and are to be used whenever they are available. These inputs consist of quoted prices in active markets for identical assets or liabilities. (ASC 820-10-35-41BB) The active market must be one in which the reporting entity has the ability to access the quoted price at the measurement date. To be considered an active market, transactions for the asset or liability being measured must occur frequently enough and in sufficient volume to provide pricing information on an ongoing basis.

A Level 1 input should be used without adjustment to measure fair value whenever possible. One should not adjust a Level 1 input except in these cases:

- When the entity has a large number of similar assets or liabilities, and it would be difficult to obtain pricing information for each individual item on the measurement date.
- When a quoted price in an active market does not represent the fair value of an asset or liability on the measurement date.
- When the quoted price needs to be adjusted for factors specific to the item.
(ASC 820-10-35-41C)

The use of Level 2 or Level 3 inputs is generally prohibited when Level 1 inputs are available.

Level 2 inputs Level 2 inputs are quoted prices for the asset or liability (other than those included in Level 1) that are either directly or indirectly observable. Level 2 inputs are to be considered when quoted prices for the identical asset or liability are not available. If the asset or liability being measured has a contractual term, a Level 2 input must be observable for substantially the entire term. These inputs include:

- Quoted prices for *similar* assets or liabilities in active markets
- Quoted prices for identical or similar assets or liabilities in markets that are *not active*
- Inputs other than quoted prices that are observable for the asset or liability (e.g., interest rates and yield curves observable at commonly quoted intervals; implied volatilities; credit spreads; and market-corroborated inputs)
(ASC 820-10-35-48)

Adjustments made to Level 2 inputs necessary to reflect fair value, if any, will vary depending on an analysis of specific factors associated with the asset or liability being measured. These factors include:

- Condition or location
- Extent to which the inputs relate to items comparable to the asset
- Volume or level of activity in the markets in which the inputs are observed.
(ASC 820-10-35-50)

Depending on the level of the fair value input hierarchy in which the inputs used to measure the adjustment are classified, an adjustment that is significant to the fair value measurement in its entirety could render the measurement a Level 3 measurement.

Level 3 inputs Level 3 inputs are unobservable inputs. These are necessary when little, if any, market activity occurs for the asset or liability. Level 3 inputs are assumptions that a market participant would use when pricing the asset or liability including assumptions about risk. (ASC 820-10-35-53) The best information available in the circumstances is to be used to develop the Level 3 inputs. This information might begin with internal data of the reporting entity. Cost/benefit considerations apply in that management is not required to "undertake all possible efforts" to obtain information about the assumptions that would be made by market participants. Attention is to be paid, however, to information available to management without undue cost and effort and, consequently, management's internal assumptions used to develop unobservable inputs are to be adjusted if such information contradicts those assumptions.

Inputs based on bid and ask prices Quoted bid prices represent the maximum price at which market participants are willing to buy an asset; quoted ask prices represent the minimum price at which market participants are willing to sell an asset. If available market prices are expressed in terms of bid and ask prices, management is to use the price within the bid-ask spread (the range of values between bid and ask prices) that is most representative of fair value irrespective of where in the fair value hierarchy the input would be classified. ASC 820 permits the use of pricing conventions such as midmarket pricing as a practical alternative for determining fair value measurements within a bid-ask spread. The use of bid prices for asset valuations and ask prices for liability valuations is permitted but not required. (ASC 820-10-35-36C and 35-36D)

Categorizing inputs Categorization of inputs as to the level of the hierarchy in which they fall serves two purposes. First, it provides the evaluator with a means of prioritizing assumptions used as to their level of objectivity and verifiability in the marketplace. Second, as discussed later in this chapter, the hierarchy provides a framework to provide informative disclosures that enable readers to assess the reliability and market observability of the fair value estimates embedded in the financial statements. (ASC 820-10-35-37)

In making a particular measurement of fair value, the inputs used may be classifiable in more than one of the levels of the hierarchy. When this is the case, the inputs used in the fair value measurement in its entirety are to be classified in the level of the hierarchy in which the lowest level input that is significant to the measurement is classified. (ASC 820-10-35-37A)

It is important to assess available inputs and their relative classification in the hierarchy prior to selecting the valuation approach or approaches to be applied to measure fair value for a particular asset or liability. The objective, in selecting from among alternative calculation approaches, would be to select the approach or combination of approaches that maximizes the use of observable inputs. (ASC 820-10-35-38)

Valuation Approaches In measuring fair value, management employs one or more valuation approaches consistent with the market approach, the income approach, and/or the cost approach. (ASC 820-10-35-24A) As previously discussed, the selection of a particular approach to measure fair value is to be based on its appropriateness to the asset or liability being measured, maximizing the use of observable inputs and minimizing the use of unobservable inputs.

In certain situations, such as when using Level 1 inputs, use of a single valuation approach will be sufficient. In other situations, such as when valuing a reporting unit, management may need to use multiple valuation approaches. When doing so, the results yielded by applying the various approaches are evaluated considering the reasonableness of the range of values. The fair value is the point within the range that is most representative of fair value in the circumstances. (ASC 820-10-35-24B)

Management is required to consistently apply the valuation approaches it elects to use to measure fair value. It would be appropriate to change valuation approaches or how they are applied if the change results in fair value measurements that are equally or more representative of fair value. Situations that might give rise to such a change would be when new markets develop, new information becomes available, previously available information ceases to be available, valuation approaches improve, or market conditions change. (ASC 820-10-35-25) Revisions that result from either a change in valuation approach or a change in the application of a valuation approaches are to be accounted for as changes in accounting estimate under ASC 250. (ASC 820-10-35-26)

Market approach The market approach to valuation uses information generated by actual market transactions for identical or comparable assets or liabilities (including a business in its entirety). The market approach often will use market multiples derived from a set of comparable transactions for the asset or liability or similar items. The evaluator needs to consider both qualitative and quantitative factors in determining the point within the range that is most representative of fair value. An example of a market approach is matrix pricing. This is a mathematical approach used primarily for the purpose of valuing debt securities without relying solely on quoted prices for the specific securities. Matrix pricing uses factors such as the stated interest rate, maturity, credit rating, and quoted prices of similar issues to develop the issue's current market yield. (ASC 820-10-55-3A through 55-3C)

Cost approach The cost approaches are based on quantifying the amount required to replace an asset's remaining service capacity (i.e., the asset's current replacement cost). A valuation approach classified as a cost approach would measure the cost to a market participant (buyer) to acquire or construct a substitute asset of comparable utility, adjusted for obsolescence. Obsolescence adjustments include factors for physical wear and tear, improvements to technology, and economic (external) obsolescence. Thus, obsolescence is a broader concept than financial statement depreciation, which simply represents a cost allocation convention and is not intended to be used as a valuation approach. (ASC 820-10- 55-3D and 55-3E)

Income Approaches Approaches classified as income approaches measure fair value based on current market expectations about future amounts (such as cash flows or net income) and discount them to an amount in measurement date dollars. Valuation approaches that follow an income approach include the Black-Scholes-Merton model (a closed-form model) and binomial or lattice models (open-form models), which use present value techniques, as well as the multiperiod excess earnings method that is used in fair value measurements of certain intangible assets such as in- process research and development. (ASC 820-10-55-3F and 55-3 G)

Fair Value Disclosures

Substantial disclosures regarding fair value are required by various ASC topics. In the preparation of the financial statements, these disclosures are often placed in different informative notes including descriptions of the entity's accounting policies, financial instruments, impairment, derivatives, pensions, revenue recognition, share-based compensation, risks and uncertainties, certain significant estimates, and so forth. ASC 820 encourages preparers to combine disclosure requirements under ASC 820 with those of other subtopics. Plan assets of a defined benefit pension plan or other postretirement plans accounted for under ASC 715 are not subject to the ASC 820 requirements and should apply the disclosure requirements in the relevant paragraphs of ASC 715. A list of the required disclosures can be found at www.wiley.com/go/GAAP2021.

52 ASC 825 FINANCIAL INSTRUMENTS

PERSPECTIVE AND ISSUES

Subtopics

ASC 825, *Financial Instruments*, contains two subtopics:

- ASC 825-10, *Overall*, which has two subsections:
  - General, which provides guidance on the fair value option and some disclosures about financial instruments
  - Fair Value Option, which provides guidance on the circumstances under which entities may choose the fair value option and the related presentation and disclosure requirements

  (ASC 825-10-05-2)
- ASC 825-20, *Registration Payment Arrangements*, which provides guidance on financial instruments subject to registration payment arrangements.

Scope and Scope Exceptions

ASC 825-10 The following items are eligible for the fair value option:

- All recognized financial assets and financial liabilities except for those listed in ASC 825-10-15-5 below.
- Firm commitments that would otherwise not be recognized at inception and that involve only financial instruments. An example is a forward purchase contract for a loan that is not readily convertible to cash. The commitment involves only financial instruments (the loan and cash) and would not be recognized at inception since it does not qualify as a derivative.
- A written loan commitment.

- Rights and obligations under insurance contracts or warranties that are not financial instruments[1] but whose terms permit the insurer (warrantor) to settle claims by paying a third party to provide goods and services to the counterparty (insured party or warranty claimant).
- A host financial instrument resulting from bifurcating an embedded nonfinancial derivative instrument from a nonfinancial hybrid instrument under ASC 815-15-25. An example would be an instrument in which the value of the bifurcated embedded derivative is payable in cash, services, or merchandise but the host debt contract is only payable in cash. (ASC 825-10-15-4)

Entities may *not* elect the fair value option for:

- Investments in subsidiaries required to be consolidated by the reporting entity
- Interests in variable interest entities required to be consolidated by the reporting entity[2]
- Employers' and plans' obligations (unfunded or underfunded liabilities) or assets (representing net overfunded positions) for:
  - Pension benefits
  - Other postretirement benefits (including health care and life insurance benefits)
  - Postemployment benefits
  - Other deferred compensation, termination, and share-based payment arrangements such as employee stock option plans; employee stock purchase plans; compensated absences; and exit and disposal activities
- Financial assets and financial liabilities under leases (this exception does not, however, apply to a guarantee of a third-party lease obligation or a contingent obligation associated with cancellation of a lease)
- Deposit liabilities, withdrawable on demand, of banks; saving and loan associations; credit unions; and other similar depository institutions
- Financial instruments that are, in whole or in part, classified by the issuer as a component of stockholders' equity (including temporary equity), such as a convertible debt security with a noncontingent beneficial conversion feature
  (ASC 825-10-15-5)

ASC 825-20 The guidance in ASC 825-20 applies to all entities and the following transactions:

- A registration payment arrangement
- An arrangement that requires the issuer to obtain or maintain a listing on the stock exchange if the remaining characteristics of a registration payment are met
  (ASC 825-20-15-1 and 15-2)

The guidance in this subtopic does *not* apply to:

- Arrangements that require registration or listing of convertible debt instruments or convertible preferred stock if the form of consideration that would be transferred to the counterparty is an adjustment to the conversion ratio.

---

[1] Insurance contracts that require or permit the insurer to settle claims by providing goods or services instead of by paying cash are not, by definition, financial instruments. Similarly, warranties that require or permit the warrantor to settle claims by providing goods and services in lieu of cash do not constitute financial instruments.

[2] Under ASC 805, consolidated variable interest entities are referred to as subsidiaries in the same manner as consolidated voting interest entities.

Arrangements in which the amount of consideration transferred is determined by reference to either:
   - An observable market other than the market for the issuer's stock
   - An observable index
- Arrangements in which the financial instrument or instruments subject to the arrangement are settled when the consideration is transferred. (ASC 825-20-15-4).

Overview

ASC 825-10-25, *The Fair Value Option*, encourages reporting entities to elect to use fair value to measure eligible assets and liabilities in their financial statements. The objective is to improve financial reporting by mitigating the volatility in reported earnings that is caused by measuring related assets and liabilities differently. Electing entities obtain relief from the onerous and complex documentation requirements that apply to certain hedging transactions under ASC 815. ASC 825-10-25 applies to businesses and not-for-profit organizations and provides management of these entities substantial discretion in electing to measure eligible assets and liabilities at fair value.

DEFINITIONS OF TERMS

Source: ASC 825-20. See Appendix A, *Definitions of Terms*, for terms relevant to this chapter: Benchmark Interest Rate, Cash Equivalents, Conduit Debt Securities, Credit Risk, Fair Value, Financial Asset (Def. 2), Financial Instrument, Financial Liability, Firm Commitment, Interest Rate Risk, Market Participants, Nonpublic Entity (Def. 4), Orderly Transaction, Public Business Entity, Publicly Traded Entity (Def. 1), Registration Payment Arrangement, Reinsurance, Reinsurance Recoverable, and Related Parties

Liability Issued with an Inseparable Third-Party Credit Enhancement. A liability that is issued with a credit enhancement obtained from a third party, such as debt that is issued with a financial guarantee from a third party that guarantees the issuer's payment obligation.

CONCEPTS, RULES, AND EXAMPLES

ASC 825-10, *Overall*

Fair Value Option—Flexibility of Application ASC 825-10 provides management with substantial flexibility in electing the fair value option (FVO). Once elected, however, the election is irrevocable unless, as discussed later in this section, a new election date occurs. The election can be made for a single eligible item without electing it for other identical items subject to the following limitations:

1. If the FVO is elected with respect to an investment otherwise required to be accounted for under the equity method of accounting, the FVO election must be applied to all of the investor's financial interests in the same entity (equity and debt, including guarantees) that are eligible items.
2. If a single contract with a borrower (such as a line of credit or construction loan) involves multiple advances to that borrower and those advances lose their individual identity and are aggregated with the overall loan balance, the FVO is only permitted to be elected to apply to the larger overall loan balance and not individually with respect to each individual advance.

3. If the FVO is applied to an eligible insurance or reinsurance contract, it is also required to be applied to all claims and obligations under the contract.
4. If the FVO is elected for an eligible insurance contract (base contract) for which integrated or nonintegrated contract features or coverages (some of which are referred to as "riders") are issued either concurrently or subsequently, the FVO must be applied to those features and coverages. The FVO is not permitted to be elected for only the nonintegrated contract features and coverages, even though they are accounted for separately under ASC 944-30.[3]

(ASC 825-10-25-7)

Other than as provided in (1) and (2) above, management is not required to apply the FVO to all instruments issued or acquired in a single transaction. (ASC 825-10-25-10) The lowest level of election, however, is at the single legal contract level. A financial instrument that is in legal form a single contract is not permitted to be separated into component parts for the purpose of electing the FVO. (ASC 825-10-25-11) For example, an individual bond is the minimum denomination of that type of debt security.

An investor in an equity security of a particular issuer may elect the FVO for its entire investment in that equity security including any fractional shares issued by the investee in connection, for example, with a dividend reinvestment plan. (ASC 825-10-25-12)

Management of an acquirer, parent company, or primary beneficiary[4] decides whether to elect the FVO with respect to the eligible items of an acquiree, subsidiary, or consolidated variable interest entity. That decision, however, only applies in the consolidated financial statements. FVO choices made by management of an acquiree, subsidiary, or variable interest entity continue to apply in their separate financial statements should they choose to issue them. (ASC 825-10-25-6)

Timing of the Election Management may elect the FVO for an eligible item on the date of occurrence of one of the following events:

- The entity initially recognizes the item.
- The entity enters into an eligible firm commitment.
- Financial assets previously required to be reported at fair value with unrealized gains and losses included in income due to the application of specialized accounting principles cease to qualify for that accounting treatment (e.g., a subsidiary subject to ASC 946 transfers a security to another subsidiary of the same parent that is not subject to the ASC).
- The accounting treatment for an investment in another entity changes because:
    - the investment becomes subject to the equity method of accounting.
    - the investor ceases to consolidate a subsidiary or variable interest entity but retains an interest in the entity.
- An event requires an eligible item to be remeasured at fair value at the time that the event occurs but does not require fair value measurements to be made at each subsequent reporting date.

---

[3] ASC 944-30-20 defines a nonintegrated contract feature in an insurance contract as a feature in which the benefits provided are not related to or dependent on the provisions of the base contract. For the purposes of applying the FVO election, neither an integrated nor a nonintegrated contract feature or coverage qualifies as a separate instrument.

[4] Under ASC 805 a primary beneficiary is referred to as a parent in the same manner as a company that consolidates a voting interest entity.

Specifically excluded from being considered an eligible event are:

- Recognition of impairment under lower-of-cost-or-market accounting, or
- Other-than-temporary impairment.[5]

(ASC 825-10-25-4)

Among the events that require initial fair value measurement or subsequent fair value remeasurements of this kind are:

- Business combinations,
- Consolidation or deconsolidation of a subsidiary or variable interest entity, and
- Significant modifications of debt, as defined in ASC 470-50, *Debt—Modifications and Extinguishments*.
  (ASC 825-10-25-5)

Financial Statement Presentation and Disclosure

A robust section on the presentation and disclosure requirements for ASC 825 can be found at www.wiley.com/go/GAAP2021.

ASC 825-20, *REGISTRATION PAYMENT ARRANGEMENTS*

Recognition and Initial Measurement

Entities must recognize registration payment arrangements as separate units of account from the financial instruments subject to those arrangements. Those financial instruments are recognized and initially measured in accordance with other applicable, relevant GAAP. Entities recognize contingent obligations to make future payments or otherwise transfer consideration under registration payment arrangements separately in accordance with ASC 450-20. (ASC 825- 20-25-1 through 25-3 and 825-20-30-1 and 30-2)

A contingent obligation to make future payments or transfer consideration is measured separately using the guidance in ASC 450-20. (ASC 825-20-30-3) Using the measurement guidance in ASC 450-20, if the transfer of consideration is probable and reasonably estimable at inception, the contingent liability is included in the allocation of proceeds from the related financing transaction. The remaining periods are allocated using applicable GAAP. (ASC 825- 20-30-4)

The issuer's share price at the reporting date is used to measure the contingent liability under ASC 450-20 if all of the following are met:

- There is a requirement to deliver shares
- The transfer is probable
  (ASC 825-20-30-5)

After inception, if the consideration becomes probable and reasonably estimable, the charge is recognized in earnings. A sale equal to change in estimate is also recognized in earnings. (ASC 825-20-35-1)

[5] Upon implementation of ASU 2016-13, item 2 changes to "Accounting for Securities under ASC 321 or ASC 326."

53 ASC 830 FOREIGN CURRENCY MATTERS

ASC 830, *FOREIGN CURRENCY MATTERS*

PERSPECTIVE AND ISSUES

Subtopics

ASC 830 contains five subtopics:

- ASC 830-10, *Overall*
- ASC 830-20, *Foreign Currency Transactions*
- ASC 830-30, *Translation of Financial Statements*
- ASC 830-250, *Statement of Cash Flows*
- ASC 830-740, *Income Taxes*

ASC 830 provides guidance about:

- Foreign currency transactions, and
- Translation of financial statements

Scope and Scope Exceptions

ASC 830 applies to all entities. ASC 830-20 does not apply to derivative instruments. Preparers should look to ASC 815 for guidance on derivatives.

Overview

To facilitate the proper analysis of foreign operations by financial statement users, transactions and financial statements denominated in foreign currencies must be expressed in a common currency (i.e., U.S. dollars). Preparing financial statements in a single currency requires the entity to recognize and measure changes in the relationship between different units of currency. The GAAP governing the translation of foreign currency financial statements and the accounting for foreign currency transactions are found in ASC 830.

The guidance in ASC 830 was issued in 1981 and has not changed significantly since that time. The guidance makes four assumptions. It assumes the reporting entity:

- Is located in the United States,
- Uses the U.S. dollar as its reporting currency,
- Is an operating company with a functional currency in U.S. dollars, and
- Provides support to its foreign operations.

However, in today's global economy, some U.S. reporting entities are merely holding companies with no significant operations. This results in the four assumptions listed above no longer being true and has created challenges in applying the guidance. To prepare consolidated financial statements, amounts denominated in foreign currencies should be:

- Remeasured in the reporting currency and/or
- Translated into the reporting currency.

These two processes are outlined in the exhibit below.

Subtopic	Process	Description of Process	Reporting Changes
ASC 830-20	Remeasurement	Used to measure amounts that are denominated in a foreign currency other than its functional currency.	Transaction gains and losses reflected in net income.
ASC 830-30	Translation	Used to translate a foreign entity's financial information to the reporting currency when the foreign entity's financial records are maintained in its functional currency.	Translation adjustments recorded in a cumulative translation account, a component of other comprehensive income.

The objectives of translation are to provide:

- Information relative to the expected economic effects of rate changes on an enterprise's cash flows and equity.
- Information in consolidated statements relative to the financial results and relationships of each individual foreign consolidated entity as reflected by the functional currency of each reporting entity.
  (ASC 830-10-10-2)

These are the steps in the process to achieve these goals:

Step 1: Determine the functional currency of each foreign entity.
Step 2: Remeasure into its functional currency the account balances of each entity not denominated in the entity's functional currency.

Step 3: Translate financial statements of foreign entities to the reporting currency of the parent company
Step 4: Evaluate whether the cumulative translation account should be released into net income.

To understand and apply the guidance in ASC 830, it is important to understand the definitions below.

DEFINITIONS OF TERMS

Source: ASC 830, *Glossaries*. See Appendix A, *Definitions of Terms*, for additional terms relevant to this topic: Net Realizable Value and Not-for-Profit Entity.

Attribute. The quantifiable characteristic of an item that is measured for accounting purposes. For example, historical cost and current cost are attributes of an asset.

Exchange Rate. The ratio between a unit of one currency and the amount of another currency for which that unit can be exchanged at a particular time.

Foreign Currency. A currency other than the functional currency of the reporting entity being referred to (for example, the U.S. dollar could be a foreign currency for a foreign entity). Composites of currencies, such as the Special Drawing Rights on the International Monetary Fund (SDR), used to set prices, denominate amounts of loans, and the like have the characteristics of foreign currency for purposes of applying ASC 830.

Foreign Currency Statements. Financial statements that employ as the unit of measure a functional currency that is not the reporting currency of the enterprise.

Foreign Currency Transactions. Transactions whose terms are denominated in a currency other than the reporting entity's functional currency. Foreign currency transactions arise when an enterprise (1) buys or sells goods or services on credit whose prices are denominated in foreign currency, (2) borrows or lends funds and the amounts payable or receivable are denominated in foreign currency, (3) is a party to an unperformed forward exchange contract, or (4) for other reasons, acquires or disposes of assets or incurs or settles liabilities denominated in foreign currency.

Foreign Currency Translation. The process of expressing in the enterprise's reporting currency amounts that are denominated or measured in a different currency.

Foreign Entity. An operation (for example, subsidiary, division, branch, joint venture, and so forth) whose financial statements are both:

1. Prepared in a currency other than the reporting currency of the reporting entity
2. Combined or consolidated with or accounted for on the equity basis in the financial statements of the reporting entity.

Functional Currency. The currency of the primary economic environment in which the entity operates; normally, the currency of the environment in which the entity primarily generates and expends cash.

Local Currency. The currency of a particular country being referred to.

Noncontrolling Interest. The portion of equity (net assets) in a subsidiary not attributable, directly or indirectly, to a parent. A noncontrolling interest is sometimes called a minority interest.

Reporting Currency. The currency used by the entity to prepare its financial statements.

Reporting Entity. An entity or group of entities whose financial statements are being referred to. Those financial statements reflect (1) the financial statements of one or more foreign operations by combination, consolidation, or equity method accounting; (2) foreign currency transactions; or (3) both.

Transaction Gain or Loss. Transaction gains or losses result from a change in exchange rates between the functional currency and the currency in which a foreign currency transaction is denominated. They represent an increase or decrease in (1) the actual functional currency cash flows realized upon settlement of foreign currency transactions and (2) the expected functional currency cash flows on unsettled foreign currency transactions.

Translation Adjustments. Translation adjustments result from the process of translating financial statements from the entity's functional currency into the reporting currency.

CONCEPTS, RULES, AND EXAMPLES

Determining the Functional Currency

Before the financial statements of a foreign branch, division, or subsidiary are translated into U.S. dollars, the management of the U.S. entity must determine which currency is the functional currency of the foreign entity. Once determined, the functional currency cannot be changed unless economic facts and circumstances have clearly changed. Additionally, previously issued financial statements are not restated for any changes in the functional currency. (ASC 830-10-45-7) The functional currency decision is crucial, because different translation methods are applied which may have a material effect on the U.S. entity's financial statements.

The FASB defines functional currency but does not list definitive criteria that, if satisfied, would with certainty result in the identification of an entity's functional currency. Rather, realizing that such criteria would be difficult to develop, the FASB listed various factors that were intended to give management guidance in making the functional currency decision. These factors include:

- *Cash flows.* Do the foreign entity's cash flows directly affect the parent's cash flows and are they immediately available for remittance to the parent?
- *Sales prices.* Are the foreign entity's sales prices responsive to exchange rate changes and to international competition?
- *Sales markets.* Is the foreign entity's sales market the parent's country or are sales denominated in the parent's currency?
- *Expenses.* Are the foreign entity's expenses incurred primarily in the parent's country?
- *Financing.* Is the foreign entity's financing primarily from the parent or is it denominated in the parent's currency?
- *Intercompany transactions.* Is there a high volume of intercompany transactions between the parent and the foreign entity?
  (ASC 810-55-5)

If the answers to the questions above are predominantly yes, the functional currency is the reporting currency of the parent entity (i.e., the U.S. dollar). If the answers are predominantly no, the functional currency would most likely be the local currency of the foreign entity, although it is possible for a foreign currency other than the local currency to be the functional currency.

Once the functional currency is determined, the entity proceeds to steps 2 or 3. The flowchart below explains how to make that decision.

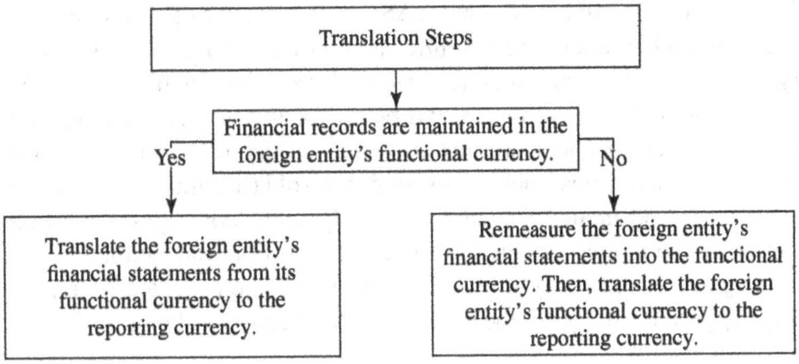

Translation When Foreign Entity Maintains Financial Records in Its Functional Currency

Current Rate Method All assets and liabilities are translated at the exchange rate at the balance sheet date. Revenues and expenses are translated at rates in effect when the transactions occur, but those that occur evenly over the year may be translated at the weighted-average rate for the year. (ASC 830-30-45-3)

The Codification recognizes the detailed record-keeping may be burdensome and, therefore, allows averages or other approximations. (ASC 830-10-55-10) Note that weighted-average, if used, must take into account the actual pace and pattern of changes in exchange rates over the course of the year, which will often not be varying at a constant rate throughout the period nor, in many instances, monotonically increasing or decreasing over the period. When these conditions do not hold, it is incumbent upon the reporting entity to develop a weighted-average exchange rate that is meaningful under the circumstances. When coupled with transactions (sales, purchases, etc.) that also have not occurred evenly throughout the year, this determination can become a fairly complex undertaking, requiring careful attention. (ASC 830-10-55-11)

The theoretical basis for the current rate method is the "net investment concept," wherein the foreign entity is viewed as a separate entity in which the parent invested, rather than being considered part of the parent's operations. The FASB's reasoning was that financial statement users can benefit most when the information provided about the foreign entity retains the relationships and results created in the environment (economic, legal, and political) in which the entity operates. Converting all assets and liabilities at the same current rate accomplishes this objective.

The rationale for this approach is that foreign-denominated debt is often used to purchase assets that create foreign-denominated revenues. These revenue-producing assets act as a natural hedge against changes in the settlement amount of the debt due to changes in the exchange rate. The excess (net) assets—which are the U.S. parent entity's net equity investment in the foreign operation—will, however, be affected by this foreign exchange risk, and this effect is recognized by the parent.

Translation When a Foreign Entity Maintains Financial Records in a Currency Other Than Its Functional Currency

Remeasurement Method The remeasurement method has also been referred to as the monetary/nonmonetary method. This approach is used when the foreign entity's accounting records are *not* maintained in the functional currency. (ASC 830-10-55-17) This method translates monetary assets (cash and other assets and liabilities that will be settled in cash) at the current rate. Nonmonetary assets, liabilities, and stockholders' equity are translated at the appropriate historical rates. The appropriate historical rate would be the exchange rate at the date the transaction involving the nonmonetary account originated. Also, the income statement amounts related to nonmonetary assets and liabilities, such as cost of goods sold (inventory), depreciation (property, plant, and equipment), and intangibles amortization (patents, copyrights), are translated at the same rate as used for the related statement of financial position translation. Other revenues and expenses occurring evenly over the year may be translated at the weighted-average exchange rate in effect during the period, subject to the considerations discussed above.

Examples

Both of these methods are illustrated below. All amounts in the following two illustrations, other than exchange rates, are in thousands.

Example of the Current Rate Method

Assume that a U.S. entity has a 100% owned subsidiary in Italy that commenced operations in 20X2. The subsidiary's operations consist of leasing space in an office building. This building, which cost one million euros, was financed primarily by Italian banks. All revenues and cash expenses are received and paid in euros. The subsidiary also maintains its accounting records in euros. As a result, management of the U.S. entity has decided that the euro is the functional currency of the subsidiary.

The subsidiary's statement of financial position at December 31, 20X2, and its combined statement of income and retained earnings for the year ended December 31, 20X2, are presented below in euros.

Italian Company
Statement of Financial Position
at December 31, 20X2
(€000 omitted)

Assets		**Liabilities and Stockholders' Equity**	
Cash	€ 100	Accounts payable	€ 60
Accounts receivable	40	Unearned rent	20
Land	200	Mortgage payable	800
Building	1,000	Common stock	80
Accumulated depreciation	(20)	Additional paid-in capital	320
		Retained earnings	40
Total assets	€ 1,320	Total liabilities and stockholders' equity	€ 1,320

Italian Company
Statement of Income and Retained Earnings
for the Year Ended December 31, 20X2
(€000 omitted)

Revenues	€ 400
Expenses (including depreciation of €20)	340
Net income	60
Retained earnings, January 1, 20X2	–
Less dividends declared	(20)
Retained earnings, December 31, 20X2	€ 40

Various exchange rates for 20X2 are as follows:

€ 1 = $1.50 at the beginning of 20X2 (when the common stock was issued and the land and building were financed through the mortgage)

€ 1 = $1.55 weighted-average for 20X2

€ 1 = $1.58 at the date the dividends were declared and paid and the unearned rent was received

€ 1 = $1.62 at the end of 20X2

Since the euro is the functional currency, the Italian Company's financial statements must be translated into U.S. dollars by the current rate method. This translation process is illustrated below.

Italian Company
Statement of Financial Position Translation
(The euro is the functional currency) at December 31, 20X2
(€/$000 omitted)

	Euros	*Exchange rate*	*U.S. dollars*
Assets			
Cash	€ 100	1.62	$162.00
Accounts receivable, net	40	1.62	64.80
Land	200	1.62	320.00
Building, net	980	1.62	1,587.60
Total assets	€1,320		$ 2,138.40
Liabilities and Stockholders' Equity			
Accounts payable	€ 60	1.62	$97.20
Unearned rent	20	1.62	32.40
Mortgage payable	800	1.62	1,296.00
Common stock	80	1.50	120.00
Additional paid-in capital	320	1.50	480.00
Retained earnings	40	See income statement	61.40
Translation adjustments	–	See computation below	51.40
Total liabilities and stockholders' equity	€ 1,320		$ 2,138.40

Italian Company
Statement of Income and Retained Earnings
Statement Translation
(The euro is the functional currency)
for the Year Ended December 31, 20X2
(€/$000 omitted)

	Euros	*Exchange rate*	*U.S. dollars*
Revenues	€ 400	1.55	$ 620.00
Expenses (including depreciation of €20 [$31.00])	340	1.55	527.00
Net income	60	1.55	93.00
Retained earnings, January 1	–	–	–
Less dividends declared	(20)	1.58	(31.60)
Retained earnings, December 31	€ 40		$ 61.40

Italian Company
Statement of Cash Flows
Statement Translation
(The euro is the functional currency)
for the Year Ended December 31, 20X2
(€/$000 omitted)

	Euros	Exchange rate	U.S. dollars
Operating activities			
Net income	€60	1.55	$93.00
Adjustments to reconcile net income to net cash provided by operating activities			
Depreciation	20	1.55	31.00
Increase in accounts receivable	(40)	1.55	(62.00)
Increase in accounts payable	60	1.55	93.00
Increase in unearned rent	20	1.58	31.60
Net cash provided by operating activities	120		186.60
Investing activities			
Purchase of land	(200)	1.50	(300.00)
Purchase of building	(1,000)	1.50	$ (1,500.00)
Net cash used by investing activities	(1,200)		(1,800.00)
Financing activities			
Proceeds from issuance of common	400	1.50	600.00
Proceeds from mortgage payable	800	1.50	1,200.00
Dividends paid	(20)	1.58	(31.60)
Net cash provided by financing activities	1,180		1,768.40
Effect of exchange rate changes on cash	N/A		7.00
Increase in cash and equivalents	100		162.00
Cash at beginning of year	0		0
Cash at end of year	€100	1.62	$62.00

Note the following points concerning the current rate method:

1. All assets and liabilities are translated using the current exchange rate at the date of the statement of financial position (€1 = $1.62). All revenues and expenses are translated at the rates in effect when these items are recognized during the period. Due to practical considerations, however, weighted-average rates can be used to translate revenues and expenses (€1 = $1.55).
2. Stockholders' equity accounts are translated by using historical exchange rates. Common stock was issued at the beginning of 20X2 when the exchange rate was €1 = $1.50. The translated balance of retained earnings is the result of the weighted-average rate applied to revenues and expenses and the specific rate in effect when the dividends were declared (€1 = $1.58).
3. Translation adjustments result from translating all assets and liabilities at the current rate, while stockholders' equity is translated by using historical and weighted-average rates. The adjustments have no direct effect on cash flows. Also, the translation adjustment is due to the net investment rather than the subsidiary's operations. For these reasons, the cumulative translation adjustments balance is reported as a component of accumulated other comprehensive income (AOCI) in the stockholders' equity section of the U.S. parent

entity's consolidated statement of financial position. This balance essentially equates the total debits of the subsidiary (now expressed in U.S. dollars) with the total credits (also in dollars). It also may be determined directly, as shown next, to verify the translation process.

4. The translation adjustments credit of $30.70 is calculated as follows for the differences between the exchange rate of $1.62 at the end of the year and the applicable exchange rates used to translate changes in net assets:

Net assets at inception (Land and buildings of $1,200,000 – Portion financed by mortgage of $800,000)	400 × ($1.62 – $1.50)	=	$ 48.00 credit
Net income	60 × ($1.62 – $1.55)	=	4.20 credit
Dividends declared	20 × ($1.62 – $1.58)	=	0.80 debit
Translation adjustment			$ 51.40 credit

5. The translation adjustments balance that appears as a component of AOCI in the stockholders' equity section is cumulative in nature. Consequently, the change in this balance during the year is disclosed as a component of other comprehensive income (OCI) for the period. In the illustration, this balance went from zero to $51.40 at the end of 20X2. In addition, assume the following occurred during the following year, 20X3:

Italian Company
Statement of Financial Position
at December 31
(€000 omitted)

	20X3	*20X2*	*Increase/(Decrease)*
Assets			
Cash	€ 200	€ 100	€ 100
Accounts receivable, net	–	40	(40)
Land	300	200	100
Building, net	960	980	(20)
Total assets	€ 1,460	€ 1,320	€ 140
Liabilities and Stockholders' Equity			
Accounts payable	€ 100	€60	€ 40
Unearned rent	0	20	(20)
Mortgage payable	900900	800	100
Common stock	80	80	0
Additional paid-in capital	320	320	0
Retained earnings	60	40	20
Total liabilities and stockholders' equity	€ 1,460	€ 1,320	€ 140

Italian Company
Statement of Income and Retained Earnings
for the Year Ended December 31, 20X3
(€000 omitted)

Revenues	€440
Operating expenses (including depreciation of €20)	340
Net income	100
Retained earnings, January 1, 20X3	40
Less: Dividends declared	(80)
Retained earnings, December 31, 20X3	€ 60

Exchange rates were:

€1 = \$1.62 at the beginning of 20×3

€1 = \$1.65 weighted-average for 20×3

€1 = \$1.71 at the end of 20×3

€1 = \$1.68 when dividends were declared in 20×3 and additional land bought by incurring mortgage

The translation process for 20X3 is illustrated below.

Italian Company
Statement of Financial Position Translation
(The euro is the functional currency)
at December 31, 20X3
(€/\$000 omitted)

	Euros	*Exchange rate*	*U.S. dollars*
Assets			
Cash	€ 200	1.71	\$342.00
Land	300	1.71	513.00
Building, net	960	1.71	1,641.60
Total assets	€ 1,460		\$ 2,496.60
Liabilities and Stockholders' Equity			
Accounts payable	€100	1.71	\$171.00
Mortgage payable	900	1.71	1,539.00
Common stock	80	1.50	120.00
Additional paid-in capital	320	1.50	480.00
Retained earnings	60	See income statement	92.00
Translation adjustments	–	See computation below	94.60
Total liabilities and stockholders' equity	€ 1,460		\$ 2,496.60

Italian Company
Statement of Income and Retained Earnings
Statement Translation
(The euro is the functional currency)
for the Year Ended December 31, 20X3
(€/\$000 omitted)

	Euros	*Exchange rate*	*U.S. dollars*
Revenues	€ 440	1.65	\$ 726.00
Expenses (including depreciation of €10 [\$12.50])	340	1.65	561.00
Net income	100	1.65	165.00
Retained earnings, January 1, 20X3	40	–	61.40
Less: Dividends declared	(80)	1.68	(134.40)
Retained earnings, December 31, 20X3	€ 60		\$ 92.00

Italian Company
Statement of Cash Flows
Statement Translation
(The euro is the functional currency)
for the Year Ended December 31, 20X3
(€/$000 omitted)

	Euros	Exchange rate	U.S. dollars
Operating activities			
Net income	€100	1.65	$ 165.00
Adjustments to reconcile net income to net cash provided by operating activities			
Depreciation	20	1.65	33.00
Decrease in accounts receivable	40	1.65	66.00
Increase in accounts payable	40	1.65	66.00
Decrease in unearned rent	(20)	1.65	(33.00)
Net cash provided by operating activities	180		297.00
Investing activities			
Purchase of land	(100)	1.68	(168.00)
Net cash used by investing activities	(100)		(168.00)
Financing activities			
Mortgage payable	100	1.68	168.00
Dividends	(80)	1.68	(134.40)
Net cash provided by financing activities	20		33.60
Effect of exchange rate changes on cash	N/A		17.40
Increase in cash and equivalents	100		180.00
Cash at beginning of year	100		162.00
Cash at end of year	€ 200	1.71	$ 342.00

Using the analysis presented before, the *change* in the translation adjustment attributable to 20X3 is computed as follows:

Net assets at January 1, 20X3	€440	($1.71 – $1.62)	=	$39.60	credit
Net income for 20X3	€100	($1.71 – $1.65)	=	6.00	credit
Dividends for 20X3	€ 80	($1.71 – $1.68)	=	2.40	debit
Total				$ 43.20	credit

The balance in the cumulative translation adjustment component of AOCI at the end of 20X3 is $94.60. ($51.40 from 20X2 and $43.20 from 20X3.)

6. The use of the equity method by the U.S. parent entity in accounting for the subsidiary would result in the following journal entries (in $000s), based upon the information presented above:

	20X2		20X3	
Original investment				
Investment in Italian subsidiary	600*		–	
Cash		600		–

** € 80 of common stock + €320 of additional paid-in capital = €400 translated at €1.50 = $600.*

Earnings pickup				
Investment in Italian subsidiary	93.00		165.00	
Equity in subsidiary income		93.00		165.00
Dividends received				
Cash	31.60		134.40	
Investment in Italian subsidiary		31.60		134.40
Translation adjustments				
Investment in Italian subsidiary	51.40		43.20	
OCI—Translation adjustments		51.40		43.20

Note that in applying the equity method to record this activity in the U.S. parent entity's accounting records, the parent's stockholders' equity should be the same whether or not the Italian subsidiary is consolidated. Since the subsidiary does not report the translation adjustments on its financial statements, care should be exercised so that it is not forgotten in the application of the equity method.

7. If the U.S. entity disposes of its investment in the Italian subsidiary, the cumulative translation adjustments balance becomes part of the gain or loss that results from the transaction and is eliminated. Guidance requires that when a parent ceases to hold a controlling interest *within* a foreign entity, the parent should apply ASC 830-30 and release any cumulative foreign translation adjustment into net income. For an equity method investment in a foreign entity, the partial sale guidance in ASC 830-40 applies.

   For example, assume that on January 2, 20X4, the U.S. entity sells its entire investment for €465,000. The exchange rate at this date is €1 = $1.71. The balance in the investment account at December 31, 20X3, is $786,600 as a result of the entries made previously.

   The following entries would be made by the U.S. parent entity to reflect the sale of the investment:

Cash (€465 × $1.71 conversion rate)	795.15	
Investment in Italian subsidiary		786.60
Gain from sale of subsidiary		8.55
AOCI—Translation adjustments	94.60	
Gain from sale of subsidiary		94.60

If the U.S. entity had sold only a portion of its investment in the Italian subsidiary, only a pro rata portion of the accumulated translation adjustments balance would have become part of the gain or loss from the transaction. To illustrate, if 80% of the Italian subsidiary was sold for €372 on January 2, 20X4, the following journal entries would be made:

Cash (€372 × $1.71 exchange rate)	636.12	
Investment in Italian subsidiary (80% × $786.60)		629.28
Gain from sale of subsidiary		6.84
AOCI—Translation adjustments (80% × $94.60)	75.68	
Gain from sale of subsidiary		75.68

An exchange rate might not be available if there is a temporary suspension of foreign exchange trading.

ASC 830-30-55 provides that, if exchangeability between two currencies is temporarily lacking at a transaction date or the date of the statement of financial position, the first subsequent rate at which exchanges could be made is to be used to implement ASC 830.

Example of the Remeasurement Method

In the previous situation, the euro was the functional currency because the Italian subsidiary's cash flows were primarily in euros. Assume, however, that the financing of the land and building was denominated in U.S. dollars instead of euros and that the mortgage payable is denominated in U.S. dollars (i.e., it must be repaid in U.S. dollars). Although the rents collected and the majority of the cash flows for expenses are in euros, management has decided that, due to the manner of financing, the U.S. dollar is the functional currency. The accounting records, however, are maintained in euros.

The remeasurement of the Italian financial statements is accomplished by use of the remeasurement method (also known as the monetary/nonmonetary method). This method is illustrated below using the same information that was presented before for the Italian subsidiary.

Italian Company
Statement of Financial Position (Remeasurement)
(The U.S. dollar is the functional currency)
at December 31, 20X2
(€/$000 omitted)

	Euros	*Exchange rate*	*U.S. dollars*
Assets			
Cash	€ 100	1.62	$162.00
Accounts receivable, net	40	1.62	64.80
Land	200	1.50	300.00
Building, net	980	1.50	1,470.00
Total assets	€ 1,320		$ 1,996.80
Liabilities and Stockholders' Equity			
Accounts payable	€60	1.62	$97.20
Unearned rent	20	1.58	31.60
Mortgage payable	800	1.62	1,296.00
Common stock	80	1.50	120.00
Additional paid-in capital	320	1.50	480.00
Retained earnings	40	(See income statement)	(28.00)
Total liabilities and stockholders' equity	€ 1,320		$ 1,996.80

Italian Company
Statement of Income and Retained Earnings (Remeasurement)
(The U.S. dollar is the functional currency)
for the Year Ended December 31, 20X2
(€/$000 omitted)

	Euros	*Exchange rate*	*U.S.dollars*
Revenues	€ 400	1.55	$ 620.00
Expenses (not including depreciation)	(320)	1.55	496.00
Depreciation expense	(20)	1.50	(30.00)
Remeasurement loss	–	See analysis below	(90.40)
Net income (loss)	60	–	(3.60)
Retained earnings, January 1	–	–	–
Less dividends declared	(20)	1.58	(31.60)
Retained earnings, December 31	€ 40		$ (28.00)

Italian Company
Remeasurement Loss
(The U.S. dollar is the functional currency)
for the Year Ended December 31, 20X2
(€/$000 omitted)

	Euros Debit	Euros Credit	Exchange rate	U.S. dollars Debit	U.S. dollars Credit
Cash	€ 100		1.62	$ 162.00	
Accounts receivable, net	40		1.62	64.80	
Land	200		1.50	300.00	
Building, net	980		1.50	1,470.00	
Accounts payable		€60	1.62		$97.20
Unearned rent		20	1.58		31.60
Mortgage payable		800	1.62		1,296.00
Common stock		80	1.50		120.00
Additional paid-in capital		320	1.50		480.00
Retained earnings		–	–		
Dividends declared	20		1.58		31.60
Revenues		400	1.55		620.00
Operating expenses	320		1.55	496.00	
Depreciation expenses	20		1.50	30.00	
Totals	€ 1,680	€ 1,680		$ 2,554.40	$ 2,644.80
Remeasurement loss				90.40	
Totals				$ 2,644.80	$ 2,644.80

Italian Company
Statement of Cash Flows (Remeasurement)
(The U.S. dollar is the functional currency)
for the Year Ended December 31, 20X2
(€/$000 omitted)

	Euros	Exchange rate	U.S. dollars
Operating activities			
Net income (loss)	€ 60	See income statement	$ 3.60
Adjustments to reconcile net income to net cash provided by operating activities			
Remeasurement loss	–	See income statement	90.40
Depreciation	20	1.50	30.00
Increase in accounts receivable	(40)	1.55	(62.00)
Increase in accounts payable	60	1.55	93.00
Increase in unearned rent	20	1.58	31.60
Net cash provided by operating activities	120		186.60
Investing activities			
Purchase of land	(200)	1.50	(300.00)
Purchase of building	(1,000)	1.50	(1,500.00)
Net cash used by investing activities	(1,200)		(1,800.00)
Financing activities			
Proceeds from issuance of common	400	1.50	600.00
Proceeds from mortgage payable	800	1.50	1,200.00
Dividends paid	(20)	1.58	(31.60)
Net cash provided by financing activities	1,180		1,768.40
Effect of exchange rate changes on cash	N/A		7.00
Increase in cash and equivalents	100		162.00
Cash at beginning of year			0
Cash at end of year	€ 100	1.62	$ 62.00

Note the following points concerning the remeasurement method:

1. Assets and liabilities that have historical cost balances (nonmonetary assets and liabilities) are remeasured by using historical exchange rates (i.e., the rates in effect when the transactions giving rise to the balance first occurred). Monetary assets and monetary liabilities, cash, and those items that will be settled in cash, are remeasured by using the current exchange rate at the date of the statement of financial position. In 20X2, the unearned rent from year-end 20X2 of €10 would be remeasured at the rate of €1 = $1.58. The unearned rent at the end of 20X2 is not considered a monetary liability. Therefore, the $1.58 historical exchange rate is used for all applicable future years. See the final Section of this chapter, titled "Accounts to Be Remeasured Using Historical Exchange Rates" for a listing of accounts that are remeasured using historical exchange rates.
2. Revenues and expenses that occur frequently during a period are remeasured, for practical purposes, by using the weighted-average exchange rate for the period. Revenues and expenses that represent allocations of historical balances (e.g., depreciation, cost of goods sold, and amortization of intangibles) are remeasured using historical exchange rates. Note that this is a different treatment as compared to the current rate method.
3. If the functional currency is the U.S. dollar rather than the local foreign currency, the amounts of specific line items presented in the reconciliation of net income to net cash flow from operating activities will be different for nonmonetary items (e.g., depreciation).
4. The calculation of the remeasurement gain (loss), in a purely mechanical sense, is the amount needed to make the dollar debits equal the dollar credits in the Italian entity's trial balance.
5. The remeasurement loss of $90.40 is reported on the U.S. parent entity's consolidated income statement because the U.S. dollar is the functional currency. When the reporting currency is the functional currency, as it is in this example, it is assumed that all of the foreign entity's transactions occurred in U.S. dollars (even if this was not the case). Accordingly, remeasurement gains and losses are taken immediately to the income statement in the year in which they occur as they can be expected to have direct cash flow effects on the parent entity. They are not deferred as a translation adjustments component of AOCI, as they were when the functional currency was the euro (applying the current rate method).
6. The use of the equity method of accounting for the subsidiary would result in the following entries by the U.S. parent entity during 20X2:

Original investment		
Investment in Italian subsidiary	600.00	
Cash		600.00
Earnings (loss) pickup		
Investment in Italian subsidiary	3.60	
Equity in subsidiary income		3.60
Dividends received		
Cash	31.60	
Investment in Italian subsidiary		31.60

Note that remeasurement gains and losses are included in the subsidiary's net income (net loss) as determined in U.S. dollars before the earnings (loss) pickup is made by the U.S. entity.

7. In economies in which—per ASC 830-10-45—cumulative inflation is greater than 100% over a three-year period, FASB requires that the functional currency be the reporting currency, that is, the U.S. dollar. Projections of future inflation cannot be used to satisfy this threshold condition. The remeasurement method must be used in this situation even though the factors indicate the local currency is the functional currency. FASB made this decision to prevent the evaporation of the foreign entity's fixed assets, a result that would occur if the local currency was the functional currency.

Cessation of Highly Inflationary Condition When a foreign subsidiary's economy is no longer considered highly inflationary, the entity converts the reporting currency values into the local currency at the exchange rates on the date of change on which these values become the new functional currency accounting bases for nonmonetary assets and liabilities. (ASC 830-10-45-15) Furthermore, ASC 830-740 states that when a change in functional currency designation occurs because an economy ceases to be highly inflationary, the deferred taxes on the temporary differences that arise as a result of a change in the functional currency are treated as an adjustment to the cumulative translation adjustments portion of stockholders' equity (accumulated other comprehensive income).

Applying ASC 740 to Foreign Entity Financials Restated for General Price Levels Price level-adjusted financial statements are preferred for foreign currency financial statements of entities operating in highly inflationary economies when those financial statements are intended for readers in the United States. If this recommendation is heeded, the result is that the income tax bases of the assets and liabilities are often restated for inflation. ASC 830-740 provides guidance on applying the asset-and-liability approach of ASC 740 as it relates to such financial statements. It discusses (1) how temporary differences are to be computed under ASC 740, and how deferred income tax expense or benefit for the year is to be determined.

With regard to the first issue, temporary differences are computed as the difference between the indexed income tax basis amount and the related price-level restated amount of the asset or liability. The consensus reached on the second issue is that the deferred income tax expense or benefit is the difference between the deferred income tax assets and liabilities reported at the end of the current year and those reported at the end of the prior year. The deferred income tax assets and liabilities of the prior year are recalculated in units of the current year-end purchasing power.

On a related matter, ASC 830-10-45-16 states that, when the functional currency changes to the reporting currency because the foreign economy has become highly inflationary, ASC 740 prohibits recognition of deferred income tax benefits associated with indexing assets and liabilities that are remeasured in the reporting currency using historical exchange rates. Any related income tax benefits would be recognized only upon their being realized for income tax purposes. Any deferred income tax benefits that had been recognized for indexing before the change in reporting currency is effected are eliminated when the related indexed amounts are realized as income tax deductions.

Application of ASC 830 to an Investment to Be Disposed of That Is Evaluated for Impairment Under ASC 830, accumulated foreign currency translation adjustments are reclassified to net income only when realized upon sale or upon complete or substantially complete liquidation of the investment in the foreign entity. ASC 830-30-45 addresses whether a reporting entity is to include the translation adjustments in the carrying amount of the investment in assessing impairment of an investment in a foreign entity that is held for disposal if the planned disposal will cause some or all of the translation adjustments to be reclassified to net income. The standard points out that an entity that has committed to a plan that will cause the translation adjustments for an equity-method investment or consolidated investment in a foreign entity to be reclassified to earnings is to include the translation adjustments as part of the carrying amount of the investment when evaluating that investment for impairment. An entity would also include the portion of the translation adjustments that represents a gain or loss from an effective hedge of the net investment in a foreign operation as part of the carrying amount of the investment when making this evaluation. (ASC 830-30-45-13)

Foreign Operations in the United States

With the world economy as interconnected as it is, entities in the United States are sometimes the subsidiaries of parent companies domiciled elsewhere in the world. The financial statements of the U.S. entity may be presented separately in the United States or may be combined as part of the financial statements in the foreign country.

In general, financial statements of U.S. companies are prepared in accordance with U.S. GAAP. However, adjustments may be necessary to conform these financial statements to the accounting principles of the foreign country of the parent entity where they will be consolidated.

Translation of Foreign Currency Transactions

According to ASC 830, a foreign currency transaction is a transaction ". . . denominated in a currency other than the entity's functional currency." Denominated means that the amount to be received or paid is fixed in terms of the number of units of a particular foreign currency regardless of changes in the exchange rate. From the viewpoint of a U.S. entity, a foreign currency transaction results when it imports or exports goods or services to or from a foreign entity or makes a loan involving a foreign entity and agrees to settle the transaction in currency other than the U.S. dollar (the functional currency of the U.S. entity). In these situations, the U.S. entity has "crossed currencies" and directly assumes the risk of fluctuating exchange rates of the foreign currency in which the transaction is denominated. This risk may lead to recognition of foreign exchange transaction gains or losses in the income statement of the U.S. entity. Note that transaction gains or losses can result only when the foreign transactions are denominated in a foreign currency. (ASC 830-20-35-1) When a U.S. entity imports or exports goods or services and the transaction is to be settled in U.S. dollars, the U.S. entity is not exposed to a foreign exchange gain or loss because it bears no risk due to exchange rate fluctuations.

Example of Foreign Currency Transaction Translation

The following example illustrates the terminology and procedures applicable to the translation of foreign currency transactions. Assume that U.S. Company, an exporter, sells merchandise to a customer in Italy on December 1, 20X2, for €10,000. Receipt is due on January 31, 20X3, and U.S. Company prepares financial statements on December 31, 20X2. At the transaction date (December 1, 20X2), the spot rate for immediate exchange of foreign currencies indicates that €1 is equivalent to $1.30. To find the U.S. dollar equivalent of this transaction, the foreign currency amount, €10,000, is multiplied by $1.30 to get $13,000. At December 1, 20X2, the foreign currency transaction is recorded by U.S. Company in the following manner:

Accounts receivable—Italy (€ denominated)	13,000	
Sales		13,000

The accounts receivable and sales are measured in U.S. dollars at the transaction date using the spot rate at the time of the transaction. While the accounts receivable is measured and reported in U.S. dollars, the receivable is denominated or fixed in euros. This characteristic may result in foreign exchange transaction gains or losses if the spot rate for the euro changes between the transaction date and the date the transaction is settled (January 31, 20X3).

If financial statements are prepared between the transaction date and the settlement date, all receivables and liabilities denominated in a currency other than the functional currency (the U.S. dollar) must be restated to reflect the spot rates in effect at the statement of financial position date. Assume that on December 31, 20X2, the spot rate for euros is €1 = $1.32. This means that the €10,000 are now worth $13,200 and that the accounts receivable denominated in euros has increased by $200. The following adjustment is recorded on December 31, 20X2:

Accounts receivable—Italy (€ denominated)	200	
Foreign currency transaction gain		200

Note that the $13,000 credit to sales recorded on the transaction date is not affected by subsequent changes in the spot rate. This treatment exemplifies the two-transaction viewpoint adopted by FASB. In other words, making the sale is the result of an operating decision, while bearing the risk of fluctuating spot rates is the result of a financing decision. Therefore, the amount determined as sales revenue at the transaction date is not altered because of the financing decisions to wait until January 31, 20X3, for payment of the account and to accept payment denominated in euros. The risk of a foreign exchange transaction loss can be avoided by (1) demanding immediate payment on December 1, 20X2, (2) fixing the price of the transaction in U.S. dollars instead of in the foreign currency, or (3) by entering into a forward exchange contract to hedge the exposed asset (accounts receivable). The fact that, in the example, U.S. Company did not take any of these actions is reflected by recognizing foreign currency transaction gains or losses in its income statement (reported as financial or nonoperating items) in the period during which the exchange rates changed. This treatment has been criticized, however, because earnings will fluctuate because of changes in exchange rates and not because of changes in the economic activities of the enterprise. The counterargument, however, is that economic reality is that earnings *are* fluctuating because the management chose to commit the reporting entity to a transaction that exposes it to economic risks and, therefore, the case can be made that the volatility in earnings faithfully represents the results of management's business decision.

On the settlement date (January 31, 20X3), assume the spot rate is €1 = $1.31. The receipt of €10,000 and their conversion into U.S. dollars is recorded as follows:

Foreign currency (€)	13,100	
Foreign currency transaction loss	100	
Accounts receivable—Italy (€ denominated)		13,200
Cash	13,100	
Foreign currency (€)		13,100

The net effect of this foreign currency transaction was to receive $13,100 in settlement from a sale that was originally measured (and recognized) at $13,000. This realized net foreign currency transaction gain of $100 is reported on two income statements—a $200 gain in 20X2 and a $100 loss in 20X3. The reporting of the gain or loss in two income statements causes a temporary difference in the basis of the receivable for income tax and financial reporting purposes. This results because the 20X2 unrealized transaction gain of $200 is not taxable until 20X3, the year the transaction was ultimately completed or settled. Accordingly, deferred income tax accounting is required to account for the effects of this temporary difference.

It is important to note that all monetary assets and liabilities of U.S. Company that are denominated in a currency other than U.S. Company's functional currency (the U.S. dollar) are required to be remeasured at the date of each statement of financial position to the extent that they are affected by increases or decreases in the exchange rate. For example, a U.S. Company whose functional currency is the U.S. dollar holds a bank account in France that is denominated in euros. At the date of each statement of financial position, by reference to the spot rate for the euro, U.S. Company would remeasure the carrying amount of its French bank account and record any resulting transaction gains and losses in the same manner as above.

Intercompany Transactions and Elimination of Intercompany Profits

Gains or losses from intercompany transactions are reported on the U.S. company's consolidated income statement unless settlement of the transaction is not planned or anticipated in the foreseeable future. In that case, which is atypical, gains and losses arising from intercompany transactions are reflected in the accumulated translations adjustments component of accumulated other comprehensive income in stockholders' equity of the U.S. entity. In the typical situation (i.e., gains and losses reported on the U.S. entity's income statement) gains and losses result whether the functional currency is the U.S. dollar or the foreign entity's local currency. When the U.S. dollar is the functional currency, foreign currency transaction gains and losses result because of one of the two situations below:

1. The intercompany foreign currency transaction is denominated in U.S. dollars. In this case, the foreign subsidiary has a payable or receivable denominated in U.S. dollars. This may result in a foreign currency transaction gain or loss that would appear on the foreign subsidiary's income statement. This gain or loss would be translated into U.S. dollars and would appear on the U.S. entity's consolidated income statement.
2. The intercompany foreign currency transaction is denominated in the foreign subsidiary's local currency. In this situation, the U.S. entity has a payable or receivable denominated in a foreign currency. Such a situation may result in a foreign currency transaction gain or loss that is reported on the U.S. parent entity's income statement.

The above two cases can be easily altered to reflect what happens when the foreign entity's local currency is the functional currency. The gain or loss from each of these scenarios would be reflected on the other entity's financial statements first (i.e., the subsidiary's rather than the parent's and vice versa).

The elimination of intercompany profits due to sales and other transfers between related entities is based upon exchange rates in effect when the sale or transfer occurred. Reasonable approximations and averages are allowed to be used if intercompany transactions occur frequently during the year.

Example of Intercompany Transactions Involving Foreign Exchange

Cassiopeia Corporation buys an observatory-grade telescope from its Spanish subsidiary for €850,000, resulting in a profit for the subsidiary of €50,000 on the sale date at an exchange rate of

$1:€0.6 (euros). The profit is eliminated at $1:€0.6. The payable to the subsidiary is due in 90 days, and is denominated in euros. On the payment date, the exchange rate has changed to $1:€0.65. Thus, rather than paying $1,416,667 to settle the payable, as would have been the case on the sale date, Cassiopeia must now pay $1,307,692 on the payable date. Cassiopeia presents the $108,975 exchange gain in its income statement in the following manner:

Sales	$ 20,000,000
Cost of sales	$ (14,000,000)
Gross profit	6,000,000
Operating expenses	(5,500,000)
Other revenues/gains (expenses/losses)	
Gain on translation of foreign currencies	(108,975)
Net income	608,975

In a separate series of transactions, the subsidiary sends a weekly shipment of telescope repair parts to Cassiopeia, totaling €48,000 of profits for the entire year. For these transactions, the exchange rate varies from $1:€0.6 to $1:€0.75. A reasonable estimate of the average exchange rate for all the transactions is $1:€1.67. Consequently, the €48,000 profit is eliminated at the $1:€1.67(= $71,642) average exchange rate.

ACCOUNTS TO BE REMEASURED USING HISTORICAL EXCHANGE RATES

- Marketable securities carried at cost (equity securities and debt securities not intended to be held until maturity)
- Inventories carried at cost
- Prepaid expenses such as insurance, advertising, and rent
- Property, plant, and equipment
- Accumulated depreciation on property, plant, and equipment
- Patents, trademarks, licenses, and formulas
- Goodwill
- Other intangible assets
- Deferred charges and credits, except policy acquisition costs for life insurance companies
- Deferred income
- Common stock
- Preferred stock carried at issuance price
- Revenues and expenses related to nonmonetary items
  - Cost of goods sold
  - Depreciation of property, plant, and equipment
  - Amortization of intangible items such as goodwill, patents, licenses, and the like
  - Amortization of deferred charges or credits, except policy acquisition costs for life insurance companies

(ASC 830-10-45-18)

54 ASC 835 INTEREST

PERSPECTIVE AND ISSUES

Subtopics

ASC 835, *Interest*, contains three Subtopics:

- ASC 835-10, *Overall*, which merely points to other topics with guidance on interest
- ASC 835-20, *Capitalization of Interest*, which provides guidance on capitalization of interest in connection with an asset investment
- ASC 835-30, *Imputation of Interest*, which provides guidance where imputation of interest is required

Scope and Scope Exceptions

All assets that require a time period to get ready for their intended use should include a capitalized amount of interest. However, accomplishing this level of capitalization would usually violate a reasonable cost/benefit test because of the added accounting and administrative costs that would be incurred. In many such situations, the effect of interest capitalization would be immaterial. Accordingly, interest cost is only capitalized as a part of the historical cost of the following types of assets (qualifying assets) when such interest is considered to be material. (ASC 835-20-15-2) Common examples include:

- Assets constructed for an entity's own use or for which deposit or progress payments are made
- Assets produced as discrete projects that are intended for lease or sale
- Equity-method investments when the investee is using funds to acquire qualifying assets for principal operations that have not yet begun
(ASC 835-20-15-5)

Many entities use threshold levels to determine whether or not interest costs related to inventory or property, plant, and equipment should be capitalized. (ASC 835-20-15-4)

The capitalization of interest costs does not apply to the following situations:

- When the effects of capitalization would not be material, compared to the effect of expensing interest.
- When qualifying assets are already in use or ready for use.
- When qualifying assets are not being used and are not awaiting activities to get them ready for use.
- When qualifying assets are not included in a statement of financial position of the parent company and its consolidated subsidiaries.
- When principal operations of an investee accounted for under the equity method have already begun.
- When regulated investees capitalize both the cost of debt and equity capital.
- When assets are acquired with grants and gifts that are restricted by the donor (or grantor) to the acquisition of those assets, to the extent that funds are available from those grants and gifts. For this purpose, interest earned on the temporary investment of those funds that is subject to similar restriction is to be considered an addition to the gift or grant.
(ASC 835-10-15-6)

Accretion costs related to exit costs and asset retirement obligations are covered by the guidance in ASC 420 or ASC 410-20. So, too, the interest cost component of net periodic pension cost falls under the ASC 715-30 guidance.

All commitments to pay (and receive) money at a determinable future date are subject to present value techniques and, if necessary, interest imputation with the exception of the following:

- Normal accounts payable due within one year
- Amounts to be applied to purchase price of goods or services or that provide security to an agreement (e.g., advances, progress payments, security deposits, and retentions) except for amounts promised in a contract with a customer
- Amounts intended to provide security for one party
- Transactions between parent and subsidiary
- Obligations payable at some indeterminable future date (e.g., warranties)
- Lending and depositor savings activities of financial institutions whose primary business is lending money
- Transactions where interest rates are affected by prescriptions of a governmental agency (e.g., revenue bonds, tax exempt obligations, etc.)
- Estimates of contractual or other obligations assumed in connection with sales of property, goods, or services

- Receivables, contract assets, and contract liabilities in contracts with customers[1] (ASC 835-30-15-3)

Overview

ASC 835 provides guidance in two instances—where interest capitalization is in connection with an investment in an asset and where imputation of interest is required.

Per ASC 835-20, the recorded amount of an asset includes all of the costs necessary to get the asset set up and functioning properly for its intended use, including interest. The principal purposes accomplished by the capitalization of interest costs are:

- To obtain a more accurate measurement of the costs associated with the investment in the asset
- To achieve a better matching of costs related to the acquisition, construction, and development of productive assets to the future periods that will benefit from the revenues that the assets generate

ASC 835-30 specifies when and how interest is to be imputed when the receivable is non-interest-bearing or the stated rate on the receivable is not reasonable. It applies to transactions conducted at arm's length between unrelated parties, as well as to transactions in which captive finance companies offer favorable financing to increase sales of related companies.

DEFINITIONS OF TERMS

Source: ASC 835. Also see Appendix A, *Definitions of Terms*, for the definitions of Contract, Contract Asset, Contract Liability, Customer, Fair Value, Finance Lease, Lease, Lessee, Public Business Entity (Def. 3), and Underlying Asset.

Activities. The term activities is to be construed broadly. It encompasses physical construction of the asset. In addition, it includes all the steps required to prepare the asset for its intended use. For example, it includes administrative and technical activities during the preconstruction stage, such as the development of plans or the process of obtaining permits from governmental authorities. It also includes activities undertaken after construction has begun in order to overcome unforeseen obstacles, such as technical problems, labor disputes, or litigation.

Capitalization Rate. Rate used to determine amount of interest to be capitalized in an accounting period.

Discount. The difference between the net proceeds, after expense, received upon issuance of debt and the amount repayable at its maturity. See Premium.

Expenditures. Expenditures to which capitalization rates are to be applied are capitalized expenditures (net of progress payment collections) for the qualifying asset that have required the payment of cash, the transfer of other assets, or the incurring of a liability on which interest is recognized (in contrast to liabilities, such as trade payables, accruals, and retainages on which interest is not recognized).

Imputed Interest Rate. The interest rate that results from a process of approximation (or imputation) required when the present value of a note must be estimated because an established exchange price is not determinable and the note has no ready market.

Intended Use. Intended use of an asset embraces both readiness for use and readiness for sale, depending on the purpose of acquisition.

[1] This item is effective upon implementation of ASU 2014-09 on revenue.

Interest Cost. Interest cost includes interest recognized on obligations having explicit interest rates, interest imputed on certain types of payables in accordance with Subtopic 835-30, and interest related to a capital lease determined in accordance with Subtopic 840–30.[2] With respect to obligations having explicit interest rates, interest cost includes amounts resulting from periodic amortization of discount or premium and issue costs on debt.

Interest Method. The method used to arrive at a periodic interest cost (including amortization) that will represent a level effective rate on the sum of the face amount of the debt and (plus or minus) the unamortized premium or discount and expense at the beginning of each period.

Premium. The excess of the net proceeds, after expense, received upon issuance of debt over the amount repayable at its maturity. See Discount.

CONCEPTS, RULES, AND EXAMPLES

ASC 835-20, *Capitalization of Interest*

Interest Cost Generally, inventories and land that are not undergoing preparation for intended use are not qualifying assets. When land is being developed, it is a qualifying asset. If land is developed for lots, the capitalized interest cost is added to the cost of the land. The capitalized interest will then be properly matched against revenues when the lots are sold. If, however, the land is developed for a building, then the capitalized interest cost is added to the cost of the building, in which case the capitalized interest will be matched against related revenues as the building is depreciated.

The amount of interest to be capitalized. Interest cost includes the following:

- Interest on debt having explicit interest rates (fixed or floating)
- Interest related to capital leases
- Interest required to be imputed on payables (i.e., those due in over one year, per ASC 835-30)

Capitalization Interest Rate The most appropriate rate to use as the capitalization rate is the rate applicable to specific new debt resulting from the need to finance the acquired assets. If there is no specific new debt, the capitalization rate is a weighted-average of the rates of the other borrowings of the entity. This reflects the fact that the previously incurred debt of the entity could be repaid if not for the acquisition of the qualifying asset. Thus, indirectly, the previous debt is financing the acquisition of the new asset and its interest is part of the cost of the new asset. The selection of borrowings to be used in the calculation of the weighted-average of rates requires judgment. The amount of interest to be capitalized is that portion which could have been avoided if the qualifying asset had not been acquired. Thus, the capitalized amount is the incremental amount of interest cost incurred by the entity to finance the acquired asset. (ASC 835-20-30-2)

If the reporting entity uses derivative financial instruments as fair value hedges to affect its borrowing costs, ASC 815-25-35-14 specifies that the interest rate to use in capitalizing interest is the effective yield that takes into account gains and losses on the effective portion of a derivative instrument that qualifies as a fair value hedge of fixed interest rate debt. The amount of interest subject to capitalization could include amortization of the adjustments of the carrying amount of the hedged liability under ASC 815, if the entity elects to begin amortization of those adjustments during the period in which interest is eligible for capitalization. Any ineffective portion of the fair value hedge is not reflected in the capitalization rate.

---

[2] Upon implementation of ASU 2016-02, Leases, this wording will change to "interest related to a finance lease determined in accordance with Topic 842."

Capitalizable Base Once the appropriate rate has been established, the base to which that rate is to be applied is the average amount of accumulated net capital *expenditures* incurred for qualifying assets during the relevant time frame. (ASC 835-20-30-3) Capitalized costs and expenditures are not the same terms. Theoretically, a capitalized cost financed by a trade payable for which no interest is recognized is not a capital expenditure to which the capitalization rate is applied. Reasonable approximations of net capital expenditures are acceptable, however, and capitalized costs are generally used in place of capital expenditures unless there is expected to be a material difference.

If the average capitalized expenditures exceed the specific new borrowings for the time frame involved, then the *excess* expenditures are multiplied by the weighted-average of rates and not by the rate associated with the specific debt. This requirement more accurately reflects the interest cost incurred by the entity to acquire the fixed asset. (ASC 835-20-30-3)

The interest being paid on the debt may be simple or compound. Simple interest is computed on the principal alone, whereas compound interest is computed on the principal *and* on any interest that has not been paid. Most fixed assets will be acquired with debt subject to compound interest.

The total amount of interest actually incurred by the entity is the ceiling for the amount of interest cost capitalized. The amount capitalized cannot exceed the amount actually incurred during the period involved. On a consolidated basis, the ceiling is defined as the total of the parent's interest cost plus that of the consolidated subsidiaries. If financial statements are issued separately, the interest cost capitalized is limited to the amount that the separate entity has incurred, and that amount includes interest on intercompany borrowings. (ASC 835-20-30-6). The interest incurred is a gross amount and is not netted against interest earned except in cases involving externally restricted tax-exempt borrowings. (ASC 835-20-30-10)

Example of Accounting for Capitalized Interest Costs

- On January 1, 20X1, Daniel Corp. contracted with Rukin Company to construct a building for $2,000,000 on land that Daniel had purchased years earlier.
- Daniel Corp. was to make five payments in 20X1, with the last payment scheduled for the date of completion, December 31, 20X1.
- Daniel Corp. made the following payments during 20X7:

January 1, 20X1	$ 200,000
March 31, 20X1	400,000
June 30, 20X1	610,000
September 30, 20X1	440,000
December 31, 20X1	350,000
	$2,000,000

- Daniel Corp. had the following debt outstanding at December 31, 20X7:

a. A 12%, four-year note dated 1/31/20X7 with interest compounded quarterly. Both principal and interest due 12/31/Y0 (relates specifically to building project).	$850,000
b. A 10%, ten-year note dated 12/31/X1 with simple interest payable annually on December 31.	$600,000
c. A 12%, five-year note dated 12/31/20X3 with simple interest payable annually on December 31.	$700,000

The amount of interest to be capitalized during 20X7 is computed as follows:

Step 1—Compute average accumulated expenditures

Average Accumulated Expenditures

Date	*Expenditure*	*Capitalization period**	*Average accumulated expenditures*
1/1/X7	$ 200,000	12/X7	$200,000
3/31/X7	400,000	9/X7	300,000
6/30/X7	610,000	6/X7	305,000
9/30/X7	440,000	3/X7	110,000
12/31/X7	350,000	0/X7	–
	$ 2,000,000		$915,000

** The number of months between the date expenditures were made and the date interest capitalization stops (December 31, 20X7).*

Because the average accumulated expenditures of $915,000 exceed the $850,000 borrowed specifically for the project, interest will be capitalized on the excess expenditures of $65,000 by using the weighted-average interest rate on the other two notes.

Step 2—Compute the weighted-average interest rate on the company's other borrowings

	Principal	Interest
10%, ten-year note	$ 600,000	$ 60,000
12%, five-year note	700,000	84,000
	$1,300,000	$144,000

$$\frac{\text{Total interest}}{\text{Total principal}} = \frac{\$144,000}{\$1,300,000} = 11.08\%\ \text{weighted-average interest rate}$$

Step 3—Compute the potential interest cost to be capitalized

The $850,000 loan is considered first because it relates specifically to the project. Interest accretes on this loan quarterly. Since interest is not due until the loan's maturity, the interest for each quarter increases the unpaid principal amount on which further quarters' interest will be accreted.

Date	Description	Interest	Principal	Balance
1/1/20X7	Loan proceeds			$ 850,000
4/1/20X7	Quarterly compound interest	$ 25,500	$ (25,500)	875,500
7/1/20X7	Quarterly compound interest	26,265	(26,265)	901,765
10/1/20X7	Quarterly compound interest	27,053	(27,053)	928,818
12/31/20X7	Quarterly compound interest	27,866	(27,866)	956,684
	Totals	$106,684	$(106,684)	

The above computations can be made using specialized present value software or standard spreadsheet software. They can also be made/proved using the following formula to compute the future value of $1 for four periods at 3% per period (12% annual rate ÷ 4 periods per year quarterly compounding) where:

FV = Future value of the present sum of $1.

i = The interest rate at which the amount will be compounded each period, and

n = The number of periods.

$$FV = (1+i)^n$$

$$= (1+.03)^4$$

$$= 1.03^4$$

$$= 1.12551$$

$$\$850{,}000 \times 1.12551 = \$956{,}684$$

$$(850{,}000)\text{principal}$$

$$\$106{,}684\ \text{interest}$$

Potential Interest Cost to Be Capitalized

Interest on the project-related loan	(\$850,000 × 1.12551) – \$850,000	=	\$106,684
Interest on remaining average accumulated expenditures	65,000 × .1108	=	7,202
	\$915,000		\$113,886

Step 4—Compute the actual interest cost for the period

12%, three-year note [(\$850,000 × 1.12551) – \$850,000]	=	\$106,684
10%, ten-year note (\$600,000 × 10%)	=	60,000
12%, five-year note (\$700,000 × 12%)	=	84,000
Total interest		\$250,684

Step 5—Compute the amount of interest cost to be capitalized

The interest cost to be capitalized is the lesser of \$113,886 (avoidable interest cost) or \$250,684 (actual interest cost), which is \$113,886. The remaining \$136,798 (\$250,684 – \$113,886) is expensed during 20X7.

Determining the Time Period for Interest Capitalization Three conditions must be met before capitalization commences:

1. Necessary activities are in progress to get the asset ready to function as intended
2. Qualifying asset expenditures have been made
3. Interest costs are being incurred
   (ASC 835-30-25-2)

As long as these conditions continue, interest costs are capitalized.

Necessary activities are interpreted in a very broad manner. They start with the planning process and continue until the qualifying asset is substantially complete and ready to function. Brief, normal interruptions do not stop the capitalization of interest costs. However, if the entity intentionally suspends or delays the activities for some reason, interest costs are not capitalized from the point of suspension or delay until substantial activities regarding the asset resume. (ASC 835-30-25-4)

If the asset is completed in parts, the capitalization of interest costs stops for each part as it becomes ready. An asset that must be entirely complete before the parts can be used capitalizes interest costs until the total asset becomes ready. (ASC 835-30-25-5)

Interest costs continue to be capitalized until the asset is ready to function as intended, even in cases where lower of cost or market rules are applicable and market is lower than cost. The required write-down is increased accordingly.

Capitalization of Interest Costs Incurred on Tax-Exempt Borrowings If qualifying assets have been financed with the proceeds from tax-exempt, externally restricted borrowings, and if temporary investments have been purchased with those proceeds, a modification is required. The interest costs incurred from the date of borrowing must be reduced by the interest earned on the temporary investment in order to calculate the ceiling for the capitalization of interest costs. This procedure is followed until the assets financed in this manner are ready. When the specified assets are functioning as intended, the interest cost of the tax-exempt borrowing becomes available to be capitalized by other qualifying assets of the entity. Portions of the tax-exempt borrowings that are not restricted are eligible for capitalization in the normal manner.

Assets acquired with gifts or grants Qualifying assets that are acquired with externally restricted gifts or grants are not subject to capitalization of interest. The principal reason for this treatment is the concept that there is no economic cost of financing when a gift or grant is used in the acquisition.

Summary of Interest Capitalization Requirements The process chart below summarizes the accounting for interest capitalization.

ASC 835-30, *Imputation of Interest*

Receivables If a receivable is due on terms exceeding one year, the proper valuation is the present value of future payments to be received, determined by using an interest rate commensurate with the risks involved at the date of the receivable's creation. In many situations the interest rate commensurate with the risks involved is the rate stated in the agreement between the payee and the debtor. However, if the receivable is noninterest-bearing or if the rate stated in the agreement is not indicative of the market rate for a debtor of similar creditworthiness under similar terms, interest is imputed at the market rate. A valuation allowance is used to adjust the face amount of the receivable to the present value at the market rate. The balance in the valuation allowance is amortized as additional interest income so that interest income is recognized using a constant rate of interest over the life of the agreement. Initial recording of such a valuation allowance also results in the recognition of an expense, typically (for customer receivables) reported as selling expense or as a contra revenue item (sales discounts).

ASC 835-30-25 divides receivables into three categories for discussion:

1. Notes issued solely for cash,
2. Notes issued for cash and rights or privileges, and
3. Notes issued in exchange for property, goods, or services.

Note Issued Solely for Cash When a note is issued solely for cash, its present value is necessarily assumed to be equal to the cash proceeds. (ASC 835-30-25-4) The interest rate is that rate which equates the cash proceeds received by the borrower to the amounts to be paid in the future. (ASC 835-30-25-5) For example, if a borrower agrees to pay $1,060 in one year in exchange for cash today of $1,000, the interest rate implicit in that agreement is 6%. A valuation

Summary of Accounting for Interest Capitalization

Capitalization of Interest during Construction

Qualifying assets
a. Assets constructed for use in operations
b. Assets for sale or lease that are constructed as discrete projects (ships, real estate), but not in inventory
c. Certain equity method investments

When to capitalize interest (all three must be met)
a. Expenditures for asset have been made
b. Activities intended to get asset ready are in progress
c. Interest cost is being incurred

Applicable interest (net of discounts, premiums, and other costs)
a. Interest obligations having explicit rates
b. Imputed interest on certain payables/receivables

Amount of interest to capitalize

Average accumulated expenditures

(Specific borrowings × Applicable interest rate) + (Other borrowings × Weighted-average interest rate*)

Qualfications
a. Amount of interest to be capitalized cannot exceed total interest costs incurred during the period
b. Interest earned on temporarily invested borrowings may not be offset against interest to be capitalized (except externally restricted tax-exempt borrowings)

$$^{*}\textit{Weighted-average interest rate} = \frac{\textit{Total interest on other borrowings}}{\textit{Average outstanding principal during period}}$$

allowance of $60 is applied to the face amount ($1,060) so that the receivable is included in the statement of financial position at its present value ($1,000).

Note Issued for Cash and Rights or Privileges When a note receivable that bears an unrealistic rate of interest is issued in exchange for cash, an additional right or privilege is usually granted, unless the transaction was not conducted at arm's length. Often when a note bearing an unrealistic rate of interest is issued in exchange for cash, an additional right or privilege is granted, such as the issuer agreeing to sell merchandise to the purchaser at a reduced rate. If there was an added right or privilege involved, the difference between the present value of the receivable and the cash advanced is the value assigned to the right or privilege. It will be accounted for as an addition to the cost of the products purchased for the purchaser/lender, and as additional revenue to the debtor. (ASC 835-30-25-6)

This treatment stems from an attempt to match revenue and expense in the proper periods and to differentiate between those factors that affect income from operations and income or expense from nonoperating sources. In the situation above, the purchaser/lender will amortize the discount (difference between the cash loaned and the present value of the note) to interest income over the life of the note, and the contractual right to purchase inventory at a reduced rate will be allocated to inventory (or cost of sales) as the right expires. The seller/issuer of the note will amortize the discount to interest expense over the life of the note, and the unearned revenue will be recognized in sales as the products are sold to the purchaser/lender at the reduced price. Because the discount is amortized on a different basis than the contractual right, net income for the period is also affected.

Example of Accounting for a Note Issued for Both Cash and a Contractual Right—Accounting by Issuer

1. Schwartz borrows $10,000 from Weiss via an unsecured five-year note. Simple interest at 2% is due at maturity.
2. Schwartz agrees to sell Weiss a car for $15,000, which is less than its market price.
3. The market rate of interest on a note with similar terms and a borrower of similar creditworthiness is 10%.

The present value factor for an amount due in five years at 10% is .62092. Therefore, the present value of the note is $6,830 [= ($10,000 principal + $1,000 interest at the stated rate) × .62092]. According to ASC 835, the $3,170 (= $10,000 – $6,830) difference between the present value of the note and the face value of the note is regarded as part of the cost/purchase price of the car. The following entry would be made by Weiss to record the transaction:

Note receivable	10,000	
Car	18,170	
Cash		25,000
Discount on note receivable		3,170

The discount on note receivable is amortized using the effective interest method, as follows:

	Effective interest (10%)	*Stated interest (2%)*	*Amortization*	*Note and interest receivable*
01/01/X1				6,830
01/01/X2	683	200	(483)	7,513
01/01/X3	751	200	(551)	8,264
01/01/X4	826	200	(626)	9,091
01/01/X5	909	200	(709)	10,000
01/01/X6	1,000	200	(800)	11,000

The entry for the first year would be:

Discount on note receivable	483	
Interest receivable	200	
Interest revenue		683

Note Issued in Exchange for Property, Goods, or Services When a note is issued in exchange for property, goods, or services and the transaction is entered into at arm's length, the stated interest rate is presumed to be fair unless:

- No interest rate is stated,
- The stated rate is unreasonable,
- The face value of the note receivable is materially different from fair value of the property, goods, or services received, or
- The face value of the note receivable is materially different from the current market value of the note at the date of the transaction.

Example of Accounting for a Note Issued for Both Cash and a Contractual Right—Accounting by Debtor and Issuer

- Miller borrows $10,000 via a noninterest-bearing three-year note from Krueger.
- Miller agrees to sell $50,000 of merchandise to Krueger at less than the ordinary retail price for the duration of the note.
- The market rate of interest on a note with similar payment terms and a borrower of similar credit-worthiness is 10%.

According to ASC 835-30, the difference between the present value of the note and the face value of the loan is to be regarded as part of the cost of the products purchased under the agreement. The present value factor for an amount due in three years at 10% is .75132. Therefore, the present value of the note is $7,513 (= $10,000 × .75132). The $2,487 (= $10,000 – $7,513) difference between the face value and the present value is to be recorded as a discount on the note payable and as unearned revenue on the future purchases by the debtor. The following entries would be made by the debtor (Miller) and the creditor (Krueger) to record the transaction:

Miller			*Krueger*		
Cash	10,000		Note receivable	10,000	
Discount on note payable	2,487		Contract right with supplier	2,487	
Note payable		10,000	Cash		10,000
Unearned revenue		2,487	Discount on note receivable		2,487

The discount on note payable (and note receivable) is to be amortized using the effective interest method, while the unearned revenue account and contract right with supplier account are amortized on a pro rata basis as the right to purchase merchandise is used up. Thus, if Krueger purchased $20,000 of merchandise from Miller in the first year, the following entries would be necessary:

Miller			*Krueger*		
Unearned revenue	995		Inventory (or cost of sales)	995	
[$2,487 × (20,000/50,000)]					
Sales		995	Contract right with supplier		995
Interest expense	751		Discount on note receivable	751	
Discount on note payable ($7,513 × 10%)		751	Interest revenue		751

The amortization of unearned revenue and contract right with supplier accounts will fluctuate with the amount of purchases made. If there is a balance remaining in the account at the end of the loan term, it is amortized to the appropriate account in that final year.

According to ASC 835, when the rate on the note is not fair, the note should be recorded at the fair market value of the property, goods, or services sold or the market value of the note, whichever is the more clearly determinable. The difference is recorded as a discount or premium and amortized to interest income. (ASC 835-30-25-10)

Example of Accounting for a Note Exchanged for Goods

- Green sells Brown inventory that has a fair market value of $8,573.
- Green receives a two-year noninterest-bearing note having a face value of $10,000.

In this situation, the fair market value of the consideration is readily determinable and, thus, represents the amount at which the note is to be recorded. The following entry would be made by Green:

Notes receivable	10,000	
Discount on notes receivable		1,427
Sales revenue		8,573

The discount will be amortized to interest expense over the two-year period using the interest rate implied in the transaction, which is 8%. The present value factor is .8573 ($8,573/$10,000). Using a present value table for amount due in two years, .8573 is located under the 8% rate.

If neither the fair value of the property, goods, or services sold nor the fair value of the note receivable is determinable, then the present value of the note must be determined using an imputed market interest rate. (ASC 835-30-25-11) This rate will then be used to establish the present value of the note by discounting all future payments on the note at that rate. General guidelines for determining the appropriate interest rate, which are provided by ASC 835, include the prevailing rates of similar instruments with debtors having similar credit ratings and the rate the debtor could obtain for similar financing from other sources. Other factors to be considered include any collateral or restrictive covenants involved, the current and expected prime rate, and other terms pertaining to the instrument. (ASC 835-30-25-12) The objective is to approximate the rate of interest that would have resulted if an independent borrower and lender had negotiated a similar transaction under comparable terms and conditions. This determination is as of the issuance date, and any subsequent changes in market interest rates are irrelevant.

Example of Accounting for a Note Exchanged for Property

- Alexis sells Brett a machine that has a fair market value of $7,510.
- Alexis receives a three-year noninterest-bearing note having a face value of $10,000.

In this situation, the fair market value of the consideration is readily determinable and, thus, represents the amount at which the note is to be recorded. The following entry by Brett is necessary:

Machine	7,510	
Discount on notes payable	2,490	
Notes payable		10,000

The discount will be amortized to interest expense over the three-year period using the interest rate implied in the transaction. The interest rate implied is 10%, because the factor for an amount due in three years is .75132, which when applied to the $10,000 face value results in an amount equal to the fair value of the machine.

Example of Accounting for a Note Exchanged to Property

- Alexis sells Brett a used machine. The fair market value is not readily determinable.
- Alexis receives a three-year noninterest-bearing note having a face value of $20,000. The market value of the note is not known.
- Brett could have borrowed the money for the machine's purchase from a bank at a rate of10%.

In this situation, the fair market value of the consideration is not readily determinable, so the present value of the note is determined using an imputed interest rate. The rate used is the rate at which Brett could have borrowed the money—10%. The factor for an amount due in three years at 10% is .75132, so the present value of the note is $15,026. The following entry by Brett is necessary:

Machine	15,026	
Discount on notes payable	4,974	
Notes payable		20,000

Bonds Issued for Cash When a note is issued solely for cash, its present value is assumed to be equal to the cash proceeds. The interest rate is that rate equating the cash proceeds to the amounts to be paid in the future. For example, a $1,000 note due in three years that sells for $889 has an implicit rate of 4% (= $1,000 × .889, where .889 is the present value factor at 4% for a lump sum due three years hence). This implicit rate, 4%, is to be used when amortizing the discount.

In most situations, a bond will be issued at a price other than its face value. The amount of the cash exchanged is equal to the total of the present values of all the future interest and principal payments. The difference between the cash proceeds and the face value is recorded as a premium if the cash proceeds are greater than the face value or a discount if they are less. The journal entry to record a bond issued at a premium follows:

Cash	(proceeds)	
Bonds payable		(face value)
Premium on bonds payable		(difference)

Example of Bonds Issued for Cash

Enterprise Autos issues $100,000 of 10-year bonds bearing interest at 10%, paid semiannually, at a time when the market demands a 12% return from issuers with similar credit standings. The proceeds of the bond issuance would be $88,500, which is computed as follows:

Present value of 20 semiannual interest payments of $5,000 discounted at 12% (6% semiannually: factor = 11.4699)	$57,300
Present value of $100,000 due in 10 years, discounted at 12% compounded semiannually (factor = .31180)	31,200
Present value of bond issuance	$88,500

The journal entry would be:

Cash	88,500	
Discount on bonds payable	11,500	
Bonds payable		100,000

Summary—ASC 835-30 ASC 835-30 specifies when and how interest is to be imputed when a debt is either noninterest-bearing or the stated rate is not reasonable. ASC 835-30 divides debt into three categories for discussion. The following diagram illustrates the accounting treatment for the three types of debt.

Accounting for Monetary Assets and Liabilities

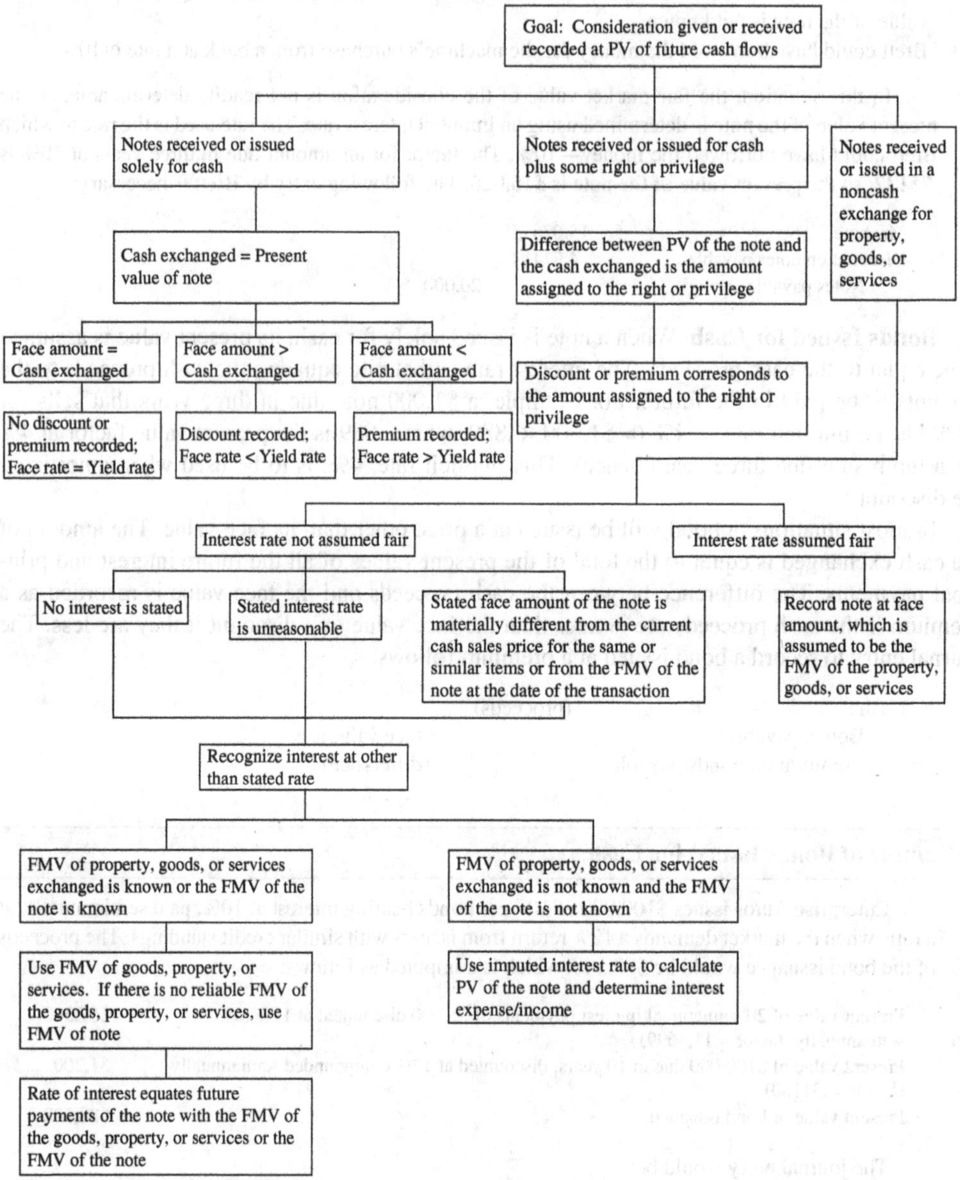

Sales of Future Revenue ASC 470-10-25 deals with the situation in which a reporting entity receives an initial payment from another party in exchange for a promised stream of royalties or other revenue-based receipts from a defined business, which could be a segment or product line of the reporting entity. Arguably, the up-front payment could be seen as an advance against the future payments, or as a borrowing by the reporting entity. The payment is not revenue to the reporting entity.

The Codification states that the initial receipt would be accounted for as either debt or deferred revenue, depending on the facts and circumstances of the transaction. It identifies six factors that would cause the amounts to be recorded as debt, rather than as deferred income. These factors are:

- The transaction does not purport to be a sale.
- The reporting entity has significant continuing involvement in the generation of the cash flows due the other party (referred to as the investor in this consensus).
- The transaction is cancelable by either party through payment of a lump sum or other transfer of assets by the entity.
- The investor's rate of return is implicitly or explicitly limited by the terms of the transaction.
- Variations in the reporting entity's revenue or income underlying the transaction have only a trifling impact on the investor's rate of return.
- The investor has any recourse to the reporting entity relating to the payments due to the investor.

  (ASC 470-10-25-2)

Amounts recorded as debt should be amortized under the interest method and amounts recorded as deferred income should be amortized under the units-of-revenue method. The proceeds classified as foreign-currency-denominated debt would be subject to recognition of foreign currency transaction (exchange) gains and losses under ASC 830-20.

Effective Interest Method

The effective interest method is the preferred method of accounting for a discount or premium arising from a note or bond. Under the effective interest method, the discount or premium is amortized over the life of the debt in such a way as to result in a constant rate of interest when applied to the amount outstanding at the beginning of any given period. Therefore, interest expense is equal to the market rate of interest at the time of issuance multiplied by this beginning figure. The difference between the interest expense and the cash paid represents the amortization of the discount or premium.

Amortization tables are often created at the time of the bond's issuance to provide amounts necessary when recording the entries relating to the debt issue. They also provide a check of accuracy since the final values in the unamortized discount or premium and carrying value columns should be equal to zero and the bond's face value, respectively.

Example of Applying the Effective Interest Method

1. A 3-year, 12%, $10,000 bond is issued at 1/1/20X1, with interest payments semiannually.
2. The market rate is 10%.

The amortization table would appear as follows:

Date	*Credit cash*	*Debit int. exp.*	*Debit prem.*	*Unamort. prem. bal.*	*Carrying value*
1/1/X1				$507.61	$10,507.61[(a)]
7/1/X1	$ 600.00[(b)]	$ 525.38[(c)]	$ 74.62[(d)]	432.99[(e)]	10,432.99[(f)]
1/1/X2	600.00	521.65	78.35	354.64	10,354.64
7/1/X2	600.00	517.73	82.27	272.37	10,272.37
1/1/X3	600.00	513.62	86.38	185.99	10,185.99
7/1/X3	600.00	509.30	90.70	95.29	10,095.29
1/1/X4	600.00	504.71[(g)]	95.29	–	10,000.00
	$3,600.00	$3,092.39	$507.61		

(a) PV of principal and interest payments at 5% for 6 periods $10,000(.74622) = $7,462.20 $ 600 (5.07569) = 3,045.41 $10,507.61
(b) $10,000.00 × .12 × one-half year
(c) $10,507.61 × .10 × one-half year
(d) $600.00 – $525.38
(e) $507.61 – $74.62
(f) $10,507.61 – $74.62 (or $10,000 + $432.99)
(g) Rounding error = $.05

Although the effective interest method is the preferred method of amortizing a discount or premium, the straight-line method may be used if the results are not materially different. The amortized portion is equal to the total amount of the discount or premium divided by the life of the debt from issuance in months multiplied by the number of months the debt has been outstanding that year. Interest expense under the straight-line method is equal to the cash interest paid plus the amortized portion of the discount or minus the amortized portion of the premium.

When the interest date does not coincide with the year-end, an adjusting entry must be made to recognize the proportional share of interest payable and the amortization of the discount or premium. Within the amortization period, the discount or premium can be amortized using the straight-line method.

If bonds or notes are issued between interest payment dates, the interest and the amortization must be computed for the period between the sale date and the next interest date. The purchaser usually pays the issuer for the amount of interest that has accrued since the last payment date. That payment is recorded as a payable by the issuer. At the next interest date, the issuer pays the purchaser as though the bond had been outstanding for the entire interest period. The discount or premium is also amortized for the short period.

Example of Note Issued between Payment Dates

On June 1, 20X1, Acme Manufacturing issues a $100,000 7% bond with a three-year life at 104 (i.e., at 104% of face value). Interest is payable on July 1 and January 1. The computation of the premium would be:

Proceeds	$104,000
Face value	100,000
Premium	$ 4,000

The entry to record the bond issuance and the receipt of interest from the purchaser would be:

Cash	106,967	
Bonds payable		100,000
Premium on bonds		4,000
Interest payable		2,967

The bonds will be outstanding for two years and seven months. An effective interest rate must be computed that will equate the present value of the future principal and interest payments to the cash received. Using a spreadsheet facilitates the trial and error process. Many calculators with financial functions also do this calculation. Alternatively, present value tables can be used to compute the value, as shown below.

First, compute the present value of the interest and principal payments as of 7/1/X1 using a guess of 5% annually.

Present value of an annuity due of $3,500 for six periods @ 2.5% = 3,500 × 5.6458 =	19,760
Present value of a single payment of $100,000 in five periods @ 2.5% = 100,000 × .88385 =	88,385
	108,145

Then, compute the present value of that result one month earlier (at June 1, 2012) using the same interest rate.

Present value of a single payment of $108,145 in one month = 108,145/[1 + (.05/12)] = 107,696
The result is more than the cash received ($106,967), so we know that the interest rate must be higher than 5%. Repeat the calculation at a 6% annual rate.

Present value of an annuity due of $3,500 for six periods @ 3% = 3,500 × 5.5797 =	19,529
Present value of a single payment of $100,000 in five periods @ 3% = 100,000 × .86261 =	86,261
	105,790
Present value of a single payment of $105,790 in one month = 105,790/[1 + (.06/12)] =	105,263

The result is less than the cash received ($106,967), so we know the rate is between 5 and 6%. By interpolation, we determine that the rate is 5.3%.

$$\frac{107,696-106,967}{107,696-105,263}\times(6\%-5\%)=.2996\%, \text{ which is added to } 5\% \text{ to get the effective rate:}$$

The amortization of the $4,000 premium would be as follows:

	Cash paid (received)	Interest at 5.3% annually	Amortization	Interest payable	Bond payable
					104,000
06/01/X1	(2,967)			2,967	104,000
07/01/X1	3,500	459	74	(2,967)	103,926
01/01/X2	3,500	2,754	746		103,180
07/01/X2	3,500	2,734	765		102,415
01/01/X3	3,500	2,714	786		101,629
07/01/X3	3,500	2,693	807		100,822
01/01/X4	103,500	2,672	822		100,000

The entry to record the first interest payment would be:

Interest payable	2,967	
Interest expense	459	
Premium on bonds	74	
Cash		3,500

Debt Issuance Costs

Costs may be incurred in connection with issuing bonds. Examples include legal, accounting, and underwriting fees; commissions; and engraving, printing, and registration costs. Debt issuance costs must be presented on the statement of financial position as a direct reduction of proceeds from debt and the costs must be amortized and reported as interest expense. (ASC 835-30-45-1 through 45-3) For a $200,000 loan with $10,000 in debt issuance costs, the transaction is recorded as:

Debit		Credit	
Cash	190,000	Long-term debt	190,000

Consistency The presentation of debt issuance costs as a direct reduction of the liability is consistent with current guidance on debt discounts. The guidance is also consistent with FASB CON 6, paragraph 237 which states:

> Debt issue cost is not an asset for the same reason that debt discount is not: it provides no future economic benefit. Debt issue cost in effect reduces the proceeds of borrowing and increases the effective interest rate and thus may be accounted for the same as debt discount.

55 ASC 840 LEASES[1]

[1] The FASB has issued ASU 2016-02, *Leases*. See the chapter on ASC 842 for more information.

PERSPECTIVE AND ISSUES

Technical Alert

See the chapter on ASC 842 for information on the new standard on leases.

Subtopics

ASC 840, *Leases*, and its subtopics establish standards of accounting and reporting by lessees and lessors for leases overall, and for specific classifications of leases. ASC 840 contains four subtopics:

- ASC 840-10, *Overall*
- ASC 840-20, *Operating Leases*
- ASC 840-30, *Capital Leases*
- ASC 840-40, *Sale-Leaseback Transactions*

Each of the subtopics contains the following subsections:

- General
- Lessees
- Lessors

Scope and Scope Exceptions

ASC 840 applies to all entities. However, to be considered a lease the right to use property, plant, or equipment must be transferred from one contracting party to the other. The definition of lease does not include contracts for services.

DEFINITIONS OF TERMS

Source: 840 *Glossary Sections*. Other terms relevant to this topic can be found in Appendix A, *Definitions of Terms*: Acquiree, Acquirer, Acquisition by a Not-for-Profit Entity, Contract, Customer, Financing Receivable, Nonprofit Entity, Revenue, Standalone Selling Price, Variable Interest, and Variable Interest Entity.

Bargain Purchase Option. A provision allowing the lessee, at his option, to renew the lease for a rental sufficiently lower than the fair rental of the property at the date the option becomes exercisable that exercise of the option appears, at lease inception, to be reasonably assured. Fair rental of a property in this context shall mean the expected rental for equivalent property under similar terms and conditions.

Bargain Renewal Option. A provision allowing the lessee, at his option, to renew the lease for a rental sufficiently lower than the fair rental of the property at the date the option becomes exercisable that exercise of the option appears, at lease inception, to be reasonably assured. Fair rental of a property in this context shall mean the expected rental for equivalent property under similar terms and conditions.

- *Capital Lease.* From the perspective of a lessee, a lease that meets any of the four lease classification criteria in ASC 840-10-25-1.
- *Transfer of ownership.* The lease transfers ownership of the property to the lessee by the end of the lease term. This criterion is met in situations in which the lease agreement provides for the transfer of title at or shortly after the end of the lease term in exchange for the payment of a nominal fee, for example, the minimum required by statutory regulation to transfer title.
- *Bargain purchase option.* This option is included in the lease.
- *Lease term.* The lease term is equal to 75% or more of the estimated economic life of the leased property. However, if the beginning of the lease term falls within the last 25% of the total estimated economic life of the lease property, including earlier years of use, this criterion shall not be used for purposes of classifying the lease.
- *Minimum lease payment.* The present value at the beginning of the lease term of the minimum lease payments, excluding that portion of the payments representing executor costs such as insurance, maintenance, and taxes to be paid by the lessor, including any profit thereon, equals or exceeds 90% of the excess of the fair value of the leased property to the lessor at lease exception over any related investment tax credit retained by the lessor and expected to be realized by the lessor. If the beginning of the lease term falls within the last 25% of the total estimated economic life of the leased property, including earlier years of use, this criterion shall not be used for purposes of classifying the lease.

Contingent Rentals. The increases or decreases in lease payments that result from changes occurring after lease inception in the factors (other than the passage of time) on which lease payments are based, excluding any escalation of minimum lease payments relating to increases in construction or acquisition cost of the leased property or for increases in some measure of cost or value during the construction or preconstruction period. The term *contingent rentals* contemplates an uncertainty about future changes in the factors on which lease payments are based.

Estimated Economic Life. The estimated remaining period during which the property is expected to be economically usable by one or more users, with normal repairs and maintenance, for the purpose for which it was intended at lease inception, without limitation by the lease term.

Estimated Residual Value of Leased Property. The estimated fair value of the leased property at the end of the lease term.

Fair Value of Leased Property. The price that would be received to sell the property in an orderly transaction on the measurement date between market participants that are not related parties.

When the lessor is a manufacturer or dealer, the fair value of the property at the inception of the lease will ordinarily be its normal selling price net of volume or trade discounts. In some cases, due to market conditions, fair value may be less than the normal selling price or even the cost of the property.

When the lessor is not a manufacturer or dealer, the fair value of the property at the inception of the lease will ordinarily be its cost net of volume or trade discounts. However, if a significant amount of time elapses between the acquisition of the property by the lessor and the inception of the lease, fair value is determined in light of market conditions prevailing at the inception of the lease. Thus, fair value may be greater or less than the cost or carrying amount of the property.

Fair value determinations made for lease classification or measurement purposes are to be performed as defined by ASC 840, not as later set forth by ASC 820, other than as pertains to business combinations accounted for under ASC 805. For acquisition accounting applications, ASC 820 is the relevant guidance to be followed.

Incremental Borrowing Rate. The rate that, at lease inception, the lessee would have incurred to borrow over a similar term the funds necessary to purchase the leased asset. This definition does not proscribe the lessee's use of a secured borrowing rate as its incremental borrowing rate if that rate is determinable, reasonable, and consistent with the financing that would have been used in the particular circumstances.

Initial Direct Costs. Only those costs incurred by the lessor that are (1) costs to originate a lease incurred in transactions with independent third parties that (a) result directly from and are essential to acquire that lease and (b) would not have been incurred had that leasing transaction not occurred, and (2) certain costs directly related to specified activities performed by the lessor for that lease. Those activities are: evaluating the prospective lessee's financial condition; evaluating and recording guarantees, collateral, and other security arrangements; negotiating lease terms; preparing and processing lease documents; and closing the transaction. The costs directly related to those activities include only that portion of the employees' total compensation and payroll-related fringe benefits directly related to time spent performing those activities for that lease and other costs related to those activities that would not have been incurred but for that lease. Initial direct costs do not include costs related to activities performed by the lessor for advertising, soliciting potential lessees, servicing existing leases, and other ancillary activities related to establishing and monitoring credit policies, supervision, and administration. Initial direct costs do not include administrative costs, rent, depreciation, any other occupancy and equipment costs and employees' compensation and fringe benefits related to activities described in the previous sentence, unsuccessful origination efforts, and idle time.

Interest Method. The method used to arrive at a periodic interest cost (including amortization) that will represent a level effective rate on the sum of the face amount of the debt and (plus or minus) the unamortized premium or discount and expense at the beginning of each period.

Interest Rate Implicit in the Lease. The discount rate that causes the aggregate present value at the beginning of the lease term of the minimum lease payments (as described in paragraph 840-10-25-4), excluding that portion of the payments representing executory costs to be paid by the lessor, together with any profit thereon and the unguaranteed residual value, accruing to the benefit of the lessor to be equal to the fair value of the leased property to the lessor at lease inception, minus any investment tax credit retained by the lessor and expected to be realized by him. If the lessor is not entitled to any excess of the amount realized on disposition of the property over a guaranteed amount, no unguaranteed residual value would accrue to its benefit.

Lease. An agreement conveying the right to use property, plant, or equipment (land or depreciable assets or both), usually for a stated period of time.

Lease Incentive. An incentive for the lessee to sign the lease, such as an up-front cash payment to the lessee, payment of costs for the lessee (such as moving expenses), or the assumption by the lessor of the lessee's preexisting lease with a third party.

Lease Inception. The date of the lease agreement or commitment, if earlier. For purposes of this definition, a commitment shall be in writing, signed by the parties in interest to the transaction, and shall specifically set forth the principal provisions of the transaction. If any of the principal provisions are yet to be negotiated, such a preliminary agreement or commitment does not qualify for purposes of this definition.

Lease Term. The fixed noncancelable term of the lease plus the following:

- Periods covered by bargain renewal options
- Periods for which failure to renew the lease imposes a penalty on the lessee in an amount such that renewal appears, at the inception of the lease, to be reasonably assured
- Periods covered by ordinary renewal options during which a guarantee by the lessee of the lessor's debt directly or indirectly related to the leased property is expected to be in effect, or a loan from the lessee to the lessor directly or indirectly related to the leased property is expected to be outstanding
- Periods covered by ordinary renewal options preceding the date that a bargain purchase option is exercisable
- Periods representing renewals or extensions of the lease at the lessor's option

However, the lease term does not extend beyond the date a bargain purchase option becomes exercisable or beyond the useful life of the leased asset.

Minimum Lease Payments. For the lessee: The payments that the lessee is or can be required to make in connection with the leased property. Contingent rental guarantees by the lessee of the lessor's debt, and the lessee's obligation to pay executory costs, are excluded from minimum lease payments (MLPs). Additionally, if a portion of the MLPs representing executory costs is not determinable from the provisions of the lease, an estimate of executory costs is excluded from the calculation of the minimum lease payments. If the lease contains a bargain purchase option, only the minimum rental payments over the lease term and the payment called for in the bargain purchase option are included in minimum lease payments. Otherwise, MLPs include the following:

- The minimum rental payments called for by the lease over the lease term.
- Any guarantee of residual value at the expiration of the lease term made by the lessee (or any party related to the lessee), whether or not the guarantee payment constitutes a purchase of the leased property. When the lessor has the right to require the lessee to purchase the property at termination of the lease for a certain or determinable amount, that amount is considered a lessee guarantee. When the lessee agrees to make up any deficiency below a stated amount in the lessor's realization of the residual value, the guarantee to be included in the MLP is the stated amount rather than an estimate of the deficiency to be made up. ASC 840 provides additional guidance regarding residual guarantees, as follows:
  - Lease provisions requiring the lessee to reimburse the lessor for residual value deficiencies due to damage, extraordinary wear and tear, or excessive usage are analogous to contingent rentals, since at the inception of the lease, the amount of the deficiency is not determinable. Therefore, these payments are not included in the MLP as residual value guarantees
  - Some leases contain provisions limiting the lessee's obligation to reimburse the lessor for residual value deficiencies to an amount less than the stipulated residual value of the leased property at the end of the lease term. In computing the MLP associated with these leases, the amount of the lessee's guarantee is limited to the specified maximum deficiency the lessee can be required to reimburse to the lessor
  - A lessee may contract with an unrelated third party to guarantee the residual for the benefit of the lessor. The MLP can only be reduced by the third-party guarantee to the extent that the lessor explicitly releases the lessee from the obligation to make up the deficiency, even if the guarantor defaults. Amounts paid by the lessee to the guarantor are executory costs and are not included in the MLP.

- Any payment that the lessee must or can be required to make upon failure to renew or extend the lease at the expiration of the lease term, whether or not the payment would constitute a purchase of the leased property.

For the lessor: The payments described above, plus any guarantee of the residual value or of the rental payments beyond the lease term by a third party unrelated to either the lessee or lessor (provided the third party is financially capable of discharging the guaranteed obligation).

Noncancelable in this context means that a lease is cancelable only if one of the following conditions is satisfied:

- A remote contingency occurs.
- The lessor grants permission.
- The lessee enters into a new lease with the same lessor.
- The lessee pays a penalty in an amount such that continuation of the lease appears, at inception, reasonably assured.

Nonrecourse Financing. Lending or borrowing activities in which, in the event of default, the collateral available to the creditor is limited to certain assets that are specifically agreed to in the loan agreement, and that collateral does not include the general assets of the debtor.

Penalty. Any requirement that is imposed or can be imposed on the lessee by the lease agreement or by factors outside the lease agreement to pay cash, incur or assume a liability, perform services, surrender or transfer an asset or rights to an asset or otherwise forego an economic benefit, or suffer an economic detriment.

Primary Beneficiary. A variable interest holder that is required to consolidate a VIE. Consolidation is required when the holder of one or more variable interests would absorb a majority of the VIE's expected losses, receive a majority of the VIE's expected residual returns, or both. If one holder would absorb a majority of the VIE's expected losses and another holder would receive a majority of the VIE's expected residual returns, the holder absorbing the majority of the expected losses is the primary beneficiary and is thus required to consolidate the VIE.

Profit or Loss on Sale. The profit or loss that would be recognized on the sale if there were no leaseback. For example, on a sale of real estate subject to Topic 360, the profit on the sale to be deferred and amortized in proportion to the leaseback would be the profit that could otherwise be recognized in accordance with Topic 360.

Profit Recognition. Any method to record a transaction involving real estate, other than the deposit method, or the methods to record transactions accounted for as financing, leasing, or profit-sharing arrangements. Profit recognition methods commonly used to record transactions involving real estate include, but are not limited to, the full accrual method, the installment method, the cost recovery method, and the reduced profit method.

Sale-Leaseback Accounting. A method of accounting for a sale-leaseback transaction in which the seller-lessee records the sale, removes all property and related liabilities from its statement of financial position, recognizes gain or loss from the sale, and classifies the leaseback in accordance with this section.

Unguaranteed Residual Value. The estimated residual value of the leased property, exclusive of any portion guaranteed by the lessee, by any party related to the lessee, or by any party unrelated to the lessee. If the guarantor is related to the lessor, the residual value is considered unguaranteed.

Unrelated Parties. All parties that are not related parties as defined above.

CONCEPTS, RULES, AND EXAMPLES

Variable Interest Entities

From the standpoint of the lessee, it is critical for the accountant to first determine whether the relationship between the entities requires consolidation as a VIE under ASC 810. This is discussed in detail in the chapter on ASC 810. If consolidation is required, the effects of the lease recorded by the parties will be eliminated in the consolidated financial statements and the lease accounting will, in effect, be moot from the standpoint of the lessee.

In essence, a VIE is an entity that, by design, is not funded with an amount of at-risk equity sufficient to enable it to sustain itself in the face of reasonably possible losses without obtaining additional support ("subordinated financial support") from existing or additional sources. In practical terms, in the context of leasing, the lessee is at risk for an amount greater than the contractual rental payments—such as for the lessor's debt arising from financing the leased property.

Determining whether an entity is a VIE involves analysis of the individual facts, circumstances, relationships, structures, risks, and rewards associated with the entity and the parties with whom it is involved. Often, especially when related parties are involved, this analysis can be performed qualitatively without laborious numeric estimates of expected variability. That is because even a superficial review of the relationships and transaction details will reveal that the entity in question is indeed a VIE, or that it clearly is not one.

In more complex situations, however, or when qualitative analysis does not yield a conclusive answer, the holder of one or more variable interests may be required to estimate the present value of the probability-weighted expected cash flows associated with the entity in order to determine the expected variability of the entity's future cash flows as well as the portion of that expected variability that is allocable to the various holders of variable interests.

For more information and examples regarding leases and consolidation, see the chapter on ASC 810.

Lease or Sale—the Interplay of Lease and Revenue Recognition Accounting

ASC 840-10-35, *Determining Whether an Arrangement Contains a Lease* ASC 840 defines a lease as "an agreement conveying the right to use property, plant, or equipment (land and/or depreciable assets) usually for a stated period of time." ASC 840-10-35 provides guidance on determining when all or part of an arrangement constitutes a lease.

Scope of ASC 840-10-35 Property, plant, or equipment, as the term is used in ASC 840, includes only land and/or depreciable assets. Therefore, inventory (including equipment parts inventory) cannot be the subject of a lease because inventory is not depreciable. Although specific property, plant, or equipment may be explicitly identified in an arrangement, it is not the subject of a lease if the arrangement can be fulfilled without using the specified property, plant, or equipment. For example, if the owner/seller is obligated to deliver a specified quantity of goods or services but can provide those goods or services using property, plant, or equipment other than that specified in the arrangement, then the arrangement does not contain a lease.

In addition, ASC 840 contains specific scope exceptions with respect to agreements concerning:

- Exploration or exploitation of natural resources (e.g., oil, gas, minerals, and timber)
- Intangible licensing rights (e.g., motion pictures, plays, manuscripts, patents, and copyrights)

Lease treatment is not precluded in situations where the owner or manufacturer of the property has extended a product warranty that includes a provision for replacement of the property if it is not operating adequately. Similarly, if the arrangement includes a provision permitting the equipment owner the right to substitute other equipment on or after a specified date, irrespective of the reason, the arrangement can still qualify as a lease.

Right to use property, plant, or equipment The right to use the specified property, plant, or equipment is conveyed if any one of the following conditions is met:

- A *party* (for the purpose of this discussion, we will refer to this party, the potential lessee, as "the recipient" of the rights) has the ability or right to operate the property, plant, or equipment or direct others to do so as the recipient specifies, while attaining or controlling more than a minor portion of the output (or service utility),
- The recipient has the ability or right to control physical access to the specified property, plant, or equipment while attaining or controlling more than a minor portion of the output (or other service utility), or
- Analysis of the relevant facts and circumstances indicates that it is remote (as that term is used in ASC 450-20) that a party (or parties) other than the recipient will attain more than a minor amount of the output (or other service utility) that will be produced or generated by the specified property, plant, or equipment during the term of the arrangement, *and* the price that the recipient will pay for the output is neither contractually fixed per unit of output nor equal to the market price per unit of output at the time delivery of the output is received.

Timing of initial assessment and subsequent reassessments The assessment of whether an arrangement contains a lease is to be made at the inception of the arrangement. A reassessment of whether the arrangement contains a lease is to be made only if (a) the contractual terms are modified, (b) a renewal option is exercised or the parties to the arrangement agree on an extension of its term, (c) there is a change in the determination as to whether or not fulfillment of the arrangement is dependent on the property, plant, or equipment that was originally specified, or (d) the originally specified property and equipment undergoes a substantial physical change. Remeasurement/redetermination is not permitted merely because of a change in an estimate made at inception (e.g., the number of expected units of output or the useful life of the equipment).

Aggregation of separate contracts There is a rebuttable presumption that separate contracts between the same parties (or related parties) that are executed on or near the same date were negotiated together as a package.

This issue also provides accounting guidance for any recognized assets and liabilities existing at the time that an arrangement (or a portion of an arrangement) either ceases to qualify as a lease or commences to qualify as a lease due to a reassessment in the circumstances as described above.

Sales with a Guaranteed Minimum Resale Value To provide sales incentives, manufacturers sometimes include in a sales contract a guarantee that the purchaser will, upon disposition of the property, receive a minimum resale amount. Upon disposition, the manufacturer either reacquires the property at the agreed-upon minimum price or reimburses the purchaser for any shortfall between the actual sales proceeds and the guaranteed amount.

ASC 605-50-60[2] states that transactions containing guarantees of resale value of equipment by a manufacturer are to be accounted for as leases and not as sales. The minimum lease

[2] Upon implementation of ASU 2014-09, this reference will change and the guidance can be found in ASC 606-10-25-30 and ASC 60 10 55 66 through 78.

payments used to determine if the criteria have been met for lessor sales-type lease accounting, described later in this chapter, are computed as the difference between the proceeds received from the transferee/lessee upon initial transfer of the equipment and the amount of the residual value guarantee on its first contractual exercise date.

If the lease is accounted for as an operating lease because it does not qualify for sales-type lease accounting (as discussed and illustrated later in this chapter), the manufacturer/lessor is to record the proceeds received at inception as a liability, which is subsequently reduced by crediting revenue pro rata from the inception of the lease until the first guarantee exercise date so that, on that exercise date, the remaining liability is the guaranteed residual amount. If the lessee elects, under the terms of the arrangement, to continue to use the leased asset after the first exercise date, the manufacturer/lessor will continue to amortize the liability for the remaining residual amount to revenue to reduce it further to any remaining guarantee, if applicable.

The foregoing prescribed accounting is followed by manufacturers even when there is dealer involvement in the transaction when it is the manufacturer who is responsible for the guarantee to the purchaser.

ASC 460-10-55-17 states that ASC 460-10-55 does not apply to these transactions irrespective of whether they are accounted for as operating leases or sales-type leases because, in either case, the underlying of such a guarantee is an asset owned by the guarantor.

Equipment Sold and Subsequently Repurchased Subject to an Operating Lease ASC 605-15-25-5 specifies that if four conditions are satisfied, a manufacturer can recognize a sale at the time its product is transferred to a dealer for subsequent sale to a third-party customer, even if this ultimate customer (the dealer's customer) enters into an operating lease agreement with the same manufacturer or the manufacturer's finance affiliate:

- The dealer must be an independent entity that conducts business separately with manufacturers and customers,
- The passage of the product from the manufacturer to the dealer fully transfers ownership,
- The manufacturer (or finance affiliate) has no obligation to provide a lease arrangement for the dealer's customer, and
- The dealer's customer is in control of selecting which of the many financing options available will be used.

Lessee Classification

For accounting and reporting purposes the lessee has two possible classifications for a lease:

1. Operating
2. Capital

The proper classification of a lease is determined by the circumstances surrounding the transaction. According to ASC 840, if substantially all of the benefits and risks of ownership have been transferred to the lessee, the lessee records the lease as a capital lease at its inception. Substantially all of the risks or benefits of ownership are deemed to have been transferred if any one of the following criteria is met:

- The lease transfers ownership to the lessee by the end of the lease term.
- The lease contains a bargain purchase option.
- The lease term is equal to 75% or more of the estimated economic life of the leased property, and the beginning of the lease term does not fall within the last 25% of the total economic life of the leased property.

- The present value of the minimum lease payments at the beginning of the lease term is 90% or more of the fair value to the lessor less any investment tax credit retained by the lessor. This requirement cannot be used if the lease's inception is in the last 25% of the useful economic life of the leased asset. The interest rate, used to compute the present value, is the incremental borrowing rate of the lessee unless the implicit rate is available and lower. For the purpose of this test, lease structuring fees or lease administration fees paid by the lessee to the lessor are included as part of the minimum lease payments. (ASC 840-10-25)

If a lease agreement meets none of the four criteria set forth above, it is classified as an operating lease by the lessee.

Lessor Classification

There are four possible classifications that apply to a lease from the standpoint of the lessor.

1. Operating
2. Sales-type
3. Direct financing
4. Leveraged

The conditions surrounding the origination of the lease determine its classification by the lessor. If the lease meets any one of the four criteria specified above for lessees and both of the qualifications set forth below, the lease is classified as either a sales-type lease, direct financing lease, or leveraged lease depending upon the conditions present at the inception of the lease.

1. Collectibility of the minimum lease payments is reasonably predictable.
2. No important uncertainties surround the amount of unreimbursable costs yet to be incurred by the lessor under the lease.

If a lease transaction does not meet the criteria for classification as a sales-type lease, a direct financing lease, or a leveraged lease as specified above, it is classified by the lessor as an operating lease. The classification testing is performed prior to considering the proper accounting treatment.

It is a common practice in equipment leasing transactions for the lessor to obtain, from an unrelated third party, a full or partial guarantee of the residual value of a portfolio of leased assets. These transactions are structured in such a manner that the third-party guarantor provides a guarantee of the aggregate residual value of the portfolio but does not individually guarantee the residual value of any of the individually leased assets included in that portfolio. To the extent that a specific leased asset's residual value exceeds the guaranteed minimum amount, that excess is used to offset shortfalls relating to other specific leased assets whose residual values are below the guaranteed minimum amount.

In ASC 840-30-S99, the SEC staff observer announced the SEC staff's position that the expected proceeds from these types of portfolio residual guarantees are to be *excluded* from minimum lease payments in computing the present value of the minimum lease payments for the purpose of determining the lessor's classification of the lease transaction. The SEC believes this treatment to be appropriate because, under the terms of this portfolio guarantee, the lessor is unable to determine, at lease inception, the guaranteed residual amount of any individually leased asset.

Distinctions among Sales-type, Direct Financing, and Leveraged Leases A lease is classified as a sales-type lease when the criteria set forth above have been met and the lease transaction is structured in such a way that the lessor (generally a manufacturer or dealer) recognizes a profit or loss on the transaction in addition to interest income. In order for this to occur, the fair value of the property must be different from the cost (carrying value). The essential substance of this transaction is that of a sale, and thus its name. Common examples of sales-type leases: (1) when a customer of an automobile dealership opts to lease a car in lieu of an outright purchase, and the release of equipment coming off an expiring lease. Note, however, that a lease involving real estate must transfer title (i.e., criterion 1 in the preceding list) by the end of the lease term for the lessor to classify the lease as a sales-type lease.

A direct financing lease differs from a sales-type lease in that the lessor does not realize a profit or loss on the transaction other than interest income. In a direct financing lease, the fair value of the property at the inception of the lease is equal to the cost (carrying value). This type of lease transaction most often involves lessor entities engaged in financing operations. The lessor (a bank, or other financial institution) purchases the asset and then leases the asset to the lessee. This transaction merely replaces the conventional lending transaction in which the borrower uses the borrowed funds to purchase the asset. There are many economic reasons why the lease transaction is considered. They are as follows:

- The lessee (borrower) is able to obtain 100% financing.
- Flexibility of use for the tax benefits.
- The lessor receives the equivalent of interest as well as an asset with some remaining value at the end of the lease term.

In summary, it may help to visualize the following chart when considering the classification of a lease from the lessor's standpoint:

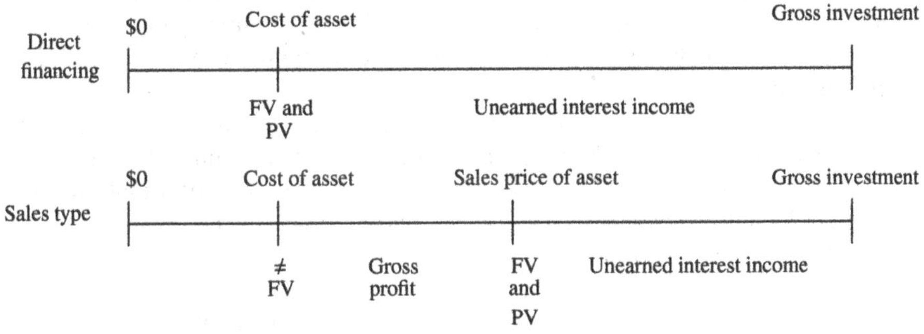

One form of a direct financing lease is a leveraged lease, which is discussed later in this chapter. This type is mentioned separately because it receives a different accounting treatment by the lessor. A leveraged lease meets all the definitional criteria of a direct financing lease, but differs because it involves at least three parties: a lessee, a long-term creditor, and a lessor (commonly referred to as the equity participant). Other characteristics of a leveraged lease are as follows:

1. The financing provided by the long-term creditor must be without recourse to the general credit of the lessor, although the creditor may hold recourse with respect to the leased

property. The amount of the financing must provide the lessor with substantial "leverage" in the transaction.

2. The lessor's net investment declines during the early years and rises during the later years of the lease term before its elimination.

Lessee Accounting

As discussed in the preceding section, there are two classifications that apply to a lease transaction from the standpoint of the lessee, operating or capital.

Operating Leases The accounting treatment accorded an operating lease is relatively simple; the rental payments are charged to expense as the payments are made or become payable. This assumes that the lease payments are being made on a straight-line basis (i.e., an equal payment per period over the lease term).

If the lease agreement calls for either an alternative payment schedule or a scheduled rent increase over the lease term, per ASC 840-20-25, the lease expense is recognized on a straight-line basis over the lease term unless another systematic and rational basis is a better representation of the actual physical usage of the leased property. In addition, the lessor may grant various incentives to the lessee during the lease term, such as a rent holiday, or allowances to fund leasehold improvements. Incentives paid to or incurred on behalf of the lessee by the lessor are an inseparable part of the lease agreement. These amounts are recognized as reductions to rental expense on a straight-line basis over the term of a lease, as described in the preceding paragraph.

In these instances, it is necessary to record either a prepaid asset or a liability depending upon the structure of the payment schedule. If the scheduled increase(s) is due to additional leased property, recognition is to be based on the portion of the leased property that is being utilized with the increased rents recognized over the years that the lessee has control over the use of the additional leased property.

Notice that in the case of an operating lease there is no recognition of the leased asset on the statement of financial position, because the substance of the lease is merely that of a rental. There is no reason to expect that the lessee will derive any future economic benefit from the leased asset beyond the lease term.

Capital Leases Recall that the classification of a lease is determined prior to the consideration of the accounting treatment. Therefore, it is necessary to first examine the lease transaction against the four criteria (transfer of title, bargain purchase option, 75% of useful life, or 90% of net fair value). Should the lease agreement satisfy one of these, it is accounted for as a capital (also referred to as financing) lease.

The lessee records a capital lease as an asset and an obligation (liability) at an amount equal to the present value of the minimum lease payments at the beginning of the lease term. For the purposes of the 90% test, the present value is computed using the incremental borrowing rate of the lessee unless it is practicable for the lessee to determine the implicit rate used by the lessor, and the implicit rate is less than the incremental borrowing rate. The incremental borrowing rate is defined as the rate at lease inception at which the lessee would have been able to borrow over a loan term equivalent to the lease term had it chosen to purchase the leased asset. If the lessee determines a secured borrowing rate that is reasonable and consistent with the financing that would have been used, then it is acceptable to use a secured borrowing rate.

The asset is recorded at the lower of the present value of the minimum lease payments or the fair value of the asset. When the fair value of the leased asset is less than the present value of the minimum lease payments, the interest rate used to amortize the lease obligation will differ from the interest rate used in the 90% test.

The interest rate used in the amortization will be the same as that used in the 90% test when the fair value is greater than or equal to the present value of the minimum lease payments. For purposes of this computation, the minimum lease payments are considered to be the payments that the lessee is obligated to make or can be required to make excluding executory costs such as insurance, maintenance, and taxes.

The minimum lease payments generally include the minimum rental payments, any guarantee of the residual value made by the lessee, and the penalty for failure to renew the lease, if applicable. If the lease includes a bargain purchase option (BPO), the amount required to be paid under the BPO is also included in the minimum lease payments.

The lease term used in this present value computation is the fixed, noncancelable term of the lease plus the following:

- All periods covered by bargain renewal options
- All periods for which failure to renew the lease imposes a penalty on the lessee
- All periods covered by ordinary renewal options during which the lessee guarantees the lessor's debt on the leased property
- All periods covered by ordinary renewals or extensions up to the date a BPO is exercisable
- All periods representing renewals or extensions of the lease at the lessor's option

Remember, if the amount computed as the present value of the minimum lease payments exceeds the fair value of the leased property at the inception of the lease, the amount recorded is limited to the fair value.

The amortization of the leased asset will depend upon how the lease qualifies as a capital lease. If the lease transaction meets the criteria of either transferring ownership, or containing a bargain purchase option, then the asset arising from the transaction is amortized over the estimated useful life of the leased property. If the transaction qualifies as a capital lease because it meets either the 75% of useful life or 90% of fair value criteria, the asset is amortized over the lease term. The conceptual rationale for this differentiated treatment arises because of the substance of the transaction. Under the first two criteria, the asset actually becomes the property of the lessee at the end of the lease term (or upon exercise of the BPO). In the latter situations, the title to the property remains with the lessor, and, thus, the lessee ceases to have the right to use the property at the conclusion of the lease term.

The leased asset is amortized (depreciated) over the lease term if title does not transfer to the lessee, while the asset is depreciated in a manner consistent with the lessee's normal depreciation policy if the title is to eventually transfer to the lessee. This latter situation can be interpreted to mean that the asset is depreciated over the useful economic life of the leased asset. The treatment and method used to amortize (depreciate) the leased asset is very similar to that used for any other long-lived asset. The amortization entry requires a debit to amortization expense and a credit to accumulated amortization. The leased asset is not amortized below the estimated residual value.

In some instances when the property is to revert to the lessor, there may be a guaranteed residual value. This is an amount that the lessee guarantees to the lessor. If the fair value of the asset at the end of the lease term is greater than or equal to the guaranteed residual amount, the lessee incurs no additional obligation. On the other hand, if the fair value of the leased asset is less than the guaranteed residual value, then the lessee must make up the difference, usually with a cash payment. The guaranteed residual value is often used as a tool to reduce the periodic payments by substituting the lump-sum amount at the end of the term that results from the guarantee. In any event the amortization must still take place based on the estimated residual value. This results in a rational and systematic allocation of the expense to the periods of usage and avoids a large loss (or expense) in the last period as a result of the guarantee.

The annual (periodic) rent payments made during the lease term are allocated between a reduction in the obligation and interest expense in a manner such that the interest expense represents the application of a constant periodic rate of interest to the remaining balance of the lease obligation. This is commonly referred to as the effective interest method.

The following examples illustrate the treatment described in the foregoing paragraphs.

Example of Accounting for a Capital Lease—Asset Returned to Lessor

1. The lease is initiated on 1/1/X1 for equipment with an expected useful life of three years. The equipment reverts to the lessor upon expiration of the lease agreement.
2. The fair value of the equipment at lease inception is $135,000.
3. Three payments are due to the lessor in the amount of $50,000 per year beginning 12/31/X1.
4. An additional sum of $1,000 is to be paid annually by the lessee for insurance.
5. The lessee guarantees a $10,000 residual value on 12/31/X3 to the lessor.
6. Irrespective of the $10,000 residual value guarantee, the leased asset is expected to have only a $1,000 salvage value on 12/31/X3.
7. The lessee's incremental borrowing rate is 10%. (The lessor's implicit rate is unknown.)

The present value of the lease obligation is as follows:

PV of guaranteed residual value	= $10,000 × 7513*	= $ 7,513
PV of annual payments	= $50,000 × 2.4869**	= 124,345
		$131,858

* *The present value of an amount of $1 due in three periods at 10% is .7513.*
** *The present value of an ordinary annuity of $1 for three periods at 10% is 2.4869.*

The first step in dealing with any lease transaction is to classify the lease. In this case, the lease term is for three years, which is equal to 100% of the expected useful life of the asset. Note that the 90% test is also fulfilled as the present value of the minimum lease payments ($131,858) is greater than 90% of the fair value (90% × $135,000 = $121,500). Thus, the lessee accounts for the lease as a capital lease.In item 7, the present value of the lease obligation is computed. Note that the executory costs (insurance) are not included in the minimum lease payments and that the incremental borrowing rate of the lessee was used to determine the present value. This rate was used because the lessor's implicit rate was not determinable.

NOTE: To have used the implicit rate it would have to have been less than the incremental borrowing rate.

The entry necessary to record the lease on 1/1/X1 is:

Leased equipment	131,858	
Lease obligation		131,858

Note that the lease is recorded at the present value of the minimum lease payments that, in this case, is less than the fair value. If the present value of the minimum lease payments had exceeded the fair value, the lease would have been recorded at the fair value.

The next step is to determine the proper allocation between interest and reduction of the lease obligation for each lease payment. This is done using the effective interest method as illustrated below.

Year	Cash payment	Interest expense	Reduction in lease obligation	Balance of lease obligation
Inception of lease				$131,858
20X1	$50,000	$13,186	$36,814	95,044
20X2	50,000	9,504	40,496	54,548
20X3	50,000	5,452	44,548	10,000

The interest is calculated at 10% (the incremental borrowing rate) of the balance of the lease obligation for each period, and the remainder of each $50,000 payment is allocated as a reduction in the lease obligation. The lessee is also required to pay $1,000 for insurance on an annual basis. The entries necessary to record all payments relative to the lease for each of the three years are shown below.

	12/31/X1		12/31/X2		12/31/X3	
Insurance expense	1,000		1,000		1,000	
Interest expense	13,186		9,504		5,452	
Lease obligation	36,814		40,496		44,548	
Cash		51,000		51,000		51,000

The leased equipment recorded as an asset must also be amortized (depreciated). The initial unamortized balance is $131,858; however, as with any other long-lived asset, it cannot be amortized below the estimated residual value of $1,000 (note that it is amortized down to the actual estimated residual value, not the guaranteed residual value). In this case, the straight-line amortization method is applied over a period of three years. This three-year period represents the lease term, not the life of the asset, because the asset reverts to the lessor at the end of the lease term. Therefore, the following entry will be made at the end of each year:

Amortization expense	43,619		
Accumulated amortization		43,619	[($131,858 – 1,000) ÷ 3]

Finally, on 12/31/X3 we must recognize the fact that ownership of the property has reverted back to the owner (lessor). The lessee made a guarantee that the residual value would be $10,000 on 12/31/14; as a result, the lessee must make up the difference between the guaranteed residual value and the actual residual value with a cash payment to the lessor. The following entry illustrates the removal of the leased asset and obligation from the lessee's accounting records:

Lease obligation	10,000	
Accumulated amortization	130,858	
Cash		9,000
Leased equipment		131,858

The foregoing example illustrated a situation where the asset was to be returned to the lessor. Another situation exists (under BPO or transfer of title) where ownership of the asset is expected to transfer to the lessee at the end of the lease term. Remember that leased assets are amortized over their useful life when title transfers or a bargain purchase option exists. At the end of the lease, the balance of the lease obligation should equal the guaranteed residual value, the bargain purchase option price, or termination penalty for failure to renew the lease.

Example of Accounting for a Capital Lease—Asset Ownership Transferred to Lessee

- A three-year lease is initiated on 1/1/X1 for equipment with an expected useful life of five years.
- Three annual lease payments of $52,000 are required beginning on 1/1/X1 (note that the payment at the beginning of the year changes the present value computation from the previous example). The lessee pays $2,000 per year for insurance on the equipment and this amount is included in the annual payments.
- The lessee can exercise a bargain purchase option on 12/31/X3 for $10,000. The expected residual value at 12/31/X3 is $18,000.
- The lessee's incremental borrowing rate is 10% (the lessor's implicit rate is unknown).
- The fair value of the leased property at the inception of the lease is $140,000.

Once again, the classification of the lease must be determined prior to computing the accounting entries to record it. This lease is classified as a capital lease because it contains a BPO. In this case, the 90% test is also fulfilled.

The present value of the lease obligation is computed as follows:

PV of bargain purchase option	= $10,000	× .7513*	= $ 7,513
PV of annual payments	= ($52,000 – $2,000)	× 2.4869**	= 136,755
			$144,268

** .7513 is the present value of an amount due in three periods at 10%.*
*** 2.7355 is the present value of an annuity due for three periods at 10%.*

Since the lessee pays $2,000 a year for insurance, this payment is treated as executory costs and excluded from the calculation of the present value of the annual payments. Note that the present value of the lease obligation is greater than the fair value of the asset. Because of this, the lease obligation must be recorded at the fair value of the leased asset:

1/1/X1 Leased equipment	140,000	
Obligation under capital lease		140,000

According to ASC 840, the allocation between interest and principal is determined so that interest expense is computed using a constant periodic rate of interest applied to the remaining balance of the obligation. If the fair value of the leased asset is greater than or equal to the present value of the lease obligation, the interest rate used is the same as that used to compute the present value (i.e., the incremental borrowing rate or the implicit rate). In cases such as this, when the present value exceeds the fair value of the leased asset, a new rate must be computed through a series of manual trial and error calculations. Alternatively, spreadsheet or loan amortization software can be used to solve for the unknown effective interest rate. In this situation the interest rate used was 13.267%. The amortization of the lease takes place as follows:

Date	Cash payment	Interest expense	Reduction in lease obligation	Balance of lease obligation
Inception of lease				$140,000
1/1/X1	$50,000	$–	$50,000	90,000
1/1/X2	50,000	11,940	38,060	51,940
1/1/X3	50,000	6,891	43,109	8,831
12/31/X3	10,000	1,169	8,831	–

The following entries are required in years 20X1 through 20X3 to recognize the payment and amortization:

		20X1		*20X2*		*20X3*	
1/1	Insurance expense	2,000		2,000		2,000	
	Obligation under capital lease	50,000		38,060		43,109	
	Accrued interest payable			11,940		6,891	
	Cash		52,000		52,000		52,000
12/31	Interest expense	11,940		6,891		1,169	
	Accrued interest payable		11,940		6,891		1,169
12/31	Amortization expense	24,400		24,400		24,400	
	Accumulated amortization		24,400		24,400		24,400
	[($140,000–$18,000)÷5years)]						
12/31	Obligation under capital lease					8,831	
	Accrued interest payable					1,169	
	Cash						10,000

Lessor Accounting

As previously noted, there are four classifications of leases with which a lessor must be concerned. They are operating, sales-type, direct financing, and leveraged.

Operating Leases As in the case of the lessee, the operating lease requires a less complex accounting treatment. The payments received by the lessor are recorded as rent revenues in the period in which the payment is received or becomes receivable. As with the lessee, if the rentals vary from a straight-line basis, the lease agreement contains a scheduled rent increase over the lease term, or the lessor grants incentives to the lessee such as a rent holiday or leasehold improvement allowance, the revenue is recorded on a straight-line basis unless an alternative basis of systematic and rational allocation is more representative of the time pattern of physical usage of the leased property. If the scheduled increase(s) is due to the lessee leasing additional property under a master lease agreement, the increase is allocated proportionally to the additional leased property and recognized on a straight-line basis over the years that the lessee has control over the additional leased property. ASC 840-20- 25 prescribes that, in this case, the total revised rent be allocated between the previously leased property and the additional leased property based on their relative fair values.

The lessor presents the leased property on the statement of financial position under the caption "Investment in leased property." This caption is shown with or near the fixed assets of the lessor, and depreciated in the same manner as the lessor's other fixed assets.

Any initial direct costs are amortized over the lease term as the related lease revenue is recognized (i.e., on a straight-line basis unless another method is more representative). However, these costs may be charged to expense as incurred if the effect is not materially different from straight-line amortization.

Any incentives made by the lessor to the lessee are treated as reductions of rent and recognized on a straight-line basis over the term of the lease.

In most operating leases, the lessor recognizes rental income over the lease term and does not measure or recognize any gain or loss on any differential between the fair value of the property and its carrying value. One exception to this rule is set forth in ASC 840-40. The exception applies when an operating lease involving real estate is not classified as a sales-type lease because ownership to the property does not transfer to the lessee at the end of the lease term. In this case, if at the inception of the lease the fair value of the property is less than its carrying amount, the lessor must recognize a loss equal to that difference at the inception of the lease.

Sales-type Leases In accounting for a sales-type lease, it is necessary for the lessor to determine the following amounts:

- Gross investment
- Fair value of the leased asset
- Cost.

Note that, following the promulgation of ASC 820, there was some confusion over the definition of fair value to be employed for purposes of lease determination and measurement. ASC 820 does not apply to ASC 840 determinations of lease classifications or measurements. However, ASC 820 is applicable to the determinations to be made in business combinations accounted for under ASC 805.

From these amounts, the remainder of the computations necessary to record and account for the lease transaction can be made. The first objective is to determine the numbers necessary to complete the following entry:

Lease receivable	xx	
Cost of goods sold	xx	
Sales		xx
Inventory		xx
Unearned interest		xx

The gross investment (lease receivable) of the lessor is equal to the sum of the minimum lease payments (excluding executory costs) plus the unguaranteed residual value. The difference between the gross investment and the present value of the two components of gross investment (minimum lease payments and unguaranteed residual value) is recorded as the unearned interest revenue. The present value is computed using the lease term and implicit interest rate (both of which were discussed earlier). The lease term used in this computation includes any renewal options exercisable at the discretion of the lessor. The resulting unearned interest revenue is to be amortized into income using the effective interest method. This will result in a constant periodic rate of return on the net investment (the net investment is the gross investment less the unearned income).

Recall from our earlier discussion that the fair value of the leased property is, by definition, equal to the normal selling price of the asset adjusted by any residual amount retained (this amount retained can be exemplified by an unguaranteed residual value, investment credit, etc.).

The adjusted selling price used for a sales-type lease is equal to the present value of the minimum lease payments. Thus, we can say that the normal selling price less the residual amount retained is equal to the PV of the minimum lease payments.

The cost of goods sold to be charged against income in the period of the sale is computed as the historic cost or carrying value of the asset (most likely inventory) plus any initial direct costs, less the present value of the unguaranteed residual value. (ASC 840-30-25-6) The difference between the adjusted selling price and the amount computed as the cost of goods sold is the gross profit recognized by the lessor at the inception of the lease (sale). Thus, a sales-type lease generates two types of revenue for the lessor:

1. The gross profit on the sale
2. The interest earned on the lease receivable.

Note that if the sales-type lease involves real estate, the lessor must account for the transaction under the provisions of ASC 360 in the same manner as a seller of the same property (see chapter on ASC 360).[3]

The application of these points is illustrated in the example below.

Example of Accounting for a Sales-type Lease

Price Inc. is a manufacturer of specialized equipment. Many of its customers do not have the necessary funds or financing available for outright purchase. Because of this, Price offers a leasing alternative. The data relative to a typical lease are as follows:

- The noncancelable fixed portion of the lease term is five years. The lessor has the option to renew the lease for an additional three years at the same rental. The estimated useful life of the asset is ten years.
- The lessor is to receive equal annual payments over the term of the lease. The leased property reverts to the lessor upon termination of the lease.
- The lease is initiated on 1/1/12. Payments are due annually on 12/31 for the duration of the lease term.
- The cost of the equipment to Price Inc. is $100,000. The lessor incurs costs associated with the inception of the lease in the amount of $2,500.
- The selling price of the equipment for an outright purchase is $150,000.
- The equipment is expected to have a residual value of $15,000 at the end of five years and $10,000 at the end of eight years.
- The lessor desires a return of 12% (the implicit rate).

The first step is to calculate the annual payment due to the lessor. To yield the lessor's desired return, the present value of the minimum lease payments must equal the selling price adjusted for the present value of the residual amount. The present value is computed using the implicit interest rate and the lease term. In this case, the implicit rate is given as 12% and the lease term is eight years (the fixed noncancelable portion plus the renewal period). Thus, the computation would be as follows:

Normal selling price – PV of residual value = PV of minimum lease payments

[3] Upon implementation of ASU 2014-09, this paragraph will be superseded.

Or, in this case,

\$150,000 – (.40388* × \$10,000 = \$4,038.80)	4.96764** × Annual minimum lease payment
	= Annual minimum lease payment
\$29,382.40	= Annual minimum lease payment

*.40388 is the present value of an amount of \$1 due in eight periods at a 12% interest rate.
**4.96764 is the present value of an annuity of \$1 for eight periods at a 12% interest rate.

Prior to examining the accounting implications of the lease, we must first determine the lease classification. Assume that there are no uncertainties regarding the lessor's costs, and the collectibility of the lease payments is reasonably assured. In this example, the lease term is eight years (discussed above) while the estimated useful life of the asset is ten years; thus, this lease is not an operating lease because the lease term covers 80% of the asset's estimated useful life. This exceeds the previously discussed 75% criterion. (Note that it also meets the 90% of fair value criterion because the present value of the minimum lease payments of \$145,961.20 is greater than 90% of the fair value [90% × \$150,000 = \$135,000].) Next it must be determined if this is a sales-type, direct financing, or leveraged lease. To do this, examine the fair value or selling price of the asset and compare it to the cost. Because the two are not equal, this is a sales-type lease.

Next, obtain the figures necessary for the lessor to record the entry. The gross investment is the total minimum lease payments plus the unguaranteed residual value, or:

$$(\$29,382.40 \times 8 = \$235,059.20) + \$10,000 = \$245,059.20$$

The cost of goods sold is the historical cost of the inventory (\$100,000) plus any initial direct costs (\$2,500) less the present value of the unguaranteed residual value (\$10,000 × .40388 = \$4,038.80). Thus, the cost of goods sold amount is \$98,461.20 (= \$100,000 + \$2,500 – \$4,038.80). Note that the initial direct costs will require a credit entry to record their accrual (accounts payable) or payment (cash). The inventory account is credited for the carrying value of the asset, in this case \$100,000.

The adjusted selling price is equal to the present value of the minimum payments, or \$145,961.20. Finally, the unearned interest revenue is equal to the gross investment (i.e., lease receivable) less the present value of the components making up the gross investment (the present values of the minimum annual lease payments of \$29,382.40 and the unguaranteed residual of \$10,000). The computation is [\$245,059.20 – (\$29,382.40 × 4.96764 = \$145,961.20) – (\$10,000 × .40388 = 4,038.80) = \$95,059.20]. Therefore, the entry necessary for the lessor to record the lease is:

Lease receivable	245,059.20	
Cost of goods sold	98,461.20	
Inventory		100,000.00
Sales		145,961.20
Unearned interest		95,059.20
Accounts payable (initial direct costs)		2,500.00

The next step in accounting for a sales-type lease is to determine the proper handling of each payment. Both principal and interest are included in each payment. Interest is recognized using the effective interest rate method so that an equal rate of return is earned each period over the term of the lease. This will require setting up an amortization schedule, as illustrated below:

Year	*Cash payment*	*Interest*	*Reduction in principal*	*Balance of net investment*
Inception of lease				$150,000.00
20X1	$ 29,382.40	$18,000.00	$ 11,382.40	138,617.00
20X2	29,382.40	16,634.11	12,748.29	125,869.31
20X3	29,382.40	15,104.32	14,278.08	111,591.23
20X4	29,382.40	13,390.95	15,991.45	95,599.78
20X5	29,382.40	11,471.97	17,910.43	77,689.35
20X6	29,382.40	9,322.72	20,059.68	57,629.67
20X7	29,382.40	6,915.56	22,466.84	35,162.83
20X8	29,382.40	4,219.57	25,162.83	10,000.00
	$235,059.20	$95,059.20	$140,000.00	

A few of the columns need to be elaborated upon. First, the net investment is the gross investment (lease receivable) less the unearned interest. Note that at the end of the lease term, the net investment is equal to the estimated residual value. Also note that the total interest earned over the lease term is equal to the unearned interest at the beginning of the lease term.

The entries below illustrate the proper accounting for the receipt of the lease payment and the amortization of the unearned interest in the first year:

Cash	29,382.40	
Lease receivable		29,382.40
Unearned interest	18,000.00	
Interest revenue		18,000.00

Note that there is no entry to recognize the principal reduction. This is done automatically when the net investment is reduced by decreasing the lease receivable (gross investment) by $29,382.40 and the unearned interest account by only $18,000. The $18,000 is 12% (implicit rate) of the net investment. These entries are to be made over the life of the lease.

At the end of the lease term the asset is returned to the lessor and the following entry is required:

Asset	10,000	
Lease receivable		10,000

Direct Financing Leases The accounting for a direct financing lease holds many similarities to that for a sales-type lease. Of particular importance is that the terminology used is much the same; however, the treatment accorded these items varies greatly. Again, it is best to preface our discussion by determining our objectives in the accounting for a direct financing lease. Once the lease has been classified, it must be recorded. To do this, the following numbers must be obtained:

- Gross investment
- Cost
- Residual value

As noted, a direct financing lease generally involves a leasing company or other financial institution and results in only interest income being earned by the lessor. This is because the fair value (selling price) and the cost are equal and, therefore, no profit is recognized on the actual lease transaction. Note how this is different from a sales-type lease that involves both a profit on the transaction and interest income over the lease term. The reason for this difference is derived from the conceptual nature underlying the purpose of the lease transaction. In a sales-type lease, the manufacturer (distributor, dealer) is seeking an alternative means to finance the sale of the product, whereas a direct financing lease is a result of the consumer's need to finance an equipment purchase through a third party. Because the consumer is unable to obtain conventional financing, he or she turns to a leasing company that will purchase the desired asset and then lease it to the consumer. Here the profit on the transaction remains with the manufacturer, while the interest income is earned by the leasing company.

Like a sales-type lease, the first objective is to determine the amounts necessary to complete the following entry:

Lease receivable	xxx	
Asset		xxx
Unearned interest		xx

The gross investment is still defined as the minimum amount of lease payments exclusive of any executory costs plus the unguaranteed residual value. The difference between the gross investment as determined above and the cost (carrying value) of the asset is to be recorded as the unearned interest income because there is no manufacturer's/dealer's profit earned on the transaction. The following entry would be made to record the initial direct costs:

Initial direct costs	xx	
Cash (or accounts payable)		xx

The net investment in the lease is defined as the gross investment less the unearned interest income plus the unamortized initial direct costs related to the lease. Initial direct costs are defined in the same way that they were for purposes of the sales-type lease; however, the accounting treatment is different. For a direct financing lease, the unearned lease (interest) income and the initial direct costs are amortized to income over the lease term to yield a constant effective rate of interest on the net investment. Thus, the effect of the initial direct costs is to reduce the implicit interest rate, or yield, to the lessor over the life of the lease.

An example follows that illustrates the preceding principles.

Example of Accounting for a Direct Financing Lease

Edwards, Inc. needs new equipment to expand its manufacturing operation; however, it does not have sufficient capital to purchase the asset at this time. Because of this, Edwards has employed Samuels Leasing to purchase the asset. In turn, Edwards (the lessee) will lease the asset from Samuels (the lessor). The following information applies to the terms of the lease:

Lease information

- A three-year lease is initiated on 1/1/X1 for equipment costing $131,858 with an expected useful life of five years. Fair value at 1/1/X2 of the equipment is $131,858.
- Three annual payments are due to the lessor beginning 12/31/X1. The property reverts to the lessor upon termination of the lease.
- The unguaranteed residual value at the end of year three is estimated to be $10,000.

- The annual payments are calculated to give the lessor a 10% return (implicit rate).
- The lease payments and unguaranteed residual value have a present value equal to $131,858 (FMV of asset) at the stipulated discount rate.
- The annual payment to the lessor is computed as follows:

PV of residual value	=	$10,000 × .7513* = $7,513
PV of lease payments	=	Selling price – PV of residual value
	=	$131,858 – 7,513 = $124,345
Annual payment	=	$\frac{\$124,345}{PV_{3}, 10\%} = \frac{\$124,345}{2.4869^{**}} = \$50,000$

**.7513 is the present value of an amount due in three periods at 10%.*
***2.4869 is the present value of an annuity of $1 for three periods at a 10% interest rate.*

- Initial direct costs of $7,500 are incurred by Samuels in the lease transaction.

As with any lease transaction, the first step must be to determine the proper classification of the lease. In this case, the present value of the lease payments ($124,345) exceeds 90% of the fair value (90% × $131,858 = $118,672). Assume that the lease payments are reasonably assured and that there are no uncertainties surrounding the costs yet to be incurred by the lessor.

Next, determine the unearned interest and the net investment in the lease.

Gross investment in lease [(3 × $50,000) + $10,000]	$160,000
Cost of leased property	131,858
Unearned interest	$28,142

The unamortized initial direct costs are to be added to the gross investment in the lease and the unearned interest income is to be deducted to arrive at the net investment in the lease. The net investment in the lease for this example is determined as follows:

Gross investment in lease	$160,000
Add: Unamortized initial direct costs	7,500
	$167,500
Less: Unearned interest income	28,142
Net investment in lease	$139,358

The net investment in the lease (Gross investment – Unearned revenue) has been increased by the amount of initial direct costs. Therefore, the implicit rate is no longer 10%. We must recompute the implicit rate. The implicit rate is really the result of an internal rate of return calculation. We know that the lease payments are to be $50,000 per annum and that a residual value of $10,000 is expected at the end of the lease term. In return for these payments (inflows) we are giving up equipment (outflow) and incurring initial direct costs (outflows) with a net investment of $139,358 ($131,858 + $7,500). The only way to manually obtain the new implicit rate is through a trial and error calculation, as set up below.

$$\frac{50,000}{(1+i)^1} + \frac{50,000}{(1+i)^2} + \frac{50,000}{(1+i)^3} + \frac{10,000}{(1+i)^3} = \$139,358$$

Where i = implicit rate of interest.

This computation is most efficiently performed using either spreadsheet or present value software. In doing so, the $139,358 is entered as the present value, the contractual payment stream and residual value are entered, and the software iteratively solves for the unknown implicit interest rate.

In this case, the implicit rate is equal to 7.008%. Thus, the amortization table would be set up as follows:

	(a) Lease payments	*(b) Reduction in unearned interest*	*(c) PV x implicit rate (7.008%)*	*(d) Reduction in initial direct costs (b – c)*	*(e) Reduction in PVI net invest. (a – b + d)*	*(f) PVI net invest. in lease* $(f)_{(n+1)} = (f)_n - (e)$
						$139,358
1.	$ 50,000	$13,186 (1)	$ 9,766	$3,420	$ 40,234	99,124
2.	50,000	9,504 (2)	6,947	2,557	43,053	56,071
3.	50,000	5,455 (3)	3,929	1,526	46,271	10,000
	$ 15,000	$28,145*	$20,642	$7,503	$129,358	

* *Rounded*

(b.1) $131,858 × 10% = $13,186

(b.2) [$131,858 – ($50,000 – 13,186)] × 10% = $9,504

(b.3) {$131,858 – [($50,000 – 9,504) + ($50,000 – 13,186)]} × 10% = $5,455

Here the interest is computed as 7.008% of the net investment. Note again that the net investment at the end of the lease term is equal to the estimated residual value.

The entry made to initially record the lease is as follows:

Lease receivable* [($50,000 × 3) + 10,000]	160,000	
Asset acquired for leasing		131,858
Unearned interest		28,142

* *Also the "gross investment in lease."*

When the payment of (or obligation to pay) the initial direct costs occurs, the following entry must be made:

Initial direct costs	7,500	
Cash (or accounts payable)		7,500

Using the schedule above, the following entries would be made during each of the indicated years:

	20X1		*20X2*		*20X3*	
Cash	50,000		50,000		50,000	
Lease receivable*		50,000		50,000		50,000
Unearned interest	13,186		9,504		5,455	
Initial direct costs		3,420		2,557		1,526
Interest revenue		9,766		6,947		3,929

* *Also the "gross investment in lease."*

Finally, when the asset is returned to the lessor at the end of the lease term, it must be recorded by the following entry:

Used asset	10,000	
Lease receivable*		10,000

* *Also the "gross investment in lease."*

Leveraged Leases One of the more complex accounting subjects regarding leases is the accounting for a leveraged lease. Just as is the case with sales-type and direct financing leases, the classification of the lease by the lessor has no impact on the classification of the lease by the lessee. The lessee simply considers whether the lease qualifies as an operating lease or a capital lease. The lessor's accounting issues, however, are substantially more complex.

To qualify as a leveraged lease, a lease agreement must meet the following requirements, and the lessor must account for the investment tax credit (when in effect) in the manner described below.

NOTE: Failure to do so will result in the lease being classified as a direct financing lease.

- The lease must meet the definition of a direct financing lease (the 90% of fair value criterion does not apply).[4]
- The lease must involve at least three parties:
  - An owner-lessor (equity participant)
  - A lessee
  - A long-term creditor (debt participant).
- The financing provided by the creditor is nonrecourse as to the general credit of the lessor and is sufficient to provide the lessor with substantial leverage.
- The lessor's net investment (defined below) decreases in the early years and increases in the later years until it is eliminated.

This last characteristic poses the accounting issue.

The leveraged lease arose as a result of an effort to maximize the income tax benefits associated with a lease transaction. To accomplish this, it was necessary to involve a third party to the lease transaction (in addition to the lessor and lessee): a long-term creditor. The following diagram[5] illustrates the relationships in a leveraged lease agreement:

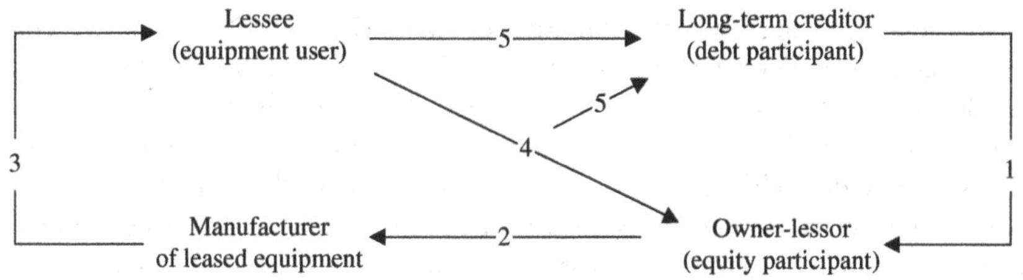

- The owner-lessor obtains long-term financing from the creditor, generally in excess of 50% of the purchase price. ASC 840 indicates that the lessor must be provided with sufficient leverage in the transaction, therefore the 50%.
- The owner then uses this financing along with his/her own funds to purchase the asset from the manufacturer.

---

[4] A direct financing lease must have its cost or carrying value equal to the fair value of the asset at the lease's inception. So even if the amounts are not significantly different, leveraged lease accounting may not be used.

[5] Adapted from "A Straightforward Approach to Leveraged Leasing" by Pierce R. Smith, *The Journal of Commercial Bank Lending,* July 1973, pp. 40–47.

- The manufacturer delivers the asset to the lessee.
- The lessee remits the periodic rent to the lessor.
- The debt is guaranteed by using either the equipment as collateral, the assignment of the lease payments, or both, depending on the demands established by the creditor.

The FASB concluded that the entire lease agreement be accounted for as a single transaction and not a direct financing lease plus a debt transaction. The feeling was that the latter did not readily convey the lessor's net investment in the lease to the user of the financial statements. Thus, the lessor records the investment as a net amount. The gross investment is calculated as a combination of the following amounts:

- The rentals receivable from the lessee, net of the principal and interest payments due to the long-term creditor
- A receivable for the amount of the investment tax credit (ITC) to be realized on the transaction
- The estimated residual value of the leased asset
- The unearned and deferred income, consisting of:
  - The estimated pretax lease income (or loss), after deducting initial direct costs, remaining to be allocated to income
  - The ITC remaining to be allocated to income over the remaining term of the lease[6]

The first three amounts described above are readily obtainable; however, the last amount, the unearned and deferred income, requires additional computations. In order to compute this amount, it is necessary to create a cash flow (income) analysis by year for the entire lease term. As described in item 4 of the preceding list, the unearned and deferred income consists of the pretax lease income (Gross lease rentals – Depreciation – Loan interest) and the unamortized investment tax credit. The total of these two amounts for all of the periods in the lease term represents the unearned and deferred income at the inception of the lease.

The amount computed as the gross investment in the lease (foregoing paragraphs) less the deferred taxes relative to the difference between pretax lease income and taxable lease income is the net investment for purposes of computing the net income for the period. To compute the periodic net income, another schedule must be completed that uses the cash flows derived in the first schedule and allocates them between income and a reduction in the net investment.

The amount of income is first determined by applying a rate to the net investment. The rate to be used is the rate that will allocate the entire amount of cash flow (income) when applied in the years in which the net investment is positive. In other words, the rate is derived in much the same way as the implicit rate (trial and error), except that only the years in which there is a positive net investment are considered. Thus, income is recognized only in the years in which there is a positive net investment.

The income recognized is divided among the following three elements:

1. Pretax accounting income
2. Amortization of investment tax credit
3. The tax effect of the pretax accounting income.

The first two are allocated in proportionate amounts from the unearned and deferred income included in the calculation of the net investment. In other words, the unearned and deferred

[6] The ITC was repealed, effective January 1, 1986. ITC was relevant only for property placed in service prior to this date. We continue to discuss these concepts because Congress has historically reinstated this credit during economic downturns.

income consists of pretax lease accounting income and ITC. Each of these is recognized during the period in the proportion that the current period's allocated income is to the total income (cash flow). The last item, the income tax effect, is recognized in income tax expense for the year. The income tax effect of any difference between pretax lease accounting income and taxable lease income is charged (or credited) to deferred income taxes.

When income tax rates change, all components of a leveraged lease must be recalculated from the inception of the lease using the revised after-tax cash flows arising from the revised income tax rates.

If, in any case, the projected cash receipts (income) are less than the initial investment, the deficiency is to be recognized as a loss at the inception of the lease. Similarly, if at any time during the lease period the aforementioned method of recognizing income would result in a future period loss, the loss is to be recognized immediately.

This situation may arise as a result of the circumstances surrounding the lease changing. Therefore, any estimated residual value and other important assumptions must be reviewed on a periodic basis (at least annually). Any change is to be incorporated into the income computations; however, there is to be no upward revision of the estimated residual value.

The following example illustrates the application of these principles to a leveraged lease.

Example of a Simplified Leveraged Lease

- A lessor acquires an asset for $100,000 with an estimated useful life of three years in exchange for a $25,000 down payment and a $75,000 three-year note with equal payments due on 12/31 each year. The interest rate is 18%.
- The asset has no residual value.
- The present value of an ordinary annuity of $1 for three years at 18% is 2.17427.
- The asset is leased for three years with annual payments due to the lessor on 12/31 in the amount of $45,000.
- The lessor uses the Accelerated Cost Recovery System (ACRS) method of depreciation (150% declining balance with a half-year convention in the year placed in service) for income tax purposes and elects to reduce the ITC rate to 4% as opposed to reducing the depreciable basis.
- Assume a constant income tax rate throughout the life of the lease of 40%.

Chart 1 analyzes the cash flows generated by the leveraged leasing activities. Chart 2 allocates the cash flows between the investment in leveraged leased assets and income from leveraged leasing activities. The allocation requires finding that rate of return, which when applied to the investment balance at the beginning of each year that the investment amount is positive, will allocate the net cash flow fully to net income over the term of the lease. This rate can be found only by a computer program or by an iterative trial and error process. The example that follows has a positive investment value in each of the three years, and thus the allocation takes place in each time period. Leveraged leases usually have periods where the investment account turns negative and is below zero.

Allocating principal and interest on the loan payments is as follows:

$$(\$75{,}000 \div 2.17427 = \$34{,}494)$$

Year	*Payment*	*Interest 18%*	*Principal*	*Balance*
Inception of lease	$–	$–	$–	$75,000
1	34,494	13,500	20,994	54,006
2	34,494	9,721	24,773	29,233
3	34,494	5,261	29,233	–

Chart 1

	A	B	C	D	E	F	G	H	I
	Rent	*Depr*	*Interest on loan*	*Taxable income (loss) (A-B-C)*	*Income tax payable (rcvbl.) Dx40%*	*Loan principal payments*	*ITC*	*Cash flow (A ± G–C E–F)*	*Cumulative cash flow*
Initial	$–	$–	$–	$–	$–	$–	$–	$(25,000)	$(25,000)
Year 1	45,000	25,000	13,500	6,500	2,600	20,994	4,000	11,906	(13,094)
Year 2	45,000	38,000	9,721	(2,721)	(1,088)	24,773	–	11,594	(1,500)
Year 3	45,000	37,000	5,261	2,739	1,096	29,233	–	9,410	7,910
Total	$135,000	$100,000	$28,482	$6,518	$2,608	$75,000	$4,000	$ 7,910	

The chart below allocates the cash flows determined above between the net investment in the lease and income. Recall that the income is then allocated between pretax accounting income and the amortization of the investment credit. The income tax expense for the period is a result of applying the income tax rate to the current periodic pretax accounting income.

The amount to be allocated in total in each period is the net cash flow determined in column H above. The investment at the beginning of year one is the initial down payment of $25,000. This investment is then reduced on an annual basis by the amount of the cash flow not allocated to income.

Chart 2

	1	2	3	4	5	6	7
	Cashflow assumption				*Income analysis*		
	Investment beginning of year	*Cash flow*	*Allocated to Investment*	*Allocated to Income*	*Pretax income*	*Income tax expense*	*Investment tax credit*
Year 1	$25,000	$11,906	$ 7,964	$3,942	$3,248	$1,300	$1,994
Year 2	17,036	11,594	8,908	2,686	2,213	885	1,358
Year 3	8,128	9,410	8,128	1,282	1,057	423	648
$32,910	$25,000	$7,910	$6,518	$2,608	$4,000		

Rate of return = 15.77%

- Column 2 is the net cash flow after the initial investment, and columns 3 and 4 are the allocation based upon the 15.77% rate of return. The total of column 4 is the same as the total of column H in Chart 1.
- Column 5 allocates column D in Chart 1 based upon the allocations in column 4. Column 6 allocates column E in Chart 1 (and, of course, is computed as 40% of column 5), and column 7 allocates column G in Chart 1 on the same basis.

The journal entries below illustrate the proper recording and accounting for the leveraged lease transaction. The initial entry represents the cash down payment, investment tax credit receivable, the unearned and deferred revenue, and the net cash to be received over the term of the lease.

The remaining journal entries recognize the annual transactions which include the net receipt of cash and the amortization of income.

	Year 1		*Year 2*		*Year 3*	
Rents receivable [Chart 1 (A – C – F)]	31,518					
Investment tax credit receivable	4,000					
Cash		25,000				
Unearned and deferred income		10,518				
Initial investment, Chart 2 (5 + 7) totals						

	Year 1		*Year 2*		*Year 3*	
Cash	10,506		10,506		10,506	
Rent receivable		10,506		10,506		10,506
Net for all cash transactions, Chart 1 (A–C–F) line by line for each year						
Income tax receivable (cash)	4,000					
Investment tax credit receivable		4,000				
Unearned and deferred income	5,242		3,571		1,705	
Income from leveraged leases		5,242		3,571		1,705
Amortization of unearned income, Chart 2 (5+7) line by line for each year						

The following schedules illustrate the computation of deferred income tax amount. The annual amount is a result of the temporary difference created due to the difference in the timing of the recognition of income for GAAP and income tax purposes. The income for income tax purposes can be found in column D in Chart 1, while the income for GAAP purposes is found in column 5 of Chart 2. The actual amount of deferred income tax is the difference between the income tax computed with the temporary difference and the income tax computed without the temporary difference. These amounts are represented by the income tax payable or receivable as shown in column E of Chart 1 and the income tax expense as shown in column 6 of Chart 2. A check of this figure is provided by multiplying the difference between GAAP income and tax income by the annual rate.

Year 1

Income tax payable	$ 2,600	
Income tax expense	(1,300)	
Deferred income tax (Dr)		$1,300
Taxable income	$ 6,500	
Pretax accounting income	(3,248)	
Difference	$ 3,252	
$3,252 × 40% = $1,300		

Year 2

Income tax receivable	$ 1,088	
Income tax expense	885	
Deferred income tax (Dr)		$1,973
Taxable loss	$ 2,721	
Pretax accounting income	2,213	
Difference	$ 4,934	
$4,934 × 40% = $1,973		

	Year 3	
Income tax payable	$ 1,096	
Income tax expense	(423)	
Deferred income tax (Dr)		$ 673
Taxable income	$ 2,739	
Pretax accounting income	(1,057)	
Difference	$,682	
$1,682 × 40% = $673		

Interpretive Guidance

Changes in income tax rates ASC 840 requires that the rate of return and allocation of income to be recalculated from the date of inception of a lease and a gain or loss recognized when an important assumption is changed. Per ASC 840-30-35, the effect on a leveraged lease of a change in the income tax rate is recognized as a gain or loss in the accounting period in which the rate changes. Deferred income taxes relating to the change are recognized in accordance with ASC 740.

Change or projected changes in the timing of cash flows relative to income taxes applicable to a leveraged lease transaction ASC 840 also provides that the projected timing of income tax cash flows attributable to a leveraged lease is to be reviewed annually during the lease term (or between annual reviews if events or changes in circumstances indicate that a change in timing either has occurred or is projected to occur in the future). Upon review, if the projected timing of the lease's income tax cash flows changes, the lessor will be required to recalculate, from the inception of the lease, the rate of return and the allocation of income to positive investment years in accordance with ASC 840-30-35. The net investment amount is adjusted to the recalculated amount with the change recognized as a gain or loss in the year that the assumptions changed. The pretax gain or loss is to be included in income from continuing operations before income taxes in the same financial statement caption in which leverage lease income is recognized with the income tax effect of the gain or loss reflected in the income tax provision or benefit.

The standard further provides that the recalculated cash flows are to exclude interest and penalties, advance payments, and deposits to the IRS (and presumably any other relevant state, local, or foreign taxing jurisdiction). The deposits or advance payments are to be included in the projected amount of the settlement with the taxing authority.

This accounting treatment is applicable only to changes or projected changes in the timing of income taxes that are directly attributable to the leveraged lease transaction. ASC 840-30-35 provides that reporting entities whose tax positions frequently vary between the alternative minimum tax (AMT) and regular tax are not required to annually recalculate the net investment in the lease unless there is an indication that the original assumptions about the leveraged lease's anticipated total after-tax net income were no longer valid.

Another factor to consider in the determination of the after-tax cash flows attributable to a leveraged lease transaction is the application of ASC 740-40-25, *Income Taxes—Recognition*. As discussed in detail in the chapter on ASC 740, the lessor is required to assess whether it is more likely than not (i.e., there is a greater than 50% chance probability) that the tax positions it takes or plans to take relative to the transaction would be sustained upon examination by the applicable taxing authorities. If the tax positions do not meet that recognition threshold, the tax benefits associated with taking those positions would be excluded from the leveraged lease calculations and, in fact, would give rise to a liability for unrecognized income tax benefits as well as an accrual for any applicable interest and penalties for all open tax years that are within the statute of limitations. This could obviously have a significant impact on the computed rate of return on the investment attributable to the years in which the net investment is positive.

If, however, the tax positions meet the recognition threshold, then they are subject to measurement to determine the maximum amount that is more than 50% probable of being sustained upon examination. The difference between the income tax position taken or planned to be taken on the income tax return (the "as-filed" benefit), and the amount of the benefit measured using the more than 50% computation, along with any associated penalties and interest, is recorded as the liability for unrecognized income tax benefits as previously described.

The only situation in which this liability, penalties, and interest would not be applicable would be if the tax positions were assessed to be highly certain tax positions, as defined in ASC 740-10-55. Under those circumstances, the entire tax benefit associated with the lease would be recognized and, of course, no interest or penalties would be recognized.

Applicability to real estate leases The foregoing discussion involved the lease of a manufactured asset. ASC 840-40 clarifies that leases that involve land and buildings or leases in a sale-leaseback transaction potentially qualify as leveraged leases if the criteria to qualify as a leveraged lease are met.

Applicability to existing assets of the lessor At the inception of a lease, the cost or carrying value and the fair value of an asset must be the same for the lease to be classified as a direct financing lease which is a necessary condition for leveraged lease treatment. The carrying amount of an existing asset before any write-down must equal its fair value in order for the lease to be classified as a leveraged lease. (ASC 840-10-55)

Real Estate Leases

Real estate leases can be divided into the following four categories:

1. Leases involving land only
2. Leases involving land and building(s)
3. Leases involving real estate and equipment
4. Leases involving only part of a building.

Leases Involving Only Land

Lessee Accounting If the lease agreement transfers ownership or contains a bargain purchase option, the lessee accounts for the lease as a capital lease, and records an asset and related liability equal to the present value of the minimum lease payments. If the lease agreement does not transfer ownership or contain a bargain purchase option, the lessee accounts for the lease as an operating lease.

Lessor Accounting If the lease gives rise to dealer's profit (or loss) and transfers ownership (i.e., title), the lease is classified as a sales-type lease and accounted for under the provisions of ASC 360-20[7] in the same manner as a seller of the same property. (ASC 840-10-25-55) If the lease transfers ownership and the criteria for both collectibility and no material uncertainties are met, but the lease does not give rise to dealer's profit (or loss), the lease is accounted for as a direct financing or leveraged lease as appropriate. If the lease does not transfer ownership, but it contains a bargain purchase option and both the collectibility and no material uncertainties criteria are met, the lease is accounted for as a direct financing, leveraged, or operating lease using the

[7] Upon implementation of ASC 2014-09, this reference will change to ASC 610-20.

same lessor classification criteria as any other lease. If the lease does not meet the collectibility and/or no material uncertainties criteria, the lease is accounted for as an operating lease.

Leases Involving Land and Building

Lessee Accounting If the agreement transfers title or contains a bargain purchase option, the lessee accounts for the agreement by separating the land and building components and capitalizing each separately. The land and building elements are allocated on the basis of their relative fair values measured at the inception of the lease. The land and building components are separately accounted for because the lessee is expected to own the real estate by the end of the lease term. The building is amortized over its estimated useful life without regard to the lease term.

When the lease agreement neither transfers title nor contains a bargain purchase option, the fair value of the land must be determined in relation to the fair value of the aggregate property included in the lease agreement. If the fair value of the land is less than 25% of the aggregate fair value of the leased property, then the land is considered immaterial. Conversely, if the fair value of the land is 25% or greater of the fair value of the aggregate leased property, then the land is considered material and the land and building must be treated separately for accounting purposes.

When the land component of the lease agreement is considered immaterial (fair value land < 25% of the total fair value), the lease is accounted for as a single unit. The lessee capitalizes the lease if one of the following applies:

1. The term of the lease is 75% or more of the economic useful life of the building.
2. The present value of the minimum lease payments equals 90% or more of the fair value of the leased real estate less any lessor investment tax credit.

If neither of the above two criteria is met, the lessee accounts for the lease agreement as a single operating lease.

When the land component of the lease agreement is considered material (fair value land ≥ 25% of the total fair value), the land and building components are separated. By applying the lessee's incremental borrowing rate to the fair value of the land, the annual minimum lease payment attributed to land is computed. The remaining payments are attributed to the building. The division of minimum lease payments between land and building is essential for both the lessee and lessor. The portion of the lease involving the land is always accounted for as an operating lease. The lease involving the building(s) must meet either the 75% or 90% test to be treated as a capital lease. If neither of the two criteria is met, the building(s) are also accounted for as an operating lease.

Computing the Minimum Lease Payments

Construction period lease payments Payments made by a lessee during construction of the leased asset and prior to the beginning of the lease term (sometimes called "construction period lease payments") are considered part of the minimum lease payments for the purpose of the 90% of fair value test. These advance payments are to be included in minimum lease payments at their future value, at the beginning of the lease term, with interest accreted using the same interest rate used to discount payments made during the lease term. (ASC 840-10-25)

If the lease is an operating lease, these payments are accounted for as prepaid rent and amortized to expense along with other rental costs over the term of the lease, normally using the straight-line method.

Residual value guarantees If the terms of the lease include a guarantee of the residual value of the leased property by the lessee, that guarantee is to be included in the minimum lease payments and, in accordance with ASC 840-10-25, is to be allocated entirely to the building. This treatment is consistently followed by both the lessee and the lessor.

Environmental indemnifications An indemnification by the lessee to the lessor that any environmental contamination that the lessee causes during the lease term does not affect the lessee's classification of the lease as capital or operating.

If the lessee's indemnification covers contamination that occurred prior to the lease term, the lessee is to consider, under the ASC 450 criteria for evaluating contingencies, whether the likelihood of loss is considered remote, reasonably possible, or probable before considering any available reimbursements available from insurance companies or other third parties. If the probability of loss is considered remote, then the indemnification does not affect the lessee's classification of the lease. If, however, the probability of loss is either reasonably possible or probable, the transaction is subject to the sale-leaseback provisions of ASC 840-40 and the lessee will be considered to have purchased, sold, and then leased back the property. A lessee providing an indemnification that meets certain criteria under ASC 460 is required to record the indemnification as a guarantee and, in addition, is subject to that pronouncement's disclosure provisions.

Lessee obligation to maintain financial covenants Leases sometimes contain financial covenants similar to those included in loan agreements that obligate the lessee to maintain certain financial ratios. Should the lessee violate these covenants, it is considered an event of default under the lease and the lessor may have a right to put the property to the lessee or require the lessee to make a payment to the lessor. In this case, for the purpose of the 90% of fair value test, the lessee includes in the minimum lease payments the maximum amount it would be required to pay in the event of default unless all of the following conditions exist:

- The default covenant provision is customary in financing arrangements,
- The occurrence of the event of default is objectively determinable and is not at the subjective whim of the lessor,
- The event of default is based on predefined criteria that relate solely to the lessee and its operations, and
- It is reasonable to assume at the inception of the lease and in considering recent lessee operating trends that the event of default will not occur.

Lessor Accounting The lessor's accounting depends on whether the lease transfers ownership, contains a bargain purchase option, or does neither of the two.

If the lease transfers ownership and gives rise to dealer's profit (or loss), the lessor classifies the lease as a sales-type lease and accounts for the lease as a single unit under the provisions of ASC 360-20 in the same manner as a seller of the same property. If the lease transfers ownership, meets both the collectibility and no important uncertainties criteria, but does not give rise to dealer's profit (or loss), the lease is accounted for as a direct financing or leveraged lease as appropriate.

If the lease contains a bargain purchase option and gives rise to dealer's profit (or loss), the lease is classified as an operating lease. If the lease contains a bargain purchase option, meets both the collectibility and no material uncertainties criteria, but does not give rise to dealer's profit (or loss), the lease is accounted for as a direct financing lease or a leveraged lease as appropriate.

If the lease agreement neither transfers ownership nor contains a bargain purchase option, the lessor should follow the same rules as the lessee in accounting for real estate leases involving land and building(s).

However, the collectibility and the no material uncertainties criteria must be met before the lessor can account for the agreement as a direct financing lease, and in no such case may the lease be classified as a sales-type lease (i.e., ownership must be transferred).

The treatment of a lease involving both land and building can be illustrated in the following examples.

Example of Lessee Accounting for Land and Building Lease Containing Transfer of Title

- The lessee enters into a ten-year noncancelable lease for a parcel of land and a building for use in its operations. The building has an estimated remaining useful life of twelve years.
- The fair value of the land is $75,000, while the fair value of the building is $310,000.
- A payment of $50,000 is due to the lessor at the beginning of each of the ten years of the lease.
- The lessee's incremental borrowing rate is 10%. (The lessor's implicit rate is unknown.)
- Ownership will transfer to the lessee at the end of the lease.

The present value of the minimum lease payments is $337,951 ($50,000 × 6.75902).[8] The portion of the present value of the minimum lease payments to be capitalized for each of the two components of the lease is computed as follows:

FV of land			$ 75,000		
FV of building			310,000		
Total FV of leased property			$385,000		
Portion of PV allocated to land	$337,951	×	75,000 / 385,000	=	$ 65,835
Portion of PV allocated to building	$337,951	×	310,000 / 385,000	=	272,116
Total PV to be capitalized					$337,951

The entry made to initially record the lease is as follows:

Leased land	65,835	
Leased building	272,116	
Lease obligation		337,951

Subsequently, the obligation will be decreased using the effective interest method. The leased building will be amortized over its expected useful life.

Example of Lessee Accounting for Land and Building Lease without Transfer of Title or Bargain Purchase Option

Assume the same facts as the previous example except that title does not transfer at the end of the lease.

The lease is still a capital lease because the lease term is more than 75% of the remaining useful life of the building. Since the fair value of the land is less than 25% of the aggregate fair value of the leased property, (75,000/385,000 = 19%), the land component is considered immaterial and the lease is accounted for as a single unit. The entry to record the lease is as follows:

Leased property	337,951	
Lease obligation		337,951

[8] 6.75902 is the present value of an annuity due for ten periods at 10%.

Assume the same facts as the previous example except that the fair value of the land is $110,000 and the fair value of the building is $275,000. Once again title does not transfer.

Because the fair value of the land exceeds 25% of the aggregate fair value of the leased property (110,000/385,000 = 29%), the land component is considered material and the lease is separated into two components. The annual minimum lease payment attributed to the land is computed as follows:

FV of land	$110,000	= $16,275
PV factor	6.75902*	

** 6.75902 is the present value of an annuity due for ten periods at 10%.*

The remaining portion of the annual payment is attributed to the building.

Annual payment	$ 50,000
Less amount attributed to land	(16,275)
Annual payment attributed to building	$ 33,725

The present value of the minimum annual lease payments attributed to the building is then computed as follows:

Minimum annual lease payment attributed to building	$ 33,725
PV factor	× 6.75902*
PV of minimum annual lease payments attributed to building	$ 227,948

** 6.75902 is the present value of an annuity due for ten periods at 10%.*

The entry to record the capital portion of the lease is as follows:

Leased building	227,948	
Lease obligation		227,948

There is no computation of the present value of the minimum annual lease payment attributed to the land since the land component of the lease is treated as an operating lease. For this reason, each year $16,275 of the $50,000 lease payment will be recorded as land rental expense. The remainder of the annual payment ($33,725) will be applied against the lease obligation using the effective interest method.

Leases Involving Real Estate and Equipment

ASC 360-20-15 states that sales of integral equipment are within the scope of ASC 360-20. Consequently, the determination of whether equipment is considered to be integral equipment has increased in importance. A determination of whether equipment to be leased is integral is also necessary for proper accounting for sales-type leases by lessors.

According to ASC 360-20-15,[9] the determination of whether equipment is integral is based on two factors:

1. The significance of the cost to remove the equipment from its existing location (which would include the costs of repairing the damage done to that location by the removal).

[9] Upon implementation of ASU 2014-09, this reference will change to 978-10-15-7*l*.

2. The decrease in value of the equipment that would result from its removal (which is, at minimum, the cost to ship the equipment to the new site and reinstall it). The nature of the equipment and whether others can use it are considered in determining whether there is further diminution in fair value. When the combined total of the cost to remove and any further diminution of value exceeds 10% of the fair value of the equipment (installed), the equipment is considered integral equipment.

ASC 360-20-15 clarifies that ASC 360-20 applies to all sales of real estate, including real estate with accompanying property improvements or integral equipment. Consistent with ASC 360-20-15, ASC 840-10-25 specifies that when evaluating a lease that includes integral equipment to determine the classification of the lease under ASC 840, the equipment is to be evaluated as real estate. ASC 840-10-25 also provides guidance on evaluating how to determine transfer of ownership of integral equipment when no statutory title registration system exists in the jurisdiction.

When real estate leases also involve equipment or machinery, the equipment component is separated and accounted for as a separate lease agreement by both lessees and lessors. "The portion of the minimum lease payments applicable to the equipment element of the lease shall be estimated by whatever means are appropriate in the circumstances." The lessee and lessor apply the capitalization requirements to the equipment lease independently of accounting for the real estate lease(s). The real estate leases are handled as discussed in the preceding two sections. In a sale-leaseback transaction involving real estate with equipment, the equipment and land are not separated.

Leases Involving Only Part of a Building

It is common to find lease agreements that involve only part of a building as, for example, when leasing a floor of an office building or a store in a shopping mall. A difficulty that arises in this situation is that the cost and/or fair value of the leased portion of the whole may not be objectively determinable.

Lessee Accounting If the fair value of the leased property is objectively determinable, then the lessee follows the rules and accounts for the lease as described in "Leases involving land and building." If the fair value of the leased property cannot be objectively determined, consider whether the agreement satisfies the 75% test. This calculation is made using the estimated remaining economic life of the building in which the leased premises are located. If the test is met (i.e., the term of the lease is 75% or more of the estimated remaining economic life of the building), the lease is accounted for as a capital lease. If the test is not met, the lease is accounted for as an operating lease.

Lessor Accounting From the lessor's position, both the cost and fair value of the leased property must be objectively determinable before the procedures described under "Leases involving land and building" will apply. If either the cost or the fair value cannot be determined objectively, the lessor accounts for the agreement as an operating lease.

Operating leases with guarantees It is important to note that, for any operating lease where the terms include a guarantee of the residual value of the leased asset, two issues require consideration:

1. Since a guarantee constitutes a variable interest in the lessor or in the leased assets, does the guarantee cause the lessee to be the primary beneficiary of the lessor that would be required to consolidate the lessor? (See discussion of ASC 810 earlier in this chapter.)
2. Is the guarantee required to be recognized as a liability at inception on the statement of financial position of the lessee under ASC 460?

Lessee-incurred real estate development or construction costs Lessees sometimes incur real estate development or construction costs prior to executing a lease with the developer/lessor. The lessee records these costs as construction in progress on its statement of financial position and any subsequent lease arrangement is accounted for as a sale-leaseback transaction under ASC 840- 40, as discussed in the following section.

Sale-Leaseback Transactions

Sale-leaseback describes a transaction where the owner of property (seller-lessee) sells the property, and then immediately leases all or part of it back from the new owner (buyer-lessor). These transactions may occur when the seller-lessee is experiencing cash flow or financing problems or because of available income tax advantages. The important consideration in this type of transaction is the recognition of two separate and distinct economic events. It is important to note, however, that in a typical sale-leaseback there is not a change in the party that has the right to use the property. First, there is a sale of property, and second, there is a lease agreement for the same property in which the original seller is the lessee and the original buyer is the lessor. This is illustrated below.

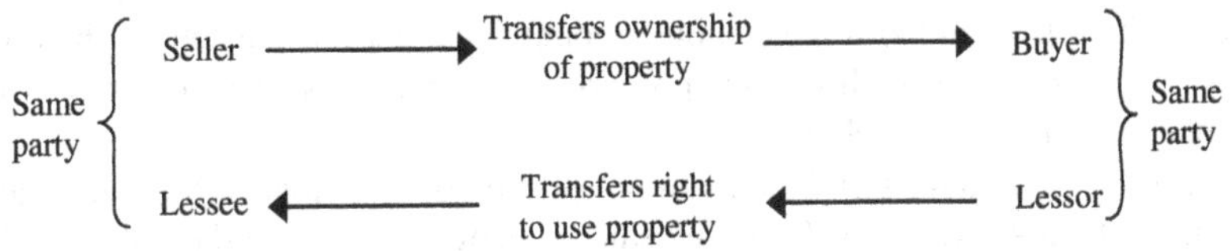

A sale-leaseback transaction is usually structured with the sales price of the asset at or above its current fair value. The result of this higher sales price is higher periodic rental payments over the lease term. The transaction is usually attractive because of the income tax benefits associated with it. The seller-lessee benefits from the higher price because of the increased gain on the sale of the property and the deductibility of the lease payments that are usually larger than the depreciation that was previously being deducted. The buyer-lessor benefits from both the higher rental payments and the larger depreciable income tax basis.

Retention of Rights to Use the Property The accounting treatment from the seller-lessee's point of view will depend upon the extent to which it retains the rights to use the property which can be characterized as one of the following:

- Substantially all
- Minor
- More than minor but less than substantially all

Retention of Rights to Use Property

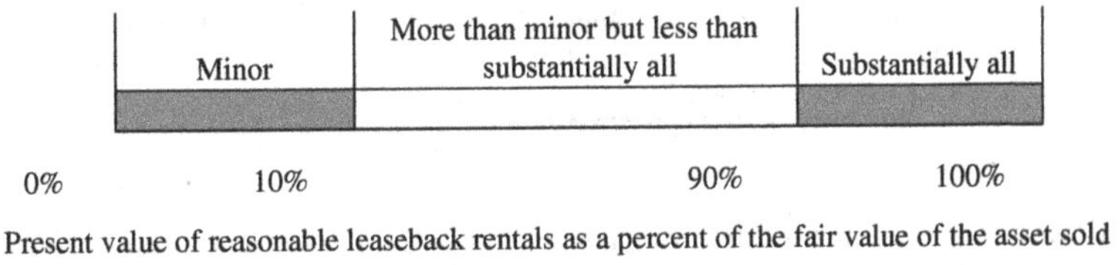

As depicted in the diagram "Retention of Rights to Use Property," the guideline for the determination of substantially all is based upon the classification criteria presented for the lease transaction. That is, if the present value of fair rental payments is equal to 90% or more of the fair value of the asset sold, the seller-lessee is presumed to have retained substantially all of the rights to use the sold property. The test for retention of minor rights would be to substitute 10% or less for 90% or more in the preceding sentence.

If substantially all the rights to use the property are retained by the seller-lessee, and the agreement meets at least one of the criteria for capital lease treatment, the seller-lessee accounts for the leaseback as a capital lease and any profit on the sale is deferred and amortized in proportion to amortization of the leased asset. If the leaseback is classified as an operating lease, it is accounted for as such, and any profit on the sale is deferred and amortized over the lease term in proportion to gross rental charges. Any loss on the sale would also be deferred unless the loss were perceived to be a real economic loss, in which case the loss would be immediately recognized and not deferred.

If only a minor portion of the rights to use are retained by the seller-lessee, the sale and the leaseback are accounted for separately. However, if the rental payments appear unreasonable based upon the existing market conditions at the inception of the lease, the profit or loss is adjusted so the rentals are at a reasonable amount. The amount created by the adjustment is deferred and amortized over the life of the property if a capital lease is involved or over the lease term if an operating lease is involved.

If the seller-lessee retains more than a minor portion but less than substantially all the rights to use the property, any excess profit on the sale is recognized on the date of the sale. For purposes of this paragraph, excess profit is derived as follows:

- If the leaseback is classified as an operating lease, the excess profit is the portion of the profit that exceeds the present value of the minimum lease payments over the lease term including the gross amount of the guaranteed residual value. The seller-lessee uses its incremental borrowing rate to compute the present value of the minimum lease payments. If the implicit rate of interest in the lease is known and lower, it is substituted for the incremental borrowing rate in computing the present value of the minimum lease payments. The present value is amortized over the lease term while that guaranteed residual is deferred until resolution at the end of the lease term.
- If the leaseback is classified as a capital lease, the excess profit is the portion of the profit that exceeds the recorded amount of the leased asset.

Executory costs are not to be included in the calculation of profit to be deferred in a sale-leaseback transaction. (ASC 840-40-30) When the fair value of the property at the time of the leaseback is less than its undepreciated cost, the seller-lessee immediately recognizes a loss for the difference. In the example below, the sales price is less than the book value of the property. However, there is no economic loss because the fair value is greater than the book value.

Sales price	Book value	FV and PV
$85,000	$90,000	$100,000

($5,000)
Artificial loss

The artificial loss is deferred and amortized as an addition to depreciation.

The diagram below summarizes the accounting for sale-leaseback transactions.

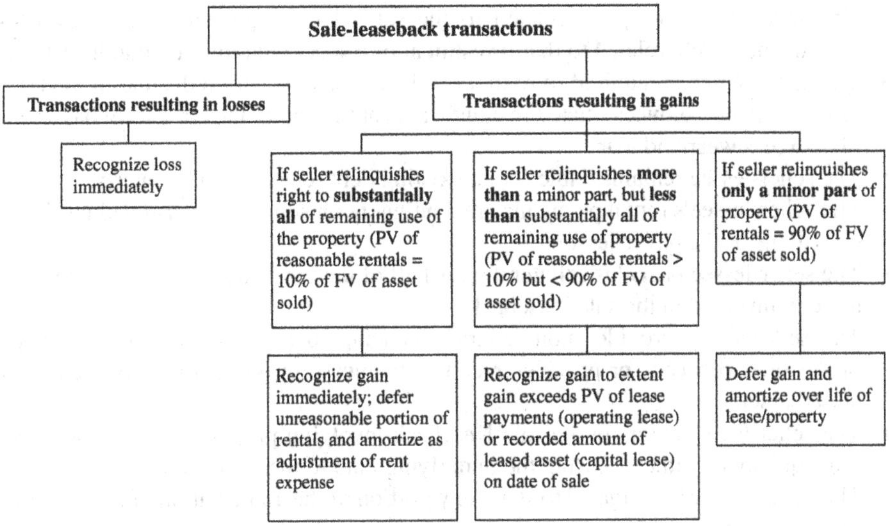

In the above circumstances, when the leased asset is land only, any amortization is recognized on a straight-line basis over the lease term, regardless of whether the lease is classified as a capital or operating lease.

The buyer-lessor accounts for the transaction as a purchase and a direct financing lease if the agreement meets the criteria of either a direct financing lease or a sales-type lease. Otherwise, the agreement is accounted for as a purchase and an operating lease.

Sale-Leaseback Involving Real Estate Three requirements are necessary for a sale-leaseback involving real estate (including real estate with equipment) to qualify for sale-leaseback accounting treatment. Those sale-leaseback transactions not meeting the three requirements are accounted for using the deposit method or as a financing. The three requirements are:

1. The lease must be a normal leaseback (i.e., it involves active use of the leased property in the seller-lessee's trade or business during the lease term).
2. Payment terms and provisions must adequately demonstrate the buyer-lessor's initial and continuing investment in the property as prescribed by ASC 360-20.
3. Payment terms and provisions must transfer all the risks and rewards of ownership as demonstrated by a lack of continuing involvement by the seller-lessee.

Adequacy of initial and continuing investment The buyer-lessor's initial investment is adequate if it demonstrates the buyer-lessor's commitment to pay for the property and indicates a reasonable likelihood that the seller-lessee will collect any receivable related to the leased property. The buyer-lessor's continuing investment is adequate if the buyer is contractually obligated to pay an annual amount at least equal to the amount of the annual payment sufficient to repay the principal and interest over no more than twenty years for land or the customary term of a first mortgage for other real estate.

Lack of continuing involvement by the seller-lessee Any continuing involvement by the seller-lessee other than normal leaseback disqualifies the lease from sale-leaseback accounting treatment. Some examples of continuing involvement other than normal leaseback include:

- The seller-lessee has an obligation or option (excluding the right of first refusal) to repurchase the property.

- The seller-lessee (or party related to the seller-lessee) guarantees the buyer-lessor's investment or debt related to that investment or a specified return on that investment.
- The seller-lessee is required to reimburse the buyer-lessor for a decline in the fair value of the property below estimated residual value at the end of the lease term based on other than excess wear and tear.
- The seller-lessee remains liable for an existing debt related to the property.
- The seller-lessee's rental payments are contingent on some predetermined level of future operations of the buyer-lessor.
- The seller-lessee provides collateral on behalf of the buyer-lessor other than the property directly involved in the sale-leaseback.
- The seller-lessee provides nonrecourse financing to the buyer-lessor for any portion of the sales proceeds or provides recourse financing in which the only recourse is the leased asset.
- The seller-lessee enters into a sale-leaseback involving property improvements or integral equipment without leasing the underlying land to the buyer-lessor.
- The buyer-lessor is obligated to share any portion of the appreciation of the property with the seller-lessee.
- Any other provision or circumstance that allows the seller-lessee to participate in any future profits of the buyer-lessor or the appreciation of the leased property.

The inclusion of a put provision in the lease as a remedy for the occurrence of an event of default under the lease including for lessee noncompliance with financial covenants violates the continuing involvement criteria in ASC 840-40 when the transaction is part of a sale-leaseback. This would necessitate accounting for the transaction using the deposit method or as a financing depending on the application of ASC 360-20 to the circumstances.

When one member of a consolidated group provides an uncensored guarantee of lease payments for another member of the same consolidated group, this is not held to be continuing involvement on the part of the consolidated group. Therefore, sale-leaseback accounting is appropriate in the consolidated financial statements. In the separate financial statements of the subsidiary/seller-lessee, however, the guarantee is a form of continuing involvement that precludes sale-leaseback accounting because the guarantee provides the buyer-lessor with additional collateral that reduces the buyer-lessor's risk of loss. (ASC 840-40-25)

An uncollateralized irrevocable letter of credit is not a form of continuing involvement that precludes sale-leaseback accounting unless a contract exists between the seller-lessee and third-party guarantor that would create collateral (e.g., right of offset of amounts on deposit). All written contracts between the seller-lessee and the issuer of the letter of credit must be evaluated to determine if other forms of collateral exist. (ASC 840-40-25)

Example of Accounting for a Sale-Leaseback Transaction

To illustrate the accounting treatment in a sale-leaseback transaction, suppose that Seller/ Lessee Corporation sells equipment that has a book value of $80,000 and a fair value of $100,000 to Buyer/ Lessor Corporation for $100,000 in cash, and then immediately leases it back under the following conditions:

- The sale date is January 1, 20X1, and the equipment has a fair value of $100,000 on that date and an estimated remaining useful life of fifteen years.

- The lease term is fifteen years, noncancelable, and requires equal rental payments of $13,109 at the beginning of each year.
- Seller/Lessee Corp. has the option to annually renew the lease at the same rental payments upon expiration of the original lease.
- Seller/Lessee Corp. has the obligation to pay all executory costs.
- The annual rental payments provide the Buyer/Lessor Corp. with a 12% return on investment.
- The incremental borrowing rate of Seller/Lessee Corp. is 12%.
- Seller/Lessee Corp. depreciates similar equipment on a straight-line basis.

Seller/Lessee Corp. will classify the agreement as a capital lease since the lease term exceeds 75% of the estimated remaining economic life of the equipment, and because the present value of the lease payments ($13,109 × 7.62817 = $100,000)[10] is greater than 90% of the fair value of the equipment. Assuming that collectibility of the lease payments is reasonably predictable and that no important uncertainties exist concerning the amount of unreimbursable costs yet to be incurred by Buyer/Lessor Corp., Buyer/Lessor Corp. will classify the transaction as a direct financing lease because the present value of the minimum lease payments is equal to the fair value of $100,000.

Seller/Lessee Corp. and Buyer/Lessor Corp. would make the following journal entries during the first year:

Upon Sale of Equipment on January 1, 20X1

Seller/Lessee Corp.			*Buyer/Lessor Corp.*		
Cash	100,000		Equipment*	80,000	
Equipment		100,000	Cash		100,000
Unearned profit on sale-leaseback		20,000			
Leased equipment	100,000		Lease receivable ($13,109 × 15)	196,635	
Lease obligations	100,000		Equipment		100,000
			Unearned interest		96,635

** Assumes new equipment; for used equipment the accumulated depreciation would also be debited to remove it.*

Supplemental guidance The following paragraphs provide supplemental guidance regarding the application of sale-leaseback accounting.

Property sold subject to seller's preexisting operating lease ASC 840-40-55 considers the situation in which the reporting entity is an investor in a partnership that owns property with respect to which the reporting entity is also a lessee under an operating lease that covers all or a portion of the property. The reporting entity sells its interest in the partnership or the partnership sells the property to an independent party with the preexisting operating lease continuing in effect.

If the leased property is within the scope of ASC 840-40 (real estate or real estate with integral equipment), ASC 840-40-55 requires recognition of the transaction as a sale-leaseback if the

[10] 7.62817 is the present value of an annuity due for fifteen periods at a 12% interest rate.

preexisting lease is significantly modified in connection with the sale. If no changes are made to the lease, or if changes are insignificant, then profit is deferred and recognized in accordance with ASC 360-20 and ASC 840-40 for real estate, property improvements, and integral equipment.

The computation of any deferred profit is not affected by the seller-lessee's prior ownership percentage in the property. In addition, exercise of renewal options or sublease provisions contained in the preexisting lease that were included in the original minimum lease term do not affect the accounting for the transaction. ASC 840-40 would apply, however, to renewal options not contained in the original minimum lease term. These renewal options would be treated as a new lease. Finally, leases between parties under common control are not considered preexisting leases for this purpose and ASC 840-40 applies unless one of the parties is a regulated enterprise such as a public utility under the provisions of ASC 980. (ASC 840-40-55)

Sale-leaseback of an asset leased to another party A variation of the previous issue arises when a leaseback involves an asset that is personal property falling outside coverage of ASC 840-40 and either (1) subject to an operating lease, or (2) subleased or intended to be subleased to another entity under an operating lease. The standard specified that the seller-lessee-sublessor is to account for the transaction by recording the sale, removing the asset from its statement of financial position, classifying the leaseback based on the normal criteria for determining lease classification, and recognizing or deferring any gain on the transaction as previously discussed. (ASC 840-40-55)

Other Lease Issues

Accounting for a Sublease A sublease is an arrangement where the original lessee re-leases the leased property to a third party (the sublessee), and the original lessee acts as a sub-lessor. Normally, the nature of a sublease agreement does not affect the original lease agreement, and the original lessee/sublessor retains primary liability to the lessor.

The original lease remains in effect, and the original lessor continues to account for the lease as before. The original lessee/sublessor accounts for the lease as follows:

1. If the original lease agreement transfers ownership or contains a BPO and if the new lease meets any one of the four specified criteria (i.e., transfers ownership, BPO, 75% test, or 90% test) and both the collectibility and uncertainties criteria, then the sublessor classifies the new lease as a sales-type or direct financing lease; otherwise it is classified as an operating lease. In either situation, the original lessee/sublessor continues accounting for the original lease obligation as before.
2. If the original lease agreement does not transfer ownership or contain a BPO, but it still qualifies as a capital lease, then the original lessee/sublessor (with one exception) applies the usual criteria in classifying the new agreement. If the new lease qualifies, the original lessee/sublessor accounts for it as a direct financing lease, with the unamortized balance of the asset under the original lease being treated as the cost of the leased property. However, the original lessee/sublessor should recognize a loss on the sublease if its carrying amount exceeds the total sublease rentals and the estimated residual value. (ASC 840-20-25) The one exception arises when the circumstances surrounding the sublease suggest that the sublease agreement was an important part of a predetermined plan in which the original lessee played only an intermediate role between the original lessor and the sub-lessee. In this situation, the sublease is classified by the 75% and 90% criteria as well as collectibility and uncertainties criteria. In applying the 90% criterion, the fair value for

the leased property is the fair value to the original lessor at the inception of the original lease. Under all circumstances, the original lessee continues accounting for the original lease obligation as before. If the new lease agreement (sublease) does not meet the capitalization requirements imposed for subleases, then the new lease is accounted for as an operating lease.

3. If the original lease is an operating lease, the original lessee/sublessor accounts for the new lease as an operating lease and accounts for the original operating lease as before.

Example of a Direct-Financing Sublease

The Silver Pick Mine obtains a $300,000 ore carrier truck under a five-year capital lease at 8% interest. Annual lease payments are $75,137. Silver Pick reduces its lease liability in accordance with the following amortization table:

Year	*Cash payment*	*Interest*	*Reduction in principal*	*Balance of net investment*
Inception				$300,000
1	$ 75,137	$24,000	$ 51,137	248,863
2	75,137	19,909	55,228	193,635
3	75,137	15,419	59,646	133,989
4	75,137	10,719	64,418	69,571
5	75,137			0
	$375,685	$75,685	$300,000	

At the end of Year 2, silver prices drop too low for ongoing mining operations to be profitable, so Silver Pic k subleases the ore carrier via a direct financing lease to the Lead Bottom Mine for the remaining three years of the lease at the same interest rate. Silver Pick should use the unamortized balance of $193,635 at the end of Year 2 as the cost basis of the sublease, but Lead Bottom negotiates a lower inception value of $160,000, resulting in the following amortization table:

Year	*Cash payment*	*Interest*	*Reduction in principal*	*Balance of net investment*
Inception				$160,000
3	$ 62,085	$12,800	$ 49,285	110,715
4	62,085	8,857	53,228	57,487
5	62,085	4,598	57,487	0
	$186,255	$26,255	$160,000	

At the inception of the sublease, Silver Pick records a loss of $39,156 to reflect the negotiated $33,635 drop in the cost basis of the sublease, from $193,635 to $160,000, as well as a reduction of sublease interest income of $5,521, also due to the reduced cost basis. The summary entry for the final three years of Silver Pick's payments under the original lease agreement and its receipts under the sublease follows:

	Years 3–5 of original lease transaction		*Total of sublease transactions*		*Variance*	
Lease liability	193,635			160,000		33,635
Interest expense	31,776			26,255		5,521
Cash		225,411	186,255		39,156	

Lease Escalations Virtually all commercial leases contain provisions obligating the lessee to pay the lessor various additional sums, often referred to as lease escalations, that supplement the specified fixed rentals. It is important that the parties to the lease properly classify these payments because the way they are characterized can affect whether the lease is accounted for in the correct manner.

Escalating base rents These are periodic increases in the fixed monthly rentals scheduled to occur at one or more points during the lease term. Escalating base rents are included in minimum lease payments.

Variations of this type of escalation occur when the fixed (or base) rent is structured at inception to include a future escalation based on the expected growth of the lessee requiring it to physically use additional portions of the premises that it was not using at inception or an actual addition or based on the lessee actually adding space or capacity.

ASC 840-20-25 prescribes the following two rules:

1. If, at the inception of the lease, the lessee takes possession of or controls the physical use of the leased property, all rentals including the escalated rents are to be recognized by the lessee and lessor as rental expense and rental revenue, respectively, on a straight-line basis commencing with the beginning of the lease term.
2. If rents escalate under a master lease agreement because the lessee obtains access to or control of additional leased property at the time of the escalation, the escalated rents are considered by the lessee and lessor as rental expense and rental revenue respectively that is attributable to the newly leased property. This additional rental expense or rental revenue is to be computed based on the relative fair values of the original leased property and the additional leased property as determined at the inception of the lease and allocated to the time periods during which the lessee controls the use of the additional leased property.

Executory costs These represent reimbursements to the lessor of costs associated with owning and maintaining the leased property. The most common executory costs are real estate taxes, insurance, and maintenance. Amounts paid by a lessee as consideration for a guarantee from an unrelated third party of the residual value are also considered executory costs. If executory costs are paid by the lessor, any lessor's profit on those costs is considered in the same manner as the actual executory costs. Executory costs are excluded from minimum lease payments.

Contingent rentals These are additional rentals due that are computed based on changes that occur subsequent to the inception of the lease in factors, other than the passage of time, on which the lease payments were based. Examples of contingent rentals include real estate rentals based on a percentage of the lessee's retail sales over a certain dollar amount (often referred to as percentage rent or overage rent) and equipment rentals based on machine hours of use. One type of escalation that many commercial leases contain is a required rent increase based on increases in an index such as the prime interest rate or the Consumer Price Index (CPI). Depending on how the terms are structured, these payments might actually consist of two elements that must be separately considered. The portion attributable to the index or rate that was in effect at the inception of the lease (considered part of the minimum lease payments) and the portion representing subsequent increases in that index or rate (considered to be contingent rentals) are illustrated in the following examples.

Example 1

A three-year lease requires fixed rentals of $1,000 per month plus $10 for every full percentage point of the prime interest rate or fraction thereof determined as of the beginning of the month. The prime interest rate at the inception of the lease is 6% and on the first day of the fourth month of the lease term the prime interest rate increased to 7%.

At lease inception, the minimum rentals are computed as follows:

$$\$1,000 + (10 \times 6 \text{ percentage points} = \$60) = \$1,060 \text{ per month} \times 36 \text{ months} = \$38,160$$

The increase in rent due at the beginning of the fourth month would be allocated as follows:

Minimum rentals:	$10 × 6 percentage points =	$60
Contingent rentals:	$10 × 1 percentage points =	10
		$70

Example 2

Same facts as Example 1, except that the lease requires the lessee to pay fixed rentals of $1,000 per month plus $10 for every full percentage point or fraction thereof that the prime interest rate determined as of the beginning of the month exceeds 6%.

At lease inception, the minimum rentals are computed as follows:

$$\$1,000 \text{ per month} \times 36 \text{ months} = \$36,000$$

The increase in rent due at the beginning of the fourth month would be allocated as follows:

Minimum rentals:		$ –
Contingent rentals:	$10 × 1 percentage point =	10
		$10

As illustrated in the examples, amounts determined to be contingent rentals are excluded from minimum lease payments.

As discussed previously, leases for retail space often contain percentage rent provisions that obligate the lessee to pay the lessor a percentage of retail sales over a certain dollar amount. These dollar thresholds are often expressed in terms of annual targets such as one-half of one percent of annual sales over $10 million. This type of lease provision raises the accounting issue of how the lessor and lessee are to account for the lease during the interim periods prior to the attainment of the contractual target.

ASC 840-10-25 and ASC 840-10-40 prescribes the accounting as follows:

Lessor:	No revenue recognition until the actual target is achieved and surpassed.
Lessee:	Recognize contingent rental expense during interim periods if it is probable that the target will be reached by the end of the fiscal year. If, subsequently, the specified target is not met, previously recorded expense is reversed at the time it becomes probable that the target will not be met.

Lessee Involvement in Asset Construction

A lessee often has substantial involvement in construction activities with respect to an asset to be leased under a long-term lease agreement. This involvement can take many forms that can include:

- Providing the construction financing directly or indirectly
- Guaranteeing the construction debt
- Serving as primary or secondary obligor under construction contracts
- Acting as the real estate developer or general contractor
- Agreeing to purchase the asset if the construction is not completed by a specified date
- Agreeing to fund construction cost overruns
- Serving as an agent of the lessor for the construction, financing, or ultimate sale of the asset
- Agreeing to a date-certain lease that obligates the lessee to commence rental payments on a certain date irrespective of whether the construction is complete by that date

Construction Period Rent Associated with Land and Building Leases In certain instances, the lessee will delay occupancy or usage of leased property until, for example, leasehold improvements have been completed. ASC 840-20-25 states that a lease conveys to the lessee the right to control the use of property, such as leased land and building, both during and after any construction period necessary to construct leasehold improvements to the property. Consequently, rental expense is required to be allocated to periods during which construction activities are occurring even though the lessee has not yet commenced operations on the premises. It further provides that the rentals allocated to the construction period are not to be capitalized as part of the cost of the leasehold improvements but rather are to be recorded as a period expense as a charge against income from continuing operations in the lessee's financial statements.

Transfer of Construction Period Risks A lessee is considered the owner of a real estate project during its construction period if the lessee bears substantially all of the construction period risks. (ASC 840-40)

Under ASC 840-40, if the lessee is determined to bear substantially all of the construction risks, it is considered to be the owner of the asset during the construction period. If that is the case, then a sale-leaseback of the asset occurs upon the completion of construction and the commencement of the lease term.

The primary test to be used in determining if a lessee has substantially all of the construction period risks is virtually the same as the 90% of fair value test for determining if a lease is to be classified as a capital lease by a lessee. Beginning with the earlier of the date of the inception of the lease or the date that the construction terms are agreed to, if at any time during the construction period the documents governing the construction project could require, under any circumstance, that the lessee pay 90% or more of the total project costs, excluding land acquisition costs, then the lessee is considered to be the owner of the real estate project during its construction period.

Even if the present value of the lessee's maximum guarantee is less than 90% of total project costs, ASC 840-40 provides six examples of when the lessee would still be considered the owner of a real estate project.

For the purposes of this 90% test, the lessee's maximum guarantee includes any payments the lessee could be required to make in connection with the construction project. The lessee's maximum guarantee includes, but is not limited to:

- Lease payments that must be made regardless of when or whether the project is complete
- Guarantees of the construction financing

- Equity investments made in the owner-lessor or any party related to the owner-lessor
- Loans or advances made to the owner-lessor or any party related to the owner-lessor
- Payments made by the lessee in the capacity of a developer, a general contractor, or a construction manager/agent that are reimbursed less frequently than is normal or customary
- Primary or secondary obligations to pay project costs under construction contracts
- Obligations that could arise from being the developer or general contractor
- An obligation to purchase the real estate project under any circumstances
- An obligation to fund construction cost overruns
- Rent or fees of any kind, such as transaction costs, to be paid to or on behalf of the lessor by the lessee during the construction period
- Payments that might be made with respect to providing indemnities or guarantees to the owner-lessor

The scope of ASC 840-40 includes government-owned property under construction and subject to a future lease of the completed improvements. (ASC 840-40-15)

Any direct or indirect financial interests of the lessee in the leased asset or in the lessor must be analyzed by the lessee to determine if:

- They require accounting recognition as a guarantee obligation under ASC 460.
- They result in the lessee holding a variable interest in the lessor or in the lessor's specified assets (the project) that potentially could require the lessee to consolidate the lessor as the primary beneficiary of a VIE or consolidate the specified assets and related liabilities (referred to as "silo" or a "virtual VIE").

If the lessee consolidates the lessor or the project, intercompany transactions and balances will be eliminated in consolidation.

Change in Residual Value

For any of the foregoing types of leases, the lessor is to review the estimated residual value at least annually. If there is a decline in the estimated residual value, the lessor must make a determination as to whether this decline is temporary or permanent. If temporary, no adjustment is required; however, if the decline is other than temporary, then the estimated residual value must be revised to conform to the revised estimate. The loss that arises in the net investment is recognized in the period of decline. Under no circumstance is the estimated residual value to be adjusted to reflect an increase in the estimate. ASC 840-30-35 clarifies that this prohibition against reflecting an increase in the estimated residual value also extends to increases in the guaranteed portions of the residual value that result from renegotiations between the parties.

Example of a Permanent Decline in Residual Value

Hathaway Corporation enters into a sales-type leasing transaction as the lessor of a fire truck. The following table shows key information about the lease:

Lease term	10 years
Implicit interest rate	8%
Lease payments	One payment per year
Normal selling price	$300,000
Asset cost	$200,000
Residual value	$50,000

After one year, immediately after the first lease payment has been received, Hathaway determines that an indicated decline in residual value from $50,000 to $30,000 is other than temporary. The calculation it originally used to determine the annual minimum lease payment follows:

$$\frac{\text{Selling price} - (\text{Present value of residual value due in 10 years at 8\% interest} \times \text{residual value})}{\text{Present value of an annuity of \$1 for 10 years at 8\% interest}}$$

$$= \frac{\$300{,}000 - (0.46319 \times \$50{,}000)}{6.71008}$$

$= \$41{,}257.33$ **Annual minimum lease payment**

Hathaway calculates the following reduction in the residual present value of the fire truck, using a multiplier of 0.5002 to obtain the present value of the residual value due in nine years at an interest rate of 8%:

Accreted original residual asset present value = ($50,000) × (Present value of 0.5002) = $25,010
Less: Revised residual asset present value = ($30,000) × (Present value of 0.5002) = $15,006
Equals net change in residual asset present value = ($10,004)

The following table shows the original and revised elements of Hathaway's lease transaction entry:

	*Initial entry**	*Revised residual value*	*Entry net of Residual value change*	
Less receivable	462,572	20,000	442,572	
Cost of goods sold	176,840		176,840	
Loss on residual reduction	10,004		10,004	
Inventory		200,000		200,000
Sales		276,840		276,840
Unearned interest		162,572	9,996	152,576

** Lease receivable = (Total minimum lease payments) + (Residual asset value) Cost of goods sold = (Inventory cost) – (Present value of residual asset value) Sales = (Present value of minimum lease payments) Unearned interest = (Lease receivable) – (Present value of minimum lease payments) – (Present value of residual asset value)*

The following amortization table tracks the net impact of these changes, resulting in a $30,000 residual value at the end of Year 10:

Year	*Cash payment*	*Interest*	*Reduction in principal*	*Balance of net investment*
Inception				$300,000
1	$ 41,257	$ 24,000	$ 17,257	282,743
Adjustment			10,004	272,739

2	41,257	21,819	19,438	253,301
3	41,257	20,264	20,993	232,308
4	41,257	18,584	22,673	209,635
5	41,257	16,770	24,487	185,148
6	41,257	14,811	26,446	158,702
7	41,257	12,696	28,561	130,141
8	41,257	10,411	30,846	99,295
9	41,257	7,943	33,314	65,981
10	41,257	5,276	35,981	30,000
	$412,570	$152,574	$270,000	

Thus, net of rounding errors, the total of all payments on the amortization table and the $30,000 revised residual value equals the revised lease receivable of $442,572. Similarly, the total of all interest payments on the amortization table matches the adjusted unearned interest entry.

Change in the Provisions of a Lease

Accounting issues arise when the lessee and lessor agree, subsequent to its inception, to change the provisions of the lease (other than by renewals or term extensions that are discussed later). If, from the standpoint of the lessee, the revised lease terms would have, at the inception of the original lease, resulted in a different lease classification (e.g., operating lease versus capital lease or vice versa), the revised agreement is considered to be a new agreement.

If the original lease was accounted for as a capital lease and the revised lease qualifies for treatment as an operating lease, they are to be accounted for as sale-leaseback transactions (discussed later in this chapter).

If the original lease was accounted for as an operating lease and the revised lease is a capital lease, then on the date of the revision, the lessee records an asset and an obligation based on the present value of the remaining lease payments (or the fair value of the leased property, if less).

Finally, if the original and revised leases are both capital leases, then the lessee adjusts the recorded asset and obligation by an amount equal to the difference between the present value of the future minimum lease payments under the revised agreement and the recorded balance of the obligation. For the purposes of this calculation, the rate of interest to be used is the rate that was used to record the lease initially. The adjustment is recognized as a gain or loss of the period in which the revision is made.

In the case of either a sales-type or direct financing lease where there is a change in the provisions of a lease, the lease is accounted for by the lessor as discussed below.

Changes in the provisions that affect the amount of the remaining minimum lease payments can result in one of the following three outcomes:

1. The change does not give rise to a new agreement. A new agreement is defined as a change that, if in effect at the inception of the lease, would have resulted in a different classification.
2. The change does give rise to a new agreement that would be classified as a direct financing lease.
3. The change gives rise to a new agreement that would be classified as an operating lease.

If either item 1 or item 2 occurs, the balance of the minimum lease payments receivable and the estimated residual value (if affected) are adjusted to reflect the effect of the change. The net adjustment is charged (or credited) to unearned income, and the accounting for the lease over its remaining term is adjusted to reflect the change.

If the new agreement is an operating lease, then the remaining net investment (lease receivable less unearned income) is written off and the leased asset is recorded by the lessor at the lower of its cost, present fair value, or carrying value. The net adjustment resulting from these entries is charged (or credited) to income of the period in which the revision is made. Thereafter, the new lease is accounted for as any other operating lease.

The lessee and the lessor may negotiate a shortened lease term and an increase in the lease payments over the revised lease term. ASC 840-20-55 observes that the nature of the modification is a matter of judgment that depends on the relevant facts and circumstances. If the modification is deemed only a change in future lease payments, the increase is amortized over the remaining term of the modified lease. On the other hand, a modification deemed a termination penalty is to be recognized in the period of modification. Termination penalties are calculated as the excess of the modified lease payments over the original lease payments that would have been required during the shortened lease term.

ASC 840-20-55 provides that consideration is to be given to (1) the length of the modified lease period compared to the remaining term of the original lease, and (2) the difference between the modified lease payments and comparable market rents in determining whether the modification is a termination penalty.

Early Termination of a Lease

Accounting for premature lease termination from the standpoints of the lessee and lessor follows.

Lessee Accounting Discontinuation of business activities in a particular location is considered an exit activity, the accounting for which is specified in ASC 420.

Operating leases In connection with lease termination, the lessee may incur (1) costs to terminate the lease prior to the end of its noncancelable term and/or (2) continuing lease costs incurred during the remainder of the lease term for which the lessee receives no economic benefit because the premises are no longer in use. On the date the lessee terminates the lease, the lessee recognizes a liability for the fair value of the termination costs. The termination date is the date that the lessee provides written notice to the lessor in accordance with the notification requirements contained in the lease or the date the lessee and lessor agree to a negotiated early termination.

The fair value of rentals that continue to be incurred under the lease during its remaining term without benefit to the lessee is recognized as a liability on the date that the lessee ceases to use the property (referred to as the cease-use date). Fair value is computed based on the remaining rentals due under the lease, adjusted for any prepaid or deferred rent under the lease, and reduced by estimated sublease rentals that are reasonable to expect for the property. The fair value measurement requires that reasonable sublease rentals be included in the computation even if the lessee does not intend to sublease the property.

In periods subsequent to the recognition of these liabilities but prior to their settlement, changes in fair value are measured using the credit-adjusted risk-free rate of interest (in essence, the lessee's incremental borrowing rate) used to initially measure the liability.

Upon initial recognition of these liabilities, the related costs are recognized in the lessee's income statement as operating expense (or income from continuing operations if no measure of operations is presented) unless required to be presented as part of discontinued operations. The cumulative effects of any subsequent period changes in liabilities that result from changes in the estimates of either the amounts or timing of cash flows are reported in the same income statement caption used to initially recognize the costs. Changes to the liabilities as a result of the passage of time increase their carrying amount and are recorded as accretion expense, which is also considered an operating expense.

Capital leases If the lease is a capital lease, it is subject to the provisions of ASC 360 with respect to long-lived assets to be disposed of other than by sale (see chapter on ASC 360) either individually (in which case the gain or loss is recorded as a component of operating expense) or as part of a disposal group (in which case the gain or loss is presented as a part of discontinued operations). During the time period between the termination date and the cease-use date, the capital lease asset continues to be classified as "held and used," is subject to impairment evaluation, and its remaining carrying value is amortized over that shortened time period.

Lessor Accounting Lessor accounting for an early lease termination is as follows.

Sales-type and direct financing leases The lessor records the leased equipment as an asset at the lower of its original cost, present fair value, or current carrying value. The difference between the remaining net investment in the lease and the amount of the adjustment to recognize the leased equipment is reflected in income of the period in which the lease is terminated.

Example of Lessor Accounting for the Early Termination of a Sales-type Lease

La Crosse Corporation enters into a sales-type leasing transaction as the lessor of a digital color copier. The following table shows key information about the lease:

Lease term	5 years
Implicit interest rate	8%
Lease payments	One payment per year
Normal selling price	$80,000
Asset cost	$50,000
Residual value	$10,000
Present value of ordinary annuity of 1 for 5 years at 8%	3.9927
Present value of 1 due in 5 years at 8%	0.6806

Based on the information in the table, La Crosse calculates an annual minimum lease payment of $18,332, which is reflected in the following amortization table:

Year	*Cash payment*	*Interest*	*Reduction in principal*	*Balance of net investment*
Inception		$80,000		
1	$18,332	$ 6,400	$11,932	68,068
2	18,332	5,445	12,887	55,181
3	18,332	4,414	13,918	41,263
4	18,332	3,301	15,031	26,232
5	18,332	2,100	16,232	10,000
	$91,660	$21,660	$70,000	

At the end of Year 3, the lessee cancels the lease. At that time, the fair value of the color copier is $35,000, which is $6,263 less than the $41,263 current carrying value indicated at the end of Year 3 in the amortization table. This change is reflected in the following table, which notes the original and revised elements of La Crosse's lease transaction:

	Initial entry		*Total of transactions for first 3 years*		*Lease cancellation entry*	
Cash			54,996			
Lease receivable	101,660			54,996		46,664
Cost of goods sold	43,194					
Inventory		50,000			35,000	
Sales		73,194				
Interest income				16,259		
Loss on early lease termination					6,263	

Lease receivable = (Total minimum lease payments) + (Residual asset value) Cost of goods sold = (Inventory cost) − (Present value of residual asset value) Sales = (Present value of minimum lease payments)
Unearned interest = (Lease receivable) − (Present value of minimum lease payments) − (Present value of residual asset value)

Operating leases Accounting for the leased asset is subject to the provisions of ASC 360. Between the termination date and the cease-use date, the leased asset continues to be presented as held-and- used and depreciated subject to an impairment evaluation that considers the likelihood and timing of replacing the tenant and market rents that would be realized. On the cease-use date, the leased asset is reclassified from held-and-used to the category of idle property and equipment with the associated temporary suspension of depreciation.

Upon receiving notice of termination, the lessor recognizes a receivable for the fair value of any termination fees to be received from the lessee as a result of early cancellation and a corresponding deferred rent liability that is recorded as an adjustment to any previously recorded deferred rent liability or prepaid rent. The remaining rental stream to be received thereafter is recognized on a straight-line basis over the remainder of the time period during which such payments were agreed to continue by adjusting any remaining prepaid rent, deferred rent, and/or unamortized initial direct costs so that they will be fully amortized by the date on which the lessee's payment obligation is fully satisfied.

Renewal or Extension of an Existing Lease

The renewal or extension of an existing lease agreement affects the accounting of both the lessee and the lessor. There are two basic situations: (1) the renewal occurs and makes a residual guarantee or penalty provision inoperative, or (2) the renewal agreement does not do the foregoing and the renewal is treated as a new agreement. The accounting treatment prescribed under the latter situation for a lessee is as follows:

- If the renewal or extension is classified as a capital lease, then the (present) current balances of the asset and related obligation are adjusted by the difference between the present value of the future minimum lease payments under the revised agreement and the (present) current balance of the obligation. The present value of the minimum lease payments under the revised agreement is computed using the interest rate in effect at the inception of the original lease.
- If the renewal or extension is classified as an operating lease, then the current balances of the asset and liability are written off and a gain (loss) recognized for the difference. The new lease agreement resulting from a renewal or extension is accounted for in the same manner as other operating leases.

Under the same circumstances, the following treatment is followed by the lessor:

- If the renewal or extension is classified as a direct financing lease, then the existing balances of the lease receivable and the estimated residual value are adjusted for the changes resulting from the revised agreement.

NOTE: Remember that an upward adjustment to the estimated residual value is not allowed.

  The net adjustment is charged or credited to unearned income.
- If the renewal or extension is classified as an operating lease, then the remaining net investment under the existing sales-type lease or direct financing lease is written off and the leased asset is recorded as an asset at the lower of its original cost, present fair value, or current carrying amount. The difference between the net investment and the amount recorded for the leased asset is charged to income of the period that includes the renewal or extension date. The renewal or extension is then accounted for prospectively as any other operating lease.
- If the renewal or extension is classified as a sales-type lease and it occurs at or near the end of the existing lease term, then the renewal or extension is accounted for as a sales-type lease.

NOTE: A renewal or extension that occurs in the last few months of an existing lease is considered to have occurred at or near the end of the existing lease term.

If the renewal or extension causes the guarantee or penalty provision to be inoperative, the lessee adjusts the current balance of the leased asset and the lease obligation to the present value of the future minimum lease payments (according to ASC 840 "by an amount equal to the difference between the present value of the future minimum lease payments under the revised agreement and the present balance of the obligation"). The present value of the future minimum lease payments is computed using the rate used in the original lease agreement.

Given the same circumstances, the lessor adjusts the existing balance of the lease receivable and estimated residual value to reflect the changes of the revised agreement (remember, no upward adjustments to the residual value). The net adjustment is charged (or credited) to unearned income.

Example of Lessor Accounting for Extension of a Sales-type Lease

Entré Computers enters into a sales-type leasing transaction as the lessor of a corporate computer system. The following table shows key information about the lease:

Lease term	6 years
Implicit interest rate Lease payments Normal selling price	10%
One payment per year	$240,000
Asset cost	$180,000
Residual value	$450,000
Present value of ordinary annuity of 1 for 6 years at 10%	4.3553
Present value of 1 due in 6 years at 10%	0.5645

Based on the information in the table, Entré calculates an annual minimum lease payment of $49,273, which is reflected in the following amortization table:

Year	*Cash payment*	*Interest*	*Reduction in principal*	*Balance of net investment*
Inception				$240,000
1	$ 49,273	$ 24,000	$ 25,273	214,727
2	49,273	21,472	27,801	186,926
3	49,273	18,692	30,581	156,345
4	49,273	15,634	33,639	122,706
5	49,273	12,270	37,003	85,703
6	49,273	8,570	40,703	45,000
	$295,638	$100,638	$195,000	

After making the Year 3 payment, the lessee requests a lease extension in order to reduce the annual payment amount. To do so, Entré extends the lease duration by two years and assumes the same residual value. Entré calculates the revised annual minimum lease payment under the assumption that the selling price is the balance of the net investment at the end of Year 3, as noted in the preceding amortization table.

$$\frac{\text{Selling price} - (\text{Present value of residual value due in 5 years at 10\% interest} \times \text{residual value})}{\text{Present value of an annuity of \$1 for 5 years at 10\% interest}}$$

$$= \frac{\$156{,}345 - (0.6209 \times \$45{,}000)}{3.7908}$$

$$= \$33{,}873 \text{ Annual minimum lease payment}$$

The revised lease payment and residual value is shown in the following amortization table, which includes both the first three years of the original lease agreement and the full five years of the lease extension agreement:

Year	*Cash payment*	*Interest*	*Reduction in principal*	*Balance of net investment*
Inception				$240,000
1	$ 49,273	$ 24,000	$ 25,273	214,727
2	49,273	21,472	27,801	186,926
3	49,273	18,692	30,581	156,345
4	33,873	15,635	18,238	138,107
5	33,873	13,811	20,062	118,045
6	33,873	11,805	22,068	95,977
7	33,873	9,598	24,275	71,702
8	33,873	7,171	26,702	45,000
	$317,184	$122,184	$195,000	

This change is reflected in the following table, which notes the original and revised elements of Entré's lease transaction:

	Initial entry*		Revised entry		Net entry required	
Lease receivable	340,638		362,184		21,546	
Cost of goods sold	154,597		154,597			
Inventory		180,000		180,000		
Sales		214,597		214,597		
Unearned interest		100,638		122,184		21,546

** Lease receivable = (Total minimum lease payments) + (Residual asset value) Cost of goods sold = (Inventory cost) − (Present value of residual asset value) Sales = (Present value of minimum lease payments) Unearned interest = (Lease receivable) − (Present value of minimum lease payments) − (Present value of residual asset value)*

Leases between Related Parties

Leases between related parties are classified and accounted for as though the parties are unrelated, except in cases where it is certain that the terms and conditions of the agreement have been influenced significantly by the fact that the lessor and lessee are related. When this is the case, the classification and/or accounting is modified to reflect the true economic substance of the transaction rather than the legal form. Under ASC 810, discussed earlier in this chapter, many related-party lessors will qualify as VIEs. When this is the case, the lessee will present consolidated financial statements that include the lessor's assets, liabilities, and results of operations. The elimination of intercompany transactions and balances will result in the rental expense and rental income being removed from the consolidated financial statements, which will instead reflect the depreciation of the leased asset and the interest expense on any related debt.

ASC 850 requires that the nature and extent of leasing activities between related parties be disclosed. ASC 810 requires the following disclosures by the primary beneficiary of a VIE:

- The nature, purpose, size, and activities of the VIE
- The carrying amount and classification of consolidated assets that collateralize the VIE's obligations
- Any lack of recourse that VIE creditors or holders of VIE beneficial interests have to the general credit of the primary beneficiary.

Indemnification Provisions in Lease Agreements

Some lease agreements contain a provision whereby the lessee indemnifies the lessor on an after-tax basis for certain income tax benefits that the lessor might lose if a change in the income tax law should occur.

An indemnification agreement of this kind is considered a guarantee that is subject to the recognition and disclosure requirements of ASC 460. Any payments that might be required under the indemnification clause are, therefore, not considered contingent rentals.

Accounting for Leases in a Business Combination

A business combination, in and of itself, has no effect upon the classification of a lease. However, if, in connection with a business combination, a lease agreement is modified to change the original classification of the lease, it is considered a new agreement and accounted for as previously discussed.

In most cases, a business combination will not affect the previous classification of a lease unless the provisions have been modified as indicated in the preceding paragraph.

The acquiring company applies the following procedures to account for a leveraged lease in a business combination:

- The classification as a leveraged lease is retained.
- The net investment in the leveraged lease is assigned a fair value (present value, net of income taxes) based upon the remaining future cash flows. Also, the estimated income tax effects of the cash flows are recognized.
- The net investment is broken down into three components: net rentals receivable, estimated residual value, and unearned income.
- Thereafter, the leveraged lease is accounted for as described in the discussion earlier in this chapter.

ASC 805 significantly alters the accounting for business combinations. It requires the use of the acquisition method, which requires that assets acquired and liabilities assumed in such a transaction be accounted for at fair values. This means, among other things, that capital leases under which the acquiree entity was obligated at the acquisition date are to be revalued at fair value at the date of the acquisition. The amounts of depreciation and interest to be recognized in subsequent periods by the acquirer will accordingly, in most instances, vary from the amounts that would have been recognized by the acquiree absent the business combination.

For example, if the fair value of the leased property under a capital lease is greater than its carrying value (the depreciated capitalized value as of that date), future amortization will be greater than would otherwise have been the case. Given that rental payments will not be altered by the acquisition transaction, this means that the effective interest cost will be reduced. A new effective interest rate will need to be computed in order to properly record the accounting implications of future rental payments, in such a circumstance. Contrariwise, if the fair value of the leased property is lower than its precombination carrying (book) value, the effective interest rate will be greater than had previously been determined.

ASC 805 states that the determination of the classification of an existing lease is generally not reassessed at the date of a business combination, and that the determination made at the lease inception is not to be reconsidered. However, if the terms of an operating lease are favorable or unfavorable compared with the market terms of leases of the same or similar items at the acquisition date, accounting ramifications must be addressed. The acquirer in such a circumstance is to recognize an intangible asset if the terms of an operating lease are favorable relative market terms, and is to recognize a liability if the terms are unfavorable relative to market terms.

An identifiable intangible asset may be associated with an operating lease, which may be objectively revealed by market participants' willingness to pay a price for the lease even if its terms are already at market. For example, a lease of gates at an airport or of retail space in a prime shopping area might provide entry into a market or other future economic benefits that qualify as identifiable intangible assets—for example, as a customer relationship. In that situation, the acquirer is to recognize the associated identifiable intangible asset(s). Under ASC 805, the identifiable intangible assets acquired in a business combination are to be recognized distinct from goodwill. An intangible asset is *identifiable* if it meets either the separability criterion or the contractual-legal criterion described by ASC 805.

If the acquiree in a business combination has assets (e.g., building or equipment) that are subject to operating leases (that is, the acquiree is a lessor), ASC 805 directs that such assets are to be recorded at fair value determined without regard to the terms of the associated leases. The extent to which the lease terms are favorable or unfavorable relative to the market at the acquisition date, however, will be reflected in the additional intangible asset or liability to be recognized by the acquirer.

Accounting for Changes in Lease Agreements Resulting from Refunding of Tax-Exempt Debt

Tax-exempt debt is often "refunded" by the issuer of the debt instruments. Refunding is a refinancing that enables the issuer (i.e., a municipality that issued bonds) to take advantage of favorable interest rates. A current refunding is effected when the debt becomes callable and the issuer issues new debt in order to use the proceeds to retire the original debt. An advance refunding is a more complex variation that occurs prior to the call date of the original instruments. It entails issuance of new tax-exempt debt at the lower interest rate with a similar maturity to the original issuance. The proceeds of the new debt are invested in a portfolio of market-traded U.S. Treasury securities and other obligations that effectively "defease" the original bonds. If, during the lease term, a change in the lease results from a refunding by the lessor of tax-exempt debt (including an advance refunding) and (1) the lessee receives the economic advantages of the refunding, and (2) the revised agreement can be classified as a capital lease by the lessee and a direct financing lease by the lessor, the change is accounted for as follows:

- If the change is accounted for as an extinguishment of debt:
  - Lessee accounting. The lessee adjusts the lease obligation to the present value of the future minimum lease payments under the revised agreement. The present value of the minimum lease payments is computed using the interest rate applicable to the revised agreement. Any gain or loss is recognized currently as a gain or loss on the extinguishment of debt in accordance with the provisions of ASC 470-50-45 (discussed in detail in the chapter on ASC 470).
  - Lessor accounting. The lessor adjusts the balance of the lease receivable and the estimated residual value, if affected, for the difference in present values between the old and revised agreements. Any resulting gain or loss is recognized currently.
- If the change is not accounted for as an extinguishment of debt:
  - Lessee accounting. The lessee accrues any costs in connection with the debt refunding that are obligated to be reimbursed to the lessor. These costs are amortized by the interest method over the period from the date of refunding to the call date of the debt to be refunded.
  - Lessor accounting. The lessor recognizes as revenue any reimbursements to be received from the lessee, for costs paid in relation to the debt refunding. This revenue is recognized in a systematic manner over the period from the date of refunding to the call date of the debt to be refunded.

Sale or Assignment to Third Parties; Nonrecourse Financing

The sale or assignment of a lease or of property subject to a lease that was originally accounted for as a sales-type lease or a direct financing lease will not affect the original accounting treatment of the lease. Any profit or loss on the sale or assignment is recognized at the time of the transaction, except under the following two circumstances:

- When the sale or assignment is between related parties, apply substance versus form provisions presented above under "leases between related parties."
- When the sale or assignment is with recourse, it is accounted for using the provisions of ASC 860.

The sale of property subject to an operating lease is not treated as a sale if the seller (or any related party to the seller) retains "substantial risks of ownership" in the leased property. A seller may retain "substantial risks of ownership" by various arrangements. For example, if the lessee defaults upon the lease agreement or if the lease terminates, the seller may arrange to do one of the following:

- Acquire the property or the lease.
- Substitute an existing lease.
- Secure a replacement lessee or a buyer for the property under a remarketing agreement. (ASC 840-20-40-3)[11]

A seller does not retain substantial risks of ownership by arrangements where one of the following occurs:[12]

- A remarketing agreement includes a reasonable fee to be paid to the seller.
- The seller is not required to give priority to the releasing or disposition of the property owned by the third party over similar property owned by the seller. (ASC 840-20-40-4)

When the sale of property subject to an operating lease is not accounted for as a sale because the substantial risk factor is present, it is accounted for as a borrowing. (ASC 840-20-40-5)[13] The proceeds are recorded by the seller as an obligation. Rental payments made by the lessee under the operating lease are recorded as revenue by the seller even if the payments are paid to the third-party purchaser. The seller accounts for each rental payment by allocating a portion to interest expense (to be imputed in accordance with the provisions of ASC 835-30), and the remainder to reduce the existing obligation. Other normal accounting procedures for operating leases are applied except that the depreciation term for the leased asset is limited to the amortization period of the obligation.

The sale or assignment of lease payments under an operating lease by the lessor is accounted for as a borrowing as described above.

Nonrecourse financing is a common occurrence in the leasing industry, whereby the stream of lease payments on a lease is discounted on a nonrecourse basis at a financial institution with the lease payments collateralizing the debt. The proceeds are then used to finance future leasing transactions. Even though the discounting is on a nonrecourse basis, the offsetting of the debt against the related lease receivable is prohibited unless a legal right of offset exists or the lease qualified as a leveraged lease at its inception.

Money-over-Money Lease Transactions

A money-over-money lease transaction occurs when an enterprise manufactures or purchases an asset, leases the asset to a lessee and obtains nonrecourse financing in excess of the asset's cost using the leased asset and the future lease rentals as collateral. ASC 840-30-55 prescribes that this series of transactions should be accounted for as follows:

- Record the purchase or manufacture of the asset,
- Record the lease as an operating, direct financing, or sales-type lease as appropriate,
- Record nonrecourse debt.

[11] Upon implementation of ASU 2014-09, this paragraph will be superseded by guidance in ASC 606.
[12] Ibid.
[13] Ibid.

The only income that is recognizable by the reporting entity in this transaction would be any manufacturer's or dealer's profit that arises if the lease is classified as a sales-type lease. With respect to the presentation in the statement of financial position, offsetting of any assets recorded as a result of the transaction with the nonrecourse debt is not permitted unless a right of setoff exists.

Wrap-Lease Transaction

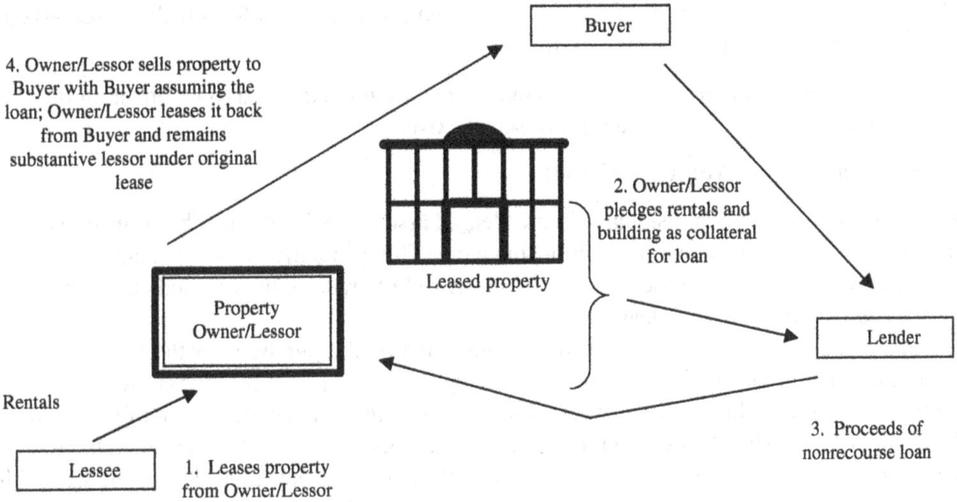

Cash Flows

Lessee pays rentals to Lessor.
Lessor pays rentals to Buyer.
Buyer pays loan principal and interest to Lender.

Wrap-Lease Transactions

A wrap-lease transaction (see diagram) occurs when a reporting enterprise:

- Purchases an asset,
- Leases the asset to a lessee,
- Obtains nonrecourse financing using the lease rentals and/or the asset as collateral,
- Sells the asset to an investor, subject to the lease and the nonrecourse debt, and
- Leases the asset back while remaining the substantive principal lessor under the original lease.

If the asset is real estate, the specialized rules with respect to sale-leaseback of real estate set forth in ASC 840-40 apply (see example of accounting for a sale-leaseback transaction in this chapter).

If the asset is personal property, the accounting would be as follows:

- The asset is removed from the accounting records of the original reporting entity
- The leaseback is classified in accordance with the normal criteria for the classification of leases
- Gain on the transaction is recognized or deferred/amortized following the criteria in ASC 840-40-25

- The reporting entity reflects the following items on its statement of financial position:
  - Any retained interest in the residual value of the leased asset
  - Gross sublease receivable
  - Note receivable from the investor
  - Nonrecourse third-party debt
  - Leaseback obligation
  - Deferred revenue related to any future remarketing rights for which the remarketing services had not yet been performed.

The sublease asset and related nonrecourse debt are not permitted to be offset on the statement of financial position unless a right of setoff exists.

Transfers of Residual Value (ASC 860)

Acquisitions of interests in residual values of leased assets may be effected by companies whose primary business is other than leasing or financing. This generally occurs through the outright purchase of the right to own the leased asset or the right to receive the proceeds from the sale of a leased asset at the end of its lease term.

In instances such as these, the rights are recorded by the purchaser at the fair value of the assets surrendered net of the present value of any liabilities assumed, unless the fair value of the residual is more objectively determinable. Increases in the estimated value of the interest in the residual (i.e., residual value accretion) to the end of the lease term are permitted to be recognized only for *guaranteed* residual values because they are financial assets. However, recognition of such increases is prohibited for *unguaranteed* residual values. A nontemporary write-down of a residual value interest (guaranteed/unguaranteed) is recognized as a loss and is not permitted to be subsequently restored. This guidance also applies to lessors who sell the related minimum lease payments but retain the interest in the residual value irrespective of whether the residual is guaranteed.

Example of the Transfer of Residual Value

Longbottom Lease Brokers obtains an interest in the residual value of a cable placer truck as a fee for its assistance in leasing the truck to a third party. The fair value of Longbottom's interest in the residual value of the truck is estimated by an appraiser to be $47,000. Since the fair value of Longbottom's interest in the residual value is the most clearly evident valuation, Longbottom uses it as the basis for the following entry:

Interest in asset residual value	47,000	
Revenue—leasing services rendered		47,000

In another transaction, Longbottom pays $32,000 for the residual value of an aerial truck. Longbottom records the transaction as follows:

Interest in asset residual value	32,000	
Cash		32,000

After six months, Longbottom appraises its interest in the residual value of both trucks, and finds that the value of the cable placer has declined from $47,000 to $41,000, while the residual value of the aerial truck has increased from $32,000 to $35,000. Longbottom uses the following entry to record the reduction of value in its cable placer truck:

Loss on interest in asset residual value	6,000	
Interest in asset residual value		6,000

Longbottom records no entry for the $3,000 increase in value of its aerial truck.

Leases Involving Government Units

Leases that involve government units (i.e., airport facilities, bus terminal space, etc.) usually contain special provisions that prevent the agreements from being classified as anything but operating leases. These special provisions, referred to as fiscal funding clauses, include the governmental body's authority to abandon a facility at any time during the lease term, thus making its economic life indeterminable. These leases also do not contain a BPO or transfer ownership. The fair value is generally indeterminable because neither the leased property nor similar property is available for sale.

However, leases involving government units are subject to the same classification criteria as nongovernment units, except when all of the following six criteria are met:

NOTE: If all six conditions are met, the agreement is classified as an operating lease by both lessee and lessor.

1. A government unit or authority owns the leased property.
2. The leased property is part of a larger facility operated by or on behalf of the lessor.
3. The leased property is a permanent structure or part of a permanent structure that normally cannot be moved to another location.
4. The lessor, or a higher governmental authority, has the right to terminate the lease at any time under the lease agreement or existing statutes or regulations.
5. The lease neither transfers ownership nor allows the lessee to purchase or acquire the leased property.
6. The leased property or similar property in the same area cannot be purchased or leased from anyone else.

If any one of the six conditions that qualify the lease for automatic operating lease treatment is not met, then the lease is evaluated to determine the likelihood of future cancellation. Using the loss contingency criteria from ASC 450, if it is remote (i.e., the chances are slight) that the lease will be canceled, then the lease agreement qualifies as a noncancelable lease and is classified the same as any other such lease with a nongovernmental lessee. Otherwise, the lease is considered to be cancelable and accounted for as an operating lease. (ASC 840-10-25)

Maintenance Deposits by Lessees

In some lease arrangements, the lessee may be required to make a deposit associated with the lessee's responsibility for the maintenance of the leased asset. Under a typical arrangement of this sort, the deposit is calculated based on a performance measure, such as hours of use of the leased asset, and is contractually required under the lease to be used to reimburse the lessee for required maintenance of the leased asset upon the completion of that maintenance. The lessor is thus contractually required to reimburse the lessee for the maintenance costs paid by the lessee, to the extent of the amounts on deposit. If the cumulative maintenance costs are less than the amount deposited, the excess may or may not be required to be returned to the lessee.

ASC 840-10-25 and ASC 840-10-35 address this issue. Maintenance deposits paid by a lessee under an arrangement accounted for as a lease that are refunded only if the lessee performs specified maintenance activities are to be accounted for as a deposit asset. Lessees must continue to evaluate whether it is *probable* that an amount on deposit will be returned to reimburse the costs of the maintenance activities incurred by the lessee. When an amount on deposit is less than probable of being returned, it is to be recognized as additional expense. When the underlying maintenance is performed, the maintenance cost is to be expensed or capitalized in accordance with the lessee's existing maintenance accounting policy.

Entities are to recognize the effect of the change as a change in accounting principle as of the beginning of the fiscal year in which this requirement is initially applied for all arrangements existing at the effective date. The cumulative effect of the change in accounting principle is to be recognized as an adjustment to the opening balance of retained earnings (or other appropriate components of equity or net assets in the statement of financial position) for that fiscal year, presented separately. The cumulative effect adjustment is the difference between the amounts recognized in the statement of financial position before initial application of this requirement and the amounts recognized in the statement of financial position at its initial application.

Leasehold Improvements

Leasehold improvements result when tangible physical enhancements are made to property by or on behalf of the lessee of real estate. By law, when improvements are made to real property and those improvements are permanently affixed to the property, the title to those improvements automatically transfers to the owner of the property. The rationale behind this is that the improvements, when permanently affixed, are inseparable from the rest of the real estate.

As a result of this automatic title transfer, the lessee's interest in the improvements is not a direct ownership interest but rather it is an intangible right to use and benefit from the improvements during the term of the lease. Consequently, the capitalized costs incurred by a lessee in constructing improvements to property that it leases represent an intangible asset analogous to a license to use them. Thus, when allocating the costs of leasehold improvements to the periods benefited, the expense is referred to as amortization (as used in the context of amortization of intangibles) and not depreciation.

A frequently encountered issue with respect to leasehold improvements relates to determination of the period over which they are to be amortized. Normally, the cost of long-lived assets is charged to expense over the estimated useful lives of the assets. However, the right to use a leasehold improvement expires when the related lease expires, irrespective of whether the improvement has any remaining useful life. Thus, the appropriate useful life for a leasehold improvement is the lesser of the useful life of the improvement or the term of the underlying lease. ASC 840-10-35-9 reinforces this concept by requiring that leasehold improvements acquired in a business combination or leasehold improvements completed well after commencement of a lease agreement be amortized over the lesser of the useful life of the leasehold improvement or a time period that includes required lease periods as well as reasonably assured lease renewal periods.

Some leases contain a fixed, noncancelable term and additional renewal options. When considering the term of the lease for the purposes of amortizing leasehold improvements, normally only the initial fixed noncancelable term is included. There are exceptions to this general rule that arise out of the application of GAAP to the lessee's accounting for the lease. If a renewal option is a bargain renewal option, then it is probable at the inception of the lease that it will be exercised and, therefore, the option period is included in the lease term for purposes of determining the amortizable life of the leasehold improvements. Additionally, under the definition of the lease term there are other situations where it is probable that an option to renew for an additional period would be exercised. These situations include periods for which failure to renew the lease imposes a penalty on the lessee in such amount that a renewal appears, at the inception of the lease, to be reasonably assured. Other situations of this kind arise when an otherwise excludable renewal period precedes a provision for a bargain purchase of the leased asset or when, during periods covered by ordinary renewal options, the lessee has guaranteed the lessor's debt on the leased property.

In deciding whether to include the period covered by a renewal option in the calculation of the amortizable life of the leasehold improvements, management of the lessee must be consistent with its own interpretation of renewal options that it included in the minimum lease payment calculations made to determine whether the lease is a capital or operating lease.

Example

Marcie Corporation occupies a warehouse under a five-year operating lease commencing January 1, 20X1, and expiring December 31, 20X5. The lease contains three successive options to renew the lease for additional five-year periods. The options are not bargain renewals, as they call for fixed rentals at the prevailing fair market rents that will be in effect at the time of exercise. When the initial calculation was made to determine whether the lease is an operating lease or a capital lease, only the initial noncancelable term of five years was included in the calculation. Consequently, for the purpose of determining the amortizable life of any leasehold improvements made by Marcie Corporation, only the initial five-year term is used. If Marcie Corporation decides, at the beginning of year 4 of the lease, to make a substantial amount of leasehold improvements to the leased property, it could be argued that it would now be probable that Marcie would exercise one or more of the renewal periods, since not doing so would impose the substantial financial penalty of abandoning expensive leasehold improvements. This would trigger accounting for the lease as if it were a new agreement and would require testing to determine whether the lease, prospectively, qualifies as a capital or operating lease.

The SEC has provided the following guidance on the proper accounting treatment by a lessee for incentives or allowances provided by a lessor to a lessee under an operating lease.[33]

1. The incentives are not permitted to be netted against the leasehold improvements they were intended to subsidize. Instead, they are to be recorded as deferred rent and amortized as reductions to lease expense over the lease term.
2. The leasehold improvements are to be recorded gross, at their cost, and amortized as discussed above.
3. The lessee's cash flow statement is to reflect the cash received from the lessor as an incentive or allowance as cash provided by operating activities and the acquisition of the leasehold improvements as cash used for investing activities.

Note that this guidance is a reasonable interpretation of GAAP as it applies to all entities, not just those subject to the jurisdiction of the SEC.

---

[14] Letter from SEC Chief Accountant to the chairman of the American Institute of Certified Public Accountants (AICPA) Center for Public Company Audit Firms (CPCAF) dated February 7, 2005; www.sec.gov/info/accountants/staffletters/ cpcaf020705.htm.

Statement of Financial Position Classification

The balance of the lease payments receivable (lessor) and the lease obligation (lessee) must be allocated between their current and noncurrent portions. First, the current portion is computed at the date of the financial statements as the present value of the lease payments (or receipts) to be paid (received) within twelve months of the date of the statement of financial position. The noncurrent portion is computed as the difference between the current portion and the balance of the lease obligation at the end of the period. The conceptual justification for this treatment is the fact that the total lease obligation is equal to the present value of the future minimum lease payments. Therefore, it follows that the current portion is the present value of the lease payments due within one year while the noncurrent portion is the present value of all other remaining lease payments.

Summary of Accounting for Selected Items (see following page)

TREATMENT OF SELECTED ITEMS IN ACCOUNTING FOR LEASES

	Lessor		Lessee	
	Operating	Direct financing and sales-type	Operating	Capital
Initial direct costs	Capitalize and amortize over lease term recognized proportion to rent revenue in (normally SL basis)	***Direct financing*:** Record in separate account Add to net investment in lease Compute new effective rate that equates gross amt. of min. lease payments and unguar. residual value with net invest. Amortize so as to produce constant rate of return over lease term ***Sales-type*:** Expense in period incurred as part of cost of sales	N/A	N/A
Investment tax credit retained by lessor	N/A	Reduces FV of leased asset for 90% test	N/A	Reduces FV of leased asset for 90% test
Bargain purchase option	N/A	Include in: Minimum lease payments 90% test	N/A	Include in: Minimum lease payments 90% test
Guaranteed residual value	N/A	Include in: Minimum lease payments 90% test Sales-type: Include PV in sales revenues	N/A	Include in: Minimum lease payments 90% test
Unguaranteed residual value	N/A	Include in: "Gross investment in lease" Not included in: 90% test Sales-type: Exclude from sales revenue Deduct PV from cost of sales	N/A	N/A
Contingent rentals	Revenue in period earned	Not part of minimum lease payments; revenue in period earned	Expense in period incurred	Not part of minimum lease payments; expense in period incurred

	Lessor		Lessee	
	Operating	*Directfinancing and sales-type*	*Operating*	*Capital*
Amortization period	Amortize down to estimated residual value over estimated economic life of asset	N/A	N/A	Amortize down to estimated residual value over lease term or estimated economic life[b]
Revenue (expense)[a]	Rent revenue (normally SL basis) Amortization (depreciation expense)	Direct financing: Interest revenue on net investment in lease (gross investment less unearned interest income) Sales-type: Dealer profit in period of sale (sales revenue less cost of leased asset) Interest revenue on net investment in lease	Rent expense (normally SL basis)[b]	Interest expense and amortization (depreciation) expense

[a] *Elements of revenue (expense) listed for the above items are not repeated here (e.g., treatment of initial direct costs).*
[b] *If lease has automatic passage of title or bargain purchase option, use estimated economic life; otherwise, use the lease term.*

56 ASC 842 LEASES

PERSPECTIVE AND ISSUES

Technical Alerts

ASU 2019-10 and ASU 2020-05, Deferrals in the Effective Dates The FASB deferred the effective date for ASU 2016-02, *Lease*, first in ASU 2019-10, *Financial Instruments—Credit Losses (Topic 326), Derivatives and Hedging (Topic 815), and Leases (Topic 842): Effective Dates*, and most recently in ASU 2020-05.

In June 2020, the FASB issued ASU 2020-05, *Revenue from Contracts with Customers (Topic 606) and Leases (Topic 842): Effective Dates for Certain Entities*. Because of the COVID-19 pandemic, the FASB in this ASU provides a deferral in the effective date for "all other" entities to fiscal years beginning after December 15, 2021 and interim periods beginning after December 15, 2022. These dates are reflected in the chart below and "all other" entities is defined in the chart.

The new standard is effective as follows:

	Public Companies	**All Other Entities**
Effective Date	Annual and interim periods in fiscal years beginning after December 15, 2018, including interim periods within those years.	Annual periods beginning on or after December 15, 2021, and interim period beginning after December 15, 2022.
Early Adoption	Yes	Yes

"Public companies" above refers to:

- Public business entities,
- Not-for-profit entities that have issued or are conduit bond obligors for securities that are traded, listed, or quoted on an exchange or over-the-counter market, and
- Employee benefit plans that files or furnishes statements with or to the SEC.

ASU 2016-02—Putting It on the Balance Sheet

NOTE: See the Technical Alert in the chapter on ASC 250 for information on SEC pre-adoption disclosures for the new standard on leases, ASU 2016-02.

Note that in order to capture comparative data, some companies will have to keep two sets of records for fiscal years beginning in 2017. Some entities may want to take advantage of the synergies between the new revenue recognition standard and the lease standard by early adopting and aligning processes.

Guidance The objective of the standard is to improve information for financial statement users by increasing transparency and comparability among organizations. To accomplish this, the standard requires:

- Lessees to recognize lease assets (right of use assets) and lease liabilities on the balance sheet,
- Lessors to align with certain changes in the lessee model and the new revenue recognition standards, and
- Lessees and lessors to disclose significant information about lease transactions.

Lessees Under ASC 842, lessees recognize all leases, other than short-term leases, on the balance sheet. Lessees recognize a right-of-use (ROU) asset and a lease liability for those leases. Compared with ASC 840 guidance, this may significantly increase reported assets and liabilities for some lessees for some leases. For the first time, under ASC 842, long-term operating leases will appear on the balance sheet as nondebt liabilities. ASC 842 offers some relief to preparers by exempting leases with terms of less than 12 months. As a consequence, some lessees may request new or renewed leases with terms less than 12 months.

Lessors Under the guidance in ASC 842, the lessor accounting model is substantially unchanged. However, lessors will have to review their systems and processes to ensure that data will be available to management for the new required disclosures. The main focus of the FASB was specifically to improve the guidance for operating leases in the financial statements of lessees. Therefore, the Board decided not to make fundamental changes to lessor accounting. However, some changes were made to lessor guidance in order to conform and align it to the new guidance for lessees and the new revenue recognition guidance, Topic 606.

Revenue from Contracts with Customers The new lease standard is aligned with the revenue recognition standard, and those familiar with that standard will see some similarities in terminology and approach.

Effective Dates See the Technical Alerts at the beginning of this chapter for deferrals of the effective dates.

Transition Like the revenue standard the leases standard provides for a transition approach using the modified retrospective transition approach. The approach must be applied to all comparative periods presented.

Practical Expedients Again, as with the revenue recognition standard, the standard setters provide practical expedients to ease the transition. The expedients must be applied consistently to all leases. The expedients include:

- An entity may elect not to reassess:
  - Whether expired or existing contracts contain leases under the new definition of a lease.
  - Lease classification for expired or existing leases.
  - Whether previously capitalized initial direct costs would qualify for capitalization under the new standard.

  (The above expedients must be elected as a package at the date of adoption.)
- Use of hindsight when determining the lease term and in assessing impairment of right-to-use assets.
- Making an accounting policy election by class of underlying asset not to separate lease components from nonlease components. Lessors can make this election if:
  - The timing and patter of transfer of the non lease component and the associated lease component are the same and
  - The lease component is classified as an operating lease on a stand-alone basis.

Entities making this election account for the nonlease components and the lease components as a single lease component.

To address concerns that it is costly to determine a discount rate, nonpublic entities may elect an accounting policy to use a risk-free rate to measure liabilities.

NOTE: For entities that have not yet adopted ASU 2016-02, the following ASUs have the same effective date as ASU 2016-02.

ASU 2018-01 In January 2018, the FASB issued ASU 2018-01, *Leases (Topic 842): Land Easements Practical Expedient for Transition to Topic 842*. The ASU adds an optional practical expedient upon transition for land easements that allows entities to continue applying their current accounting policy for certain land easements that exist on or expired before the ASU 2018-01's effective date, which is the same as the new leases standard.

ASU 2018-10 In July 2018, the FASB issued ASU 2018-10, *Codification Improvements to Topic 842, Leases*. The ASU amends the following areas:

- Residual value guarantees
- Rate implicit in the lease
- Lessee reassessment of lease classification
- Lessor reassessments of lease term and purchase option
- Variable lease payments that depend on an index or a rate
- Investment tax credits
- Lease term and purchase option
- Transition guidance for amounts previously recognized in business combinations

- Certain transition adjustments
- Transition guidance for leases previously classified as capital leases under ASC 840
- Transition guidance for modifications to leases previously classified or direct financing or sales-type leases under ASC 840
- Transition guidance for sale and leaseback transactions
- Impairment of net investment in the lease
- Unguaranteed residual asset
- Effect of initial direct costs on rate implicit in the lease
- Failed sale and leaseback transaction

The changes are incorporated in this volume when appropriate.

ASU 2018-11 In July 2018, the FASB issued ASU 2018-11, *Leases (Topic 842) Targeted Improvements*. The ASU clarified:

- Transition requirements for initial adoption. See the transition requirements.
- Separating components of a contract

The added guidance on separating components of a contract provides lessors with a practical expedient. It permits, by class of underlying asset, lessors to not separate nonlease components from the associated lease component. Instead, the lessor may account for those components as a single component if the nonlease components otherwise would be accounted for under the revenue guidance in ASC 606 and both of the following conditions are met:

- The timing and pattern of a transfer of the nonlease components and associated lease component are the same
- The lease component, if accounted for separately, would be classified as an operating lease (ASC 842-10-15-42A)

Certain disclosures are required, and those are included in Appendix B.

ASU 2018-20 In December 2018, the FASB issued ASU 2018-20, *Narrow-Scope Improvements for Lessors*. To help lessors apply ASU 2016-02, the FASB issued amendments that permit lessors to make an accounting policy election not to evaluate whether sales taxes, and other similar taxes imposed by a governmental authority on a specific lease revenue-producing transaction are the primary obligations of the lessor as owner of the underlying leased asset. If the lessor makes that election, it may exclude those taxes from the measurement of lease revenue and associated expense.

The ASU requires lessors to:

- Exclude lessor costs paid directly by lessees to third parties on the lessor's behalf from variable payments and thus lease revenue
- Include in the measurement of variable lease revenue and the associated expense lessor costs that are paid by the lessor and reimbursed by the lessee

When lessors allocate variable payments to lease and nonlease components, the ASU clarified that lessors are required to follow the recognition guidance in ASU 2016-02 for the lease component and other guidance for the nonlease component.

Certain disclosures are required and are included in Appendix B.

ASU 2019-01 In March 2019, the FASB issued ASC 2019-01, *Leases (Topic 842) Codification Improvements*. The FASB clarified

- The fair value of the underlying asset by lessors that are not manufacturers.
- The presentation of sale-type and direct-financing leases on the statement of cash flows, and
- The transition disclosures under ASC 250.

These changes are incorporated in this chapter and in Appendix B as appropriate.

Subtopics

ASC 842 contains five subtopics:

- ASC 842-10, *Overall,* that establishes the principles for reporting the amount, timing, and uncertainty of cash flows.
- ASC 842-20, *Lessee,* which addresses accounting by lessees for finance and operating leases.
- ASC 842-30, *Lessor,* that addresses accounting by lessors for sales-type, direct financing, and operating leases.
- ASC 842-40, *Sale and Leaseback Transactions,* that addresses accounting for sale and leaseback transactions for leases accounted for under any of the above subtopics.
- ASC 842-50, *Leveraged Lease Arrangements,* that provides guidance for leases defined as leveraged leases.

Scope

ASC 842 applies to all leases. Because a lease conveys the right to control the use of an identified asset for a period of time in exchange for consideration, ASC 842 does not apply to leases of:

- Intangible assets,
- Biological assets, such as timber,
- Inventory,
- Assets under construction, or
- Leases to explore for and use minerals, oil, natural gas, and other similar resources.
  (ASC 842-10-15-1)

Determining Whether a Lease Is Present in the Contract

The critical determination in applying the scope guidance is whether a contract contains a lease. A lease is present in the contract if the contract includes:

- An identified asset, that is,
  - The asset is explicitly or implicitly specified.
  - The supplier has no practical ability to substitute or would not economically benefit from substituting.
- The right to control the use of the asset during the term of the lease, that is,
  - The lessee has the ability to obtain substantially all economic benefit from the use of the asset.
  - The lessee has decision-making authority over the use of the asset.
    (ASC 842-10-15-9, 15-10, 15-20, and 15-17)

Economic Benefit from the Use of the Asset A portion of an asset is an identified asset if it is physically distinct. Examples include a floor of a building or a pipeline that connects a single customer to a large pipeline. However, if the portion is not physically distinct, like a capacity portion of a fiber optic cable, it is not an identified asset unless the portion represents substantially all of the asset, giving the customer substantially all of the economic benefit. (ASC 842-10-15-16) When evaluating "substantially all," the entity should consider the economic benefits of the customer's right to use the asset as defined in the contract. For example, is the lease of a vehicle confined to a geographic area or number of miles? (ASC 842-10-15-18)

Direct the Use of the Asset The Codification identifies two subsections where the customer has the right to direct the use of the identified asset throughout the period of the leases:

- The customer can direct how and for what purpose the asset is used and
- The decisions about use are predetermined, for example, by the terms of the lease or the design of the asset, and at least one of the following exists:
  - The customer can operate the asset without the supplier having the right to change the operating instructions, or
  - The customer designed the asset in a way that predetermines its use.

(ASC 842-10-15-20 and 15-21)

Once an entity concludes that a contract contains a lease, the entity must identify the separate lease components. The right to use an underlying asset is considered a separate component from any other components if:

- The lessee can benefit from the right of use either on its own or together with other resources readily available to the lessee, and
- The right of use is neither:
  - Highly dependent nor
  - Highly interrelated with other rights to use underlying assets in the contract.

If each right to use significantly affects the other, they are considered highly dependent or highly interrelated. (ASC 842-10-15-28)

Where the lease involves land and other assets, even if the conditions in ASC 842-10-15-28 are met, the entity accounts for the right to use land as a separate lease component. The only exception is if the accounting effect would be insignificant. (ASC 842-10-15-29)

Components of a contract include only those items that transfer a good or service to the lessee. Thus, the following are not components of a contract:

- Administrative taxes to set up a contract or initiate the lease
- Reimbursement or payment of the lessor's costs

(ASC 842-10-15-30)

Nonlease components are accounted for under the relevant guidance. Each separate lease component is accounted for separately from the nonlease components unless the lessee elects the accounting policy in ASC 842-10-15-37 or in ASC 842-10-15-42A. (ASC 842-10-15-31)

Lessee Unless the lessor elects the practical expedient in ASC 842-10-15-42A, the next step in the process is to allocate the consideration to the separate lease and nonlease components by:

- Determining the relative standalone price of the lease and nonlease components based on their observable standalone prices or, if not available, an estimate of the standalone prices
- Allocating the contract's consideration on a relative standalone price basis to the separate contract components

(ASC 842-10-15-33)

As a practical expedient, a lessee may elect, by class of underlying asset, not to separate nonlease from lease components. Instead, the lessee would account, as a single lease component, for each separate lease component associated with that lease component. (ASC 842-10-15-37)

Lessor Unless electing the accounting policy in ASC 842-10-15-42A, the lessor should allocate the contract's consideration to the separate lease and nonlease components. Capitalized costs should be allocated to the related separate lease or nonlease components. (ASC 842-10-15-38) The lessor may elect to exclude from the contract consideration, and from variable payments not included in the contract consideration, all taxes that are imposed on and concurrent with a specific lease revenue. Excluded from the election are taxes assessed on a lessor's total gross receipts or on the lessor as owner of the underlying asset. Excluded from the consideration, and from variable payments not included in the contract consideration, are all leases within the scope of the election. (ASC 842-10-15-39A)

A lessor may, as a practical expedient, elect by class of underlying asset to not separate nonlease from lease components. Instead, the lessor should account for the lease and nonlease components as a single component if the nonlease components would otherwise be accounted for under ASC 606 and:

- The timing and scope of the lease and nonlease components are the same and
- If accounted for separately, the lease component would be accounted for as an operating lease.
  (ASC 842-10-15-42A)

Those familiar with the revenue recognition standard will recognize the concepts discussed above. Below is a flowchart of the decision-making process for determining if a lease is present in the contract.

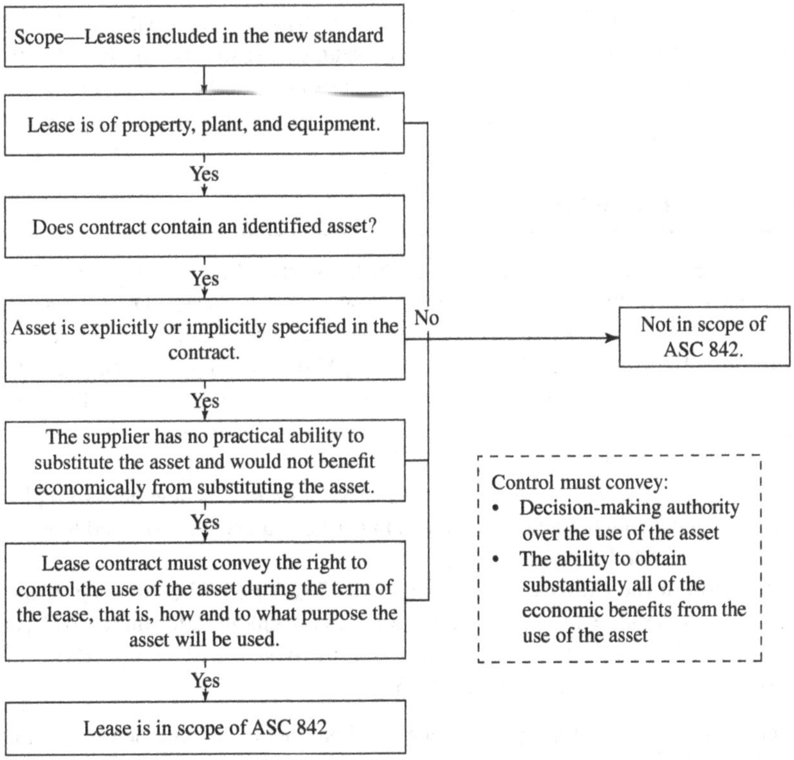

OVERVIEW

Lease transactions became enormously popular over the years as businesses sought new ways to finance long-lived assets. Leasing offers two attractive advantages: typically100% financing, coupled very often with off-the-books obligations.

There are several economic reasons why the lease transaction is considered a viable alternative to outright purchase:

- The lessee (borrower) is frequently able to obtain 100% financing.
- Income tax benefits may be available to one or both of the parties.
- The lessor receives the equivalent of interest as well as an asset with some remaining residual value at the end of the lease term.

A lease agreement involves at least two parties, a lessor and a lessee, and an asset that is to be leased. The lessor is the party that agrees to provide the lessee with right to use an asset for a specified period of time in return for consideration.

The lease transaction derives its accounting complexity from the number of alternatives available to the parties involved. Leases can be structured to allow differing assignments of income tax benefits associated with the leased asset to meet the objectives of the transacting parties. Leases can be used to transfer ownership of the leased asset, and they can be used to transfer control of the assets. In any event, the substance of the transaction dictates the accounting treatment, irrespective of its legal form. The lease transaction is probably the best example of the accounting profession's substance-over-form argument. If the transaction effectively transfers the control of the asset to the lessee, then the substance of the transaction is that of a sale and, accordingly, it is recognized as such for accounting purposes even though the transaction is legally structured as a lease.

DEFINITIONS OF TERMS

Acquiree, Acquirer, Acquisition by a Not-for-Profit Entity, Business, Business Combination, Commencement Date of the Lease (Commencement Date), Contract, Direct Financing Lease, Fair Value (Def. 2), Inventory, Lease, Lease Liability, Lease Payments, Lease Receivable, Lease term, Legal Entity, Lessee, Lessor, Leveraged Lease, Market Participants, Net Investment in the Lease, Not-for-Profit Entity, Operating Lease, Orderly Transaction, Penalty, Probable (Def. 2), Public Business Entity, Related Parties, Remote, Right-of-Use Asset, Sales-type Lease, Sublease, Underlying Asset, and Unguaranteed Residual Asset.

Advance Refunding. A transaction involving the issuance of new debt to replace existing debt with the proceeds from the new debt placed in trust or otherwise restricted to retire the existing debt at a determinable future date or dates.

Consideration in the Contract—Lessees. ASC 842-10-15-35 contains guidance for what constitutes the consideration for lessees. At the commencement date, the consideration in the contract for a lessee includes all of the payments relating to the use of the underlying asset during the lease term as described in ASU 842-10-30-5:

- Fixed payments, including in substance fixed payments, less any lease incentives paid or payable to the lessee (see paragraphs 842-10-55-30 through 55-31).
- Variable lease payments that depend on an index or a rate (such as the Consumer Price Index or a market interest rate), initially measured using the index or rate at the commencement date.

- The exercise price of an option to purchase the underlying asset if the lessee is reasonably certain to exercise that option (assessed considering the factors in paragraph 842-10-55-26).
- Payments for penalties for terminating the lease if the lease term reflects the lessee exercising an option to terminate the lease.
- Fees paid by the lessee to the owners of a special-purpose entity for structuring the transaction. However, such fees shall not be included in the fair value of the underlying asset for purposes of applying paragraph 842-10-25-2(d).
- For a lessee only, amounts probable of being owed by the lessee under residual value guarantees (see paragraphs 842-10-55- 34 through 55-36).

The consideration also includes all of the following payments that will be made during the lease term:

- Any fixed payments (for example, monthly service charges) or in substance fixed payments, less any incentives paid or payable to the lessee, other than those included in
- Any other variable payments that depend on an index or a rate, initially measured using the index or rate at the commencement date
  (ASU 842-10-15-35)

Consideration in the Contract—Lessors. The consideration in the contract for a lessor includes all of the amounts described in paragraph 842-10-15-35 and any other variable payment amounts that would be included in the transaction price in accordance with the guidance on variable consideration in Topic 606 on revenue from contracts with customers that specifically relates to either of the following:

- The lessor's efforts to transfer one or more goods or services that are not leases.
- An outcome from transferring one or more goods or services that are not leases.

Any variable payment amounts accounted for as consideration in the contract shall be allocated entirely to the nonlease component(s) to which the variable payment specifically relates if doing so would be consistent with the transaction price allocation objective in paragraph 606-10-32-28.

Discount Rate for the Lease. For a lessee, the discount rate for the lease is the rate implicit in the lease unless that rate cannot be readily determined. In that case, the lessee is required to use its incremental borrowing rate. For a lessor, the discount rate for the lease is the rate implicit in the lease.

Economic Life. Either the period over which an asset is expected to be economically usable by one or more users or the number of production or similar units expected to be obtained from an asset by one or more users.

Effective Date of the modification. The date that a lease modification is approved by both the lessee and the lessor.

Finance Lease. From the perspective of a lessee, a lease that meets one or more of the criteria in paragraph 842-10-25-2.

Fiscal Funding Clause. A provision by which the lease is cancelable if the legislature or other funding authority does not appropriate the funds necessary for the governmental unit to fulfill its obligations under the lease agreement.

Incremental Borrowing Rate. The rate of interest that a lessee would have to pay to borrow on a collateralized basis over a similar term an amount equal to the lease payments in a similar economic environment.

Initial Direct Cost. Incremental costs of a lease that would not have been incurred if the lease had not been obtained.

Lease modification. A change to the terms and conditions of a contract that results in a change in the scope of or the consideration for a lease (for example, a change to the terms and conditions of the contract that adds or terminates the right to use one or more underlying assets or extends or shortens the contractual lease term).

Period of Use. The total period of time that an asset is used to fulfill a contract with a customer (including the sum of any nonconsecutive periods of time).

Rate Implicit in the Lease. The rate of interest that, at a given date, causes the aggregate present value of (a) the lease payments and (b) the amount that a lessor expects to derive from the underlying asset following the end of the lease term to equal the sum of (1) the fair value of the underlying asset minus any related investment tax credit retained and expected to be realized by the lessor and (2) any deferred initial direct costs of the lessor. However, if the rate determined in accordance with the preceding sentence is less than zero, a rate implicit in the lease of zero shall be used.

Residual Value Guarantee. A guarantee made to a lessor that the value of an underlying asset returned to the lessor at the end of a lease will be at least a specified amount.

Selling Profit or Selling Loss. At the commencement date, selling profit or selling loss equals:

- The fair value of the underlying asset or the sum of the
- Lease receivable and
- Any lease payments prepaid by the lessee, if lower; minus
- The carrying amount of the underlying asset net of any unguaranteed residual asset; minus
- Any deferred initial direct costs of the lessor.

Stand-alone Price. The price at which a customer would purchase a component of a contract separately.

CONCEPTS, RULES, AND EXAMPLES

Lease Classification

Under ASC 840, the classification of a lease determines whether or not it is on the balance sheet. Under ASC 842, because all leases are generally on the balance sheet, the classification of a lease determines how entities measure and present lease income and expenses and cash flows.

Lessees classify leases as either

- Operating or
- Financing leases.

Lessors retain the ASC 840 classifications:

- Sales-type
- Direct financing
- Operating leases

However, the leveraged lease classification is eliminated. Lessors should account for leveraged leases existing at the implementation date under the guidance in ASC 840.

For sales-type leases, in order to derecognize the asset and record revenue, collection of payments must be probable. Under ASC 840, the presence of upfront profit is the major difference between a sales-type lease and a direct finance lease. When upfront profit is present, the arrangement is a sales-type lease.

In a sales-type lease, the lessee needs to obtain control over the leased asset in order for the lessor to recognize upfront revenue and profit.

For a lease that otherwise would be a direct financing lease, collectibility uncertainties require that the lease be classified as an operating lease. In ASC 842, control is the key factor in lease classification. If the lease payments criterion has been met, as least in part, by the third party residual value guarantee, the lease is classified as a direct financing lease.

Lessees should classify a lease as a finance lease, and lessors should classify a lease as a sales-type lease when the lease meets any of these criteria at lease commencement:

- The lease transfers ownership of the underlying asset to the lessee by the end of the lease term.
- The lease grants the lessee an option to purchase the underlying asset that the lessee is reasonably certain to exercise.
- The lease term is for the major part of the remaining economic life of the underlying asset. However, if the commencement date falls at or near the end of the economic life of the underlying asset, this criterion should not be used for purposes of classifying the lease.
- The present value of the sum of the lease payments and any residual value guaranteed by the lessee that is not already reflected in the lease payments in accordance with paragraph 842-10-30-5(f) equals or exceeds substantially all of the fair value of the underlying asset reduced by any related investment tax credit retained by the lessor and expected to be realized by the lessor.
- The underlying asset is of such a specialized nature that it is expected to have no alternative use to the lessor at the end of the lease term.
(ASC 842-10-25-2)

If none of the above criteria applies, a lessee classifies the lease as an operating lease and the lessor classifies the lease as a direct finance lease or an operating lease. The lessor classifies the lease as an operating lease unless both of the following criteria are met, in which case the lessor classifies the lease as a direct financing lease:

- The present value of the sum of the lease payments and any residual value guaranteed by the lessee that is not already reflected in the lease payments in accordance with paragraph 842-10-30-5(f) and/or any other third party unrelated to the lessor equals or exceeds substantially all of the fair value reduced by any related investment tax credit retained by the lessor and expected to be realized by the lessor of the underlying asset, and
- It is probable that the lessor will collect the lease payments plus any amount necessary to satisfy a residual value guarantee.
(ASC 842-10-25-3)

The FASB clarified that for lessors who are not manufacturers or dealers, the fair value of the underlying asset at the commencement of the lease is its cost. The costs should reflect volume or trade discounts. However, if there is a significant amount of time between acquisition of the asset and commencement of the lease, the lessor should apply fair value. (ASC 842-30-55-17A)

Reassessment

Lessees must reassess the lease term if a triggering event occurs that:

- Is under the lessee's control or
- An option is exercised/not exercised as planned.

Any necessary reassessment should be made as of the date the reassessment is required. Examples of that date include a change in the lease term. Changes to the lease term should lead to a reassessment of lease classification and remeasurement of the right-of-use asset and the lease liability. As a result, on an updated remeasurement date, assumptions such as the discount rate and variable rents based on a rate or index will be updated. (ASC 842-10-25-1)

Modifications

A lease modification is a change to the terms and conditions of a lease:

- That was not part of the original lease and
- That results in a change in scope or consideration.
  (ASC 842-10-20)

If the modification that grants the lessee an additional right of use priced at market, a separate lease results. That lease should be classified at the lease modification date. (ASC 842-10-25-8) If the modification does not result in a separate lease, the entity should reassess the classification of the lease or of the effective date of the modification. (ASC 842-10-25-9)

Subsequent Measurement

If a lessor changes its assessment regarding the possibility of exercising an option to extend a lease or actually exercises an option to terminate, the lessor should account for the exercise of that option as a lease modification. (ASC 842-10-35-3)

A lessee is required to remeasure the lease payment if any of the following occur:

a. The lease is modified
b. A contingency affecting variable lease payments is resolved so that those payments meet the definition of lease payments. A change in a reference index or a rate used to calculate variable lease payments is not considered a resolution of a contingency
c. A change in:
   - Lease term
   - Assessment of whether a lessee is reasonably certain to exercise an option to purchase an underlying asset
   - Amounts probable of being owned by the lessee under residual value guarantees (ASC 842-10-35-4)

If one of the events listed above under "a" or "c" occur or when a change unrelated to a reference index or rate under "b" above is resolved, variable lease payments dependent on an index or rate must be remeasured using the index or rate current as of the date the measurement is required. (ASC 842-10-35-5)

Significant Changes in ASC 842

Definition of a Lease Under ASC 842, an arrangement contains a lease only when it conveys the right to control the use of an identified asset. Under ASC 840, an arrangement may contain a lease if the customer takes substantially all of the output over the term of the arrangement. Control is not required.

Lease Accounting ASC 842 eliminates the use of explicit "bright lines" when classifying a lease. It does, however, provide one bright line approach to help determine whether the lease is for a major portion of the asset's life. This when payments represent substantially all of the assets value in the 75% and 90% thresholds provided in ASC 840. (ASC 842-10-55-2)

In ASC 842, expense related to an operating lease is recognized on a straight-line basis. Under ASC 840, operating leases are off-balance sheet.

ASC 842 calls for the lessee to use a display approach to place lease obligations on the balance sheet:

Lease liability = the present value of remaining payments, using a discount rate calculated on the basis of information available at commencement date of the lease.

Right of use asset for an operation lease = The lease liability

+ or – unamortized initial direct costs
= or – prepaid/accrued lease payments

Remaining balance of the lease incentives received.

The display approach is discussed later in this chapter.

Collectibility uncertainties Under ASC 840, a lease with uncertainties related to collectability cannot be classified as a sales-type lease. This changes with ASC 842. Where collectability of the lease payments plus any amount necessary to satisfy a lessee residual value guarantee is not probable for a sales-type lease, the entity accounts for the lease as follows:

- Lease payments received are recognized as a deposit liability rather than income.
- Generally, the underlying asset is not derecognized until collectibility of the remaining amounts becomes probable.

Significant variable lease payments ASC 842 permits leases with predominantly variable payments to be classified as sale-type or direct financing leases.

Definition of initial direct costs ASC 842's definition is narrower than under current GAAP. The new definition is incremental costs of a lease that would not have been incurred had the lease not been obtained and excludes:

- Legal fees
- Costs of evaluating the prospective lessee's financial condition
- Costs of negotiating lease terms and conditions
- General overhead expenses

Those expenses must be expensed as incurred. This change may have the effect of some lessors recognizing more expenses before the lease begins, and it may create higher margins on lease income earned over the lease term.

Property taxes and insurance are not considered components of a contact. They are not payments for a service provided by the lessor. Therefore, they are part of lease payments. This is a change from ASC 840 guidance where those items are executory costs rather than minimum lease payments.

Allocation of consideration to lease and non lease components ASC 842 only applies to accounting for leases. So, if an entity has a lease that has a nonlease component, like a service component, that component is accounted for under the new revenue recognition standard. (Also see "Practical Expedients" section above.)

The lessor may have executory costs to cover ownership of the underlying asset, like property taxes or insurance. Those costs do not represent payment for a good or service and, as mentioned above, under ASC 840 are excluded from lease accounting. Under ASC 842, such costs are allocated to the lease and nonlease components in the same manner as all other payments in the contract.

Sale-leaseback accounting ASC 842 brings sale-leaseback transactions onto the balance sheet by requiring seller-lessees to recognize a right-of-use asset and a lease liability for the leaseback.

Under ASC 840, a failed sale for the seller-lessee is not accounted for as a failed purchase by the buyer-lessor. ASC 842 requires buyer-lessors to evaluate whether they have purchased the underlying asset based on the transfer of control guidance in the new revenue recognition standard. The buyer-lessor must also account for a failed purchase as a financing arrangement.

Under ASC 842, a sale and leaseback transaction qualifies as a sale only if:

- It meets the sale guidance in the ASC 606,
- The leaseback is not a finance lease or a sales-type lease, and
- If there is a repurchase option:
  - The repurchase price is at the asset's fair value at the time of exercise and
  - Alternative assets that are substantially the same as the transferred asset are readily available in the marketplace.

(ASC 842-40-25-1 through 25-3)

If the transaction does not meet the qualifications for sale under the revenue recognition guidance, the seller-lessee accounts for it as a financing transaction. Purchase options preclude sale accounting unless:

- The strike price of the repurchase option is the fair value of the asset at the option exercise date, *and*
- Assets that are substantially the same as the underlying asset are readily available in the marketplace.

If the sale-leaseback transaction qualifies as a sale of the underlying asset, the seller-lessee recognizes the entire gain from the sale at the time of sale as opposed to recognition over the leaseback terms. The gain is the difference between the selling price and the carrying value of the amount of the underlying asset. The sale-leaseback guidance is the same for all assets, including real estate.

Build-to-suit lease guidance While ASC 840's guidance is built on a risks and rewards model, the guidance in ASC 842 is built on control and ownership during the construction period is based on the control model. ASC 842 states that a lessee is the owner for accounting purposes of an asset under construction if it controls the asset before the lease commencement date.

The rules for determining control of an asset will likely result in fewer instances where the lessee is deemed the accounting owner of an asset during the construction period. Under ASC 840, build-to-suit assets and liabilities may have remained in the balance sheet after the end of the construction period. When those entities transition to the new guidance, many will be able to derecognize those assets.

Presentation—Using the Display Approach

To allow preparers to leverage existing standards and processes, the FASB designed the display approach for recognizing operating leases on the balance sheet. Using this approach, preparers can maintain their existing records and systems, use the information to create a period end journal entry that conforms to the guidance in ASC 842, and then reverse the entry at the start of the next period. The following exhibit illustrates the journal entries.

Sample journal entries under the display approach for 12/31/X2:

Right of use asset
Accrued rent
    Lease liability—current
    Lease liability—long-term
    Prepaid rent
    Deferred initial direct costs—current
    Deferred initial direct costs—long-term

Sample journal entries under the display approach for 1/1/X3:

Lease liability—current
Lease liability—long-term Prepaid rent
Deferred initial direct costs—current
Deferred initial direct costs—long-term
    Right of use asset
    Accrued rent

Disclosures Under ASC 842

The standard significantly expands qualitative and quantitative disclosures. The lessor's disclosures include:

- Qualitative information:
  - Information about the nature of variable payment arrangements and termination, renewal or purchase options
  - Information about how the lessor manages residual asset risk, including about residual value guarantees and other means of limiting that risk
  - Significant accounting judgments and estimates
- Quantitative information:
  - Maturity analysis of lease receivables for sales-type and direct financing leases and of lease payments for operating leases
- Table of lease income, showing:
  - Selling profit or loss recognized at lease commencement and interest income for sales-type and direct financing leases
  - Operating lease income
  - Variable lease income

The lessee's disclosures include:

- Qualitative:
  - Nature of lease, such as terms and conditions of variable lease payments, extension and termination options, purchase options, and residual value guarantees
- Quantitative:
  - Operating lease costs
  - Amortization of finance lease right-of-use assets, and interest on finance lease liabilities
  - Variable lease cost
  - Weighted-average discount rate
  - Maturity analysis of lease liabilities

- Significant judgments
  - Such as whether a contract contains a lease, stand-alone price for lease and nonlease components, and the discount rate for the entities' leases
  - Information about the nature of leases

Implementation Considerations

As part of its change management approach to the new standard, management will want to have a robust implementation plan. When implementing its project plan, management should consider the following steps:

- Review existing leases.
- Evaluate the ability of current systems to collect and maintain all the data necessary for compliance. IT systems must capture data for the proper period or date related to disclosures.
- Identify where more judgment is required. Implement processes and controls to make sure adequate processes and controls are in place. Also make sure adequate documentation is in place to respond to auditors or regulators.
- Determine whether the standard affects other areas, such as:
  - Taxation
  - Debt covenant compliance. Debt covenants are often based on a measure of net income. Entities must be careful not to unintentionally violate an agreement. Debt covenants may have to be modified in preparation for change, while keeping their original intent.
- Review standard leases and determine if language should be changed. The standard introduces some new terms and those should be considered.
- Review lease terms. Entities may want to make changes to better align with the standard.
- Analyze how implementation affects net income and communicate it internally, but also to stakeholders.
- Evaluate the need for training at all levels: audit committees, management, operational units.

57 ASC 845 NONMONETARY TRANSACTIONS

PERSPECTIVE AND ISSUES

Subtopics

ASC 845, *Nonmonetary Transactions*, has only one subtopic:

- ASC 845-10, *Overall*, which includes five subsections:
  - General
  - Purchases and sales of inventory with the same counterparty
  - Barter transactions
  - Exchanges involving monetary consideration

  (ASU 845-10-05-1)

Scope and Scope Exceptions

Several variants of noncash transactions are governed by ASC 845. ASC 845-10-15-4 lists scope exceptions. The following types of transactions are *not* treated as nonmonetary transactions:

1. A business combination accounted for by an entity according to the provisions of ASC 805 or a combination accounted for by a not-for-profit entity according to the provisions of ASC 958-805.

2. A transfer of nonmonetary assets solely between entities or persons under common control, such as between a parent and its subsidiaries or between two subsidiaries of the same parent, or between a corporate joint venture and its owners.
3. Acquisition of goods or services on issuance of the capital stock of an entity under ASC 718-10.
4. Stock issued or received in stock dividends and stock splits.
5. A pooling of assets in a joint undertaking intended to find, develop, or produce oil or gas from a particular property or group of properties.
6. The exchange of a part of an operating interest owned for a part of an operating interest owned by another party that is subject to ASC 932-360-55-6.
7. The transfer of a financial asset within the scope of ASC 860-10-15.
8. Involuntary conversions specified in ASC 610-30-15-2.[1]
9. The transfer of goods or services in a contract with a customer within the scope of ASC 606 in exchange for noncash consideration.
10. The transfer of a nonfinancial asset within the scope of ASC 610-20 in exchange for noncash consideration. Noncash consideration promised in exchange for a nonfinancial asset that is a noncontrolling ownership interest is within the scope of ASC 845.[2] (ASC 845-10-15-4)

The guidance in the *Purchases and Sales of Inventory with the Same Counterparty* subsections does not apply to inventory purchase and sales arrangements that are accounted for as derivatives under Topic 815, or involve exchanges of software or exchanges of real estate. (ASC 845-10-15-8)

The guidance in the *Exchanges Involving Monetary Consideration* subsections does not apply to transfers between a joint venture and its owners. (ASC 845-10-15-14)

The guidance in the *Exchanges of a Nonfinancial Asset for a Noncontrolling Ownership Interest* subsections does not apply to the following types of transfers:

- Transfers between a joint venture and its owners
- Capital contributions of real estate in return for an unconsolidated real estate investment (for guidance, see Subtopic 970-323)
- A deconsolidation of a subsidiary that is a business or nonprofit activity that is within the scope of Subtopic 810-10 (see paragraph 810-10-40-3A)
- A derecognition of a group of assets that constitutes a business or nonprofit activity that is within the scope of Subtopic 810-10 (see paragraph 810-10-40-3A) (ASC 845-10-15-21)

Overview

ASC 845, *Nonmonetary Transactions*, addresses those transactions in which no money changes hands. These transactions are most commonly associated with exchanges of fixed assets, but can also involve other items, such as inventory, liabilities, and ownership interests. They can also involve one-way, or nonreciprocal, transfers.

This chapter sets forth the basic structure and concepts of nonmonetary transactions, including the concept of commercial substance, rules regarding similar and dissimilar exchanges, involuntary conversions, and how to handle exchanges that include a certain amount of monetary consideration.

[1] Upon implementation of ASU 2014-09 on revenue, this citation changes to ASC 610-30-15-2).
[2] Items 10 and 11 are effective upon implementation of ASU 2014-09.

DEFINITIONS OF TERMS

Source: ASC 845-10-20. Also see Appendix A, *Definitions of Terms*, for other terms related to this Topic: Contract, Customer, Nonprofit Activity, Not-for-Profit Entity, Owners, and Revenue.

Exchange. A reciprocal transfer between two entities, resulting in one entity acquiring assets or services or satisfying liabilities by surrendering other assets or services or incurring other obligations.

Monetary Assets and Liabilities. Monetary assets and liabilities are assets and liabilities whose amounts are fixed in terms of units of currency by contract or otherwise. Examples are cash, short- or long-term accounts and notes receivable in cash, and short- or long-term accounts and notes payable in cash.

Nonmonetary Assets and Liabilities. Assets and liabilities other than monetary ones. Examples are inventories; investments in common stocks; property, plant, and equipment; and liabilities for rent collected in advance.

Nonreciprocal Transfer. A transfer of assets or services in one direction from an entity to its owners (whether or not in exchange for their ownership interests) or another entity, or from its owners or another entity to the entity. An entity's reacquisition of its outstanding stock is an example of a nonreciprocal transfer.

Owners. Used broadly to include holders of ownership (equity interests) of investor-owned entities, mutual entities, or not-for-profit entities. Owners include shareholders, partners, proprietors, or members or participants of mutual entities. Owners also include owner and member interests in the net assets of not-for-profit entities.

Productive Assets. Productive assets are assets held for or used in the production of goods or services by the entity. Productive assets include an investment in another entity if the investment is accounted for by the equity method but exclude an investment not accounted for by that method. Similar productive assets are productive assets that are of the same general type, that perform the same function, or that are employed in the same line of business.

CONCEPTS, RULES, AND EXAMPLES

Types of Nonmonetary Transactions

There are three types of nonmonetary transactions identified in ASC 845:

1. Nonreciprocal transfers with owners—Examples include dividends-in-kind, nonmonetary assets exchanged for common stock, split-ups, and spinoffs.
2. Nonreciprocal transfers with nonowners—Examples include charitable donations of property either made or received by the reporting entity and contributions of land by a state or local government to a private enterprise for the purpose of construction of a specified structure.
3. Nonmonetary exchanges—Examples include exchanges of inventory for productive assets, exchanges of inventory for similar products, and exchanges of productive assets. (ASC 845-10-05-3)

General Rule

The primary accounting issue in nonmonetary transactions is the determination of the amount to assign to the nonmonetary assets or services transferred to or from the reporting entity.

The general rule is to:

- Value the transaction at the fair value of the asset *given up*, unless the fair value of the asset *received* is more clearly evident, and
- Recognize gain or loss on the difference between the fair value and carrying value of the asset.

ASC 820 provides the guidance for fair value and provides that when one of the parties to a nonmonetary transaction could have elected to receive cash in lieu of the nonmonetary asset, the amount of cash that would have been received may be the best evidence of the fair value of the nonmonetary assets exchanged. The fair value of the asset surrendered should be used to value the exchange unless the fair value of the asset received is more clearly evident of the fair value. (ASC 845-10-30-1)

Modification of the General Rule

ASC 845-10-30-3 states that under certain circumstances a nonmonetary exchange should be measured based on the recorded amount (after reduction for any impairment) of the nonmonetary asset relinquished, and not on the fair values of the exchanged asset, if any of the following conditions apply:

1. The fair value of neither the asset received nor the asset relinquished is determinable within reasonable limits.
2. The transaction is an exchange of a product or property held for sale in the ordinary course of business for a product or property to be sold in the same line of business to facilitate sales to customers other than the parties to the exchange.
3. The transaction lacks commercial substance.

NOTE: ASC 845 states that a transfer of a nonmonetary asset will not qualify as an exchange if the transferor has substantial continuing involvement in the transferred assets that result in the transferee not obtaining the usual risks and rewards associated with ownership of the transferred assets.

Commercial Substance

As explained in ASC 845-10-30-4, a nonmonetary exchange is subjected to a test to determine whether or not it has "commercial substance." An exchange has commercial substance if cash flows change as a result of the exchange. If determined to have commercial substance, the exchange is recorded at the fair value of the transferred asset. If the transaction is determined not to have commercial substance, the exchange is recognized using the recorded amount of the exchanged asset or assets, reduced for any applicable impairment of value.

To determine commercial substance, management estimates whether, after the exchange, the reporting entity will experience changes in its expected cash flows:

1. Because of changes in amounts, timing, and/or risks (these factors are collectively referred to as the "configuration" of the expected future cash flows), *or*
2. Because the entity-specific value of the assets received differs from the entity-specific value of the assets transferred.

If the changes in either of these criteria are significant relative to the fair values of the assets exchanged, the transaction is considered to have commercial substance. *Entity-specific value* is a concept defined in CON 7 that substitutes assumptions that an entity makes with respect to its own future cash flows for the corresponding assumptions that marketplace participants would make with respect to cash flows. The commercial substance criterion is *not* met if a transaction is structured to achieve income tax benefits or in order to achieve a specific outcome for financial reporting purposes.

Recognition of Gains or Losses Entities should recognize losses incurred on all exchanges whether or not they have commercial substance. This is so that assets are not overstated. If an exchange has commercial substance, any gain should be recognized immediately. If an exchange has no commercial substance, the entity recognizes the gain through lower depreciation expense or when it sells the asset. However, if cash or "boot" is received, the entity may recognize a portion of the gain even if there is no commercial substance.

Nonreciprocal Transfers

The valuation of most nonreciprocal transfers is based upon the fair value of the nonmonetary asset (or service) given up, unless the fair value of the nonmonetary asset received is more clearly evident. This will result in recognition of gain or loss on the difference between the fair value assigned to the transaction and the carrying value of the asset surrendered.

The valuation of nonmonetary assets distributed to owners of the reporting entity in a spin-off or other form of reorganization or liquidation is based on the recorded amounts, again after first recognizing any warranted reduction for impairment. Other nonreciprocal transfers to owners are accounted for at fair value if

- The fair value of the assets distributed is objectively measurable, and
- That fair value would be clearly realized by the distributing reporting entity in an outright sale at or near the time of distribution to the owners.
  (ASC 845- 10-30-10)

Example of Accounting for a Nonreciprocal Transfer with a Nonowner

1. Jacobs Corporation donated depreciable property with a book value of $10,000 (cost of $25,000 less accumulated depreciation of $15,000) to a charity during the current year.
2. The property had a fair value of $17,000 at the date of the transfer.

The transaction is valued at the fair value of the property transferred, and any gain or loss on the transaction is recognized on the date of the transfer. Thus, Jacobs recognizes a gain of $7,000 ($17,000–$10,000) in the determination of the current period's net income. The entry to record the transaction would be as follows:

Charitable donations	17,000	
Accumulated depreciation	15,000	
Property		25,000
Gain on donation of property		7,000

Note that the gain on disposition of the donated property is reported as operating income in accordance with ASC 420 and is not to be presented in the "other income" section of the income statement.

Example of an Exchange Involving No Boot

Company presidents Able and Baker agree to swap copiers, since each needs certain printing features only available on the other company's copier. Able's copier has a book value of $18,000 (cost of $24,000 less depreciation of $6,000). Both copiers have a fair value of $24,000. In testing for the commercial substance of the transaction, there is no difference in the fair values of the assets exchanged, nor are Able's future cash flows expected to significantly change as a result of the transfer. Under ASC 845, exchanges of assets that do not alter expected future cash flows are deemed to lack commercial substance, and are accounted for at book value. As a result of the trade, Able has the following *unrecognized* gain:

Fair value of Able copier given to Baker	$ 24,000
Book value of Able copier given to Baker	18,000
Total gain (unrecognized)	$ 6,000

The entry by Able to record this transaction is as follows:

Fixed assets—Office equipment; Copier received from Baker	18,000	
Accumulated depreciation—Office equipment; Copier given	6,000	
Fixed assets—Office equipment; Copier given		24,000

Able elects to depreciate its newly acquired copier over four years with an assumed salvage value of zero, which computes to monthly depreciation of $375. If Able had recorded the fair value of the incoming copier at $24,000, this would have required a higher monthly depreciation rate of $500. Thus, the unrecognized gain on the transaction is actually being recognized each month through reduced depreciation charges.

Able immediately exchanges its newly acquired copier for one owned by Charlie. However, the fair value of the copier owned by Charlie is $30,000, as compared to the $24,000 fair value of Able's copier (which is being carried at $18,000, the carryforward basis of its predecessor). In testing for the commercial substance of the transaction, there is determined to be a significant difference in the entity-specific values of the assets exchanged, so in accordance with the provisions of ASC 845 Able must record a gain on the transaction based on the difference in the fair values of the exchanged assets. This is done with the following entry:

Fixed assets—Office equipment; Copier received from Charlie	30,000	
Fixed assets—Office equipment; Copier received from Baker		18,000
Gain on disposal of office equipment		12,000

Note that the full gain from both exchanges is now being recognized, since the carryforward book value of the original copier was used as the book value of the first-acquired trade, and that carryforward amount is now being compared to the fair value of the latest trade.

Able elects to depreciate the newly acquired copier over four years with no salvage value, resulting in monthly depreciation of $625.

After ten months, Able trades his newly acquired copier to Echo. The book value has now dropped to $23,750 (cost of $30,000 less depreciation of $6,250); however, due to technology advances, its fair value has declined to $20,000. This final trade has no commercial substance, in the ASC 845-defined sense, since cash flows will not materially vary between the use of these two machines. Thus, in general, under ASC 845, fair value accounting would not be employed in an exchange of similar assets lacking commercial substance; Able is required to recognize an impairment loss under ASC 360-10-40-4 if the fair value of the asset being disposed of is less than its carrying amount. Were this not done, the new asset would be recognized at an amount in excess of its realizable amount (fair value). Able has incurred the following impairment loss resulting from the transaction, which must be fully recognized in the current period:

Fair value of Able copier given to Echo	$ 20,000
Book value of Able copier given to Echo	(23,750)
Total impairment loss (recognized)	$ (3,750)

The entry by Able to record this transaction is as follows:

Fixed assets—Office equipment; Copier received from Echo	$ 20,000	
Accumulated depreciation—Office equipment; Copier received from Charlie	6,250	
Impairment loss on asset disposed of	3,750	
Fixed assets—Office equipment; Copier received from Charlie		30,000

Nonmonetary Exchanges That Include Monetary Consideration (Boot)

A single exception to the nonrecognition rule for an exchange without commercial substance occurs when the exchange involves both a monetary and nonmonetary asset being exchanged for a nonmonetary asset. The monetary portion of the exchange is termed *boot*. When boot is at least 25% of the fair value of the exchange, the exchange is considered a monetary transaction. In that case, both parties record the exchange at fair value. When boot received is less than 25%, only the boot portion of the earnings process is considered to have culminated. The portion of the gain applicable to the boot is considered realized and is recognized in the determination of net income in the period of the exchange by the receiver of the boot. The payor does not record a gain. (ASC 845-10-25-6) The payor records the asset received at the monetary consideration received plus the recorded amount of the nonmonetary asset surrendered. Any loss in the exchange is recorded. (ASC 845-10-30-6)

The formula for the recognition of the gain in an exchange involving boot of less than 25% of fair value is expressed as follows:

$$\frac{\text{Boot}}{\text{Boot} + \text{Fair value of nonmonetary asset received}} \times \text{Total gain indicated} = \text{Gain recognized}$$

Example of an Exchange Involving No Commercial Substance and Boot

Amanda Excavating exchanges one of its underutilized front loaders with Dorothy Diggers, another excavator, for a bulldozer.

These assets are carried on the respective companies' statements of financial position as follows:

	Amanda (front loader)	*Dorothy (bulldozer)*
Cost	$75,000	$90,000
Accumulated depreciation	7,500	15,000
Net book value	$67,500	$75,000
Fair (appraised) value	$60,000	$78,000

The terms of the exchange require Amanda to pay Dorothy $18,000 cash (boot). Boot represents approximately 23% of the fair value of the exchange computed as follows:

	Amount	*Percent of total*
Fair value of front loader	$60,000	77%
Cash consideration (boot)	18,000	23%
Total consideration	$78,000	100%

Note that as the payer of boot, Amanda does not recognize a gain. As a receiver of boot that is less than 25% of the fair value of the consideration received, Dorothy recognizes a pro rata gain that is computed as follows:

Total gain = $78,000 consideration – $75,000 net book value of bulldozer = $3,000

Portion of gain to be recognized by Dorothy

$$\frac{\$18,000\,\text{boot}}{\$18,000\,\text{boot} + \$60,000\,\text{fair value of nonmonetary asset received} = \$78,000}$$

$$= 23\% \times \$3,000\,\text{gain} = \$690\,\text{gain recognized}$$

The accounting entries to record this transaction by Amanda and Dorothy are as follows:

	Amanda		*Dorothy*	
	Debit	*Credit*	*Debit*	*Credit*
Excavating equipment	10,500			32,310
Accum. depreciation—excavating equipment	7,500		15,000	
Cash		$18,000	18,000	
Recognized gain	–	–	–	690
	18,000	$18,000	33,000	33,000

Amanda records the increase in the carrying value of its excavating equipment to account for the difference between the $78,000 fair value of the bulldozer received and the $67,500 carrying value of the front loader exchanged. The accumulated depreciation on the front loader is reversed since, from the standpoint of Amanda, it has no accumulated depreciation on the bulldozer at the date of the exchange.

Dorothy records the cash received, removes the previously recorded accumulated depreciation on the bulldozer, records the $690 gain attributable to the boot as computed above, and records the difference as an adjustment to the carrying value of its excavating equipment.

After recording the entries above, the carrying values of the exchanged equipment would be as follows:

	Amanda (bulldozer)	*Dorothy (front loader)*
Net book value exchanged	$67,500	$ 75,000
Cash paid (received)	18,000	(18,000)
Gain recognized		$ 690
Carrying value of asset received	$85,500	$ 57,690

To summarize, if boot is 25% or more of the fair value of an exchange, the transaction is considered a monetary transaction. In that case, both parties record the transaction at fair value. If the boot is less than 25%, the payer of the boot does not recognize a gain and the receiver of the boot must follow the pro rata recognition guidance in ASC 845-10-30-6. See the following section for rules regarding exchanges with boot involving real estate.

Gain on a *monetary* exchange that involves transfer by one entity of its ownership of a controlled asset, group of assets, or business to another entity in exchange for a noncontrolling ownership interest in the other entity is accounted for consistent with the guidance above for similar *nonmonetary* exchanges.

Exchanges of Real Estate Involving Monetary Consideration (Boot)[3]

A transaction that involves the exchange of similar real estate and boot of 25% or more of the fair value of the exchange is recorded with two separate components, a monetary component and a nonmonetary component. The allocation is made based on the relative fair values of the monetary and nonmonetary portions at the time of the transaction. (ASC 845-10-25-7) The party that receives the boot accounts for the monetary component of the transaction under ASC 360-20 as the equivalent of a sale of an interest in the underlying real estate and the nonmonetary component of the transaction based on the recorded amount (reduced, if applicable, for any impairment in value) of the nonmonetary asset relinquished. For the party that pays the boot, the monetary component is accounted for as an acquisition of real estate, and the nonmonetary component is accounted for based on the recorded amount (reduced, if applicable, for any impairment in value).

Inventory Purchases and Sales with the Same Counterparty

Some enterprises sell inventory to another party from whom they also acquire inventory in the same line of business. These transactions may be part of a single or separate arrangements and the inventory purchased or sold may be raw materials, work-in-process, or finished goods. These arrangements require careful analysis to determine if they are to be accounted for as a single exchange transaction under ASC 845, *Nonmonetary Transactions*, and whether they are to be recognized at fair value or at the carrying value of the inventory transferred.[4]

Determining Whether Transactions Constitute a Single Exchange ASC 845-10-15-6 states that inventory purchases and sales with the same counterparty are to be treated as a single transaction when:

1. An inventory transaction is legally contingent upon the occurrence of another inventory transaction with the same counterparty, *or*
2. Two or more inventory purchase and sale transactions involving the same counterparties are entered into in contemplation of one another and are combined.

In determining whether transactions were entered into in contemplation of one another, FASB provides the following indicators, which are neither all-inclusive nor determinative (ASC 845-10- 25-4):

1. The counterparties have a specific legal right of offset of their respective obligations.
2. The transactions are entered into simultaneously.

---

[3] This guidance is superseded when ASU 2014-09 is implemented.

[4] This guidance does not apply to arrangements accounted for as derivatives under ASC 815, or to exchanges of software or real estate.

3. The terms of the transactions were "off-market" when the arrangement was agreed to by the parties.
4. The relative certainty that reciprocal inventory transactions will occur between the counterparties.

Measurement of the Exchange When management has determined that multiple transactions between the same counterparties within the same line of business are to be treated as a single exchange transaction, the measurement of the transaction depends on the type of inventory items exchanged. The rules are summarized in the following table:

Nonmonetary Exchanges of Inventory Within the Same Line of Business*

Type of inventory transferred to counterparty	*Type of inventory received from counterparty*	*Accounting treatment*
Finished goods	Raw materials or work-in-process	Recognize the transaction at fair value of the asset if: • Fair value of the asset is determinable within reasonable limits, and • Transaction has commercial substance per ASC 845-10-30-4) If these conditions are not met, recognize at the carrying value of the inventory transferred.
Raw materials or work-in-process	Raw materials, work-in-process or finished goods	Recognize the transaction at the carrying value of the inventory transferred.
Finished goods	Finished goods	
(ASC 845-10-30-15 and 30-16)		

* *Items in this table do not fall under the guidance of ASC 845-10-30-3 discussed previously for an exchange transaction to facilitate sales to customers for the entity transferring the finished goods.*

Example of Counterparty Inventory Transfers

Shapiro Optics Corporation (SOC) manufactures lenses for cameras, binoculars, and telescopes.

Farber Products, Inc. (FPI) is a manufacturer of digital cameras. FPI internally manufactures many of the individual parts used in its cameras including all of the electronic circuitry, and the viewfinders. FPI does not have the expertise or capacity to design and manufacture lenses or camera housings, which it accordingly purchases from external suppliers.

SOC has been a long-time supplier of lenses to FPI and due to their strong business relationship, SOC wishes to purchase electronic components from FPI similar to those that FPI uses in its camera circuit boards. SOC plans to use those components as raw materials in a popular line of telescopes it manufactures. The parties negotiate and execute an agreement with the following terms:

1. FPI agrees to purchase a specified number of lenses from SOC over a two-year period.
2. At least weekly, at its discretion, FPI can settle its payable to SOC by either paying the obligation in cash, or by shipping electronic components to SOC of equivalent value.
3. SOC is obligated to accept the components in lieu of cash, should FPI choose to settle the outstanding balance in that manner.

Historically, based on its manufacturing capacity and its cash management policies, FPI has settled these transactions by shipping components and SOC has accepted those components and used them in manufacturing its telescopes. Upon delivery of its lenses to FPI, SOC reasonably expects that it will receive electronic components from FPI in return.

These transfers are to be treated as a single, nonmonetary transaction, since:

1. The agreement that governs both the purchase transactions and their settlement is evidence that they were entered into simultaneously.
2. There is a strong likelihood that each time FPI purchases lenses it will also ship components in a reciprocal inventory transaction.
3. By accepting settlement of its receivable from FPI in components rather than in cash, SOC is, in effect, allowing the offset of its receivable from FPI with its payable to FPI for its purchase of components.

From the perspective of SOC, it is relinquishing its lenses, which are accounted for in its financial statements as finished goods inventory, and exchanging the lenses for electronic components, which are accounted for as raw materials used in the production of its telescopes. Assuming the transaction passes the commercial substance test (ASC 840-10-30-4), SOC will account for the nonmonetary exchange at fair value.

Exchange of Product or Property Held for Sale for Productive Assets

An exchange of goods held for sale in the ordinary course of business for property and equipment to be used in the production process, even if they pertain to the same line of business, is recorded at fair value.

Barter Transactions

Through third-party barter exchanges, many commercial enterprises exchange their goods and services to obtain barter credits that can be used in lieu of cash to obtain goods and services provided by other members of the barter exchange.

If it subsequently becomes apparent that either of the following conditions exist, the reporting entity should recognize an impairment loss on the barter credits:

1. The carrying value of any remaining barter credits exceeds their fair value, or
2. It is probable that the entity will not use all of the remaining barter credits.
   (ASC 845-10-30-19)

If an exchange involves transfer or assumption of an operating lease for barter credits, impairment of the lease is to be measured as the amount of remaining lease costs (the discounted future rental payments plus the carrying amount of unamortized leasehold improvements) in excess of the fair value of the discounted amount of the probable future sublease rentals for the remaining lease term. (ASC 845-10-30-20)

Summary

The situations involving the exchange of nonmonetary assets are summarized in the diagram on the following page.

Nonmonetary Transactions

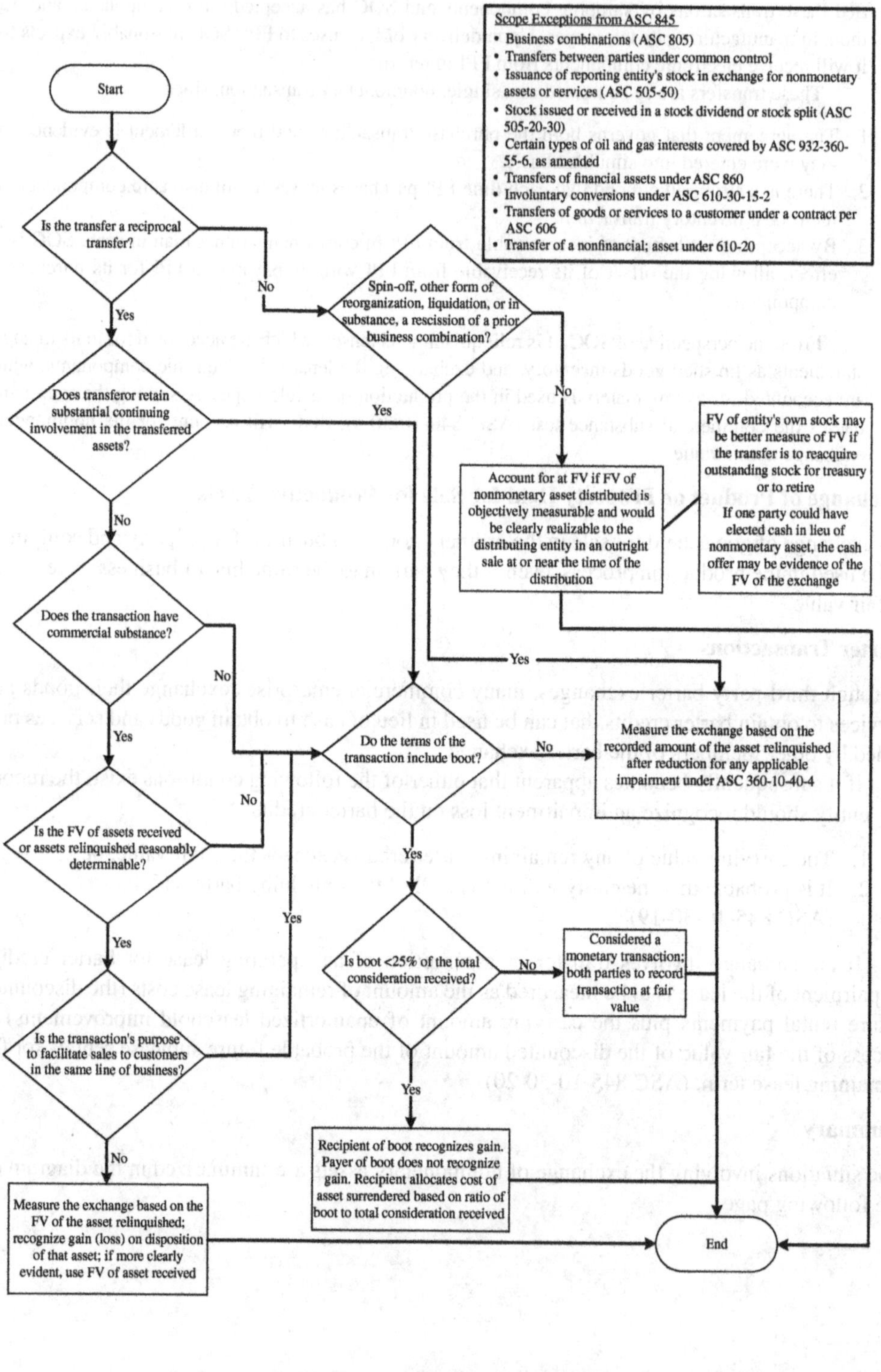

58 ASC 848 REFERENCE RATE REFORM

TECHNICAL ALERT

In March 2020, the FASB issued ASU 2020-04, *Reference Rate Reform (Topic 848): Facilitation of the Effects of Reference Rate Reform.* The ASU was issued in response to concerns about structural risks of the interbank offered rates and the risks of cessation of LIBOR and is designed to provide relief from the potential accounting burden when transitioning from reference rates, like LIBOR, that may be discontinued. FASB stakeholders raised concerns about contract modifications, hedge accounting, and the volume of contracts, such as debt agreements, leases, and derivatives.

If certain criteria are met, the ASU's changes offer optional expedients and exceptions for applying the Codification to the contract, hedging relationships, and other matters. ASC 848 is unique in that the guidance sunsets in 2022. When certain benchmark rates are discontinued, contracts will be modified. The optional expedients and exceptions can be applied to contract modifications and hedging relationships entered into or evaluations made until December 31, 2022.

Effective Dates

The amendments are effective as of March 12, 2020 through December 31, 2022. Once elected for a Topic or an Industry Subtopic, the amendments must be applied prospectively for all eligible contract modifications for that Topic or Industry Subtopic.

- Contract modifications
  - An entity may elect to apply the guidance to contract modifications as of any date from the beginning of the interim period that includes or is subsequent to March 12, 2020, or it may apply the guidance prospectively from a date within an interim period that includes or is subsequent to March 12, 2020, up to the date the financial statements are available to be issued.
- Hedge accounting
  - The guidance related to hedges may be applied to eligible hedging relationships that either existed on or were entered into after the beginning of the interim period that includes March 12, 2020 (that is, January 1, 2020 for a calendar-year entity).

- If an entity has not adopted the amendments in ASU 2017-12, *Derivatives and Hedging (Topic 815): Targeted Improvements to Accounting for Hedging Activities,* it is eligible to apply only certain of the optional expedients provided in ASC 848 for hedging relationships.

Sunset Provision

- The guidance in ASC 848 may not be applied to contract modifications made after December 31, 2022 or to new hedging relationships entered into after that date.
- In addition, the new guidance may not be applied to hedging relationships for periods after December 31, 2022, although hedging relationships existing at December 31, 2022 that apply the following expedients should retain those expedients through the end of the hedging relationship:
  - Expedient used to recognize in earnings the components excluded from the assessment of effectiveness in ASC 848-30-25-12.
  - Expedient used to determine the rate to discount cash flows associated with the hedged item, as well as expedient used for any adjustment to the cash flows for the designated term or the partial term of the designated hedged item in a fair value hedge, in ASC 848-40-25-6.
  - Expedient used to not periodically evaluate the conditions in ASC 815-20-25-104(d) and (g) when using the shortcut method for a fair value hedge in ASC 848-40-25-8.

PERSPECTIVE AND ISSUES

Subtopics

ASU 848 contains five Subtopics:

- ASU 848-10, *Overall*
- ASU 848-20, *Contract Modifications,* provides optional expedients for contract modifications resulting from reference rate reform
- ASU 848-30, *Hedging—General*
- ASU 848-40, *Fair Value Hedges*
- ASU 848-59, *Cash Flow Hedges*

(ASC 848-10-05-1)

DEFINITIONS OF TERMS

ASC 848 contains one term in its Glossary: Financial Statements Are Available to Be Issued. That definition can be found in Appendix A, *Definitions of Terms.*

CONCEPTS, RULES, AND EXAMPLES

ASC 848-10, *Overall*

Scope ASC 848 applies to all entities and, if elected, to contracts or other transactions that reference LIBOR or a reference rate that is expected to be discontinued as a result of reference rate reform. (ASC 848-10-15-2 and 15-3)

A reference rate is expected to be discontinued if any one of the following three conditions exists:

1. The reference rate administrator or its regulatory supervisor has announced its intention to discontinue the reference rate.
2. A significant number of market participants (or market participants representing a significant number of transactions) take the initiative to move away from the reference rate.
3. The method to calculate the reference rate is either fundamentally restructured or relies on another rate that is expected to be discontinued.
(ASC 848-10-15-4)

Subsequent Measurement Entities have the option to use a one-time election to:

- Sell or transfer held-to-maturity (HTM) debt securities or
- Both sell and transfer HTM to available-for-sale (AFS) or trading categories.

At the time of application of the election, the debt securities must:

- Reference a rate in the scope of ASC 480-10-15-3 and
- Be classified as HTM before January 1, 2020.

The election to sell and/or transfer HTM debt securities may be made at any time on or before December 31, 2022. (ASC 848-10-35-1)

Transfers of HTM debt securities are recognized as of the date the entity makes the transfer decision and are measured under the guidance on debt and equity security investments in ASC 320-10-35-10 through 35-16, requiring the entity to measure the transferred security at fair value. The sale or transfer of HTM debt securities will not have any effect on the entity's assertion regarding its intent and ability to hold the remaining HTM debt securities. (ASC 848-10-345-2)

ASC 848-20, *Contract Modifications*

Scope and Scope Exceptions The guidance in ASC 848-20 applies only to a contract modification whose terms:

- Directly replace LIBOR or a reference rate that is expected to be discontinued as a result of reference rate reform.
- Modify contract terms that change or have the potential to change the amount or timing of contractual cash flows, and is related to the replacement of LIBOR or another reference rate that is expected to be discontinued as a result of reference rate reforms.
(ASC 848-20-15-2)

If a term is modified that changes or has the potential to change contractual cash flow, but is *unrelated* to reference rate reform, the guidance in ASC 848-20 does *not* apply. (ASC 848-20-15-3) An entity may adopt the guidance in this Subtopic even if contract modifications do not change the amount or timing of contractual cash flows, as long as they are made contemporaneously with modifications related to reference rate reform. (ASC 848-20-15-4)

The Codification offers examples of contract modifications that are considered either related or unrelated to reference rate reform.

- Examples of changes to terms that are related to the replacement of a reference rate:
  - Changes to the referenced interest rate index (for example, a change from London Interbank Offered Rate [LIBOR] to another interest rate index)

- ◦ Addition of or changes to a spread adjustment
- ◦ Changes to the reset period, reset dates, day-count conventions, business-day conventions, payment dates, payment frequency, and repricing calculation
- ◦ Changes to the strike price of an existing interest rate option (including an embedded interest rate option)
- ◦ Addition of an interest rate floor or cap that is out of the money on the basis of the spot rate at the time of the amendment of the contract
- ◦ Addition of a prepayment option for which exercise is contingent upon the replacement reference interest rate index not being determinable in accordance with the terms of the agreement
- ◦ Addition of or changes to contractual fallback terms that are consistent with fallback terms developed by a regulator or by a private-sector working group convened by a regulator
- ◦ Changes to terms (including those in the examples in paragraph 848-20-15-6) that are necessary to comply with laws or regulations or to align with market conventions for the replacement rate

(ASC 848-20-15-5)

Examples of changes to terms that are generally *unrelated* to the replacement of a reference rate in accordance with paragraph 848-20-15-3 include the following:

- Changes to the notional amount or maturity date
- Changes from a referenced interest rate index to a stated fixed rate
- Changes to the loan structure (for example, changing a term loan to a revolver loan)
- The addition of an underlying or variable unrelated to the referenced rate index (for example, addition of payments that are indexed to the price of gold)
- The addition of an interest rate floor or cap that is in the money on the basis of the spot rate at the time of the amendment of the contract
- A concession granted to a debtor experiencing financial difficulty
- The addition or removal of a prepayment or conversion option except for the addition of a prepayment option for which exercise is contingent upon the replacement reference interest rate index not being determinable in accordance with the terms of the agreement.
- The addition or removal of a feature that is intended to provide leverage
- Changes to the counterparty except in accordance with paragraphs 815-20-55-56A, 815-25-40-1A, and 815-30-40-1A
- Changes to the priority or seniority of an obligation in the event of a default or a liquidation event
- The addition or termination of a right to use one or more underlying assets in a lease contract
- Changes to renewal, termination, or purchase option provisions in a lease contract

(ASC 848-20-15-6)

When modifying a contract, an entity might add or amend contractual fallback terms. If the new fallback terms are consistent with those developed by a regulator or by a private-sector working group convened by a regulator, then the addition or amendment of the fallback terms is presumed to be related to reference rate reform. (ASC 848-20-15-7) If the fallback terms added are inconsistent with those developed by a regulator or by a private-sector group convened by a regulator, then an entity should assess whether the new terms include, or have the potential to include, a term that is unrelated to reference rate reform in determining whether the modification is within the scope of ASC 848. (ASC 858-20-15-8)

A contract modification that directly replaces a reference rate index with a stated fixed rate is unrelated to reference rate reform. However, a replacement rate that is equal to the last published rate of a discontinued interest-rate index is not considered a stated fixed rate (that is, the replacement can be considered related to reference rate reform). (ASC 848-20-15-9)

Subsequent Measurement The election to apply the guidance in ASC 848-20 to contract modifications should be applied to all contract modifications that are accounted for within the scope of an ASC Topic or Industry Subtopic. For example:

- If an entity elects to account for modifications to lease contracts within the scope of ASC 842, *Leases* (ASC 840 prior to the adoption of ASU 2016-02) in accordance with ASC 848-20, then all lease contract modifications within the scope of ASC 848-20 will be subject to the guidance in ASC 848-20.
- If an insurance entity applies the guidance in this Subtopic to modifications of a contract accounted for in accordance with Topic 310 on receivables, it shall apply the guidance in this Subtopic to all modifications of contracts accounted for in accordance with Industry Subtopic 944-310 that meet the scope of paragraphs 848-20-15-2 through 15-3. The entity does not need to apply the guidance in this Subtopic to contracts within the scope of other Industry Subtopics of Topic 944 that meet the scope of paragraphs 848-20-15-2 through 15-3.
(ASC 848-20-35-1)

ASC 828-20 provides optional expedients for accounting for modifications of contracts accounted for in accordance with the following Topics that meet the scope of paragraphs 848-20-15-2 through 15-3:

- ASC 310 on receivables
- ASC 470 on debt
- ASC 840 or 842 on leases

Following is a summary of expedients under ASC 848 arranged by Codification topics.

- ASC 310, Receivables
If the entity elects the optional expedient, the entity treats the modification as minor in accordance with ASC 310- 20-35-10 and the effective interest rate is adjusted prospectively. (ASC 848-20-35-6)
- ASC 470, *Debt*
If the entity elects the optional expedient, the entity treats the modification as not substantial and it is accounted for prospectively by adjusting the effective interest rate in accordance with ASC 470-50.
(ASC 848-20-35-8)
- ASC 842 and ASC 840, *Leases*
The modification does not require lessees or lessors to reassess lease classification and the discount rate, to remeasure lease payments, or to make other reassessments or remeasurements that are required for a contract modification that is not accounted for as a separate contract. The lease is accounted for as a continuation of the existing lease.
(ASC 848-20-35-11)

Following is a summary of potential outcomes of applying ASC 848-20-35-4 to contract modifications that meet the scope of ASC 848-20-15-2 and 15-3, but are not within the scope of ASC 848-20-35-4.

- ASC 815-15, *Derivatives and Hedging: Embedded Derivatives*
  The modification does not require entities to reassess the original conclusion about whether the contract contains an embedded derivative that is clearly and closely related to the economic characteristics and risks of the host contract under ASC 815-15-25-1(a). (ASC 848-20-35-14)
- ASC 815-10, *Derivatives*
  The modification does not require entities to reassess whether the modified instrument is a hybrid instrument and whether it includes a financing element under the guidance in ASC 815-10-45-11 through 45-15. The modified instrument continues to be accounted for and presented in the same manner as the instrument before modification.
- ASC 944, *Financial Services*
  The modification does not require entities to reassess whether the insurance contract is substantially unchanged in accordance with ASC 944-30. The post-modification contract continues to be accounted for and presented in the same manner as the pre-modification contract.
- ASC 606, *Revenue from Contracts with Customers*
  The modification does not require entities to reassess the contract under modification guidance in ASC 606-10-25-10 through 25-13. The change in cash flows resulting from variability in the new reference rate is accounted for in the same manner as the variability that resulted from the original reference rate.
- ASC 810, *Consolidation*
  The modification is not a reconsideration event and, therefore, does not require a reporting entity to reconsider whether the counterparty to the contract is a variable-interest entity. (ASC 848-20-55-2)

ASC 848-30, *Hedging*

ASC 848-30 allows the following optional expedients for different types of hedging relationships, which entities will generally elect on a hedge-by-hedge basis:

- For all types of hedging relationships (that is, fair value hedges, cash flow hedges, and net investment hedges):
  - The hedging relationship may continue without dedesignation of the hedging relationship if changes to the contractual terms of the hedging instrument, the hedged item, or the forecasted transaction are made due to reference rate reform.
  - If a component that is affected by reference rate reform is excluded from the assessment of hedge effectiveness, the entity can change the systematic and rational method used to recognize the excluded component in earnings. In addition, if the changes to a hedging instrument's contractual terms change the fair value of the excluded component, that change in fair value may be recognized in current earnings in the same income statement line item used to present the earnings' effect of the hedged item.

  (ASC 848-30-25-12 and 25-13)

- For a cash flow hedge:
  - An entity may change to the method of assessing hedge effectiveness documented at hedge inception. This would not require dedesignation of the hedging relationship if both:
    - The hedging instrument, hedged item, or hedged transaction references LIBOR or another rate that is expected to be discontinued, and
    - The new method designated for assessing hedge effectiveness is an optional expedient specified in ASC 848-50.

  (ASC 848-30-25-8)
- For a fair value hedge: If the entity makes a change to either the proportion of a designated hedging instrument or the proportion of the hedged item, the entity would not be required to dedesignate of the hedging relationship.
  (ASC 848-30-25-9a)
- For fair value and cash flow hedges: A change to the designated hedging instrument to combine and jointly designate two or more derivative instruments or proportions of those instruments in a hedging relationship would not require dedesignation of the hedging relationship.
  (ASC 848-30-25-9b)

ASC 848-40, *Fair Value Hedges*

ASC 848-40 allows the following optional expedients, which can be individually elected on a hedge-by-hedge basis. (ASC 848-40-25-1)

- A change to the designated benchmark interest rate that is expected to be impacted by the reference rate reform to a different eligible benchmark interest rate under ASC 815-20 would not require dedesignation of the hedging relationship if the hedge is expected to be highly effective. The guidance permits an entity to apply a method to change the designated benchmark interest rate that either adjusts the hedged item's cumulative fair value hedge-basis adjustment or maintains the cumulative basis adjustment. If the approach elected results in a change to the cumulative fair value hedge-basis adjustment, that change should be recognized in current earnings in the same income statement line item where the hedged item's effect on earnings is presented. The method applied to change the designated benchmark interest rate should be applied consistently across similar fair value hedging relationships.
- Entities that apply fair value hedge accounting using the shortcut method for assessing hedge effectiveness may disregard certain conditions for applying the shortcut method in determining whether a hedge continues to qualify for the shortcut method when certain changes are made to the contractual terms of the hedging instrument.

ASC 848-50, *Cash Flow Hedges*

ASC 848-50 permits the following optional expedients, which can be individually elected on a hedge-by-hedge basis for cash flow hedging relationships if the hedging instrument or hedged item includes a rate that is expected to be discontinued due to reference rate reform:

- Entities may disregard changes in the designated hedged interest rate risk when assessing whether the hedged forecasted transaction is probable, and may continue to apply hedge accounting if either the hedge remains highly effective or the entity elects to apply an optional expedient to subsequently assess hedge effectiveness under ASC 848-50-35.

- Entities may disregard certain conditions for (1) determining whether a cash flow hedge qualifies for the shortcut method to assess hedge effectiveness, (2) applying the simplified hedge accounting approach for eligible private companies, and (3) determining the presumption of perfect effectiveness in applying the change-in-variable-cash-flows method and the hypothetical derivative method.
- Entities may make certain adjustments to the quantitative methods of assessing hedge effectiveness described in ASC 815-30-35-10 through 35-32.
- An entity may make certain adjustments to the critical terms of a perfectly effective hypothetical hedging instrument to match the hedging instrument when assessing effectiveness based on an option's terminal value in accordance with ASC 815-20-25-126.
- For cash flow hedges of portfolios of forecasted transactions, an entity may disregard the requirement that the group of individual transactions must share the same risk exposure for which they are designated as being hedged.

59 ASC 850 RELATED-PARTY DISCLOSURES

PERSPECTIVE AND ISSUES

Subtopic

ASC 850 contains one subtopic:

- ASC 850-10, *Overall*, which sets forth the disclosure requirements, certain significant related party transactions, and control relationships

Scope

ASC 850 applies to all entities.

DEFINITIONS OF TERMS

Source: ASC 850-20. Also see Appendix A, *Definitions of Terms*, for another term related to this topic: Related Parties.

Affiliate. A party that, directly or indirectly through one or more intermediaries, controls, is controlled by, or is under common control with an entity.

Control. The possession, direct or indirect, of the power to direct or cause the direction of the management and policies of an entity through ownership, by contract, or otherwise.

Immediate Family. Family members who might control or influence a principal owner or a member of management, or who might be controlled or influenced by a principal owner or a member of management, because of the family relationship.

Management. Persons who are responsible for achieving the objectives of the entity and who have the authority to establish policies and make decisions by which those objectives are to be pursued. Management normally includes members of the board of directors, the chief executive officer, chief operating officer, vice presidents in charge of principal business functions (such as sales, administration, or finance), and other persons who perform similar policy-making functions. Persons without formal titles also may be members of management.

Principal Owners. Owners of record or known beneficial owners of more than 10% of the voting interests of the entity.

CONCEPTS, RULES, AND EXAMPLES

Disclosures

According to ASC 850, *Related-Party Disclosures*, financial statements are required to disclose material related-party transactions other than compensation arrangements, expense allowances, or other similar items that occur in the ordinary course of business.

A related party is essentially any party that controls or can significantly influence the management or operating policies of the company to the extent that the company may be prevented from fully pursuing its own interests. Related parties include affiliates, investees accounted for by the equity method, trusts for the benefit of employees, principal owners, management, and immediate family members of owners or management.

Transactions with related parties must be disclosed even if there is no accounting recognition made for such transactions (e.g., a service is performed without payment). Disclosures are not permitted to assert that the terms of related-party transactions were essentially equivalent to arm's-length dealings unless those claims can be substantiated. If the financial position or results of operations of the reporting entity could change significantly because of common control or common management, disclosure of the nature of the ownership or management control is required, even if there were no transactions between the entities.

The disclosures include:

1. The nature of the relationship
2. A description of transactions and the effects of those transactions reflected in the financial statements for each period for which an income statement is presented
3. The dollar amount of transactions for each period for which an income statement is presented and the effects of any change in the terms of such transactions as compared to the terms used in prior periods
4. Amounts due to and from related parties as of the date of each statement of financial position presented, together with the terms and manner of settlement.

See Appendix B, Disclosure and Presentation Checklist for Commercial Businesses. (www.wiley.com/go/GAAP2021).

60 ASC 852 REORGANIZATIONS

PERSPECTIVE AND ISSUES

Subtopics

ASC 852, *Reorganizations*, contains two subtopics:

- ASC 852-10, *Overall*, which provides guidance for entities that have filed petitions in the Bankruptcy Court and expect to reorganize under Chapter 11
- ASC 852-20, *Quasi-Reorganizations*

Scope and Scope Exceptions

ASC 852-10 applies to all entities except governmental organizations but does *not* apply to debt restructurings outside of Chapter 11 and reorganizations consisting of liquidation or adoption of plans of liquidation under the Bankruptcy Code.

ASC 852-20 applies only to "readjustments in which the current income, or retained earnings or accumulated deficit account, or the income account of future years is relieved of charges that would otherwise be made against it." (ASC 852-20-15-2) Further, it does not apply to:

a. "Quasi-reorganizations involving only deficit reclassifications
b. Charges against additional paid-in capital in other types of readjustments such as readjustments for the purpose of correcting erroneous credits made to additional paid-in capital in the past
c. Financial reporting for entities that enter and intend to emerge from Chapter 11 reorganization, at the time of such reorganization."
(ASC 852-20-15-3)

Overview

Entities expected to reorganize as going concerns under Chapter 11 of the Bankruptcy Code employ so-called fresh start accounting if:

1. The "reorganization value of the assets of the emerging entity immediately before the date of confirmation is less than the total of all postpetition liabilities and allowed claims, and

2. Holders of existing voting shares immediately before confirmation receive less than 50 percent of the voting shares of the emerging entity."
   (ASC 852-10-45-19)

DEFINITIONS OF TERMS

Source: 851-10-20

Bankruptcy Code. A federal statute, enacted October 1, 1979, as title 11 of the United States Code by the Bankruptcy Reform Act of 1978, that applies to all cases filed on or after its enactment and that provides the basis for the current federal bankruptcy system.

Bankruptcy Court. The United States Bankruptcy Court is an adjunct of the United States District Courts. Under the jurisdiction of the District Court, the Bankruptcy Court is generally responsible for cases filed under Chapters 7, 11, 12, and 13 of the Bankruptcy Code.

Chapter 7. A liquidation, voluntarily or involuntarily initiated under the provisions of the Bankruptcy Code, that provides for liquidation of the business or the debtor's estate.

Chapter 11. A reorganization action, either voluntarily or involuntarily initiated under the provisions of the Bankruptcy Code, that provides for a reorganization of the debt and equity structure of the business and allows the business to continue operations. A debtor may also file a plan of liquidation under Chapter 11.

Emerging Entity. An entity (sometimes referred to as the reorganized entity), that has had its plan confirmed and begins to operate as a new entity.

Petition. A document filed in a court of bankruptcy, initiating proceedings under the Bankruptcy Code.

Plan of Reorganization. An agreement formulated in Chapter 11 proceedings under the supervision of the Bankruptcy Court that enables the debtor to continue in business. The plan, once confirmed, may affect the rights of undersecured creditors, secured creditors, and stockholders as well as those of unsecured creditors. Before a plan is confirmed by the Bankruptcy Court, it must comply with general provisions of the Bankruptcy Code. Those provisions mandate, for example, that the plan is feasible, the plan is in the best interest of the creditors, and, if an impaired class does not accept the plan, the plan must be determined to be fair and equitable before it can be confirmed.

Reorganization Items. Items of income, expense, gain, or loss that are realized or incurred by an entity because it is in reorganization.

Reorganization Proceeding. A Chapter 11 case from the time at which the petition is filed until the plan is confirmed.

Reorganization Value. The value attributed to the reconstituted entity, as well as the expected net realizable value of those assets that will be disposed of before reconstitution occurs. Therefore, this value is viewed as the value of the entity before considering liabilities and approximates the amount a willing buyer would pay for the assets of the entity immediately after the restructuring.

Trustee. A person appointed by the Bankruptcy Court in certain situations based on the facts of the case, not related to the size of the entity or the amount of unsecured debt outstanding, at the request of a party in interest after a notice and hearing.

CONCEPTS, RULES, AND EXAMPLES

Corporate Bankruptcy and Reorganizations

Entities Operating under and Emerging from Protection of the Bankruptcy Laws The going concern assumption is one of the basic postulates underlying generally accepted accounting principles and is responsible for, among other things, the historical cost convention in financial reporting. For entities that have entered bankruptcy proceedings, however, the going concern assumption is no longer of central importance.

ASC 852 provides financial reporting standards for entities undergoing and emerging from reorganization under the bankruptcy laws. Under its provisions, assets are presented at estimated realizable values. Liabilities are set forth at the estimated amounts to be allowed in the statement of financial position, and liabilities subject to compromise are distinguished from those that are not. Furthermore, the Codification requires that in both the statements of income and cash flows, normal transactions be differentiated from those that have occurred as a consequence of the entity's being in reorganization. While certain allocations to the latter category are rather obvious, such as legal and accounting fees incurred, others are less clear. For example, the Codification suggests that if the entity in reorganization earns interest income on funds that would normally have been used to settle obligations owed to creditors, such income will be deemed to be income arising as a consequence of the bankruptcy action.

Another interesting aspect of ASC 852 is the accounting for the emergence from reorganization (known as confirmation of the plan of reorganization). The ASC provides for "fresh start" financial reporting in such instances. This accounting is similar to that applied in acquisitions, with the total confirmed value of the entity upon its emergence from reorganization being analogous to the purchase price in an acquisition. In both cases, this total value is allocated to the identifiable assets and liabilities of the entity, with any excess being allocated to goodwill. In the case of entities emerging from bankruptcy, goodwill (called reorganization value in excess of amounts allocable to identifiable assets) is measured as the excess of liabilities existing at the plan confirmation date, computed at present value of future amounts to be paid, over the reorganization value of assets. Reorganization value is calculated with reference to a number of factors, including forecasted operating results and cash flows of the new entity.

ASC 852 applies *only* to entities undergoing formal reorganization under the Bankruptcy Code. Less formal procedures may still be accounted for under quasi-reorganization accounting procedures.

Quasi-Reorganizations

Generally, this procedure is applicable during a period of declining price levels. It is termed "quasi" since the accumulated deficit is eliminated at a lower cost and with less difficulty than a legal reorganization.

Per ASC 852-20, the procedures in a quasi-reorganization involve the:

1. Proper authorization from stockholders and creditors where required
2. Revaluation of assets to their current values: all losses are charged to retained earnings, thus increasing any deficit
3. Elimination of any deficit by charging paid-in capital:

a. First, additional paid-in capital to the extent it exists.
b. Second, capital stock when additional paid-in capital is insufficient: the par value of the stock is reduced, creating the extra additional paid-in capital to which the remaining deficit is charged.

(ASC 852-20-25-4)

No retained earnings may be created by a reorganization. Any excess created by the reduction of par value is credited to "Paid-in capital from quasi-reorganization."

ASC 852-20-10-2 requires that retained earnings be titled for ten years (less than ten years may be justified under exceptional circumstances) after a quasi-reorganization takes place. A title similar to "since quasi-reorganization of June 30, 20XX" is appropriate.

61 ASC 853 SERVICE CONCESSION ARRANGEMENTS

PERSPECTIVE AND ISSUES

Subtopic

ASC 853, *Service Concession Arrangements*, contains one subtopic:

- ASC 853-10, *Overall*, which addresses the accounting for service concession arrangements between a public sector entity grantor and an operating entity where the operating entity operates the grantor's infrastructure

Scope

ASC 853 applies to the accounting:

- By operating entities
  - Of a service concession arrangement
  - Under which a public-sector entity grantor enters into a contract with an operating entity
  - To operate the grantor's infrastructure

The operating entity also may provide the construction, upgrading, or maintenance services of the grantor's infrastructure. (ASC 853-10-15-2)

It is important to note that a service concession arrangement within the scope of ASC 853 must meet *both* of the following conditions:

a. The grantor controls or has the ability to modify or approve the services that the operating entity must provide with the infrastructure, to whom it must provide them, and at what price.
b. The grantor controls, through ownership, beneficial entitlement, or otherwise, any residual interest in the infrastructure at the end of the term of the arrangement.
(ASC 853-10-15-3)

Scope Exception A service concession arrangement meeting the scope criteria in Topic 980 on regulated operations should apply the guidance in Topic 980.

Overview

ASC 853 addresses a narrow issue and limits the scope of the guidance to arrangements in which the grantor is a public-sector entity.

DEFINITIONS OF TERMS

See Appendix A, *Definitions of Terms*, for terms relevant to this topic: Not-for-Profit Entity, Public Business Entity

CONCEPTS, RULES, AND EXAMPLES

Accounting for Service Concession Arrangements

The topic has two main provisions:

- Service concession arrangements in scope are accounted for in accordance with ASC 606 to recognize revenue on construction, upgrade, or operation services. The grantor is the customer for ASC 853 service concession arrangements. Operating entities should look to other Topics to account for other aspects of service concession arrangements. (ASC 853- 20-25-1)
- The infrastructure involved in the arrangements should not be recognized as the operating entity's property, plant, and equipment. Service concession arrangements within the scope of ASC 853 are not within the scope of ASC 840 or ASC 842. (ASC 853-10-25-2)

Service Concession Arrangements The infrastructure that an entity operates may be airports, roads, bridges, hospitals, prisons, and so forth. The operating entity may also provide construction or maintenance services to the grantor's infrastructure. A key feature of a service concession arrangement is that it is generally for the public good. The operator usually receives payment for the services performed over a specified time. The operator may have the right to charge users of the infrastructure. The arrangement may include unconditional guarantees for guaranteed minimum payments.

Economic Substance The grantor controls or has the ability to modify or approve the services provided and the price charged for the service. The grantor controls any residual interest in the infrastructure at the end of the term. This control is important in deciding the economic substance of the transaction and the reason why it is not appropriate for the operating entity to recognize a lease or property, plant, and equipment. (ASC 853-10-05-01 and 05-02)

62 ASC 855 SUBSEQUENT EVENTS

PERSPECTIVE AND ISSUES

Subtopic

ASC 855, *Subsequent Events*, consists of one subtopic:

- ASC 855-10, *Overall*, which provides guidance for events or transactions occurring after the balance sheet date

Scope and Scope Exceptions

ASC 855 applies to all entities and all transactions except for those covered in other Codification Topics.

Overview

ASC 855 describes the circumstances under which an entity should recognize events or transactions in its financial statements that occur subsequent to the balance sheet date, but before the financial statements are available to be issued. This can have a potentially significant impact on loss contingencies.

DEFINITIONS OF TERMS

Source: ASC 855-20. See Appendix A, *Definitions of Terms*, for other terms related to this topic: Conduit Debt Securities, Financial Statements Are Available to Be Issued, Financial Statements Are Issued, and (SEC) Filers.

Revised Financial Statements. Financial statements revised only for either of the following conditions:

a. Correction of an error
b. Retrospective application of U.S. GAAP

Subsequent Events. Events or transactions that occur after the balance sheet date but before financial statements are issued or are available to be issued. There are two types of subsequent events:

a. The first type consists of events or transactions that provide additional evidence about conditions that existed at the date of the balance sheet, including the estimates inherent in the process of preparing financial statements (that is, recognized subsequent events).
b. The second type consists of events that provide evidence about conditions that did not exist at the date of the balance sheet but arose subsequent to that date (that is, nonrecognized subsequent events).

CONCEPTS, RULES, AND EXAMPLES

Types of Subsequent Events

The statement of financial position is dated as of the last day of the fiscal period, but a period of time usually elapses before the financial statements are issued. During this period, significant events or transactions may have occurred that materially affect the company's financial position. These events and transactions are called subsequent events. The omission of disclosure of significant events occurring between the date of the statement of financial position and issuance date of the financial statements could mislead the reader who is otherwise unaware of those events.

SEC filers and conduit bond obligors for conduit debt securities traded in a public market are required to evaluate subsequent events through the date the financial statements are issued. All other entities must evaluate subsequent events through the date the financial statements are *available* to be issued. (ASC 855-10-25-1A and 25-2)

There are two types of subsequent events, which relate to when the event or transaction occurred and determine the accounting treatment:

1. *Existing conditions.* Additional evidence may arise about a condition that existed as of the balance sheet date. If so, recognize these changes within the financial statements.
2. *Subsequent events.* Evidence may arise about conditions that did not exist as of the balance sheet date, but which occurred later. Entities should not recognize these changes within the financial statements.

The following table presents a variety of sample situations occurring after the balance sheet date but before the financial statements are available to be issued, and that apply to these two types of subsequent events:

Event	*Accounting Treatment*
Litigation is settled for an amount different from the recorded liability	(1)
Loss of assets due to a natural disaster	(2)
Changes in estimated credit losses on receivables from conditions arising after the balance sheet date	(2)
Changes in the fair value of assets or liabilities	(2)
Issuing significant guarantees	(2)
(ASC 855-10-55-1 and 55-2)	

1. *Recognize within the financial statements if they are not yet available to be issued.*
2. *Do not recognize until the next reporting period.*

Presentation and Disclosure The *Disclosure and Presentation Checklist for Commercial Businesses* at www.wiley.com/go/GAAP2021 contains ASC 855 presentation and disclosure requirements.

63 ASC 860 TRANSFERS AND SERVICING

PERSPECTIVE AND ISSUES

Subtopics

ASC 860 contains four subtopics:

- ASC 860-10, *Overall*, which together with the other three Subtopics provides guidance on transfers and servicing of financial assets and transfers of servicing rights.
- ASC 860-20, *Sales of Financial Assets*, provides guidance on a transfer that satisfies the conditions for a sale and if a transferor regains control of assets previously sold.
- ASC 860-30, *Secured Borrowings and Collateral*, provides guidance for secured borrowings with a transfer of collateral.
- ASC 860-50, *Servicing Assets and Liabilities*, provides guidance for servicing assets and for servicing liabilities.
  (ASC 860-10-05-2)

Scope and Scope Exceptions

ASC 860 applies to all entities and to transfers and servicing of noncash financial assets. A transfer includes:

- Selling a receivable,
- Transferring a receivable to a trust, or
- Using a receivable as security for a loan.

A transfer does *not* include:

- The origination of a receivable,
- The settlement of a receivable, or
- The restructuring of a receivable in a troubled debt restructuring.
  (ASC 860-10-15-2 and 20-20)

Those transactions are transfers involving the issuer of the receivable.
Among the types of transfers of financial assets for which ASC 860 provides guidance are:

- All loan participations
- Transfers of equity method and cost-method investments (ASC 860-10-55-3)
- Financial instruments
- Financial assets
- Collateral
- Transfers of receivables with recourse (factoring with recourse)
- Transfers of options to repurchase individual financial assets
- Transfers of receivables with servicing retained
- Transfers of lease receivables under sales-type and direct financing leases
- Putting a receivable into a securitization trust
- Repurchase agreements
- Dollar rolls
- Securities lending transactions
- Posting a receivable as collateral
- Banker's acceptances
  (ASC 860-10-55-43)

ASC 860-10-15-4 *excludes* the following items from the scope of ASC 860:

- Except for transfers of servicing assets (see ASC 860-50-40) and for the transfers noted in the following paragraph, transfers of nonfinancial assets
- Transfers of unrecognized financial assets, for example, lease payments to be received under operating leases
- Transfers of custody of financial assets for safekeeping
- Contributions
- Transfers of in substance nonfinancial assets
- Investments by owners or distributions to owners of a business entity
- Employee benefits subject to the provisions of ASC 712
- Leveraged leases subject to ASC 840 (ASC 842 upon implementation)
- Money-over-money and wrap-lease transactions involving nonrecourse debt subject to ASC 840 (ASC 842 upon implementation)

The guidance in ASC 860-30 applies to transactions in which cash is obtained in exchange for financial assets with an obligation for an opposite exchange later, such as repurchase agreements, dollar rolls, and securities lending transactions. (ASC 860-30-15-3)

The guidance in ASC 860-50 applies to transactions:

- In which servicing assets are obtained and servicing liabilities are incurred, including transactions in which loans are transferred and servicing retained by the transferor, and in which servicing assets are transferred with loans retained by the transferor.
(ASC 860-50-15-3)

Overview

Transfers with continuing involvement raise questions about whether the assets have been sold or remain as assets. (ASC 860-10-05-4) ASC 860 describes the proper accounting for sales of financial assets to third parties and the use of financial assets as collateral in secured borrowings. Importantly, ASC 860 sets forth the guidelines for a transferor to derecognize transfers from the transferor's statement of financial position. This chapter also includes ASC 860's standards for repurchase agreements and securities lending. Although those two types of transfers usually involve investments, the guidance is contained in ASC 860 because the same underlying theory—the financial components approach—is used for those transactions as is used for transfers involving receivables.

Transfers of financial assets may involve a sale or a transfer where the transferor has some continuing involvement with the transferred financial assets. Arrangements where the transferor has continuing involvement include:

- Servicing arrangements, such as resource and guarantee arrangements
- Agreements to purchase or redeem transferred financial assets
- Options written or held
- Pledges of collateral
- The transferor's beneficial interest in the transferred financial asset
(ASC 860-10-05-4)

ASC 860 covers:

- Securitizations
- Factoring

- Transfers of receivables with recourse
- Securities lending transactions
- Repurchase agreements
- Loan participations
- Banker's acceptances
  (ASC 860-10-05-6)

DEFINITIONS OF TERMS

Source: ASC 860 and Master Glossary. Also see Appendix A, *Definitions of Terms*, for additional terms relevant to this topic: Affiliate, Beneficial Interests, Derivative Financial Instrument, Financial Asset (Def. 2), Financial Instrument, Financial Liability, In-substance Nonfinancial Asset, Loan Originations Fees, Not-for-Profit Entity, Public Business Entity, Recourse, Remote, and Repurchase Agreement.

Agent. A party that acts for and on behalf of another party. For example, a third-party intermediary is an agent of the transferor if it acts on behalf of the transferor.

Bankruptcy-Remote Entity. An entity that is designed to make remote the possibility that it would enter bankruptcy or other receivership.

Collateral. Personal or real property in which a security interest has been given.

Consolidated Affiliate. An entity whose assets and liabilities are included in the consolidated, combined, or other financial statements being presented.

Continuing Involvement. Any involvement with the transferred financial asset that permits the transferor to receive cash flows or other benefits that arise from the transferred financial assets or that obligates the transferor to provide additional cash flows or other assets to any party related to the transfer.

Derecognize. Remove previously recognized assets or liabilities from the statement of financial position.

Fixed Participation Method. Liquidation method used to allocate principal payments on the receivables in a trust to the investors, under which all principal payments on the receivables in the trust are allocated to the investors based on their respective participation interests in the credit card receivables in the trust at the end of the reinvestment period.

Floating Participation Method. Liquidation method used to allocate principal payments on the receivables in a trust to the investors, under which principal payments allocated to the investors are based on the investors' actual participation interests in the receivables in the trust each month. Each month, investors' participation interests in the credit card receivables in the trust are redetermined for that month's allocation of principal payments.

Freestanding Call Option. A call option that is neither embedded in nor attached to an asset subject to that call option.

Liquidation Method. The method used to allocate the principal payments on the receivables in a trust to the investors.

Loan Participation. A transaction in which a single lender makes a large loan to a borrower and subsequently transfers undivided interest in the loan to groups of banks or other entities.

Loan Syndication. A transaction in which several lenders share in lending to a single borrower. Each lender loans a specific amount to the borrower and has the right to repayment from the borrower. It is common for groups of lenders to jointly fund those loans when the amount borrowed is greater than any one lender is willing to lend.

Money-over-Money Lease. A transaction in which an entity manufactures or purchases an asset, leases the asset to a lessee, and obtains nonrecourse financing in excess of the asset's cost using the leased asset and the future lease rental as collateral.

Participating Interest. From the date of the transfer, it represents a proportionate (pro rata) ownership interest in an entire financial asset. The percentage of ownership interests held by the transferor in the entire financial asset may vary over time, while the entire financial asset remains outstanding as long as the resulting portions held by the transferor (including any participating interest retained by the transferor, its consolidated affiliates included in the financial statements being presented, or its agents) and the transferee(s) meet the other characteristics of a participating interest. For example, if the transferor's interest in an entire financial asset changes because it subsequently sells another interest in the entire financial asset, the interest held initially and subsequently by the transferor must meet the definition of the participating interest.

Repurchase Financing. A repurchase agreement that relates to a previously transferred financial asset between the same counterparties (or consolidated affiliates of either counterparty) that is entered into contemporaneously with, or in contemplation of, the initial transfer.

Repurchase-to-Maturity Transaction. A repurchase agreement in which the settlement date of the agreement to repurchase a transferred financial asset is at the maturity date of that financial asset and the agreement would not require the transferor to reacquire the financial asset.

Revolving-Period Securitizations. Securitizations in which receivables are transferred at the inception and also periodically (daily or monthly) thereafter for a defined period (commonly three to eight years), referred to as the revolving period. During the revolving period, the special-purpose entity uses most of the cash collections to purchase additional receivables from the transferor on prearranged terms.

Securitization. The process by which financial assets are transformed into securities.

Seller. A transferor that relinquishes control over financial assets by transferring them to a transferee in exchange for consideration.

Setoff Right. A common law right of a party that is both a debtor and a creditor to the same counterparty to reduce its obligation to that counterparty if that counterparty fails to pay its obligation.

Standard Representations and Warranties. Representations and warranties that assert the financial asset being transferred is what it is purported to be at the transfer date.

Transfer. The conveyance of a noncash financial asset by and to someone other than the issuer of that financial asset.

A transfer includes the following:

- Selling a receivable
- Putting a receivable into a securitization
- Posting a receivable as collateral

A transfer excludes the following:

- The origination of a receivable
- Settlement of a receivable
- The restructuring of a receivable into a security in a troubled debt restructuring

Transferee. An entity that receives a financial asset, and interest in a financial asset, or a group of financial assets from a transferor.

Transferor. An entity that transfers a financial asset, and interest in a financial asset, or a group of financial assets that it controls to another entity.

Transferred Financial Assets. Transfers of any of the following:

- An entire financial asset
- A group of entire financial assets
- Participating interest in an entire financial asset

Unilateral Ability. A capacity for action not dependent on the actions (or failure to act) of any other party.

CONCEPTS, RULES, AND EXAMPLES

ASC 860-10, *Overall*

If receivables or other financial assets are transferred to another entity and the transferor has no continuing involvement with the transferred assets or with the transferee, it is clear that:

- A sale has taken place,
- The asset should be derecognized, and
- A gain or loss on the sale is to be measured and recognized.

However, in some situations, the transferor may have some form of continuing involvement with the transferred assets. It may:

- Sell the receivables with recourse for uncollectible amounts,
- Retain an interest in the receivables, or
- Agree to service the receivables after the sale.

The more control that the transferor retains over the receivables, the more the transfer appears to be in substance a secured borrowing rather than a sale. ASC 860 establishes the criteria and procedures used to determine whether a transfer of financial assets is a sale or a secured borrowing.

In a sale or other transfer, financial assets and liabilities may be disaggregated into components, which become separate assets and liabilities. (ASC 860-10-05-5) ASC 860 uses a financial components approach in which a single financial asset is viewed as a mix of component assets (controlled economic benefits) and component liabilities (obligations for probable future sacrifices of economic benefits). The focus is on who controls the components, and, therefore, the economic benefits of the asset, and whether that control has changed as a result of a given transfer:

- If the transferor has surrendered control of the transferred assets, the transfer is a sale, and the assets should be derecognized.
- If the transferor retains control of the transferred assets, the transfer is a secured borrowing, with the asset pledged as collateral to secure an obligation of the transferor, and derecognition is not appropriate.

Derecognition of financial liabilities by a debtor can be properly reflected only if the obligation is extinguished, which requires that either:

- The debt is retired (paid off) or
- The debtor is legally released from being the primary obligor by either the counterparty or by judicial action (e.g., in bankruptcy proceedings).

Transferors and transferees should use symmetrical reporting, that is, account for transfers of financial assets in a similar way.

The conditions for sale, transfer, and derecognition are discussed in the following sections.

Conditions for a Sale of a Financial Asset A transfer of financial assets (or a component of a financial asset) is recognized as a sale if the transferor surrenders control over those assets in exchange for consideration. The conditions for accounting as a sale a transfer of an entire financial asset, a group of entire financial assets, or a participating interest in an entire financial asset where control has been surrendered are described in ASC 860-10-40-5:

a. *Isolation of transferred financial assets.* The financial assets transferred are beyond the reach of the transferor and its affiliates, its creditors, potential bankruptcy trustees, or other receivers. This is achieved only if the transferred financial assets would be beyond the reach of the powers of a bankruptcy trustee or other receiver for the transferor or any of its consolidated affiliates included in the financial statements being presented. For multiple-step transfers, an entity that is designed to make remote the possibility that it would enter bankruptcy or other receivership (the "bankruptcy-remote entity") is not considered a consolidated affiliate for purposes of performing the isolation analysis. Notwithstanding the isolation analysis, each entity involved in the transfer is subject to the applicable GAAP guidance on whether it must be consolidated.
b. *Pledge or exchange rights.* This condition is met if:
    - Each transferee (or—if the transferee is an entity whose sole purpose is to engage in securitization or asset-backed financing activities, and if it is constrained from pledging or exchanging the assets it receives—each third-party holder of its beneficial interests) has the right to pledge or exchange the assets (or beneficial interests) it received, and
    - If no condition, does both of the following:
        1. Constrains the transferee (or third-party holder of its beneficial interests) from taking advantage of its right to pledge or exchange, and
        2. Provides more than a trivial benefit to the transferor.
c. *Effective control.* The transferor or its consolidated affiliates included in the financial statements being presented, or its agents, does not maintain effective control over the transferred financial assets or the third-party beneficial interests related to those transferred assets. A transferor maintains effective control if, for example:

    1. An agreement both entitles and obligates the transferor to repurchase or redeem the financial assets before their maturity,
    2. The transferor has the ability, other than through a clean-up call, to unilaterally cause the holder to return specific financial assets and that ability conveys more than trivial benefit, or
    3. An agreement permits the transferee to require the transferor to repurchase the transferred financial assets at a price that is so favorable to the transferee that it is probable that the transferee will require this to occur.

A repurchase to maturity transaction is accounted for as a secured borrowing as if the transferor maintains effective control. (ASC 860-10-40-5A)

Exchange of One Form of Beneficial Interest for Another Control is not surrendered to the extent that the consideration received is a beneficial interest in these very same transferred assets. For example, a transferor's exchange of one form of beneficial interests in a trust for an equivalent, but different, form in the same transferred financial assets cannot be accounted for as a sale. (ASC 860-10-55-16) If the trust initially issued the beneficial interests, the exchange is not even considered to be a transfer under ASC 860.

Isolation of Transferred Financial Interests ASC 810-10-40-5a above requires isolation of transferred assets as a condition of sale.

The existence of setoff rights does not impede the finding of a "true sale." (ASC 860-10-40-6A) In practice, while setoff rights may exist for the transferor and transferee, if either the obligor under the transferred financial asset (e.g., debtor under transferred receivable) or the transferor entity enters bankruptcy, the transferee might have only an unsecured claim, notwithstanding the nominal right of setoff.

An entity must assess all available evidence to determine if transferred assets would be beyond the reach of the powers of a bankruptcy trustee (or equivalent). (ASC 860-10-40-8) It is not relevant to this determination that the possibility of bankruptcy is remote at the date of the transfer. Instead, the transferor must endeavor to isolate the assets in the event of bankruptcy, however unlikely that eventuality may be. (ASC 860-10-55-23c) In many cases, transferors use two transfers to isolate the transferred assets.

- First, the transferor transfers the assets to a wholly owned corporation that is designed in a way that prevents the transferor or its creditors from reclaiming the assets (or makes the possibility that they can reclaim them remote).
- Second, the wholly owned corporation transfers the assets to a trust. The trust is prevented from undertaking any business other than management of the assets and from incurring any liabilities. (Thus, there are no creditors to force bankruptcy of the trust.) (ASC 860-10-55-23a and 23b)

A determination that the transferred assets are beyond the reach of a bankruptcy trustee may require a legal opinion regarding the application of the laws of the relevant jurisdiction. (ASC 860-10-55-18A and 55-18B) Such legal opinions commonly address whether a "true sale" has occurred, and in practice different attorneys may reach different conclusions regarding a given transaction.

Isolation of Transferred Assets Assets transferred by a bank or other financial institution that is subject to possible receivership by the FDIC can be considered isolated from the transferor even if the FDIC or another creditor can require their return, provided that the return can only occur in receivership, after a default, and in exchange for a payment of, at a minimum, principal and interest earned at the contractual yield to the date the investors are paid. (That rule does not apply to situations in which the transferor can require return of the assets in exchange for payment of principal and interest earned at the contractual yield to the date the investors are paid. In those cases the assets are not isolated from the transferor.) (ASC 860-10-55-24A and 24B)

Transference of Rights to Pledge or Exchange Transferred Financial Assets A transferee has control of transferred assets if there is the unconstrained right to both pledge and exchange the assets. (ASC 860-10-40-5b) In actual practice it may be more difficult to discern whether the transferee has control if it can pledge the transferred assets but cannot sell them. The key to a determination of control by a transferee with the right to pledge *or* exchange the assets rests on whether the transferee obtains all or most of the cash inflows that are the primary economic benefits of the pledged or exchanged assets.

Meaning of "Participating Interest." The FASB substantially limits sale accounting, by stipulating that sale accounting can be applied only if transfers are of entire financial assets, a group of financial assets, or of a portion of those assets only if the transferor and transferee proportionately share in all the rights, risks, and benefits of the entire asset. Thus, it is difficult to employ sale accounting (and thus to recognize gains on such sales) when transferring less than an entire financial asset (or group of assets). (ASC 860-10-40-4D)

The concept of a *participating interest* is used to denote a portion of a financial asset that is transferred, meeting criteria for sale accounting. If a given financial asset is divided into components prior to transfer, the transfer can be accounted for as a sale only if the components meet the criteria for being participating interests (see criteria, below). It is not appropriate to apply surrender of control criteria unless the component (or entire asset or group of assets) being transferred meets the definition of participating interests. If the definition of participating interest is satisfied, *and* if control is surrendered, only then will sale accounting be validly applied. (ASC 860-10-40-6A)

ASC 860-10 establishes the definition of a *participating interest* to describe when it would be appropriate to evaluate a transferred portion of a financial asset for sale accounting treatment. For sales of partial interests in financial assets, it is only appropriate to apply the sale accounting conditions if the transferor and transferee proportionately share in all of the rights, risks, and benefits of the entire financial asset.

As discussed above, a transfer can only be treated as a sale if the transferor has surrendered control over the financial asset. If a portion, rather than the entire asset, is transferred, the transferor retains a participating interest, the character of which will determine whether sale treatment is warranted. If an entity transfers part of a financial asset and retains another portion of that asset, gain can be recognized on the portion sold only, and then only if all components qualify as participating interests; gain can be recognized, in such situations, only on the components transferred, assuming control is relinquished. However, if the entire asset (or group) is transferred in circumstances where sale accounting is warranted, and then, after first relinquishing control, the transferor obtains a beneficial interest in the transferred asset, the gain recognized on the transfer will be based on the entire transfer.

The FASB has provided specific guidance on the definition of a portion of a financial asset that would be eligible for sale accounting. According to ASC 860-10-40-6A, participating interest must have *all* of the following characteristics:

- From the date of the transfer, the participating interest represents a proportionate (pro rata) ownership interest in an entire financial asset. The percentage of ownership interests held by the transferor in the entire financial asset may vary over time, while the entire financial asset remains outstanding, as long as the resulting portions held by the transferor (including any participating interest retained by the transferor, its consolidated affiliates, or its agents) and the transferee(s) meet the other characteristics of a participating interest.

  For example, if the transferor's interest in an entire financial asset changes because it subsequently sells another interest in the entire financial asset (a piecemeal transfer of its interests to others), the interests held initially and subsequently by the transferor will meet the definition of a participating interest.
- From the date of the transfer, all cash flows received from the entire financial asset are divided proportionately among the participating interest holders according to their respective shares of ownership. Cash flows that are allocated as compensation for services performed (e.g., for loan servicing), if any, may not be included in that determination provided those cash flows are not subordinate to the proportionate cash flows of the

participating interest and are not significantly above an amount that would fairly compensate a substitute service provider, should one be required, which includes any profit that would be demanded by a market participant.

Also, any cash flows received by the transferor as proceeds of the transfer of the participating interest are to be excluded from the determination of proportionate cash flows, provided that the transfer does not result in the transferor receiving an ownership interest in the financial asset that permits it to receive disproportionate cash flows.

- The rights of each participating interest holder (including the transferor, in its role as a participating interest holder) have the same priority of cash flow, and no participating interest holder's interest is subordinated to the interest of another participating interest holder. Priority is not subject to change in the event of bankruptcy or other receivership of the transferor, the original debtor, or any other participating interest holder. Participating interest holders can have no recourse to the transferor (or its consolidated affiliates or its agents) or to each other, other than for the standard representations and warranties, ongoing contractual obligations to service the entire financial asset and administer the transfer contract, and contractual obligations to share in any setoff benefits received by any participating interest holder. Thus, no participating interest holder can be entitled to receive cash before any other participating interest holder under its contractual rights as a participating interest holder.

  Note, however, that if a participating interest holder also is the servicer of the entire financial asset, and receives cash in its role as servicer, that arrangement would not violate the requirement that all participating interest holders share the same priority.
- No party has the right to pledge or exchange the entire financial asset unless all participating interest holders agree to pledge or exchange the entire financial asset.

If all the foregoing conditions are satisfied, the transfer of a portion of the entire financial asset would be accounted for as a sale, if control is relinquished. If one or more of the foregoing conditions are not met, however, the transfer would be accounted for as a lending transaction.

Transferor's Right to Pledge or Exchange Transferred Financial Assets

If a transferor imposes conditions on a transferee's right to pledge or exchange a financial asset, the entity must exercise judgement to assess:

- Whether the condition results in a constraint and
- Whether the constraint provides a more-than-trivial benefit to the transferor (ASC 860-10-40-15)

There is a presumption that a condition imposed by the transferor that constrains the transferee provides more than a trivial benefit. (ASC 860-10-40-16) Following are examples of conditions that constrain the transferee and are presumed to provide the transferor with more than trivial benefits.

- A provision that prohibits selling or pledging a transferred loan receivable
- Transferor-imposed contractual constraints that *narrowly* limit timing or terms
- Some rights or obligations to reacquire transferred financial assets or beneficial interests, including:
  - A freestanding call option written by that transferee to the transferor
  - A call option to repurchase third-party beneficial interest at the price paid plus a stated return, provided the transferred financial assets are not readily obtainable in the market place
  - A call option written by the transferee to the transferor that is sufficiently deep in the money

- A freestanding forward purchase-sale contract between the transferor and the transferee on transferred financial assets not readily available in the market place (ASC 860-10-40-17)

Generally, the following would *not* preclude accounting as a sale:

- The right of first refusal,
- Prohibition of a sale to competitors,
- The requirement to obtain transferor permission that will not be unreasonably withheld (judgment is necessary in this case) to sell or pledge,
- Regulatory limitation,
- Illiquidity, such as in the case of the absence of an active market, and
- Freestanding rights to reacquire transferred assets if readily attainable. (ASC 860-10-40-18)

Agreements that constrain the transferee from pledge or exchange are to be accounted for as secured borrowings.

If the transferor maintains effective control, the transfer is accounted for as a secured borrowing and not as a sale. The transferor must not be able to unilaterally take back the transferred assets. Therefore, an attached call option, a forward purchase contract, or a removal of accounts provision will in many cases defeat the determination that a sale has taken place. The transferor cannot take back the transferred assets even through the liquidation of the transferee. (ASC 860- 10-40-21)

Effective Control through Both a Right and an Obligation A transferor maintains effective control over the transferred assets, and thus cannot account for the transfer as a sale, if a repurchase or redemption agreement meets all of the following conditions:

- The financial assets covered by the agreement are the same or substantially the same as the transferred assets. In order to meet this condition, the assets transferred and those to be repurchased or redeemed must meet all of the following conditions:
  - The same primary obligor or, in the case of government-guaranteed instruments, the same guarantor and terms of the guarantee. (If the asset is debt guaranteed by a sovereign government, central bank, government-sponsored enterprise, or agency thereof, the guarantor and the terms of the guarantee must be the same.)
  - Identical form and type providing the same risks and rights.
  - The same maturity, or, in the case of mortgage-backed pass-through or pay-through securities, have similar remaining weighted-average maturities that provide approximately the same market yield.
  - Identical contractual interest rates.
  - Similar assets as collateral.
  - The same aggregate unpaid principal amount or principal amounts that are within accepted "good delivery" standards for the type of security being transferred.
- The redemption or repurchase agreement requires repurchase or redemption of the financial assets prior to maturity at a fixed or determinable price.
- The agreement is entered into simultaneously with, or in contemplation of, the transfer. (ASC 860-10-40-24)

If it is initially impracticable to measure the fair value of an asset or liability but it later becomes practicable, the transferor does not remeasure the asset or liability (or the gain or loss) under ASC 860 unless it is a servicing asset or liability. However, adjustment of the carrying value may be required by other standards, such as ASC 320.

Transfers of Receivables with Recourse Classic factoring involves the outright sale of receivables and, notwithstanding the existence of a "holdback" intended to deal with returns and allowances, are accounted for as sales. However, some entities have such a poor history of uncollectible accounts that factors are only willing to purchase their accounts if a substantial fee is collected to compensate for the risk. If the company believes that the receivables are of a better quality than the factor has assessed them, a way to avoid excessive factoring fees is to sell these receivables with recourse. This variation of factoring is, in substance, an assignment of receivables with notification to the affected customers (whereas traditional assignment does not include notification of debtors).

Structure of transfer In a transfer of receivables with recourse, the transferor is obligated to make payments to the transferee or to repurchase receivables sold upon the occurrence of an uncertain future event. (ASC 860-10-05-15) Typically, recourse provisions compensate the transferee for uncollectible accounts (sometimes amounts over a defined threshold), but they can also be written to compensate the transferee for such uncertain future events as prepayments of receivables subject to discounts or that are interest bearing, merchandise returns, or other events that change the anticipated cash flows from the receivables.

The effect of a recourse provision on the application of ASC 860's surrender of control provisions may vary by jurisdiction and by the level of recourse provided. For example, in some jurisdictions, full recourse will not place the receivables beyond the reach of the transferor and its creditors, while a limited recourse provision may have this result. Thus, some transfers of receivables with recourse will meet the criteria of ASC 860 and be accounted for as sales; other transfers will fail the criteria and be accounted for as secured borrowings. The remaining discussion in this section relates to scenarios where the arrangement qualifies for sales treatment. (ASC 860-10-55-46)

Computing gain or loss In computing the gain or loss to be recognized at the date of a transfer of receivables that meets the criteria of ASC 860, the borrower (transferor) must take into account the anticipated chargebacks from the transferee. This action requires an estimate by the transferor, based on its past experience. Adjustments are to be made at the time of sale to record the recourse obligation for the estimated effects of any bad debts, prepayments by customers (where the receivables are interest-bearing or where cash discounts are available), and any defects in the eligibility of the transferred receivables. In computing this recourse obligation, the transferor is to consider all probable credit losses over the life of the transferred receivables. The recourse obligation is to be measured at its fair value on the date of sale. (ASC 860-10-55- 46)

A present value method is acceptable for estimating fair value if the timings of the future cash flows are reasonably estimable. In applying a present value method, the estimated future cash flows are to be discounted using a discount rate at which the liability could be settled in an arm's- length transaction (i.e., a risk-adjusted rate versus a risk-free rate). Subsequent accruals to adjust the discounted amount are to be discounted at the interest rate inherent in determining the initial recourse obligation. ASC 860 expresses a preference for the use of the CON 7 probability-weighted expected cash flow model over the more traditional discounting of the single point estimate of the most probable or most likely cash flows. This model is discussed and illustrated in Chapter 1.

Example of Accounting for the Transfer of Receivables with Recourse

- Thirsty Corp. enters into an agreement with Rich Company to sell a group of its receivables with a face value of $200,000 on which a 5% allowance for uncollectible accounts has been recorded. Rich Company (the factor) will charge 20% interest computed on the weighted-average time to maturity of the receivables of thirty-six days and a 3% fee. A 5% holdback will also be retained.
- Generally, 40% of Thirsty's customers take advantage of a 2% cash discount.
- The factor accepts the receivables subject to recourse for nonpayment.
- In this jurisdiction, the transfer qualifies as a sale.

Under ASC 860, Thirsty must record the recourse liability. It has accepted the obligation for all credit losses and has, in effect, guaranteed the receivables. The recourse obligation is measured as the estimate of uncollectibles (5% of face value).

The entry required to record the sale is:

Cash	180,055	
Allowance for bad debts	10,000	
Interest expense (200,000 × .20 × 36/365)	3,945	
Factoring fee (200,000 × .03)	6,000	
Factor's holdback receivable [$10,000/($10,000 + $190,000) × $190,000]	9,500	
Loss on sale of receivables	2,100	
Due to factor for discounts (200,000 × .40 × .02)		1,600
Accounts receivable		200,000
Recourse obligation		10,000
Simplified, the entry is:		
Cash	180,055	
Allowance for bad debts	10,000	
Factor's holdback receivable (9,500 – 1,600)	7,900	
Loss on sale of receivables (3,945 + 6,000 + 2,100)	12,045	
Accounts receivable		200,000
Recourse obligation		10,000

The accounts receivable net of the allowance for uncollectible accounts (a valuation allowance) is removed from the transferor's accounting records, as it has been sold. Previously accrued bad debts expense is not reversed, however, as the transferor still expects to incur that expense through the recourse provision of the factoring agreement. (Alternatively, the bad debts expense could have been reversed and the new charge to loss on sale will have to be increased by $10,000.) The loss on sale of receivables is the sum of the interest charged by the factor ($3,945), the factor's fee ($6,000), the expected chargeback for cash discounts to be taken ($1,600), and the difference between the holdback receivable at face value and at carrying value ($500). The factor's holdback receivable is a retained interest in the receivables transferred, and it is measured by allocating the original carrying amount ($190,000) between the assets sold ($190,000) and the assets retained ($10,000).

If, subsequent to the sale of the receivables, the actual experience relative to the recourse terms differs from the provision made at the time of the sale, a change in an accounting estimate results. It is accounted for prospectively, as are all changes in accounting estimates, and therefore will be reflected as an additional gain or loss in the subsequent period. These changes are not to be deemed corrections of errors or other retroactive adjustments.

If the above facts apply, but the transfer does not qualify as a sale, the borrower's entry will be:

Cash	180,055	
Interest expense (or prepaid)	3,945	
Factoring fee	6,000	
Factor borrowing payable		190,000

In a secured borrowing, the accounts receivable continue to be recognized by the borrower. Both the accounts receivable and the factor borrowings payable must be cross-referenced on the face of the statement of financial position or in the notes to the financial statements. The accounting for the collateral under ASC 860 depends upon the terms of the collateral agreement. Accounting for collateral is discussed later in this chapter.

ASC 860-20, *Sales of Financial Assets*

This Subtopic provides guidance for transfers of financial assets that satisfy the conditions in ASC 860-10-40-5 listed earlier in this chapter. (ASC 860-20-05-1) Any participating interest(s) obtained, other assets obtained, and any liabilities incurred should be recognized and initially measured at fair value.[1] (ASC 860-20-30-2)

Measuring Assets and Liabilities after Completion of a Transfer Financial assets, except for instruments that are within the scope of Subtopic 815-10, that can contractually be prepaid or otherwise settled in such a way that the holder would not recover substantially all of its recorded investment, should be subsequently measured like investments in debt securities classified as available for sale or trading under ASC 320. Examples of such financial assets include interest-only strips, other beneficial interests, loans, or other receivables. Interest-only strips and similar interests that meet the definition of securities are included in the scope of ASC 320. Therefore, all relevant provisions of ASC 320 should be applied. (ASC 860-20-35-2)

Sale of a Participating Interest When a transfer of a participating interest that satisfies the conditions above in ASC 860-10-40-05 has been completed, the transferor (*seller*) should:

- Allocate the previous carrying amount of the entire financial asset between the participating interests sold and the participating interest that continues to be held by the transferor, on the basis of relative fair values as of the date of the transfer;
- Derecognize the participating interest(s) sold;
- Recognize and initially measure at *fair value* servicing assets, servicing liabilities, and any other assets obtained and liabilities incurred in the sale;

[1] Upon implementation of ASU 2016-13, this guidance makes an exception for a purchased financial asset with credit deterioration and a beneficial interest that meets the criteria in paragraph 325-40-30-1A. In those cases, entities should apply the guidance in ASC 326 on measurement of credit losses to determine the initial amortized cost basis.

- Recognize in earnings any gain or loss on the sale; and
- Report any participating interest or interests that continue to be held by the transferor as the difference between the previous carrying amount of the entire financial asset and the amount derecognized (i.e., the initial amount is allocated book value).
  (ASC 860-20-40-1A)

Sale of an Entire Financial Asset or Group of Entire Financial Assets If, instead of a participating interest, the entire financial asset or group of financial assets is transferred, in a manner that complies with the requirements (as set forth above) for sale accounting, then the transferor (seller) is required to:

- Derecognize all transferred financial assets;
- Recognize and initially measure at fair value servicing assets, servicing liabilities, and any other assets obtained (including a transferor's beneficial interest in the transferred financial assets) and liabilities incurred in the sale; and
- Recognize in earnings any gain or loss on the sale.

The transferee furthermore is to recognize all assets obtained and any liabilities incurred and initially measure them at fair value (which, in the aggregate, presumptively equals the price paid). (ASC 860-20-40-1B)

If the transfer is accounted for as a secured borrowing, there is no adjustment to carrying value and no gain recognition.

Accrued Interest Receivable ASC 860-20-55-18 states that:

> *The right to receive the accrued interest receivable, if and when collected, is transferred to the securitization trust. Generally, if a securitization transaction meets the criteria for sale treatment and the accrued interest receivable is subordinated either because the asset has been isolated from the transferor (see paragraph 860-10-50-5) or because of the operation of the cash flow distribution (or waterfall) through the securitization trust, the total accrued interest receivable should be considered to be one of the components of the sale transaction. Therefore, under the circumstances described, the accrued interest receivable asset should be accounted for as a transferor's interest. It is inappropriate to report the accrued interest receivable related to securitized and sold receivables as loans receivable or other terminology implying that it has not been subordinated to the senior interest in the securitization.*

When loans (mortgages and other) are sold to securitization trusts, the debtors are not informed that ownership has been transferred, and they will continue to make monthly (or other) payments to the original creditor. Often the transferor retains servicing.

ASC 860-30, *Secured Borrowing and Collateral*

This Subtopic provides guidance on secured borrowings with transfers of collateral. (ASC 860-30-01-1)

ASC 860-30-35-2 provides subsequent measurement guidance for pledged assets required to be reclassified that are accounted for as secured borrowings. For those assets, the transferor should follow the same measurement principles as before the transfer.

ASC 860-50, *Servicing Assets and Liabilities*

Interests Retained by the Transferor Interests in transferred assets that are not a part of the proceeds of a sale are considered retained interests that are still under the control of the transferor. Retained interests include:

- Participating interests for which control has not been given up by the transferor,
- Servicing assets and liabilities, and
- Beneficial interests in assets transferred in a securitization in a transaction that can be accounted for as a sale.

In general, the more extensive an interest that the transferor of assets retains, the less likely the transaction will be classified as a sale and the more likely the transaction will be classified as a secured borrowing. The primary reason for this result is that in a true sale, the transferor no longer bears the risks or reaps the rewards associated with the transferred assets. If a determination cannot be made between classification as proceeds of a sale or as retained interests, the asset is classified as proceeds and measured at fair value.

In practice, retained interests are usually comprised of one or both of two items: the spread between the average yield on the assets securitized and the cost of the debt issued by the securitization trust, and any overcollateralization provided. Regarding the spread in yields, it is often the case that trusts can issue debt securities at a lower cost than could the transferring entity, for reasons that may include the lower risk attaching to trust instruments, which are isolated from the transferor's overall credit risk. Indeed, this is one of the major attractions of employing a securitization structure. Typically the excess of the yields on the assets placed into securitization over the costs of servicing the debt issued by the securitization trust, less credit losses and other costs incurred, revert to the transferor at the termination of the securitization. Since this event may be many years in the future, the current value of this residual interest, to the transferor, must be measured on a present value (i.e., discounted) basis, which then accretes over the term to final maturity.

Overcollateralization is the other principal residual interest held by transferors. To enhance the creditworthiness of the securities issued by the trust, it is commonly found that placing a surfeit of collateral (i.e., the underlying mortgage or other loans) into the trust (say, $100 of loans receivable for each $90 of debt to be issued by the trust) will result in a significantly reduced net interest cost incurred by the trust, and hence a greater yield spread that will ultimately revert to the transferor. Additionally, an overcollateralization structure will garner a better rating for the trust securities, making them more readily marketable (in addition to having lower coupon rates), thus insuring the ability to fully fund the trust. Alternatives to the use of an overcollateralization structure include the purchase of credit insurance and arranging for a standby letter of credit. Only overcollateralization results in a residual interest being retained by the transferor, however.

Servicing assets and servicing liabilities are measured by allocating the carrying value of the transferred assets before the transfer between the assets sold (if any) and the assets retained based on their relative fair values on the date of transfer. ASC 860-50-35 specifies that the carrying value allocated should be exclusive of any amounts included in an allowance for loan losses. Any gain recognized upon a partial sale of a loan is not to exceed the gain that would be recognized if the entire loan were sold. If the transferor retains a servicing contract, a portion of the carrying value is allocable to either a servicing asset retained or a servicing liability. If the initial measure is zero, the servicing contract does not result in a servicing asset or liability. (ASC 860-50-30-2)

Relative fair value determinations should incorporate assumptions regarding interest rates, defaults, and prepayments that marketplace participants would make, as well as the expected timing of cash flows. (ASC 860-50-30-3 and 30-4) This allocation must be applied to all transfers that have retained interests, regardless of whether they qualify as sales. It should be noted that this fair value allocation may result in a relative change in financial reporting basis unless the fair values are proportionate to their carrying values. Thus, the gain or loss from any sale component could also be affected.

The retained interests continue to be the transferor's assets, since control of these assets has not been transferred. Thus, the retained interest is considered continuing control over a previously owned asset (although the form may have changed). It is not to be remeasured at fair value, nor is a gain or loss recognized on it.

Example—Sale of Partial Interest in Receivables

Facts Given

Receivables' fair value	$16,500
Receivables' book value	15,000

Seller sells 80% of receivables and agrees to service them. The benefits of servicing are just adequate to compensate for the servicing, thus there is no servicing asset or liability to be recognized.

	FV	*80% FV*	*20% FV*	*Allocated 80% BV**	*Allocated 20% BV**
Receivables sold	$16,500	$13,200		$12,000	
Retained amount (20%)			$3,300		$3,000

**Allocated based on the relative fair values.*

Seller's Journal Entry

Cash	13,200	
Receivables		12,000
Gain		1,200

Seller reports retained amount at $3,000, which is defined by book value, not fair value.

Example—Sale of Loans with Various Types of Retained Interests

Facts Given Applicable to All Examples Below (Each Example Is Independent)

Loans' fair value and amount of cash proceeds	$16,500
Loans' book value	15,000
Fair value of recourse obligation	(900)
Fair value of call option* on portfolio of $16,500	800
Fair value of interest rate swap on portfolio of $16,500	700

** An option that permits the seller/transferor to repurchase the same or similar loans.*

Seller's Journal Enties

1. Sale only

Cash	16,500	
Loans		15,000
Gain		1,500

2. Sale with recourse obligation

Cash	16,500	
Loans		15,000
Recourse obligation		900
Gain		600

3. Sale with recourse obligation and call option to purchase the loans sold or similar loans

Cash	16,500	
Call option	800	
Loans		15,000
Recourse obligation		900
Gain		1,400

4. Sale with recourse obligation, call, and swap (seller provides floating interest rate return although the underlying loans are at fixed interest rate terms)

Cash	16,500	
Call option	800	
Interest rate swap	700	
Loans		15,000
Recourse obligation		900
Gain		2,100

5. Partial sale with recourse obligation, call, and swap. Seller sells 80% of loans.

	FV	80% FV	20% FV	Allocated 80% BV*	Allocated 20% BV
Loans	$16,500	$13,200		$11,579	
Call	800	640		561	
Swap	700	560		491	
Recourse obligation	(900)	(720)		(631)	
Retained amount (20%)			$3,420		$3,000
	$17,000	$13,680	$3,420	$12,000	$3,000

Cash	13,200	
Call	640	
Swap	560	
Loans		12,000
Recourse obligation		720
Gain		1,680

Seller reports retained amount of receivables at $3,000, at book value.

**Allocated based on the relative fair values.*

In some transfers of receivables, the transferor provides credit enhancement (similar to a recourse provision) by retaining a beneficial interest that absorbs the credit risk. If there is no liability beyond the transferor's retained subordinated interests, the interest obtained is initially measured at allocated carrying value based on relative fair value, and no recourse liability is necessary. The interest would be subsequently measured like other retained interests held in the same form. (ASC 860-20-25-6)

Cash reserve accounts and subordinated beneficial interests created as credit enhancements are retained interests and are accounted for as such even if the seller collects the proceeds and deposits a portion in the cash reserve account. (New asset credit enhancements such as financial guarantees and credit derivatives are measured at the fair value of the amount to benefit the transferor.) ASC 860-10-35-8 provides guidance on estimating fair values and should be used in the case of credit enhancements.

One possible method of estimating fair value of a credit enhancement is the *cash-out method.* Using that method, cash flows are discounted from the date the credit enhancement asset becomes available to the transferor (i.e., when the cash in the credit enhancement account is expected to be paid out to the transferor). The present value can be computed using an expected present value technique with a risk-free rate or a "best estimate" technique with an appropriate discount rate. Among other transferor assumptions, time period of restrictions, reinvestment income, and potential losses due to uncertainties must be included. ASC 860 does not provide guidance concerning subsequent measurement of credit enhancements.

The Nature of Servicing Servicing of financial assets can include such activities as:

- Collecting payments (principal, interest, and escrows)
- Paying taxes and insurance from escrows
- Monitoring delinquencies
- Foreclosing
- Investing funds temporarily prior to their distribution
- Remitting fees to guarantors, trustees, and service providers
- Accounting for and remitting distributions to holders of beneficial interests (ASC 860-50-05-3)

Although inherent in holding most financial assets, servicing is a distinct asset or liability only when separated contractually from the underlying financial asset. Servicers' obligations are contractually specified. Servicing is subject to significant risks due to the effects of change in interest rates and debtors' propensity for prepayment of the related obligations. As the likelihood of prepayment (known as *prepayment speed*) increases, the value of the servicing asset decreases, and vice versa.

Transferors will most commonly retain the right and obligation to perform this servicing, and will be paid a certain fee to do so, often a small percentage (say, one-quarter of 1%) of the principal amount of loans being serviced. In some cases third parties will buy the right to service loans, or, in other situations, the transferor will retain servicing and purchase rights to service yet other loans. If the fee for providing servicing exceeds the expected cost of doing so, the right to service will be a valuable asset, which will trade for a positive price. In other circumstances, a party (generally the transferor) will have to perform servicing for a fee that will not cover expected costs, in which case a servicing liability exists.

Adequate compensation for servicing is determined by the marketplace. (See "Definitions of Terms" section at the beginning of this chapter.) The concept of adequate compensation is judged by requirements that would be imposed by a new or outside servicer. It includes profit demanded by the marketplace and does not vary with the specific servicing costs of the servicer. (ASC 860- 50-30-3) Thus, it would not be acceptable to use a given servicer's cost plus a profit margin to estimate the fair value of a servicing asset or liability to be recognized by that particular servicer.

Other changes in economic conditions may also impact the value of servicing arrangements. Some entities having servicing contracts will attempt to hedge these risks by holding financial assets, the value of which will move in the opposite direction of the servicing contracts.

Typically, the benefits are more than adequate compensation for the servicing and the servicing contract results in an asset. The benefits to be reaped by the servicer include:

- Fees
- Late charges
- A portion of interest
- Other income, including float
  (ASC 860-50-05-4)

If the above benefits are not expected to provide adequate compensation, the contract results in a liability. (ASC 860-50-30-2) With regard to the sale of assets, a servicing liability would reduce the net proceeds and would affect the gain or loss calculation.

Accounting for Servicing Servicing assets are recognized initially at fair value (ASC 860-50-30-1) if arising out of the transfer of the entire financial asset or group of financial assets, or a participating interest in financial assets, or if associated with purchased servicing rights unrelated to the assets transferred. (ASC 860-50-25-1) If financial assets are transferred to an unconsolidated affiliate in a sale transaction, and the transferor retains servicing and obtains debt securities (from the securitization process) that are properly classified as held-to-maturity, the servicing rights may be reported either as a separate asset or combined with the debt instruments held. (ASC 860-50-25-4)

Once a servicing asset is recognized, the asset must be expensed over the expected period over which serving income will be realized. Similarly, if a loss on servicing is anticipated, the liability must be taken into income over the appropriate time horizon. One of two acceptable methods can be employed:

1. *Amortization method*: Amortize servicing assets or servicing liabilities in proportion to and over the period of estimated net servicing income (if servicing revenues exceed servicing costs) or net servicing loss (if servicing costs exceed servicing revenues), and assess servicing assets or servicing liabilities for impairment or increased obligation based on fair value at each reporting date; or
2. *Fair value measurement method*: Measure servicing assets or servicing liabilities at fair value at each reporting date and report changes in fair value of servicing assets and servicing liabilities in earnings in the period in which the changes occur.
   (ASC 860-50-35-1)

A reporting entity that elects to subsequently measure a class of separately recognized servicing assets and servicing liabilities at fair value should apply that election prospectively to all new and existing separately recognized servicing assets and servicing liabilities within those classes that a servicer elects to subsequently measure at fair value. (ASC 860-50-35-3) This election cannot be applied on a contract-by-contract basis.

The method chosen can vary by class of servicing, so a given entity may be using both amortization and fair value methods simultaneously. (ASC 860-50-35-2) However, all servicing in a given class must be accounted for consistently, and cannot be changed after being elected. (ASC 860-50-35-4) For purposes of this requirement, a class of servicing assets and servicing liabilities is identified based on:

- The availability of market inputs used in determining the fair value of servicing assets or servicing liabilities,
- An entity's method for managing the risks of its servicing assets or servicing liabilities. (ASC 860-50-35-5)

Example—Sale of Receivables with Servicing Asset Retained by Transferor

Facts

Receivables' fair value, without servicing	$16,500
Receivables' book value	15,000
Servicing asset of $16,500 portfolio	800

Partial sale of receivables with servicing asset (i.e., excess of servicing fees anticipated over cost to provide services) retained. Seller sells 80% of receivables.

	FV	*80% FV*	*20% FV*	*Receivables allocated 80% BV**	*Receivables allocated 20% BV**
Receivables sold	$16,500	$13,200		$12,000	
Servicing asset**	800	640			
Retained amount (20%)	______	______	$3,460	______	$3,000
	$17,300	$13,840	$3,460	$12,000	$3,000

**Allocated based on the relative fair values.*
***Initially measured at fair value, per ASC 860-50-35.*

Journal Entry

Cash	13,200	
Servicing asset	640	
Receivables		12,000
Gain		1,840

Seller reports retained receivables at $3,000 (book value) and the servicing asset at its fair value of $640.

Example—Sale of Receivables with Servicing Liability Retained by Transferor

Facts Given

Receivables' fair value, without servicing	$16,500
Receivables' book value	15,000
Servicing (liability) for $16,500 portfolio	(500)

Partial sale of receivables with servicing liability (i.e., excess cost to provide servicing over fees anticipated) retained. Seller sells 80% of receivables.

	FV	*80% FV*	*20% FV*	*Receivables allocated 80% BV**	*Receivables allocated 20% BV**
Receivables sold	$16,500	$13,200		$12,000	
Servicing liability**	(500)	(400)			
Retained amount (20%)			$3,300		$3,300
	$16,000	$12,800	$3,300	$12,000	$3,000

**Allocated based on the relative fair values.*
***Initially measured at fair value, if practicable, per ASC 860-50-35.*

Journal Entry

Cash	13,200	
Servicing liability		400
Receivables		12,000
Gain		800

Seller reports retained receivables at $3,000 (book value) and the servicing obligation at its fair value of $400.

Amortization Method—Measurement of Impairment or Increased Obligations The entity should evaluate and measure impairment of servicing assets as follows:

- Stratify recognized servicing assets based on predominant risk (asset size, type, interest rate, term, location, date of organization, etc.).
- Recognize impairment through a valuation allowance for individual stratum in the amount of the excess of carrying value over fair value.
- Adjust the valuation allowances to reflect subsequently needed changes. Excess fair value for a stratum is not recognized.
(ASC 860-50-35-9)
- If amortization of servicing liabilities is employed, it is done in proportion to and over the period of net servicing loss (excess of servicing costs over servicing revenues). In cases where subsequent changes have increased the fair value of the servicing liability above the carrying value, an increased liability and a loss are recognized. (ASC 860-50-35-11)

Example—Sale of Receivables with Servicing Asset Retained

Facts Given Applicable to Both Examples Below (Each Example Is Independent)

Receivables' fair value	$16,500
Receivables' book value	15,000
Servicing asset fair value on portfolio of $16,500	700
Recourse obligation on portfolio of $16,500	(900)

1. Receivables sold, with servicing asset retained, no recourse obligation on receivables.

Journal Entry

Cash	16,500	
Servicing asset	700	
Receivables		15,000
Gain on transfer		2,200

2. Partial sale of receivables with servicing asset retained and recourse obligation. Seller sells 80% of receivables.

	FV	*80% FV*	*20% FV*	*Allocated 80% BV**	*Allocated 20% BV**
Receivables sold	$16,500	$13,200		$12,000	
Servicing asset	700	560			
Recourse obligation	(900)	(720)			
Retained amount (20%)			$3,300		$3,000
	$16,300	$16,040	$3,300	$12,000	$3,000

*Allocated based on the relative fair values of the receivables sold and retained.

Journal Entry

Cash	13,200	
Servicing asset	560	
Receivables		12,000
Recourse obligation		720
Gain on transfer		1,040

Seller reports retained receivables at $3,000 (book value) and servicing asset at $560, the fair value of servicing the 80% of the portfolio that has been transferred.

The foregoing example presumes that the recourse obligation does not obviate the ability to apply sale accounting for the asset transferred. While this is possible under specific circumstances, it is less likely to be acceptable under the revised ASC 860 provisions than it would have been under preamendment GAAP.

Servicing versus Interest-Only Strip Rights to future income from serviced assets that exceed contractually specified servicing fees are accounted for as a servicing asset, an interest-only strip, or both, depending on whether the servicer would continue to receive the value of the right to future income if a replacement servicer started servicing the assets. Generally, the value of the right to receive future cash flows from ancillary sources such as late fees is included with the servicing asset if retention of the right depends on servicing being performed satisfactorily. (ASC 860-50-25-7)

An interest-only strip does not depend on satisfactory performance of servicing, and any portion that would continue to be received if servicing were shifted to a replacement servicer would be accounted for separately as a financial asset. ASC 860-50-35 specifies that interest-only strips or other interests that continue to be held by the transferor in securitizations, loans, other receivables, or other financial assets that can be prepaid or otherwise settled in such a way that the entity might not recover its investment are to be subsequently remeasured as an investment in debt securities classified as available-for-sale or trading under ASC 320. (ASC 860-20-35-2)

Example of Rights to Future Income from Serviced Assets

The NorthStar Bank sells a portion of its loan portfolio, but retains the obligation to service the loans and the rights to a portion of any future interest income. Accounting for the servicing asset will be on the amortization method permitted by ASC 860-50-35. NorthStar records a servicing asset of $148,000 and an interest-only strip receivable of $68,000 (based on the fair value of its retention of a portion of interest proceeds) as part of the sale transaction. The total book value of loans sold is $3,000,000, for which it receives total payment of $2,900,000. The entry to record these assets as part of the sale is:

Servicing asset	148,000	
Interest-only strip receivable	68,000	
Cash	2,900,000	
Loans		3,000,000
Gain on transfer of receivables		116,000

The $3,000,000 of loans to be serviced will be contractually terminated at different times, so the estimated net servicing income and related amortization of the servicing asset will decline in accordance with the following schedule:

	Year 1	*Year 2*	*Year 3*	*Year 4*	*Year 5*
Estimated net servicing income	$120,000	$109,000	$82,000	$53,000	$19,000
Percent of total estimated servicing income	31%	28%	21%	14%	6%
Annual amortization of servicing asset	$ 45,880	$ 41,440	$31,080	$20,720	$8,880

Thus, the entry to record amortization of the servicing asset in Year 1 follows:

Amortization—servicing asset	45,880	
Servicing asset		45,880

NorthStar retains a portion of the interest income to which it is due under the original loan sale agreement. The initial interest income retention is for $23,000, and is recorded as follows:

Cash	23,000	
Interest-only strip receivable		23,000

At the beginning of Year 4, NorthStar sells its servicing business to a third party, but retains the interest-only strip receivable, whose balance has now declined to $17,500. The entry to eliminate the remaining unamortized balance of the servicing asset, covering Years 4 and 5, follows:

Amortization—servicing asset	29,600	
Servicing asset		29,600

Since the interest-only strip receivable is no longer dependent on NorthStar's satisfactory servicing activities, it shifts the remaining balance of this receivable into an available-for-sale investment account, as shown in the following entry:

Investment in debt securities—available-for-sale	17,500	
Interest-only strip receivable		17,500

Derecognition—Do Transferred Servicing Rights Qualify as a Sale? Some organizations transfer servicing rights on loans to third parties. ASC 942 provides criteria to be considered when evaluating whether the transfer qualifies as a sale, the first three of which are cited by reference to ASC 860-50-40.

- Has the seller received written approval from the investor (if required)?
- Is the buyer a currently approved seller/servicer and not at risk of losing approved status?
- If the sale is seller-financed:
  - Has the buyer made a nonrefundable deposit large enough to demonstrate a commitment to pay the remaining sales price?
  - Does the note receivable from the buyer provide full recourse to the buyer?
- Is the seller adequately compensated in accordance with a subservicing agreement for any short-duration, temporary servicing provided?
- Has title passed?
- Have substantially all risks and rewards of ownership been irrevocably passed to the buyer?
- Are any protection provisions retained by the seller considered minor and are they reasonably estimable?
  (ASC 860-50-40-2 and 40-3)

These criteria apply to transfers of servicing rights relating to loans previously sold and to transfers of servicing rights related to loans retained by the transferor. If the loans have been retained by the transferor, the carrying amounts sold should be allocated at the date of sale between the servicing rights and the loans retained using relative fair value. (ASC 860-50-40-6).

Changes Resulting in Transferor Regaining Control of Financial Assets Sold If a transferor is required to re-recognize financial assets in which it holds a beneficial interest because the transferor's contingent right (for example, a removal of accounts provision, known as ROAP, or other contingent call option on the transferred financial assets) becomes exercisable, sales treatment is precluded. The transferor continues to account for its beneficial interest in those assets apart from the re-recognized assets. That is, the beneficial interest is not combined with and accounted for with the re-recognized assets. A sale may be recognized upon the exercise of a ROAP or similar contingent right with respect to the "repurchased" portion of the transferred assets that were sold if the ROAP or similar contingent right held by the transferor is not accounted for as a derivative under ASC 815 and is not at-the-money. The exercise would result in a recombination of the beneficial interest with the repurchased assets. (ASC 860-10-40-12 and 40-13)

If a transferor is required to re-recognize financial assets because the securitization entity becomes nonqualifying, no gain or loss is recognized with respect to the "repurchase" by the transferor of the financial assets originally sold that remain outstanding in the securitization entity (or the portion thereof, if the transferor retained a partial interest in those assets). The fair value of the re-recognized assets will equal the fair value of the liability assumed by the transferor, because the transferor is contractually required to pass on all of the cash flows from the re-recognized assets to the securitization entity for distribution in accordance with the contractual documents governing the securitization entity. The transferor continues to account for its beneficial interest in those assets, if any, apart from the re-recognized assets.

Under no circumstances is a valuation allowance initially recorded for assets (loans) that are re-recognized at their fair value.

The accounting for the servicing asset related to the previously sold financial assets does not change because the transferor, as servicer, is still contractually required to collect the asset's cash flows for the benefit of the securitization entity and otherwise service the assets. The transferor continues to recognize the servicing asset and assess it for impairment as required by ASC 860-20-55.

Sales-Type and Direct Financing Lease Receivables Lessors' lease receivables are composed of two components: lease receivables and residual values. Lease receivables are requirements for lessees to pay cash, and thus are financial assets subject to ASC 860 if transferred. Residual values represent the salvage value of the underlying asset at the end of the lease term. If the residual value is guaranteed at the commencement of the lease, the right is a financial asset subject to ASC 860 if transferred. If the residual value is not guaranteed (or if it is guaranteed after the inception of the lease), transfers of that residual value are not subject to ASC 860. When entities sell lease receivables, the gross investment of the lease is allocated between lease payments, residual values guaranteed at inception, and residual values not guaranteed at commencement. (ASC 860-10-55-6) If the reporting entity retains servicing rights, it also records a servicing asset or liability if appropriate.

Example of Sale of Interest in Lease Payments

Lucky Leasing sells a senior interest in the guaranteed cash flows of a financing lease for $12,200. It retains a subordinated interest in the guaranteed cash flows and the residual value that is not guaranteed. The lease has the following components:

	Face value	*Present value*
Lease receivable	$ 8,350	$ 7,000
Guaranteed residual value	7,000	5,875
Residual value not guaranteed	1,400	1,175
Total investment in lease	$16,750	$14,050

The present values are computed using the implicit lease rate. The fair value of the subordinated interest retained is $1,200. Lucky Leasing receives no explicit compensation for servicing the lease, but it estimates that the benefits of servicing are just adequate to compensate it for its servicing responsibilities (that is, there is no servicing asset or liability). The allocation of the carrying amount for the interest sold is as follows:

	Fair value	*Allocated cost*
Senior interest sold	$12,200	$11,722
Subordinated interest retained	1,200	1,153
Totals	$13,400	$12,875

The entry to record the sale would be as follows:

Cash	12,200	
Subordinated interest	1,153	
Residual value	1,175	
Net investment in lease		14,050
Gain on sale		478

Securitizations

Entities that generate a large number of similar receivables, such as mortgages, credit card receivables, or car loans, sometimes securitize those receivables. Securitization is the transformation of the receivables into securities that are sold to other investors. (ASC 860-10-05-7) For example, mortgages can be converted into mortgage-backed securities, which entitle the investors to receive specific cash flows generated by the mortgages. With an established market, issuance of the securities can cost less than using the receivables as collateral for a borrowing. Transfers in securitization transactions must be evaluated for sale accounting treatment by the criteria in ASC 860, and must be evaluated for consolidation by the usual GAAP criteria applicable to variable interest entities, set forth at ASC 810. If consolidation of the securitization entity is necessitated by the circumstances, gain cannot be recognized on the transfer.

Note that securitizations may still be treated as transfers warranting sale treatment, and thus gain recognition if justified by the facts, but the strict criteria this may be more difficult to achieve.

In a typical securitization, the transferor (also called issuer or sponsor) forms a securitization mechanism (a separate corporation or a trust) to buy the assets and to issue the securities. (ASC 860-10-05-7) The securitization mechanism then generates beneficial interests in the assets or resulting cash flows that are sold to investors with the sales proceeds used to pay the transferor/sponsor for the transferred assets. The form of the securities chosen depends on such things as the nature of the assets, income tax considerations, and returns to be received. The securities issued by the securitization entity may consist of a single class of interests with the characteristics of equity or multiple classes of interests, some having debt characteristics and others equity characteristics.

For example, a transferor originates long-term loans and accumulates them on its statement of financial position (referred to as warehousing). When the group of loans reaches a sufficient size, the loans are sold to a securitization entity. During the accumulation phase, the transferor finances the cost of holding the loans with prearranged lines of credit, known as warehouse lines. Often the transferor hedges the price risk of the loans as they await sale. This is referred to as an *on-statement-of-financial-position warehousing.*

Alternatively, a transferor may use a properly structured *off-statement-of-financial-position warehousing* to securitize assets. In an off-statement-of-financial-position warehouse, the transferor creates a temporary securitization vehicle. A bank typically extends credit to the securitization vehicle in the form of a variable-funding note. Using the proceeds of the note, the vehicle acquires loans from the transferor as they are originated. The principal of the note increases, up to a ceiling, as the transferor transfers additional loans to the securitization vehicle. When the loans have reached the ceiling amount of the note, the bank puts the note back to the securitization vehicle, forcing the vehicle to sell the loans to a permanent securitization entity to raise the cash to pay the note.

Payments by the securitization mechanism are usually classified as pay-through, pass-through, or revolving-period. In a *pay-through*, cash flows from the assets pay off the debt securities. The assets are essentially collateral. In a *pass-through*, undivided interests are issued and the investors share in the net cash flows. In a *revolving-period*, undivided interests are issued, but until liquidation, the net cash flows are split between buying additional assets and paying off investors. During the reinvestment period, principal repayments are reinvested in additional receivables generated by the debtors whose receivables were securitized. Under ASC 860-10-05, any gain recognized by the transferor/sponsor on the sale of credit card or other receivables to a securitization entity is limited to amounts relating to receivables existing at the date of sale. This prevents the transferor/sponsor from recognizing additional gains on transfers that are anticipated to occur during the specified reinvestment period.

In computing gain or loss on the initial transfer, the transferor/sponsor recognizes costs estimated to be incurred for all future servicing activities, including the costs of servicing the receivables that the sponsor expects to sell to the vehicle during the reinvestment period. If the initial sale results in a gain, the costs associated with the receivables to be sold during the reinvestment period may be recorded as an asset and allocated to expense using a systematic and rational method over the initial and reinvestment periods.

Various financial components arise from securitizations. Examples include servicing contracts, interest-only strips, retained interests, recourse obligations, options, swaps, and forward contracts. All controlled assets and liabilities must be recognized under ASC 860. The following examples presume that sale criteria under amended ASC 860 are met, but it is important to bear in mind that this is a facts and circumstances determination that must be made in each situation.

Example of a Securitization Debt Involving Four Classes of Securities

Principal of loans held by the securitizer/transferor	$10,000,000
Accrued interest on loans held by the securitizer/transferor	230,000
Deferred origination costs of loans held by the securitizer/transferor	100,000
Deferred origination fees of loans held by the securitizer/transferor	(200,000)
Loss allowance on loans held by the securitizer/transferor	(250,000)
Net carrying amount of loans	$ 9,880,000

Classes of securities issued and prices:

	Principal	*Price*	*Fair value*
Class A	$9,000,000	100	$ 9,000,000
Class B	1,000,000	90	900,000
Interest-only strip (retained)	150,000		150,000
Residual class (retained)			100,000
Total fair value			$10,150,000

Servicing is retained by the transferor and has a fair value of $75,000

Transaction costs are $100,000

Proceeds are $9,800,000 ($9,000,000 Class A + $900,000 Class B – $100,000 costs)

Allocation of carrying value:

	Fair value	*Percent*	*Allocation*	*Sold*	*Retained*
Class A	$ 9,000,000	88.0	$8,696,332	$ 8,696,332	
Class B	900,000	8.8	869,633	869,633	
Interest-only strip	150,000	1.5	144,939		$144,939
Residual class	100,000	1.0	96,626		96,626
Servicing	75,000	.7	72,470		72,470
Total	$10,225,000	100.0	$9,880,000	$ 9,565,965	$314,035

The entry to record the sale would be as follows:

Cash	9,800,000
Interest-only strip	144,939
Residual class	96,626
Servicing asset	72,470

Loan loss allowance	250,000	
Deferred origination fees	200,000	
Loans receivable		$10,000,000
Interest receivable		230,000
Deferred origination costs		100,000
Gain on sale of loans		234,035

The entry to mark the securities retained to fair value under ASC 320 would be:

Interest-only strip	5,061	
Residual class	3,374	
Comprehensive income (unless trading)		8,435

Just as it is necessary to distinguish new assets, which are recorded at fair value, from retained interests, which are recorded at allocated carrying value, when accounting for a transfer to another enterprise, it is necessary to do so when accounting for a transfer to a securitization entity. In certain securitization transactions, more than one transferor contributes assets to a single securitization entity. A transferor treats the beneficial interests it receives in a securitization that commingles assets from more than one transferor as:

- New assets, to the extent that the sources of the cash flows to be received by the transferor are assets transferred by another entity
- Retained interests, to the extent that the sources of the cash flows are assets transferred by the transferor
- New assets, to the extent that any derivatives, guarantees, or other contracts were entered into by the securitization entity to "transform" the transferred assets.

After a securitization, the beneficial interests held by the transferor either are in the form of securities that are accounted for under ASC 320 or are required to be accounted for as available- for-sale securities in accordance with ASC 860. Thus, the transferor must classify the beneficial interests into one of the ASC 320 categories. If beneficial interests held by the transferor after the transfer convey rights to the same cash flows as the transferor was entitled to receive from securities that it transferred to the securitization entity, the ASC 320 classification of the beneficial interests is the same as the securities held before the transfer. For example, if prior to the transfer the debt securities were accounted for as available-for-sale securities in accordance with ASC 320, the beneficial interests are to be classified as available-for-sale securities if the transferor receives the cash flows from those securities via its beneficial interest. In contrast, if the transferred assets were not ASC 320 securities prior to the transfer but the beneficial interests were issued in the form of debt securities that have readily determinable fair values, then the transferor has the opportunity to decide the appropriate ASC 320 classification at the date of the transfer. (ASC 860-10-55-77)

Revolving-period securitizations present some unique issues because they contain an implicit forward contract to sell new receivables during the revolving period. The forward contract may become valuable to the transferor or burdensome depending upon how interest rates and market conditions change. The value of the implicit forward contract arises from the difference between the rate promised to the holders of the beneficial interests and the market rate of return on similar investments. For example, if the agreed-upon rate to holders is 5% and the market rate is 7%, the forward contract's value to the transferor is 2% of the amount of the investment for each year remaining in the revolving period, after the initially transferred receivables are collected. When receivables are sold to a revolving-period securitization trust, gain or loss recognition is limited to receivables that exist and have been sold. Similarly, servicing assets or liabilities are limited to servicing receivables that exist and have already been transferred. As proceeds from collection of the receivables are used to purchase new receivables for the trusts, each additional transfer is treated as a separate sale, with its own gain or loss calculation. Those additional transfers also can result in recognition of additional servicing assets and liabilities.

ASC 860 does not address the accounting for desecuritization of securities into loans or other financial assets. ASC 320-10-25 addresses that issue. It states that the guidance in ASC 860 is to be extended by analogy to desecuritizations. Thus, the transfer of securities or beneficial interests in a securitized pool of financial assets in which the transferor receives in exchange only the financial assets underlying those securities or beneficial interests would not be accounted for as a sale.

Example of Revolving Period Securitizations

The Mason-Dixon Auto Sales Company enters into a revolving-period securitization agreement to sell $100,000 of its car loan receivables each month to the Meridian Securitization Trust for a four-year period. Meridian guarantees a 5% rate of return to its investors for the entire four-year period. Mason-Dixon will continue to service all receivables sold to Meridian. If Mason-Dixon can create new car loans at interest rates greater than 5%, then it can recognize the difference between the actual interest rate and the rate issued to Meridian's investors as an interest-only strip.

At the end of the first month, Mason-Dixon sells $100,000 of principal on car loan receivables to Meridian, as well as $600 of accrued interest on the loans. Thus, the net carrying amount of the loans sold is $100,600. Mason-Dixon retains receivables servicing, which has a fair value of $6,000, as well as an interest-only strip receivable that recognizes the difference between the 5% guaranteed interest rate paid to Meridian's investors and the average 7% actual interest rate on the loan receivables, which has a fair value of $8,000 at the sale date.

The initial sale includes transaction costs of $5,000, which are deducted from the cash paid by Meridian to Mason-Dixon. The following entry by Mason-Dixon records the sale transaction:

Cash	95,600	
Interest-only strip receivable	8,000	
Servicing asset	6,000	
Loans receivable		100,000
Interest receivable		600
Gain on sale of loans		9,000

At the end of the next month, Mason-Dixon sells another $100,000 of receivables to Meridian, as well as $350 of accrued interest on the loans. Thus, the net carrying amount of the second group of loans is $100,350. The lower accrued interest is due to a drop in the actual interest rate on this second block of loans, which averages 4% and is below the 5% guaranteed Meridian's investors. The fair value of the servicing asset associated with these loans is $6,000. The following calculation allocates the fair value of the various elements of the transaction to the net carrying amount of the loans:

	Fair value	*Percent*	*Allocation*
Loans	$100,000	98.0	$ 98,343
Interest-only strip	(4,000)	(3.9)	(3,914)
Servicing asset	6,000	5.9	5,921
Totals	$102,000	100.0	$100,350

This second sale also includes transaction costs of $5,000, which are deducted from the cash paid to Mason-Dixon. The following entry records the sale transaction:

Cash	95,350	
Servicing asset	6,000	
Loss on sale of loans	3,000	
Interest-only strip receivable		4,000
Loans receivable		100,000
Interest receivable		350

Repurchase Agreements Repurchase agreements are used to obtain short-term use of funds. (ASC 860-10-05-9) Under the terms of a repurchase agreement the transferor transfers financial assets to a transferee in exchange for cash. Concurrently, the transferor agrees to reacquire the financial assets at a future date for an amount equal to the cash exchanged and an interest factor. Many repurchase agreements are for short terms, often overnight.

It is necessary to determine whether the repurchase agreement meets the requirements described in the section earlier in this chapter, "Effective Control through Both a Right and an Obligation." Usually the critical determination is whether the repurchase agreement gives the transferor effective control over the transferred assets. That determination is made by applying the criteria described in the section entitled, "Effective control." In most cases, if the repurchase is required prior to the maturity of the security transferred and the cash transferred is sufficient to repurchase the assets if the transferee defaults, the transferor retains effective control and the agreement is accounted for as a collateralized borrowing. For example, fixed-coupon and dollar-roll repurchase agreements, and other contracts under which the securities to be repurchased need not be the same as the securities sold, qualify as borrowings if the return of substantially the same securities as those transferred is assured. However, if a transferor does not maintain control over the transferred assets and other criteria in ASC 860 are met, the transfer is accounted for as a sale and a forward commitment. ASC 860-20-55, discussed earlier in this chapter, addresses situations where a transferee transfers the assets back to the transferor in a repurchase financing arrangement, which (depending on meeting criteria specified) may or may not interfere with derecognition of the assets by the original transferor.

Example of a Repurchase Agreement

Mighty Manufacturing has $1,995,000 excess cash that it desires to invest for a 7-day period. It transfers the cash to Lion Bank in exchange for $2,000,000 of commercial paper. At the end of the 7-day period, Lion Bank agrees to repurchase the commercial paper for $1,996,500. Mighty Manufacturing does not have the right to sell or pledge the commercial paper during the 7-day period.

The entries to record the origination of the agreement are as follows:

Mighty Manufacturing			*Lion Bank*		
Investment	1,995,000		Cash	1,995,000	
Cash		1,995,000	Short-term payable		1,995,000

The entries to record the termination of the agreement seven days later are as follows:

Mighty Manufacturing			*Lion Bank*		
Cash	1,996,500		Short-term payable	1,995,000	
Investment		1,995,000	Interest expense	1,500	
Interest income		1,500	Cash		1,996,500

Securities Lending Transactions Broker-dealers and other financial services companies initiate securities lending transactions when they need to obtain specific securities to cover a short sale or a customer's failure to deliver securities sold. The transferor/lender provides the securities to the transferee/borrower in exchange for "collateral," usually in an amount greater than the fair value of the borrowed securities. This collateral is commonly cash but could alternatively be other securities or standby letters of credit.

When the collateral is cash, the transferor/lender invests the cash during the period that the security is loaned. The investment return on the cash collateral is larger than the fees paid by the lender under the agreement (the rebate). Because the cash collateral is usually valued daily and adjusted frequently for changes in the market value of the underlying securities, the transaction has very low credit risk.

In determining whether to account for a securities lending transaction as a sale or a secured borrowing, the same criteria used for other asset transfers are applied. Many securities lending transactions are accompanied by an agreement that entitles and obligates the transferor/lender to repurchase or redeem the transferred assets before their maturity. Thus, the transferor maintains effective control over the securities lent. If that is the case, the transaction is accounted for as a secured borrowing. The following is an example of a securities lending transaction accounted for as a secured borrowing:

Example—Securities Lending Transaction (30 Days)

Fair value of loaned security	$16,500
Book value of loaned security	16,500
Collateral (cash)	16,995
Transferor/lender's return from investing cash	5%
Transferor/lender's rebate to transferee/borrower	4%

Transferor/lender's journal entries
At date of loan:

Securities pledged	16,500	
Securities		16,500
To record transfer of securities as a loan		
Cash	16,995	
Loan agreement payable		16,995
To record receipt of cash collateral		
Money market instrument	16,995	
Cash		16,995
To invest cash collateral		

At end of 30 days:

Cash	17,065	
Interest income		70
Money market instrument		16,995
To transfer cash from money market and record interest earned		
Securities	16,500	
Securities pledged		16,500
To record securities returned by transferee/borrower		
Loan agreement payable	16,995	

Interest rebate	56	
Cash		17,051
To return cash collateral and pay rebate		

Accounting for Collateral Accounting for collateral depends both on whether the secured party has the right to sell or repledge the collateral and on whether the debtor has defaulted. Ordinarily, the transferor should carry the collateral as an asset and the transferee does not record the pledged asset.

The collateral provisions of ASC 860 apply to all transfers (repurchase agreements, dollar-roll, securities lending, etc.) of financial assets pledged as collateral and accounted for as a secured borrowing. The provisions do not apply to the accounting for cash in secured borrowing transactions.

If the secured party (transferee) has the right to sell or repledge the collateral, then the debtor (transferor) reclassifies the asset used as collateral and reports it in the statement of financial position separately from other assets not similarly encumbered. That is, the debtor (transferor) continues to hold the collateral assets as its own, and the secured party (transferee) does not recognize the collateral asset. If the secured party (transferee) sells the collateral, it recognizes the proceeds from the sale and the obligation to return the collateral to the debtor (transferor).

Although collateral is required to be reclassified and reported separately by the transferor if the transferee has the right to sell or repledge the collateral, that requirement does not change the transferor's measurement of the collateral. The same measurement principles are to be used as before the transfer and the collateral is not derecognized. The subsequent measurement of the transferee's obligation to return the collateral in securities borrowing and resale agreement transactions is not addressed by ASC 860.

If the transferor defaults and is not entitled to the return of the collateral, it is to be derecognized by the transferor. If not already recognized, the transferee records its asset at fair value.

Example of Accounting for Collateral

Deep Water Marine enters into a loan arrangement with Key West Bank for $4,700,000, using one of its submersibles as collateral. The loan terms are monthly interest payments at an annual rate of 9%, followed by a balloon payment in five years for the entire amount of the principal. The submersible has a book value of $4,250,000, net of accumulated depreciation of $500,000, and a fair value of $4,650,000. Deep Water misses its first loan payment, so the parties renegotiate the loan agreement, allowing Key West the right to resell the submersible. Deep Water records this change by separately listing the submersible in the property, plant, and equipment section of its statement of financial position in the following manner:

Equipment used as collateral with right of sale (net of accumulated depreciation of $500,000)	$4,250,000

Two months after the loan initiation date, Deep Water defaults on the note and enters bankruptcy proceedings, so Key West takes possession of the submersible. Deep Water records the default with the following entry:

Loan payable	4,700,000	
Accrued interest payable	70,500	
Accumulated depreciation	500,000	
Fixed assets—equipment		4,750,000
Gain on loan defaults		520,500

Foreclosure of the Deep Water loan is certain. The estimated cost to sell the submersible is a 2% commission, or $93,000, which Key West includes in the following entry to record its ownership of the submersible ($4,650,000 fair value net of $93,000 commission):

Repossessed assets	4,557,000	
Bad debt expense	213,500	
Interest receivable		70,500
Loans receivable		4,700,000

Key West sells the submersible for $4,500,000, net of all sales costs. It records the transaction with the following entry:

Cash	4,500,000	
Loss on asset sale	57,000	
Repossessed assets		4,557,000

64 ASC 900s SPECIALIZED INDUSTRY GAAP

CONTRACTORS—FEDERAL GOVERNMENT (ASC 912)

PERSPECTIVE AND ISSUES

ASC 912 governs the accounting and income recognition issues related to:

- Cost-plus-fixed-fee contracts
- Contracts terminated for the convenience of the government
- Fixed-price war and defense of supply contracts (ASC 912-10-15-3)

The fees under government cost-plus-fixed-fee contracts are recognized as income on the basis of partial performance if there is reasonable assurance of realization. Fees are also accrued as they become billable unless this accrual is not reasonably related to the proportionate performance of total work to be performed.

DEFINITIONS OF TERMS

See Appendix A, *Definitions of Terms*, for additional terms relevant to this topic: Contract, Contract Asset. Source: Terms are from ASC 912, *Glossary*.

Contract. A legal agreement obligating a contractor (referred to as the "general contractor" or "prime contractor") to provide products or services to the U.S. government. The term also refers to subcontracts obligating subcontractors to indirectly perform in a similar manner under the supervision and control of the prime contractor.

Contractors. In the context of this discussion, contractors are enterprises that sell products or services to the U.S. government pursuant to a formal contract. The relationship to the government can be direct (a prime contract between the enterprise and the government) or indirect (a subcontract between the enterprise and a prime contractor).

Cost-Plus-Fixed-Fee Contracts. A contract under which the contractor is reimbursed for costs plus the provision for a fixed fee. (ASC 912-10-20)

Disposal Credits. Amounts deducted from the contractor's termination claim receivable by reason of the contractor's retention, or sale to outsiders, of some or all of the termination inventory for which the claim was made. In the circumstance of items retained, either as scrap or for use by the contractor, the amount of the credit is determined by agreement between the contractor and a representative of the government. (ASC 912-310-25-4)

No-Cost Settlements. A contractor whose contract is terminated may prefer to retain the termination inventory for use in other production or for disposal at the contractor's risk. For these or other reasons the contractor may prefer to make no claim against the government or a higher-tier contractor. In such no-cost settlements there is no sale of inventory or other items to the government and no occasion to accrue any profit arising from the termination. The costs otherwise applicable to the contract shall be given their usual treatment in the accounts. Items of inventory or other property retained, having been previously recorded, require no charge to purchases but shall be treated in accordance with the usual procedures applicable to such assets. (ASC 912-310-25-5)

Subcontractor's Claims. Those obligations of a contractor to a subcontractor that arise from the subcontractor's costs incurred through transactions that were related to a contract terminated but did not result in the transfer of billable materials or services to the contractor before termination. (FASB ASC Master Glossary)

CONCEPTS, RULES, AND EXAMPLES

Cost-plus-fixed-fee contracts (CPFFC) are used for the manufacture and delivery of products, the construction of plants and other facilities, and for management and other services. The amount of the flat-fee payment is usually determined by the ratio of the actual expenditures to the total estimated expenditures. CPFFC may be cancelled and terminated by the government. If this occurs, the contractor is entitled to reimbursement for expenditures and an appropriate portion of the fixed fee. All federal government contracts and contract modifications negotiated on the basis of cost with commercial entities are required to follow the cost principles mandated by Federal Acquisition Legislation and Regulations in pricing negotiated contracts and contract modifications. (ASC 912-20-05-2)

Advances in CPFFC are generally intended to assist the contractor in financing its costs. Thus, in general, advances are treated as liabilities and are not offset against contract receivables. Advances are permitted to be offset against contract receivables only when there is an expectation that the advances will be applied against those specific charges. Any such offsets require disclosure in the financial statements.

Terminated Defense Contracts

These "convenience terminations" contracts are contracts terminated for the convenience of the government. (ASC 912-20-05-4)

Material termination claims are separately captioned in the revenues section of the contractor's statement of income. (ASC 912-20-45-5) When inventory is reacquired by the contractor after including it in a termination claim, it is recorded as a purchase. (ASC 912-330-25-1) The credit is applied against the termination claim receivable. (ASC 912-310-35-1)

ENTERTAINMENT—BROADCASTERS (ASC 920)

PERSPECTIVE AND ISSUES

ASC 920 provides accounting and reporting standards for broadcasters. (ASC 920-10-05-1) Ordinarily, license fees are paid in installments over a period generally shorter than the license period. The agreement usually contains a separate license for each program in the package. The license expires at the earlier of the last telecast allowed or the end of the license period. The licensee pays the required fee whether or not the rights are exercised. If the licensee does not exercise the contractual rights, the rights revert to the licensor with no refund to the licensee. ASC 920 provides overall guidance and guidance on intangibles—goodwill and other, liabilities, and commitments.

DEFINITIONS OF TERMS

Source: ASC 920, *Glossaries*. Also see the following terms in Appendix A: Film Group, Films.

Broadcaster. An enterprise or an affiliated group of enterprises that transmits radio or television program material. (ASC 920-10-20)

Daypart. An aggregation of programs broadcast during a particular time of day (e.g., daytime, evening, late night) or programs of a similar type (e.g., sports, news, children's shows). Broadcasters generally sell access to viewing audiences to advertisers on a day part basis. (ASC 920-350-20)

License Agreement. A typical license agreement for program material (e.g., features, specials, series, or cartoons) covers several programs (a package) and grants a television station, group of stations, network, pay television, or cable television system (licensee) the right to broadcast either a specified number or an unlimited number of showings over a maximum period of time (license period) for a specified fee. (ASC 920-230-20)

Network Affiliation Agreement. A broadcaster may be affiliated with a network under a network affiliation agreement. Under the agreement the station receives compensation for the network programming that it carries based on a formula designed to compensate the station for advertising sold on a network basis and included in the network programming. (ASC 920-10-20)

CONCEPTS, RULES, AND EXAMPLES

Accounting for License Agreements

A broadcaster accounts for a license agreement for program material as a purchase of rights. Thus, an asset and a liability are recorded for the program rights purchased and the liability incurred when the license period begins and the broadcaster has met the following requirements:

- Knows or can reasonably determine the cost of each program
- Has accepted the program material according to the license agreement
- Has access to the program for the first telecast (unless an agreement with another licensee prevents the telecast)
(ASC 920-350-25-2)

The asset is capitalized and the liability reported at either the gross amount of the liability for program rights or, alternatively, at the fair value of the liability. If a present value technique is used to measure fair value, the difference between the gross and net liability must be accounted for as interest. (ASC 920-405-30-1) Under either method, the capitalized costs are allocated to each program within a package based on the relative value of each program to the broadcaster. The asset recorded acquired for program material should be presented separately from films.

The asset is separated into current and noncurrent portions based on expected time of program usage. The liability is likewise segregated according to the payment maturities. (ASC 920-405-45-1)

Amortizing Capitalized Costs

The capitalized costs of license agreements, including agreements in a film group, are amortized to expense as the program rights are used; generally based on the estimated number of program telecasts. However, licenses granting the right to unlimited broadcasts of programs such as cartoons are amortized over the license period, since the number of telecasts may be indeterminable. (ASC 920-350-35-1)

Feature programs and program series require specific treatment. Feature programs are amortized program-by-program, unless amortization as a package produces approximately the same result. Syndicated programs are amortized as a series. If the broadcaster considers the first showing to be more valuable than reruns, the series is amortized using an accelerated method. If each showing is equally valuable, straight-line amortization is used. (ASC 920-350-35-2)

Impairment If the license agreement is part of a film group, the entity should review it for impairment by:

1. Determining whether a film is part of a film group where it is expected to be monetized on its own or with other films and/or license agreements.
2. Assessing whether there is a significant change to the monetization strategy.
(ASC 920-350-3-2A and 926-350-3B and 35-3C)

The impairment review should be done whenever events or circumstances indicate that the fair value of a film predominantly monetized on its own or a film group may be less than its amortized costs. (ASC 926-350-12)

Example of Accounting for Program License Agreements

On July 31, 20X1, Lakie Media Company executed a license agreement for three movies, which it plans to televise on its local television station. The agreement allows the broadcast of each movie twice during the license period. Lakie is a calendar year-end company. The appropriate rate for imputing interest is 12%. Additional facts and assumptions are as follows:

License period				*First telecast*		*Second telecast*	
Film	*From*	*To*	*Film availability date*	*Date*	*% of Total revenue*	*Date*	*% of Total revenue*
A	10/1/X1	9/30/X3	9/1/X1	3/1/X2	60%	6/1/X3	40%
B	10/1/X1	9/30/X3	9/1/X1	5/1/X2	70%	7/1/X3	30%
C	11/1/X1	8/31/X3	10/1/X1	6/1/X2	75%	8/1/X3	25%

Payment terms and discounted present value data are as follows (Films A and B were acquired as a package):

Film(s)	*Payment*		*Discount period**	
	Date	*Amount*	*From*	*To*
A & B	7/31/X1	$ 1,000		
	12/31/X1	6,000	10/1/X1	12/31/X1
	12/31/X2	6,000	10/1/X1	12/31/X2
		13,000		
C	12/31/X2	3,750	11/1/X1	12/31/X2
$		$16,750		

* *Discounted from the first day of the license period to the date of payment.*

Based on management's estimates of expected advertising revenues, Film A represents 70% and Film B 30% of the total package A and B.

Present Value Approach When each film's license period begins, an asset and a liability are recorded at the present value of the liability. Since the first three payments apply to the package of films A and B, the $12,027 combined present value (see the amortization schedule below) must be allocated to these films according to the 70%/30% assumption stated above.

Film	*Asset and liability recognized*	
A	$ 8,419	($12,027 × 70%)
B	3,608	($12,027 × 30%)
	12,027	
C	3,283	
	$15,310	

In this case, all costs are capitalized in 20X1 because all of the films' licensing periods begin in that year (assuming the three conditions are met).

The amount capitalized as an asset is amortized according to the percentage of revenues to be earned each year from each film. Interest is accrued on the unpaid balance of the liability for each film. Note that for films A and B, the unpaid balance at December 31, 20X1, is $11,027 ($12,027 – the $1,000 down payment).

Amortization Schedules—Annual Compounding

Description	*Date*	*Payment*	*Interest at 12%*	*Principal*	*Balance*
Films A and B					
Down payment	7/31/X1	$ 1,000.00	–	$1,000.00	–
Discounted obligation	10/1/X1				$11,027.23
Payment	12/31/X1	6,000.00	$ 329.91	5,670.09	5,357.14
Payment	12/31/X2	6,000.00	642.86	5,357.14	–
		13,000.00	972.77	12,027.23	
Film C					
Original obligation	11/1/X1				3,283.44
Accrued interest	12/31/X2	–	64.77	(64.77)	3,348.21
Payment	12/31/X2	3,750.00	401.79	3,348.21	–
		3,750.00	466.56	3,283.44	
		$16,750.00	$1,439.33	$15,310.67	

	20X1	*20X2*	*20X3*	*Total*
Amortization of film rights				
Film A				
($12,027 × 70% =) $8,419 × 60%		$ 5,051		
($12,027 × 70% =) $8,419 × 40%			$3,368	$ 8,419
Film B				
($12,027 × 30% =) $3,608 × 70%		2,526		
($12,027 × 30% =) $3,608 × 30%			1,082	3,608
				12,027
Film C				
$3,283 × 75%		2,462		
$3,283 × 25%			821	3,283
Total amortization of film rights		$10,039	$5,271	15,310
Interest expense per amortization schedule				
Films A and B	$ 330	$643		973
Film C	65	402		467
	$ 395	$ 1,045		1,440
				$16,750

Gross Method Costs are capitalized at the gross amount of the liability.

Film	*Asset and liability recognized*	
A	$ 9,100	($13,000 × 70%)
B	3,900	($13,000 × 30%)
C	3,750	
	$16,750	

Again, since the license period for all the films begins in 2012, the assets and liabilities are recognized in that year.

Under the gross approach, no interest is accrued on the unpaid liability. Thus, the only expense recognized is the amortization of the program cost.

	Year of expense recognition				*Total*
Film	*20X2*		*20X3*		
A	$ 5,460	(1)	$3,640	(4)	$ 9,100
B	2,730	(2)	1,170	(5)	3,900
C	2,813	(3)	937	(6)	3,750
	$11,003		$5,747		$16,750

(1) $9,100 × 60% (4) $9,100 × 40%
(2) $3,900 × 70% (5) $3,900 × 30%
(3) $3,750 × 75% (6) $3,750 × 25%

Accounting for Network Affiliation Agreements

A broadcaster may be affiliated with a network under a network affiliation agreement. (ASC 920-10-20) Program costs, a major expense of television stations, are generally lower for a network affiliate than for an independent station because an affiliate does not incur program costs for network programs.

Upon termination of a network affiliation agreement, immediate replacement, or an agreement to replace the affiliation, the broadcaster will recognize a loss measured by the unamortized cost of the previous affiliation less the fair value of the new affiliation. No gain is recognized if the fair value exceeds the unamortized cost. If the terminated affiliation is not replaced, its unamortized cost is charged to expense. (ASC 920-350-40-1)

Reporting and Disclosure

The capitalized cost of program rights is reported in the statement of financial position at the lower of unamortized cost or fair value of package, series, program-by-program, series, or day-part basis. (ASC 920-350-30-3) Either on the balance sheet or in the notes, the asset related to rights acquired under a license agreement for program material is presented separately from films accounted for under ASC 926-20. (ASC 350-45-1) Network affiliation agreements are reported in the statement of financial position as intangible assets. (ASC 920-350-45-2)

ENTERTAINMENT—CABLE TELEVISION (ASC 922)

PERSPECTIVE AND ISSUES

ASC 922 provides accounting and reporting guidance for costs and expenses for the cable television industry. (ASC 922-10-05-1) These standards apply to cable television systems in the prematurity period. See the Definitions of Terms section below for a description of the prematurity period.

DEFINITIONS OF TERMS

Source: Terms are from ASC 922, *Glossary*.

Cable Television Plant. The cable television plant refers to the equipment required to render service to subscribers including:

- *Head-end.* This includes the equipment used to receive signals of distant television or radio stations, whether directly from the transmitter or from a microwave relay system. It also includes the studio facilities required for operator-originated programming, if any.
- *Cable.* This consists of cable and amplifiers (which maintain the quality of the signal) covering the subscriber area, either on utility poles or underground.
- *Drops.* These consist of the hardware that provides access to the main cable, the short length of cable that brings the signal from the main cable to the subscriber's television set, and other associated hardware, which may include a trap to block particular channels.
- *Converters and descramblers.* These devices are attached to the subscriber's television sets when more than twelve channels are provided or when special services are provided, such as "pay cable" or two-way communication.

(ASC 922-350-20)

Direct Selling Costs. Direct selling costs include commissions, the portion of a salesperson's compensation other than commissions for obtaining new subscribers, local advertising targeted for acquisition of new subscribers, and costs of processing documents related to new subscribers acquired. Direct selling costs do not include supervisory and administrative expenses or indirect expenses, such as rent and other facilities costs.

Prematurity Period. During the prematurity period, the cable television system is partially under construction and partially in service. The prematurity period begins when revenue from the first subscriber is recognized. Its end will vary with circumstances of the system but will be determined based on plans for completion of the first major construction period or achievement of a specified predetermined subscriber level at which no additional investment will be required for other than cable television plant. The construction period of a cable television system varies with the size of the franchise area, density of population, and difficulty of physical construction. The construction period is not completed until the head-end, main cable, and distribution cables are installed, and includes a reasonable time to provide for installation of subscriber drops and related hardware. During the construction period, many system operators complete installation of drops and begin to provide service to some subscribers in some parts of the system while construction continues. Providing the signal for the first time is referred to as energizing the system. (ASC 922-350-20)

Subscriber-Related Costs. Costs incurred to obtain and retain subscribers including costs of billing and collection, bad debts, and mailings; repairs and maintenance of taps and connections; franchise fees related to revenues or number of subscribers; general and administrative system costs, such as salary of the system manager and office rent; programming costs for additional channels used in the marketing effort or costs related to revenues from, or number of subscribers to, per channel or per program service; and direct selling costs. (ASC 922-720-20)

CONCEPTS, RULES, AND EXAMPLES

ACCOUNTING DURING THE PREMATURITY PERIOD

Before the first subscriber revenue is recognized by the cable company, the beginning and end of the prematurity period must be established by management. This period generally is presumed not to exceed two years. Once the prematurity period has been established, it may not be changed except in highly unusual circumstances. (ASC 920-360-25-1)

Separate accounting is required for any portion[1] of a cable television system that is in the prematurity period and that is distinct from the rest of the system. This distinction is made if the portion is characterized by a majority of the following differences:

- Accounting (e.g., separate forecasts, budgets, etc.)
- Investment decisions (e.g., separate ROI, breakeven, etc.)
- Geographical (e.g., separate franchise area)
- Mechanical (e.g., separate equipment)
- Timing (e.g., separate inception of construction or marketing) (ASC 922-360-25-3)

If the portion meets these requirements, it will be charged costs of the entire system only if these costs are directly traceable to that portion. (ASC 922-360-25-4) Separate projections are also developed for that portion.

During the prematurity period, costs incurred for the plant are capitalized as usual. (ASC 922-360-25-5) General and administrative expenses and subscriber-related costs are considered period costs. Subscriber-related costs are costs incurred to obtain and retain subscribers to the cable television system. Initial installation costs are capitalized and depreciated over a period that does not exceed the period used to depreciate the cable plant. (ASC 922-360-25-7)

System costs that will benefit the cable system upon completion (e.g., programming costs), and that will remain fairly constant despite changes in the number of subscribers, are separated into amounts benefiting current operations (which are expensed currently) and amounts allocable to future operations (which are capitalized). These amounts are evaluated separately for recoverability. (ASC 922-360-35-1) The current depreciation expense is determined by multiplying the

[1] The word "segment" has been used by some television enterprises. However, since ASC 280 uses segment in a different context, the FASB uses the word "portion" instead of "segment" to refer to the part of a cable television system that is still in the prematurity period. (ASC 922-360-25-2)

total monthly system costs by a fraction calculated each month during the prematurity period as follows:

Current portion of system costs benefiting future periods	=	The numerator is the greatest of: a) Average # of subscribers expected that month as estimated at beginning of prematurity period; b) Average # of subscribers assuming straight-line progress towards estimated # of subscribers at end of prematurity period; or c) Average # of actual subscribers ——— The denominator is the total # of subscribers expected at end of prematurity period

(ASC 922-360-35-3)

Depreciation and amortization during the prematurity period are determined as follows:

Depreciation and amortization expense	=	Monthly depreciation and amortization of total capitalized costs expected on completion of the prematurity period (using depreciation method to be used at completion of prematurity period)	×	Fraction used to determine monthly system costs to be expensed currently (See above for calculation)

During the prematurity period, interest cost is capitalized using an interest capitalization rate as described in ASC 835-20. The amount of interest cost to be capitalized is determined as follows:

Interest cost capitalized = Interest capitalization rate × Average amount of qualifying assets during the period capitalized
(ASC 922-835-25-1)

ASC 835-20-15-2 describes which assets qualify for interest cost capitalization. (See the chapter on ASC 835 for more information.) The amount of capitalized interest cost may not exceed actual interest cost for the period.

Franchise Application Costs A cable television franchise is a right granted by a municipality to provide service to its residents. The treatment of franchise application costs depends upon whether or not the application is successful. If successful, the application costs are capitalized and amortized as intangible assets over the life of the franchise agreement. (ASC 922-350-25-3) If unsuccessful or abandoned, all application costs are charged to expense.

ENTERTAINMENT—CASINOS (ASC 924)

PERSPECTIVE AND ISSUES

There is some form of legalized gambling in most states, as well as on Native American land and on riverboats. (ASC 924-10-05-3) Legalized gambling includes betting for horse racing, dog racing, lotteries, and jai alai. Gambling has become a considerable revenue stream for resort operators who also provide other services to attract gamblers.

Additional guidance can be found in the GASB codifications for gaming entities classified as governmental. Note that the AICPA publishes an audit and accounting guide, *Gaming*.

DEFINITIONS OF TERMS

Source: ASC 924-10-20

Base Jackpot. The fixed, minimum amount of the payout from a slot machine for a specific combination.

Chips. Money substitutes issued by a gaming entity and used by its patrons for wagering.

Slot Machine. A type of mechanical or electrical apparatus used in connection with gaming.

CONCEPTS, RULES, AND EXAMPLES

A casino typically exchanges cash from patrons for its gaming chips. When a casino has an obligation to pay the jackpot, it records a liability. (ASC 924-405-25-2) The casino calculates the amount of this liability by determining the difference between the total chips placed in service and the actual amount of chips in custody. (ASC 924-405-25-1)

For base jackpots from slot machines or other games, an entity may be able to avoid a payout. If so, the entity does not have to record a liability until the entity is subject to pay. (ASC 924-405-55-1)

Some wagering contracts by bettors have known or knowable odds at the time the bet is placed. These are known as fixed-odds contracts. The issuer of fixed-odds wagering contracts should account for them under ASC 606 on revenue and not under ASC 815 on derivatives and hedging. (ASC 924-815-25-1)

ENTERTAINMENT—FILM (ASC 926)

PERSPECTIVE AND ISSUES

Overview

The production, sale, licensing, and distribution of motion pictures (and television series) are fraught with uncertainties. The industry is speculative in nature with studios routinely investing multimillion dollar sums in the hope that the production will achieve critical acclaim and that moviegoers will flock to the box office, purchase licensed merchandise tied to the film and its characters, and purchase or rent copies of the film. Due to the uncertainties involved in estimating the revenues that will be recognized and costs that will be incurred over a film's life, an acceptable estimation methodology is required to achieve proper matching of costs and revenues and accurately reflect the results of the film's financial performance. This methodology is provided in ASC 926, *Entertainment—Films*.

DEFINITIONS OF TERMS

Source: ASC 926, *Glossary*. Also see Appendix A, *Definitions of Terms*, for other terms relevant to this topic: Contract, Film Group, Films, Firm Commitment, Revenue, and Spot Rate.

Cross-Collateralized. A contractual arrangement granting distribution rights to multiple films, territories, and/or markets to a licensee. In this type of arrangement, the exploitation results of the entire package are aggregated by the licensee in determining amounts payable to the licensor.

Distributor. The owner or holder of the rights to distribute films. Excluded from this definition, for the purposes of applying ASC 926, are entities that function solely as broadcasters, retailers (such as video stores), or movie theaters.

Exploitation Costs. All direct costs incurred in connection with the film's distribution. Examples include marketing, advertising, publicity, promotion, and other distribution expenses.

Film Costs. Film costs include all direct negative costs incurred in the physical production of a film, including allocations of production overhead and interest capitalized in accordance with ASC 835-20. Examples of direct negative costs include costs of story and scenario; compensation of cast members, extras, directors, producers, and miscellaneous staff; costs of set construction and operations, wardrobe and accessories; costs of sound synchronization; rental facilities on location; and postproduction costs such as music, special effects, and editing.

Film Prints. The materials containing the completed audio and video elements of a film which are distributed to a theater to exhibit the film to its customers.

Market. A distribution channel located within a certain geographic territory for a certain type of media, exhibition, or related product. Examples include theatrical exhibition, home video (laser disc, videotape, DVD), pay television, free television, and the licensing of film-related merchandise.

Nonrefundable Minimum Guarantee. Amount to be paid by a customer in a variable fee arrangement that guarantees an entity a minimum fee on that arrangement. This amount applies to payments paid at inception, as well as to legally binding commitments to pay amounts over the license period.

Overall Deal. An arrangement whereby an entity compensates a creative individual (e.g., producer, actor, or director) for the exclusive or preferential use of that party's creative services.

Participation Costs. Frequently, persons involved in the production of a film are compensated, in part or in full, with an interest (referred to as a *participation*) in the financial results of the film. Determination of the amount of compensation payable to the participant is usually based on formulas (participations) and by contingent amounts due under provisions of collective bargaining agreements (residuals). The recipients of this compensation are referred to as participants and the costs are referred to as participation costs. Participations may be paid to creative talent (e.g., actors or writers), or to entities from whom distribution rights are licensed.

Producer. An individual or enterprise that is responsible for all aspects of a film and has a financial interest in a film. Although the producer's role may vary, his or her responsibilities include administration of such aspects of the project as initial concept, script, budgeting, shooting, postproduction, and release.

Sale. The transfer of control of the master copy of a film and all of the associated rights that accompany it.

Set for Production. A film qualifies as being set for production when all of the following conditions have been met: (1) management with relevant authority authorizes (implicitly or explicitly) and commits to funding the film's production; (2) active preproduction has begun; and the start of principal photography is expected to begin within six months.

Significant Changes to a Film. Changes that are additive to a film; that is, the creation of new or additional content after the film is initially available to the customer. For example, reshooting a scene or creating additional special effects are significant changes.

Territory. A geographic area in which a film is exploited, usually a country. In some cases, however, a territory may be contractually defined as countries with a common language.

CONCEPTS, RULES, AND EXAMPLES

ASC 926, *Entertainment—Films,* provides the authoritative guidance with respect to accounting for arrangements to sell, license, or exhibit films. The term "film" is generic and includes intellectual property produced on traditional celluloid film as well as videotape, digital, or other video-recording formats. The content or format of films includes (1) feature films, (2) television series, (3) television specials, and (4) similar products (including animated films and television programming). The guidance in the standard applies to producers and distributors who own or hold rights to distribute or exploit films. (ASC 926-10-15-2) The standard does not apply to the following specialized industries or applications that have their own specialized GAAP:

- The recording industry (ASC 928)
- Cable television (ASC 922)
- Broadcasters (ASC 920)
- Computer software to be sold, leased, or otherwise marketed (ASC 985-20)
- Entertainment and educational software products (ASC 985-705).
  (ASC 924-10-15-3)

Costs and Expenses—Components

Costs associated with the production and bringing to market of a film can be categorized as one of the following:

- Film costs
- Participation costs
- Manufacturing costs
  (ASC 926-10-05-1)

Film Costs Film costs are presented separately on the entity's statement of financial position from the rights acquired under a license agreement for program materials under ASC 920-350. See the section on ASC 920 earlier in this chapter. (ASC 926-20-45-2) They consist of

- Direct negative costs
- Production overhead
- Overall deal costs
- Rights to film properties
- Production period interest capitalized in accordance with ASC 835-20

Direct negative costs include the cost of adaptation or development of the property; compensation of the cast, directors, producers, extras, and other staff members; costs of set construction and operations, wardrobe and accessories; costs of sound synchronization; on-location rental facilities; and postproduction costs such as music, special effects, and editing. Production overhead includes allocation of costs of individuals or departments with exclusive or significant responsibility for the production of films. However, production overhead does not include general and administrative expenses, the costs of certain overall deals, or charges for losses on properties sold or abandoned. (ASC 926-20-25-2) The amortization of film costs is explained later in this section. Rights to film properties costs include costs to acquire the rights to intellectual property, for example, film rights to books or stage plays, or original screenplays.

Participation Costs Participation costs are contingent compensation paid to creative talent such as actors or writers, or to entities from whom the distribution rights are licensed, such as the publisher of a novel on which a screenplay is based (these recipients are referred to as participants). (ASC 926-10-20) Participation costs are accrued using the individual-films-forecast computation method. This method accrues expenses at the same rate that current period actual revenue (numerator) bears to estimated remaining unrecognized ultimate revenue as of the beginning of the current fiscal year (denominator). This method should yield a constant rate of profit over the ultimate period. (ASC 926-405-25-1) See the section below for more information.

Exploitation Costs The advertising cost component of exploitation costs is accounted for in accordance with ASC 720-35, that is, they are expensed as incurred or the first time the advertising takes place except for costs described in ASC 720-35-25-1A. (ASC 926-720-25-1) All other exploitation costs, including marketing costs, publicity, promotion, and other distribution expenses, are expensed as incurred. (ASC 926-720-25-3)

Manufacturing Costs The cost of making theatrical film prints is charged to expense over the period benefited. The cost of manufacturing and/or duplication of products to be held for sale such as videocassettes and digital video discs is charged to expense on a unit-specific basis when the related product revenue is recognized. Unsold inventories should be evaluated at the date of each statement of financial position, for net realizable value and obsolescence. (ASC 926-330-35-1)

Costs and Expenses—Amortization of Film Costs and Accrual of Participation Costs

For a film that is predominantly monetized on its own, amortization of capitalized film costs and accrual (expensing) of participation costs commences when the film is released and the entity begins to recognize revenue from the film. The method used to compute the amortization of film costs and the accrual of participation costs is called the individual-film-forecast-computation method. (ASC 926-20-35-1) This method amortizes film costs using the following formula:

$$\frac{\text{Current period actual revenue}}{\text{Estimated remaining unrecognized ultimate revenue as of the beginning of the fiscal year}} \times \text{Unamortized film costs at the beginning of the fiscal year} = \text{Film cost amortization for the fiscal year}$$

Similarly, participation costs are accrued and expensed using the following formula:

$$\frac{\text{Current period actual revenue}}{\text{Estimated remaining unrecognized ultimate revenue as of the beginning of the fiscal year}} \times \text{Unaccrued ultimate participation costs at the beginning of the fiscal year} = \text{Amount of participation costs to be accrued (expensed) for the fiscal year}$$

Irrespective of the above calculation, participation costs are subject to special rules. The liability is only accrued if it is probable that there will be a sacrifice of assets to settle the entity's obligation under the participation agreement. In addition, at the date of each statement of financial position, accrued participation costs must at least equal the amounts that the entity is obligated to pay at that date.

Using this formulaic approach, in the absence of a change in estimate, the entity would earn a constant rate of profit over the ultimate period for each film before considering exploitation costs, manufacturing costs, and other period costs. (ASC 926-20-35-1)

It is, of course, likely that the actual results will vary from the estimates and that the estimates will require review and refinement. At each reporting date, the entity reviews and revises estimates of ultimate revenue and ultimate participation costs to reflect the most current information available to it. As a result of this review, the denominator is revised to include only the remaining ultimate revenue at the beginning of the fiscal year of change. In this way, these changes in estimate are accounted for prospectively as of the beginning of the fiscal year of the change. The numerator is unaffected by the change since it is based on actual results. The entity uses this revised denominator in the fraction applied to the net unamortized film costs and to the film's unaccrued ultimate participation costs. The difference between expenses determined using the new estimates and any amounts previously recorded as expense during that fiscal year are charged (or credited) to the income statement in the period (e.g., quarter) during which the estimates are revised.

Ultimate Revenue In general, ultimate revenue to be included in the denominator of the fraction includes estimates of revenue to be recognized by the entity from the exploitation, exhibition, and sale of a film in all markets and territories. (ASC 926-20-35-4) There are, however, certain limitations that apply to the determination of ultimate revenue:

1. The period over which ultimate revenue for a film may be estimated is limited to ten years following the date of the film's initial release. Ultimate revenue excludes estimates of amounts related to the sale of rights for periods after this period. The period over which ultimate revenue for an episodic television series may be estimated is limited to ten years from the date of delivery of the first episode or, if the series is still in production, five years from the date of delivery of the most recent episode, if later. For previously released films acquired as part of a film library, the period over which ultimate revenue may be estimated is limited to twenty years from the date of acquisition of the library. A film must have been initially released at least three years prior to the acquisition date of the film library in order to be categorized as part of the library for the purposes of applying this limitation.
2. Ultimate revenue includes estimates of revenue for a market or territory only if persuasive evidence exists that such revenue will occur, or if an entity can demonstrate a history of recognizing such revenue in that market or territory. Ultimate revenue includes estimates of revenue from newly developing territories only if an existing arrangement provides persuasive evidence that the entity will realize the revenue.
3. Ultimate revenue includes estimates of revenue from licensing arrangements with third parties to market film-related products only if there is persuasive evidence that such revenue from that arrangement will occur for that particular film (e.g., a signed contract to receive a nonrefundable minimum guarantee or nonrefundable advance) or if the entity can demonstrate a history of recognizing such revenue from that form of arrangement.
4. Ultimate revenue includes estimates of the portion of the wholesale or retail revenue from an entity's sale of peripheral items (such as toys and apparel) attributable to the exploitation of themes, characters, or other contents related to a particular film only if the entity can demonstrate a history of recognizing revenues from that form of exploitation in similar kinds of films. Ultimate revenue should not include estimates of the entire amount of wholesale or retail revenue from an entity's sale of peripheral items.

5. Ultimate revenue excludes estimates of revenue from unproven or undeveloped technologies.
6. Ultimate revenue excludes estimates of wholesale promotion or advertising reimbursements to be received from third parties. These reimbursements are accounted for as an offset against exploitation costs.
7. Ultimate revenue excludes estimates of amounts related to the sale of film rights for periods after those identified in 1 and 2 above.
(ASC 926-20-35-5)

Ultimate revenue should not be discounted to present value unless a significant financing component is identified in a contract where an entity promises to grant a license within the scope of ASC 606. (ASC 926-20-35-6)

Ultimate revenue does not include amounts representing projections of future inflation. (ASC 926-20-35-7) The portion of ultimate revenue that is expected to be received in a foreign currency is valued at current spot rates. (ASC 926-20-35-8)

Example of Individual Film Forecast Computation Method

Paula Pictures incurred film costs and earned revenues from its motion picture, Arachno-Man, as follows:

	Year1	Year2
1. Film cost, including capitalized interest (FC)	$15,000	
2. End-of-year estimate of ultimate revenue (UR)	36,000	$30,000
3. Remaining ultimate revenue at beginning of year* (RUR)	–	11,000
4. Actual recognized revenues for the year (ER)	19,000	5,000
5. End-of-year estimate of ultimate participation costs (UPC)	3,600	3,000
6. Actual participation costs for the year (APC)	1,600	500

* *Revised estimate of ultimate revenue less actual revenue recognized from date of release through the beginning of the year.*

The individual film forecast computation method is applied as follows:

Year 1

Film cost amortization:

$$\frac{\$19{,}000\text{ ER}}{\$36{,}000\text{ UR}} \times \$15{,}000\text{ FC} = \$7{,}917\text{ Film cost amortization}$$

Accrual of participation costs:

$$\frac{\$19{,}000\text{ ER}}{\$36{,}000\text{ UR}} \times \$3{,}600\text{ UPC} = \$1{,}900\text{ Accrued participation costs}$$

Year 2

Film cost amortization:

$$\frac{\$5{,}000\text{ ER}}{\$11{,}000\text{ RUR*}} \times \$7{,}083\text{** Unamortized film costs} = \$3{,}220\text{ Film cost amortization}$$

* *Computed as Year 2 revised estimate of ultimate revenue of $30,000 less actual revenue recognized in prior year of $19,000.*

** *Computed as film cost of $15,000 less prior amortization expense recognized of $7,917.*

Accrual of participation costs:

$$\frac{\$5{,}000\text{ ER}}{\$11{,}000\text{ RUR}} \times \$1{,}100\text{ Remaining ultimate participation costs***} = \$500$$

*** *Computed as Year 2 revised estimate for ultimate participation costs of $3,000 less the prior year accrued amount of $1,900.*

Valuation of Unamortized Film Costs

Unamortized film costs must be tested for impairment when there is an indication that the fair value of a film predominantly monetized on its own or a film group may be less than unamortized costs. (ASC 926-20-35-12) Consistent with the rules for recognizing impairment of long-lived assets in ASC 360, guidance in ASC 926-20 offers examples of events or changes in circumstances that indicate that the entity must assess whether the fair value of the film (whether it has been completed or is still in production) is less than the carrying amount of its unamortized film costs:

- An adverse change in the expected performance of the film prior to its release
- Actual costs substantially in excess of budgeted costs
- A change in the predominate monetization strategy of a film that results in the film being predominately monetized with other films and/or license agreements
- Substantial delays in completion or release schedules
- Changes in release plans, such as a reduction in the initial release pattern
- Insufficient funding or resources to complete the film and to market it effectively
- Actual performance subsequent to release fails to meet prerelease expectations (ASC 926-20-35-12A)

Upon making the comparison between the film's fair value and its unamortized costs, any excess of the unamortized costs over the fair value should be written off as an operating expense on the income statement. Amounts written off may not be subsequently restored. (ASC 926-20-35-13) The fair value of a film is often estimated using a traditional discounted cash flow model.

The limits regarding the number of years of revenue to include in the determination of ultimate revenue do not apply to the estimation of future cash flows associated with the film for the purpose of determining the film's fair value. (ASC 926-20-35-14) Factors to be considered by management in estimating future cash inflows for a film include:

- The film's performance in prior markets, if previously released
- The public's perception (the popularity and market appeal) of the film's story, cast, director, or producer

- Historical results of similar films
- Historical results of the cast, director, or producer on prior films
- The running time of the film

In addition to estimating the film's or film group's fair value, management must estimate future costs to complete the film or film group (if any), future exploitation and participation costs, and other necessary cash outflows necessary to achieve the estimated cash inflows. (ASC 926-20-35-15)

When using the traditional discounted cash flow method to estimate fair value, the estimates of future cash inflows and outflows represent management's best estimates of the most likely cash flows. The discount rate used is adjusted to consider the level of risk inherent in investing in a project of this nature. (ASC 926-20-35-16)

When using the expected cash flow approach to estimate fair value (which is preferred and encouraged by ASC 360), all possible relevant future cash inflows and outflows are probability-weighted by period and the estimated average for each period used. In employing this method, the discount rate is risk-adjusted as described above only if the probable expected cash flows have not already been risk-adjusted. (ASC 926-20-35-17) Guidance for applying these two estimation techniques is contained in CON 7, discussed in detail in Chapter 1.

If an impairment loss is attributable to a film group, it should only reduce the carrying amount of a film or license agreement in that group. The loss is allocated on a pro rata basis. If, however, the fair value of individual films and license agreements can be estimated without undue burden, those films should not be reduced below their fair value. (ASC 926-20-35-19)

ENTERTAINMENT—MUSIC (ASC 928)

PERSPECTIVE AND ISSUES

ASC 928 offers accounting and reporting guidance for the music industry. In this industry, business is transacted through license agreements, contractual arrangements entered into by an owner (licensor) of a music master or copyright. License agreements are modifications of the compulsory provisions of the copyright law. The licensor grants the licensee the right to sell or distribute recordings or sheet music for a fixed fee paid to the licensor or for a fee based on sales. This section presents the proper accounting by both the licensor and the licensee for license agreements in the music industry and for artist compensation costs, for compensation paid to artists in the form of royalties, and for the costs of producing record masters. (ASC 928-10-05-1)

DEFINITIONS OF TERMS

Source: ASC 928, *Glossary*

Advance Royalty. An amount paid to music publishers, producers, songwriters, or other artists in advance of their earning royalties from recording or sheet music sales. These amounts are based on contractual terms and are generally nonrefundable.

License Agreements. Contractual arrangements entered into by an owner (licensor) of a master or music copyright and a licensee that grant the licensee the right to sell or distribute recordings or sheet music for a fixed fee paid to the licensor or for a fee based on sales.

Minimum Guarantee. An amount paid in advance by a licensee to a licensor for the right to sell or distribute recordings or sheet music.

Record Master. The master tape resulting from the performance of the artist. It is used to produce molds and tapes for use in making cartridges, cassettes, DVDs, and reel tapes. The costs of producing a master include (1) the cost of the musical talent (musicians, vocal background, and arrangements); (2) the cost of the technical talent for engineering, directing, and mixing; costs for the use of the equipment to record and produce the master; and (4) studio facility charges. Under the standard type of artist contract, the media company bears a portion of the costs and recovers a portion of the cost from the artist out of designated royalties earned. However, either party may contractually agree to bear all or most of the cost.

Royalties. Amounts paid to producers, songwriters, or other artists for their participation in making recordings and to sheet music publishers for their copyright interest in music.

CONCEPTS, RULES, AND EXAMPLES

Accounting by Licensors

Fees Paid In some cases the licensee pays a minimum guarantee, which is an amount paid in advance to a licensor for the right to sell or distribute recordings or sheet music. A minimum guarantee is first recorded by the licensor as a liability and then amortized to income as the license fee is earned. If the amount of the fee that is earned is indeterminable, then straight-line recognition of revenue from the guarantee is required over the license period. (ASC 928-405-25-1)

Cost of Artist Compensation Royalties are paid to producers, songwriters, or other artists for their participation in making recordings and to music publishers for their copyright interest in music. Amounts for artists are determined by the terms of personal service contracts negotiated between the artists and media companies and usually are determined based upon a percentage of sales activity and license fee income, adjusted for estimated sales returns. Publishing royalties are generally based on copyright or other applicable laws. Royalties are recorded as a period expense of the licensor.

Advance royalties are recorded as assets if the licensor expects that the artist's recording will be successful enough to provide for full recovery of the advance from future royalties due the artist. (ASC 928-340-25-1) As royalties are subsequently earned by the artist, the capitalized advance is charged to expense. The advance must be apportioned between current and noncurrent assets according to how soon each portion is expected to be charged to expense. If it later appears that the advance will not be fully recovered from subsequent royalties earned by the artist, then the unrecoverable portion is charged to expense in the period in which the loss becomes apparent. (ASC 928-340-35-1)

Cost to Produce Masters The portion of the cost that is paid by the media company is recorded as an asset if the company expects that sales of the artist's recording will be successful enough to provide for full recovery of the accumulated costs. If this is not the case, then these costs are expensed. Costs to produce masters that are recoverable from the artist's royalties are treated as advanced royalties by the media company. (ASC 928-340-25-2 and 25-3) Any amount capitalized is amortized over the useful life of the recording in a manner that relates the costs to estimated net revenue to be recognized. (ASC 928-340-35-2)

Accounting by Licensees

When a licensee pays a minimum guarantee in advance, the guarantee is recorded as an asset and then amortized to expense according to the terms specified in the license agreement. If it later appears that the minimum guarantee is not fully recoverable through use of the rights received under the agreement, then the unrecoverable portion is charged to expense. (ASC 928- 340-35-3)

EXTRACTIVE ACTIVITIES—OIL AND GAS (ASC 932)

PERSPECTIVE AND ISSUES

Oil and gas producing activities are those activities that involve the acquisition of mineral interests in properties, exploration, development, and production of crude oil, including condensate and natural gas liquids, and natural gas. The successful efforts method of accounting adheres to a traditional historical cost basis. Property acquisition costs, whether the property is proved or unproved, are capitalized as incurred. For other costs incurred under this method, a direct relationship between the costs incurred and specific reserves discovered is required before costs are permitted to be capitalized. Under the successful efforts method, costs that cannot be directly related to the discovery of specific oil and gas reserves are expensed immediately as incurred, analogous to research and development. (ASC 932-360-25-3) Oil and gas producing companies are also subject to the requirements of ASC 410 regarding the recognition of asset retirement obligations.

The use of the successful efforts method is preferred, but not required by GAAP. An oil and gas producing company is permitted to use, as an alternative to the successful efforts method, a prescribed form of the full cost method permitted by the SEC. All enterprises are required to disclose the method used for accounting for costs incurred and the method of disposition used for capitalized costs. (ASC 932-235-50-1) The SEC requires additional disclosures for publicly traded companies and also provides guidance (SAB 106) on ensuring that the expected cash flows associated with asset retirement obligations are not double-counted in making computations under the full cost method.

For an enterprise that uses the full cost method of accounting, assets being depreciated, depleted, or amortized are considered to be in use in the earning activities of the enterprise and, consequently, do not qualify for interest capitalization. However, assets employed in ongoing exploration or development activities but that are not yet engaged in earning activities and not presently being depreciated, depleted or amortized, are subject to interest capitalization. (ASC 932-10-S99-1)

Exploratory wells or tests that are in progress at the end of the period present unique accounting issues. If, subsequent to the end of the period, but before the financial statements are issued, a well or test is found to be unsuccessful, the incurred costs, less salvage value, are expensed. Retroactively restated financial statements are not permitted.

DEFINITIONS OF TERMS

Source: ASC 932, *Glossary*. Also see Appendix A, *Definitions of Terms*, for other terms relevant to this topic: Conduit Debt Securities, Consolidated Financial Statements, Contract, Customer, Noncontrolling Interest, Parent, Publicly Traded Company, and Subsidiary.

Condensate. Condensate is a mixture of hydrocarbons that exists in the gaseous phase at original reservoir temperature and pressure but when produced is in the liquid phase at surface pressure and temperature.

Development Project. A development project is the means by which petroleum resources are brought to the status of economically producible. As examples, the development of a single reservoir or field, an incremental development in a producing field, or the integrated development of a group of several fields and associated facilities with a common ownership may constitute a development project.

Economically Producible. The term economically producible, as it relates to a resource, means a resource that generates revenue that exceeds, or is reasonably expected to exceed, the costs of the operation. The value of the products that generate revenue shall be determined at the terminal point of oil- and gas-producing activities.

Exploration. Exploration involves both of the following:

a. Identifying areas that may warrant examination
b. Examining specific areas that are considered to have prospects of containing oil and gas reserves, including drilling exploratory wells and exploratory-type stratigraphic test wells

Oil- and Gas-Producing Activities. Paragraph 932-10-15-2A defines the term oil- and gas-producing activities.

Production. Production involves lifting the crude oil and natural gas to the surface; extracting saleable hydrocarbons, in the solid, liquid, or gaseous state from oil sands, shale, coalbeds, or other nonrenewable natural resources that are intended to be upgraded into synthetic oil or gas; gathering, treating, field processing (as in the case of processing gas to extract liquid hydrocarbons), and field storage.

The oil and gas production function shall be regarded as ending at a terminal point, which is the outlet valve on the lease or field storage tank. If unusual physical or operational circumstances exist, it may be appropriate to regard the terminal point for the production function as:

a. The first point at which oil, gas, or gas liquids, natural or synthetic, are delivered to a main pipeline, a common carrier, a refinery, or a marine terminal.
b. In the case of natural resources that are intended to be upgraded into synthetic oil or gas, if those natural resources are delivered to a purchaser before upgrading, the first point at which the natural resources are delivered to a main pipeline, a common carrier, a refinery, a marine terminal, or a facility that upgrades such natural resources into synthetic oil or gas.

Properties. Mineral interests in properties (hereinafter referred to as properties), which include all of the following:

a. Fee ownership or a lease
b. Concession
c. Other interest representing the legal right to produce or a revenue interest in the production of oil or gas subject to such terms as may be imposed by the conveyance of that interest.

Properties also include:

a. Royalty interests
b. Production payments payable in oil or gas
c. Other nonoperating interests in properties operated by others

Properties include those agreements with foreign governments or authorities under which an entity participates in the operation of the related properties or otherwise serves as producer of the underlying reserves (see paragraph 932-235-50-7); but properties do not include other supply agreements or contracts that represent the right to purchase (as opposed to extract) oil and gas.

Properties are classified as proved properties or unproved properties.

Proved Properties. Proved properties are properties with proved reserves.

Reserves. Reserves are estimated remaining quantities of oil and gas and related substances anticipated to be economically producible, as of a given date, by application of development projects to known accumulations. In addition, there must exist, or there must be a reasonable expectation that there will exist, the legal right to produce or a revenue interest in the production, installed means of delivering oil and gas or related substances to market, and all permits and financing required to implement the project.

Reserves should not be assigned to adjacent reservoirs isolated by major, potentially sealing, faults until those reservoirs are penetrated and evaluated as economically producible. Reserves should not be assigned to areas that are clearly separated from a known accumulation by a nonproductive reservoir (that is, absence of reservoir, structurally low reservoir, or negative test results). Such areas may contain prospective resources (that is, potentially recoverable resources from undiscovered accumulations).

Resources. Resources are quantities of oil and gas estimated to exist in naturally occurring accumulations. A portion of the resources may be estimated to be recoverable, and another portion may be considered to be unrecoverable. Resources include both discovered accumulations and undiscovered accumulations.

Saleable Hydrocarbons. Hydrocarbons that are saleable in the state in which the hydrocarbons are delivered.

Unproved Properties. Unproved properties are properties with no proved reserves.

Scope

Oil- and gas-producing activities include:

- The search for crude oil, including condensate and natural gas liquids, or natural gas in their natural states and original locations
- The acquisition of property rights or properties for the purpose of further exploration or for removing the oil or gas
- The construction, drilling, and production activities necessary to retrieve oil and gas from their natural reservoirs, including the acquisition, construction, installation, and maintenance of field gathering and storage systems, such as:
    - Lifting the oil and gas to the surface
    - Gathering, treating, and field processing (as in the case of processing gas to extract liquid hydrocarbons).
- Extraction of saleable hydrocarbons, in the solid, liquid, or gaseous state, from oil sands, shale, coalbeds, or other nonrenewable natural resources that are intended to be upgraded into synthetic oil or gas, and activities undertaken with a view to such extraction. (ASC 923-10-15-2A)

ASC 932 does not address:

- Refining, marketing, or transportation issues
- Processing of produced oil, gas, or natural resources that can be turned into synthetic oil or gas by an entity that is not the producer of the resources
- Activities relating to the production of natural resources other than oil, gas, or natural resources from which synthetic oil and gas can be extracted
- The production of geothermal steam

- Accounting for interest on funds borrowed to finance an entity's oil- and gas-producing activities
  (ASC 932-10-15-3)

CONCEPTS, RULES, AND EXAMPLES

The following is a discussion of the recommended treatment of oil and gas activities as per ASC 932. (Note that this treatment is recommended, but not required.)

The costs of the special types of assets used in oil and gas producing activities are capitalized when incurred. Some examples include:

- Mineral interests in properties:
  - Unproved—Properties with no proved reserves
  - Proved—Properties with proved reserves
- Wells and related equipment and facilities
- Support equipment and facilities
- Uncompleted wells, equipment, and facilities
  (ASC 926-360-25-6)

Costs associated with drilling exploratory wells or exploratory-type stratigraphic wells related directly to specific oil and gas reserves are capitalized until it is determined that the well has proved reserves at which time the capitalized costs are reclassified to wells and related equipment and facilities. (ASC 932-360-25-3) If, however, proved reserves are not found, the capitalized drilling costs of the well are charged to expense. When drilling is completed if it is determined that the well has reserves but those reserves cannot be classified as proved, the reporting enterprise will continue to capitalize drilling costs if (1) the reserves found are sufficient to justify completion of the well as a producing well, and (2) the reporting enterprise is making sufficient progress assessing the reserves and the economic and operating viability of the project. (ASC 932-360-35-18)

These costs are amortized as reserves are produced and, along with lifting (production) costs, are classified as costs of production. (ASC 932-360-35-2) Periodically, unproved properties are evaluated for impairment. The impairment model used for drilling and mineral rights is not the same model set forth in ASC 350 for intangible assets, but rather is based on the level of established reserves. (ASC 932-350-35-8) If impaired, a loss is recognized.

Acquisition costs incurred to obtain oil and gas properties through purchase, lease, etc. are capitalized. (ASC 932-360-25-7)

Geological and geophysical costs, unproved properties' carrying costs, and the costs of dry hole and bottom hole contributions are expensed. Drilling costs are capitalized until a determination has been made as to the success of the well. If successful, these costs are transferred to uncompleted wells, related equipment, and facilities. The cost of drilling, less residual value, is charged to expense if proved reserves are not found.

Development costs are incurred in order to:

- Get access to and prepare well locations
- Drill and equip development wells
- Set up production facilities
- Provide better recovery systems
  (ASC 932-360-25-13)

These costs are capitalized as uncompleted equipment and facilities until drilling or construction is completed. (ASC 932-360-25-14)

The cost of support equipment is capitalized and depreciated. This depreciation, along with other operating costs, is allocated to exploration, development, or production costs, as appropriate. (ASC 932-360-25-15)

Production involves different costs ranging from lifting to field storage. These costs, together with depreciation, depletion, and amortization of capitalized acquisition, exploration, and development costs, are part of the cost of the oil and gas produced. (ASC 932-360-25-15)

Unproved properties are reclassified to proved properties upon discovery of proved reserves. When proved reserves are found, the costs capitalized as uncompleted wells, equipment, and facilities are reclassified as completed wells, equipment, and facilities. (ASC 932-360-35-2) Capitalized costs are amortized or depleted by the unit of production method. Estimated residual values must be considered when determining amortization and depreciation rates. (ASC 932-360-35-3)

Any information that becomes available between the end of the period and the date when the financial statements are issued should be considered in the evaluation of conditions existing at the date of the statement of financial position. With respect to the costs of a company's wells, related equipment, facilities, and the costs of related proved properties, the provisions for impairment as outlined in ASC 360 are applicable.

FINANCIAL SERVICES—DEPOSITORY AND LENDING (ASC 942)

PERSPECTIVE AND ISSUES

ASC 942 provides accounting guidance for entities, including:

- Finance companies, including finance company subsidiaries
- Depository institutions insured by either the FDIC or the National Credit Union Share Insurance Fund
- Banks
- Thrifts
- Credit unions
- Savings and loan associations
- Corporate credit unions
- Mortgage companies
  (ASC 942-10-15-2 and 15-3)

It also is applicable to the financing activities of manufacturers, retailers, wholesalers, and other business enterprises.

DEFINITIONS OF TERMS

Source: ASC 942, *Glossary*. Also see Appendix A to this volume for additional terms relevant to this Topic: Cash, Commitment Fees, Fair Value, Market Participants, Orderly Transactions, Reinsurance Recoverable, Related Parties.

Accretable Yield. In the context of loans acquired in transfers, the cash flows expected to be collected in excess of the initial investment.

Carrying Amount. The face amount of the interest-bearing asset plus (or minus) the unamortized premium (or discount).

Debt-Equity Swap. A debt-equity swap is an exchange transaction of a monetary asset for a nonmonetary asset.

General Reserve. Used in the context of the special meaning this term has in regulatory pronouncements and in the U.S. Internal Revenue Code.

Incremental Direct Costs. Costs to originate a loan that (1) result directly from and are essential to the lending transaction, and (2) would not have been incurred by the lender had that lending transaction not occurred.

Long-Term Interest-Bearing Assets. For purposes of this section, these are interest-bearing assets with a remaining term to maturity of more than one year.

Net-Spread Method. Under this method, the acquisition of a savings and loan association is viewed as the acquisition of a leveraged whole rather than the acquisition of the separate assets and liabilities of the association.

Nonaccretable Difference. In the context of loans acquired in a transfer, the excess of contractual cash flows over the amount of expected cash flows.

Origination Fees. Fees charged to the borrower in connection with the process of originating, refinancing, or restructuring a loan. This term includes, but is not limited to, points, management, arrangement, placement, application, underwriting, and other fees pursuant to a lending or leasing transaction and also includes syndication and participation fees to the extent they are associated with the portion of the loan retained by the lender.

Pretax Accounting Income. Represents income or loss for a period, exclusive of related income tax expense, determined in conformity with generally accepted accounting principles.

Taxable Income. Represents pretax accounting income (1) adjusted for reversal of provisions of estimated losses on loans and property acquired in settlement of loans, gains or losses on the sales of such property, and adjusted for permanent differences, and (2) after giving effect to the bad debt deduction allowable by the U.S. Internal Revenue Code assuming the applicable tax return were to be prepared based on such adjusted pretax accounting income.

CONCEPTS, RULES, AND EXAMPLES

Accounting Guidance

Receivables

Loans to financially troubled creditors At times, bank loans to financially troubled countries meet the conditions in ASC 326-20 on financial instruments measured at amortized cost for recording of credit losses. If so, banks should establish loan loss allowances for such loans by charges to income. (ASC 942-310-35-1)

An entity may receive payments on a loan on which the accrual of interest was suspended. In that case, the entity must determine whether the payment is:

- A reduction of the principal balance or
- Interest income.

If the ultimate collectibility of the entire or partial amount is in doubt, the payment should be applied to reduce the principal to the extent it reduces doubt. (ASC 942-310-35-2)

When a country normalizes relations with the international financial community and becomes current with payments, the creditor may recognize receipt of interest payments as income, assuming the loss allowance is adequate. (ASC 942-310-35-3)

Debt-equity swap programs ASC 942-310 specifically addresses accounting for debt-equity swap programs. (ASC 942-310-05-1) Fees and transactions involved in a debt-equity swap should be charged to expense as incurred. (ASC 942-310-25-2)

Creditors should recognize a loss if the fair value of the equity investment or net assets in a debt-equity swap is less than the recorded investment in the loan. The loss should be recorded as of the date the transaction is agreed to. The loss generally should be charged to the allowance for loan losses account. (ASC 942-310-35-5) Loss recoveries or gains should not be recorded until investment or assets received are realized in unrestricted cash. (ASC 942-310-35-6)

Customer's liabilities on acceptances It may be necessary to provide for uncollectible amounts for customer's acceptance liabilities. (ASC 942-310-35-8)

Investments Accretion for debt securities should run from the purchase date to the maturity date, unless other guidance applies. (ASC 942-320-35-1)

Federal Home Loan Bank or Federal Reserve Bank stock Federal Home Loan Bank and Federal Reserve Bank stock should be classified as a restricted investment security, carried at cost and evaluated for impairment. (ASC 942-325-25-1 and 35-1) Impairment is evaluated based on the ultimate recoverability of par value. Temporary declines in value are not recognized. (ASC 942-325-35-3) Cash and stock dividends received on Federal Home Loan Bank stock is reported as income. (ASC 942-325-35-2)

Regular-way securities Regular-way purchases and sales of securities are recorded on the trade date. (ASC 942-325-25-2)

National Credit Union Share Insurance Fund (NCUSIF) Deposits Due to unique legal and operational aspects of the credit union share insurance fund, credit unions report amounts placed in their deposit insurance fund as an asset if such amounts are fully refundable. (ASC 942-325-25-3) Banks and thrifts expense payments to their deposit insurance fund as incurred. This is because of differences in how the funds operate.

Credit unions must review refundability of Share Insurance Fund deposits and premiums for impairment taking into consideration the financial condition of the credit union and the insurance fund. (ASC 942-325-35-4a) If the equity of the NCUSIF exceeds normal operating levels, the National Credit Union Administrator must reduce its equity by making distributions to credit unions. (ASC 942-325-35-4b)

If the NCUSIF waives insurance premiums, it is industry practice to net imputed earnings on the insurance deposits against imputed premium expense rather than presenting them gross. (ASC 942-325-35-4c)

Liabilities

Short sales of securities Obligations incurred on short sales are reported as liabilities and usually titled securities sold, not yet purchased. (ASC 942-405-25-1)

Deposits The liability for deposits received is recognized when the deposits are received. The deposit float is recorded both as an asset and a liability. (ASC 942-405-25-3)

Other Expenses An institution should report the Financing Corporation (FICO) assessment as a period cost when incurred. (ASC 942-720-25-1)

Income Taxes and Bad-Debt Reserves Both stock and mutual savings and loan associations are required by regulatory authorities to place a portion of their earnings into a general reserve as protection for depositors. Savings and loan associations are allowed by the IRS to maintain a bad-debt reserve and to deduct any additions to their reserve in determining taxable income. Since this method differs from the method for determining bad debt expense, pretax accounting income and taxable income will differ. (ASC 942-740-05-2)

Presentation and Disclosure

In addition to the guidance in ASC 942, preparers should also consult SEC Regulation S-X:

- Rule 9-02 for the applicability of general rules on Regulation S-X Articles 1, 2, 3, 3A, and 4 (ASC 942-10-S45-1)
- Rule 9-03 for balance sheet disclosures
- Rule 9-04 for income statement disclosures

Balance Sheet Entities covered by ASC 942 should disclose restrictions on the use or availability of certain cash balances. Examples of these are:

- Deposits with a Federal Reserve Bank, Federal Home Loan Bank, or corresponding financial institutions to meet reserve requirements
- Deposits under formal compensating balance agreement
  (ASC 942-210-50-1)

Liabilities ASC 942-405-55-1 requires that the savings accounts deposited in a credit union must be unequivocally listed as a liability for a credit union to be in compliance with the Codification. The statement of financial condition must present savings accounts either as the first item in the liabilities and equity section or as a separate subtotal before total liabilities. (ASC 942-405-55-2)

Debt Significant categories of borrowings should be presented as separate line items on the balance sheet. (ASC 942-470-45-1) Transfers of mortgages accounted for under ASC 860 should be classified as debt on the balance sheet and classified separately from advances, other notes payable, and subordinated debt. (ASC 942-470-15-2) The entity should disclose in the notes for debt:

- The title or nature of the agreement or both
- The interest rate
- Payment terms
- Maturity date
- Conversion features
- Redemption features
- Whether it is senior or subordinated
- Restrictive covenants
  (ASC 942-470-50-3)

Equity

Regulatory capital—banks and savings institutions At a minimum, banks and savings institutions should disclose the following in the notes:

a. A description of regulatory capital requirements for:
   1. Those for capital adequacy purposes and
   2. Those established by the prompt corrective action provisions of Section 38 of the Federal Deposit Insurance Act.
b. The actual or possible material effects of noncompliance with such requirements.
c. Whether the entity is in compliance with the regulatory capital requirements, including, the following with respect to quantitative measures:
   1. The entity's required and actual ratios and amounts of regulatory capital, which may include Tier 1 leverage, which may include Common Equity Tier 1 leverage, Tier 1 risk-based, and total risk-based capital, and (for savings institutions) tangible capital.

2. Factors that may significantly affect capital adequacy such as potentially volatile components of capital, qualitative factors, and regulatory mandates.

d. As of each balance sheet date presented, the prompt corrective action category in which the entity was classified as of its most recent notification.

e. As of the most recent balance sheet date, whether management believes any conditions or events since notification have changed the institution's category.
(ASC 942-505-50-1)

Institutions should also present disclosures for any state-imposed capital requirements that are more stringent than or significantly different from federal requirements. (ASC 942-505-50-1A)

For the disclosure in ASC 942-505-50-1(c) above, "adequately capitalized" or "undercapitalized" entities, should:

- Present the minimum amounts and ratios the institution must have to be categorized as *adequately capitalized* under the prompt corrective action framework and
- Should include the effect of any supervisory action that has been imposed.

The amounts disclosed under ASC 942-505-50-1(c) may be presented in either narrative or tabular form. The percentages disclosed should be those applicable to the entity. Entities with CAMELS ratings of 1 that are not anticipating or experiencing significant growth and have well-diversified risk are required to maintain a minimum leverage ratio of 3.0 percent. An additional 100 to 200 basis points are required for all but these most highly rated entities. If the institution has been advised that it must meet capital adequacy levels that exceed the statutory minimums, those higher levels should be disclosed. Such institution-specific requirements also shall be the basis for management's assertion in paragraph 942-505-50-1(c) about whether the entity is in compliance. (942-505-50-1B)

Under federal regulations, a bank or savings institution is considered to be within a given capital category as of the most recent date of any of the following:

- The date the institution filed a regulatory financial report
- The date a final regulatory examination report is delivered to the institution
- The date the institution's primary regulator provides written notice of the entity's capital category or that the institution's capital category has changed
(942-505-50-1C)

If any of the conditions in the following paragraph exist, the possible material effects of such conditions and events on amounts and disclosures in the financial statements should be disclosed. (942-505-50-1D)

The guidance in the preceding paragraph applies if any of the following conditions exist:

- The entity is not in compliance with capital adequacy requirements
- The entity is considered less than adequately capitalized under the prompt corrective action provisions
(942-505-50-1E)

Other regulatory limitations may exist despite compliance with minimum regulatory capital requirements. To the extent such limitations could materially affect the economic resources of the institution and claims to those resources, they shall similarly be disclosed in the notes to financial statements. (942-505-50-1F)

Disclosures for Holding Companies The disclosures required by ASC 942-505-50-1 through 50-1F should be presented for all significant subsidiaries of a holding company. In addition, bank holding companies should present the disclosures required by ASC 942-505- 50-1 through 50-1F as they apply to the holding company, except for disclosure required by ASC 942-505-50-1(d). Savings institution holding companies are not subject to regulatory capital requirements separate from those of their subsidiaries. Bank holding companies are not subject to the prompt corrective action provisions of the Federal Deposit Insurance Act. (ASC 942-505-50-1G)

Credit Unions A credit union or corporate credit union within the scope of ASC 942-10-15-2, at a minimum, should disclose the following in the notes to the financial statements:

a. A description of the regulatory requirements for:
    1. Capital adequacy purposes and
    2. Prompt corrective action.
b. The actual or possible material effects of noncompliance with those requirements.
c. Whether the entity is in compliance with the regulatory capital requirements,
d. The prompt corrective action category in which the institution was classified.
e. If, as of the most recent balance-sheet date or date financial statements are issued or are available to be issued, the institution is not in compliance with capital adequacy requirements, the possible material effects of such conditions on amounts and disclosures in the financial statements.
f. Whether after the balance sheet date and before the financial statements are issued or are available to be issued, management believes any events or changes have occurred to change the institution's prompt corrective action category.
(ASC 942-505-50-1H)

Disclosures should be presented for any state-imposed capital requirements that are more stringent than or significantly different from federal requirements. (ASC 942-505-50-2)

Branches of Foreign Institutions Branches of foreign financial institutions should disclose requirements to maintain capital-equivalent deposits and, depending on facts and circumstances, supervisory-mandated reserves. Quantitative disclosure shall be made, highlighting mandated deposit or reserve requirements and actual balances in those reserve or deposit accounts at the balance sheet date(s) reported. (ASC 942-505-50-3)

Further, if an uncertainty exists related to a parent that creates a higher-than-normal risk as to the viability of a branch or subsidiary, then that matter shall be adequately disclosed in the notes to the financial statements of the branch or subsidiary. If factors do not exist that indicate a higher than normal amount of risk or uncertainty regarding parent capital and other regulatory matters, then disclosures of capital and supervisory issues of the parent would not be required. (ASC 942-505-50-4)

Trust Operations If an institution is subject to capital requirements based on trust assets under management, the entity should include in the notes to the financial statements a discussion of:

- The existence of these requirements,
- Ramifications of failure to meet them, and
- A measurement of the entity's position relative to imposed requirements
(ASC 942-505-50-5)

Financial Instruments

Off-balance-sheet credit risk For financial instruments with off-balance-sheet credit risk, except for those instruments within the scope of ASC 815, an entity should disclose all of the following information:

a. The face or contract amount
b. The nature and terms, including, at a minimum, a discussion of the:
   1. Credit and market risk of those instruments
   2. Cash requirements of those instruments
   3. Related accounting policy according to ASC 235-10
c. The entity's policy for requiring collateral or other security to support financial instruments subject to credit risk
d. Information about the entity's access to that collateral or other security
e. The nature and a brief description of the collateral or other security supporting those financial instruments
   (ASC 942-825-50-1)

Deferred Taxes If a deferred tax liability is not recognized because of exceptions to comprehensive recognition of deferred taxes related to a savings and loan institution's bad-debt reserve for financial reporting, all of the following should be disclosed:

- Description of the types of temporary differences
- The types of evens that would cause the temporary differences to become taxable
- The cumulative amount of each type of temporary difference
- The amount of the deferred tax liability for temporary differences that is not recognized in accordance with ASC 740-10-25-3,25-5, 25-18 and 942-740-25-1 through 25-3 (ASC 942-740-50-1)

Consolidations If a bank does not consolidate a trust in a trust-preferred arrangement, the bank or holding company should report:

- Its debt issues to the trust and
- Its equity-method investment in the common stock of the trust (ASC 942-810-45-1)

Income Statement See SEC Regulation S-X Rule 9-04.

Statement of Cash Flows Banks, savings institutions, and credit unions are not required to report gross cash receipts and payments for the following:

- Deposits placed with other financial institutions
- Withdrawals of deposits
- Time deposits accepted
- Repayments of deposits
- Loans made to customers
- Principal collections of loans (ASC 942-230-45-1)

If an enterprise is part of a consolidated enterprise, net cash receipts and payments of the enterprise should be reported separate from the gross cash receipts and payments of the consolidated enterprise. (ASC 942-230-45-2)

Principal payments received under sales type and direct financing leases should be classified with investing activities. (ASC 942-230-45-4[2])

FINANCIAL SERVICES—INSURANCE (ASC 944)

PERSPECTIVE AND ISSUES

Technical Alert

In August 2018, the FASB issued Accounting Standards Update 2018-12, *Financial Services—Insurance (Topic 944) Targeted Improvements to the Accounting for Long-Duration Contracts.*

Guidance ASU 2018-12 applies to all insurance entities that issue long duration contracts as defined in ASC 944. The amendments do not apply to holders (or policyholders) of long duration

- contracts and
- noninsurance entities.

The changes affecting ASC 944 include:

Assumptions used to measure the liability for future policy benefits for traditional and limited- payment contracts.

- The amendments require an insurance entity to
  - review and, if there is a change, update the assumptions used to measure cash flows at least annually and
  - update the discount rate assumption at each reporting date.

  (ASC 944-40-35-5)
- The provision for risk of adverse deviation and premium deficiency (or loss recognition) testing are eliminated.
  (ASC 944-30-35-5)
- The change in the liability estimate as a result of updating cash flow assumptions is required to be recognized in net income. The change in the liability estimate as a result of updating the discount rate assumption is required to be recognized in other comprehensive income. The amendments require that an insurance entity discount expected future cash flows at an upper-medium grade (low-credit-risk) fixed-income instrument yield that maximizes the use of observable market inputs.
  (ASC 944-40-35-6A)

Measurement of market risk benefits.

- The ASU requires that an insurance entity measure all market risk benefits associated with deposit (or account balance) contracts at fair value. The portion of any change in fair value attributable to a change in the instrument specific credit risk is required to be recognized in other comprehensive income.
  (ASC 944-40-30-19C)

[2] This paragraph is effective upon implementation of ASU 2016-02.

Amortization of deferred acquisition costs.

- The ASU simplifies the amortization of deferred acquisition costs and other balances amortized in proportion to premiums, gross profits, or gross margins.
- The changes require that those balances be amortized on a constant level basis over the expected term of the related contracts.
- (ASC 944-30-35-3A)
- Deferred acquisition costs are required to be written off for unexpected contract terminations but are not subject to an impairment test.
  (ASC 944-30-35-3B)

Disclosures An insurance entity must disclose:

- Disaggregated rollforwards of beginning to ending balances of the liability for future policy benefits, policyholder account balances, market risk benefits, separate account liabilities, and deferred acquisition costs.
  (ASC 944-30-50-6)
- Information about significant inputs, judgments assumptions, and methods used in measurement, including changes in those inputs, judgments, and assumptions, and the effect of those changes on measurement.

Effective Dates In October 2019, the FASB issued ASU 2019-09 changing the effective date of ASU 2108-12. The new effective dates are financial statements of SEC files, excluding smaller reporting companies, for fiscal years beginning after December 15, 2021, and after December 15, 2023, for all other entities.[3]

Overview To apply the guidance in ASC 944, it is necessary to determine the type of insurance contract:

- Short-duration
- Long-duration, including:
  - Traditional fixed and variable annuity and life insurance contracts
  - Universal life-type contracts
  - Nontraditional fixed and variable annuity and life insurance contracts
  - Participating life insurance contracts
  - Group participatory pension contracts
- Reinsurance
- Financial guarantee

The two major types of insurance companies are life and property and casualty. Each category is further subdivided into stock companies and mutual associations. Due to the regulated nature of the insurance industry, financial reporting may be in conformity to statutory accounting principles (SAP) or GAAP. Furthermore, publicly held companies subject to SEC accounting rules will account for certain transactions and events in other manners dictated by those requirements. While accounting principles under GAAP are broadly applicable to all types of insurance companies (including those dealing in such specialized products as mortgage insurance, title insurance, and reinsurance), the nature of the estimation process (such as for claims liabilities) differs substantially depending upon the character of the risks assumed.

[3] On July 9, 2020, the FASB issued an alert that they are proposing a one-year delay in the effective date. Preparers should consult FASB.org for the latest information.

The main contrasts between SAP and GAAP arise from the more conservative nature of SAP, which is a reflection of the insurance regulatory agencies' concern with protection of the policyholders' interests, and hence with the liquidity and solvency of the insurance companies. Accordingly, under SAP certain costs, such as policy acquisition expenses, are written off as incurred; certain nonliquid assets, such as property and furniture, are not recognized; and claims liabilities are very conservatively estimated. In contrast to this essentially short-term perspective, financial statements prepared on the GAAP basis are more concerned with the value of the companies' investments and net worth on a going concern basis.

The primary source of insurance industry GAAP is ASC 944, *Financial Services—Insurance*. Insurance contracts are categorized as short duration (which includes most property and liability insurance) or long duration (which includes most life, mortgage, and title insurance). Nominal insurance contracts that are effectively investment contracts, however, are not accounted for as insurance.

ASC 944 discusses those aspects of accounting and auditing unique to life and health insurance entities, and contains significant discussions of statutory accounting practices (SAP), which comprise laws, regulations, and administrative rulings adopted by various states that govern the operations and reporting requirements of life insurance entities. It does not reflect SAP under the National Association of Insurance Commissioners (NAIC) codification project.

The ASC also addresses the classification and valuation of liabilities, as well as disclosures for nontraditional annuity and life insurance contracts issued by insurance enterprises. Several of the conclusions reached on these topics are discussed later in this section.

CONCEPTS, RULES, AND EXAMPLES

Premium Income

Premium income is recognized differently for short- and long-duration contracts. For short-duration contracts, premium income is recognized over the contract term in proportion to the amount of insurance provided. (ASC 944-605-25-1) In the case of long-duration contracts, revenue is accrued as the premiums become due from policyholders, except for contracts that provide benefits over a term longer than the premium payment term (such as twenty-year life policies), in which case income is recognized over the longer period during which benefits may be provided. (ASC 944-605-25-3)

Financial Guarantee Insurance Financial guarantee insurance (and reinsurance) contracts are contracts issued by insurers that provide protection to the holder of a financial obligation, such as a municipal bond or an asset-backed security, from a financial loss in the event of a default. A financial guarantee insurance contract obligates the insurer to pay a claim upon the occurrence of an event of default. Insurers are to recognize a liability for unearned premium revenue at the inception of a financial guarantee insurance contract in an amount equal to the present value of the premiums due or, if certain criteria are met and used, expected to be collected over the period of the financial guarantee insurance contract. The insurance enterprise is to determine the present value of the premiums due or expected to be collected using a discount rate that reflects the risk-free rate at the inception of the contract, based on the insurance contract period unless the insurer is permitted to consider prepayments. The discount is to be accreted on the premium receivable through earnings over that same period. (ASC 944-310-30-2)

The discount rate used is to be updated to a current risk-free rate only when prepayment assumptions change. When an *expected period* is used to measure the unearned premium revenue, the insurer is to adjust the prepayment assumptions when those assumptions change. The adjustment to the unearned premium revenue will equal the adjustment to the premium receivable, and thus there will be no effect on earnings at the time of the adjustment. (ASC 944-310-35-5) If the premium receivable has an expected credit loss, it must be adjusted in accordance with ASC 326 measured at amortized cost with a charge against earnings. (ASC 944-310-35-6)

The insurer will recognize a claim liability on a financial guarantee insurance contract when it expects that a claim loss will exceed the unearned premium revenue for that contract based on the present value of expected net cash outflows to be paid under the insurance contract. (ASC 944-40-25-42)

Reinsurance Contracts Another specialized topic area pertinent to insurance companies is that of reinsurance, which is addressed by ASC 944. It requires that reinsurance receivables, including amounts related to claims incurred but not reported, be reported as assets, consistent with the manner in which liabilities relating to the underlying reinsured contracts are accounted for. (ASC 944-310-25-2)

ASC 944-605 addresses accounting for foreign property and liability reinsurance, and concludes that except for special circumstances, only the periodic method is acceptable in accounting for foreign reinsurance premiums. (ASC 944-605-25-18) ASC 944-505-50 requires specific disclosures for foreign reinsurance accounted by the open-year method. (ASC 944-605-50-1d)

Surplus Notes ASC 944-470 affects accounting by certain insurance companies that issue a security known as surplus notes. It requires that these instruments be accounted for as debt and included in the liabilities caption of the statement of financial position. (ASC 944-470-25-1) Furthermore, interest must be accrued and recognized as an expense over the term of the notes, whether or not payment of interest and/or principal has been approved by the insurance commissioner. (ASC 944-470-35-1) However, disclosure is required as to the state insurance commissioner's ability to approve any interest or principal payments. (ASC 944-470-50-1)

Demutualizations ASC 944-805 addresses demutualizations (whereby formerly mutually owned insurers issue stock), as well as the formation of insurance holding companies (MIHC). A key concern is the accounting for the *closed block* of assets and liabilities, and of earnings allocable to the closed block. This pertains to mechanisms designed to protect the adjustable policy features and dividend expectations of participating life insurance policyholders from the competing interests of stockholders. Typically, the plan of demutualization describes how the closed block will operate. The closed block assets and cash returns on those assets will not inure to the stockholders of the demutualized company; instead, all cash flows from these assets will be used to benefit the closed block policyholders. The insurance enterprise remains obligated to provide for minimum guarantees under the participating policy, and it is consequently possible under certain circumstances that additional "stockholder" funds will have to be used to meet the contractual benefits of the closed block policyholders. The assets designated to the closed block are subject to the same liabilities, with the same priority in the case of insolvency or in liquidation, as assets outside the closed block. In many situations, commissions and other expenses (including management expenses) of operating and administering the closed block will not be charged to the closed block. Unless the state insurance department consents to an earlier termination, the closed block will continue in effect until the date on which none of the policies in the closed block remains in force.

Alternatives to the closed block have arisen in practice encompassing, for a number of types of contracts, various mechanisms believed by the insurance enterprise and state insurance regulators to be appropriate in the specific circumstances. Closed block alternative mechanisms have been used in lieu of closed blocks for certain participating life contracts to commit to the insurance regulator that the insurance company will continue to follow its established dividend practices. Closed block alternative mechanisms also have been used to protect nonguaranteed elements of participating and nonparticipating insurance contracts such as interest credits on deferred annuities and adjustable premiums on adjustable premium term business. In some instances, the methodology and limitations defined in the agreements with the state insurance regulators have considered only specific profit components, such as mortality experience on a block of term insurance or investment spreads on a block of annuities, and in other instances have considered virtually all components of product profitability. Where there is a limitation on the profits that may inure to the stockholders, there generally is a formal agreement between the insurance company and the insurance regulators that defines (1) the contracts covered by the limitation, (2) the profit limitation calculation, and (3) the timing and manner (for example, as policy dividends, reduced premiums, or additional benefits) in which amounts that may not be distributed to stockholders are to be distributed to policyholders.

ASC 944 addresses the classification and valuation of liabilities as well as disclosures for nontraditional annuity and life insurance contracts issued by insurance enterprises. The requirements are set forth in the following paragraphs.

An insurance entity that owns the assets and is contractually obligated to pay the liabilities should include in its financial statements separate account assets and liabilities. (ASC 944-80-25-1)

ASC 944-80-25-3 below applies if:

- The separate account is recognized legally
- The separate account assets, supporting the contract liabilities, are insulated legally from the general account liabilities, meaning the contract holder is not subject to insurer default risk to the extent of the assets held in the separate account
- The insurer is obligated by contractual, statutory, or regulatory requirements to invest the contract holder's funds within the separate account as directed by the contract holder in designated investment alternatives or following specific investment objectives or policies
- Investment performance, net of contract fees and assessments, or regulatory requirements, is passed through to the contract holder
  (ASC 944-80-25-2)

The portion of separate account assets representing contract holder funds should be measured at fair value (ASC 944-80-30-1) and reported in the insurance enterprise's financial statements as a summary total, with an equivalent summary total for related liabilities, if the separate account arrangement meets all the specified criteria in ASC 944-80-25-2. (ASC 944-80-25-3 and 45-3) If the arrangement does not meet the criteria:

- Assets representing contract holder funds should be accounted for as general account assets,
- Any related liability should be accounted for as a general account liability, and
- Revenue and expense related to such arrangements should be recognized within the respective revenue and expense lines in the statement of operations.
  (ASC 944-80-25-4)

Assets underlying an insurance enterprise's proportionate interest in a separate account do not represent contract holder funds, and thus are not to be separately reported and valued. (ASC 944-80-25-6) If a separate account arrangement meets the criteria in ASC 944 and:

- The terms of the contract allow the contract holder to invest in additional units in the separate account, or

- The insurance enterprise is marketing contracts that permit funds to be invested in the separate account,
- The assets underlying the insurance enterprise's proportionate interest in the separate account should be accounted for in a manner consistent with similar assets held by the general account that the insurance enterprise may be required to sell.

(ASC 944-80-25-8 and 25-9)

If the enterprise's proportionate interest in the separate account is less than 20% of the separate account, and all of the underlying investments of the separate account meet the definition of securities in ASC 320-10 and ASC 321-10, or the definition of cash and cash equivalents, the enterprise may report its portion of the separate account value as an investment in equity securities classified as trading under ASC 320. (ASC 944-80-25-11) If the criteria are met, ASC 944-80-25-6 through 25-9 may also be applied. (ASC 944-80-25-10)

Assets transferred from the general account to a separate account should be recognized at fair value to the extent of third-party contract holders' proportionate interest in the separate account if the separate account arrangement meets the criteria in ASC 944-80-25-2. Any gain related to the third-party contract holder's proportionate interest should be recognized immediately in earnings of the general account of the insurance enterprise, if the risks and rewards of ownership have been transferred to contract holders using the fair value of the asset at the date of the contract holder's assumption of risks and rewards. (ASC 944-80-40-1) A guarantee of the asset's value or minimum rate of return or a commitment to repurchase the asset would indicate that the risks of ownership have not been transferred, and no gain can be recognized. If the separate account arrangement does not meet the criteria in the codification, the transfer generally should have no financial reporting effect (that is, general account classification and carrying amounts should be retained). In certain situations loss recognition may be appropriate.

The basis for determining the balance that accrues to the contract holder for a long-duration insurance or investment contract that is subject to ASC 944 is the accrued account balance. The accrued account balance equals:

- Deposit(s) net of withdrawals;
- Plus amounts credited pursuant to the contract;
- Less fees and charges assessed;
- Plus additional interest (for example, persistency bonus); and
- Other adjustments, such as appreciation or depreciation recognized under the codification, to the extent not already credited.

(ASC 944-40-25-14)

For contracts that have features that may result in more than one potential account balance, the accrued account balance should be the highest contractually determinable balance that will be available in cash or its equivalent at contractual maturity or the reset date, without reduction for future fees and charges. (ASC 944-40-25-22) The accrued account balance should not reflect any surrender adjustments (for example, fair value annuity adjustments, surrender charges, or credits). For contracts in which amounts credited as interest to the contract holder are reset periodically, the accrued balance should be based on the highest crediting rate guaranteed or declared through the reset date. (ASC 944-40-25-24)

For a contract not accounted for under ASC 815 that provides a return based on the total return of a contractually referenced pool of assets either through crediting rates or termination adjustments, the accrued account balance should be based on the fair value of the referenced pool of assets (or applicable index value) at the date of the statement of financial position, even if the related assets are not recognized at fair value. (ASC 944-40-25-19)

To determine the accounting under ASC 944 for a contract that contains death or other insurance benefit features, the enterprise should first determine whether the contract is an investment or universal-life-type contract. (ASC 944-20-15-26) A rebuttable presumption is that a contract has significant mortality risk where the additional insurance benefit would vary significantly in response to capital markets volatility. The determination of significance should be made at contract inception, other than at transition, and should be based on a comparison of the present value of expected excess payments (that is, insurance benefit amounts and related incremental claim adjustment expenses in excess of the account balance) to be made under insurance benefit features to the present value of all amounts expected to be assessed against the contract holder (revenue).

For contracts classified as insurance contracts that are not accounted for under ASC 815 and have amounts assessed against contract holders each period for the insurance benefit feature that are assessed in a manner that is expected to result in profits in earlier years and subsequent losses from that insurance benefit function, a liability should be established in addition to the account balance to recognize the portion of such assessments that compensates the insurance enterprise for benefits to be provided in future periods in accordance with the guidance in the codification. (ASC 944-40-25-26 and 25-27)

If a reinsurer assumes the insurance benefit feature, it should assess the significance of mortality and morbidity risk within the reinsurance contract according to the guidance in ASC 944, regardless of whether there is an account balance. (ASC 944-40-25-35) The reinsurer should determine the classification of the reinsurance contract as an investment contract or as an insurance contract at the inception of the reinsurance contract. (ASC 944-40-25-36) For reinsurance contracts, the mortality or morbidity risk could be deemed other than nominal even if the original issuer did not determine mortality or morbidity to be other than nominal. (ASC 944-40-25-37) Similarly, the issuer of a contract that provides only an insurance benefit feature that wraps a noninsurance contract, for example, a guaranteed minimum death benefit related to a mutual fund balance, should evaluate its contract in the same manner. (ASC 944-40-25-39) A reinsurer or issuer of the insurance benefit features of a contract should calculate a liability for the portion of premiums collected each period that represents compensation to the insurance enterprise for benefits that are assessed in a manner that is expected to result in current profits and future losses from the insurance benefit function. That liability should be calculated using the methodology described in ASC 944. (ASC 944-40-25-41)

Contracts may provide for potential benefits in addition to the account balance that are payable only upon annuitization, such as annuity purchase guarantees, guaranteed minimum income benefit (GMIB), and two-tier annuities. Insurance enterprises should determine whether such contract features should be accounted for under the provisions of ASC 815. If the contract feature is not accounted for under the provisions of ASC 815, an additional liability for the contract feature should be established if the present value of expected annuitization payments at the expected annuitization date exceeds the expected account balance at the expected annuitization date in accordance with the guidance in ASC 944. (ASC 944-40-25-40)

Sales inducements provided to the contract holder, whether for investment or universal-life-type contracts, should be recognized as part of the liability for policy benefits over the period for which the contract must remain in force for the contract holder to qualify for the inducement or at the crediting date, if earlier, in accordance with the codification. No adjustments should be made to reduce the liability related to the sales inducements for anticipated surrender charges, persistency, or early withdrawal contractual features. (ASC 944-40-25-12)

Sales inducements that are recognized as part of the liability under ASC 944, that are explicitly identified in the contract at inception, and that meet the criteria specified in the codification should be deferred and amortized using the same methodology and assumptions used to amortize capitalized acquisition costs.

Costs Associated with Acquiring or Renewing Insurance Contracts

Only the following costs incurred in the acquisition of insurance contracts can be capitalized and subsequently amortized:

- Incremental direct costs of successfully acquiring or renewing insurance contracts; these are costs that result directly from the contract transactions and are essential to the contract and would not have been incurred if the contract acquisition had not occurred.
- Costs directly related to underwriting, policy issuance, medical and inspection, and sales force contract selling for successfully acquired or renewed insurance contracts. (ASC 944-30-25-1A)

All other costs, such as market research, training, administration, and product development, should be treated as period costs. Entities should treat all administrative expenses as period costs.

Capitalized acquisition costs should be charged to expense on a constant-level basis recognized under ASC 944-605. (ASC 944-30-35-3A)

Deferred Acquisition Costs for Insurance Contract Modifications or Exchanges

ASC 944-30 addresses the accounting for deferred acquisition costs related to the internal replacement of selected insurance and investment contracts. An internal replacement is a modification of an insurance product's benefits, features, rights, or coverages (described hereafter as *benefits*) by a variety of means, including the extinguishment and replacement of a contract.

If an internal replacement occurs and the rights and obligations of the parties are essentially unchanged, then the replacement contract is considered a continuation of the replaced contract. In this case, the replaced contract's unamortized deferred acquisition costs, unearned revenue liabilities, and deferred sales inducement assets should continue to be recognized as part of the replacement contract. (ASC 944-30-35-24) Also, costs incurred in connection with such a replacement are charged to expense as incurred.

A contract change must meet all of the following criteria in order to be considered a continuation of the replaced contract—if any condition is not met, the change is treated as a substantially changed contract:

- The insured event, risk, or period of coverage has not changed.
- The contract holder's investment return rights have not changed.
- Either there is no change in the insurance premium, or a premium reduction is matched by a corresponding reduction in benefits.
- Net of distributions, there is no net reduction in contract value.

- There is no change in contractual participation or dividend features.
- There is no change in the contract's amortization method or revenue classification. (ASC 944-30-35-37)

If benefits replacement results in a substantially changed contract, then the replaced contract is considered extinguished, in which case unamortized deferred acquisition costs, unearned revenue liabilities, and deferred sales inducement assets from the replaced contract should not be deferred as part of the replacement contract. (ASC 944-30-40-1 and 40-2)

If a contract is accounted for as a long-duration participating contract, the estimated gross profit of the replacement contract is treated as a revision of the replaced contract's gross profit when determining the amortization of deferred acquisition costs, deferred sales inducement assets, and the recognition of unearned revenues. If a contract is accounted for as nonrefundable fees, the cash flows of the replacement contract revise the cash flows of the replaced contract for purposes of calculating the interest rate amortization of unamortized deferred acquisition costs and deferred sales inducement assets.

The guidance above does not apply to contract modifications resulting from an election by the contract holder that was within the original contract, as long as:

1. The election followed the terms of the original contract,
2. The election is not subject to any underwriting,
3. The insurance provider cannot decline the coverage or adjust contract pricing, and
4. The benefit had been accounted for since the contract inception. (ASC 944-30-35-26)

The guidance above also does not apply if a contract feature is nonintegrated (it provides coverage that is priced solely for the incremental benefits coverage, and does not alter other components of the contract), in which case it should be accounted for as a separately issued contract. (ASC 944-30-35-31 through 33)

Present Value of Future Profits

ASC 944-20-S99 notes that industry practice is to amortize the present value of future profits (PVP) using an interest method with accrual of interest added to the unamortized balance. In the past, there has been some diversity in the application of this method in practice, and so the codification mandates that the interest rate used to amortize PVP should be the liability or contract rate. It also states that changes in estimates of future gross profits on contracts should be accounted for as a catch-up adjustment. And finally, PVP and any related liability should be subject to the premium deficiency test required in ASC 944-60.

ASC 944-20 includes criteria for the recognition and amounts of assets and liabilities by the assuming and ceding enterprises, respectively, and accounting for changes in coverage during the reinsurance period. A number of conditions are identified, satisfaction of which is necessary for a contract to be treated as reinsurance, and in their absence such contracts are to be accounted for by the deposit method. (ASC 944-20-25-4)

ASC 944-605-25 states that recognition of an unearned revenue liability representing amounts that have been assessed to compensate insurers for services to be performed over future periods is a requirement under ASC 944. (ASC 944-605-25-6) Importantly, this liability is not to be used to inappropriately level or smooth out gross profit over the term of the contract or produce a level gross profit from the mortality benefit over the life of the contract.

FINANCIAL SERVICES—INVESTMENT COMPANIES (ASC 946)

PERSPECTIVE AND ISSUES

Scope

ASC 946 provides incremental guidance to those entities that meet the assessment guidelines to be deemed investment companies. All entities regulated under the Investment Company Act of 1940 are in the scope of ASC 946. (ASC 946-10-15-4) Other entities must assess the characteristics of an investment company outlined below, taking into account the entities' purpose and design. (ASC 946-10-15-5) The fundamental characteristics of an investment company are that it:

- Obtains funds from one or more investors.
- Provides the investors with investment management services.
- Commits to its investors that its business purpose and only substantive activities are investing the funds solely for returns from capital appreciation, investment income, or both.
- Does not obtain or have the objective of obtaining returns or benefits from an investee or its affiliates that are not normally attributable to ownership interests or that are other than capital appreciation or investment income.
  (ASC 946-10-15-6)

Typical characteristics of an investment company are:

- It has more than one investment and investor.
- Investors are not related parties of the parent, if any, or the investment manager.
- Ownership interests are in the form of equity or partnership interests.
- It manages substantially all of its investments on a fair value basis.
  (ASC 946-10-15-7)

Entities that do not possess one or more of the characteristics above may still be investment companies. (ASC 946-10-15-8)

REASSESSMENT OF INVESTMENT COMPANY STATUS

If an entity makes the assessment and judges that it is an investment company, it should account for the effect of the change from the date of the change, recognizing the effect as a cumulative effect adjustment. (ASC 944-10-25-3) Entities that make the assessment and come to the conclusion that they are no longer an investment company discontinue applying the guidance and account for the effect of the change prospectively in accordance with other topics. (ASC 946-10-25-2)

DEFINITIONS OF TERMS

Source: Terms are from ASC 946, *Glossary*. Other terms relevant to this topic can be found in Appendix A, *Definitions of Terms*, including Affiliate, Control Def. 1, Fair Value, Market Participants, Orderly Transaction, Parent, and Related Parties.

Front-End Load. A sales commission or charge payable at the time of purchase of mutual fund shares.

Net Asset Value per Share. Net asset value per share is the amount of net assets attributable to each share of capital stock (other than senior equity securities, that is, preferred stock) outstanding at the close of the period. It excludes the effects of assuming conversion of outstanding convertible securities, whether or not their conversion would have a diluting effect.

CONCEPTS, RULES, AND EXAMPLES

Several types of investment companies exist: management investment companies, unit investment trusts, collectible trust funds, investment partnerships, certain separate accounts of life insurance companies, and offshore funds. Management investment companies registered under or regulated by the Investment Company Act of 1940 include open-end funds (mutual funds), closed-end funds, special-purpose funds, venture capital investment companies, small business investment companies, and business development companies.

Accounting Policies

The accounting policies for an investment company result from the company's role as a vehicle through which investors can invest as a group. These policies are largely governed by the SEC, Small Business Administration, and specific provisions of the Internal Revenue Code relating to investment companies.

Investments—Debt and Equity Securities

Security purchases and sales are generally recorded at the trade date; therefore, the effects of all securities trades entered into by the investment company to the date of the financial statements are included in the financial report. (ASC 946-320-25-1)

Investment companies subsequently report investment securities at fair value in accordance with the guidance in ASC 825. (ASC 946-320-35-1)

Investment companies record dividend income on the ex-dividend date, not on the later record or payable date. The rationale for this treatment is that the market price of market securities may be affected by the exclusion of the declared dividend. Additionally, investment companies record a liability for dividends payable on the ex-dividend date because mutual fund shares are purchased and redeemed at prices equal to or based on net asset value. If investors purchase shares between the declaration and ex-dividend dates they are entitled to receive dividends; however, investors purchasing shares after the ex-dividend date are not entitled to receive dividends. (ASC 946-320-25-4)

Open-end investment companies often employ the practice of equalization. This theory states that the net asset value of each share of capital stock sold comprises the par value of the stock, undistributed income, and paid-in capital and other surplus. When shares are sold or repurchased, the investment company calculates the amount of undistributed income available for distribution to its shareholders. Based on the number of shares outstanding, the investment company determines the per share amount; this amount is credited to an equalization account when shares are sold. Conversely, the equalization account is charged when shares are repurchased.[4]

Accounting for High-Yield Debt Securities

The accounting by creditors for investments in *step bonds* and *payment-in-kind (PIK)* bonds, if these qualify as *high-yield* securities, is addressed by the ASC 946. Step interest bonds are

---

[4] See *Investment Companies–Audit and Accounting Guide*, Copyright 2019, American Institute of Certified Public Accountants.

generally unsecured debentures that pay no interest for a specified period after issuance, then pay a stipulated rate for a period, then a higher rate for another period, etc., until maturity. Thus, they combine some of the characteristics of zero-coupon bonds with some features of current interest bonds. PIK bonds pay some or all interest in the form of other debt instruments (*baby* or *bunny* bonds), which in turn may also pay interest in the form of baby bonds. All babies mature at the due date of the parent bond.

ASC 946-320 concludes that for PIK and step bonds:

- The interest method should be used to determine interest income;
- A reserve against income should be established for interest income not expected to be realized;
- The cost plus any discount should not exceed undiscounted future cash collections. (ASC 946-320-35-10 through 35-13)

Accounting for Expenditures of Defaulted Debt Securities

For defaulted debt securities, any interest receivable written off that had been recognized as income constitutes a reduction of income. Write-offs of purchased interest increase the cost basis and represent an unrealized loss until the security is sold. (ASC 946-320-35-17 and 35-18) *Capital infusions* are accounted for as an addition to the cost basis, while related "workout expenditures" are recorded as unrealized losses. Any ongoing expenditures to protect the value of the investment are recorded as operating expenses. (ASC 946-320-35-14 through 16)

Exemptions from the Requirement to Provide a Statement of Cash Flows

The following conditions must be met for an investment company to be exempted from providing a statement of cash flows:

- The entity's investments are carried at fair value and classified as Level 1 or Level 2 measurements per ASC 820.
- The entity had little or no debt, based on average debt outstanding during the period, in relation to average total assets.
- The entity provides a statement of changes in net assets.
  (ASC 230-10-15-4)

Commodity Pools

ASC 946-210 stipulates that investment partnerships, which are commodity pools subject to regulation by the Commodity Exchange Act of 1934, are subject to its guidance. Thus, notwithstanding the rapid turnover common among such pools, the financial statements must include a schedule of investments. (ASC 946-210-50-4)

Taxes

Investment companies that distribute all taxable income and taxable realized gains qualifying under Subchapter M of the Internal Revenue Code are not required to record a provision for federal income taxes. If the investment company does not distribute all taxable income and taxable realized gains, a liability should be recorded at the end of the last day of the taxable year. The rationale for recording on the last day of the year is that only shareholders of record at that date are entitled to credit for taxes paid.[5]

---

[5] Ibid.

Foreign Currency Matters

ASC 946-830 concludes that transactions denominated in a foreign currency must originally be measured in that currency. (ASC 946-830-45-2) Reporting exchange rate gains and losses separately from any gain/loss on the investment due to changes in market price is allowable but not required. (ASC 946-830-45-4)

Balance Sheets

ASC 946-20-25-3 requires investment companies with enhanced 12b-1 plans or board-contingent plans for which the board has committed to pay costs to recognize a liability and the related expense, for the amount of excess costs. This liability should be discounted at an appropriate current rate if the amount and timing of cash flows are reliably determinable and if distribution costs are not subject to a reasonable interest charge. Excess costs are recorded as a liability because the fund has assumed an obligation to pay the 12b-1 fee after the termination of the plan to the extent that the distributor has excess costs.

Presentation ASC 946-210 affects the required presentation of certain contracts held by investment companies if these are fully benefit-responsive. Both the fair values of the contracts, segregated between guaranteed investment contracts and so-called wrapper contracts, and the contract (guaranteed) values, must be displayed in the investment company's statement of financial position.

A contract is deemed fully benefit-responsive if *all* five conditions set forth by the ASC are met. These conditions are defined as:

- The contract is negotiated directly between the fund and the issuer, and it prohibits the fund from assigning or selling the contract or its proceeds to another party without the consent of the issuer.
- Either (a) the repayment of principal and interest credited to participants in the fund is guaranteed by the issuer of the investment contract, or (b) the fund provides for prospective interest crediting rate adjustments to participants in the fund on a designated pool of investments held by the fund, provided that the terms of the agreement with participants in the fund specify that the crediting interest rate cannot be less than zero. The risk of decline in the interest crediting rate below zero must be transferred to a financially responsible third party through a *wrapper* contract. If an event (e.g., decline in creditworthiness of the contract issuer or wrapper provider) has occurred that may affect the realization of full contract value for a particular investment contract, the contract no longer is to be considered fully benefit-responsive.
- The terms of the contract require all permitted participant-initiated transactions with the fund to occur at contract value with no conditions, limits, or restrictions. Permitted participant-initiated transactions are those transactions allowed by the underlying defined-contribution plan, such as withdrawals for benefits, loans, or transfers to other funds within the plan.
- Events that limit the ability for the fund to transact at contract value with the issuer (e.g., premature termination of the contracts by the plan, plant closings, layoffs, plan termination, bankruptcy, mergers, and early retirement incentives) must be *probable* of *not* occurring.
- The fund itself must allow participants reasonable access to their funds.
  (ASC 946-210-20)

Statements of financial position of investment companies must report separately investments, including guaranteed investment contracts, at fair value, and wrapper contracts, also at fair value. The statement of financial position must also display an additional account to bring the total assets being reported to contract amounts—that is, the amounts at which participants can transact with the fund. (ASC 946-210-45-15)

Additionally, the following information must be disclosed in footnotes to the financial statements for each investment contract, and be reconciled to corresponding line items on the statement of financial position:

- The fair value of the wrapper contract and the fair value of each of the corresponding underlying investments;
- Adjustment from fair value to contract value (if the investment contract is fully benefit-responsive); and
- Major credit ratings of the issuer or wrapper provider.
  (ASC 946-210-45-18)

In order to be considered within the scope of the guidance in ASC 946-210-45-15 through 45-18, any portion of the net assets of the investment company that is not held by participants in qualified employer-sponsored defined-contribution plans as of the effective date are not permitted to increase due to gross contributions, loan repayments, or transfers into the fund. (ASC 946-210-45-18A)

ASC 946-210-50 pertains to investment partnerships that are exempt from SEC registration under the Investment Company Act of 1940. Specifically, the statement requires that the financial statements include a condensed schedule of securities that categorizes investments by type, country or geographic region, and industry; discloses pertinent information concerning investments comprising greater than 5% of net assets; and aggregates any securities holdings less than the 5% of net assets threshold. (ASC 946-210-50-6) The statement of operations for nonpublic investment companies shall be presented in conformity with requirements for public investment companies so as to reflect their comparable operations. The financial statements shall also present management fees and disclose their computation.

Disclosures for Fully Benefit-Responsive Investment Contracts Expanded disclosures are mandated for investment companies having fully benefit-responsive contracts, as follows:

- A description of the nature of the investment contracts, how they operate, and the methodology for calculating the crediting interest rate, including the key factors that could influence future average crediting interest rates, the basis for and frequency of determining credit interest-rate resets, and any minimum crediting interest rate under the terms of the contracts. This disclosure should explain the relationship between future crediting rates and the amount reported on the statement of financial position representing the adjustment of the portion of net assets attributable to fully benefit-responsive investments from fair value to contract value.
- A reconciliation between the beginning and ending balance of the amount presented on the statement of financial position that represents the difference between net assets at fair value and net assets for each period in which a statement of changes in net assets is presented. This reconciliation should include:
  - The change in the difference between the fair value and contract value of all fully benefit-responsive investment contracts, and
  - The increase or decrease due to changes in the fully benefit-responsive status of the fund's investment contracts.

- The average yield earned by the entire fund (without regard to the interest rate credited to participants in the fund) for each period for which a statement of financial position is presented.
- The average yield earned by the entire fund with an adjustment to reflect the actual interest rate credited to participants in the fund covering each period for which a statement of financial position is presented.
- Two different sensitivity analyses:
  - The effect on the weighted-average crediting interest rates calculated at the latest date of a statement of financial position and the next four reset dates, under two or more scenarios where there is an immediate hypothetical increase or decrease in interest rates, with no change to the duration of the underlying investment portfolio and no contributions or withdrawals. These scenarios should include, at a minimum, immediate hypothetical changes in market yields equal to one-quarter and one-half of the current yield.
  - The effect on the weighted-average crediting interest rates calculated at the latest date of a statement of financial position and the next four reset dates, under two or more scenarios where there are the same immediate hypothetical changes in market yields in the first analysis, combined with an immediate hypothetical 10% decrease in the net assets of the fund due to participant transfers, with no change to the duration of the portfolio.
- A description of the events which limit the ability of the fund to transact at contract value with the issuer (for example, premature termination of the contracts by the plan, plant closings, layoffs, plan termination, bankruptcy, mergers, and early retirement incentives), including a statement that the occurrence of such events is probable or not probable.
- A description of the events and circumstances that would allow issuers to terminate fully benefit-responsive investment contracts with the fund and settle at an amount different from contract value. (ASC 946-210-50-14)

FINANCIAL SERVICES—MORTGAGE BANKING (ASC 948)

PERSPECTIVE AND ISSUES

Mortgage banking guidance comprises two activities:

1. The origination or purchase of mortgage loans and subsequent sale to permanent investors, and
2. Long-term servicing of the mortgage loan.

To the extent that mortgage banking activities discussed in this section may be undertaken by subsidiaries or divisions of commercial banks or savings institutions, the same accounting and reporting standards apply. Normal, nonmortgage lending of those enterprises, however, is accounted for in accordance with the lender's normal accounting policies for such activities.

DEFINITIONS OF TERMS

Source: ASC 948, *Glossary*

Affiliated Entity. An entity that directly or indirectly controls, is controlled by, or is under common control with another entity; also, a party with which the entity may deal if one party has the ability to exercise significant influence over the other's operating and financial policies.

Current (Normal) Servicing Fee Rate. A servicing fee rate that is representative of servicing fee rates most commonly used in comparable servicing agreements covering similar types of mortgage loans.

Federal Home Loan Mortgage Corporation (FHLMC). Often referred to as *Freddie Mac*, FHLMC is a private corporation authorized by Congress to assist in the development and maintenance of a secondary market in conventional residential mortgages. FHLMC purchases and sells mortgages principally through mortgage participation certificates (PC) representing an undivided interest in a group of conventional mortgages. FHLMC guarantees the timely payment of interest and the collection of principal on the PC.

Federal National Mortgage Association (FNMA). Often referred to as *Fannie Mae*, FNMA is an investor-owned corporation established by Congress to support the secondary mortgage loan market by purchasing mortgage loans when other investor funds are limited and selling mortgage loans when other investor funds are available.

Gap Commitment. A commitment to provide interim financing while the borrower is in the process of satisfying provisions of a permanent loan agreement, such as obtaining a designated occupancy level on an apartment project. The interim loan ordinarily finances the difference between the floor loan (the portion of a mortgage loan commitment that is less than the full amount of the commitment) and the maximum permanent loan.

Government National Mortgage Association (GNMA). Often referred to as *Ginnie Mae*, GNMA is a U.S. governmental agency that guarantees certain types of securities (mortgage-backed securities) and provides funds for and administers certain types of low-income housing assistance programs.

Internal Reserve Method. A method for making payments to investors for collections of principal and interest on mortgage loans by issuers of GNMA securities. An issuer electing the internal reserve method is required to deposit in a custodial account an amount equal to one month's interest on the mortgage loans that collateralize the GNMA security issued.

Mortgage-Backed Securities. Securities issued by a governmental agency or corporation (e.g., GNMA or FHLMC) or by private issuers (e.g., FNMA, banks, and mortgage banking entities). Mortgage-backed securities generally are referred to as mortgage participation certificates or pass-through certificates (PC). A PC represents an undivided interest in a pool of specific mortgage loans. Periodic payments on GNMA PC are backed by the U.S. government. Periodic payments on FHLMC and FNMA PC are guaranteed by those corporations and are not backed by the U.S. government.

Mortgage Banking Entity. An entity that is engaged primarily in originating, marketing, and servicing real estate mortgage loans for other than its own account. Mortgage banking entities, as local representatives of institutional lenders, act as correspondents between lenders and borrowers.

Permanent Investor. An entity that invests in mortgage loans for its own account, for example, an insurance entity, commercial or mutual savings bank, savings and loan association, pension plan, real estate investment trust, or FNMA.

CONCEPTS, RULES, AND EXAMPLES

Mortgage Banking Activities

A mortgage banking entity (MBE) acts as an intermediary between borrowers (mortgagors) and lenders (mortgagees). MBE activities include purchasing and originating mortgage loans for sale to permanent investors and performing servicing activities during the period that the loans are outstanding. The mortgage loans offered for sale to permanent investors may be originated by the MBE (in-house originations); purchased from realtors, brokers, or investors; or converted from short-term, interim credit facilities to permanent financing. The common technique used by the MBE to market and sell the loans is referred to as securitization because the mortgage loans receivable are pooled and converted to mortgage-backed securities and sold in that form.

MBEs customarily retain the rights to service the loans that they sell to permanent investors in exchange for a servicing fee. (ASC 948-10-05-7) The servicing fee, normally a percentage of the mortgage's outstanding principal balance, compensates the MBE for processing of mortgagor payments of principal, interest and escrow deposits, disbursing funds from the escrow accounts to pay property taxes and insurance on behalf of the mortgagor, and remitting net proceeds to the permanent investor along with relevant accounting reports.

The MBE classifies mortgage loans that it holds as either (1) held-for-sale, or (2) held for long-term investment.

Loans Held-for-Sale Mortgage loans held for sale are reported at the lower of amortized cost or fair value as of the date of the statement of financial position. Any excess of amortized cost over fair value is accounted for as a valuation allowance, changes in which are included in income in the period of change. (ASC 948-310-35-1 and 35-2)

If a held-for-investment mortgage loan is transferred into the held-for-sale category, the entity should reverse any previous credit losses. The loan is transferred at its amortized cost basis and then determines if a valuation allowance is necessary. (ASC 948-310-35-2A)

Loan Origination Fees Loan origination fees and related direct costs for loans held for sale are capitalized as part of the related loan and amortized, using the effective yield method. However, fees and costs associated with commitments to originate, sell, or purchase loans are treated as part of the commitment, which is a derivative accounted for under ASC 815.

Loan origination fees and costs for loans held for investment are deferred and recognized as an adjustment to the yield. (ASC 948-310-25-3)

Determination of Cost Basis The following matters must be considered with respect to the cost basis used for the purposes of the lower of amortized cost or fair value determination:

- If a mortgage loan has been identified as a hedged item in a fair value hedge under ASC 815, the amortized cost basis used reflects adjustments to the loan's carrying amount for changes in the loan's fair value attributable to the risk being hedged. (ASC 948-310-35-1)
- Purchase discounts on mortgage loans reduce the cost basis and are not amortized as interest revenue during the period that the loans are held for sale. (ASC 948-310-35-2)
- Capitalized costs attributable to the acquisition of mortgage servicing rights associated with the purchase or origination of mortgage loans are excluded from the cost basis of the mortgage loans. (ASC 948-310-35-6)

Determination of Fair Value The fair value of mortgage loans held for sale is determined by type of loan. At a minimum, separate determinations are made for residential and commercial loans. Either an aggregate or individual loan basis may be used in determining the lower of amortized cost or fair value for each type of loan. Fair values for loans subject to investor purchase commitments (committed loans) and loans held for speculative purposes (uncommitted loans) must be determined separately as follows:

- For committed loans, market value is defined as fair value.
- For uncommitted loans, fair value is based on quotations from the principal market in which the MBE normally operates or in the absence of such a market, in the most advantageous market, considering:
  - Market prices and yields sought by the MBE's normal market outlets,
  - Quoted Government National Mortgage Association (GNMA) security prices or other public market quotations of rates for long-term mortgage loans, and
  - Federal Home Loan Mortgage Corporation (FHLMC) and Federal National Mortgage Association (FNMA) current delivery prices.

  (ASC 948-310-35-3)

Loans Held as Long-Term Investments If a mortgage loan is transferred from the held-for-sale classification to the held-for-long-term investment classification, the entity should reverse the valuation allowance through a credit to earnings. The loan is then transferred at its amortized cost basis. Following the guidance in ASC 326-20 upon implementation of ASU 2016-13, the entity determines whether a credit loss allowance is necessary. (ASC 948-310-35-5A)

Mortgage-Backed Securities The securitization of mortgage loans held-for-sale is accounted for as a sale of the mortgage loans and purchase of mortgage-backed securities.

Classification and valuation After the securitization of a held-for-sale mortgage loan, any mortgage-backed securities retained by the MBE are classified under the provisions of ASC 320. As is the case with the MBE's mortgage loans held for investment, the MBE must have both the intent and ability to hold the mortgage-backed securities for the foreseeable future or until maturity in order to classify them as held-to-maturity. If the MBE had committed to sell the securities before or during the securitization process, the securities are required to be classified under the trading category. (ASC 948-310-35-3A) Mortgage-backed securities held by a not-for-profit entity are stated at fair value under ASC 958-320.

The fair value of uncommitted mortgage-backed securities collateralized by the MBE's own loans is ordinarily based on the market value of the securities. If the trust holding the loans may be readily terminated and the loans sold directly, fair value of the securities is based on the market value of either the loans or the securities, depending on the entity's intentions. Fair value for other uncommitted mortgage-backed securities is based on published yield data.

Servicing Fees Servicing fees are usually based on a percentage of the outstanding principal balance of the mortgage loan. When a mortgage loan is sold with servicing rights retained, the sales price must be adjusted if the stated rate is materially different from the current (normal) servicing fee rate so that the gain or loss on the sale can be determined. (ASC 948-10-05-7) The adjustment is:

$$\text{Adjustment} = \text{Actual sales price} - \begin{array}{c}\text{Estimated sales price}\\ \text{obtainable if normal servicing}\\ \text{fee rate had been used}\end{array}$$

This adjustment allows for recognition of normal servicing fees in subsequent years.

The adjustment and any recognized gain or loss is determined as of the sale date. If estimated normal servicing fees are less than total expected servicing costs, then this loss is accrued on the sale date as well.

Sales to Affiliated Entities

When mortgage loans or mortgage-backed securities are sold to an affiliated entity, the carrying amount of the assets must be adjusted to lower of amortized cost or fair value as of the date that management decides that the sale will occur. This date is evidenced by formal approval by a representative of the affiliated entity (purchaser), issuance of a purchase commitment, and acceptance of the purchase commitment by the seller. Any adjustment is charged to income. (ASC 948-310-30-1)

If a group of (or all) mortgage loans are originated specifically for an affiliate, then the originator is an agent of the affiliated entity. In this case, the loans are transferred at the originator's cost of acquisition. This treatment does not apply to *right of first refusal* or similar contracts in which the originator retains all risks of ownership. (ASC 948-310-30-2)

Issuance of GNMA Securities

An issuer of GNMA securities who elects the internal reserve method must pay one month's interest cost to a trustee. This cost is capitalized (at no greater than the present value of net future servicing income) and amortized. (ASC 948-340-25-1)

Loan and Commitment Fees and Costs

Mortgage bankers may pay or receive loan and commitment fees as compensation for various loan administration services. These fees and costs are accounted for as described in the following paragraphs.

Other Expenses Services Rendered Fees paid to permanent investors for specific services rendered by third parties as part of a loan origination (e.g., appraisal fees) are recognized when the services are performed. (ASC 948-720-25-1)

FINANCIAL SERVICES—TITLE PLANT (ASC 950)

PERSPECTIVE AND ISSUES

ASC 950-350, *Financial Services—Title Plant,* presents accounting and reporting standards for costs relating to the construction and operation of title plants. A title plant comprises a record of all transactions or conditions that affect titles to land located in a specified area. The length of time spanned by a title plant depends upon regulatory requirements and the time frame required to gather sufficient information to efficiently issue title insurance. (ASC 950-350-05-3) Updating occurs frequently as documentation of the current status of a title is added to the title plant. (ASC 950-350-05-5)

This guidance applies to entities such as title insurance companies, title abstract companies, and title agents that use a title plant in their operations. (ASC 950-350-15-1)

DEFINITIONS OF TERMS

Source: ASC 950, *Glossary*. See Appendix A for additional terms relevant to this topic: Contract, Customers, and Revenue.

Backplant. A title plant that antedates the period covered by its existing title plant.

Title Plant. A historical record of all matters affecting title to parcels of land in a particular geographic area. The number of years covered by a title plant varies, depending on regulatory requirements and the minimum information period considered necessary to issue title insurance policies efficiently.

CONCEPTS, RULES, AND EXAMPLES

Acquisition Costs

The standard provides that costs directly incurred to construct a title plant should be capitalized when the entity can use the title plant to do title searches and that such capitalized costs are not normally depreciated. The statement also requires that the costs of maintaining a title plant and of doing title searches be expensed as incurred. (ASC 950-350-25-1 and 25-2)

The cost of constructing a title plant includes the cost of obtaining, organizing, and summarizing historical information pertaining to a particular tract of land. Costs incurred to assemble a title plant are to be capitalized until the record is usable for conducting title searches. Costs incurred to construct a backplant (a title plant that predates the time span of an existing title plant) must also be capitalized. However, an entity may capitalize only those costs that are directly related to and traceable to the activities performed in constructing the title plant or backplant. (ASC 950-350-30-1)

The purchase of a title plant or backplant, or an undivided interest therein (the right to its joint use) is recorded at cost as of the date acquired. If the title plant is acquired separately, it is recorded at the fair value of consideration given. (ASC 950-350-30-2)

Capitalized title plant costs are not amortized or depreciated unless an impairment in the carrying amount of the title plant occurs. (ASC 950-350-35-1) The following events or changes in circumstances can indicate that the carrying amount may not be recoverable. An impairment may be indicated by the following circumstances (not intended to be an exhaustive list):

- Changing legal or statutory requirements
- Economic factors, such as changing demand
- Loss of competitive advantage
- Failure to maintain an up-to-date title plant
- Circumstances that indicate obsolescence, such as abandonment of title plant (ASC 950-350-35-2)

The provisions of ASC 360 apply to any such impairment. See chapter on ASC 360 for a complete discussion of this topic. (ASC 950-350-35-3)

Operating Costs

Costs of title plant maintenance and of conducting title searches are required to be expensed currently. (ASC 950-350-25-2)

Once a title plant is operational, costs may be incurred to convert the record from one storage and retrieval system to another or to modify the current storage and retrieval system. These costs may not be capitalized as title plant. However, they may be separately capitalized and amortized using a systematic and rational method. (ASC 950-350-25-3 and 4)

Reporting Title Plant Sales

The sale of a title plant is to be reported separately. The amount to be reported is determined by the circumstances surrounding the sale as follows:

Terms of sale	*Amount reported*
a. Sale of title plant and waiver of all rights to future use	As gain or loss—Amount received less adjusted cost of title plant in accordance with ASC 610-20
b. Sale of undivided ownership interest (rights to future joint use)	As gain or loss—Amount received less pro rata portion of adjusted cost of title plant
c. Sales of copies of title plant or the right to use it	As revenue recognized—If a contract with a customer, in accordance with ASC 606. Otherwise, as gain or loss, in accordance with ASC 610-20

(ASC 950-350-40-1)

FRANCHISORS (ASC 952)

PERSPECTIVE AND ISSUES

Technical Alert

Maintenance Update 2017-09 simplifies the guidance for ASC 952 and consolidates all of it into ASC 952-10.

Overview

Franchising has become a popular growth industry with many businesses seeking to sell franchises as their primary income source and individuals seeking to buy franchises and become entrepreneurs. How to recognize transactions that arise in connection with the continuing relationship between the franchisor and franchisee are prime accounting issues.

ASC 952, *Franchisors*, offers incremental guidance for franchisors. (ASC 952-10-05-1 and 10-1)

DEFINITIONS OF TERMS

Source: ASC 952, *Glossary*. See Appendix A for additional terms relevant to this topic: Contract, Customer.

Continuing Franchise Fee. Consideration for the continuing rights granted by the franchise agreement and for general or specific services during its term.

Franchise Agreement. A written business agreement that meets the following principal criteria:

- The relation between the franchisor and franchisee is contractual, and an agreement confirming the rights and responsibilities of each party is in force for a specified period.
- The continuing relation has as its purpose the distribution of a product or service, or an entire business concept, within a particular market area.

- Both the franchisor and the franchisee contribute resources for establishing and maintaining the franchise. The franchisor's contribution may be a trademark, a company reputation, products, procedures, labor, equipment, or a process. The franchisee usually contributes operating capital as well as the managerial and operational resources required for opening and continuing the franchised outlet.
- The franchise agreement outlines and describes the specific marketing practices to be followed, specifies the contribution of each party to the operation of the business, and sets forth certain operating procedures with which both parties agree to comply.
- The establishment of the franchised outlet creates a business entity that will, in most cases, require and support the full-time business activity of the franchisee.
- Both the franchisee and the franchisor have a common public identity. This identity is achieved most often through the use of common trade names or trademarks and is frequently reinforced through advertising programs designed to promote the recognition and acceptance of the common identity within the franchisee's market area.

The payment of an initial franchise fee or a continuing royalty fee is not a necessary criterion for an agreement to be considered a franchise agreement.

Franchisee. The party who has been granted business rights (the franchise) to operate the franchised business.

Franchisor. The party who grants business rights (the franchise) to the party (the franchisee) who will operate the franchised business.

CONCEPTS AND RULES

Scope

ASC 952 applies to:

- Incremental industry guidance
- Entities that meet the definition above of franchisors
- Costs associated with franchising activities
- Transactions between the franchisor and franchisee
  (ASC 952-10-15-1 through 15-3)

Costs

Indirect regular and recurring costs that are incurred no matter what the sale level are expensed as incurred. These usually are regular and recurring costs that bear no relationship to sales. Guidance for incremental costs of obtaining a contract with a customer can be found in ASC 340-40. (ASC 952-310-25-1 and 25-2)

Presentation

Where practicable, the costs associated with franchisor-related outlets should be presented separately from those related to franchised outlets. (ASC 952-10-45-1)

Disclosure

If the franchisor has experienced significant changes to franchisor-owned outlets, it should disclose:

- Franchises sold
- Franchises purchased
- Franchised outlets in operation
- Franchisor-owned outlets in operation
  (ASC 952-10-50-1)

The franchisor should also disclose:

- The nature of all significant commitments and obligations from franchise agreements
- A description of the services the franchisor has agreed to provide for agreements that have not yet been substantially performed
  (ASC 952-10-50-2)

NOT-FOR-PROFIT ENTITIES (ASC 958)[6]

PERSPECTIVE AND ISSUES

Overview

Not-for-profit entities have several characteristics that distinguish them from business entities. First, and perhaps foremost, not-for-profit entities exist to provide goods and services without the objective of generating a profit. Rather than obtaining resources by conducting exchange transactions at a profit or from capital infusions from owners, a not-for-profit organization obtains most resources from others that share its desire to serve a chosen mission—an educational, scientific, charitable, or religious goal. Although not-for-profit organizations can be "owned" or controlled by another, the ownership interest is unlike that of business entities because the "owner" cannot remove resources from the entity for personal use or gain; the resources must be used for a mission-related purpose. Examples of not-for-profit entities are: churches and religious entities, colleges and universities, health care entities, libraries, museums, performing arts entities, civic or fraternal entities, federated fund-raising entities, professional and trade associations, social clubs, research entities, cemeteries, arboretums, and zoos.

Specifically excluded from the list of not-for-profit entities are all investor-owned entities and entities that exist to provide dividends, lower costs, or other economic benefits directly and proportionately to their members, participants, or owners, such as mutual insurance companies, credit unions, farm or utility cooperatives, and employee benefit plans. (ASC 958-10-15-5) Further, some not-for-profit entities are governmental and are required to follow the standards of the Governmental Accounting Standards Board (GASB). Governmental entities are outside of the scope of this publication. Readers instead should refer to *Wiley GAAP for Governments 2018*.

ASC 958, *Not-for-Profit Entities*, applies specifically to not-for-profit entities that are nongovernmental entities. (ASC 958-10-05-01)

[6] See the chapter on ASC 350 for information on ASU 2019-06 and its extension of the private company goodwill alternative to not-for-profit entities.

All authoritative pronouncements in the FASB Codification apply to not-for-profit entities unless the pronouncement specifically excludes not-for-profit entities from its scope. Certain standards apply specifically to not-for-profit entities. Because those standards are particularly relevant to the transactions of not-for-profit entities they are discussed in this chapter.

This chapter contains a highly summarized discussion of accounting and reporting standards for not-for-profit entities. Readers who desire a more in-depth discussion should refer to *Wiley Not-for-Profit GAAP*.

DEFINITIONS OF TERMS

Source: ASC 958. See Appendix A, *Definitions of Terms*, for other terms related to this topic: Contribution, Donor-Imposed Condition, Not-for-Profit Entity, Promise to Give, Public Business Entity.

Agent. An entity that acts for and on behalf of another. Although the term agency has a legal definition, the term is used broadly to encompass not only legal agency, but also the relationships described in Topic 958. A recipient entity acts as an agent for and on behalf of a donor if it receives assets from the donor and agrees to use those assets on behalf of or transfer those assets, the return on investment of those assets, or both to a specified beneficiary. A recipient entity acts as an agent for and on behalf of a beneficiary if it agrees to solicit assets from potential donors specifically for the beneficiary's use and to distribute those assets to the beneficiary. A recipient entity also acts as an agent if a beneficiary can compel the recipient entity to make distributions to it or on its behalf.

Collections. Works of art, historical treasures, or similar assets that meet the following three criteria: (1) they are held for public exhibition, education, or research in service to the public rather than for financial gain; (2) they are protected, kept unencumbered, cared for, and preserved; and (3) they are subject to a policy requiring that the organization use the proceeds from the sale of an item to acquire another item for the collection.

Collections generally are held by museums, botanical gardens; libraries; aquariums; arboretums; historic sites; planetariums; zoos; art galleries; nature, science, and technology centers; and similar educational, research, and public service organizations that have those divisions; however, the definition is not limited to those entities nor does it apply to all items held by those entities.

Designated Net Assets. Unrestricted net assets subject to self-imposed limits by action of the governing board. Designated net assets may be earmarked for future programs, investment, contingencies, purchase or construction of fixed assets, or other uses.

Donor-Imposed Restriction. A donor stipulation (donors include other types of contributors, including makers of certain grants) that specifies a use for a contributed asset that is more specific than broad limits resulting from the following:

- The nature of the not-for-profit entity (NFP)
- The environment in which it operates
- The purposes specified in its articles of incorporation or bylaws or comparable documents for an unincorporated association

Some donors impose restrictions that are temporary in nature, for example, stipulating that resources be used after a specified date, for particular programs or services, or to acquire buildings or equipment. Other donors impose restrictions that are perpetual in nature, for example, stipulating that resources be maintained in perpetuity. Laws may extend those limits to investment returns from those resources and to other enhancements (diminishments) of those resources. Thus, those laws extend donor-imposed restrictions.

Endowment Fund. An established fund of cash, securities, or other assets to provide income for the maintenance of a not-for-profit entity (NFP). The use of the assets of the fund may be with or without donor-imposed restrictions. Endowment funds generally are established by donor-restricted gifts and bequests to provide a source of income in perpetuity or for a specified period. See Donor-Restricted Endowment Fund.

Alternatively, an NFP's governing board may earmark a portion of its net assets as a Board-Designated

Intermediary. Although in general usage the term intermediary encompasses a broad range of situations in which an entity acts between two or more other parties, in this usage, it refers to situations in which a recipient entity acts as a facilitator for the transfer of assets between a potential donor and a potential beneficiary (donee) but is neither an agent or trustee nor a donee and donor.

Natural Expense Classification. A method of grouping expenses according to the kinds of economic benefits received in incurring those expenses. Examples of natural expense classifications include salaries and wages, employee benefits, professional services, supplies, interest expense, rent, utilities, and depreciation.

Net Assets. The excess or deficiency of assets over liabilities of a not-for-profit entity, which is divided into two mutually exclusive classes according to the existence or absence of donor-imposed restrictions. See Net Assets with Donor Restrictions and Net Assets without Donor Restrictions.

Net Assets with Donor Restrictions. The part of net assets of a not-for-profit entity that is subject to donor-imposed restrictions (donors include other types of contributors, including makers of certain grants).

Net Assets without Donor Restrictions. The part of net assets of a not-for-profit entity that is not subject to donor-imposed restrictions (donors include other types of contributors, including makers of certain grants).

Spending Rate. The portion of total return on investments used for fiscal needs of the current period, usually used as a budgetary method of reporting returns of investments. It is usually measured in terms of an amount or a specified percentage of a moving average market value. Typically, the selection of a spending rate emphasizes the use of prudence and a systematic formula to determine the portion of cumulative investment return that can be used to support fiscal needs of the current period and the protection of endowment gifts from a loss of purchasing power as a consideration in determining the formula to be used.

Trustee. An entity that has a duty to hold and manage assets for the benefit of a specified beneficiary in accordance with a charitable trust agreement. In some states, not-for-profit entities (NFPs) are organized under trust law rather than as corporations. Those NFPs are not trustees as defined because, under those statutes, they hold assets in trust for the community or some other broadly described group, rather than for a specific beneficiary.

CONCEPTS, RULES, AND EXAMPLES

Complete Set of Financial Statements

Financial statements are intended to help donors, creditors, and others who provide resources to a not-for-profit organization assess the services provided by the not-for-profit organization and its ability to continue to provide those services. The statements should also help them assess whether management has properly discharged its stewardship responsibilities and whether it has performed satisfactorily in its other management duties. (ASC 958-205-05-3)

ASC 958, *Not-for-Profit Entities,* requires all not-for-profit entities to present:

- A statement of financial position,
- A statement of activities,
- A statement of cash flows
  (ASC 958-205-05-5)

In most ways, the content and format of those financial statements are similar to the financial statements prepared by business enterprises. However, three major differences between not-for-profit entities and business enterprises cause differences in the content and format of financial statements of not-for-profit entities.

First, there is no profit motive in the nonprofit sector, and thus no single indicator of performance comparable to a business enterprise's net income or bottom line. In fact, the best indicators of the performance of a not-for-profit organization are generally not measurable in dollar amounts but rather in the reader's qualitative judgment about the effectiveness of the organization in achieving its mission. Nevertheless, dollars are the language of financial reporting. Information to help assess performance is provided in financial statements (1) by reporting revenues and expenses gross rather than net, and (2) by classifying expenses based on the mission-related programs and supporting activities they sustain, rather than by their natural classifications (salaries, utilities, depreciation, etc.).

Second, because the bottom line of a not-for-profit organization's statement of activities is not a performance measure, but simply a change in net assets for the reporting period, there is no need for not-for-profit entities to distinguish between components of comprehensive income as business enterprises do. All revenues, expenses, gains, and losses are reported in a single statement rather than being divided between an income statement and a statement of other comprehensive income.

Third, not-for-profit entities receive contributions, a type of transaction that is without counterpart in business enterprises. Those contributions often are subject to donor-imposed restrictions which can affect the types and levels of service that a not-for-profit organization can offer. Because donor-imposed restrictions are prevalent, recurring, and, in some cases, permanent, financial reporting by not-for-profit entities needs to reflect the nature and extent of donor-imposed restrictions and changes in them that occur during the reporting period.

Net Assets and Changes in Net Assets

Statement of Financial Position The statement of financial position should report totals for:

- Assets
- Liabilities
- Net assets
- Net assets with donor restrictions
- Net assets without donor restrictions
  (ASC 958-210-45-2)

The nature and extent of donor-imposed restrictions are reported in the statement of financial position, either on the face of the statement or in the notes, by distinguishing between the portions of net assets with donor restrictions and unrestricted net assets. (ASC 958-210-45-6)

Disclosures are required to explain the differences in the nature of donor restrictions and how and when the resources can be used. Deficiencies in endowments and lapsing of restrictions have simplified accounting guidance. Entities have to disclose:

- The extent to which the balance sheet comprises financial assets
- The one-year liquidity of those assets, and
- Any limitations on their use.
  (ASC 958-210-50-1A)

Statement of Activities Changes in donor-imposed restrictions are reported in the statement of activities. The organization's revenues, expenses, gains, and losses for the period are classified into the two classes of net assets so that the statement of activities reports amounts for the change in restricted net assets and the change in unrestricted net assets, as well as the change in net assets in total. (ASC 958-220-45-1) Transactions and events that do not change the net assets of the organization as a whole, but only their classification, are reported separately as reclassifications. Reclassifications are events that simultaneously increase one class of net assets and decrease another. For example, unrestricted net assets increase and restricted net assets decrease when the purchase of a long-lived asset fulfills a donor-imposed restriction to acquire long-lived assets with the gift (sometimes referred to as a release of restrictions). (ASC 958-220-45-3)

Fund Accounting Not-for-profit entities often use fund accounting as a tool for tracking compliance with donor-imposed restrictions and internal designations. Fund accounting is a system of recording resources whose use is limited either by donors, granting agencies, governing boards, law, or legal covenants. A separate fund (a self-balancing group of accounts composed of assets, liabilities, and net assets) is maintained for each purpose limitation. For external reporting, a fund may be classified entirely in one net asset class or it may need to be allocated among two or three classes. (For an example of the allocations necessary to restate a fund balance to net asset classes, see the discussion of endowment funds in "Investments" below.)

Investments and Endowment Funds

If an equity security with readily determinable fair value is acquired through a contribution, it is recognized as an asset and as revenue or a gain in the period received. (ASC 958-321-25-1)

Entities report other investments at:

- Cost upon acquisition if they are purchased or
- Fair value if they are a contribution or received through an agency transaction.
  (ASC 958-325-30-1)

Endowment Funds Many of the investments held by not-for-profit entities are held as the investments of endowment funds. Endowment funds generally are established by gifts from donors who desire to provide support for the organization permanently (a permanently restricted endowment fund) or for a specified period of time (a term endowment fund). In addition, a governing board may determine that certain resources be invested and that only the return generated be spent by the organization. These board-designated amounts are referred to as quasi-endowment funds or funds functioning as endowment. The net assets of an endowment fund are classified in accordance with the restrictions placed on the resources by donors, if any. Because a donor can place different restrictions on each source of the net assets (original gift, investment gains and losses, and investment income), each source must be examined separately to achieve the proper classification.

Each source is unrestricted unless its use is restricted by the donor or by a law that extends the donor's restriction to the source. Thus, the net assets of an endowment fund created by the governing board from a large unrestricted bequest (or from unrestricted net assets) are classified as unrestricted because no donor was involved in the transaction of creating the endowment fund and all amounts transferred to that fund are free of donor-imposed restrictions.

In contrast, assume that a donor contributes $50,000 to a museum and stipulates that the gift be invested in perpetuity and the investment income be used to purchase works of art. The donor further stipulates that any gains on the investment be added to the original gift and invested in perpetuity. The donor's original gift ($50,000) increases restricted net assets because of the stipulation that the gift be invested in perpetuity. The income earned by the investment of the gift increases restricted net assets. When works of art are purchased, the restriction on net assets resulting from the income is fulfilled and the net assets are reclassified to unrestricted net assets. The realized and unrealized gains from investment of the gift increase restricted net assets because the donor required that those gains also be reinvested in perpetuity.

In most cases, the classification of the original gift and the investment income is straightforward because donors explicitly state the time and purpose restrictions on them. Classification of gains and losses on the investments is not as clearly determinable unless the donor explicitly states how gains are to be used and whether losses must be restored immediately from other sources, from future gains on the investments, or not at all. However, donors are often silent in their agreements about those matters.

Unless stated otherwise in the gift instrument, a not-for-profit organization should classify the assets in an endowment fund as donor-restricted assets until they are appropriated for expenditure by the organization, unless the gift instrument states otherwise. This is in accordance with the stipulation in subsection 4(a) of UPMIFA. (ASC 958-205-05-10)

According to ASC 958-205-50-1, a not-for-profit organization, whether or not subject to UPMIFA, should disclose information that will enable users of its financial statements to understand the net asset classification, net asset composition, changes in net asset composition, spending policies, and related investment policies of its endowment funds. Therefore, at a minimum, the following disclosures should be made:

- A description of the governing board's interpretation of the law that supports the organization's net asset classification of donor-restricted endowment funds, including its interpretation of the ability to spend from underwater endowment funds.
- A description of the organization's endowment spending policies, including its interpretation of the ability to spend from underwater endowment funds.
- A description of the organization's endowment investment policies.
- The make-up of the organization's endowment by net asset class at the end of the period. These amounts should be presented in total, as well as by endowment fund and should separately show donor-restricted endowment funds from board-designated endowment funds.
- A reconciliation of the beginning and ending balance of the organization's endowment, in total and by net asset class.
  (ASC 958-205-50-1B)
- Information about the net assets of its endowment funds such as:
  - The aggregate amount of the deficiencies for all donor-restricted endowment funds where the fair value of the assets at the reporting date is less than the level required in the donor stipulations or law.

  (ASC 958-205-50-2(c))

Split-Interest Agreements

A split-interest agreement is an arrangement in which a donor transfers assets to a not-for- profit organization or to a charitable trust and requires that the benefits of ownership of those assets be split among two or more beneficiaries. (ASC 958-220-20) Charitable gift annuities, annuity trusts, charitable remainder unitrusts, charitable lead trusts, and pooled (or life) income funds are examples of split-interest agreements. ASC 958 provides guidance for reporting the initial gifts that create these funds and the annual adjustments necessary to report them properly. Accounting for split-interest gifts is a complex area; the following discussion is highly summarized and preparers should consult the Codification for more guidance

Revocable Agreements Revocable split-interest agreements are not accounted for as intentions to give unless the not-for-profit organization receives the assets. Assets received by a not-for-profit organization that acts as trustee under a revocable agreement are recognized as refundable advances at their fair value. Contribution revenue for the assets received is recognized when:

- The agreement becomes irrevocable or
- The assets are distributed to the NFP for its unconditional use
  (ASC 958-30-25-2)

Irrevocable Agreements Not-for-profit entities are required to report their interests in irrevocable split-interest agreements when the NFP is notified of the existence of the split-interest agreement. If another party, such as a bank, holds the assets and the NFP is the beneficiary and has unconditional rights to receive all or a portion of the cash flows, a not-for-profit organization recognizes its interest as an asset and contribution revenue and measures its interest at fair value, usually based on the present value of the cash flows to be received. (ASC 958-30-25-17)

If the donor explicitly grants the recipient organization variance power, the recipient organization, rather than the beneficiary, recognizes contribution revenue and the NFP does not recognize potential distributions until it has unconditional rights. (ASC 958-30-25-18) Variance power is the unilateral power to direct the transferred assets to an entity other than the specified beneficiary. Unilateral power means that the recipient organization does not have to contact the donor, the beneficiary, or any other interested party in order to substitute a different beneficiary. Variance power must be granted by the instrument transferring the assets.

If the not-for-profit organization holds the assets and is also a beneficiary of the agreement, it reports the fair value of the assets received from the donor as its assets and reports the actuarially computed present value of the payments to be made to other beneficiaries as its liability. The difference between the two amounts is the contribution received by the not-for-profit organization. (ASC 958-30-25-4) Each year thereafter, the liability to the beneficiaries is recomputed based on revaluations of the amounts to be paid, the expected lives of the beneficiaries, and other relevant actuarial assumptions. (ASC 958-30-35-6)

Presentation The net assets resulting from most split-interest agreements are classified as restricted because they are subject to time restrictions and purpose restrictions. The net assets are time-restricted either because the distributions are not yet due (when amounts are held by a third party) or because the contribution amount cannot be used by the not-for-profit organization until the death of the beneficiary or some other future specified date. The net assets are classified as restricted if the donor has permanently restricted the organization's use of the assets. (For example, the donor requires that the not-for-profit organization use the remaining assets to create a permanent endowment fund at the end of the agreement.) Similarly, if upon the establishment of the agreement the organization can immediately spend the contribution portion without restriction, as is the case for some gift annuities, the net assets would be classified as unrestricted. (ASC 958-30-45-2)

Transfers Received as an Agent, Trustee, or Intermediary If the recipient organization and the specified beneficiary are financially interrelated entities, the recipient organization reports contribution revenue and the specified beneficiary recognizes its interest in the net assets of the recipient organization using a method similar to the equity method of accounting for investments in common stock. Entities are financially interrelated if the relationship between them has both of the following characteristics:

1. One organization has the ability to influence the operating and financial decisions of the other, and
2. One organization has an ongoing economic interest in the net assets of the other. (ASC 958-20-05-1)

The ability to influence the operating and financial decisions of the other can be demonstrated in several ways:

1. The entities are affiliates as defined in ASC 850, *Related-Party Disclosures*,
2. One organization has considerable representation on the governing board of the other,
3. The charter or bylaws of one organization limit its activities to those that are beneficial to the other, or
4. An agreement between the entities allows one organization to actively participate in the policymaking processes of the other.
(ASC 958-20-15-2)

An ongoing economic interest in the net assets of another is a residual right to the other organization's net assets that results from an ongoing relationship. A common example of financially interrelated entities is a foundation that exists to raise, hold, and invest assets for a specific beneficiary that it supports.

Contributions Received for a Financially Interrelated Beneficiary In general, a recipient organization reports a liability if it accepts assets from a donor and agrees to use those assets on behalf of or transfer those assets to another organization or individual specified by the donor. (ASC 958-20-25-1) When it subsequently spends the assets on behalf of the beneficiary or transfers the assets, their return, or both to the beneficiary, the nonprofit organization reduces the liability it recorded earlier. If the assets received from the donor are donated materials, supplies, or other nonfinancial assets, the recipient organization may choose either to:

1. Report the receipt of the assets as liability to the beneficiary concurrent with recognition of the assets received, or
2. Not to report the transaction at all.

The choice is an accounting policy that must be applied consistently from period to period and disclosed in the notes to the financial statements.

In addition to establishing standards for contributions transferred to beneficiaries via agents, trustees, and intermediaries, ASC 958-20 sets standards for transfers that take place in a similar manner but are not contributions because the terms of the transfer or the relationships between the parties make the transfer revocable, repayable, or reciprocal. Transfers are recognized by the recipient organization as liabilities if one or more of the following situations are present:

1. The transfer is subject to the transferor's right to redirect the transferred assets to another beneficiary,
2. The transfer is accompanied by the transferor's conditional promise to give,
3. The transferor controls the recipient organization and specifies an unaffiliated beneficiary, or
4. The transferor specifies itself or its affiliate as the beneficiary of a transfer that is not an equity transaction.

Equity transactions An equity transaction is a transfer that has all of the following terms:

1. The transferor specifies itself or its affiliate as beneficiary,
2. The transferor and the recipient organization are financially interrelated entities, and
3. Neither the transferor nor its affiliate expects payment of the transferred assets (although payment of investment return is allowable).
   (ASC 958-20-25-4)

Equity transactions are reported by the recipient organization as a separate line item in the statement of activities.

ASC 958-360, *Not-for-Profit Entities—Property, Plant, and Equipment*, requires the depreciation of land, buildings, and equipment used by not-for-profit entities. (ASC 958-360-35-1) An exception to that requirement is provided for certain works of art, historical treasures, and similar assets. Depreciation need not be recognized if a not-for-profit organization can demonstrate both:

1. That an asset individually has cultural, historical, or aesthetic value worth maintaining in perpetuity, and
2. That the organization has the ability to protect and preserve that value essentially undiminished.
   (ASC 958-360-35-3)

Depreciation expense is a natural expense classification that must be allocated to programs and supporting activities in reporting expenses by functional classification.

Revenue Recognition

Exchange transactions are accounted for using the guidance of other applicable topics, such as ASC 606. (ASC 958-605-25-1)

Example of Donated Capital

A board member of the for-profit Adirondack Boys' Club (ABC) donates land to the organization that has a fair market value of $1 million. ABC records the donation with the following entry:

Land	1,000,000	
Revenue—donations		1,000,000

The same board member donates one year of accounting labor to ABC. The fair value of services rendered is $75,000. ABC records the donation with the following entry:

Salaries—accounting department	75,000	
Revenue—donations		75,000

The board member also donates one year of free rent of a local building to ABC. The annual rent in similar facilities is $45,000. ABC records the donation with the following entry:

Rent expense	45,000	
Revenue—donations		45,000

Finally, the board member pays off a $100,000 debt owed by ABC. ABC records the donation with the following entry:

Notes payable	100,000	
Revenue—donations		100,000

Following the closing of the fiscal period, the effect of all the foregoing donations will be reflected in Adirondack's retained earnings account.

With some exceptions, ASC 958-605, *Not-For-Profit Entities—Revenue Recognition*, requires contributions to be recognized as revenue or gains at the time of the gift and measured at the fair value of the contributed assets. Conditional transfers are not recognized as contribution revenues until the conditions are substantially met. (ASC 958-605-25-2) Donor-imposed restrictions do not change the timing of recognition of a contribution. Donor-imposed restrictions, or the absence of them, affect only a contribution's classification as an increase in restricted net assets or unrestricted net assets.

Donor-imposed conditions, however, affect the timing of recognition. Because a contribution is an unconditional transfer, a transfer of assets subject to donor-imposed conditions is not a contribution yet, although it may become one at a future date. A donor-imposed condition has:

- One or more barriers that must be overcome before a recipient is entitled to the assets transferred or promise and
- A right of return to the contribution for assets transferred or reduction, settlement, or cancellation of liabilities or a right of release of the promisor from its obligation. (ASC 958-605-25-5A)

Thus, making the distinction between donor-imposed restrictions and donor-imposed conditions is very important to the timing of recognition. If a donor's stipulations do not clearly state whether a gift depends on a stated stipulation and the ambiguity cannot be resolved by communicating with the donor or by examining the circumstances surrounding the gift, a transfer is presumed to be conditional. (ASC 958-605-25-5E)

Promises to Give

Unconditional promises to give Unconditional promises to give cash or other assets are recognized in financial statements when the promise is made and received, provided that there is sufficient evidence in the form of verifiable documentation (written, audio, or video). (ASC 958- 605-25-8) If payments of the promises are due in future periods, the promise has an implied time restriction that expires on the date the payment is due. Thus, unless circumstances surrounding the receipt of the promise indicate that the donor intended the gift to support the current period's activities, unconditional promises increase temporarily restricted net assets. A present value technique is used to measure unconditional promises to give, although short-term promises (due in less than one year) may be reported at net realizable value.

Conditional promises to give Conditional promises are not recognized as revenue until the conditions are substantially met; however, they are required to be disclosed in notes to the financial statements. (ASC 958-605-25-11)

Contributions held by others In a manner similar to recognizing promises to give, a beneficiary recognizes contributions held on its behalf by an agent, trustee, or intermediary. For example, if the assets held by the agent were transferred subject to a condition that is not yet met, the beneficiary does not recognize its potential rights to the assets held by the agent. If a beneficiary has an unconditional right to receive cash flows from a charitable trust or other pool of assets, the beneficiary recognizes its rights when the beneficial interest is created and measures the rights using the present value of the estimated expected cash flows. However, if the beneficiary and the agent, trustee, or intermediary are financially interrelated entities, the beneficiary reports its rights to the assets held using a method similar to the equity method of accounting for investments. (ASC 958-20-25-2) (For further discussion, see "Transfers Received as an Agent, Trustee, or Intermediary" in this section.)

Works of Art, Historical Treasures, and Similar Items An organization that maintains works of art, historical treasures, and similar assets in collections, as defined, does not recognize gifts of items that are added to its collections unless it also capitalizes its collections. (ASC 958-605-25-19) However, gifts that are not added to collections or items given to entities that do not maintain collections in accordance with the definition are recognized as revenues and measured at the fair value of the assets received. (ASC 958-605-25-18)

Reporting Expenses

Expenses are recognized in the statement of activities as decreases in unrestricted net assets. Financing an expense with donor-restricted resources does not make the expense restricted; instead, it releases the restriction on the restricted resources, causing a reclassification to be reported in the statement of activities.

Expenses must be reported by functional classifications either on the face of the statement of activities or in the notes to the financial statements. The functional classifications describe the major classes of program services and supporting activities of an organization. (ASC 958-720-45-2) Program services are the mission-related activities of the organization that result in goods and services being distributed to clients, customers, or members. They are the activities that are the major purpose of and the major output of the organization. For example, a not-for-profit organization with the mission of enhancing the lives of the community's senior citizens might have senior center, home visits, transportation services, and home maintenance as its program expense classifications. Supporting activities are all activities of a not-for-profit organization other than program services. Fund raising expenses and management and general are two common supporting activity classifications. (ASC 958-720-20)

ASC 958-205 encourages, but does not require, most not-for-profit entities to provide an analysis of expenses by natural classification. Information about expenses by natural expense classifications (salaries, benefits, rent, depreciation, and so forth) can help readers of the financial statements understand the mix of fixed and discretionary costs incurred by the organization. Only voluntary health and welfare entities are required to report information about expenses by both functional and natural classification. Those entities must provide that information in a matrix format in a statement of functional expenses. (ASC 958-205-45-6)

Joint Activity Many not-for-profit entities solicit contributions as part of conducting activities that also serve their program or management and general functions. For example, an organization that has a mission of reducing the incidence of cancer might conduct a direct mail campaign and include in an envelope a listing of lifestyle changes that will lessen the risks of cancer and a request for contributions. When a fund-raising activity is conducted in conjunction with an activity that serves a program or other support purpose, the activity is referred to as a joint activity. Users of the financial statements of not-for-profit entities are particularly interested in the extent to which the organization is able to minimize its fund-raising and management and general costs. Because neither of these types of costs directly benefit the beneficiaries of the organization's programs, successful entities attempt to minimize them as a percent of the organization's support and revenue. Since the effectiveness of the management of a not-for-profit organization is often judged on operating metrics of this nature, there is a natural incentive for management to maximize the portion of the costs of these joint activities that is characterized as program expenses.

ASC 958-720 establishes standards for reporting the costs of joint activities. It begins with the presumption that the costs of a joint activity are reportable as fund-raising expenses. To overcome that presumption, three criteria must be met:

1. Purpose,
2. Audience, and
3. Content.

If all three of the criteria are met, the costs of a joint activity should be charged as follows:

- Costs identifiable with a particular function are charged to that function.
- Joint costs are allocated between fund-raising and the appropriate program or management and general function.
  (ASC 958-720-45-29)

Joint costs are the costs of conducting joint activities that are not directly identifiable with a particular component of the activity. (ASC 958-720-20) Joint costs might include the costs of salaries, professional fees, paper, printing, postage, event advertising, telephones, broadcast airtime, and facility rentals.

Determining whether all three criteria are met is complicated because the purpose and audience criteria have additional tests within them. The purpose test includes a call to action test, a compensation or fees test, a similar scale and same medium test, and another evidence test. The audience criterion includes a prior donor test, an ability and likelihood to contribute test, and a need to use or reasonable potential for use test. Failure of one of the additional tests often causes the activity to fail the criterion.

If any of the three criteria is not met, all costs of the joint activity must be reported as fund-raising expense. "All costs" includes the costs that would have been considered program or management and general if they had been incurred in a different activity. There is an exception to the rule that all costs are charged to fund-raising expense if one or more of the criteria is not met. The costs of goods or services provided in an exchange transaction (sometimes referred to as a quid pro quo contribution) that is part of the joint activity are charged to cost of goods sold rather than fund-raising expense. For example, the costs of direct donor benefits, such as the value of items sold at a fund-raising auction or meals served at a fund-raising dinner, are not charged to fund-raising expenses. (ASC 958-720-45-29)

ASC 958-720 requires that the method used to allocate the joint costs be rational and systematic and that it result in a reasonable allocation of costs. The method selected should be applied consistently given similar facts and circumstances. No particular method of allocation is required by the standard, but three allocation methods are illustrated: the physical units method, the relative direct cost method, and the standalone joint-cost-allocation method. (ASC 958-720-45-54)

Entities that allocate joint costs are required to disclose the types of activities in which joint costs have been incurred, a statement that the costs have been allocated, and the total amount of joint costs allocated, and the portion of joint costs allocated to each functional expense category. The standard also encourages disclosure of the amount of joint costs for each type of joint activity. (ASC 958-720-50-2)

Mergers and Acquisitions

ASC 958-805 establishes standards for determining whether a combination of not-for-profit entities is a merger or an acquisition, describes the carryover method of accounting (for a merger) and the acquisition method of accounting (for an acquisition), and notes related disclosures. (ASC 958-805-05-4 and 05-5)

Combinations in which the acquiring entity is a not-for-profit organization, unlike combinations in which the acquiring entity is a business entity, cannot be assumed to be an exchange of commensurate value. Acquired not-for-profit entities lack owners who are focused on receiving a return on and return of their investment. Moreover, the parent or governing body of an acquired organization may place its mission effectiveness ahead of achieving maximum price when negotiating a combination agreement. Thus, when two not-for-profit entities combine, it will be necessary to determine:

- If there was an exchange of commensurate value (in which case, standards similar to ASC 850 would be applied) or
- If there is a contribution inherent in the transaction that would be reported in accordance with ASC 958-605.

If there is a contribution inherent in the transaction, it would be measured as the excess of the net fair values of the identifiable assets acquired and the liabilities assumed over the fair value of the consideration exchanged. If the acquired entity is a business enterprise, the contribution inherent in a combination would be measured as the excess of the fair value of the acquired business enterprise over the cost of that business enterprise. The primary difference is that no goodwill would be recognized in most contributions of not-for-profit entities, although it would be in the contributions of business entities.

In the rare cases in which the sum of the fair values of the liabilities assumed exceeds the sum of the fair values of the identifiable assets acquired, the acquiring organization would initially recognize that excess as an unidentifiable intangible asset (goodwill).

In a merger, where two or more not-for-profit entities cede control to a new entity, the *carry-over method* is used. (ASC 958-805-25-3) Under this method, the initial financial statements of the combined entities carry forward the assets and liabilities of the combining entities, measured at their carrying amounts, less the effects of any intra-entity transactions. (ASC 958-805-25-6) There is no recognition of changes in fair value. The financial history of the new entity created by the merger begins on the merger date—it does not report the prior financial results of the preceding merged entities. Key merger disclosures include the reasons for the merger, the amounts of any significant adjustments made to conform the individual accounting policies of the merged entities, and the amounts of any intra-entity balance eliminations.

An acquisition by a not-for-profit entity is accounted for using the *acquisition method*. If this method is used, there are a few exceptions to the recognition principle in ASC 805. The acquirer cannot recognize an acquired donor relationship as an intangible asset. (ASC 958-805-25-22) So, too, if the not-for-profit acquirer has a policy of not capitalizing collections (works of art, historical treasures, or similar assets), then the acquirer does not recognize those items as assets at acquisitions added to the collection. Instead, the acquirer recognizes the cost of the collection items purchased as a decrease in the appropriate class of net assets in the statement of activities and as a cash outflow for investing activities and does not recognize the fair value of collection items contributed. (ASC 958-805-25-23) For conditional promises to give, the not-for-profit acquirer recognizes either:

- The conditional promise only if the conditions on which it depends are substantially met as of the acquisition date, or
- A transfer of assets with a conditional promise to contribute them as a refundable advance unless the conditions have been substantially met as of the acquisition date. (ASC 958-805-25-26)

Key acquisition disclosures include the reasons for the acquisition, the factors that make up either goodwill recognized or the equivalent amount charged to expense, and the fair value of consideration transferred. (ASC 958-805-50-11)

If an acquirer expects the operations of the acquiree to be supported primarily by contributions and returns on investments, then it should recognize as an expense on the acquisition date the amount that would otherwise be recognized as a goodwill asset. This situation arises when an acquiree's contributions and returns on investments are expected to significantly exceed all other sources of revenue. (ASC 958-805-25-29)

In an acquisition, there is an *inherent contribution received*, because the acquirer receives net assets from the acquiree without any corresponding transfer of consideration. (ASC 958-805-25-31)

The Reporting Entity

The financial statement preparer must consider the applicability of ASC 958-810 in determining the reporting entity. That subtopic provides guidance on reporting investments in majority-owned for- profit subsidiaries, investments in common stock in which the not-for-profit organization owns a 50% or less voting interest, and certain relationships with other not-for-profit entities.

If a not-for-profit entity has a controlling financial interest through direct or indirect ownership of majority voting interest in a for-profit entity that is other than a limited partnership, it follows the standards in ASC 810. (ASC 958-810-25-2) If that is not the case, but the not-for- profit entity has control of a related, but separate NFP, through a majority voting interest in the board of the other NFP, ASC 810 should also be followed. (ASC 958-810-25-3)

Control of a related, but separate, not-for-profit entity in which the reporting entity has an economic interest may take forms other than a majority ownership interest, sole corporate membership, or majority voting interest in the board of the other entity. For example, control may be through contract or affiliation agreement. In circumstances such as these, consolidation is permitted but not required. Consolidation is, however, encouraged if *both* the following criteria are met:

- The reporting entity controls a separate not-for-profit entity that it has an economic interest in, and that control is not control through either of the following means:

- A controlling financial interest in the other not-for-profit through direct or indirect ownership of a majority voting interest
- A majority voting interest in the board of the other not-for-profit

- Consolidation would be meaningful.
(ASC 958-810-25-4)

If a not-for-profit entity has significant influence over the operating and financial policies of the investee (generally owns 20% or more but less than 50% of the voting interest), it either follows the standards in ASC 323 or reports the investment at fair value. (ASC 958-810-25-4C)

Different combinations of control and economic interest determine the appropriate accounting for relationships with other not-for-profit entities, as shown in the following table. Control is defined for this purpose as the direct or indirect ability to determine the direction of management and policies through ownership, contract, or otherwise. (ASC 958-810-20) Economic interest is defined as an interest in another entity that exists if:

1. The other entity holds or utilizes significant resources that must be used for the purposes of the reporting organization, either directly or indirectly by producing income or providing services, or
2. The reporting organization is responsible for the liabilities of the other entity. (ASC 958-810-20)

Control?	*Economic interest?*	*Accounting Treatment*
Yes, via ownership of a majority voting interest	Yes	Consolidate.
Yes, via ownership of a majority voting interest	No	Consolidate.
Yes, via majority voting interest in the board of the other entity, as a majority owner	Yes	Consolidate.
Yes, via majority voting interest in the board of the other entity, as a majority owner	No	Consolidation is prohibited, and disclosure required.
Yes, via a contract or an affiliation agreement	Yes	Consolidation is permitted, but not required.
Yes, via a contract or an affiliation agreement	No	Consolidation is prohibited, and disclosure required.
No	Yes	Consolidation is prohibited, and disclosure required.
No	No	Consolidation is prohibited. No disclosure required.

Certain disclosures are necessary if consolidated statements are not presented. If consolidated statements are not presented when consolidation is permitted, but not required, the not-for-profit organization must disclose the identity of the other organization, the nature of the relationship, and summarized financial data in addition to the information required by ASC 850. (ASC 958-810-50-4) If consolidation is prohibited, the not-for-profit organization must disclose the information required by ASC 850.

PLAN ACCOUNTING (ASC 960, ASC 962, ASC 965)

PERSPECTIVE AND ISSUES

Employee benefit plans have become increasingly important and diverse. Using assets that are segregated from the plan sponsor, they provide benefits to employees and former employees in accordance with a plan agreement. The provisions of the plan agreement deal with such matters as eligibility, entitlement to benefits, funding, plan amendments, operation and administration, allocation of responsibilities among the fiduciaries, and fiduciaries' ability to delegate duties. A few examples of employee benefit plans are pension plans, profit-sharing plans, stock bonus plans, 401(k) plans, 403(b) plans, disability plans, health care plans, life insurance plans, unemployment benefit plans, tuition assistance plans, dependent care plans, and cafeteria/flexible benefit plans. For accounting and reporting purposes, the plans are divided into three major types: defined benefit pension plans, defined contribution pension plans, and health and welfare benefit plans.

Employee benefit plans that are sponsored by and provide benefits to the employees of state and local governmental entities are outside of the scope of this publication. Readers should instead refer to *Wiley GAAP for Governments 2020*.

All authoritative pronouncements apply to employee benefit plans unless the pronouncement specifically excludes them from its scope. Certain authoritative pronouncements apply specifically to employee benefit plans. Because those pronouncements are particularly relevant to the transactions of employee benefit plans, they are discussed in this chapter.

ASC 960, ASC 962, and ASC 965 set standards for defined benefit pension plans, defined contribution pension plans, and health and welfare benefit plans, respectively. In addition to providing accounting and reporting guidance for the plans, they provide summaries of statutory rules and regulations applicable to employee benefit plans and illustrative financial statements.

ASC 960, *Plan Accounting—Defined Benefit Pension Plans*, is the principal standard involving the accounting and reporting of employee benefit plans. ASC 960 applies only to ongoing plans, not to plans that are terminated or expected to be terminated. The codification describes the objectives of plan financial statements and the necessary components of a complete set of plan financial statements.

ASC 962, *Plan Accounting—Defined Contribution Pension Plans,* provides the requirements for defined contribution pension plans. Relevant information for defined contribution plans is different from defined benefit plans because plan participants bare the investment risk and, therefore, have a greater vested interest. (ASC 962-10-05-4)

ASC 965, *Plan Accounting—Health and Welfare Benefit Plans*, provides the standards for health and welfare benefit plans. It divides the diverse universe of plans into two major types: defined benefit health and welfare plans and defined contribution health and welfare plans. It requires defined benefit health and welfare plans to use certain provisions of ASC 715, to measure benefit obligations. In addition, it applies many of the measurement and disclosure provisions of ASC 960 to health and welfare plans.

ASC 965-205-05 specifies the accounting for and disclosure of 401(h) features of defined benefit pension plans that offer medical benefits to retirees in addition to the normal retirement benefits.

This section presents a highly summarized discussion of accounting and reporting standards by employee benefit plans. This chapter does not describe an employer's requirements for reporting information about employee benefit plans. That information is described in the chapters on ASC 710-718.

DEFINITIONS OF TERMS

Source: ASC 960, *Glossary*

Accumulated Plan Benefits. Future benefit payments that are attributable under the provisions of a pension plan to employees' service rendered to the benefit information date. Accumulated plan benefits comprise benefits expected to be paid to any of the following:

- Retired or terminated employees or their beneficiaries
- Beneficiaries of deceased employees
- Present employees or their beneficiaries

Benefits. The monetary or in-kind benefits or benefit coverage to which participants may be entitled under a pension plan or health and welfare plan (which can include active, terminated, and retired employees or their dependents or beneficiaries). Examples of benefits may include, but are not limited to, health care benefits, life insurance, legal, educational, and advisory services, pension benefits, disability benefits, death benefits, and benefits due to termination of employment.

Health and Welfare Benefit Plan. Plans that provide benefits such as medical, dental, visual, or other health care, insurance, disability, vacation, education, or dependent care.

Liquidation. The process by which an entity converts its assets to cash or other assets and settles its obligations with creditors in anticipation of the entity ceasing all activities. Upon cessation of the entity's activities, any remaining cash or other assets are distributed to the entity's investors or other claimants (albeit sometimes indirectly). Liquidation may be compulsory or voluntary. Dissolution of an entity as a result of that entity being acquired by another entity or merged into another entity in its entirety and with the expectation of continuing its business does not qualify as liquidation.

Net Assets. The residual interest in the assets of an employee benefit plan that remains after deducting its liabilities. The liabilities of a plan do not include its accumulated plan benefits (defined benefit pension plans) or its benefit obligation (defined benefit health and welfare plans).

Noncontributary Plan. A pension or other postretirement benefit plan under which participants do not make contributions.

CONCEPTS, RULES, AND EXAMPLES

In addition to varying by basic type (defined benefit plan, defined contribution plan, and health and welfare benefit plan), employee benefit plans vary by operating and administrative characteristics. Plans established by one employer or a group of controlled corporations are referred to as single employer plans. Alternatively, plans can include the employees of many employers who are related in some way, often by all being parties to a collective-bargaining agreement. Those plans are referred to as multiemployer plans. A plan can be either contributory or noncontributory. A contributory plan requires both the employer and the participants to fund (contribute to) the cost of the future benefits. In a noncontributory plan, the participants do not fund any part of the cost of the future benefits. Insured plans are funded through insurance contracts. Self-funded plans are funded through contributions and investment return. Split-funded plans are funded by a combination of insurance contracts, contributions, and investment return.

Complete Set of Financial Statements

The primary objective of a plan's financial statements is to provide the information necessary to assess the plan's ability to pay benefits when due. Thus, financial statements must include information about the plan's resources, the results of transactions and events that changed the plan's resources, the stewardship of management over the plan's resources, and any other facts necessary to understand the information provided.

A complete set of financial statements includes:

- A statement of net assets available for benefits as of the end of the plan year (statement of financial position equivalent), and
- A statement of changes in net assets available for benefits for the plan year ended (income statement equivalent).

In addition, defined benefit plans must include information about the actuarial present value of accumulated benefits and the effects of changes in the accumulated benefits. That information can appear either as additional financial statements or in the notes to financial statements. (ASC 960-205-45-1, ASC 962-205-45-1, and ASC 965-205-45-1)

ASC 230-10-15-4 exempts defined benefit pension plans from the requirement that a statement of cash flows be provided. Other employee benefit plans are also exempted if they report similar to defined benefit pension plans, including ASC 960's requirement to report plan investments at fair value. Although not required, presentation of a statement of cash flows is encouraged if it would provide useful information about the plan's ability to pay future liabilities, as would be the case if the plan either holds illiquid investments or purchases investments using borrowed funds. (ASC 960-205-45-6)

Statement of Net Assets Available for Benefits

ASC 960-325-35 requires defined benefit pension plans to report all investment contracts, including guaranteed investment contracts issued by insurance companies, at fair value. (ASC 960-325-35-1) Only contracts that incorporate mortality or morbidity risk (insurance contracts) may be reported at contract value.

Most plan investments are reported at fair value. If there is an active market, quoted market prices are used. If market quotations are not available, investments are valued "in good faith" by the plan's trustees and administrator. The selling price of similar investments or discounted cash flows can be useful in estimating fair value. The use of an independent expert may be necessary for the valuation of certain investments. Investment contracts with an insurance company, bank, or other financial institution are reported at fair value. Only insurance contracts—contracts that incorporate mortality or morbidity risk (defined benefit pension plans) or that are fully benefit-responsive (defined contribution plans and health and welfare plans)—may be reported at contract value, and then only if the plan reports at contract value in its annual report filed with government agencies. Contract value is the *only* measure required by ASC 962 and ASC 965 for fully benefit-responsive investment contracts, which maintains the relevant information while reducing the cost and complexity of reporting for fully benefit-responsive investment contracts. The financial statements should identify plan investments by type of investment and indicate how fair value was determined.

The Codification provides an expedient that allows employers to measure defined benefit plan assets on a month-end date that is nearest to the employer's fiscal year-end ("alternative measurement date"). This is allowed when the fiscal period does not coincide with a month-end and should be applied consistently from year-to-year. (ASC 960-325-35-4) Employers who elect the expedient are required to:

- Disclose contributions, distributions, or significant events occurring between the alternative measurement date and the plan's fiscal year-end, and
- Disclose the use of the practical expedient, the alternative measurement date, and the date used to measure investment-related accounts.
(ASC 960-325-50-4 and 50-5, ASC 962-325-50-2A and 2B, and 965-325-50-1B and 1C)

Disclosure of the original cost of investments in the basic financial statements is neither required nor prohibited. (ASC 960-325-50-3 and ASC 962-325-50-2)

Contributions receivable include those due as of the reporting date from participants, employers, withdrawing employers of a multiemployer plan, and other sources (such as a state or federal government in the case of a grant or subsidy). Receivables arise from formal commitments of an employer, legal requirements, or contractual requirements. The receivables should be reduced by an allowance for uncollectible amounts if warranted.

Long-lived assets (such as buildings, equipment, furniture and fixtures, and leasehold improvements) that are used in the plan's operations are presented at cost less accumulated depreciation or amortization.

Statement of Changes in Net Assets Available for Benefits

The statement of changes in net assets available for benefits is a comprehensive income statement that includes all recognized transactions and events that change the net assets available for benefits. At a minimum, the statement is to include separate amounts for:

- Contributions from:
  - Employer(s)—separating cash from noncash contributions
  - Participants, including those transmitted by the plan sponsor
  - Other identified sources.
- Net appreciation or depreciation (realized and unrealized amounts may be combined) in fair value for each significant class of investment, presented by:
  - Investments measured by quoted market prices
  - Investments measured by some other means.
- Investment income (not including appreciation or depreciation in fair value).
- Payments to plan participants for benefits, excluding amounts paid by insurance contracts that are not included in plan assets.
- Payments to insurance companies to purchase contracts that are excluded from plan assets.
- Administrative expenses.
- Other changes, if necessary, with appropriate description(s).

Interests in Master Trusts

Employee benefit plans must report an interest in a master trust as a separate item on the statement of net assets. The plans must also report the changes in value of that interest in a separate line in the statement of changes in net assets available for benefits. The guidance also requires the plan to:

- Disclose the master trust's investments and other assets and liabilities
- Disclose the dollar amount of its interest in those balances
- Present investment measured at fair value by general type of investment
(ASC 960-205-45-7, ASC 962-205-45-10 and 8C, and ASC 965-205-45-11)

The plan must also disclose for investments in a master trust.

- Net appreciation or depreciation in the fair value of investments
- Investment income
  (ASC 960-325-50-7, ASC 962-325-50-7, ASC 965-325-50-5)

The notes should include:

- Description basis used to allocate
  - Net assets
  - Total investment income
- For plans with an individual interest in the master trust, the percentage interest is the master trust
  (ASC 960-325-50-8, ASC 962-325-50-8, ASC 965-325-50-6)

The plan should also include a note presenting investments in a master trust measured at fair value by general type of investments and the dollar amount of that investment. (ASC 960-325-50-9 and 50-10, ASC 962-325-50-8A and 50-8B, ASC 965-325-50-7, and 50-8) The master trust's other assets and liabilities and the amount of the plan's interest in both should be disclosed. (ASC 960-325-50-10 and 50-11, ASC 962-325-50-8C, ASC 965-325-50-9)

Risks and Uncertainties

Employee benefit plans must disclose the information required by ASC 275, *Risks and Uncertainties*. Risks that are unique to employee benefit plans include:

- A significant industry downturn that could cause employees to retire early in order to avoid being laid off, especially if the plan's participants are concentrated within a particular industry or with a single employer.
- Likelihood that an employer will significantly increase pension or health and welfare benefits in order to avoid a union walkout.
- A planned downsizing that is expected to offer early retirement to employees.
- Investments in the stock of the employer.

Defined Benefit Plans (ASC 960)

In addition to the statement of net assets available for benefits and the statement of changes in net assets available for benefits, defined benefit pension plans must provide information about the actuarial present value of accumulated plan benefits and changes in the actuarial present value of accumulated plan benefits. The information can be included as separate financial statements or as schedules in the notes to the financial statements.

Accumulated plan benefits include the present value of future benefits to retired or terminated employees or their beneficiaries, to beneficiaries of deceased employees, and to present employees or their beneficiaries. Whenever possible, plan provisions are to govern the measurement of accumulated plan benefits. If the benefits earned in each year are not determinable from the plan's provisions, a formula for measurement is provided in ASC 960. When calculating accumulated plan benefits, an ongoing plan is to be assumed, analogous to the going concern assumption used in preparing GAAP financial statements of other types of entities. Thus, interest rates used for discounting expected future payments are based on rates of return on investments for the benefit deferral period, and employee turnover and employee mortality are considered.

The information provided in the financial statements for accumulated plan benefits should include net assets available for benefits in enough detail to identify significant changes during the year. (ASC 960-30-45-1) The minimum information should include:

- Net appreciation or depreciation in fair value
- The investment income
- Contributions from the employer segregated between cash and noncash
- Contributions from participants
- Contributions from other identified sources
- Benefits paid to participants
- Payments to insurance entities to purchase contracts excluded from plan assets
- Administrative expenses
- Other changes
  (ASC 960-30-45-2)

If the provisions of the defined benefit plan include a postretirement medical benefit component that is funded in accordance with IRC §401(h), ASC 960-30-45-4 through 45-10 specifies the presentation rules with respect to the §401(h) component. These specialized rules are necessary due to legal requirements regarding the separate accounting for and funding of these arrangements.

Defined Contribution Plans (ASC 962)

Types of Defined Contribution Plans The three general types of defined contribution plans are:

- Profit-sharing plans,
- Money purchase pension plans, and
- Stock bonus plans.

A profit-sharing plan is a plan that is neither a pension plan, as defined in the Internal Revenue Code, nor a stock bonus plan. Employer contributions to a profit-sharing plan are to be either discretionary or based on a fixed formula. Although the plan is called a profit-sharing plan, the contributions need not be made from the profits of the plan sponsor.

A money purchase plan is a benefit plan that bases employer contributions on a fixed formula that is unrelated to profits.

A stock bonus plan is a plan that makes its distributions to participants in the stock of the employer unless the participant chooses otherwise.

Within these three categories of plans are more specialized plans, such as 401(k) plans, 403(b) plans, savings plans, employee stock ownership plans, target benefit plans, and Keogh plans.

Distinguishing Characteristics of a Defined Contribution Plan The three primary attributes that distinguish a defined contribution plan from a defined benefit plan are:

1. Employer contributions are determined at the discretion of the employer or according to a contractual formula, rather than being actuarially determined.
2. Individual accounts are maintained for each plan participant, rather than a single account in which all participants partake.
3. Benefits are determined based on the amount accumulated in a participant's account at the time he or she retires or withdraws from the plan, rather than being defined in the plan agreement. If vested, the account's value is either paid to the participant or used to purchase an annuity for the participant.

The liabilities of a defined contribution plan include:

- Refunds of excess contributions,
- Income taxes payable by the plan, or
- Other expenses.

These should be deducted to arrive at net assets available for benefits. (ASC 962-205-45-4)

Presentation of Net Assets of an Investment Company ASC 946-210-45 specifies that, if the net assets of an investment company contain fully benefit-responsive investment contracts, those assets shall be reported at their contract values, because that is the amount participants in the fund would receive if they were to initiate withdrawals under the terms of the plan. An asset is considered fully benefit-responsive if:

1. The investment contract is between the fund and the issuer and prohibits the fund from assigning or selling the contract without issuer permission,
2. The issuer is obligated to repay principal and interest, or a financially responsible third party assures that the interest rate will not drop below zero,
3. All permitted participant-initiated transactions occur at contract value, and
4. An event that would limit the fund's ability to transact at contract value with the issuer is not probable.

The Codification also specifies disclosure requirements for this scenario.

Reporting Loans to Participants by Defined Contribution Pension Plans ASC 962-310 requires that loans to the participants in an entity's defined contribution pension plan be classified as notes receivable. (ASC 962-310-45-2) These loans should be reported separately from plan investments. The proper measurement of these loans is their unpaid principal balances, plus all accrued but unpaid interest. This requirement keeps entities from recording such loans at their fair value. The reason for making this distinction is that U.S. GAAP requires most investments by a pension plan to be recorded at their fair values, which would normally include loans to plan participants. By recording these loans as notes receivable, rather than investments, the fair value recordation requirement no longer applies.

HEALTH AND WELFARE BENEFIT PLANS (ASC 965)

Health and welfare plans stipulate a determinable benefit amount, which may take the form of a payment directly to the participant or a payment to a third party (such as a service provider or an insurance company) on the participant's behalf. These benefits may be provided upon retirement of the participant or during the postemployment period between termination of employment and retirement. Factors such as length of employment, age, and salary level determine the level of benefits to be provided. The contributions from the employer may be determined actuarially, by actual claims paid, or by a formula established by the plan sponsor. Regardless of the manner in which the plan is funded, the plan is a health and welfare benefit plan if its purpose is to provide a defined benefit.

Like defined benefit pension plans, health and welfare benefit plans must include information in their financial statements about the actuarial present value of benefit obligations earned by having performed past service. A benefit obligation for postemployment benefits for current participants should be recognized if all of the following conditions are met:

1. The participants' rights to receive benefits are attributable to services already rendered.
2. The participants' benefits vest or accumulate.

3. Payment of benefits is probable.
4. The amount can be reasonably estimated.
   (ASC 965-30-25-3)

If conditions 1 and 2 are not met, the obligation is recognized if the event that gives rise to the liability has already occurred and the amount can be reasonably estimated. (ASC 965-30-25-4)

The benefit obligations are measured as of the end of the plan year and include the actuarial present value of:

- Claims payable
- Claims incurred but not reported (IBNR)
- Insurance premiums due
- Accumulated eligibility credits and postemployment benefits, net of amounts currently payable
- Postretirement benefits for retired participants and their beneficiaries, other plan participants who are eligible to receive benefits, and participants who are not yet eligible to receive benefits
  (ASC 965-50-35-1)

Benefit obligations of health and welfare benefit plans, similar to accumulated plan benefits of defined benefit pension plans, do not appear as liabilities on the statement of net assets available for benefits. Instead, they are presented either as a separate financial statement, on the face of another financial statement, such as the statement of net assets available for benefits, or in the notes to the financial statements. Regardless of the location selected, the information about benefit obligations is required to be presented in its entirety in the same location.

A reconciliation, presented as a separate statement, on the face of another financial statement, or in the notes to the financial statements, is to identify significant factors comprising the change in the benefit obligation from the beginning of the year to the end. (ASC 965-30-50-45-4) The changes are classified into at least three categories:

1. Amounts currently payable, which includes claims payable, claims IBNR, and premiums due insurance companies,
2. Accumulated eligibility credits and post-employment benefits, net of amounts currently payable, and
3. Postretirement benefit obligations, net of amounts currently payable and claims IBNR.
   (ASC 965-30-45-5)

The information for each category is to include, at a minimum, the effects of:

1. Plan amendments
2. Changes in the nature of the plan, such as a merger or a spin-off
3. Changes in actuarial assumptions
4. Benefits accumulated during the year
5. Benefits paid during the year
6. Interest component (from amortizing the discount)
7. Other changes
   (ASC 965-30-45-6 and 45-7)

The last four items can be combined into a single "other changes" line. ASC 965-205-50-1 requires the following additional disclosures:

- A description of the plan agreement
- A description of the significant plan amendments
- The funding policies
- Any changes made to the funding policy during the year
- The policy regarding the purchase of contracts with insurance entities that are excluded from plan assets
- Amounts and types of securities included in plan assets
- Significant real estate or other transactions jointly involving the plan and the sponsor, the plan administrator, employers, and employee organizations
- Unusual or infrequent events or transactions that occurred after the financial statement date but before the financial statements are issued or available to be issued
- Material lease commitments
- Other commitments
- Contingent liabilities
- The assumed health care cost-trend rate used to measure the cost of benefits for the next year
- If the plan provides past retirement health benefits, the effect of a one percent increase in the assumed health care cost-trend rates for each future year
- Modification of the existing cost-sharing provisions in the substantive plan
- The existence and nature of any commitment to increase monetary benefits provided by the plan and their effect on the financial statements
- Termination provisions and priorities
- Restrictions in plan assets
  (ASC 965-205-50-1)

Defined contribution health and welfare are plans must also disclose the accounting policy and disposition of forfeited nonvested accounts. (ASC 965-205-50-1)

Defined contribution health and welfare plans, like other defined contribution plans, maintain an account for each participant that determines the amount of benefits that the participant will eventually receive. The terms of a defined contribution health and welfare plan agreement determine the contribution that will be made by the employer or participant into each account. Defined contribution health and welfare plans do not report information about benefit obligations because a plan's obligation is limited to the amounts accumulated in the participants' accounts.

Government Regulations

Pursuant to the requirements of ERISA, the federal government oversees the operating and reporting practices of employee benefit plans. ERISA establishes minimum standards for participation, vesting, and funding. It defines the responsibilities of plan fiduciaries and standards for their conduct. It requires plans to annually report summarized plan information to plan participants.

The Department of Labor (DOL) and the Internal Revenue Service (IRS) are authorized to issue regulations establishing reporting and disclosure requirements for employee benefit plans that are subject to ERISA. Each year, plans are required to report certain information to the DOL, the IRS, and the Pension Benefit Guaranty Corporation (if applicable). For many plans, the information is reported using Form 5500, which includes financial statements prepared in conformity with GAAP and additional supplementary financial schedules.

Various provisions of the Internal Revenue Code apply to employee benefit plans. If an employee benefit plan qualifies under Section §401(a) of the Code, certain favorable tax treatments apply. For example, if a plan is qualified, the plan sponsor receives current deductions for contributions to the plan, and the plan participants do not pay income taxes on those contributions or the accumulated earnings on them until benefits are distributed to them. In addition, plan participants may receive favorable tax treatment on the distributions. Qualified plans are exempt from income taxes, except for taxes on unrelated business income. Nonqualified plans, which generally provide benefits selectively only to a few key employees, are not entitled to those favorable treatments.

Terminating Plans

If the liquidation of a plan is imminent before the end of the plan year, the plan is a terminating plan, even if another plan will replace the terminated plan. (ASC 960-40-20) A terminating plan may continue to operate for as long as necessary to pay accrued benefits. Prominent disclosure of the relevant circumstances is necessary in all financial statements issued by the plan after the decision to terminate is made. Financial statements of a terminating plan are prepared on the liquidation basis of accounting for plan years ending after the determination that the termination is imminent. The liquidation basis for accumulated plan benefits (defined benefit pension plans) and benefit obligations (defined benefit health and welfare plans) may differ from the actuarial present value of benefits for an ongoing plan. For example, certain or all benefits may become vested upon plan termination.

REAL ESTATE—GENERAL (ASC 970)

PERSPECTIVE AND ISSUES

ASC 970, *Real Estate—General*, specifies the accounting for various costs in acquiring and developing real estate projects. It does not apply to:

- Real estate developed by an entity for its own use rather than for sale or rental
- Initial direct costs of leases (discussed in the chapter on ASC 842)
- Costs directly related to manufacturing, merchandising, or service activities rather than real estate activities
- Rental operations in which the predominant rental period is less than a month. (ASC 970-10-15-8 and 15-9)

ASC 970 does address the accounting for costs of real estate whether rented or sold.

DEFINITIONS OF TERMS

See Appendix A for additional terms relevant to this topic: Contract, Corporate Joint Venture, Kick-out Rights (Voting Interest Entity definition), Net Realizable Value, Noncontrolling Interest.

Amenities. Features that enhance the attractiveness or perceived value of a time-sharing interval. Amenities include golf courses, utility plants, clubhouses, swimming pools, tennis courts, indoor recreational facilities, and parking facilities.

Common Costs. Costs that relate to two or more units within a real estate project.

Costs Incurred to Rent Real Estate Projects. Costs related to real estate rental activities, including: costs of model units and their furnishings, rental facilities, semipermanent signs, rental brochures, advertising, grand openings, and rental overhead including rental salaries.

Costs Incurred to Sell Real Estate Projects. Costs related to the sale of real estate, including: model units and their furnishings, sales facilities, sales brochures, legal fees for preparation of prospectuses, semi-permanent signs, advertising, grand openings, and sales overhead including sales salaries.

Incidental Operations. Revenue-producing activities engaged in during the holding or development period to reduce the cost of developing the property for its intended use, as distinguished from activities designed to generate a profit or a return from the use of the property.

Incremental Costs of Incidental Operations. Costs that would not be incurred except in relation to the conduct of incidental operations. Interest, taxes, insurance, security, and similar costs that would be incurred during the development of a real estate project regardless of whether incidental operations were conducted are not incremental costs.

Incremental Revenue from Incidental Operations. Revenues that would not be earned except in relation to the conduct of incidental operations.

Indirect Project Costs. Costs incurred after the acquisition of the property, such as construction administration, legal fees, and various office costs, that clearly relate to projects under development or construction.

Phase. A contractually or physically distinguishable portion of a real estate project (including time-sharing projects). That portion is distinguishable from other portions based on shared characteristics such as:

- Units a developer has declared or legally registered to be for sale
- Units linked to an owners' association
- Units to be constructed during a particular time period
- How a developer plans to build the real estate project

Preacquisition Costs. Costs related to a property that are incurred for the express purpose of, but prior to, obtaining that property. Examples may be costs of surveying, zoning or traffic studies, or payments to obtain an option on the property.

Project Costs. Costs clearly associated with the acquisition, development, and construction of a real estate project.

Relative Fair Value before Construction. The fair value of each land parcel in a real estate project in relation to the fair value of the other parcels in the project, exclusive of value added by on-site development and construction activities.

CONCEPTS, RULES, AND EXAMPLES

Other Assets and Deferred Costs—Real Estate Project Costs

Preacquisition Costs

Payments are generally capitalized if they relate to an option to obtain the real property or if all of the following conditions are met:

- Costs are directly identified with the property.
- Costs would be capitalized if the property already were acquired.
- Acquisition of the option or property is probable. The purchaser wants the property and believes it to be available for sale and has the ability to finance its acquisition.
  (ASC 970-340-25-3)

Once capitalized, these costs are project costs that, if not receivable in the future, or if the property is not acquired, are to be recognized as expense. (ASC 970-340-25-4)

Taxes and Insurance

Real estate taxes and insurance are capitalized as property costs only when the property is undergoing activities necessary to get the property ready for its intended use. After the property is substantially complete and ready for its intended use such items are expensed. (ASC 970-340-25-8)

Property, Plant, and Equipment—Project Costs

If project costs are recognized as an asset under the guidance in ASC 340-40-25-1 through 25-8, then the recognized asset is capitalized as a cost of the project. (ASC 970-360-25-2) Indirect costs that relate to several projects are capitalized and allocated to these projects. (ASC 970-360-25-3)

Amenities

The costs in excess of anticipated proceeds of amenities that are to be sold or transferred in connection with the sale of individual units are treated as common costs of the project.

The costs of amenities that are to be sold separately or retained by the developer are capitalized with those costs in excess of estimated fair value treated as common costs. Fair value is determined as of the expected date of substantial physical completion and the amounts allocated to the amenity are not to be revised later. The sale of the amenity results in a gain or loss when the selling price differs from the fair value less accumulated depreciation. (ASC 970-340-25-9)

Costs of amenities are allocated among land parcels benefited for which development is probable. The fair value of a parcel is affected by its physical characteristics, its highest and best use, and the time and cost required to make such use of the property. (ASC 970-340-25-10) Before completion and availability for use, operating income or loss is an adjustment to common costs. After such date, operating income or loss is included in the income statement. (ASC 970-340-25-11)

Incidental Operations

Revenue from incidental operations is netted with the costs of such operations and any excess of incremental revenue over incremental costs reduces capitalized project costs. If such costs exceed revenues, the excess is recognized as expense as incurred. (ASC 970-340-25-12)

Allocation of Costs

Capitalized costs are allocated by specific identification. If this is not feasible, then costs prior to construction are allocated by the relative fair value of each parcel before construction and construction costs are allocated by the relative sales value of each unit. If estimation of relative values is impractical, allocation may be based on square footage or another area method, or by using other appropriate methods. (ASC 970-360-30-1)

Revisions of Estimates

Estimates and cost allocations should be reviewed at the end of each period until the project is substantially complete and available for sale. Costs are revised and reallocated as necessary for material changes in current estimates. Changes in estimate are reported following the guidance in ASC 250-10-45 and 10-50. (ASC 970-340-35-1)

Abandonment and Change in Use

Abandonment of a project requires all capitalized costs to be expensed and not reallocated to other components of the project or other projects. (ASC 970-360-40-1) Real estate donated to governmental units is not deemed abandoned and its costs are treated as project common costs. (ASC 970-360-35-1)

Changes in use made according to a formal plan require that costs incurred and expected to be incurred that exceed the estimated value of the required project (when substantially complete and ready for intended use) be charged to expense. (ASC 970-360-35-2)

Selling Costs

Costs incurred to sell should be evaluated for capitalization in accordance with ASC 340- 40-25-1 through 25-8. (ASC 970-340-25-13)

Rental Costs

Costs incurred to rent real estate projects under operating or direct financing leases and reasonably expected to be recoverable from future rental operations are capitalized. This excludes initial direct costs as defined and described in accounting for leases. Costs that do not qualify for capitalization are expensed as incurred. (ASC 970-340-25-16)

Capitalized costs are amortized over the term of the lease, other than initial direct costs, if directly related to a specific operating or direct financing lease, or over the period of expected benefit. Amortization begins when the project is substantially completed and available for occupancy. Estimated unrecoverable amounts are expensed when it is probable that the lease will be terminated. (ASC 970-340-35-2)

A project is substantially completed and available for occupancy when tenant improvements are completed or after one year from the end of major construction activity. (ASC 970-340-25-19) Then normal operations take place with all revenues and costs (including depreciation and other amortized costs) recognized in the income statement. (ASC 970-340-25-18) If part of a project is occupied but other parts are not yet complete, completed portions are considered separate projects. (ASC 970-340-25-17)

Real Estate Special Assessments The laws of various states permit the formation of Tax Increment Financing Entities (TIFEs). Although their structure and characteristics differ between jurisdictions, TIFEs are generally special taxing districts established to finance and operate infrastructure owned by the municipality, such as roads, water mains, electric lines, sewers, and the like. These infrastructure improvements are used to revitalize a discrete geographic area by facilitating the private development of adjoining residential and commercial real estate. The TIFE or, absent a TIFE, the municipality typically issues bonds to finance the construction of the infrastructure improvements. (ASC 970-470-05-2) The bonds may offer investors favorable after-tax yields by qualifying for tax-exempt status under IRC §141. Generally, the bonds are repaid from special assessments specifically designated for this purpose by the TIFE (or the municipality) such as user fees, tolls, sales taxes, real estate taxes, hotel bed taxes, and the like.

Besides paying for the debt service, these special assessments also fund ongoing operating costs, such as routine infrastructure repairs and maintenance. The infrastructure improvements made with the bond proceeds directly benefit the adjoining property owners and, in fact, the terms of these arrangements are often jointly negotiated between residential and commercial real estate developers and the municipality as an inducement to the developers to invest in a local development project.

Depending on an analysis of the specific facts and circumstances, including the relevant statute, ordinance, bond indenture, and other legal documents, the property owner or developer may potentially be required to record:

- A liability for a special assessment by the TIFE or municipality if that assessment is levied on each individual property owner at an amount that is fixed or determinable and that covers a determinable period of time.
- A guarantee liability under ASC 450 if, for example, it has:
  - Contractually agreed to cover all or a portion of any shortfalls in the required annual debt service of the bond obligations of the issuing TIFE or municipality.
  - Pledged company assets as collateral for the bond obligations.
  - Provided a letter of credit or other credit enhancements to support all or a portion of the bond obligations.
    (ASC 970-470-25-1)

REAL ESTATE—RETAIL LAND (ASC 976)

PERSPECTIVE AND ISSUES

The purpose of ASC 976 is to present the guidelines that need to be considered when reporting on retail land sales that are sales, on a volume basis, of lots that are subdivisions of large tracts of land. These sales are characterized by small down payments and a sales contract for the balance. ASC 976 provides guidance on receivables, inventory, and cost of sales and services for the transaction listed in the scope section below. (ASC 976-10-05-2)

DEFINITIONS OF TERMS

Lien. A claim or charge a creditor has on property which serves as security for payment of debt by the debtor.

CONCEPTS, RULES, AND EXAMPLES

Real Estate—Retail Land

ASC 976 Scope ASC 976 provides guidance for all entities that sell, on a volume basis, lots that are subdivisions of large tracts of land. (ASC 976-10-15-3)

ASC 976 does not apply to sales of:

- Lots to builders
- Homes, buildings, and parcels of land to builders and owners
- Corporate stock of entities with substantial real estate
- Partnership interests
- Time-sharing interests if the sales are in substance sales of real estate
- Options to purchase real estate
  (ASC 976-10-15-4)

Receivables

If a contract is canceled, the receivable balances are charged to the allowance for contract cancellation. (ASC 976-310-35-1)

Disclosure

Entities with retail land sales should disclose for each of the five years following the date of the financial statements:

- Estimated total costs
- Estimated dates of expenditures for improvements for major areas where sales are being made
- Recorded obligations for improvements
(ASC 976-330-50-1)

REAL ESTATE TIME-SHARING ACTIVITIES (ASC 978)

PERSPECTIVE AND ISSUES

Overview

A major segment of the real estate industry has evolved in recent decades to market and sell time-shares, whereby parties acquire the right to use property (typically, resort condominiums or other vacation-oriented property) for a fixed number of weeks per year (known as intervals). While a vast variety of property types and transaction structures exist, there are certain common features and complexities that have challenged the accounting profession. Time-sharing transactions are characterized by the following:

- Volume-based, homogeneous sales
- Seller financing
- Relatively high selling and marketing costs
- Upon default, recovery of the time-sharing interval by the seller and some forfeiture of principal by the buyer
(ASC 978-10-05-5)

Time-share transactions are should be accounted for as nonretail land sales, while time-share transactions are excluded from certain provisions otherwise applicable to incidental rental operations.

DEFINITIONS OF TERMS

Source: ASC 978, Glossary. Other terms found in Appendix A: Fair Value, Market Participants, Orderly Transactions, Related Parties

Fixed Time. A time-sharing arrangement in which ownership is passed through a deed and the buyer purchases a specific period (generally, a specific week) during the year.

Floating Time. A time-sharing arrangement in which ownership is passed through a deed but the buyer is not limited to a specific period (generally, a specific week) during the year.

Fractional Interest. A partial ownership interest in real estate that typically includes larger blocks of time on an annual basis (for example, three weeks or more).

Interval. The specific period (generally, a specific week) during the year that a time-sharing unit is specified by agreement to be available for occupancy by a particular customer. Also denoted Time-Sharing Interest or Time-Share.

Phase. A contractually or physically distinguishable portion of a real estate project (including time-sharing projects). That portion is distinguishable from other portions based on shared characteristics such as:

- Units a developer has declared or legally registered to be for sale
- Units linked to an owners' association
- Units to be constructed during a particular time period
- How a developer plans to build the real estate project

Points. Purchased vacation credits that a buyer may redeem for occupancy at various sites. The number of points redeemed depends on such factors as unit type and size, site location, and season.

Project. A time-sharing development; some projects may be completed in a single phase, such as a single, one-story building containing several time-sharing units. Other projects may be completed in several phases, for example:

- A hotel that is being converted to time-sharing units one floor at a time while the unconverted units continue to be rented
- A number of buildings, each containing several time-sharing units, being built on a piece of property over an extended period of time

Tenancy-for-Years. A time-sharing arrangement in which a customer has a qualified right to possession and use of a time-sharing interval for a certain number of years, after which it reverts to the seller or a third party. Also known as estate-for-years or term-for-years.

Time-Share. See Interval.

Time-Sharing. An arrangement in which a seller sells or conveys the right to occupy a dwelling unit for specified periods in the future. Forms of time-sharing arrangements include but are not limited to fixed and floating time, interval ownership, undivided interests, points programs, vacation clubs, right-to-use arrangements such as tenancy-for-years arrangements, and arrangements involving special-purpose entities. In this context, an undivided interest is a time-sharing arrangement that involves a tenant-in-common interest in a condominium unit or entire improved property, and in which the interest holder is assigned a specific period (generally, a specific week). The interest holder is also assigned a specific unit if the undivided interest is in the entire improved property.

Time-Sharing Interest. See Interval.

Time-Sharing Special-Purpose Entity. An entity, typically a corporation or a trust, to which a seller transfers time-sharing real estate in exchange for the entity's stock, membership interests, or beneficial interests.

CONCEPTS, RULES, AND EXAMPLES

Scope

ASC 978 provides guidance for a seller's accounting for real estate time-sharing transactions, including:

- Fee simple transactions in which nonreversionary title and ownership of the real estate pass to the buyer or an SPE
- Transactions in which title and ownership of all or a portion of the real estate remain with the seller

- Transactions in which title and ownership of all or a portion of the real estate pass to the buyer and subsequently revert to the seller or transfer to a third party
- Transactions by a time-share reseller
(ASC 978-10-15-3)

Incidental Operations

Rental and other operations during holding periods, including sampler programs and minivacations, should be accounted for as incidental operations. This requires that any excess of revenue over costs be recorded as a reduction of inventory costs. (ASC 978-330-35-3)

VIES and Other Complex Structures

The accounting treatment for more complex time-sharing structures such as time-sharing special-purpose entities (variable interest entities [VIEs]), points systems, and vacation clubs should be determined using the same profit recognition guidance as for simpler structures, provided that the time-sharing interest has been sold to the end user. For statement of financial position presentation purposes, a VIE should be viewed as an entity lacking economic substance and established for the purpose of facilitating sales if the VIE structure is legally required for purposes of selling intervals to a class of nonresident customers, and the VIE has no assets other than the time-sharing intervals and has no debt. In those circumstances, the seller should present on its statement of financial position as time-sharing inventory the interests in the VIE not yet sold to end users. (ASC 978-810-25-3) Entities should look to the following for guidance: ASC 810, 323, and 321. (ASC 978-810-25-4)

REGULATED OPERATIONS (ASC 980)

PERSPECTIVE AND ISSUES

Although various businesses are subject to regulatory oversight to greater or lesser degrees, as used in GAAP the term regulated operations refers primarily to public utilities, whose ability to set selling prices for the goods or services they offer is constrained by government actions. Generally, the regulatory process has been designed to permit such enterprises to recover the costs they incur, plus a reasonable rate of return to stockholders. However, given the political process of rate-setting by regulatory authorities, and the fact that costs such as those for plant construction have escalated, the ability to recover all costs through rate increases has become less certain. For this and other reasons, specialized GAAP has been promulgated.

CONCEPTS, RULES, AND EXAMPLES

These accounting principles apply to regulated enterprises only if they continue to meet certain criteria, which relate to the intended ability to recover all costs through the rate-setting process. When and if these conditions are no longer met, due to deregulation or a shift to rate-setting which is not based on cost recovery, then application of the specialized GAAP should terminate.

Asset Recognition

If certain costs are not recognized for current rate-setting purposes, but it is probable that the costs will be recovered through future revenue, then these costs can be capitalized even though a nonregulated enterprise would be required to expense these costs currently. (ASC 980-340-25-1) Deferred costs can include an imputed cost of equity capital, if so accounted for rate-setting purposes, even though this would not normally be permitted under GAAP. Thus, the regulatory process can result in the accounting recognition of an asset that would not otherwise be recognized by a commercial enterprise. If at any time it becomes apparent that the incurred cost will not be recovered through generation of future revenue, that cost is to be charged to expense. (ASC 980-340-40-1) If a regulator subsequently excludes specific costs from allowable costs, the carrying value of the asset recognized is to be reduced to the extent of the excluded costs. Should the regulator allow recovery of these previously excluded costs or any additional costs, a new asset is to be recognized and classified as if these costs had been initially included in allowable costs.

Imposition of Liabilities

In other situations, the regulatory process can result in the accounting recognition of a liability. This usually occurs when regulators mandate that refunds be paid to customers, which must be accrued when probable and reasonably estimable, per ASC 450, *Contingencies*. Furthermore, regulatory rates may be set at a higher level, in order to recover costs expected to be incurred in the future, subject to the caveat that such amounts will be refunded to customers if it later becomes apparent that actual costs incurred were less than expected. In such cases, the incremental rate increase related to recovery of future costs must be accounted for as a liability (unearned revenue), until the condition specified is satisfied. Finally, regulators may stipulate that a gain realized by the utility will be returned to customers over a specified future period; this will be accounted for by accrual of a liability rather than by recognition of the gain for accounting purposes. (ASC 980-405-25-1)

Abandonment

Accounting for abandonments is also stipulated for regulated enterprises. If an abandonment occurs or becomes probable, any costs which are probable of not being recovered are required to be written off as a loss. (ASC 980-360-35-1) Furthermore, if the return on the investment that will be recoverable will not be equal to the normal rate of return, then an additional loss accrual must be recognized currently. This loss is measured by the difference between the projected future revenues, discounted at the enterprise's incremental borrowing rate, and the remaining costs to be recovered. The amount of loss to be recognized obviously depends on the enterprise's estimate of time to elapse until rate increases are effective, and the length of time over which the increases will remain in effect. These estimates may change over time, and the effect of revisions in the estimate will be reflected in earnings in the periods the new estimates are made. (ASC 980-360-35-3)

The carrying value of the costs of an abandoned plant is increased during the period from the abandonment until recovery occurs through rate increases as promised by the regulatory authorities. If full return of investment is anticipated, the cost of abandoned assets is accreted at the rate (the enterprise's overall cost of capital) permitted for rate-setting purposes. If partial or no return on investment is expected, the asset value is accreted at the same rate that was used to compute the loss accrual, which is the enterprise's incremental borrowing rate. During the recovery period, the costs of the abandoned plant are amortized. If full return on investment is expected, this amortization is to be computed on the same basis as is permitted for rate-setting purposes. If partial or no return is expected, amortization is recognized in amounts that provide a constant rate of return on the unamortized balance of the investment in the costs of the abandoned plant.

Accounting for Liabilities Related to Asset Retirement Obligations

Historically, and particularly since the advent of nuclear energy generation, public utilities have faced the problem of accounting for costs which are expected to be incurred attendant upon the retirement from service of the generating facilities. Environmental and other laws and regulations typically mean that very substantial costs have to be borne, in order to dispose of waste, restore the land (not merely the power generating facility site, but, in the case of coal-fired plants, restoration of the strip mining locations), and ameliorate other problems. These issues are addressed by ASC 410-20, *Asset Retirement Obligations*.

The chapter on ASC 410 presents a detailed examination of ASC 410-20, and that discussion is not duplicated here. In brief, this pronouncement establishes standards for measuring the future cost to retire an asset and recognizing it in the financial statements as a liability and correspondingly, as part of the depreciable cost of the asset. ASC 410-20 applies to legal obligations associated with the retirement of tangible long-lived assets that result from their acquisition, construction, development, and/or normal operation. It does not apply to situations where moral suasion is to be applied to encourage cleanup efforts, even if the reporting entity has a history of making such voluntary gestures. However, the principle of "promissory estoppel" does create legal obligations even absent contractual or statutory requirements, in some cases.

If costs, such as those related to nuclear decommissioning, are legal obligations, the present value of the future expenditures is recognized as an added cost of the asset, and as a liability, at acquisition. Further cost accretion is required due to the passage of time. Depreciation charges are based on the recorded cost of the asset, including the estimated future retirement costs. Changes in estimates, which are inevitable, are handled differently if they are increases versus decreases, as described in the chapter on ASC 360.

Accounting for Deregulation and "Stranded Costs"

The utilities industries have undergone varying degrees of deregulation. This has significant effects on the financial reporting of many of the entities operating in these industries, since under GAAP many had recognized regulatory assets and regulatory liabilities which will no longer be recognizable once full deregulation occurs. Also, certain costs may no longer be recoverable in a deregulated environment, transforming certain assets into *stranded costs*.

When deregulation legislation has been enacted affecting all or a portion of the entity's operations, it is to cease applying ASC 980 to the affected operations. In cases in which the effects of deregulation are imposed by means of a rate order, such an order would have to be sufficiently detailed so that the entity would be able to determine how it will be affected. Regulatory assets would not, however, be immediately written off; instead, an evaluation of regulatory cash flows would be conducted to determine whether an impairment had occurred and to determine whether the portion of the business from which the regulatory cash flows are derived is still subject to ASC 980. Only if the asset is impaired (applying ASC 360 criteria) or if ASC 980 is no longer applicable would the asset be written off before being recovered. Similarly, regulatory liabilities would not be reclassified into income until the obligation is eliminated by the regulatory authority.

A related concern is whether the new regulatory assets or liabilities must be given recognition to reflect expenses and obligations that will arise from the portion of the business being deregulated. The same "source of cash flow" type of analysis noted above is to be applied to make these determinations. Thus, a cost or obligation is recognized as a regulatory asset or liability, respectively, once it is expensed or incurred after ASC 980 is applied to that portion of the operations, if it has been designated for recovery or settlement, respectively, via regulated cash flows. (ASC 980-20-35-6)

Revenue

ASC 980-605-25 addresses the treatment of additional revenues of rate-regulated utility companies that are to be billed in the future under alternative revenue programs. It identifies two types of alternative revenue programs, defined as Type A and Type B. (ASC 980-605-25-1) The revenues from alternative revenue programs are to be recognized when the events permitting billing of the revenues have occurred and three specific criteria that are discussed in the abstract are met. (ASC 980-605-25-4)

Also, rate-regulated utilities recognizing revenues from an alternative revenue program that do not meet the conditions of this consensus must amend the plan or change the program to meet the conditions.

Compensation—Retirement Benefits

ASC 980-715-25 holds that, if the regulator includes other postemployment benefits (OPEB), costs in rates on a pay-as-you-go basis, the regulatory asset relating to the cost under ASC 715 is not to be recognized. (ASC 980-715-25-4) Further, the regulatory asset for a rate-regulated enterprise is to recognize the difference between ASC 715 costs and the OPEB costs if future revenue will at least offset the deferred cost and meet four specific criteria, which are discussed in the standard. (ASC 980-715-25-4)

Regarding the accounting for regulatory assets, ASC 980-715-25-8 states that a rate-regulated enterprise that fails to initially meet the asset recognition criteria can recognize a regulatory asset for other postemployment benefits costs in a future period when applicable criteria are met.

SOFTWARE (ASC 985)

PERSPECTIVE AND ISSUES

Overview

As technology has come to play a more important role in businesses, increasing levels of activity have been devoted to the development of computer software. This involves a number of undertakings:

- Software licensed, purchased, or leased from others for internal use
- Software obtained from others for resale in the normal course of business (either on a standalone basis or as part of a larger product)
- Software developed internally for sale to others
- Software developed internally for the developer's own use

Software can be licensed, purchased, or leased and can reside on the user's hardware or be "hosted" by an application service provider (ASP) and leased to the user for remote use over the Internet. A growing set of accounting standards deal with some, but not all, of these issues.

Scope ASC 985 applies to computer software to be sold, leased, or otherwise marketed as a separate product or as part of a product or process. However, it does not apply as follows:

- ASC 985-20, 985-330, 985-350, 985-705, and 985-730 do not apply to software created for internal use.

- ASC 985-20, 985-330, 985-350, 985-705, and 985-730 do not apply to arrangements to deliver software or a software system, either alone or together with other products or services, requiring significant production, modification, or customization of software. Preparers should consult the guidance in ASC 606 on ASC 340-40.
(ASC 985-10-15-3)

ASC 350-40 addresses accounting for the costs of software acquired from others, or developed internally, for internal use. For guidance to help determine whether software is developed for internal use or is subject to a plan to be marketed externally, see ASC 350-40-15-2 through 15-2C and ASC 350-40-15-5.

In addition to the scope limitations above, ASC 985-20 does not apply to research and development assets acquired in a combination or acquisition. (ASC 985-20-15-3) Software subject to a hosting arrangement is within the scope of ASC 985-20 if:

- The customer has the right to take possession of the software at any time during the hosting period without significant penalty and
- It is feasible for the customer to either run the software on its own hardware or contract with another party unrelated to the vendor to host the software.
(ASC 985-20-15-5)

DEFINITIONS OF TERMS

Source: Terms are from ASC 985, *Glossary*. Also see the following terms in Appendix A: Business, Contract, Customer Hosting Arrangement, Not-for-Profit Entity, Revenue.

Coding. Generating detailed instructions in a computer language to carry out the requirements described in the detail program design. The coding of a computer software product may begin prior to, concurrent with, or subsequent to the completion of the detail program design.

Customer Support. Services performed by an enterprise to assist customers in their use of software products. Those services include any installation assistance, training classes, telephone question and answer services, newsletters, on-site visits, and software or data modifications.

Detail Program Design. The detail design of a computer software product that take product functions, features, and technical requirements to their most detailed, logical form and enable coding of the product.

Maintenance. Activities undertaken after the product is available for general release to customers to correct errors or keep the product updated with current information. Those activities include routine changes and additions.

Product Design. A logical representation of all product functions in sufficient detail to serve as product specifications.

Product Enhancement. Improvements to an existing product that are intended to extend the life or improve significantly the marketability of the original product. Enhancements normally require their own product design and may require a redesign of all or part of the existing product.

Testing. Performing the steps necessary to determine whether the coded computer software product meets function, feature, and technical performance requirements set forth in the product design.

Working Model. An operative version of the computer software product that is completed in the same software language as the product to be ultimately marketed, performs all the major functions planned for the product, and is ready for initial customer testing (usually referred to as beta testing).

CONCEPTS, RULES, AND EXAMPLES

Costs of Software Developed Internally for Sale or Lease

A separate set of accounting issues arise in connection with the costs of computer software developed internally for lease or sale to others. The principal issue relates to the point in the development process at which development efforts are no longer characterized as research and development (R&D). The costs of R&D activities are required to be expensed currently as discussed in the chapter on ASC 730. The determination of this milestone has important accounting significance because specified costs incurred subsequent to the completion of R&D may be deferred (i.e., inventoried) and later reclassified as cost of sales as the finished products are sold or leased.

ASC 985 established the concept of technological feasibility to demarcate the point at which it is proper to begin to defer costs. According to this standard, all costs of development are considered research and development costs and must be expensed until technological feasibility has been established. (ASC 985-20-25-1) This point is reached when all the necessary planning, designing, coding, and testing activities have been completed, to the extent these activities are necessary to establish that the product in question can meet its design specifications. Design specifications, in turn, may include such product aspects as functions, features, and technical performance requirements. (ASC 985-20-25-2)

If the process of creating the software involves a detail program design, evidence of having achieved technological feasibility includes having performed these steps:

- The product design (the logical representation of the product) and detailed program design have been completed. This step includes having demonstrated that the necessary skills, hardware, and software technologies are accessible to the entity for completion of product development.
- The detailed program design has been documented and traced to product specifications, thus demonstrating completeness and consistency.
- The detailed program design has been reviewed for any high-risk elements, such as unproven functions or product innovations, and any such high-risk elements have been resolved through coding and testing.
  (ASC 985-20-25-2a)

If the software development effort does not involve creation of a detailed program design, then the following steps would require completion to demonstrate technological feasibility:

- A product design and working model of the software have been completed.
- The completeness of the working model and its consistency with the product design have been confirmed by testing.
  (ASC 985-20-25-2b)

If all the foregoing steps in either of the above listings have been completed as applicable, then technological feasibility has been demonstrated, and if all research and development activities for the other components of the product have been completed, qualifying costs of producing product masters incurred thereafter are capitalized as production costs. (ASC 985-20-25-4) Such costs include additional coding and testing activities that occur after the establishment of technological feasibility. The costs of producing product masters include not only the master copy of the software itself but also related user documentation and training materials and coding and testing performed after establishing technological feasibility. (ASC 985-20-25-3) Capitalized production costs may include allocated indirect costs (e.g., occupancy costs related to programmers). General and administrative expenses should not be allocated. (ASC 985-20-25-5)

Other costs, such as product duplication, training material publication, and packaging, are capitalized as inventory on a unit-specific basis and expensed as cost of sales when product sales revenues are recognized. (ASC 985-330-25-1 and 40-1)

Capitalization of software costs ceases once the product is available for general release to customers of the entity. Period costs, such as maintenance and ongoing customer support efforts, are expensed as incurred. (ASC 985-20-25-6)

The capitalized production costs must be amortized, beginning when the product is first available for general release to customers. (ASC 985-20-35-3) Amortization is computed on a product-by-product basis, which means that costs related to development of earlier products cannot be "rolled forward" into the costs of newer products, thereby delaying expense recognition. Periodic amortization must be the greater of

1. An amount determined with reference to total estimated future gross revenues to be generated by the product, or
2. An amount computed on a straight-line basis with reference to the product's expected life cycle.

(ASC 985-20-35-1 and 35-2)

If adjustments are recognized, the written-down amount becomes the new cost basis for further amortization purposes, as well as for comparison to net realizable value in the following period. (ASC 985-20-35-4)

Example of Amortization of Capitalized Computer Software Development Costs

Assume total costs of $30,000 have been capitalized at the point product sales begin. Management estimates that the product will eventually generate revenues of $5,100,000 over a period of four years. For the current period (1/2 of a year), revenues of $600,000 have been earned. Capitalized costs of $3,750 must be amortized, which is the greater of the pro rata amount based on estimated total revenues to be derived from product sales [($600,000 ÷ $500,000) × $30,000 = $3,529] or the amount determined on a straight-line basis ($30,000 ÷ 4 × 1/2 = $3,750).

Software Revenue Recognition Provision for Losses

If it is probable that the transaction price allocated to an unsatisfied performance delegation under the guidance in ASC 606 will result in a loss, the entity should recognize the loss under the guidance in ASC 450.

Product May Not Equate with Delivery of Software Services to be provided commonly involve significant production, modification, or customization of the software. Thus, physical delivery of the software might not constitute the delivery of the final product contracted for, absent those alterations, resulting in the requirement that such arrangements be accounted for as construction-type or production-type contracts in conformity with ASC 606-35. (ASC 985-605-25-2)

APPENDIX A
DEFINITIONS OF TERMS

(**Note:** Items with an asterisk are pending implementation of ASU 2016-02, *Leases*)

Acquiree. Topics 805, 840, 842, 958. The business or businesses that the acquirer obtains control of in a business combination. This term also includes a nonprofit activity or business that a not-for-profit acquirer obtains control of in an acquisition by a not-for-profit entity.

Acquirer. Topics 805, 842, 954, 958. The entity that obtains control of the acquiree. However, in a business combination in which a variable interest entity (VIE) is acquired, the primary beneficiary of that entity always is the acquirer.

Acquisition by a Not-for-Profit Entity. Topics 270, 350, 420, 450, 460, 730, 740, 805, 815, 820, 840, 842, 954, 958, 985. A transaction or other event in which a not-for-profit acquirer obtains control of one or more nonprofit activities or businesses and initially recognizes their assets and liabilities in the acquirer's financial statements. When applicable guidance in Topic 805 is applied by a not-for-profit entity, the term "business combination" has the same meaning as this term has for a not-for-profit entity. Likewise, a reference to business combinations in guidance that links to Topic 805 has the same meaning as a reference to acquisitions by not-for-profit entities.

Acquisition Date. Topics 450, 740, 805, 954, 958. The date on which the acquirer obtains control of the acquiree.

Acquisition, Development, and Construction Arrangements. Topics 310, 810, 840, 970. Acquisition, development, or construction arrangements, in which a lender, usually a financial institution, participates in expected residual profit from the sale or refinancing of property.

Affiliate. Def. 1. Topics 850, 860, 946, 454, 958. A party that, directly or indirectly through one or more intermediaries, controls, is controlled by, or is under common control with an entity.

Amortized Cost Basis. Topics 310, 320, 326, 470. The amount at which an investment is acquired, adjusted for accretion, amortization, collection of cash, previous other-than-temporary impairments recognized in earnings (less any cumulative-effect adjustments), foreign exchange, and fair value hedge accounting adjustments.

Asset Groups. An asset group is the unit of accounting for a long-lived asset or assets to be held and used, which represents the lowest level for which identifiable cash flows are largely independent of the cash flows of other groups of assets and liabilities.

Available-for-Sale Securities. Topics 220, 320, 326. Investments not classified as either trading securities or as held-to-maturity securities.

Bargain Purchase Option.* A provision allowing the lessee, at his option, to purchase the leased property for a price that is sufficiently lower than the expected fair value of the property at the date the option becomes exercisable that exercise of the option appears, at lease inception, to be reasonably assured.

Bargain Renewal Option.* A provision allowing the lessee, at his option, to renew the lease for a rental sufficiently lower than the fair rental of the property at the date the option becomes exercisable that exercise of the option appears, at lease inception, to be reasonably assured. Fair rental of a property in this context shall mean the expected rental for equivalent property under similar terms and conditions.

Benchmark Interest Rate. Topics 815, 820. A widely recognized and quoted rate in an active financial market that is broadly indicative of the overall level of interest rates attributable to high-credit-quality obligors in that market. It is a rate that is widely used in a given financial market as an underlying basis for determining the interest rates of individual financial instruments and commonly referenced in interest-rate-related transactions.

In theory the benchmark interest rate should be a risk-free rate (that is, has no risk of default). In some markets, government borrowing rates may serve as a benchmark. In other markets, the benchmark interest rate may be an interbank offered rate.

Beneficial Interests. Topics 325, 805, 810, 820, 860. Rights to receive all or portions of specified cash inflows received by a trust or other entity, including, but not limited to, all of the following:

- Senior and subordinated shares of interest, principal, or other cash inflows to be passed-through or paid-through
- Premiums due to guarantors
- Commercial paper obligations
- Residual interests, whether in the form of debt or equity.

Benefit Formula. Def. 2. Topic 715. The basis for determining benefits to which participants may be entitled under a postretirement benefit plan. A plan's benefit formula specifies the years of service to be rendered, age to be attained while in service, or a combination of both that must be met for an employee to be eligible to receive benefits under the plan. A plan's benefit formula may also define the beginning of the credited service period and the benefits earned for specific periods of service.

Benefits. Topics 715, 960, 962, 965. The monetary or in-kind benefits or benefit coverage to which participants may be entitled under a pension plan or other postretirement benefit plan, including health care benefits; life insurance; legal, educational, and advisory services; pension benefits; disability benefits; death benefits; and benefits due to termination of employment.

Business. Topics 205, 270, 350, 360, 420, 450, 460, 505, 610, 730, 740, 805, 810, 815, 820, 840, 842, 845, 954, 958, 985. Paragraphs 805-10-55-3A through 55-6 and 805-10-55-8 through 55-9 define what is considered a business. For more information on this pending content, see the Technical Alert and other information in the chapter on ASC 805.

Business Combination. Topics 850, 805, 810, 820, 842, 958. A transaction or other event in which an acquirer obtains control of one or more businesses. Transactions sometimes referred to as true mergers or mergers of equals also are business combinations. See also Acquisition by a Not-for-Profit Entity.

Call Option. Topics 260, 718. A contract that allows the holder to buy a specified quantity of stock from the writer of the contract at a fixed price for a given period. See Option and Purchased Call Option.

Cash. Topics 210, 230, 610, 860, 942. Consistent with common usage, cash includes not only currency on hand but demand deposits with banks or other financial institutions. Cash also includes other kinds of accounts that have the general characteristics of demand deposits in that the customer may deposit additional funds at any time and also effectively may withdraw funds at any time without prior notice or penalty. All charges and credits to those accounts are cash receipts or payments to both the entity owning the account and the bank holding it. For example, a bank's granting of a loan by crediting the proceeds to a customer's demand deposit account is a cash payment by the bank and a cash receipt of the customer when the entry is made.

Cash Consideration. Topics 605, 705, 908. Cash payments and credits that the customer can apply against trade amounts owed to the vendor. In addition, as indicated in Section 505-50-25, consideration in the form of equity instruments is recognized in the same period or periods and in the same manner (that is, capitalize versus expense) as if the entity had paid cash for the goods or services or used cash rebates as a sales discount instead of paying with or using the equity instruments. Accordingly, guidance with respect to cash consideration is applicable to consideration that consists of equity instruments (regardless of whether a measurement date has been reached).

Cash Equivalents. Topics 210, 230, 320, 610, 715, 830, 958. Cash equivalents are short-term, highly liquid investments that have both of the following characteristics:

- Readily convertible to known amounts of cash
- So near their maturity that they present insignificant risk of changes in value because of changes in interest rates

Generally, only investments with original maturities of three months or less qualify under that definition. Original maturity means original maturity to the entity holding the investment. For example, both a three-month U.S. Treasury bill and a three-year U.S. Treasury note purchased three months from maturity qualify as cash equivalents. However, a Treasury note purchased three years ago does not become a cash equivalent when its remaining maturity is three months. Examples of items commonly considered to be cash equivalents are Treasury bills, commercial paper, money market funds, and federal funds sold (for an entity with banking operations).

Change in Accounting Principle. Topics 250, 270, 805. A change from one generally accepted accounting principle to another generally accepted accounting principle when there are two or more generally accepted accounting principles that apply or when the accounting principle formerly used is no longer generally accepted. A change in the method of applying an accounting principle also is considered a change in accounting principle.

Combined Financial Statements. Topics 810, 958. The financial statements of a combined group of commonly controlled entities or commonly managed entities presented as that of a single economic entity. The combined group does not include the parent.

Commencement Date of the Lease (Commencement Date).* Topics 210, 255, 310, 410, 815, 450, 460, 740, 805, 815, 842. The date on which a lessor makes an underlying asset available for use by a lessee. See paragraphs 842-10-55-19 through 55-21 for implementation guidance on the commencement date.

Commitment Fees. Topic 320, 942. Fees charged for entering into an agreement that obligates the entity to make or acquire a loan or to satisfy an obligation of the other party under a specified condition. Commitment fees include fees for letters of credit and obligations to purchase a loan or group of loans and pass-through certificates.

Common Stock. Topics 260, 323. A stock that is subordinate to all other stock of the issuer. Also called common shares.

Component of an Entity. Topics 205, 320, 360, 715. A component of an entity comprises operations and cash flows that can be clearly distinguished, operationally and for financial reporting purposes, from the rest of the entity. A component of an entity may be a reportable segment or an operating segment, a reporting unit, a subsidiary, or an asset group.

Comprehensive Income. Topics 205, 220, 815, 954. The change in equity (net assets) of a business entity during a period from transactions and other events and circumstances from nonowner sources. It includes all changes in equity during a period except those resulting from investments by owners and distributions to owners. Comprehensive income comprises both of the following:

- All components of net income
- All components of other comprehensive income

Conditional Contribution. A contribution that contains a donor-imposed condition.

Conduit Debt Securities. Topics 105, 220, 280, 360, 405, 715, 805, 820, 830, 855, 954, 958. Certain limited-obligation revenue bonds, certificates of participation, or similar debt instruments issued by a state or local governmental entity for the express purpose of providing financing for a specific third party (the conduit bond obligor) that is not a part of the state or local government's financial reporting entity. Although conduit debt securities bear the name of the governmental entity that issues them, the governmental entity often has no obligation for such debt beyond the resources provided by a lease or loan agreement with the third party on whose behalf the securities are issued. Further, the conduit bond obligor is responsible for any future financial reporting requirements.

Consolidation. Topic 958. The presentation of a single set of amounts for an entire reporting entity. Consolidation requires elimination of intra-entity transactions and balances.

Contingency. Topics 450, 460, 805. An existing condition, situation, or set of circumstances involving uncertainty as to possible gain (gain contingency) or loss (loss contingency) to an entity that will ultimately be resolved when one or more future events occur or fail to occur.

Contract. Topics 210, 230, 235, 255, 270, 275, 310, 340, 350, 360, 410, 420, 430, 440, 450, 460, 470, 505, 605, 606, 610, 705, 718, 720, 740, 805, 808, 810, 815, 820, 835, 840, 842, 845, 860, 910, 912, 926, 932, 954, 958, 970, 974, 980, 985. An agreement between two or more parties that creates enforceable rights and obligations.

Contract Asset. Topics 270, 606, 610, 740, 805, 835, 912, 954. An entity's right to consideration in exchange for goods or services that the entity has transferred to a customer when that right is conditioned on something other than the passage of time (for example, the entity's future performance).

Contract Liability. Topics 270, 430, 605, 606, 610, 835, 954. An entity's obligation to transfer goods or services to a customer for which the entity has received consideration (or the amount is due) from the customer.

Contribution. An unconditional transfer of cash or other assets to an entity or a settlement or cancellation of its liabilities in a voluntary nonreciprocal transfer by another entity acting other than as an owner. Those characteristics distinguish contributions from exchange transactions, which are reciprocal transfers in which each party receives and sacrifices approximately equal value; from investments by owners and distributions to owners, which are nonreciprocal transfers between an entity and its owners; and from other nonreciprocal transfers, such as impositions of taxes or legal judgments, fines, and thefts, which are not voluntary transfers. In a contribution transaction, the value, if any, returned to the resource provider is incidental to potential public benefits. In an exchange transaction, the potential public benefits are secondary to the potential proprietary benefits to the resource provider. The term *contribution revenue* is used to apply to transactions that are part of the entity's ongoing major or central activities (revenues), or are peripheral or incidental to the entity (gains). See also Inherent Contribution.

Note: The following definition is pending content, effective upon implementation of ASU 2018-08.

An unconditional transfer of cash or other assets, as well as unconditional promises to give, to an entity or a reduction, settlement, or cancellation of its liabilities in a voluntary nonreciprocal transfer by another entity acting other than as an owner. Those characteristics distinguish contributions from:

a. Exchange transactions, which are reciprocal transfers in which each party receives and sacrifices approximately commensurate value.
b. Investments by owners and distributions to owners, which are nonreciprocal transfers between an entity and its owners.
c. Other nonreciprocal transfers, such as impositions of taxes or legal judgments, fines, and thefts, which are not voluntary transfers. In a contribution transaction, the resource provider often receives value indirectly by providing a societal benefit, although that benefit is not considered to be of commensurate value. In an exchange transaction, the potential public benefits are secondary to the potential direct benefits to the resource provider. The term contribution revenue is used to apply to transactions that are part of the entity's ongoing major or central activities (revenues), or are peripheral or incidental to the entity (gains). See also Inherent Contribution and Conditional Contribution.

Control. Def. 1. Topics 310, 850, 946. The possession, direct or indirect, of the power to direct or cause the direction of the management and policies of an entity through ownership, by contract, or otherwise.

Control. Def. 2. Topics 954, 958. The direct or indirect ability to determine the direction of management and policies through ownership, by contract, or otherwise.

Control. Def. 3. Topic 805. The same as the meaning "controlling financial" interest in ASC 810-10-15-8.

Corporate Joint Venture. Topics 320, 740, 845, 970. A corporation owned and operated by a small group of entities (the joint venturers) as a separate and specific business or project for the mutual benefit of the members of the group. A government may also be a member of the group. The purpose of a corporate joint venture frequently is to share risks and rewards in developing a new market, product, or technology; to combine complementary technological knowledge; or to pool resources in developing production or other facilities. A corporate joint venture also usually provides an arrangement under which each joint venturer may participate, directly or indirectly, in the overall management of the joint venture. Joint venturers thus have an interest or relationship other than as passive investors. An entity that is a subsidiary of one of the joint venturers is not a corporate joint venture. The ownership of a corporate joint venture seldom changes, and its stock is usually not traded publicly. A noncontrolling interest held by public ownership, however, does not preclude a corporation from being a corporate joint venture.

Cost Recovery Method. Def. 1. Topic 360. Under the cost recovery method, no profit is recognized until cash payments by the buyer, including principal and interest on debt due to the seller and on existing debt assumed by the buyer, exceed the seller's cost of the property sold.

Cost Recovery Method. Def. 2. Topic 944. A revenue recognition method under which premiums are recognized as revenue in an amount equal to estimated claim costs as insured events occur until the ultimate premium is reasonably estimable, and recognition of income is postponed until that time.

Credit Risk. Topics 815, 820. For purposes of a hedged item in a fair value hedge, credit risk is the risk of changes in the hedged item's fair value attributable to both of the following:

a. Changes in the obligor's creditworthiness
b. Changes in the spread over the benchmark interest rate with respect to the hedged item's credit sector at inception of the hedge

For purposes of a hedged transaction in a cash flow hedge, credit risk is the risk of changes in the hedged transaction's cash flows attributable to all of the following:

a. Default
b. Changes in the obligor's creditworthiness
c. Changes in the spread over the contractually specified interest rate or the benchmark interest rate with respect to the related financial asset's or liability's credit sector at inception of the hedge

Credit Derivative. Topics 460, 815. A derivative instrument that has both of the following characteristics:

1. One or more of its underlyings are related to any of the following:
    - The credit risk of a specified entity (or a group of entities)
    - An index based on the credit risk of a group of entities
2. It exposes the seller to potential loss from credit-risk-related events specified in the contract.

Examples of credit derivatives include, but are not limited to, credit default swaps, credit spread options, and credit index products.

Current Assets. Topics 210, 310. Current assets is used to designate cash and other assets or resources commonly identified as those that are reasonably expected to be realized in cash or sold or consumed during the normal operating cycle of the business.

Current Tax Expense (or Benefit). Topics 323, 740. The amount of income taxes paid or payable (or refundable) for a year as determined by applying the provisions of the enacted tax law to the taxable income or excess of deductions over revenues for that year.

Customer. Def. 1. A party that has contracted with an entity to obtain goods or services that are an output of the entity's ordinary activities in exchange for consideration.

Debt. A receivable or payable (collectively referred to as debt) represents a contractual right to receive money or a contractual obligation to pay money on demand or on fixed or determinable dates that is already included as an asset or liability in the creditor's or debtor's balance sheet at the time of the restructuring.

Debt Security. Def. 1. Topics 220, 310, 320, 325, 326, 715, 740, 958. Any security representing a creditor relationship with an entity. The term debt security also includes all of the following:

- Preferred stock that by its terms either must be redeemed by the issuing entity or is redeemable at the option of the investor
- A collateralized mortgage obligation (or other instrument) that is issued in equity form but is required to be accounted for as a nonequity instrument regardless of how that instrument is classified (that is, whether equity or debt) in the issuer's statement of financial position
- U.S. Treasury securities
- U.S. government agency securities
- Municipal securities
- Corporate bonds
- Convertible debt
- Commercial paper
- All securitized debt instruments, such as collateralized mortgage obligations and real estate mortgage investment conduits
- Interest-only and principal-only strips

The term debt security *excludes* all of the following:

- Option contracts
- Financial futures contracts
- Forward contracts
- Lease contracts
- Receivables that do not meet the definition of security and, so, are not debt securities, for example:
    - Trade accounts receivable arising from sales on credit by industrial or commercial entities

- ◦ Loans receivable arising from consumer, commercial, and real estate lending activities of financial institutions

Defensive Intangible Asset. Topics 350, 805. An acquired intangible asset in a situation in which an entity does not intend to actively use the asset but intends to hold (lock up) the asset to prevent others from obtaining access to the asset.

Defined Benefit Plan. Topics 715, 960, 965, 980. A defined benefit plan provides participants with a determinable benefit based on a formula provided for in the plan.

- Defined benefit health and welfare plans—Defined benefit health and welfare plans specify a determinable benefit, which may be in the form of a reimbursement to the covered plan participant or a direct payment to providers or third-party insurers for the cost of specified services. Such plans may also include benefits that are payable as a lump sum, such as death benefits. The level of benefits may be defined or limited based on factors such as age, years of service, and salary. Contributions may be determined by the plan's actuary or be based on premiums, actual claims paid, hours worked, or other factors determined by the plan sponsor. Even when a plan is funded pursuant to agreements that specify a fixed rate of employer contributions (for example, a collectively bargained multiemployer plan), such a plan may nevertheless be a defined benefit health and welfare plan if its substance is to provide a defined benefit.
- Defined benefit pension plan—A pension plan that defines an amount of pension benefit to be provided, usually as a function of one or more factors such as age, years of service, or compensation. Any pension plan that is not a defined contribution pension plan is, for purposes of Subtopic 715-30, a defined benefit pension plan.
- Defined benefit postretirement plan—A plan that defines postretirement benefits in terms of monetary amounts (for example, $100,000 of life insurance) or benefit coverage to be provided (for example, up to $200 per day for hospitalization, or 80% of the cost of specified surgical procedures). Any postretirement benefit plan that is not a defined contribution postretirement plan is, for purposes of Subtopic 715-60, a defined benefit postretirement plan. (Specified monetary amounts and benefit coverage are collectively referred to as benefits.)

Defined Contribution Plan. Topics 715, 962, 965. A plan that provides an individual account for each participant and provides benefits that are based on all of the following: amounts contributed to the participant's account by the employer or employee; investment experience; and any forfeitures allocated to the account, less any administrative expenses charged to the plan.

- Defined contribution health and welfare plans—Defined contribution health and welfare plans maintain an individual account for each plan participant. They have terms that specify the means of determining the contributions to participants' accounts, rather than the amount of benefits the participants are to receive. The benefits a plan participant will receive are limited to the amount contributed to the participant's account, investment experience, expenses, and any forfeitures allocated to the participant's account. These plans also include flexible spending arrangements.
- Defined contribution postretirement plan—A plan that provides postretirement benefits in return for services rendered, provides an individual account for each plan participant,

and specifies how contributions to the individual's account are to be determined rather than specifies the amount of benefits the individual is to receive. Under a defined contribution postretirement plan, the benefits a plan participant will receive depend solely on the amount contributed to the plan participant's account, the returns earned on investments of those contributions, and the forfeitures of other plan participants' benefits that may be allocated to that plan participant's account.

Derivative Financial Instrument. Topic 860. A derivative instrument that is a financial instrument.

Derivative Instrument. Topics 210, 815, 860. Paragraphs 815-10-15-83 through 15-139 define the term derivative instrument.

Direct Financing Lease.* From the perspective of a lessor, a lease that meets none of the criteria in paragraph 842-10-25-2 but meets the criteria in paragraph 842-10-25-3(b). (See the chapter on ASC 842 for more information.)

Direct Guarantee of Indebtedness. Topic 460. An agreement in which a guarantor states that if the debtor fails to make payment to the creditor when due, the guarantor will pay the creditor. If the debtor defaults, the creditor has a direct claim on the guarantor.

Direct Loan Origination Costs. Topic 310. Direct loan origination costs represent costs associated with originating a loan. Direct loan origination costs of a completed loan shall include only the following:

- Incremental direct costs of loan origination incurred in transactions with independent third parties for that loan
- Certain costs directly related to specified activities performed by the lender for that loan Those activities include all of the following:
    - Evaluating the prospective borrower's financial condition
    - Evaluating and recording guarantees, collateral, and other security arrangements
    - Negotiating loan terms
    - Preparing and processing loan documents
    - Closing the transaction

The costs directly related to those activities shall include only that portion of the employees' total compensation and payroll-related fringe benefits directly related to time spent performing those activities for that loan and other costs related to those activities that would not have been incurred but for that loan. See Section 310-20-55 for examples of items.

Discount Rate Adjustment Technique. Topics 410 and 820. A present value technique that uses a risk-adjusted discount rate and contractual, promised, or most likely cash flows.

Disposal Group. Topics 305, 360, 610, 958. A disposal group for a long-lived asset or assets to be disposed of by sale or otherwise represents assets to be disposed of together as a group in a single transaction and liabilities directly associated with those assets that will be transferred in the transaction. A disposal group may include a discontinued operation along with other assets and liabilities that are not part of the discontinued operation.

Dividends. Topic 323. Dividends paid or payable in cash, other assets, or another class of stock and does not include stock dividends or stock splits.

Donor-Imposed Condition. A donor stipulation (donors include other types of contributors, including makers of certain grants) that represents a barrier that must be overcome before the recipient is entitled to the assets transferred or promised. Failure to overcome the barrier gives the contributor a right of return of the assets it has transferred or gives the promisor a right of release from its obligation to transfer its assets.

Dropdown. Topics 260, 805. A transfer of certain net assets from a sponsor or general partner to a master limited partnership in exchange for consideration.

Effective Interest Rate. Topics 230, 310, 326. The rate of return implicit in the loan, that is, the contractual interest rate adjusted for any net deferred loan fees or costs, premium, or discount existing at the origination or acquisition of the loan.

Note: The following definition of Effective Interest Rate is pending content; it is effective upon implementation of ASU 2016-13.

The rate of return implicit in the financial asset, that is, the contractual interest rate adjusted for any net deferred fees or costs, premium, or discount existing at the origination or acquisition of the financial asset. For purchased financial assets with credit deterioration, however, to decouple interest income from credit loss recognition, the premium or discount at acquisition excludes the discount embedded in the purchase price that is attributable to the acquirer's assessment of credit losses at the date of acquisition.

Employee. Def. 1. Topic 960. A person who is presently sending service.

Employee. Def. 2. Topics 505, 718. An individual over whom the grantor of a share-based compensation award exercises or has the right to exercise sufficient control to establish an employer–employee relationship based on common law as illustrated in case law and currently under U.S. Internal Revenue Service (IRS) Revenue Ruling 87-41. A reporting entity based in a foreign jurisdiction would determine whether an employee–employer relationship exists based on the pertinent laws of the jurisdiction. Accordingly, a grantee meets the definition of an employee if the grantor consistently represents that individual to be an employee under common law. The definition of an employee for payroll tax purposes under the U.S. Internal Revenue Code includes common law employees. Accordingly, a grantor that classifies a grantee potentially subject to U.S. payroll taxes as an employee also must represent that individual as an employee for payroll tax purposes (unless the grantee is a leased employee as described below). A grantee does not meet the definition of an employee solely because the grantor represents that individual as an employee for some, but not all, purposes. For example, a requirement or decision to classify a grantee as an employee for U.S. payroll tax purposes does not, by itself, indicate that the grantee is an employee, because the grantee also must be an employee of the grantor under common law.

A leased individual is deemed to be an employee of the lessee if all of the following requirements are met:

- The leased individual qualifies as a common law employee of the lessee, and the lessor is contractually required to remit payroll taxes on the compensation paid to the leased individual for the services provided to the lessee.

- The lessor and lessee agree in writing to all of the following conditions related to the leased individual:
  - The lessee has the exclusive right to grant stock compensation to the individual for the employee service to the lessee.
  - The lessee has a right to hire, fire, and control the activities of the individual. (The lessor also may have that right.)
  - The lessee has the exclusive right to determine the economic value of the services performed by the individual (including wages and the number of units and value of stock compensation granted).
  - The individual has the ability to participate in the lessee's employee benefit plans, if any, on the same basis as other comparable employees of the lessee.
  - The lessee agrees to and remits to the lessor funds sufficient to cover the complete compensation, including all payroll taxes, of the individual on or before a contractually agreed-upon date or dates.

A nonemployee director does not satisfy this definition of employee. Nevertheless, nonemployee directors acting in their role as members of a board of directors are treated as employees if those directors were elected by the employer's shareholders or appointed to a board position that will be filled by shareholder election when the existing term expires. However, that requirement applies only to awards granted to nonemployee directors for their services as directors. Awards granted to those individuals for other services shall be accounted for as awards to nonemployees.

Employee Stock Ownership Plan. Topics 260, 480, 718. An employee stock ownership plan is an employee benefit plan that is described by the Employee Retirement Income Security Act of 1974 and the Internal Revenue Code of 1986 as a stock bonus plan, or combination stock bonus and money purchase pension plan, designed to invest primarily in employer stock. Also called an employee share ownership plan.

Equity Security. Def. 1. Topics, 320, 321, 360, 958. Any security representing an ownership interest in an entity (for example, common, preferred, or other capital stock) or the right to acquire (for example, warrants, rights, forward purchase contracts, and call options) or dispose of (for example, put options and forward sale contracts) an ownership interest in an entity at fixed or determinable prices. The term equity security does not include any of the following:

- Written equity options (because they represent obligations of the writer, not investments)
- Cash-settled options on equity securities or options on equity-based indexes (because those instruments do not represent ownership interests in an entity)
- Convertible debt or preferred stock that by its terms either must be redeemed by the issuing entity or is redeemable at the option of the investor.

Equity Security. Def. 2. Topic 715. Any security representing an ownership interest in an entity (for example, common, preferred, or other capital stock) or the right to acquire (for example, warrants, rights, forward purchase contracts, and call options) or dispose of (for example, put options and forward sale contracts) an ownership interest in an entity at fixed or determinable prices. However, the term does not include convertible debt or preferred stock that by its terms either must be redeemed by the issuing entity or is redeemable at the option of the investor.

Equity Shares. Topic 480. Equity shares refers only to shares that are accounted for as equity.

Event. Topics 323, 718, 740, 805. A happening of consequence to an entity. The term encompasses both transactions and other events affecting an entity.

Expected Cash Flow. Topics 815, 820. The probability-weighted average (that is, mean of the distribution) of possible future cash flows.

Expected Return on Plan Assets. Topic 715. An amount calculated as a basis for determining the extent of delayed recognition of the effects of changes in the fair value of plan assets. The expected return on plan assets is determined based on the expected long-term rate of return on plan assets and the market-related value of plan assets.

Fair Value. Def. 1. Topics 505, 718. The amount at which an asset (or liability) could be bought (or incurred) or sold (or settled) in a current transaction between willing parties, that is, other than in a forced or liquidation sale.

Fair Value. Def. 2. Topics 205, 230 255, 275, 310, 320, 321,326, 360, 410, 460, 470, 480, 505, 605, 715, 718, 805, 810, 815, 820, 825, 835, 842, 940, 942, 944, 946, 948, 958, 962, 965, 978. The price that would be received to sell an asset or paid to transfer a liability in an orderly transaction between market participants at the measurement date.

Film Group. Topics ASC 920 and 926. The unit of account used for impairment testing for a film or a license agreement for program material when the film or license agreement is expected to be predominantly monetized with other films and/or license agreements instead of being predominantly monetized on its own. A film group represents the lowest level for which identifiable cash flows are largely independent of the cash flows of other films and/or license agreements.

Films. Topics ASC 920 and 926. Feature films, television specials, television series, or similar products (including animated films and television programming) that are sold, licensed, or exhibit.

Financial Asset. Topics 230, 270, 310, 325, 326, 805, 810, 820, 825, 860, 940, 958. Cash, evidence of an ownership interest in an entity, or a contract that conveys to one entity a right to do either of the following:

- Receive cash or another financial instrument from a second entity.
- Exchange other financial instruments on potentially favorable terms with the second entity.

Financial Instrument. Topics 260, 480, 505, 815, 820, 825, 954. Cash, evidence of an ownership interest in an entity, or a contract that both:

- Imposes on one entity a contractual obligation either:
  - To deliver cash or another financial instrument to a second entity, or
  - To exchange other financial instruments on potentially unfavorable terms with the second entity
- Conveys to that second entity a contractual right either:
  - To receive cash or another financial instrument from the first entity, or
  - To exchange other financial instruments on potentially favorable terms with the first entity.

The use of the term "financial instrument" in this definition is recursive (because the term financial instrument is included in it), though it is not circular. The definition requires a chain of contractual obligations that ends with the delivery of cash or an ownership interest in an entity. Any number of obligations to deliver financial instruments can be links in a chain that qualifies a particular contract as a financial instrument.

Contractual rights and contractual obligations encompass both those that are conditioned on the occurrence of a specified event and those that are not. All contractual rights (contractual obligations) that are financial instruments meet the definition of asset (liability) set forth in FASB Concepts Statement No. 6, *Elements of Financial Statements*, although some may not be recognized as assets (liabilities) in financial statements—that is, they may be off-balance-sheet—because they fail to meet some other criterion for recognition.

For some financial instruments, the right is held by or the obligation is due from (or the obligation is owed to or by) a group of entities rather than a single entity.

Financial Liability. Topics 815, 820, 825, 860. A contract that imposes on one entity an obligation to do either of the following:

- Deliver cash or another financial instrument to a second entity
- Exchange other financial instruments on potentially unfavorable terms with the second entity

Financial Statements Are Available to Be Issued. Topics 105, 205, 805, 810, 815, 820, 855. Financial statements are considered available to be issued when they are complete in a form and format that complies with GAAP and all approvals necessary for issuance have been obtained, for example, from management, the board of directors, and/or significant shareholders. The process involved in creating and distributing the financial statements will vary depending on an entity's management and corporate governance structure as well as statutory and regulatory requirements.

Financial Statements Are Issued. Topics 205, 805, 855. Financial statements are considered issued when they are widely distributed to shareholders and other financial statement users for general use and reliance in a form and format that complies with GAAP. (U.S. Securities and Exchange Commission [SEC] registrants also are required to consider the guidance in paragraph 855-10-S99-2.)

Financing Receivable. Topics 270, 310, 326, 840. A financing arrangement that has both of the following characteristics:

- It represents a contractual right to receive money in either of the following ways:
  - On demand
  - On fixed or determinable dates
- It is recognized as an asset in the entity's statement of financial position.

See paragraphs 310-10-55-13 through 55-15 for more information on the definition of financing receivable, including a list of items that are excluded from the definition (for example, debt securities).

Firm Commitment. Def. 2. Topics 470, 815, 825. An agreement with an unrelated party, binding on both parties and usually legally enforceable, with the following characteristics:

- The agreement specifies all significant terms, including the quantity to be exchanged, the fixed price, and the timing of the transaction. The fixed price may be expressed as a specified amount of an entity's functional currency or of a foreign currency. It may also be expressed as a specified interest rate or specified effective yield. The binding provisions of an agreement are regarded to include those legal rights and obligations codified in the laws to which such an agreement is subject. A price that varies with the fair value of the item that is the subject of the firm commitment cannot qualify as a fixed price. For example, a price that is specified in terms of ounces of gold would not be a fixed price if the fair value of the item to be purchased or sold under the firm commitment varied with the price of gold.
- The agreement includes a disincentive for nonperformance that is sufficiently large to make performance probable. In the legal jurisdiction that governs the agreement, the existence of statutory rights to pursue remedies for default equivalent to the damages suffered by the nondefaulting party, in and of itself, represents a sufficiently large disincentive for nonperformance to make performance probable for purposes of applying the definition of a firm commitment.

Firm Purchase Commitment. A firm purchase commitment is an agreement with an unrelated party, binding on both parties and usually legally enforceable, that meets both of the following conditions:

- It specifies all significant terms, including the price and timing of the transaction.
- It includes a disincentive for nonperformance that is sufficiently large to make performance probable.

Freestanding Financial Instrument. Topics 480 and 718. A financial instrument that meets either of the following conditions:

- It is entered into separately and apart from any of the entity's other financial instruments or equity transactions.
- It is entered into in conjunction with some other transaction and is legally detachable and separately exercisable.

Gain Contingency. Topic 450. An existing condition, situation, or set of circumstances involving uncertainty as to possible gain to an entity that will ultimately be resolved when one or more future events occur or fail to occur.

Goodwill. Topics 350, 805, 958. An asset representing the future economic benefits arising from other assets acquired in a business combination or an acquisition by a not-for-profit entity that are not individually identified and separately recognized. For ease of reference, this term also includes the immediate charge recognized by not-for-profit entities in accordance with ASC 958-805-25-29.

Grant Date. (Topics 606 and 718) The date at which grantor and grantee reach a mutual understanding of the key terms and conditions of a share-based payment award. The grantor becomes contingently obligated on the grant date to issue equity instruments or transfer assets to a grantee who renders the services or purchases goods or services as a customer. Awards made under an arrangement that is subject to shareholder approval are not deemed to be granted until that approval is obtained, unless approval is essentially a formality (or perfunctory)—for example, if management and the members of the board of directors control enough votes to approve the arrangement. Similarly, individual awards that are subject to approval by the board of directors, management, or both are not deemed to be granted until all such approvals are obtained. The grant date for an award of equity instruments is the date that a grantee begins to benefit from, or be adversely affected by, subsequent changes in the price of the grantor's equity shares. ASC 718-10-25-5 provides guidance on determining the grant date. See Service Inception Date.

Holding Gain or Loss. The net change in fair value of a security. The holding gain or loss does not include dividend or interest income recognized but not yet received or write-downs for other-than-temporary impairment.

Note: The following definition of Holding Gain or Loss is pending content effective upon implementation of ASU 2016-13.

The net change in fair value of a security. The holding gain or loss does not include dividend or interest income recognized but not yet received, writeoffs, or the allowance for credit losses.

Hosting Arrangement. Topics 350, 985. In connection with the licensing of software products, an arrangement in which an end user of the software does not take possession of the software; rather, the software application resides on the vendor's or a third party's hardware, and the customer accesses and uses the software on an as-needed basis over the Internet or via a dedicated line.

Upon implementation of ASU 2018-15 (see chapter on ASC 350 for more information):

In connection with the processing and using of software products, an arrangement in which the customer of the software does not currently have possession of the software; rather, the customer accesses and uses the software on an as-needed basis.

Income from Continuing Operations. Topic 255. Income after applicable income taxes but excluding the results of discontinued operations, the cumulative effect of accounting changes, translation adjustments, purchasing power gains and losses on monetary items, and increases and decreases in the current cost or lower recoverable amount of nonmonetary assets and liabilities.

Income Tax Expense (or Benefit). Topics 323, 740. The sum of current tax expense (or benefit) and deferred tax expense (or benefit).

Income Taxes. Topics 323, 718, 740, 805, 852. Domestic and foreign federal (national), state, and local (including franchise) taxes based on income.

Indirectly Related to the Leased Property.* The provisions or conditions that in substance are guarantees of the lessor's debt or loans to the lessor by the lessee that are related to the leased property but are structured in such a manner that they do not represent a direct guarantee or loan. Examples include a party related to the lessee guaranteeing the lessor's debt on behalf of the lessee, or the lessee financing the lessor's purchase of the leased asset using collateral other than the leased property.

Inherent Contribution. Pending content: Effective upon implementation of ASU 2018-12. A contribution that results if an entity voluntarily transfers assets (or net assets) or performs services for another entity in exchange for either no assets or for assets of substantially lower value and unstated rights or privileges of a commensurate value are not involved.

Initial Investment. Topic 320. The amount paid to the seller plus any fees paid or less any fees received.

Initial Market. Topic 926. The first market of a film's exploitation in each territory, whether that market is a broadcast or cable television network, first-run syndication, or other.

Installment Method. Topic 360. The installment method apportions each cash receipt and principal payment by the buyer on debt assumed between cost recovered and profit. The apportionment is in the same ratio as total cost and total profit bear to the sales value.

Intangible Asset Class. Topics 350, 805. A group of intangible assets that are similar, either by their nature or by their use in the operations of an entity.

Intangible Assets. Topics 350, 610, 805, 958. Assets (not including financial assets) that lack physical substance. (The term intangible assets is used to refer to intangible assets other than goodwill.)

Integral Equipment. Topics 360, 978. Integral equipment is any physical structure or equipment attached to the real estate that cannot be removed and used separately without incurring significant cost.

The aggregate of those items of tangible personal property that have any of the following characteristics:

- Held for sale in the ordinary course of a business
- In process of production for such sale
- To be currently consumed in the production of goods or services to be available for sale

The term inventory embraces goods awaiting sale (the merchandise of a trading concern and the finished goods of a manufacturer), goods in the course of production (work in process), and goods to be consumed directly or indirectly in production (raw materials and supplies). This definition of inventories excludes long-term assets subject to depreciation accounting, or goods which, when put into use, will be so classified. The fact that a depreciable asset is retired from regular use and held for sale does not indicate that the item should be classified as part of the inventory. Raw materials and supplies purchased for production may be used or consumed for the construction of long-term assets or other purposes not related to production, but the fact that inventory items representing a small portion of the total may not be absorbed ultimately in the production process does not require separate classification. By trade practice, operating materials and supplies of certain types of entities such as oil producers are usually treated as inventory.

Interest Rate Risk. Topics 815 and 820. For recognized variable-rate financial instruments and forecasted issuances or purchases of variable-rate financial instruments, interest rate risk is the risk of changes in the hedged item's cash flows attributable to changes in the contractually specified interest rate in the agreement. For recognized fixed-rate financial instruments, interest rate risk is the risk of changes in the hedged item's fair value attributable to changes in the designated benchmark interest rate. For forecasted issuances or purchases of fixed-rate financial instruments, interest rate risk is the risk of changes in the hedged item's cash flows attributable to changes in the designated benchmark interest rate.

Investee. Topic 323. An entity that issued an equity instrument that is held by an investor.

Investor. Topic 323. A business entity that holds an investment in voting stock of another entity.

Issued, Issuance, or Issuing of an Equity Instrument. (Topics 505 and 718) An equity instrument is issued when the issuing entity receives the agreed-upon consideration, which may be cash, an enforceable right to receive cash, or another financial instrument, goods, or services. An entity may conditionally transfer an equity instrument to another party under an arrangement that permits that party to choose at a later date or for a specified time whether to deliver the consideration or to forfeit the right to the conditionally transferred instrument with no further obligation. In that situation, the equity instrument is not issued until the issuing entity has received the consideration. The grant of stock options or other equity instruments subject to vesting conditions is not considered to be issuance.

Lease. Topics 210, 230, 255, 270, 310, 350, 360, 410, 420, 440, 450, 460, 470, 606, 740, 805, 810, 815, 835, 846, 842, 860, 958, 970, 974. An agreement conveying the right to use property, plant, or equipment (land and/or depreciable assets) usually for a stated period of time.

Lease.* A contract, or part of a contract, that conveys the right to control the use of identified property, plant, or equipment (an identified asset) for a period of time in exchange for consideration.

Lease Liability.* Topics 230, 805, 842. A lessee's obligation to make the lease payments arising from a lease, measured on a discounted basis.

Lease Modification.* Topics 310, 470, 842. A change to the terms and conditions of a contract that results in a change in the scope of or the consideration for a lease (for example, a change to the terms and conditions of the contract that adds or terminates the right to use one or more underlying assets or extends or shortens the contractual lease term).

Lease Payments.* Topics 230, 255, 310, 410, 440, 460, 805, 810, 842. See paragraph 842-10-30-5 for what constitutes lease payments from the perspective of a lessee and a lessor. For more information, see the chapter on ASC 842.

Lease Receivable.* Topics 255, 310, 805, 842, 860. A lessor's right to receive lease payments arising from a sales-type lease or a direct financing lease plus any amount that a lessor expects to derive from the underlying asset following the end of the lease term to the extent that it is guaranteed by the lessee or any other third party unrelated to the lessor, measured on a discounted basis.

Lease Term. Topics 230, 255, 310, 360, 410, 460, 805, 840, 842, 860, 958, 970. The fixed noncancelable lease term plus all of the following, except as noted in the following paragraph:

- All periods, if any, covered by bargain renewal options.
- All periods, if any, for which failure to renew the lease imposes a penalty on the lessee in such amount that a renewal appears, at lease inception, to be reasonably assured.

- All periods, if any, covered by ordinary renewal options during which any of the following conditions exist:
  - A guarantee by the lessee of the lessor's debt directly or indirectly related to the leased property is expected to be in effect.
  - A loan from the lessee to the lessor directly or indirectly related to the leased property is expected to be outstanding.
- All periods, if any, covered by ordinary renewal options preceding the date as of which a bargain purchase option is exercisable.
- All periods, if any, representing renewals or extensions of the lease at the lessor's option.

The lease term shall not be assumed to extend beyond the date a bargain purchase option becomes exercisable.

The following definition of Lease Term is pending implementation of AU 2016-02. The noncancelable period for which a lessee has the right to use an underlying asset, together with all of the following:

- Periods covered by an option to extend the lease if the lessee is reasonably certain to exercise that option
- Periods covered by an option to terminate the lease if the lessee is reasonably certain not to exercise that option
- Periods covered by an option to extend (or not to terminate) the lease in which exercise of the option is controlled by the lessor

Legal Entity. Topics 610, 810, 842, 954, 958. Any legal structure used to conduct activities or to hold assets. Some examples of such structures are corporations, partnerships, limited liability companies, grantor trusts, and other trusts.

Lending Activities. Topic 310. Lending, committing to lend, refinancing or restructuring loans, arranging standby letters of credit, syndicating loans, and leasing activities are lending activities.

Lessee.* Topics 210, 230, 255, 270, 310, 360, 410, 440, 450, 460, 740, 805, 810, 815, 835, 842, 860, 958, 970. An entity that enters into a contract to obtain the right to use an underlying asset for a period of time in exchange for consideration.

Lessor.* Topics 210, 230, 255, 270, 310, 360, 410, 440, 450, 460, 740, 810, 815, 842, 860, 958. An entity that enters into a contract to provide the right to use an underlying asset for a period of time in exchange for consideration.

Leveraged Lease.* Topics 210, 255, 310, 740, 805, 840, 842. From the perspective of a lessor, a lease that was classified as a leveraged lease in accordance with the lease's guidance in effect before the effective date and for which the commencement date is before the effective date.

Liability Issued with an Inseparable Third-Party Credit Enhancement. Topics 820 and 825. A liability that is issued with a credit enhancement obtained from a third party, such as debt that is issued with a financial guarantee from a third party that guarantees the issuer's payment obligation.

Loan Commitment. Topics 326, 815. Loan commitments are legally binding commitments to extend credit to a counterparty under certain prespecified terms and conditions. They have fixed expiration dates and may either be fixed rate or variable rate. Loan commitments can be either of the following:

- Revolving (in which the amount of the overall line of credit is reestablished upon repayment of previously drawn amounts)
- Nonrevolving (in which the amount of the overall line of credit is not reestablished upon repayment of previously drawn amounts).

Loan commitments can be distributed through syndication arrangements, in which one entity acts as a lead and an agent on behalf of other entities that will each extend credit to a single borrower. Loan commitments generally permit the lender to terminate the arrangement under the terms of covenants negotiated under the agreement. This is not an authoritative or all-encompassing definition.

Loan Origination Fees. Topics 310, 360. Origination fees consist of all of the following:

- Fees that are being charged to the borrower as prepaid interest or to reduce the loan's nominal interest rate, such as interest buy-downs (explicit yield adjustments).
- Fees to reimburse the lender for origination activities.
- Other fees charged to the borrower that relate directly to making the loan (for example, fees that are paid to the lender as compensation for granting a complex loan or agreeing to lend quickly).
- Fees that are not conditional on a loan being granted by the lender that receives the fee but are, in substance, implicit yield adjustments because a loan is granted at rates or terms that would not otherwise have been considered absent the fee (for example, certain syndication fees addressed in paragraph 310-20-25-19).
- Fees charged to the borrower in connection with the process of originating, refinancing, or restructuring a loan. This term includes, but is not limited to, points, management, arrangement, placement, application, underwriting, and other fees pursuant to a lending or leasing transaction and also includes syndication and participation fees to the extent they are associated with the portion of the loan retained by the lender.

Long-Term Obligations. Topic 470. Long-term obligations are those scheduled to mature beyond one year (or the operating cycle, if applicable) from the date of an entity's balance sheet.

Loss Contingency. Topics 450, 460, 958. An existing condition, situation, or set of circumstances involving uncertainty as to possible loss to an entity that will ultimately be resolved when one or more future events occur or fail to occur. The term loss is used for convenience to include many charges against income that are commonly referred to as expenses and others that are commonly referred to as losses.

Management. Topics 820 and 850. Persons who are responsible for achieving the objectives of the entity and who have the authority to establish policies and make decisions by which those objectives are to be pursued. Management normally includes members of the board of directors, the chief executive officer, chief operating officer, vice presidents in charge of principal business functions (such as sales, administration, or finance), and other persons who perform similar policy-making functions. Persons without formal titles also may be members of management.

Mandatorily Redeemable Financial Instrument. Topics 480 and 815. Any of various financial instruments issued in the form of shares that embody an unconditional obligation requiring the issuer to redeem the instrument by transferring its assets at a specified or determinable date (or dates) or upon an event that is certain to occur.

Market Participants. Topics 321, 326, 805, 820, 842, 946. Buyers and sellers in the principal (or most advantageous) market for the asset or liability that have all of the following characteristics:

- They are independent of each other, that is, they are not related parties, although the price in a related-party transaction may be used as an input to a fair value measurement if the reporting entity has evidence that the transaction was entered into at market terms.
- They are knowledgeable, having a reasonable understanding about the asset or liability and the transaction using all available information, including information that might be obtained through due diligence efforts that are usual and customary.
- They are able to enter into a transaction for the asset or liability.
- They are willing to enter into a transaction for the asset or liability, that is, they are motivated but not forced or otherwise compelled to do so.

Market Risk Benefit Note: The following definition is pending content. A contract or contract feature in a long-duration contract issued by an insurance entity that both protects the contract holder from other-than-nominal capital market risk and exposes the insurance entity to other-than-nominal capital market risk.

Merger of Not-for-Profit Entities. Topics 740, 805, 815, 954, 958. A transaction or other event in which the governing bodies of two or more not-for-profit entities cede control of those entities to create a new not-for-profit entity.

Most Advantageous Market. Topics 820 and 948. The market that maximizes the amount that would be received to sell the asset or minimizes the amount that would be paid to transfer the liability, after taking into account transaction costs and transportation costs.

Multiemployer Plan. Subtopic 715-80. A pension or postretirement benefit plan to which two or more unrelated employers contribute, usually pursuant to one or more collective-bargaining agreements. A characteristic of multiemployer plans is that assets contributed by one participating employer may be used to provide benefits to employees of other participating employers since assets contributed by an employer are not segregated in a separate account or restricted to provide benefits only to employees of that employer. A multiemployer plan is usually administered by a board of trustees composed of management and labor representatives and may also be referred to as a joint trust or union plan. Generally, many employers participate in a multiemployer plan, and an employer may participate in more than one plan. The employers participating in multiemployer plans usually have a common industry bond, but for some plans the employers are in different industries and the labor union may be their only common bond. Some multiemployer plans do not involve a union. For example, local chapters of a not-for-profit entity (NFP) may participate in a plan established by the related national.

Multiple-Employer Plan. Subtopics 715-30 and 715-60. A pension plan or other postretirement benefit plan maintained by more than one employer but not treated as a multiemployer plan. Multiple-employer plans are generally not collectively bargained and are intended to allow participating employers, commonly in the same industry, to pool their plan assets for investment purposes and to reduce the cost of plan administration. A multiple-employer plan maintains separate accounts for each employer so that contributions provide benefits only for employees of the contributing employer. Multiple-employer plans may have features that allow participating employers to have different benefit formulas, with the employer's contributions to the plan based on the benefit formula selected by the employer.

Mutual Entity. Topics 350, 805. An entity other than an investor-owned entity that provides dividends, lower costs, or other economic benefits directly and proportionately to its owners, members, or participants. Mutual insurance entities, credit unions, and farm and rural electric cooperatives are examples of mutual entities.

Net Asset Value per Share. Topics 820 and 946. Net asset value per share is the amount of net assets attributable to each share of capital stock (other than senior equity securities; that is, preferred stock) outstanding at the close of the period. It excludes the effects of assuming conversion of outstanding convertible securities, whether or not their conversion would have a diluting effect.

Net Income. Topics 305, 220. A measure of financial performance resulting from the aggregation of revenues, expenses, gains, and losses that are not items of other comprehensive income. A variety of other terms such as net earnings or earnings may be used to describe net income.

Net Investment in the Lease.* Topics 255, 805, 842. For a sales-type lease, the sum of the lease receivable and the unguaranteed residual asset. For a direct financing lease, the sum of the lease receivable and the unguaranteed residual asset, net of any deferred selling profit.

Net Periodic Pension Cost. Topic 715. The amount recognized in an employer's financial statements as the cost of a pension plan for a period. Components of net periodic pension cost are service cost, interest cost, actual return on plan assets, gain or loss, amortization of prior service cost or credit, and amortization of the transition asset or obligation existing at the date of initial application of Subtopic 715-30. The term net periodic pension cost is used instead of net pension expense because part of the cost recognized in a period may be capitalized along with other costs as part of an asset such as inventory.

Net Periodic Pension Cost. Topic 715. (This definition is pending implementation of ASU 2017- 07.) The amount recognized in an employer's financial statements as the cost of a pension plan for a period. Components of net periodic pension cost are service cost, interest cost, actual return on plan assets, gain or loss, amortization of the transition asset or obligation existing at the date of initial application of Subtopic 715-30. The term net periodic pension cost is used instead of net pension expense because part of the cost recognized in a period may be capitalized as part of an asset such as inventory.

Net Periodic Postretirement Benefit Cost. Topic 715. The amount recognized in an employer's financial statements as the cost of a postretirement benefit plan for a period. Components of net periodic postretirement benefit cost include service cost, interest cost, actual return on plan assets, gain or loss, amortization of prior service cost or credit, and amortization of the transition obligation or asset.

Net Realizable Value. Topics 270, 275, 330, 360, 830, 905. Estimated selling prices in the ordinary course of business, less reasonably predictable costs of completion, disposal, and transportation.

Noncancelable Lease Term. Note: This definition is superseded by ASU 2016-02. That portion of the lease term that is cancelable only under any of the following conditions:

- Upon the occurrence of some remote contingency
- With the permission of the lessor
- If the lessee enters into a new lease with the same lessor
- If the lessee incurs a penalty in such amount that continuation of the lease appears, at inception, reasonably assured

Noncontrolling Interest. Topics 240, 260, 323, 350, 480, 610, 740, 805, 810, 815, 845, 932, 942, 958, 970, 974. The portion of equity (net assets) in a subsidiary not attributable, directly or indirectly, to a parent. A noncontrolling interest is sometimes called a minority interest.

Nonfinancial Asset. Topics 805, 810, 820, 958. An asset that is not a financial asset. Nonfinancial assets include land, buildings, use of facilities or utilities, materials and supplies, intangible assets, or services.

Nongovernmental Entity. Topics 105, 958. An entity that is not required to issue financial reports in accordance with guidance promulgated by the Governmental Accounting Standards Board or the Federal Accounting Standards Advisory Board.

Nonperformance Risk. Topics 815 and 820. The risk that an entity will not fulfill an obligation. Nonperformance risk includes, but may not be limited to, the reporting entity's own credit risk.

Nonprofit Activity. Topics 205, 350, 360, 610, 805, 810, 840, 845, 954. An integrated set of activities and assets that is capable of being conducted and managed for the purpose of providing benefits, other than goods or services at a profit or profit equivalent, as a fulfillment of an entity's purpose or mission (for example, goods or services to beneficiaries, customers, or members). As with a not-for-profit entity, a nonprofit activity possesses characteristics that distinguish it from a business or a for-profit business entity.

Nonpublic Entity. Def. 1. Topics 105, 220, 350, 360, 405, 820, 830, 954. Any entity that does not meet any of the following conditions:

a. Its debt or equity securities trade in a public market either on a stock exchange (domestic or foreign) or in an over-the-counter market, including securities quoted only locally or regionally.
b. It is a conduit bond obligor for *conduit debt securities* that are traded in a public market (a domestic or foreign stock exchange or an over-the-counter market, including local or regional markets).

c. It files with a regulatory agency in preparation for the sale of any class of debt or equity securities in a public market.
d. It is required to file or furnish financial statements with the Securities and Exchange Commission.
e. It is controlled by an entity covered by criteria (a) through (d).

Nonpublic Entity. Def. 2. Topics 480, 718. Any entity other than one that meets any of the following criteria:

- Has equity securities that trade in a public market either on a stock exchange (domestic or foreign) or in an over-the-counter market, including securities quoted only locally or regionally
- Makes a filing with a regulatory agency in preparation for the sale of any class of equity securities in a public market
- Is controlled by an entity covered by the preceding criteria

An entity that has only debt securities trading in a public market (or that has made a filing with a regulatory agency in preparation to trade only debt securities) is a nonpublic entity.

Nonpublic Entity. Def. 3. Topic 715-20. Any entity other than one with any of the following characteristics:

a. Whose debt or equity securities trade in a public market either on a stock exchange (domestic or foreign) or in the over-the-counter market, including securities quoted only locally or regionally
b. That is a conduit bond obligor for conduit debt securities that are traded in a public market (a domestic or foreign stock exchange or an over-the-counter market, including local or regional markets)
c. That makes a filing with a regulatory agency in preparation for the sale of any class of debt or equity securities in a public market
d. That is controlled by an entity covered by a or c

Conduit debt securities refers to certain limited-obligation revenue bonds, certificates of participation, or similar debt instruments issued by a state or local governmental entity for the express purpose of providing financing for a specific third party (the conduit bond obligor) that is not a part of the state or local government's financial reporting entity. Although conduit debt securities bear the name of the governmental entity that issues them, the governmental entity often has no obligation for such debt beyond the resources provided by a lease or loan agreement with the third party on whose behalf the securities are issued. Further, the conduit bond obligor is responsible for any future financial reporting requirements.

Nonpublic Entity. Def. 4. Topic 825. Note this definition is superseded upon implementation of ASU 2016-01. Any entity that does not meet any of the following conditions:

- Its debt or equity securities trade in a public market either on a stock exchange (domestic or foreign) or in the over-the-counter market, including securities quoted only locally or regionally.

- It is a conduit bond obligor for conduit debt securities that are traded in a public market (a domestic or foreign stock exchange or an over-the-counter market, including local or regional markets).
- It files with a regulatory agency in preparation for the sale of any class of debt or equity securities in a public market.
- It is controlled by an entity covered by the preceding criteria.

Nonpublic Entity. Def. 5. Topics 715, 740. An entity that does not meet any of the following criteria:

- Its debt or equity securities are traded in a public market, including those traded on a stock exchange or in the over-the-counter market (including securities quoted only locally or regionally).
- It is a conduit bond obligor for *conduit debt securities* that are traded in a public market (a domestic or foreign stock exchange or an over-the-counter market, including local or regional markets).
- Its financial statements are filed with a regulatory agency in preparation for the sale of any class of securities.

Nonreciprocal Transfer. Def. 1. Topics 810, 845, 972. Nonreciprocal transfer is a transfer of assets or services in one direction, either from an entity to its owners (whether or not in exchange for their ownership interests) or to another entity, or from owners or another entity to the entity. An entity's reacquisition of its outstanding stock is an example of a nonreciprocal transfer.

Not-for-Profit Entity. Topics 105, 205, 260, 270, 310, 323, 326, 340, 350, 360, 606, 715, 720, 740, 805, 810, 815, 830, 842, 845, 853, 860, 954, 958, 985. An entity that possesses the following characteristics, in varying degrees, that distinguish it from a business entity:

- Contributions of significant amounts of resources from resource providers who do not expect commensurate or proportionate pecuniary return
- Operating purposes other than to provide goods or services at a profit
- Absence of ownership interests like those of business entities

Entities that clearly fall outside this definition include the following:

- All investor-owned entities
- Entities that provide dividends, lower costs, or other economic benefits directly and proportionately to their owners, members, or participants, such as mutual insurance entities, credit unions, farm and rural electric cooperatives, and employee benefit plans

Operating Cycle. Topics 210, 470. The average time intervening between the acquisition of materials or services and the final cash realization constitutes an operating cycle.

Operating Lease. Topics 450, 805, 840, 842, 970. From the perspective of a lessee, any lease other than a capital lease. From the perspective of a lessor, a lease that meets the conditions in paragraph 840-10-25-43(d).

The following definition of Operating Lease is pending implementation of ASU 2016-02: From the perspective of a lessee, any lease other than a finance lease. From the perspective of a lessor, any lease other than a sales-type lease or a direct financing lease.

Operating Segment. Topics 280, 350, 360. A component of a public entity. See Section 280-10- 50 for additional guidance on the definition of an operating segment.

Option. Topics 260, 718. Unless otherwise stated, a call option that gives the holder the right to purchase shares of common stock from the reporting entity in accordance with an agreement upon payment of a specified amount. Options include, but are not limited to, options granted to employees and stock purchase agreements entered into with grantees. Options are considered securities. See Call Option.

Orderly Transaction. Topics 321, 326, 820, 842, 946. A transaction that assumes exposure to the market for a period before the measurement date to allow for marketing activities that are usual and customary for transactions involving such assets or liabilities; it is not a forced transaction (for example, a forced liquidation or distress sale).

Ordinary Course of Business. Def. 1. Topics 810, 958, 970. Decisions about matters of a type consistent with those normally expected to be events or transactions that would necessitate such decisions will occur. The ordinary course of business does not include self-dealing transactions.

Other Comprehensive Income. Topics 220, 815, 954. Revenues, expenses, gains, and losses that under generally accepted accounting principles (GAAP) are included in comprehensive income but excluded from net income.

Owners. Topics 805, 810, 845. Used broadly to include holders of ownership interests (equity interests) of investor-owned entities, mutual entities, or not-for-profit entities. Owners include shareholders, partners, proprietors, or members or participants of mutual entities. Owners also include owner and member interests in the net assets of not-for-profit entities.

Parent. Topics 220, 323, 480, 610, 740, 810, 932, 942, 946. An entity that has a controlling financial interest in one or more subsidiaries. (Also, an entity that is the primary beneficiary of a variable interest entity.)

Participant. Topics 715, 960. Any employee or former employee, or any member or former member of a trade or other employee association, or the beneficiaries of those individuals, for whom there are pension plan benefits or other accumulated plan benefits.

Participating Rights VIE Definition. Topic 810. The ability to block the actions through which a reporting entity exercises the power to direct the activities of a VIE that most significantly impact the VIE's economic performance.

Penalty. Topic 842. Any requirement that is imposed or can be imposed on the lessee by the lease agreement or by factors outside the lease agreement to do any of the following:

- Disburse cash.
- Incur or assume a liability.
- Perform services.

- Surrender or transfer an asset or rights to an asset or otherwise forego an economic benefit, or suffer an economic detriment. Factors to consider in determining whether an economic detriment may be incurred include, but are not limited to, all of the following:
  - The uniqueness of purpose or location of the underlying asset
  - The availability of a comparable replacement asset
  - The relative importance or significance of the underlying asset to the continuation of the lessee's line of business or service to its customers
  - The existence of leasehold improvements or other assets whose value would be impaired by the lessee vacating or discontinuing use of the underlying asset
  - Adverse tax consequences
  - The ability or willingness of the lessee to bear the cost associated with relocation or replacement of the underlying asset at market rental rates or to tolerate other parties using the underlying asset

Pension Benefits. Topics 715, 960. Periodic (usually monthly) payments made pursuant to the terms of the pension plan to a person who has retired from employment or to that person's beneficiary.

Performance Condition. Topics 606 and 718. A condition affecting the vesting, exercisability, exercise price, or other pertinent factors used in determining the fair value of an award that relates to both of the following:

- Rendering service or delivering goods for a specified (either explicitly or implicitly) period of time
- Achieving a specified performance target that is defined solely by reference to the grantor's own operations (or activities) or by reference to the grantee's performance related to the grantor's own operations (or activities).

Attaining a specified growth rate in return on assets, obtaining regulatory approval to market a specified product, selling shares in an initial public offering or other financing event, and a change in control are examples of performance conditions. A performance target also may be defined by reference to the same performance measure of another entity or group of entities. For example, attaining a growth rate in (EPS) that exceeds the average growth rate in EPS of other entities in the same industry is a performance condition. A performance target might pertain either to the performance of the entity as a whole or to some part of the entity, such as a division or to the performance of the grantee if such performance is in accordance with the terms of the award and relates solely to the grantor's own operations (or activities).

Performance Obligation. Topics 270, 275, 340, 460, 605, 606, 610, 840, 912, 940, 985. A promise in a contract with a customer to transfer to the customer either:

- A good or service (or a bundle of goods or services) that is distinct
- A series of distinct goods or services that are substantially the same and that have the same pattern of transfer to the customer

Plan Assets. Def. 2. Topics 715, 960. Assets—usually stocks, bonds, and other investments that have been segregated and restricted, usually in a trust, to provide for pension benefits. The amount of plan assets includes amounts contributed by the employer, and by employees for a contributory plan, and amounts earned from investing the contributions, less benefits paid.

Plan assets ordinarily cannot be withdrawn by the employer except under certain circumstances when a plan has assets in excess of obligations and the employer has taken certain steps to satisfy existing obligations. Assets not segregated in a trust or otherwise effectively restricted so that they cannot be used by the employer for other purposes are not plan assets even though it may be intended that such assets be used to provide pensions. If a plan has liabilities other than for benefits, those nonbenefit obligations may be considered as reduction of plan assets. Amounts accrued by the employer but not yet paid to the plan are not plan assets. Securities of the employer held by the plan are includable in plan assets provide they are transferable.

Preliminary Project State. Topic 350. When a computer software project is in the preliminary project stage, entities will likely do the following:

- Make strategic decisions to allocate resources between alternative projects at a given point in time. For example, should programmers develop a new payroll system or direct their efforts toward correcting existing problems in an operating payroll system?
- Determine the performance requirements (that is, what it is that they need the software to do) and systems requirements for the computer software project it has proposed to undertake.
- Invite vendors to perform demonstrations of how their software will fulfill an entity's needs.
- Explore alternative means of achieving specified performance requirements. For example, should an entity make or buy the software? Should the software run on a mainframe or a client server system?
- Determine that the technology needed to achieve performance requirements exists.
- Select a vendor if an entity chooses to obtain software.
- Select a consultant to assist in the development or installation of the software.

Principal Market. Topics 820 and 948. The market with the greatest volume and level of activity for the asset or liability.

Private Company. Topics 323, 350, 805, 810, 815. An entity other than a public business entity, a not-for-profit entity, or an employee benefit plan within the scope of Topics 960 through 965 on plan accounting.

Probable. Def. 1. Topic 840. As used in paragraph 25 of FASB Concepts Statement No. 6, Elements of Financial Statements, that which can reasonably be expected or believed on the basis of available evidence or logic but is neither certain nor proved *(Webster's New World Dictionary of the American Language*, 2d college ed. [New York Simon and Schuster 1982], p. 1132).

Probable. Def. 2. Topics 205, 310, 323, 325, 360, 450, 460, 470, 606, 705, 715, 718, 730, 815, 842, 944, 985. The future event or events are likely to occur.

Promise to Give. A written or oral agreement to contribute cash or other assets to another entity. A promise carries rights and obligations—the recipient of a promise to give has a right to expect that the promised assets will be transferred in the future, and the maker has a social and moral obligation, and generally a legal obligation, to make the promised transfer. A promise to give may be either conditional or unconditional.

Public Business Entity. Topics 105, 205, 230, 260, 270, 310, 323, 326, 330, 340, 350, 360, 606, 715, 718, 740, 805, 810, 815, 820, 825, 835, 842, 853, 860, 944, 958. A public business entity is a business entity meeting any one of the criteria below. Neither a not-for-profit entity nor an employee benefit plan is a business entity.

- It is required by the U.S. Securities and Exchange Commission (SEC) to file or furnish financial statements, or does file or furnish financial statements (including voluntary filers), with the SEC (including other entities whose financial statements or financial information are required to be or are included in a filing).
- It is required by the Securities Exchange Act of 1934 (the Act), as amended, or rules or regulations promulgated under the Act, to file or furnish financial statements with a regulatory agency other than the SEC.
- It is required to file or furnish financial statements with a foreign or domestic regulatory agency in preparation for the sale of or for purposes of issuing securities that are not subject to contractual restrictions on transfer.
- It has issued, or is a conduit bond obligor for, securities that are traded, listed, or quoted on an exchange or an over-the-counter market.
- It has one or more securities that are not subject to contractual restrictions on transfer, and it is required by law, contract, or regulation to prepare U.S. GAAP financial statements (including footnotes) and make them publicly available on a periodic basis (for example, interim or annual periods). An entity must meet both of these conditions to meet this criterion.

An entity may meet the definition of a public business entity solely because its financial statements or financial information is included in another entity's filing with the SEC. In that case, the entity is only a public business entity for purposes of financial statements that are filed or furnished with the SEC.

Public Entity. Topics 280, 805, 954, 958. A business entity or a not-for-profit entity that meets any of the following conditions:

- It has issued debt or equity securities or is a conduit bond obligor for conduit debt securities that are traded in a public market (a domestic or foreign stock exchange or an over-the-counter market, including local or regional markets).
- It is required to file financial statements with the Securities and Exchange Commission (SEC).
- It provides financial statements for the purpose of issuing any class of securities in a public market.

Public Entity. Def. 1. Topic 740. An entity that meets any of the following conditions:

- Its debt or equity securities are traded in a public market (a domestic or foreign stock exchange) or an over-the counter market, including securities quoted only locally or regionally.
- It is a conduit bond obligor for conduit debt securities that are traded in a public market (a domestic or foreign stock exchange) or an over-the-counter market, including local or regional markets.
- Its financial statements are filed with a regulatory agency in preparation for the sale of any class of securities.

Public Entity. Def. 2. Topics 470, 718. An entity that meets any of the following criteria:

- Has equity securities that trade in a public market, either on a stock exchange (domestic or foreign) or in an over-the-counter market, including securities quoted only locally or regionally.
- Makes a filing with a regulatory agency in preparation for the sale of any class of equity securities in a public market.
- Is controlled by an entity covered by the preceding criteria. That is, a subsidiary of a public entity is itself a public entity.
- An entity that has only debt securities trading in a public market (or that has made a filing with a regulatory agency in preparation to trade only debt securities) is not a public entity.

Publicly Traded Company. Topics 220, 270, 325, 825. A publicly traded company includes any company whose securities trade in a public market on either of the following:

- A stock exchange (domestic or foreign)
- In the over-the-counter market (including securities quoted only locally or regionally), or any company that is a conduit bond obligor for conduit debt securities that are traded in a public market (a domestic or foreign stock exchange or an over-the-counter market, including local or regional markets)

Additionally, when a company is required to file or furnish financial statements with the SEC or makes a filing with a regulatory agency in preparation for sale of its securities in a public market it is considered a publicly traded company for this purpose.

Conduit debt securities refer to certain limited-obligation revenue bonds, certificates of participation, or similar debt instruments issued by a state or local governmental entity for the express purpose of providing financing for a specific third party (the conduit bond obligor) that is not a part of the state or local government's financial reporting entity. Although conduit debt securities bear the name of the governmental entity that issues them, the governmental entity often has no obligation for such debt beyond the resources provided by a lease or loan agreement with the third party on whose behalf the securities are issued. Further, the conduit bond obligor is responsible for any future financial reporting requirements.

Publicly Traded Entity (or Public Entity). Topic 715. Any entity that does not meet the definition of a nonpublic entity.

Purchased Call Option. Topic 260. A contract that allows the reporting entity to buy a specified quantity of its own stock from the writer of the contract at a fixed price for a given period. See Call Option.

Purchased Financial Assets with Credit Deterioration. Acquired individual financial assets (or acquired groups of financial assets with similar risk characteristics) that as of the date of acquisition have experienced a more-than-insignificant deterioration in credit quality since origination, as determined by an acquirer's assessment. See paragraph 326-20-55-5 for more information on the meaning of similar risk characteristics for assets measured on an amortized cost basis.

Pushdown Accounting. Topic 805. Use of the acquirer's basis in the preparation of the acquiree's separate financial statements.

Put Option. Topic 260. A contract that allows the holder to sell a specified quantity of stock to the writer of the contract at a fixed price during a given period.

Reacquisition Price of Debt. Topic 470. The amount paid on extinguishment, including a call premium and miscellaneous costs of reacquisition. If extinguishment is achieved by a direct exchange of new securities, the reacquisition price is the total present value of the new securities.

Readily Determinable Fair Value. Def. 2. Topics 320, 321, 820, 825, 944, 958. An equity security has a readily determinable fair value if it meets any of the following conditions:

- The fair value of an equity security is readily determinable if sales prices or bid-and-asked quotations are currently available on a securities exchange registered with the U.S. Securities and Exchange Commission (SEC) or in the over-the-counter market, provided that those prices or quotations for the over-the-counter market are publicly reported by the National Association of Securities Dealers Automated Quotations systems or by OTC Markets Group Inc. Restricted stock meets that definition if the restriction terminates within one year.
- The fair value of an equity security traded only in a foreign market is readily determinable if that foreign market is of a breadth and scope comparable to one of the U.S. markets referred to above.
- The fair value of an equity security that is an investment in a mutual fund or in a structure similar to a mutual fund (that is, a limited partnership or a venture capital entity) is readily determinable if the fair value per share (unit) is determined and published and is the basis for current transactions.

Reasonably Possible. Topics 275, 450, 470, 840, 944. The chance of the future event or events occurring is more than remote but less than likely.

Recorded Investment. Topics 310, 320, 815. The amount of the investment in a loan, which is not net of a valuation allowance, but which does reflect any direct write-down of the investment. However, if a loan is a hedged item in a fair value hedge, the amount of that loan's recorded investment should include the unamortized amount of the cumulative fair value hedge adjustments.

Recourse. Topics 310, 860, 978. The right of a transferee of receivables to receive payment from the transferor of those receivables for any of the following:

- Failure of debtors to pay when due
- The effects of prepayments
- Adjustments resulting from defects in the eligibility of the transferred receivables.

Registration Payment Arrangement. Topics 460, 480, 505, 815, 825. An arrangement with both of the following characteristics:

It specifies that the issuer will endeavor to do either of the following:

File a registration statement for the resale of specified financial instruments and/or for the resale of equity shares that are issuable upon exercise or conversion of specified financial instruments and for that registration statement to be declared effective by the U.S. Securities and Exchange

Commission (SEC) (or other applicable securities regulator if the registration statement will be filed in a foreign jurisdiction) within a specified grace period.

Maintain the effectiveness of the registration statement for a specified period of time (or in perpetuity).

It requires the issuer to transfer consideration to the counterparty if the registration statement for the resale of the financial instrument or instruments subject to the arrangement is not declared effective or if effectiveness of the registration statement is not maintained. That consideration may be payable in a lump sum or it may be payable periodically, and the form of the consideration may vary. For example, the consideration may be in the form of cash, equity instruments, or adjustments to the terms of the financial instrument or instruments that are subject to the registration payment arrangement (such as an increased interest rate on a debt instrument).

Reinsurance. Topics 340, 405, 450, 460, 720, 805, 810, 825, 944. A transaction in which a reinsurer (assuming entity), for a consideration (premium) assume all or part of a risk undertaken originally by another insurer (ceding entity). For indemnity reinsurance, the legal rights of the insured are not affected by the reinsurance transaction and the insurance entity issuing the insurance contract remains liable to the insured for payment of policy benefits. Assumption or novation reinsurance contracts that are legal replacements of one insurer by another extinguish the ceding entity's liability to the policyholder.

Reinsurance Recoverable. Topics 825, 944. All amounts recoverable from reinsurers for paid and unpaid claims and claim settlement expenses, including estimated amounts receivable for unsettled claims, claims incurred but not reported, or policy benefits.

Related Parties. Topics 310, 321, 326, 460, 715, 718, 730, 810, 820, 842, 850, 946, 958. Related parties include:

- Affiliates of the entity
- Entities for which investments in their equity securities would be required, absent the election of the fair value option under the Fair Value Option Subsection of Section 825-10-15, to be accounted for by the equity method by the investing entity
- Trusts for the benefit of employees, such as pension and profit-sharing trusts, that are managed by or under the trusteeship of management
- Principal owners of the entity and members of their immediate families
- Management of the entity and members of their immediate families
- Other parties with which the entity may deal if one party controls or can significantly influence the management or operating policies of the other to an extent that one of the transacting parties might be prevented from fully pursuing its own separate interests
- Other parties that can significantly influence the management or operating policies of the transacting parties or that have an ownership interest in one of the transacting parties and can significantly influence the other to an extent that one or more of the transacting parties might be prevented from fully pursuing its own separate interests

Remote. Topics 205, 450, 840, 842, 860, 944. The chance of the future event or events occurring is slight.

Reporting Unit. Topic 350. The level of reporting at which goodwill is tested for impairment. A reporting unit is an operating segment or one level below an operating segment (also known as a component).

Repurchase Agreement. Topics 860, 940. An agreement under which the transferor (repo party) transfers a financial asset to a transferee (repo counterparty or reverse party) in exchange for cash and concurrently agrees to reacquire that financial asset at a future date for an amount equal to the cash exchanged plus or minus a stipulated interest factor. Instead of cash, other financial assets sometimes are exchanged. Some repurchase agreements call for repurchase of financial assets that need not be identical to the financial assets transferred.

Reseller. Def. 2. Topics 330, 605, 705. Any entity that purchases another vendor's products for resale, regardless of whether that entity is a distributor or wholesale, a retailer, or other type of reseller.

Residual Value. Topic 350. The estimated fair value of an intangible asset at the end of its useful life to an entity, less any disposal costs.

Retirement. Topic 410. The other-than-temporary removal of a long-lived asset from service. This term encompasses sale, abandonment, recycling, or disposal in some other manner. However, it does not encompass the temporary idling of a long-lived asset. After an entity retires an asset, that asset is no longer under the control of that entity, no longer in existence, or no longer capable of being used in the manner for which the asset was originally acquired, constructed, or developed.

Retrospective Application. Topic 250. The application of a different accounting principle to one or more previously issued financial statements, or to the statement of financial position at the beginning of the current period, as if that principle had always been used, or a change to financial statements of prior accounting periods to present the financial statements of a new reporting entity as if it had existed in those prior years.

Revenue. Topics 235, 270, 275, 340, 350, 360, 410, 430, 460, 470, 605, 606, 610, 705, 720, 740, 808, 810, 820, 810, 845, 910, 912, 926, 932, 940, 950, 954, 958, 978, 980, 985. Inflows or other enhancements of assets of an entity or settlements of its liabilities (or a combination of both) from delivering or producing goods, rendering services, or other activities that constitute the entity's ongoing major or central operations. (New ASC 606 Definition)

Reverse Repurchase Agreement Accounted for as a Collateralized Borrowing. Topics 210, 860. A reverse repurchase agreement accounted for as a collateralized borrowing (also known as a reverse repo) refers to a transaction that is accounted for as a collateralized lending in which a buyer-lender buys securities with an agreement to resell them to the seller-borrower at a stated price plus interest at a specified date or in specified circumstances. The receivable under a reverse repurchase agreement accounted for as a collateralized borrowing refers to the amount due from the seller-borrower for the repurchase of the securities from the buyer-lender. In certain industries, the terminology is reversed; that is, entities in those industries refer to this type of agreement as a repo.

Right-of-Use Asset.* Topics 230, 360, 805, 842. An asset that represents a lessee's right to use an underlying asset for the lease term.

Sale-Leaseback Accounting. Topics 360, 840. **Note:** This definition is superseded upon implementation of ASU 2016-01. A method of accounting for a sale-leaseback transaction in which the seller-lessee records the sale, removes all property and related liabilities from its balance sheet, recognizes gain or loss from the sale, and classifies the leaseback in accordance with the Lessees Subsections of Subtopic 840-40.

Sales-Type Lease. From the perspective of a lessor, a lease that meets either of the conditions in paragraph 840-10-25-43(a). This definition of Sales-Type Lease is pending implementation of ASU 2016-02: From the perspective of a lessor, a lease that meets one or more of the criteria in paragraph 842-10-25-2. (See the chapter on ASU 842 for more information.)

Securities and Exchange Commission (SEC) Filer. Topics 326, 350, 805, 855. An entity that is required to file or furnish its financial statements with either of the following:

- The Securities and Exchange Commission (SEC)
- With respect to an entity subject to Section 12(i) of the Securities Exchange Act of 1934, as amended, the appropriate agency under that Section

Financial statements for other entities that are not otherwise SEC filers whose financial statements are included in a submission by another SEC filer are not included within this definition.

Securities and Exchange Commission Registrant. Topics 480, 718. An entity (or an entity that is controlled by an entity) that meets any of the following criteria:

- It has issued or will issue debt or equity securities that are traded in a public market (a domestic or foreign stock exchange or an over-the counter market, including local or regional markets).
- It is required to file financial statements with the SEC.
- It provides financial statements for the purpose of issuing any class of securities in a public market.

Securities Industry and Financial Markets Association (SIFMA) Municipal Swap Rate. Topic 815. The fixed rate on a U.S. dollar, constant-notional interest rate swap that has its variable-rate leg referenced to the Securities Industry and Financial Markets Association (SIFMA) Municipal Swap Index with no additional spread over the SIFMA Municipal Swap Index on that variable-rate leg. That fixed rate is the derived rate that would result in the swap having a zero fair value at inception because the present value of fixed cash flows, based on that rate, equates to the present value of the variable cash flows.

Security. Def. 1. Topics 260, 505. The evidence of debt or ownership or a related right. It includes options and warrants as well as debt and stock.

Security. Def. 2. Topics 320, 321, 326, 860, 958. A share, participation, or other interest in property or an entity of the issuer or an obligation of the issuer that has all of the following characteristics:

- It is either represented by an instrument issued in bearer or registered form or, if not represented by an instrument, is registered in books maintained to record transfers by or on behalf of the issuer.
- It is of a type commonly dealt in on securities exchanges or markets or, when represented by an instrument, is commonly recognized in any area in which it is issued or dealt in as a medium for investment.
- It is either one of a class or series or, by its terms, is divisible into a class or series of shares, participations, interests, or obligations.

Service Condition. Topics 606 and 718. A condition affecting the vesting, exercisability, exercise price, or other pertinent factors used in determining the fair value of an award that depends solely on an employee rendering service to the employer for the requisite service period or a nonemployee delivering goods or rendering services to the grantor over a vesting period. A condition that results in the acceleration of vesting in the event of a grantee's death, disability, or termination without cause is a service condition.

Settlement of a Pension or Postretirement Benefit Obligation. Topics 205, 715. A transaction that is an irrevocable action, relieves the employer (or the plan) of primary responsibility for a pension or postretirement benefit obligation, and eliminates significant risks related to the obligation and the assets used to effect the settlement.

Share-Based Payment Arrangements. (ASC 260, 718) An arrangement under which either of the following conditions is met:

a. One or more suppliers of goods or services (including employees) receive awards of equity shares, equity share options, or other equity instruments.
b. The entity incurs liabilities to suppliers that meet either of the following conditions:
   1. The amounts are based, at least in part, on the price of the entity's shares or other equity instruments. (The phrase at least in part is used because an award may be indexed to both the price of the entity's shares and something other than either the price of the entity's shares or a market, performance, or service condition.)
   2. The awards require or may require settlement by issuance of the entity's shares.

The term shares includes various forms of ownership interest that may not take the legal form of securities (for example, partnership interests), as well as other interests, including those that are liabilities in substance but not in form. Equity shares refers only to shares that are accounted for as equity.

Also called share-based compensation arrangements.

Sponsor. Def. 1. Topics 730, 810. An entity that capitalizes a research and development arrangement.

Sponsor. Def. 2. Topics 960, 962. In the case of a pension plan established or maintained by a single employer, the employer; in the case of a plan established or maintained by an employee entity, the employee entity; in the case of a plan established or maintained jointly by two or more employers or by one or more employers and one or more employee entities, the association, committee, joint board of trustees, or other group of representatives of the parties that have established or that maintain the pension plan.

Spot Rate. Topics 815, 926, 946. The exchange rate for immediate delivery of currencies exchanged.

Standalone Selling Price. Topics 606, 705, 820, 840. The price at which an entity would sell a promised good or service separately to a customer.

Standby Letter of Credit. Topics 310, 326. A letter of credit (or similar arrangement however named or designated) that represents an obligation to the beneficiary on the part of the issuer for any of the following:

- To repay money borrowed by or advanced to or for the account of the account party
- To make payment on account of any evidence of indebtedness undertaken by the account party
- To make payment on account of any default by the account party in the performance of an obligation

A standby letter of credit would not include the following:

- Commercial letters of credit and similar instruments where the issuing bank expects the beneficiary to draw upon the issuer and which do not guarantee payment of a money obligation
- A guarantee or similar obligation issued by a foreign branch in accordance with and subject to the limitations of Regulation M of the Federal Reserve Board

Stock Dividend. Topics 260 and 505. An issuance by a corporation of its own common shares to its common shareholders without consideration and under conditions indicating that such action is prompted mainly by a desire to give the recipient shareholders some ostensibly separate evidence of a part of their respective interests in accumulated corporate earnings without distribution of cash or other property that the board of directors deems necessary or desirable to retain in the business. A stock dividend takes nothing from the property of the corporation and adds nothing to the interests of the stockholders; that is, the corporation's property is not diminished and the interests of the stockholders are not increased. The proportional interest of each shareholder remains the same.

Sublease.* Topics 805, 842. A transaction in which an underlying asset is leased by the lessee (or intermediate lessor) to a third party (the sublessee) and the original (or head) lease between the lessor and the lessee remains in effect.

Subsidiary. Topics 220, 260, 323, 480, 610, 810, 845, 932, 942. An entity, including an unincorporated entity such as a partnership or trust, in which another entity, known as its parent, holds a controlling financial interest. (Also, a variable interest entity that is consolidated by a primary beneficiary.)

Time of Restructuring. Topics 310, 470. Troubled debt restructurings may occur before, at, or after the stated maturity of debt, and time may elapse between the agreement, court order, and so forth, and the transfer of assets or equity interest, the effective date of new terms, or the occurrence of another event that constitutes consummation of the restructuring. The date of consummation is the time of the restructuring.

Time Value. Topics 718, 815. The portion of the fair value of an option that exceeds its intrinsic value. For example, a call option with an exercise price of $20 on a stock whose current market price is $25 has intrinsic value of $5. If the fair value of that option is $7, the time value of the option is $2 ($7 – $5).

Trading. Topics 320, 815. An activity involving securities sold in the near term and held for only a short period of time. The term trading contemplates a holding period generally measured in hours and days rather than months or years. See paragraph 948-310-40-1 for clarification of the term trading for a mortgage banking entity.

Transaction. Topic 815. An external event involving transfer of something of value (future economic benefit) between two (or more) entities.

Transaction Price. Topics 270, 275, 340, 450, 606, 610, 985. The amount of consideration to which an entity expects to be entitled in exchange for transferring promised goods or services to a customer, excluding amounts collected on behalf of third parties.

Troubled Debt Restructuring. Topics 310, 326, 470. A restructuring of a debt constitutes a troubled debt restructuring if the creditor for economic or legal reasons related to the debtor's financial difficulties grants a concession to the debtor that it would not otherwise consider.

Unconditional Purchase Obligation. Topics 440, 470, 815. An obligation to transfer funds in the future for fixed or minimum amounts or quantities of goods or services at fixed or minimum prices (for example, as in take-or-pay contracts or throughput contracts).

Underlying. Topics 460, 810, 815, 946. A specified interest rate, security price, commodity price, foreign exchange rate, index of prices or rates, or other variable (including the occurrence or nonoccurrence of a specified event such as a scheduled payment under a contract). An underlying may be a price or rate of an asset or liability but is not the asset or liability itself. An underlying is a variable that, along with either a notional amount or a payment provision, determines the settlement of a derivative instrument.

Underlying Asset.* Topics 210, 230, 255, 270, 310, 360, 410, 440, 450, 460, 740, 805, 815, 835, 842, 860, 958, 970. An asset that is the subject of a lease for which a right to use that asset has been conveyed to a lessee. The underlying asset could be a physically distinct portion of a single asset.

Unguaranteed Residual Asset.* Topics 255, 805, 842, 860. The amount that a lessor expects to derive from the underlying asset following the end of the lease term that is not guaranteed by the lessee or any other third party unrelated to the lessor, measured on a discounted basis.

Unit of Account. Topic 820. The level at which an asset or a liability is aggregated or disaggregated in a topic for recognition purposes.

Useful Life. Topics 350, 842. The period over which an asset is expected to contribute directly or indirectly to future cash flows.

Variable Interest Entity. Topics 805, 810, 842. A legal entity subject to consolidation according to the provisions of the Variable Interest Entities subsections of Subtopic 810-10.

Variable Interests. Topics 610, 810. The investments or other interests that will absorb portions of a variable interest entity's (VIE's) expected losses or receive portions of the entity's expected residual returns are called variable interests. Variable interests in a VIE are contractual, ownership, or other pecuniary interests in a VIE that change with changes in the fair value of the VIE's net assets exclusive of variable interests. Equity interests with or without voting rights are considered variable interests if the legal entity is a VIE and to the extent that the investment is at risk as described in paragraph 810-10-15-14. Paragraph 810-10-25-55 explains how to determine whether a variable interest in specified assets of a legal entity is a variable interest in the entity. Paragraphs 810-10-55-16 through 55-41 describe various types of variable interests and explain in general how they may affect the determination of the primary beneficiary of a VIE.

Variable Lease Payments.* Topics 410, 450, 460, 815, 842. Payments made by a lessee to a lessor for the right to use an underlying asset that vary because of changes in facts or circumstances occurring after the commencement date, other than the passage of time.

Vendor. Topics 330, 605, 705. A service provider or product seller, such as a manufacturer, distributor, or reseller.

Warrant. Topic 260. A security that gives the holder the right to purchase shares of common stock in accordance with the terms of the instrument, usually upon payment of a specified amount.

Weather Derivative. Topics 460, 815. A forward-based or option-based contract for which settlement is based on a climatic or geological variable. One example of such a variable is the occurrence or nonoccurrence of a specified amount of snow at a specified location within a specified period of time.

With Cause. Topics 810, 958. With cause generally restricts the limited partners' ability to dissolve (liquidate) the limited partnership or remove the general partners in situations that include, but that are not limited to, fraud, illegal acts, gross negligence, and bankruptcy of the general partners.

Without Cause. Topics 810, 958. Without cause means that no reason need be given for the dissolution (liquidation) of the limited partnership or removal of the general partners.

Working Capital. Topics 210, 470. Working capital (also called net working capital) is represented by the excess of current assets over current liabilities and identifies the relatively liquid portion of total entity capital that constitutes a margin or buffer for meeting obligations within the ordinary operating cycle of the entity.

Appendix B
DISCLOSURE AND PRESENTATION CHECKLIST FOR COMMERCIAL BUSINESSES

In order to make this checklist as useful as possible to the end user, it has been posted to: www.wiley.com/go/GAAP2021. The password is Flood2021. It is saved as a Word document.

INDEX